Costs & Funding following the Civil Justice Reforms: Questions & Answers

8th Edition

Published in 2022 by Thomson Reuters, trading as Sweet & Maxwell.
Thomson Reuters is registered in England & Wales, Company No.1679046.
Registered Office and address for service:
5 Canada Square, Canary Wharf, London, E14 5AQ

For further information on our products and services, visit www.sweetandmaxwell.co.uk
Printed in Great Britain by CPI Grp Ltd, Croydon
Typeset by Cheshire Typesetting Ltd, Cuddington, CW8 2BS

No natural forests were destroyed to make this product; only farmed timber was used
and re-planted.

A CIP catalogue record for this book is available from the British Library.

ISBN (White Book) 978-041410-317-7
ISBN (Standalone) 978-0-41410-252-1

Thomson Reuters, the Thomson Reuters Logo and Sweet & Maxwell ® are trademarks of
Thomson Reuters.

Costs & Funding following the Civil Justice Reforms: Questions & Answers

Contributors

Peter Hurst LLB MPhil FCIArb, General Editor. Peter was the Senior Costs Judge of England & Wales, at the Royal Courts of Justice, from 1992 to 2014. During a judicial career which has spanned thirty years, he was also Judicial Taxing Officer of the House of Lords from 2002 to 2009 and of the United Kingdom Supreme Court from 2009 to 2014 and also of the Judicial Committee of the Privy Council from 2002 to 2014. He sat not only as a costs judge in the SCCO but also as a recorder in civil and criminal matters, including costs appeals from District Judges. He sat as an assessor with High Court Judges dealing with numerous costs appeals. He was invited to sit with the Court of Appeal as an assessor when that Court was dealing with difficult or complex costs appeals. He joined 39 Essex Chambers as a door tenant in December 2014. He is now an arbitrator, mediator and expert on costs and funding issues.

He is the author of *Civil Costs* (Sweet & Maxwell Litigation Library)—the sixth edition published in 2018—and *Criminal Costs* (OUP). He was, until retirement, a member of the Senior Editorial Board of *Civil Procedure* (the *White Book*, Sweet & Maxwell) as well as being an editor contributing the commentary on all the costs rules and practice directions. He is now an advisory editor of the *White Book*.

Simon Middleton was appointed a District Judge in 2004 and a Regional Costs Judge at the inception of the scheme in 2005. He has sat in both the Midlands and the Western regions. Before his appointment he was a solicitor with Higher Court (Civil Advocacy) qualification.

Simon was a member of the Judicial College tutor team for six years. In that capacity he was a member of the team charged with delivering education on the April 2013 reforms. Subsequently he was one of the Course Directors appointed for civil education. In that role he was responsible for, amongst other things, the training offered on case and costs management.

Simon has written and lectured extensively on the subject of costs and case and costs management.

Roger Mallalieu QC is a barrister at 4 New Square specialising in matters relating to costs, litigation funding and civil procedure. He routinely ranks as one of the leaders in the field of costs law of all types and has appeared in a considerable number of the leading cases in the area. He is regularly instructed on important test issues and appears regularly in the Court of Appeal and other higher courts on such matters.

Judith Ayling QC is a barrister at 39 Essex Chambers, where she completed pupillage in 1999 following a career in academic publishing. She took silk in 2021. She specialises in costs, clinical negligence and personal injury. She is regularly instructed in high-value cases and cases where novel and difficult points of law arise.

She is a member of the executive committee of the Personal Injuries Bar Association.

Nicola Greaney is a barrister at 39 Essex Chambers, where she completed pupillage in 2000. She specialises in costs, clinical negligence, Court of Protection and public law. She is regularly instructed in cases raising difficult points of law which cross-over her practice areas. She is a member of the Bar Council's Remuneration Committee.

Shaman Kapoor is a barrister at 39 Essex Chambers where he specialises in costs, litigation funding, common law and commercial litigation. He is a qualified Mediator, sits as a Deputy District Judge, and teaches as a lead Advocacy Tutor for Lincoln's Inn. He is a regular speaker at the leading seminars on costs and is highly regarded in the directories.

Publisher's Note

Costs & Funding following the Civil Justice Reforms: Questions & Answers is a unique book. Produced in conjunction with Practical Law, it tackles common practitioner questions on the effects of the 2013 Jackson reforms on costs and funding. It not only states the law, as set out in the latest legislation, court rules, forms and case law, but also identifies and, where possible, tackles issues and inconsistencies. The authors answer questions on topics ranging from funding of litigation, case and costs management and proportionality to settlement offers, QOCS and summary assessment. As well as updating the existing questions and answers, the 8th edition adds a significant number of new questions and answers, and much of the commentary is revised in light of new and ongoing case law and legislation in the fast-evolving costs and funding landscape post-Jackson.

Subscribers to the White Book Service 2022 receive this book gratis as part of their subscription. It is generally up-to-date to 25 February 2022 and to the Civil Procedure (Amendment) Rules 2022 (SI 2022/101) and the 140th CPR Update.

As this edition went to press, the Court of Appeal refused permission to appeal in *PGI Group Ltd v Thomas* [2022] EWCA Civ 233. Whilst a decision on an application for permission to appeal, it merits mention here because the text comments on the 1st instance decision and, more importantly, because Coulson LJ considered the case of *Kazakhstan Kagazy Plc v Zhunus* [2015] EWHC 33 (TCC) and concluded that "there may be cases in which the reasonable and necessary costs required to enable the claimant to fight the case through to trial were disproportionate, and would therefore justify a CCO in a lesser amount. Indeed, that is more than just a theoretical possibility (which is how the judge wrongly described it): that principle is enshrined in r.44.3(2)(a), which provides for such a result in terms (even though it is concerned primarily with assessment after the event, not limiting the incurring of such costs in the first place by way of a CCO). So in principle, a costs budget or a CCO could be set at a sum that was less than the reasonable and necessary costs to be incurred, because that sum might still be disproportionate." This conclusion confirms the position that has always been advanced in this text (see paras. 3-04, 3-16, 3-17 and 4-84), but was slightly qualified in this edition as a result of the 1st instance decision.

This book is not possible without the time, help and expertise of the author team: we welcome Judith Ayling QC, Nicola Greaney and Shaman Kapoor to the team, who have joined Peter Hurst, Simon Middleton and Roger Mallalieu QC. The publisher wishes to thank them for their hard work, co-operation and speed with which they have updated the new edition, an impressive achievement in itself. This project was the result of collaboration between the Dispute Resolution team at Practical Law and the author team and it would not have got off the ground without either of them.

We welcome any feedback—please email *whitebook@sweetandmaxwell.co.uk*.

Contents

List of Questions

I. Case management

Chapter 5 **Part 36 and Other Settlement Offers Including ADR and Costs Consequences**

B. Content requirements for Part 36 offers (CPR r.36.5)

Q7. Can a valid Part 36 offer include settlement terms which (if accepted), impose conditions; require a defendant to do something other than pay money; or provide for interest to run after the end of the relevant period?
Can a Part 36 offer include a sum for future loss? In this case, the future loss is in the form of continuing loss of rental income? (CPR rr.2.1, 36.2(2), 36.5(4).   350

Q8. The topic of making offers and content requirements attracted the largest number of questions as it did in the previous editions.
(i) I act for a defendant in proceedings in which summary judgment has been awarded in my client's favour. Indemnity costs have been awarded to my client and the costs are to be summarily assessed. The summary assessment is to take place at a separate hearing from that in which judgment was awarded. Can I make a Part 36 offer to the claimant in relation to the payment by him of my client's costs?
(ii) We act for a defendant who has accepted the claimant's Part 36 offer to settle the claim. The defendant has paid the settlement sum under the Pt 36 Agreement to the claimant, and the costs are now being assessed. Can the claimant make another Part 36 offer in relation to those costs, given that the defendant is already liable for the assessed costs under the original Pt 36 Agreement?
(iii) Can a claimant make a Part 36 offer to accept nothing (zero pounds)?
(iv) Is it possible to make a pre-action Part 36 offer and then commence legal proceedings before the relevant period has expired? If B makes a pre-issue Part 36 offer to A in relation to an unpaid invoice, is there a risk that A may issue proceedings, incurring solicitors and possibly counsel's fees, and then accept the offer before the end of the relevant period, so that B has to pay A's costs? If so, presumably this is something that should be explained to B?
(v) Is it possible to make a valid Part 36 offer with a set figure payable in respect of costs? I want the offer to be inclusive of a set amount of costs, but the costs are not fixed, and I do not want them to be subject to standard assessment.
(vi) Can a pre-action Part 36 offer be valid if it states that each party must bear its own costs? If the defendant makes a Calderbank offer that includes a condition that the claimant pays the defendant's costs or even that both parties pay their own costs, is there any reason why the claimant cannot reject the offer but then make exactly the same proposal in the form of a Part 36 offer? Would it make any difference if the Part 36 offer was exactly the same except that it did not refer to the costs consequences?

(vii) Will a claimant's Part 36 offer still constitute a valid offer if it is for an unliquidated amount (such as, for example, the settlement sum being 50% of a deceased person's net estate)? Can an offer to accept a percentage of the equity in a property (rather than a set amount of money because the value/sale price of the property is not known) be a valid Part 36 offer? Where A and B are in dispute in relation to a piece of land owned by A, can B make a valid Part 36 offer to acquire A's land? I am conscious that a Part 36 offer should be an offer to pay a single sum of money (CPR r.36.6), but what if that single sum of money is in the form of an offer to purchase something from the opponent? I note the payment timescale set down by CPR r.36.14(6) but if the offer was an offer to pay money in return for land, clearly it may not be possible to conclude the transfer within 14 days of acceptance.

(viii) Can a defendant's Part 36 offer be valid where the defendant does not have the finances to pay the amount contained in the offer?

(ix) Can confidentiality terms be included in a Part 36 offer and if so, will that affect the costs consequences if the claim does not settle?

(x) Where a defendant has made a Part 36 offer in proceedings, and the claimant then makes a Part 36 counteroffer, and neither offer is accepted, what are the costs consequences?   350

Q9. Where there's more than one claimant, in his Part 36 offer must the defendant apportion the settlement sum he offers between each claimant?

I'm trying to find out if there is a case or any legislation that states that Part 36 offers to more than one claimant need to be apportioned between the offerees? For example, if a Part 36 offer of £50,000 is made to two claimants, do you have to specify that it's 50/50 for each, or, say, 70% for one and 30% for the other (CPR r.36.5)?   355

Q10. In a case where there is no counterclaim and the claimant makes a Part 36 offer, does that offer need to state whether it takes into account any counterclaim given that there is no counterclaim in existence? (CPR r.36.5(1)(e))   356

C. Time when a Part 36 offer may be made or accepted

Q11. i. What is the position when a Part 36 offer is made pre-action and accepted after the issue of proceedings, but before the proceedings have been served on the defendant, where service has been reserved for up to four months?

ii. After our client (the claimant) issued proceedings, the defendant filed an acknowledgement of service and then accepted the claimant's pre-action Part 36 offer. What is the best way to record the settlement—is there any reason why we cannot use a Tomlin Order?

iii. If a Part 36 offer is expressly rejected (in writing), can the party then change their mind and accept the Part 36 offer (within the relevant period)? (CPR r.36.7)

iv. Where a defendant makes a pre-action Part 36 offer, the relevant period expires, the claimant issues proceedings and only then does the claimant accept the Part 36 offer, will the claimant be entitled to its pre-action costs? 356

Q12. Will a Part 36 offer still have effect if it is made during a stay of proceedings which were for reasons other than to allow for settlement of the case? (CPR r.36.7).Whilst I understand that accepting the Part 36 offer will stay the proceedings in accordance with CPR r.36.14(1), when will the stay come into force? Will the claim be automatically stayed upon deemed service of the notice of acceptance of the Part 36 offer? Can a party to litigation make a Part 36 offer during a period of stay of the claim? If it can, then when does the relevant period commence and end, and can that offer be accepted within the period of stay? 358

Q13. Where a party (represented by solicitors) has served a Part 36 offer by email (when you have neither expressly nor by implication confirmed that you accept service by email), are you under any obligation to inform that party that you do not accept service by email? Where a Part 36 offer has been made, is there a duty or an obligation on the offeree, to bring to the attention of the offeror, any potential defects which may render the offer non-compliant with CPR Pt 36? 359

Q14. What would the costs consequences be if a claimant makes a Part 36 offer to settle less than 21 days before the trial date, the trial is then postponed by a month and the claimant obtains a judgment at least as advantageous as the offer at the postponed trial? Would the Pt 36 costs consequences apply and if so, from what date? Alternatively, would the court consider the offer when deciding what order to make about costs under CPR r.44.3 (as would otherwise have been the case)? Is the court's permission required to accept a Part 36 offer after a summary judgment application hearing has been heard (but before the handing down)? CPR r.36.11(3)(d) provides that the court's permission is required to accept a Part 36 offer if a trial is in progress but summary judgment does not fall under the definition of "trial". 360

Q15. We (the claimant) have made a Part 36 offer on Form N242A sent via email to the defendant's solicitor. This has not been acknowledged by the defendant's solicitor, and the timescale has expired. The defendant's solicitors have not formerly said that they accept service via email but also have not said that they have not in response. We have previously served via email our directions questionnaire and draft directions without complaint. Is it still a

(i) Can they withdraw their offer within the relevant period
without permission of the Court?
(ii) Having withdrawn their offer, do they lose the costs protection
of that offer?
If an offeror serves a notice of withdrawal of a (pre-claim) Part
36 offer before expiry of the relevant period, does that notice
take effect immediately to make the Part 36 offer incapable of
acceptance, or does the withdrawal notice take effect only after the
relevant period has expired, thereby meaning that the Part 36 offer
remains capable of acceptance by the offeree during the relevant
period?
At the first CMC, we intend to ask the Court to allow for the claim
value to be increased. Are we, in the meantime, allowed to make a
Part 36 offer to the defendant, stating a figure which is above the
current claim value? 365

Q20. What is the position where a Part 36 offer is withdrawn
at the same time as the claimant purports to accept it?
(CPR rr.36.9, 36.10) 365

Q21. The defendant has made a Part 36 offer which it wishes to vary
following a query from the claimant. There are still 20 days left in
the "relevant period". What are the costs consequences of this and
does the relevant period commence again once a varied Part 36
offer is made? 366

Q22. If a Part 36 offer is not withdrawn, it continues to run.
However, would this Part 36 offer be seen to be rejected if the
other side makes its own Part 36 offer?
If the matter goes to trial and the judge finds that an amount is
due which is more than the claimant's original Part 36 offer but
less than the varied offer, what are the implications? Do the Pt 36
costs consequences still follow, based on the original Part 36 offer,
or is it only the increased figure that is relevant, meaning that
there would be no Pt 36 costs consequences? 367

*F. Part 36 offer acceptance requirements (CPR rr.36.11, 36.12)/Disclosure
of Part 36 offer (CPR r.36.16)*

Q23. Where there has been a split trial or a trial of preliminary
issues, what is the position with regard to Part 36 offers which may
have been made? (CPR r.36.12)
Can a defendant accept a Part 36 offer after the claimant has won
a liability trial, bearing in mind CPR r.36.12, and what would the
costs consequences be? 368

Q24. My client received the Part 36 offer on Monday 14 August. The
relevant period stated in the offer is "within 21 days of service"
what is the final date for accepting the offer and how is it
calculated? 370

has not complied with that settlement. No proceedings have been commenced. To obtain a County Court Judgment, must I commence proceedings?

Q31. I act for a proposed claimant in a dispute where legal proceedings have yet to be issued. The proposed defendant has served a Part 36 offer by Form N242A which states that the defendant will be liable for the claimant's costs in accordance with CPR r.36.13. CPR r.36.13 states the claimant will be entitled to the costs of proceedings including their recoverable pre-action costs. Does this mean my client can only recover pre-action costs as part of the costs of any proceedings? If this is so, can we agree that the pre-action costs are recoverable and if so, if the amount cannot be agreed can we issue costs only proceedings pursuant to Pt 8A to have the court adjudicate upon costs? (CPR r.36.13)   375

Q32. If a defendant accepts a claimant's Part 36 offer after proceedings have been issued, is a consent order to dispose of the proceedings necessary?

I understand that generally speaking, there is no need for there to be a consent order if a settlement results from acceptance of a Part 36 offer. Am I right? If so, are there any significant exceptions from this general proposition? (CPR r.36.13(1)).

Where a Part 36 offer is accepted to settle a dispute, should the parties also draw up and sign a separate settlement agreement or enter into a consent order?

Is there any benefit in a defendant making a Part 36 offer in relation to costs after the claimant has discontinued the claim? If a defendant accepts the claimant's Part 36 offer, can the claimant require the defendant then to enter into a separate settlement agreement?   376

Q33. CPR r.36.2 provides that a Part 36 offer may be made in a counterclaim or additional claim, and it includes a reminder that CPR r.20.2 and CPR r.20.3 provide that counterclaims and other additional claims are treated as claims. With that in mind, if a defendant makes a Part 36 offer in relation to its counterclaim, which is accepted within the relevant period (RP), does that mean that the defendant is automatically "entitled to the costs of the proceedings" (that is, the costs relating to both the original claim and the counterclaim) under CPR r.36.13(1)? (CPR r.36.13(7))   377

Q34. Where a defendant entered into a consent order agreeing to pay costs on the indemnity basis in respect of the claimant's application for summary judgment on part only of its claim, and the defendant then made a Part 36 offer in full and final settlement of the whole claim, if the claimant accepted the Part 36 offer within the relevant period, would the defendant pay the claimant's costs on the standard basis pursuant to CPR r.36.13 or

Q44. Can a Pt 20 defendant make a Part 36 offer? We have a case where the claimant is suing the first defendant (D1), the claimant is also suing the second defendant (D2), and D1 is suing D2, who they brought in as a Pt 20 defendant. D2 wishes to make a Part 36 offer, but is it possible for one Part 36 offer to encompass both claims?

How can you best use Pt 36 in multi-party disputes? We act for Party A in an action against Party B. Party B has issued Pt 20 proceedings against Party C. Our client wishes to resolve the claim by making a Part 36 offer to settle the entire action, including the Pt 20 proceedings, on terms that my client will accept a small sum in settlement from Party B, and that Party B will discontinue against the Pt 20 defendant (who is a Litigant in Person (LiP) and therefore has no costs consequences). There is a connection between Party A and Party B (CPR r.36.2(1), CPR rr.36.5, 36.15). 389

Q45. Our client is a defendant to a multi-party disease claim. For commercial reasons they would like to make a Part 36 offer for their portion of the claim and costs only. In what circumstances would CPR r.36.15 apply to a disease claim such as this? And if the offer were accepted by the claimant how would the court deal with the "common costs"? 390

Q46. i. We are one of two defendants in High Court proceedings. The claimant's solicitors have made a Part 36 offer to us which states, "We are prepared to settle the entire proceedings on the following terms". Those terms are payment by our client of £200,000. Obviously, if accepted, costs would also be payable. The same letter has also been sent to the other defendant. Can either of the defendants accept the offer and thus settle the entire proceedings, and then agree between them how to divide up the payment?

ii. Our client issued a claim against two defendants who are jointly and severally liable for the entire debt stemming from a hire agreement. We would now like to make a Part 36 offer to the defendants. Should that offer be in the form of a joint Part 36 offer, given there is joint and several liability, or separate Part 36 offers for the full amount addressed to each of the defendants?

iii. I am acting for two defendants who have instructed me to make a Part 36 offer to the claimant. Will I be required to complete a separate Part 36 form for each defendant? The claims against each are identical.

iv. Can three out of four defendants make a joint Part 36 offer apportioning the liability as between them?

v. In a negligence claim against multiple defendants each considered to have caused the resulting harm in varying ways, can a Part 36 be offered to each defendant for different amounts

Chapter 6   Qualified One-Way Costs Shifting

claim has been struck out (no court permission needed) or if it is fundamentally dishonest (court permission needed). We do not have sufficient time to obtain written consent from each and every defendant in a consent order but in any event consider that we would be QOCS protected even by serving a notice of discontinuance. 461

Q18. CPR r.44 relating to QOCS states that it will not apply if the claimant has disclosed no reasonable grounds for bringing the proceedings. What is the position where during the course of the court proceedings medical evidence comes to light which is not supportive of causation which means the claim may have to be withdrawn/discontinued? At the time proceedings were issued it was believed there were reasonable prospects/grounds for bringing the claim. Would the claimant still have the benefit of QOCS or would they automatically be liable for the defendant's costs due to filing a notice of discontinuance? 462

C. QOCS and settlement offers

Q19. In respect of CPR r.44.14 (1) relating to QOCS, can an order for costs be made up to the extent of any damages when a Calderbank offer has been made, or does this rule only apply when a Part 36 offer has been made (i.e. this rule does not apply to Calderbank offers)? 463

Q20. I'm the claimant in a claim to which QOCS applies and in which the defendant has recently made a generous Part 36 offer. If I don't accept the offer and, at trial, my claim fails completely, will I have to pay the defendant's costs? 464

Q21. What should practitioners do in the light of Cartwright? Should claimants not use Part 36 offers? Should settlements be recorded in Tomlin orders? If acting for the defendant, is it advisable to seek to bring a counterclaim even if there is little basis for it? 464

D. QOCS and set-off

Q22. A claimant loses a personal injury claim and a costs order is made in the usual way but the judge also finds fundamental dishonesty and thus allows enforcement of the costs order totalling £7,000.00. The claimant appeals against the finding of fundamental dishonesty, but not the loss of the claim, and wins and so the finding of fundamental dishonesty is quashed and the claimant is awarded costs of the appeal of £12,000.00. The original order against the claimant in respect of the costs of losing the personal injury claim remains in place but is now unenforceable. Could the defendant, successful in the primary

We act for the claimant and the defendant filed and served an acknowledgement of service but failed to file and serve a defence. The claim relates to unpaid commission of £25,000. The debt was originally disputed in the acknowledgment of service. In terms of costs, we are aware that our costs for filing Form N225 will be fixed (£35). Will our costs for issuing the claim be fixed costs? As a side note, the court allocated this case to the multi-track.

ii. We act for the claimant in a matter. We have obtained default judgment against the defendant, after previously making an unaccepted Part 36 offer. My query is, are we able to recover our costs pursuant to Pt 36 or Pt 45?

iii. If your claim is for a sum in excess of say £25,000 and you wish to obtain default judgement and costs to be assessed in the absence of agreement, can you do this on a request or must C make an application?

iv. If I have issued a claim for over £40,000 and the defendants then fail to acknowledge the claim and I make a request for judgment, would fixed costs still apply? Would this still be the case where I incurred costs over £4,000? If Fixed Costs do apply, what grounds would I potentially have in trying to persuade the court to apply discretion and how would I go about making such an application?   529

Q15. We act for the claimant in a personal injury claim. The case was settled on the basis that the defendant agreed to pay the claimant's costs on a standard basis to be assessed if not agreed. I understand that there has been a recent court decision that determined that by reason of the procedure adopted by the claimant when issuing the claim, the defendant only had to pay fixed costs. However, there is a private agreement between the claimant and the defendant that the defendant pays standard costs. Can the parties contract out of a fixed costs regime? In the event that a Part 36 offer is accepted by a defendant in a low value personal injury claim (where QOCS and fixed costs regime apply), would the claimant be entitled to recover under the Pt 36 regime only its fixed costs or the entirety of its costs on an indemnity basis? Further, if the defendant chooses to make a Part 36 offer and it is accepted, would the defendant only have to pay the claimant's fixed costs or its actual costs (on the standard basis)?   531

Q16. On an application for possession of residential property, following the service and expiry of a s.8 notice, my understanding is that fixed costs apply in the event the proceedings are undefended. However, is the successful claimant that obtained a possession and money order (for arrears) and fixed costs able to bring fresh proceedings (for breach of contract) against the tenant to recover the balance of the solicitors' costs that he has incurred in bringing the possession proceedings but not recovered? The tenancy agreement provides that all costs associated with recovering rent will be payable by the tenant. I am aware of the following case where, under the small claims track, legal costs have been awarded, above the fixed costs usually permitted, as they were claimed under a contractual obligation (a clause in a lease) *Chaplair Ltd v Kumari* [2015] EWCA Civ 798 (27 July 2015). Are there any appeals/cases since that have set a different precedent, where the legal costs have been limited to the fixed costs in small claims cases, even when there was a contractual obligation? 534

Q17. Are there any fixed costs we can charge for making an Order for Sale Claim? 535

B. Fixed costs and multi-party situations (where fixed costs may not apply equally)

Q18. Where a claim is made against more than one defendant, one of whom admits the debt and judgment is obtained under CPR r.14.4(3), while the other defendant does not respond and judgment in default is obtained under CPR r.12.4(1), is the claimant entitled to two sets of fixed costs given that there are two defendants and judgment has been obtained on two different bases? (CPR r.45.1)
Can two or more claimants both claim fixed costs i.e. two or more sets? 535

Q19. What is the court's approach to legal costs for a general claim on the fast track before trial, e.g. costs of a summary judgment application or other interim application? Are costs of those not fixed and subject to summary assessment? Do judges routinely summarily assess such costs? 536

C. Getting the court to order more than fixed costs

Q20. If a fast track hearing is to be decided in writing with another hearing to decide costs at a later date: 1. Can another statement of costs be filed? 2. Can a new or revised costs bundle be filed? 3. Does the fast track fixed trial cost apply to both hearings or to each hearing? 536

Q21. Can you/how do you get more than fixed costs? Can you give some guidance/authorities regarding when the court will order otherwise than fixed costs under CPR r.45 in a case where the fixed costs provisions should otherwise apply?
Is it possible for costs be assessed when requesting default judgment or are only fixed costs allowed pursuant to CPR r.45? 537

Chapter 8   Assessments of Costs and Payments on Account of Costs

Table of Cases

Table of Statutes

Table of Statutory Instruments

Introduction

In Chapter 1 of the 7th Edition of this work we stated that there were still   1–01
numerous issues connected with costs and funding generally and, more
particularly, connected with the 2013 Jackson/civil litigation reforms, to be
resolved by the Civil Procedure Rule Committee and the courts. At the time we
were looking forward to the coming into force of the Civil Liability Act 2018
and the Whiplash Injury Regulations. There was also the Fixed Recoverable
Costs Consultation which closed on 6 June 2019. What we had not anticipated was a speech by Sir Geoffrey Vos MR to the Association of Costs Lawyers
Annual Conference on the 25 November 2021.

Speech by Sir Geoffrey Vos MR

The MR began by saying   1–02

> *"The costs world is of growing importance in the civil justice system, but has been
> somewhat left to its own devices. I fear that costs has been seen by too many as
> something of a niche specialist activity. For my part, I feel that that approach is
> no longer possible."*

He continued that there were four main overarching developments:

> *"First, the rapidly advancing digital online civil justice system epitomised by the
> personal injury portal, handling some 600,000 cases per annum, the Whiplash
> portal, and the new Online Damages Claims system. Costs will not be immune
> from the welcome and necessary changes that digitisation brings.*
> *Secondly, the introduction of a new Guide to the Summary Assessment of Costs
> which came into force on 1 October 2021 . . . when I introduced the current
> Guide, I promised another review within 2 years. I have, however, already asked
> the Civil Justice Council to embark on a review of costs issues at all levels, includ-
> ing Guideline Hourly Rates.*
> *Thirdly, since Sir Terence Etherton MR asked Mr Justice Stephen Stewart to under-
> take his review of the Guide in 2019, there have been radical changes to ways of
> working in the legal profession, . . . Lawyers can now mostly work happily and
> effectively from home without needing an office, and undertake many court hear-
> ings and most client meetings successively on Zoom or Teams.*
> *Fourthly, the Government has just indicated that it intends to bring forward many
> of the remaining recommendations as to fixed recoverable costs made by Lord
> Justice Jackson in his report published in 2017. . ."*

Dealing with the new Guide to Summary Assessment the MR emphasised   1–03
that the guideline rates are not scale figures – they are guidelines; a starting
point; nothing more. And they are broad approximations. He thought some

attribute more significance to them. He concluded by saying that the GHR do not operate as a capping exercise. Rather, they provide a common starting point and a cross-check for busy judges when assessing costs.

The MR then turned his attention to the future:

> *"What the future holds for those specialising in costs within the civil justice system? So far as Guideline Hourly Rates are concerned, . . . they need to be updated annually or at least every two years . . . we should also look more closely at their regional focus now that many lawyers work from home and give advice by Zoom or Teams.*
>
> *. . . there is an immediate need for an holistic consideration of a number of inter-connected issues.*
>
> *First, the move from mostly face-to-face hearings to a mixture of video and remote hearings alongside some face-to-face hearings may affect the way we look at costs recovery in different situations.*
>
> *Secondly, . . . costs recovery will look very different in the online space, with the implementation of an entirely digital online justice system for civil . . . cases . . . the system that is currently being developed and implemented as part of the HMCTS Reform Programme . . . will have integrated mediated interventions at every stage and will be more accessible to litigants in person and provide greater access to justice.*
>
> *Thirdly, the government's decision to increase the applicability of fixed recoverable costs will have far-reaching effects on the kinds of cases where summary and detailed assessment is needed. . . . we need to look again at how the fixed recoverable costs regime (after its extension) interacts and harmonises with the old world of summary and detailed assessment by costs judges.*
>
> *Fourthly, . . . we should undoubtedly take another look at costs budgeting now that considerable experience of its pros and cons has been obtained by judges, costs judges, and practitioners alike . . .*
>
> *Fifthly, I have for some time been concerned about the seemingly unlimited costs incurred in lengthy cases in the Business and Property Courts and elsewhere in the system. I think that "money no object" litigation needs careful consideration in the modern environment, because:*
>
> *(i) it utilises scarce court resources that may be better devoted elsewhere;*
>
> *(ii) it is sometimes undertaken for overseas parties with no obvious connection with the jurisdiction;*
>
> *(iii) is not always undertaken proportionately; and*
>
> *(iv) it is not always driven by motivations that are compatible with the objectives of our justice system . . .*
>
> *. . . our judges should be the masters of our justice system, and should be astute to ensure that it is used for the ends of justice and not for any ulterior purposes.*
>
> *Sixthly, . . . the development and use of pre-action portals, artificial intelligence*

and the blockchain[1] requires us to take a fresh look at the costs of civil litigation more generally . . . the UK Jurisdiction Taskforce, that I chair, has developed its Digital Dispute Resolution Rules that apply English law to on-chain digital relationships and smart contracts. They are ground-breaking in that they allow for arbitral or expert dispute resolution in very short periods, arbitrators to implement decisions directly on-chain using a private key, and the optional anonymity of the parties. More importantly for present purposes, they show the way to more streamlined dispute resolution at lower cost in a digital era."

The MR concluded: 1–04

"It is, I think, extremely important that we take the opportunity now, to consider whether the ways in which we handle costs and costs shifting are fit for a modern justice system, delivering dispute resolution digitally . . . The way things are done in a digital justice system will be different. Indeed, . . . the disputes we resolve will be different. But lawyers will continue to be a valuable and important part of the system. They must ensure, though, that they add value. This means that lawyers and costs professionals will not support outdated practices that can be undertaken more cheaply and effectively with the aid of technology. They will be striving for technologically enabled systems that reduce costs for the litigants and expedite dispute resolution for all.
Proportionate, speedy and cost-effective dispute resolution is an admirable goal. It dramatically reduces economic drag caused by lengthy drawn out disputes, and improves the psychological health of litigants. In many fields the stress and upset caused by litigation reduces productivity and thereby harms the economy."

In answer to questions at the conference, the MR said:

- He agreed that costs law was complex. However, that was bad for litigation. It was not fit for purpose and change would come. The online rules would assist this. The costs position should be more straightforward. This does not mean that there will not be cases where costs will be assessed.
- If we don't change the way we do costs, then we will fail the system. The Civil Justice Council (CJC) Review is a big job. But he does not want it to be like previous reviews and take ages to implement and then, when implemented, be out of date. It needs to be agile.

Previous Reviews of Civil Justice and Costs
There have, of course, been previous attempts to improve practice and pro- 1–05
cedure as well as the way in which costs are dealt with. After the Second World War the government set up a committee on Supreme Court Practice and Procedure ("the Evershed Committee") and as a result of the recommendations made by that committee between 1951 and 1953 a wholesale revision of the rules was undertaken, culminating in the Rules of the Supreme Court

---

[1] A blockchain is a distributed database that is shared among the nodes of a computer network.

1965. The statutory instrument revoked all the previous rules and orders made since 1883 thus providing a fresh starting point. The Supreme Court Cost Rules 1959 were incorporated into the 1965 Rules (RSC Order 62). Order 62 itself, in common with all other Orders, underwent a certain amount of piecemeal amendment over the years but in 1986 as a result of a judgment by Sir Robert Megarry V-C who referred to it as "an ungodly jumble" the Order was completely revised.

The Royal Commission on Legal Services was set up in 1976 under the chairmanship of Lord Benson. The Commission reported in 1979 and made a total of 369 recommendations 26 of which related to lawyers' charges. The Commission was not instructed to question the rule that costs should follow the event. Its recommendations, essentially, were that costs should be awarded on a more generous basis than before and that the former bill of costs prescribed for submission to taxing masters should be simplified. A working party on the simplification of taxation (detailed assessment) (the Horne Report) resulted in the fundamental revision of RSC Order 62 with effect from 1 April 1986.

A further Civil Justice Review was established in February 1985 "to improve the machinery of civil justice in England and Wales by means of reforms in jurisdiction procedure and court administration and in particular to reduce delay, cost and complexity". The report was presented to Parliament by the Lord Chancellor in June 1988. The review body made 91 recommendations, although the report noted that the cost of litigation was often quite disproportionate to the amount involved in the claim, and that fear of costs was one of the greatest deterrents to using the courts, because of the uncertainty of knowing what the case was likely to cost. Only three recommendations relating specifically to costs were made:

(i)   there should be a single cost regime for the High Court and County Court;
(ii) solicitors and barristers should be encouraged and expected to provide information to the public by way of stated rates per case or per hour;
(iii) the prohibition on contingency fees and other forms of incentive scheme should be open to re-examination.

It is not clear why the review body did not address in greater depth the problems of costs but it seems that the hope was that by updating and streamlining procedures and making provision for small claims to be dealt with speedily in the County Court the problems in relation to costs would diminish.

The recommendations made by the review body in relation to costs were not in fact addressed until Lord Woolf undertook his Access to Justice Review giving his Final Report in July 1996. Lord Woolf's proposals came under further scrutiny from Sir Peter Middleton in his Review of Civil Justice and Legal Aid in 1997, which he carried out at the request of the Lord Chancellor, Lord Irvine. Lord Woolf's reforms addressed reforms of principle and reforms of practice; his intention was to reduce the scale of costs by controlling what was required of the parties in the conduct of proceedings. He wished to make the amount of costs more predictable and more proportionate to the nature of the dispute and to make the court's powers in respect of costs orders a more effective incentive for responsible behaviour and a more compelling deterrent against unreasonable behaviour. He felt that if litigants were themselves supplied with more information as to costs, they would exercise greater control over the expenses which were incurred by their lawyers on their behalf.

It was not until 26 April 1999 that the Civil Procedure Rules came into force. The Costs Rules stayed in force until 1 April 2013 when Sir Rupert Jackson's reforms came into force and this book came into being.

Professor Adrian Zuckerman has stated on a number of occasions[2] that every attempt to reform the law of costs has resulted in costs increasing. Perhaps, on this occasion, the outcome will be different.

Funding

2021 could perhaps be described as the year Damages Based Agreements   1–06
(DBAs) came to fruition. The key case of the year came early in 2021 with the Court of Appeal's decision in *Zuberi v Lexlaw Ltd*[3] and the positive news for those wishing to make more effective use of DBAs continued with that court's decision in *DAF Trucks Deutschland GmbH v Road Haulage Association Ltd (RH)* and *UK Trucks Claim Ltd (UKTC)*.[4] Whilst problems remain and it would still be preferable to see effective revision of the governing legislation, the potential to make effective use of DBAs without unnecessary risk of such agreements being held to be unenforceable has greatly increased since the last edition. These issues – and other developments in the area of funding – are considered in detail in **Ch.2**.

Costs Budgeting

The MR, in his speech appears to be echoing what Senior Costs Judge Gordon-   1–07
Saker said in his speech to the Costs Law Reports Conference on 23 September 2021:

> "*Costs management hit the headlines with the judgment of Master Davison in Smith v W Ford & Sons that "QB masters, Chancery masters and costs judges do not necessarily share this defendant's expressed confidence that costs budgeting controls costs better, or more effectively, than detailed assessment". It may be that the time has come to review the criteria for costs management. The government has decided to extend costs budgeting to heavy JRs. So costs budgeting is not going away. But is it needed in every multi-track case up to £10m?*"

Cavanagh J has expressed the view that it would be extremely unlikely in future that the pre-condition for making a costs capping order (CCO) in CPR

---

[2] See his book *Zuckerman on Civil Procedure* 4th Ed.
[3] [2021] EWCA Civ 16.
[4] [2021] EWCA Civ 299.

r.3.19(5)(c) (whether the risk that costs would be disproportionately incurred could be controlled by costs budgeting or by a detailed assessment) would be met, as costs budgeting was a more sophisticated and nuanced way of setting a costs figure than a CCO. In the particular case, 31 Malawian women who had been employed by a Malawian company to work on its plantations alleged that they had been raped or subjected to sexual assault and sexual harassment by male employees. The defendant was an English domiciled parent of the company. If the claimants succeeded, the likely level of damages was £310,000. The estimated total costs if the case proceeded to trial was in excess of £5.6 million. The defendant applied for a CCO limiting the recoverable future costs to £150,000. The application was refused. The court stated that the reasons for declining to impose a CCO were equally reasons for declining to impose a costs budget in the sum of £150,000.[5]

Costs budgeting is dealt with in **Ch.4.**

Settlement

1–08 The courts have been encouraging parties to engage in ADR for some years by imposing costs sanctions on parties who unreasonably refuse to mediate, even on those that are ultimately successful in the litigation. There is now a momentum growing for a re-evaluation of whether ADR should be compulsory. The view was expressed in *Halsey v Milton Keynes General NHS Trust*[6] that compulsory ADR would breach Art.6 of the European Convention on Human Rights but the CJC has looked at the issue in a recent report "Compulsory ADR" (June 2021)[7] and expressed a more nuanced view, taking account of recent ECtHR jurisprudence, as well as the fact that compulsory ADR is a feature of other legal systems within the Council of Europe and beyond.[8]

The CJC has invited consideration of the issue by the legislature or appellate courts as soon as possible. Sir Geoffrey Vos MR and Chair of the CJC has endorsed the report, which "opens the door to a significant shift towards earlier resolution of claims" and has asked the CJC to consider further how ADR can best be incorporated into HMCT's court reform programme for delivering online justice. In the future, it may no longer be apposite to describe dispute resolution as "alternative", the focus should be on "resolution" rather than "dispute".

ADR, as well as Part 36 and other settlement offers, are dealt with in **Ch.5.**

QOCS

1–09 Probably the most important decision under this heading is the Supreme Court's judgment in *Ho v Adelekun*,[9] reversing the Court of Appeal's decision in the same case, *Ho v Adelekun*.[10] The decision is considered in **Ch.6.**

---

[5] *Thomas v PGI Group Limited* [2021] EWHC 2776 (QB), Cavanagh J.
[6] EWCA Civ 576.
[7] *https://www.judiciary.uk/wp-content/uploads/2021/07/Civil-Justice-Council-Compulsory-ADR-report-1.pdf.*
[8] Italy, Ontario, Australia and Greece.
[9] [2021] UKSC 43.
[10] [2020] EWCA Civ 517.

Fixed Recoverable Costs

The Civil Procedure (Amendment No. 2) Rules 2021 amended the Civil Proce-   **1–10**
dure Rules 1998 (S.I. 1998/3132). The amendments give effect to, or are
consequential upon—

(a) changes to Part 26 of the Civil Procedure Rules regarding the alloca-
    tion of personal injury claims arising from road traffic accidents which
    occur on or after 31 May 2021 to the small claims track and fast track;
(b) new Practice Direction 27B: Claims Under the Pre-Action Protocol for
    Personal Injury Claims Below the Small Claims Limit in Road Traffic
    Accidents – Court Procedure; and
(c) the Pre-Action Protocol for Personal Injury Claims Below the
    Small Claims Limit in Road Traffic Accidents ("the RTA Small
    Claims Protocol").

The Whiplash Injury Regulations 2021 specify, by way of a tariff, the total
amount of damages for pain, suffering and loss of amenity that a court may
award for road traffic accident ("RTA") related whiplash injuries of up to two-
years duration and any minor psychological injuries suffered on the same
occasion. The Regulations permit the court to award a maximum uplift of
20% on those damages in exceptional circumstances.

These Regulations further specify the medical evidence that must be
provided before a regulated person (defined in s.9 of the Civil Liability Act
2018) may invite a payment in settlement of, or offer payment to settle, or
make or accept a payment in settlement of, an RTA related whiplash injury
claim.

The minutes of the Civil Procedure Rule Committee for November 2021
record that Robert Wright (Ministry of Justice (MoJ) Costs Policy) explained:

> "[T]hat the Government published its response to Extending Fixed Recoverable
> Costs in Civil Cases on 6th September 2021, which followed the 2019 consulta-
> tion on the recommendations in Sir Rupert Jackson's report on FRC in 2017.
> The overall intention is to define the scope and parameters of FRC (and the asso-
> ciated changes), while outlining the new procedures that will ensure cases are
> appropriately allocated and managed within the new FRC architecture . . .
> The parts of the CPR of particular relevance to the extension of FRC are, broadly,
> in (i) Part 26 (Case Management, Preliminary Stage), (ii) Part 28 (The Fast
> Track), (iii) Part 29 (The Multi-track), and (iv) Part 45 (Fixed Costs). Other parts
> of the CPR inevitably also apply, including certain Practice Directions associated
> with these rules.
> Given the complexity of costs related reforms . . . the policy view is to commence
> a complete re-draft of CPR Part 45 to simplify and streamline the rules. This
> should ensure that the objectives of clarity and proportionality in civil litigation
> are appropriately reflected in the rules . . .
> MoJ are also considering certain policy issues, as outlined in the consulta-
> tion response, including whether further changes need to be made in respect of

> *recoverable Disbursements and Qualified One Way Costs Shifting (QOCS), in order to ensure the integrity of the extended FRC regime . . .*
> *The intention is to implement the extension of FRC in October 2022 and the MoJ is keen to work in collaboration with the CPRC to ensure the smooth delivery of these reforms."*

The Minutes noted that the CJC was considering further work on costs (presumably the review required by the MR), but this should not delay the Fixed Recoverable Costs (FRC) reforms.

1–11   The implementation of the remaining recommendations as to FRC will have the effect of introducing fixed recoverable costs for all fast track cases worth up to £25,000 and most cases valued at between £25,000 and £100,000 in an extended fast track. This will, therefore, significantly reduce the number of cases to which both Guideline Hourly Rates and the costs management regime will apply.

FRC are dealt with in **Ch.7**.

The government has also indicated a desire to extend the use of FRC in other cases not covered in its consultation and response, such as clinical negligence claims and immigration judicial reviews. There may therefore be further developments. Clinical negligence cases were excluded from the government's consultation, as the government had already asked the Civil Justice Council to consider a bespoke process for low value clinical negligence cases. We await further developments in that regard. As to judicial review, the government proposes costs budgeting for all "heavy" judicial review cases (where the costs of a party are likely to exceed £100,000). Courts will have the discretion to make a costs management order, either on their own or on the application of either party.

Guideline Hourly Rates

1–12   The CJC's Final Report on guideline hourly rates (GHR), prepared by Mr Justice Stewart and his working group was published on 30 July 2021. The details and implications of the Report are dealt with in **Ch.8**.

Solicitor-client costs

1–13   The reforms proposed by Sir Rupert Jackson, and enacted in part in 2013 and subsequently, did not directly address the question of solicitor-client costs. However, for a variety of reasons, they have had a considerable knock-on effect. 2021 saw the continuation of the growth in solicitor-client disputes, particularly relating to the deductions of success fees and unrecovered costs from damages in low value personal injury litigation. Hanging over all of this in 2021 was the pending appeal in the case of *Belsner v Cam Legal Services Ltd*, with Mr Justice Lavender's important judgment having been handed down in late 2020. The second appeal in that case was due to be heard by the Court of Appeal in February 2022, but was adjourned to be heard by the 31 July 2022 on the second day when the Court of Appeal decided that the ramifications of the case were more profound than originally appeared. The area is undoubtedly one which is likely to see further important developments in 2022 and these matters are considered further in **Ch.9**.

The Department of Health and Social Care is seeking views on proposals to **1–14** introduce a mandatory FRC scheme for lower value clinical negligence claims regarding medical treatment provided by NHS, non-profit and private healthcare providers in England and Wales. The aim of the proposed scheme is to enable more claims to be resolved quickly, at lower, more proportionate cost and before going to court. The consultation runs until 11.45 pm on 24 April 2022.

The Civil Procedure (amendment) Rules 2022 (SI 2022/101), come into force on 6 April 2022.

The Rules amend the Civil Procedure Rules 1998 (S.I. 1998/3132) by—

- amending Part 1 to remove the word "new" from the opening words which describe the Rules as a "new procedural code";
- amending Part 2 to revise the definition of "filing" and insert a new definition of "MyHMCTS" in relation to the introduction of a system to allow notices of change of solicitor (as defined in rule 6.2(d)) to be filed at the court online. Amendments are also made to CPR r.42.2(3) to accommodate this new online system;
- substituting Part 10 with a revised Part on acknowledgment of service;
- substituting Part 12 with a revised Part on default judgment;
- amending Part 26 to increase from £1,000 to £1,500 the small claims track limit for non-road traffic accident related personal injury claims and making consequential amendments to Parts 16, 27 and 45;
- amending Part 39 in response to the judgement in *Brearley v Higgs & Sons (A Firm)* [2021] EWHC 1342 (Ch) to extend the breadth of rule 39.2(4) to bring all instances in which the court may exercise a jurisdiction to anonymise under the same procedural provision;
- amending Part 47 to exclude from the powers of an authorised costs officer the power to impose a sanction for delay in requesting detailed assessment proceedings (the power to impose a sanction for delay in commencing detailed assessment proceedings is already excluded);
- amending Parts 52 and 54 in consequence of new Practice Direction 54D (*Planning Court claims and appeals to the Planning Court*), which consolidates provisions to be found elsewhere in practice directions regarding the Planning Court;
- amending Part 65 to include provision for ensuring that the respondent is made aware of the opportunity to obtain legal representation and to apply for legal aid.

The UK Supreme Court has refused permission to appeal two costs cases: *Lejonvarn v Burgess* on 13 December 2021 (Permission to appeal be refused because the application does not raise an arguable point of law. The application is totally without merit. The respondent should be awarded her costs on the indemnity basis.); and *Deepchand v Sooben* on 15 December 2021, (permission to appeal be refused because the application does not raise an arguable point of law of general public importance.)

CHAPTER 2

Funding Litigation

Introduction

The introduction of the Legal Aid, Sentencing and Punishment of Offenders   2–01
Act 2012 (LASPO) and associated secondary legislation has had a significant
impact on the funding of litigation. Some aspects, in particular the greater
restrictions on availability of public funding, are beyond the scope of this
section.

This section will instead focus on the changes to funding arrangements
available to litigants, in particular conditional fee agreements (CFAs),
damages-based agreements (DBAs) and policies of after-the-event insurance
(ATE).

Lord Justice Jackson's Final Report contained detailed and inter-related proposals for the means of funding litigation. These included:

- emphasising the benefits of public funding and stressing the "vital necessity" to avoid any further cutbacks in its availability or eligibility;[1]
- recommendations for the encouragement of take up of before-the-event
  insurance in certain circumstances;[2]
- and perhaps most notably; a recommendation for the abolition of between
  the parties recovery of ATE premiums,[3] allied to the introduction of qualified one-way costs shifting for certain litigants; and a recommendation
  for the abolition of the between the parties recoverability of success fees
  in CFAs,[4] in turn allied to a 10% increase in awards for general damages,
  the enhancement of Part 36 benefits for claimants and the capping of
  success fees chargeable by solicitors in personal injury claims.

Whilst, broadly, Jackson LJ's package of reforms in relation to CFAs, ATE insurance, and QOCS was adopted, his call for public funding not to be further
restricted was not, and the reforms of funding introduced did not always
follow his precise recommendations.

This can be seen in particular in relation to QOCS, where Jackson LJ's proposal for a means-tested model similar to that applicable to public funding
costs protection was not adopted,[5] but also in relation to DBAs, where the
reforms introduced have not had the desired effect in practice of making a
new form of funding widely available to litigants.

---

[1] Final Report, p.70.
[2] Final Report, p.79.
[3] Final Report, p.89.
[4] Final Report, p.112.
[5] For further details, see Ch.6 on QOCS.

The transitional provisions in relation to the abolition of between the parties' recovery of success fees and ATE premiums gave rise to problems of their own. These became particularly apparent in circumstances where, for one reason or another, there was some need to vary or change the funding arrangement after 1 April 2013 in circumstances where that arrangement was first entered into prior to that date, or in other related cases where a claimant might appear to be caught between the "old" and "new" regimes. This, in turn has had a significant impact on questions relating to the availability of QOCS, which has only added to the uncertainty in this area arising out of considerable argument over the precise application and interpretation of the QOCS provisions.

These issues will be considered further below.

In February 2019, the MoJ published its review of the implementation of Pt 2 of LASPO. The review did not encompass matters such as costs management, proposed changes to fixed recoverable costs or areas where the LASPO reforms were yet to be or have not yet been implemented (such as privacy and publication claims or mesothelioma claims).

It was clear from that review[6] that the Government considered Pt 2 of LASPO to be achieving its principal aim of reducing the cost of civil litigation and that substantial revision to those reforms is unlikely at this stage, though the door was at least left open for a review of the position in relation to DBAs. In that regard, considerable work has been undertaken by way of an independent review, commissioned by the MoJ and led by Nicholas Bacon QC and Professor Rachael Mulheron QC, including the publication by them of a draft set of revised regulations[7] and, in June 2021, following a consultation process (and following the *Zuberi* decision[8]), the production of a Supplementary Report which has been submitted to the Ministry of Justice for further consideration. Whilst the Court of Appeal's important decision in *Zuberi* may have provided something of a case-law based cure for at least some of the perceived problems with the regulations and may have resulted in a material increase in the use of DBAs, it is not an adequate substitute for properly drafted and transparent regulations.

The precise details of the Bacon/Mulheron review are beyond the scope of this work, at least unless and until their proposals reach the stage of being adopted by the MoJ as draft legislation. However, the project has very widespread support, including from Sir Rupert Jackson. Whilst there remain some issues to be debated, not least because of the parameters within which the project had to be conducted, the need for reform of the present regulations seems clear and the very detailed and careful work by Mr Bacon QC and Professor Mulheron QC seeks to resolve many of the perceived problems. It

---

[6] *https://assets.publishing.service.gov.uk/government/uploads/system/uploads/attachment_data/file/777039/post-implementation-review-of-part-2-of-laspo.pdf.*
[7] *https://www.qmul.ac.uk/law/research/impact/dbarp/.*
[8] *Zuberi v Lexlaw Ltd* [2021] EWCA Civ 16.

will hopefully be met with a similar commitment by the MoJ to press ahead with such reforms.

Further changes may come in those areas identified above which have been expressly left outside the scope of the review.

Conditional fee agreements

Section 44 of LASPO amended s.58A(6) of the Courts and Legal Services Act 1990 to provide that a costs order may no longer include provision requiring another party to pay part of the successful party's success fee. This was a simple reversal of the position prior to 1 April 2013.

Whilst certain changes were made to s.58 in relation to the specific requirements for a CFA in personal injury claims,[9] the basic circumstances in which a CFA could be entered into, its basic requirements and the type of cases where such an agreement was lawful were not amended by LASPO.

Accordingly, the effect of the amendment to s.58A(6) was apparently simple. Where success fees had formerly been recoverable in principle between the parties, they are now no longer recoverable where new CFAs are entered into in respect of proceedings, save in relation to a limited, and diminishing, category of excepted cases. Since s.58(A)(6) was brought into force in relation to publication and privacy proceedings with effect from the 6 April 2019, the category of excepted proceedings where success fees continue to be recoverable for new claims is now a category of one – mesothelioma claims. In all other claims where a CFA with a success fee is entered into, such success fees will have to be paid by the client, with no prospect of any between the parties' recovery.

It is perhaps worth noting at this point that this does not necessarily mean that it will always be impermissible to recover a success fee in litigation. The case of *Hirachand*[10] illustrates that in certain, limited, circumstances a success fee, or at least part of the same, may be recoverable as part of "reasonable financial provision" from a deceased's estate under the Inheritance (Provision for Family & Dependents) Act 1975 or, in financial relief proceedings, under s.25 of the Matrimonial Causes Act 1973. This is essentially on the basis that in such cases the court is assessing a party's financial needs and must take into account that party's debts. A success fee (as with other legal costs) may be part of that debt which must then be taken into account in ensuring adequate provision. This does not breach the legislative policy enshrined in s.58A(6) since the success fee is not being recovered as an item of costs under a costs order. Having noted this potential situation, however, the remainder of this text will work on the assumption of the more general position which is that success fees are not recoverable post LASPO as an item of between the parties costs save, now, in mesothelioma claims.

2–02

---

[9] These are the "specified claims" under s.58(4A)(b) by virtue of art.2 of the Conditional Fee Agreements Order 2013 (SI 2013/689).

[10] *Hirachand v Hirachand* [2021] EWCA Civ 1498.

It is important to note that the fundamental principle in s.58(1) of the Act, that a CFA which does not satisfy all of the conditions applicable to it by virtue of s.58 shall be unenforceable, remains unchanged.

Equally, Lord Justice Jackson's clear recommendation that the indemnity principle should be abrogated,[11] at least in part to limit the scope for satellite litigation in relation to issues of enforceability of retainers, was rejected. The call was repeated in early 2015,[12] and in September 2015 the Civil Justice Council Working Group on DBA Reform made a reasoned recommendation for its abolition, at least in the context of DBAs, but recognised that this was closely tied to the question of the abolition of the principle more generally, which was "a thorny policy issue" and one where the Government has shown a marked disinclination to intervene.[13] These calls remain unheeded and at present there does not appear to be any intention to abrogate the indemnity principle (save to the extent already seen in relation to fixed costs, which has resulted from judicial development through case law rather than legislative intervention).

The DBA Reform Project's proposals appear to recognise that the indemnity principle is here to stay for the foreseeable future. The adoption of a "success fee" model in the redrafted regulations produced both by the CJC and the Bacon/Mulheron review identified above (that is to say a model where the solicitor, under a DBA, is entitled to recoverable profit costs, plus a DBA "payment" on top, the latter not being recoverable from the opponent) is, in part at least, expressly adopted in order to try to mitigate challenges to the DBA by reference to the indemnity principle.

However, whilst the indemnity principle appears to be here to stay, and remains a powerful argument to prevent costs recovery in appropriate circumstances, in some areas, at least, its relevance will be diminished in light of the proposed, but delayed, expansion of the scheme of fixed costs (addressed in **Ch.7**). It is now trite law that the indemnity principle does not apply to a between the parties claim for profit costs which are themselves fixed by the CPR.[14]

Such fixed costs regimes aside, a failure to comply with the requirements of s.58, including the post-April 2013 requirements imposed by the new s.58(4A) and (4B) in relation to personal injury CFAs, will leave the litigant, and their solicitor, exposed to the well-rehearsed arguments that the agreement is unenforceable and that accordingly no costs under the CFA may be recovered between the parties. 2021 saw the essentially unsuccessful appeal from yet another reported example of a case where the CFA (in fact three CFAs) were

[11] Final Report, Ch.5 para.4.1.
[12] *http://www.judiciary.gov.uk/wp-content/uploads/2014/10/litigation-post-jackson-world.pdf.*
[13] CJC, *The Damages-Based Agreements Reform Project—"Drafting and Policy Issues"*, 2 September 2015, Ch.23.
[14] See *Butt v Nizami* [2006] EWHC 159 (QB); [2006] 1 W.L.R. 3307, as approved in *Kilby v Gawith* [2008] EWCA Civ 812; [2009] 1 W.L.R. 853 and a number of further subsequent Court of Appeal decisions.

held to be unenforceable for breaches of s.58 of the 1990 Act, with the effect that the solicitor's profit costs were unrecoverable from the client.[15]

The removal of the between the parties recovery of success fees does not appear to have resulted in a material reduction in the appetite or ability of paying parties to take such points. For the reasons already identified, there remain strong reasons to pursue such arguments where parties are acting on CFAs and DBAs and there is at least some reason to believe that there has not been compliance with the relevant legislation. However, one indirect consequence of the fact that solicitors are now expected to look to their clients for payment of success fees has been that the client has an increased interest in pursuing arguments as to enforceability which, until the 2013 reforms, had primarily been the business of paying party opponents. The period post-April 2013 has seen a significant rise in solicitor-client disputes, particularly in relation to lower value and personal injury claims, often concerning challenges to success fees and other deductions from clients' damages. It is in the nature of such litigation that once challenges are brought on one aspect of the solicitor's fees, additional disputes, including as to the enforceability of retainers, tend to arise. These issues are considered further in **Ch.9** dealing with the effects of the Jackson Reforms on solicitor-client costs.

The final point to note in relation to issues of general application is that s.58(5) of the 1990 Act remains untrammelled. This is the section that provides that where the CFA is a non-contentious business agreement under s.57 of the Solicitors Act 1974, s.58(1) does not render it unenforceable. The scope of this was considered in detail by the then Senior Costs Judge in 2010 in an authoritative judgment[16] and the ability to use CFAs (and now DBAs) which are not subject to the restrictions of ss.58 and 58AA for what might be termed non-contentious business is a valuable option, particularly in the commercial sphere and particularly in light of the problems, referred to below, in relation to the implementation of DBAs. The drafting and use of such agreements, however, is an area which needs to be approached carefully and is considered further in **Ch.9**.

Arguments as to the enforceability of CFAs, whether pre- or post-LASPO, arising out of poor or unclear drafting continue to arise. 2018 saw two Court of Appeal decisions giving helpful guidance on the correct approach to construction of such documents.[17] In 2019, Kelyn Bacon QC, sitting as a judge of the High Court, held that a CFA which did not expressly make clear that it was not a contentious business agreement was indeed a CBA. As such, the solicitor could not bring a debt claim in relation to the fees under the CBA without first subjecting the CFA to scrutiny under s.65 of the Solicitors Act 1974 as to whether it was fair and reasonable and should be enforced.[18] The court

---

[15] *The Winros Partnership v Global Energy Horizons Corporation* [2021] EWHC 3410 (Ch).
[16] *Tel-Ka Talk Ltd v Revenue and Customs Commissioners* [2011] S.T.C. 497; [2011] S.T.I. 267.
[17] *Malone v Birmingham Community NHS Trust* [2018] EWCA Civ 1376; [2018] 3 Costs L.R. 627 and *Radford v Frade* [2018] EWCA Civ 119; [2018] 1 Costs L.R. 59.
[18] *Healys LLP v Partridge & Partridge* [2019] EWHC 2471 (Ch); [2019] Costs L.R. 1515.

declined to comment on whether an express statement that the CFA was not a CBA (as is contained in the Law Society standard model personal injury CFA) would have been effective. This issue continued to trouble the courts in 2021 – and once again, the fact that it remains such a difficult issue to identify whether something is or is not a CBA, which is fundamental in then identifying what rights the client has, is a further example of the need for reform in this area. *Cardium Law Ltd*[19] is another example of a CFA being considered to be a CBA. In *Acupay Systems LLC v Stephenson Harwood LLP*[20], Master Leonard rejected an argument that a CFA was a CBA on the essential basis that, whilst following *Wilson*[21] the fact that the description a document gives itself is not necessarily determinative, where the parties have clearly agreed that the CFA is not a CBA such an agreement may – and in this case did – determine the issue. These issues are considered further in **Ch.9**.

However, the issues in those cases and issues generally concerning the enforceability (or not) of CFAs are unrelated to the implementation of the LASPO reforms and are not considered further here, save to note that in the case of *Radford*[22] the important Privy Council decision of *Kellar*[23]—which held that where a party changes funding arrangements after the making of a costs order, the party paying the costs cannot be held to any new arrangement which increases their costs liability—was affirmed.[24]

Transitional provisions

2–03   The transitional provision provided for by s.44(6) states that:

> *"The amendment made by [the subsection] does not prevent a costs order including provision in relation to a success fee payable by a person ("P") under a conditional fee agreement entered into before [1 April 2013] if—*
>
> (a) *the agreement was entered into specifically for the purposes of the provision to P of advocacy or litigation services in connection with the matter that is the subject of the proceedings in which the costs order is made, or*
>
> (b) *advocacy or litigation services were provided to P under the agreement in connection with that matter before the commencement day."*

This ensured that the court retains its discretion to allow a between the parties success fee where the CFA was entered into before 1 April 2013. The one proviso is that the CFA relates to a specific matter which is the subject of the proceedings before the court or advocacy or litigation services were in fact provided under the CFA before 1 April 2013.[25] Certain issues that have arisen

---

[19] *Cardium law Ltd v Kew Holdings Ltd* [2021] EWHC 1299 (Ch).

[20] SCCO, 25 June 2021.

[21] *Wilson v the Specter Partnership* [2007] EWHC 133 (Ch).

[22] *Radford v Frade* [2018] EWCA Civ 119; [2018] 1 Costs L.R. 59.

[23] *Kellar v Williams* [2004] UKPC 30; [2005] 4 Costs L.R. 559.

[24] In that regard see also the first instance judgment of Master James in *Dial Partners LLP v Eastern Airways International Ltd* unreported 16 January 2018 SCCO.

[25] The latter part of this provision appears primarily directed to the position in relation to collective conditional fee agreements (CCFAs). Such an agreement may have been entered into prior to 1 April 2013, but may cover all claims of

in relation to the transitional provisions are addressed under the heading "Implementation issues" below.

Mesothelioma claims

In addition, s.48 of the Act contained a specific saving provision which sus-   2–04
pended the implementation of s.44 of the Act (and s.46 in relation to ATE premiums) in relation to diffuse mesothelioma claims, thereby allowing for the continued between the parties recovery of success fees (and ATE premiums) in such claims. Section 48 expressly provides that ss.44 and 46 cannot be introduced in relation to such claims until the Lord Chancellor has carried out a review and published a report into the effect of those sections on such claims.

On 4 December 2013, following such a review, the Government announced that ss.44 and 46 were to be brought into force and the exception was to be removed and success fees (and ATE premiums) would cease to be recoverable between the parties in such claims. However, in October 2014 the High Court[26] ruled that the consultation process leading to that decision had been flawed and that the decision had to be quashed, leading to the Government announcing that there would be a further review of whether or not to remove the exception. That review was due to take place "towards the end of" the period to April 2018,[27] but does not appear yet to have been completed. What that review will say if and when it takes place and, accordingly, if and when the mesothelioma exception will be lifted, remains to be seen. Much time has now passed and at present, there appears to be no ministerial intention to implement ss.44 and 46 in relation to mesothelioma claims. As noted, the post-implementation review of Pt.2 of LASPO expressly did not deal with this issue.

Publication and privacy proceedings

Implementation of s.44 was also "suspended" in relation to publication and   2–05
privacy proceedings and insolvency proceedings.[28] In respect of publication and privacy proceedings, this was intended to be only until further, related, reforms, including the possible extension of QOCS to such claims, initially anticipated in October 2013 and then April 2014, were introduced.

---

a particular type a solicitor is undertaking for a particular client or funder. The agreement may therefore cover claims in respect of matters which had not even arisen prior to 1 April 2013. If the transitional provision simply focused on the date of the funding arrangement, the CCFA could be used to ensure the ongoing recovery of additional liabilities even in respect of post-April 2013 instructions. Accordingly, in such circumstances, it is not the date of the CCFA which is relevant (because the CCFA did not relate to a specific matter which is the subject of proceedings) but rather whether the legal representative had started to provide services in respect of that specific matter before 1 April 2013. This point appears to have been overlooked, or at least not clearly addressed, by the Court of Appeal in *Catalano v Epsley-Tyas Development Group Ltd* [2017] EWCA Civ 1132; [2017] 4 Costs L.R. 769 at [29].
[26] *R. (Whitson) v Secretary of State for Justice* [2014] EWHC 3044 (Admin); [2015] 1 Costs L.R. 35.
[27] Written Statement by Lord Faulks, Minister for Civil Justice, HLWS410, 17 December 2015.
[28] See Legal Aid, Sentencing and Punishment of Offenders Act 2012 (Commencement No.5 and Saving Provision) Order 2013 (SI 2013/77) (which also contains a secondary and essentially superfluous provision also suspending operation of the sections in relation to diffuse mesothelioma claims).

However, the position remained under review.

There was a pressing need for a settled position to be reached in relation to the recoverability of additional liabilities in such claims. It was in precisely such a claim that the European Court of Human Rights held, over eleven years ago, that the exposure on the part of a media defendant to such additional liabilities constituted a breach of art.10 of the Convention.[29]

Although the Supreme Court, in *Coventry v Lawrence*,[30] rejected a challenge in a non-media claim that additional liabilities incurred under pre-April 2013 CFAs and ATE breached art.6 or art.1 of the First Protocol to the Convention, the continued recoverability of such additional liabilities in media claims unsurprisingly provoked fresh challenge on the basis of art.10.

2–06   In three cases heard together, *Times Newspapers Ltd v Flood; Miller v Associated Newspapers Ltd; Frost v MGN Ltd*,[31] the Supreme Court dismissed three newspaper publishers' appeals against the recoverability of additional liabilities. However, the terms in which they did so were far from an endorsement of the present regime. In *Flood* and *Miller*, the Government appears to have only been saved from the very real risk of finding that, as a general rule, a requirement for a publisher to pay a success fee and ATE premium would breach the publisher's art.10 rights by virtue of the Government not being a party to the appeals.

On an individual basis, in *Miller* and *Flood,* any such breach would have had to be balanced against the individual claimants' rights under art.1 of the First Protocol, given the legitimate expectation they had that they could rely on the existing statutory provisions as to recoverability. That art.1 right would have trumped the art.10 breach (but would not, of course, have resolved the position as between the Government and the publishers). In the *Frost* case, MGN's conduct in illegally obtaining the relevant information in the first place negated any weight to be attached to the publisher's art.10 rights.

Miller and *Flood* therefore contained both an endorsement of the ECHR decision in *MGN Ltd v UK* and a clear warning that the continuation of the present system was likely to breach the Convention.

Article 10 aside, whilst *Coventry* appears to have largely disposed of the art.6 point, there may be issues, in particular in relation to those instances where between the parties recoverability has been preserved post-April 2013, where arguments in this regard remain. Moreover, whether the ECHR would agree with the Supreme Court's analysis, particularly given its decision in the *Naomi Campbell* case,[32] if given the opportunity, must be open to argument and therefore, whilst parties are likely to be very wary of further challenges on this ground, they cannot be entirely ruled out.

2–07   By virtue of the Legal Aid, Sentencing and Punishment of Offenders Act 2012 (Commencement No.13) Order 2018 (SI 2018/1287), with effect from

---

[29] *MGN Ltd v UK* [2011] 1 Costs L.O. 84; [2011] E.M.L.R. 20.
[30] *Coventry v Lawrence* [2015] UKSC 50; [2015] 1 W.L.R. 3485.
[31] *Times Newspapers Ltd v Flood; Miller v Associated Newspapers Ltd; Frost v MGN Ltd* [2017] UKSC 33; [2017] 1 W.L.R. 1415.
[32] *MGN Ltd v UK* [2011] 1 Costs L.O. 84; (2011) 53 E.H.R.R. 5.

the 6 April 2019, s.44 of LASPO (but not s.46 in relation to ATE insurance – see further below) was brought into force in respect of publication and privacy proceedings. This therefore had the effect that success fees are no longer recoverable in relation to publication and privacy proceedings where the CFA was entered into on or after 6 April 2019, but that the premiums for policies of ATE insurance remain recoverable (subject to assessment). It is therefore a hybrid of the position that applies generally under LASPO in other cases (where neither success fees nor ATE are recoverable) and that which applied pre-LASPO (where both were). The 2018 ministerial statement which accompanied the reform noted that the ATE exception was likely to remain in place "for the time being" on the basis that "after the event insurance discourages weaker cases as these are unlikely to be insured". This suggests that the MoJ perceives the ATE market in such claims to work in a more robust way, exercising a greater degree of scrutiny of the merits of such claims on an individual claim basis, than was the case with the mass market provision of ATE in personal injury claims prior to April 2013.

Costs shifting will remain the norm in publication and privacy proceedings and there will be no QOCS type regime introduced.

It remains unclear whether these amendments will satisfy the concerns identified in the cases referred to above. In particular, it will be important to see how the courts approach the assessment of ATE premiums. On the basis of the present legislation, such assessment is governed by the pre-April 2013 case law and rules, since an ATE premium in a publication and privacy case is treated as a pre-commencement funding arrangement (PCFA) pursuant to CPR r.48.2. No specific new provisions have been introduced.

This is in contrast to the other main area where ATE premiums remain recoverable, namely the limited recoverability permitted in relation to clinical negligence claims pursuant to the Recovery of Costs Insurance Premiums in Clinical Negligence Proceedings (No.2) Regulations 2013. In that circumstance, the Court of Appeal held back in 2017 that such premiums are subject to the "new" post-April 2013 test of proportionality, though unfortunately its call for the Civil Procedure Rule Committee to issue guidance as to recoverability appears not to have been heeded.[33]

If the recoverability of ATE premiums in publication and privacy claims is left to the pre-April 2013 case law, there is likely to be further scope for argument as to whether such a provision infringes the right to free speech in light of the cases referred to above. Further, whilst transitional provisions are always necessary where substantial procedural reform takes place, it is unsatisfactory that the ongoing recoverability of ATE premiums in such cases will continue to be governed by rules which have been revoked for all other purposes.

---

[33] *Peterborough & Stamford Hospitals NHS Trust v McMenemy* [2017] EWCA Civ 1941; [2018] 1 W.L.R. 2685.

Insolvency proceedings

2–08   In respect of insolvency proceedings, the implementation was originally intended to be postponed until April 2015 only. However, it was further suspended pending further consideration of the "appropriate way forward" and was finally removed by virtue of the Legal Aid, Sentencing and Punishment of Offenders Act 2012 (Commencement No.12) Order 2016 (SI 2016/345). Sections 44 and 46 of the 2012 Act were therefore brought into effect in relation to insolvency proceedings with effect from the 6 April 2016.

Where a CFA is entered into or an ATE policy is taken out in relation to insolvency proceedings on or after that date, the additional liability is not recoverable between the parties.

2–09   It should, in any event, be noted that the insolvency exception was a narrow one and only applied to officeholders or companies in administration bringing proceedings under the Insolvency Act 1986—see the Legal Aid, Sentencing and Punishment of Offenders Act 2012 (Commencement No.5 and Saving Provisions) Order 2013 (SI 2013/77). Other cases which might fall within a general description of "insolvency" claims did not benefit from the exception and were subject to the general removal of between the parties recoverability of additional liabilities—see *Re Hartmann Capital*.[34]

Such (now very) limited exceptions aside, therefore, the key point remains that where the CFA was entered into before the respective commencement dates for the types of proceedings concerned (1 April 2013 for the majority), the success fee continues to be recoverable in principle. If entered into on or after that date the success fee is irrecoverable from the paying party.

Personal injury claims—additional requirements

2–10   Section 44 of LASPO amended ss.58 and 58A of the Courts and Legal Services Act 1990 to impose additional conditions on CFAs, including the requirement that in certain classes of case, primarily personal injury claims (but for the time being excluding mesothelioma claims), the success fee does not exceed a maximum limit expressed as a percentage of certain types of damages.[35]

There is a strange circularity in the Conditional Fee Agreements Order 2013 ("the 2013 Order") in that the types of cases in respect of which the cap on the success fee imposed by s.58(4)(c) applies—personal injury claims—are expressly specified in the Order (see art.4). However, art.6 provides that art.4[36] does not apply to publication, privacy and insolvency proceedings. Given that they are not specified in art.4, art.4 could not apply to them in any event, so this part of art.6 serves no purpose. It is assumed that art.6 was phrased in this way in anticipation of the success fee cap possibly being extended to cover other proceedings (in particular, mesothelioma proceedings), if and

---

[34] *Re Hartmann Capital* [2015] EWHC 1514 (Ch); [2015] Bus. L.R. 983.
[35] As set out in the Conditional Fee Agreements Order 2013 (SI 2013/689).
[36] And art.5, which sets the maximum percentage success fee in cases covered by art.5.

when success fees in such claims are no longer recoverable between the parties (though given that such claims could then simply be specified under art.4, the wording of art.6(2) remains something of a mystery).

As noted above, the insolvency "exception" was lifted with effect from the 6 April 2016 and the publication and privacy exception with effect from the 6 April 2019. However, neither of these sets of proceedings have been added to the list under art.4 and therefore, as with all proceedings which may be the subject of a CFA other than personal injury claims, the only statutory limitation on the success fee that may be specified as payable by the client under a CFA in proceedings other than personal injury proceedings is that the percentage success fee payable by the client cannot exceed 100% maximum of the fees otherwise chargeable. There is no other "cap" on the success fee that may be charged.

For a claim involving personal injury, the key restriction in relation to a post-April 2013 CFA is contained in art.5 of the 2013 Order, which must be read in conjunction with s.58(4B) of the 1990 Act.

The success fee in any such agreement must be limited to a maximum of 25% of specified classes of damages awarded in the proceedings, in respect of proceedings at first instance. Note, the express reference in s.58(4B)(b) is to damages "awarded" and not to damages actually recovered.

The specified classes of damages are general damages for pain, suffering and loss of amenity and damages for pecuniary loss, other than future pecuniary loss, in both cases net of any sums recoverable as CRU (Compensation Recovery) (art.5(2)).

Accordingly, under such a CFA, the success fee, which cannot be recovered between the parties, cannot exceed 25% of the damages for general damages and past pecuniary loss (net of CRU).

It is important not to confuse the cap on the quantum of the success fee **2–11** with the percentage of the success fee itself. The maximum percentage success fee, that is to say the maximum percentage by which the solicitors' base fees may be multiplied, remains at 100%, in all claims where a CFA is permissible, including personal injury claims. The 25% cap operates as a financial limit on how much of the success fee the client may be charged and is an additional limitation which applies in personal injury claims only.

If the amount of damages for general damages and past loss awarded is sufficiently high, or the amount of base fees to which the success fee is to be applied, or the percentage success fee itself is sufficiently low, then the full success fee may be payable, because it is less than the cap. Where, however, the success fee calculated at the applicable percentage on the base fees payable under the agreement exceeds 25% of the prescribed damages, then the amount of the success fee must be limited accordingly if the CFA is to be enforceable.

The interaction of the maximum limit on the percentage success fee (100%) with the separate cap on the maximum fee chargeable gives rise to a risk of error, particularly in relation to CFAs which cover appeal proceedings.

This is because, under art.5(1)(b) of the 2013 Order, the cap on the maximum success fee is lifted from 25% to 100% in relation to proceedings other than at first instance. It is important to note that this is still a cap. It is merely that the effect of the cap in this situation is that the maximum success fee is limited to the full amount of the net damages for general damages and past loss, rather than only 25% of that sum. This 100% (of specified damages) cap is separate and distinct from the 100% (of base fees) limit on the success fee itself—though the presence of two separate limiting percentages on the success fee in the applicable statutory provisions has, unsurprisingly, led to some confusion and presents a clear drafting risk. It also creates difficulties of explanation for clients, particularly less sophisticated ones with less experience of legal matters. As discussed in **Ch.9**, one of the parallel developments in the years since 2013 has been the growing judicial emphasis on the concept of "informed consent" in the solicitor-client relationship. The full implications of CFAs already create difficulties in this regard and the inclusion of caps and, in particular, of a second cap for different types of proceedings referring to a different percentage, will not make the job of explaining these matters any easier, with consequent risks for both solicitor and client.

2–12   As a matter of practice, it would appear that many practitioners have chosen to ignore the ability to have a higher cap on the success fee where the CFA covers appellate proceedings. This is no doubt because of the concerns about ensuring that the agreement is fully compliant with both limitations where it covers both first instance and appellate proceedings and because of the danger of a simple error leading to the entire CFA being deemed unenforceable. Careful drafting is needed and the simpler and safer, if potentially less remunerative, course adopted by many appears to be to simply apply the 25% cap alone throughout.

The applicable cap under the 2013 Order is inclusive of VAT—that is to say that the maximum success fee chargeable, including VAT, should not exceed the 25% limit. Peculiarly, this is not specified within art.5, but rather is explained in the Explanatory Note to the Order which, as it states, is not part of the Order itself. Despite this further regulatory anomaly and the potential argument therefore that VAT is not required to be included in the cap, the authors consider it would be optimistic at best and unwise in practice to ignore the intended effect and to seek to make the client liable for VAT in addition to the 25% capped success fee, simply on the basis that a patent drafting error in the Order appears to permit it.

It is generally accepted that the cap should include any success fee payable to counsel (including VAT) under any CFA in relation to the same matter between the solicitor and counsel. However, as a result of what appears to be a further drafting oversight, neither the 2013 Order nor s.58 of the 1990 Act, as amended, specify this. As a result, it is open to argument that reference to "the success fee" specified under s.58(4B) of the 1990 Act, which is to be subject to the 25% "cap", is to the success fee chargeable under the CFA with the client (that is to say the solicitor's success fee), and that any success fee chargeable under any separate CFA (for example between the solicitor and counsel) is subject to a separate, but identical (and therefore additional) maximum limit. That does not appear to have been the intention, but is an argument left open by the apparent drafting anomaly.

Notification and advice requirements

Prior to April 2013, the between the parties notification requirements in rela-   2–13
tion to additional liabilities were contained in CPR r.44.15, CPR PD 44 para.19 and CPR PD 47 para.32. These were replaced (and effectively removed) as part of the general substitution of CPR rr.44–48[37] and have no effect in rela- tion to the majority of funding arrangements entered into on or after 1 April 2013. However, they have continued effect in relation to pre-commencement funding arrangements[38] (as do the former provisions of CPR rr.43–48 gener- ally, for example in relation to the between the parties assessment of success fees) by virtue of CPR r.48.1.

Accordingly, care had to be taken in the event, for example, of a claimant who entered into a pre-April 2013 CFA where a letter before claim was not sent until sometime later, or, where proceedings were not issued for some considerable time, to ensure that the proper notification had been given as required by the "old" rules. Similarly, in the perhaps more likely situation of assessment of costs where the funding arrangement is a pre-April 2013 CFA (or there is a pre-April 2013 ATE premium) the requirements of old CPR 47 PD para.32 must be observed if the between the parties recoverability of the additional liabilities is not to be jeopardised.

In that regard, note should be taken of the case of *Springer*[39] in which the Court of Appeal decided that the requirement under the Practice Direction on Pre-Action Conduct to give pre-issue notification of a funding arrangement which exposed the paying party to paying additional liabilities required such notification to be given "as soon as possible" after the funding arrangement was entered into, including where appropriate, before sending the letter of claim. Failure to do so risked the additional liabilities being irrecoverable for the period of default. By a quirk of the transitional arrangements, this obliga- tion does not appear to survive April 2013 in respect of pre-commencement funding arrangements.

It is also important to note that additional liabilities in excepted pro-   2–14
ceedings, such as publication and privacy claims where the CFA was entered into before 6 April 2019, continued to fall within the definition of pre-commencement funding arrangements and therefore continued to be subject to these notification requirements.

---

[37] Effected by CPR r.16 of the Civil Procedure (Amendment Rules) 2013 (SI 2013/262).
[38] As defined in CPR r.48.2, which broadly means a CFA or ATE policy entered into prior to 1 April 2013 (or a CCFA where, in the individual case in which costs are being considered, work was begun in relation to that case under the CCFA prior to 1 April 2013) or a CFA or ATE in one of the "excepted" categories, such as diffuse mesothelioma claims, publication and privacy proceedings (entered into before 6 April 2019) and insolvency proceedings (entered into prior to 6 April 2016).
[39] *Springer v University Hospitals of Leicester NHS Trust* [2018] EWCA Civ 436; [2018] 4 W.L.R. 61.

However, by yet another quirk, ATE premiums in clinical negligence claims under the post-April 2013 regime allowing for limited recovery of the same[40] are not pre-commencement funding arrangements (as the Court of Appeal confirmed in *Peterborough & Stamford Hospitals NHS Trust v McMenemy*[41]) and are therefore not subject to the "old" notification requirements under CPR rr.44 and 47. Again, this appears to be something of an oversight and the Court of Appeal in *McMenemy* expressly invited the CPRC to look at the issues surrounding the recoverable elements of such premiums and whether there was a need to introduce some further rules and guidance in relation to them. This has not yet been done. If it is done, such rules and guidance may impose further requirements on notification. In any event, despite any rule-based requirement, it remains good practice to provide notification of the fact that such a policy has been taken out, not least to limit arguments as to whether it is reasonably recoverable in principle at the successful conclusion of a case.

The confusion which surrounded the correct interpretation of the "new" CPR r.3.9 following the Court of Appeal's decision in *Mitchell*[42] pending clarification in *Denton*[43] led to a much stricter approach being taken towards any breaches of these notification requirements and the application of old CPR r.44.3B.

That strict approach has now been moderated in light of *Denton*, as seen, for example, in *Caliendo*.[44] The existence of the strict approach did result in some clarification of the scope of the sanctions under CPR r.44.3B being provided in *Long v Value Properties Ltd*,[45] which may be material in cases of such breaches in relation to pre-April 2013 funding arrangements.[46]

Implementation issues

2–15   Resolving issues surrounding implementation and transitional provisions appears largely to have been left as a matter for the courts. There were a number of appellate cases addressing some of the difficult issues that arose concerning the construction and operation of the transitional provisions and related cases arising out of the implementation of the 2013 reforms. There are a number of remaining issues and further appellate guidance may yet follow.

One of the key topics concerned issues relating to changes of funding around the time of the introduction of LASPO and in relation to the transfer and assignment of CFAs.

---

[40] Under the Recovery of Costs Insurance Premiums in Clinical Negligence Proceedings (No.2) Regulations 2013 (SI 2013/739).
[41] *Peterborough and Stamford Hospitals NHS Trust v McMenemy* [2017] EWCA Civ 1941; [2018] 1 W.L.R. 2685.
[42] *Mitchell v News Group Newspapers Ltd* [2013] EWCA Civ 1537; [2014] 1 W.L.R. 795.
[43] *Denton v TH White Ltd* [2014] EWCA Civ 906; [2014] 1 W.L.R. 3926.
[44] *Caliendo v Mischon De Reya* [2014] EWHC 3414 (Ch); [2014] 6 Costs L.O. 935.
[45] *Long v Value Properties Ltd* [2014] EWHC 2981 (Ch); [2015] 3 All E.R. 419.
[46] In that case, it was made clear that the sanction of disallowance of the success fee under CPR r.44.3B(1)(d) for late service of the relevant information in relation to the CFA in detailed assessment proceedings was limited to the loss of the success fee for the period of the default, rather than there being a disallowance of the entire success fee for the whole case, as had previously generally been thought to be the case.

In relation to the former, the core issue related to the reasonableness of claimants incurring additional liabilities—and seeking to recover the same from an unsuccessful opponent—where those claimants had available to them an alternative form of funding which would not have involved any additional liability.

Consideration of the case law supports anecdotal evidence that there were a substantial number of claims, particularly clinical negligence claims, where there was a change of funding—commonly from public funding to a CFA/ATE arrangement—shortly prior to 1 April 2013.

In theory, such cases should not involve any new issue of principle. The issue of the choice of funding is one of reasonableness and the broad principles have been relatively well established since *Sarwar*.[47] However, LASPO and the number of cases involving a change of funding in early 2013 appear to have thrown the issue into sharp focus. In three conjoined appeals, under the name of *Surrey v Barnet and Chase Farm Hospitals NHS Trust*[48] the Court of Appeal addressed issues concerning changes from public funding to CFAs in circumstances where the client had not been fully advised that by doing so the client would lose the right to the 10% general damages uplift[49] as a result of the change, if the claim was successful.

The court overturned the first appellate decision of Mr Justice Foskett and restored the first instance decisions which had held that the choice had been unreasonable. The judgment reaffirmed that the test to be applied was the *Sarwar* test of whether the choice of funding made by the claimant was an objectively reasonable one having regard to the individual circumstances of the particular claimant and that, in examining the reasons for the choice, if those reasons were made up of advice given by the solicitor and that advice was flawed, the choice was likely to be unreasonable. The decision in *Surrey* does not have the consequence of meaning that all such changes in funding are unreasonable, merely that the court must carefully scrutinise the reasons given for the choice when deciding whether it is objectively reasonable. Where, on a standard basis assessment, there was a doubt, the benefit of the doubt went to the paying party in accordance with the express terms of CPR r.44.3.

Change of funding cases continue to trouble the courts and a number of cases were decided at first instance or at first appellate level in 2019. None added to the principles established in *Surrey* and accordingly they are not considered in detail here. Perhaps only two points are of note. Firstly, the pattern of such claims indicates that the *Surrey* decision created a very difficult environment for claimants who sought to justify the reasonableness of the choice to switch funding arrangements shortly prior to the introduction of LASPO. The majority of the decided cases resulted in the additional liabilities

---

[47] *Sarwar v Alam* [2001] EWCA Civ 1401; [2002] 1 W.L.R. 125.
[48] *Surrey v Barnet and Chase Farm Hospitals NHS Trust* [2018] EWCA Civ 451; [2018] 1 W.L.R. 5831.
[49] *Simmons v Castle* [2012] EWCA Civ 1039; [2013] 1 W.L.R. 1239.

being disallowed, though there were occasional successes for the claimant.[50] Secondly, in *XDE* the Court of Appeal was asked to reconsider the question of the reasonableness of a change in funding in a case where the solicitors had been instructed on a CFA "lite" and in circumstances where the most common flaw in such cases – a failure to advise the client that the change would mean losing the 10% *"Simmons"*[51] enhancement to general damages – was not present.[52] The Court of Appeal took the opportunity to confirm that the *Surrey* principles did not only apply to *"Simmons"* cases and that a CFA lite was not so obviously superior to legal aid that it obviated the need for proper advice as to the respective benefits of the two regimes. Whilst the number of cases where these issues remain should now be limited, given the passage of time, it is likely that those remaining will be cases of high value or complexity where substantial costs may turn on the quality of advice given.

In *Hyde v Milton Keynes Hospital NHS Foundation Trust*,[53] the Court of Appeal gave guidance on the law where a solicitor ceases to act for a publicly funded client and swaps to a private fee-paying arrangement (in that case a CFA) but fails to discharge the public funding certificate. The defendant's argument (rejected at first instance and on first appeal) was that the continued existence of the certificate covering the proceedings meant that any private retainer was unlawful. The Court of Appeal rejected this argument and confirmed that the existence of the certificate was evidential and not conclusive. Where, on other evidence, the court could be satisfied the solicitor was not engaged in "topping up" and that the intention had been to replace one form of funding with another, there was no illegality and costs were recoverable on the basis of the CFA.

2–16 In relation to the transfer and assignment of CFAs, the common scenario where this occurred was where a personal injury claimant had entered into a pre-commencement funding arrangement, as defined in s.44(6) of LASPO, but wished to change firms after that date. By virtue of the strict wording of the transitional provision, the claimant was not entitled to QOCS protection if he or she entered into a new, post-LASPO agreement with the new firm of solicitors. Equally, if he or she entered into a new, post-LASPO, agreement, the success fee under the new agreement would prima facie be irrecoverable and the claimant may have been exposed to a deduction from any damages in respect of that success fee.

These issues were considered by the Court of Appeal in two related cases in 2017, *Catalano*[54] and *Budana*[55] and also received some attention from the Supreme Court in *Plevin*.[56]

[50] See, for example, *AB v Mid Cheshire Hospitals NHS Trust* [2019] EWHC 1889 (QB); [2019] Costs L.R. 1197.
[51] *Simmons v Castle* [2012] EWCA Civ 1288.
[52] *XDE v Middlesex University Hospitals NHS Trust* [2020] EWCA Civ 543, [2020] 1 W.L.R 2680.
[53] *Hyde v Milton Keynes Hospital NHS Foundation Trust* [2017] EWCA Civ 399; [2017] 3 Costs L.O. 391.
[54] *Catalano v Espley-Tyas Development Group Ltd* [2017] EWCA Civ 1132; [2017] 4 Costs L.R. 769.
[55] *Budana v Leeds Teaching Hospitals NHS Trust* [2017] EWCA Civ 1980; [2018] 1 W.L.R. 1965.
[56] *Plevin v Paragon Personal Finance Ltd* [2017] UKSC 23; [2017] 1 W.L.R. 1249.

In all three cases, the courts had to wrestle with the general point identified above, namely that there appeared to be the potential for a claimant to be "stuck" with the benefits (recoverability of additional liabilities) and detriments (no QOCS) of the old scheme and yet, by virtue of some apparent change in funding, to be also fixed, in part at least, with some of the detriments of the new scheme (loss of recoverability) whilst not also having the benefits of the new scheme (QOCS).

The broad answer, in all three cases, was to find that the apparent change in funding was not really a change at all, at least for the purpose of the transitional provisions. Once the claimant was pinned to the pre-LASPO scheme, by virtue of having a pre-LASPO CFA or ATE policy, the claimant would usually remain in that scheme for the duration of his or her claim and therefore any varied funding arrangement would usually be treated as a pre-LASPO funding arrangement.

So, in *Plevin*, the challenge was to a post-LASPO extension to a pre-LASPO CFA, in order to cover appeals, and to post-LASPO top-ups of pre-LASPO ATE premiums (for the same purpose). The Supreme Court held in each case that unless the intention had been to replace completely the original funding arrangements with new ones (which the court held was not the intention) then the "further" funding arrangements were still part of the pre-LASPO regime and remained recoverable.

In *Catalano*, the claimant's approach had been somewhat different. The claimant had originally entered into a pre-LASPO CFA for a noise-induced hearing loss claim. However, the claimant had not been able to obtain ATE. Accordingly, post-April 2013 the claimant sought to terminate the CFA, so as to enter into a post-LASPO CFA and argued that in such circumstances she was not precluded from the benefit of QOCS by CPR r.44.17 because it should be interpreted as only disapplying QOCS where any pre-LASPO CFA was "unterminated".

The Court of Appeal rejected this argument and held that once services had been provided under the original CFA, the claimant came within the transitional provision of CPR r.44.17 and QOCS would not apply to the proceedings even if the CFA was terminated. This is consistent with the *Plevin* approach that once the claimant is tied to the pre-LASPO regime, that remains the position—at least in so far as the proceedings are the same.

However, what is less clear is the dicta at [27] of the judgment in *Catalano* where the court held that "success fees can continue to be recovered as costs".

This appears to suggest that had Mrs Catalano been successful in her case, she would have been able to recover the success fee under her CFA, despite having expressly terminated the pre-LASPO CFA and having entered into a new post-LASPO CFA, which would presumably have contained the post-LASPO cap on success fees and which is likely to have contained a statement that the success fee was irrecoverable between the parties. Where the indemnity principle would feature in such a case is a matter that the court does not appear to have been addressed on.

In *Budana*, the Court of Appeal finally grappled with the question of how a solicitor's retainer and, in particular, a CFA can be transferred from one firm to another and, in particular, whether such agreements are capable of assignment and what the effect is where there is a transfer of a pre-LASPO CFA post-April 2013.

The judgments bear reading in full. By a 2:1 majority, the court held that the purported assignment of the CFA in this case was, in fact, a novation, with a new agreement coming into being. Accordingly, the argument that as a matter of contract law this was simply a continuation of the original, "assigned" agreement failed and the High Court authority of *Jenkins*, to contrary effect, was overruled.[57] However, unanimously, the court ruled that this was immaterial since, for the purposes of the transitional provisions and s.44(6) of LASPO, the success fee under that novated agreement remained a success fee payable under a pre-April 2013 CFA. That had been the intention of the parties and to order otherwise would leave the claimant with an imbalance between the old and new regimes.

The court's decision was applied in the High Court decision in *Warren v Hill Dickinson LLP*[58] and appears to have been welcomed by the courts as providing a practical solution to the problem of transfer of retainers even if it required a particularly purposive construction of the transitional provisions.

2–17   There is greater clarity of reasoning in *Budana* as to why the success fee under an apparently new post-April 2013 agreement remains recoverable as a pre-April 2013 success fee than is to be found in the obiter dictum to the same effect in the starker circumstances of *Catalano*. In addition, there will be a wide number of variations on the facts. Whilst passage of time since the introduction of LASPO means that the number of such cases has greatly diminished, there may yet be further cases where the courts will have to grapple with whether they can properly be satisfied that the ostensibly "new" arrangement is in fact to be treated for the purposes of the statutory provisions as an "old" one, even if contract law would indicate a contrary conclusion and also with whether the additional liability is nevertheless recoverable in light of other issues, such as the indemnity principle. Inevitably, if such cases do arise, they are likely to involve substantial claims for costs.

The consistent threads that can be drawn from the cases appear to be:

(i) that wherever possible the courts will be keen to make the transitional provisions work in a harmonious fashion, so that a claimant in any given set of proceedings is either wholly in the pre-LASPO camp or the post-LASPO camp unless the claimant has done something to indicate a clear intention to the contrary;[59]

---

[57] *Jenkins v Young Brothers Transport Ltd* [2006] EWHC 151 (QB); [2006] 1 W.L.R. 3189.
[58] *Warren v Hill Dickinson LLP* [2018] EWHC 3322 (QB); [2018] 6 Costs L.R. 1377.
[59] See further the Court of Appeal's decision in *BNM v MGN Ltd* [2017] EWCA Civ 1767; [2018] 1 W.L.R. 1450 which is consistent with this analysis.

(ii) that as a matter of generality, where the claimant has started out in the pre-LASPO camp, that is where the claimant will remain—at least in so far as the same proceedings are concerned—and attempts by the claimant to jump into the post-LASPO camp (for example to obtain QOCS where it becomes obvious that the claim will fail) are themselves likely to fail.

There remain some unresolved issues in this area, though they diminish with the passage of time. Not least is the vexed question of what the position is where the need for a change in funding arrangements is caused not by a change of solicitors, or by a desire by a claimant to change funding, but by a post-LASPO change in the identity of the claimant. For example, in the case of a claimant who dies, where the claim (perhaps already issued) is to be pursued by a personal representative on behalf of the estate. In such cases, is the "new" claimant to be regarded as a pre-LASPO claimant? If not, is the effect that the entire proceedings now lose any pre-LASPO protection, such as the recoverability of additional liabilities? Or is each claimant looked at individually? The transitional provisions do not address these issues, nor do cases such as *Catalano* or *Budana*. Further appellate clarification is likely to be necessary in the absence of clarification by the CPRC.

In *Morgan v Singh*[60] the judge dismissed an appeal against a finding that a personal representative in such a situation did have the benefit of QOCS as a "new" claimant.

Among the issues to be looked at by the Civil Justice Council working group 2–18 on the impact of the Jackson Reforms is the question of problems arising out of changes in the client's or the lawyer's status or basis of instruction in cases which straddle April 2013. No recommendations in this regard have yet been made and considerable uncertainty remains in this area, but the courts' approach in the above cases gives some structure to the likely nature of any recommendations if required. The passage of time is likely to mean that the number of cases where this is an issue will diminish, though in those that remain the costs in dispute may be substantial.

After the event insurance

Section 46 of LASPO introduced s.58C of the Courts and Legal Services Act 2–19 1990 with the effect of repealing s.29 of the Access to Justice Act 1999 (and s.47 LASPO repealed the similar s.30 of the 1999 Act in relation to the "notional" premiums charged by bodies such as trade unions). These legislative changes had the effect of preventing the between the parties recovery of ATE premiums where such policies were taken out on or after 1 April 2013.

Again, this tied in (in personal injury claims) with the introduction of QOCS, in that the existence of a pre-LASPO ATE policy prevents the claimant being eligible for QOCS protection.

---

[60] (HHJ Robinson, Sheffield County Court) Blog post, Arguments on the provisions and application of CPR 44.13–17: *Anne Morgan (on behalf of herself and of the estate of Mr Christopher John Morgan) v Dr Chongtham Singh.*

As with success fees, exceptions existed allowing for continued between the parties recoverability in mesothelioma, publication and privacy, and insolvency proceedings. Such exceptions were subject to the same process of review and possible revocation in due course (with the insolvency exception having ended with effect from 6 April 2016). As noted, in relation to publication and privacy proceedings, the exemption in relation to ATE (but not success fees which ended with effect from 6 April 2019) continues, at least for now. Accordingly, the cost of premiums for policies of ATE insurance remain recoverable in principle in three categories of cases – mesothelioma claims, publication and privacy proceedings and (to a limited extent) clinical negligence claims. Unhelpfully, the legislative basis for the recoverability in each of the three types of proceedings is different.

In terms of the revocation of recoverability in more general proceedings, it is worth noting that the wording of the general transitional provision is different from that in relation to success fees, in that pursuant to s.58C of the 1990 Act, the amendments (i.e. the revocation of between the parties recoverability) do not apply "in relation to a costs order made in favour of a party who took out a costs insurance policy in relation to the proceedings before [1 April 2013[61]]".

Accordingly, the test is whether "a" costs insurance policy was taken out in relation to the proceedings prior to 1 April 2013. The apparent effect is that the amendments (that is to say, the revocation of recoverability) do not apply at all where this is the case. It seems open to argument, therefore, that, provided the claimant has taken out a single pre-April 2013 ATE policy in respect of the proceedings, the claimant is entitled to seek to recover between the parties any (reasonably incurred) ATE premiums for any subsequent policies – whether with the same insurer or otherwise – in respect of the same proceedings.

This issue was not wholly resolved in the case of *Plevin*, which concerned the recoverability of premiums for "top-ups" to an ATE policy to cover appeals. Those top-ups were obtained after April 2013. The prime focus was on whether, for the purpose of the transitional provisions, the appeals were to be regarded as part of the same proceedings. The Supreme Court held that they were. Accordingly, the premiums for the top-ups remained recoverable.

Whilst, therefore, the Supreme Court did not deal specifically with the question of whether, where a claimant has entered into one ATE policy in relation to a case pre-April 2013, the premium for a further but different policy post-April 2013 will be recoverable (assuming it relates to the same proceedings), the answer to that question seems highly likely to be yes. Not only is this consistent with the wording of the transitional provision and the outcome in *Plevin*, it is also consistent with the approach taken by the Court of Appeal in the CFA cases of *Catalano* and *Budana*, above. The claimant is tied

---

[61] Or 6 April 2016 in the context of insolvency proceedings. References in this section to April 2013 should be read as referring to April 2016 where the claim in question is an insolvency proceeding within the meaning of the Act.

to the "old" regime in respect of those proceedings and accordingly, further funding arrangements in relation to those proceedings are likely to be treated in some way as continuations or extensions of "old" pre-LASPO funding arrangements and not "new" arrangements, in order to prevent the claimant being stuck between two regimes (for example by being unable to recover the cost of additional policies, but at the same time not having QOCS protection against the costs the claimant wishes to insure against).

A saving provision relating to the continued between the parties recover-   2–20
ability of ATE premiums in very limited circumstances in clinical negligence claims was provided by s.58C of the 1990 Act and the Recovery of Costs Insurance Premiums in Clinical Negligence Proceedings (No.2) Regulations 2013 (SI 2013/739). These allow for the continued recovery between the parties of ATE premiums in clinical negligence claims in certain circumstances, namely where:

- the claim has a value in excess of £1,000; and
- the insured risk relates to liability for the cost of an expert's report on issues of liability or causation.

The recoverable premium is limited to the cost of such a limited policy or, if the policy is wider, to the part of the premium that can be identified as relating to that part of the risk identified above.

The process of implementation of the clinical negligence exception was not a smooth one, with the original statutory instrument being found to be unhelpfully drafted, and possibly ultra vires. The second version does not appear to have addressed all of these problems and, in particular, there appears to be a tension between the authority delegated to the Lord Chancellor to make provision for continued recoverability, under s.58C of the 1990 Act, and the precise provision he has made under the 2013 Regulations. Some of these issues were addressed by the court in *Nokes*[62] and were further addressed in an appeal in a County Court appellate case named *Axelrod*,[63] heard in December 2015. Further cases seeking to resolve some of the ambiguities created by the implementation provisions may yet arise, though the position in relation to the recoverability of such premiums appears to have calmed in recent years following the Court of Appeal decisions referred to below.

The legacy of recoverable ATE premiums in the clinical negligence context   2–21
initially led to a continuation of the additional liability costs wars. This was fuelled by the combination of this continued element of recoverability with the introduction of the new, and apparently more robust, post-April 2013 test on proportionality. In turn, this led to arguments as to whether such new tests apply at all to these premiums and then whether the arguably generous approach to the between the parties recoverability of ATE premiums

---

[62] *Nokes v Heart of England Foundation NHS Trust* [2015] EWHC B6 (Costs).
[63] *Axelrod v University Hospitals of Leicester NHS Trust* unreported 28 January 2016 County Court (Chester).

established by the Court of Appeal in *Rogers v Merthyr Tydfil CBC*[64] no longer applied and, in particular, whether a court was entitled, or bound, to have regard to "the needs of the insurance market" when deciding whether a premium was proportionate.

In *BNM v MGN Ltd*,[65] the Court of Appeal dealt with some of the legacy issues relating to the assessment of additional liabilities generally. In doing so, it confirmed that where such additional liabilities are pre-commencement funding arrangements (PCFAs) within the meaning of CPR rr.48.1 and 48.2, such additional liabilities are to be assessed on the basis of the "old" rules and the new test of proportionality does not apply. This will apply to all PCFAs, so covers not merely CFAs and ATE policies entered into pre-April 2013, but would, for example, apply to such funding arrangements in relation to a diffuse mesothelioma claim for as long as the exemption for funding arrangements for such cases continues. This is so even where the base costs in such a case are subject to the new test of proportionality – another unhelpful example of how the rule changes potentially lead to old and new versions of the rules still applying within the same case.

Following *BNM*, in *Peterborough & Stamford Hospitals NHS Trust v Maria McMenemy*[66] the Court of Appeal addressed the first stage of challenges in relation to the specific issues concerning the limited clinical negligence exemption for post-April 2013 ATE premiums. A number of issues were decided.

Firstly, it was held that such premiums are subject to assessment as to their reasonableness and proportionality, despite the regulations arguably not providing for the same and despite the lack of any specific rules providing for such assessment. The assessment takes place in accordance with CPR r.44.2, though the Court of Appeal invited the CPRC to consider whether any specific rules or guidance in this regard should be (re)introduced (none have yet been).

Secondly, it was held that such policies are not PCFAs under CPR r.48.1; they are a new category of recoverable cost. Accordingly, and in contrast with additional liabilities under PCFAs, they are subject to the new test of proportionality.

Thirdly, the court upheld the pre-April 2013 approach to the question of whether it was reasonable to take out such policies at an early stage of proceedings. The perceived benefits of block rating of such policies were held to outweigh the apparent requirement in the rules to consider the reasonableness of taking out such insurance on a case by case basis.

Issues as to the quantum of such premiums and the application of the test of proportionality were then addressed in a second round of test cases, led by *Demouilpied v Stockport NHS Foundation Trust* and *West v Stockport NHS Foundation Trust*.[67] That case authoritatively resolved the question of the

---

[64] *Rogers v Merthyr Tydfil CBC* [2006] EWCA Civ 1134; [2007] 1 W.L.R. 808.
[65] *BNM v MGN Ltd* [2017] EWCA Civ 1767; [2018] 1 W.L.R. 1450.
[66] *Peterborough & Stamford Hospitals NHS Trust v Maria McMenemy* [2017] EWCA Civ 1941; [2018] 1 W.L.R. 2685.
[67] *West v Stockport NHS Foundation Trust* [2019] EWCA Civ 1220; [2019] 1 W.L.R. 6157.

correct approach. The court held firstly that the *Rogers* approach did, in general terms, continue to apply to the assessment of block-rated ATE premiums.

Secondly, that when considering (new) proportionality, the court was entitled to take into account the wider issues concerning the needs of the market in providing such policies. However, the impact of proportionality on the assessment of such premiums was more fundamentally resolved by the more general guidance the court gave in that case on the application of the new test of proportionality and, in particular, its conclusions that "inevitable" or "unavoidable" costs were proportionate. Given that the court held that an ATE premium was such an inevitable or unavoidable cost (subject to the reasonableness of its cost), proportionality had no real part to play in the assessment of such premiums and, to a large extent, the pre-April 2013 position was restored in relation to these "rump" ATE premiums.

Day to day issues as to the reasonableness and proportionality of ATE premiums which are recoverable under PCFAs continue to present themselves, see for example the decision of Foskett J in *Surrey* (above), where he upheld first instance decisions to reduce premiums on a broad brush basis (that decision not being part of the second appeal to the Court of Appeal) and also the much more receiving party friendly decision of *Percy v Anderson-Young*.[68] Permission to appeal to the Court of Appeal was granted but the matter does not appear to have been pursued in light of the outcome in *West*.

Issues as to the operation of the "old" tests of reasonableness and proportionality to such premiums are beyond the scope of this chapter, save to note that the arguments as to precisely when a judge can intervene to reduce a premium on assessment may continue.

Finally, as noted above, s.46 of LASPO preventing recovery of ATE premiums as an item of between the parties costs has not been and, it appears at least for now, will not be brought into force in relation to publication and privacy proceedings. Accordingly, ATE premiums remain recoverable in such cases on established principles and as a "pre commencement funding arrangement" (in contrast with the "rump" residual recoverable clinical negligence ATE premiums, which are not PCFAs).

The fact that ATE premiums remain recoverable in publication and privacy proceedings, but not other proceedings, appears to have been a material factor in the way in which some claims have been presented. For example, a claim for breach of confidence or misuse of private information is a publication or privacy proceeding and therefore the ATE premium is, in principle, recoverable as an item of costs. A data protection claim is not (see the definitions in the Legal Aid, Sentencing and Punishment of Offenders Act 2012 (Commencement No.5 and Saving Provision) Order 2013). Accordingly, there may be a temptation to seek to at least include a claim for breach of confidence or misuse of private information in a data protection claim to seek to benefit from such recoverability. The potential difficulties in doing so were

---

[68] *Percy v Anderson-Young* [2017] EWHC 2712 (QB); [2018] 1 W.L.R. 1583.

highlighted in the *Warren* judgment[69] in which claims for breach of confidence and misuse of private information were struck out from a claim concerning an incident in which cybercriminals compromised the personal date of the defendant's customers, leaving only the data protection claim.

Damages-Based Agreements (DBAs)

2–22   The introduction of DBAs was long-awaited. DBAs had, of course, been permissible for some time prior to April 2013 in relation to employment tribunal matters and the more general use of a contingency fee arrangement—that is to say, one where remuneration was based in whole or part on a share of the proceeds of litigation—was and is permissible under s.57 of the Solicitors Act 1974 in relation to non-contentious business matters. The proposed introduction of a regulated form of arrangement whereby the solicitor's payment would be directly proportionate to the client's recovery, in general litigation, was seen by many, if not all, as a positive step in widening the available forms of funding.

Unfortunately, the precise method of their introduction was widely criticised as being too narrow and restrictive, with the result that, at least until recently, there appears to have been very limited use of DBAs in circumstances where they were prohibited prior to April 2013.

The widening of the permissibility of DBAs in contentious business was achieved by virtue of s.45 of LASPO, amending the existing s.58AA of the 1990 Act, with effect from 1 April 2013. By virtue of s.58AA(4), a DBA is now permissible in all matters save those which cannot presently be the subject of an enforceable CFA (primarily criminal and family matters).

As with CFAs, a DBA must comply with the conditions imposed by the permitting statute. If it fails to do so, it is unenforceable. Again, as with CFAs, an exception exists for agreements which fall under s.57 of the Solicitors Act 1974, that is to say non-contentious business agreements (NCBAs).[70] This exemption for NCBAs is important and should not be overlooked. It allows the continued and more flexible use of contingency fee arrangements without the problems identified below in relation to the DBA regulations 2013, provided that the arrangement only applies to non-contentious business. The introduction of regulated DBAs in contentious business in 2013 appears to have sparked an increased interest in contingency fee arrangements generally, but it would be an error to assume that all contingency fee arrangements must comply with the Damages-Based Agreement Regulations 2013 ("the DBA Regulations").

---

[69] *Warren v DSG Retail Ltd* [2021] EWHC 2168 (QB).
[70] 2016 saw a rare and significant decision in relation to the use of "contingency fee arrangements" in the form of non-contentious business agreements and therefore used outside the context of proceedings. In *Bolt Burdon Solicitors v Tariq* [2016] EWHC 1507 (QB); [2016] 4 W.L.R. 112 the High Court upheld the validity of a 50% contingency fee and gave some useful guidance on how the court would approach challenges to such fees. The Court of Appeal refused permission for an appeal against that decision [2016] EWCA Civ 845.

Indeed, following the Court of Appeal's decision in *Zuberi*[71] (and subject to statutory reform), and perhaps somewhat to the surprise of some, the scope of what is regulated by s.58AA of the 1990 Act and the DBA Regulations 2013 is rather more narrow than had been commonly anticipated. The majority judgment held that a DBA is only that part of the contract which provides for a share of recoveries. Any residual part of the contract which provides for any other form of remuneration or payment of expenses, assuming it is not based on a share of recoveries, is not a DBA and is not subject to s.58AA or the DBA Regulations 2013.

Accordingly, it is entirely possible for a solicitor to have a retainer which, whilst ostensibly a single contract, in fact is subject to two different layers of regulation. For example, a retainer which provided for payment of fees (presumably, though not necessarily, discounted below the usual rate) in the event of failure of the case, but for payment of part of the recoveries (possible in addition to the fees) in the event of success. Only that part which provided for payment of a percentage of recoveries is subject to s.58AA and the DBA Regulations 2013. The balance would either be a simple matter of contract or, presumably, if it involved differing payments in specified circumstances, would be subject to the CFA Order 2013.

References in the legislation to a DBA – and therefore references below to a DBA – must now be understood as referring only to that part of the contract of retainer which provides for payment as a part of recoveries.

Beyond the basic requirements of the part of the agreement being in writing and not relating to prohibited classes of proceedings, the amended s.58AA provides that for such a DBA to be enforceable it must comply with the requirements of the Damages-Based Agreements Regulations 2013 (SI 2013/609) (DBA Regulations 2013). It is therein that the problems are said to lie.

Jackson LJ had proposed that, in order for a DBA to be "valid", there should be a requirement for a client to receive specific and independent advice before it was signed.[72] The recommendation was not implemented—primarily it would appear out of concerns that it might lead to a return to the sort of between the parties arguments over enforceability and adequacy of advice which had been a feature of the Conditional Fee Agreements Regulations 2000 (SI 2000/692) (CFA Regulations 2000). However, there are certain requirements for the provision of information in relation to DBAs in employment matters (set out in reg.5 of the DBA Regulations 2013). Presumably, such advice is thought to be more desirable and, perhaps more importantly, less likely to lead to indemnity principle arguments of the type which were notoriously prevalent in relation to CFAs generally as a result, in particular, of the specific advice requirements under the (now revoked) CFA Regulations 2000, given the limited scope for between the parties costs recovery before the Employment Tribunal.

2–23

---

[71] [2021] EWCA Civ 16.
[72] Final Report, p.133.

The basic provisions in relation to DBAs in employment matters have not changed as a result of the 2013 reforms and the remainder of this section will therefore focus on the requirements in non-employment matters.

The effect of the DBA Regulations 2013 is that a solicitor is entitled to agree with their client that they shall be paid by way of a percentage of the damages ultimately recovered by the client. Such "payment", as defined by reg.1 of the DBA Regulations 2013, must be net of any between the parties costs recovered or recoverable by way of profit costs or counsel's fees (reg.4)—the so-called "Ontario" model. In other words, the solicitor cannot enjoy the benefit of both the "payment" from the client and the between the parties costs recovery, but must allow such between the parties costs recovery to reduce the client's liability to make the "payment".

In addition, the solicitor is permitted to charge expenses (disbursements) to the client (other than counsel's fees) on top of the percentage fee (again, with credit being given against that charge for any between the parties costs recovered or recoverable in respect of such disbursements) (reg.4(1)(b)).

The DBA Regulations 2013 include a requirement for any DBA (other than one in relation to employment proceedings) to contain a cap on the amount of the client's recovered damages which may be used to pay the solicitor's fee under the DBA. In proceedings generally, the sum is 50% (inclusive of VAT) (reg.4(3)—and unlike the CFA Order, the regulation does expressly mention VAT as being included). Put simply, the maximum the client can be charged is 50% of their damages to cover both the solicitors' and counsels' fees (including VAT) together with any other expenses on top.

2–24 In personal injury claims there is a stricter limit, with the cap being restricted to 25% of the same classes of damages as apply in relation to the cap on a success fee under a CFA, namely, general damages and damages for pecuniary loss other than future pecuniary loss (reg.4(2)).

This latter restriction appeared to pose a potential, though not necessarily insuperable, obstacle to the use of a DBA in personal injury litigation. With a post-April 2013 CFA, the success fee is capped at 25% of the prescribed classes of damages. However, there is no cap on base fees (other than their reasonableness) and counsel's fee can be charged in addition to the base fees and success fee (though counsel's success fee is probably included in the cap).

With a DBA, however, the total percentage fee (excluding non-counsel expenses but, including counsel's fee), is capped at 25% of the same classes of damages. Whilst there will be cases where the figures are such that a DBA is still attractive, the most valuable heads of loss in a large personal injury case are usually future losses (care, loss of earnings, etc.) and not past losses or general damages and the limitation of the total fee under a DBA to a fraction of those heads of loss has the potential to limit their attractiveness and suitability in all but a small minority of cases.

This appears to be consistent with the intention behind the introduction of such agreements. In its initial assessment in relation to the post-implementation review of Pt 2 of LASPO,[73] the MoJ noted that:

> *"It is worth emphasising that DBAs were intended as an additional form of funding in appropriate cases, not an alternative form of funding in every case. DBAs may therefore be more suited to niche areas, where damages are high relative to the costs, or where costs are not recoverable. For this reason, and given the prevalence of CFAs, it was unlikely that DBAs would be suitable for, say, fast-track or multi-track PI claims."*

Whether that obstacle remains following the Court of Appeal's decision in *Zuberi* remains to be seen. Assuming that no legislative reform follows to alter the effect of the judicial construction of s.58AA of the 1990 Act and the DBA Regulations 2013, then there is now nothing (bar the client's willingness to agree on an informed basis) to prevent solicitors agreeing with their client that there shall be some form of payment of basic charges (whether contingent on success or not), either in addition to the payment of the percentage success fee or as a fallback reduced payment in the event of failure. In particular, the decision in *Zuberi* appears to open up the way for solicitors to use DBAs to provide a "top-up" on success to otherwise contingent basic charges, but in a way whereby the "top-up" is more directly proportionate to the level of certain types of recovery than is possible with a CFA.

The decision in *Zuberi* is possibly the most significant decision in the area of costs and funding since the 2013 reforms. The case itself concerned whether or not it was possible for a DBA "retainer" to include a provision whereby the client could be liable for fees on some other basis (in that case, a simple and conventional hourly rate basis for work done) in the event of early termination by the client, or whether such provision would render the agreement unenforceable.

The Court of Appeal concluded that such an arrangement was permissible. The DBA Regulations 2013 and s.58AA did not prevent such an arrangement. Whilst the regulations were open to contrary interpretation, the decision in this regard was not unexpected and cured one of the principal problems with DBAs.

However, it was the second part of the decision – where the Court of Appeal was divided – that was most significant. In considering the first issue, the court considered the more fundamental question of "what is a DBA" – and therefore what was (and was not) regulated by the DBA Regulations 2013 and s.58AA of the 1990 Act. The answer of the majority was that a DBA was only those provisions which dealt with the payment out of recoveries. Any other provisions of the retainer – and in particular any other provisions dealing with payment, for example, by way of an hourly rate (whether in addition to or as

---

[73] *https://assets.publishing.service.gov.uk/government/uploads/system/uploads/attachment_data/file/719140/pir-part-2-laspo-initial-assessment.pdf.*

an alternative to the DBA payment in certain circumstances) was not a DBA and accordingly was not regulated by the DBA Regulations 2013 or s.58AA.

Those provisions are then left to the more conventional forms of control – what a client is willing to agree to and assessment, if required, under s.70 of the Solicitors Act 1974. Of course, some parts may be subject to their own further regulation – for example a provision for contingent payment of an hourly rate fee in addition to or as an alternative to the DBA payment would be prima facie subject to the CFA Order 2013. It would now, therefore, appear to be possible to have a retainer which is subject, in parts, to both the CFA Order 2013 and the DBA Regulations 2013. An interesting question would arise whether the whole retainer was subject to the CFA regime, or whether each part was only separately subject to its own specific system of regulations, with the overall retainer then potentially being subject to assessment under s.70 of the 1974 Act.

The full implications of the decision remain to be seen. It is possible that the legislature might consider that the effect of the court's decision goes too far. There are strong indicators that the government did not intend to permit hybrid DBAs, let alone go as far as the Court of Appeal now appears to have done. It is certainly arguable that the preferable course would now be for the MoJ to grasp the considerable work done by Mr Bacon QC and Professor Mulheron QC and to provide a revised and comprehensive system of regulation and guidance for DBAs, designed to work in tandem with the system of regulation for CFAs and solicitor-client retainers generally.

However, in the interim and assuming that the Court of Appeal's decision remains untouched, the effect appears to have been a considerable increase in appetite for the use of retainers including some form of DBA payment. Whether this will provide the enhanced access to justice originally intended or will create substantial problems of its own remains to be seen.

Between the parties costs recovery with a DBA

2–25 CPR r.44.18 provides that the fact of a DBA will not affect between the parties costs recovery and that between the parties costs shall be assessed in accordance with CPR r.44.3. The rule itself is somewhat vague in this regard, and the limited use of DBAs to date means that its scope has yet to be properly tested.

However, it is generally understood that it is intended to result in between the parties costs being assessed on a "conventional" basis, that is to say on the basis of an hourly rate and time spent basis.

What is clear is that the between the parties costs will not be assessed by reference to the "payment" the client is liable to pay the solicitor under the DBA, save that, as noted below, such payment may act as an indemnity principle "cap" on the opponent's total liability. Accordingly, clients entering into a DBA must be made expressly aware that there is likely to be a fundamental difference (and often a shortfall) between the payment due under the DBA (and any related terms of retainer) and the equivalent sum in profit costs an opponent is likely to be ordered to pay if the claim succeeds. This would be particularly so if the DBA payment is used as a "top-up" to conventional base fees where it may well be that the DBA element is simply not recovered as an item of between the parties cost.

The between the parties assessment is likely to involve the court identifying a "notional" hourly rate where none has been contractually agreed, much as occurs in between the parties assessments in publicly funded cases. It may be advisable for a solicitor in such a case to record, at the outset, the hourly rate that the firm would have charged had it not been acting under a DBA and the reasons which would have supported charging such a rate (assuming no hourly rate charge is being made in any event).

It also means that a solicitor who believed that acting on a DBA would allow the firm to avoid having to conduct detailed time recording would be wrong. Not only would a lack of detailed time recording hamper any between the parties costs recovery, it could be very unfortunate were the DBA to be challenged on a solicitor-client basis.

As noted previously, the indemnity principle has not been disapplied, despite Jackson LJ's recommendation. This is expressly reflected in CPR r.44.18(2)(b) which recites that a party may not recover more by way of costs than the total amount payable under the DBA.

Accordingly, if the "notional/conventional" between the parties costs in a case exceed the sum payable under a DBA, then the between the parties costs recovery will be limited to the DBA sum (together with any additional contractual liability the client may have to base costs under a "hybrid" arrangement.) However, if the "notional/conventional" between the parties costs are less than the total sum payable under the retainer (the DBA payment plus any other liability), then because the assessment is conducted on that "notional" basis, the between the parties costs recovery will be limited to that conventional sum.

Problems with DBAs

Some issues have already been highlighted above. The decision in *Zuberi* has provided a cure to some of these problems. Specific problems were previously identified in earlier editions of this work. They are repeated below, updated in light of *Zuberi*, since it may assist consideration of that decision and the present position: 2–26

- The wording of para.4 of the DBA Regulations 2013, and in particular the definition of "payment", which appeared to prevent the use of hybrid DBAs. That is to say, it appeared to prevent the agreement allowing the legal representative to be paid anything by way of profit costs other than the percentage share of damages if the case is won or nothing if the case is lost. Hybrid or discounted DBAs would allow for the solicitor to charge a low hourly rate, win or lose, with a percentage share of damages on success. Discounted CFAs have been popular in commercial litigation, where a client is able and prepared to pay something win or lose, but wishes to share the risk with the solicitor. Hybrid DBAs would potentially be popular for offering the same opportunity whilst tying the reward directly to the amount of recovery. The drafting appeared to prevent such agreements and the wording of the regulations appeared to mean that such agreements would be unenforceable. That impression was emphasised by the fact that when asking the Civil Justice Council to consider some technical revisions to the DBA Regulations 2013 in November 2014, the MoJ appeared to rule out revising them to permit (or to make clear that they already permitted) hybrid DBAs. The then Master of the Rolls referred to the Government having decided to "not permit hybrid DBAs".[74] Lord Justice Jackson called for the Government to rethink its position in this regard and gave cogent reasons why the position should be reconsidered.[75] That reconsideration had yet to take place at the time of the *Zuberi* decision in the Court of Appeal. However, that decision now appears to open the door to such hybrids – indeed to a far wider variety of hybrids on a far less regulated basis than had been proposed, for example, by Mr Bacon QC and Professor Mulheron QC. Their proposals had sought to introduce a regulated and controlled form of hybrids through amendment of the DBA Regulations 2013. The whole agreement would remain a DBA, but the ability to take discounted hourly rate payments in the event of failure would be permitted. The Court of Appeal's decision removes all bar the part of the retainer which deals with payment out of recoveries from regulation under the DBA Regulations 2013 at all. This is a seismic shift and whilst it apparently cures this problem, whether it will create others will only become apparent over the coming years.

- The wording of para.4 also appeared to create a problem with using a DBA in a form similar to a CFA "lite". That is to say, a DBA which included a provision allowing for the solicitor to retain between the parties costs in full in the event that the between the parties costs payable on the hypothetical hourly rate/time spent basis (the "Ontario model") exceed the sum which would otherwise be payable under the agreement on a simple percentage of damages basis. There seemed no particular reason why such an agreement should not be permissible if CFA lites are to remain permissible. It would not require an opponent to pay more than a reasonable and proportionate sum. At the same time, the prospect of enhanced between the parties recovery would facilitate the greater use of DBAs on a solicitor-client basis. Once again, it would appear that the Court of Appeal's decision in *Zuberi* now appears to clear the way for such agreements, though the precise boundaries between the interaction of the DBA Regulations 2013 and the CFA Order 2013 may give rise to interesting legal arguments.

---

[74] http://www.judiciary.gov.uk/related-offices-and-bodies/advisory-bodies/cjc/working-parties/civil-justice-council-cjc-to-look-at-damages-based-agreements-revisions/.
[75] http://www.litigationfutures.com/news/jackson-outlines-two-pronged-strategy-promote-dbas.

- The Regulations appear to require the legal representative's fee to be calculated only by reference to damages "ultimately recovered" by the client (reg.1), whilst at the same time requiring the solicitor to give credit for any between the parties costs (profit costs or counsel's fees) which are "paid or payable" to the client (reg.4). In other words, the legal representative bears the risk of the opponent's insolvency, having to give credit for between the parties costs payable, even if not received, whilst only being able to charge the client the percentage fee where damages are actually received. The same applies to disbursements. This still appears to be the case post-*Zuberi*, though the ability to have other mechanisms for payment alongside the DBA payment means that this may be less problematic.

- The latter point ties into a further, related issue, namely that the way the present DBA scheme is drafted effectively requires a DBA to be based on the solicitor being paid a percentage of sums actually recovered. The regime does not appear to admit of or allow for a solicitor to be paid on the basis of some other benefit obtained or retained by the client – for example, for a DBA to be used on the basis that the solicitor will be paid a percentage of the value of an asset that a successful defendant client retains. This problem was highlighted in the case of *Tonstate Group*,[76] in which a DBA which was said to allow for the solicitor to be paid on such a basis was held to be unenforceable for want of compliance with the Regulations. Once again, the Bacon/Mulheron report contains proposals to address this issue, allowing for the DBA payment to be calculated by reference to the "financial benefit" to the client and not merely as a percentage of sums actually recovered. Unless and until these or similar proposals are taken forward, DBAs are unlikely to be of use other than in cases where a successful claim is likely to result in the actual payment of monies to a client.

- The Regulations did not contain any provisions for payment on termination of the agreement. There appeared to be nothing preventing the agreement providing that, if the client instructs another firm and subsequently wins the claim, the "payment" under the agreement will be payable in full (or indeed in part). However, the restriction on permitting any other form of "payment" was said to prevent the rendering of a different form of charge, for example on an hourly rate basis or otherwise, if the client simply "walked away" or if the firm felt obliged to cease acting and, in particular, it appeared to prevent the solicitor from providing for some non-contingent charge (that is to say, one not dependent on the client's ultimate success in the case) being made.

The latter point, in particular, gave rise to a number of issues. One of the core issues that was to arise for consideration in the dispute between *Harlequin*

---

[76] *Tonstate Group Ltd v Wojakovski* [2021] EWCH 1122 (Ch).

Property (SVG) Ltd and *ELS Legal* arising out of the *Harlequin Property (SVG) Ltd v Wilkins Kennedy* litigation was understood to relate to the enforceability of DBAs entered into by both the solicitors and counsel and, in particular, whether provisions in those agreements relating to payment in the event of termination rendered the agreements unenforceable. Unfortunately—for those seeking guidance—the matter settled mid-trial in mid-2017 and no judgment on the issues was given.

However, any remaining concerns in this regard were dissipated by the Court of Appeal's decision in *Zuberi* in January 2021. Put simply, a termination provision of this type is permissible for one of two reasons. The first, according to the unanimous judgment of the court, is simply that there is nothing in the DBA Regulations 2013 preventing it. The absence of reference to such a provision does not mean it is not permitted, rather that it is not prevented (and indeed is not regulated, at least by these Regulations). The second reason – which was that of the majority only – is that any provision other than the specific provision dealing with the payment out of recoveries and any express limitations related to that, is simply not regulated by the DBA Regulations 2013. It may be regulated by other regulations (for example the CFA Order 2013) and may be subject to assessment under s.70 of the Solicitors Act 1974, but it is not prevented by or regulated by the DBA Regulations 2013 and, most fundamentally therefore, its presence does not render such an agreement unenforceable for non-compliance with those Regulations.

The inhibiting effect of the concerns in relation to DBAs and the poorly drafted Regulations —and the uncertainty created to date by such issues— was enhanced by the continuing treatment of DBAs and CFAs in litigation as islands of legality in a sea of illegality whereby, if the requirements of s.58AA and s.58 respectively are not fully complied with, the agreement is unenforceable. In conjunction with the continued application of the indemnity principle, this exposes the solicitor to a risk that if the DBA departs in any material fashion from the strictures of the Regulations, the agreement will be unenforceable and no payment at all will be permitted.

2–27   It is not clear to what extent these restrictions were intended (though it now seems clear that the non-permissibility of hybrid DBAs, at least, was intentional). However, the combined effect of all of these factors had resulted in very limited use of DBAs. The effective removal of many of these problems following the *Zuberi* decision appears to have resulted in a substantial increase in the use of such agreements – and, in particular, in the use of novel hybridised agreements of various types which are likely to go well beyond the sort of agreements that the likes of Mr Bacon QC and Professor Mulheron QC had been calling for. The introduction of DBAs was intended to enhance access to justice. To date, there had been little evidence that this had happened. The potential now exists for this to occur, though the risk of abuse has probably also increased and it is likely that, in due course, at least some such agreements will fall to be closely scrutinised on solicitor-client assessments and in other disputes.

In addition to matters identified above, a particular issue arose with commercial third-party funding. Section 58AA(3) of the 1990 Act, as amended by LASPO, provides that a DBA includes an agreement of that type entered into between a person providing claims management services and the recipient of those services. "Claims management services" were given the same definition as in Pt 2 of the Compensation Act 2006. With effect from 29 November 2018, this was amended to refer to the similar definition now in s.419A of the Financial Services and Markets Act 2000. Whilst there are minor differences in the wording, both definitions provide that "claims management services" means "advice or other services in relation to the making of a claim". This is a very wide definition and on its face it appeared that, for example, the provision of third-party funding for a claim would be the provision of an "other service" in respect of the claim.

Since the funder was being rewarded for that funding by a payment which (usually) was determined by reference to the amount of the financial benefit obtained (s.58AA(3)(a)(ii) of the 1990 Act), such a funding arrangement was arguably prima facie a DBA and had to comply with the DBA Regulations 2013 or be unenforceable. Not only would a non-compliant agreement mean that the funder could not rely on the agreement to recover its reward in the event of a successful claim, but the use of an agreement which was contrary to statute in order to bring a claim would possibly give rise to arguments as to whether the claim should be stayed.[77]

This was also a particular problem in opt-out collective proceedings in the Competition Appeal Tribunal, since DBAs are expressly unenforceable if they relate to such proceedings (s.47C(8) of the Competition Act 1998).

Given that opt-out collective proceedings almost invariably require third-party funding in order to be brought, if it was correct that such agreements fell within the definition of a DBA in s.58AA then such agreements would not be lawful and were likely to prove a major obstacle to certification of any proposed class representative who relied on such an agreement as part of their funding plan.

Given the importance of the point in such proceedings, it is perhaps unsurprising that the point crystallised in a case before the CAT (*UK Trucks Claim Ltd v Fiat Chrysler Automobiles N.V.*[78]). In that case, the argument to the effect that such an agreement was a DBA was rejected.

Shortly before the decision in the CAT, a decision to the apparently opposite effect, accepting the argument that such an arrangement was a DBA, was given in *Meadowside Building Developments Ltd v 12–18 Hill Street Management Co Ltd*.[79] *Meadowside* does not appear to be subject of an application for permission to appeal. The Tribunal in the *Trucks* case was not referred to

---

[77] Though note that the Court of Appeal has been reluctant to hold that the use of an unlawful or champertous funding arrangement should prevent the claim itself proceedings—see for example *Faryab v Smyth* (CA) unreported 28 August 1998 and *Stocznia Gdanska SA v Latreefers Inc* [2000] C.P.L.R. 65.

[78] *UK Trucks Claim Ltd v Fiat Chrysler Automobiles N.V* [2019] CAT 26.

[79] *Meadowside Building Developments Ltd v 12–18 Hill Street Management Co Ltd* [2019] EWHC 2651 (TCC).

Meadowside before giving judgment, but in rejecting an application for permission to appeal, the CAT held that *Meadowside* was not in conflict with its own judgment because the actions of the funders in each case were different and those in *Meadowside* had been managing the claim generally.

The issue was authoritatively disposed of by the Court of Appeal in March 2021.[80] The Court noted that s.58B Courts & Legal Services Act 1990 contained express provision (though not yet brought into force) for regulation of litigation funding. The idea that this was also regulated, effectively through the back door, by s.58AA and s.419 of the Financial Services & Markets Act 2000 ("FSMA") did not make sense. The advice or other services provided (including financial services and assistance) must be of a claims management nature, and pure commercial non-party funding was not (though, as in *Meadowside*, if a non-party went further then they may well fall into the definition). Put simply, commercial third-party funding does not come within the scope of the DBA Regulations.

Once again, the Mulheron/Bacon proposals proposed making clear that litigation funding agreements were excluded from the scope of the DBA Regulations 2013. Indeed, that review, which reconsidered the legislative provisions surrounding DBAs, continues to provide a clear opportunity both to clarify the residual uncertainties and to revise the Regulations such that DBAs may be subject to properly codified and coherent statutory control. It is unsatisfactory that fundamental questions, such as whether third-party funding arrangements must comply with such legislation, are left to judicial interpretation, when the issues are ones which could be shortly and expressly dealt with in the legislation.

2–28   In terms of the scope for revising the DBA Regulations 2013, as mentioned above, the Civil Justice Council (CJC) Working Group was asked to look at a number of technical issues. These were:

- dividing into two sets the existing regulations with employment tribunal regulations (as per the 2010 regime) separated from regulations for civil litigation proceedings;
- changing the regulations so that defendants will be able to use DBAs, by widening the application of the regulations where the party receives a specified financial benefit (rather than restricting them to receiving a payment);
- reviewing whether the regulations should contain provisions on terminating the DBA;
- clarifying that different forms of litigation funding cannot be used during a case when a DBA is being used to fund litigation; and

---

[80] *DAF Trucks Deutschland GmbH v Road Haulage Association Limited (RH) and UK Trucks Claim Ltd* (UKTC) [2021] EWCA Civ 299.

- clarifying that the lawyer's payment can only come from damages, and the payment should be a percentage of the sum ultimately received (not awarded or agreed).

The CJC's report was published in September 2015[81] and focused primarily on the issue of hybrid DBAs.

The report contained 45 recommendations, which are not repeated here. It noted that the inability to enter into what it described as "concurrent hybrid DBAs"—that is to say a hybrid DBA as described above, as opposed to the ability to have separate, consecutive retainers (perhaps first a conventional retainer and then a DBA) has had an "incredibly chilling effect" on the take up of DBAs, but ultimately concluded that the introduction of such arrangements, whether generally or only in relation to certain practice areas, remained a policy decision for the Government. As noted above, that view now appears to have been superseded by the Court of Appeal's decision in *Zuberi*.

Other recommendations included changes to make DBAs more available for use by defendants, an increase in the 25% DBA cap for personal injury claims to 50% for defendants, and greater freedom as to the "trigger points" for payment of the DBA fee and for the effect of early termination of DBAs. The CJC's call for further modifications to try and improve the use of DBAs was supported by the then Master of the Rolls.

As already noted, the operation of DBAs forms an express part of the ongoing review of Pt 2 of LASPO and that review includes consideration of whether there should be any amendment to the DBA Regulations 2013, whether in accordance with the recommendations of the CJC or otherwise. The Mulheron/Bacon Review Program has been referred to above and the in-depth work undertaken there merits close attention by anyone interested in this area, but its finer detail is beyond the scope of this work.

Third-party funding/litigation funding

The general operation of third-party funding arrangements and matters such as the voluntary Code of Conduct for Litigation Funders published by the CJC in its most recent form in November 2011 and the potential liability of third-party funders to adverse costs orders is beyond the scope of this text. A summary of the relevant background to the operation of third-party funding as at the time of its writing may be found in Ch.11 of Lord Justice Jackson's Final Report.

2–29

However, there are a number of decisions which are of particular note.

In 2016, in *Excalibur Ventures LLC v Texas Keystone Inc*,[82] the Court of Appeal upheld the judgment of Sir Christopher Clarke by which he had held that the

---

[81] The Damages-Based Agreements Reform Project: Drafting And Policy Issues—*https://www.judiciary.gov.uk/wp-content/uploads/ 2015/09/dba-reform-project-cjc-aug-2015.pdf*.

[82] *Excalibur Ventures LLC v Texas Keystone Inc* [2016] EWCA Civ 1144; [2017] 1 W.L.R. 2221.

professional funders of the failed litigation were liable on a joint and several liability basis to pay the other party's costs on an indemnity basis.

The case breaks no new ground on the core approach to the making of a non-party costs order against commercial funders, set out by the Court of Appeal in 2005 in *Arkin v Borchard Lines Ltd.*[83] However, in addition to reaffirming those principles, it did also provide clarity on two important points. Firstly, whilst a commercial funder (in the absence of impropriety or the funding arrangement being champertous) will not normally be held liable for adverse costs in a sum greater than the amount of funding that particular funder provided (the so-called "Arkin cap"), when considering how to calculate that cap, the court will not only take into account the level of funding the funder provided for the litigant's own costs and disbursements, but will also take into account any money the funder advanced to allow the litigant to provide security for costs. Both are to be regarded as "funding" for the purposes of the cap. This potentially widens the scope of a funder's exposure.

Secondly, the court made clear that a funder can be ordered to pay adverse costs under a non-party costs order on the indemnity basis where the circumstances of the case generally warrant such an order, even where the funder's own conduct, in isolation, would not. The fact that costs are awarded on the indemnity basis does not lift the Arkin cap. The funder's maximum exposure is still limited by the cap, but the fact that it may be liable for costs on the indemnity basis means that its exposure within that cap is likely to be higher. This is likely to be particularly important given the increased impact of the proportionality test post-April 2013. Put simply, the gap between costs on the standard basis and on the indemnity basis (where the proportionality test does not apply—see CPR r.44.3) is likely to widen. It is also important, in the context of the funding of larger cases, in light of the greater use of costs budgeting. The relative certainty that a funder would have been able to take from the fact that an opponent party's costs were budgeted is removed if the funder is potentially exposed to a non-party costs order on the indemnity basis, since the limitation in CPR r.3.18 only applies to costs awards on the standard basis.

Both aspects of the judgment are likely to increase the care with which sensible litigation funders consider whether a case is suitable for funding and are also likely to increase the cost of such funding. The former point seems to have been an outcome that the judges at both first instance and on appeal considered not merely an acceptable, but a desirable consequence of their judgments.

2–30   The need for such care was emphasised in 2017 by the decision of Mr Justice Foskett in *Bailey v GlaxoSmithkline UK Ltd.*[84] In that case, the court was considering an application for security for costs against a litigation funder. The

---

[83] *Arkin v Borchard Lines Ltd* [2005] EWCA Civ 655; [2005] 1 W.L.R. 3055. It is notable, in passing, that Lord Justice Jackson's recommendation in Ch.11 of the Final Report that the Arkin cap should be lifted such that commercial funders are generally liable for all (reasonable and proportionate) adverse costs if the case is lost was not adopted.
[84] *Bailey v GlaxoSmithkline UK Ltd* [2017] EWHC 3195 (QB); [2018] 4 W.L.R. 7.

funder accepted it was vulnerable to such an application, but contended that the security order should not exceed the Arkin cap. The funder was not a member of the Association of Litigation Funders and was balance sheet insolvent. Foskett J made the often-overlooked point that the ratio in *Arkin* strictly only applies where the funder merely contributes to a share of the costs risk, rather than underwriting the whole risk, and that in the latter situation it may be open to argument that the cap does not apply. In such circumstances, he was not prepared, at an interlocutory stage, to limit the amount of security on the assumption that the cap would apply, since to do so would undermine the protection to be afforded by an order for security if the cap was held not to apply.

Whilst the *Bailey* case may be of particular relevance to those cases where the funding arrangement is less conventional, it serves to highlight the danger of assuming the Arkin cap will always apply.

The limitations of the Arkin cap were authoritatively exposed in the Court of Appeal's decision *in Chapelgate Credit Opportunity Master Fund Ltd v Money.*[85] In that case, the funder was ordered to pay the opponent's costs without limitation by reference to the amount of their funding – the Arkin cap. They appealed. The Court of Appeal made clear that the application of the Arkin cap was not a binding issue of legal principle in all funded cases. It was, instead, a factor – albeit usually a very significant one – in considering in all the circumstances whether and to what extent it was just to order a funder to pay the opponent's costs directly. However, it had to be balanced against other matters, including the fact that the funder may have been able to protect itself (by either securing itself or ensuring the funded clients secured adequate ATE cover), the extent to which the funder had funded the whole claim (even if subject to a financial limit on the amount of funding) or only part of the claimants' costs, the size of the funder's potential return and all the circumstances of the case. Only if the judge went beyond the bounds of reasonably exercising their discretion as to what was just in all the circumstances would the court intervene. Here, the judge had not done so and the appeal seeking to limit liability to the Arkin cap failed.

A further example of a funder's liability not being limited by the Arkin cap may be seen in *Laser Trust v CFL Finance Ltd,*[86] a case in which the litigation funder was found to have "control of an extraordinarily high order" over the proceedings.

In the *RBS Rights litigation*, security was ordered against a third-party funder. For present purposes, perhaps the most notable part of the case is the earlier judgment[87] whereby Hildyard J held that he had power to order disclosure of details of a third-party funding arrangement, but that whilst he also had such power in relation to an ATE policy, it would not usually be appropriate to order

---

[85] [2020] EWCA Civ 246 (unreported elsewhere).
[86] [2021] EWHC 1404 (Ch).
[87] [2017] EWHC 463 (Ch).

disclosure of the latter at an interim stage. See further, in this context and in the specific context of opt out collective actions in the Competitions Appeals Tribunal (where funding may be an important interim issue due to the need for the proposed class representative to obtain certification), the recent decision of the Tribunal in *Kent v Apple*,[88] in which disclosure of the quantum of ATE premiums was refused on the basis, inter alia, that such disclosure might inform the opponent of the assessment of risk by the claimant's insurer.

In *Premier Motorauctions Ltd v Pricewaterhousecoopers LLP*,[89] the Court of Appeal gave some much-needed guidance on the relevance of the existence of ATE to a security for costs application. The precise terms of the same are outside the scope of this section, but the guidance in this regard is welcome.

More closely related to the other subject matter of this chapter is the decision in *Essar Oilfield Services Ltd v Norscot Rig Management Pvt Ltd*.[90] HHJ Waksman QC held that an arbitrator's general powers under s.59(1)(c) of the Arbitration Act 1996 included the power to award to the successful party the costs that party had incurred in obtaining third-party funding—in effect, the "reward" that the party had paid to the funder in return for the provision of that funding (and potentially other associated costs).

That award was on the basis that s.59(1)(c) allows an award of "legal or other costs".[91] It was accepted that third-party funding costs were not a "legal" cost and that such costs were not traditionally capable of being the subject of an award of costs in litigation, pursuant to s.51 of the Senior Courts Act 1981, CPR r.44.2 or any of the conventional routes to an award of "costs" within proceedings. However, the judge accepted the submission that "other" costs under s.59(1)(c) was wide enough to include such costs and that it was therefore within the tribunal's discretion to allow such costs if it considered it appropriate to do so.

The decision makes no inroads on the well-established principle that funding costs are not recoverable in litigation. However, it does create a radical difference between the potential costs recovery in an arbitration under the 1996 Act in comparison with those in litigation.

The decision in *Essar* has been the subject of much interest and some criticism. It would appear ripe for consideration at higher appellate level. However, the High Court refused permission and as a result s.68(4) of the 1996 Act operates as a bar on any further appeal. This is unfortunate and a more authoritative decision on this important issue would be welcome.

Some support for the decision in *Essar* may be thought to be found in the decision of the CAT in *Merricks v Mastercard Inc*.[92] In that case, the tribunal held that a proposed representative claimant's potential liability to a

---

[88] *Kent v Apple Inc* [2021] CAT 37.
[89] *Premier Motorauctions Ltd v Pricewaterhousecoopers LLP* [2017] EWCA Civ 1872; [2018] 1 W.L.R. 2955.
[90] *Essar Oilfield Services Ltd v Norscot Rig Management Pvt Ltd* [2016] EWHC 2361 (Comm); [2017] Bus. L.R. 227.
[91] As to "legal" costs, see inter alia *London Scottish Benefit Society v Chorley* [1884] 13 Q.B.D. 872.
[92] *Merricks v Mastercard Inc* [2017] CAT 16; [2018] Comp. A.R. 1.

third-party funder was capable of coming within the definition of "costs or expenses" incurred by a party in connection with proceedings. However, the relevance of the decision in *Merricks* is likely to be limited to the (nevertheless important) issue of funding arrangements in the CAT. The judgment rested on the specific definition in s.47C(6) of the Competition Act 1998 and the tribunal made clear, at [113], that the issue it was considering was whether a liability to a third-party funder could be seen as costs or expenses within that definition for the purpose of seeing whether the representative claimant would be able to claim that sum from unclaimed damages, rather than any question of allowing the sum to be recovered as a between the parties cost. Nevertheless, both cases do illustrate that the effect of LASPO in preventing recoverability of additional liabilities in litigation generally may not extend to tribunals where the principles of costs recovery are not based on the same legislation.

In principle, the logic of the *Essar* decision could also be used to argue   2–31 that success fees—now expressly irrecoverable in litigation by virtue of s.44 of LASPO —are nevertheless recoverable in principle in proceedings under the Arbitration Act 1996. However, this would appear to run into the barrier that s.58A(4) of the Courts and Legal Services Act 1990 contains a very wide definition of "proceedings", which is wide enough to encompass proceedings under the 1996 Act and s.58(6) (as amended by the 2012 Act), thereby prohibiting an award of costs in any such proceedings from including payment of the success fee. The point may, however, raise its head again in a similar context in the CAT where, particularly in light of the decision in *Merricks* (above), successful CAT claimants in collective actions may seek to argue that ATE premiums, DBA fees and/or the funder's reward are all in some way recoverable as "costs or expenses", though for the reasons given such arguments appear difficult in light of the definition of costs in r.104 of the CAT Rules.

The position in relation to ATE premiums under the Arbitration Act is less clear. The revocation of s.29 Access to Justice Act 1999 by s.46 of the 2012 Act does not appear to lead to the same sort of positive prohibition on recovery as part of a costs order under the 1996 Act as s.58A(6) of the 1990 Act does with success fees. *McGraddie v McGraddie*[93] makes clear that an ATE premium cannot be recovered between the parties, absent the receiving party being able to identify express statutory provision permitting the same. It remains to be seen, however, whether the provision in s.59(1)(c) of the 1996 Arbitration Act allowing the tribunal to award "other costs" will be considered to be wide enough to allow the award of an ATE premium.

The use of third-party funding in England and Wales has developed incrementally through precedent, rather than having been the subject of specific statutory approval or regulation. As a result, and as the use of such funding grows, there are likely to be further cases in the near future exploring the boundaries of its use.

---

[93] *McGraddie v McGraddie* [2015] UKSC 1; [2015] 1 W.L.R. 560.

Questions and answers

A. *Transfer and variation of funding*

Q1. Is it possible to assign a pre-LASPO CFA and to retain between the parties recoverability of success fees?

2–32 This issue has now been largely resolved by the case of *Budana*, above. The Court of Appeal accepted that the rights under a CFA were assignable. This was never in doubt. It rejected the application of the "conditional benefit" analysis which had formed the basis of the earlier High Court decision of *Jenkins* as an answer to the more difficult question of whether the burdens under a CFA were assignable and ultimately accepted that the overall effect of the transfer of the contract was a novation.

However, the court then went on to hold that the overall effect of the attempted assignment and the various contractual documents created was that the novated agreement continued, for the purposes of s.44 of LASPO and the particular proceedings, to be a PCFA and accordingly the success fee under the new agreement remained recoverable. Although not expressly addressed, this would appear also to resolve any argument that the novated agreement must comply with the CFA Order 2013 (SI 2013/689) in order to be enforceable.

Accordingly, where the parties to the CFA clearly intended the transferred agreement to give continued effect to their vested rights and obligations under the original CFA, the court will treat the new agreement as a PCFA, regardless of the fact that it is a novation and not an assignment.

Whilst there is some remaining room for argument, the simple answer therefore seems to be that it is not possible usually to assign both the benefit and burden of a CFA, but that in the context of LASPO transitional arrangements this will not matter since, provided the parties' intentions are clear, the court will treat the novated agreement as a continuation of the pre-April 2013 agreement in any event.

Q2. What is the effect on recoverability of the success fee of assigning a pre-April 2013 CFA post-April 2013?

2–33 This is largely covered by the above. For the reasons set out in *Budana*, it is unlikely to be correct to refer to the CFA as having been assigned, whatever label is put on it. However, provided the parties to the CFA and to the transfer have manifested an intention that they would like the transferred CFA to continue as if it was the original CFA, the court is likely to construe the transferred or novated CFA as still being a PCFA and therefore the success fee as still being recoverable.

Indeed, if the dicta towards the end of the *Catalano* case is to be taken at face value, it may be the position that even where the parties expressly state an intention to abandon wholly a pre-April 2013 CFA and enter into a new post-April 2013 CFA with the express intention of that not being a

PCFA, the court will nevertheless treat the new CFA as being a PCFA, with a recoverable success fee. Although this would be a surprising outcome and one which requires going rather further than *Budana* (which is based on the idea of giving effect to the parties' intentions), it arises out of the court's desire to try and ensure that an individual claimant in an individual set of proceedings is only ever either a pre-LASPO or a post-LASPO claimant. Once a claimant is tied to the pre-LASPO regime (with no QOCS, for example) by having received services under a PCFA of some kind in relation to that case, it appears that the courts will take a very flexible approach towards the issue of any change in funding arrangements in order to try and ensure that the claimant remains at all times a pre-LASPO claimant—not receiving the benefit of QOCS, but continuing to have the benefit of recoverability of additional liabilities in relation to whatever funding arrangements are entered into.

Inevitably, such an approach will lead to a number of practical problems when applied to the facts of individual cases and when it is applied to other aspects of the post-LASPO regulatory regime. For example, does this mean that where a pre-LASPO claimant enters into a post-LASPO CFA (rather than simply attempting to transfer the old agreement) the new agreement need not comply with the consumer protection aspects of the CFA Order 2013, since those are really only intended to address the problems caused by the loss of recoverability? Such problems will have to be addressed when they arise. However, the general tenor of the judgments in *Budana, Catalano* and *Plevin* suggests that the courts will be prepared to take a very purposive approach to statutory construction wherever possible to achieve a satisfactory outcome.

Q3. Do you think the exceptional circumstances which applied in *Jenkins v Young Brothers Transport* to allow the assignment of a CFA might apply in the following circumstances: One part of an LLP was trading under the name of SS until the LLP demerged, at which point the SS business and trading name was transferred to SL Ltd. The LLP continued to trade as a separate entity, but the SRA has treated SL Ltd as a successor practice rather than a new practice. Can or should SL Ltd:

- **Enter into new CFAs with all its clients (in which case how will costs incurred prior to the transfer be dealt with and, in particular, what will happen to any recoverable success fees under pre-April 2013 CFAs)?**
- **Novate or assign the existing CFAs?**
- **Rely on having told its clients of the change of legal entity?**

See the preceding two answers. *Jenkins* is no longer good law (nor is it required in light of *Budana*) on the issue of assignment. Given the passage of time since 2013, it is anticipated that in the vast majority of cases any arrangements relating to transfer of pre-April 2013 arrangements have already been made. What

2–34

will now be important is how they are interpreted in light of *Budana*. For the reasons given above, provided the intention of the contracting parties is clear, the likely outcome is that the court will treat any attempt at transferring pre-April 2013 CFAs post-April 2013 as being one which means that the transferred agreement continues to be a PCFA, with a recoverable success fee, regardless of any black letter law classification of the transfer as a novation and not an assignment. For any transfers yet to take place, the question of which of the identified courses of action would be best on the facts of the individual case is a matter of detailed advice which is beyond the scope of this text, save to note that the description of such a transfer as an assignment is probably wrong, but what is much more important than the label is recording the parties intention that the transferred agreement shall continue as a PCFA.

Q4. My client instructed me prior to 1 April 2013, but I was not able to offer a CFA until later. Is it possible to backdate the CFA to the date of first instruction?

2–35 The first point is that the use of the term "backdating" is dangerous and has been the subject of repeated judicial criticism. It suggests some form of deception and that the date on the written document does not reflect the date on which it was entered into. This should never happen. If an agreement is intended to have retrospective effect, it should expressly state the date on which it was entered into and expressly state the earlier date from which it is said to apply. Note also the High Court's comments in this regard in the decision of *O'Brien*.[94]

As to agreeing a CFA "retrospectively" so that it can benefit from pre-LASPO principles of recoverability, this would not seem possible. Section 44(6) of LASPO provides that the amendments do not apply if the relevant CFA was "entered into" prior to 1 April 2013. Here, the agreement would be entered into after that date, but with retrospective effect. There seems no contractual reason why the agreement would not have retrospective effect, but it would not turn the CFA into a pre-LASPO CFA and the success fee would be irrecoverable. Note that the claimant's position here is materially different to that in *Budana*. The claimant is not "tied" to the pre-LASPO regime and has QOCS and the various other benefits available to him or her. There is no reason therefore for the court to adopt a favourable construction in this situation allowing the claimant's post-LASPO CFA to be treated as a PCFA. This might be different if, for example, the claimant had taken out a pre-LASPO ATE policy.

---

[94] *O'Brien v Shorrock* [2015] EWHC 1630 (QB); [2015] 4 Costs L.O. 439 and see also the decision in *Pentecost v John* [2015] EWHC 1970 (QB); [2015] 4 Costs L.O. 497.

Q5. Can you amend a CFA in advance of detailed assessment? If so, what is the risk of doing so?

It is assumed that by referring to "in advance of detailed assessment" the question is referring to the "window" between the conclusion of the substantive action/making of the costs order in the successful receiving party's favour and the hearing of the detailed assessment of the costs so awarded.

2–36

If so, the position is that there is no contractual or legislative bar to amending a CFA, though any amendment would have to comply with usual contractual principles as well as ensuring that the amended agreement satisfied the requirements of s.58 of the Courts and Legal Services Act 1990, the CFA Order 2013 (SI 2013/689), and any applicable consumer legislation. However, the practical effect is that any such amendment is highly unlikely to have any effect on the between the parties costs.

In *Kellar v Williams*,[95] the Privy Council confirmed that, whilst such an agreement could be amended by agreement between the parties to the agreement after the costs order had been made, the paying party opponent would be entitled to disregard the amendment to the extent that it resulted in any increase in the paying party's liability over and above what that liability would have been but for the amendment.

Although *Kellar* is "only" a Privy Council decision and is therefore not binding on courts in England & Wales, it has been regularly cited and followed by those courts and was expressly accepted by the Court of Appeal in *Radford*.[96] *Radford* is therefore now binding Court of Appeal authority that a variation of a retainer which has the effect of increasing a paying party's liability above that which would otherwise have arisen will not be allowed to stand (on a between the parties basis) where it is made after the time at which the costs become payable in principle.

The key problem with such an amendment, therefore, is that it will not achieve its intended aim, assuming that aim is to cure some defect which was not perceived prior to the completion of the substantive claim for the purpose of between the parties costs recovery.

Q6. Is it possible to vary a pre-April 2013 CFA and still recover the success fee?

In principle, this seems possible. A variation does not change the date of the original agreement. However, in practice, it may depend on the variation. If the variation was seen in some way to offend the broad principle against the between the parties recoverability of additional liabilities incurred after 1 April 2013 then there would be a substantial risk of it being disallowed. To take an extreme example, if the pre-April CFA had provided for a 5% success fee, but was varied after the 1 April 2013 to include a 100% success fee on a retrospective basis, the court might well disallow the success fee, though it

2–37

---

[95] *Kellar v Williams* [2004] UKPC 30; [2005] 4 Costs L.R. 559.
[96] *Radford v Frade* [2018] EWCA Civ 119; [2018] 1 Costs L.R. 59.

could probably do so (subject to the facts) on the simple basis that even if the success fee was recoverable in principle, the increase was unreasonable on a between the parties basis.

Variation is sometimes confused with issues of construction or rectification of CFAs. Where there is some doubt as to the precise meaning of terms in a CFA, these may be resolved by reference to standard principles of construction and this simply involves identifying the true terms of the original agreement. This would have no effect on the recoverability of any success fee under the CFA. Similarly, where it can be established that the written terms do not properly record the true intention of the parties, it may be possible for the CFA to be rectified. Again, rectification is not variation—it is simply ensuring that the written document properly records the true terms as originally agreed but imperfectly recorded, and this would probably not affect the recoverability of any success fee. Variation may not always be the only, or best, solution to perceived problems with a pre-April 2013 CFA.

Radford v Frade[97] is a good example of the difficulties that can be faced where the CFA, as originally drafted, later turns out to be less than ideally drafted for the particular case. As well as providing a good illustration of the sort of approach the court will take to the construction of a CFA in such circumstances, it also provides a sound illustration of the *Kellar v Williams* point mentioned in the answer to Q5 above, namely that an attempt to correct the CFA after the conclusion of the case is likely to fail on a between the parties basis. In *Radford*, as in the *Oyston*[98] case referred to therein, it is arguable that where the court is referring to rectification, it is, in fact, referring to poorly or mis-described attempts to vary the agreement, since rectification does not involve making any change to the original agreement. The appellant in *Radford* was unsuccessful in seeking to persuade the court not to follow *Kellar* and the judgment now helpfully provides Court of Appeal authority on what was previously "only" a Privy Council judgment.

Q7. In a number of reported cases where a claimant moved from legal aid funding to a pre-Jackson CFA, the court has disallowed the recovery of success fees and additional liabilities where in principle they were recoverable, but allowed other costs to be recovered. The result seems fair enough, but on what legal basis did the court specifically disallow some costs but not others? Wasn't the CFA either valid or invalid?

2–38   No. The leading case on this issue is the decision of the Court of Appeal in *Surrey v Barnet & Chase Farm Hospitals NHS Trust*.[99] The issue in these cases is not (usually) one of enforceability (or validity) of the CFA. Rather, the issue is one of reasonableness. Put simply, the paying party accepts (broadly) that the claimant would have incurred some costs in pursuing his or her successful

---

[97] *Radford v Frade* [2018] EWCA Civ 119; [2018] 1 Costs L.R. 59.
[98] *Oyston v Royal Bank of Scotland* unreported 16 May 2006 SCCO; (2006) 103(25) L.S.G. 29.
[99] *Surrey v Barnet & Chase Farm Hospitals NHS Trust* [2018] EWCA Civ 451, [2018] 1 W.L.R. 5831.

case, but contends that it was unreasonable to choose a CFA in place of public funding and therefore the additional cost involved—the success fee and any ATE premium—were unreasonably incurred. If the paying party is correct, reasonable base costs remain payable (subject to assessment and any other arguments).

The basis of the argument is commonly that the advice provided by the solicitor to the client as to the choice of funding methods was objectively unreasonable, having regard to the subjective characteristics and particular circumstances of the individual concerned at the time the particular funding arrangement was entered into. However, the effect would be the same if the argument was that the client made an unreasonable choice despite receiving appropriate advice from their solicitors. As the Court of Appeal noted, the real issue is what were the reasons for the change of funding and were those reasons reasonable, on an objective basis, having regard to the individual circumstances of the claimant concerned.

These situations—where, if the argument is correct, the base costs are still recoverable but the additional liabilities are lost—may be contrasted with the sort of arguments that were run in respect of CFAs which had to comply with the Conditional Fee Agreement Regulations 2000 (revoked with effect from November 2005), where a failure to give proper advice as to alternative forms of funding could be held to be a breach of reg.4 of the regulations, with the effect that the CFA would be held to be unenforceable in its entirety, with consequent non-recoverability of base costs as well as additional liabilities.

Whilst most such arguments as to enforceability (as opposed to reasonableness) ceased following the revocation of the 2000 regulations, they do still arise occasionally in specific narrow contexts, as seen in cases such as *Hyde v Milton Keynes NHS Foundation Trust*.[100] The Court of Appeal's decision in *Hyde*, upholding the two first instance decisions and rejecting the technical challenge by the paying party may be seen as a firm indication that such challenges will only succeed where the legislative provisions plainly require the funding arrangement to be held to be unenforceable.

Q8. In the light of the *Surrey* decision, do you think challenges by paying parties to additional liabilities in cases where there has been a change of funding are likely to increase or are they going away?

The *Surrey* case (and related cases) relate to a particular phenomenon, namely changes of funding from a form of funding which did not give rise to any additional liability (commonly public funding) to one with additional liabilities (a CFA, usually supported by ATE). That phenomenon is limited in time in light of the fundamental changes introduced in April 2013 which mean that, in the majority of cases, additional liabilities are no longer recoverable between the parties where the funding arrangement was entered into on or after 1 April 2013 (though the long tail of such cases has probably been extended by the

2–39

---

[100] *Hyde v Milton Keynes NHS Foundation Trust* [2017] EWCA Civ 399.

decisions in *Plevin*, *Budana* and *Catalano* which will lead to some apparently post-April 2013 funding arrangements in fact being treated as pre-April 2013 arrangements with recoverable additional liabilities). Accordingly, such challenges are likely to reduce in number by virtue of the passage of time regardless of the outcome in *Surrey*.

Whilst *Surrey* gives helpful guidance by clearly restating the applicable principles, the outcome of such cases will generally turn on the facts of the individual case. A switch from public funding to a CFA in one case may well be unreasonable, as in *Surrey*. In another, it may well be reasonable. The outcome of *Surrey* is likely to encourage investigation of these issues by paying parties, particularly since the cases where such matters may remain live are likely to be the larger, more costly, cases. However, their success or failure will depend on individual facts.

Q9. Is a pre-April 2013 ATE policy premium still recoverable if the policyholder changes solicitors post-April 2013? Should the policy be "assigned" to the new firm?

2–40   An ATE policy is a contract between the claimant and the insurer. Provided the policy is not voided or terminated by virtue of the change of solicitor (and this is often the case, particularly with policies issued by the solicitor under delegated authority) then the policy remains in place and, as a pre-April 2013 policy, the premium charged for it remains recoverable in principle between the parties.

There should be no question of "assignment" of the policy to the new firm. Neither the new firm nor the old one are likely to be parties to the contract of insurance. In any event, post-*Plevin*, the court is likely to look favourably on any suggestion that a "transferred" ATE policy remains a pre-LASPO policy regardless of the precise nature of the contractual arrangement which has to be reached between the claimant and ATE insurer.

B. Conditional Fee Agreement terms

Q10. Is it possible to recover pre-action costs in a CFA?

2–41   There are really two parts to this question. First, is it possible to have a CFA with a client covering pre-action costs. The answer to that is generally "yes", provided the scope of the work covered by the CFA, as defined in the agreement itself, is sufficiently widely drawn. In the vast majority of CFAs used for typical forms of litigation, the CFA covers all work, both pre and post-issue, without difficulty.

The second part is whether those pre-action costs are recoverable between the parties. The answer to this has nothing to do with the terms of the CFA itself, save that the CFA must impose a liability for such costs on the client in order to avoid a breach of the indemnity principle and therefore non-recoverability. The answer will instead lie in the terms of the costs order or agreement reached between the parties. If that order or agreement imposes a liability for such costs on the opponent, then those costs will be recoverable between the parties subject to assessment in the usual way.

Q11. Are costs recoverable under a CFA in relation to work done in the Magistrates Court? Is a success fee recoverable in such circumstances?
This depends on the nature of the proceedings, rather than the venue. CFAs are 2–42
made lawful by s.58 of the Courts and Legal Services Act 1990 (as amended). Section 58(3)(b) requires that a CFA must not relate to proceedings which cannot be the subject of an enforceable CFA.

Those proceedings are specified by s.58A(1) and, in short, are criminal proceedings (except proceedings under s.82 of the Environmental Protection Act 1990) and family proceedings (further defined in s.58A(2)). Provided the proceedings concerned are not within these catogories, they may be subject to an enforceable CFA and costs may be recovered under that CFA, subject to the relevant applicable costs rules of the forum concerned.

In relation to success fees, s.58(4) operates in the reverse fashion. Rather than making the agreement enforceable save in relation to excepted proceedings, s.58(4) requires that a CFA which provides for a success fee must relate to proceedings of a specified type in order to be enforceable.

However, in a piece of circuitous legislation, art.3 of the Conditional Fee Agreements Order 2000[101] provides that all proceedings which can be subject of an enforceable CFA are specified as proceedings in respect of which the CFA may include a success fee.

That deals with enforceability. However, recoverability between the parties of such success fees was abolished for all agreements entered into on or after 1 April 2013 save for limited categories in respect of which the amendments to s.58 were not introduced (now only mesothelioma and privacy and defamation claims (entered into prior to 6 April 2019 for the latter)). Save for such claims, success fees under a CFA are not recoverable, pursuant to s.58A(6) of the 1990 Act. Accordingly, whilst the CFA may be enforceable in relation to the Magistrates Court proceedings (assuming they are not criminal or family proceedings) and base costs may be recovered on success, the success fee will be irrecoverable.

Q12. Is it possible to charge a fixed fee (if successful) under a no win, no fee agreement? If so, would this be a CFA or a DBA?
The short answer is yes, it is possible and yes, it would probably be a CFA. 2–43
The key definitional features of a CFA are identified in s.58(2) of the Courts & Legal Services Act 1990. They say nothing about the arrangements having to be for payment on an hourly rate basis. What is key is whether the agreement provides for the fees or expenses, or any part of them, to be payable only in specified circumstances. If so, that contingent element of payment makes the agreement a CFA.

---

[101] Conditional Fee Agreements Order 2000 (SI 2000/823).

What differentiates that arrangement from a DBA is when the agreement provides both that a payment of some or all of the fees is only to be made if the client obtains a specified financial benefit from the case and that the amount of the payment to the solicitor is determined by reference to the amount of the financial benefit (s.58AA(3)). Such an arrangement is a DBA. It is important to note that both elements are required. The first element may be present in a CFA – for example, the CFA may say that some or all of the fees are only payable if the client receives damages of at least £x. Nevertheless, that arrangement remains a CFA, not a DBA. It is only where the agreement provides that the amount of the solicitor's reward is determined by direct reference to the benefit (for example, and most commonly, that the solicitor shall be entitled to x% of the damages) that that part of the agreement (but not the remainder of it) becomes a DBA.

Whilst unusual, there is nothing in principle in the legislation to prevent a fixed fee (or part of it) being contingent on success, or indeed a success fee being charged on that contingent element of the fixed fee. Unless the amount of the fixed fee was determined by reference to the amount of proceeds of the litigation, such an arrangement would remain a CFA. It may require careful drafting, but in principle is permissible.

Q13. Do you need to name all defendants in a CFA?

2–44   No. What is necessary is to ensure that the CFA adequately identifies what claim or claims the CFA covers so that the parties to the agreement can be sufficiently certain as to its scope. That may be achieved, for example, by identifying the underlying matter which gives rise to the claim (for example an accident in which the claimant was involved on a particular date) and that the agreement covers the claimant's claim for damages arising out of that accident against any opponent who might be identified.

There have been a large number of reported cases where parties have encountered difficulties as a result of a CFA identifying the potential defendants to a claim too narrowly and failing to notice during the lifetime of the claim that the CFA may need to be amended to reflect additional defendants who have subsequently been identified. Perhaps the best-known examples are *Malone v Birmingham NHS Trust*,[102] where the CFA was held to be wide enough to cover the claim against the Trust despite naming the Home Office as the defendant and *Engeham v London and Quadrant Housing Trust Ltd*,[103] where the claimant managed to recover her costs despite a similar problem. Parties should be wary of undue reliance on *Engeham*. If anything, it emphasises the point that errors in the naming of defendants to a CFA may be fatal to a claim for costs—the claimant in *Engeham* was only successful in recovering her costs by way of a secondary argument having decided not to appeal before the Court of Appeal the decision of the judges below that the CFA, properly

---

[102] *Malone v Birmingham NHS Trust [2018]* EWCA Civ 1376; [2018] 3 Costs L.R. 627.
[103] *Engeham v London and Quadrant Housing Trust Ltd* [2015] EWCA Civ 1530; [2016] 3 Costs L.O. 357.

construed, did not name the relevant defendant. However, *Malone* is a much
more positive decision from a receiving party's perspective and illustrates, correctly that the court's main function is to seek to identify the intention of the
parties and that, where it is plain that there has been poor drafting, the court
will examine the factual matrix rather than focussing on an unduly narrow
textual analysis.

Experience suggests that adopting an approach of limiting the CFA to a
single, specifically identified, defendant at the outset may be an unwise practice. However, there will be cases where it is helpful or advisable to specifically
name the potential defendants, in particular where the intention is to ensure
that the solicitor is only bound to act in relation to certain specific matters
and is not bound to pursue a claim against other potential defendants unless
the solicitor later expressly agrees to do so. In such circumstances, the solicitor needs to make sure that it has robust processes in place to ensure that any
necessary variation to the CFA is agreed with the client, in writing, before any
work on the additional aspect of the claim is undertaken.

**Q14. My client entered into a CFA prior to 1 April 2013, but has now died.
I wish to offer the personal representatives a CFA to continue the claim.
Will I be able to recover the success fee?**

It is a moot point whether the original CFA is automatically assigned to the 2–45
personal representatives on the death of the client. Certain contracts are so
assigned by operation of law on death (unless the contract provides otherwise). However, personal contracts are generally an exception to this and it is
arguable whether a CFA falls into this category.

Equally, there is no reason in principle why the CFA should not expressly
provide for the consequences on death of the client, including for its continuation in relation to the remaining claim, subject to instruction by the personal representative. There is nothing preventing the (now) deceased making
contractual provision to bind their personal representatives on their death,
though such provision is rare in CFAs.

However, despite both of those points, the most common scenario is for
CFAs, particularly personal injury CFAs, to provide expressly that the agreement ended on the death of the client. The Law Society standard model prior
to April 2013, expressly so provided. If such a CFA was used, then there is no
need to consider whether it is arguable in law that the CFA persists, because
the issue has been expressly addressed in the CFA. It does not.

In summary, therefore, there are certain circumstances, depending on the
terms of the original CFA and how it is categorised by a court, where there
may be arguments that the original CFA may continue in some way, though
this could only be determined by reference to the specific terms of the CFA. If
the CFA is a standard Law Society model (or one of the many variants based
thereon) or if these specific circumstances do not apply, then it will be necessary to consider whether any new CFA—which is likely, ostensibly, to be a
post-LASPO CFA—should be seen to be a pre-LASPO CFA.

There may be scope for argument in light of *Budana* and *Catalano* as to whether, in certain circumstances, a personal representative taking over such a case should be entitled to have any funding arrangement treated as a PCFA. However, this may depend on (i) whether the personal representative is treated as a new claimant and/or (ii) whether the proceedings following death are to be regarded as different proceedings for the purpose of the transitional provisions, and therefore whether the personal representative has the benefit of QOCS protection.

As cases such as *Plevin*, above, illustrate, the court's general approach is wherever possible to treat a claimant in respect of particular proceedings as always being either a pre-LASPO claimant, with recoverable additional liabilities but no QOCS protection, or a post-LASPO claimant, with no recoverable additional liabilities but QOCS protection. However, there may be valid grounds for contending that there is a clearer distinction post-death.

It is unsatisfactory that the position is unclear and remains unresolved so long after the April 2013 rule changes. Cases on the point may yet reach appellate level at some point in the future.

For an interesting and detailed analysis of some of the issues surrounding the effect of death on a CFA and the use of the Law Society standard "death" clause see *Higgins v Evans*.[104]

Q15. We wish to enter into a CFA with our client whereby in addition to the success fee being capped as required by s.58 of the Courts and Legal Services Act 1990 and the CFA Order 2013, the total costs payable under the agreement will also be capped as a percentage of the damages. We have been told that this means our agreement is a contingency fee agreement, or DBA, and must comply with the DBA Regulations 2013. Is this correct?

2–46   No. As a matter of pure terminology, any agreement where the right to or amount of payment depends on the outcome of the case is probably a form of contingency fee agreement. However, that loose terminology has been replaced by the specific terminology of conditional fee agreements and damages based agreements used in ss.58 and 58AA.

A CFA whereby the fees payable under the CFA are not calculated by reference to the damages awarded, but where there is an overall cap on the amount that can be paid by reference to the damages is a CFA. It is not a DBA. The key distinction is that the cap is precisely that. If the fees payable are less than the cap, then the fees payable are those fees, as calculated on a conventional basis and not as a percentage of damages. The cap merely operates as an overall limit, rather than as the method of calculation of the fees.

A DBA, by contrast, is that part (and only that part) of an agreement where the fee payable is determined as a percentage of the damages recovered. It is not a cap, but rather the primary method of determination of the applicable fee.

---

[104] *Higgins v Evans* [2019] EWHC 2809 (QB).

Prior to the introduction of recoverable success fees, the Law Society model CFA used to provide for a cap on the success fee payable under the CFA. The new provisions for personal injury CFAs operate on a similar model. The agreements remain CFAs and this principle applies even if the capping effect is extended beyond the success fee to the fees generally.

Q16. Is it possible to get around the limits on the recoverability of success fees in CFAs by agreeing a CFA with no success fee but higher base costs, given that firms are free to negotiate the level of their fees with clients?
The loss of recoverable success fees has required many firms to reconsider **2–47** their approach to charging clients. In such circumstances, it is open to a firm to conclude that, on a solicitor-client basis, in order to provide services to their clients and maintain a profitable business, it is necessary to charge a higher hourly rate than the firm would previously have charged.

Care should be taken, however, to avoid a situation where the client is being charged a higher hourly rate for the case in specified circumstances than would have been charged but for those specified circumstances. Such an arrangement would amount to the charging of a success fee in accordance with the definition in s.58(2)(b) of the Courts and Legal Services Act 1990. Not only would the success fee element be irrecoverable between the parties—even if described as being part of the basic charges—but the inclusion of a success fee element would risk the whole agreement being declared unenforceable, especially in a personal injury case.

Whilst as noted, it remains open to a firm to charge a higher hourly rate post-LASPO, on a between the parties basis the court must still be satisfied that the hourly rate is reasonable. The charging of hourly rates which have increased to compensate for the non-recoverability of success fees is unlikely to be seen as a valid basis for allowing such rates between the parties. Success fees were intended to be revenue-neutral—the success fee in the successful cases paying for the loss of costs in the unsuccessful ones—even if that may not have been how it worked in practice. The LASPO changes were not intended to alter that model, but merely to shift the burden of the success fee to the client. The loss of recoverability therefore does not provide any valid between the parties justification for an increase in the basic hourly rate.

Fundamental to ensuring recoverability of costs from the client is ensuring that the client is properly informed as to the nature of the proposed arrangements such that he or she is able to make an informed choice—see *Herbert v HH Law* Ltd and related cases discussed in **Ch.9**.[105] The more unusual the arrangement, the more important it is that this is fully and clearly explained to the client.

Q17. We were acting for a personal injury client on a CFA basis with a success fee element. Due to the actions of the client, we had to terminate

---

[105] *Herbert v HH Law Ltd* [2019] EWCA Civ 527; [2019] 1 W.L.R. 4253.

the retainer. There are outstanding costs and disbursements allocated to the file. We told the client that we would wait for payment until the matter was concluded, after which the success fee element would also be payable if the client was successful. The client has now instructed a new firm of solicitors and the new firm is asking for a final bill of costs. Of course, we cannot include the success fee as this is based on whether the client is successful in the future. Are we under an obligation to provide a final bill and what are the implications of our lien over the papers?

2–48   The standard Law Society CFA terms (last updated in 2014 and currently not published and under review) in this situation provide that the firm has the choice, as the question suggests, of charging basic charges and disbursements at the time of the termination of the retainer or only charging basic charges, disbursements and success fees if the claimant goes on to win the claim for damages. Note, this is different to the terms which apply in some other circumstances, where the client is required to pay the basic charges and disbursements forthwith, with the success fee being payable in addition if the claim is won.

Assuming the terms here are as per those standard terms, the solicitor appears to have elected to follow the latter course, in which case the client has no liability, save for disbursements (which are payable in any event) unless and until the claim is won.

The firm is not therefore in a position to provide the client with a bill of costs at this stage. Disbursements could be billed—and it is now clear that disbursements may be the subject of a separate and discrete statute bill.[106] However, base charges and success fees cannot.

Provided sums due remain outstanding the firm has a valid lien over the papers. It is unclear whether this would extend to the position where the sums are only contingently payable and it is certainly open to argument, in the situation identified above, that payment of disbursements would be sufficient to allow the client to demand delivery up of his papers.

Note care should be taken—the precise terms of the CFA will be crucial and many other forms of CFA impose materially different terms in relation to the client's liability where the client has failed to keep to their responsibilities.

Q18. Is it possible to enter into a CFA before investigating the strengths and weaknesses of the case and then terminate the CFA if the client does not have a reasonable prospect of success and still charge the client for carrying out the investigation?

2–49   It is not uncommon for CFAs to provide that the solicitor may end the CFA if the prospects of success change, though this is commonly on the basis that the solicitor will only be entitled to expenses/disbursements if they do so. The question assumes a more basic position, namely that of entering into a CFA before any investigation of the merits and then being able to discontinue the

---

[106] See the case of *Slade v Boodia* [2018] EWCA Civ 2667; [2019] 1 W.L.R. 1126.

CFA and charge the client for the work done to date. The short answer is that such an agreement would not be in contravention of s.58 of the Courts and Legal Services Act 1990 or the CFA Order 2013. The client would, however, need to be given a very clear explanation of what the effect of the agreement was and care would need to be taken to ensure that the agreement was not in breach of the Consumer Rights Act (see, in particular, Sch.2 and terms such as those identified in paras 3 and 7).

Further, the solicitor's ability to "walk away" and still be paid if the merits of the claim turned out to be poor would be material to the reasonableness of any success fee the solicitor sought to claim if the case proceeded and was successful. By entering into such an arrangement, the solicitor has reduced the risk that it would otherwise have been exposed to, had it entered into a more conventional CFA at the outset.

Ultimately, however, provided the proposed arrangement is properly explained to the client and the client is willing to enter into the arrangement then such an arrangement would not be unlawful.

Q19. Is it permissible for a law firm to enter into a CFA with its client that provides that if the law firm ends the agreement and the client continues the claim and wins, the client remains liable to pay the firm's basic charges, disbursements and success fee when the claim is concluded? We have a potential client who entered into a CFA with such a provision and the law firm then decided that it no longer wished to continue acting for the client as they considered there to be insufficient prospects of success.

This question appears to be almost the mirror image of the previous question. 2–50 In principle, such an arrangement is possible, though as discussed above it is unusual for the client to be left liable for basic charges, disbursements and success fees where it is the solicitor who "walks away", unless this is because the client has not kept to his or her responsibilities. Absent a very clear explanation of these matters to the client and their informed consent, there would be a real doubt as to whether such terms were reasonable and enforceable. In addition, consideration should be given to whether the CFA is, in fact, a contentious business agreement, in which case s.65 of the Solicitors Act 1974 would provide the client with a direct route to test the fairness and reasonableness of the agreement. See also Sch.2 para.7 of the Consumer Rights Act 2015.

Q20. We wish to enter into a discounted CFA with our client whereby we would be paid 70% of our standard rates if the client loses, and 100% of our standard rates if it wins, plus a success fee. We know that the success fee is no longer recoverable from the unsuccessful party, but would the 30% balance between the discounted and standard fees be recoverable from an unsuccessful opponent or would this be treated as part of/like the success fee?

In principle, yes. The hourly rates would be subject to assessment between 2–51 the parties. Assuming those rates were reasonable, and assuming the CFA was otherwise properly drafted, then on success the "full" hourly rates would be recoverable. The leading case on discounted CFAs is still *Gloucestershire CC v Evans*[107] and the dicta in that case support the proposition that when considering the enforceability of such a discounted CFA the court will not usually seek to go behind the statement in the CFA that the "full" rates are the rates that would have applied if the matter had not been conducted on a CFA. Assuming proper drafting and absent a clear case of a sham arrangement, therefore, the court will not usually be receptive to arguments that there is a "disguised" success fee. However, as noted, the court can still decide whether those rates are reasonable.

Q21. Can a law firm enter into a CFA with a client in a contentious matter which covers the pre-action period but not any subsequent period if proceedings are issued?

2–52   The legislation in relation to CFAs is not prescriptive in relation to such matters. In principle, therefore, this is possible. Care would, however, need to be taken to ensure that the CFA was well-drafted, in particular, to impose and preserve a liability (contingent or otherwise) on the client if the scope of work covered by the CFA came to an end without success having yet been achieved and to provide for an appropriate transition to an alternative form of funding. Care would also need to be taken to ensure that the client was given a full and clear explanation of the CFA and any related funding arrangement and to ensure that the agreement (in the case of a consumer) complied with the Consumer Rights Act 2015.

Q22. We generally use DBAs for pre-action work where we believe that the case will settle and court proceedings will not be required, and we use a CFA from the outset where we consider court action is likely. Due to the uncertainties regarding DBAs, we do not use DBAs for court proceedings. In an ongoing case, we have used a DBA for a debt claim, believing it would settle, but we are now looking at having to issue court proceedings. The DBA is expressly limited to attempts to recover the debt and excludes the issue of proceedings. Can we now disregard the DBA and enter into a CFA with our client, which provides that it retrospectively covers the work already undertaken, or does the DBA preclude us from doing this and effectively mean that we cannot recover costs for the time incurred to date against the proposed defendant and we must start afresh with a CFA for the court proceedings, so that only costs incurred from the date of the CFA are potentially recoverable from the other party?

2–53   The practice of using one form of retainer for non-contentious business and a different one if the work becomes contentious, sometimes with the latter than retrospectively replacing the earlier, is not uncommon. To take the example in the question – and as noted in the text above – provided the retainer was

---

[107] *Gloucestershire CC v Evans* [2008] EWCA Civ 21; [2008] 1 W.L.R. 1883.

limited to non-contentious work, it need not even be a DBA in the strictest sense of having to comply with the DBA Regulations 2013. It could be a Non-Contentious Business Agreement. However, to answer the question, provided both parties to the DBA are in agreement, there is no particular reason why they could not agree that such agreement shall no longer be of effect and that, instead, the remuneration for the case, both in respect of work done and to be done, shall be determined in accordance with some different agreement. Care must be taken to ensure that there is adequate consideration passing for the new agreement and that it complies with all necessary contractual and regulatory formalities. Difficulties tend to arise where this is done in circumstances where the effect may be to increase the opponent's liability if a costs order is made in due course, and plainly any such agreement (i) must not be a sham and (ii) must be reasonable if it is to allow for between the parties recovery.

Finally, in this regard, it is worth noting that in light of the Court of Appeal's decision in *Zuberi*, it is probably inappropriate to refer to a whole agreement as a DBA. A DBA, as a legal term, is only that part of the agreement which provides for payment out of recoveries. The balance of the agreement is not a DBA (though it could, for example, be a CFA).

Q23. We entered into a CFA with a client who has since passed away. Her husband is her personal representative and will be continuing her claim. What do we need to do to novate her CFA and insurance policy to her husband now she is deceased?

The authors are not able to give advice for use in specific cases. However, in general, the answer to a question of this type will turn on the particular terms of the CFA in question. Many CFAs, particularly those based on the Law Society standard personal injury model, expressly provide that on the death of the claimant the CFA ends. The terms commonly further provide that the firm may then offer a fresh CFA to the personal representatives to continue to pursue the claim as an estate claim, but only provide the estate agrees to pay the base costs and success fee under the original CFA if the claim succeeds (or similar terms). In these circumstances, the terms are express, the CFA has ended and there is therefore no CFA to novate to the personal representatives. What is required is a new funding arrangement and some discussion or agreement about payment of any fees and expenses under the old one.

2–54

Some CFAs expressly provide that the CFA will not end on death, but will continue for the benefit of the estate, subject (depending on the particular terms) to some form of election or agreement on the part of either the estate, the solicitors or both. In such circumstances, the continuation of the CFA should be automatic, subject to any conditions, for example, in relation to any election being complied with. Again, in this situation, the terms of the CFA will dictate the outcome. This time, the CFA will expressly continue for the benefit of the estate and again there is unlikely to be any need for a novation.

C. After the event insurance

Q24. If a staged premium ATE policy was incepted prior to 1 April 2013, but the further staged premiums are only incurred after that date, will the further premiums be recoverable?

2–55 In an early edition of this book, the answer was said to be "probably". Staged premiums were a common feature of litigation and their use had been expressly approved by the courts in cases such as *Rogers v Merthyr Tydfil CBC*.[108] Their existence and use was well known at the time of the amendment of the rules and it would have been simple for the rule to provide that only the stages incurred prior to 1 April 2013 would be recoverable, if that had been the intention. Instead, s.58C of the 1990 Act refers to "a policy of insurance" having been "taken out" prior to 1 April 2013 and the taking out of a staged policy would appear to satisfy that requirement, with the effect that subsequent premiums under the policy remain recoverable in principle.

Following the Supreme Court's decision in *Plevin*, above, the answer may now be stated to be "almost certainly", provided they relate to the same proceedings. In *Plevin*, the court was concerned with post-LASPO top-up premiums to allow appeals to be covered. The court held that these were to be regarded as PCFAs (or more accurately as part of the existing PCFA) despite the point that for some costs purposes at least appeals are regarded as separate proceedings. The court held that that distinction did not apply to ss.44 and 46 of LASPO. If a top-up premium is to be regarded as part of the existing PCFA where taken out for an appeal, there seems to be no reason why it should not be so regarded for a reasonably required top-up for the case itself.

The point may yet be tested, however, if there has been abuse of the system with policies being incepted on a wide-scale basis for nominal premiums merely to get them "on the books" prior to 1 April 2013 and then substantial premiums being later charged when the case is properly evaluated. Whether this has occurred and how the courts will approach claims for premiums in such cases remains to be seen. It may be that in order to succeed in such a case a paying party would need to establish that the original policy was, in fact, a sham.

Q25. Would an increased premium on a pre-1 April 2013 ATE policy be payable by a losing defendant? i.e. is the increased premium payable or only the original premium amount?

2–56 See the preceding answer. On the plain wording of s.58C of the 1990 Act, a further (part) premium payable under a policy incepted prior to the 1 April 2013 would appear to be recoverable in principle. *Plevin* strongly supports this position.

---

[108] *Rogers v Merthyr Tydfil CBC* [2006] EWCA Civ 1134; [2007] 1 W.L.R. 808.

Q26. In a clinical negligence case, where a claimant obtains a breach and causation report and the defendant then admits liability, could the claimant recover the cost of the premium if it then obtained ATE insurance in relation to obtaining a quantum report?

Yes, in principle. The recoverability of a premium under the Recovery of Costs Insurance Premiums in Clinical Negligence Proceedings (No.2) Regulations 2013 (SI 2013/739) is not contingent on whether or not the claimant takes out some other ATE insurance in respect of other aspects of the case. However, the premium (or part of the premium) that is recoverable is only that premium (or part thereof) that relates to the cost of obtaining reports on liability and causation. The premium or part premium for the ATE insurance in respect of the other aspects of the case is not recoverable. Such premiums are subject to assessment as to their reasonableness and proportionality, applying the new, post-April 2013 test of proportionality—see *McMenemy*[109] and *West*— though the decision in *West* means that proportionality will have little impact on the assessment of such a premium and the main issue will be the reasonableness of the premium which, in a block-rated case, will be considered applying the established *Rogers* criteria.

2–57

Q27. A firm acted for two claimants, one of whom was insolvent. It entered into an ATE policy before April 2016, planning to rely on the insolvency exemption to LASPO if successful, so that it could recover the ATE premium from the defendant. Would the fact that only one of the claimants was insolvent prevent the firm from relying on the insolvency exemption? If they were allowed to recover the ATE premium from the defendant, would it be reduced to 50% to reflect the fact that only one of the claimants was insolvent?

This point is open to argument. The saving provision in art.4 of the Legal Aid, Sentencing and Punishment of Offenders Act 2012 (Commencement No.5 and Saving Provision) Order 2013 (SI 2013/77) provides that the amendments removing recoverability of additional liabilities "do not apply to . . . proceedings" of various types. The order does not provide that the amendments do not apply to particular claimants.

2–58

This suggests that, provided the proceedings themselves are within the exception, any of the parties to the proceedings may rely on that exception, regardless of whether they are one of the identified classes of legal persons referred to in the order.

However, the underlying premise in the exception appears to have been to allow particular officeholders and companies being wound up or entering into administration to benefit from the continued availability of funding arrangements with recoverable additional liabilities. Accordingly, a purposive construction of the order may exclude parties other than those identified within the order from its operation.

---

[109] *Peterborough and Stamford Hospitals NHS Trust v McMenemy* [2017] EWCA Civ 1941; [2018] 1 W.L.R. 2685.

Such a purposive approach would appear to be consistent with cases such as *Budana* and *Plevin* which place heavy emphasis on the packaged nature of the changes introduced in April 2013 and on ensuring that the courts try to interpret the relevant provisions to give effect to the identifiable intention of the legislature, even if that means placing a strained construction on those provisions.

If one party is excluded from the operation of the exemption, it will not necessarily follow that only 50% (or indeed as much as 50%) of the premium will be recoverable. It may be that the remaining party is able to show that all or the majority of the cost of the premium would have been incurred by it in any event and that it is liable for that premium in full (whether jointly and severally with the other party or otherwise). The precise outcome is likely to be fact dependent.

Q28. If a claimant with a pre-1 April 2013 ATE insurance policy is successful at first instance, an appeal is granted and a top-up of the ATE premium (after 1 April 2013) is required to cover the appeal, is a post-1 April 2013 ATE top-up premium or, alternatively, the premium for a new policy to cover the appeal recoverable from the other side if the appeal is successful?

2–59   Yes. See *Plevin v Paragon Personal Finance Ltd*.[110] This was the very issue resolved by the Supreme Court in that case. The Supreme Court distinguished the Court of Appeal decision of *Hawksford Trustees*[111] which held that appeals were to be regarded as separate proceedings for the purposes of s.29 of the Access to Justice Act 1999, noting the different legislative purpose of LASPO and the need to ensure that a claimant who was in the pre-LASPO "camp" did not suffer the dis-benefits (loss of recoverability) where it had been reasonable to take out a later top-up policy and the need for the same had only arisen post-LASPO.

Q29. Does "old" CPR r.44.12B still apply to proceedings in publication cases, such that a defendant who admits liability and offers to settle before or within 42 days of notification of an ATE premium, will not incur liability for payment of the claimant's ATE insurance premium if the matter settles without court proceedings?

2–60   Yes. Rule 44.12B which was introduced in October 2009 is a "provision relating to funding arrangements" within "old" CPR rr.43 to 48 and it continues in effect by virtue of CPR r.48.1(1). It is for that reason that it remains in the *White Book* Volume 2 as part of the pre-April 2013 General Rules About Costs and is likely to continue to apply to any ATE premium in a publication and privacy case for as long as the publication and privacy exemption to the removal of recoverability remains. As noted above, whilst success fees

---

[110] *Plevin v Paragon Personal Finance Ltd* [2017] UKSC 23; [2017] 1 W.L.R. 1249.
[111] *Hawksford Trustees Jersey Ltd v Stella Global UK Ltd* [2012] EWCA Civ 987; [2012] 1 W.L.R. 3581.

have ceased to be recoverable in relation to funding agreements in publication and privacy cases where the agreement was entered into after April 2019, ATE premiums continue to be recoverable. Since the chosen mechanism for maintaining, at least for now, the recoverability of ATE premiums was simply to continue with not bringing into force s.46 of LASPO (rather than introducing any new, specific regimes such as that which applies in clinical negligence claims), an ATE premium in such a case remains a PCFA. CPR r.44.12B therefore continues to apply – again a rather unhelpful and potentially confusing position which may operate as a trap for the unwary.

D. Issue and notification

Q30. Our client entered into a CFA and ATE insurance policy before April 2013 in relation to insolvency proceedings. Since then, another party has been added as a party to the CFA and ATE insurance policy. Are we required to notify the defendants of this variation to the CFA and ATE insurance? If so, how do we notify them and do we need to file the notice? Assuming this case falls within the insolvency exception (which some, but not all, insolvency cases will do) then the April 2013 date is a red herring. The correct question is whether the funding arrangements were entered into on or before 5 April 2016.   2–61

In relation to the addition of parties to an existing CFA, the notification requirements under the former CPR PD 47 para.32.5, as preserved in operation by CPR r.48.1, require notification to be given where "a claimant [or defendant] has entered into a [relevant] funding arrangement". Accordingly, the matter should be looked at from the perspective of each individual party. The additional party here has now entered into a relevant funding arrangement by joining the existing CFA and notice should be given by way of a fresh N251 in respect of that particular party. It may be appropriate, depending on the facts, to provide additional information to make clear, for example, the date from which the client's liability under that arrangement runs if it is otherwise unclear.

If the case is not within the insolvency exception, or if the later joining party was added to the CFA on or after 1 April 2016, then the later joining party will (probably) fall foul of s.58A(6) of the Courts and Legal Services Act 1990 and s.44(6) LASPO and will not be able to recover any additional liabilities, despite the CFA having been entered into earlier by the other party.

Q31. Is there a long stop date whereby a party who has entered into a pre-April 2013 funding arrangement in relation to a claim must issue proceedings?
No (save, of course, for the general law of limitation in respect of that party's claim). However, the funding arrangement must relate to the "matter that is the subject matter of the proceedings in which the costs order is made". Accordingly, if the claim subsequently brought is seen to relate to a different   2–62

matter, then any additional liabilities will not be recoverable (and indeed there may be an issue as to what retainer in fact covers the proceedings that have been issued, with potential consequences between the parties as a result of the application of the indemnity principle and on a solicitor-client basis).

Q32. Is a notice of funding required for a DBA?

2–63   No. The requirements for notices of funding in (old) CPR r.44 were revoked with effect from 1 April 2013. They continue to apply in relation to pre-April 2013 funding arrangements and in the excepted cases where additional liabilities remain recoverable, as referred to in the main text (as do the requirements relating to provision of information about additional liabilities on detailed assessments in CPR PD 47 para.32) and should be complied with fully in respect of such arrangements (see CPR r.48.1). This includes the provision under the "old" CPR PD 44 para.19.3 whereby there is a requirement to provide notice of change if the information previously provided is no longer accurate. Accordingly, if there is a change in relation to a pre-April 2013 CFA or ATE which means information provided in respect of those arrangements is no longer accurate, the opposing party should be notified accordingly.

Q33. We are acting for the claimant in a litigation matter. The defendant's solicitors have asked us to confirm how the litigation is being funded. Is there any obligation on our client to provide this information?

2–64   There is no procedural obligation to provide this information. However, it is well established that the court may order a party to provide information in relation to its funding arrangements where the court accepts that to do so would serve a proper purpose. For example, the court has ordered a party to provide details of the identity of third-party funders where to do so would serve the purpose of allowing a party to consider whether to bring an application for security for costs pursuant to CPR r.25.14.[112] It might take a similar approach for the purposes of an application for third-party costs pursuant to s.51 of the Senior Courts Act 1981.

Accordingly, where there is a legitimate purpose to be served by the request and the information or documentation requested is not privileged (a question, in relation to funding arrangements, which is still not satisfactorily resolved, but in practice may often be dealt with by redaction of privileged information from a document), there is at least some risk that a court would order that the information be provided.

The court is likely to scrutinise closely whether such a legitimate purpose exists at the time the application is made. See, for example, the judgment of HHJ Keyser QC in *Dawnus Sierra Leone Ltd v Timis Mining Corp Ltd*[113] where the court concluded that an application for disclosure of the identity of the

---

[112] *Wall v Royal Bank of Scotland Plc* [2016] EWHC 2460 (Comm); [2017] 4 W.L.R. 2 and *Raiffeisen Zentralbank Osterreich Ag v Crossseas Shipping Ltd* [2003] EWHC 1381 (Comm).
[113] *Dawnus Sierra Leone Ltd v Timis Mining Corp Ltd* [2016] EWHC B19 (TCC).

third-party funder was premature—on the evidence available the funder did not appear to be operating for commercial gain, and therefore the disclosure was not needed for the purpose of considering any CPR r.25.14 application. It was also premature in relation to any potential application under s.51 of the Senior Courts Act 1981 since such matters would only usually arise at the end of the case.

However, even in that case, the application was only refused because the defendant (who was bringing a counterclaim) had disclosed both that it had third party funding and the basic nature of that funding.

See further the *RBS Rights Litigation* and Mr Justice Hildyard's judgment.[114] In that case, the court accepted (on a security for costs application) that it had jurisdiction to order disclosure of details of third-party funding and indeed of ATE insurance, though noted that the details of an ATE policy would not normally be relevant (unless, of course, a party relied on it as a basis for security not being awarded). The court also noted that the terms of an ATE policy were unlikely to be privileged, save to the extent that any redaction was necessary to ensure that any references to legal advice were removed. On the facts, disclosure of relevant details of the third-party funding was ordered, but disclosure of details of the ATE was not.

Q34. Where there are ongoing court proceedings and the defendant knows that the claimant has the benefit of some BTE legal expenses cover, is the defendant entitled to ask for a copy of the policy or for details as to what is and what is not covered?
This would be unlikely unless, as indicated above, there is a clear legiti-   2–65
mate purpose for doing do, for example if such information was likely to be directly relevant to an application for security for costs and the BTE policy was advanced as a basis for such an application not being warranted. This would not usually arise in the context of most claims by individuals resident in this jurisdiction whose claims may be supported by BTE insurance.

Absent such a consideration, a court is unlikely to see any legitimate purpose in such a demand for information. The real purpose would appear to be to allow the defendant to quantify its potential ability to recover costs from the claimant (whether directly or by indemnity from the insurer) in the event that the defence to the claim was successful. Absent a legitimate context such as a security for costs application, this is no more than a request for details of a claimant's financial resources and is not something a court is likely to consider to be a legitimate line of enquiry at this stage.

---

[114] *Re RBS Rights Issue Litigation* [2017] EWHC 463 (Ch); [2017] 1 W.L.R. 3539.

Q35. If you are notified that the opponent has a CFA in place, are you entitled to see a copy of it, given that you will be liable to meet those costs where liability is not contested?

2–66   This question is effectively the mirror image of the preceding one. Without repeating the previous answer, therefore, the short answer is that it is open to the court to order disclosure of details of funding arrangements where some immediate interlocutory purpose would be served by such disclosure, but it will be rare that this is established in relation to a CFA. In addition to the issues generally surrounding disclosure of funding arrangements, referred to above, there are particular issues with CFAs, particularly at the interim stage. Firstly, they may either be privileged documents themselves, or contain or refer to privileged material – an issue neatly sidestepped by the Court of Appeal in *Hollins*.[115] Secondly, even if not, they may well contain confidential information which it is not appropriate to have disclosed, particularly at an interim stage (for example, the reasons for setting the success fee at a particular level, or what the trigger for a "win" is, particularly if that may be tied to beating offers etc). It may sometimes be necessary to refer to or disclose particular parts of a CFA at an interim stage in order to satisfy a court that there is a present liability to costs in order to recover interim costs awards, but any such disclosure is likely to be both (i) voluntary (the receiving party could always choose simply to not seek immediate payment and await the outcome of the case) and (ii) limited.

Q36. What information does a winning party have to provide about its funding arrangements to the losing party?

2–67   This depends. If the funding arrangement is a pre-commencement funding arrangement (PCFA) within the meaning of CPR r.48.1 – that is to say, in very broad terms, a CFA or ATE policy entered into before s.44–46 of LASPO came into effect in respect of the particular type of proceedings (1 April 2013 for most cases), then the relevant provisions of CPR rr.43–48 and the Costs Practice Direction will apply, as they applied prior to April 2013.

Those provisions required that, within the context of a detailed assessment, a party seeking to claim an additional liability from the other party provide certain details of the underlying arrangement – see old CPR 47 PD 32. Old CPR 44.3B imposed a sanction for any failure to provide such information within the detailed assessment proceedings, though the effective bite of such a sanction (at least in respect of success fees) was limited by the decision in *Long v Value Properties Ltd*.[116]

Old CPR 47 PD 32 was introduced as a practical solution to the guidance provided by the Court of Appeal in *Hollins* at [71].[117] An unvarnished reading of that paragraph would lead to the conclusion that the Court of Appeal had

---

[115] *Hollins v Russell* [2003] EWCA Civ 718, [2003] 1 W.L.R 2487.
[116] [2014] EWHC 2981(Ch).
[117] *Hollins v Russell* [2003] EWCA Civ 718, [2003] 1 W.L.R 2487.

decided that in any case where a receiving party's case was funded by way of CFA, that party should ordinarily be put to their election under what is now CPR 47 PD 13.13 to disclose their CFA or to rely on other evidence to satisfy the court that (i) they had an enforceable CFA and (ii) were entitled to any additional liability they claimed. In practice, following the introduction of CPR 47 PD 32,[118] compliance with the more limited requirements of that PD were usually held to suffice, unless the information disclosed as a result gave rise to a genuine issue which warranted further disclosure.

Following the revocation of the recoverability of additional liabilities (and therefore, in post LASPO CFAs, the application of old CPR 47 PD 32), the question remains as to whether a receiving party can be required to disclose its CFA within assessment proceedings, even where no success fee is claimed. This would be because, unlike the position with ATE premiums (where they are now largely irrelevant to the paying party's liability to pay costs), the question of whether the CFA (or indeed a DBA) is enforceable may well be relevant to the question of whether the paying party has any liability at all – see paras 64 and 69 of *Hollins*.

CPR 47 PD 5.11 requires a receiving party to set out, in their bill of costs, a brief explanation of any agreement or arrangement between the receiving party and their legal representatives which affects the costs claimed in the bill. The use of the word "affects" admits of an argument that where no success fee is claimed there is no need, under this provision, to set out that the case is CFA funded, since the fact of the CFA does not affect the costs claimed. However, in practice this provision is more likely to be interpreted as requiring a party to set out a brief explanation of any funding arrangement which potentially affects the costs claimed – for example, a CFA or DBA, since if either was unenforceable this would mean no, or only reduced, costs were payable.

In practice, therefore, there is probably some obligation on a receiving party to at least set out the core nature of its funding arrangement. Once this is done, it is unlikely that a court would ordinarily then require further information to be provided – or put the receiving party to its election – unless the paying party was able to indicate some genuine issue giving rise to a concern that the funding arrangement might be unenforceable.

Q37. What information does a losing party have to provide about its funding arrangements to the winning party?
The answer to this question is likely to ultimately turn on the question of relevance or "legitimate purpose" and to be approached in a similar way to arguments about disclosure of such information during the claim, the fundamental difference being that by this stage, the court will know who has won and lost and, therefore, there may be a stronger basis for seeking disclosure from a losing party than at the interim stage, without the risk of such a demand

2–68

---

[118] Which now remains relevant and of application only to pre-commencement (of LASPO) funding arrangements.

being dismissed as being "premature". Furthermore, any question of information potentially being privileged may have fallen away by this point.

The precise information which might be ordered to be disclosed will depend on all of the circumstances of the case, but the court has ample powers, in the context for example of an application for non-party costs under s.51, to order disclosure of relevant material. Whether such an order will be granted – and the scope of the same – is highly fact dependent.

Q38. If a claimant involved in a contractual dispute enters a CFA in June 2020, must the claimant serve a completed notice of funding (form N251) on the defendant even though the success fee is not potentially recoverable from the defendant?

2–69 See the answer to **Q32**. There is no procedural obligation to provide this information and the N251 procedure and related rules no longer apply to such funding arrangements.

Q39. How can a party discover if the other side has a CFA? Should a party disclose a CFA to the other party?

2–70 This is largely addressed in **Q37**. There is no obligation to disclose a CFA to the other party, or even that is the basis of funding, during the course of proceedings. The nature of funding may become relevant in certain circumstances (for example in response to an application for security for costs), but even in those circumstances it would be unusual for there to be disclosure of the CFA. In any event, in such circumstances, disclosure is not ordered by the court. Instead, the position is that the party who is subject to the application for security may raise certain matters (commonly the availability of ATE insurance) as a "defence" to the application. If that person does so, then the court will attach little weight to the point unless they provide disclosure of relevant documentation. Accordingly, it is not the court which orders disclosure, rather the disclosure is volunteered by the party to assist their responding to the application.

Outside these situations, or other situations such as where a party is seeking certification as a class representative in the Competitions Appeal Tribunal, it is difficult to see why the question of the method of funding would be a relevant issue during the conduct of the case, let alone on what basis the court would consider itself able to order disclosure of such documentation.

Q40. Where a claimant entered into a CFA prior to 1 April 2013 and provided written notice (a letter) to the defendant of such CFA, but then failed to file/serve form N251 upon issue of the claim, what are the consequences?

2–71 Where a CFA is a pre-April 2013 CFA the full rigour of the pre-April 2013 CPR Pts 43 to 48 apply, as expressly provided for by CPR r.48.1.

To provide a full recitation of all of the applicable provisions and case law in relation to the giving of notifications of funding and related information before, during and after proceedings (for example, within the context of detailed assessments) would result in an unduly lengthy answer. However, in short, the failure referred to in the question would mean that the claimant was in breach of the pre-April 2013 CPR 44 PD 19.2, as a consequence of which, pursuant to the pre-April 2013 CPR r.44.3B(1)(c) and (d) (if the failure to give notice also related to an ATE premium), the claimant's success fee would be disallowed for the period of any default (i.e. from when the notice should have been given until it was, in fact, given) and any ATE premium would be disallowed. This would all be subject to any application for relief from sanction.

Given the fact that notice appears to have been given, but not in the proper form, there would appear to be a reasonable argument that relief should be granted, but it is not possible to say without consideration of the precise facts. See, for example, *Forstater v Python (Monty) Pictures Ltd*.[119]

These principles also apply to any of the "excepted" cases such as insolvency related proceedings (provided the CFA was entered into before 6 April 2016), publication and privacy proceedings (provided the CFA was entered into before 6 April 2019) or mesothelioma claims where success fees remained recoverable after the 1 April 2013. Per CPR r.48.2(1)(b), such agreements are "pre-commencement funding arrangements", even where entered into on or after 1 April 2013 and are therefore subject to the rigours of the pre-April 2013 notice provisions and consequent sanctions for non-compliance.

Q41. Where a CFA in one of the excepted cases (where the success fee is still recoverable) is entered into and the proceedings are issued on the same day but only served four months later and we realise that we haven't served a notice of funding some weeks after service, what advice would you give? For example, should a formal application seeking relief be made?

The first point to note is that the question may involve wider considerations   2–72
than those which are immediately apparent. Although the provisions on providing notices of funding, as continued in force in such cases by virtue of CPR r.48.1(1), relate to the date of issue and service, it is open to argument whether it is still a requirement to provide such notice at an earlier date. The requirement to do so, contained in the previous version of the Practice Direction on Pre-Action Conduct, has not been replicated in the current version of the Practice Direction and CPR r.48.1(1) does not continue the application of the old version for these purposes. This is likely to have been an oversight, but nevertheless seems clearly to be the position. Accordingly, it is not clear whether the requirement to provide notification of a relevant funding arrangement "as soon as possible and in any event either within seven days of entering into the funding arrangement concerned or, where a claimant

---

[119] *Forstater v Python (Monty) Pictures Ltd* [2013] EWHC 3759; [2014] 1 Costs L.R. 36.

entered into a funding arrangement before sending a letter before claim, in the letter before claim" still applies.

Best practice would be to follow that course in any event. In the event of non-compliance with a relevant provision, best practice would be to remedy the provision as soon as the error is noted. This could be done by providing the necessary notice, inviting the opponent to agree that relief from sanction should be granted in respect of any breach, where appropriate by inviting the opponent to agree that it will not take the point on assessment and that a formal application need not be made. In the event that the opponent does not agree, a prompt application for relief should be issued, even if it is then agreed that the hearing of the application may be adjourned pending the outcome of the claim or any detailed assessment proceedings. In some cases, where the sums at risk are substantial, it may be appropriate to proceed to determination of the application without delay.

Q42. Is a claimant entitled to recover the success fee under their "pre-1 April 2013" CFA from the defendant, where the claim was only commenced and the funding was only notified after 1 April 2013? Please explain why the amendment to s.58A(6) does not apply to CFAs entered into prior to 1 April 2013, in circumstances where the funding is notified after 1 April 2013?

2–73 Yes. The amendment to s.58(A)(6) of the Courts and Legal Services Act 1990 does not apply to CFAs entered into prior to 1 April 2013 by virtue of the express provision at s.44(6) LASPO—subject to satisfying the precise terms of that section.

Q43. In the excepted cases, where a success fee is still recoverable: Do you have to provide a notice of funding when issuing proceedings, even if it will be allocated to the small claims track? What date do you give in the N251 notice of funding when the matter is funded by a collective conditional fee agreement (CCFA)? Is it the date of the CCFA with the insurer or the date of the subsequent signed retainer with the insured client?

2–74 The answer to the first question is "yes" unless you are willing to accept that any additional liabilities potentially claimable from the opponent if the case succeeds are to be surrendered. Whilst, in a case likely to be allocated to the small claims track, this might seem to be an inevitable consequence of the general costs limitations, there is no certainty at the time of issue that a claim will be allocated to or will remain in that track, or that there may not be circumstances under CPR r.27.14 where costs might be sought despite such allocation. Accordingly, not serving an N251 may be shutting out a potential claim for additional liabilities.

In relation to the second question, the N251 requires the date of the agreement. That is the date of the CCFA. There is no reason why additional information cannot be provided if this would appear to be sensible and the bare information required by the N251 might risk misleading the other party or a court.

Q44. In insolvency proceedings, where a CFA and ATE insurance policy were taken out in February 2016, what are the requirements regarding service of the notice of funding? Is there a requirement to apply the old CPR r.44.15 (which requires that a party who intends to recover an additional liability must notify the court and the other parties) or are these rules now superseded?

See the previous answers to Q32 and Q33. The notification provisions pursu-   2–75
ant to CPR r.44.15 are continued in force in relation to "pre-commencement funding arrangements" by CPR r.48.1 and specifically, in relation to insolvency proceedings, by CPR r.48.2(1)(b). The requirements to provide notice (save probably that which was contained under the pre-April 2013 version of the Practice Direction on Pre-Action Conduct) continue to apply and should have been complied with (and in a case started under a pre-April 2016 insolvency CFA should continue to be complied with).

Q45. Where two CFAs (one with solicitor and one with counsel) were entered into pre-1 April 2013 and notice of funding was only served in relation to the first one (solicitor) is that okay because CPR 47 PD 19.3(2)(a) says further notification is not required where notice has already been given that the party has entered into a CFA with a legal representative and during the currency of that agreement either of them enters into another such agreement with an additional legal representative? Will the success fee on the second CFA still be recoverable?

Yes. Assuming all other notice requirements have been complied with, coun-   2–76
sel's success fee will remain recoverable in principle. As the question notes, CPR 47 PD 19.3(2)(a) (as it was pre-April 2013 and with continuing effect for any CFAs entered into before that date and also for CFAs after that date in certain types of proceedings which benefited from a LASPO exemption—by virtue of CPR r.48.1) expressly provides that where proper notification has been given of a CFA between solicitor and client, notification is not required of a subsequent CFA between the solicitor and an additional legal representative—in this case counsel. It should be noted that this only applies where counsel's CFA follows that of the solicitor. If, for example, the solicitor was on a conventional, non-CFA, retainer but counsel entered into a CFA, then notice would have to be given of the CFA with counsel.

E. Third-Party Funding

Q46. Are parties required to notify an opponent that they are being funded by a third-party litigation funder?

See the answer to Q21 above. There is no rule-based obligation to provide   2–77
such information, but it would be open to the court to order disclosure of the

fact and any relevant and appropriate details of such funding if a legitimate purpose was served by doing so.

Although beyond the scope of this text, it is certainly arguable that a general obligation to disclose the presence of such funding may be established in the context of proceedings under the Arbitration Act 1996. Not only have arbitration tribunals shown a willingness to order such disclosure, but if the decision in *Essar Oilfield Services Ltd v Norscot Rig Management Pvt Ltd*[120] is correct, and the costs of obtaining third-party funding are recoverable as a "non-legal" cost in the arbitration, then it seems highly likely that the tribunal will expect the fact of such funding—and therefore the risk of liability for such additional adverse costs—to have been notified in advance and may consider a failure to provide such advance notification as a reason to refuse to award such costs under its broad discretion.

Such an issue does not arise outside the context of arbitrations since (at present at least) it is settled law that the costs of third-party funding are not a recoverable cost between the parties.

There may be other specific proceedings – such as opt out collective proceedings in the Competition Appeal Tribunal – where disclosure of aspects of funding arrangements is, in practice, required (at least into a confidentiality ring) if the proposed class representative is to be able to satisfy the Tribunal as to certification.

Q47. When third-party funding is used in an arbitration, under what circumstances could costs be awarded against third-party funders and how could the tribunal cost orders against the funders be made enforceable against the funders (given that funders are not a party to the arbitration)?

2–78 Due to the consent-based nature of an arbitration, a tribunal will not usually have any power to regulate the conduct of a third party which is providing funding for that arbitration or to make any order for costs against it. The costs provisions of the Arbitration Act 1996 (ss.59 to 65) do not contain any provision for the making of a costs order against a third party akin to that to be found in s.51 of the Senior Courts Act 1981 and, as the Court of Appeal has made clear in a very different context,[121] it is necessary to identify a specific statutory power or alternatively, in the context of arbitrations, a specific contractually binding provision giving a tribunal power to bind a third party to such an order before such an order may be made.

It therefore appears that, absent the third party becoming "bound" in some way to the arbitration, there is no scope for a third-party funder in an arbitration to be made subject to a direct order for costs against it. There is, therefore, something of an irony in the fact that it is in the arbitration context that it has been held that the cost of obtaining third-party funding is a recoverable

---

[120] *Essar Oilfield Services Ltd v Norscot Rig Management Pvt Ltd* [2016] EWHC 2361 (Comm); [2017] Bus. L.R. 227.
[121] See *Darroch v Football Association Premier League Ltd* [2016] EWCA Civ 1220; [2017] 4 W.L.R. 6.

cost—see *Essar Oilfield Services Ltd,* above. It appears arguable that the apparent inability to make a direct order against such a funder would not merely be a reason to reach a contrary view, but also would potentially support an argument that third-party funding should either not be permitted or should be subject of greater restrictions within the arbitration context than in the general litigation context.

At the very least, there would appear to be an argument that if a party is to seek to recover third-party funding costs if successful, on the *Essar* principle, then:

- either they and/or the funder should be prepared to submit to some earlier order or agreement providing some security to the opposing party that, in the event of their succeeding, they would either have some greater security for their costs recovery than would otherwise have been the case;
- or the funder should submit to an order or agreement that the opposing party would have some direct right against the funder for at least some of their costs, if awarded in that party's favour.

The tribunal's scope for seeking to "encourage" such an agreement would appear to lie in its discretionary ability to refuse to award the third-party funding costs at the conclusion of the claim in the absence of such agreement. Whether this is the approach that will be taken or, if not, what alternative approach might be adopted remains to be seen.

Q48. Do third-party funders have access to inspect documents disclosed to the claimant whose action they are funding?

This is a matter for the agreement between the funder and the litigant. As a matter of generality, a litigation funding agreement should set out whether and if so to what extent the funder may provide input into any decisions as to settlement of a case. Equally, a funder will usually not have any rights to exercise any kind of direct control over the case—particularly if that funder does not want to be vulnerable to the Arkin cap on its potential liability for adverse costs being disapplied.   2–79

However, both as part of the process of reaching initial agreement with the funder to provide funding in the first place and as part of the ongoing monitoring of the funded claim, the funder may require sight of certain documents in relation to the case. The precise classes of documents which would fall to be disclosed at either stage are a matter for agreement between the funder and the litigant.

F. Conditional fee agreements and success fees

Q49. How should the success fee be calculated in a post-April 2013 CFA?

The short answer is that it should be calculated in the same way as a success   2–80
fee under a pre-April 2013 CFA was, but of course with a recognition that it is

the client that will be paying the success fee with no prospect of between the parties recovery.

The slightly longer answer is that the maximum success fee which may be payable under a CFA remains at 100%. In setting the success fee, the solicitor is entitled to have regard to those matters set out at the revoked CPR 43 PD 11.7 and 11.8. In addition, the solicitor is entitled to take into account matters such as the delay in payment under a CFA (a matter which could be used to justify the success fee on a solicitor-client basis prior to April 2013 but not on a between the parties basis). The main component of the success fee is likely to remain the risk of losing and not being paid, and in that regard the traditional "ready reckoner" remains useful.

Ultimately, however, the issue is one of agreeing a reasonable success fee with the client in light of the terms and conditions of the CFA, the risks to which it exposes the solicitor of not being paid their base fees in whole or part, any additional financial burden placed on the solicitor, such as the arrangements for paying disbursements and the likely delay in payment overall, and the application of these matters to the facts of the case.

It is important to explain the success fee clearly and properly to the client and to ensure their informed agreement. It is vital that the client is informed that the success fee is not recoverable between the parties in any circumstances, even if the claim is won, and will remain payable by the client.

It should be emphasised that the assessment of risk should usually relate to the risks of the individual case. The MoJ confirmed in its initial assessment as part of the post-implementation review of Pt 2 of LASPO[122] that the intention of the reforms was to return to the original concept of each case being individually risk assessed, rather than to introduce a basis of assessing the success fee across a basket of cases. It referred to in Lord Mackay's speech (as Lord Chancellor) when the Courts and Legal Services Act 1990 was originally being passed through the House:

> "My understanding of this system is that you do not subsidise other cases: the success fee is dependent on the chances of success in your case. It is a factor which is dependent on a probability of success that works into the success fee. It is not dependent on other cases; it is dependent on the precise potential for winning that exists in the case that you have in hand."

This is not to say that the success fee in one case does not, in practice, provide a cross subsidy. Provided cases are being properly screened and risk assessed, across a large basket of cases the system of success fees should still operate on a broadly revenue neutral basis – that is to say, with success fees on successful cases compensating for unrecovered base fees on unsuccessful cases.

---

[122] *https://assets.publishing.service.gov.uk/government/uploads/system/uploads/attachment_data/file/719140/pir-part-2-laspo-initial-assessment.pdf.*

If a different approach is to be adopted, such as applying a single, standardised success fee to all cases of a particular type, then it is vital that this is clearly and fully explained to the client—see *Herbert v HH Law Ltd*.

Q50. A CFA was entered pre-April 2013 and therefore falls under the old rules. An interim hearing was won by the applicant and the applicant would therefore like to apply for a detailed cost assessment against the losing party for their costs in the application. However, the success in the interim hearing, has not triggered "success" under the terms of the CFA (and the CFA itself does not include a clause relating to interim hearings). Could you advise whether it is therefore possible to still seek base costs from the losing party (not the additional liability) or whether this would fall foul of the indemnity principle? Research so far points to old CPR 47 PD 32.3 which states that if a party is seeking detailed assessment without any additional liability they do not need to provide information about CFAs etc.

The reference to old CPR 47 PD 32.3 misses the point. In order to recover any costs between the parties (save where those costs are fixed), the receiving party must be able to satisfy the court that the indemnity principle is not breached. The standard N260 Statement of Costs for Summary Assessment contains a statement, which the receiving party's solicitor is required to sign, confirming that the costs claimed in the statement do not exceed the costs which the receiving party is liable to pay in respect of the work which the statement covers.

2–81

In the unusual situation envisaged above (it being more common that CFAs generally provide for the client to be liable for interim costs where such an award is made), the solicitor would be unable to sign the statement and would be unable to claim the costs at that stage. This would probably be a "good reason"[123] for the court not to undertake summary assessment. A summary assessment at that point would not be able to include these costs which might, in fact, be payable and recoverable if the client ultimately succeeds on the claim. See further *Arkin v Borchard Lines Ltd*.[124]

As the question notes, even if costs recovery was allowed at the interim stage, this would be of base costs only and the success fee would have to be the subject of detailed assessment or agreement at the end of the case. There have been reports of astute judges on detailed assessments checking the CFA to see if the claimant had indeed been entitled, under the CFA, to seek recovery of base costs in relation to interim awards and where it has been discovered that they were not, of the success fee on those base costs being disallowed as a sanction. Whether this is a common practice or whether such a sanction is an appropriate sanction in the circumstances is beyond the scope of this supplement. More fundamentally, as noted above, such recovery should not

[123] See CPR PD 44 para.9.2.
[124] *Arkin v Borchard Lines Ltd (Costs)* [2001] C.P. Rep. 108; [2002] U.K.C.L.R. 150.

be sought unless the solicitor can sign the certificate to confirm the claimant is entitled to the same at that time and, as is now trite law, the signature of such a statement by a solicitor, as an officer of the court, is an important matter which should not be undertaken lightly.

Q51. If the solicitor has entered into a pre-April 2013 CFA, but counsel's CFA with the solicitor post-dates April 2013, is counsel's success fee recoverable between the parties?

2–82   The point is arguable. The wording of s.44(6) refers to the between the parties recovery of a success fee under a CFA not being prevented if the agreement was entered into before 1 April 2013. It would seem to fit with the spirit and intent of the changes and the wording of the statute (and CPR r.48.2) that each agreement is looked at individually. The solicitor's success fee would be recoverable in principle, but counsel's would (probably) not be.

Support for the contrary argument may be drawn from the cases of *Plevin*, *Budana* and *Catalano*. In the situation envisaged above, the claimant has few of the benefits of the post-LASPO regime (save, perhaps, that the CFA Order 2013 would require there to be a cap on the success fee chargeable by counsel if the case was a personal injury case). Despite having none of the other "balancing" benefits, the claimant would be unable to recover counsel's success fee. Whether that would be sufficient to persuade the court to take a very purposive approach to s.44(6) of LASPO and CPR r.48.2 remains to be seen, but the prospects of such an approach have undoubtedly increased in light of the higher judicial decisions in 2017.

Q52. I have a client who is acting under a CFA in defamation proceedings. The CFA is pre-April 2019 and accordingly a success fee is recoverable. He now wants to instruct counsel. Can counsel claim a success fee under the solicitor's CFA?

2–83   See the preceding question. The issue of principle is no different. This is one of the remaining, unanswered, questions arising out of the LASPO transitional provisions, whether in relation to personal injury cases in 2013 or insolvency and publication and privacy proceedings with their later commencement dates for s.44 LASPO. A strict and literal construction supports the point that this is a different agreement and not an agreement entered into before the relevant commencement date and therefore the success fee is not recoverable. However, this would leave the claimant with a foot in both "camps". It must, however, be noted that in publication and privacy proceedings the effect of having a foot in both camps is less stark. In particular, ATE premiums remain recoverable and the claimant would not be left in the position (as with personal injury claims) of being denied QOCS because of the CFA with the solicitor (since there is no QOCS), but yet also being denied recoverability of any ATE premium. It may be, therefore, that were this point to be argued in a defamation case the court might be more inclined to take a more literal approach to the rules than it would in a similar personal injury case.

Q53. What is the effect on the success fee where a CFA relating to a group claim was entered into before 1 April 2013, but some of the claimants were added after that date?

The answer to this is unclear. The transitional provisions in relation to the 2–84
recoverability of success fees in s.44 of LASPO are statutory provisions and do
not admit of a discretion (indeed, their express effect is to remove any discretion to allow a success fee in respect of cases covered by s.44).

Accordingly, and despite the possible temptation to do so, a court managing a GLO probably cannot simply exercise a discretion to decide how to treat such a situation (for example by reference to s.51 of the Senior Courts Act 1981) but is limited to considering the particular CFA and how it interacts with the provisions of s.44(6).

Section 44(6) appears to require the court to look not merely at the date of the CFA but at whether the CFA was entered into for the purposes of providing services to a specific person in relation to the subject matter of the claim or, if not entered into for a specific person (for example, a CCFA), whether services were provided, before 1 April 2013, to the specific person in whose favour the costs order has been made.

The CCFA analogy appears the most apt here and there must be a substantial likelihood that the later joining claimants will be held not to be able to recover the success fee in respect of their claims. This may involve some question of a pro-rata division of any success fee payable on common costs. The quid pro quo would be that the later joining claimants would benefit from QOCS (if it is a personal injury claim). Such an approach would therefore be consistent with the "all or nothing" approach to transitional provisions identified by the Court of Appeal and Supreme Court in cases such as *Plevin* and *Budana*.

However, alternative approaches are possible and it is conceivable, given that the potential claimants in a GLO could be seen as being a limited and identifiable class of persons, that a court might conclude that the test under CPR r.44.6(a) was satisfied in respect of all claimants when the CFA was first entered into and accordingly a success fee is recoverable in respect of all claimants.

The precise outcome will be heavily affected by the terms of the CFA, the precise circumstances of the case, the terms of any related documentation, such as costs sharing agreements, and the court's approach to the interpretation of s.44(6), which at present is uncertain.

Q54. Where a firm had an insolvency case on a CFA with a success fee and had ATE insurance in place, and then the Government removed the exemption from LASPO for insolvency-related cases, presumably the success fee and premium will still be recoverable from the other side if the claim is successful even if it wasn't issued before the exemption was removed?

The answer to this is largely covered by **Q28** and **Q29**. The key date is the 2–85
date on which the funding arrangement was entered into, provided it properly relates to the claim that was issued. The insolvency exception ended

with effect from the 6 April 2016. The same transitional provisions as applied to the core changes in 2013 (namely ss.44(6) and 46(3) of the 2012 Act in respect of success fees and ATE premiums respectively) expressly apply to these changes.[125] Accordingly, provided the CFA and ATE are incepted before the date fixed for the ending of recoverability (6 April 2016, therefore on or before 5 April 2016), the additional liabilities will continue to be recoverable.

As noted in the commentary above, in any insolvency case care should be taken to ensure that the case falls within the narrow scope of the exemption. Not all "insolvency" cases will.

Q55. I understand that for an ATE insurance premium to be recoverable from the other side in insolvency proceedings it must have been put in place before 6 April 2016. Is it also necessary to have given notice of funding to the other side before 6 April 2016?

2–86 See the answer to the preceding question and **Q28** and **Q29**. Provided the funding arrangement was entered into on or before 5 April 2016, the insolvency "exemption" will apply. However, as noted, the pre-April 2013 provisions of CPR Pts 43 to 48 will apply to such an arrangement and the obligation to provide notice of funding in relation to it. Those provisions do not require notice to be given before 6 April 2016. Provided notice is given in accordance with the requirements of those sections—for example by giving of a notice of funding when filing or serving the claim form, even if that is not due until after 6 April 2016—then the additional liabilities will be recoverable in principle, subject to any assessment as to quantum.

Q56. We note that insolvency proceedings were excluded from ss.44 and 46 of LASPO where proceedings in England and Wales were brought by:

- **A person acting in the capacity of a liquidator of a company in creditors' voluntary liquidation (CVL) or compulsory liquidation; a trustee in bankruptcy; or an administrator.**
- **A company that is in: CVL; compulsory liquidation; or administration.**

What is the situation if you acted for an insolvency practitioner outside the jurisdiction (the insolvent company also being outside the jurisdiction) who brought a claim in England and Wales against a company based in England and Wales for monies owed? If you entered into a CFA with the client in these circumstances, would the success fee be recoverable from the other side if your client is successful?

2–87 The situation described appears to fall outside the scope of art.4 of the Legal Aid, Sentencing and Punishment of Offenders Act 2012 (Commencement No.5 and Saving Provision) Order 2013 (SI 2013/77). Accordingly, any

---

[125] See art.2 of the Legal Aid, Sentencing and Punishment of Offenders Act 2012 (Commencement No.12) Order 2016 (SI 2016/345).

additional liabilities are unlikely to be recoverable. This will therefore be unaffected by the ending of the insolvency exception with effect from 6 April 2016 since such additional liabilities were never part of the exception in the first place.

Q57. What are the rules on recoverability of success fees in a defamation matter and, assuming that recoverability is allowed, does the success fee have to be capped in any way?

By virtue of art.4(b) of the Legal Aid, Sentencing and Punishment of Offenders 2–88 Act 2012 (Commencement No.5 and Saving Provision) Order 2013 (SI 2013/77) the commencement of the provisions removing the recoverability of additional liabilities was suspended in respect of publication and privacy proceedings. Accordingly, success fees were recoverable in principle in such cases in the same way as before April 2013. This changed with effect from 6 April 2019 and where the CFA is entered into on or after that date in respect of such proceedings the success fee will no longer be recoverable.

Whether pre- or post-6 April 2019, there is no statutory provision imposing a cap on the success fee other than the 100% maximum percentage set by the Lord Chancellor pursuant to s.58(4)(c) and art.4 of the Conditional Fee Agreements Order 2000 (SI 2000/823). This would appear to be the case even if an element of the damages claimed in the publication and privacy proceedings is for personal injury (provided that the cause of action remains one of those identified in the statutory definitions of publication and privacy proceedings). What has changed is the ability to seek to recover the success fee, in whole or part, from the opponent.

Q58. The Legal Aid, Sentencing and Punishment of Offenders Act 2012 (Commencement No.5 and Saving Provision) Order 2013 defines "publication and privacy proceedings" as meaning proceedings for—

(a) **defamation;**
(b) **malicious falsehood;**
(c) **breach of confidence involving publication to the general public;**
(d) **misuse of private information; or**
(e) **harassment, where the defendant is a news publisher.**

Accordingly, success fees and ATE premiums may be recoverable in all of these types of publication and privacy proceedings. Would recoverability be allowed if the claim is a "mixed claim", including publication and privacy elements and other elements not falling within the definition of "publication and privacy proceedings"? How should a CFA relating to such a situation be structured?

The first point to note is that, where the CFA is entered into on or after 6 April 2–89 2019, the success fee will no longer be recoverable from the opponent. ATE premiums remain recoverable in principle.

Subject to the above, neither s.58/s.58A of the 1990 Act nor the Legal Aid, Sentencing & Punishment of Offenders Act 2012 (Commencement No. 5 & Saving Provision) Order 2013 ("the commencement order") deal with the question of "mixed" proceedings, in contrast, for example, to CPR r.44.16(1)(b) in relation to QOCS. Section 58A(6) prevents the court allowing the recoverability of a success fee under a CFA generally. Article 4 of the 2013 Order provides that the amendment to s.58A preventing such recovery does not apply to "publication and privacy proceedings".

It is, perhaps, again notable that the expression used is not "proceedings which include a publication or privacy claim"—which would be similar to the definition in CPR r.44.12 which identified which claims are subject to QOCS. Accordingly, the fact that the proceedings include such a claim is not the determinative factor. The ability to recover the success fee is limited to "publication and privacy proceedings".

Precisely how this would operate in practice if there was one set of proceedings which included both a claim relating to publication and privacy and a related claim for another matter is undecided. One option would be for the court to treat the entire proceedings as being exempted from the LASPO amendment, and the success fee recoverable in full. However, this would tend to encourage the use of a publication or privacy claim as a "Trojan horse" to obtain the ability to recover additional liabilities which would otherwise be irrecoverable. The more likely and sensible outcome would be for the court to seek to identify that part of the proceedings which could properly be identified as publication and privacy proceedings, and to allow the success fee on that element, but not on the remainder. This would, however, be likely to lead to practical difficulties of identifying what part of the costs related to which part of the proceedings.

It is not clear how many such mixed claims will exist in practice. It is important here to draw a distinction between proceedings, for example for misuse of private information or harassment, where part of the damage suffered is a personal injury (for example psychiatric harm) and true "mixed claims" where there are distinct causes of action. The former is much more likely than the latter and, in those circumstances, it seems tolerably clear that since the proceedings would still be publication and privacy proceedings – even though they included an element of damages for personal injury – then the prohibition on recovery would not apply (at least until s.44 was brought into force in respect of such claims with effect from 6 April 2019).

It may remain an issue in relation to ATE premiums, given that they remain recoverable in principle between the parties in publication and privacy proceedings, but for the reasons given it is suggested that the concern is probably more theoretical than practical.

Peculiarly, if the above analysis is correct, an oddity is created. The CFA Order 2013, at art.6, provides that the need for a cap on the success fee in personal injury proceedings does not apply to CFAs entered into "in relation to" certain classes of proceedings, including publication and privacy proceedings.

Accordingly, where the publication and privacy proceedings include a claim for damages for personal injury, a species of (partly) personal injury claims where the success fee does not have to be capped by reference to the damages is created.

Q59. Privacy cases are "excepted" and so the success fee and ATE insurance premium are recoverable (provided the CFA was entered into before 6 April 2019). This includes breach of confidence/misuse of private information claims. However, most misuse of privacy claims/breach of confidence claims form part of a mixed claim which includes a claim for breach of the DPA as well, and sometimes personal injury in the form of a recognised psychiatric injury as a result of that breach. How would recoverability work in (1) a mixed claim which included a misuse of private information and data protection breach claim; and (2) a mixed claim the same as (1) but which also alleged personal injury had resulted?

The answer to this question largely follows from the above. Whilst no certainty can be offered unless and until either the regulations are clarified or there is an authoritative decision on the point, if the personal injury has resulted from the misuse of private information then the claim is likely to be considered to be a publication and privacy proceeding and therefore exempt from the prohibition on the recoverability of success fees. The position where a DPA claim is included is more contentious. The definition of "publication and privacy proceedings" in the commencement order appears to be a limited and exclusive definition which does not include DPA claims. As noted above, the definition also does not refer to the exempted proceedings being ones which "include" a claim of the specified type (which might allow for a more expansive interpretation) but rather as proceedings "for" the specified cause of action. It is therefore arguable that it is the inclusion of the DPA claim, and not the fact of a personal injury, which might lead to a need to "split" the proceedings in some way to determine the recoverability of the additional liabilities. *Warren v DSG Retail Ltd* [2021] EWHC 2168 provides an illustration of the dangers of seeking to use publication and privacy proceedings to bring a claim which is, in reality, a data protection claim with a view to benefitting from the recoverability of ATE premiums in the former.

Q60. Given that success fees in CFAs entered into from 1 April 2013 are not recoverable in English civil litigation (apart from in the excepted cases), are they recoverable in arbitrations? Nothing in the Arbitration Act or LCIA Rules appears to preclude an arbitrator awarding a success fee under a CFA.

It is entirely correct that neither the Arbitration Act 1996 nor the rules of any of the main institutions deal directly with the issue of the recoverability of success fees.

The lawfulness of such arrangements will be determined by reference to the law of the country in which the arrangement is entered into, the law of the

2–90

2–91

place of arbitration and the law of the country where any award (including costs) would be enforced.

Assuming the question relates to whether a success fee would be awarded in principle in what might loosely be termed an "English" arbitration, following *Benaim UK Ltd v Davies Middleton & Davies Ltd*[126] it was generally accepted that such additional liabilities may be awarded in principle. However, whether such an award would be made in practice and, if so, whether the amount awarded would be at the level sought is very much within the discretion of the tribunal and in practice tends to be far less certain than would be the position in court proceedings.

Following the LASPO changes it is strongly arguable that success fees are no longer recoverable in arbitrations. Section 58A(4) of the Courts and Legal Services Act 1990 makes clear that the reference to proceedings under s.58 is wide enough to include an arbitration. Pursuant to the amended s.58(6) of the Act, "a costs order made in proceedings [which appears to include an arbitration] may not include provision requiring the payment by one party of all or part of a success fee". Accordingly, and subject to the transitional provisions, there would appear to be a strong case for contending that success fees are no longer recoverable within arbitrations within the English and Welsh jurisdictions.

This throws into stark light the effect of the decision in *Essar* (see main text and Q37 above) to allow the recoverability of third-party funding costs.

Q61. What is the current position with regard to the question of whether the recoverability of pre-April 2013 additional liabilities is compatible with the European Convention on Human Rights?

2–92   This is addressed in the main text above. In *Coventry*, the Supreme Court rejected the argument that additional liabilities permitted by primary and secondary legislation and subject to the test of reasonableness and, where applicable, proportionality on assessment amounted to an unwarranted interference with a party's rights under art.6 or art.1 of the First Protocol to the European Convention on Human Rights. That issue now appears to be conclusively determined in relation to general litigation. In *Flood, Frost* and *Miller,* the Supreme Court dealt with the specific issue of the balance between a media defendant's rights under art.10 of the Convention, and those of a litigant under art.1 of the First Protocol. As is set out in the main text, in two of those cases the court affirmed that a requirement to pay a success fee or ATE premium would normally be a breach of art.10 rights, but left a final decision open on the basis that the Government was not a party to the proceedings. However, as between the litigants, that breach was not sufficient to warrant a disallowance between the parties of the additional liabilities because this would have interfered with the individual litigants' legitimate expectations of recovery, based on the continued application of the statutory regime of

---

[126] *Benaim UK Ltd v Davies Middleton & Davies Ltd* [2004] EWHC 737 (TCC); (2004) 154 N.L.J. 617.

recoverability, and therefore would interfere with those litigants' rights under art.1 of the First Protocol. Accordingly, on a between the parties basis any breach of art.10 did not prevent recoverability.

Q62. What procedure must claimant solicitors follow in a personal injury case involving a child in order to obtain payment of the success fee under the CFA from (i) the defendant and/or (ii) the damages paid to the child.

The obvious starting point is that the success fee is not recoverable from the   2–93
defendant following the April 2013 rules changes in any case where the CFA was entered into on or after 1 April 2013.

As to seeking recovery of the same from the child's damages, the procedure is as set out in CPR rr.21.12 and 46.4. Where the only issue is the payment of the success fee, a simplified procedure for summary assessment of the success fee applies (see CPR r.46.4(5)). Strictly, the procedure is that of an application by the Litigation Friend seeking payment of the success fee as an item of costs out of the claimant's damages. The detailed procedure set out in CPR 21 PD 11 should be followed, including provision to the court of a copy of the CFA and the (or any) risk assessment.

As is noted in the main body of the text, amendments to this procedure were introduced in April 2019 to require the application to include a copy of any bill of costs rendered by the solicitor to the Litigation Friend and/or a breakdown of the costs claimed. This applies even where the costs claimed are limited to the success fee, for the obvious reason that the success fee is simply a percentage of the base costs and the court will wish to see how the base costs are made up in order to decide if the sum claimed by way of success fee is reasonable.

It makes no difference that the success fee is limited to a percentage of general damages and past pecuniary loss. The "cap" on the success fee is simply a cap and again the court will wish to seek how the base costs and then the success fee pre-cap are calculated before being able to decide whether the capped sum is reasonable.

G. Damages-Based Agreements

Q63. What exactly is a hybrid DBA, and what is the difference between a concurrent hybrid DBA and a sequential hybrid DBA?

There is no statutory definition of a hybrid DBA. It is a term that has devel-   2–94
oped amongst practitioners and is discussed in the CJC Working Committee Report and the Bacon/Mulheron explanatory note. It is broadly understood to refer to a DBA which provides for some element of payment to the solicitor other than the pure, all or nothing, contingent payment anticipated by reg.4 of the DBA Regulations 2013. Perhaps the closest comparator is with a discounted CFA, where the solicitor receives an element of payment, whether or not the case is won or lost, but with a higher payment in the event of success.

A sequential hybrid DBA is generally understood to refer to the situation where the solicitor initially agrees some form of non-DBA retainer, but then agrees at a later stage to switch to a DBA arrangement, but more widely refers to any situation where there is a DBA for one or more stages of a case and a different form of funding for other stages. In the most common, chronologically sequential, arrangement, the DBA when applied might retrospectively cover all work done, or may be limited only to future work. In either case, because the DBA itself does not provide for any payment to the solicitor other than the contingent payment in respect of the work it covers, it is not thought to fall foul of the apparent prohibition on hybrid arrangements under the DBA Regulations 2013 and the MoJ's terms of reference to the CJC Working Party appear to support this conclusion.[127]

A concurrent hybrid DBA is the sort of DBA described at the start of this answer—that is to say one that provides for both the contingent DBA payment and some other form of payment under a single agreement in relation to the same work or stage. For the reasons given above, it was generally understood that such arrangements were not permitted. The apparent inability to enter into such arrangements is believed to be one of the major reasons for the limited use of DBAs since April 2013. However, matters have now changed.

These matters form part of the MoJ's post-implementation review of Pt 2 of LASPO. However, the most significant development in this regard is the Court of Appeal's January 2021 decision in *Zuberi* (considered in detail above). In light of that, references to a "DBA" should now be understood to be references only to the part of the agreement that governs payment as a percentage of sums recovered. The rest of the retainer is not a DBA (or at least is not regulated under the DBA Regulations 2013). In such circumstances, it is probably more correct to refer to such an arrangement as a "hybrid retainer", with part being a DBA and the other parts being something else (that something else possibly being a conventional retainer, a discounted retainer or some form of CFA arrangement).

Q64. A firm is acting for a client on a pre-April 2013 hybrid CFA in ongoing litigation. The client's circumstances change and he asks whether the firm would be willing to change its funding arrangement with him to a DBA. Is there any guidance on whether this is possible and, if so, what the implications would be? (As DBA's do not currently allow the solicitor to charge anything until the client receives a financial benefit, would the firm have to repay any fees he has paid under the hybrid CFA?)

2–95 In light of the Court of Appeal's decision in *Zuberi*, the premise of this question is now incorrect. The DBA regulations 2013 only regulate that part of the agreement which deals with payment out of recoveries. The remaining parts

---

[127] See the Working Party's summary of the position at p.26 of its report: *https://www.judiciary.gov.uk/wp-content/uploads/2015/09/dba-reform-project-cjc-aug-2015.pdf*.

of a client's retainer are not regulated by and not rendered unenforceable by those regulations.

As explained in the previous answer, even on a literal interpretation and before the recent Court of Appeal decision, s.58AA of the 1990 Act and reg.4 of the 2013 Regulations do not seek to restrict anything other than the terms of payment under the DBA itself. Prima facie, therefore, they do not prevent what was described in the previous answer as a "sequential hybrid DBA" and this would include an arrangement whereby the solicitor initially agreed a CFA and then subsequently entered into a retainer including a DBA element in circumstances where the client remained liable, on success, for payments under both agreements, provided the two agreements (and in particular the DBA) did not cover the same work.

It would appear that the potential for abuse, whether with sequential arrangements of this kind or indeed concurrent ones is one to be addressed by virtue of the client's rights under s.70 of the Solicitors Act 1974 to seek assessment of the solicitor's charges.

Q65. I am acting for a client who has a "good" claim worth several million pounds. We have not yet issued proceedings, and we are hoping to avoid doing so (having proposed ADR and made an offer to settle liability). The general principle agreed with the client is for our fees to be 20% + VAT of the amount received, plus expenses. I am aware that under a DBA we have to pay counsel's fees, but otherwise the client pays disbursements. I have several questions in this regard:

- **Is it necessary to enter into a DBA before proceedings have been issued, or can we have a two-stage arrangement whereby we enter into an agreement with the client now which provides that we will contribute 20% of expenses incurred by the client, including for counsel fees, and if the matter settles before proceedings are issued, then the "success fee" of 20% + VAT is payable by the client plus 80% of the expenses. If proceedings are issued, then that arrangement would be replaced by a formal DBA. Is such a two-stage arrangement permitted?**
- **Whilst I understand the cap on fees must include VAT, where the success fee is 20% + VAT, is it necessary to state that the success fee is 24% (including VAT) or can we refer to it as 20% + VAT, as that would still be below the 50% cap?**
- **In terms of counsel's fees, we will seek to agree an arrangement with them either on a CFA or a DBA basis, but is there any restriction on agreeing a capped fee with counsel in relation to actual proceedings or trial work, rather than advice?**

In response to the first point, no it is not necessary to enter into a DBA pre-issue. It is permissible to have a non-contentious business agreement—subject   2–96 to compliance with the requirements of s.57 of the Solicitors Act 1974, but with such agreement "falling away" in the event that proceedings are issued and replaced with a DBA, or other lawful arrangement covering all past and future work. The proposed arrangement appears to be for a damages-based fee of 20% in the event of pre-proceedings success, with the client in addition paying 80% of all expenses incurred. Such an arrangement may be included within a non-contentious business agreement. Such an arrangement would, however, not satisfy the requirements of the DBA Regulations 2013 if that arrangement was continued to cover contentious work because the treatment of expenses does not appear to comply with the Regulations (and the need to comply with various other requirements of the Regulations would also have to be considered).

It appears to be perfectly permissible to refer to the fee as 20% plus VAT provided that it is made clear that the total fee, including VAT, cannot in any circumstances exceed the 50% cap.

There is no restriction on agreeing a specific fee with counsel, capped or otherwise, in relation to any aspect of the case. However, the important point to note is that whatever lawful arrangement is agreed with counsel, be it a DBA, CFA, fixed or capped fee or a simple hourly rate, the solicitor is required to cover those fees out of the DBA percentage agreed with the client.

Q66. If you enter into a DBA, with say the percentage figure being 40% of the client's damages, does that percentage include disbursements and counsel's fees?

2–97   See the main text above and reg.4(1) of the DBA Regulations 2013. The payment under the DBA is inclusive of any sum payable in respect of counsel's fees. In other words, the DBA fee the solicitor is entitled to, which (including VAT) cannot exceed 50% of the damages recovered (and to which a lesser cap applies in personal injury claims) includes any sums due to counsel and counsel must then be paid by the solicitor out of that fee. However, the client may be required in addition to pay any other expenses on top of the DBA fee.

Q67. If a DBA is terminated, would the lawyer be entitled to charge the client at the normal hourly rates for the work done up to the date of termination or would charging the client on this basis fall foul of the DBA Regulations 2013 reg.4(1) and (3) which provide that lawyers cannot require the client to make any payment for legal services unless and until they make a recovery of damages?

2–98   The longer answer to this in earlier editions may now be replaced by a much shorter "yes, such a provision is permissible in principle" in light of the Court of Appeal's decision in *Zuberi*, discussed in detail above. Only that part of the retainer which requires payment out of recoveries is regulated by the DBA Regulations 2013. A provision for reasonable payment in the event of termination is neither prohibited by those regulations, even if governed by them (according to the unanimous view of the Court of Appeal), nor is in fact regulated by them in any event (according to the majority).

Q68. What is the authority or rule which specifies that if a DBA in a non-employment matter does not comply with the DBA Regulations 2013, it will not be enforceable?

Section 58AA(2) of the Courts and Legal Services Act 1990 provides that a 2–99 DBA relating to any matter (employment or non-employment) which does not satisfy the conditions specified in subs.(4) shall be unenforceable. The conditions in subs.(4) include "such other requirements as to [the DBA's] terms and conditions as are prescribed. Amongst the prescribed conditions are the relevant sections of the DBA Regulations 2013. In addition, subs.4(b) prescribes that, if regulations so provide," the agreement must not provide for a payment above the prescribed amount or for a payment above an amount calculated in a prescribed manner. The DBA Regulations 2013 contain prescriptions of this kind which must therefore be complied with if the agreement is not to be unenforceable by force of clear and unambiguous primary statutory legislation.

For reasons discussed above, the lack of enforceability is likely to only relate to the part of the agreement that provides for payment out of recoveries, since that is probably the only part that is regulated by the regulations.

Q69. Under the DBA Regulations 2013, a party can recover costs from the other side based on normal costs recovery principles, but subject to the indemnity principle. Given then that the lawyer may not be entitled to any costs until actual recoveries are made at the end of a case, does this not cause a problem with seeking costs from the other side at interim hearings as the case progresses? Appropriate drafting of the DBA might seek to get around this but it would seem that such drafting would be a highly complex task with various pitfalls. For example, if the DBA provided that sums would immediately become due to the solicitor as and when costs are recovered from the other side, are those costs considered part of the ultimate recovery from the client and to be deducted and as a kind of payment on account, or would the solicitor be entitled to those costs plus the agreed success percentage? Wouldn't that breach the DBA Regulations 2013?

Yes, this does cause a problem. It is one of the issues addressed by the CJC 2–100 Working Group's report and, more recently, is expressly addressed by the draft revised regulations produced by Bacon/Mulheron. For the reasons given in the question, the inclusion within the DBA of some sort of immediate right to payment may well breach the prohibition under reg.4 (which does not apply in employment matters) on any payment other than the specified contingency payment under the regulations and expenses. It is one of the matters that may be addressed in any future amendment to the Regulations.

Q70. Where we and the claimant have entered into a Damages-Based Agreement, and made a Part 36 offer to the defendant, how might the Part 36 costs consequences interact with our DBA?

2–101   In the same way, in principle, as with any other case. As noted in the text, CPR 44.18 expressly provides that where there is a DBA, recoverable costs are to be assessed in accordance with CPR r.44.3 and, in effect, as if a conventional retainer was in place. Applying that approach, there should be no difficulty in applying the benefits under CPR r.36.17(4) if the matter goes to trial and the claimant betters his or her own offer.

H. Consumer Regulations

Q71. Do the doorstep selling regulations, which aim to protect consumers when they sign contracts in certain circumstances, apply to CFAs? If so, in what kind of circumstances would they apply?

2–102   Such regulations apply to contracts entered into between consumers and traders. Solicitors are traders for these purposes—see the Court of Appeal's decision in *Cox v Woodlands Manor Care Home Ltd*[128] for an example of the application of the point and the potentially draconian effects of non-compliance.

The Court of Appeal's decision in *Kupeli*[129] in relation to the 2008 Regulations looked at the question of when a meeting involving a solicitor at which clients enter into retainers is an "excursion organised by the trader away from his business premises". The court's conclusion—that on the facts of that case there was no such excursion and that the agreements were therefore not caught by the Regulations—was no doubt welcome news to the claimant solicitors, but insofar as it is of wider relevance it also serves to underline that had the Regulations applied then the harsh consequences of non-compliance as seen in *Cox* may have been unavoidable.

Fortunately, the most draconian version of these regulations (the Cancellation of Contracts made in a Consumer's Home or Place of Work etc. Regulations 2008 (SI 2008/1816)) were replaced with effect from June 2014 with the apparently less draconian, but far more complex Consumer Contract (Information, Cancellation and Additional Charges) Regulations 2013 (SI 2013/3134), so contracts entered into from that date are less vulnerable to being found unenforceable for non-compliance.

The precise circumstances in which the Regulations apply are set out in the Regulations themselves and their precise operation and implications will have to be the subject of case law. However, once again, they apply to contracts entered into by traders, including solicitors, with consumers. Different requirements apply depending on where the contract was entered into, but it should be noted that at least some regulation applies, even where the contract was entered into at the solicitor's offices (contrast the 2008 Regulations).

---

[128] *Cox v Woodlands Manor Care Home Ltd* [2015] EWCA Civ 415; [2015] 3 Costs L.O. 327.
[129] *Kupeli v Cyprus Turkish Airlines* [2017] EWCA Civ 1037; [2017] 4 Costs L.O. 517.

There is a helpful practice note provided by the Law Society,[130] but the effect on non-compliance can potentially be severe and any solicitor regularly dealing with consumers as defined should consider the Regulations closely and seek advice where necessary.

Q72. Does the failure to send out a cancellation notice invalidate a CFA under the Consumer Contract Regulations 2013?
There are three types of consumer contracts under the 2013 Regulations— Distance, On Premises and Off Premises. An On Premises contract is one which is not a Distance or Off Premises contract. Cancellation notices are required for Distance and Off Premises contracts, but not for On Premises contracts.

2–103

The effect of failure to provide a cancellation notice differs depending on whether it is a Distance or Off Premises contract. For example, a failure to do so in relation to an Off Premises contract is a criminal offence (reg.19).

A consumer is not bound by the contract until all of the required information, including the cancellation notice, has been provided (regs 10 and 13). The precise effect of this is unclear. Regulation 31 addresses the issue in the context of the information required under Sch.2 (which includes the consumer being informed of the rights and procedures in relation to cancellation) by, in effect, providing that the cancellation period shall continue on a rolling basis up to a maximum of 12 months and 14 days after the contract has been made, thereby extending the client's rights to "walk away". However, reg.31 only concerns the information under Sch.2, it is not clear if this same "backstop" applies where the client is not given a cancellation notice at all, as opposed to not being told of his rights and procedures in relation to cancellation (though in practical terms the two will often amount to the same thing). In the presence of a complete failure to provide any cancellation notice, it must be open to argument that the client is simply never bound by the contract at all.

I. Proportionality

Q73. Given that the pre-April 2013 rules on recoverability of additional liabilities continue to apply to PCFAs, does the old test of proportionality also continue to apply when assessing those additional liabilities?
In some earlier editions of this chapter the answer given was "probably". Courtesy of the Court of Appeal's decision in *BNM v MGN Ltd*[131] the answer is now a definitive "yes".[132] The *BNM* case is analysed in detail in Ch.3. Note, however, that this does not apply to ATE premiums claimed under the Recovery of Costs Insurance Premiums in Clinical Negligence Proceedings (No.2) Regulations 2013 (SI 2013/739), where, equally definitively, the answer

2–104

---

[130] At: *http://www.lawsociety.org.uk/support-services/advice/practice-notes/consumer-contracts-regulations-2013/*.
[131] *BNM v MGN Ltd* [2017] EWCA Civ 1767; [2018] 1 W.L.R. 1450.
[132] See further **Ch.3, Q14** where these issues are considered in more detail.

is that they are subject to the new test of proportionality, but that test has little practical effect.[133]

J. Funding costs

Q74. Can you charge your client for the costs of: (i) negotiating and drafting a CFA (the case of *Motto v Trafigura Ltd*,[134] suggests not?) However, the case is pre-Jackson and suggests that you cannot because the client is not yet your client—arguably the situation is different where the client is an existing client at the pre-action stage of proceedings); (ii) negotiating and entering into an ATE policy and keeping the insurers updated during the proceedings; (iii) negotiating and entering into a third party funding agreement and keeping the funders updated during the proceedings.

2–105   The ratio in *Motto* is not entirely clear and the questioner is correct to identify that, at least as far as setting up a CFA is concerned, the core of the ratio relates to the fact that the "client" is only a potential client until terms of business are agreed. However, at [113] and [114] Lord Neuberger went on to deal with reporting to insurers. He accepted that the dividing line was blurred, but regarded such costs, incurred after the client was indeed a client, as the wrong side of the blurred line and as being costs which were collateral to the litigation (and therefore not recoverable) rather than costs of (and incidental to) the litigation.

There is clearly some scope for further argument. However, on the basis of *Motto*, it would appear likely that all three categories of costs identified in the question fall the wrong side of the blurred line of recoverability.

K. Other issues

Q75. Does the 10% uplift to damages as provided for in *Simmons v Castle*[135] apply in cases where the parties are publicly funded?

2–106   Yes. The 10% uplift to damage for pain, suffering and personal injury in respect of personal injury and all other torts provided for by the Court of Appeal in *Simmons* applies to all cases save where the claimant falls within the ambit of s.44(6) of LASPO, that is to say where a claimant has a pre-commencement CFA with a recoverable success fee. A claimant with public funding will be outside s.44(6) and therefore will benefit from the uplift.

Q76. If a claimant beats their Part 36 offer at trial, are the costs consequences of CPR r.36.17(4)(d) recoverable from a non-party if an application under CPR r.46.2 is successful?

2–107   The answer to this question is unclear. The court's ability to make a non-party costs order is based on the wide discretion available to it under s.51 of the

---

[133] See the Court of Appeal's decision in *Peterborough and Stamford Hospitals NHS Trust v Maria McMenemy* and *West v Stockport NHS Trust*.
[134] *Motto v Trafigura Ltd* [2011] EWCA Civ 1150; [2012] 1 W.L.R. 657.
[135] *Simmons v Castle* [2012] EWCA Civ 1288; [2013] 1 W.L.R. 1239.

Senior Courts Act 1981 and requires the court to take into account all the circumstances. This would allow the court, for example, to make an order that the non-party pay the costs on the indemnity basis, even if its own conduct had not been unreasonable, where it bore some responsibility for the continuation of the case and where the party that was conducting the case (for whose conduct the non-party bore some responsibility) had behaved unreasonably—see *Excalibur Ventures LLC v Texas Keystone Inc.*[136]

However, CPR r.36.17 is not based on the exercise of any general discretion under s.51 Senior Courts Act 1981, but is a rule-based provision providing a specific set of benefits only in those specified circumstances. CPR r.36.17 does not, however, provide that where the claimant betters their own offer, the defendant shall be ordered to pay the identified benefits unless it is unjust to do so. Instead, it provides that the court must order "that the claimant is entitled to" those benefits. This is wide enough to admit of the argument that, for example, if the defendant was unable to pay and the claimant was able to persuade the court to make a non-party costs order against a third party, then justice (which is the ultimate touchstone for such an order) requires that the claimant's "entitlement" be the same against that non-party as it would have been against the defendant, though since the court would be exercising a discretion under s.51 it would not be bound to make such an order (and arguably could not do so in respect of the 10% additional sum).

It seems unlikely that it was the intention of the drafters of CPR r.36 to provide a route by which such benefits could be sought against a party other than the offeree (the defendant). Moreover, it is certainly open to argument that the 10% additional sum is not a "cost" and therefore is outside the court's discretion under s.51 of the Senior Courts Act 1981. Put another way, to use the language of the question, it is not a "costs consequence", but an additional sum awarded on the basis of a specific rule—CPR 36—which does not directly apply to the exercise of the court's general discretion under s.51 of the 1981 Act. As already noted, it would be open to the court to award indemnity basis costs under s.51 (in appropriate circumstances) without having to resort to CPR r.36.17. Accordingly, it is only likely to be where the claimant was unable to obtain indemnity basis costs for other reasons and sought those and/or the additional sum or a high level of interest through CPR r.36.17 that this argument would arise, since it is only those aspects that are prima facie outside the scope of s.51. In such circumstances, it may be that in any event the court would not consider it just, in all the circumstances, that the non-party be subject to these additional burdens, even if it considered that jurisdictionally it was able to award them. Unless and until the point is tested in court it is not possible to give a more definitive answer.

---

[136] *Excalibur Ventures LLC v Texas Keystone Inc* [2016] EWCA Civ 1144; [2017] 1 W.L.R. 2221.

CHAPTER 3

Proportionality

Introduction

The terms of reference for the costs review conducted by Sir Rupert Jackson[1]   3–01
were "to make recommendations in order to promote access to justice at proportionate cost". The need for change was acknowledged in the foreword to
the final report, which stated:

> "In some areas of civil litigation costs are disproportionate and impede access to
> justice. I therefore propose a coherent package of interlocking reforms, designed to
> control costs and promote access to justice."

Inevitably, therefore, proportionality lay at the core of the 2013 package of
reforms—it permeated into every aspect of the civil litigation process. The
overriding objective was amended to include specific reference to proportionality, costs and case management are determined by it, most assessments
of costs are subject to it and proposed extensions to fixed recoverable costs
regimes are based upon it. However, almost nine years on from the April 2013
amendments to the Civil Procedure Rules, proportionality still provokes more
debate, more controversy and more concern than any other aspect of the
reforms. What does it mean, when does it arise, and what impact does it have
on litigation?

Proportionality—the concept

Proportionality is not a new concept. Whilst the amended overriding objec-   3–02
tive[2] refers to "dealing with a case at proportionate cost", the previous
version, from introduction in 1999, defined "dealing with a case justly" by reference, amongst other things, to proportionate cost. However, in reality, prior
to April 2013, proportionality only had a retrospective role at the conclusion
of a case, at the time of the assessment of costs. Where it was suggested that
the costs claimed were disproportionate, the Court of Appeal required the
assessing judge to determine that issue at the outset of the assessment adopting the *Lownds v Home Office*[3] two-stage approach:

> "In other words what is required is a two-stage approach. There has to be a
> global approach and an item by item approach. The global approach will indi-
> cate whether the total sum claimed is or appears to be disproportionate having
> particular regard to the considerations which Pt. 44.5(3) states are relevant. If the

---

[1] Review of Civil Litigation Costs: Final Report, December 2009.
[2] CPR r.1.1: "These Rules are a new procedural code with the overriding objective of enabling the court to deal with
cases justly and at proportionate cost."
[3] *Lownds v Home Office* [2002] EWCA Civ 365; [2002] 1 W.L.R. 2450.

costs as a whole are not disproportionate according to that test then all that is normally required is that each item should have been reasonably incurred and the cost for that item should be reasonable. If on the other hand the costs as a whole appear disproportionate then the court will want to be satisfied that the work in relation to each item was necessary and, if necessary, that the cost of the item is reasonable."

Immediately it is apparent that such an approach does not genuinely meet the requirement of dealing with a case at proportionate cost. Even if the first stage of *Lownds* resulted in a finding that the costs were disproportionate, the court could not change the way it had dealt with the case procedurally. Instead, all it could do was to reduce the amount of costs recoverable between the parties. Even this retrospective ability to reduce the recoverable costs did not lead to proportionality in its purest sense, as there was no certainty that necessarily incurred costs were proportionate—in essence, the imposition of the "necessarily incurred" test seemed more a sanction for incurring disproportionate costs than any genuine attempt to reduce the costs to a level that was proportionate. Indeed, in giving his judgment in *Lownds*, Lord Woolf had hinted at the purists' position on proportionality when commenting:

"If, because of lack of planning or due to other causes, the global costs are disproportionately high, then the requirement that the costs should be proportionate means that no more should be payable than would have been payable if the litigation had been conducted in a proportionate manner."

Something more was needed to ensure that cases are managed so that no more is spent as the case progresses than is proportionate.

This is a theme to which Sir Rupert Jackson returned in his 2017 Supplemental Report[4] in which he described the "holy grail" as a system "in which the actual costs of each party are a modest fraction of the sum in issue and the winner recovers those modest costs from the loser". However, he immediately made a practical qualification, stating:

"What is achievable in the real world? The best that can be achieved is:

. . .

(iii) to restrict recoverable costs to that which is 'proportionate' as defined in the new proportionality rule".

Proportionality—what does it mean and when does it arise?

3–03 The 2013 reforms sought to provide that "something more" within the context of what was achievable by requiring the court to:

- deal with each case "at proportionate cost" (CPR r.1.1(1))—which includes allotting to it an appropriate share of the court's resources, while taking into account the need to allot resources to other cases (CPR r.1.1(2)(e));

---

[4] *Review of Civil Litigation Costs: Supplemental Report Fixed Recoverable Costs*, July 2017.

- ensure that every case management decision is made taking account of the costs involved in each procedural step (CPR r.3.17);
- set costs budgets that are proportionate (CPR PD 3E (Costs Management) para.12);
- determine whether or not to grant relief from sanction by giving particular weight to the need for litigation to be conducted at proportionate cost (CPR r.3.9); and
- undertake standard basis assessments of costs on the principle that only proportionate costs will be awarded, even if that means reasonably or necessarily incurred costs are disallowed. CPR r.44.3(2)(a) signals the demise of the *Lownds* test at assessment, reversing the timetable for consideration of proportionality (although this clearly defined separation of process may, in some instances, elide following the decision in *West v Stockport NHS Foundation Trust.*[5]) The court will assess those costs that are reasonably incurred and reasonable in amount and, following *West*, where appropriate it may undertake the assessment of the proportionality of an item at the same time. It will then step back and determine if the resultant figure is proportionate. If it is not, then the court will reduce the costs to the sum it determines is the proportionate figure, guarding against the risk of double deduction in respect of those items that it has already subjected to a proportionality reduction. This cross-check of proportionality is to be undertaken by an initial determination of whether the overall sum is proportionate by reference to the factors at CPR r.44.3(5) and any wider circumstances under CPR r.44.4(1). If that total figure is found to be proportionate, then no further assessment is required. If the court regards the overall figure as disproportionate, then a further assessment is required. That should not be line-by-line, but should instead consider various categories, such as disclosure or expert's reports, or specific periods where particular costs were incurred, or particular parts of the profit costs. The court will consider each category to determine whether the costs incurred are disproportionate. If they are, then the court will make such reduction as is appropriate—see *West* at [90] and [92].

Of course, the court can only fulfil the function set out above by reference to the proportionate costs for a claim and, if then appropriate, for a particular category, type or period of costs (leading to the prospect of argument over the specific parameters of these in any given case, which will be determined by an exercise of judicial discretion). How does it determine that sum? The simple answer is by reference to the 2013 proportionality test. Six and a half years on from the introduction of the 2013 reforms, guidance emerged from the Court of Appeal in *West* which makes it clear that this is by consideration of CPR r.44.3(5), which contains the definition of proportionate costs, and CPR r.44.4(1), which requires the court, when assessing if costs are proportionately

---

[5] *West v Stockport NHS Foundation Trust* [2019] EWCA Civ 1220; [2019] 1 W.L.R. 6157.

and reasonably incurred. to have regard to "all the circumstances". We say that CPR r.44.3(5) contains the definition of proportionate costs. However, in *West,* the court concluded that the provision was not exhaustive. Accordingly, costs will be proportionate if they are so by reference to CPR r.44.3(5), which provides that:

> *"Costs incurred are proportionate if they bear a reasonable relationship to:*
> *(a) the sums in issue in the proceedings;*
> *(b) the value of any non-monetary relief in issue in the proceedings;*
> *(c) the complexity of the litigation;*
> *(d) any additional work generated by the conduct of the paying party; and*
> *(e) any wider factors involved in the proceedings, such as reputation or public importance;*
> *(f) any additional work undertaken or expense incurred due to the vulnerability of a party or any witness."*

However, even if costs are not proportionate when determined under this provision, they may still be by a consideration of "wider circumstances" under CPR r.44.4(1). It seems likely that when considering the costs sought for approval (for costs management purposes) or assessment, the court will apply CPR r.44.3(5) first and only move on to the "wider circumstances" if the costs are not proportionate under CPR r.44.3(5). In contrast, if the court concludes that the costs sought are not proportionate, then in determining what is the proportionate sum, the court will have to consider both CPR r.44.3(5) and the "wider circumstances", for if these considerations lead to different figures, it will be the higher that is approved/assessed.

Accordingly, as a starting point, the court must identify which of the factors listed in CPR r.44.3(5) are relevant to any case and, having done so, relate that to a costs figure. It is this step that many critics of the process see as unsatisfactory (see the different approaches to whether or not some mathematical calculation and/or "weighting" of the factors in CPR r.44.3(2)(a) is required, in *May v Wavell Group Plc*[6] and *Reynolds v One Stop Stores Ltd*[7]—considered in more detail in **Q5** below). Critics view the process as an entirely unscientific one—as the factors do not readily equal a sum in pounds and pence. Adding in the broad concept of the "wider circumstances" makes the criticism more vocal. The simple answer from those proponents of the process is that there is no "absolute" answer, but, as with many exercises of judicial discretion, there is a range of answers and, provided the discretion has been exercised properly, none within that range are wrong. This is nothing new. Indeed, if different judges were asked to assess the same bill of costs at the conclusion of a claim, the likelihood is that there would be as many different figures as there were judges assessing the bill, but, again on the proviso that those judges had properly exercised their discretion, none of the assessments would be "wrong".

---

[6] *May v Wavell Group Plc* unreported 22 December 2017 County Court (Central London) HHJ Dight CBE.
[7] *Reynolds v One Stop Stores Ltd* unreported 21 September 2018 County Court (Norwich and Cambridge) HHJ Auerbach.

It is for this reason that in the 15th Implementation Lecture on 29 May 3–04 2012 the then Master of the Rolls, Lord Neuberger, stressed the case-sensitive nature of proportionality and anticipated little case law on the topic:

> *"While the change in culture should reduce the scope of costs assessments at the conclusion of proceedings, it will not obviate the need for a robust approach to such assessments. Again the decision as to whether an item was proportionately incurred is case-sensitive, and there may be a period of slight uncertainty as the case law is developed.*
>
> *That is why I have not dealt with what precisely constitutes proportionality and how it is to be assessed. It would be positively dangerous for me to seek to give any sort of specific or detailed guidance in a lecture before the new rule has come into force and been applied. Any question relating to proportionality and any question relating to costs is each very case-sensitive, and when the two questions come together, that is all the more true. The law on proportionate costs will have to be developed on a case by case basis. This may mean a degree of satellite litigation while the courts work out the law, but we should be ready for that, and I hope it will involve relatively few cases."*

It is hard to see what further guidance is either necessary or likely other than in extremely general terms. Unnecessary because the very flexibility of the definition makes it hard to think of any case where relevant features impacting on costs do not fall to be taken into account within one of the five factors or the "wider circumstances". Unlikely, because each case is fact sensitive, the ambit of judicial discretion is wide and any decision falling outside the parameters would only define proportionality in a very broad sense in that specific case. This view was confirmed by Sir Rupert Jackson in his May 2016 lecture "The Future for Civil Litigation and the Fixed Costs Regime,"[8] in which he stated:

> *"There has been much debate about whether a PD should provide supplementary guidance . . . Unfortunately any attempt to draft a PD which supplements those five general rules (44.3(5)) with another set of general rules, albeit more specifically focused, is doomed to fail. If a PD were to give more detailed guidance it would inevitably be lengthy. The PD would be helpful in some cases and confusing in others. There would be arguments about its interrelationship with rule 44.3(5). No legislator can foresee all the vagaries of litigation. Any detailed PD would generate satellite litigation. Then we would have rule 44.3(5) + a lengthy PD + an encrustation of case law, followed up inevitably by much learned commentary by the academic community. Surely we are better off without all that?"* para.2.2.

Even when expressing disappointment that the Court of Appeal had not been able to provide some anticipated guidance (which it has now in *West*), Sir

---

[8] Westminster Legal Policy Forum *"The future for civil litigation and the fixed costs regime"* May 2016.

Rupert Jackson referred to this as being in respect of the application of the rule to different scenarios.[9]

Accordingly, beyond defining proportionality within discretionary parameters in any given case, any comments will be of a general nature, e.g. in *CIP Properties (AIPT) Ltd v Galliford Try Infrastructure Ltd*[10] where Coulson J (as he then was) commented that:

> *"Costs budgets are generally regarded as a good idea and a useful case management tool. The pilot schemes (including the one here in the TCC) have worked well. They are not automatically required in cases worth over £2 million or £10 million, principally because the higher the value of the claim, the less likely it is that issues of proportionality will be important or even relevant. A claimant's budget of £5 million might well be disproportionate to a claim valued at £9 million, but such a level of costs is probably not disproportionate to a claim worth £50 million."*[11]

and in *Savoye v Spicers Ltd,*[12] a case concerning enforcement of an adjudication, Akenhead J concluded that:

> *"... for the purposes of costs assessment, the Court should have regard when assessing proportionality and the reasonableness of costs, in the context of the current case or type of case to the following:*
>
> *(a) The relationship between the amount of costs claimed for and said to have been incurred and the amount in issue. Thus, for example, if the amount in issue in the claim was £100,000 but the costs claimed for are £1 million, absent other explanations the costs may be said to be disproportionate."*

Whilst the court in *Kazakhstan Kagazy Plc v Zhunus*[13] purported to define what is "reasonable and proportionate" as "... the lowest amount (of costs) which it (a party) could reasonably have been expected to spend in order to have its case conducted and presented proficiently, having regard to all the circumstances", this appears to overlook the provisions of CPR r.44.3(2)(a), which is not considered in the judgment and which could not be clearer, that proportionality trumps reasonableness. Accordingly, any attempt to define proportionality by equating it to, or by any measurable reference to, reasonableness appears to overlook this procedural provision. In any event, this decision was concerned with payments on account of costs and not the assessment of recoverable costs. In *Thomas v PGI Group Ltd* [14] the court declined to express a view, because it did not need so to do in reaching its conclusion (that it would not be disproportionate, after the application of CPR r.44.3(5) and 44.3 to

---

[9] Cambridge Law Faculty *"Was it all worth it?"* March 2018. Note also that the article to which Sir Rupert Jackson referred in this lecture (at para.3.18), as providing some practical guidance, itself deals with proportionality in specific contexts—see Civil Procedure News Issue 4/2018 "Proportionality in Practice".

[10] *CIP Properties v Galliford Try Infrastructure* [2014] EWHC 3546 (TCC); [2015] 1 All E.R. (Comm) 765.

[11] The reference to £2 million and £10 million being to the respective versions of CPR r. 3.12 in place from 1 April 2013 and 22 April 2014.

[12] *Savoye v Spicers Ltd* [2015] EWHC 33 (TCC); [2015] 1 Costs L.R. 99.

[13] *Kazakhstan Kagazy Plc v Zhunus* [2015] EWHC 404 (Comm).

[14] *Thomas v PGI Group Ltd* [2021] EWHC 2776 (QB).

this case, for the claimants' costs to be budgeted at a figure which represented the amount that was necessary for them to proceed to litigate the case), on whether, as the claimant contended, standard basis costs (i.e. those both reasonable and proportionate) equate to the minimum costs required for a party to litigate a claim efficiently, or, as the defendant submitted, there are cases in which the minimum sum required for a claimant to fight a case would be disproportionate. Cavanagh J left open the following questions for a case in which they arise for determination, stating that potentially they raise an issue of public importance:

- whether costs can ever be disproportionate, even though they are no more than the minimum costs which the party needs to spend in order to bring the case to trial;
- if so, in what circumstances; and
- again, if so, how should a court decide what the proportionate figure should be? In particular, may a judge, on proportionality grounds, reduce a costs budget or impose a Costs Capping order, simply because the judge disapproves of the claimant's decision to proceed with the litigation, e.g. because the sum claimed is much smaller than the anticipated costs and there are no vindication issues?

(See **Q6** below for more detailed consideration of the link between reasonableness and proportionality and **Qs 7, 8** and **9** below for further analysis of the effect of CPR 44.3(2)(a))

Those seeking certainty are, in effect, wishing for something akin to a form of fixed fee regime for all cases. Given the variety of claims, it is almost inevitable that any regime of fixed fees would be set with a very broad brush. As stated in previous editions, "be careful for what you wish", for it leads in only one direction. Indeed, Sir Rupert Jackson concluded his consideration of the concerns expressed about CPR r.44.3(5) in his May 2016 lecture as follows:

> *"The best way to satisfy the requests for clarification is to convert the five identified factors into hard figures: In other words, a fixed costs regime."* para.2.3.

It is interesting, but not surprising, that Sir Rupert recognised the force of the argument advanced during the preparation of his Supplemental Report on fixed recoverable costs[15], that the breadth of the character of multi-track cases rendered them unsuitable for a "one size fits all" rigid costs matrix.[16] This reinforces the argument that the case sensitive nature of any particular proceedings prevents more specific guidance on proportionality. However, that fixed fee certainty appears imminent for most multi-track cases with a value not exceeding £100,000, as the Ministry of Justice response to its own

---

[15] *Review of Civil Litigation Costs Supplemental Report Fixed Recoverable Costs.*
[16] *Review of Civil Litigation Costs Supplemental Report Fixed Recoverable Costs*, Ch.7 para.1.2.

consultation on Sir Rupert Jackson's recommendations in his 2017 supplemental report[17], is to accept them almost entirely and to work with the Civil Procedure Rules Committee to bring about their implementation. The minutes of the November 2021 meeting of the Civil Procedure Rules Committee suggest that the intention is for implementation in October 2022.

Proportionality—exceptions to, or qualifications upon, it

3–05 Despite stressing that its decision did not seek to revive *Lownds*, the Court of Appeal conclusion in *West*, that when the court considers proportionality those items of cost which are fixed and unavoidable, or which have an irreducible minimum, without which the litigation could not have been progressed, "are to be left out of account" ([81] and [82]), does resonate uncomfortably with the recovery of necessary costs. This is particularly so of cost items deemed to have an irreducible minimum. In respect of fixed and unavoidable items of costs (e.g. court fees) the conclusion is irrefutable. Whether they need to be removed from the proportionality assessment or included within it and deemed proportionate, matters not, the outcome is the same as their incurrence is mandatory and at prescribed levels. However, it is far harder to reconcile the recovery of items of costs of an irreducible minimum with CPR r.44.3(2)(a). Removing from the proportionality account those items reasonably incurred which have irreducible minimums, regardless of amount, is difficult to distinguish from the recovery of necessary costs. In addition, this suggestion creates uncertainty and scope for disproportionate argument. It provides a financial incentive to exclude items from the constraints of proportionality. As a result, it seems inevitable that arguments will abound as to whether certain expenditure is an irreducible minimum and should be excluded (e.g. in the context of particular experts' fees, where an expert is reasonably required under CPR Pt 35 and this is what the expert charges so there is no choice other than to incur this item of cost)—see further consideration of this at **Q10**. The effect of the introduction of items with an irreducible minimum will depend upon how widely that description is interpreted by the courts.

Perhaps more challenging is that part of the Court of Appeal decision which suggests that the exclusion of certain items will not, in fact, impact on the overall level of costs. In [84] and [85] of *West* the court provides an example to illustrate this and an explanation for the approach as follows:

> "84. *This ought not to disadvantage the paying party. Take as an example a claim that was settled for £10,000 but where the costs were £50,000, of which £5,000 was made up of the recoverable element of the ATE insurance premium. In those circumstances, when working through the various categories of cost to assess proportionality, the judge may have some overall figure in mind that would*

---

[17] Extending Fixed Recoverable Costs in Civil Cases September 2021.

be proportionate. That figure will remain unchanged: the reductions to achieve it will simply be by reference to other elements of cost, not the ATE insurance premium...

85. We recognise that this means that, when undertaking the proportionality exercise, it is those elements of cost which are not inevitable or which are not subject to an irreducible minimum which will be vulnerable to reduction on proportionality grounds in order that the final figure is proportionate. Such costs are, however, likely to be costs which have been incurred as a result of the exercise of judgement by the solicitor or counsel. Those are precisely the sorts of costs which the new rules as to proportionality were designed to control."

We are not convinced that this can be so. The approach propounded at [85] to negate the adverse impact on overall proportionality of allowing an item of costs that is of an irreducible amount, sits unhappily with the approach to proportionality under CPR rr.44.3(5) and 44.4(1). If all other items of costs are reasonable and all categories, types and periods of costs are proportionate, on what basis, and from which costs may the court make a reduction to achieve overall proportionality, when the total figure is only disproportionate because of the allowance of an item deemed to be of an irreducible minimum cost and, so, excluded from proportionality considerations?

Proportionality—the effect on litigation

For a more detailed consideration of the effect on litigation see **Ch.4—Case and Costs Management**. In essence though, proportionality will arise at all stages of a case, as any case management decision engages the overriding objective, which includes the obligation to deal with a case at proportionate cost, regardless of any additional burdens imposed by specific provisions. This applies to all claims, regardless of track and regardless of value, even where there is a fixed cost regime in place. The court, and the parties, should have proportionality in mind whether they are dealing with the lowest value small claim or the highest value multi-track. It follows that any party seeking any specific case management direction must be prepared to justify it in the context of a consideration of the factors at CPR r.44.3(5) and the "wider circumstances" of the case.

3–06

The discretion offered by the flexible definition of proportionality means that it can be adapted to meet the diverse considerations of all claims, which is just as well as, despite Sir Rupert Jackson's original recommendation and the Supplemental Report, fixed fees have yet to be introduced for non-personal injury fast track claims and for any multi-track claims. Unless and until Sir Rupert Jackson's recommendation to introduce fixed fees across the fast track is implemented, and without costs management in that track, a significant emphasis in those claims remains on proportionality after the costs have been spent under CPR r.44.3(2)(a) at assessment.

This discretion means that, provided that the court has considered the factors in CPR r.44.3(5) and identified any relevant "wider circumstances" when reaching any decision on proportionality, it will have made no error of principle and so appealing any decision will be extremely difficult.[18]

Questions and answers

A. *The proportionality test*

Q1. How do the transitional provisions governing the change in April 2013 relate to proportionality at assessment?

3–07   Three possible scenarios arise—two of which are straightforward and the other presents some practical difficulties.

CPR r.44.3(7) makes it clear that the "new" proportionality provisions— namely the new definition of proportionality at CPR r.44.3(5) and the cross-check at CPR r.44.3(2)(a) do not apply:

- at all to a case which was commenced before 1 April 2013; and
- to those bits of work done on a case prior to 1 April 2013, where the case was commenced after 31 March 2013.

Amongst other issues that arose in the case of *Harrison v University Hospitals Coventry and Warwickshire NHS Trust*[19] was the question of what was meant by "commenced". This arose in the context of a claim form being sent to the court by DX on 27 March 2013, being date- stamped as received at court on 2 April 2013 and being issued on 9 April 2013. In the lead judgment Davis LJ was clear that in CPR r.44.3(7) "commenced" meant "issued", stating:

> "In my view, therefore, it is plain that a case is 'commenced' for the purposes of CPR 44.3 (7)(a) when the relevant proceedings are issued by the court." para.62.

This transitional provision leads to three scenarios as follows:

1. In cases commenced before 1 April 2013, *Lownds v Home Office*[20] still applies and if proportionality is challenged at assessment it must be dealt with at the outset, by reference to what were the "seven pillars of wisdom" at CPR r.44.5(3) and which are now the first seven of eight "pillars" at CPR r.44.4(3). The outcome will be that the costs are either assessed against a necessarily or reasonably incurred test.
2. In cases which are commenced after 31 March 2013 and no work is done on that case prior to that date, then the new provisions apply to all the costs.
3. In cases where the claim is commenced after 31 March 2013 but some work is done before that date, the *Lownds* approach must be adopted in

---

[18] See, for example *Malmsten v Bohinc* [2019] EWHC 1386 (Ch); [2019] 4 W.L.R. 87 in which the court restated that "as costs involve a substantial discretion vested in the judge making the order, and because appeals about costs inevitably inflate costs, appeals against costs orders are rare and the appellate court should discourage such appeals".

[19] *Harrison v University Hospitals Coventry and Warwickshire NHS Trust* [2017] EWCA Civ 792; [2017] 1 W.L.R. 4456.

[20] *Lownds v Home Office* [2002] EWCA 365; [2002] 1 W.L.R. 2450.

respect of the work done prior to 1 April 2013 and the new test to all the work after 31 March 2013.

It is the last of the three scenarios above that presents challenges. Parties seeking assessment of costs, whether by summary or detailed assessment, will need to ensure that the costs pre and post-1 April 2013 are clearly separated. From 6 April 2016 there is a requirement under CPR PD 47 para.5.8(7) to divide a bill for detailed assessment into parts matching the relevant proportionality test where the transitional arrangements provide that both the "old" and "new" provisions apply under 3. above. However, there is no procedural requirement for separate Forms N260 that would similarly divide between the costs under the "old" and the "new" test in a summary assessment. Although the incidence of costs falling within the "old" and the "new" test declines with each passing year, and this problem will resolve itself with the passage of time, until then, as the court will require this information, it seems sensible that practitioners should produce two Forms N260. Experience to date suggests that this approach has not routinely been adopted. The risks that remain if there are not separate N260s for the relevant periods are that:

- It is not proportionate to adjourn off the summary assessment to another date or for written submissions and the court may be forced to do the best it can on the information available. This may result in the court concluding that if a party has not troubled to separate out the two periods, the sanction (and proportionate way forward) is to assess all the costs under the new test.
- The court does adjourn and demands a re-drawn Form N260, but does not permit any recovery of costs for so doing.

If there are separate Forms N260 or separate parts of the bill, (and, as stated above, under CPR PD 47 para.5.8(7) the bill must be divided into the relevant "proportionality test" period for any of the costs to be assessed on the "standard basis"), the court's function is invidious. It must do one proportionality determination at the beginning (for the pre-1 April 2013 costs) and one at the end (for the post-31 March 2013 costs). However, both exercises are artificial, because the court cannot aggregate the costs of both parts to do the exercise under each discrete test. To do so would be to ignore the clear language of CPR r.44.3(7). Instead, the court will have to identify the work undertaken in each period and apply the relevant test to determine the proportionality of that work.

A review of Points of Dispute suggests that proportionality remains routinely raised at the outset and that, even now, *Lownds* is still relied upon occasionally when, in fact, the costs are exclusively under the post-31 March 2013 proportionality test and CPR r.44.3(2)(a) applies.

Q2. Which proportionality provision applies to appeal proceedings in a case where the case commenced before 1 April 2013?

3–08   Appeals are part of a case. They arise within a case, challenging a decision made within that case. Accordingly, in the example given where the case was commenced before 1 April 2013, the costs of the appeal fall under the "old" *Lownds* proportionality test. The fact that the appeal may take place many years after 1 April 2013 is of no relevance, as the transitional provision is based exclusively upon the date of commencement of the case.

Q3. Does the court look at the sums reasonably claimed or the sums recovered when determining "the sums in issue in the proceedings" under CPR r.44.3(5)(a)?

3–09   Obviously at the time that proportionality is considered for the purposes of budget setting and case management, the court does not know what sums will ultimately be recovered. At that stage, the determination must be based on what is claimed less what is admitted—which emphasises the importance of realistic valuation (how often does the statement of value on a claim form limit to a particular sum, but the subsequent schedule of loss attached to later served particulars of claim reveal that the alleged losses are significantly higher than that sum, but there is no application to increase the statement of value?). If there is an argument, namely that the claim is exaggerated, then all that does is confirm that the sums claimed are in issue (and remember the wording of CPR r.44.3(5)(a) is *"the sums in issue in the proceedings"*). It might seem attractive to the court, if it considers a claim to be inflated, to adopt what if considers to be a more realistic value under CPR r.44.3(5)(a) when budgeting. However, unless the court strikes out part of the claim, if it adopts this course, then it ignores the fact that the defendant must still meet the larger claim and its proportionate budget should recognise this. This may explain why the wording of this provision does not refer to sums claimed, but to sums in issue. Of course, if the court thinks that part of the claim will be easily defeated, it can reflect this in its proportionality determination under CPR r.44.3(5)(c) in any event.

At the conclusion of the claim the court will know what sum was recovered. The fact that the sum may be less than was claimed does not, of itself, necessarily alter the determination of proportionality. The fact that one sum was claimed and one was recovered does not mean that the original sum was not in issue (e.g. the claim may be one where breach, causation and quantum were hotly contested and the case settles for a fraction of the sum claimed, but with no admission of liability or a case where there has been a finding of contributory negligence). When the claimant's costs are being considered, the key is that it was reasonable to pursue the claim as stated. Again, though, the court must be astute to the position of a defendant who has successfully defeated a claim and has been awarded costs. To approach CPR r.44.3(5)(a) at the assessment stage on any basis other than that the entire sum claimed was in issue would be to approach the question of the defendant's proportionate costs incorrectly. As stated above, the fact that part of the claim was seen off easily can be reflected when the court considers CPR r.44.3(5)(c).

If, for example, it emerges that the claim was exaggerated, but the claimant still obtains an award of some costs, then in cases costs managed, this may well be a "good reason" to depart from the budget as that will have been set on a basis that the claimant knew was wrong. In non-budgeted cases, conduct can be considered when assessing the reasonable costs under CPR r.44.4 and the "real" value is likely to apply on the proportionality "cross-check". If, as a result of the exaggeration, the defendant secures some form of costs award, it is right that the defendant's budget reflected the proportionate work that it did as the "exaggerated" element of the claim was plainly in issue.

In contrast, if the claimant recovers a lower sum than that claimed, but it was reasonable to pursue the higher sum e.g. if there was a complicated causation argument where the defendant's expert evidence was preferred or where the case turned on a factual dispute and the court preferred the evidence of the defendant's witnesses, then it is likely that will not alter "the sums in issue" for the purpose of proportionality and so will not represent a "good reason" to depart from the budget in costs managed cases and will not influence proportionality in non-budgeted cases.

In practice, in these scenarios, the limited recovery is likely to sound in the award of costs itself, with something less than a full costs order being made under CPR rr.44.2(4)(b) and 44.2(6) or a partial costs award to the defendant. The court must be astute to avoid "double jeopardy", although as is clear from *Ultraframe v Fielding*[21] conduct may be considered both on the award and the assessment of costs.

Q4. Why is only the conduct of the paying party included in the definition?
This question really arises at two stages—at case/costs management and at assessment. It is important, though, when considering the question to remember the full wording of this factor. It is not conduct generally, which falls to be considered, but only conduct of the paying party which generates additional work.

3–10

i. At the case/costs management stage
At the costs management stage the rationale is that the past conduct of the paying party may inform the budgeting process by explaining to the court why the incurred costs of the receiving party are higher than might be expected (in that it has generated extra work). This is because CPR r.3.17(3)(b) requires the court to take into account incurred costs when determining the budgeted (future) costs. If the conduct of the paying party has inflated the incurred costs of the receiving party, then if that conduct is not taken into account the budgeted costs may be insufficient.

3–11

---

[21] *Ultraframe v Fielding* [2006] EWCA Civ 1660. A reminder of the risk of "double jeopardy" can be found In *Amey LG Ltd v Cumbria County Council* [2016] EWHC 2946 (TCC).

There is no need to make express reference to the conduct of the receiving party as that will, inevitably and implicitly, be taken into account in the court's general consideration under CPR r.44.3(5) of what is a proportionate sum. As an example, if the court's determination is that, applying CPR r.44.3(5) the relevant factors in a particular claim are amount in issue and complexity and that this translates into an overall proportionate spend on the disclosure phase of £10,000, but the incurred costs are already £10,000, then the court will approve the budgeted costs at £0. If part of the incurred £10,000 arose as a result of conduct, it can be seen that is has implicitly been taken into account as that party has no more budget to spend on any outstanding proportionate work ordered within the disclosure phase. In addition, budget approval requires the court also to consider reasonableness under CPR rr.44.4(3) and 44.4(3)(a) requires account to be taken of conduct. Adopting this approach, the court can also control the conduct of the receiving party going forward by proportionate budgeting, taking account of incurred costs, and by case management. So, if unreasonable and/or disproportionate costs have been incurred by a party as a result of its own conduct up to costs management, it may find its budget going forward suffers as a result.

In other words, the court's directions should preclude the possibility of conduct generating additional work. The court sets and manages the progression of the case. If a party persists in conduct that is likely to generate additional work, then the other party may always apply under CPR r.3.15A to vary the budget as a result of that conduct, pointing, if appropriate to CPR PD 3E para.13 or seek discrete costs sanctions on any applications that arise outside the budget under CPR r.3.17(4), relying on the stark warnings given by the Court of Appeal about non-co-operation in *Denton v TH White*,[22] which resonate beyond the specific scenario which was under consideration:

> *"The court will be more ready in the future to penalise opportunism. The duty of care owed by a legal representative to his client takes account of the fact that litigants are required to help the court to further the overriding objective."*[23]

However, part of this analysis (that which sees a party's budgeted costs take into account additional work generated already by the conduct of the other party), requires the court to identify at costs management, which is the paying and which is the receiving party. This was a point considered in *Group Seven Ltd v Nasir*.[24] The court concluded that at the costs management stage the court should assume that each party will be the receiving party when its budgeted costs are set. It also found that the conduct of some of the defendants up to the costs case management conference suggested some future procedural difficulties for other parties. As a result of these conclusions, the court indicated that it would consider allowing the costs of future applications to

[22] *Denton v TH White* [2014] EWCA Civ 906; [2014] 1 W.L.R. 3926.
[23] At [43].
[24] *Group Seven Ltd v Nasir* [2016] EWHC 620 (Ch); [2016] 2 Costs L.O. 303.

ensure compliance by those defendants as contingent budgeted costs of the other parties finding that:

> *"Rule 44.3(5)(d) refers to the relationship of the costs to any additional work generated by the paying party. That rule applies where an order for costs has been made and one knows who the paying party is. At the costs budget stage, there is not yet an order that anyone pay the budgeted costs but I consider that the question of proportionality should be judged on the hypothetical basis that the party who has prepared the budget turns out to be the receiving party ... as to future costs, I would be prepared to allow Group Seven and ETS sums for contingencies to reflect the possibility that there will be future procedural difficulties which might be attributable to a lack of cooperation from some of the Defendants."*

ii. At the assessment stage

The reason that the conduct of the receiving party does not form part of the   3–12
definition at assessment seems more complicated. Whilst it is likely that such conduct will already have been taken into account by the court when making the award of costs—see CPR r.44.2(4)(a)—that is by no means certain, as it may not always be obvious at that stage whether certain conduct has generated additional costs. However, conduct is also taken into account at the assessment—see CPR r.44.4(3). Both these provisions, though, relate to the conduct of the parties. So, if the argument is that conduct has already been considered, then that ought also to apply to the conduct of the paying party, but that remains expressly referred to in the proportionality factors.

Explanations may be that:

- the conduct has already, implicitly, been taken into account at the budgeting stage (see the example given above); and
- it is difficult to imagine a situation where any additional costs of the receiving party generated by the conduct of that party survive the test of whether they are reasonably incurred or reasonable in amount and, as such, have already been disallowed by the time that the court does the proportionality cross-check.

In contrast, the receiving party's additional costs caused by the paying party's conduct will survive the test of whether they were reasonably incurred and reasonable. If the court does not remind itself under CPR r.44.3(5)(d) when undertaking the CPR r.44.3(2)(a) cross-check, that these reasonably incurred and reasonable in amount costs include those extra costs caused by the conduct of the paying party, there is a danger that the overall sum is deemed disproportionate and the paying party escapes the consequences of its actions.

Q5. Are the six factors in CPR r.44.3(5) listed in order of their importance? Is some degree of weighting attached to these factors to translate them

into a mathematical calculation of the proportionate sum for the costs in any given case?

3–13   In *May v Wavell Group Plc*[25] the appellate court noted that the costs judge had failed to base the final figure on a "specific mathematical calculation", nor given a "specific explanation of how the weighting of the various factors resulted in the final figure". In contrast in *Reynolds v One Stop Stores Ltd*,[26] the court rejected the claimant's submission that:

> "... the Judge must decide what weight to attach to each of the factors in the Rule 44.3(5) list, and thereby arrive at a particular figure for a reduction of the provisional total in some mathematically-reasoned way."

and accepted the defendant's submission that CPR r.44.3(5):

> "... confers a discretion on the assessing Judge. It does not require a mathematical process to be followed, nor could it: a judgment about proportionality is inherently qualitative, though it must find its expression as a numerical result. Nor, similarly, does the rule require the Judge to identify and attach a particular numerical weighting to each of the Rule 44.3(5) factors."

The court did not accept that the rules required it "to apply any particular mathematical formula or algorithm", nor "to assign to each factor a precise numerical weighting, scoring it in some way, or performing any other kind of mathematical calculation". This approach accords with the view we have advocated previously. Under CPR r.44.3(5), proportionality is determined by reference to a reasonable relationship with specified factors. There is no precise formula, indeed, as we have said, there is no one correct figure. The exercise is one of discretion. However, when assessing proportionality clearly the court must offer a sufficiently principled and reasoned consideration of the factors to justify the figure reached. This conclusion chimes with the approach to determinations of proportionality articulated by the Court of Appeal in *West v Stockport NHS Foundation Trust*,[27] which simply referred to an assessment by reference to CPR rr.44.3(5) and 44.4(1) ("wider circumstances") without ascribing any hierarchy to the factors to be considered, in a process it described as leading to reductions which will be "clear and transparent for both sides".

B. The relationship between proportionality, reasonableness and necessity

Q6. Is there any distinction between proportionality and reasonableness in reality?

3–14   The answer, as an exercise of semantic interpretation of the CPR, is yes, because throughout the CPR the two are referred to separately—see for example CPR

---

[25] *May v Wavell Group Plc* unreported 22 December 2017 County Court (Central London) HHJ Dight CBE.
[26] *Reynolds v One Stop Stores Ltd* unreported 21 September 2018 County Court (Norwich and Cambridge) HHJ Auerbach.
[27] *West v Stockport NHS Foundation Trust* [2019] EWCA Civ 1220; [2019] 1 W.L.R. 6157.

PD 3E para.12 which requires the court to approve budgets for phases that are "reasonable and proportionate" and CPR r.44.3(2)(a) which clearly draws a distinction between the two. Indeed, it is the latter provision that makes it clear that some costs may be reasonable, but not proportionate. As the court said in *Group Seven Ltd v Nasir*[28]:

> "... proportionality can result in the non-recovery of costs even where they are otherwise reasonable costs and even where they are necessary costs".

In practice, there will be cases where the court, having assessed the reasonable costs, then applies the CPR r.44.3(5) factors to the proportionality cross-check under CPR r.44.3(2)(a) and determines that those costs are also proportionate—indeed, the court's assessment of proportionality might be at a higher figure than the reasonable costs for a variety of reasons (e.g. because of limits imposed by the contractual retainer). There will also be cases where the same cross-check and consideration of any "wider circumstances" reveals the reasonable costs are still disproportionate. Indeed, sometimes, as per *West v Stockport NHS Foundation Trust*[29] it may be possible to conclude an item is also plainly disproportionate whilst undertaking the assessment of reasonableness. Perhaps the better answer, therefore, is, not necessarily so. This sits happily with the words of Lord Woolf MR in *Lownds v Home Office*,[30] that there may be an overlap between issues of reasonableness and those of proportionality to the extent that reasonableness may be a condition of proportionality.

Q7. Is the effect of proportionality to prescribe that in a case about money, the costs cannot exceed the sums in dispute? Can costs exceed the value of a claim and still be proportionate? Is proportionality just about the value of the claim? What guidance is there for a determination of proportionality of costs in non-monetary claims?

Before 1 April 2013, there was an acceptance within the CPR that there were cases where the proportionate cost would exceed the sum in issue. Section 11 of the then Costs Practice Direction expressed it in these terms:

3–15

> "11.1 In applying the test of proportionality the court will have regard to rule 1.1(2)(c). The relationship between the total of the costs incurred and the financial value of the claim may not be a reliable guide. A fixed percentage cannot be applied in all cases to the value of the claim in order to ascertain whether or not the costs are proportionate.
>
> 11.2 In any proceedings there will be costs which will inevitably be incurred and which are necessary for the successful conduct of the case. Solicitors are not required to conduct litigation at rates which are uneconomic. Thus in a modest claim the proportion of costs is likely to be higher than in a large claim and may even equal or possibly exceed the amount in dispute."

---

[28] *Group Seven Ltd v Nasir* [2016] EWHC 620 (Ch); [2016] 2 Costs L.O. 303.
[29] *West v Stockport NHS Foundation Trust* [2019] EWCA Civ 1220.
[30] *Lownds v Home Office* [2002] EWCA Civ 365; [2002] 1 W.L.R. 2450.

What is immediately clear is that 11.2 accorded precedence to "necessary" costs. Work that was necessary informed the assessment of proportionality. This is no longer the situation, for CPR r.44.3(2)(a) expressly gives primacy to proportionality, even if that means that necessary costs (and by implication necessary work) are not recoverable. This does no more than codify the comments at Ch.3 para.5.10 of Sir Rupert Jackson's Final Report[31] under the bold heading "Costs do not become proportionate because they were necessary". It is for this reason that we make the comments that we do about *Kazakhstan Kagazy Plc v Zhunus*[32] in para.**3–04** above (see **Q8** below). It remains to be seen what effect, if any, the introduction of the fixed and unavoidable or irreducible minimum items of costs in *West v Stockport NHS Foundation Trust*[33] has on the revival of necessary costs (considered further at **Q10** below).

Does this mean that costs can never exceed the amount in dispute? The answer must surely be no, but not because a certain amount of work is necessary in any given claim, but, instead, because CPR r.44.3(5) does not limit the relationship between proportionality and costs solely to the amount in issue. If there are other relevant factors, then those inform the determination of the proportionate sum. This, again, illustrates the flexibility of the definition that enables it to apply to all circumstances. The Final Report concluded, when making the recommendation for the new definition of proportionality, that:

> "*Proportionality of costs is not simply a matter of comparing the sum in issue with the amount of costs incurred, important though that comparison is. It is also necessary to evaluate any non-monetary remedies sought and any rights which are in issue, in order to compare the overall value of what is at stake in the action with the costs of resolution.*"[34]

Notwithstanding this, it is likely to be rare indeed for costs to exceed the sums in dispute. As Stuart-Smith J observed in *GSK Project Management Ltd v QPR Holdings Ltd*[35]:

> "*My starting point is that a case would have to be wholly exceptional to render a costs budget of £824,000 proportionate for the recovery of £805,000 plus interest.*"

This confirms that where the only relevant factor under CPR r.44.3(5) is the sum in issue, it is difficult to envisage a court determining that it is proportionate for the parties to spend more than this sum in determining the dispute.

It is also clear that CPR r.44.3(5) and any wider circumstances under CPR r.44.1 extend beyond merely monetary value. It follows that in non-monetary claims the court will determine proportionality by reference to any other factors that apply under CPR r.44.3(5) and any wider circumstances.

---

[31] *Review of Civil Litigation Costs: Final Report*, December 2009.
[32] *Kazakhstan Kagazy Plc v Zhunus* [2015] EWHC 404 (Comm).
[33] *West v Stockport NHS Foundation Trust* [2019] EWCA Civ 1220; [2019] 1 W.L.R. 6157.
[34] Ch.3 para.5.5.
[35] *GSK Project Management Ltd v QPR Holdings Ltd* [2015] EWHC 2274 (TCC); [2015] B.L.R. 715.

Q8. Is the case of *Kazakhstan Kagazy Plc v Zhunuss*[36] the touchstone regarding proportionality—namely that it defines what is "reasonable and proportionate" as ". . . the lowest amount (of costs) which it (a party) could reasonably have been expected to spend in order to have its case conducted and presented proficiently, having regard to all the circumstances"?

No, on a strict reading of the rules. See the commentary at para.**3–04** and **3–16** **Q7** above. CPR r.44.3(2)(a) is clear that reasonable costs may be disallowed if they are disproportionate. It matters not that these costs may be at the very bottom of the bracket that the court deems reasonable. What matters is that the costs must bear a reasonable relationship to the factors at CPR r.44.3(5) or to the "wider circumstances" of the claim. If they do not, then they are disproportionate even if a party could not reasonably have spent less to have a case conducted and presented proficiently.[37] (See **Q10** below for consideration of whether this is qualified by the decision in *West v Stockport NHS Foundation Trust*.[38])

It is important to note that *Kazakhstan Kagazy Plc v Zhunuss* was a short decision in which the court was concerned only with determining the extent of a payment on account of costs. It was not assessing the costs, which would have required detailed consideration of CPR r.44.3(5) and CPR r.44.3(2)(a) (of pertinence is that neither of these provisions is mentioned). Indeed, Leggatt J (as he was then) expressly concluded in general terms that the costs claimed were neither reasonable nor proportionate and that the reasonable and proportionate costs could only properly be determined by a detailed assessment.

We said no strictly according to the rules. However, the question of "whether costs can ever be disproportionate, even though they are no more than the minimum costs which the party needs to spend in order to bring the case to trial" arose in the case of *Thomas v PGI Group Ltd*.[39] The court did not need to determine the issue, in the light of its other decisions. It declined to offer substantive comment on the question but, by indicating that that this raised an issue of potential public importance, seems to suggest that the answer may not be quite so clear as we believe the position to be. (See para.**3–04** for further consideration of this case).

Q9. In the case of *Stocker v Stocker*,[40] Mr Justice Warby observed: "I readily acknowledge the importance of ensuring that the costs budgeting process does not result in a party being unable to recover the costs necessary to

---

[36] *Kazakhstan Kagazy Plc v Zhunus* [2015] EWHC 404 (Comm); 158 Con. L.R. 253.
[37] This case is referred to in the appeal decision in *May v Wavell* unreported 22 December 2017 County Court (Central London) HHJ Dight CBE. It may be that this, in part, informed his conclusion doubting "that the proper interpretation of the rules requires or indeed entitles a costs judge at the end of an item by item assessment to impose a very substantial reduction on the overall figure without regard to the component parts". See [56] of the judgment and para.3–03 above and Q5 above where this case is considered in more detail.
[38] *West v Stockport NHS Foundation Trust* [2019] EWCA Civ 1220; [2019] 1 W.L.R. 6157.
[39] *Thomas v PGI Group Ltd* [2021] EWHC 2776 (QB).
[40] *Stocker v Stocker* [2015] EWHC 1634 (QB); [2015] 4 Costs L.R. 651.

assert their rights." Does this mean that proportionate costs can never be less than those that are necessary?

3–17 No. CPR r.44.3(2)(a) makes this quite clear:

> *"Costs which are disproportionate in amount may be disallowed or reduced even if they were reasonably or necessarily incurred."*

In fact, the extract quoted in the question needs to be put in context. It comes at the conclusion of a paragraph considering "purely financial proportionality". Of course, costs are proportionate if they bear a reasonable relationship to the six factors at CPR r.44.3(5) and, if necessary, any "wider circumstances" of the case and not simply the sums in issue in the proceedings. However, Warby J did acknowledge the difficulty "to cut radically, at a stroke, the costs of this class of litigation" (libel claims), suggesting overtly that this would need to be a gradual process. However, that said, he had no hesitation in concluding that "the defendant's global costs figure is clearly considerably out of proportion to what is at stake and the nature of the issues, and should be substantially reduced for that reason".

Perhaps it depends on the how the question is framed – see **Q8** above and the suggestion in *Thomas v PGI Group Ltd*[41] that the question "whether costs can ever be disproportionate, even though they are no more than the minimum costs which the party needs to spend in order to bring the case to trial" may still need a definitive answer from the higher courts. Notwithstanding this our answer remains the same. It is challenging to see an interpretation that decides "minimum spend" is anything other than "necessary costs". If that is so, then CPR r.44.3(2)(a) provides an unequivocal answer – the court may determine the costs to be disproportionate.

Q10. Does the decision in *West v Stockport NHS Foundation Trust* reintroduce the recovery of necessary costs? In any event, does the decision lessen the restriction imposed by the constraints of proportionality?

3–18 The court itself was at pains to stress that its decision was not a reintroduction of *Lownds v Home Office*,[42] stating that:

> *"As should be apparent, leaving particular items out of account when considering proportionality because they are both reasonable and an unavoidable expenditure does not re-introduce the Lownds test, by which necessity always trumped proportionality. Most costs will still be subject to the proportionality requirement."* [86]

Implicit in this statement is an acknowledgement that the decision does create a position that necessity (and the necessary costs linked to it) will sometimes trump proportionality in respect of discrete items of costs. To this extent the decision, inevitably, reintroduces the recovery of some necessary costs, but by taking those out of the proportionality account altogether, avoids a direct

---

[41] *Thomas v PGI Group Ltd* [2021] EWHC 2776 (QB).
[42] *Lownds v Home Office* [2002] EWCA Civ 365; [2002] 1 W.L.R. 2450.

conflict with CPR r.44.3(2)(a) and the "proportionate cost" element of the overriding objective. It is here that the challenge for the future lies. What elements of costs are the court prepared to leave out of the proportionality account to enable access to justice (see [80] and [81])? The court described these at [82] as "those items of cost which are fixed and unavoidable, or which have an irreducible minimum, without which the litigation could not have been progressed." How far does this definition extend?

We have no issue with the exclusion of court fees and VAT. The former is sums prescribed by the state and, as a result, many had previously taken the view that, as a result, they must be proportionate. Treating them this way or leaving them out of account, makes no difference to the end result. It is arguable that VAT is not an item of costs anyway. It is consequential upon costs. It does not appear in the definition of costs at CPR r.44.1, instead, having its own separate definition in that rule. It is expressly excluded from Precedent H. It matters not, for again, where it arises, VAT is unavoidable. As Marcus Smith J said in *Malmsten v Bohinic*[43]:

> "*Equally, the inclusion of VAT confuses rather than assists. The fact is that VAT is – when payable – not an option, but an inevitable cost to the receiving party.*" [61]

The potential difficulty lies in [91] of the judgment in *West*. It is here that the court discusses the exclusion from proportionality of the unavoidable elements of costs. In so doing it lists examples, which conclude with the words "...and the like". Whilst we can understand the court not wishing to provide a definitive and exclusionary list, we expect these three words to occupy further court time as parties seek to argue that a particular step (and the accompanying item of costs it generates) is necessary to enable access to justice and so is excluded from considerations of proportionality.

So far as the second question is concerned see the analysis at para.3–05 above. It would appear from [84] of the judgment in *West* that the Court of Appeal believes that assessing judges ought still to be able to achieve the overall proportionate figure they have in mind even though some items of costs will no longer be available for reduction. This belief is predicated on the basis that the court will make those deductions necessary to achieve the overall proportionate figure from the items remaining susceptible to the CPR r.44.3(2)(a) cross-check. As we have set out in para.3–05 we are not convinced that this is so. If the outcome is to be, as it must, reasoned and principled, reductions cannot be made from categories, types or periods of costs unless they are disproportionate. If they are not, then there is no possibility of reducing them to offset the fact that certain costs are irreducible, in an attempt to achieve an overall proportionate figure. Indeed, this suggestion seems a curious one on a semantic level. If the fixed and unavoidable and irreducible costs are to be taken out of account for proportionality, then

---

[43] *Malmsten v Bohinic* [2019] EWHC 1386 (Ch); [2019] 4 W.L.R. 87, Marcus Smith J sitting with Master Rowley as an assessor.

surely the overall views of proportionality held by assessing judges should also exclude them.

C. The extent of proportionality considerations

Q11. Is proportionality to be applied in all cases, or, as some wish to suggest, is it really for the small to medium value claims, where disproportionate costs are more likely?

3–19 Whilst costs management is limited to those claims specifically referred to in CPR r.3.12, and any other claims where the court orders it, this does not limit the all-encompassing relevance of proportionality. It is part of the overriding objective and, as such, all case management decisions must be made against the obligation on the court to deal with cases at proportionate cost whatever the value of a claim. This is reinforced by CPR r.3.17(1), which provides that:

> *"When making any case management decision, the court . . . will take into account the costs in each procedural step."*

Chapter 4 considers the effect of proportionality on obvious case management decisions, but the effect is more wide-ranging than that. By way of example, in *Agents Mutual Ltd v Gasgoine Halman Ltd*[44] the court considered proportionality in the context of an application for security for costs, describing some of the costs as "seriously disproportionate".

Even in those cases where the filing of Precedent H is required and the court chooses not to make a costs management order, the rules on the relevance of that budget at assessment have been strengthened. CPR PD 44 rr.3.6 and 3.7 reiterate and expand previous provisions. They enable the assessing court, where there is a difference of 20% or more between the costs claimed and those shown in a budget, to:

- Restrict the recoverable costs where reliance has been placed on the budget by the paying party to what is reasonable even if that results in a sum less than that which would otherwise be proportionate and reasonable.
- Regard the difference between the costs claimed and those in the budget as evidence that the costs claimed are unreasonable or disproportionate, even where no reliance on the budget is established.

Proportionality also has a role to play in fast track (including fixed fee) and small claims track cases. Indeed, cases that might previously have been allocated to multi-track (e.g. because the time estimate for trial exceeded one day) may now be allocated to fast track with directions targeted to reduce the time estimate to one day and cases that are over the small claim track limit may now be allocated to that track as the consent of the parties to this is no longer required. In both these tracks, directions will be targeted to ensure

---

[44] *Agents Mutual Ltd v Gasgoine Halman Ltd* [2016] EWHC 2315 (Ch); [2017] U.K.C.L.R. 269.

that the cases are dealt with proportionately (and that includes the amount of court time that they occupy). This link between proportionate costs and a proportionate amount of work was recognised by Sir Rupert Jackson in his Supplemental Report, when he acknowledged that in his proposed intermediate track, the fixed fees should be accompanied by control of the amount of work to be undertaken.[45] Whilst the Ministry of Justice has set its face against the introduction of an intermediate track,[46] we would expect the case management rules applicable to those cases within any extended fixed costs regime to ensure that cases are managed proportionately.

So far as assessments of costs are concerned, in respect of those that fall under the new proportionality regime (see **Q1** above), then the court must apply the proportionality cross-check under CPR r.44.3(2)(a) as the "court will only allow costs which are proportionate". It is no longer a case of proportionality only arising if raised by the paying party.

Q12. What relevance, if any, does proportionality have in cases where an order for costs is made on the indemnity basis?

Proportionality is still relevant before the costs order is made, as the court will have case managed on a proportionate basis. Where the order for indemnity costs has significance is on the assessment of the amount of recoverable costs. When conducting an assessment on the indemnity basis under CPR r.44.4(1)(b), the court must decide whether costs were unreasonably incurred or unreasonable in amount—it is not required to consider proportionality. Albeit that the rule number may have changed (from CPR r.44.4(3)) this does not alter the provision in place before April 2013. However, where the change in outcome is marked is in cases where a costs management order has been made. This is because CPR r.3.18, which provides that the court will not depart from the last approved or agreed budget at assessment unless there is "good reason", expressly only applies to cases where the court is assessing costs on the "standard basis".

3–20

Whilst Coulson J (as he then was) in *Elvanite Full Circle Ltd v AMEC Earth & Environment*[47] suggested that even where there was an order for indemnity costs, the budget should be the starting point, it must be remembered that he was considering a budget prepared under CPR PD 51G. The budget form (Form HB) did not require any certification suggesting that the budget was constrained in any way by proportionality—in other words it was probably a fair reflection of all the costs that the client was likely to incur and so represented an approximation of indemnity costs. Now the budget does require a certification linking the sums included to those that are proportionate as is set out in CPR PD 22 (Statements of Truth) para.2.2A:

---

[45] Review of Civil Litigation Costs: Supplemental Report Fixed Recoverable Costs, July 2017 Ch.7 para.4.1.
[46] Extending Fixed Recoverable Costs in Civil Cases September 2021.
[47] *Elvanite Full Circle Ltd v AMEC Earth & Environment* [2013] EWHC 1643 (TCC); [2016] 4 W.L.R. 186.

> *"This budget is a fair and accurate statement of incurred and estimated costs which it would be reasonable and proportionate for my client to incur in this litigation."*

As a result, the link between the budget sum and indemnity costs relied upon by Coulson J is no more. Whilst it is worth noting that he reiterated the same view, albeit in the context of a determination of a payment on account, in *The Governor & Company of the Bank of Ireland v Watts Group* Plc,[48] in *Lejonvarn v Burgess*,[49] he revisited the issue in the Court of Appeal and accepted that there was an "absence of an overlap between the cost budgeting regime on the one hand, and an order for indemnity costs on the other" before concluding, with generous and laudable humility, that:

> *"In principle, the assessment of costs on an indemnity basis is not constrained by the approved cost budget, and to the extent that my obiter comments in Elvanite or Bank of Ireland v Watts suggested the contrary, they should be disregarded."* [93]

The fact that an order for indemnity costs does result in an "escape" from the constraints of a costs management order seems clear from the Court of Appeal in the judgment of Dyson MR and Vos LJ in *Denton v TH White*.[50] The relevant section of the judgment was considering sanctions in costs for non-cooperation between the parties. It dealt with indemnity costs as a possibility and said this:

> *"If the offending party ultimately loses, then its conduct may be a good reason to order it to pay indemnity costs. Such an order would free the winning party from the operation of CPR rule 3.18 in relation to its costs budget."*

CPR PD 47 para.5.8(8) provides additional support for the view that the budget is not relevant, even as a starting point, on an assessment on the indemnity basis. The requirement to divide the bill into the budget phases and within them between the incurred and budgeted costs only applies on an assessment on the standard basis. Whilst the requirement to serve and file a breakdown in the form of Precedent Q or equivalent is not so limited (CPR PD 47 para.5.2(f)), it would be curious if the intention of the rule-makers was that the budget was to remain relevant on a detailed assessment, but essential information to enable easy identification of the specific work undertaken that took the costs over those budgeted, was removed from the bill (as it would not be readily apparent what work had been attributed to each phase, as Precedent Q only provides a limited snapshot by reference to total costs and not by identification of specific work).

In addition, if a party who has fallen foul of CPR r.3.14 and whose budgeted costs have been approved as future court fees only, subsequently recovers

---

[48] *The Governor & Company of the Bank of Ireland v Watts Group Plc* [2017] EWHC 2472 (TCC).
[49] *Lejonvarn v Burgess* [2020] EWCA Civ 114.
[50] *Denton v TH White* [2014] EWCA Civ 906; [2014] 1 W.L.R. 3926.

costs on the indemnity basis, then clearly the budget has no link, even as a starting point, with the ultimate determination of the amount of costs due.

Given that CPR PD 3E para.12 requires that budgeted costs are set by consideration of proportionality and CPR r.44.3 provides that on an assessment of costs under the indemnity basis proportionality does not play a part, what is clear is that even if the budgeted costs form the starting point on an indemnity basis assessment (and for the reasons set out above our view is that they do not), departure is likely to be routine by highlighting to the assessing judge a) the constraints imposed by the statement of truth when preparing the budget and b) the role required of the costs managing judge under CPR PD 3E para.12.

It is clear from this that there is a greater benefit to a receiving party of an order for indemnity costs than was the case before the 2013 reforms. However, the test for whether an order for indemnity costs is merited has not altered and parties should not be seeking indemnity costs orders inappropriately in an attempt to escape the strictures of CPR r.3.18. As Coulson J observed in *Elvanite Full Circle Ltd v AMEC Earth & Environment*, when explaining his rationale for the budget being the starting point:

> "There is a concern that, if an order for indemnity costs allows a receiving party to ignore the costs management order, then that will encourage successful parties to argue for indemnity costs every time."[51]

It is worth noting that when assessing costs on the indemnity basis in *Louis Dreyfus Company Suisse S.A. v International Bank of St.Petersburg (Joint-Stock Company)*[52] the court reminded itself of the words of Leggatt J (as he then was) in *Kazakhstan Kagazy Plc v Zhunus*[53], rather confirming the point we make above at para. **3–04** and **Qs 7** and **8** above, that that case resonates more with the determination of reasonable costs, rather than those that are proportionate.

Q13. Is proportionality a "fixed sum" throughout the life of a claim?
This depends entirely on the specific features of any claim, e.g. an assessment   **3–21** of proportionality is made at the costs management stage in a claim where two heads of loss are pursued, each with a considerable value. After disclosure, it becomes apparent that one head of loss is unsustainable and the claimant discontinues that part of the claim. At that stage, plainly the sum in issue has altered. In those circumstances, there has been a significant development for the purposes of CPR r.3.15A and we would expect the parties either to agree revised budgets or, in the absence of agreement, to seek the approval of the court to revised budgets on the basis that what was proportionate for the claim as originally presented is not for the claim that then remains (remember

[51] Above at [30].
[52] *Louis Dreyfus Company Suisse S.A. v International Bank of St.Petersburg (Joint-Stock Company)* [2021] EWHC 1039 (Comm).
[53] *Kazakhstan Kagazy Plc v Zhunus* [2015] EWHC 404 (Comm).

that revision where there is a significant development is expressly referred to as "upwards or downwards" in CPR r.3.15A(1)). In other words, the proportionality of a claim may alter throughout its course.

However, this does not mean that as a matter of routine the court will revisit earlier decisions on proportionality. Many saw the decision to grant permission to appeal in *Troy Foods v Manton*[54] as opening the door to revisiting proportionality in costs managed cases at subsequent assessment. This interpretation overlooks some important points as follows:

- This was simply a decision on whether to permit an appeal. As such it is not a binding authority.
- The case was within the pilot scheme under what was CPR PD 51G. At para.4.2 of the practice direction, the objective of costs management was said to be "to control the costs of litigation in accordance with the overriding objective". The overriding objective was in its pre-April 2013 form without specific reference to dealing with a case at proportionate costs. Whilst para.1.3 of the Practice Direction made a reference to proportionate costs it did so in the context of the relevance of costs already incurred. Nowhere in the Practice Direction did it state that the court was expressly charged with setting the budget by reference to proportionality.
- The costs managing judge appeared to have applied a test of approving the budget "provided it was not so unreasonable as to render it obviously excessive or, as he put it, "grossly disproportionate". Accordingly, permission was given on the basis that it was arguable the judge had applied the wrong test and been overgenerous as a result.
- When setting a budget under the costs management provisions of CPR r.3 and PD 3E, the court is required to budget phases by reference to what is "reasonable and proportionate". In other words, the court has assessed the proportionality of any phases budgeted already.

Some have taken the comments of the Court of Appeal at [52] in *Harrison v University Hospitals Coventry and Warwickshire NHS Trust*[55] to suggest that under CPR r.44.3(2)(a), the court may, at the end of the assessment, determine an overall proportionality figure below the budgeted costs (see, for example, *Reynolds v One Step Store Ltd* considered at para.3–03 above and Q5 above). We have always advocated that whilst the court must still step back under CPR r.44.3(2)(a) at the end of an assessment involving budgeted costs and consider proportionality, the court may not, in the absence of good reason, reach a conclusion that results in a total less than the budgeted costs as these have already been determined to be proportionate by the court. This is on the basis that this follows the strict wording of CPR r.3.18, which is specific rule dealing with the link between budgeted costs and the assessment process. The

---

[54] *Troy Foods v Manton* [2013] EWCA Civ 615; [2013] 4 Costs L.R. 546.
[55] *Harrison v University Hospitals Coventry and Warwickshire NHS Trust* [2017] EWCA Civ 792; [2017] 1 W.L.R. 4456.

debate surrounding the comments in *Harrison* is considered in more detail in Q16, below. However, our view remains unchanged. Accordingly, unless something has occurred that amounts to a "good reason" why there should be a departure from costs budgeted as reasonable and proportionate, then the determination of proportionality has already taken place in respect of those costs and the CPR r.44.3(2)(a) cross-check at the end of an assessment cannot reduce the overall costs assessed to less than the budgeted costs.

Q14. Can a claim, or part of a claim, be struck out as the remedy sought is disproportionate to the costs and the use of court time?
This is a question addressed recently by Mann J in *Various Claimants v MGN Ltd*.[56] The court was satisfied that such a jurisdiction exists in general terms under the provisions of CPR rr.3.1(2)(k) (the court may exclude an issue from consideration) and CPR r.3.4(2)(b) (that a statement of case is an abuse of the court's process or is otherwise likely to obstruct the just disposal of proceedings). Although the court declined to make the order sought in this case, such orders have been made previously (see for example *Schellenberg v BBC*[57] and *Dow Jones & Co Inc v Jameel*[58]). In the former, cited in the latter, Eady J specifically linked outcome with the consideration of proportionality, both as to costs and allocation of court resources, asking whether the claim was "worth the candle":

3–22

> *"It is necessary to apply the overriding objective ... and in particular to have regard to proportionality. Here there are tens of thousands of pounds of costs at stake and several weeks of court time. I must therefore have regard to the possible benefits that might accrue to the claimant as rendering such a significant expenditure potentially worthwhile. ... I am afraid I cannot accept that there is any realistic prospect of a trial yielding any tangible or legitimate advantage such as to outweigh the disadvantages for the parties in terms of expense, and the wider public in terms of court resources."*

Clearly, as evidenced by the decision in *Various Claimants v MGN* and the relative dearth of reported cases of strike out on the grounds of proportionality, the fact that the court may have the jurisdiction does not mean that it will exercise it. In most cases, the court will control proportionality by way of case and, where appropriate, costs management. This was essentially the view taken by the Court of Appeal in *Sullivan v Bristol Film Studios Ltd*:[59]

> *"The mere fact that a claim is small should not automatically result in the court refusing to hear it at all. If I am entitled to recover a debt of £50 I should, in principle, have access to justice to enable me to recover it if my debtor does not pay. It would be an affront to justice if my claim were simply struck out. The real*

---

[56] *Various Claimants v MGN Ltd* [2020] EWHC 553 (Ch).
[57] *Schellenberg v BBC* [2000] EMLR 296.
[58] *Dow Jones & Co Inc v Jameel* [2005] EWCA Civ 75.
[59] *Sullivan v Bristol Film Studios Ltd* [2012] EWCA Civ 570.

question, to my mind, is whether in any particular case there is a proportionate procedure by which the merits of a claim can be investigated. In my judgment it is only if there is no proportionate procedure by which a claim can be adjudicated that it would be right to strike it out as an abuse of process."

Essentially, the consideration comes back to the application of the overriding objective and as Briggs J (as he then was) stated in *Sectorguard plc v Dienne plc:*[60]

"It is now well established, in the light of the new culture introduced by the CPR, and in particular with the requirements of proportionality referred to in CPR 1.1(2) as part of the overriding objective, that it is an abuse of process to pursue litigation where the value to the litigant of a successful outcome is so small as to make the exercise pointless, viewed against the expenditure of court time and the parties' time and money engaged by the undertaking..."

D. The practical implications of CPR r.44.3(2)(a) at assessment

Q15. At what stage of the assessment proceedings does the court apply the provisions of CPR r.44.3(2)(a)?

3–23   This is a question that has previously been considered in the lower courts, e.g. in the cases of *May v Wavell Group Plc*[61] and *Reynolds v One Stop Stores Ltd.*[62] Both cases identified that CPR r.44.3(2)(a) contains no guidance as to the stage when it is to be applied. Reference has also been made both to the words of Sir Rupert Jackson in his *Review of Civil Litigation Costs: Final Report* para.5.13:

"The court should first make an assessment of reasonable costs, having regard to the individual items in the bill. . .The court should then stand back and consider whether the total figure is proportionate. If the total figure is not proportionate, the court should make an appropriate reduction"[63]

and to the judgment of the Court of Appeal in *Harrison*, explicitly envisaging the proportionality cross-check to be a "step back" after determining the reasonable costs:

"I add that where, as here, a costs judge on detailed assessment will be assessing incurred costs in the usual way and also will be considering budgeted costs (and not departing from such budgeted costs in the absence of 'good reason') the costs judge ordinarily will still, as I see it, <u>ultimately</u> have to look at matters in the round and consider whether the resulting aggregate figure is proportionate, having regard to CPR 44.3 (2)(a) and (5)"[64] (our emphasis)

---

[60] *Sectorguard plc v Dienne plc* [2009] EWHC 2693 (Ch).
[61] *May v Wavell Group Plc* unreported 22 December 2017 County Court (Central London) HHJ Dight CBE.
[62] *Reynolds v One Stop Stores Ltd* unreported 21 September 2018 County Court (Norwich and Cambridge) HHJ Auerbach.
[63] Review of Civil Litigation Costs: Final Report, December 2009 para.5.13. This paragraph comes with an equally clear footnote: *"The test of proportionality does not, however, replace the requirement for the court to consider the bill on an item by item basis. The application of any reduction for proportionality should only take place when each item on the bill has been assessed individually."* [FN 62].
[64] *Harrison v University Hospitals Coventry and Warwickshire NHS Trust* [2017] EWCA Civ 792; [2017] 1 W.L.R. 4456 at [52].

The definitive answer has now been provided by the Court of Appeal as part of the general guidance offered in *West v Stockport NHS Foundation Trust*[65] and is set out at [88]–[90] as follows:

> "*88. First, the judge should go through the bill line-by-line, assessing the reasonableness of each item of cost. If the judge considers it possible, appropriate and convenient when undertaking that exercise, he or she may also address the proportionality of any particular item at the same time. That is because, although reasonableness and proportionality are conceptually distinct, there can be an overlap between them, not least because reasonableness may be a necessary condition of proportionality. . .This will be a matter for the judge. It will apply, for example, when the judge considers an item to be clearly disproportionate, irrespective of the final figures.*
>
> *89. At the conclusion of the line-by-line exercise, there will be a total figure which the judge considers to be reasonable (and which may, as indicated, also take into account at least some aspects of proportionality). That total figure will have involved an assessment of every item of cost, including court fees, the ATE premium and the like.*
>
> *90. The proportionality of that total figure must be assessed by reference to both r.44.3(5) and r.44.4(1). If that total figure is found to be proportionate, then no further assessment is required. If the judge regards the overall figure as disproportionate, then a further assessment is required. That should not be line-by-line, but should instead consider various categories of cost, such as disclosure or expert's reports, or specific periods where particular costs were incurred, or particular parts of the profit costs.*"

In other words, proportionality may be considered, where possible, appropriate and convenient, when considering the reasonableness of individual items, and must be considered in respect of the total figure assessed as reasonable, but guarding against any further reduction in respect of items already reduced as disproportionate. In practice, as the determination of reasonableness and proportionality are distinct exercises based on different criteria, we would still expect the majority of assessments to leave the determination of proportionality until after the reasonable costs have been determined.

Q16. If there is no "good reason" to depart from the budgeted costs on assessment, how does the court apply the proportionality "cross-check" under CPR r.44.3(2)(a) at the end of the assessment?

Our view has always been, and remains, that at the end of the assessment the court will have determined the reasonably incurred and reasonable in amount sum of the non-budgeted costs (i.e. those incurred before the costs management order which were not agreed) and these must then be added to the budgeted costs (as amended to include the higher or lesser sum allowed for any specific phase where the court has determined there to be a "good

3–24

---

[65] *West v Stockport NHS Foundation Trust* [2019] EWCA Civ 1220; [2019] 1 W.L.R. 6157.

reason" to depart from the budgeted costs for that phase). The proportionality cross-check is then applied, but on the basis that this cannot reduce the overall costs to less than the budgeted costs, for, as is set out above in answer to **Q13**, those costs were subject to a determination of proportionality at the time the budget was set and the wording of CPR r.3.18 precludes departure from this sum. Accordingly, if the total of the assessed costs is not proportionate, then the court must reduce the costs to a level that is proportionate, but that cannot be less than the budgeted costs. For example, if the total of the budgeted costs for the "to be incurred" part of the phases budgeted, whether by agreement between the parties, approval of the court or a combination of both, is £50,000 (and there is no "good reason" to depart from the component parts of this sum on any phase) and the total for the assessed non budgeted costs is £30,000, but the court determines that the combined sum of £80,000 is disproportionate, then the proportionate figure that the court assesses under CPR r.44.3(2)(a) is somewhere between £50,000 to £80,000. It cannot be less than £50,000.

However, as set out above in **Q13**, there is an argument that comments made by Davis LJ in *Harrison v University Hospitals Coventry and Warwickshire NHS Trust*,[66] suggest that the court may, without needing to identify good reason, undertake a proportionality determination under CPR r.44.3(2)(a) of the combination of both non-budgeted and budgeted costs and conclude that the proportionate figure is less than even the budgeted costs. The comments are those cited in **Q13** above and are found in [52] of the judgment:

> *"I add that where, as here, a costs judge on detailed assessment will be assessing incurred costs in the usual way and also will be considering budgeted costs (and not departing from such budgeted costs in the absence of 'good reason') the costs judge ordinarily will still, as I see it, ultimately have to look at matters in the round and consider whether the resulting aggregate figure is proportionate . . ."*

We do not see that this comment alters what we have previously stated the position to be. The alternative argument relies on there being no qualification in [52] limiting any reduction to the budgeted costs, as opposed to a positive affirmation that CPR r.44.3(2)(a) permits the court to revisit the proportionality of budgeted costs. That CPR r.44.3(2)(a) requires the court at the end of an assessment to step back and undertake a cross-check of the sum assessed to ensure that the sum bears a reasonable relationship to the factors at CPR r.44.3(5)(a)–(e) is uncontroversial. However, there is nothing in the explanation of this requirement by Davis LJ that suggests that the court, in undertaking its function, may reduce the costs as a result of this CPR r.44(3)(2)(a) exercise to a sum less than the budgeted costs. Indeed, our view is supported if one reads the judgment as a whole. It is patently apparent that the court was astute to the fact that budgeted costs have already been subjected

---

[66] *Harrison v University Hospitals Coventry and Warwickshire NHS Trust* [2017] EWCA Civ 792; [2017] 1 W.L.R. 4456.

to a determination of proportionality—see [31]–[33], and, in particular, the comment at [32] that:

"In this regard, it is also in my view particularly important overall to bear in mind that a judge who is being asked to approve a budget at a costs management hearing must take into account, in assessing each budgeted phase, considerations both of reasonableness and of proportionality."

In addition, the judgment is clear that it is "wholly obvious that it was indeed designed to be one of the prospective benefits of cost budgeting that the need for, and scope of, detailed assessments would potentially be reduced."[67] A sentiment hard to reconcile with the view of those who suggest that in the same judgment the Court of Appeal was opening the door to the uncertainty of a second bite of the proportionality cherry as a matter of routine in all cases where the court has made a costs management order in respect of budgeted costs.

However, in *Reynolds*,[68] in reliance on [52] of *Harrison*, the court concluded that "the budgeted costs are susceptible to proportionality review under CPR r.44.3(2)(a), notwithstanding that, "upon initial consideration", the court will not depart from the budget without good reason". If this is simply indicating that the good reason to depart from the costs management order for specific phases is because the proportionality assessment made at the costs management conference is no longer valid because of changes in circumstances, then we do not disagree, but suggest that the decision must be articulated by reference to "good reason". If, however, as it seems, this passage is intended to suggest that even in the absence of there being a good reason to depart from the budget, the court may reduce the budgeted costs simply by reliance on CPR r.44.3(2)(a), then this seems to ignore the effect of CPR r.3.18, which appears to be the specific rule dealing with the effect of a costs management order at detailed assessment. As the Court of Appeal in *West* has made clear that a proportionality deduction ought not to be a "global" one, but, instead, should relate to "categories, types and periods of costs", then it is impossible to see a reduction of a budgeted phase (assuming the phases fall to be described as categories) below the level of the budgeted costs by this proportionality exercise, as anything other than a direct contradiction of CPR r.3.18. This is because the court will, then, inevitably, have departed from the last or agreed budgeted costs without "good reason", even if it purports to do so by some form of reduction by category. In other words, if after the application of the CPR r.44.3(2)(a) cross-check the overall sum assessed is less than the budgeted costs, then clearly there must have been a departure from one or more phases of the budget, without "good reason". This must also be the position if the overall sum assessed is less than the overall budgeted costs, even if the

---

[67] *Harrison v University Hospitals Coventry and Warwickshire NHS Trust* [2017] EWCA Civ 792; [2017] 1 W.L.R. 4456 at [34].
[68] *Reynolds v One Stop Stores Ltd* unreported 21 September 2018 County Court (Norwich and Cambridge) HHJ Auerbach at [54].

proportionality reduction has taken types and periods of costs that do not match the phases (e.g. counsel's fees), as by definition some budgeted costs in one or more phases must have been reduced even if the specific phase cannot be identified.

Notwithstanding the decision in *Reynolds*, our view remains that if there is no good reason to depart from the last agreed or approved budget, then, whilst the court will look at the totality of costs (the assessed or agreed incurred and the budgeted) under CPR r.44.3(2)(a), the proper application of CPR r.3.18 prevents the reduction of costs for a budgeted phase and the overall proportionate sum being determined at less than the total of the budgeted costs.

Under CPR r.44.4(2)—which is set out in the judgment, but not expressly considered within it—the court "in particular" is charged with giving effect to any orders already made. A costs management order is one such order. It has been made by a specific determination of the proportionality and reasonableness of the costs. Giving effect to it means that the only "escape route" is surely that provided expressly in the rules at CPR r.3.18—"good reason".

A compelling reason for this to be so, is that if this is not the case, then the status of the budgeted costs is removed, raising the obvious question of the purpose then of investing time and costs in the budgeting process. Equally, easier escape from the constraints of the budgeted costs than is provided under CPR r.3.18 appears to undermine one of the key purposes of the exercise—the provision of as much certainty to the parties as to their potential costs exposure at as early a stage in the proceedings as possible. As Coulson J (as he then was) said in *MacInnes v Gross*[69]:

> *"One of the main benefits to be gained from the increased work for the parties (and the court) in undertaking the detailed costs management exercise at the outset of the case is the fact that, at its conclusion, there will be a large amount of certainty as to what the likely costs recovery will be."*

This may be a matter of semantics. We struggle to envisage a situation arising where a review of the CPR r.44.3(5) factors and any "wider circumstances" under CPR r.44.3(2)(a) at assessment that merits a reduction of the overall costs to a sum below the budgeted costs, will not also amount to a "good reason" to depart from the budgeted costs of a phase/phases under CPR r.3.18.

Q17. If the effect of CPR r.44.3(2)(a) is that the sum to be allowed on an assessment is that which is proportionate, why does the court trouble first with undertaking an assessment of what is reasonably incurred and reasonable in amount?

3–25   There are a number of reasons why the court must first assess the reasonable sum. These are:

---

[69] *MacInnes v Gross* [2017] EWHC 127 (QB).

- Because that is what the combined effect of CPR rr.44.4(1)(a) and 44.3(2) require of the court (this sits happily with the approach referred to by Jackson LJ in his final report—see **Q15** above).
- The effect of the indemnity principle. The increasing use of fixed fee solicitor and client retainers and pressure on hourly rates means that there may well be cases where the proportionate sum exceeds the reasonable sum. However, to proceed straight to the proportionality assessment would lead to the assessment of a sum that exceeds the permitted recovery under the retainer. Linked to the point above is that it is also not sufficient in such a situation to say that as the costs claimed are less than the proportionate sum, they then should be allowed in full. This is because, as said above, proportionality does not necessarily equal reasonableness (see **Q6** above). The court must be satisfied under CPR r.44.4(1)(a) that the costs are both proportionate and reasonable. There may still be items of costs that were unreasonably incurred or unreasonable in amount even if the overall sum is proportionate. Those items should not be allowed, even if that means the eventual sum assessed is reduced still further from what may be the proportionate sum. In these cases, proportionality acts as a cap and not as fixed costs.
- That, as seen under **Q4** above, the question of the conduct of the parties demands an assessment of what is reasonable by looking at items where it is said that this has generated additional costs. It is only the assessment of reasonableness that introduces the conduct of the receiving party and informs the court as to whether the conduct of the paying party sounds in the proportionality determination.

Q18. In cases where a CFA was entered into before 1 April 2013, but proceedings are not issued until after 31 March 2013 are additional liabilities included for the purpose of the proportionality cross-check under CPR r.44(3)(2)(a)?

This question arises out of the proportionality transitional provisions at CPR r.44.3(7) (considered in detail in **Q1**). In *BNM v MGN Ltd*[70] the Senior Costs Judge determined that whilst CPR r.48.1 preserved both the pre-1 April 2013 provisions of the then CPR rr.43–48 and those parts of the then costs practice direction that related to funding arrangements, the old proportionality rule, then at CPR r.44.4(2), was not a provision relating to funding arrangements. As a result, he concluded that:

3–26

> "*31. A consequence of the reduction of the base costs to a proportionate figure will be that the success fee, a percentage of those base costs, also reduces. It would be absurd and unworkable to apply the new test of proportionality to the base costs, but the old test of proportionality to the success fee.*

---

[70] *BNM v MGN Ltd* EWHC B13 (Costs).

32. Ringfencing and excluding additional liabilities from the new test of proportionality would be a significant hindrance on the court's ability to comply with its obligation under CPR 44.3(2)(a) to allow only those costs which are proportionate."

The matter did not end there. A number of the other SCCO judges took a different view e.g. in the cases of *King v Basildon and Thurrock University Hospitals NHS Foundation Trust*[71] and *Savings Advice Ltd v EDF Energy Customers Plc.*[72] The counter-argument that additional liabilities should not be considered under CPR r.44.3(2)(a) was neatly summarised by Master Rowley in *King* as follows (and his reasoning was adopted in *Savings Advice Ltd*):

"20. In my view, the reforms arising from the reports of Sir Rupert Jackson, enshrined in LASPO 2012 and the recasting of CPR as of April 2013, sought to produce a completely new regime from that date. No longer would success fees and ATE premiums be recoverable from the opponent save for very limited cases such as in BNM itself. Costs incurred by the parties would be subject to the more stringent proportionality test and elsewhere in the rules, cases would be subject to prospective cost control through budgeting. Part 48 sought to preserve, as if in aspic, the pre-April 2013 regime for cases which had begun before that date until such cases concluded.

21. Furthermore, the purpose of the Jackson reforms in initiating sea change could have resulted in Parliament disallowing the recoverability of success fees and ATE premiums from 1 April 2013. But it did not do so and has allowed the run off of recoverable success fees and premiums in the main and the continued recovery of success fees or premiums in particular instances. It seems to me that the fact that additional liabilities are still allowed for by the provisions of CPR Rule 48.1 simply means that they remain in existence. It does not mean that they have to be assessed in aggregate with the base fees using a test which has no recognition of additional liabilities. This is particularly so when aggregation will render those additional liabilities effectively irrecoverable in practice."

Fortunately, much-needed clarity and certainty have now been provided by the Court of Appeal decision in *BNM v MGN Ltd.*[73] The Court of Appeal concluded that:

- as the definition of costs in CPR r.44.1 no longer includes additional liabilities, then the proportionality provisions at CPR r.44.3(2)(a) and CPR r.44.3(5) cannot "catch" them as these provisions relate to costs as defined under CPR r.44.1.
- as the "old" definition of costs included reference to additional liabilities and this rule is mentioned in CPR PD 48 para.3.1 and as the "old"

---

[71] *King v Basildon and Thurrock University Hospitals NHS Foundation Trust* [2016] EWHC B32 (Costs).
[72] *Savings Advice Ltd v EDF Energy Customers Plc* [2017] EWHC B1 (Costs).
[73] *BNM v MGN Ltd* [2017] EWCA Civ 1767; [2018] 1 W.L.R. 1450.

proportionality test applies to costs falling within the "old" definition of costs, then the old proportionality rules is one that relates to funding arrangements (even though it is not expressly mentioned in CPR PD 48) and so is preserved.

The result is that the answer to the question posed is that the "old" proportionality test applies to recoverable additional liabilities, except where that additional liability is a recoverable ATE premium on a post-April 2013 clinical negligence case.

Note that this exclusion of additional liabilities from the current definition of costs appears to raise consequential (and we suggest, unexpected) issues on other provisions where the process and outcome is determined by reference to a level of costs (see **Ch.8, Q21** and **Q22**).

Q19. Is the court obliged to/must the court consider proportionality during a provisional assessment if the paying party has not raised this in its Points of Dispute?

CPR r.47.15(4) provides that a provisional assessment will be based on the information contained in the bill and the supporting papers and the contentions set out in Precedent G (the points of dispute and the reply). This suggests that the court should not consider proportionality when undertaking a provisional assessment where it has not been raised as an issue in the points of dispute. However, CPR r.44.3(2)(a) is clear that where the court is assessing costs on the standard basis it will only allow costs which are proportionate. This is an absolute requirement imposed upon the court and contains no qualification in application. This provision is reinforced by CPR PD 44 para.9.10, which prevents the court approving disproportionate costs. It is clear, therefore, that whether a paying party challenges the proportionality of the costs, the court must consider this issue. We suspect that this is more a theoretical than practical question, for we have never encountered points of dispute that do not raise the issue of proportionality.

3–27

E. Proportionality, outcomes and the solicitor-client relationship

Q20. Is there not a risk that similar claims will have different outcomes because of the determination by separate case managing judges of what is proportionate in a particular case?

Yes—there is such a risk and this is something that advisors should stress to their clients when giving them the best view they can as to the likely reasonable and proportionate costs (see **Q24** below). It is also why evidence of what was budgeted in any given case is of no more than general guidance at best of what might be budgeted in a similar case. The determination of proportionality will dictate what case management directions are given. Different determinations will lead to different directions, e.g. permission for an expert in one case and not in another. However, that does not mean that the judges

3–28

are necessarily "wrong", simply that one has exercised discretion in another way from the other. Of course, that happens, and legitimately so, regardless of proportionality, on a daily basis in all courts—not just on procedural matters, but on factual disputes of a similar nature. Whilst there is judicial discretion there will be instances where there are a number of outcomes—none of which are "wrong". This question ought to be linked, however, with consideration of whether the risk is justified as an attempt to curb disproportionate costs and to promote access to justice. It is too early to say whether the drive to introduce proportionality will achieve this aim.

However, it is surely unarguable that a system that provides transparency of the "recoverable costs" at large at an early stage will focus the attention of the parties and enable them to make decisions and give their legal representatives instructions on a more informed basis as to how they wish a claim pursued or defended, than a system where they find out the exact extent of the other party/parties' costs only when they are ordered to pay them and find out the shortfall between their legal fees and the exact amount of those that they may recover from the other party at assessment, after the costs have been spent.

Q21. How useful are the comments in cases such as *CIP Properties (AIPT) Ltd v Galliford Try Infrastructure Ltd*,[74] *GSK Project Management Ltd v QPR Holdings Ltd*[75] and *Stocker v Stocker*[76] in setting benchmarks for proportionality?

3–29   As set out at para.**3–04** above, proportionality, other than in terms of very general (and relatively obvious) observations, is case and fact-specific. Accordingly, whilst some general guidance may emerge from authorities—such as those set out in para.**3–04** and **Q7** and **Q8** above—proportionality in each individual case will depend upon the outcome of the consideration of the CPR r.44.3(5) factors and, if necessary, following the decision in *West v Stockport NHS Foundation Trust*[77] any "wider circumstances" in that specific case.

What does emerge, by way of reinforcement, is that when preparing budgets parties should remember the wording of the statement of truth on Precedent H and the requirement at CPR PD 22 (Statements of Truth) para.2.2A (see **Q12** above) for the costs set out in the budget to be a statement of the proportionate incurred and estimated costs. Failure to do so is likely to result in unfavourable comment and possible costs sanctions, as occurred in *GSK Project Management Ltd* where Stuart-Smith J imposed a costs order upon the claimant for producing a "grossly excessive" costs budget.

Q22. Can legal representatives look to the sums budgeted as proportionate at costs management or allowed as proportionate at assessment of

---

[74] *CIP Properties (AIPT) Ltd v Galliford Try Infrastructure Ltd* [2015] EWHC 481 (TCC); [2015] 1 All E.R. (Comm) 765.
[75] *GSK Project Management Ltd v QPR Holdings Ltd* [2015] EWHC 2274 (TCC); [2015] B.L.R. 715.
[76] *Stocker v Stocker* [2015] EWHC 1634 (QB); [2015] 4 Costs L.R. 651.
[77] *West v Stockport NHS Foundation Trust* [2019] EWCA Civ 1220; [2019] 1 W.L.R. 6157.

costs in previous cases as evidence of what will be deemed proportionate in another case?

There is no doubt that previous determinations of what is proportionate in a particular type of case will be informative. However, they will neither be determinative nor definitive. This is for the reasons set out in the answers to Q20 and Q21 above. Each case will be fact- specific and subject to a discretionary proportionality assessment. Even in cases based on the same factual matrix judges may legitimately reach different assessments of the proportionate costs by a reasoned and principled application of CPR r.44.3(5) and CPR r.44.1. As the court said in *Group Seven v Nasir*,[78] when considering the relationship between costs and the sums in issue "the decided cases do not give much direct help when considering this relationship." At best, as the court did in that case, previous decisions might be useful for general guidance purposes only (perhaps setting likely brackets).

3–30

Q23. To what extent does a budget insulate a client from the court's application of the proportionality test?

It must be remembered that the costs management exercise itself involves consideration of proportionality, with the court applying the factors at CPR r.44.3(5) and considering any "wider circumstances" of the case when approving budget costs (see CPR PD 3E para.12). Thereafter, subject to any departures to the budget permitted for good reason under CPR r.3.18, and assuming that our analysis of *Harrison v University Hospitals Coventry and Warwickshire NHS Trusts*[79] (see Q16 above) is correct, and is applied, then the budgeted costs are insulated from revision under the CPR r.44.3(2)(a) proportionality cross-check. In fact, this question reinforces our analysis as the relative certainty provided in respect of budgeted costs was something that the Court of Appeal stressed in *Harrison* when rejecting the argument that a budget was only a cap, stating that:

3–31

> "It is difficult to see the sense or fairness in that. Nor does this argument show much appreciation for the position of the actual parties to the litigation—not just the prospective paying party but also the prospective receiving party—who need at an early stage in the litigation to know, as best they can, where they stand . . ."

It would be curious if, having stressed the importance of the certainty provided to parties by knowing the budgeted costs of each other, the Court of Appeal endorsed a further consideration of the proportionality of these costs as a matter of routine.

---

[78] *Group Seven v Nasir* [2016] EWHC 620 (Ch); [2016] 2 Costs L.O. 303.
[79] *Harrison v University Hospitals Coventry and Warwickshire NHS Trust* [2017] EWCA Civ 792; [2015] 4 Costs L.R. 651.

Q24. Given the fact that only general guidance has emerged from the courts, how can a solicitor best offer advice to a client on what is likely to be deemed the proportionate cost of any specific case?

3–32   The solicitor-client relationship is considered in more detail in Ch.9. However, what is clear is that solicitors must tailor their advice on costs to clients at the outset to the key provisions of the CPR relating to recoverability of costs, stressing that:

- the court emphasis on proportionality means that they will only recover reasonable and proportionate costs if awarded costs (but equally will only be liable for reasonable and proportionate costs if an award of costs is made against them);
- CPR r.44.3(2)(a) means that clients may not recover costs that are reasonable and/or necessary to pursue/defend claims if the court decides that these are not proportionate;
- they (the solicitors) may have to sign a statement of truth on a budget certifying reasonable and proportionate costs and, this may, because of CPR rr.44.3(5), 44.4(1) and 44.3(2)(a), be for a lesser sum than they think clients may need to spend to have the best chance of achieving the desired outcome;
- the best advice they can give applying the relevant test in respect of proportionality under CPR rr.44.3(5) and 44.4(1), rather than by reference to what they think the clients reasonably and/or necessarily need to spend, is in the region of £x to £y;
- the best advice they can give on solicitor-client costs is £z (or £x to £y if they think the two are the same) so that an informed decision may be made as to any shortfall (reinforcing the distinction between the two at the outset);
- the proportionality assessment may change as the claim evolves (e.g. complexities perceived at the outset may fall away or unexpected ones may arise) and clients will be informed if such a situation occurs when further advice will be given.

The key is to be realistic when considering proportionality. It is clear from authorities emerging that there are a number of cases where budgets have been deemed disproportionate (and significantly so). This suggests that there remains a difference in the way in which some solicitors and the courts are approaching CPR rr.44.3(5), 44.4(1) and 44.3(2)(a). Whilst solicitors may not be able to identify precisely the figure that the court will decide is proportionate, it should be possible, by analysis of these procedural provisions, to give a bracket within which the court figure will fall. At the very least, as Master Rowley suggested in *May v Wavell Group Plc*,[80] and notwithstanding the outcome of the appeal in that case,[81] clients should be informed that "even if successful, they will receive no more than a contribution to the costs that will be incurred".

---

[80] *May v Wavell Group Plc* [2016] EWHC B16 (Costs).
[81] Whilst the amount assessed as proportionate was increased from £35,000 plus VAT to £75,000 plus VAT, it is worth remembering that the amount sought in the bill was in excess of £200,000.

CHAPTER 4

Case and Costs Management

Introduction
Although the title of this chapter suggests that case and costs management **4-01** are two separate exercises, in reality, they are two sides of the same coin. As Sir Rupert Jackson commented in his Final Report:

> "First, case management and costs management go hand in hand. It does not make sense for the court to manage a case without regard to the costs which it is ordering the parties to incur. The Rubicon was crossed on 26th April 1999, when the court assumed under the CPR wide powers and responsibilities for case management."[1]

This link is something to which Sir Rupert Jackson returned in May 2015,[2] when acknowledging that the court was adopting various approaches to case and costs management in practice, and concluding that:

> "The objective of the 2013 civil justice reforms is to enable the court to manage each case so that it proceeds at proportionate cost" para.7.2.

and

> "In my view the norm shall be for the court to do both case management and costs management at a single hearing" para.7.5.

He confirmed this view formally in *Jamadar v Bradford Teaching Hospitals NHS Foundation Trust*.[3]

The April 2013 amendments to the CPR inextricably linked both in CPR r.3.12(2), when defining the purpose of costs management as being "that the court should manage both the steps to be taken and the costs to be incurred by the parties to any proceedings" and in CPR r.3.17 (now r.3.17(1) and (2)) which strengthened the link between the two by requiring the court to have regard to any available budgets and to take account of costs when making any case management decision. In fact, it may be artificial to talk of both case and costs management as, in those cases where costs management orders are standard (see below), the latter is simply part of the former.

In this chapter, we shall consider the procedural changes made to the pre-April 2013 case management provisions of the CPR and the costs management rules that were introduced in April 2013 (and have been amended subsequently as part of the ongoing implementation and evolving procedural

---

[1] *Review of Civil Litigation Costs: Final Report*, December 2009, Ch.40 para.7.1.
[2] *"Confronting costs management"* 13 May 2015.
[3] *Jamadar v Bradford Teaching Hospitals NHS Foundation Trust* [2016] EWCA Civ 1001; [2016] 5 Costs L.R. 809.

reform process) separately, and then illustrate how they combine in a seamless practical application.

In his Final Report, Sir Rupert Jackson asked if costs management was worth the candle. He answered the question in the affirmative giving two reasons in support of that answer. The first is set out above. The other reason was:

"Secondly, I am in full agreement with the Law Society's view that costs management, if done properly, will save substantially more costs than it generates."[4]

Presented with the same question two years after the introduction of the April 2013 amendments, Sir Rupert Jackson remained as emphatic, stating unequivocally[5]:

"The first and most important conclusion to be drawn from the experience of the last two years is the same as that which was drawn from the pilots. Costs management works." para.2.1.

In his Supplemental Report[6] in July 2017, Sir Rupert Jackson noted that the requirement for extended fixed recoverable costs schemes had been reduced as a result of the costs management experience, noting that the regime was "working distinctly better than it was two years ago".[7] It must be noted that the view of the current Master of the Rolls is that whether or not this is so, the costs management regime merits further consideration now "that considerable experience of its pros and cons has been obtained by judges, costs judges and practitioners alike"[8]. Whilst that work may be in hand, obviously, this text is written on the basis of how the regime currently operates. However, clearly readers should be astute to the possibility that change has been implemented post publication.

What we believe has become clear is that changes made to case management cannot work in isolation and "proper" costs management is essential to the success of the 2013 reforms, to ensure that cases are dealt with justly and at proportionate cost.

The changes made to the CPR case management provisions in 2013

4–02   The principal procedural change that affects and informs all case management decisions (and informs costs management decisions) was the change to the overriding objective at CPR r.1.1 to introduce the obligation to deal with a case "at proportionate cost". All the other changes were designed to achieve this objective. These were:

---

[4] *Review of Civil Litigation Costs: Final Report*, December 2009, Ch.40 para.7.1.
[5] *"Confronting costs management"* 13 May 2015.
[6] *Review of Civil Litigation Costs: Supplemental Report Fixed Recoverable Costs.*
[7] *Review of Civil Litigation Costs: Supplemental Report Fixed Recoverable Costs*, Ch.6 para.5.1. Sir Rupert Jackson reiterated this in his "Was it all worth it" lecture on 5 March 2018 lecture at the Cambridge Law Faculty at para.3.15.
[8] A view expressed in his address to The Association of Costs Lawyers at its annual conference in November 2021.

1. Enforcing stricter compliance with court orders, rules and practice directions (both in CPR rr.1.1(2)(f) and 3.9).
2. Replacing allocation questionnaires with directions questionnaires designed to provide more relevant case information (CPR r.26.3).
3. A greater discretion to the court when determining the track to which to allocate claims and an increase to the small claims limit (CPR r.26.6(3) and the removal of what was CPR Pts 26.7(3), 27.14(5) and (6)).
4. The encouragement to use standardised directions to ensure consistency and facilitate the production of orders (CPR r.29.1(2)).
5. More targeted disclosure provisions (CPR r.31.5(3)–(8)).
6. More prescriptive powers in respect of witness statements (CPR r.32.2(3)).
7. The provision of more information about any expert evidence proposed (CPR r.35.4).
8. The option to hear the oral evidence of experts concurrently (CPR PD 35 para.11).
9. Increasing the incentive for claimants to make realistic settlement proposals (CPR r.36.17(4)(d)).
10. The introduction of costs management (CPR r.3.12–3.18 and CPR PD 3E).

From 1 October 2015, the court has also expressly been given the power to hear an early neutral evaluation with the express aim of helping the parties to settle a case (by an extension of the broad jurisdiction under CPR r.3.1(2)(m))—recognising that this may result in earlier and more proportionate resolution. This provision has taken on greater importance following the decision of the Court of Appeal in *Lomax v Lomax*,[9] that there is:

> *"no reason to imply into subparagraph (m) any limitation on the court's power to order an ENE hearing to the effect that the agreement or consent of the parties is required. Indeed,. . .such an interpretation would be inconsistent with elements of the overriding objective, in particular the saving of expense and allotting to cases an appropriate share of the court's resources, and would, therefore, be contrary to rule 1.2(b)".*

In his review of his decade of procedural reform work in March 2018,[10] Sir Rupert Jackson identified two areas where he believed further work was required:

- Guidance on the application of the proportionality rule[11] (see **Ch.3** for detailed consideration of this)
- Disclosure—accepting that the introduction of the "disclosure menu" at CPR r.31.5(7) had not worked well. This and the proposed sweeping further reforms proposed by the working group chaired by Gloster LJ,

---

[9] *Lomax v Lomax* [2019] EWCA Civ 1467; [2019] 1 W.L.R. 6527.
[10] "Was it all worth it" lecture on 5 March 2018 lecture at the Cambridge Law Faculty.
[11] At para.3.18.

which are still being refined and remain the subject of a pilot in the Business and Property Courts,[12] are both considered below at para.4–09.

1. Enforcing stricter compliance with court orders, rules and practice directions (both in CPR rr.1.1(2)(f) and 3.9)

4–03 In the Final Report, Jackson LJ identified the change of culture that was required, commenting:

> "*First, the courts should set realistic timetables for cases and not impossibly tough timetables in order to give an impression of firmness. Secondly, courts at all levels have become too tolerant of delays and non-compliance with orders. In so doing they have lost sight of the damage which the culture of delay and non-compliance is inflicting upon the civil justice system. The balance therefore needs to be redressed.*"[13]

In the pre-April 2013 case of *Fred Perry (Holdings) Ltd v Brands Plaza Trading Ltd*,[14] the Court of Appeal gave an indication of the imminent alteration of emphasis, leaving no doubt that a wind of change was blowing:

> "*The Rule Committee has recently approved a proposal that the present rule 3.9(1) be deleted . . . It is currently anticipated that this revised rule will come into force on 1st April 2013. After that date litigants who substantially disregard court orders or the requirements of the Civil Procedure Rules will receive significantly less indulgence than hitherto.*"[15]

4–04 Whether the warnings went unheeded or whether some practitioners failed to appreciate quite how much less indulgence was to be afforded by the court is unclear, but from November 2013, and the decision in *Mitchell v News Group Newspapers Ltd*,[16] until July 2014, and the clarification provided in *Denton v TH White*[17] the court reverberated to the sounds of applications for relief from sanctions and the disappointed cries of those whose applications were dismissed. *Denton* has clarified that the court should approach these applications in three stages:

- Stage 1 requires an evaluation of the breach. The Court of Appeal made it clear that this must be looked at in isolation—concentrate solely on the seriousness and significance of this breach. If there have been other failures/misconduct by the defaulting party, those must be ignored at this stage, but may merit consideration at stage 3. The court then moves on to stages 2 and 3. If it has concluded that there is not a serious or significant breach, then stages 2 and 3 may not occupy much court time, but if there

---

[12] See CPR PD 51U.
[13] *Review of Civil Litigation Costs: Final Report*, December 2009, Ch.39 para.6.5.
[14] *Fred Perry (Holdings) Ltd v Brands Plaza Trading Ltd* [2012] EWCA Civ 224; [2012] 6 Costs L.R. 1007.
[15] Jackson LJ, at [4].
[16] *Mitchell v News Group Newspapers Ltd* [2013] EWCA Civ 1537; [2014] 1 W.L.R. 795.
[17] *Denton v TH White* [2014] EWCA Civ 906; [2014] 1 W.L.R. 3926.

has been a serious or significant breach then the final two stages take on a greater importance.

- Stage 2 involves consideration of whether there was good reason for the breach. The Court of Appeal declined to produce an "encyclopaedia" of what might constitute "good reason". This will be fact-specific. However, *Mitchell* at [41] sets out some examples.
- Stage 3 At this stage the court considers "all the circumstances of the case", but, remembering that the two factors specifically mentioned in CPR r.3.9 carry "particular weight" (although Jackson LJ dissented, on the basis that the two factors were mentioned to draw attention to them, but that they carried no weight above any others). It is worth noting that the Court of Appeal specifically drew attention to the fact that the importance of complying with rules, practice directions and orders had received insufficient emphasis in the past stating:

"The court must always bear in mind the need for compliance with rules, practice directions and orders, because the old lax culture of non-compliance is no longer tolerated."

It is clear from the extract above that those who think that the position has reverted to what it was on 31 March 2013 remain due for an unpleasant shock. For those who pointed to the dissenting judgment of Jackson LJ in *Denton* to counter this, his comments in the preface to the *White Book* 2015[18] left no room for uncertainty. He accepted the majority judgment as the correct construction of CPR r.3.9 and added:

"It is very important that in the euphoria with which some have greeted Denton, we do not slip back into the 'old culture of non-compliance' . . ."

The decision of the Court of Appeal in *Jamadar v Bradford Teaching Hospitals NHS Foundations Trust*[19] reinforces this message as, with echoes of the decision in *Mitchell*, the Court of Appeal upheld a refusal to grant relief from the sanction of CPR r.3.14. A more recent affirmation by the Court of Appeal of the change of approach to the granting of relief from sanction can be found in *Diriye v Bojaj*[20] [2020] EWCA Civ 1440.

As such, it is clear that whilst first instance decisions on CPR r.3.14 (and more generally CPR r.3.9) still abound, some granting relief and some not, the higher authorities leave no doubt that those failing to comply with orders, rules and practice directions cannot expect the same degree of leniency of pre-April 2013. (See **Q101** below for further consideration of this culture change.)

If evidence from an even higher authority of a shift towards compliance is required, it was provided in *Prince Abdulaziz Bin Mishal Bin Abdulaziz Al Saud v Apex Global Management Ltd*,[21] where the Supreme Court, whilst at pains

4–05

---

[18] The *White Book* 2015 Preface p.xvi.
[19] *Jamadar v Bradford Teaching Hospitals NHS Foundation Trust* [2016] EWCA Civ 1001; [2016] 5 Costs L.R. 809.
[20] *Diriye v Bojaj* [2020] EWCA Civ 1400.
[21] *Prince Abdulaziz Bin Mishal Bin Abdulaziz Al Saud v Apex Global Management Ltd* [2014] UKSC 64; [2014] 1 W.L.R. 4495.

to reiterate that generally case management and CPR are the domain of the Court of Appeal, confirmed that:

> *"The importance of litigants obeying orders of court is self-evident. Once a court order is disobeyed, the imposition of a sanction is almost always inevitable if court orders are to continue to enjoy the respect which they ought to have . . . One of the important aims of the changes embodied in the Civil Procedure Rules and, more recently, following Sir Rupert Jackson's report on costs, was to ensure that procedural orders reflected not only the interests of the litigation concerned, but also the interests of the efficient administration of justice more generally."*[22]

So, whilst the change may not be as dramatic as *Mitchell* suggested, relief will still be granted more sparingly than previously.

Hand in hand in *Denton* with guidance on relief was:

(i) an entreaty by the Court of Appeal (coupled with costs threats if ignored) for parties to co-operate and not use court rules as technical trip wires. This links to the amendment made to CPR r.3.8 in April 2014 to add a provision at CPR r.3.8(4) enabling parties to agree extensions to the period for compliance with orders, rules and practice directions that specify the consequences of a failure to comply, provided that this does not jeopardise any hearing. This costs threat was carried out in *Viridor Waste Management v Veolia Environmental Services*.[23] The court concluded that the defendant had taken an opportunistic and unreasonable advantage of late service of particulars of claim in opposing the application for relief from sanction. As a consequence, the defendant was subjected to an indemnity costs order; and

(ii) a reminder to members of the judiciary to ensure that "the directions that they give are realistic and achievable". The Court of Appeal acknowledged that it was of no use to set a timescale so tight that it was obvious that it could not be met, stressing that "the court must have regard to the realities of litigation in making orders in the first place". This harks back to the extract from Jackson LJ's Final Report quoted above, in which he stressed that the court should set realistic timetables for cases and not impossibly tough timetables in order to give an impression of firmness (see above and the Final Report Ch.39 para.6.5).

The then Master of the Rolls had cause to re-visit his comments in (i) above in *R. (Idira) v The Secretary of State for the Home Department*[24] and left no doubt, in so doing, that *Denton* did not represent a return to the pre-*Mitchell* regime, stressing that absence of prejudice did not inevitably lead to relief being granted, saying:

---

[22] At [23]–[25].
[23] *Viridor Waste Management v Veolia Environmental Services* [2015] EWHC 2321 (Comm).
[24] *R. (Idira) v The Secretary of State for the Home Office* [2015] EWCA Civ 1187; [2016] 1 W.L.R. 1694.

"At para.43 in Denton, this court said that parties should not 'adopt an unco-operative attitude in unreasonably refusing to agree extensions of time and in unreasonably opposing applications for relief from sanctions'. It added: 'it is unacceptable for a party to try to take advantage of a minor inadvertent error . . .'. I would emphasise the words 'unreasonably' and 'minor inadvertent'. A party is not required to agree to an extension of time in every case where the extension will not disrupt the time-table for the appeal or will not cause him to suffer prejudice. If the position were otherwise, the court would lose control of the management of the litigation."

Similarly, the fact that refusal to grant relief will cause significant prejudice to the party in default does not mean that relief should be granted. In *Sinclair v Dorsey & Whitney*[25] a professional negligence claim said to be valued at £30 million was struck out for breach of an unless order to provide security for costs. An application for relief was dismissed on application of the *Denton* three-stage test. The fact of prejudice was insufficient when considered in all the circumstances and giving particular weight to the two factors in CPR r.3.9.

The decision of the Supreme Court in the ill-fated case of *Thevarajah v Riordan*[26] (two visits to the Court of Appeal and this one to the Supreme Court), confirmed, if confirmation was needed, that compliance with the terms of an unless order after the date set for compliance does not amount to a material change in circumstance as required pursuant to *Tibbles v SIG Plc*[27] (one of the factors necessary to support an application under CPR r.3.1(7) for the court to vary or revoke an order).

2. Replacing allocation questionnaires with directions questionnaires designed to provide more relevant case information (CPR r.26.3)

Directions questionnaires should assist the court with determining proportion-ate case management decisions. More information is required about proposed expert evidence and, unless there is a valid explanation for being unable to do so, the court should police the requirement to provide details of witnesses and the issue(s) to which their evidence will be addressed. Questionnaires that suggest that this information is "to be advised" or "to be confirmed" should receive short shrift and their authors may find themselves the recipients of orders, including "unless orders" to provide the information or a satisfactory explanation of why it cannot be provided or face the consequences (e.g. being unable to rely upon any witness evidence without permission of the court). The directions questionnaires in the Damages Claims Portal pilot under CPR PD 51ZB have been adapted still further to consider issues of witness support that may arise.

4-06

---

[25] *Sinclair v Dorsey & Whitney Ltd* [2015] EWHC 3888 (Comm); [2016] 1 Costs L.R. 19.
[26] *Thevarajah v Riordan* [2015] UKSC 78; [2016] 1 W.L.R. 76.
[27] *Tibbles v SIG Plc* [2012] EWCA Civ 518; [2012] 1 W.L.R. 2591.

3. A greater discretion to the court when determining the track to which to allocate claims and an increase to the small claims limit (CPR rr.1.1 and 26.6(3) and the removal of what was CPR Pts 26.7(3), 27.14(5) and (6))

4–07 The court must take account of proportionality when allocating. Accordingly, those claims that might previously have been allocated to the multi-track simply because of time estimate (e.g. where the value is within fast track limits and none of the other CPR r.44.3(5) proportionality factors or wider circumstances justify allocation to the multi-track, but there are a number of witnesses) are now likely to be allocated to fast track with a restriction on the evidence that may be adduced to ensure the claim is disposed of within a day. Similarly, the omission of CPR Pt 26.7(3), which prevented a court allocating a claim to the small claims track if the value exceeded the limit for that track without the agreement of all parties, seemed designed to enable the court to allocate more claims to the limited "fixed fee on issue" regime of that track.

This aim was bolstered by the removal of previous provisions (CPR r.27.14(5) and (6)), which enabled parties agreeing to allocation to the small claims track to include an agreement that fast track costs would still apply and that any appeal would carry the costs consequences as if it had been a fast track claim. These provisions are no more and so whether a claim with a fast track value is allocated to the small claims track with or without the consent of the parties, the limited small claims track costs allowances prevail.

At the same time the proportion of claims proceeding in the small claims track was increased with the financial scope of that track doubling to £10,000 (save for personal injury and housing disrepair claims with a claim for specific performance of repairs, where the financial limit remained unaltered at £1,000—although the introduction of CPR r.26.6(ii)(aa) in 2021 has subsequently seen the increase of scope to £5,000 for most road traffic accident personal injury claims).

4. The encouragement to use standardised directions to ensure consistency and facilitate the production of orders (CPR r.29.1(2))

4–08 The proliferation of different forms of directions up and down the country was identified by Sir Rupert Jackson as a source of unnecessary cost. If the same form of order is used in all courts, then the parties can use them as a starting point when discussing proposed directions as they will not be confronted by "local" variations, there will be consistency of orders produced, less risk that a direction will be overlooked or that a direction will be phrased ambiguously (not to be underestimated given the potential sanction for non-compliance) and the final order will be easier for the court to generate. Accordingly, he recommended that:

> "... *a menu of standard paragraphs for case management directions should be prepared for each type of case of common occurrence and made available to all district judges both in hard copy and online. These standard directions should*

then be used by district judges as their starting point in formulating initial case management directions."[28]

CPR r.29.1(2) was introduced to achieve this by linking to a raft of standard orders. However, the uptake appears to have been distinctly lukewarm. Many individual courts and parties still prefer their own form of directions. The standard directions always seem to be under review, but in the meantime, some courts are insisting that draft directions are filed adopting the standard template orders and others are not. It seems likely that the move to a digital court process for unspecified ("damages") claims will see a greater emphasis placed on standardisation. Until then, it is hard to see how practitioners can be faulted by the court if they use the standard orders under CPR r.29.1(2) as the provision does state that these "should" be taken as the starting point.

5. More targeted disclosure provisions (CPR r.31.5(3–8))

In the 7th Implementation Lecture,[29] Sir Rupert Jackson referred to the costs of the disclosure process in these terms: **4–09**

> *"Even in medium-sized actions where all the documents are in paper form, disclosure can be a major exercise which generates disproportionate costs."*

The resultant attempt to curb the costs of this phase of litigation can be found at CPR r.31.5. This introduced the "disclosure report" (Form N263), which was designed to facilitate discussion between the parties as to the appropriate disclosure order prior to the first case management conference and to inform the court, in general terms, of the types of documents involved, by whom and where they are held, how electronic documents are stored, the costs of "standard disclosure" and what disclosure order is suggested. CPR r.31.5(7) sets out a menu of possible disclosure options. It is no surprise that other than a catch-all provision, "standard disclosure" was listed as the last of the disclosure options. The pre-amble to the menu stresses that the court will decide which option to order "having regard to the overriding objective and the need to limit disclosure to that which is necessary to deal with the case justly". The reference to the overriding objective plainly imposes the requirement for proportionality.

CPR r.31.5(1) and (2) combine to exclude personal injury claims from the disclosure "menu". Standard disclosure remains the "norm" in these claims, but with a residual discretion to the court to order otherwise (which it should exercise where appropriate—e.g. by limiting to the issue of limitation, liability, quantum etc. as appropriate.)

The 7th Implementation Lecture left little doubt as to the importance of the revised disclosure provisions:

---

[28] Ch.39 para.5.3.
[29] 7th Implementation Lecture: "Controlling the Costs of Disclosure", 24 November 2011.

"The order made at the first CMC concerning disclosure will have a profound impact on the future course of the case and also upon the final costs of the litigation. Therefore, this issue merits careful thought and analysis when the parties initially and the court ultimately are making their selection from the menu of possible disclosure orders."

Notwithstanding the exhortation to select from the menu after careful thought and analysis, anecdotal evidence suggests that "standard disclosure" is the type almost always suggested in Form N263, perhaps unsurprisingly, as the requirement to cost this form of disclosure and it being the default disclosure option in the standard orders under CPR r.29.1(2), steer parties towards it. Sir Rupert Jackson recognised this when reverting to the topic in his "Disclosure" lecture in October 2016[30] and answering with a resounding "no" the question he posed himself of whether everyone was using the new rules properly. He added, by way of comment:

"Parties frequently agree standard disclosure, seemingly without considering whether other options may be preferable, and the courts accept their agreements. It would be to the public benefit if all involved in the disclosure process gave more attention to the full range of options before simply proposing or agreeing to standard disclosure."

In his Supplemental Report, Sir Rupert Jackson accepted that the picture that emerged from the budget consideration exercise that formed part of the evidence gathering process for his recommendations, supported the observation of the London Solicitors Litigation Association that a more robust case management approach should be adopted by the court and that the onus is on the judiciary "proactively to challenge parties where they have failed to explore and agree a proportionate approach to disclosure"[31] (an illustration of the court doing precisely this may be found in *Bank Mellat v HM Treasury*,[32] in which the court, dealing with a dispute concerning 2,500 transactions, limited disclosure initially by way of a sampling exercise to 10% of these transactions selected at random, recognising the cost consequence of ordering disclosure in all the transactions. The court accepted that once that disclosure had been considered further disclosure might be required.)

A "disclosure working group" was established, chaired by Gloster LJ. In the October 2016 lecture, Sir Rupert Jackson suggested that this group might want to consider "whether what is needed is a culture change rather than a rule change". The working group reported in November 2017. The group concluded that the existing provisions give rise to a number of concerns, as follows:

---

[30] "Disclosure" Lecture at the Law Society's Commercial Litigation Conference, 10 October 2016.
[31] *Review of Civil Litigation Costs: Supplemental Report Fixed Recoverable Costs*, Ch.3 para.2.12.
[32] *Bank Mellatt v HM Treasury* [2017] EWHC 2409 (Comm).

- disclosure has increased, often to unmanageable proportions;
- neither the professions nor the judiciary have made adequate use of CPR r.31(5)(7);
- the existing rule is aimed at paper and not electronic disclosure;
- disclosure orders are not sufficiently focused on issues;
- the parties do not engage sufficiently before the first case management conference in relation to disclosure; and
- searches are often far wider than is necessary.

The working group conclusion was that only a wholesale change of approach, with a new rule and guidelines, could address these concerns and that what was required was a new CPR Pt 31 and accompanying practice direction. The working group drafted an appropriate rule and recommended that there should be a pilot in the Business and Property Courts in London, Birmingham, Bristol, Cardiff, Leeds, Manchester, Newcastle and Liverpool and subsequent evaluation to assess the impact in practice. Following further consultation, a mandatory two-year pilot introduced by CPR PD 51U in these courts commenced on 1 January 2019. This has subsequently been extended until 31 December 2022, but with the Civil Procedure Rules Committee minutes from June 2020 being clear that this should not be taken as an endorsement or otherwise of this disclosure scheme. We have said previously that although this is only a pilot, given the acknowledgement that CPR r.31.5(7) appears not to be working, there seemed an inevitability that extension to other courts would follow. However, there has been criticism of the pilot procedure and the fashion in which it has been adopted by some parties. The outcome of the pilot seems less clear as a consequence. Further amendments to the procedural requirements were introduced in both April and November 2021. The pilot and its success is considered in more detail in **Qs 106** and **107** below

Until/unless there is any change, and for those cases not falling within the pilot, then even if standard disclosure is to remain more routinely used than had been envisaged under the reforms (and this may not be the case as the focus on disclosure may result in a greater reluctance amongst the judiciary to accept this as the default), the definition of standard disclosure that appears at CPR r.31.6 merits repetition as it is far narrower than many appear to think:

> "*31.6 Standard disclosure requires a party to disclose only—*
> *(a) the documents on which he relies; and*
> *(b) the documents which—*
>   *(i) adversely affect his own case;*
>   *(ii) adversely affect another party's case; or*
>   *(iii) support another party's case; and*
> *(c) the documents which he is required to disclose by a relevant practice direction.*"

Tales of trial judges inundated with bundles based on "standard disclosure" from which they are taken to only a few pages may be apocryphal, but do not be surprised if some judges add to an order for standard disclosure "as defined by CPR r.31.6" and costs manage more restrictively as a result.

6. More prescriptive powers in respect of witness statements (CPR r.32.2(3)).

4–10   The court has always had the power to control evidence under CPR r.32.1. However, the specific reference in CPR r.32.2(3) to the ability of the court to give directions identifying and limiting the issues upon which factual evidence is to be given, identifying specific witnesses and limiting the length and format of statements, gives the court the ability to case manage factual evidence in a proportionate way. The identity of witnesses and the facts to which their evidence will be directed should be readily available from Section F of the Directions Questionnaire. Notwithstanding this, draft directions and orders still routinely make no attempt to limit evidence whether by number of witnesses or length of statements. Given that proportionate trial time estimates require strict control of evidence it appears inevitable that this case management provision should be used in all cases. Even if the number of witnesses listed in directions questionnaires appears reasonable and proportionate, expect the court still to impose a limit as this prevents further witnesses, whose evidence may only emerge later or whose names have been left out of Section F, being relied upon without a further order of the court.

An early illustration of the use of this provision was in *MacLennan v Morgan Sindall (Infrastructure) Plc*.[33] The court was concerned with a significant claim for loss of earnings in a severe brain injury claim. This element of loss raised four broad issues upon which the claimant wished to call 43 witnesses. The defendant sought an order under CPR r.32.2(3) limiting the number to eight. In the end, the court made an order restricting the number of witnesses to 28 and identifying those issues with which the witnesses would deal.

In December 2019 the Witness Evidence Working Group published its final report[34] in respect of cases in the Business and Property Courts. Of note, in the context of costs restriction, is that although some of the proposals of the working group may, at first blush, suggest an increase in expenditure, the conclusion reached was that perceived costs savings by restriction of evidence in chief to the content of witness statements might be illusory (due to the front-loading of costs—which, itself, may deter settlement—and because of the increased time spent at trial on cross-examination (see paras.18 and 19)). The recommendations made by the Working Group received the endorsement of the Business and Property Courts Board and have been implemented in CPR PD 57AC, with the MoJ CPR website explaining that the changes are "to ensure that witness statements reflect the facts of the case at trial as opposed to a narrative".

---

[33] *MacLennan v Morgan Sindall (Infrastructure) Plc* [2013] EWHC 4044 (QB); [2014] 1 W.L.R. 2462 Green J.
[34] *Factual witness evidence in trials before the Business and Property Courts* December 2019.

7. The provision of more information about any expert evidence proposed (CPR r.35.4).

It is curious that almost nine years after the introduction of CPR r.35.4, any   **4–11**
party still completes a directions questionnaire and attends a subsequent case
management conference, indicating that expert evidence is required without
providing details of the expert, the issues that the expert will address and the
likely cost of the expert. Curious because:

- this information is a pre-requisite to the court giving permission for expert
  evidence. CPR r.35.4(2) makes the provision of this information mandatory (qualified to the extent that the name is required where reasonably
  practicable) when applying for permission to rely upon expert evidence
  in any type of claim;
- notwithstanding the failure to provide this information, some parties
  still feel able to complete the costs budget providing details of what the
  reasonable and proportionate expenditure on the expert phase will be—
  inserting figures for the expert—at a stage when the expert has not even
  been identified and the extent of that expert's remit not determined.

There is a real risk that if this information is not available, the court will simply
not give permission. This means that in those cases that are costs managed,
they will be costs managed without provision for permission for that/those
expert(s) whom the party in default seeks to rely upon, with inevitable implications on the expert phase of the budget. If the party in default sees the way
the wind is blowing and does not pursue the application for permission at the
case management conference, but, instead, seeks to rely on a subsequent free-
standing application, it is likely to confront difficulties as the rectification of a
previous failure is unlikely to be viewed as a "significant development" for the
purpose of budget variation under CPR r.3.15A. Even if the court were minded
to entertain the subsequent application and permit the expert evidence, this
would mean consequential recasting of the directions and variations of costs
budgets at considerable expense. It is not difficult to envisage what the costs
order in respect of that additional expenditure would be!

If the intention behind failing to provide the name of the expert witness is
to enable "expert shopping" (meaning in this context, to avoid having to disclose the unfavourable report of a named expert before having any prospect of
being permitted to move on to another expert), then it should be noted that
even when courts do permit expert evidence when they are not able to name
the expert at the time of the order, they are drafting orders to prevent this.
A common order in such circumstances is to permit reliance on the expert
evidence from an unnamed expert in a specific discipline provided that, as
well as service of the report by a set date, "the name of the expert is provided
in writing to all parties and the courts by 4.00pm [y days] and that thereafter
this order is read as though that name appears in it". In other words, reliance
upon the report is conditional upon naming the expert within a limited time

period and the order will then expressly be read to provide for permission for the named expert only.

8. The option to hear the oral evidence of experts concurrently (CPR PD 35 para.11).

4–12 CPR PD 35 (Experts and Assessors) para.11 provides the court with the option of taking expert evidence concurrently and sets out, subject to judicial discretion to alter the process, the procedure to adopt. In reality, though, the process is inevitably case and judge specific.

The Civil Justice Council produced a report on concurrent expert evidence in 2016,[35] which, at p.10, illustrated the breadth of case type in which concurrent expert evidence had been used. Interestingly, one area where the report recommended further work was in respect of the costs savings achieved by concurrent expert evidence, as of those providing evidence to the Council a relatively low percentage were of the view that there was necessarily any saving, although, curiously in the light of this, the same evidence revealed that time at trial was saved by adopting this process. The report made recommendations for amendment to CPR PD 35 para.11. Sir Rupert Jackson, in a lecture in June 2016, concluded with the hope that the use of concurrent expert evidence would increase as the benefits became more widely appreciate.[36] The Council recommendations have not all been adopted by the Civil Procedure Rules Committee. However, changes were made to CPR PD 35 para.11 to provide that the judge will initiate discussion if concurrent expert evidence is to be taken and to set out in more detail how that process may proceed in practice (CPR PD 35 para.11(4)). The amendments also provide guidance for the court on control of oral expert evidence when it is not taken concurrently (e.g. experts sequentially on an issue-by-issue basis). The amendments stress the importance of consideration of an agenda for the taking of expert evidence and that if ordered it should, understandably, be based on the areas of disagreement identified in the experts' joint statement.

Whether the amendments address the challenging issue of ensuring that the parties feel they have had a sufficient opportunity to advance the expert evidence that they wish in this format (a point highlighted in the Civil Justice Council report[37]) is a moot point. The substance of CPR PD 35 para.11.4(2) largely mirrors that in its predecessor provision. Whilst it removes the limiting reference concerning cross-examination and re-examination, the restrictions in CPR PD 35 para.11.4(2)(a), (b) and (c) have the same effect.

Albeit in a more general context (that of experts and site inspections), the case of *Hatton v Connew*[38] is a reminder of the need for the court to take expert evidence in an appropriate fashion which is fair to the parties.

---

[35] CJC, *Concurrent Expert Evidence and "Hot-Tubbing" in English Litigation since the "Jackson Reforms"*, 25 July 2016.
[36] CJC, *Concurrent Expert Evidence—A Gift from Australia*, 29 June 2016.
[37] CJC, *Concurrent Expert Evidence and "Hot-Tubbing" in English Litigation since the "Jackson Reforms"*, 25 July 2016 p.50.
[38] *Hatton v Connew* [2013] EWCA Civ 1560.

9. Increasing the incentive for claimants to make realistic settlement proposals (CPR r. 36.17(4)(d)).

Giving the lead judgment in *Fox v Foundation Piling Ltd*,[39] Jackson LJ high-   **4–13**
lighted one of the major reasons that cases that ought to resolve without the
expense of a trial failed so to do:

> *"A not uncommon scenario is that both parties turn out to have been over-opti-
> mistic in their Part 36 offers. The claimant recovers more than the defendant
> has previously offered to pay, but less than the claimant has previously offered to
> accept."*[40]

Therefore, it was not a surprise that CPR Pt 36 was amended to increase the
incentive for the parties to adopt more realistic valuations to encourage earlier
settlement. That amendment comes in the form of CPR r.36.17(4)(d). If a
claimant makes a relevant Part 36 offer, then in addition to the "established"
consequences (an entitlement to indemnity costs and increased interest on
both the substantive award and the costs), there will be an award of an additional amount, unless the court thinks it unjust to make such an award. The
additional amount is 10% of the damages awarded up to £500,000 and that
sum plus 5% of the damages awarded that are over £500,000, with a cap on
the additional amount of £75,000.

The re-written CPR r.36 from April 2015 also contains an incentive at CPR
r.36.23 for an offeree to accept an offer where the offeror has fallen foul of the
provisions of CPR r.3.14 by failing to file a costs budget—this is to avoid the
situation where the "risk" to the offeree is limited solely to future court fees.[41]

Part 36 is considered in more detail in **Ch.5**.

10. The introduction of costs management (CPR rr.3.12–3.18 and CPR PD 3E).

In the Final Report, Sir Rupert Jackson described costs management in these   **4–14**
terms:

> *"(i) The parties prepare and exchange litigation budgets or (as the case proceeds
> amended budgets).*
> *(ii) The court states the extent to which those budgets are approved.*
> *(iii) So far as possible, the court manages the case so that it proceeds within the
> approved budgets.*
> *(iv) At the end of the litigation, the recoverable costs of the winning party are
> assessed in accordance with the approved budget."*[42]

In essence, these four characteristics form the basis of the regime introduced
at CPR rr.3.12–3.18 and at CPR PD 3E. However, the implementation and
regulation of costs management has proven, and is proving, more challenging

---

[39] *Fox v Foundation Piling Ltd* [2011] EWCA Civ 790; [2011] C.P. Rep. 41.
[40] At [46].
[41] See Q79 below for further consideration of this.
[42] *Review of Civil Litigation Costs: Final Report*, December 2009, Ch.40 para.1.4.

than the simple assertion of the regime's principles. To facilitate the under-standing and practical application of the regime, it is simplest to approach it under the following five headings:

A. Which cases are subject to costs management?
B. What procedural requirements are imposed on the parties in respect of costs management?
C. How does the court "costs manage"?
D. Variation of budgets and applications outside the budget.
E. The effect of a costs management order on subsequent assessment.

A. Which cases are subject to costs management?

4–15   During the nine years of its existence, there has been substantial revision of the rules regulating which types of cases are covered by the costs management regime. The current provisions relate to those cases issued after 22 April 2014, but incorporate some further amendments from April 2016 in respect of those who are children, as defined by CPR r.21, at the time of the making of the claim and those with a limited life expectancy (five years or less). In summary, the regime applies to:

- All CPR Pt 7 where the amount claimed or the limit in the statement of value is less than £10,000,000 (CPR r.3.12(1)(a) and (b)) save (i) where the party was a child at the time that the claim was made (note that this exclusion covers those parties who cease to be a child during the proceedings unless the court orders otherwise), (ii) where the claimant has a limited or severely impaired life expectancy (CPR PD 3E (Costs Management) para.1) and the court disapplies costs management (iii) where the court orders otherwise (CPR r.3.12(1)(e)) (iv) where proceedings are subject to fixed or scale costs.
- Any other proceedings (including applications) where the court so orders (CPR r.3.12(1A)). CPR r.3.13(3) sets out the procedure that will apply where costs management is proposed by either the court of its own motion or the parties in cases not otherwise within the scheme and CPR PD 3E para.3 sets out the types of case that are particularly suitable, but which are not otherwise within the regime.

If the initial form of CPR r.3.15 was deemed less than prescriptive as to when the court should costs manage, the current version leaves little room for doubt. The court will make a costs management order in cases where a costs budget has been filed and served unless it can be satisfied that the litigation can be conducted justly and at proportionate costs in accordance with the overriding objective without such an order being made. Given that the court cannot make this assessment until it has seen the budgets, it is hard to imagine why the court will not always be making costs management orders, because either the budgets are plainly disproportionate, immediately triggering court concern, or they are obviously proportionate, in which case, to ensure that costs stay that way, and as it will take no time to do, it seems prudent that the court would make a costs management order in the terms of those parts of the Precedent H that it is permitted to budget. Whilst there remains an "opt-out" for the court in CPR r.3.12(1)(e), this is surely a provision to be used sparingly, otherwise it risks undermining the regime and may result in both forum shopping (for those keen to avoid budgeting) and the suggestion of "local practice directions". (See **Q3** below in respect of developments in some Chancery claims that would otherwise fall within the costs management regime.

In *Wright v Rowland*[43] the court declined to costs manage certain phases of the defendants' budgets because there were disputes between the parties as to the complexity of the claim, whether there was a reputational issue and whether the defendants should have separate representation. The court was concerned that these disputes would only be resolved at trial, and that therefore the prospective budgeting exercise raised the risk that the defendants" costs might be set too high or too low, depending upon which party's submissions it adopted when budgeting. Those phases were left for detailed assessment. However, such an approach is likely to be a rare occurrence as, in most cases, the court will be able to record the basis of its analysis of the CPR r.44.3(5) factors and any "wider circumstances" under CPR r.44.4(1) upon which a budget is set (i.e. its preliminary conclusion on complexity, whether there were reputational issues etc.), recognising that if, subsequently, it becomes clear that those conclusions are not sustainable and, with hindsight were not sustainable at the time of the costs management hearing, parties may apply to vary under CPR r.3.15A and/or rely on "good reason" in seeking to depart from the budgeted costs at an assessment under CPR r.3.18.

The level of prescription imposed by CPR r.3.15 saw the one area of potential disagreement between Sir Rupert Jackson and Lord Dyson (then MR) in their respective "Confronting costs management" lectures in May 2015. Jackson LJ envisaged the possibility of courts not case managing if they lacked the resources to do so other than at the risk of delay and disruption to the particular case before them and other cases generally. Dyson MR perceived a risk that the "lack of resources" card might be "played" in many cases with costs management becoming the exception and not the "norm". What is clear is that agreements between the parties to avoid the costs management regime will need to be well reasoned to survive the rigorous consideration that they merit.

Litigants in person are exempted from the obligation to file and exchange costs budgets (CPR r.3.13(6)), although they must be served with the budget of any other represented party and clearly are entitled to make representations about the budget at any costs management hearing. (See **Q2** below considering whether the court may order litigants in person to file and exchange

---

[43] *Wright v Rowland* [2016] EWHC 2206 (Comm); [2016] 5 Costs L.O. 713.

budgets.) Note that from January 2019 the *Chancery Guide* contains a provision at para.17.13 that the court may order a litigant in person to serve a budget and CPR r.3.13(3)(a) now certainly permits this.

Costs management has been applied beyond the constraints of CPR r.3.12. In *Vattenfall AB v Prysmian SPA*[44] [2021] CAT 3, the Competition Appeal Tribunal concluded that "properly prepared costs budgets are a useful case management tool, particularly where questions of proportionality arise" and that the court should consider whether "the greater cost scrutiny which they facilitate is a proportionate response to the proper control of the costs of the litigation".

B. What procedural requirements are imposed on the parties in respect of costs management?

4–16   In general terms under CPR r.3.13, the parties (other than litigants in person) in receipt of a notice of provisional allocation to the multi-track (CPR r.26.3(1)) where the statement of the value of the claim is less than £50,000, must exchange and file a budget in Precedent H with their directions questionnaires. In all other multi-track cases Precedent H must be exchanged and filed 21 days before the first case management conference or, if the case is one not automatically subject to costs management under CPR r.3.12, the budget must be exchanged and filed by any date specified by the court. Failure to comply results in the automatic sanction under CPR r.3.14, namely that the defaulting party is treated as having filed a budget comprising only applicable court fees. The effect of this for any party subject to a costs management order on this basis is that only future court fees may be budgeted. Previously we have said that the situation relating to incurred costs is clear from the wording of the costs management provisions – namely that those incurred at the time of the costs management order remain recoverable, either because they have been agreed or because, absent agreement, a costs management order only relates to budgeted costs, which are "the costs to be incurred" (CPR r.3.15). However, in *Ali v Channel 5 Broadcast Ltd*[45] the court had to decide whether the limitation of recovery to 50% under CPR r.36.23 applied to all recoverable costs after the date of breach of CPR r.3.13 or only of those costs after the costs management hearing. The court concluded that once there was a breach of CPR r.3.14 then the restriction applied to all recoverable costs after the breach. As set out in **Q20** below this seems an interesting conclusion (and, perhaps, provides for a more far-reaching interpretation of the costs management rules, as a whole, than was envisaged by the court). For the reasons set out in the answer to **Q20**, there is certainly an argument that the sanction should be construed more narrowly.

It is important to stress that CPR r.3.14 is concerned with the amount of costs and not the award of costs. In other words, a failure to comply with

---

[44] *Vattenfall AB v Prysmian SPA* [2021] CAT 3.
[45] *Ali v Channel 5 Broadcast Ltd* [2018] EWHC 840 (Ch); [2018] 2 Costs L.R. 373.

CPR r.3.13, invocation of the sanction under CPR r.3.14 and the subsequent restricted budget approved by the court, does not prevent a costs order ultimately being made in favour of the defaulting party, it simply limits, on a standard basis assessment, the amount of costs that can be recovered under such an order. This is as true under "deemed" costs orders as it is on those expressly made by the court (subject to the provisions of CBR r.36.23 considered above at para.**4–13** and below at **Q78**).

For those thinking that post-*Denton*, the likelihood of relief from this sanction is high, the case of *Jamadar v Bradford Teaching Hospitals NHS Foundations Trust*[46] should come as a stark reminder of the danger of non-compliance (see para.**4–05** above). The contrasting cases of *Lakhani v Mahmud*[47] (budget one day late and the decision not to grant relief from sanction was upheld) and *Mott v Long*[48] (budget 10 days late, relief from sanction granted, but with the defaulting defendants to pay the costs of the application for relief), do no more than confirm the fact-specific discretionary nature of decisions on relief from sanction and the uncertainty of outcome and serve to reinforce the need to comply. What does come as a surprise, nine years on, is that the court is still dealing with applications for relief following a failure to comply with CPR r.3.13.

The budget must be in the form of Precedent H attached to CPR PD 3E Where the budgeted costs do not exceed £25,000 or where the statement of value in the claim form is less than £50,000, then only page 1 of the Precedent H should be completed. There have been three important cases that seek to test the prescription of this requirement. In *Bank of Ireland v Philip Pank Partnership*[49] the claimant failed to include the full wording of the statement of truth, although the budget was signed and dated by the legal representative. The court found that this omission did not render the budget a nullity and as such, the claimant had complied with the requirement to file and exchange its budget. Instead, the Precedent H was simply subject to an irregularity. In the second case, *Americhem Europe Ltd v Rakem Ltd*,[50] the same judge found that the failure to have a budget signed by a senior legal representative (it was signed by a costs draftsman) also did not render a budget a nullity, again amounting to no more than an irregularity. The judge, having noted that this was the second occasion when he had to deal with a mere irregularity in budget form, took the opportunity to cite from the judgment of Leggatt J (as he then was) in *Summit Navigation Ltd v Genrali Romania Asigurare*[51] as follows:

---

[46] *Jamadar v Bradford Teaching Hospitals NHS Foundation Trust* [2016] EWCA Civ 1001; [2016] 5 Costs L.R. 809.
[47] *Lakhani v Mahmud* [2017] EWHC 1713 (Ch); [2017] 1 W.L.R. 3482.
[48] *Mott v Long* [2017] EWHC 2130 (TCC); [2017] B.L.R. 566.
[49] *Bank of Ireland v Philip Pank Partnership* [2014] EWHC 284 (TCC); [2014] 2 Costs L.R. 301 Stuart-Smith J.
[50] *Americhem Europe Ltd v Rakem Ltd* [2014] EWHC 1881 (TCC); 155 Con. L.R. 80 Stuart-Smith J.
[51] *Summit Navigation Ltd v Genrali Romania Asigurare Reasigurare SA* [2014] EWHC 398 (Comm); [2014] 1 W.L.R. 3472 Leggatt J (as he then was).

> *"But, as the Master of the Rolls emphasised . . . it is not the aim of the reforms to turn rules and compliance into 'trip wires' . . ."*

The third case is, in our view[52], unsurprisingly, less forgiving. In *Page v RCG Restaurants Ltd,*[53] the claimant believed that a staged management approach to the case was required and so, without any prior order to this effect, filed and served an incomplete budget (one that assumed a second costs case management conference and which did not include any figures for the trial preparation or trial phases). It was also headed "Interim Budget", although understandably what name was given to the document was not found to be determinative of the nature of that document. For a number of reasons, the court concluded that by filing a materially incomplete budget, the claimant could not properly be regarded as having filed a budget for the purposes of CPR r.3.14 and, as a result, the terms of that provision were engaged (although the claimant subsequently obtained some partial relief from sanction in respect of phases that had been agreed). However, more limited budgets, extending to only part of the proceedings, may be produced where the court so orders in substantial cases. (CPR r.3.13(4)).

The use of the wording "budgeted costs" in CPR PD 3E para.4(b), when identifying those cases where only p.1 of Precedent H is required, raised a conundrum which seemed to be overlooked by the Civil Procedure Rules Committee when revising the rules from October 2020. However, subsequent commentary has resulted in revision to provide clarity by replacing "budgeted costs" with clarification that the reference to £25,000 in that paragraph is to the total costs in Precedent H (i.e. both incurred and estimated costs).[54] This is considered in **Q14** below.

As of April 2016, parties who have exchanged costs budgets (so not litigants in person) must file an agreed budget discussion report (Precedent R— the format of which was revised in October 2016 and again in April 2019) no later than seven days before the CCMC (CPR r.3.13(2)). This must set out the figures agreed for each phase and the figures offered where there is no agreement of a phase with a brief summary of the grounds of dispute (CPR PD 3E para.11). (See **Q42** for consideration of the detail required in Precedent R). The decision of Coulson J in *Findcharm Ltd v Churchill Group Ltd*[55] leaves no doubt that:

- Precedent R was designed to facilitate efficient costs management; and
- those producing unrealistic Precedents R are abusing the costs management system.

---

[52] Unsurprising in our view given the content of the Q & A at **Ch.4 Q24** of the 4th edition of this text (which, in redrafted form appears at Q28 below).
[53] *Page v RCG Restaurants Ltd* [2018] EWHC 2688 (QB); [2018] 5 Costs L.O. 545.
[54] Civil Procedure News 9/2020. Changes to the Costs Management Provisions in force from October 2020, CPRC Minutes November 2020 and 127th CPR Update – Practice Direction Amendments.
[55] *Findcharm Ltd v Churchill Group Ltd* [2017] EWHC 1108 (TCC); 172 Con. L.R. 117.

Parties would do well to note the closing sentence of the judgment:

> *"Because of the critical need to ensure that the Precedent R process is carefully and properly adhered to by the parties to civil litigation, I will arrange for this short Judgment to be put on BAILII."*

It seems that the warning went unheeded by the defendant in *Red and White Bus Services Ltd v Phil Anslow Ltd,*[56] leading Birss J a) to conclude that he was "not at all attracted by the Precedent R produced by the defendant' and b) to set his own overall proportionate figure without recourse to the Precedent R.

If the court makes a costs management order, then CPR r.3.15(7) requires a party to re-file and re-serve the budget in the form approved by the court. In fact, some courts are budgeting either electronically using the first page of the budget in a self-calculating form so that the budget recalculates as the hearing progresses (or some other form of simple summary spreadsheet, e.g. the table set out in the schedule in Chancery Form CH.40) or manually using the first page of the budget and recalculating at the end. In those cases, to reduce costs and ensure absolute clarity of the outcome of the costs management exercise, the courts are simply attaching the first page of each budget (or the simple summary spreadsheet) as costs managed to the directions order and dispensing with the requirement at CPR r.3.15(7), saving the time and resource of re-filing and re-serving. This also ensures that at the end of the CCMC, everyone is clear as to the outcome.

The preparation of the Precedent H itself is assisted by guidance on what   **4–17** work to insert in which phases within the form. This guidance is, as of 1 October 2020, incorporated in CPR PD 3E within a table referred to in para.6 and included at para.10. In the process of this incorporation, the curiosity of the inclusion of further work on budgets in the PTR phase has been removed. This related to the provisions of the pilot costs management schemes pre-2013 and its removal was long overdue.

In general terms, the table does identify the allocation of work amongst the phases of Precedent H. All costs incurred, even those pre-action, which are attributable to a phase of the budget should be inserted in the "incurred" columns in the specific phase (except, curiously, settlement discussions, advising on settlement and Part 36 offers, which are included within the pre-action phases) and all work to be incurred should be inserted in the "estimated" columns in the specific phases.

One obvious lacuna in the guidance relates to work that has already commenced post-issue, such as on an interim application, which by definition is not contingent, but which does not fit neatly into any of the phases, e.g. applications for interim payments, security for costs, etc. Remembering that the budget should inform the other parties and the court, there is a danger that the exercise becomes one of form over substance. However, the difficulty of where to include this work has become harder from April 2016. This is

---

[56] *Red and White Bus Services Ltd v Phil Anslow Ltd* [2018] EWHC 1699 (Ch); [2018] 4 Costs L.O. 425.

because before this date this type of work was often included as a contingency (even though that is not strictly correct as it is certain, rather than antici-pated, costs), which enabled the court to see the sum already incurred on the application and the estimated sum to be incurred. Courts often took the view that so long as this work was clearly identified, and the budget attributed incurred and estimated expenditure transparently, it did not really matter that this was included as a contingency even though it was already a reality. That option no longer exists, as the amendments to the Precedent H in April 2016 understandably removed the incurred costs column from the contingency phase. This leaves the conundrum of whether to insert this work somewhere in Precedent H and, if so, where (this is considered further in **Q34** and **Q35** below).

In addition, the amendments made in October 2020 continue to contain the occasional inconsistency with the rules and a disconnect between Precedents H and S:

- Why is specific disclosure excluded from the disclosure phase when it is one of the types of disclosure order mentioned in the menu of orders at CPR r.31.5(7)? The answer, presumably, is that the original guidance pre-dated the change to CPR r.31.5(7) and this has been overlooked on subsequent revisions. Whatever the reason, it is unhelpful when the court is encouraging parties to move away from the default position of standard disclosure. As Sir Rupert Jackson saw disclosure as one of the most expen-sive phases of litigation and continues to encourage the proper use of the range of disclosure orders by parties and courts alike,[57] it makes no sense that if the table is followed when the court makes an order under CPR r.31.5(7)(b), it does not budget the costs. If, as with non-party disclosure, it is deemed a contingent cost, this too appears illogical. This is because CPR r.31.5(7)(b) envisages a request for specific disclosure being made with disclosure of a party's own list. Accordingly, the time between case management order and compliance with the disclosure order is minimal. The notion that at the CMC this might be only a contingency is not credible. However, even if it is a contingency the court must budget it, so uncertainty over the proportionate expenditure cannot be the reason for it being excluded from the phase. As the court must budget it anyway, why not do it within the phase within which it most naturally arises— namely disclosure? Another option is to regard specific disclosure as not reasonably to fall within the budget and so it falls to be dealt with under CPR r.3.17(4). However, it is hard to argue that something is reasonably not included when it is what the court is ordering to take place! The final option is to treat any subsequent request for specific disclosure as a "significant development in the litigation" justifying a budget variation under CPR r.3.15A. Again, it is difficult to see the occurrence of something

---

[57] "Disclosure" Lecture at the Law Society's Commercial Litigation Conference, 10 October 2016.

the court has ordered as a "significant development". What makes the table even more confusing is that it suggests that work considering the scope of disclosure by other parties and undertaking investigations having reviewed that disclosure (which may well involve consideration of whether specific disclosure is required) should be included in this phase.

- Why does Precedent H require pre-action "settlement discussions, advising on settlement and Part 36 offers" in the pre-action phase, whereas Precedent S makes no distinction in the ADR/Settlement phase between those costs incurred pre and post-action?

C. How does the court "costs manage"?

The only provisions in respect of the form of the budgeting exercise itself are in CPR rr.3.12, 3.15, 3.17 and PD 3E para.12. Together these provide that: **4–18**

- The court costs manages "to be incurred costs" (budgeted costs) either by recording the agreement of the parties or, in the absence of agreement, by approving costs.[58] Save when undertaking a variation of a budget,[59] the court cannot costs manage costs already incurred unless the parties agree.[60] Amendment to remove what was CPR PD 3E para.7.4 and move part of that to CPR r.3.17(3)(a) in October 2020 reintroduced the scope for argument that the court could costs manage the costs case management conference itself, as the rule provided that the court may not approve costs incurred "before the date of any costs management conference". Subsequently, it transpired that the deletion in the moving process was unintended and further amendment of the wording of CPR r.3.17(3age was made to provide that the court "may not approve costs incurred up to and including the date of any costs management hearing".
- The April 2017 CPR amendments introduced a new CPR r.3.15(4). In fact, this merely codifies what the court was already able to do, namely, make recitals by recording comments about incurred costs. What is new is the fact that these "are to be taken into account in any subsequent assessment proceedings" (which is repeated at CPR r.3.18(c))—see **Q91** for further consideration of what this means in practical terms.
- CPR r.3.13(1)(b) means that there is no longer any risk of significant delay between the preparation of the budget and the costs management hearing, save where the claim form statement of value is less than £50,000 (and the delay there should be shorter, because one would expect the budgets to be lower and therefore the hearing to require a lesser time estimate, which ought to mean an earlier hearing date). However, if there is delay in listing in those cases, parties may consider filing and

---

[58] CPR r.3.15(2)(a) and (b).
[59] CPR r.3.15A(6).
[60] CPR r.3.15(2)(c) permits a costs management order in respect of agreed incurred costs.

exchanging updated budgets and making an application to be heard at the costs management for permission to rely on the updated budgets at that hearing. However, in this situation the court is likely to expect to see the same figure in the grand total on page 1 as in the earlier budget—for all that has changed is that the passage of time means that some costs that were estimated in the future have now been incurred and so the incurred costs have gone up, but by the same amount as the originally "estimated" costs have reduced, unless during that "delay period" the assumptions upon which the budget was originally prepared have altered. In all cases, the parties must discuss their respective budgets and must file an agreed budget discussion report (Precedent R) seven days before the CCMC.

- Whilst the court can only make a costs management order recording the extent of any agreement on incurred costs, these costs are still relevant to the wider costs management process. CPR r.3.17(3)(b) provides that the court may record its comments on incurred costs and, more importantly, may take these into account when considering the reasonableness and proportionality of all subsequent costs. This means that when determining the sum to budget for costs "to be incurred" for a phase, the court's decision will be informed by the amount already spent e.g. if the court concludes that the reasonable and proportionate sum for the disclosure phase is £8,000 and £6,000 has already been incurred, the budget for the phase will be £2,000. The treatment of incurred costs has arisen in a number of cases,[61] has proved challenging, has resulted in a variety of approaches being adopted by the court and is considered in more detail in the Q&A section of this chapter.[62]
- When undertaking the budgeting exercise, the court is only charged with setting a total sum which is reasonable and proportionate for each phase of the proceedings. The court is expressly not required to do a detailed assessment, nor to fix or approve hourly rates, and the underlying detail in the budget is provided "for reference purposes to assist the court in fixing the budget". In other words, the court simply sets one figure per phase for the future costs of that phase.
- The parties may agree budgets or discrete phases of the budgets. If they do this, then the court either makes a costs management order in respect of these costs recording the extent of the agreement or elects not to make a costs management order. Some see this as a curious provision. Whilst parties are to be encouraged to co-operate and narrow issues, the apparent inability of the court to interfere with agreement of what it may see as disproportionate costs seems an odd fetter in the pursuit of proportionality. If the court manages the case on a different basis from that upon which the parties have based their agreement of budgets, then the court will

---

[61] E.g. in *CIP Properties (AIPT) v Galliford Try Infrastructure Ltd (Costs No.2)* [2015] EWHC 481(TCC); [2015] 2 Costs L.R. 363 and *Yeo v Times Newspapers Ltd* [2015] EWHC 209 (QB); [2015] 2 Costs L.O. 243.
[62] See Q53 to Q55 for further consideration of this.

expect the parties to revisit the budgets (as the basis upon which agreement has been reached has been altered). If, however, the proportionate case management directions are in line with those upon which agreement of budgets was reached, then the court either makes a costs management order in line with the agreement or makes no costs management order. Remember that costs (and costs liabilities to another party) are those of the client. Any agreement of all or part of a budget requires client approval, which is why access to the client during, or very specific instructions from the client before, a costs management hearing is essential.

In other words, the precise mechanics of costs management are not prescribed. However, it is imperative that the exercise itself does not become disproportionate. The adoption of the broad brush of setting one total sum per phase as required under CPR r.3.15(8) combined with the avoidance of arguments that are of the type routinely raised at the assessment stage, seems to meet this requirement, both in respect of the proportionality of the exercise for the parties and for the court in allocating its resources between cases. The use of this approach was endorsed by Jacob J in *Yirenki v MOD*,[63] where the court allowed an appeal against the decision of a master, who had approved a budget leaving scope for later dispute on hourly rate and other matters in these qualified terms:

> "*Save that the parties reserve their positions as to incurred costs and as to hourly rates, the Master approved the budgets subject to the proviso that it remains open to them to dispute those matters (and to that extent the figure for each phase) at a detailed assessment. . ."*

The appellate court was clear that the function of the court was to set one figure per phase that was reasonable and proportionate, leaving it for the parties to determine how to spend this budgeted sum. One of the various "vices" of the master's decision identified by the court was the uncertainty that would result from a qualified budget approval. Jacob J recognised the importance of certainty, stating:

> "*The ultimate aim of the cost budgeting exercise is that both the receiving and the paying party should know where they stand: they know the figure is fixed and cannot be changed absent good reason. That also has a knock-on advantage in that since the parties know where they stand at the start, it increases the probability that a detailed assessment with all its complexity and possible cost is avoided."* At [17].

The approach certainly matches the intention of the exercise as articulated by Sir Rupert Jackson in his "Confronting Costs Management" lecture in May 2015 when he said this:

---

[63] *Yirenki v MOD* [2018] EWHC 3102 (QB); [2018] 5 Costs L.R. 1177, which cited the commentary in this paragraph in the 4th edition of this text with approval.

> *"At the conclusion of the exercise the court should approve a single total figure for each phase of the proceedings. The party is then free to spend that sum as it sees fit. The court should not specify rates or numbers of hours. That adds to the length of CCMCs and is unnecessary micro-management."*[64]

The introduction of what was CPR PD 3E para.7.10 from April 2016, and is now found within CPR r.3.15(8), served to reinforce this and ought to have tolled the death knell for the arguments of those keen that the court should set an hourly rate and multiply it by an amount of time (despite the fact that CPR PD 3E para.7.3, as was, already disavowed this process).

D. Variation of budgets and applications outside the budget

4–19   Significant changes to the costs management provisions in respect of budget variation were introduced as of 1 October 2020. These are found at CPR r.3.15A, which provides that:

- Revision is mandatory if there is a significant development in the litigation that warrants it and may result in budgets being increased or decreased (see **Q79** below for consideration of what amounts to a "significant development".)
- A proposed revised budget must be submitted to all other parties and the court promptly. Arguably, the proposed revision needs to be sent to all other parties before the court, as CPR r.3.15A(4) requires the documents to be filed at court to include an explanation of the points of difference if they have not been agreed.
- The revision must be shown on the new Precedent T (which readily identifies under which phases revision is being sought and by how much.)
- A party must certify that, if the variation sought is an increase, the additional costs did not appear in the previous approved/agreed budget or any earlier permitted variation to it.
- Precedent T, the last approved/agreed budget and an explanation of any disagreement between the parties on the sought variation, must be submitted to the court promptly.
- The court may approve, vary or disallow the proposed variation, or may list for a further costs management conference (in other words permitting the court to deal with variation as a paperwork exercise, but presumably with the usual right to challenge any decision by an application to vary or set aside within seven days of receipt of the order.)
- As part of this process the court may vary costs related to the variation that have been incurred prior to the date of the order for variation, but after the costs management order. As budgets can go down as well as up, it will be interesting to see if situations emerge where the court is asked to consider a downward variation of costs previously budgeted and incurred

---

[64] "Confronting costs management", May 2015, para.3.4.

under this provision. The provision permitting variation of incurred costs at CPR r.3.15A(6) is not drafted in such a way to exclude this possibility. Whilst, this may be seen as theoretical, perhaps service of surveillance evidence that necessitates variation of directions and budgets may provide a window of opportunity to downward variation of incurred costs.

It is important to note that this is not an open door to variation. A party so seeking must make out its case on there being a significant development that warrants revision, and that party must act promptly. Whether the approach of the court to "promptly" will be as strict as it has been post-March 2013 in respect of the same requirement when applying to set aside judgment under CPR 13.3(2) is unlikely, as an application to vary is not directly linked to the relief from a sanction. However, it seems realistic to expect the court to be restrictive in its interpretation of "promptly". As variation removes an element of costs certainty and informed decision making, the court is likely to demand expedition of application.

E. The effect of a costs management order on subsequent assessment

We have been consistent in saying that CPR r.3.18 clearly sets out that on a standard basis assessment, the court will not depart from the last approved or agreed budget for each phase without "good reason".   **4–20**

This provision applies to summary and detailed assessments. On a straight-forward reading of this rule unless there is "good reason", the budgeted costs will be assessed as budgeted and any assessment will focus on the non-budgeted costs. Curiously, given its clarity, an argument emerged that this provision was not as transparent as it appeared. This argument was rejected by Carr J in *Merrix v Heart of England NHS Foundation*,[65] when hearing the appeal from the decision that had set the hare running and which subsequently received short shrift in the Court of Appeal in *Harrison v University Hospitals Coventry and Warwickshire NHS Trust*.[66] In summary, having professed that he was "a bit bemused by some of the aspects of the arguments advanced before us", Davis LJ, unsurprisingly found that the wording of CPR r.3.18 is as clear as most had always assumed it to be, stating:

> "37. The appellant's argument requires that the word 'budget', as used in the then version of the Rule, merely connotes an available fund. But given that 'good reason' is, as conceded, required if the amount claimed on detailed assessment exceeds the approved budget that of itself surely carries with it the notion that the word 'budget' comprehends a figure. Moreover, the words 'depart from' are wide—or, to put it another way, open-ended . . . had the intention really been that good reason is required only in instances where the sum claimed exceeds the approved budget then the Rule could easily and explicitly have said so. Further,

---

[65] *Merrix v Heart of England NHS Foundation* [2017] EWHC 346 (QB); [2017] 1 W.L.R. 3399.
[66] *Harrison v University Hospitals Coventry and Warwickshire NHS Trust* [2017] EWCA Civ 792; [2017] 1 W.L.R. 4456.

the Rules in any event provide elsewhere for costs capping cases: it seems odd indeed to include a further variant of costs capping by this route. Yet further, and as indicated above, the appellant's argument bases itself almost entirely on the perceived advantages to the paying party with scant, if any, regard to the position of the receiving party: who no doubt will have placed a degree of reliance on the CMO. From the perspective of the receiving party it is all too easy to see that the paying party is indeed seeking to 'depart from' the approved budget in endeavouring to pay less than the budgeted amount.

38. There is also nothing, in my view, in CPR 44.4 (3)(h) to tell against this interpretation. In fact, to read that sub-rule as requiring the approved or agreed budget to be considered only as a guide or factor and no more would involve a departure from the specific words of CPR 3.18. In this respect, it is in fact to be noted that the words of CPR 3.18 (a) positively mandate regard to the last approved or agreed budgeted cost for each phase of the proceedings. The two Rules are perfectly capable of being read together.

39. Consequently, since the meaning of the wording is clear and since it cannot be maintained that such a meaning gives rise to a senseless or purposeless result, effect should be given to the natural and ordinary meaning of the words used in CPR 3.18. In truth, that natural and ordinary meaning is wholly consistent with the perceived purposes behind, and importance attributed to, costs budgeting and CMOs."

The decisions in *Merrix* and *Harrison* are referred to at **Qs 89** and **96** below.

Whilst the clear meaning of CPR r.3.18 has been affirmed, there is still one further issue to mention before attention can turn to the challenging aspect of that provision—namely "what constitutes "good reason""? This is whether the CPR r.44(3)(2)(a) proportionality cross-check can apply to reduce budgeted costs even where there is no good reason to depart from the sums set by phase. Our view is that it cannot and the reasoning behind this assertion is set out in full at **Ch.3 Q16**. Turning then to "good reason" and the question posed earlier in this paragraph. There is no guidance to help answer this in the rules. This is unsurprising as this must be a contextual determination. Indeed, the issue arose in passing in *Harrison* and Davis LJ offered the following comment:

"As to what will constitute 'good reason' in any given case I think it much better not to seek to proffer any further, necessarily generalised, guidance or examples. The matter can safely be left to the individual appraisal and evaluation of costs judges by reference to the circumstances of each individual case."

However, Davis LJ was keen to stress that for costs management to be purposeful:

"Costs judges should . . . be expected not to adopt a lax or over-indulgent approach to the need to find 'good reason': if only because to do so would tend to subvert one of the principal purposes of costs budgeting and thence the overriding objective. Moreover, while the context and the wording of CPR r.3.18 (b) is different from

*that of CPR r.3.9 relating to relief from sanctions, the robustness and relative
rigour of approach to be expected in that context (see Denton v TH White Ltd) can
properly find at least some degree of reflection in the present context."*

In other words, the "good reason" hurdle is a high one.

One of the first reported authorities on CPR r.3.18 and departure from a
budget in general terms and not in a specific situation (for an example of the
latter see **Q96** below), presented more questions than answers. In *Simpson v
MGN Ltd*[67] it was argued that where a party had exceeded its budget and there
was no good reason for this, the inevitability was that under CPR r.3.18(b)
the costs over and above the budget would not be recoverable. However,
the court concluded that neither CPR r.3.18 nor CPR PD 3E prescribed an
automatic sanction in this circumstance. Instead, the court adopted what it
described as a just and proportionate sanction which involved "an assessment which makes every assumption against the party which has failed to
submit an amended budget, and properly compensates the defendant for the
additional costs involved". It is arguable that whether CPR r.3.18(a) and (b)
include a sanction is of academic interest only, as, on the simple construction
referred to above, and approved in *Harrison* (above), they combine to preclude
departure from the agreed/approved budget for any phase, whether upwards
or downwards, in the absence of good reason. What is clear is that decisions
will be entirely contextual based on the specific facts of a particular case and
departures for "good reason" are likely to be rare, as is clear from the guidance
to costs judges by Davis LJ in *Harrison*, referred to above.

An illustration of the simplification of the assessment process as a result of
a costs management order can be found in *Sony Communications International
AB v SSH Communications Security Corp*,[68] where the parties accepted that as the
budgeted costs had, by definition, already been determined to be reasonable
and proportionate, there was no need for a detailed assessment and the court
should undertake a summary assessment in which it could consider departure
from the budget on the basis of good reason (e.g. because the receiving party
had actually spent less on a phase and that would be a breach of the indemnity principle or because the budget for a phase had been exceeded and the
receiving party sought an upwards departure).

However, there remain areas of difficulty. One arises where the court determines that there is "good reason" to depart from a phase. How then does
the court assess that phase, by a reversion to a line-by-line assessment or by
a further determination of a reasonable and proportionate sum by way of a
total figure? This issue arose in *Barts Health NHS Trust v Salmon*,[69] in which to
allow the budgeted sum would have been a breach of the indemnity principle

[67] *Simpson v MGN Ltd* [2015] EWHC 126 (QB); [2015] 1 Costs L.R. 139.
[68] *Sony Communications International AB v SSH Communications Security Corp* [2016] EWHC 2985 (Pat); [2016] 4 W.L.R. 186.
[69] *Barts Health NHS Trust v Salmon* unreported 17 January 2019 County Court at Central London HHJ Dight.

as that sum had not been spent. The judge referred back to *Harrison* and concluded that:

> *"In my judgment, having regard to what was said by Lord Justice Davis in the Harrison judgment, the fact that the sum claimed is lower than the budgeted figure, because of the indemnity principle, is itself capable of being a good reason. Awarding the lower figure would be, in my judgment, a departure from the budget, which requires a good reason to be established: in this case, once that had been done it was open to the paying party to challenge the figure which was then being claimed by the receiving party, and they did not have to assert a further good reason to enable the court to do so."* ([22])

There seems nothing controversial in the conclusion that a breach of the indemnity principle, when it has not been disapplied, represents a "good reason". However, the court continued to explore the consequences flowing from a finding of "good reason", concluding only by identifying the options without reaching a final view. It decided that once a good reason has been established, and the court is given the right to depart from the budget, it will assess the costs of that phase in the usual way, and, in that respect, it is left to the good sense and expertise of the costs judge to undertake that assessment in an appropriate and, insofar as possible, practical way, whether line-by-line or in a more broad-brush way.

Perhaps more controversially, the court determined that once the court has found that there is a "good reason" to depart from the budget, neither the receiving party nor the paying party needs to establish a further good reason within CPR r.3.18 if they wish to persuade the costs judge to make a further or different adjustment to the bill for the phase in which "good reason" has arisen. In other words, if the initial "good reason" would lead to a specific reduction (e.g. in the example of a limit on recovery imposed by the indemnity principle, down to the level of the costs actually incurred), that is not the end of the matter, as once a "good reason" is established, the court is not constrained by the consequence of that "good reason" in the extent of the departure from the budgeted costs. There have been other, non-binding, first instance decisions to the contrary, but authority is still awaited on this point. Our view is that the "good reason" is specific and deductions from the budget should only be based on that reason. (See **Q99** for further detailed consideration both of budgets and the indemnity principle and the effect of a finding of "good reason".)

In any event, the provision at CPR r.3.18 does not apply to costs assessed on the indemnity basis. There was initially some suggestion within the pilot schemes that the budgets still formed the starting point for an assessment on the indemnity basis (see *Elvanite Full Circle Ltd v Amec Earth & Environmental (UK) Ltd*,[70] which advanced this proposition and *Kellie v Wheatley & Lloyd*

---

[70] *Elvanite Full Circle Ltd v Amec Earth & Environmental (UK) Ltd* [2013] EWHC 1643 (TCC); [2016] 4 W.L.R. 186 Coulson J.

Architects Ltd[71] which disagreed with that approach). This is not the position as proportionality has no place in an indemnity basis assessment and budgets have been produced and set by specific reference to proportionality. Whilst Coulson J (as he then was) repeated his view from *Elvanite* in *The Governors and Company of the Bank of Ireland v Watts Group Plc*[72] (when considering a payment on account), in our view any doubt was resolved by the Court of Appeal in *Denton v TH White*.[73] When referring to the consequence of an indemnity based costs order, the Master of the Rolls described it as follows:

> "*If the offending party ultimately loses, then its conduct may be a good reason to order it to pay indemnity costs. Such an order would free the winning party from the operation of CPR rule 3.18 in relation to its costs budget.*"[74]

Our view was confirmed by the decision of the Court of Appeal in *Lejonvarn v Burgess*,[75] in which Coulson LJ cited *Kellie* with approval to explain the "absence of an overlap between the cost budgeting regime on the one hand, and an order for indemnity costs on the other" before concluding, with generous and laudable humility, that:

> "*In principle, the assessment of costs on an indemnity basis is not constrained by the approved cost budget, and to the extent that my obiter comments in Elvanite or Bank of Ireland v Watts suggested the contrary, they should be disregarded.*"([93])

Q94 below sets out specific factors that militate against the budget being the starting point in an assessment on the indemnity basis. (See also **Ch.3 Q12** for a more detailed consideration of CPR r.3.18 and assessments on the indemnity basis)

The fact that an order for indemnity costs sees "escape" from the constraints **4–21** of the budget is not a reason for an increase in applications for such orders. The principles surrounding when the court will make an order for indemnity costs have not altered (save by the identification in *Denton* of a specific type of conduct that might merit such an award).

However, an indemnity costs award arising under CPR r.36.17(4)(b) presents unique challenges. A claimant is entitled to indemnity basis costs from "the date on which the relevant period expired" (relevant period is defined in CPR r.36.3(g)). This means that for some part of the litigation costs are constrained by the budget (absent "good reason") and, for another part, the budget becomes irrelevant. However, the chance of the date when this transition takes place falling neatly at the end of a phase of Precedent H so it is clear which parts of the budget remain wholly relevant is slim (not non-existent,

---

[71] *Kellie v Wheatley & Lloyd Architects Ltd* [2014] EWHC 2886 (TCC); [2014] B.L.R. 644 HHJ Keyser QC.
[72] *Governors and Co of the Bank of Ireland v Watts Group Plc* [2017] EWHC 2472 (TCC); [2017] B.L.R. 626 at [16].
[73] *Denton v TH White* [2014] EWCA Civ 906; [2014] 1 W.L.R. 3926.
[74] Para.43 majority judgment.
[75] *Lejonvarn v Burgess* [2020] EWCA Civ 114.

e.g. if the relevant period expired just before trial it may be possible to identify the phases clearly).

What happens in this situation where only part of the phase falls to be assessed on the standard basis? Sadly, the answer is not clear. It is arguable that as the court is not looking at a phase exclusively on the standard basis, then CPR r.3.18 has no application at all or if it does, then this is a "good reason" to depart from the budget. However, this potentially presents a windfall to the receiving party beyond the ordinary benefit of an indemnity costs order. Even if this is the position, the court is still required to undertake an assessment in part on the standard basis and in part on the indemnity basis and the proportionality cross-check pursuant to CPR r.44.3(2)(a) continues to apply to the standard basis costs. Does this mean that bills where there is a relevant CPR r.36 offer will need to be split between dates as well as, within the new format bill, phases matching the Precedent H? Certainly, Precedent Q of the Costs Precedents provides no assistance with the division of phases between those on a standard and those on an indemnity basis. In addition, CPR PD 47 para.5.8(8) only requires the bill to be divided into parts to match the phases (and between the incurred and budgeted costs) where the costs are to be assessed on the standard basis. In other words, for those costs to be assessed on the indemnity basis it may not be apparent to the assessing judge how those costs even relate to the Precedent H phases. At the moment, questions abound and there are no clear answers.

Those accepting a CPR Part 36 offer, but then seeking an order for costs on the indemnity basis (in order to escape from the confines of a budget), should take note of the decision in *Courtwell Properties Ltd v Greencore PF (UK) Ltd*,[76] in which Akenhead J stated:

> "*In cases where the parties have settled through the Part 36 procedure or otherwise but leave the judge to decide costs, particularly where indemnity costs are claimed, parties must act in a proportionate way. There can be few if any cases in which there should in effect be a trial of all or some of the settled issues in the case. Where the indemnity cost application depends on evidence which is likely to involve material conflicts of evidence, the applicant party needs to think long and hard about whether it is appropriate to pursue the application.*"[77]

Case and costs management in harmony

4–22 Having identified the key case management amendments and the costs management provisions, the practical link between the two becomes obvious. By requiring the court to costs manage by phases (which broadly equate to the procedural steps on the way to trial), the court is able to tailor the directions to the reasonable and proportionate cost of the respective phases. This should result in the court:

---

[76] *Courtwell Properties Ltd v Greencore PF (UK) Ltd* [2014] EWHC 184 (TCC); [2014] 2 Costs L.O. 289 Akenhead J.
[77] At [42].

- Selecting the appropriate form of disclosure from the options at CPR r.31.5(7), which includes the possibility of dispensing with disclosure altogether, or, where appropriate, CPR PD 51U.
- Controlling the number of witnesses, the issues they may address and the length of their statements (CPR r.32.2(3)).[78]
- Controlling the extent of expert evidence by number, by reliance on jointly instructed experts, by specific identification of the issues upon which they may report and by the use of concurrent, immediately sequential or conventional (all one party's witnesses first and then all the other party's witnesses) evidence at trial.
- Conducting ongoing case and costs management preventing claims changing fundamentally in nature without court intervention. Any variation in the budget is linked to "significant developments in the litigation". It is hard to imagine many such developments that do not require further court case management directions. At such a stage the ongoing control of the parties' budgets required by CPR r.3.15(3) and the requirement at CPR r.3.17(1) for the court to take account of the costs in each procedural step, combine so that the court must determine the extent, if at all, to which it is prepared to permit the claim to change course.
- Limiting the trial length. In a sense, one should start here for the assessment of proportionality dictates the trial length and all other directions must then be crafted to ensure that the trial can be completed within that period. Inevitably this informs the court's decisions on the matters listed above.
- Conducting a summary, rather than detailed, assessment at the conclusion of the trial. In some cases, the "costs of the costs" are disproportionate. One way to avoid this is for the court to undertake more assessments on a summary basis.

What is clear from the consideration of case and costs management above is that this has presented new challenges to both the judiciary and court users (albeit that the exact nature of some of those challenges required and continues to require procedural rule and/or jurisprudential clarification). All must now be astute to ensure that rules, practice directions and orders are followed and to "cut the cloth" proportionately. For the court, this may mean deciding cases on more limited evidence than might previously have been available. For the professions this, inevitably, places a far greater emphasis on familiarity, and compliance, with rules, practice directions, court orders and the management of client expectations. For the parties, they have to co-operate with timescales and temper their expectation of a case being dealt with justly to what outcome can be achieved at a proportionate cost.

---

[78] At the time of writing a working group chaired by Popplewell J is undertaking a review within the Commercial Court as to how factual witness is taken in the Business and Property Courts—including both the effectiveness and efficiency of the current approach of witness statements standing as evidence in chief.

Questions and answers

A. The scope of the costs management scheme

Q1. How prescriptive is the wording of CPR r.3.12(1) and (1A)? In particular can the court costs manage cases that fall within the definition of those outside the scheme and when may the court exclude cases from the regime under CPR r.3.12(1)(e)?

4–23   The wording of CPR r.3.12(1) and (1A) allows the court flexibility, both of an inclusionary and exclusionary nature.

Under CPR r.3.12(1A) it may bring into the costs management regime other proceedings. Although a case involving consideration of the provisions in force from 1 April 2013 until 22 April 2014, Coulson J (as he then was) considered the question of extension of the regime in *CIP Properties (AIPT) Ltd v Galliford Try Infrastructure Ltd*.[79] In this case, the claim was put in the region of £18,000,000—so in excess of both the £2,000,000 cut off in place until 22 April 2014 and the £10,000,000 cut off since that date. He concluded that the provision at CPR r.3.12(1A), and in particular the reference to "any other proceedings", did indeed extend to multi-track claims worth £10,000,000 or more, stating:

> "I take the view that the exercise of the court's discretion under CPR 3.12(1) is unfettered. There is nothing in the CPR to suggest otherwise. This discretion extends to all cases where the claim is for more than £2 million (old regime) and £10 million (new regime) . . . There is no presumption against ordering budgets in claims over £2 million or £10 million, and no additional burden of proof on the party seeking the order."[80]

Coulson J recognised that to have concluded otherwise would have left the court's hands tied and the system open to abuse by claimants wishing to avoid the costs management regime simply valuing their claims at £1 more than the cut off.

The fact that the regime is sufficiently flexible to permit costs management in cases not strictly within the provisions is, in any event, borne out by the express provision in CPR r.3.13(3) This allows the court, whether on the application of the parties or of its own initiative, to require costs budgets where the parties are not required to file budgets under CPR rr.3.12 and 3.13. CPR PD 3E para.2 sets out examples of cases strictly outside the regime where it may be particularly appropriate to costs manage. The fact that the £10 million limit is not a bar is reinforced by the inclusion in CPR PD 3E para.2 of personal injury and clinical negligence cases where the value exceeds that sum.

---

[79] *CIP Properties (AIPT) Ltd v Galliford Try Infrastructure Ltd* [2014] EWHC 3546 (TCC); [2015] 1 All E.R. (Comm) 765 Coulson J.
[80] At [27].

The reverse position is envisaged by CPR r.3.12(1)(e), which permits the court to disapply the regime in multi-track Pt 7 claims that would otherwise fall within the provisions.

If the court does not do so prior to the deadline for filing and exchanging budgets, then the court must make a decision not to costs budget based on CPR r.3.15(2)—namely that it is satisfied that the litigation can be conducted justly and at proportionate cost in accordance with the overriding objective without a costs management order.

Cases where the court disapplies the regime before the filing and exchange of budgets ought to be rare (save for example where temporary exclusions are given, such as that which was given to clinical negligence claims before the Queen's Bench Masters). The reason for this is that it is hard to see how the court can reconcile the obligation imposed on it by the overriding objective and, more specifically, by CPR r.3.17(1) (to take into account the costs of each procedural step) without any information about costs.

If the parties wish to persuade the court that a case is not suitable for costs management then they should apply before the expiry of the time for filing and exchanging budgets both to disapply the regime and, in the alternative, for an extension of time to file and exchange budgets until a date after the determination of the application in the event that the primary application is refused. If they do this and the court dismisses the application to disapply the costs management provisions, then the parties are dealing with an application to extend time and not an application for relief from the sanction under CPR r.3.14 (see consideration of *Hallam Estates v Baker*[81] in **Q27** below).

In *Sharp v Blank*,[82] the court had to grapple with whether a claim fell within the costs management regime. The situation arose where a claimant indicated on the claim form that the claim had a value of over £25,000 (and so complied with CPR r.16.3(2)(b)(iii)), gave no value in the "amount claimed" box on the claim form, but it subsequently transpired that the claim had a value in excess of £10 million. On the face of the rules, the court concluded this type of case was strictly caught by the costs management provisions, even though it was known by the time of the case management hearing that the claim value exceeded £10 million. Nugee J concluded that it might be useful for CPR r.16.3 to require confirmation of whether a claim exceeds £10 million, which would avoid this situation arising, but then used "unless the court otherwise orders" in CPR r.3.13 to dispense with budgets in the particular case.

Q2. Can the court order a litigant in person to file and serve a Precedent H?
The starting point is that CPR r.3.13(1) require all parties other than litigants in person to file and exchange budgets. As a result, litigants in person do not fall within the costs management regime in Section II of CPR r.3 without

4–24

[81] *Hallam Estates v Baker Ltd* [2014] EWCA Civ 661; [2014] C.P. Rep. 38.
[82] *Sharp v Blank* [2015] EWHC 2685 (Ch).

something more. In cases where all parties are litigants in person, then the answer to this question is "yes". CPR r.3.13(3)(a) provides that the court:

"may, on its own initiative or on an application, order the parties to file and exchange costs budgets in a case where the parties are not otherwise required by this section to do so."

As the parties are not required so to do by CPR r.3 Section II, then clearly the court may make an order under this provision.

On a strict interpretation of the rules the position is far less clear where at least one party is represented. This is because CPR r.3.13(3) uses the plural. As a represented party is required to file and exchange a budget, then the requirement in CPR r.3.13(3) that the "parties are not...required...to do so" is not met. Can the court order a party to file a budget under any other procedural provision? There is certainly a procedural argument that suggests not under CPR r.3 Section II. This is that:

- CPR r.3.13(1) does not provide an enabling provision. The words "unless the court otherwise orders" only permit the court to disapply the requirement on all non-litigant in person parties to file and exchange budgets or to vary the time within which they must do so. In other words, this rule simply requires all non-litigant in person parties in cases falling within the regime (as set out in CPR r.3.12) to file and exchange budgets "unless the court orders otherwise" and prescribes the time when they are to do so, "unless the court orders otherwise".
- CPR r.3.12(1A) does not assist as it is not the proceedings that are excepted from the costs management regime, but a particular party.

The last point best illustrates the unsatisfactory nature of this argument (as why should the court (a) be precluded from ordering a litigant in person to file and exchange a budget where the other party is represented, but could impose the regime if all parties are litigants in person or (b) be permitted to exercise its discretion in any case where costs management does not automatically apply, but not in cases within the regime under CPR r.3.12?).

We suspect that the court will, in appropriate cases, wish to have the ability to order litigants in person to file and serve costs budgets to enable it to consider costs managing part of the costs, whether by preferring a procedural interpretation of CPR r.3.13(3)(a) that permits this in all cases, whether all or only some of the parties are litigants in person or by exercising its power under CPR r.3.1(2)(ll). Certainly the *Chancery Guide* now states that the court may order a litigant in person to serve a budget.

As stated above, there is a practical difficulty supporting the exclusion of litigants in person from the costs management regime. It stems from the fact that budgets are not set by rate multiplied by time (see para.**4–18** above and **Q61** below). Instead the court sets a sum per phase that is reasonable and proportionate under CPR rr.44.4(3) and 44.3(5). However, this will necessarily not equate to what a litigant in person will recover because such a party is limited to £19 per hour, actual financial loss or a combination of both and in any case the total cannot exceed two-thirds of that which would have been allowed if that party were legally represented. The costs management exercise is expressly not a detailed assessment and does not involve CPR r.46.5 (express provisions for litigant in person costs). Accordingly, when dealing with litigant in person costs there seems an inevitability that any budget set by reference to CPR rr.44.4(3) and 44.3(5) must be revisited under "good reason" in CPR r.3.18 as the budget will not have taken account of the constraints imposed by CPR r.46.5. As a result, in many cases the time and cost involved in budgeting litigant in person costs seem destined to be wasted. However, this simply means that the court must be selective in deciding when to order a litigant in person to file and serve a budget. Examples of cases where it may be appropriate are those where:

- It is clear that the litigant in person proposes to incur direct access fees and other fees for legal services and expert assistance.
- The detail provided will inform the court to enable it to case manage proportionately.
- Transparency of costs will be of assistance to the other party/ies.

Two of these factors arose in *CJ & LK Perk Partnership v RBS*.[83] In a case where counsel under the Direct Access scheme would be "dipping in and out of the case", the court had to consider the practicalities of requiring a LiP to provide realistic figures, against the benefit to the represented party of costs transparency. In this case, the balance came down against ordering a budget.

A final point is that if the court does order a litigant in person to file and exchange a budget then, unless it also makes a further specific order to the contrary, CPR r.3.13(2) still applies, leading to the curious position of that party not having to file a Precedent R (budget discussion report) in respect of any represented party's budget, but any represented party having to file Precedent R in respect of the litigant in person's budget.

Q3. Do the costs management provisions at CPR rr.3.12–3.18 apply to cases in the Chancery Division (now part of the Business and Property Courts)?

Yes, in principle, they do in respect of those claims that fall within CPR r.3.12.   **4–25**
The *Chancery Guide* contains a chapter on case and costs management (Ch.17) that applies save in respect of claims in the Patents Court, claims in either of the Shorter Trials or the Flexible Trials schemes (CPR PD 57AB) and claims in the Financial List (CPR r.63A). **Q13** below considers separately why parties might want the court to consider costs managing within the Shorter Trials Scheme as para.2.56 of CPR PD 57AB, which excludes the provision of CPR r.3.12, expressly permits the parties to agree to costs management. Remember

---

[83] *CJ & LK Perk Partnership v RBS* [2020] EWHC 2563 (Comm).

also that CPR r.3.12 excludes CPR r.8 claims from automatically coming within the costs management regime and, as many Chancery claims will fall within CPR r.8, that will, inevitably, reduce the incidence of costs management in these cases.

Q4. Can parties agree to dispense with costs management? If a CPR Part 7 case of no monetary value has been allocated to the multi-track, can the parties agree to dispense with costs management? If parties wish to seek a stay when responding with the directions questionnaire in those claims where Precedents H are due to be exchanged and filed with that document, do they still need to exchange and file Precedents H?

4–26   Whilst it is open to parties to agree to dispense with costs management, they will still need to persuade the court to do so. As a general rule, expect the court to approach such an agreement with caution. In *Agents Mutual Ltd v Gasgoine Halman*,[84] notwithstanding a consent order made in the Chancery Division dispensing with costs management, this was found not to have effect in the Competition Appeals Tribunal. The judge also found that even if there were an agreement in the tribunal to dispense with costs management that would not be determinative, but merely a factor to consider.

The fact that a claim may have no monetary value does not alter the position. Indeed, such claims may still be costs intensive and so ideally suited for costs management.

If parties wish to seek dispensation from costs management, then to avoid preparing, filing and exchanging Precedent H they must apply to dispense with/defer costs management before the date prescribed for compliance or find themselves caught by the provisions of CPR r.3.14. For the reason given in **Q1** above in relation to the court's obligation under CPR rr.1.1 and 3.17, it is difficult to see any situation where the court would dispense with Precedents H. Once Precedents H are filed and exchanged, then the parties will have to satisfy the court under CPR r.3.15(2) (see **Q1** above). If successful in persuading the court at this stage, the parties should remember that CPR PD 44 para.3 then applies in respect of the costs budgets that were filed.

Following on from the above, unless and until the court has dispensed with the requirement for Precedents H or extended the time for their exchange and filing, parties must comply with the provisions of CPR r.3.13. Accordingly, in the situation set out in the final question, the parties must exchange and file Precedents H with the directions questionnaire unless an order has been made extending the time for compliance. If an application for such an order has been made before the time expires then this will be treated as an application for an extension rather than an application for relief from sanction (see **Q27** and *Hallam Estates Ltd v Baker*[85]). However, obviously, if the extension is subsequently refused, then CPR r.3.14 applies.

---

[84] *Agents Mutual Ltd v Gasgoine Halman* [2016] CAT 20; [2017] Comp. A.R. 47.
[85] *Hallam Estates Ltd v Baker* [2014] EWCA Civ 661.

Q5. Does costs management apply to the disposal stage of a claim after the entry of a default judgment for damages to be decided by the court? Strictly, a disposal hearing is defined in CPR PD 26 (Case Management— Preliminary Stage: Allocation and Re-Allocation) para.12.4 as a hearing that will not exceed 30 minutes and at which the court will not take oral evidence. Such claims are not allocated to track (unless they are within the small claims limit and are allocated to that track—see CPR PD 26 para.12.3(2)). Accordingly, claims listed for disposal are not allocated to the multi-track and they do not fall within the costs management regime under CPR r.3.12.   4–27

However, parties often refer to a disposal hearing when, in fact, they mean a trial on quantum where the final hearing will exceed 30 minutes and at which oral evidence will be given. These cases should be allocated. If they are allocated to the multi-track, then, as CPR r.7 multi-track cases, the costs management provisions apply. In such cases there may not be any requirement to file directions questionnaires under CPR r.26.3. Instead, the file may be referred to the district judge on entry of the judgment for damages to be decided to give directions. Prior to the introduction of costs management, the district judge might have ordered the filing of directions questionnaires, listed the claim for case management conference or given directions as a paper exercise. The likelihood now is that the last of those options is unlikely to occur in cases where allocation is to the multi-track. Accordingly, parties should be astute to when a Precedent H is triggered under the provisions of CPR r.3.13 in these cases. **Qs 14–19**, below, provide more detailed consideration of relevant time limits, but this does not cover the situation where the statement of value of the claim is for less than £50,000, but there is no requirement to file a directions questionnaire, as neither CPR r.3.13(1)(a) nor (b) appear to envisage this situation. It seems that if the court still requires a directions questionnaire by express order then CPR r.3.13(1)(a) will apply in this situation, but if it does not, then there is no direct provision, although if the court orders a case management hearing without expressly ordering a Precedent H, it would still be prudent to comply with CPR r.3.13(1)(b) (see *Jamadar* at para.4–05 above). If the statement of value of the claim is for £50,000 or more, then CPR r.3.13(1)(b) certainly applies.

Q6. In a multi-track case under CPR Part 7 where the stated value on the claim form is £50,000 or more, but does not exceed £10 million, where in all other respects it is a case that falls within the costs management regime in CPR r.3.12, but where the case management directions were given in the course of the disposal of an interim application, so that there has been no listed case management conference, do the costs management provisions apply and, if so, when will the requirement to file and exchange Precedent H arise? Do the costs management provisions apply in a CPR Part 7 allocated to the multi-track, which falls within CPR r.3 Section II where there was no requirement to file and exchange Precedents H with

the directions questionnaire and where directions through to trial have been given on paper, but there is no costs management order?

4–28 The answer to both questions is "yes", assuming that the court has not made an order dispensing with its inclusion, as these are cases that fall within the costs management regime under CPR r.3.12. However, because of the stated value and the fact that there has been no formal CMC, there has been no trigger for the requirement to file and exchange budgets under CPR r.3.13(1) in either case. Leaving aside for the moment that it is difficult to envisage this situation arising, given the fact that it is unclear how the court has managed to give directions without consideration of any budgets to inform it of the proportionality of the steps that it has ordered, then the parties should apply for a costs management hearing or seek an order expressly disapplying costs management. CPR r.3.16 allows for hearings to be convened solely for costs management. Obviously, this will be far from ideal as by the time the court hears the application some costs will have already been spent on the ordered directions and so, in the absence of agreement of those incurred costs, the court will not be able to costs manage them.

The reason this situation is difficult to envisage is that both claims fall within the costs management regime. Accordingly, in the absence of the court "otherwise ordering" under CPR r.3.12(1)(e), then in the first example both the parties and the court should have been aware of the need to undertake this exercise. Regarding the second example it is rare indeed for the substantive directions to and including trial in multi-track cases to be approved as a paper exercise. In addition the application of both CPR rr.1.1 and 3.17(1) when considering the directions, ought to have operated as a reminder of the requirement to consider costs management. The mandatory wording of CPR r.3.12 relating to its application, and the parties' duties owed to the court, are such as to require them to seek either an order dispensing with costs management or a costs management hearing.

Notwithstanding that a hearing defined under CPR r.3.16 as a costs management conference may not be the same thing as a "first case management conference" under CPR r.3.13(1)(b) and (2), in the absence of any specific order being made on listing of the costs management conference, it would seem appropriate to file and exchange budgets and deal with Precedent R in accordance with those provisions of the CPR.

Q7. a) Do the provisions apply to a claim brought under CPR r.8, where the court has expressly listed a CMC? b) Where a CPR r.8 claim has been listed for a costs and case management conference does this mean that a Precedent H should be filed and exchanged, and, if so, when?

4–29 a) No, unless the court has also expressly made an order requiring the parties to file and exchange costs budgets. As set out in the text above, the costs management provisions from April 2014 do not apply to CPR r.8 claims (see CPR r.3.12(1)). Whilst the court retains a discretion under CPR r.3.12(1A) and CPR r.3.13(3) to bring claims that would not otherwise be subject to costs management into the regime, this would require an express order.

The court may convene a directions hearing before giving directions in CPR r.8 claims (see CPR PD 8 para.6.4). If no order for costs budgets has been made, the description of the hearing as a "case management conference" rather than as a directions hearing carries no significance other than to distinguish the hearing from a final one.

b) Strictly the answer remains the same, namely that a CPR r.8 claim does not fall within the provisions of CPR r.3 Section II. Similarly, the fact that the case has been listed for a costs and case management conference does not, of itself, bring the claim within the costs management regime. A specific order that Section II applies is required under CPR r.3.12(2). Listing for a costs and case management conference is not such an order. Indeed, whilst Section II refers separately to a case management conference and a costs management conference, It does not mention a costs and case management conference. However, counsel of caution suggests that the best course may be to query with the court whether it intended to list for a costs and case management hearing, rather than a case management hearing, and, if so, to query whether an order has been made to apply the Section II regime. Those more cautious may go further and file and exchange a budget just in case, but that incurs cost in a situation where, strictly that is unnecessary. As directions questionnaires do not form part of the CPR r.8 procedure, then those deciding to file and exchange Precedent H should do so not later than 21 days before the costs and case management hearing.

Q8. Do Landlord and Tenant Act 1954 lease renewal claims automatically fall within the costs management regime?
It is important to remember that Landlord and Tenant Act 1954 (the statute) claims are split into two distinct types. The first is those where the claim is unopposed and the second is where the claim is opposed. We shall look at each separately.   **4–30**

An unopposed claim is defined by CPR r.56.3.2(b) as being where the grant of a new tenancy is not opposed (although there may be disagreement as to the precise terms). CPR r.56.3(3) provides that where the claim is an unopposed one, then CPR r.8 procedure must be adopted. Under CPR r.3.12 such a claim does not automatically fall within the costs management regime (although, curiously, as a matter of routine, parties tend to include a superfluous direction dispensing with the costs management regime!).

An opposed claim is defined by CPR r.56.3(2)(c) as one where a new tenancy is opposed under s.24 of the statute or where the claim is for termination of the tenancy under s.29 of the statute. CPR r.56.3(4) provides that where the claim is an opposed one, then CPR r.7 procedure must be adopted. The question then is whether or not the claim is allocated to the multi-track. The likelihood is that it will be, as, even if it is allocated to the fast track, district judges cannot hear these claims (see CPR PD 2B para.11.1(a)). If it is allocated to the multi-track then as a CPR r.7 claim in that track it is within the regime unless it is one of the exceptions. The only one of relevance is CPR r.3.12(1)(b) as this is a non-monetary claim. However, non-monetary claims only come within the exception from the regime if the claim form contains a statement of value of £10 million or more. As this is unlikely, then it appears that most opposed renewals do automatically fall within the costs management regime. Amongst other issues, this immediately creates the potential for tension between CPR r.3.13(4) that requires the Precedent H to extend to cover the whole proceedings (unless the court orders otherwise) and CPR PD 56 (Landlord and Tenant Claims and Miscellaneous Provisions about Land) para.3.16, which provides that unless the circumstances of the case render it unreasonable to do so, any grounds of opposition shall be tried as a preliminary issue—suggesting that initially Precedent H should be limited to the costs of the preliminary issue. In these circumstances, it may be prudent to seek a specific direction that Precedent H may be so limited before the date for filing and exchanging Precedent H expires. The risk is that the court finds such an application unnecessary, but the wasted costs will be significantly less than those lost if the sanction in CPR r.3.14 is applied.

Q9. Must parties file and exchange Precedents H in possession claims under CPR r.55 which the court concludes are genuinely disputed on grounds which appear substantial, which the court then allocates to the multi-track and lists for a CMC?

4–31   No. Possession claims are issued under CPR r.55 and CPR r.55.3(5), PDA 55 para.1.5 and CPR PD 4 (Forms) provide that claim Form N5 (claim form for possession of property) must be used. Accordingly, the claim is not a CPR r.7 claim and its allocation to multi-track does not automatically bring it within the costs management regime. However, the court may still exercise its discretion under CPR PD 3E ordering parties to file and exchange budgets, but this will be by a specific order to that effect. Obviously, if the court orders the claim to proceed as a CPR r.7 claim, allocates to the multi-track and lists for a CMC then Precedents H will be required, for as a CPR r.7 claim this will be caught by CPR r.3.12.

Q10. Are claims where the claimant has a limited or severely impaired life expectation (defined as five years or less of life remaining) excluded from the costs management regime without the need for any court order to that effect?

4–32   No. These claims do not fall within the exceptions expressly set out in CPR r.3.12(1). However, CPR PD 3E para.1 states that in such claims the court will ordinarily disapply costs management. This suggests that the court is required to specify that the regime will not apply and practitioners should not simply assume that it will not apply. If there is no specific order in a case disapplying the provisions of Section II of CPR r.3, parties would be well advised either to raise this with the court before any date under CPR r.3.13(1) expires or comply by filing and exchanging budgets in accordance with that provision.

Q11. What should parties do when the notice of provisional allocation under CPR r.26.3 is to the multi-track, but one or more of them believes that the appropriate allocation is to the small claim or fast track? What should parties do when the notice of provisional allocation under CPR r.26.3 is to the small claim or fast track, but one or more of them believes that the appropriate allocation is to the multi-track?

The risk of ignoring the consequence of the provisional allocation to multi-track in claims where the statement of value of the claim is less than £50,000 and simply filing a directions questionnaire with proposed directions seeking allocation to the fast track but without a Precedent H, or, in claims with a stated value on the claim form of £50,000 or more, failing to file one 21 days before the CCMC, is that if the court concludes that the provisional allocation was appropriate, then there is a breach of CPR r.3.13 and the consequences of CPR r.3.14 apply. A more prudent approach is to file a consent application (if all parties agree that the provisional allocation is inappropriate) or an "on notice" application (if all parties do not agree that the provisional allocation is inappropriate) prior to the date for filing and exchanging costs budgets, seeking an extension of the time for so doing until a date to be fixed after determination of the appropriate track at an allocation hearing. This avoids the potentially wasted expense of producing a Precedent H if subsequently the court allocates other than to the multi-track, but means that the argument is one of extension of time for compliance under CPR r.3.13 and not relief from the sanction of CPR r.3.14 if the court maintains the provisional allocation to multi-track.

4–33

However, one of the major criticisms of the costs management regime is that there is a significant delay between the listing and hearing of a CCMC. If there is an argument on appropriate allocation the court will need to convene an allocation hearing and then, if it decides to allocate to the multi-track, at that juncture list a CCMC. The scope for delay is obvious. One way to ameliorate this without pre-determining what the decision of the court may be on allocation is to suggest that the court lists a short allocation hearing as soon as possible and, in the same request, ask it to list a separate full CCMC as soon as possible after the allocation hearing (allowing time for Precedents H to be filed and exchanged, if the outcome of the allocation hearing renders them relevant, after the allocation hearing but before the CCMC). If the allocation hearing results in allocation to the small claim or fast track, then the CCMC may be vacated. If the allocation hearing results in allocation to the multi-track, there will only be a short delay between this decision and the CCMC. This may be easier to arrange in some courts than others (as quite often the time can be backed or there is always box work so the vacation of a CCMC does not result in a disproportionate waste of court time). Certainly, some courts are already adopting this approach in this situation.

What of the reverse situation, where the provisional allocation is to small claim or fast track, but one or more parties believes the appropriate track is actually the multi-track. This raises similar, but not the same, problems. If all parties agree that multi-track is appropriate, but the claim is for less than £50,000, the parties might still be well advised to file a consent application with the directions questionnaires (DQ) seeking an order extending time for filing and exchanging Precedents H until after the court has made an allocation decision. This may also be the sensible approach by any party seeking allocation to the multi-track where this is not agreed. If the court subsequently allocates to the multi-track, there can be no criticism, then, that the party/ies seeking this ought to have filed and exchanged Precedent H with its/their DQ. The court can then resolve allocation on paper (with any party disagreeing having the right to apply to vary this) or list for an allocation hearing (with any application to extend the time for filing and exchange of budgets listed at the same time). If the court allocates to the fast track, whilst the costs of an application may have been wasted, these will be far less than the costs expended upon the purposeless preparation of Precedent H. Again, the party/ies seeking allocation to the multi-track might wish to encourage the court to list a separate full CCMC as soon as possible after the allocation hearing, before waiting for the outcome of that hearing (allowing time for Precedents H to be filed and exchanged and for Precedents R to be filed, if the outcome of the allocation hearing renders them relevant, after the allocation hearing but before the CCMC), so that if allocation is to the multi-track, delay post allocation before the CCMC is reduced.

Q12. Does the fact that a party has a contractual right to indemnity costs against the other party mean costs management is not applicable or pointless because the claimant has a contractual right to claim costs under *Gomba Holdings (UK) Ltd v Minories Finance Ltd (No.2)*?[86] Does a lender arguing that it does not need to file a costs budget as, in the event that it is successful and the charge is upheld, there is a clause in the charge relating to an indemnity for costs need to request permission from the court not to file a cost budget?

4-34 Whilst the position of the contractual costs of a mortgagee may be somewhat different from those parties holding contractual rights to costs in other situations, these questions seem directed to those cases where, in one form or another, there is a contractual right to costs on an indemnity basis between the parties in favour of one party, which is known about at the time that costs management would ordinarily arise.

The position is really a matter for the court. Whilst there is merit in avoiding the time and expense of budgeting by not costs managing the costs of the party who will rely upon the contractual obligation, the court still has a duty to case manage proportionately. Knowing what that party sees as the

---

[86] *Gomba Holdings (UK) Ltd v Minories Finance Ltd (No.2)* [1993] Ch. 171; [1992] 3 W.L.R. 723.

proportionate expenditure for the directions it advances will assist the court in determining the proportionate procedural approach to adopt. By so doing the court may, incidentally, reduce the costs due under the contract, as the directions proposed may not be proportionate and the effect of a different procedural route to trial may well limit what is reasonably incurred and reasonable in amount under the contractual entitlement.

However, we stress that this is a matter for the court. Unless and until an order has been made exempting a party from the costs management provisions that would otherwise apply, that party must comply. Accordingly, a party seeking to be exempted on the basis of a contractual right to indemnity costs, must apply to the court to disapply the costs management provisions and should do so before the expiry of the time for compliance (see *Hallam v Baker Estates*[87] at **Q27** below).

Q13. The Shorter Trials Scheme now under CPR PD 57AB disapplies CPR r.3.12 and the costs management regime unless the parties agree otherwise (CPR PD 57AB para.2.56). Why might parties wish to opt-in?

Ignoring the larger debate raised by this question of the merits of the costs management regime generally (and for those interested in this, Jackson LJ set out seven benefits in his "Confronting costs management" lecture in May 2015[88]), there may be case-specific reasons for departure from the general rule in the shorter trials scheme pilot. Certainly, the scheme is designed to avoid protracted disputes and ensure proportionate directions (e.g. as to disclosure, witness statements, experts, interim applications, trial, summary assessment and appeals), by robust prescribed case management and determination at various stages on paper, where appropriate. These address some of the perceived "ills" that costs management is designed to prevent and the general rule avoids the expense of the costs management exercise. However, there may still be valid reasons that parties opt for costs management. The three most significant seem to be:

4–35

- The clients may wish this to ensure that the shorter trials scheme provides "up front" certainty as to potential costs exposure.
- Linked to this, reinforcing the lack of certainty, is that no costs management exposes all the costs to the CPR r.44.3(2)(a) proportionality cross-check on summary assessment after the costs have been incurred. This may result in the receiving party recovering a lesser amount than expected as proportionality "trumps" both reasonable and necessary expenditure. In other words, whilst work may have been reasonably or necessarily incurred under a specific direction, if the total, when judged retrospectively against the relevant factors at CPR r.44.3(5) and any wider

---

[87] *Hallam Estates v Baker Ltd* [2014] EWCA Civ 661; [2014] C.P. Rep. 38.
[88] "Confronting costs management" May 2015 paras 2.2–2.12.

circumstances at CPR r.44.4(1), is deemed disproportionate, the costs will be reduced to that sum which is determined to be proportionate.

- CPR PD 57AB paras 2.57 and 2.58 require parties to file and exchange costs schedules containing "sufficient detail of the costs incurred in relation to each applicable phase identified by Precedent H to the costs budgeting regime . . .". In other words, the parties must record time by phase in any event so that they can produce this detail at the conclusion of the claim. As such the only real saving is the initial costs of budgeting and the costs of managing expenditure under the budget. In some cases, this saving may not seem proportionate when viewed against the uncertainty referred to in the two points above.

B. The time for filing and exchanging Precedent H

Q14. When is a party required only to complete page 1 of Precedent H? When considering the stated value of the claim under CPR PD 3E para.4(b), does this include interest and/or costs.

4–36 After a couple of attempts in the October 2020 amendments to the costs management provisions and then the 127th CPR Update – Practice Direction Amendments, the position is finally clear. CPR PD 3E para.4(b) provides that page 1 only is required *where a party's total costs* (incurred and estimated) in Precedent H do not exceed £25,000 or the value of the claim as stated on the claim form is less than £50,000.

The stated value of the claim does not include interest or costs claimed. CPR r.2.3(1) provides that "statement of value" is to be interpreted in accordance with CPR r.16.3, which in turn states that the claimant must disregard the possibility of awards of interest and costs when stating the value claimed in the claim form.

Q15. In respect of those cases where the value of the claim is less than £50,000 and a party fails to file and exchange Precedent H by the date set out in the CPR r.26.3(1) notice, but does file and exchange it by the extended date given in the further notice under CPR r.26.3(7A), does CPR r.3.14 apply?

4–37 Until the April 2016 amendments to the provisions of CPR r.3.13, this situation posed a procedural trap for the unwary in all multi-track claims within the costs management regime. However, that trap has now gone because:

- In those cases where the stated value on the claim form is £50,000 or more the time for filing and exchange of Precedents H is no longer linked to the time for filing directions questionnaires.
- In those claims where the statement of value of the claim is less than £50,000, the trigger for filing and exchanging budgets is the filing of the directions questionnaire and so any extension of time for filing the

directions questionnaire provides an automatic extension of time for filing of the Precedent H.

Q16. Can the parties agree to extend the times prescribed in CPR r.3.13 for the filing and exchange of Precedents H by using CPR r.3.8(4)?
It is essential to look at the two "triggers" for filing and exchanging Precedents 4–38 H separately as follows:

- In respect of claims where the statement of value of the claim is less than £50,000 the position is not straightforward and produces a different outcome depending upon whether it is the notice under CPR r.26.3(1) or that under CPR r.26.3(7A) that the parties wish to vary.
  (i) CPR r.26.3(1) notice—CPR r.26.3(6A) states categorically that the time for compliance with a notice under CPR r.26.3(1) may not be varied by agreement between the parties. CPR r.3.8(4) only applies where a party is required to do something within a time specified by a rule and that rule imposes a sanction for failure to comply. In this situation there has been non-compliance with CPR r.26.3(1) and the sanction is imposed by CPR r.26.3(7A). Is the rule CPR r.26.3 and are 3(1) and 3(7A) sub-rules within it? The answer seems to be yes. Although there is no definition of "rule" in the CPR, when it refers to a rule it seems to do so to, for example, all of CPR r.26.3. However, does the provision permitting agreement under CPR r.3.8(4) take precedence over the bar to agreement in CPR r.26.3(6A)? The answer is that specific rules take precedence over general rules. CPR r.26.3(6A) is a specific rule and CPR r.3.8(4) is a general rule. As such it would seem that the period cannot be extended by agreement and that CPR r.3.8(4) does not apply to the time for compliance with CPR r.26.3(1).
  (ii) CPR r.26.3(7A) notice—CPR r.26.3 contains no bar to an extension of the time provided under CPR r.26.3(7A) and, therefore, it seems to fall squarely within the provisions of CPR r.3.8(3) and (4) and the parties may agree to an extension. However, parties so doing would be well advised to notify the court as otherwise the court may well respond to any subsequently filed directions questionnaires and Precedents H with a letter saying that the claim, defence and any counterclaim have been struck out. Parties should also note that CPR r.26.3(7A) is only engaged when the claim is one for money (whether specified or unspecified) in the County Court – see CPR r.26.2A(1).
- In respect of claims where the statement of value of the claim is £50,000 or more where the trigger for filing and exchanging is 21 days before the first CCMC, a sanction is applied by CPR r.3.14 and so CPR r.3.8(3) and (4) do apply. However, this is qualified by CPR r.29.5. Whilst it is arguable that at this stage the claim may not have been formally allocated (as opposed to a provisional allocation), the reality is that court approval will

be required if the variation that the parties agree impacts upon the date fixed for the CCMC (CPR r.29.5(1)(a)). Parties should also be astute to the fact that the ability to agree a variation of the time for Precedents H is also constrained by the provision at CPR r.3.13(2) to file a "budget discussion report" seven days before the CCMC.

Q17. Does filing by email satisfy the requirement in CPR r.3.13 to file a budget?

4–39   CPR r.5.5, and by direct reference, CPR PD 5B (Communication and Filing of Documents by E-Mail) permit filing of documents at court by email provided this is of a file type permitted under the list of specified documents in the guidance referred to at CPR PD 5B para.1.3(a).

Accordingly, in principle, a party may file Precedent H by email. However, there are some qualifications in the practice direction. CPR PD 5B para.2.2 deals with the High Court and para.2.3 deals with the County Court. The court may refuse to accept a document if a party fails to comply with the provisions in those sub-rules. CPR PD 5B paras 3, 4 and 5 impose further technical specifications and other provisions with which a party must be familiar. Given the sanction in CPR r.3.14 for late filing, it is important to note CPR PD 5B paras 4.2 and 4.3 which provide:

> "4.2 Where an e-mail, including any attachment, is sent pursuant to this practice direction and the e-mail is recorded by HMCTS e-mail software as received in court at or after 4.00pm and before or at 11.59pm—
> (a) the date of receipt of the e-mail will be deemed to be the next day the court office is open;
> . . .
> (c) any document attached to that email will be treated as filed on that date.
> 4.3 It remains the responsibility of the party sending an application or other document to the court pursuant to this practice direction to ensure that it is received or filed within the applicable time limits, taking into account the operation of this practice direction."

In addition, CPR PD 5B does not apply to those cases:

- In the "Electronic Working Pilot Scheme", originally running for two years from November 2015, but currently extended until 6 April 2023. These cases are covered by the provisions of CPR r.51 PDO, which takes precedence where it conflicts with the provisions of CPR PD 5B.
- Started under Money Claims online if the claim has not been sent to a County Court hearing centre.
- Issued or transferred to those courts listed at CPR PD 5B para.1.2(a).

Q18. If a CPR r.7 claim seeks non-monetary relief when must Precedent H be filed and exchanged (in other words which of the provisions in CPR r.3.13 applies)? If a CPR r.7 claim seeks non-monetary relief and the total

costs (incurred and estimated) exceed £25,000 should page 1 only or a full Precedent H be filed and exchanged?
Under CPR r.3.13 whether Precedent H must be filed and exchanged with the directions questionnaire or 21 days before the first case management conference depends upon the stated value of the claim in the claim form. However, CPR r.16.3 only requires a statement of value to be included in claims for money. Accordingly, it may be thought that there is no specific provision for the filing and exchange of Precedent H in CPR r.7 non-monetary claims. However, as non-monetary CPR r.7 claims fall within the costs management regime plainly some sense must be made of CPR r.3.13 as it applies to these claims. One interpretation is that as a non-monetary claim has a value of nil, it is, therefore, less than £50,000 and Precedent H should be filed and exchanged with the directions questionnaire. However, another, and in our view better, interpretation relies upon the express wording of CPR r.3.13(1)(a). This expressly refers not to the value of the claim, but to the stated value on the claim form. As there is no stated value on the claim form in non-monetary claims, then, by definition, there is no statement that the value is less than £50,000. As such CPR r.3.13(1)(a) does not apply and by a process of elimination CPR r.3.13(1)(b) applies—requiring filing and exchange no later than 21 days before the first case management conference. We would hope that whichever interpretation is adopted by parties, provided that one limb of CPR r.3.13(1) is satisfied, any court taking a different view of the application of this rule to non-monetary CPR r.7 claims, will require little persuasion to grant relief from any perceived sanction under CPR r.3.14.

4–40

Our interpretation also leads to the conclusion that where a party's total costs exceed £25,000, but there is no stated value on the claim form, then the full precedent H should be filed and exchanged as there is no statement on the claim form that the value is less than £50,000. Accordingly, the neither of the triggers for completing page one only in CPR PD 3E para. 4(b) are met.

Q19. If the claim has a stated value on the claim form of less than £50,000, but there is a counterclaim of £50,000 or more, which part of CPR r.3.13 applies to the time for filing and exchanging Precedents H?
In the example given in the question the court is dealing with a counterclaim by the defendant against the claimant. In this situation CPR r.20 does not require the counterclaiming defendant to issue a claim form, instead the procedure at CPR r.20.4 applies. Accordingly, as CPR r.3.13(1)(a) expressly refers to the value of the claim on the claim form, it would seem that the value of the counterclaim does not inform the decision. The Precedents H must be filed and exchanged with the directions questionnaires.

4–41

However, the position is more challenging where a defendant makes an additional claim other than a counterclaim against an existing party or a claim for contribution/indemnity against a person who is already a party. This is because a claim form is required in those additional claims (see CPR r.20.7(2)). The key provision is CPR r.20.3(1), which specifies that such an additional claim shall be treated as if it were a claim. This means that if the additional claim is treated as a claim and has a stated value on the claim form of £50,000 or more, then the Precedents H in the additional claim fall due under CPR r.3.13(1)(b). Where does this leave the claimant and the defendant in respect of Precedents H in the original claim? As the original claim and the additional claim are separate claims, it seems that Precedents H in the original claim remain caught by the CPR r.3.13(1)(a) provision. In other words, the time for filing of Precedents H differs between the claim and the additional claim. This is a curious outcome, particularly where the issues overlap and the defendant has produced one Precedent H to cover the costs of both defence of the claim and the pursuit of the additional claim—see **Q37** below for further consideration of this situation in an additional claim.

Q20. Does the sanction in CPR r.3.14 take effect from the date by which a party was required to file its costs budget or from the date that the court makes the costs management order?

4–42   This point arose in *Ali v Channel 5 Broadcast Ltd*[89] (see para.4–16) above. The court decided that the sanction in CPR r.3.14 applied to all recoverable costs after the time of the breach (in other words, including to costs incurred between breach and the costs management order). There is support for the conclusion reached in *Ali* in a comment made by the court in *Page v RGC Restaurants Ltd*.[90] Amongst other issues confronting the court in *Page*, was the question of whether agreement of parts of a budget overrides the sanction in CPR r.3.14 (see **Q21** for consideration of this). When determining this issue, the court noted that:

> *"Once the time for filing a budget had expired, and Mr Page had not complied with that requirement, then unless and until the court ordered otherwise the only 'budgeted costs' within the meaning of CPR r.3.15 . . . were the applicable court fees."*

In other words, the court temporally linked the breach of the requirement to file a budget with the imposition of the sanction.

Whilst there is a logic to the conclusion that it is the fact of breach itself, rather than the time at which the budget becomes relevant, namely the time when the court costs manages based on a restricted budget, this interpretation raises an interesting outcome by extension—namely that the date, rather than the fact, of the breach is also irrelevant, as CPR r.3.14 refers to the budget (both incurred and estimated costs) being treated as containing applicable court fees only. This would mean that all incurred costs are also subject to the sanction. This is a challenging interpretation as the budget is filed to enable the court to manage costs "to be incurred" and the effect of a costs management order under CPR r.3.18 only applies to costs so managed under CPR

---

[89] *Ali v Channel 5 Broadcast Ltd* [2018] EWHC 840 (Ch); [2018] 2 Costs L.R. 373.
[90] *Page v RCG Restaurants Ltd* [2018] EWHC 2688 (QB); [2018] 5 Costs L.O. 545.

r.3.15(2)(a) and (b). In any event, even on the more limited sanction imposed in *Ali*, it seems curious that under a provision stated in CPR r.3.12 to have as its purpose the management of "costs to be incurred", the court cannot make a costs management order (other than by recording an agreement) in respect of incurred costs, but can retrospectively restrict their recovery. Albeit, in the context of "approved costs", CPR r.3.17(3)(a) expressly prevents the court costs managing costs before the date of any costs management hearing (save in the limited circumstances under CPR r.3.15A(6)). All CPR r.3.14 does is state that a party is treated as having filed a budget restricted to future court fees. It does not expressly confer on the court a jurisdiction, in such circumstances, to costs manage between the date of breach and the date of the costs management conference. It was said in *Ali* that it would undermine the purpose of CPR r.3.14 if it had no effect on costs between the date of breach and the date of costs management. It may be that the amendment to CPR PD 3E 7.4, which is repeated in CPR r.3.17(3) expressly to exclude from those costs that may be budgeted by approval, those costs incurred before the date of any costs management hearing, removes the concern of undermining the purpose of CPR r.3.14, as restricting the sanction to the costs after the costs management hearing sits squarely with the clearly defined scope of the court's costs management powers at the CCMC.

Q21. Does the sanction in CPR r.3.14 apply even to those phases of the budget agreed by the other party?

In *Page v RGC Restaurants* (see **Q20** above), the court considered this question. In this case the claimant was found to have filed and served an incomplete budget and the court concluded that the sanction in CPR r.3.14 applied. However, following the service of the incomplete budget and prior to the court finding this to be a breach of CPR r.3.13 (a point taken by the Master at the CMC and not by the parties), and, therefore, engaging CPR r.3.14, the defendant had agreed certain phases of the claimant's budget. The question for the court was whether CPR r.3.14 overrode a contractual agreement and the provisions of CPR r.3.15(2)(a). The claimant argued that CPR r.3.14 was designed to protect the other parties and that it contained nothing to enable the court to override an agreement between the parties subsequent to the breach. The defendant submitted that nothing in the rules stated CPR r.3.14 could be displaced by agreement. The court concurred with the defendant stating:

4–43

"... on the ordinary use of language CPR r.3.15(2)(a) is not engaged once CPR r.3.14 has taken effect. Once the time for filing a budget had expired, ... then unless and until the court ordered otherwise the only 'budgeted costs' within the meaning of CPR r.3.15 ... were the applicable court fees. ... The sanction in CPR r.3.14 is so important that disapplication of the sanction should not automatically result from the mere fact that figures are agreed. In these circumstances I am not persuaded [by the] contention that CPR r.3.15 trumps CPR r.3.14. I do not accept that the negotiations between the parties resulted in a contract. But even

if they had resulted in a contract, it seems to me that a contract made for costs management purposes must give way to overriding provisions in relevant rules, practice directions and orders. Nevertheless, I recognise that the costs management provisions create a tension between the importance, in the public interest, of forcing parties to grapple with potential costs consequences on the one hand, and principles of freedom of contract on the other under which parties should, unless the costs management provisions require otherwise, be able to reach agreement as to costs consequences."

However, the court left open an argument as to whether, once the sanction in CPR r.3.14 had taken effect, an agreement between the parties could override that provision, stating:

". . . in circumstances where the parties are aware that the sanction in CPR r.3.14 has taken effect, but nevertheless reach a new agreement intended to supersede that sanction, then it might be arguable that under CPR r.3.18 on assessment the court is to have regard to the new agreed budget in place of the deemed budget under CPR r.3.14. The argument is not straightforward, however, and as it does not arise in the present case I do not think it is desirable to say more about it."

Q22. Does CPR r.3.14 apply to any failure to file a costs budget? Where the court has costs managed by stages and has fixed a further CCMC, when must the parties file and exchange updated Precedents H? Is an application required for relief or can a party subject to the sanction within CPR r.3.14 ask the court to "order otherwise" at the CCMC?

4–44   A strict interpretation of CPR r.3.14 reveals that it applies to failure to comply with any requirement to file a budget and not just to the preliminary requirement to do so under CPR r.3.13—"Unless the court otherwise orders, any party which fails to file a budget despite being required to do so . . ." Accordingly, any procedural requirement or order of the court for the filing of a costs budget carries the sanction of CPR r.3.14 (However, see **Q67** below for consideration of whether this is correct in respect of the requirement to re-file a budget after a costs management order under CPR r.3.15(7)). The practical outcome where this occurs before any costs management order has been made is simple—the defaulting party is limited in the terms of CPR r.3.14. However, what if the failure arises after a costs management order has been made e.g. where the court is costs managing by stage, where the court orders amended budgets to determine the effect on proportionality of any proposed further direction or after there is a discontinuance or admission of part of the claim and the costs will reduce?

This presents a number of options and to date there is no guidance on this. The options are:

- The sanction applies only to all costs from the date of the breach—so any budgets set are varied to reduce them from the date of breach to future court fees only. However, this may be a complicated exercise when the breach arises in mid stage of many of the phases and there will need to be agreement or assessment of how much of the permitted budget had been spent at the time of default. This increases the likelihood of detailed assessment—defeating one objective of costs management. In addition, this has the effect of "varying" a previous order, as applying the sanction to future costs, means that any budget the court may have already set for those phases is reduced.

- The sanction applies only to the costs directly linked to the significant variation in the litigation. This is simple if the development would ordinarily lead to increased budgets. The defaulting party's budget is only increased by any further and additional court fees. However, this approach does not work where the significant development should result in a reduction in costs—not only because there are unlikely to be any further court fees, but, more importantly, because the purpose of the amended budgets was to enable the court to revise budgets downwards in the light of the development that alters the reasonableness and pro-portionality assessment going forward anyway. Accordingly, the failure to file the budget leads to no sanction as the outcome should be the same as if the party had filed a reduced budget removing these costs anyway (albeit that the court is deprived of the clear information to make this decision).
- The sanction applies retrospectively and the previously set budgets are void. This sanction would appear to breach the provisions of CPR r.3.12 and CPR r.3.15 that costs management can only be of costs "to be incurred".

On balance, the first option appears both the most logical and the one that seems to fit the closest with the costs management mechanism, but higher court authority appears inevitable at some stage.

For consideration of whether a party subject to the sanction of CPR r.3.14 may seek variation of its budget under CPR r.3.15A see **Q81**, which also sug-gests that the sanction of CPR r.3.14 is limited to the specific failure to file a budget and not to earlier or later requirements to file budgets/amended budgets.

Note that CPR r.3.14 expressly applies to a failure to file and not to a failure to exchange a cost budget.

Turning to the second question, where the court has ordered updated budgets, it would be usual for the court to include specific directions as CPR r.3.13 does not apply in this situation. Normally, time permitting, we would expect an order that follows the provisions of CPR r.3.13(1)(b) and (c), namely that Precedents H are filed and exchanged 21 days before the further CCMC and Precedents R must be filed no later than seven days before the restored CCMC. If the order listing the further CCMC is silent on times for filing and exchanging both Precedents H and R (and this would be surprising as it sug-gests that the court, and, if it was an order made at a hearing, the parties, overlooked this fundamental requirement), then the parties may agree these, but in default of agreement may wish to apply to the court for a timetable or, as a last resort, choose to adopt the timings in CPR r.3.13(1)(b) and (c). The order for updated budgets arguably engages CPR r.3.14 even though it does not prescribe a date, as it fixes the further CCMC, so it is clear that the court anticipates the budgets being available for that hearing, for it to be purposeful. In other words, the one absolute in this unusual (and unlikely) scenario is that budgets must be filed and exchanged before the further CCMC.

If a party has fallen foul of CPR r.3.14 and wishes the court to grant relief from its sanction, then a timeous application for relief is the sensible and recommended route. However, in *Manchester Shipping Ltd v Balfour Shipping Ltd*[91] the court concluded that whilst such an approach would be well advised in certain cases, it is not so in others (in this case there was an imminent case management conference and the defaulting party indicated that it would raise the issue at that hearing, rather than by specific application. The court referred to the commentary at para.3.14.2 of the White Book which states:

> "*A party in default of r.3.14 need not make a separate application for relief from sanctions under r.3.9. Instead, it may seek to invoke the saving provision in r.3.14 itself ('Unless the court otherwise orders') by seeking to persuade the court to adopt that course at the hearing convened for costs management purposes.*"

Q23. CPR r.3.13(1)(b) refers to Precedent H being filed and exchanged no later than 21 days before the first case management conference. How is that time period calculated? If the first case management conference is listed for 30 July 2021, by what date must Precedent H be filed and exchanged?

4–45 The April 2013 amendments to the CPR did not alter the relevant provision for the calculation of time. That is found at CPR r.2.8(2), which provides:

> "*2.8*
>
> (1) *This rule shows how to calculate any period of time for doing any act which is specified—*
>   (a) *by these Rules;*
>   (b) *by a practice direction; or*
>   (c) *by a judgment or order of the court.*
> (2) *A period of time expressed as a number of days shall be computed as clear days.*
> (3) *In this rule 'clear days' means that in computing the number of days—*
>   (a) *the day on which the period begins; and*
>   (b) *if the end of the period is defined by reference to an event, the day on which that event occurs are not included.*"

---

[91] *Manchester Shipping Ltd v Balfour Shipping Ltd* [2020] EWHC 164 (Comm).

This rule continues to provide some examples. However, perhaps the easiest way to answer this question is by the specific example given in the second part of the question. If one assumes that CPR r.3.13(1)(b) applies and the first case management conference is listed for Friday 30 July 2021, then the last date for filing and exchanging budgets is Thursday 8 July 2021. Neither 8 July nor 30 July are counted, but there are 21 intervening (clear) days.

Remember that CPR r.2.8(5) specifies that if the last date for doing any act at the court office is a day upon which the court is closed that act shall be done in time if done on the next day upon which the court office is open. Accordingly, if the last date for filing the budget is a Saturday, Sunday or another day when the court is closed, there will still be compliance if it is filed the next day that the court is open. However, this saving provision in CPR r.2.8(5) only applies to acts to be done at the court office and does not apply to service. The prudent will wish to avoid any potential problems by ensuring that in such a situation the budget is both filed and served before the weekend or other day on which the court is closed.

C. The content of Precedent H

Q24. Does the budget have to be on Precedent H or can parties produce their own forms provided that they recognisably contain the same information?
CPR PD 3E is clear: a budget must be in the form of Precedent H annexed   4–46
to CPR PD 3E unless the court otherwise orders. This degree of prescription contrasts with the more flexible language adopted by the CPR when "suggesting" the use of a particular Form e.g. in CPR PD 44 para.9.5(3) "The statement of costs should follow as closely as possible Form N260." This interpretation is supported by the fact that CPR PD 3E para.4(b) refers expressly to P.1 of Precedent H when considering budgeted costs not exceeding £25,000 or where the statement of value is below £50,000. Note also that the same PD provision requires the Precedent H to be in landscape format and an easily legible typeface. A final and more general point on this topic, is that experience shows that even when use of a particular form is recommended, but not mandatory, problems often arise for those who devise and use their own version. Unless there is a very good reason, counsel of caution is to adopt the recommended version of a form—this avoids the risk of omitting an essential piece of information.

Q25. How does Precedent H accommodate the fact that hourly rates will increase during a claim? Should parties insert blended rates to reflect the average hourly estimated for each fee earner for each phase of the work (e.g. if it is estimated 10 hours work will be done at £200 per hour, 10 hours at £225 per hour and 10 hours at £250 per hour, should 30 hours be inserted at £225 per hour)? Given that Precedent H makes a clear distinction in the disbursements section of each phase between the fees of

leading and junior counsel, does this mean that a party is constrained to use the level of counsel identified in Precedent H once the budget is set?

4–47 These linked questions all arise because of the format of Precedent H, in that:

- although the court is not charged with setting the budget for the phases by an exercise of hourly rate multiplied by time, the completion of the spreadsheet effectively operates in this way;
- the spreadsheet limits the opportunities to insert hourly rate and so it is difficult to insert the specific hourly rate envisaged for certain aspects of work, where, during the life of a claim the fee earner rates are expected to increase.
- precedent H distinguishes between leading and junior counsel.

Hourly rates

As the budget is not set by a calculation of hourly rate multiplied by time (see **Qs 59–62** below and *Yirenkyi v Ministry of Defence*[92]), there is a compelling argument that Precedent H should be amended to remove these elements and the form should simply give a global sum that the party completing it suggests is reasonable and proportionate for each phase. For those cases that currently require more than completion of p.1 of the form, the court would still benefit from the disbursement breakdown and the assumptions upon which the figures are based. There is a clear logic to this as the court does not micromanage how the budget that is agreed or approved is spent—that is for the parties and their legal representatives to determine—instead, it simply sets a total sum per phase. If Precedent H was so amended, then this problem arising from insertion of hourly rate would be removed.

However, on the basis that the format of Precedent H does require an exercise in hourly rate multiplied by time in its preparation, the issue of rates altering within the duration of a claim is a very real one. Obviously, it only arises in respect of "estimated costs" as "incurred costs" are inserted by way of a lump sum, following a calculation using whatever hourly rates have been charged on each item of work incurred to reach one overall total. So far as "estimated costs" are concerned, this was a point that was considered by Master Rowley in the SCCO in *Tucker v Griffiths*[93] (which was considered, but distinguished from the situation where hourly rates higher than those chargeable to the client had been used in calculating incurred costs in *MXX v United Lincolnshire NHS Trust*[94]). On this point he concluded:

> *"The costs that are necessarily estimated for work yet to be done can quite properly, in my view, be subject to calculation using an hourly rate which acknowledges*

---

[92] *Yirenkyi v Ministry of Defence* [2018] EWHC, 2 November (QB) Jacobs J.
[93] *Tucker v Griffiths* unreported 19 May 2017 SCCO Master Rowley.
[94] *MXX v United Lincolnshire NHS Trust* [2019] EWHC 1624 (QB); [2019] Costs L.R. 1151.

that increases upon the current hourly rate are likely to be imposed by the solicitor before the case concludes."[95]

This sits entirely happily with the certification on Precedent H in respect of estimated costs, which is, in this context, that the budget is a fair and accurate statement of estimated costs. Increases in hourly rate are envisaged and so an estimation quite properly includes them.

Another approach, avoiding a blended rate for estimated costs, is to insert the same fee earners more than once, but with different rates to reflect expected changes to hourly rate, in the hourly rate boxes and then attribute the work to be done in the phases between these different rates. If there are not sufficient boxes for this in the "Rate per hour" column, then insert new entire rows and reformat the calculation boxes across the spreadsheet to ensure that it remains self-calculating to include the totals in the new rows.

However, we remain of the view that the best approach is to remove hourly rates and time from Precedent H completely and require parties simply to insert global figures for the reasonable and proportionate estimated costs.

Counsel

The budget for a phase is not set by way of a breakdown between costs and disbursements (CPR r.3.15(8) and *Yirenkyi v Ministry of Defence*[96]), so the court should not be descending to the detail of the level of counsel to be used. In addition, it is not for the court to compel a party to use a particular level of counsel. All the court is doing by way of costs management is setting a reasonable and proportionate sum that, absent "good reason", a party will recover in the event of a costs order in their favour. If the client chooses to stay within the budget, it is entirely up to the client, no doubt in consultation with legal representatives, to decide how to spend that budget. As the budget was not set on an assumption of use of a level of counsel, but by what is the reasonable and proportionate figure by consideration of CPR r.44.3(5), r.44.4(1) and r.44.4(3), there is nothing to prevent a client who had planned to use junior counsel deciding to instruct senior counsel, or, indeed, vice versa. Of course, clients are not constrained in how much they choose to spend on a phase anyway, as that is a matter of what is agreed between the client and the solicitor and they may choose to spend more than they will recover. Accordingly, clients may decide to use leading counsel even though the costs will exceed the recoverable sum under the budget and the application of CPR r.3.18. No tactical advantage is gained by specifying in Precedent H that leading counsel will be used and then using junior counsel or vice versa, because the budget set by the court should be the same in both scenarios – namely the reasonable and proportionate sum by reference to the procedural provisions to which we have referred above.

---

[95] At [36].
[96] *Yirenkyi v Ministry of Defence* [2018] EWHC, 2 November (QB) Jacobs J.

Q26. At what stage should parties complete the section of Precedent H that quantifies the costs of the costs management exercise?

4-48 It always seemed strange that the previous Guidance Note required the costs of budgeting to be inserted in the two boxes available on p.1 of Precedent H, as soon as the final budget figure had been approved by the court. This was because those figures are, in part, based on incurred costs, which, save where a costs management order has been made by agreement under CPR r.3.15(2)(c) have been neither agreed nor assessed. The figures are, therefore, far from certain immediately after costs budgeting. This anomaly was removed in the October 2020 revision to the CPR r.3 Section II and its PD, 3E. Under CPR PD 3E para.8, the figures to be inserted in the two boxes after the court has approved the costs budget, are now described as the "maximum figures", acknowledging that ultimate recovery may be a lesser sum. It remains a curiosity that this provision only applies to "approved" costs budgets. Why should the figures not be inserted when all or parts of the costs budget are agreed? In any event the actual figure that is recoverable cannot be calculated until the incurred costs are quantified, by subsequent assessment or by agreement.

That quantification process is now found at CPR r.3.15(5), which provides as follows:

"(5) Save in exceptional circumstances—
(a) *the recoverable costs of initially completing Precedent H (the form to be used for a costs budget) shall not exceed the higher of—*
    (i) *£1,000; or*
    (ii) *1% of the total of the incurred costs (as agreed or allowed on assessment) and the budgeted costs (agreed or approved); and*
(b) *all other recoverable costs of the budgeting and costs management process shall not exceed 2% of the total of the incurred costs (as agreed or allowed on assessment) and the budgeted (agreed or approved) costs".*

Framing the calculation in this way may act as an incentive to continue to assessment where the percentage may be a not inconsiderable sum. Even in those cases where the initial cap of £1,000 applies and there are no other recoverable costs attributable to the budgeting and costs management process, it is worth remembering that this is not a fixed fee. However, given the amount, even in the event of an argument that it should be less than the cap, this alone is unlikely to result in a detailed assessment.

Q27. Should a party file its Precedent H on the basis of the way in which it thinks the claim should progress, e.g. if it thinks a split trial is appropriate should the budget be completed on that basis? If the parties disagree upon the directions required in a claim, how is this reflected in their Precedents H to enable the court to make an informed decision and to be able to budget appropriately?

4-49 CPR r.3.13(4) is clear on this. The court may direct that budgets are limited initially to part of the proceedings and subsequently extended to cover the whole of proceedings. Accordingly, unless the court has so directed, the budget must cover the whole proceedings. This means that any party which proposes to seek costs management of part only of the proceedings has two options. The first is to file and exchange a budget of the whole proceedings and then seek a direction before the case management conference that budgets are filed and exchanged on the additional alternative basis. The second is to apply before the time expires for budgets to be filed and exchanged under CPR r.3.13 for an extension of time to file budgets and for a direction that budgets should be limited initially to a discrete part of the proceedings.

The advantage of the first approach is that the party has complied with CPR r.3.13 and does not face sanction under CPR r.3.14. The disadvantage is that if the court agrees that the claim proceeds with budgeting of part only, then the parties may have incurred the cost of preparing two budgets instead of one.

The advantage of the second approach is that if the court agrees with it, then one or both parties may have saved the cost of preparing two budgets at this stage. The disadvantage is that whilst a prospective application will be treated as one for an extension of time and not as one involving relief from sanctions (see *Hallam Estates v Baker*),[97] in this age of robust case management, it is a brave course to adopt.[98] This is particularly so following the decision of the Court of Appeal in *Jalla v Shell International Trading and Shipping Co. Ltd*[99], in which the Court of Appeal concluded that there would be cases where although the relief from sanction regime is not directly applicable (there being no breach of an unless order), the application of the general principles identified in *Denton v T H White Ltd*[100] are relevant, by analogy, when considering the overriding objective. However, there is still no doubt that this approach is better than filing and exchanging a full budget and raising the possibility of limited costs management only at the case management hearing when the court will then have difficulties deciding whether that is proportionate (without knowing the cost of so doing) and costs managing if it agrees (e.g. the court accepts that it is just and proportionate that there should be a preliminary trial on liability, but the budgets are not readily divisible between costs on liability and costs on quantum).

Interestingly, CPR PD 3E para.9 suggests that the trial of a preliminary issue may be dealt with as a contingency in the budget. In practical terms it is hard to see how this could be done in an informative way, as to do so would have the court budgeting one figure under one contingency phase for all the work to be incurred to the end of the preliminary point, rather than by the identified phases in Precedent H. As such it would be difficult, if not impossible, for the court to determine the proportionality by phases

---

[97] *Hallam Estates v Baker Ltd* [2014] EWCA Civ 661; [2014] C.P. Rep. 38.
[98] The answer to this point was cited to the court in *Page v RCG Restaurants Ltd* [2018] EWHC 2688 (QB) (see Qs 20 and 21 above). Walker J commented at [123] that the answer given was consistent with his conclusion on the question of whether an incomplete budget satisfied the requirement in CPR PD 3E para.6(a).
[99] *Jalla v Shell International Trading and Shipping Co. Ltd* [2021] EWCA Civ 1559.
[100] *Denton v T H White Ltd* [2014] [EWCA Civ 906.

to enable it to manage the steps to be incurred in the preliminary issue proportionately.

Some courts may want to see three budgets to enable a decision to be made as to whether it is just and proportionate to order a split trial as follows:

- A budget for the whole proceedings without a split trial.
- A budget for the costs of the preliminary issue.
- A budget for the costs of the remainder of the proceedings if a split trial is ordered, but the preliminary issue does not dispose of the proceedings.

CPR PD 3E para.9 also includes a new provision within the costs management regime. It governs how parties approach the costs associated with a particular direction sought, but which is disputed. The provision specifies that:

"Costs which are disputed (such as the need for a particular expert) should be set out in the appropriate phase of the budget and if necessary marked as disputed."

However, there is a practical concern with this provision. The court remains charged with budgeting a phase by a total sum that is within the bracket of what is reasonable and proportionate, rather than by an exercise of time multiplied by rate (for that is the territory of an assessment and micro-management). If the costs attributable to a disputed direction are subsumed within a phase, rather than clearly identifiable within a discrete contingency, how is each party and the court to know how much of the overall sum for a phase relates to this direction? Take the example given of an expert. What if the budget is prepared on the basis of a direction sought for two experts, but the use of only one is agreed and, subsequently, permitted by the court? How does the court know what the estimated costs are for one expert only? It is easy, in this situation, to identify the actual disbursement sum, but the costs are an unspecified amount of the overall costs of the phase. Whilst PD 3E para.9 concludes this provision with the words "and if necessary marked as disputed" what does this mean? Ideally, it will be taken to mean that, save where the disputed direction generates the entirety of the costs for a phase, the assumptions box for the relevant phase must identify both the dispute and how much of the estimated disbursements and costs respectively relate to this dispute.

Q28. Does the introduction of the electronic bill of costs and forms of time recording to enable this to be used to record all work against the discrete phases, lead to Precedent H being completed to include all costs— including those of a solicitor-client nature? Does a costs management order apply to solicitor-client costs?

4–50   The answer is "no" to both questions. The court has no role in budgeting solicitor and client costs—those remain a matter of contractual retainer. J-Codes and other time recording against phase systems should enable representatives to record time against the specific phases of the Precedent H and should simplify both the production of Precedent H and the management of any budget set by a costs management order. So far as the court is concerned the use of this method of time recording ought to enable easier comparison of the budgeted costs and the sum spent on each phase budgeted if there is a challenge on any subsequent assessment in respect of a breach of the indemnity principle in connection with any budgeted costs. It also enables ready comparison of time recorded as against the non-budgeted incurred costs set out in the bill at later assessments. This is relevant as the court may have set budgeted costs for a phase predicated by the incurred costs taking account of CPR r.3.17(3)(b). If it transpires that the incurred costs were understated in the budget, then that might be a "good reason" to depart from the budgeted costs (e.g. by specific reference to incurred costs of £4,000 for a phase, the court has budgeted the estimated costs at £3,000. Had the court known that in fact the incurred costs were £6,000 it might have only budgeted the estimated costs at £1,000, having taken the view that £7,000 was the overall reasonable and proportionate sum for the entirety of that phase).

This type of time recording should also make it easier for a party to identify the costs attributable to any free-standing application that falls outside a budget under CPR r.3.17(4).

The electronic bill became mandatory for all costs incurred in CPR r.7 claims, with limited exceptions, after 6 April 2018 (see **Ch.8** at para.8–08 for more detail).

In respect of the second question, the effect of a costs management order may impact on solicitor-client costs, but that depends entirely on how the retainer is drafted and is a consequence, rather than the purpose, of costs management. (See **Ch.9** for more detailed consideration of solicitor-client costs).

Q29. Do the costs allocated to contingencies count when determining whether budgeted costs exceed £25,000[101] and, in consequence, in determining whether only p.1 of the Precedent H needs to be completed?
As the budget must be in the format of Precedent H and that form includes   4–51
contingencies and, as any contingencies that the court includes in the costs management order it makes plainly form part of the budget, it follows that the sums included by parties as contingencies in Precedent H count towards the total budgeted costs and even if, absent these, the budgeted costs would not exceed £25,000, the full Precedent H must be completed.

Q30. Should applications to enforce compliance with case management decisions be included in the contingency section of Precedent H?
The instinctive answer is that such applications should not be in the budget   4–52
at all. The reason is simple. The court makes orders with which the parties are required to comply. To include as a contingency an application to enforce

---

[101] See **Q14** for consideration of this figure.

compliance means, following CPR PD 3E para.9 of the Guidance Notes on Precedent H, that a party believes that such an application is more likely than not. In other words, anyone including such a contingency is, in effect, saying to the court that, on the balance of probabilities, its orders will be breached. One might expect the court to respond that an order of the court is an order of the court with which there should be compliance and it is not prepared to countenance non-compliance. However, in *Group Seven Ltd v Nasir*[102] the court indicated that it:

> *"would be prepared to allow . . . sums for contingencies to reflect the possibility that there will be procedural difficulties which might be attributable to a lack of cooperation from some of the defendants".*

It should be noted, though, that this comment was made against a backdrop of alleged procedural difficulties and delay that had already been encountered. In essence, therefore, the court could, quite properly apply the para.6 test and conclude that future problems were more likely than not. In most cases this is unlikely to be the case and an anticipatory budget for applications to address breach of orders will be exception and not the "norm".

On a practical level there is a sound reason not to include the possibility of these applications as a contingency. It is that the parties (and therefore the court) does not know how many applications may be required, making it challenging to budget a reasonable and proportionate sum—opening up the possibility, uncertainty and expense of interim applications to vary or arguments on assessment on "good reason". This difficulty is avoided if these applications are not included as contingencies and instead, if and when they arise, are dealt with under CPR r.3.17(4) as freestanding applications outside and additional to the budget.

Q31. How detailed should be the assumptions upon which the budget is based?

4–53   The length of assumptions accompanying Precedent H has been an acknowledged area of contention since inception of the costs management regime. The minutes of the July 2015 meeting of the Civil Procedure Rules Committee revealed that "An attempt should be made to limit the amount of detail provided by way of schedules of assumptions". The result was the clearer steer to proportionality in the then revised Precedent H guidelines, which stated unambiguously that "brief details only are required in the box beneath each phase". This wording now appears in CPR PD 3E para.10. Remember that the court is also likely to have both the directions questionnaire and draft directions from all parties, which should serve to reinforce assumptions under which the parties propose to progress the claim. What is clear is that attached breakdowns of costs that render the Precedent H far more akin to a bill for a prospective detailed assessment are clearly contrary to requirements and

---

[102] *Group Seven Ltd v Nasir* [2016] EWHC 620 (Ch); [2016] 2 Costs L.O. 303.

should be things of the past. The October 2020 revisions to the costs management regime made this even clearer with CPR PD 3E para.10 warning that "additional documents should only be prepared in exceptional circumstances". This same provision concludes with a stark health warning, that if the additional document is disregarded by the court then the cost of its preparation may be disallowed (as this must be a cost of initially completing Precedent H, then this must be when considering the costs provided for by CPR r.3.15(5).

Q32. Is the fact that the assumptions area under pre-action costs is greyed out an indication that it should not be completed, notwithstanding that assumptions for this phase are still contained in the table after para.10 in CPR PD 3E?
Whilst CPR PD 3E refers to assumptions, the table after para.10 merely iden-   **4–54** tifies where, within Precedent H, various items of work should appear. This is reinforced by CPR PD 3E para.6, which introduces the table. There is no express requirement to include assumptions in the Pre-Action phase. As a result, there seems no contradiction between the table and the format of Precedent H.

However, there may be cases where a party may wish to provide some form of explanation for the costs incurred in the Pre-Action phase. In **Ch.3 Q4** at para.**3–10** we have considered the situation where the conduct of another party has caused greater costs to be incurred than might otherwise be expected in a particular case. As incurred costs will inform the budgeted costs under CPR r.3.17(3)(b) the party whose costs have been so increased may want to explain this to the court. If the increase arises in the Pre-Action phase, then this may be one of the few occasions where a party files an additional document with the Precedent H to explain this.

Q33. Do parties who are required to file and exchange budgets using only page 1 of Precedent H (i.e. claims where the costs do not exceed £25,000— see Q18 above for further consideration of the meaning of this—or the value of the claim as stated on the claim form is less than £50,000) need to provide assumptions upon which the budget is based? If assumptions are required in these cases where should they be inserted in Precedent H? If not required, how will the court know the basis upon which the budget is predicated?
CPR PD 3E para.10(b) is clear. Written assumptions are not normally required   **4–55** by the court in these cases. It is for this reason that the short form Precedent H does not provide any room for the insertion of assumptions. However, there appears to be a tension between CPR PD 3E para.4(b), which makes it mandatory in this situation for parties to use p.1 only, and the insertion of the word "normally" in the Practice Direction, which suggests that parties may be asked to provide the assumptions in cases "out of the norm". Perhaps the tension is eased by an interpretation that recognises that the para.4(b) requirement is

one imposed on the parties, but para.10(b) is a requirement imposed by the court. Whilst there is no specific reference in Section II of CPR r.3 to the court having jurisdiction to make an order that a party must file a "full" budget, where the PD only requires use of p.1, there is certainly an argument that the court could make such an order under either CPR r.3.1(2)(ll) or (m) which provide that the court may:

> *"(ll) order any party to file and exchange a costs budget;*
> *(m) take any other step or make any other order for the purpose of managing the case and furthering the overriding objective . . ."*

If the court does make an order requiring assumptions, where, then, should those be inserted? Assuming that the order of the court does not require a "full" budget, but simply that assumptions are provided, there is no reason why the court cannot order that these are filed and exchanged as a separate document. Parties should still be astute to CPR PD 3E para 10(a) indicating the detail required.

If no assumptions are ordered the court should still have a clear idea of the basis upon which budgets are based from the information provided in parties' directions questionnaires, the draft directions filed, any disclosure report, accompanied by any electronic documents questionnaire and CPR r.35.4 information relating to permission for any expert evidence.

Q34. If work has already been undertaken on an interim application at the time that Precedent H must be prepared, should this work be reflected in the budget, and, if so, where? If an application has been disposed of by the court before preparation of Precedents H should these costs appear in the budget, and, if so, in which phase?

4–56 CPR PD 3E refers to the table that appears after para.10. This table identifies what type of work should appear under which phase in a budget. However, as considered in para.**4–17** above the table contains a few curiosities. There are also some omissions and the first question highlights one of them. Although one might consider that it is challenging to describe as a contingency something that has already happened (i.e. a decision has already been made to make an application and costs have been incurred consequent upon that decision), it seems that the CPR PD 3E para.9 leads to that conclusion. This provides that:

> *"The 'contingent cost' sections of this form should be used for anticipated costs which do not fall within the main categories set out in this form. Examples might be the trial of preliminary issues, applications to amend, applications for disclosure against third parties or (in libel cases) applications re meaning. Costs which are disputed (such as the need for a particular expert) should be set out in the appropriate phase of the budget and if necessary marked as disputed. Only costs which are more likely than not to be incurred should be included."*

Application of this guidance leads to the following conclusions:

- Costs associated with the application are anticipated (whilst some have been incurred, some remain to be incurred).
- Costs associated with the application are more likely than not to be incurred (again, some have already been incurred, giving a clear steer that more will be).
- This application does not fall into another section of Precedent H.

This, in turn, appears to lead, inexorably, to the conclusion that this application sits firmly within the contingent cost sections of Precedent H.

The only alternative is that the application comes within CPR r.3.17(4), namely that it is an interim application which is not reasonably included in the budget and so the costs will be dealt with outside of and additional to the budget. Many have viewed this provision and its predecessor (previously para.7.9 of PD 3E) as referring to applications that were made after the budget has been prepared and which were neither anticipated nor more likely than not to occur at that time. For this provision to assist "If interim applications are made which reasonably, were not included in a budget . . ." would have to be interpreted to extend to non-inclusion on the basis that there is nowhere for them to appear in the budget.

Assuming that such an application does fall within the contingent cost sections, then as of April 2016, a further problem arises. Until the April 2016 amendment to Precedent H, there was an incurred column in the contingent cost sections. This is no longer the case and the contingent cost sections permit entry of detail only in respect of estimated costs. Where should the "incurred costs" appear? There is no ready answer to this. However, it is essential that the court has the "incurred" and "estimated" information separately so that it (a) may use the "incurred" information under CPR r.3.17(3)(b) to inform what "estimated costs" it budgets and (b) knows what the "estimated costs" are, to ensure that it does not inadvertently budget the entire phase (both incurred and estimated). One solution, and it is accepted that this does not sit happily with CPR PD 3E para.4(a), is to put both incurred and estimated costs in the estimated costs section of the phase but in the assumptions under the phase explain this and provide the breakdown between incurred and estimated. At least this way the court has all the information that it needs to budget the phase properly (although the court must then be astute to ensure that the costs management order expressly records the budgeted estimated costs and records somewhere the incurred costs which informed this decision, so that it is clear later, particularly on any subsequent assessment, what was budgeted and what was incurred and not budgeted). However, we stress that adopting this approach means that Precedent H is not compliant with CPR PD 3E para.4(a). Accordingly, a prudent party may consider that an application pursuant to the "otherwise order" provision in PD 3E para.4(a) is necessary to avoid any possible sanction (e.g. CPR r.3.14) for non-compliance. Albeit in a different context the question of sanction is considered below at **Q35**.

Does the same position assist, when an application has been made and concluded prior to the preparation of the budget as envisaged in the second question? It is hard to describe this as in anyway contingent and this situation does not sit happily within the conclusion to the analysis of CPR PD 3E para.9 above. Assuming that "concluded" means that the costs of the application have also been determined, whether by an order in favour of one party, or by no order for costs, then our view is that these costs are left out of the budget completely. They were the costs within a discrete application that has been determined as have the costs of that application. The tabular Guidance in CPR PD 3E does not provide a home for them within Precedent H. Of course, the order on that application will be available to the court at the time of costs management, so it will be astute to the fact of the application and its outcome, which may be relevant to its consideration of CPR r.44.3(5) and wider circumstances under CPR r.44.4(1). (See **Q88** below)

Q35. The table in CPR PD 3E identifying where to insert items of work in Precedent H is brief and it is not always clear where certain items of work should be included. Is there any sanction for inserting items in what the court may regard as the wrong phase of the budget? If a party does not agree a specific direction sought by another party (e.g. the instruction of an expert in a particular discipline should it include the costs associated with such a direction as a contingency in case the court makes such an order?

4–57 The decisions in *Bank of Ireland v Philip Pank Partnership*[103] and *Americhem Europe Ltd v Rakem Ltd*[104] suggest that the court may treat insertion of items in the wrong place in the budget as irregularities rather than things that render the budget a nullity.

Obviously, parties should follow the Precedent H guidance but where it is not clear there is a real danger that the process of completing the Precedent H becomes one of form rather than substance. The document should inform the parties and the court to enable the parties to reach agreement or raise any issues of contention and to enable the court to case and costs manage properly. If it is not clear where to insert specific work and the cost incurred and to be incurred on that (such as in the first scenario in **Q34** above) surely to be purposeful the key is to ensure that wherever it is included it, and the costs attributable to it, are clearly identified, even if, as set out in **Q34** above, that means being creative. At least by so doing the expenditure is in the budget and the costs attributable to it are set out separately – assisting the court under CPR r.3.17(3), as what has already been spent informs what costs should be budgeted going forward. We repeat that a prudent party may wish to seek court permission to do this in advance of the date for filing and exchange to avoid any possibility of a sanction being imposed.

---

[103] *Bank of Ireland v Philip Pank Partnership* [2014] EWHC 284 (TCC); [2014] 2 Costs L.R. 301 Stuart-Smith J.
[104] *Americhem Europe Ltd v Rakem Ltd* [2014] EWHC 1881 (TCC); 155 Con. L.R. 80 Stuart-Smith J.

The second question is linked to the necessity of including work within the correct phase. From October 2020 CPR PD 3E para.9 contains the directive not to include "costs which are disputed" as a contingency, but in the appropriate phase of the budget. An example is given of the need for a particular expert. The wording might have been clearer. It is the underlying case management direction sought (which generates the costs), which is disputed, rather than, necessarily, the costs, for a party may object to a particular direction, but agree the costs associated with it, if the court makes such an order. However, the effect is obvious. In the example given in the question, the cost should be included in the expert phase.

However, there is also a practical concern with this amendment. The court remains charged with budgeting a phase by a total sum that is within the bracket of what is reasonable and proportionate, rather than by an exercise of time multiplied by rate (for that is the territory of an assessment and micro-management). If the costs attributable to a disputed direction are subsumed within a phase, rather than clearly identifiable within a discrete contingency, how is each party and the court to know how much of the overall sum for a phase relates to this disputed direction? Take the example given of an expert. What if the budget is prepared on the basis of a direction sought for two experts, but the use of only one is agreed and, subsequently, permitted by the court? How does the court know what the estimated costs are for one expert only? It is easy, in this situation, to identify the actual disbursement sum, but the costs are an unspecified amount of the overall costs of the phase. Whilst PD 3E para.9 concludes this provision with the words 'and if necessary marked as disputed' what does this mean? Ideally, it will be taken to mean that, save where the disputed direction generates the entirety of the costs for a phase, the assumptions box for the relevant phase must identify both the dispute and how much of the estimated disbursements and costs respectively relate to this dispute.

Q36. Is it better for a party to over-estimate costs in the budget filed and exchanged, on the basis that it is then likely to see a higher budget set and less likely to need to go back to the court asking for the budget to be varied under CPR r.3.15A? Conversely, if a party recognises that it is likely to be the paying party is underestimation better, trying to persuade the court to reduce the budgets of all parties to that level to limit the potential liability for costs or limit the work that can be undertaken, making the outcome of the claim less certain as a result?

The simple answer to the related questions above is that the parties must   4–58
complete Precedent H in a fashion that enables them to sign the statement of truth set out in CPR PD 22 para.2.2A. As is clearly set out in CPR PD 22 para.5 and, by cross-reference, CPR r.32.14, the consequence of verifying the budget by statement of truth knowing that the Precedent H does not give a fair and accurate statement of incurred and estimated costs that it would be reasonable and proportionate for the client to incur, is possible proceedings

for contempt of court. Representatives should be extremely wary of adopting "tactical budgets"—whether high or low. They ought also to be aware that as the court will form its own view of what is reasonable and proportionate, it will recognise budgets that are artificially and/or unrealistically high or low for whatever reasons (see for example [27] of the judgment in *Red and White Services Ltd v Phil Anslow Ltd*).[105]

As an aside, it is clear from the decision of Coulson J (as he then was) in *Findcharm Ltd v Churchill Group Ltd*[106] that the court will similarly not look favourably on unrealistic Precedents R (see para.4–16 above for further consideration of this case).

Q37. If a defendant brings an additional claim against a party other than the claimant, does the defendant need to produce two budgets—one for the defence of the claim and one for the pursuit of the additional claim— or will one total budget suffice? If the defendant brings a claim against a party other than the claimant, does the claimant have to exchange its budget with the additional party (and vice versa)?

4–59   There is no clear guidance on this. However, the situation did arise and was considered by Coulson J (as he then was) in *CIP Properties (AIPT) Ltd v Galliford Try Infrastructure Ltd*[107] (see **Q1** above). In that case, one of four additional parties suggested that the defendant should provide separate costs budgets for the defence of the claim and for the discrete claims against each additional party. The response of the defendant was that the costs overlapped, with some costs being common costs, and that to do separate budgets would be "unworkable, impractical and expensive". Coulson J concluded that as it was a case where it would be difficult to identify what of the overall costs would be spent on the defence and what on the additional claims, it would be unfair and disproportionate to order separate budgets. He cited with approval the judgment of Master Kaye QC in *Lotus Cars Ltd v Mechanica Solutions Inc*.[108] In multi-party litigation, the Master had concluded that:

> *". . . where the management of cases is to be treated as common and is dealt with accordingly, there is no sensible reason why the costs budgeting should always be considered separately and some good reasons why it should not".*

What seems clear is that each case is likely to be fact-specific, but that where the issues overlap inextricably then the court is unlikely to order separate budgets. (See **Q19** above for consideration of when Precedent H should be exchanged and filed in an additional claim.)

So far as the second question is concerned, CPR r.3.13(1) provides that all parties must exchange party budgets. CPR r.20.10(1) makes it clear that a

---

[105] *Red and White Services Ltd v Phil Anslow Ltd* [2018] EWHC 1699 (Ch); [2018] 4 Costs L.O. 425.
[106] *Findcharm Ltd v Churchill Group Ltd* [2017] EWHC 1108 (TCC); 172 Con. L.R. 117.
[107] *CIP Properties (AIPT) Ltd v Galliford Try Infrastructure Ltd* [2014] EWHC 3546 (TCC); [2015] 1 All E.R. (Comm) 765 Coulson J.
[108] *Lotus Cars Ltd v Mechanica Solutions Inc* [2014] EWHC 76 (QB) Master Kaye QC.

person on whom an additional claim is served becomes a party to the proceedings "if he is not a party already". As a result, the additional party becomes one of the parties for the purposes of CPR r.3.13(1) and so the claimant and the additional party must exchange budgets.

Q38. If a number of defendants are represented by the same solicitors, should separate budgets be prepared for each such defendant?
The answer to this depends upon the nature of the retainer and the claim/s   **4–60**
that is/are being brought. If these defendants have filed one common defence, then it seems both reasonable and proportionate that they should file and exchange one budget as their interests obviously coincide. Any costs incurred are in respect of all these defendants and so it is unnecessary to separate them out as any subsequent order for costs in their favour would be made in respect of them all. However, there are some claims where the same firm, but a different fee earner, represents different defendants. This is where there is no conflict of interest between these defendants, but the claims against them stand or fall on their own. A classic illustration of this is in historic industrial disease claims. The claim against each defendant is free standing, but there may be no conflict between different defendants. In such cases then clearly there should be separate budgets for each defendant as the court will need to make costs management orders identifying the agreed or approved budget for each defendant.

Q39. Should the costs of surveillance evidence be included in a budget? If not, if surveillance evidence is subsequently obtained, should applications be made under CPR r.3.15A to amend the budgets?
In *Purser v Hibbs*[109] the court concluded that a defendant should be allowed   **4–61**
to recover the costs of surveillance evidence, notwithstanding that those costs had not been included in the costs budget on the basis there was "good reason" for those costs not to have been included in the budget at all. The court noted the absence of any reference to this type of evidence in either Precedent H or the guidance upon it. The rationale for the decision was that alerting a fraudulent claimant to the possibility of covert surveillance evidence would discourage judicious use of such evidence and the court did not wish to do so. As a result, when the evidence showed the claimant to be exaggerating injuries there was "good reason" to allow recovery in excess of the budget figure. In fact, the court had already decided to award these costs on the indemnity basis, rendering their lack of inclusion in the budget of academic interest only for, as a result, the requirement for "good reason" under CPR r.3.18 did not arise on subsequent assessment anyway as it only applies to a standard basis assessment. Accordingly, the defendant would not have been constrained by the budgeted figures (see para.4–20 above). It is also arguable that the guidance and the Precedent H do cover this situation without requiring express

---

[109] *Purser v Hibbs* [2015] EWHC 1792 (QB) HHJ Moloney QC.

reference, as this type of evidence falls within both disclosure and witness statement evidence.

In any event, *Purser* only deals with half the story (this is not intended to be a criticism, because it only had to do so). The reason for this is that the court in *Purser* was determining the award of costs after the claimant accepted the defendant's CPR r.36 offer on receipt of the surveillance evidence, but outside the relevant period for acceptance. As the parties could not agree the incidence of costs, the court had to determine them under what is now CPR r.36.13(4) and (5). However, what of the situation where surveillance evidence is served, but the claim continues? The admission of the evidence is surely a significant development in the litigation pursuant to CPR r.3.15A and as a result that provision requires parties to revise budgets. At this stage there is no "secrecy" requirement—the evidence has been served. In that situation, one would expect both parties to apply for a prospective variation of budgets (regardless of the obligation to do so under CPR r.3.15A), because they want prospective approval of additional costs, rather than find themselves arguing "good reason" under CPR r.3.18 at a later date. The claimant's solicitor will want to view the evidence and take instructions, parties will want to put the evidence to experts, ask questions and review answers, counsels' views may be sought, the evidence may impact on any settlement work and it is likely to affect the trial time estimate. Accordingly, service of surveillance evidence should be accompanied (by the defendant) and swiftly followed (by the claimant) by service of revised budgets, an attempt to agree these, and, failing that, by applications to the court for variation of the budgets set. If revision is not sought it seems unlikely that the court will conclude that the costs related to surveillance after disclosure of it either fall outside the budget or that there is a "good reason" to depart from the original budget at any subsequent assessment on the standard basis as there seems no logical explanation for why parties would not seek prospective variation. This is particularly so when the service of surveillance evidence necessitates an application to the court anyway for variation of, or additional, case management directions.

How does the court approach this evidence and any costs budget variation going forward, assuming, if the evidence is served outside the time set for disclosure and witness statement evidence, that the court permits the "late" evidence by any appropriate grants of relief from sanction or retrospective extensions of time and the parties seek budget variation? This involves consideration of CPR r.1.1 (to manage cases justly and at proportionate cost), CPR r.3.17(1) (taking into account the cost of any procedural step), CPR r.3.15(3) (if a costs management order has been made the court will thereafter control the parties' budgets) and CPR r.3.15A (the court may approve, vary or disallow the proposed variations to the budget). When undertaking this exercise, the court will be astute to the fact that any previous determination of the relevant proportionality factors under CPR r.44.3(5) may require revision because this evidence may engage CPR r.44.3(5)(c) and (e)—a timely reminder that proportionality is a flexible concept and may vary during the lifetime of a claim. The court will then determine, against the proportionality factors, the extent to which it is just and proportionate to permit the evidence and, if so, the reasonable and proportionate costs that should be added to the relevant phases of the budgets.

Previously we have said that the court cannot budget those costs already incurred on surveillance evidence by the time of its disclosure. However, CPR r.3.15A(6) now permits the court to vary the budget for costs related to that variation (in this instance the use of surveillance evidence), which have been incurred prior to the order for variation, but after the costs management order. Although CPR r.3.15A(4) requires that particulars of variation must be submitted promptly, it is certainly arguable that in this context a variation is submitted promptly if the evidence is disclosed as soon as it is reasonable to do so and is accompanied by the particulars. Accordingly, this may be a situation where the retrospective budgeting period is a lengthy one. Of course, there is a cut-off as the court cannot, under CPR r.3.15A, vary the budget to include any costs expended on the surveillance prior to the costs management order.

D. Preparation for the CCMC

Q40. Some courts are asking parties to produce a composite summary enabling comparison of the parties' budgets. Is there a specified precedent form for this? If not, what format should be used for that summary?
Some courts do like to see a one-page summary of the respective budgets in all cases (the *Chancery Guide* at para.17.12 did require one but this provision has now been deleted). Others are happy simply to look at the respective pages 1 of the Precedents H for comparison, or only order such a summary in specific cases (e.g. where there are a large number of parties). As a result, a summary should not be filed routinely unless one is expressly requested by the court. Where a summary is ordered there is no prescribed precedent form within the CPR. There is also no prescribed form of order and so parties should ensure that they comply with any specific requirements for a summary in any order requesting one. If the order is simply something to the effect that:

4–62

> "*The claimant/defendant must file and serve a one-page summary of the Precedent H of all parties to enable the Court to compare budget totals for each phase*",

and is silent as to format, then provision of this information in a tabular form such as that below may be thought suitable. Contingencies have not been included as the parties' contingencies may not be the same and so there is no useful comparison to be made. If they are and there is, then these can be added (also adding to what the contingency relates). Columns can be added for each additional party. A total column is included as the court may find this informative when considering the proportionality of a particular case management direction for any given phase.

Phase	Claimant	Defendant	Total
Pre-action costs			
Issue/statements of case			
CMC			
Disclosure			
Witness statements			
Expert reports			
PTR			
Trial preparation			
Trial			
Settlement			

(See **Q41** below for consideration of other requirements imposed by some courts before the CCMC.)

Q41. A number of courts are issuing detailed directions when listing a CCMC. Are these necessary and should they be standardised? One of the directions is for a breakdown of pre-action costs. Why is this required, is provision of this automatic under the CPR and what form should it take?

4–63   This was a topic considered by Sir Rupert Jackson in his May 2015 "Confronting costs management" lecture.[110] He concluded that it ought to be possible to create a standard order, distilling the best from those orders that had emerged from the (then) two and three-quarter years' experience acquired by the judiciary. This has not taken place. What is essential is that any order is proportionate to the needs of the specific case. In many cases, a light touch only will be necessary e.g. those judges who budget and create case management orders electronically will require the Precedents H and draft directions in electronic and alterable form (and self-calculating in respect of the budgets). Even when there is a "standard order" only those parts of it pertinent to the individual case should be used. The danger of a tick box form is that there is a temptation to tick all the boxes in every case. If concerns over the costs of the costs management process are to be addressed, directions must be targeted proportionately and this demands that whilst the form of any orders used should be standardised, it should not be mandatory to issue the orders.

An order that is sometimes included when the court lists the CCMC is for a party to file and serve a breakdown of the pre-action costs. There is no procedural requirement for this within CPR r.3 Section II, which is why the court has expressly ordered it. This order is likely to be generated by what appears to be an unexpectedly, and not readily explicable, high spend in the pre-action

---

[110] "Confronting costs management", May 2015, para.8.1.

costs phase. Given that the table in CPR PD 3E requires (with the exception of settlement work) phase work undertaken pre-issue to be incorporated into Precedent H as incurred work within a discrete phase, the court will generally expect the costs in the pre-action phase to be comparatively low. If they are not, and there is no obvious reason for this, the court will want an explanation. A breakdown is a good way of obtaining this. There is no set form, unless the order specifies one. If it does not, what is required is more than simply providing a Form N260 type breakdown. The court will want to know what specific work has been done (amongst other things to ensure that no work that ought to have been costed within a phase has been included here either instead of as incurred costs in another phase, or in duplication of what also appears in the incurred element of another phase). As a result, the breakdown will require some detail and must enable the court to understand the work undertaken and the amount spent on it.

Q42. How detailed should be the summary in Precedent R of the reasons why a phase of the budget is not agreed?
The answer comes by way of a combination of the procedural provisions at **4–64** CPR PD 3E paras.11(c) and 12 and CPR r.3.15(8). The first of the three provisions mentioned could not be clearer. Precedent R "must set out a brief summary of the grounds of dispute" (our emphasis). The reference made to CPR PD 3E para.12 is simply a reminder that the court is expressly not undertaking a detailed assessment and CPR r.3.15(8) stresses that the court is not descending to the detail of setting hourly rates (and therefore is not prescribing time). Accordingly, this document must not be viewed as Points of Dispute. The document is intended to allow both the party whose budget is being commented upon and the court to understand, at a glance, which phases are contentious and why. Whilst Precedent R is in Excel format (and so the boxes will expand), it may be informative that the spreadsheet is published on only one page.

There have been a few cases where parties have used Precedent R to reply to the other party's Precedent R! Those documents have received short shrift. There is no provision in the rules permitting the filing of any formal document in reply.

Q43. If a party has failed to comply with CPR r.3.13 (either by not filing and exchanging a Precedent H at all, or by doing so outside the time provided for so doing, and the sanction in CPR r.3.14 applies, is there still a requirement for the other party to file and exchange Precedent R? If one party agrees the costs of another is it still required to file and serve a Precedent R? How does CPR r.3.13(2) apply in a case where a party is a litigant in person? Who is the "paying party" in the penultimate column of Precedent R? Does Precedent R need to be signed and, if so, by whom?
The requirement to file and exchange Precedent R is prescribed by CPR **4–65** r.3.13(2), which, for this purpose, states:

"In the event that a party files and exchanges a budget under (1) above, all other parties. . .must file an agreed budget discussion report. . ."

Here, a party to whom the CPR r.3.14 sanction applies has not filed and exchanged a budget under CPR r.3.13(1). Accordingly, the obligation on the other party to file Precedent R is not triggered. So, the answer to the first question is "no". The wording of CPR r.3.13(2) is also why there is no obligation to file a Precedent R when the other party is a litigant in person, because that party has not filed and exchanged a budget under the provisions of CPR r.3.13. Of course, if the court has ordered a Precedent H to be filed and exchanged by a litigant in person (see **Q2**), then CPR r.3.13(2) applies. However, what if a party in default has subsequently filed and served Precedent H outside the time allowed for so doing under CPR r.3.13(1)) and has applied for relief from sanction and this is to be heard at the listed CCMC (and so there is a chance that the court may grant relief at that hearing)? Late service and filing alone does not prompt the requirement to file precedent R as Precedent H has still not been filed and exchanged as required under CPR r.3.13(1). However, it may be prudent for the other party to file and serve a Precedent R in response commenting on that budget, even if it opposes the granting of relief (this will clearly not be possible where the party opposing relief wishes to rely on the argument that the Precedent H has been served too late for it to consider the budget properly in advance of the CCMC). This is so that if relief is granted, then the CCMC can still be effective. Of course, if relief is opposed, then filing and service of the Precedent R should be "without prejudice" to the primary contention that the defaulting party's budget is limited to future court fees only.

CPR r.3.13(2) creates more of a problem where a budget has been filed and exchanged by one party, but it is agreed by the other. Strictly, the procedural provision makes it mandatory for the party agreeing the budget to file a Precedent R. However, if this is simply going to say "agreed" against each phase that falls to be budgeted, it is hard to see there being any point taken if, instead, a letter is filed at court confirming agreement. It would be sensible to state in the letter if the agreement extends to incurred costs. Obviously, the party whose budget is agreed should also be notified of this formally, so that time and cost is not expended preparing to "defend" a budget that is not in dispute.

Whilst Precedent R is fairly self-explanatory, for those unfamiliar with it and who are uncertain as to whose figures to insert where, the following table may be of use:

Column B	Insert the other party's incurred costs figures for each phase. Note that occasionally there may be incurred costs to insert within some of those phases marked as N/A, if costs management occurs late in the claim
Column C	Insert the total of the other party's estimated costs for each phase

Column D	Insert the time element of the other party's estimated costs for each phase
Column E	Insert the disbursement element of the other party's estimated costs for each phase
Column F	Insert your total offer for the other party's estimated costs
Column G	Insert the time element of your offer for the other party's estimated costs for each phase
Column H	Insert the disbursement element of your offer the other party's estimated costs for each phase
Columns I and J	Insert a brief summary which identifies the reasons why your offer on any phase is lower than the estimated costs of the other party

To answer the penultimate question directly, when completing Precedent R, the party completing it and commenting on the other party's budget, is the "paying party" for this exercise.

There is no requirement for Precedent R to be certified. CPR PD 3E para.11 encourages the use of Precedent R and there is no statement of truth/certification on that form. This is in contrast to both Precedents H and T, which do have statements of truth/certifications. However, the fact that Precedent R does not require certification does not insulate the author of it from criticism and sanction – see *Findcharm Ltd v Churchill Group Ltd*[111] considered at para.4–16 and Q36 above.

Q44. Why does Precedent R contain the pre-action phase as costs in that phase can never be budgeted costs?
Even though Precedent R as amended continues to include the pre-action phase, it is now completed in such a way that makes it abundantly clear that it is not a phase for budgeting. Whilst we are not privy to the reasoning that saw its retention in this altered format, it does serve a useful purpose. In order to budget, the court should do so in an overall context. The approach we favour involves setting out a bracket of figures that the court views as the overall range of proportionate and reasonable costs at the commencement of the costs management process. Leaving the pre-action costs phase in Precedent R avoids these being overlooked when undertaking this exercise or on an overall cross-check at the end of the CCMC if the court has budgeted using Precedent R.

This question does afford an opportunity to highlight a couple of concerns with Precedent R, as follows:

4–66

---

[111] *Findcharm Ltd v Churchill Group Ltd* [2017] EWHC 1108 (TCC).

1. Given that the court may make a costs management order in respect of agreed "incurred costs", and given that, under CPR r.3.17(3)(b), incurred costs are taken into account on a phase when approving estimated costs, it would be useful to have a column in Precedent R (logically next to the incurred costs column) that enables the court to see at a glance whether the incurred costs for a particular phase are agreed (perhaps the column could be headed "Are incurred costs agreed?" with a Y/N deletion option going down the column); and

2. As some cases are costs managed late and only when a couple of phases (or, indeed parts of them) remain outstanding, we would prefer the PTR and Trial Preparation phases not to have "na" in the incurred costs column (see for example *Hegglin v Person(s) Unknown, Google Inc*,[112] considered at **Q75**) Whilst it is possible to overwrite these boxes, in current form it just gives the impression that they are never relevant.

Q45. Should the discussions that the parties have when attempting to agree the costs budgets be without prejudice?

4–67   CPR r.3.13(2) requires the parties (other than a litigant in person) to file an agreed "budget discussion report" (Precedent R) at least seven days before the CCMC, setting out an "open position". However, as with any discussions, there is nothing to prevent both "open" and "without prejudice" proposals being made in an attempt to reach agreement over budgets or certain phases within the budgets.

Q46. Is there a sanction if a party fails to agree a budget discussion report (Precedent R) or fails to file this?

4–68   The wording of CPR r.3.13(2) is curious. It does not specify that a party must serve Precedent R on all other parties, but this is surely implicit in the requirement that the form filed is "agreed". Obviously, it cannot be agreed unless the party agreeing it has had the opportunity to see it to consider it! One practical problem that this raises, is that there is, therefore, no provision for the time by which it is to be served—the only time constraint is that by which it must be filed (no later than seven days before the first CCMC).

Of course, this begs the question: what is an agreed budget discussion report? Presumably, the party whose budget is the subject of the form simply notes the content and either accepts proposals in respect of certain phases so that an amended final version may be filed or confirms that the form accurately reflects the measure of agreement and disagreement.

What can be done if one party either does not serve Precedent R or does so allowing insufficient time for the other party to consider it with a view to agreeing it more than seven days before the first CCMC? There is no automatic sanction applied to CPR r.3.13(2) and there has been no authority on this subject. Whilst it might be thought that an obvious sanction linked to

---

[112] *Hegglin v Person(s) Unknown, Google Inc.* [2014] EWHC 3793 (QB); [2015] 1 Costs L.O. 65.

the breach is for the court to refuse to permit the party in breach to "challenge" the budget, this sits entirely unhappily with the court's obligation to manage the costs to be incurred under CPR rr.3.12(2) and 3.15(1), its more general obligation to consider the costs of any case management decision under CPR r.3.17(1) and the obligation under the overriding objective to deal with cases at proportionate cost. Another possible sanction that is unlikely to be imposed, for the same reason, is to accept the compliant party's Precedent R comments on the defaulting party's budget.

More likely, therefore, is the imposition of some form of delay sanction in the form of an order that the defaulting party pays all or part of the costs of the CCMC or that, if it subsequently recovers costs, then the costs associated with the production of budgets under CPR r.3.15(5)(a) are disallowed. There is some logic to the second of these options, particularly where there is a complete failure to comply with CPR r.3.13(2), as the likelihood is that the CCMC will take more time as neither the court nor the other party/parties will know in advance which, if any, phases are agreed. Some support for the imposition of a costs sanction may be derived by analogy from the decision in *Findcharm v Churchill Group Ltd*,[113] in which the court imposed an indemnity costs order on the defendant for filing a wholly unrealistic Precedent R.

Another option might be to apply to the court for an "unless order". However, the time between making this and the CCMC will, necessarily, be brief and it may not be possible for the court to deal with this before the CCMC (either in terms of not dealing with it or there being enough time for any extended compliance). Again, the issue arises as to the appropriate sanction.

The final possibility is for the CCMC to be adjourned to afford time for compliance with an adverse costs order against the defaulting party. However, a decision to adjourn is a case management one and compensating one party in costs overlooks CPR r.1.1(2)(e) as this will waste court time that has been allocated to this case. Given the demands on court time one must expect the court to be loath to adjourn an, often long-awaited, CCMC.

The same difficulties emerge where a party serves its Precedent R in good time, but the other party neither engages in any discussions nor indicates any response and so the party serving the Precedent R has no idea if it is "agreed". In those circumstances, it seems the best course is to ensure that the form is still filed no later than seven days before the CCMC, but indicating that it is not agreed with an explanation for why that is the case. The same options (and difficulties) arise in connection with any sanction for non-compliance.

E. Approval and agreement of budgets

Q47. If one party puts in an absurdly low budget is it advisable for the other party to agree it or will this suggest an acceptance that any costs

---

[113] *Findcharm v Churchill Group Ltd* [2017] EWHC 1108 (TCC); 172 Con. L.R. 117.

above that level are not reasonable and proportionate and so prejudice its own budget which is significantly higher?

4-69   Yes, it is advisable to agree it. This will not prevent submissions being made to the court, both in Precedent R and orally, that such a budget is artificially low, that it has been agreed because that is in the other party's best interest to limit potential exposure to "between the parties" costs in the event of a subsequent adverse costs order, but that budget has no relevance whatsoever to what the reasonable and proportionate costs of the other party may be. Courts will be astute to the possibility of tactical budgeting (whether high or low). Indeed, this is one reason why a budget comparison summary (see **Q40** above) may not only be unhelpful, but can present an utterly misleading picture when viewed in isolation, in some cases.

Q48. CPR PD 3E para.5 includes a specific reference to CPR rr.44.3(5) and 44.4(3) and states that when deciding the reasonable and proportion- ate costs the court will include in its consideration "where and the cir- cumstances in which the work was done as opposed to where the case is heard". What is the significance of this reference?

4-70   The reference to the two CPR provisions is because these are, respectively, the procedural provisions that define whether costs are proportionate and whether costs are reasonable and CPR PD 3E para.12 requires the court to set budgets by reference to reasonableness and proportionality. Although they have been put in chronological order, as they follow a reference to reasonable and proportionate costs it may have made this link easier to understand if they had been inverted so it was clear that CPR r.44.3(5) referred to propor- tionality and CPR r.44.4(3) to reasonableness.

The words at the end are an extension of CPR r.44.4(3)(g). However, the tenses used do not sit happily with the task of budget setting, which is about prospective costs, and seem to resonate more with a retrospective assessment of costs ("was done"). However, as these words appear in the PD for use in prospective costs budgeting, they should be interpreted purposively. Doing so, it seems likely that these words have been inserted to deal with the pos- sibility of forum shopping—where representatives are based in one location, but issue proceedings out of another, where, for example, hourly rates are higher or lower, resulting in a budget that is artificially high or low. However, as budgets are not set by reference to hourly rate and as the court is astute to tactical budgeting arguments,[114] forum shopping should not result in any benefit in any event. Linked to this, it is worth remembering that CPR PD 29 (The Multi-Track) para.2.6A already compels parties in claims in specialist lists to justify in detail why these should be heard in London and not in regional specialist courts where the dispute arises in a region outside London.

---

[114] See, for example, *CIP Properties (AIPT) Ltd v Galliford Try* [2015] EWHC 481 (TCC); [2015] 1 All E.R. (Comm) 765 at [24].

In passing, it is worth noting those who seek to argue that CPR r.3.18 and the decision in *Harrison v University Hospitals Coventry and Warwickshire NHS Trust*[115] does not exclude a reconsideration of proportionality of the budgeted costs under CPR rr.44.3(2)(a) and 44.4(1) at the end of any assessment will need to surmount the hurdle that on a standard basis assessment costs allowed are those which are reasonable and proportionate, but as the budget has been set by reference to both of these any attempt to revisit them may be seen as an attempt to ask the assessing court to adopt an appellate function, which it does not have (see **Q90** below for further consideration of this).

Q49. Does the introduction of costs management mean that the court is rarely likely to dispense with a case/costs management conference and deal with directions and budgets as a paper exercise?
Clearly having a case/costs management hearing introduces delay and expense to cases (although as parties and courts become accustomed to the discipline this appears to be lessening). If the court is able to undertake this work as a paperwork exercise that would be the preferable course[116] (indeed Sir Rupert Jackson in his Final Report was at pains to stress that only case management hearings that had a purpose should be listed). However, unless the case management directions and budgets are agreed and the court is prepared to approve both (see the *Queen's Bench Guide* at para.10.23, which envisages this), then it is difficult to envisage how a hearing can be dispensed with at this stage. Even if the court does undertake the exercise on paper, clearly any party may apply to vary or set aside the order made. It is hoped that as the regime continues to settle in and the experience of practitioners and judges alike grows, then an increasing number of budgets and proposed directions will lend themselves to a paper determination. In the meantime, parties should seek to narrow as many issues as possible and the requirement for "budget discussion reports" at CPR r.3.13(2) does appear to have assisted in this process, leading to more agreements and enabling the judge to "target" preparation in advance of the CCMC. If there is early and significant agreement the parties should inform the court of this as soon as possible as that will reduce the required hearing time for a case management conference, which may both expedite the listing of the hearing (as a shorter time estimate ought to lead to earlier court availability) and reduce the cost of the hearing. It is fair to observe that the introduction of CPR r.3.13(1)(b) has meant that in many cases Precedents H are filed and exchanged later and mean that CCMC time estimates have to be set on a "worst case assumption", allowing sufficient time for both case and costs management and the chances of the court dealing with the matter as a paper exercise are reduced.

4–71

---

[115] *Harrison v University Hospitals Coventry and Warwickshire NHS Trust* [2017] EWCA Civ 792; [2017] 1 W.L.R. 4456.
[116] See para.10.2.9 of the *Queen's Bench Guide* 2018, which envisages such a situation (albeit, presumably, assuming that the court accepts the assumptions upon which the budgets were agreed match the directions which it proposes to order).

Parties should remember, in any event, that they are under a duty to endeavour to agree appropriate directions (CPR r.29.4).

Where it is not possible to dispense with a hearing, the parties should, at least, consider whether a telephone case/costs management hearing is feasible (subject to the court being prepared to accommodate this). In many cases, there is an argument to be made that a hearing by telephone is more proportionate (e.g. where the advocates are not local to the hearing centre). However, whilst CPR PD 23A para.6.2(c) suggests that a case management conference will be by telephone unless the court orders otherwise, this is in respect of hearings up to an hour long. Many case/costs management hearings are listed for longer than this (although this does not prevent the court deciding to hear the conference by telephone). It may be that adaptation of court practice in response to the Covid 19 pandemic will have persuaded more courts to adopt telephone hearings.

As a final point on this, it is worth remembering the content of CPR r.3.16(2), dealing with costs management conferences, which provides that:

> *"Where practicable, costs management conferences should be conducted by telephone or in writing."*

Q50. Does the court give the directions first and subsequently costs manage?

4–72   As costs management and case management go hand-in-hand, the two cannot be separated. If the case management directions are set without reference to the costs, with the budgeting exercise conducted afterwards, then all the court is doing when costs managing is pricing directions that have been given. The consequence is that if the court subsequently determines that a particular direction cannot be budgeted proportionately, there is nothing it can do as the direction has already been given. In contrast, if the two are done hand-in-hand, the proportionate expenditure informs the appropriate direction. In this respect it is curious that the *Chancery Guide*[117] suggests that normally directions are dealt with first and costs management afterwards, but with the directions only likely to be informed by the budgets. In simple terms, the danger of setting the directions and then costing them is that the directions ordered are those that the court determines are needed in the particular case. However, CPR r.44.3(2)(a) makes it clear that proportionality trumps need and the overriding objective "to deal with a case at proportionate cost" applies to any case management decision. The court should be giving directions that see the case dealt with proportionately and that assessment can only be made by dealing with the directions and the relevant phase of the budget simultaneously. This was a theme on which Sir Rupert Jackson commented in "Confronting costs management"[118], concluding that the proportionate cost for a phase

---

[117] Chancery Guide para.17–16.
[118] "Confronting costs management", May 2015, paras 7.4–7.6.

inevitably determined the proportionate case management direction for that phase.[119] This approach is one that the Court of Appeal implicitly approved in *Jamadar v Bradford Teaching Hospitals NHS Foundation Trust*[120] when highlighting that case and costs management should take place simultaneously. This might mean that the court's preliminary view of the proportionate direction needs to be revised if the cost associated with it is not proportionate e.g. a more limited disclosure order may have to be adopted to ensure proportionality of spend on that phase. It may also mean that the court's preliminary view of proportionality needs to be revised as it understands more of the case (usually in the context of complexity under CPR r.44.3(5)(c)) and that more extensive and costly directions are required in consequence.

Q51. The *Chancery Guide* at para.17.16 suggests that the court cannot manage incurred costs. Is that correct? If so, does that mean that CPR r.3.15(2)(c) is disapplied in the Chancery Division?
CPR r.3.15(2)(c) applies in all cases that fall with the Section II of CPR r.3.   **4–73**
Whilst the *Chancery Guide* has been updated since the introduction of CPR r.3.15(2)(c), which permits the court to make a costs management order in respect of any agreed incurred costs, it seems that this has simply been overlooked or the word "manage" in para.17.16 is used in a more active sense i.e.to refer to approval, rather than recitation of agreement.

Q52. Should costs lawyers attend CCMCs?
This must be for the client to decide (recognising that the costs of attendance   **4–74**
form part of the capped costs under CPR r.3.15(5)). In principle, there is no reason why a costs lawyer/costs draftperson should not attend, provided that this person has rights of audience. It remains the case that some CCMCs are attended by counsel/solicitor and a costs lawyer/draftperson. Views differ, but, provided only one of the advocates addresses the court on each point, there appears to be nothing wrong with this approach. Indeed, there has long been a history of costs counsel and a costs lawyer/draftperson attending detailed assessment with the former addressing the court on substantive points of principle and then handing over to the costs lawyer/draftperson for the minutiae of assessing actual sums. This begs the question of whether a costs lawyer/draftperson is necessary at the CCMC as the court will not be undertaking anything approaching an assessment. The appropriate person to attend is the one best able to address the court on proportionality and how this translates into the reasonable and proportionate directions and budget for each phase. In other words, the advocate must understand the synthesis between the two.

---

[119] An illustration of this is given by Jackson LJ in his Law Society Disclosure Lecture on 10 October 2016 when he said: "Since the court should be doing case and costs management together, it can a) adjust the level of disclosure to fit with the budgets and/or b) set the budgets to take account of the level of disclosure ordered."
[120] *Jamadar v Bradford Teaching Hospitals NHS Foundation Trust* [2016] EWCA Civ 1001; [2016] 5 Costs L.R. 809.

Q53. The court seems to have adopted a number of approaches to dealing with incurred costs where these are not agreed. Is it possible to discern clear guidance on the treatment of these costs in the budgeting exercise?

4–75 There is no doubt that the treatment of incurred costs is difficult and that the court has adopted different approaches to try to address this. The difficulty is that in the absence of agreement of incurred costs, the court cannot make costs management orders in respect of them. However, it is required to take these into account when considering the reasonableness and proportionality of all subsequent costs. This presents a number of problems, the most obvious of which are:

- What if the incurred costs already exceed the sum that the court considers a reasonable and proportionate sum for the entire claim?
- What if the incurred costs on a certain phase which is incomplete exceed the sum that the court considers a reasonable and proportionate sum for the entire phase?
- What if the court sets the budget for a phase by determining the reasonable and proportionate sum for that phase, deducts from it the amount that has been incurred and budgets the difference for the "costs to be incurred", but at assessment the assessing judge allows less than the full amount of the incurred costs?

These specific problems are addressed in more detail in the answers to **Q55**, **Q56** and **Q57** below. However, they have caused the court to grapple with how best to treat incurred costs against the backdrop of case-specific situations.

In *Yeo v Times Newspapers Ltd* the court considered the position when it was presented with substantial costs incurred prior to the costs management hearing. It set out CPR PD 3E para.7.4 (now CPR r.3.17(3)) and concluded that comments on those costs "briefly recorded at the time the budget is approved" would greatly assist the parties and the court at the conclusion.

The problem was more acute in *CIP Properties (AIPT) Ltd v Galliford Try Infrastructure Ltd*. The court was confronted by a budget that it considered "unreliable", that had been "deliberately manipulated" and which revealed both the incurred and estimated costs to be disproportionate. Challenged by the extent of the incurred costs, but to ensure that the overall costs were limited to those that he determined to be reasonable and proportionate, Coulson J (as he then was) adopted a mechanism that enabled him to control all the costs whilst recognising the problem of the assessing judge taking a different view to his in respect of incurred costs. His solution was to limit the recoverable incurred costs per phase, but to devise an off-setting calculator so that if the assessing judge allowed more than that sum, then an equivalent amount should be deducted from the estimated spend budgeted. In other words, regardless of how ultimately the costs are divided between those incurred and those budgeted, the claimant will be limited to the overall sum permitted by this mechanism. This raises a number of issues e.g. can the costs managing judge prospectively limit recoverable costs on a subsequent assessment of non-budgeted costs (para.98 plainly refers to "assessed costs"), the extent to which, if at all, the costs managing judge may off-set incurred costs in one phase against budgeted costs in another phase (para.97(a) expressly offsets incurred costs on the pre-action phase against future costs generally), the extent to which the court can effectively set a budget for a phase to include both incurred and estimated costs by adopting the set-off formula used by the court when CPR r.3.12 and CPR r.3.15 are clear that budgets are in respect of "costs to be incurred" and whether the effect of setting a total sum (para.98) precludes arguments under "good reason" or the exercise by the assessing judge of discretion on "good reason" for the budgeted sums to be increased on assessment (the effect of which anyway would seem simply to be a £ for £ off-set against incurred sums). This approach has subsequently been adopted in *GSK Project Management Ltd v QPR Holdings Ltd*.

The simple answer to the question is that "guidance" on the treatment of incurred costs comes from CPR r.3.17(3). However, it is clear from the above that the court is still grappling with the question of how to implement this fairly on a practical level. Further authority seems inevitable. In the meantime, the answers to the subsequent three questions attempt to address some of the issues that arise.

Q54. Are incurred costs relevant to the overall costs at the budgeting stage or only relevant on a phase by phase basis?
This picks up on the previous answer. CPR r.3.17(3) refers to incurred costs   **4–76** without reference to specific phases. Although the judgment does not overtly say so, it may be that it is the absence of an express link between CPR r.3.17(3) and individual phases that was relied upon by the court in *CIP Properties (AIPT) Ltd v Galliford Try* (see above) to justify off-setting of the incurred expenditure on one phase against the "to be incurred" budget on another phase (e.g. the off-set at para.97(a) of any pre-action costs subsequently assessed above £680,000 against the prospective budgeted figures in other phases— albeit without specifying any particular phase). Difficulties with adopting this approach have been mentioned above. However, this narrower question highlights what appear to be insurmountable procedural hurdles to the adoption of a general off-set. These are that:

- Costs management orders are made in respect of budgets which are set by what is reasonable and proportionate for individual phases. Accordingly, a formula that may operate, albeit retrospectively, to reduce what has been determined as the reasonable and proportionate sum for a specific phase to a sum less than that by an off-set of incurred costs from another phase, means that in those instances where the off-set operates, the court has not set the budget as required under CPR para.12.
- At assessment on the standard basis, by a combination of CPR r.44.3(1) and (2)(a), the receiving party may only recover those costs which are

reasonable and proportionate. CPR r.3.18 is clear that the court looks at whether there should be a departure from the budget by reference to the last agreed/approved sums for each phase. As the agreed/approved sums for those phases budgeted have been expressly determined by reference to the same criteria (under CPR PD 3E para.12), how can it be a "good reason" under CPR r.3.18 (or, indeed, correct under CPR r.44.3) to reduce budgeted costs on one phase by an off-set from another phase?

Although it did not arise in *CIP Properties (AIPT) Ltd v Galliford Try*, it is conceivable that this situation could arise in reverse adopting this formula. This would happen where a party actually recovers less at subsequent assessment for incurred costs than the court had assumed it would when ordering the general inter phase off-set. The same problems arise, albeit in reverse. The budget for a particular phase would be retrospectively varied to a sum over that which was reasonable and proportionate for that phase or the court would have to assess the sum for the budgeted costs for that phase in excess of the reasonable and proportionate sum.

As stated above, depending upon how the court articulates its decision and with properly drafted recitals reflecting this in the costs management order, there is a possibility of applying a later off-set between incurred and budgeted costs within a phase, resulting in either an addition or a deduction to the budgeted sum for "good reason", if the assessing judge is so minded. However, for the reasons set out above these options are not available when the off-set is between different phases.

However, this does not mean that overall incurred costs have no relevance. Clearly when the court undertakes its initial determination of overall reasonableness and proportionality, to inform the reasonable and proportionate case management directions and budgets for the discrete phases, the total "incurred costs" will determine how much of the overall figure remains.

Q55. What happens if the total incurred costs means that even with the most proportionate case management possible it is not possible to budget costs "to be incurred" at a level that, when added to those "incurred costs", comes within the court's overall assessment of reasonableness and proportionality?

4–77 As discussed in response to the previous two questions this is a real, rather than merely theoretical, problem. There are a number of possible outcomes as follows:

- The court declines to make a costs management order (as was the decision of Coulson J [as he then was] in *Willis v MRJ Rundell and Associates Ltd*[121]). Whilst this leaves all of a budget exposed to the subsequent

---

[121] *Willis v MRJ Rundell and Associates Ltd* [2013] EWHC 2923 (TCC); [2013] 6 Costs L.R. 924.

proportionality cross-check at any subsequent assessment under CPR r.44.3(2)(a), it does mean that the court has lost one of the vital tools out of its robust case management armoury. In reality, even with robust case management and the provisions of CPR PD 44 para.3 (which deals with the relevance of filed budgets in cases where no costs management order is made), the costs incurred by the end are likely to be even higher than those in the budget and it will be more challenging to manage the case in accordance with the overriding objective. In addition, as noted by Birss J in *Red and White Services Ltd v Phil Anslow Ltd,* after concluding the budgets to be disproportionate:

> *"Simply to send this case away on the footing that the costs budgets are disproportionate helps nobody. Also, simply to decline to make a costs management order also helps neither side and, indeed, in some ways could just make the situation worse by prolonging uncertainty."*

- The one occasion where declining to costs manage may be less challenging is if the case managing judge is also to be the assessing judge on any subsequent assessment (an option for the District Bench). Trenchant comments and recitals to the case management order justifying the fact no costs management order has been made and giving a view of what the case managing judge determined to be the overall proportionate figure, coupled with the fact both parties know that the same judge will conduct any subsequent detailed assessment, may encourage greater cost control going forward, recognising the inevitability of outcome on assessment of increased expenditure. This may also avoid the need for an assessment as the parties will know what is likely to happen at any subsequent assessment when the assessing judge undertakes the CPR r.44.3(2)(a) proportionality cross-check at the end (a figure not dissimilar to that indicated at the case management conference).
- The court adopts the approach of Warby J in *Yeo v Times Newspapers Ltd*[122] and records as recitals comments on "incurred costs". He adopted this route adding, by way of explanation, that to do so ". . . is likely to help the parties reach agreement without detailed assessment later on if these reasons are briefly recorded at the time the budget is approved".
- The court adopts the approach of Coulson J (as he then was) in *CIP Properties (AIPT) Ltd v Galliford Try* as set out above in **Q53**. In *GSK Project Management Ltd v QPR Holdings Ltd*[123] this is precisely what the court did. As noted above this approach does raise interesting challenges. It is right to record that the problem of "incurred costs" in *CIP* presented far more of a challenge on costs management than they did in *Yeo*. In *CIP* the "incurred costs" totalled £4,226,768.16. At the end of the costs management exercise, adopting his off-set formula across the phases, the total

[122] *Yeo v Times Newspapers Ltd* [2015] EWHC 209 (QB); [2015] 1 W.L.R. 3031.
[123] *GSK Project Management Ltd v QPR Holdings Ltd* [2015] EWHC 2274 (TCC); [2015] B.L.R. 715.

that the court decided would ultimately be recoverable was £4,280,000. As the pre-action phase spend was over £1.3 million and as the total sum Coulson J "allowed" overall in those phases where there was an incurred sum was always less than the incurred sum, the extent of his difficulty in costs management is obvious.

- Another way is a variation of the *CIP* approach, but one that may be seen to sit more comfortably within the existing rules. It extends the recitals approach advocated in *Yeo*. Under this approach the court first indicates and recites its view of overall reasonableness and proportionality of each party's costs. The court then case and costs manages by phases. In those phases where the "incurred costs" already equal/exceed what the court decides is the reasonable and proportionate sum for that phase, nothing is budgeted and the court recites its finding on the reasonable and proportionate overall sum for the phase. In those phases where the "incurred costs" do not equal or exceed the overall reasonable and proportionate figure for that phase, the court budgets the difference and recites its view on the overall reasonable and proportionate sum for that phase. This does leave matters to the assessing judge and, as such, is less prescriptive than the *CIP* approach, but provides a formula that sits happily with the budgeting by phase requirement, does not remove the assessing judge's discretion on arguments on "good reason", provides clarity of intended outcome from the costs managing judge to the assessing judge and provides a mechanism to ensure that the overall costs are ultimately proportionate. Remember that the assessing judge will apply CPR r.44.3(2) (a) and any "wider circumstances" under CPR r.44.4 as a cross-check at the end of any assessment. Whilst this cannot apply to budgeted costs, as they have already been set by reference to proportionality (see **Ch.3, Q16** for further consideration of this point), all costs incurred (and, therefore, not budgeted) at the time of the costs management order are subject to the cross-check. Armed with this clear order and forewarned of the likely outcome of any assessment, it will be a brave party, or one armed with genuine "good reason" on any particular phase, who accepts the challenge of an assessment.

Q56. If there has been a significant front-loading of the costs so that by the time of the costs management hearing the costs already spent exceed what the court regards as the overall proportionate expenditure on the claim, can the court set a budget going forward of nil?

4–78   No. As set out above, the reason for this is that the budget is not set as an overall sum. It is set by phase under CPR r.3.15(8). Accordingly, even if the court concludes that the incurred sum to date exceeds that which is proportionate to have dealt with the entire claim, it must look at the budget on a phase by phase basis. This may mean that the budget for certain phases may be set at nil if the court thinks the incurred sum under that phase already equals or exceeds the reasonable and proportionate cost for the entire phase. This is because CPR r.3.17(3)(b) requires the court to take costs already incurred "into account when considering the reasonableness and proportionality of all subsequent costs". However, there will be other phases, such as PTR, trial preparation and trial, where plainly there will be no incurred costs at the CCMC stage and it would be wrong, as the budget is set by reference to the reasonable and proportionate costs for each phase, for the court to budget these phases at nil.

Of course, as noted in the answers to Q53 to Q55 above, the court may also record its comments on the costs incurred before the date of any budget to assist the court at any later assessment when it considers the non-budget-related costs. The addition of CPR r.3.15(4) and CPR r.3.18(c) in the April 2017 amendments reinforces the ability to make recitals and stresses that those that are made shall be taken into account on any subsequent assessment.

Q57. What can be done to avoid the potential injustice of the court setting a phase budget by basing this on an overall view of the reasonable and proportionate sum for that phase, deducting the incurred costs and budgeting the difference, only for the assessing judge then to reduce the incurred costs undermining the basis upon which the budget was set?
This has already been identified above as a real risk of setting budgets by reference to the overall reasonableness and proportionality of a phase. However, the final suggested approach in the answer to Q55 (above) may provide the solution. If the court adopts that approach, then it will be clear to the assessing judge the basis upon which the budget was set, both within the context of overall reasonableness and proportionality and on a phase basis. Of course, the assessing judge is not bound by the costs managing judge's recitals, but if the assessing judge allows less for the incurred costs than the costs managing judge included when setting the budget this may open the door for the receiving party to argue that there is a "good reason" under CPR r.3.18 to depart from the budget for that phase. By way of illustration take a case where the costs managing judge determined that the overall (incurred and estimated costs) reasonable and proportionate sum for a phase was £15,000, and taking account of the incurred costs of £5,000 under CPR r.3.17(3), set the budgeted costs at £10,000. If the assessing judge only allows £3,000 for the incurred costs, to achieve the outcome upon which the costs managing judge based the calculation of budgeted costs (the overall sum for the phase of £15,000 less the incurred costs for the phase of £5,000), then there is an argument that there is "good reason" to depart from the budget, increasing the budgeted costs for the phase by the sum deducted from the incurred costs of the phase on assessment, namely £2,000. This preserves the discretion of the assessing judge, which it is arguable that the *CIP* approach does not, but also gives effect to the basis upon which the budgeted costs were calculated.

4–79

Q58. Should parties coming to the first CCMC to debate their respective budgets do so on the basis that it is the appropriate occasion on which to contest the costs in the budgets (both incurred and estimated) as per [44] of *Sarpd Oil International Ltd v Addax Energy SA*?[124]

4–80　No. The major decisions of *SARPD Oil* have been reversed by a combination of rule change (amendments to CPR r.3.15(2)(c), CPR r.3.18(c) and CPR r.3.17(3)(a)) and case law (*Harrison v University Hospitals Coventry and Warwickshire NHS Trust*[125]—although the court believed that rule change was not required). The court can only costs manage incurred costs if they are agreed. Whilst they are relevant to the approval of budgeted costs under CPR r.3.17(3)(b), that does not mean when considering the reasonableness and proportionality of the budget, the CCMC is the forum to contest costs in the same way that takes place at a detailed assessment. CPR PD 3E para.12 expressly provides that the costs management exercise is not a detailed assessment, but rather an exercise in considering whether the budgeted costs fall within a range of reasonable and proportionate costs leading to the approval of total figures only for each phase of the budget taking account of the incurred costs.

Q59. Should the court set hourly rates as part of the budgeting exercise?

4–81　Curiously, there still appears to be a divergence of approach on this topic. Curiously, because the straightforward answer is that not only is the court not required to set hourly rate when costs managing but it should expressly not do so (see para.**4–18**, CPR r.3.15(8) and *Yirenki v MOD*).[126] Since inception of the costs management regime CPR PD 3E para.7.3 historically specifically stated that the court sets "total figures for each phase of the proceedings". This provision has (as of October 2020) been elevated to the rules at CPR r.3.15(8), which concludes that "it is not the role of the court in the costs management hearing to fix or approve the hourly rates claimed in the budget". There are those who still favour the setting of hourly rates and suggest that the court can only set a total figure by reference to an hourly rate or that, implicit in the budgeting of a phase is an approval of an hourly rate. Costs management undertaken in accordance with CPR 3 Section II involves no such exercise (save that noting a particularly high or low rate may go some way to explaining why the total figures in a given budget are above or below those that the court considers to be proportionate).

　　There is a clear logic to CPR r.3.15(8). Remember that hourly rate in isolation is worthless. It is only relevant if it is multiplied by an amount of time. However, hours multiplied by time smacks of what is "needed", which brings us back to CPR PD 3E para.12, as the court is not charged with setting a budget to allow necessary work—instead it is charged with setting a budget for each phase that

---

[124] *Sarpd Oil International Ltd v Addax Energy SA* [2016] EWCA Civ 120; [2016] C.P. Rep. 24.
[125] *Harrison v University Hospitals Coventry and Warwickshire NHS Trust* [2017] EWCA Civ 792; [2017] 1 W.L.R. 4456.
[126] *Yirenki v MOD* [2018] EWHC 3102 (QB); [2018] 5 Costs L.R. 1177.

is reasonable and proportionate, which in turn involves CPR r.44.3(2)(a) and the fact that proportionality trumps reasonableness and necessity.

There are a number of other reasons why setting the budget by reference to an hourly rate is inappropriate for those still attracted to this approach despite the clear and reinforced provisions of CPR r.3. These reasons are:

- It is too prescriptive. It is for the legal representatives and the client to determine how to spend the sum budgeted for a phase. If the budget is set by a specific hourly rate, then the court is effectively saying that that particular fee earner must do that amount of work. This is micro-management taken to an extreme. Setting a total figure enables the representatives and, more importantly, the client, to decide who does what work and what work is contracted out to counsel.

- If the budget is set by reference to hourly rate it opens doors for arguments at assessment as to whether, in fact, a fee earner commanding that rate actually undertook the phase work in question. If the answer is no, then that may be "good reason" to depart from the budget. One of the aims of costs management is to reduce the incidence and cost of subsequent costs assessment, not to increase both by further micro examination These arguments do not arise if the budget is simply a total sum for the phase.

- If an hourly rate is set and at the end of the case, on assessment, a different hourly rate is set for the non-budgeted work (as the hourly rate set for the budget cannot be determinative in respect of the non-budgeted costs as the court has no power to budget them under CPR rr.3.12 and 3.15 other than by recording agreement), then immediately that opens the door to one or other party to argue "good reason" to depart from the budget, submitting that the budget was set on the "wrong" hourly rate. This is precisely what occurred in *RNB v London Borough of Newham*.[127] The court reduced the hourly rate for incurred (non-costs managed costs) at detailed assessment. It then determined that this reduction amounted to a good reason to depart downwards from the budget, as Precedent H had included the same rates for estimated costs. In fact, a more compelling argument, in this situation, is one that results in the exact opposite outcome. This is that a reduction, for whatever reason, in non-costs managed incurred costs may present a good reason to increase the approved budgeted costs. This is because the approved budgeted costs will have been set taking into account incurred costs under CPR r.3.17(3)(b). A reduction in those incurred costs to reflect a lower hourly rate, may mean that the court has "under-budgeted" future costs by deducting incurred costs as set out in Precedent H from what it regarded as the

---

[127] *RNB v London Borough of Newham* [2017] EWHC B15 (Costs). It is worth noting that there are other decisions from the SCCO that have rejected the argument that a reduction in hourly rates is a "good reason" to depart from budgeted costs under CPR r.3.18, e.g. *Nash v Ministry of Defence* [2018] EWHC B4 (Costs) and *Jallow v Ministry of Defence* [2018] EWHC B7 (Costs).

overall reasonable and proportionate sum for each phase when calculating the budgeted costs to be approved (see **Q57** above and **Q64** below for further consideration of this topic).

- Setting rate and then determining the time by which to multiply it has all the hallmarks of a detailed assessment, which CPR PD 3E para.12 specifically cautions the court against undertaking when costs managing.
- The amount of court time taken to determine rate and then the time by which to multiply it renders the budgeting exercise disproportionate—both for the parties and for the court.
- There is a very real risk that parties/representatives will "forum shop" in cases with no requirement to proceed in a particular court venue.

In summary, CPR r.3.15(8) and CPR PD 3E para.12 do not require the court to set hourly rates—indeed r.3.15(8) makes it perfectly plain that the position is quite the reverse—it is expressly not the role of the costs manager to fix or set hourly rates. Accordingly, it is curious (and misses the point of costs management) that it appears that some costs management orders are made "subject to hourly rate being determined at subsequent assessment" or "reserving argument on hourly rate on budgeted costs to subsequent assessment" or even with a discussion of hourly rate at all (see **Qs 60** and **92** below for more detailed explanation of this). The emphasis is on a far simpler, less time-consuming and more proportionate process. One aim of costs management is to reduce the incidence of, and time taken on, subsequent assessments of costs. Setting a rate within the budget seems designed to encourage more contested assessments and to defeat this aim. This also requires assessing judges to understand the process of costs management, namely that rate has not been used in the approval of budgeted costs.

Q60. Are the parties able to agree budgets or specific phases, but state that this is qualified on the basis that arguments on the hourly rate informing that agreement are reserved to subsequent agreement or assessment?

4–82   Whilst parties may reach such an agreement, the real question is whether the court will be prepared to record such an agreement as a costs management order under CPR r.3.15(2)(a) and (c).

Under CPR 3.15(2)(a) we would expect the court to decline to record such an agreement. In simplistic terms, there is no agreement of the budgeted sums, as any sum is qualified in a way that leaves them at large (in the same way that approving a budget subject to rates is flawed—see **Q59** above and **Q92** below). Such an agreement neither provides certainty for the clients, nor necessarily reduces the incidence of subsequent assessments, both of which form part of the rationale underlying costs management. CPR r.3.15(2)(b) requires the court to approve budgeted costs where these are not agreed. As an agreement qualified in a way that provides no certainty of the actual sum agreed, leaves the budgeted costs unagreed, then, in our view the court must step in and approve the budget. In this situation we would expect the court to put the party agreeing the budget on this basis to an election—either agree the budgeted costs without qualification or accept that the court will approve the budgeted costs under CPR r.3.15(b) and will start with a clean sheet when so doing (i.e. the qualified agreement does not feature and the court simply fulfils its function to approve as set out in CPR PD 3E para.12).

Under CPR r.3.15(2)(c) we would expect the court to decline to make a formal costs management order (as again the incurred costs are not agreed, because they are subject to a qualification that prevents certainty of the actual sum). However, the likelihood is that the court will make a recital recording the qualified agreement, so that the narrowing of the extent of any subsequent assessment is noted.

Q61. If the court does not set the budget by reference to hourly rates and time, then why does Precedent H require this information and, linked to this, what does "the underlying detail in the budget for each phase used by the party to calculate the totals claimed is provided for reference purposes only to assist the court in fixing a budget" in CPR r.3.15(8) mean?
This is a very fair point. Whilst this text has always maintained that CPR PD   4–83
3E para.7.3 was clear that the court does not set hourly rate and this was subsequently bolstered by CPR PD 3E para.7.10 (and these provisions are now at CPR r.3.15(8) and PD 3E para.12), why does Precedent H require a breakdown, which simply serves to reinforce the "old" approach to costs—set a rate and multiply it by an amount of time? It is arguable that a form that makes those completing it focus on reasonableness and proportionality in the round is far more likely to achieve the desired effect. On that basis Precedent H could be reduced to just the first page in all cases as some have suggested.

However, that is not the position, and CPR r.3.15(8) considers the "underlying detail". This suggests that some courts may be assisted by this detail. An example of this may be where the parties' budgets are poles apart, but their proposed directions are similar and the court is endeavouring to discern a reason for this. In other words, there may be cases where some of the detail assists, but at the end of the day the court will not set rates, will not prescribe the amount of time to be taken, but will simply budget a reasonable and proportionate sum and leave it to the parties to manage the budgets. A review of CPR PD 3E para.7.3 (now para.12) suggests that this was always the role of the court. However, given the apparent inconsistency of approach, notwithstanding that provision, the unqualified confirmation in CPR PD 3E para.7.10 (now found in CPR r.3.15(8)), that the court does not set rate is a welcome one. Removing the unnecessary focus on rates and time dramatically reduces the hearing length of CCMCs, making the costs management process itself a proportionate one. As a result, it is both disappointing and inexplicable to be seeing authorities that suggest that considerations of hourly rate and time have driven the budgeting process.

Q62. How can the court set the budget without assessing prospectively the work that is required and the appropriate hourly rate(s) at which that work should be done? Is the budget set as the lowest amount of costs which a party can reasonably expect to spend in order to have its case conducted and presented proficiently, having regard to all the circumstances?

4–84   The court is not charged when setting a budget with "assessing", giving the word its customary meaning in a costs context. The court is also not charged with determining what work is necessary. What the court is charged with doing, is determining the just and proportionate case management directions and whether the budgeted costs for a phase of these directions "fall within the range of reasonable and proportionate costs". This inevitably involves a decision based on the definition of proportionality at CPR r.44.3(5) and any "wider circumstances" under CPR r.44.4. It is against the backdrop of this decision that the court determines whether the sum sought for a phase is reasonable and proportionate and, if it is not, whether there is a more suitable case management direction and what total sum should be substituted. When looked at in these stark terms, it is clear why a detailed analysis of hourly rate and time does not inform the outcome. The court simply determines the work to be done by reference to reasonable and proportionate expenditure (with the latter having the final say under CPR r.44.3(2)(a)) to deal with a case justly and at proportionate cost. It is for that reason that case and costs management have to go hand in hand, so that the directions ordered only permit work that can be undertaken at proportionate cost and, on the other side of the coin, the court is not expecting the presentation of a case in a fashion that the proportionate budget does not permit. The latter is as important as the former. Proportionality applies equally to the manner in which the claim will be conducted within the monetary constraints that it imposes.

It is for the reasons set out above that we believe that the answer to the second question is no, as a matter of strict interpretation of the rules, in particular the qualification of the overriding objective in CPR r.1 by reference to proportionate costs and the primacy of proportionality (over reasonable and necessary costs) in CPR r.44.3(2)(a) – see **Ch.3 Q8** for detailed consideration of this and in particular the commentary on *Thomas v PGI Group Ltd*.[128]

Q63. If the court is budgeting only be reference to a global sum and not taking account of the respective hourly rates, surely this means that a party who has agreed a lower hourly rate retainer will be able to do more work than one with a higher hourly rate? If so this appears unfair.

4–85   Yes—a party with a lower hourly rate retainer is, in theory, able to undertake more work than one with a higher hourly rate. However, there are relevant factors that militate against the apparent unfair consequence:

---

[128] [2021] EWHC 2776 (QB).

- The court determines the appropriate proportionate case management directions. These inevitably define the extent of work that may be undertaken, e.g. limits on the number of factual witnesses, the amount of disclosure, the length of trial, etc.
- If the budget is set globally, then it is for a party to determine how to spend that money. Remember, costs are the client's and the budget is the client's to spend—see **Ch.9** below. The budget "set" by the court will have to be explained to the client. Professional obligations on legal representatives may dictate that the way that sum is spent necessitates that the case plan is re-visited (e.g. does the client wish the work to be done by a lower level fee earner or is the client happy to have the higher level fee earner for less time or for the same amount of time, but in the knowledge that some of that cost will, inevitably be irrecoverable from the other party? Does the client want a less expensive expert/counsel or lesser input from the expert/counsel?). In certain instances, this may mean that the client seeks alternative representation. What this does highlight is the importance of the retainer, both at the outset and on any variation, in defining precisely what work will be done for what remuneration. There is no doubt that the introduction of budgets reiterates the ongoing importance of managing client expectation, particularly in terms of any restraints that the case and costs management orders impose on a client's instructions. This is considered in the Q&A sections of **Chs 3 and 9.**

However, at the end of the day, it is for each client to negotiate the retainer with the legal representatives. If one negotiates a lower rate than another, then any consequences based on the differential rate stem from the choice of the solicitor client retainer and not from any costs management order.

Q64. If the court does set the hourly rate in the budget what happens if, at assessment, the assessing court sets a different hourly rate for the non-budgeted work?

This should not happen as CPR r.3.15(8) categorically states that setting rate is not the role of the costs managing judge and CPR PD 3E para.12 is clear as to how the court approves a figure as the budgeted costs for a phase. Accordingly, any attempt by one party to persuade the costs managing judge to do so should be resisted. If rates are set then this may open the door to arguments that there is "good reason" to depart from the budget. (See the answers to **Qs 59 and 60** and consideration of *RNB v London Borough of Newham*[129] above, for the unnecessary mischief that this may cause. In *MXX v United Lincolnshire NHS Trust*[130] that part of the appeal on assessment which challenged the findings on the effect of the improper or unreasonable conduct of the claimant's solicitors, who had overstated an hourly rate in Precedent

4–86

---

[129] *RNB v London Borough of Newham* [2017] EWHC B15 (Costs).
[130] *MXX v United Lincolnshire NHS Trust* [2019] EWHC 1624 (QB); [2019] Costs L.R. 1151.

H, would have been unnecessary or so much easier to resolve, if hourly rate had not formed part of the budget setting process. In fact, if the budget for a phase is set using a combination of CPR PD 3E para.12 and CPR r.3.17(3)(b), by determination of the overall reasonable and proportionate sum and deducting from it the sum already incurred on that phase, then any over-statement of incurred costs whether by inflation of hourly rate or otherwise, contains an in-built sanction, because it means that the budget has been set at too low a level—see Q57 above.) Other possible consequences are that the length of summary assessments increase, that this persuades the trial judge to order a detailed assessment instead of assessing summarily in a fraction of the time and at a fraction of the cost and that there is an increased incentive for a paying party to take its chances on a detailed assessment. All fly in the face of a desire to make decisions about "the costs of the costs" simpler and proportionate.

Q65. What, if anything, can the court do when the parties agree budgets or phases of the budgets in sums that the court thinks are disproportionate? Is the offer made by the other party in Precedent R the benchmark below which the court cannot go if the offer is not accepted?

4–87   One of the curiosities of the costs management regime is that CPR r.3.15 clearly envisages that the parties may agree all or part of the budgets and that if they do so, the court is left with the options of making no costs manage-ment order at all or making a costs management order recording the extent of the agreement (and approving a budget in respect of any phases not agreed).

However, CPR r.3.12(2) makes it clear that the function of the court is to manage both the steps and the costs to be incurred. Accordingly, if the court takes the view that the case management approach of the parties upon which the budget agreement is based is not proportionate, then the court must give proportionate directions. This is reinforced by the duty on the court imposed by CPR r.3.17(1) to take account of the cost of any procedural step and by the overriding objective.

It is unlikely that an agreed budget will remain so if the assumptions upon which the agreement was reached are altered, e.g. if the disclosure phase is agreed on the basis of an order for standard disclosure, but the court permits only a more limited form of disclosure, is a party really likely to maintain the agreement? This means that representatives at court must have ready access to the client during the case management hearing (if the client is not present) so that further instructions may be taken. Of course, if the parties have agreed what the court perceives to be proportionate case management directions, but have simply agreed figures more than the court thinks are proportion-ate, then there genuinely is nothing that the court can do to interfere with the agreement, other than to decline to make a costs management order and recite the reason for this decision. However, not making a costs management order in this situation flies in the face of the requirement at CPR r.3.15(2) as the court cannot be satisfied that the litigation can be conducted justly and at proportionate cost in accordance with the overriding objective in the absence of such an order.

On the other side of the coin is the situation where costs for a phase have not been agreed and the court thinks that the rejected offer put by one party to another in Precedent R is disproportionate. Can the court approve a figure below the offer? The answer is that it can. This was confirmed by the court in *Gray v Commissioner of Police for the Metropolis*[131] in which Lambert J dismissed a suggestion to the contrary with brevity:

> "... I find that the Judge was not required to spell out why the figure which she allowed for witness statements was less than the figure offered by the Defendant. The reason is obvious: the figure offered by the Defendant was not the proportionate figure. It goes without saying that, if a Defendant (or any party) makes an offer, that offer does not become the benchmark below which the cost cannot be budgeted." [27]

(Contrast to CPR r.3.15A, which does permit the court to vary or disallow a proposed variation of the budget without qualification. In other words, this power applies whether or not the proposed variation is agreed). See also **Q80** below.

Q66. How important is the breakdown between disbursements and solicitors' fees in an approved/agreed budget?

Whilst the format of Precedent H requires a division between profit costs and various types of disbursement, CPR PD 3E para.12 simply requires the court to set the budget for phases by way of total figures. Accordingly, many courts are not breaking down the sum budgeted for a specific phase between profit costs, counsel, experts and other disbursements, and for good reason. The rationale for this is that it is for the solicitor and the client to agree how the sum for a phase is to be spent. Solicitors may model this in many ways for the client to choose, e.g. where the proposed budget has been reduced by the court, the client may agree to place less reliance than had been envisaged on counsel or the same amount of reliance, but with the solicitors then using a less expensive fee earner.

Another difficulty of the court being too prescriptive about how the total sum for a phase is spent, is that it reduces the flexibility for the solicitor and client, e.g. if the budget for the pre-trial review is based on a division between solicitor and counsel on the assumption that counsel will attend the PTR and, in fact, the solicitor and the client agree that the solicitor will conduct that hearing, is that then "good reason" to depart from the budget that was based on counsel attending? As one aim of costs budgeting is to reduce the number of assessments, this is better achieved by the court setting one figure for each phase and leaving the solicitor and client to decide how to spend that sum. Remember that the court is not sanctioning, for example, use of counsel or

4–88

---

[131] *Gray v Commissioner of Police for the Metropolis* [2019] EWHC 1780 (QB); [2019] Costs L.R. 1105.

a particular fee earner with a set hourly rate at a specific stage: it is instead simply determining what is the reasonable and proportionate' sum of costs for each phase.

Having said all the above, there is no doubt that the breakdown in the Precedent H may inform the court of the case plan upon which the filed budget is predicated and so influence the decision as to what is the reasonable and proportionate overall sum for a phase. This was the view expressed in *Yirenkyi v Ministry of Defence*,[132] with the court stating that these details, amongst others:

"...feed in to the identification of a reasonable and proportionate figure. They do not feed in to a finding as to the specific number of hours which are to be spent in the future, or a finding as to specific figure for disbursements to be incurred in the future."

Q67. Should parties re-file budgets after the CCMC when a costs management order has been made under CPR r.3.15? When doing so, does the re-filed and re-served budget need to be re-signed? Are orders that simply record a costs management order in a total sum for the entire budget appropriate?

4–89   Whilst the answer is simple, as CPR r.3.15(7) imposes an obligation upon the parties to do precisely this, it is worth stressing that if the court has made a costs management order that makes it plain from the face of the order, or any attached pages 1 of the budgets or other spreadsheets, which phases of the Precedent H have been budgeted, and in what amount, the court should be asked, if it does not automatically so do, to dispense with the requirements of CPR r.3.15(7) as they are superfluous and disproportionate in that situation (see, for example, Chancery Form CH.40, which provides that amended budgets should not be filed where a spreadsheet showing the budgeted sum per phase is a schedule to the costs management order). The purpose of this provision is to ensure that there is a clear record of what phases have been budgeted and in what amount. If this information is readily available on the court file and to the parties without them going to the expense of compliance with CPR r.3.15(7) so much the better.

In those cases where the court does not discharge the obligations of the parties under CPR r.3.15(7), the budget does not need to be re-signed. It is being refiled and re-served simply to reflect the figures that have been approved or agreed by way of costs management order. It should be annexed to the order that approves/records as agreed the budgeted costs.

Too often a costs management order simply recites that "The court has budgeted the claimant's costs in the sum of £x and the defendant's costs in sum of £y". This has the potential to cause many problems. These are as follows:

---

[132] *Yirenkyi v Ministry of Defence* [2018] EWHC 3102; [2018] 5 Costs L.R. 1177, 2 November (QB) Jacobs J.

234

- Often the sum inserted is the total of incurred and estimated costs and there has been no agreement of incurred of costs and so the reference to budgeted costs is incorrect.
- Even if the total is that of the budgeted costs, the budget is set by phases and not by overall total.
- Unless there is a copy of Pages 1 of the respective budgets or another form of spreadsheet identifying the specific phases budgeted and the amount approved/agreed for each phase budgeted, then any judge later dealing with either variation of budget or assessment will be presented with difficulties undertaking their functions.

If the court has budgeted using page 1 of Precedent H a simple order that identifies the phases budgeted and enables ready calculation of the amount approved/agreed is as follows:

"The court has made a costs management order in respect of the parties' costs in accordance with the attached pages 1 of Precedent H, with the phases budgeted those where the total for the phase is in bold typeface (if budgeting electronically)/ is marked with an asterisk (if budgeting manually) and the budget for the phase is the total less the incurred costs"

The pages 1 are then attached to the case management order and there is clarity of position for any future reference.

This leads to another point so obvious that it surprises us that it needs to be made. When filing draft directions in advance of a costs case management hearing, it is noticeable how many solicitors take the trouble to prepare Precedents H and R, but omit to make provision for a costs management order.

F. Post costs management order general issues

Q68. Can a budget be varied when it is noted that the sum calculated incorporates a mathematical error?
This issue arose in the case of in *Broom v Archer*[133] unreported 28 March *2018* **4–90**
QBD (TCC), in which an arithmetical error was noted in the budget some months after the CCMC. The parties had failed to comply with the then requirement in CPR PD 3E para.7.7 (now CPR r.3.15(7)) to re-file and re-serve the budget in the form approved or agreed. The court lamented the drain on judicial resources in dealing with the matter and suggested that had the parties complied with the obligation, then the error would have become apparent at an earlier juncture. As a result of the failure to comply with the procedural requirements after the CCMC, the court decline to rectify the error, although the budget was varied for other reasons.

---

[133] *Broom v Arche* unreported 28 March 2018 QBD (TCC) Fraser J.

Q69. What sanction is there if a party fails to re-file the budget under CPR r.3.15(7), in particular does this failure engage the sanction in CPR 3.14?

4–91 The requirement at CPR r.3.15(7) is temporally open-ended. No time-period is specified for compliance, other than that the re-cast budget must be re-filed and re-served after the budgeted costs have been approved or recorded as agreed. As the re-cast budget must be attached to the court order containing the costs management order, then clearly the re-filing and re-service cannot take place until the sealed court order is received by the parties. Although one might assume that the intention is that the re-cast budget should then be filed and served promptly so that any dispute as to its accuracy in reflecting the court order can be resolved whilst it is still relatively fresh and so that it is then readily available to inform any subsequent applications to vary or any assessment process, strictly a party can comply with the obligation at any time after the CCMC. For this reason, whilst we accept that CPR r.3.15(7) creates an obligation to file a budget and CPR r.3.14 applies to any failure by a party to file a budget when required to do so, it is difficult to see when CPR r.3.14 would ever be engaged in this situation.

Far more likely is that the court will apply case-specific sanctions if the failure to comply with CPR r.3.15(7) causes later difficulties. In other words, the sanction applied will be directly linked to the consequences of the breach e.g. see **Q68** above, which deals with the limited circumstances where failure to comply with CPR r.3.15(7) resulted in a failure to identify an arithmetical error.

Q70. Can the parties agree to vary their budgets from that recorded by the court in a costs management order, where there has been no "significant development" in the litigation, but both are unhappy with the amount budgeted by the court? Is it possible to ask the court to disapply the costs budgeting regime after a costs management order has been made?

4–92 The simple answer to the first question is "no". Once a costs management order has been made by the court, it may only be varied where there are significant developments (see CPR r.3.15A). The fact that all parties may be unhappy with the costs management order made is not a significant development. The remedy of the parties in such a situation would be to seek to appeal the costs management order. This is reinforced by CPR r.3.15(3) which places an obligation upon the court having set a budget to control the parties' budgets thereafter.

In the situation raised by the second question variation does not arise. The party is not asking the court to vary a budget, but, instead, to revoke the costs management order entirely. The jurisdiction of the court to revoke orders is strictly circumscribed. The relevant rule is that at CPR r.3.1(7). In summary there would need to be a material change in circumstances after the costs management order was made, the facts on which it was made were misstated or there has been a genuine error (see *Tibbles v SIG Plc*[134]). Accordingly, decisions will be case-specific. However, it is hard to think of a situation where the CPR r.3.1(7) would apply to a costs management order (other than, perhaps, that the court applies the sanction in CPR r.3.14, erroneously believing that no Precedent H has been filed in time, but it subsequently emerges that it was filed in time).

Q71. Once a budget has been set, should solicitors be monitoring the budgets?

Although the answer to this question is so obvious it ought not to need answering, it leads to a slightly different and more important issue. The answer to the basic question is yes. However, merely monitoring the budget is insufficient in isolation. The more important issue arises if one substitutes the word "managing" in place of "monitoring". Simply watching as the budget for a phase dissipates is largely purposeless, it simply identifies when the money has been spent regardless of whether there has been compliance with the phase direction. What is needed is a planned expenditure within the budget. This requires consideration immediately after the CCMC of how the directed phase work is to be undertaken within the budgets set for the phases (assuming that the client is not prepared to fund additional work over and above the budget in the knowledge that it will be irrecoverable "between the parties"). This must be followed by management to ensure that the directed phase work is completed within budget as planned. Accordingly, it comes as no surprise that some firms are/are considering engaging project managers accustomed to delivering work within budgetary constraint. There are software packages of varying degrees of sophistication that will enable alerts when time has been recorded matching specific percentages of a phase budget to enable a regular stocktake.

4–93

Q72. Upon taking over instructions for a client from another firm, it is clear that the "incurred costs" for the pre-action phase in the Precedent H filed and exchanged by that firm are considerably lower than the amount of costs that the client paid that firm for work done during that period. Whilst estimating future costs may be somewhat speculative, is there any explanation for why the incurred costs in Precedent H differ from "actual costs" incurred? Is a party able to include in its Precedent H costs incurred when instructing a previous firm of solicitors?

The answer to both questions is "yes, but...".

4–94

There is an explanation why the costs in the budget were lower than those incurred by the client, although whether it applies to a particular budget is fact specific both as to the terms of the solicitor and client retainer and as to whether the costs incurred are reasonable and proportionate. The explanation is that the Precedent H is meant to be prepared as a fair and accurate

---

[134] *Tibbles v SIG Plc* [2012] EWCA Civ 518.

statement of incurred and estimated costs which it would be reasonable and proportionate for the client to incur. This is the wording of the statement of truth under CPR PD 22 para.2.2A that appears on the Precedent H. In other words, regardless of the costs actually incurred by the client at the time of the preparation of Precedent H, only those that are reasonable and proportionate should be included. Of course, this does not preclude the actual billed/incurred costs and those appearing in the Precedent H coinciding, but that should only occur if the representative signing the statement of truth on that form is satisfied that those costs are reasonable and proportionate.

The client has incurred those costs with the previous solicitors that were instructed and so may, if the current firm is satisfied that it was reasonable and proportionate to have incurred them, include them within the appropriate phases in Precedent H.

Q73. What if a client still wants the legal representatives to incur costs that the court has not allowed within the budget?

4–95   Remember that the costs management exercise is concerned with recoverable costs "between the parties" only. The basis of retainer remains a contractual issue between the solicitor and the client—see **Ch.9**. To that extent, provided that the retainer permits it and the expenditure is agreed, the client is not constrained in what costs are actually incurred by the budget set by the court. So, for example, the client may still choose to engage counsel whose brief fees will mean that the client inevitably exceeds the budgeted sum for the trial phase. This is entirely the prerogative of the client provided he/she realises that there will be a shortfall between expenditure incurred and recovery of costs even if he/she is awarded the costs—see Q75 and the reference to CPR r.46.9(3)(c) below, particularly in the light of the decision in *Belsner v Cam Legal Services Ltd*[135] about specific informed consent from a client. This is all the more important in the County Court as a result of s.74(3) of the Solicitors Act 1974 which provides:

> "*The amount which may be allowed on the assessment of any costs or bill of costs in respect of any item relating to proceedings in the county court shall not, except in so far as rules of court may otherwise provide, exceed the amount which could have been allowed in respect of that item as between party and party in those proceedings, having regard to the nature of the proceedings and the amount of the claim and of any counterclaim.*"

However, clearly, the case management directions that the court has given do impose an inevitable constraint. For example, if the court has limited a party to a set number of named expert witnesses, then there is no purpose in the client insisting upon the instruction of further experts as their evidence cannot be relied upon in court.

---

[135] *Belsner v Cam Legal Services Ltd* [2020] EWHC 2755 (QB).

In summary, as Sir Rupert Jackson stated in his *Preface and Guide to the Civil Justice Reforms* in the *White Book* 2014:

"Within the confines of the directed procedure any party is free to waste its own money if it wishes to do so."

Q74. Does the statement of truth on the budget prevent a solicitor recovering more than the budget from the client?

The answer to the first question is no, subject to the appropriate wording of any specific solicitor and client fee retainer (the qualification is because in County Court proceedings, s.74(3) of the Solicitors Act 1974 limits costs to those which could have been recovered from another party in the absence of any agreement to the contrary).   4–96

CPR PD 22 para.2.2A makes it clear that the budget is concerned with reasonable and proportionate costs. Proportionality has no place in solicitor-client assessments (which are effectively on the indemnity basis).

However, plainly a solicitor should inform the client of the budgeted sum so that the client is aware of the limit on those costs that may be recovered from another party in the event a costs order is made in the client's favour. This should enable the client to give informed instructions after the budget has been set. CPR r.46.9(3)(c) makes clear that on any assessment of solicitor and client costs, costs are assumed to be unreasonably incurred if they are of an unusual nature or amount and the solicitor did not tell the client that as a result they might be irrecoverable (see **Q73** above).

Q75. What is the position if a Pt 7 claim commences as a fast track claim, but subsequently it becomes apparent that the claim is undervalued and needs to be re-tracked to the multi-track, but it is not within one of the costs management exceptions in CPR r.3.12(1)?

This is not an uncommon scenario—particularly in personal injury proceedings where the prognosis is uncertain at the time of allocation. Whilst the court is not constrained by a statement of value or allocation as to what sum it may award (see CPR r.16.3(7)), plainly the claimant must apply to amend the statement of value and to seek re-allocation. In any event, the increase in value is likely to result in a need to be linked with an application for further substantive directions (e.g. change of trial time estimate/trial window/further expert evidence, etc.).   4–97

As the costs management provisions apply to all multi-track CPR r.7 claims (subject to the exceptions detailed in CPR r.3.12(1)), then the effect of any re-allocation is to bring the claim within the costs management provisions. As such, it would be prudent for the claimant to attach a Precedent H to the application (and if the application is by consent for the defendant to do likewise). In any event, expect the court to order Precedents H to be filed and exchanged when listing the application or before it considers any consent order if the parties have not already provided them. This is not only because the court wishes to consider costs managing, but also because of the provisions of CPR r.3.17(1). Re-allocation is a case management decision and the court will need to know the cost consequence of any decision it takes.

If the application comes very late in the claim and the only variations to the existing case management directions are the amendment to statement of value, re-allocation and fresh trial window, it may be appropriate to include in the application a request that the court exercises its power under CPR r.3.12(1)(c) not to costs manage. This would be on the basis that the cost of the exercise may, in context, be disproportionate as the costs and steps to be incurred at that stage are limited. Of course, this argument is something of a double-edged sword, as the court may take the view that as such, the costs management exercise will not occupy much court time and can be dealt with promptly and proportionately and as preparation for trial and trial are usually two of the most expensive phases of the budget (if not the most expensive), the exercise is still worthwhile and necessary. In the case of *Hegglin v Person(s) Unknown, Google Inc*[136] the court was confronted with an application to cap costs ten days before the commencement of the trial. Edis J declined to do so, based on the late stage of the proceedings and the procedural threshold for making such orders, but, instead, exercised costs management powers under CPR r.3.15 to budget the trial and some outstanding work on an expert's report (see **Q105** below). Similarly, in *Arcadia Group Ltd v Telegraph Media Group Ltd*[137] the court costs managed even though only the PTR, Trial Preparation and Trial phases remained.

Q76. Is a party who was acting in person at the costs management conference (and so has no budget), but who subsequently instructs solicitors, required to exchange and file a Precedent H? If a party changes solicitors are the new solicitors bound by the budget?

4–98 Strictly the answer to the first question is that there is no procedural provision that requires the party to serve and file a budget in this situation. However, in practice the position is not quite as simple as this initial answer suggests as there are a number of potential triggers for a Precedent H in this situation. These are as follows:

- Whilst the court file is unlikely to be referred to a judge simply because a party has become represented and a notice of acting is filed, experience suggests that frequently solicitors coming on record make applications for directions at the same time. If the file is referred to the judge to consider listing of any such application it is likely that the court will take the opportunity to order the filing and service of a Precedent H, triggering the possibility of costs management. Remember that under CPR r.3.16 a hearing may be convened by the court solely for purpose of costs management.

---

[136] *Hegglin v Person(s) Unknown, Google Inc* [2014] EWHC 3793 (QB); [2015] 1 Costs L.O. 65 Edis J.
[137] *Arcadia Group Ltd v Telegraph Media Group Ltd* [2019] EWHC 96 (QB); [2019] 1 Costs L.O. 169.

- It is arguable that the instruction of solicitors by a party previously unrepresented is a significant development in the litigation for any other party who is subject to a costs management order already (e.g. representation may shorten the trial or any application made by the new representatives, if successful, would have an effect on the budget previously set). This would engage CPR r.3.15A for the budgeted party and it is hard to see that if the court had to be involved in respect of any variation of budgets it would not also wish to budget the costs of the party who had previously been a litigant in person.
- Any other party who was subject to a budget might apply to the court to make a costs management order in respect of the previously unrepresented party's costs under CPR r.3.16 (see above). This seems likely as otherwise any budgeted party may feel prejudiced by having to conduct litigation within the parameters of a budget, whilst the previously unrepresented party would not be so constrained.
- All parties may want a budget set so that the "recoverable costs" are known at this stage and the parties may then make decisions about the litigation fully informed about the costs consequences i.e. knowing what, if anything, will be the shortfall between recoverable and solicitor-client costs if a costs order is secured and what the liability will be for the other party's costs if there is an adverse costs order.

So far as the second question is concerned, the court has made a costs management order. Unless there is a significant development in the litigation (and a change of representation itself does not amount to this), then the budget is binding. This does not prevent the new solicitors seeking to approach the claim in a different way and using CPR r.3.15A to try to vary the budget. The fact that they are "new" solicitors does not alter the approach of the court to variation under CPR r.3.15A.

Q77. In multi-track claims which have not been subject to costs budgets, are parties under an obligation to file a costs estimate with the Pre-Trial Checklist ("PTCL")?

CPR PD 29 para.8.1(1) requires a PTCL to be in Form N170. Guidance at the   4–99
beginning of the N170 suggests that in cases not costs managed an estimate of costs is required. However, it is clear from the wording used (reference to costs estimates and reference to these being provided in accordance with the provisions of the CPR) that the guidance is an unhappy and unwelcome failure to take account of the revised CPR. The provisions relating to budgets are to be found at CPR rr.3.1(7)(ll), 3.12–3.18, 3.20, PD 3E, PD 3F and CPR PD 44 para.3. These do not contain any requirement for an estimate at the time of PTCL (and neither does CPR r.29—other than by cross-reference to Form N170 in the PD as referred to above).

The result is that there appears little reason for the reference to "an estimate of costs" in cases not costs managed in Form N170. By this stage, directions will have been given and so the estimate is unlikely to inform the route the claim takes to trial. In addition, the provisions of CPR PD 44 para.3 do not apply as the estimate is not "a budget in accordance with" CPR PD 3E. It is also not clear what form the estimate should take as one is not prescribed. The requirements set out in Form N170 become even less clear in the (apparently incomplete) final sentence on estimates, which provides:

"In substantial cases, these should be provided in compliance with CPR."

This version of Form N170 is well into its eighth year. It is clearly ripe for update and correction.

As an aside, but supportive of the view that the procedural requirements for costs estimates have not kept pace with the changing rules, CPR PD 28 para.6.1(4), which applies to fast track cases also requires a costs estimate with the pre-trial checklist, but states this to be in accordance with s.6 of the Costs PD. That PD ceased to exist nearly nine years ago. It seems that this PD is also long overdue a continuity check.

Finally, it seems that the clock may be about to stop on nine years and counting of confusion. The minutes of the open meeting of the Civil Procedure Rules Committee in May 2021 reveal this exchange:

"Question 10 Form N170 & Costs Form N170 (Listing Questionnaire (Pre-Trial Checklist)) states in section F that the parties must attach 'an estimate of costs' to the N170 but this reference would appear to relate to the pre-April 2013 CPR costs regime and the old costs Practice Direction. Is there any plan for this form to be updated?
Answer 10 On behalf of Master Cook, the Chair confirmed that there are indeed plans to update this form. The question raises an important issue which the Forms Sub-Committee are keen to address, which is to ensure that necessary changes to the Forms are addressed when changes are made to CPR."

Notwithstanding what is set out above, it appears some estimates of costs are still required outside the CPR, e.g. para.9 of the PTCL information appearing at App.2 of the *Commercial Court Guide* and which parties must complete under para.D13.1 of the guide.

Q78. What is the purpose of the reference in CPR r.36.23 to CPR r.36.17(4)–(b)?

4–100   CPR r.36.23 provides a limited "automatic" relief from the sanction of CPR r.3.14 if an offeror pursuant to CPR r.36 is subject to the constraints imposed by CPR r.3.14. In the three situations set out in CPR r.36.23 (namely under CPR r.36.13(5)(b), 36.17(3)(a) and 36.17(4)(b)), the offeror may still be able to recover 50% of the costs assessed for those costs otherwise subject to the sanction and any other recoverable costs (i.e. those that were incurred at the time of the failure to file Precedent H). The rationale is clear. It is to provide the offeree with an incentive to accept the offer (the incentive being some adverse costs risk if the offer is a good one).

However, why does CPR r.36.23 expressly refer to CPR r.17(4)(b) because that provision is one specifically awarding the claimant costs on the indemnity basis? Having secured such an award of costs one might think that the sanction under CPR r.3.14 falls away anyway, because the constraints imposed on recoverable costs as a result of an approved or agreed budget by CPR r.3.18 expressly only apply to costs awards "between the parties" on the standard basis (see para.4–20 above and Q93 below). Accordingly, one might assume that any budget set on the basis of what is deemed under CPR r.3.14 to be in the budget (namely future court fees) ceases to be relevant on an indemnity basis award of costs. On this interpretation the provision seems designed to cover the period from the date the budget is set at future court fees only until the date from which the indemnity basis costs order runs. However, if that is the intention why link the provision to CPR r.36.17(4)(b) expressly, which already offers a solution for the particular period covered by that provision and not to CPR r.36.17(1) more generally?

Another construction is that CPR r.36.23 is a "freestanding" procedural sanction designed to constrain the effect of an award of indemnity costs where there has been a breach of CPR r.3.13, so that the award of indemnity costs under CPR r.36.17(4)(b) does not provide an unqualified escape route for a claimant. In other words, it is a specific rule, the 50% is not expressed to be 50% of what would have been budgeted and therefore CPR r.3.18 is not engaged at all. This would mean that CPR r.36.23 provides a benefit where the offeror comes before the court under either CPR r.36.13(5)(b) or 36.17(3)–(a), but a sanction if the offeror is a claimant coming before the court under CPR r.36.17(4)(b). However, this would mean that a claimant whose costs are constrained under CPR r.3.14 who secures an indemnity basis costs award outside the CPR r.36 regime is in a better situation than one who secures the award under CPR r.36.17(4)(b)—a curious outcome when CPR r.36 is designed to promote settlement.

On balance, given that CPR r.36.23 does not refer to the 50% being linked to what would have been budgeted, instead being an assessed sum outside of the budget, and because it expressly refers to a specific rule for indemnity costs that the rule-makers would have realised gives "relief" from CPR r.3.14 without the need for any further provision, the arguments for the latter of these two constructions appear more compelling. However, with an increasing number of "costs managed" cases coming to fruition and with this provision having been in place for approaching seven years, it cannot be long before some authorities emerge from the Higher Courts to provide guidance on the purpose of this discrete provision.

A final option is that the reference to CPR r.36.17(4)(b) in 36.23 is one made in error. However, it must be assumed that this is not so and that it reflects the intention of the rule- makers. Unless and until it is removed it raises the issues set out above.

G. Variation of budgets and freestanding costs orders

Q79. What is a significant development for the purposes of CPR r.3.15A?

4–101 There is no formal definition of "significant development". No doubt the reason for this is that the interpretation has to be sufficiently flexible to enable the court to consider the position in the specific context of the case before it. Much has been made of the decision in *Churchill v Boot*[138] in which Picken J refused permission to appeal the decision of the QB Master not to permit variation of the claimant's budget in circumstances where the claimant argued that each of:

- the doubling in the size of the claim;
- the adjournment of the trial; and
- there being further disclosure,

amounted to a "significant development". However, in fact, this decision simply confirms the "case-specific" approach to be adopted. The court concluded that:

- a doubling of the size of the claim does "not necessarily" amount to a significant development (and in any event, this was something that could have been anticipated at the time of costs management);
- whilst adjournment of a trial could amount to a significant development, it did not in this case; and
- the issue of further disclosure was something apparent before the costs management order.

In other words, these were not significant developments in this case as they were known about and/or should have been considered at the time of the costs management order. A similar view was taken in *Seekings v Moores*,[139] where the court refused variations to a number of phases on the basis that work should have been anticipated when the budget was agreed and, unsurprisingly, where the party had brought the additional costs on himself by failing to give the best particulars available and clarify his case in response to a request for further information.

Similarly, in *Chalfont St. Peter Parish Council v Holy Sisters Trustees Inc*[140] the court refused a late application to vary as the party applying was not being required to do anything that it had not known it would need to do to meet the allegations against it. There was nothing that had caused substantially more work than that which should have always been foreseeable as part of the case.

---

[138] *Churchill v Boot* [2016] EWHC 1322 (QB); [2016] 4 Costs L.O. 559.
[139] *Seekings v Moores* [2019] EWHC 1476 (Comm); [2019] Costs L.R. 689.
[140] *Chalfont St. Peter Parish Council v Holy Cross Sisters Trustees Inc* unreported 29 January 2019 (QBD) Sir Alistair MacDuff.

More recently, under the amended provisions at CPR r.3.15A in *Persimmon Homes Ltd v Osborne Clark LLP*,[141] where the assumptions upon which Precedent H has been prepared were out of date by the time of costs and case management, but this was not raised before the court or with the other parties, and the court gave tailored directions (particularly in respect of disclosure) and set the budget, informed by what appeared to be the relevant Precedent H figures, the court concisely summarised the requirements of a variation in these terms, usefully highlighting that which does not fall within the constraints of CPR r.3.15A:

"It is for the party seeking the variation to provide sufficient information and evidence with their application to satisfy the court that the variation is not simply an attempt to address a miscalculation or an overspend or to claw back previously disallowed costs." Para 118

By way of contrast, the court permitted a variation to the claimant's budget in *Zeromska-Smith v United Lincolnshire Hospitals NHS Trust*[142] where there appeared to have been a misunderstanding when agreeing directions and it only became apparent when the defendant served its psychiatric evidence, eight months after its receipt, that there was a denial that the claimant had suffered any psychiatric injury.

As a gloss on *Persimmon Homes Ltd* (above), in *Thompson v NSL Ltd*,[143] the court concluded that there may be cases (and this was one of them) where the trigger for a revision happened between drafting Precedent H and the costs management conference, but the effect of the significant development was not clear enough to justify a revised budget at the hearing and, so, a later revision of the budget was permitted, once it became apparent that the development did trigger a need to vary the budget.

Some other examples of developments that the court may consider significant are given in para.4–19 above.

Q80. Can the court make retrospective orders in respect of revisions of budgets under CPR r.3.15A to enable it to fulfil its function under CPR r.3.15(3)? Exactly what scope is there for retrospective revision of budgets? Does the replacement of CPR PD 3E para.7.6 by CPR 3.15A deal with how the two provisions interact? Why does Precedent T only seek one figure for variation, rather than a division of the variation costs between those already incurred and those to be incurred arising from the significant development? Does a party have to file a revised Precedent H with the Precedent T?

---

[141] *Persimmon Homes Ltd v Osborne Clark LLP* [2021] EWHC 831 (Ch).
[142] *Zeromska-Smith v United Lincolnshire Hospitals NHS Trust* [2019] EWHC 630 (QB).
[143] *Thompson v NSL Ltd* [2021] EWHC 679(QB).

4–102 The answer to the first question is yes. The new CPR r.3.15A(6) provides that:

> *"Where the court makes an order for variation, it may vary the budget for costs related to that variation which have been incurred prior to the order for variation but after the costs management order."*

However, it is important to note that this is only possible if the court does make an order for variation. In other words, if the court does not consider there to have been a significant development, or that there has been, but this does not warrant a variation of the budget, a party cannot seek retrospective validation of costs under CPR r.3.15A(6). In theory, it could still apply to recover these costs at a later assessment under the "good reason" provision in CPR r.3.18. In theory, because it is difficult to foresee a situation where the court has decided that there is no significant development that warrants revision, but accepts that there is good reason to depart. One situation may be where a receiving party has been forced to incur costs over the budgeted sum for a phase in response to what the paying party says is a significant development that warrants variation, the court accepts that there is a significant development, but not one that warrants variation and, so, unless there is a permitted departure from the budget for "good reason" the receiving party will be left out of pocket as a result of the paying party's conduct.

The new procedure set out in CPR r.3.15A, which requires court approval of any variation, removes the previous anomaly that permitted variation without court intervention, which sat unhappily with the obligation on the court under CPR r.3.15(3) to control the parties' budgets in respect of recoverable costs once it had made a costs management order. Now, under CPR 3.15A(5):

> *"The court may approve, vary or disallow the proposed variations, having regard to any significant developments which have occurred since the date when the previous budget was approved or agreed, or may list a further costs management hearing."*

As retrospective variation is permitted by CPR r.3.15A(6), the court does not require a division of the variation costs between those costs already incurred and those still to be incurred as the court will, if it decides there has been a significant development in the litigation justifying variation, permit a variation by way of one figure that is reasonable and proportionate. It is, therefore, unsurprising that the variation column in Precedent T requires only one figure per phase for the entire costs (up or down) associated with the variation.

The extent of permitted retrospection remains seems to be a matter for determination. This is unsurprising as promptness under CPR r.3.15A(d) will be case-specific. However, there are some early general steers. In *Cranstoun v Notta*[144] the court suggested that "the promptness (or otherwise) with which a variation is sought may well reflect on whether the revision is or is not in

---

[144] *Cranstoun v Notta* [2021] EWHC 133 (Ch).

respect of a significant development". Certainly, CPR r.3,15A is not designed to permit "budget repair" when the work in question has been undertaken and the party simply failed to deal with revision timeously nor, as in *Persimmon Homes Ltd v Osborne Clark*,[145] where the assumptions upon which Precedent H has been prepared are out of date by the time of costs and case management, but this is not raised before the court or with the other parties, and the court makes a specific direction informed by what appear to be the relevant budget figures. As Master Kaye observed:

> "It is for the party seeking the variation to provide sufficient information and evidence with their application to satisfy the court that the variation is not simply an attempt to address a miscalculation or an overspend or to claw back previously disallowed costs."

Q81. Can a party who is subject to the sanction of CPR r.3.14 vary its budget if there is a significant development in the litigation pursuant to CPR r.3.15A?

Yes it can. Unsurprisingly, the court has confirmed that if there is a significant development leading to increased costs in a claim where one party has fallen foul of CPR r.3.14 and has had a budget set at future costs only, that party will be able to seek an upward variation for the additional work linked to the significant variation (see *Asghar v Bhatti*).[146] Unsurprisingly because the provision at CPR r.3.15A is dealing with variation. The original budget (whether set under CPR r.3.14 or CPR r.3.15) will not have included anything for the unforeseen significant development in the litigation and therefore the original budget should be varied to provide for this.

4–103

Q82. Can a party make repeated variations to its budget? Is agreement of budgets to be approached differently under CPR r.3.15(2)(b) and CPR r.315A?

Yes, if that is appropriate. Under CPR r.3.15A a party must (a semantic change from the previous provision, which used the word "shall") revise its budget if significant developments in the litigation warrant this. Accordingly, provided that there are a number of significant developments, then there is no reason why there should not be repeated attempts to vary. What a party may not do is to make repeated attempts to vary in respect of the same alleged significant developments. If a variation is submitted to the court, which finds that there is, in fact, no significant development or finds that there is a significant development but either that this does not justify revision of the budget or not to the level that the party wishes, any dissatisfied party may appeal the decision of the court in the usual way under CPR r.52 (recognising that it will be rare indeed for an appellate court to interfere with a discretionary case management decision).

4–104

---

[145] *Persimmon Homes Ltd v Osborne Clark LLP* [2021] EWHC 831 (Ch).
[146] *Asghar v Bhatti* [2017] EWHC 1702 (QB); [2017] 4 Costs L.O. 427.

This leads neatly on to a consideration of the effect of agreement of budgets. Does agreement between the parties carry less weight on variation than when the court sets the first budget? CPR r.3.15A(5), gives the court the jurisdiction to approve, vary, or disapprove a variation (and this provision is not expressly limited to variations that are not agreed). Although "approve" in CPR r.3.15(2)(b) refers to where there is no agreement, in practical terms there is no difference between approval or agreement under CPR r.3.15(2), as the effect is that the court makes a costs management order with the consequence set out in CPR r.3.18. Accordingly, both CPR r.3.15A(5) and CPR r.3.15(2) provide that where the parties are in agreement and, on variation, assuming the court is prepared to endorse the agreement by way of approval, the jurisdiction is the same. Similarly, the court may "disapprove" of an agreement expressly under CPR r.3.15A(5) and may do so under CPR r.3.15(2), by simply exercising its discretion not to make a costs management order. However, what CPR r.3.15(2) does not permit the court to do and which CPR r.3.15A(5) does permit it to do, is to vary the agreed sum where the basis upon which it was agreed has not been altered by the directions that the court has given (e.g. the expert phase is agreed on the basis of two experts per party and that is what the court permits), whereas it seems that CPR r.3.15A(5) does permit this (and so in the example given, may give a direction for two experts per party on an application based on a significant development in the litigation, but can vary the agreed variation to budget sum for this significant development).

Q83. If an appeal is launched against a decision on an interim application that falls within a discrete phase (e.g. against an order in respect of permission for expert evidence) does CPR r.3.15A apply and should budgets be revised and submitted to the court for approval of the proposed variation?

4–105   Precedent H itself makes it clear that the costs of any appeals are excluded. Accordingly, unless the appellate court decides to costs manage the appeal under the provisions of CPR r.3.12(1A) and so orders, there is no requirement either to file and exchange budgets for the appeal itself or to seek revision of the existing budget in the substantive proceedings simply to budget the appeal. However, where the substantive appeal requiring determination raises issue of proportionality (e.g. should an additional expert have been permitted) the appellate court may require revised budgets to enable it to determine the issue (see CPR r.1.1 and CPR r.3.17). In any event, if the consequence of the appeal, whether allowed or dismissed, is to have an effect on the budgets set for the substantive litigation, then variation of those existing budgets does arise e.g. the appeal results in permission for another expert, for strike out of, or judgment on, part only of the claim. This latter point raises the issue of whether the appellate court undertakes any budget revision required or refers this back to the first instance case managing court. If the appeal allowed is one such as in respect of additional expert evidence, the appellate court has had the revised budgets to enable it to determine the issue of proportionality, then it is likely to be proportionate for it to undertake the revision. If the appeal is one such as summary judgment in part, that does not require consideration of the costs consequences and which, in any event, completely alters the complexion of the case (and, inevitably in consequence, the budget set), then adjourning the revision to the case managing judge, seems more appropriate.

Q84. It seems that some parties are not applying to vary budgets, but instead prefer to wait to argue "good reason" to depart from the budget at any subsequent assessment. Is this because it is easier to depart from a budget retrospectively when the work, which has by then been done, may be simpler to justify than to vary prospectively when the work proposed may be seen to be speculative?

As noted under **Q80** above, a party is obliged to revise its budgeted costs if significant developments in the litigation warrant this. CPR r.3.15A is prescriptive Accordingly, any party choosing to ignore this and seeking to argue "good reason" at any subsequent assessment does so contrary to mandatory requirements in the CPR. Whilst it is for the court in each individual case to determine whether the "good reason" requirement for departure from a budget under CPR r.3.18 is met, it is difficult to imagine that a deliberate decision to defer could ever constitute "good reason".

It is also challenging to imagine many significant developments in litigation that do not require court intervention, regardless of budgetary considerations, by way of further case management decision. As the court is under an obligation pursuant to CPR r.1.1, CPR rr.3.15(3) and CPR r.3.17 to control costs and ensure that case management decisions are made against a backdrop of whether a step is proportionate, it should not be possible for directions that result in or follow a significant development in the litigation to be determined without consideration of the budgetary implications at that juncture. It follows from this that any application for any additional case management directions that will result in or follow a significant development in the litigation, after a budget has been set, should be accompanied by a Precedent T setting out the implications on the budget set, if the additional direction/s is/ are granted. Any respondent to such an application, whether opposing it or not, whose budget will be affected if the court makes the direction/s sought, ought to submit its own Precedent T to ensure that its budget will also be varied if the court accepts that there is a significant development justifying additional work for which the last agreed/approved budget does not provide. Indeed, any party opposing a variation on the basis that any significant development should not lead to a specific direction (e.g. permitting an expert) or does not warrant budget revision on the grounds of proportionality, would be well advised to submit its own Precedent T anyway, so that it can demonstrate to the court the disproportionality of the direction sought. In this situation the court will still want to know potential cost implications of any decision,

4–106

to inform it when determining under the provisions set out above, whether to make the order sought.

The suggestion that work (and, more precisely, the costs associated with it) may be easier to justify with the benefit of hindsight, also risks overlooking the provisions of CPR r.44.3(2)(a)—namely that considerations of proportionality trump both reasonable and necessary work. Accordingly, unless the application of CPR r.44.3(5) leads to a different conclusion than it did when the budget was set, the fact that more work might have been necessary or reasonable is irrelevant.

(See **Q80** above for further consideration of the link between CPR rr.3.15A and 3.18)

Q85. Can parties vary budgets by agreement without court involvement or must the court approve any variation for it be effective? If so, what options are available to the court? How should "promptly" be interpreted in CPR r.3.15A(2)? Does CPR 3.15A require a formal application to the court?

4–107 The previous procedural provision regulating variation of budget permitted this to occur without court scrutiny or approval (although, with limited exceptions, variations tend to require court involvement in any event, by way of direction orders). However, this is no longer the position. CPR r.3.15A(2) is clear that, whether agreed or not, revised budgets must be submitted to the court after being submitted to the other party/ies. This must be done promptly (r.3.15A(4)). The court has a number of options on receipt of Precedent T. These are as follows:

- To approve the variation as sought.
- To approve a variation, but in a varied amount.
- To disallow the variation.
- To list for a costs management conference.

This requirement for court approval is consistent with the obligation imposed on the court by CPR r.3.15(3) to "control the parties" budgets in respect of recoverable costs" once it has made a costs management order and represents a departure from the procedure on initial costs management, when the court cannot interfere with agreed budgets, unless it does not case manage in line with the assumptions that informed the agreed budget or it chooses not to make a case management order.

CPR r.3.15A(4) does not appear to require a formal application, providing only an obligation to submit documents to the court:

"(4) The revising party must submit the particulars of variation promptly to the court, together with the last approved or agreed budget, and with an explanation of the points of difference if they have not been agreed."

Prompt submission of the particulars of the revision is vital. However, when submitting this, the party seeking variation is obliged under CPR r.3.15A(4) to do so with an explanation of the points of difference if the variations have not been agreed. This suggests that the party seeking variation must first afford any other parties the opportunity to agree the revisions or to state why they are not agreed. The rules provide no time scale for the consideration by any other party and no definition of promptly in this context. However, there can be no doubt that to satisfy the requirements for prompt submission, tight timescales will have to be imposed on any other parties' consideration of a proposed variation. If these are not complied with, then our view is that it will be better to submit the proposed variation to the court with an accompanying explanation that it is not known if the variation is agreed, explaining why there is no compliance with CPR r.3.15A(4) in respect of points of difference, than to wait for a response and risk falling foul of the requirement to submit promptly.

Q86. If a costs management order has been made in a case but not long afterwards a party makes a potentially determinative application for summary judgment (SJ), should the parties apply promptly for the budgets to be revised? Suppose that they do, but the hearing for SJ is likely to come on before the application to revise costs budgets can be heard, what should they do? Could the potential respondent to the SJ application not justifiably seek, in such circumstances, an order that the costs thrown away by this change of tack by the applicant be paid by it in any event?

These questions raise two issues. The first relates to contingencies and the second to the relationship between budgets and CPR r.3.17(4). Dealing with those in turn:

    4–108

1) Depending upon the temporal proximity the position may be different for the applicant and the respondent to the application.
    • The applicant: This seems to be an example of when something (the application) was more likely than not to occur at the time of the budget, and so ought to have been included as a contingency. If it ought to have been in the budget as a contingency, it raises the interesting question of whether the failure to include it means that the applicant to the application can neither seek budgetary variation because it is not, for that party, a significant development in the litigation (as it knew at budget setting time it was going to issue the application imminently) nor, if successful on the application, seek a freestanding order for costs of the application outside the budget (considered in more general terms below) as it is not an interim application made that, reasonably, was not included in the budget. The fact that the application itself may fall within a fixed costs regime (e.g. a CPR r.24 application) offers no assistance either, as it is only if the proceedings (as opposed to the application) are subject to fixed costs that there is an exclusion from costs management under CPR r.3.12(1)(c).

- The respondent: Obviously the respondent's budget did not include in it anything for the application, as it was not in a position to determine whether it was more likely than not to occur. As a result, CPRr.3.17(4) applies (see below) to any costs to which the respondent may become entitled, as it reasonably did not include this in the budget.

2) If the application was not "more likely than not to occur" at budget setting time and so was reasonably not included in either budget, then CPR r.3.17(4) applies. As such costs of the application will be dealt with at the end of the application and fall outside the budget. In other words, any costs awarded to a party will be in addition to, and freestanding of, any costs under the budget.

Q87. What sort of applications fall within the provisions of CPR r.3.17(4)? How does this link with the provisions for contingencies in the budget and budget variation?

4–109   CPR r.3.17(4) sets out those costs that will fall outside the budget. It refers to interim applications "which reasonably were not included in a budget". CPR PD 3E para.9 provides clear guidance on those costs which are contingent. CPR r.3.15A sets out the pre-condition for variation ("significant development in the litigation"). These comments link to the definition of contingent costs in the Precedent H guidance. The result is this:

- If something is more likely than not to occur at the time of the costs management order, but is not certain and so does not fit into another phase under-estimated costs, it should be included as a contingency. Parties need to be astute to whether a budgeted contingency becomes a reality as otherwise they may overlook that some of the contingencies never came to fruition for the purpose of "good reason" to depart from the budget (as the fact that a contingency for which budgetary provision was made did not occur, must surely be a "good reason" for departing from the budget).
- If the cost relates to an application that was not reasonably included in the budget at the time of the costs management order, it falls within CPR r.317(4) e.g. an application to enforce compliance with directions, and that cost is outside the budget and the costs of that application fall to be determined and then assessed as part of the determination of the application, which is entirely free-standing and independent of the budget.
- If something representing a significant development in the litigation arises (other than an application which is either more likely than not to occur at the time of costs management or which it was reasonable not to include in the budget), then the costs fall to be dealt with under CPR r.3.15A as a revision to the budgets.

Q88. When preparing Precedent H how should a party deal with the costs incurred in an application that has already been made and disposed of

with an order for costs? Should these be in as a contingency? Should they be in Precedent H at all?

Whilst this question might have been included in Section C above (and the same answer is given within **Q34**, we have included it here as a separate question because it links to comments on CPR r.3.17(4). Even though these are costs that have already been incurred, the court has already made a costs order within a freestanding application. It matters not whether that was an order that (a) one side pay the costs of another (b) quantified or did not quantify those costs or (c) provided for costs in the case, our view is that these fall outside the costs management regime and are additional to the budget.

4–110

H. The relevance of a budget at a subsequent assessment

Q89. What is the effect of a costs management order at an assessment of costs on the standard basis?

We have always adopted the position that CPR r.3.18 is clear and that there can be no departure, whether upwards or downwards, from the last agreed or approved budget for a phase unless there was a "good reason". However, there was a concerted challenge to this position in 2016 and 2017 which was rejected both by Carr J in *Merrix v Heart of England NHS Foundation*[147] and, subsequently, and in short order, by the Court of Appeal in *Harrison v University Hospitals Coventry and Warwickshire NHS Trust*,[148] with Davis LJ stating:

4–111

> "... since the meaning of the wording is clear and since it cannot be maintained that such a meaning gives rise to a senseless or purposeless result, effect should be given to the natural and ordinary meaning of the words used in CPR 3.18. In truth, that natural and ordinary meaning is wholly consistent with the perceived purposes behind, and importance attributed to, costs budgeting and CMOs."

Accordingly, the position is as we have stated—namely that the budgeted cost for a phase is a precise sum and that any departure (upwards or downwards) from the last agreed or approved budgeted cost for a phase at an assessment may only be on the basis of "good reason". (See **Ch.3, Q12** and para.**4–20** for further consideration of these decisions).

Q90. If the court makes a costs management order pursuant to CPR r.3.15(2)(c) what is the effect of this at any subsequent assessment of costs on the standard basis?

One might be forgiven for thinking that the answer is easy, as CPR r.3.18 is headed "Assessing costs on the standard basis where a costs management order has been made". After all, in the scenario in the question, a costs management order has been made under CPR r.3.15(2)(c). Unfortunately, the answer is not

4–112

---

[147] *Merrix v Heart of England NHS Foundation* [2017] EWHC 346 (QB); [2017] 1 W.L.R. 3399.
[148] *Harrison v University Hospitals Coventry and Warwickshire NHS Trust* [2017] EWCA Civ 792; [2017] 1 W.L.R. 4456.

so simple, as CPR r.3.18(a) limits the consequence at CPR r.3.18(b)—namely that the court will not depart from the figure unless satisfied that there is a good reason to do so—to "budgeted costs". "Budgeted costs" are defined in CPR r.3.15(1) as "the costs to be incurred". In fact, there is no reference at all in CPR r.3.18 to costs management orders in respect of agreed incurred costs and no provision elsewhere in Section II of CPR r.3 that provides the answer. Does this mean that there is no escape from the agreement of incurred costs or that there is, but the escape route is not founded on "good reason" (in which case it begs the question of what is it founded upon)? The argument for interpreting the silence in the rules as an indication that there is no escape from the agreed figures for incurred costs is that the party agreeing them has not done so undertaking a prospective exercise that involves an element of uncertainty as there is when dealing with costs to be incurred. Instead, it has made a decision with the benefit of hindsight based on known information. However, this is not entirely satisfactory. Take, for example, the case where significant sums have been incurred on expert evidence at the time of the preparation of Precedent H. Is it fair that a party that agrees those incurred costs cannot later seek to resile from that agreement if, subsequent to the agreement, the nature of the case alters to render that expert evidence superfluous, allowance is made for this in the award of costs by a percentage costs order, which still permits recovery of that percentage of the agreed incurred costs?

The argument for interpreting the silence in the rules as an indication that there is an escape from the agreed figures is the obvious one that CPR r.3.18 deals with the consequences of a costs management order and does not specify any consequence for those orders made under CPR r.3.15(2)(c) and could, and should, have done had that been the rule-makers intention.

Unless and until there is higher authority on this, we prefer the former interpretation because:

- It makes CPR r.3.15(2)(c) purposeful (because if there is no consequence what is the point of the court being permitted to make a costs management order in respect of these costs anyway); and
- If a party can depart from an agreement that leads to an order one would expect there to be some form of prescription in respect of the circumstances in which it can do so.

Rather than leave CPR r.3.15(2)(c) orders without express outcome, which opens the door to expensive argument upon this, it would be helpful if the CPR expressly addressed this point and provided clarity and certainty of the consequence (which might, of course, result in neither of the interpretations above being adopted, but instead see agreed incurred costs included in CPR r.3.18(a)).

Q91. CPR r.3.15(4) states that the court "may record on the face of any case management order any comments it has about the incurred costs

which are to be taken into account in any subsequent assessment proceedings". CPR r.3.18(c) makes it clear that if those assessment proceedings are on the standard basis the court will take those comments into account. What does "take into account" mean in these provisions?

Whilst CPR r.3.15(4) and CPR r.3.18(c) were added in April 2017, what was **4–113** CPR PD 3E para.7.4 (and is now found at both CPR r.3.15(4) and CPR r.3.17(3) (b)) already permitted the court to record comments on incurred costs, but with no specified consequence. However, there is no guidance as to what "take into account" means in this context. That said, to those involved with costs, it is a familiar phrase in the CPR. CPR r.44.4, dealing with assessment of amount of costs, is headed "Factors to be taken into account in deciding the amount of costs". It seems clear from this, that this is but another factor amongst all the circumstances that the assessing judge will take into account when exercising judicial discretion to assess the reasonableness and proportionality of the incurred costs. This interpretation is in line with that expressed by the Chief Chancery Master in *Richard v BBC*[149] who stated that the requirement to "take into account" a comment "falls someway short of it being binding on the Costs Judge" who, having taken the comment into account, is entitled to disagree with it. It is worth noting that in the same decision the Chief Master concluded that the court should exercise a degree of caution before making a comment. A view mirrored, unsurprisingly in the *Chancery Guide*, which states that "the power to make comments about incurred costs is likely to be used sparingly".[150] (See **Q55** which suggests a specific instance when recitals/comments on incurred costs might be appropriate.)

Q92. Is the budget "without prejudice" to any subsequent assessment?

There is no provision in the rules for applying a "without prejudice" qualifica- **4–114** tion beyond "good reason" to a costs management order, it is not part of the costs management regime and seems, simply to add time and costs to the case management process for no purpose.

Adopting this approach seems to deprive the parties of the certainty that CPR r.3.18 provides, involves everyone in an exercise that may well prove futile and seems to act as a clear encouragement to pursue costs issues further at assessment. Accordingly, such an approach seems contrary to the specific costs management provisions and the overriding objective (a view endorsed by the Court of Appeal in *Harrison v University Hospitals Coventry and Warwickshire NHS Trust*[151] when considering the purposes and prospective benefits of costs management).

Anecdotally, it appears some parties are trying to agree budgets subject to reserving the right to argue about the hourly rate at a subsequent assessment. As budgeted costs (to be incurred costs) are either agreed or are not agreed,

---

[149] *Richard v BBC* [2017] EWHC 1666 (Ch).
[150] *Chancery Guide* para.17.16.
[151] *Harrison v University Hospitals Coventry and Warwickshire NHS Trust* [2017] EWCA Civ 792; [2017] 1 W.L.R. 4456.

parties advancing this position should expect to be given fairly short shrift by the court. They are likely to find themselves deciding between maintaining the agreement on the budget, but without the qualification, or electing to have the court approve the budget. (See **Qs 59** and **60** above for further reference to this).

Q93. Can you explain how an award of costs on the standard basis differs from an award of costs on the indemnity basis in circumstances where a costs budget is in place?

4–115   The difference stems from the respective definitions of standard basis and indemnity basis costs in CPR r.44.3. Under the former, costs will only be allowed if costs are reasonably incurred and reasonable and proportionate in amount. Under the latter, costs will be allowed if they are reasonably incurred and reasonable in amount. In other words, there is no consideration of the proportionality of the costs under an award of indemnity basis costs. As costs budgets are set under CPR PD 3E para.12 on the basis of setting a figure within the range of reasonable and proportionate costs, it immediately becomes apparent that a budget cannot be relevant on an indemnity basis assessment as it has been set taking account of something that does not arise under the indemnity basis. This is why CPR r.3.18 expressly only applies to standard basis assessments. Accordingly, on a standard basis assessment, CPR r.3.18 applies and there may only be departure from those costs budgeted if there is "good reason", whilst on an indemnity basis assessment CPR r.3.18 does not apply, the budget does not operate as any constraint on recovery of costs and the court simply allows those costs reasonably incurred and reasonable in amount, with the benefit of any doubt going to the receiving party (which is also not something that the court applies on budgeting). If there was any uncertainty, this has been removed by the Court of Appeal decision in *Lejonvarn v Burgess*[152] (see para.**4–20** above in which the court confirmed that "In principle, the assessment of costs on an indemnity basis is not constrained by the approved cost budget. . .") It is obvious that the potential differential between costs on the standard basis and those on the indemnity basis in budgeted cases may, where the costs incurred exceed the budgeted sum, be significant.

Q94. If an award of indemnity costs is made and CPR r.3.18 does not apply, does the budget still form the starting point for the assessment of costs?

4–116   No—see para.**4–20** and **Q93** above. Instead, the starting point is that CPR r.3.18 only applies on standard basis assessments. In effect, this provides the explanation for the short answer given. However, to provide greater clarity there are three obvious justifications linked to the same underlying principle. These are:

---

[152] *Lejonvarn v Burgess* [2020] EWCA Civ 114.

- The statement of truth on the Precedent H makes it clear that the form should only include "incurred and estimated costs which it is reasonable and proportionate" for that party to incur. However, on an indemnity basis assessment proportionality has no part to play and, so, using a budget based on a Precedent H, which was prepared taking account of proportionality, as the starting point for an assessment which takes no account of it is immediately and obviously flawed.
- Under CPR PD 3E para.12 any budget set by the court will be one within the range of "reasonable and proportionate costs". Accordingly, the budgeted figures have been set taking account of proportionality which has no place on an indemnity basis assessment.
- On an indemnity basis assessment the benefit of any doubt as to whether costs were reasonably incurred or reasonable in amount is given to the receiving party. This is not something that has been applied at the budgeting stage.

If there remained any doubt, the comments of Dyson MR cited in para.**4–20** should dispel it. (See also **Ch.3 Q12**, which also considers this point.)

There is a real danger if the court were to send out a message that the budget is the starting point for an indemnity basis assessment. That danger is that parties will ignore the proportionality qualification in the certification on Precedent H and include higher costs, hoping that if they start the budgeting process higher they will come out higher and if then they obtain an indemnity costs order, even if the budget is taken as the starting point, the end result is still more likely to equate to a realistic approximation of indemnity basis costs. This may not lead to higher costs, as we would hope that the court's decision on proportionate costs for budgeting purposes would be unaltered by unrealistically high Precedent H figures, but, at the very least, it is likely to lead to more challenging and longer costs management hearings. There is also a risk that the court may be sufficiently troubled by unrealistic Precedent H figures, that this, perhaps understandably, infects its views on reasonableness and proportionality, resulting in a less generous approval of the appropriate figures for budgeted costs.

It is to be hoped that the Court of Appeal's decision in *Lejonvarn* (considered above at **Q93** and para.**4–20**) will mark the end of this debate.

Q95. (1) What effect will a "costs sanction" for unreasonable conduct, as suggested by the Court of Appeal in *Denton v TH White*,[153] have on a costs budget? (2) What does oppressive behaviour mean in CPR PD 3E para.13?

(1) At [42] of the majority judgment the Court of Appeal said this: 4–117

> "*The court will be more ready in the future to penalise opportunism . . . Heavy costs sanctions should, therefore, be imposed on parties who behave unreasonably in refusing to agree extensions of time or unreasonably oppose applications for*

---

[153] *Denton v TH White* [2014] EWCA Civ 906; [2014] 1 W.L.R. 3926.

relief from sanctions. An order to pay the costs of the application under rule 3.9 may not always be sufficient. The court can, in an appropriate case, also record in its order that the opposition to the relief application was unreasonable conduct to be taken into account under CPR r.44.11 when costs are dealt with at the end of the case. If the offending party ultimately wins, the court may make a substantial reduction in its costs recovery on grounds of conduct under rule 44.11. If the offending party ultimately loses, then its conduct may be a good reason to order it to pay indemnity costs. Such an order would free the winning party from the operation of CPR r.3.18 in relation to its costs budget."

Accordingly, it is clear that the "costs sanction" envisaged may be relevant to budgets set in two scenarios:

1. If the offending party subsequently becomes the receiving party on an assessment, then the unreasonable opposition may be a "good reason" to depart from the budget relying upon the provisions at CPR rr.44.11(1)(b) and 44.11(2)(a).
2. If the offending party subsequently becomes the paying party, then an award of costs on the indemnity basis may follow and, as has already been stated, this means that the provisions of CPR r.3.18 do not apply (as that rule is limited to where the court is assessing on the standard basis).

In both situations, the effect may be substantial—in the first limiting and in the second increasing costs recovery.

In a more general conduct/budget context, remember that CPR PD 3E para.13 enables a party to "apply to the court if it considers that another party is behaving oppressively in seeking to cause the applicant to spend money disproportionately on costs and the court will grant such relief as may be appropriate."

(2) There is no authority on this point. However, we suspect that any application of this provision will be case-specific and provide little guidance. Indeed, the relevant provision at CPR PD 3E para.13 gives a very clear explanation of its operation. The behaviour is that which seeks to cause another party to spend money disproportionately on costs. At the risk of over-simplification, we suspect that the answer is that you will know oppressive behaviour when you encounter it.

Q96. What guidance is there on what may constitute "good reason" under CPR r.3.18 to enable a departure from a budget at assessment?

4–118 Authorities on this topic are limited. However, that is not surprising for as Davis LJ observed in *Harrison v University Hospitals Coventry and Warwickshire NHS Trust*[154]:

---

[154] *Harrison v University Hospitals Coventry and Warwickshire NHS Trust* [2017] EWCA Civ 792; [2017] 1 W.L.R. 4456.

"As to what will constitute 'good reason' in any given case I think it much better not to seek to proffer any further, necessarily generalised, guidance or examples. The matter can safely be left to the individual appraisal and evaluation of costs judges by reference to the circumstances of each individual case." [44]

In other words, each case and each decision will be fact-specific. Obviously, some "good reason" departures from the budget are obvious, e.g. where a budgeted contingency does not arise or where a claim is resolved before a specific phase has commenced (and so the indemnity principle applies as no cost has been spent on that phase). Beyond these, counsel of caution must be to seek prospective variation under CPR r.3.15A whenever it is appropriate, rather than to run the gauntlet of arguing "good reason" at assessment. Further comments made by Davis LJ in *Harrison* reinforce this:

"Where there is a proposed departure from budget—be it upwards or downwards— the court on a detailed assessment is empowered to sanction such a departure if it is satisfied that there is good reason for doing so. That of course is a significant fetter on the court having an unrestricted discretion: it is deliberately designed to be so. Costs judges should therefore be expected not to adopt a lax or over-indulgent approach to the need to find 'good reason': if only because to do so would tend to subvert one of the principal purposes of costs budgeting and thence the overriding objective." At [44].

An illustration of the court finding there to be good reason in specific circumstances arises in the case of *Barkhuysen v Hamilton*.[155] Whilst awarding costs on the indemnity basis, and so there was no practical effect of considering departure from the budget (as CPR r.3.18 only applies to standard basis assessments), the court accepted that conduct of litigation, increasing costs beyond the budgeted amount by the generation of work beyond that contemplated within the budget, was "good reason" under CPR r.3.18, as, indeed, was a change of trial venue. Although *Simpson v MGN Ltd*[156] saw a departure from the budget, this case provided no guidance on "good reason" as the court found that there was no "good reason"—see para.4–20 above and Q98 below.

Q97. Can a trial judge ordering a detailed assessment of the costs of a party subject to a costs management order, give guidance to the assessing judge on what may be "good reason" to depart from the budget set?
This issue was mentioned in passing in *Capital for Enterprise Fund A LP v Bibby Financial Services Ltd*.[157] The judge concluded that even if, which he doubted, the trial judge had jurisdiction to indicate that it would be appropriate for there to be a departure from a budget, such power should only be used in exceptional circumstances. In *Car Giant Ltd v The Mayor and Burgesses of the*   4–119

155 *Barkhuysen v Hamilton* [2016] EWHC 3371 (QB); [2016] 6 Costs L.R. 1217.
156 *Simpson v MGN Ltd* [2015] EWHC 126 (QB); [2015] 1 Costs L.R. 139.
157 *Capital For Enterprise Fund A LP v Bibby Financial Services Ltd* [2015] 6 Costs L.R. 1059.

London Borough of Hammersmith[158] the court accepted that it had the jurisdiction, but indicated that a court should be slow to exercise that jurisdiction. The difficulty that this causes is one of possible inconsistency. This arises where an assessing judge is not assisted by any indication from the trial judge and so does not take certain information into account, but if the trial judge conducted a summary assessment then that information from the trial relevant to departure for "good reason" under CPR r.3.18 would be before the court. It is arguable that the court in *Capital for Enterprise Fund ALP* took too narrow a view of its function. If it could have used "trial information" to assist it on a summary assessment, why should that not be before the assessing judge on a detailed assessment: it is the same information and surely carries the same relevance whoever assesses the costs? The indication in *Car Giant Ltd* ". . . that there might be cases where the trial judge has a particular view of costs or on an aspect of costs, having conducted the trial or where he has had to decide an issue which is directly relevant to the assessment of costs" and that should be conveyed to the assessing judge is preferable. This view is supported by established authority that trial judges should assist assessing judges with relevant information (e.g. in the context of the application of the conduct provisions under CPR r.44.2 (trial judge) and CPR r.44.4 (assessing judge)—see for example *Ultraframe (UK) Ltd v Fielding*[159] and *Drew v Whitbread Plc*[160]) and there appears no discernible reason why the position should be any different in this situation.

Q98. Does CPR r.3.18(b) prescribe an automatic sanction where the receiving party has failed to amend its budget prospectively and can show no "good reason" for this failure or, as is suggested in *Simpson v MGN Ltd* (see para.4–20 and Q96 above), is it for the court, applying the overriding objective, to determine what the just and proportionate sanction should be?

4–120   In *Simpson* the court concluded that CPR r.3.18(b) did not provide a sanction and so, even where there was no "good reason" to depart from the last approved or agreed budget, that did not mean that the receiving party was automatically precluded from recovering in excess of the budgeted sum. An alternative view was expressed in *Sony Communications International Ab v SSH Communications Security Corp.*[161] The Court of Appeal in *Harrison v University Hospitals Coventry and Warwickshire NHS Trust*[162] has provided the definitive answer. Whether one calls the provision a sanction or not (and we have always regarded the provision as having an inbuilt sanction) matters not, as the effect of the rule is that in the absence of "good reason" there shall be no

---

[158] *Car Giant Ltd v The Mayor and Burgesses of the London Borough of Hammersmith* [2017] EWHC 464 (TCC); [2017] 2 Costs L.O. 235.
[159] *Ultraframe (UK) Ltd v Fielding* [2006] EWCA Civ 1660; [2007] C.P. Rep. 12 at [34].
[160] *Drew v Whitbread Plc* [2010] EWCA Civ 53; [2010] 1 W.L.R. 1725.
[161] *Sony Communications International AB v SSH Communications Security Corp* [2016] EWHC 2985 (Pat); [2016] 4 W.L.R. 186.
[162] *Harrison v University Hospitals Coventry and Warwickshire NHS Trust* [2017] EWCA Civ 792; [2017] 1 W.L.R. 4456.

departure upwards or downwards from the last agreed or approved budget for a phase. It is challenging to see this as anything but a sanction.

Q99. Can the budgeted sum exceed the sum due from that party to the solicitor under the contractual retainer, and, if so, is this a permitted breach of the indemnity principle? Is the indemnity principle a "good reason" to depart from the budget?
The budgeted sum may exceed the sum provided for within the retainer. **4–121** However, the fact that the court makes a costs management order does not mean that those costs are recoverable from another party regardless of the indemnity principle. Indeed, the amendment to the original statement of truth on Precedent H was, in part at least, to address the problem where specific fee retainers made completion of the budget difficult (e.g. in-house lawyers, fixed fee cases, cases run under DBAs, etc.).

Breach of the indemnity principle would be a "good reason" under CPR r.3.18 to depart from the budget (see comments on this at Q96 and para.4–20 above). However, this may prove a more challenging exercise than it seems at first sight. Imagine the case where the fee retainer is a fixed fee for all work or a damages-based agreement where there is simply "the payment" which cannot be calculated until the end of the claim. How does the solicitor apportion between the phases of Precedent H in those situations? Client retainers may need to be drafted in creative fashion to enable this apportionment and to meet any challenge under "good reason", e.g. that apportionment of the overall fixed fee/the payment is a matter for the solicitor provided that the work that has been agreed to be done under the retainer is undertaken. It is likely that as these cases work through the system, the court will be confronted with the challenges that they present and authority will emerge.

We have said previously, and still do (both here, in Q96 and para.4–20 above), that a failure to spend all the sum agreed/approved for a completed phase under a costs management order is a "good reason" to depart from a budget. There are different views e.g. see *Utting v City College Norwich*.[163] To an extent this difference of opinion matters not, for, by a different route, we reach the same outcome as in those cases – namely that the sum allowed on assessment is the sum actually spent by the party.

The reason we approach the matter slightly differently is because of the strict wording of CPR r.3.18. This is crystal clear. The court at assessment "will not depart from such approved or agreed budgeted costs unless satisfied that there is good reason to do so" (our emphasis). Assume that a party has an approved budget of £10,000 for the expert phase and the case management direction for that phase permits one expert each, that all the work anticipated for that phase has been undertaken (and so the phase is a completed one), but the party has spent only £8,000 on the phase. In its bill, the party claims £8,000 not £10,000, because it is constrained to do so by

---

[163] *Utting v City College Norwich* [2020] EWHC B20 (Costs).

the indemnity principle (remembering that these are budgeted and not fixed costs). CPR r.3.18 must apply, as the sum sought by the party is, self-evidently, a departure from the approved budget for the phase. The court may only assess a different sum than that approved upon there being a "good reason". The "good reason" is the indemnity principle. Does that mean that having found there to be "good reason" then the whole phase is subject to assessment on an item-by-item basis in the conventional way, which was what the court concluded in *Barts Health NHS Trust v Salmon*?[164] No. In our view, CPR r.3.18 is equally clear that the departure from the budget is by reference to the "good reason". Accordingly, in the example given up, the "good reason" is the constraint on costs imposed by the indemnity principle and the departure from the approved budget as a result of that "good reason", is a reduction from the budgeted sum of £10,000 of £2,000, leaving the assessed sum at £8,000. Remember that the court has already determined £10,000 to be reasonable and proportionate expenditure for the phase, therefore it is not open to a paying party to seek to erode the reduced sum (which, we believe addresses the concern that by concluding that the indemnity principle is a "good reason" this would somehow reopen arguments about the budget sum originally set, act as an incentive for detailed assessments and take away the certainty of budgets).

In conclusion, our view on the strict wording of CPR r.3.18, is that any departure (up or down) can only be on the basis of "good reason" and that the consequence of a finding of "good reason" sees a departure from the budgeted sum that is linked to that "good reason".

Q100. In a case where there has been a costs management order, is a breakdown of the costs claimed for each phase of the proceedings required when commencing detailed assessment proceedings when the assessment of costs is to be on the indemnity basis?

4–122 The simple answer is yes. A breakdown (and Precedent Q of the costs precedents is a model of such a form) must be served unless the information required is already provided in an electronic bill. This is because this is a requirement both under CPR r.47.6 and CPR PD 47 para.5.2(f). What purpose this breakdown serves is hard to imagine, as on an indemnity basis assessment CPR r.3.18, which sets out the relevance of the budget at assessment, does not apply as its provisions are limited to a standard basis assessment (see **Q93** above). We suspect that CPR r.47.6(1)(c) and CPR PD 47 para.5.2(f) should contain a qualification that they only apply where the order under which the court will be assessing the costs was one made on the standard basis. We say this because CPR PD 47 para.5.8(8), which is a section of the PD under the heading "Form and contents of bills of costs—general" and which requires bills in cases subject to a costs management order to be split into parts identifying the separate phases and, within those parts, between the incurred and

---

[164] *Barts Health NHS Trust v Salmon* unreported 17 January 2019 County Court at Central London HHJ Dight.

budgeted costs—applied to electronic bills under CPR PD 47 para.5.A3, which requires the incorporation of a form comparable to the Funding and Parts Table in Precedent S—is expressly limited to those cases where the costs order is on the standard basis.

To avoid the cost of compliance a receiving party in this position might consider contacting the paying party in advance of the time for commencement of the detailed assessment proceedings seeking agreement to a consent order providing that this requirement is waived. In the absence of agreement, an application ought to be made prospectively to dispense with the requirement. It seems prudent that this is dealt with by consent order even if the paying party agrees as CPR PD 47 para.5.2(f) is a mandatory provision. Accordingly, it may be wise to obtain the court's formal approval.

Of course, this still leaves the difficulty where there are both standard and indemnity bases costs orders and no clear phase division to match the temporal division.

I. Case management

Q101. Does the decision of the Court of Appeal in *Denton v TH White*[165] mean that relief from sanction will be granted provided that there is no prejudice to any other party that cannot be compensated by a costs order and that a trial date can still be met?
No, not necessarily. All cases will be fact-specific. The Court of Appeal has set out a clear three-stage approach to applications under CPR r.3.9 and it is the application of that which will determine the outcome of each specific request for relief. As such that may mean that in some cases the fact that there is no prejudice to the other party and a trial date can be met will, in all the circumstances, result in relief and in others it will not.

4–123

Whilst *Denton* clearly provides those seeking relief with a greater prospect of success than *Mitchell*, it is clear from the phraseology adopted by the court in *Denton* that there is not to be a return to the approach of pre-1 April 2013 as set out in the quote from the judgment in the text. Instead, as is stated in the judgment of the majority, what is required:

> "*is a more nuanced approach . . . Anything less will inevitably lead to the court slipping back to the old culture of non-compliance which the Jackson reforms were designed to eliminate.*"[166]

It is also important to remember that whilst *Denton* may have clarified and amplified the judgment in *Mitchell*, much of what that latter case determined remains pertinent and the actual facts of *Mitchell*, and the conclusion reached on those facts, still represents a far more robust approach to non-compliance than prior to 1 April 2013. If there was any doubt about that it is dispelled by

---

[165] *Denton v TH White* [2014] EWCA Civ 906; [2014] 1 W.L.R. 3926.
[166] At [38].

the decisions of the Court of Appeal in *Jamadar v Bradford Teaching Hospitals NHS Foundation Trust*[167] and the more recent restatement in *Diriye v Bojaj*[168] (see para.4–05 above). In the second of these two cases the Court of Appeal dealt directly with the pre and post-April 2013 approach to relief:

> *"If a breach was required adversely to affect the court timetable before it could be called serious or significant, that would be uncomfortably and unacceptably close to the pre-CPR regime, where the defaulting party could get away with repeated breaches of court orders simply because the other side could not show that they had suffered specific prejudice as a result. That is not now the law."* [50].

That this is a restatement and continuation of a theme can be seen from the earlier comments of the Court of Appeal in *R. (Idira) v The Secretary of State for the Home Department*[169] when it stressed:

> *"A party is not required to agree to an extension of time in every case where the extension will not disrupt the time-table for the appeal or will not cause him to suffer prejudice. If the position were otherwise, the court would lose control of the management of the litigation."*

This was also the approach adopted by the court in *BMCE Bank International PLC v Phoenix Commodities PVT Ltd*,[170] when the court rejected the notion that an undertaking to pay any additional costs caused by the late service and filing of a budget, so avoiding any prejudice to the other party, would, in isolation, result in relief being granted. Instead, the court applied the more nuanced approach required and considered this as simply part of the circumstances to consider, stating:

> *"I reject any suggestion, that the mere giving of the undertaking offered is some form of trump card or weighs so heavily in the weight of the balance of all the circumstances so as to outweigh all other factors. It is a matter that regard is to be had to, as I have done, as part of a consideration of all the circumstances."*

Similarly, the fact that refusal to grant relief will cause significant prejudice to the party in default does not mean that relief should be granted. In *Sinclair v Dorsey & Whitney*[171] a professional negligence claim said to be valued at £30 million was struck out for breach of an unless order to provide security for costs. An application for relief was dismissed on application of the *Denton* 3 stage test. The fact of prejudice (in terms of the lost opportunity to pursue such a claim) was insufficient when considered in all the circumstances and giving particular weight to the two factors in CPR r.3.9.

---

[167] *Jamadar v Bradford Teaching Hospitals NHS Trust* [2016] EWCA Civ 1001; [2016] 5 Costs L.R. 809.
[168] *Diriye v Bojaj* [2020] EWCA Civ 1440.
[169] *R. (Idira) v The Secretary of State for the Home Office* [2015] EWCA Civ 1187; [2016] 1 W.L.R. 1694.
[170] *BMCE Bank International PLC v Phoenix Commodities PVT Ltd* [2018] EWHC 3380 (Comm); [2018] 6 Costs L.O. 767.
[171] *Sinclair v Dorsey & Whitney Ltd* [2015] EWHC 3888 (Comm); [2016] 1 Costs L.R. 19.

Q102. Does the decision in *British Gas Trading Ltd v Oak Cash and Carry Ltd*[172] impact on the likelihood of relief from sanction being granted under CPR r.3.9?

In this case, the defence was struck out because the defendant failed to file its pre-trial checklist by the date specified in the case management order and then failed to comply with an "unless order" requiring filing by a later date and providing for strike out unless there was compliance. The claimant applied for judgment in default of defence and the entry of this triggered an application for relief by the defendant almost five weeks after the strike out. Relief was granted at first instance. This decision was overturned on appeal and the defendant appealed to the Court of Appeal, which dismissed the appeal. The importance of the Court of Appeal's decision is that it clarified that at the first stage of the *Denton* test for relief, the court should recognise that the breach of the "unless order" is not a free-standing breach and should look at both the original breach which led to the "unless order" and the breach of the "unless order" when considering whether the breach is serious or significant. Having clarified this, Jackson LJ drew the inevitable conclusion that breach of an "unless order" was a pointer towards both seriousness and significance because:

4-124

- it evidences breach of more than one obligation to do the same specific task; and
- the importance of compliance has been highlighted to the defaulting party by the very fact that an "unless order" has been made.

To answer the question, the effect of the decision is that parties applying for relief from sanction after the breach of an "unless order" start from the position that there is a pointer towards the breach being treated as serious or significant that does not exist where the breach is of what the court described as an "ordinary" order (i.e. not an "unless order").

Q103. Does the emphasis on proportionality impact on the situation where a claim falls within fast track financial limits, but the number of witnesses is such that the time needed for trial exceeds one day?

Indeed it does. Many of these cases would have been allocated to the multi-track based on the trial time estimate prior to 1 April 2013. Since that date, allocation must be viewed against the revised overriding objective and the court must determine whether allocation to the multi-track is proportionate. It will do so by reference to the revised overriding objective, the CPR r.44.3(5) factors and any "wider circumstances" under CPR r.44.4(1). The mere fact that the number of witnesses that the parties wish to call would mean that the trial will exceed one day is not determinative in isolation. If there is that number of witnesses because of the complexity of the claim or because there are issues

4-125

---

[172] *British Gas Trading Ltd v Oak Cash and Carry Ltd* [2016] EWCA Civ 153; [2016] 1 W.L.R. 4530.

of public importance or reputation, then that may justify allocation to the multi-track as proportionate. If no such factors exist, then the court is likely to allocate to the fast track. This will be in conjunction with effective case management using the powers that the court has under CPR r.32.2(3) to control the extent of witness evidence permitted and its powers under CPR r.39.4 (and, by cross-application, CPR r.28.6(1)(b)) to timetable the trial to ensure that the trial does not exceed one day. In such a case, parties may expect the trial timetable to limit the time allocated for opening the case (if permitted), cross examination, closing submissions and judicial consideration, judgment delivery, award of costs and summary assessment under any award. In other words, parties may have to select their "best" evidence and their "best" cross examination points. As Sir Rupert Jackson stated in the Final Report:

> *"The essence of proportionality is that the ends do not necessarily justify the means."*[173]

Remember that not only will allocation to the multi-track incur the parties in further expenditure, but also that CPR r.1.1(2)(e) expressly includes in the definition of "dealing with a case justly and at proportionate cost" the allocation of court resources and the express requirement to take account of the resource needs of other cases. Allocation to multi-track simply to accommodate a longer trial time erodes the judicial time available for other cases.

Q104. Do the case management rules apply as much to litigants in person as to represented parties?

4–126 Prior to 1 October 2015 the answer was yes, with the exception of the costs management provisions (as litigants in person are not required to prepare Precedents H under CPR r.3.13(6)—but see **Q2** above). However, from 1 October 2015 CPR r.3.1A has added a discrete provision relating to case management and the taking of evidence in claims involving litigants in person. The rule applies where at least one party is unrepresented (CPR r.3.1A(1)) and requires the court to have regard to the fact that at least one party is unrepresented when exercising any case management function. This includes the court adapting the standard directions under CPR r.29.1(2) (para.**4–08** above) and adopting any procedure that it considers appropriate to further the overriding objective. When taking evidence, the court may ascertain from an unrepresented party matters about which a particular witness may be able to give evidence and upon which that witness should be cross examined and may put to that witness or cause to be put to that witness such questions as appear to the court to be proper. What this means in practice remains to be seen. However, it seems likely that in terms of case management, properly interpreted, any alterations to usual procedure/directions in any particular case by the application of this rule will apply equally to represented and unrepresented parties in that particular claim.

---

[173] Ch.3, para.5.3.

Although not limited to litigants in person or parties, anyone conducting civil litigation through the courts should ensure they are aware of the Civil Justice Council Final Report "Vulnerable witnesses and Parties within Civil Proceedings—February 2020". As a result of this paper, from 6 April 2021 CPR r.1.1(2)(a) has been amended to include the requirement that consideration must be given to ensure that parties "can participate fully in proceedings, and that parties and witnesses can give their best evidence". There is a new accompanying PD at CPR PD 1A, which makes "provision for how the court is to give effect to the overriding objective in relation to vulnerable parties or witnesses".

Q105. Will cost capping under CPR Pt 3 Section III be ordered more rarely?
It seemed that costs capping had run its course. In his May 2015 "Confronting   **4–127**
costs management" lecture there is a record of only one question put to Sir Rupert Jackson that evening. It was: *"Is there now any place for costs capping?"*. His answer was unequivocal: "No. In my view the costs capping rules should be repealed". Reports of the CPRC meeting in July 2015 suggested that this was to happen. However, they were granted an 11th-hour reprieve and remain.

However, it is difficult to see how costs capping has a future in those cases where the costs management regime applies (see *Hegglin v Person(s) Unknown, Google Inc*[174] considered at **Q75** above and more recently *Thomas v PGI Group Ltd*[175]). By definition, a costs management order ensures that the costs budgeted are proportionate, as that is the basis upon which they have been set under CPR PD para.12. As the court in the costs capping regime can only apply a cap to future costs, then where costs management is available a party will never be able to satisfy the requirement of CPR r.3.19(5)(b), that without a cap there is a substantial risk that costs will be disproportionately incurred, because if they can do so, the court is inexorably drawn back to the requirement in CPR r.3.15(1) that it must costs manage where budgets have been filed and exchanged unless it is satisfied that the litigation can be conducted justly and at proportionate cost in accordance with the overriding objective.

It would be nonsensical to look at costs capping in those cases where the court exercises its discretion under CPR r.3.12(1)(e) to exclude cases that would otherwise fall within the costs management regime. This would fly in the face of the decision not to costs manage in the first place.

The relevance of costs capping in cases where the court chooses not to make a costs management order or which fall outside the regime is, at first blush, unaltered by costs management. However, in cases outside the regime where the court is concerned at the level of costs and the likelihood of these being adequately controlled by case management and subsequent assessment,

---

[174] *Hegglin v Person(s) Unknown*, Google Inc [2014] EWHC 3793 (QB); [2015] 1 Costs L.O. 65 Edis J.
[175] *Thomas v PGI Group Ltd* [2021] EWHC 2776 (QB).

the court may choose to exercise its discretion under CPR r.3.12(1A) to costs manage, rather than to costs cap. As the budget to be filed and served in an application for costs capping will be in the format of Precedent H (see CPR PD 3F para.2) and as the court will have to assess the costs for the purpose of imposing a cap anyway (CPR PD 3F para.4.1), it may determine that costs management is preferable to costs capping. This also avoids the difficulty presented by the "exceptional circumstances" threshold set for costs capping. As a result, it may be that a party seeking a costs cap may wish to link the application to one for costs management under CPR r.3.13(3)(a).

Obviously, if the court is to consider costs management as an alternative to costs capping it will require Precedents H from all parties and will need to exercise its discretion under CPR r.3.20(3)(a) to ensure that it has these when dealing with a multi-party claim.

A point of interest arises in respect of the subsequent relevance of budgets where a claim is not subject to the costs management regime, but where, in the course of an unsuccessful application for costs capping, Precedents H are filed and served. Are these budgets of relevance at any subsequent assessment of costs? Strictly under CPR PD 44 para.3.1 only budgets filed under CPR PD 3E are relevant when considering the provisions relating to a 20% or more difference between budget and eventual costs claimed. As the budget in a costs capping application has been filed under CPR PD 3F it seems that these provisions do not apply. It does seem curious that the provisions of CPR PD 44 para.3 have been limited and do not apply to all budgets filed under any rule, practice direction or court order.

The question is limited to CPR Pt 3 Section III. Amendments have been made to CPR Pt 46 to introduce the discrete costs capping regime in Judicial Review cases at Section VI.

Q106. What changes were implemented to the disclosure provisions at CPR Pt 31 under the Business and Property Courts disclosure pilot pursuant to CPR PD 51U? Has the pilot proven successful?

4–128   For those cases that fall within the pilot (see CPR PD 51U paras 1.2 – subject to para.1.4), the disclosure provisions apply, save in respect of existing orders that will not be disturbed unless set aside or varied. In addition, the pilot disclosure provisions will continue to apply after the end of the pilot period to any proceedings to which it applied. The pilot provisions have been subject to significant amendment. The most recent amendments found in the 136th CPR update in force from 1 November 2021 introduce a simplified and less onerous procedure for "Less Complex Claims" and include revisions to the Disclosure Review Document and to disclosure lists. As amendment seem to occur frequently (in the context of the pilot duration), there can be no substitute for referring to the PD and the various appendices to it for the detail of the disclosure regime under CPR PD 51U.

So far as the success of the pilot is concerned, it seems that this has not been unqualified. Not only has there been some judicial guidance on the conduct expected within the pilot (see *McParland & Partners Ltd v Whitehead*[176] and *AAH Pharmaceuticals Ltd v Jhoots Healthcare Ltd*,[177] but concerns were raised within the third Interim report on the pilot by Professor Mulheron.[178] The report has been considered by the Disclosure Working Group, which suggested amendments to the Pilot scheme and the Disclosure Review Document for consideration by the Civil Procedure Rules Committee. The recommendations were accepted by the Civil Procedure Rules Committee and as a result, the 127th CPR Update – Practice Direction Amendments, included revision of CPR PD 51U to reflect them. Subsequently, as indicated above, further substantive amendments have been made in the 136th CPR update at the suggestion of the Disclosure Working Group. The CPRC has extended the pilot until 31 December 2022, but when making the previous extension it did so explicitly on the basis that so doing "does not endorse the success or otherwise of the scheme".

Q107. How do the costs management provisions apply to the pilot disclosure provisions?
The first point to make is that an inevitability of the pilot disclosure provision is an intent to make the disclosure process more proportionate. In this **4–129** respect, the disclosure provisions sit entirely happily with costs management, as case management tools to operate as prospective controls on costs. Indeed, the disclosure certificate at the end of the Disclosure Review Document (DRD) refers to an awareness that in completing the document, if unrepresented, the signatory is aware that the burden and costs of disclosure are reasonable and proportionate in the context of the proceedings and, if represented, that the client has been informed of the overriding objective obligation to ensure this and of the costs of the disclosure model sought. There is genuine concern that the aim of the provisions has not been met and that the requirements under the pilot scheme have actually increased the cost of the disclosure phase.

CPR PDU 51 para.22 sets out the costs provisions under the disclosure pilot. These are as follows:

"*22.1 The parties are required to provide an estimate of what they consider to be the likely costs of giving the disclosure proposed by them in the Disclosure Review Document, and the likely volume of documents involved, in order that a court may consider whether such proposals on disclosure are reasonable and proportionate (as defined in paragraph 6.4). These estimated costs may be used by the court in the cost budgeting process.*
22.2 In cases where the cost budgeting scheme applies, if it is not practical to complete the disclosure section of Form H in relation to disclosure prior to the court making an order in relation to disclosure at the case management conference, the

---

[176] *McParland & Partners Ltd v Whitehead* [2020] EWHC 298 (Ch).
[177] *AAH Pharmaceuticals Ltd v Jhoots Healthcare Ltd* [2020] EWHC 2524 (Comm).
[178] Disclosure Pilot Monitoring in the Business and Property courts 3rd Interim Report – an analysis of questionnaire feedback from legal practitioners 25 February 2020, Professor Mulheron.

*parties may notify the court that they have agreed to postpone completion of that
section of Form H until after the case management conference. If they have agreed
to postpone they must complete the disclosure section within such period as is
ordered by the court after an order for disclosure has been made at the case management conference. Where possible the court will then consider (and if appropriate, approve) that part of the cost budget without an oral hearing."*

Clearly, the pre-case management conference work required on disclosure
means that there will be incurred costs on this phase. However, those will
have been spent on a process designed to ensure overall proportionality of
the phase. It is, therefore, unsurprising that the court should be able to make
a reasonable and proportionate decision on disclosure without all the detail
that would normally appear in the disclosure phase of Precedent H. In any
event, the DRD includes a section for the parties to estimate the cost of the
extended disclosure sought by any party,[179] and they should be in a position
to explain how these estimates were arrived at and to provide more information as to the impact upon them of any particular request for extended disclosure.[180] Accordingly, for those cases within the costs management regime, the
Practice Direction removes the obligation on parties to compete the disclosure
phase of Precedent H prior to the case management conference if that is not
practical and if the parties agree on this. If there is no agreement then either
this phase must be completed or, presumably the party seeking to defer completion may apply for an order to this effect, and if so, should apply before
the date for filing and exchange of Precedent H so that the court is then
considering an application to extend and not one directly for relief from the
sanction of CPR r.3.14 (see *Hallam v Baker Estates*[181], *Jalla v Shell International
Trading and Shipping Co. Ltd*[182] and **Q27** above). If the parties do agree to defer,
then once an order for disclosure has been made the parties must complete
this phase of Precedent H within such period as the court orders, on the basis
that they will then be in a better informed position as to the likely costs.[183]
Whilst this may seem contrary to the inextricable link between case and costs
management, requiring the two to be done together, in fact the court will
have had sufficient information in general terms at the CMC to inform the
reasonable and proportionate direction based on the information and costs
estimates in the DRD. Deferring the formal costs management process enables
the parties to provide the detail for simply the selected mode of disclosure,
aware of the court's views as to proportionality.

Finally, on the issue of costs, it is worth highlighting that CPR PD 51U para
6.6 contains this caution:

---

[179] Disclosure Review Document s.2 para.10 and Disclosure Review Document in "Less Complex Claims" at s.5.
[180] Disclosure Review Document s.2 paras.11 and 12.
[181] *Hallam v Baker Estates* [2014] EWCA Civ 661; [2014] 4 Costs L.R. 660.
[182] *Jalla v Shell International Trading and Shipping Co. Ltd* [2021] EWCA Civ 1559.
[183] CPR PD 51U para.22.2.

"*Disclosure Models should not be used in a way that increases cost through undue complexity.*"

This directive was echoed by the Chancellor of the High Court in the case of *McParland & Partners Ltd v Whitehead*,[184] when he took the opportunity to give general guidance on the disclosure pilot, including that:

"*It is clear that some parties to litigation in all areas of the Business and Property Courts have sought to use the Disclosure Pilot as a stick with which to beat their opponents. Such conduct is entirely unacceptable, and parties can expect to be met with immediately payable adverse costs orders if that is what has happened. No advantage can be gained by being difficult about the agreement of Issues for Disclosure or of a DRD, and I would expect judges at all levels to be astute to call out any parties that fail properly to cooperate as the Disclosure Pilot requires.*"

Q108. Why has the court proceeded to allocation of a case before the defendant to an additional claim has filed its directions questionnaire? Does this mean that the value and issues raised in the additional claim and the defence to it have been ignored for the purpose of allocation?
CPR r.20.3(2)(c) expressly disapplies CPR Pt 26 (Case management – preliminary stage) in respect of additional claims. As the requirement to file a directions questionnaire arises under CPR Pt 26, then, clearly, an additional party does not need to file such a document. However, this does not mean that the court ignores the additional claim when allocating to track. This is because CPR r.26.8(1)(e) requires the court, when deciding upon the track for a claim, to have regard, amongst a number of factors, to: **4–130**

"*the value of any counterclaim or other Part 20 claim and the complexity of any matters relating to it.*"

Q109. Do listing questionnaires have to be exchanged?
No. Neither CPR rr.28.5 (fast track) nor 29.6 (multi-track) require service, only filing. Whilst both CPR PDs 28 and 29 recommend the parties exchange listing questionnaires before their filing to ensure that the court is not provided with conflicting information, they do not contain any express obligation to do so, either before or after filing. However, it is conceivable that if a listing hearing is convened by the court Ie of a discrepancy between the parties' listing questionnaires and one party has not exchanged the document with the other prior to its filing and that would have resolved this discrepancy, then a costs sanction may arise in respect of the costs of the hearing. **4–131**

---

[184] *McParland & Partners Ltd v Whitehead* [2020] EWHC 298 (Ch).

CHAPTER 5

Part 36 and Other Settlement Offers Including ADR and Costs Consequences

Introduction

This chapter deals both with Part 36 offers and with other methods of achiev-   5–01
ing settlement; and is divided into two sections, the first dealing with Pt 36
and the second with methods of settlement other than Pt 36.

Section 1 Pt 36

Background to Pt 36

The Civil Procedure (Amendment No.8) Rules 2014 (SI 2014/3299), which   5–02
came into force on 6 April 2015, contain an entirely new version of Pt 36 in
Sch.1. There are also consequential amendments to other Parts. The intention
of the new Pt 36 is to align the rules with the case law developed since the Part
was last amended.

Transitional provisions

The current version of Pt 36 applies in its entirety only in relation to Part 36   5–03
offers made on or after 6 April 2015, save that CPR r.36.3 (definitions), CPR
r.36.11 (acceptance of a Part 36 offer), CPR r.36.12 (acceptance of a Part 36
offer in a split trial case) and CPR r.36.16 (restriction on disclosure of a Part 36
offer) also apply in relation to any Part 36 offer where the offer is made before
6 April 2015, but a trial of any part of the claim or any issue arising in it starts
on or after 6 April 2015.[1]

CPR Pt 36 after 5 April 2015

Section I of Pt 36 contains a self-contained procedural code about offers to   5–04
settle made pursuant to the procedure set out in that Part. Section I contains
general rules about Part 36 offers. Section II contains rules about offers to
settle where the parties have followed the Pre-Action Protocol for Low Value
Personal Injury Claims in Road Traffic Accidents (the RTA Protocol) or the Pre-
Action Protocol for Low Value Personal Injury (Employers' Liability and Public
Liability) claims (the EL/PL Protocol) and have started proceedings under Pt 8
in accordance with CPR PD 8B.[2]

---

[1] Civil Procedure (Amendment No.8) Rules 2014 (SI 2014/3299), CPR r.18(1) and (2).
[2] CPR r.36.1.

Under Section I, any party to an action may make an offer to settle in whatever way that party chooses, but if the offer is not made in accordance with CPR r.36.5 (form and content of a Part 36 offer) it will not have the consequences specified in Section I.[3] Where an offer does not comply with the requirements set out in CPR r.36.2, it is not a Part 36 offer.[4]

A Part 36 offer may be made in respect of the whole or part of any issue that arises in a claim, counterclaim or other additional claim, or an appeal or cross-appeal from a decision made at a trial.[5] Counterclaims and other additional claims are treated as claims, and references to a claimant or a defendant include a party bringing or defending an additional claim.[6]

The definition section of Pt 36 makes it clear that a trial means any trial in a case whether it is a trial of all the issues or a trial of liability, quantum or some other issue in the case. A trial is in progress from the time when it starts until the time when judgment is given or handed down. A case is decided when all issues in the case have been determined, whether at one or more trials.[7] CPR r.36.3 also defines the relevant period, as to which see para.5–06 below.

5–05   Except where a Part 36 offer is made in appeal proceedings, it has effect only in relation to the costs of the proceedings in respect of which it is made and not in respect of any appeal in those proceedings. Composite first instance and appeal offers to settle are not permissible and separate offers must be made. If a Part 36 offer is made in appeal proceedings the references in the rules to, e.g. claimant/defendant are replaced by corresponding terms, e.g. appellant/respondent.[8]

In personal injury proceedings, the claimant at first instance had been awarded damages which failed to beat two Part 36 offers made by the defendant. The claimant was held liable for the costs incurred from the date of expiry of the first offer. On appeal, the total damages award was increased to an amount in excess of the first Part 36 offer, although less than the second. The Court of Appeal revised the first instance costs decision ordering the claimant to pay the costs from the date of expiry of the second Part 36 offer. With regard to the costs of the appeal, the court held that the claimant had already been penalised in costs for having failed to accept the defendant's offers and the second offer had not been open for acceptance after May 2014. It had therefore been necessary for the claimant to pursue the appeal in order to improve his position. The claimant was awarded his costs subject to two exceptions relating to specific categories of costs.[9]

---

[3] CPR r.36.2.
[4] See *Thewlis v Groupama Insurance Co Ltd* [2012] EWHC 3 (TCC); [2012] B.L.R. 259; [2012] 5 Costs L.O. 560. Rule 44.2 (4)(c) requires the court to consider any admissible offer to settle made by a party which is drawn to the court's attention, and which is not an offer to which costs consequences under Pt 36 apply.
[5] CPR r.36.2(3).
[6] CPR rr.20.2 and 20.3.
[7] CPR r.36.3.
[8] CPR r.36.4(1) and (2).
[9] *Pawar v JSD Haulage Ltd* [2016] EWCA Civ 551.

Form and content of a Part 36 offer

A Part 36 offer must: 5–06

(a) be in writing;
(b) make clear that it is made pursuant to Pt 36;
(c) specify a period of not less than 21 days within which the defendant will be liable for the claimant's costs, where a Part 36 offer is accepted in accordance with CPR r.36.13 or, where Section IIIA of Pt 45 applies, in accordance with CPR r.36.20 if the offer is accepted;
(d) state whether it relates to the whole of the claim or part of it or to an issue that arises in it and if so, to which part or issue; and
(e) state whether it takes into account any counterclaim.[10]

A Part 36 offer may be made at any time including before the commencement of proceedings. Such an offer is made when it is served on the offeree.[11] The period of 21 days specified in (c) above or such longer period as the parties agree in the case of an offer made not less than 21 days before trial, is known as "the relevant period". Where an offer is made less than 21 days before a trial, the relevant period is the period up to the end of the trial.[12] A Part 36 offer may be made using Form N242A. If the other party is legally represented the notice must be served on the legal representative.[13]

In proceedings between a local authority and a waste disposal company, the local authority was successful. An issue arose as to whether the local authority's Part 36 offer was valid. The offer stated that if it was accepted within 21 days of the date of the offer letter (7 March 2019), the defendant would be liable to pay the claimant's costs in accordance with CPR r.36.13. The defendant argued that the offer did not comply with CPR r.36.5(1)(c) because it was sent by email at 4:54pm and was therefore "made" on 8 March 2019. The relevant period accordingly expired 20 days from the date the offer was made. The court, applying *C v D*,[14] construed the statement that the relevant period ran for "21 days of the date of this letter" as meaning that the 21 days ran from 8 March 2019, i.e. the date the offer was made. This was consistent with the claimant's intention to make a Part 36 offer and ensured that the offer was effective. In the light of the defendant's unreasonable failure to engage with the Part 36 offer and its conduct in pursuing a defence and large counterclaim based on unwarranted allegations of lack of good faith, false allegations and a compromised expert witness, interest was

---

[10] CPR r.36.5(1).
[11] CPR r.36.7. In *Best v Luton and Dunstable Hospital NHS Foundation Trust* [2021] EWHC B2 (Costs), a clinical negligence case, the defendant accepted the claimant's part 36 offer of £475,000 to settle the costs. The claimant then made a £52,000 Part 36 offer in relation to the costs of assessment, which she bettered by £6,120 at the assessment and so sought the usual benefits of beating the offer. The costs judge held that a part 36 offer cannot be made in relation to the costs of detailed assessment proceedings. If it could, this would open the way potentially to an indefinite cycle of part 36 offers and new detailed assessment proceedings.
[12] CPR rr.36.3(g) and 36.5(2).
[13] CPR r.36.7 and see CPR PD 36 para.1.1.
[14] [2011] EWCA Civ 646.

awarded at the maximum rate of 10% above base rate from the date of expiry of the Part 36 offer, together with indemnity costs from that date and interest on those costs at 10% above base rate.[15] Where a letter containing a Part 36 offer stated that the offer was to be accepted within "21 days (the relevant period), being by 4pm on 19 July 2019 or any time thereafter", when the relevant period ended on 22 July, this did not render the offer ineffective, because a reasonable recipient of the letter, knowing it was intended to be a Part 36 offer, would have realised the mistake. The inclusion of the words "or at any time thereafter" did not deprive the offer of its intended effect because Part 36 did not require acceptance of an offer to be time-limited.[16] The Court of Appeal has said that whilst a purported Part 36 offer could be so lacking in clarity as not to be a Part 36 offer at all, an offer could be a valid Part 36 offer if it left more unresolved than a contractual offer, and left some matters to be defined, especially the mechanics of payment.[17]

The Court of Appeal has upheld a decision to award costs to a defendant in low-value personal injury RTA proceedings where the claimant had made two Part 36 offers. CPR r.36.5(1)(d) requires that the offer state whether it relates to all or part of a claim, or the issue to which it relates, The claimant had made two Part 36 offers, one to accept on condition that liability be admitted, 90% of the claim for damages and interest to be assessed if not agreed; and the second to agree the question of liability on the basis that the claimant accept 90% of the claim for damages and interest, to be assessed if not agreed. At trial the claimant recovered damages for whiplash damages but not for a back injury for which damages had also been sought. Accepting either offer would have meant the defendant admitting liability for both injuries, and unable to dispute causation for the back injury. As he was only found liable for the whiplash injury, he had beaten both offers. Properly understood the offers had addressed liability and causation, and both heads of damage. The natural meaning of "the claim for damages" required a concession as to liability and causation for both injuries.[18]

As to interest, CPR r.36.5(4) provides that a Part 36 offer which offers to pay or offers to accept a sum of money will be treated as inclusive of all interest until the relevant period expires. A new provision, CPR r.36.5(5), which came into effect on 6 April 2021, provides that a Part 36 offer may make provision for accrual of interest after the relevant period, and if it does not, then it shall be treated as inclusive of all interest up to the date of acceptance if it is later accepted. CPR r.36.14(5)(b) provides that any stay arising on the acceptance of a Part 36 offer will not affect the power of the court to deal with any question of costs (including interest on costs) relating to the proceedings.[19]

---

[15] *Essex County Council v UBB Waste (Essex) Ltd (No. 3)* [2020] EWHC 2387 (TCC), Pepperall J.

[16] *King Security Systems Ltd v King* [2021] EWHC 653 (Ch); [2021] 3 WLUK 331; [2021] Costs L.R. 191.

[17] *Adams v Options UK Personal Pensions LLP* [2021] EWCA Civ 1188.

[18] *Seabrook v Adam* [2021] EWCA Civ 382; [2021] 4 W.L.R 54; [2021] Costs L.R. 505.

[19] See: *King v City of London Corp* [2019] EWCA Civ 2266; [2020] 1 W.L.R. 1517; [2020] 3 All E.R. 643 [2019] Costs L.R. 2197; and Q27 below.

A sub-contractor made, what was stated to be, a Part 36 offer to a contractor and, when it was accepted, sought to recover the costs of two sets of adjudication proceedings. The sub-contractor, who was the claimant, argued that its own offer did not comply with CPR r.36.13(4)(b) and (5) since it purported to exclude the court's power to determine liability for costs in circumstances where the offer was accepted after the 21 days and, therefore, precluded the court from deciding what was just in the particular circumstances of the case. The court held that the claimant's argument was an artificial one and that the offer was a valid Part 36 offer with the result that it could recover the costs of the proceedings but not the costs of the adjudication. Even if the offer had not been a valid Part 36 offer, it would have made no difference. The offer letter had expressly referred to Pt 36 which presupposed that there would be court proceedings in respect of which the offer was designed to operate. Accordingly, even if it was not a Part 36 offer, it was still an offer made in relation to the costs of the proceedings as set out in CPR r.36.13(1). A party seeking to recover a sum awarded by an adjudicator was not entitled to the legal costs incurred in the adjudication itself. The Housing Grants, Construction and Regeneration Act 1996 provided that costs incurred in adjudication were not recoverable. It followed that if a successful party could not recover its costs in the adjudication itself, it could not recover them in enforcement proceedings. Although the "costs of proceedings" included "recoverable pre-action costs", those costs would not normally include the costs of separate stand-alone alternative dispute resolution proceedings such as adjudication.[20]

Where the two parties had entered into an agreement for the eventual defendant to provide structural engineering advice on two properties owned by the claimant, and negligence proceedings were commenced, at the time when the Part 36 offer was made the claim only related to property 1. Later, the claimant amended the claim to include property 2. The defendant then accepted the claimant's Part 36 offer "in full and final settlement of the whole of this claim", on the basis that the offer now encompassed the claim relating to both properties. The claimant argued that the offer was only ever and remained in relation to property 1. At first instance, the judge held that the effect of acceptance was only to compromise the claim in relation to property 1, such that the claim in relation to property 2 continued. Jefford J agreed and dismissed the defendant's appeal.[21]

Where a claimant had accepted a Part 36 offer made jointly by all defendants in relation to part of the proceedings and the offer expressly stated that it did not concern the counterclaim, a defendant sought summary judgment on its counterclaim arguing that the offer covered all allegations of wrongdoing on which the claimant's defence to the counterclaim was founded. The court concluded that the acceptance of the defendants' offer did not prevent the

---

[20] *Wes Futures Ltd v Allen Wilson Construction Ltd* [2016] EWHC 2863 (TCC); 170 Con. L.R. 121; [2016] 6 Costs L.R. 1083 Coulson J.
[21] *Bentley Design Consultants v Malcolm Sansom* [2018] EWHC 2238 (TCC); [2018] 6 Costs L.O. 743, Jefford J.

claimants from relying in their defence to the counterclaim on facts alleged as part of the settled claim.[22]

In a hard fought employment claim, the defendants accepted the claimant's Part 36 offer relating to their counterclaim (which alleged misconduct against the claimant). The court found, however, that this did not settle the misconduct allegations which were repeated in the defence. The judge, applying *Marathon Asset Management,* above, found that what had been settled was a matter of contractual construction. The counterclaim was independent of the defence and the claimant had not stated that the offer was to compromise entirely the misconduct allegations.[23]

In a clinical negligence case, the defendant health trust's conduct of the litigation was held to be out of the norm. It had made various offers to settle, but ultimately the claimant made a Part 36 offer to accept 95% of the full value of her claim. This offer was rejected two days before the expiration of the relevant period. The defendant did not respond to invitations to alternative dispute resolution. Its witness statements, expert's reports and joint statements were served late. The claimant had to apply to the court to order the defendant to comply with certain case management directions. The Part 36 offer had not lapsed and was not withdrawn. The defendant accepted it over 12 months after the offer had been made. The costs payable by the defendant from the end of the relevant period until the date of acceptance were ordered to be paid on the indemnity basis.[24]

Withdrawing or changing the terms of a Part 36 offer generally

5–07 A Part 36 offer may only be withdrawn or its terms changed if the offeree has not previously served notice of acceptance. The offeror may withdraw the offer or change its terms by serving written notice of the withdrawal or change of terms on the offeree.[25] CPR r.36.10 makes provision about when permission is required to withdraw or change the terms of an offer before the expiry of the relevant period. Subject to that, notice of withdrawal or change of terms takes effect when it is served on the offeree.[26]

Provided that the offeree has not previously served notice of acceptance, after expiry of the relevant period the offeror may withdraw the offer or change its terms without the permission of the court, or the offer may be automatically withdrawn in accordance with its terms. Where the offeror changes the terms of the offer to make it more advantageous to the offeree, the improved offer will be treated not as the withdrawal of the original offer, but as the making of a new Part 36 offer on the improved terms, and provided that the new offer is not made less than 21 days before the start of the trial,

---

[22] *Marathon Asset Management LLP v Seddon* [2016] EWHC 2615 (Comm) Leggatt J.
[23] *Comberg v Vivopower International Services Ltd* [2020] EWHC 2438 (QB), Freedman J.
[24] *Holmes v West London Mental Health Trust* [2018] 4 Costs L.R. 763 HHJ Gore QC.
[25] See CPR r.36.17(7) as to the costs consequences following judgment of an offer which is withdrawn.
[26] CPR r.36.9(1), (2) and (3).

the relevant period will be 21 days or such longer period (if any) identified in the written notice of change of terms.[27]

CPR r.36.9(4)(b) provides that an offer may be automatically withdrawn after the expiry of the relevant period in accordance with its terms. This is both the effect and apparent intention of the rule—a Part 36 offer can now include within it a provision by which the offer is automatically withdrawn (and therefore time limited)—though it must still usually be open for a minimum of 21 days and CPR r.36.9(4)(b) cannot be used until that relevant period has passed. This alters the position under the previous version of Pt 36, as confirmed in *C v D*.[28]

Where, under the previous version of Pt 36, the offer was not a Part 36 offer (because the solicitors' letter did not specify any period for acceptance for the purposes of the rule) that was fatal.[29] It was difficult to see how the court could award additional interest unless the offer complied with Pt 36 and in the absence of a true Part 36 offer any claim for indemnity costs would have to be justified on the relevant general principles. The impact of the offer on costs was properly to be considered not as if it had complied with Pt 36 when it had not, but as part of the court's general discretion as to costs under Pt 44.[30]

Following a collision at sea, the claimant offered to settle liability 60/40 in favour of the claimant. The offer was said to be made in accordance with CPR r.61.4(10)–(12) and/or Pt 36. The offer was subsequently withdrawn two months before trial, when the claimant offered to settle on a two-thirds/one-third basis. At trial, liability was apportioned 60/40 in favour of the claimant. In relation to costs, the court decided that there was a line of authority starting before the CPR but continuing after it, indicating that where an offer had been withdrawn which should have been accepted, it would not be unjust to award the offeror all of its costs, because, had the offer been accepted, no further costs would have been incurred thereafter (see *Bristol and West Building Society v Evans Bullock & Co*).[31] The mere fact that an offer had been withdrawn did not necessarily deprive the offer of effect on the question of costs. The defendant should have accepted the offer when it was available, or should have appreciated the costs risk and taken protective steps by making a realistic Part 36 offer itself. The fact that the offer was withdrawn two months before trial did not make it unjust to order that the claimant should get all their costs from 21 days after the offer was made. Prior to that the defendant should pay 60% of the claimant's costs, and the claimant should pay 40% of the defendant's costs.[32]

---

[27] CPR r.36.9(4) and (5).

[28] *C v D* [2011] EWCA Civ 646; [2012] 1 W.L.R. 1962; [2012] 1 All E.R. 302; [2011] 5 Costs L.R. 773.

[29] *Onay v Brown* [2009] EWCA Civ 775; [2010] 1 Costs L.R. 29 and *C v D* [2011] EWCA Civ 646; [2012] 1 W.L.R. 1962; [2012] 1 W.L.R. 1962; [2012] 1 All E.R. 302; [2011] 5 Costs L.R. 773.

[30] *Carillion JM Ltd v PHI Group Ltd* [2012] EWCA Civ 588; [2012] C.P. Rep. 37; [2012] 4 Costs L.O. 523.

[31] *Bristol and West Building Society v Evans Bullock & Co* [1996] C.L.Y. 695.

[32] *Owners and/or Bareboat Charterers and/or Sub Bareboat Charterers of the Ship Samco Europe v Owners of the Ship MSC Prestige* [2011] EWHC 1656 (Admlty); [2011] 2 C.L.C. 679 Teare J.

The court gave judgment on a claim for damages arising out of a restriction of competition contrary to the Treaty on the Functioning of the European Union ("TFEU") Preamble, Article 101. The court held that the claimant had sustained losses as a result of the operation of a cartel and was entitled to damages. In a subsequent judgment, the court dealt with the question of costs. The claimant submitted that the party who writes the cheque at the end of the day is the unsuccessful party and the party receiving the cheque is the successful party. Marcus Smith J stated:

"4. I confess that I am not sure that the definition of success is so easy a concept, at least in this case. In this case, there was, from the outset, a binding finding against ABB. I refer to the Commission's decision which found the existing existence of the cartel which found that ABB was party to that cartel and which found that the BritNed Interconnector was a cartelised project pursuant to that cartel. In a very real sense, therefore, quantum was substantially the only issue before the Court. Absent one of the two factors that I list below, it was, one might well say, inevitable that ABB would be writing a cheque to BritNed. It does not, therefore, axiomatically follow that simply because a payment was ordered in this case, that ABB was the loser."

The two factors were, first, that it was open to the court to find there was no overcharge and no loss to BritNed at all (a contention which failed), although the outcome of the litigation in monetary terms was closer to ABB's case than to BritNed's. The second factor was the existence of a Part 36 offer. ABB had made a Part 36 offer which was withdrawn after trial but before judgment. The existence of the offer was no more than a factor to be taken into account in the court's decision as to costs. The judge continued:

"12. In terms of who writes the cheque, it is clear. . . that BritNed is the winner. Against this, however, a number of points must be noted:
1. In terms of expectation, BritNed was substantially the loser in this case when measured by reference to its own Pt 36 offer of €135m. BritNed recovered under 10% of this amount. . .
2. What is more, ABB made an offer, which remained open throughout the trial, that BritNed failed to beat.
3.The case on overcharge advanced by BritNed substantially failed. . .
4. It was a consequence of the failure, in relative terms, of BritNed's overcharge claim that the lost profit claim failed. So far as the regulatory cap issue was concerned, it might have to be said that that was something of a score draw for the parties. On the fourth issue, BritNed lost on the compound interest claim, but in terms of the time spent, this was a relatively minor issue."

The court went on to reject making an issues-based costs order. The overcharge claim had been central to BritNed's case and their analysis was not accepted, whereas ABB's analysis was. The court indicated that if it were to award BritNed its costs, it would be on the basis of a discount of 40% to reflect the relative failure on the overcharge claim. The court also had to take into account the withdrawn Part 36 offer, and concluded that the existence of the offer was not enough, when quantification was so difficult, to reverse the incidence of costs. Accordingly, ABB was not awarded its costs, but the court considered that the making of a commercial offer early on that was not beaten by BritNed meant that it would be unjust for ABB to pay any of BritNed's costs. Each party had to bear its own costs.[33]

Withdrawing or changing the terms of a Part 36 offer before the expiry of the relevant period

Where the offeree has not previously served notice of acceptance and the offeror serves notice of withdrawal of the offer or changes in its terms to be less advantageous to the offeree before the expiry of the relevant period, if the offeree has not served notice of acceptance of the original offer by the expiry of the relevant period, the offeror's notice has effect on the expiry of that period; if the offeree serves notice of acceptance of the original offer before the expiry of the relevant period, that acceptance has effect unless the offeror applies to the court for permission to withdraw the offer or to change its terms within seven days of the offeree's notice of acceptance, or, if earlier, before the first day of trial. If such an application is made, the court may give permission for the original offer to be withdrawn or its terms changed if satisfied that there has been a change of circumstances since the making of the original offer and that it is in the interests of justice to give permission.[34]

5–08

Where the offeror seeks permission of the court to withdraw a Part 36 offer or to change its terms to be less advantageous to the offeree before expiry of the relevant period, the permission of the court must, unless the parties agree otherwise, be sought by making a Pt 23 application which must be dealt with by a judge other than the trial judge or at a trial or other hearing provided that it is not to the trial judge.[35]

In litigation concerning the alleged anti-competitive effect of the multilateral interchange fee (MIF) paid by acquirers to issuers of debit and credit cards, the defendants made a Part 36 offer one week before trial which began on 14 November. The "relevant period" under CPR r.36.3 was therefore the duration of the trial, which was scheduled to end in March 2017. In parallel litigation involving most of the same claimants and the same expert witness, of which all parties were aware, judgment was handed down during the course of the trial. The claimants applied under CPR r.36.11 for permission to accept the offer. The defendants sought permission to withdraw it, arguing that it had become apparent that the claimants' case was very weak and that the legal outlook had changed significantly following the judgment.

CPR r.36.10(3) not only applied to an offeror's application for permission to withdraw an offer made during the relevant period, where a notice of

---

[33] *BritNed Development Ltd v ABB AB, ABB Ltd* [2018] EWHC 3142 (Ch); [2018] 6 Costs L.O. 807 Marcus Smith J.
[34] CPR r.36.10.
[35] CPR PD 36 para.2.

acceptance could be served without the court's permission, but also applied indirectly where the offeree needed the court's permission to accept an offer when a trial was in progress. The court would hold the offeror to the terms of its offer unless there had been such a change of circumstances since the making of the offer that it would be unjust to do so. The judgment in the parallel case had not changed the legal landscape and did not constitute a sufficient change in circumstances to make it unjust for the claimants to accept the offer. It involved a different group of defendants with different MIFs; it was a decision on its own facts; and it did not constitute binding precedent for the instant action. The parties had known that the judgment was likely to be forthcoming during the trial but had decided to go ahead with the trial rather than waiting to see its effect. To change the legal landscape, there would almost certainly have to be a binding decision of a higher court, probably the Supreme Court, settling the position on a general basis for some time to come on a fundamental point adverse to the claimant. There was nothing unjust about the defendants being held to the offer, particularly as the court had a more general discretion in relation to costs. The claimants were entitled to accept the offer with immediate effect. However, they were not entitled to all their costs up to the date of acceptance: they had not needed three months to consider the offer and the CPR did not envisage an offeree having a "free ride" on costs for such a period whilst it watched the ebb and flow of the action. The claimants could reasonably have been expected to respond by 28 November (which would normally have been the end of the relevant period). The court could take account of the fact that the claimants had deliberately chosen not to accept the offer whilst watching how the proceedings progressed. The claimants would be awarded their costs up to 28 November but should pay the defendants' costs from that date.[36]

Acceptance of a Part 36 offer

5–09   Acceptance of a Part 36 offer is effected by serving written notice of acceptance on the offeror. Except where the permission of the court is required (see below) or in a split trial case, a Part 36 offer may be accepted at any time unless it has already been withdrawn, whether or not the offeree has subsequently made a different offer.[37]

A claimant who was already in breach of an unless order requiring him to serve certain documents purported to accept a Part 36 offer. On appeal it was held that a claim that had been struck out (under the unless order) was at an end, therefore the claimant could not have accepted the Part 36 offer once he was in breach of the order, as his claim had, in substance, been brought to an end.[38]

---

[36] *Retailers v Visa* also known as Application in Private [2017] EWHC 3606 (Comm); [2018] 6 Costs L.R. 1203 Sir Jeremy Cooke).
[37] CPR r.36.11(1) and (2).
[38] *Joyce v West Bus Coach Services Ltd* [2012] EWHC 404 (QB); [2012] 3 Costs L.R. 540 Kenneth Parker J.

The court's permission is required to accept a Part 36 offer where a trial is in progress. Where a claimant originally declined to accept a Part 36 offer, but later, during trial, decided to accept (because the trial was going less well than expected), the court refused permission to the claimant to accept the offer, as it would be unjust to impose settlement on a reluctant defendant.[39]

In the phone hacking litigation a claimant sought a declaration that he was entitled to accept and had accepted the defendant's Part 36 offer which had been made in September 2014. The application was made the day before the trial was due to start in July 2017. In the course of the application before Mann J it was accepted by the defendant that the claimant had accepted the September 2014 Part 36 offer and so the debate was focused on the costs consequences of that acceptance. Since the offer predated 6 April 2015, the costs consequences were governed by an earlier version of CPR r.36.10(4) and (5). The court followed the decision in *SG (A Child) v Hewitt (Costs)*[40] which held:

> *"The court had to make the normal order unless it considered it unjust to do so and in deciding whether it was unjust, it had to take into account all the circumstances of the case including the four matters expressly set out in CPR r.36.14(4)."*

Those matters were

(a) the terms of any Part 36 offer;
(b) the stage in the proceedings when any Part 36 offer was made including, in particular, how long before trial started the offer was made;
(c) the information available to the parties at the time when the Part 36 offer was made; and
(d) the conduct of the parties with regard to the giving or refusing to give information for the purposes of enabling the offer to be made or evaluated.

During the course of the proceedings the defendant had made later higher offers including one of £100,000. The claimant also sought permission to accept the higher non-Part 36 offer but that application failed. Based on the claimant's conduct, the court ordered costs on the indemnity basis to the defendant from the expiry of the relevant period until the date of acceptance. The judge concluded:

> *"On 22 June 2016 the parties met in a without prejudice meeting to discuss various cases including Mr Jordan's. So far as Mr Jordan's case is concerned his representatives offered to settle at £160,000 and the defendant offered £100,000. Two things emerge from that. The one of lesser importance is that Mr Jordan's offer to settle of £160,000 makes it even odder that he should take £15,000 and costs burden immediately before trial. The more significant one is that it demonstrates that Mr Jordan could have settled at more than £90,000 in June 2016.*

---

[39] *Houghton v Donoghue (t/a Haulage and Plant Hire Ltd)* [2017] EWHC 1738 (Ch); [2017] 5 Costs L.R. 857 Morgan J.
[40] *SG (A Child) v Hewitt (Costs)* [2012] EWCA Civ 1053; [2013] 1 All E.R. 1118; [2012] 5 Costs L.R. 937.

> *That justifies the defendants in saying in correspondence that they would have agreed an increase in their £80,000 offer to £90,000 in July 2017 had Mr Jordan proposed it, and that as a result Mr Jordan should bear the costs since July. It makes it even more apparent that the costs since then were down to Mr Jordan, though of course my actual decision relates to the costs over the longer period going back to the September 2014 Pt 36 offer."*[41]

In a claim for libel and malicious falsehood the claimants put their special damages at £21.5 million. The defendant made a Part 36 offer of £125,000 in May 2016. The claimants accepted the offer in February 2017. The court found that if the claimants had provided information about their special damages at an earlier date the defendant would have made its offer earlier. Having considered the factors under CPR r.36.17(5)(d) the court awarded the defendant its costs on the indemnity basis from 11 January 2016, the notional expiry date of the offer, had the defendant been able to make it earlier. The claimants' pursuit of the pleaded claim after the offer was wholly disproportionate and the unexplained acceptance of an offer so different from the pleaded case was highly unreasonable.[42]

5–10   A father whose son had been killed as a passenger in a car accident, in which the driver was also killed, claimed dependency, bereavement and funeral costs, accepted a pre-proceedings Part 36 offer of £12,185 for the "whole of the claim". On the same day an e-mail was sent stating that the acceptance was in respect of the funeral expenses only and that the dependency claim would continue. The claimant sought to bring a dependency claim on his own behalf and in respect of the deceased's mother and two sisters. That claim was defended on the basis that the whole of the claim under the Fatal Accidents Act 1976 had been the subject of a binding contract of compromise. The claimant appealed against a preliminary ruling that his dependency claim against the defendant had been settled by way of acceptance of the Part 36 offer.

On appeal the court held that it was correct that bereavement damages were not payable because the deceased was aged 18 when he died. It could not, however, sensibly be argued that by accepting the offer, the claimant was effectively warranting that there were no other dependants. It was conceded that the Act did not apply to the circumstances of the appeal because no action had been commenced at the time of acceptance of the Part 36 offer. Furthermore, the Act did not undermine the substantive position in law that each dependant had a separate claim.

The Part 36 offer had been expressed to be in respect of the "whole of the claim", but the only claim which had been raised in the correspondence was the claimant's. The acceptance of the offer was therefore limited to the claimant's individual claim in its entirety. It did not extend to claims which might

---

[41] *Jordan v MGN* [2017] EWHC 1937 (Ch); [2017] 4 Costs L.R. 687 Mann J.
[42] *Optical Express Ltd v Associated Newspapers Ltd* [2017] EWHC 2707 QB; [2017] 6 Costs L.O. 803 Warby J. See also: *Knibbs v Heart of England NHS Foundation Trust* unreported 23 June 2017 QBD.

or might not have followed from other alleged dependants. The claimant's attempt thereafter to bring a dependency claim was valid only in his capacity as administrator of the estate on behalf of the other alleged dependants. His own claim fell to be struck out on the basis that he accepted the Part 36 offer which, on its face, related to the whole of his claim.[43]

The approval of the court is needed for acceptance of a Part 36 offer on behalf of a child or protected party, see CPR r.21.10; the Court of Appeal has held that a child's litigation friend's acceptance of a Part 36 offer is not binding until approved; and the High Court has held that where a longstanding Part 36 offer had been accepted by a protected party in the hours before his death, the other party could still withdraw it before the settlement had been approved.[44]

Acceptance of a Part 36 offer made by one or more but not all defendants

The court's permission is required to accept a Part 36 offer where an offer is made by one or more but not all defendants (subject to the exceptions set out below):

5–11

- a defendant in personal injury claims who has made a Part 36 offer has stated that it is intended to include any deductible amounts, the relevant period has expired and further deductible amounts have been paid to the claimant since the date of the offer;
- an apportionment is required under CPR r.41.3A in proceedings under the Fatal Accidents Act 1976 and Law Reform (Miscellaneous Provisions) Act 1934; or
- a trial is in progress.

Where the court gives permission, unless all the parties have agreed the costs, the court must make an order dealing with costs and may order that the costs consequences set out in CPR r.36.13 (costs consequences of acceptance of a Part 36 offer) apply.[45]

In the case of Part 36 offers made by one or more, but not all, of a number of defendants, if they have been sued jointly or in the alternative, the claimant may accept the offer, if the claimant discontinues the claim against those defendants who have not made the offer, and those defendants give written consent to the acceptance of the offer. If the claimant alleges that the defendants have a several liability, the claimant may accept the offer, and continue with the claims against the other defendants if entitled to do so. In any other

---

[43] *Kore v Brocklebank* [2019] EWHC 3491 (QB); [2019] Costs L.R. 2173, Turner J.

[44] *Drinkall v Whitwood* [2003] EWCA CIv 1547; and *Wormald v Ahmed* [2021] EWHC 973 (QB), though it should be noted that in *Wormald* the final decision was reserved pending further steps to be taken by the parties, and so is of doubtful authority. There was also the potential for an appeal on the point of principle. Following this initial judgment the parties compromised the claim.

[45] CPR r.36.11(3) and (4).

case the claimant must apply to the court for an order permitting acceptance of the Part 36 offer.[46]

Acceptance of a Part 36 offer in a split trial case

5–12   Where there has been a trial but not all the issues in the case have been determined,[47] a Part 36 offer, which relates only to parts of the claim or issues that have already been decided, can no longer be accepted. Subject to that proviso, and unless the parties agree, any other Part 36 offer cannot be accepted earlier than seven clear days after judgment is given or handed down in that trial.[48]

In a split trial case the court decided that where there was a split liability/quantum trial, the appropriate course was to address costs only after quantum had been resolved, because it was only then that the court could determine who had been successful and whether the Part 36 offer affected the costs order that should be made; given the findings on liability, there would have to be a further hearing for an account of profits and/or an inquiry as to damages.[49]

The Court of Appeal has clarified that where a Calderbank offer, rather than Part 36 offer, has been made covering the whole dispute in a split trial, the court is not bound to treat the offer as equivalent to a Part 36 offer and defer ruling on costs until all stages of the litigation have concluded. In a petition for unfair prejudice under s.994 of the Companies Act 2006 a split trial had been ordered, with liability to precede valuation. Following the liability trial, the judge gave a separate costs judgment when he knew that a Calderbank offer had been made but had not been told by whom, when or in what terms. The appellant (M) contended that the court should treat the offer as equivalent to a Part 36 offer to displace the presumption that costs be awarded at this stage. The judge rejected this analysis and M appealed. The Court of Appeal held that M's analysis was not consistent with the broad language of CPR r.44.2, which differed from CPR r.36, which was self-contained and did not govern or limit the broader discretion under CPR r.44.2, which expressly both confers a broad discretion on the court and makes the existence, scope and effect of admissible offers one of the factors to be taken into account in exercising that broad discretion. Further, M's analysis was not consistent with the policy underpinning CPR r.44.2, and nothing in the case law under CPR r.36 or r.44.2 compelled the conclusion for which M argued. [50]

Costs consequences of acceptance of a Part 36 offer

5–13   Subject to the exceptions set out below, where a Part 36 offer is accepted within the relevant period, the claimant will be entitled to the costs of the

---

[46] CPR r.36.15(1)–(4).
[47] Within the meaning of CPR r.36.3(e).
[48] CPR r.36.12 and also see CPR r.36.3.
[49] *Lifestyle Equities CV v Sportsdirect.com Retail Ltd (No.2)* [2018] EWHC 962 (Ch) HHJ Pelling QC. See also *Original Beauty Technology v G4K Fashion Ltd* [2021] EWHC 954 (Ch); [2021] Costs L.R. 445, David Stone sitting as a Deputy Judge of the High Court, 28 April 2021.
[50] *McKeown v Langer* [2021] EWCA Civ 1792.

proceedings (including their recoverable pre-action costs) up to the date on which notice of acceptance was served on the offeror.[51]

Where a defendant's Part 36 offer relates to part only of the claim and the claimant abandons the balance of the claim at the time of serving notice of acceptance within the relevant period, the claimant will only be entitled to the costs of that part of the claim unless the court orders otherwise.[52]

Where a Part 36 offer, which was made less than 21 days before the start of the trial, is accepted; or, which relates to the whole of the claim and is accepted after expiry of the relevant period; or, subject to the previous paragraph, a Part 36 offer which does not relate to the whole of the claim is accepted at any time; the liability for costs must be determined by the court unless the parties have agreed the costs.[53]

Where the offer has been accepted after expiry of the relevant period but the parties are unable to agree the liability for costs, the court must, unless it considers it unjust to do so, order that the claimant be awarded costs up to the date on which the relevant period expired and that the offeree pay the offeror's costs for the period from the date of expiry of the relevant period to the date of acceptance. In considering whether it would be unjust to make the orders specified, the court must take into account all the circumstances of the case including the matters listed in CPR r.36.17(5) (see para.5–16 below, costs consequences following judgment). The claimant's costs include any costs incurred in dealing with the defendant's counterclaim if the Part 36 offer states that it takes it into account.[54]

In phone hacking litigation, the claimant made a Part 36 offer in respect of which the relevant period was 21 days. On the 22nd day, the defendant accepted the offer on the express basis that the court would be invited to deal with the extent to which it would have to pay costs. The defendant's argument was that the court should disallow the claimant's costs from a particular date on the basis that she had not engaged properly in a settlement process. The court held that the defendant was entitled to invoke CPR r.36.13(4) and have the costs determined by the court. On the facts, the defendant failed to establish that the claimant had failed to engage, falling so far short of the standards which the courts expected of litigants, in terms of willingness to negotiate, that it could discharge the burden of showing that it would be unjust to apply the normal Part 36 consequences. The claimant was awarded all the costs of the proceedings.[55] At the annual open Civil Procedure Rules Committee meeting it was said *Pallett* (and the earlier Court of Appeal decision of *Dutton v Minards*[56]) are examples of tactical use of Part 36, to avoid the presumption of costs, and the Lacuna Sub-Committee was of the same view:

---

[51] CPR r.36.13(1).
[52] CPR r.36.13(2).
[53] CPR r.36.13(4).
[54] CPR r.36.13(5) to (7).
[55] *Pallett v MGN Ltd* [2021] EWHC 76 (Ch), Mann J.
[56] [2015] EWCA Civ 984; [2015] 6 Costs L.R. 1047.

the point has been sent to the CPR Costs Sub-Committee for further consideration, though a solution may be difficult to fashion (and it might be said that the difficulty of overcoming the "unjust" threshold is sufficient in itself).

In a personal injury action, the claimant failed to disclose the fact that she had obtained a franchise in a playgroup organisation and had run workshops for a year. The defendant became aware of the playgroup and informed the claimant's solicitors. The defendant made a Part 36 offer which was not accepted within the 21-day period. On acceptance of the offer out of time, the defendant was ordered to pay the claimant's costs only up to the date that the claimant had begun to mislead the defendant with regard to her disability. The court found that the claimant's attempt to run a playgroup did not amount to evidence that her disability was fabricated, otherwise the defendant would not have made an unconditional Part 36 offer. The case was not one of gross exaggeration, although the judge at first instance had been entitled to describe the claimant's conduct as dishonest and misleading, the judgment did not address the fact that the Part 36 offer was unconditional rather than a Calderbank offer, and that it had been made with knowledge of the claimant's non-disclosure. The Court of Appeal held that it was highly unlikely to be unjust to apply the default rule, where the claimant had accepted a Part 36 offer out of time, provided that nothing emerged from the facts to show that the defendant's assessment of the risks and benefits involved in making the offer had been significantly upset, contradicted or misinformed (see *Tiuta Plc v Rawlinson & Hunter (A Firm)*).[57] Accordingly, even though the claimant's material non-disclosure was dishonest and misleading, the respondent/defendant was ordered to pay the claimant's costs, up to the end of the relevant period.[58]

Despite the variation in wording between old CPR r.36.10(5) and the new CPR r.36.13(5) and in particular the reference to whether it is "unjust" to disapply the normal costs consequences, the new rule has not materially changed the proper approach to be taken by the court when deciding how to deal with costs where there has been a late acceptance of a Part 36 offer. The appropriate test is whether, bearing in mind the factors listed under CPR r.36.17(5), the usual costs rules should be departed from because it would be unjust to apply it in the particular circumstances of the case. In the particular case, the claimant was found to have grossly exaggerated her damages claim and the court ordered that the costs payable by the claimant to the defendant should include the defendant's reasonable costs of collecting the surveillance evidence, even though this had not been included in the defendant's approved budget (see **Ch.4, Q39** for further consideration of this topic).[59]

It is for the offeree to satisfy the court that it is unjust for the court to make the normal order. The court must take into account all the circumstances of

---

[57] *Tuita Plc v Rawlinson & Hunter (A Firm)* [2016] EWHC 3480 (QB).
[58] *Tuson v Debbie Murphy* [2018] EWCA Civ 1461; [2018] Costs L.R. 733.
[59] *Purser v Hibbs* [2015] EWHC 1792 (QB), HHJ Moloney QC.

the case including the matters set out in CPR r.36.17(5). It is open to the court to depart from the normal costs rule in CPR r.36.13(5). Where a young boy had suffered frontal lobe damage in a road traffic accident, it was material that the inherent uncertainty in prognosis would have resolved well before the limitation period expired so that the child did not need to commence proceedings before the position was clear. The defendant had made a pre-action Part 36 offer in full and final settlement; the claimant accepted the offer after the date of its expiry. The court approved the settlement, but at first instance it was held that the defendant should be entitled to its costs from the date of acceptance. The Court of Appeal held that the judge's conclusion did not give weight to the particular features of the claimant's case, the consequence of omitting to give weight to the matters that were in the claimant's favour was that the normal rule dominated when it should not have done. In the circumstances it was unjust to make the normal costs order, and the claimant was awarded his costs throughout.[60]

The Court of Appeal has held, in different circumstances, that the fact that there had been uncertainty regarding the claimant's prognosis was part of the usual risks of litigation, and the purpose of Pt 36 was to shift the risk to the offeree if he did not accept the offer within the relevant period. There was nothing to distinguish the case from one involving the usual risks of litigation. The court was unable to detect anything rendering the usual costs order unjust.[61]

In a claim for disputed commission, the defendants offered the claimants £25,000 plus their reasonable costs. The claimants did not accept the offer. The claimants ultimately made a Part 36 offer to settle for £18,000. The defendants deliberately accepted it one minute after the expiry of the 21-day relevant period. As a result, the claim settled but the automatic costs consequences under CPR r.36.10(1) (now CPR r.36.13(1)) were avoided. The parties could not agree with costs and the defendants argued that the claimants should have accepted their higher offer which had been made 15 months earlier. The judge found that the defendants had elected to accept the offer rather than reminding the claimants of their earlier offer which had never been withdrawn. A decisive factor was that the value of the claim net of the counterclaim was uncertain because of the defendant's unwillingness to disclose the strengths and weaknesses of their case. It was accordingly not unjust to apply the presumption that the defendant should pay the claimant's costs. The first instance decision was upheld on appeal.[62]

In a clinical negligence action, the claimant accepted the defendant's Part 36 offer eight months after the relevant period had expired. The defendants argued that an order that the claimant should be awarded costs until the expiry of the offer and to pay the defendant's costs from that date until the

---

[60] *SG (A Child) v Hewitt (Costs)* [2012] EWCA Civ 1053; [2013] 1 All E.R. 1118; [2012] 5 Costs L.R. 937.
[61] *Briggs v CEF Holdings Ltd* [2017] EWCA Civ 2363; [2018] 1 Costs L.O. 23.
[62] *Dutton v Minards* [2015] EWCA Civ. 984; [2015] 6 Costs L.R. 1047.

date of acceptance would be unjust, since the claimant had failed in relation to the vast majority of his pleaded case, namely causation. The court held that there was nothing unjust in making the normal order under Pt 36. The difficulty with the defendant's arguments was that it had the means and opportunity to protect itself in respect of the costs that it was going to have to incur in relation to causation, yet it had chosen, when making its offer, to frame it as a settlement of the whole claim. When its offer was not accepted it had not made any revised offer excluding causation. The court found that the claimant had acted unreasonably in rejecting the offer and pursuing the action to within two weeks of trial. Accordingly, for the period when the claimant had to pay the defendant's costs, the costs would be on the indemnity basis.[63]

Unaccepted offers

Restriction on disclosure of a Part 36 offer

5–14   A Part 36 offer is treated as being "without prejudice except as to costs". The fact that such an offer has been made must not be communicated to the trial judge until the case has been decided. This restriction does not apply where:

- the defence of tender before claim has been raised;
- the proceedings have been stayed following the acceptance of a Part 36 offer;
- the offeror and offeree agree in writing that it should not apply; or
- although the case has not been decided, any part of it or issue in it has been decided, and the Part 36 offer relates only to parts or issues which have been decided.

Where a part or issue has been decided, the trial judge may be told whether or not there are Part 36 offers other than those relating to the parts or issues which have been decided, but must not be told any of the terms of the other offers unless any of the above exceptions apply to them.[64]

CPR r.36.16 does not apply to the situation where a Part 36 offer has been accepted. It refers to a Part 36 offer being made and for that fact to be withheld from the judge. Once an offer has been accepted, there is no longer an offer, there is a binding compromise and Pt 36 makes no reference to that situation. But that does not mean that the material may be freely referred to. It has to be relevant, and if there is possible prejudice from its disclosure it is within the court's discretion to prevent it. However, the prejudice would have to be very heavy to outweigh its relevance.[65]

The court declined to make a costs order in favour of a claimant following a trial on liability, where the defendants had made CPR Part 36 offers to

---

[63] *ABC (A Protected Party) v Barts Health NHS Trust* [2016] EWHC 500 (QB); [2016] 2 Costs L.R. 271 HHJ McKenna.
[64] CPR r.36.16(1)–(4).
[65] *Richard v BBC* [2018] EWHC 2504 (Ch) Mann J.

the claimant which did not relate only to the issues which had been determined, and the contents of which were not known to the court. The costs were reserved until a later stage when the court could be told the terms of the Part 36 offers and take them into account when deciding what order to make in respect of costs.[66]

CPR r.52.22(1) has been amended to read:

"Unless the appeal court otherwise orders, the fact that a Part 36 offer or payment into court has been made must not be disclosed to any judge of the appeal court who is to hear or determine (a) an application for permission to appeal; or (b) an appeal, until all questions (other than costs) have been determined."[67]

For a discussion about how a Part 36 offer is dealt with on judgment in default, see **Ch.7, Q15**.

Costs consequences following judgment

Save where Section IIIA of Pt 45 applies,[68] where, upon judgment being 5–15 entered, (i) a claimant fails to obtain a judgment more advantageous than the defendant's Part 36 offer, or (ii) judgment against the defendant is at least as advantageous to the claimant as the proposals contained in the claimant's Part 36 offer, the court must, unless it consider it unjust to do so, where (i) applies: order that the defendant is entitled to costs (including any recoverable pre-action costs) from the date on which the relevant period expired, and interest on those costs.[69] The provision does not apply to a soft tissue injury claim to which CPR r.36.21 applies.

Where (ii) applies the court must, unless it considers it unjust to do so, order that the claimant is entitled to:

(a) interest on the whole or part of any sum of money (excluding interest) awarded, at a rate not exceeding 10% above base rate for some or all of the period starting with the date on which the relevant period expired;
(b) costs (including any recoverable pre-action costs) on the indemnity basis from the date on which the relevant period expired;
(c) interest on those costs at a rate not exceeding 10% above base rate; and
(d) provided that the case has been decided and there has not been a previous order under this provision, an additional amount, which may not exceed £75,000, calculated by applying the prescribed percentage set out in the rule to an amount which is:

---

[66] *Interactive Technology Corp Ltd v Ferster* [2017] EWHC 1510 (Ch) Morgan J.
[67] Civil Procedure (Amendment) Rules 2020. SI 2020/82. The explanatory memorandum states: "The amendment makes it clear that the court may have a hearing of both substantive issues and costs issues and that in such circumstances the usual restrictions on informing the court of a Part 36 offer (to settle the claim) is removed."
[68] See CPR r.36.21.
[69] In relation to any money claim or any money element of a claim, "more advantageous" means better in money terms by any amount however small and "at least as advantageous" is to be construed accordingly—CPR r.36.17(1)–(3).

> (i) the sum awarded to the claimant by the court; or
>
> (ii) where there is no monetary award, the sum awarded to the claimant by the court in respect of costs.[70]

The prescribed percentage where the amount awarded by the court is up to £500,000 is 10% of the amount awarded. Where the amount awarded by the court is above £500,000, the prescribed percentage is 10% of the first £500,000 and (subject to the limit of £75,000) 5% of any amount above that figure.[71]

In a construction dispute the claimants made a Part 36 offer in the sum of £875,000 to settle two claims in the proceedings. They succeeded at trial on one claim, failed on the other and narrowly bettered their offer. The claimants beat their Part 36 offer by £4,847 and sought an order in accordance with CPR r.36.17(4) including an additional amount of £65,123.77.

The court found that it would not be unjust to apply the provisions of CPR r.36.17. The terms of the offer were clear. The Part 36 offer was made at a very early stage in the proceedings, after the letter of claim but before the issue of the formal claim. By that time, extensive investigations and remedial works had been concluded. The parties had sufficient information to make an informed judgment as to the merits of the case. The offer was at a level that indicated it was a genuine attempt to settle the dispute. Accordingly the claimants were entitled to an enhanced rate of interest on damages and costs from the date of expiry of the offer. The defendant's conduct was not unreasonable and the court awarded 6% above base rate (the mid-point between the 2% agreed on damages and the maximum of 10%). The claimants were entitled to the additional sum of £65,123.77, and also entitled to have their costs on the indemnity basis.

The court found that the fact that the claimants beat the Part 36 offer by a very small margin did not displace the CPR r.36.17 regime: CPR r.36.17(1)(b). Further, the general provisions of CPR Pt 44 did not apply where the costs consequences of a Part 36 offer applied: CPR r.44.2(4)(c). The court was, however, persuaded that it would be unjust to order the defendant to pay the costs of what was known as "the underpass claim" and ordered the defendant pay 85% of the claimants' costs on the indemnity basis.[72]

The award of enhanced interest on the costs (CPR r.36.14(3)(c)) (now CPR r.36.17(4)(c))—*McPhilemy v Times Newspapers Ltd (Abuse of Process)*[73] did not oblige the court to decide that the rate of enhanced interest on costs should achieve a fairer result for the claimant than would otherwise have been the case. That said, the award was not purely compensatory. Many of the factors applicable to the rate of enhanced interest on damages would apply in relation to costs, though some would be different and the court might have to

---

[70] CPR r.36.17(3) and (4). And see: *Marathon Asset Management LLP v Seddon* [2017] EWHC 479 (Comm); [2017] 2 Costs L.R. 255 Leggatt J.

[71] CPR r.36.17(4).

[72] *Hochtief (UK) Construction Ltd v Atkins Ltd* [2019] EWHC 3028 (TCC), O'Farrell J.

[73] *McPhilemy v Times Newspapers Ltd (Abuse of Process)* [2001] EWCA Civ 871; [2001] E.M.L.R. 34.

consider whether the costs had been reasonably incurred. Moreover, the defendant had ignored a proper offer and run up costs thereafter, and the judge had failed to consider that costs had largely been incurred in relation to a dishonest and unreasonable defence. The correct rate of enhancement was 10% (see [43]–[45]).[74]

In a claim where there was no issue over quantum and quite clearly no defence, the claimant made an offer to accept 99.7% of the claim. The defendant did not accept the offer, but eventually admitted the claim. The court took into account the fact that the defendant had been unable, by reason of its insolvency, to pay the sum offered. On the facts, the court held that the offer was a genuine offer to settle under CPR r.36.17(5)(e). It would, however, be unjust to apply some of the consequences set out in CPR r.36.17(4) having regard to the defendant's insolvency. In the circumstances, two of the four possible orders should apply, such that the defendant should pay the claimant's costs of the proceedings on the indemnity basis, and interest on the principal sum owed at a rate of 8%, as from the date the offer expired.

The Commercial Court has given judgment on the appropriate rates of interest on costs and damages to be awarded to a claimant that had beaten its own Part 36 offers. For the compensatory rate of interest on damages, the appropriate base rate was three month LIBOR, the standard reference rate for borrowing, the appropriate percentage above base rate was 2%, producing a blended rate of both elements. Taking all relevant factors into account, the enhanced rate of interest on damages was set at 5% above LIBOR. As to costs, the court decided that the rate of interest should be the compensatory rate applied to damages, namely three month LIBOR plus 2%. The court considered *OMV Petrom SA v Glencore International AG* (above) and suggested it had limitations in that it was a case on extreme facts which resulted in an enhanced rate of 10% above base rate.[75]

Where a claimant made an offer to accept a specific sum including interest, in sterling, and subsequently obtained judgment in US dollars, the Commercial Court declined to allow the successful claimant the Pt 36 enhancements, for the period between expiry of the "relevant period" and the date of judgment, since the difference in the value of the judgment was a direct consequence of the fall in sterling following the referendum vote to leave the EU. The judge stated it would be "adventitious and inconsistent with the principle of risk allocation which underlies Pt 36" to penalise the defendant for not accepting the offer.[76]

Following a road traffic accident which occurred in Spain, the claimant, suing the Motor Insurers Bureau, was successful and beat its own Part 36 offer.

---

[74] *OMV Petrom SA v Glencore International AG* [2017] EWCA Civ 195; [2017] 1 W.L.R. 3465; [2018] 1 All E.R. 703; [2018] 1 All E.R. (Comm) 210; [2017] 2 Lloyd's Rep. 93; [2017] 2 Costs L.R. 287.

[75] *Assetco Plc v Grant Thornton UK LLP* [2019] EWHC 592 (Comm); [2019] 1 Costs L.R. 197, Bryan J. The judge exercised his power under CPR PD 47 para.5.1(a)(iii) to waive the requirement for the claimant to submit an electronic bill of costs.

[76] *Novus Aviation Ltd v Alubaf Arab International Bank BSC (c)* [2016] EWHC 1937 (Comm); [2016] 4 Costs L.R. 705 Leggatt J.

The claimant was successful in all but two issues of his claim which related to care costs and future costs. He called expert evidence on Spanish law and on care requirements. The defendant sought an issue-based costs order to reflect the issues upon which the claimant had lost. The court, relying on *Pigot v Environment Agency*[77] held that the fact that a successful party had not been successful on every issue did not of itself justify an issue-based costs award. The claimant had been advancing alternative arguments, one more ambitious than the other. He had succeeded on the less ambitious one, but the evidence of the experts had not been wasted. It was not appropriate to make an issue-based order. The defendant was also ordered to pay interest at 6% and costs on the indemnity basis.[78]

A claimant who had succeeded in his personal injury claim against the Ministry of Justice sought costs. The defendant had asked for a 30% reduction as the claimant had not succeeded in establishing a number of allegations. However, the defendant had failed on most of its case. The court held that on any fair reading of the judgment, the claimant had succeeded and was awarded the whole of the costs of the trial. However, the defendant should have its costs of successfully defending the claimant's abuse of process application. The claimant claimed to be entitled to further costs under CPR r.36.17 since the judgment against the defendant was at least as advantageous to the claimant as the Part 36 offer. The defendant maintained that, but for a change in the discount rate, the claimant would not have exceeded the judgment at trial. The second offer had been a genuine offer to settle. There was no injustice if the costs consequences of CPR r.36.17(4) were applied. The claimant had done better than the second offer by a significant amount. The defendant was ordered to pay the claimant additional interest on the sum awarded, at 8.5%. An additional award of 10% of the judgment was made. The defendant was also ordered to pay the claimant's costs on the standard basis up to July 2016 and thereafter on the indemnity basis because the Ministry of Justice had refused to engage in mediation. The Ministry's reasons for refusal were not accepted by the court.[79]

A successful claimant beat its Part 36 offer and the parties agreed an order including the damages and interest, and also the additional amount payable under Part 36. The defendants, however, resisted an order for costs on the indemnity basis. The defendants' argument was that the claimant's costs budget was approved in March 2018 when the claim form indicated that the total value of the claim would exceed £50,000 but would not exceed £100,000. The total damages, interest and additional amount was £19,746.37. The defendants argued that an order for costs on the indemnity basis would preclude the costs judge from having regard to proportionality and that it would be unjust to make such an order for that reason, since the costs budget

---

[77] [2020] EWHC 1444 (Ch); [2020] Costs LR 825.
[78] *Scales v Motor Insurers Bureau* [2020] EWHC 1749 (QB); [2020] Costs LR 771, Cavanagh J.
[79] *Marsh v Ministry of Justice* [2017] EWHC 3185 (QB) Thirlwall LJ.

had been based on an inflated valuation of the claim. During the course of the proceedings, a direction had been given that all parties had to consider settling by any means of alternative dispute resolution. The defendant had indicated that it did not intend to engage in settlement negotiations and remained confident in the strength of its defence. The court held that the reasons given for refusing to engage in mediation were inadequate. The court stated: "No defence, however strong, by itself justifies a failure to engage in any kind of alternative dispute resolution". The fact that costs on the indemnity basis did not involve a consideration of proportionality was part of the incentive for parties to make and accept Part 36 offers.[80]

Where an unsuccessful defendant was required to pay an additional amount, having previously rejected the claimant's Part 36 offer to accept a sum lower than that awarded, no interest was payable on the additional amount. The wording of CPR r.36.17(4)(d) indicated that that amount was in addition to the award and interest set out in CPR r.36.17(4)(a). If interest were payable on the additional amount, the rule would have said so.[81]

A claimant was employed by defendant accountants working in Dubai from 2008 until 2014. The claimant was the internal audit partner responsible for the audit of a Dubai company. He discovered that the company was engaged in irregularities involving the import of gold bullion. The claimant had a reasonable suspicion that the company was involved in money laundering. This was accepted by the defendants at trial.

At trial the defendants based in London were ordered to pay $10.8 US million for loss of earnings to the claimant although he was not employed by the London part of the defendants. His actual employers were not based in the UK and not party to the proceedings.

The claimant made two Part 36 offers. The parties agreed that the judge could be told about these offers.

The first was an offer to settle for £8.5 million, including any tax liability the claimant may incur in consequence of receipt of the sum, which would be borne by the claimant. The second was made about twelve months later, to settle for £5 million, also including any tax liability incurred from receipt of the sum. It was agreed that the claimant beat the second offer and that the normal Part 36 consequences should apply. However, the defendants questioned whether, the claimant had beaten the first offer. On the facts the judge found that the claimant had beaten the first offer and it was not unjust to impose the normal Part 36 consequences of the claimant having beaten it at trial.

The court awarded costs on the indemnity basis from the expiry of the first offer together with an additional amount of £75,000. The court also awarded interest on past losses at 7% and interest on costs at 6.5%.[82]

---

[80] *DSN v Blackpool Football Club Limited* [2020] EWHC 670 (QB); [2020] Costs LR 359, Griffiths J.
[81] *FZO v (1) Adams, (2) Haringey London BC* [2019] EWHC 1286 (QB); [2019] Costs L.R. 437, Cutts J. The substantive judgment was upheld on appeal [2020] EWCA Civ 180.
[82] *Rihan v Ernst and Young Global Ltd*, [2020] EWHC1380 (QB) Kerr J.

None of the above consequences apply to a Part 36 offer which has been withdrawn, which has been changed so that its terms are less advantageous to the offeree—where the offeree has beaten the less advantageous offer, or which was made less than 21 days before trial unless the court has abridged the relevant period.[83]

Where the defendants in a personal injury action had done almost nothing to seek a compromise after rejecting the claimant's Part 36 offer, but the claimant's solicitors were acting under an old-style conditional fee agreement, 4% above base rate was the appropriate rate of interest payable under CPR r.36.17(4)(c) on indemnity costs ordered against the defendants after they lost on liability.[84]

Where a claimant made a successful Part 36 offer the court had to deal with the question of interest under CPR r.36.17(4). The judge stated:

> "18 In my judgment the appropriate rate of interest is 8% which matches the judgment rate of interest. To the extent one can apply analysis and logic to a discretionary figure, I am influenced in coming to this conclusion by the thought that the claimant should be entitled to be treated as if it had been in the position of a judgment creditor now that it has more than vindicated itself by the recovery under my judgment when compared to what was advantageously offered to the defendant by the Part 36 offer.
>
> 19 The essential thrust of CPR 36.17(4), in such circumstances and assuming normality prevails, is to put the rejected offeror into a different, superior class of judgment creditor in relation to the period beginning with the expiry of his offer. And the essential basis for that can be said to be the reflection, in hindsight, that the litigation should by then have been concluded with recognition of his entitlement. It is clear that the claimant may be awarded interest at a rate which proves to be more than compensatory. In modern times it might be said that judgment rate of 8% produces, at least in some cases, an element of over-compensation. Whether or not that is so, I have concluded in this case that it is right to award that rate to the claimant for the period of its superior entitlement as if it was then entitled under a judgment rather than simply looking to the court's discretion for the recovery of a less generous commercial or compensatory rate over the pre-judgment period. Therefore, Mr De Waal, I am going to say it is interest at the rate of 8% per annum both under (a) and (c)."[85]

5–16   In considering whether it would be unjust to make the orders referred to above, the court must take into account all the circumstances of the case including:

---

[83] CPR r.36.17(7).
[84] *Bruma v Hassan* [2018] EWHC 248 (QB) HHJ Curran QC.
[85] *Kivells Ltd v Torridge DC* [2019] EWHC 3210 (TCC); [2019] Costs L.R. 1987, HHJ Russen QC. See also *Essex CC v Davies* [2019] EWHC 3443 (QB), Saini J where the court upheld an award of 10% above base rate in a case where the claimant had beaten its own Part 36 offer.

(a) the terms of any Part 36 offer;
(b) the stage in the proceedings when any Part 36 offer was made, including in particular how long before the trial started the offer was made;
(c) the information available to the parties at the time when the Part 36 offer was made;
(d) the conduct of the parties with regard to the giving of or refusal to give information for the purposes of enabling the offer to be made or evaluated; and
(e) whether the offer was a genuine attempt to settle the proceedings.[86]

Where the court awards interest under these provisions and also awards interest on the same sum and for the same period under any other power, the total rate of interest must not exceed 10% above base rate.[87]

There is no limit to the circumstances which could make it unjust that the ordinary consequences under CPR r.36.17 should follow. Where an action had been about restoration of reputation and the conduct of the defendant's disciplinary procedures the court ordered the costs to lie where they fell.[88]

In a claim for false imprisonment and assault the claimant was successful and was awarded damages of £2,750, but the judge at first instance found that it would be unjust to apply the provisions of CPR r.36.17 and made no order for costs. The claimant appealed.

Prior to the trial the defendant had made a Part 36 offer to settle for £4,000 and to provide a letter of apology. That offer was refused. The claimant made a Part 36 offer to settle for £5,000 provided the defendant admitted liability for the matters alleged in the claim. He subsequently made an offer to settle for the same amount provided that the defendant admitted unlawful arrest and removed all records of his arrest and harassment warning and that his DNA, fingerprints and custody photographs were deleted. The defendant refused that offer. The claimant then made a Part 36 offer to settle for nil damages and an admission of liability and reasonable costs. The defendant invited the claimant to attend a without prejudice discussion but the claimant did not respond.

On appeal the defendant argued that the claimant's offer was not a genuine Part 36 offer since it included a proposal as to costs, which negated any concession and disregarded the defendant's earlier offers. The appeal court found that there was no realistic prospect that the claimant would ever obtain the admission he wanted from the defendant by pre-trial negotiation and settlement. The fact that the appellant had given up all claim to a financial remedy was a significant concession indicative of a genuine Part 36 offer. That offer did engage the provisions of CPR r.36.17 and accordingly meant that the appellant was entitled to his costs from the expiry of the relevant period.

---

[86] CPR r.36.17(5).
[87] CPR r.36.17(6).
[88] *Smith v Trafford Housing Trust* [2012] EWHC 3320 (Ch); (2012) 156(46) S.J.L.B. 31 Briggs J.

It would be unjust not to apply CPR r.36.17 and follow its provisions in the usual way. The claimant's failure to respond to the offer of a without prejudice discussion, was not capable of having any direct effect on the course of the litigation. The appeal succeeded in relation to the appellant's costs incurred from the end of the relevant period. He was entitled to costs on the indemnity basis for that period, together with the other entitlements set out in CPR r.36.17(4) from that date. The part of the order as to no costs before that date remained unaltered.[89]

Two claimants had succeeded in their claim for misuse of private information but failed to beat a Part 36 offer made by the defendant. The defendant's failure in the offer to provide an apology or agree to a statement being made in open court did not make it unjust to impose the usual costs consequences of failing to beat a Part 36 offer. Among other things, there was no settled practice that claimants in cases of misuse of private information were entitled to an apology or an agreed statement in open court. The court rejected the claimants' submission that the defendant's Part 36 offer to pay two claimants a single sum of money jointly was not a valid Part 36 offer by relying on CPR r.36.11(3)(c). The court found that the claims, though technically distinct, were parallel claims by a married couple, arising out of the same events. The claimants "presented a united front" throughout the litigation and could have agreed a division of the sum offered. The claimants were awarded their costs up to the end of the relevant period of a second, improved, offer, but were ordered to pay the defendant's costs thereafter. The defendant, having failed to file or serve a costs budget was entitled to only 50% of its assessed costs.[90]

Joint liquidators of a company obtained judgment against one of two respondents which exceeded their Part 36 offer. At trial, the liquidators were awarded an amount greater than their Part 36 offer and the claim against the second respondent was dismissed. The liquidators sought a costs order requesting the full consequences under CPR r.36.17(4). The respondents argued that the Part 36 offer had been made jointly to the respondent and not severally, and it had not been open to the first respondent to accept it without the second respondent also doing so, and so it would be unjust for the costs consequences to apply. The court accepted that the first respondent could not accept the offer without the second respondent also doing so. Acceptance by the second respondent would have made her liable for paying damages and costs for which she was not liable. Had the first respondent accepted the offer, it would have rendered him liable for all the costs, including those regarding an unsuccessful claim against the second respondent. These factors took the case out of the norm and it would be unjust for the costs consequences in CPR r.36.17(4) to apply. An issues-based order and detailed assessment would be impractical and disproportionate. A percentage order was appropriate. The

---

[89] *MR v Commissioner of Police of the Metropolis* [2019] EWHC 1970 (QB); [2019] Costs L.R. 1441, McGowan J.
[90] *Ali v Channel 5 Broadcast Ltd* [2018] EWHC 840 (Ch); [2018] 2 Costs L.R. 373 Arnold J.

first respondent was ordered to pay 50% of the liquidators' costs. The second respondent was entitled to all her costs on the standard basis.[91]

The High Court upheld the decision of the County Court that the defendants should bear the usual Part 36 consequences when the claimant had made a Part 36 offer of £1 and beaten it when the trial judge awarded nominal damages of £10. The offer had been a genuine offer to settle, the "unjust" test is a high hurdle and the defendants failed to surmount it: they were ordered to pay costs on the indemnity basis from the end of the relevant period and indemnity costs thereafter, with interest on the sum awarded.[92]

The High Court has found that it would be unjust for the claimant to recover the CPR r.36.17(4) enhancements where she had only bettered her Part 36 offer because she was permitted to adduce evidence served late and without good reason. Although the defendant had not objected to the introduction of that evidence at the time, the court found that that did not prevent the defendant from arguing at the costs stage that it would be unjust for the claimant to recover the CPR r.36.17(4) enhancements. Whilst none of the factors set out in CPR r. 36.17(4) themselves led to a conclusion that the enhancements should not be recovered, "all the circumstances" had to be taken into account, the defendant produced worked figures which showed that without the evidence the claimant would not have beaten the Part 36 offer, and had the defendant objected to its introduction, the claimant would have had to seek relief from sanctions.[93] The facts of this case are highly unusual, and the general principle is firmly that those seeking to persuade the court not to award the enhancements where a Part 36 offer has been beaten at trial face an uphill battle.

The importance of making an effective Part 36 offer by a defendant faced with a claim that it considers to be over-valued was emphasised by the Court of Appeal in a claim for an account for breach of fiduciary duty brought by a company against an individual alleged to have taken advantage of an opportunity to obtain a personal interest in an investment vehicle used to acquire and develop new technology to access oil and gas reserves.[94] The Court of Appeal held that the company was the "winner" and entitled to its costs (subject to some deductions to reflect parts of the claim on which it had not succeeded) because an account had been awarded (for $3 million and £1.67 million, even though this amounted to just 1.6% of the claim value, thereby overturning the first instance decision of no order. Mr Gray (the defendant) could have protected himself by making a Part 36 offer for a much smaller sum. This was not a case where the company had dishonestly exaggerated its claim; indeed,

---

[91] *Bramston (1), Harris (2) (as Joint Liquidators of IT Protect Ltd) v Pye(1), Mantague(2)*, [2020] EWHC 14 October (Ch); Judge Barber.
[92] *Shah v Shah* [2021] EWHC 1668 (QB).
[93] *Head v Culver Heating Co Ltd* [2021] EWHC 1235 (QB), Johnson J.
[94] *Global Energy Horizons v Gray* [2021] 2 WLUK 63;[2021] Costs L.R. 133.

the enquiry hearing had been necessary by reason of the dishonest account put forward by Mr Gray.

5–17   The correct approach in determining whether a judgment award is more advantageous than a Part 36 offer is:

> ". . . to ensure that the offer or the Judgment sum is adjusted by eliminating from the comparison the effect of interest that accrues after the date when the relevant offer could have been accepted."[95]

In a construction dispute, the claimant Jockey Club made a Part 36 offer to settle liability on the basis that the defendant should pay 95% of damages to be assessed. The defendant did not respond to this offer and the claimant amended its particulars of claim to set out the quantified costs of the repairs. The court directed a split trial. The defendant subsequently conceded liability and preliminary liability issues were settled by consent in the claimant's favour. The club, accordingly, claimed its costs on the indemnity basis as it had beaten its own Part 36 offer. The court held that there was no possibility of contributory negligence so that a decision that the defendant should pay 95% of the damages was not one which was open to the court. It was, however, not necessary for a Part 36 offer to reflect an outcome that would be possible at trial. The court accepted that the claimant's offer was a genuine attempt to settle and whilst the 5% discount was very modest it was not derisory. Accordingly, the offer had to be given effect unless it would be unjust. It would be unjust to order indemnity costs from 21 days after the offer given that the defendant has just learned of a major increase in the claim but the claimant was entitled to costs on the indemnity basis from the earliest date after which the defendant should have been equipped to assess the claim on liability. On the facts this was four months after the offer.[96]

In a clinical negligence trial the claimant was successful on liability. Before trial, the claimant had made a Part 36 offer to accept 90% of the value of the claim. The "relevant period" expired one working day before the trial began. The offer had not been accepted. The claimant argued that he had achieved an outcome at least as advantageous as his offer.

The costs consequences set out in CPR r.36.17 had to be ordered unless the court considered it unjust to do so. The court had to take account of whether the offer was a genuine attempt to settle the proceedings. The defendant argued that an assessment of the risks of the litigation as being only 10% was a significant under-evaluation and could not have been a genuine attempt to settle. That kind of argument could hardly ever succeed. How one side perceived the risks in a particular case would almost invariably be different from the way the other side perceived them. A judge should not ordinarily carry out the exercise of determining how the case should have looked to the

---

[95] *Purrunsing v A'Court and Co* (A Firm) [2016] EWHC 1528 (Ch); [2016] C.I.L.L. 3861 HHJ Pelling QC. See also *Blackman v Entrepose UK* [2004] EWCA Civ 1109; [2005] C.P. Rep. 7; [2005] Costs L.R. 68.
[96] *Jockey Club Racecourse Ltd v Willmott Dixon Construction Ltd* [2016] EWHC 167 (TCC); [2016] 4 W.L.R. 43; [2016] 1 Costs L.R. 123 Edwards-Stuart J.

offeror before the offer was made. That would be almost akin to embarking on a mini-trial in the post-trial situation. There was no reason to doubt that the offer to accept 90% had been made because the claimant's team regarded the claim as very strong, but was prepared to offer a modest discount to secure absolute certainty of obtaining substantial compensation. A discount of 10% was not a token amount, particularly at a time when the level of damages in serious cases was very significant. The offer should have been regarded as a genuine offer of settlement and it did not militate against ordering the normal consequences for the claimant having achieved more than his Part 36 offer. The judge had been given a lot of information about the position taken by each side during without prejudice negotiations. The information had not been of any value during the costs hearing, and in most cases it would not assist in deciding whether an offer was a genuine offer of settlement. The content of privileged discussions should generally remain privileged.[97]

The additional amount

In a subsequent judgment Foskett J declined to award the claimant an additional amount under CPR r.36.17(4) as not all the issues in the case had been decided. Given that the claimant was a protected party and any additional sum awarded should be for his benefit, it would not be right to take action that would preclude the possibility of obtaining an enhanced award. No order for an additional sum would be made until all issues in the case had been determined.[98]

    5–18

In proceedings where the defendants were in breach of their duty, but the claimant failed on primary causation, the defendants claimed costs, approximately one-third of which were incurred in expert's fees on technical tax points which were lost. The defendants relied on their Part 36 offer made prior to trial which had not been accepted by the claimants. The court held that the general principles for determining an order for costs were subject to the operation of CPR Pt 36, in particular CPR r.36.17. The starting point was that the defendants had been successful and were entitled to their costs. However, those costs did not reflect success on the issues for which they had been incurred. The defendants were awarded 50% of their costs for the period before the Part 36 offer expired and the whole of their costs from the date of the offer expiring. The offer ought to have been accepted and the trial avoided.[99]

Solicitors sued under a non-contentious business, contingency fee agreement and the defendants were ordered to pay the full amount of the claim plus

---

[97] *JMX (A Child) v Norfolk and Norwich Hospitals NHS Foundation Trust* [2018] EWHC 185 (QB); [2018] 1 Costs L.R. 81 Foskett J.

[98] *JMX v Norfolk and Norwich Hospitals NHS Foundation Trust (No.2)* [2018] EWHC 675 (QB); [2018] 2 Costs L.R. 285 Foskett J.

[99] *Altus Group (UK) Ltd v Baker Tilly Tax and Advisory Services LLP* [2015] EWHC 411 (Ch); [2015] 2 Costs L.R. 267 HHJ Keyser QC.

contractual interest. They were further required to pay under CPR r.36.17(4)(d) an additional amount of 10% of the judgment. Three issues arose:

(i) whether an additional amount was payable in respect of the contractual interest award;
(ii) the rate of interest payable on costs incurred prior to judgment; and
(iii) the amount to be paid on account of costs.

The parties agreed that the interest rate prior to judgment was 4% above base rate from the date on which the work was done or the liability for the disbursement was incurred, or 9 March 2015 whichever was the later. Payment on account of 80% of the approved costs budget was ordered to be paid. With regard to the additional amount, the sum awarded by way of interest was a contractual entitlement. As such, it was part of a "specific sum" awarded to the claimant and was thus part of the sum in respect of which the additional amount was to be calculated.[100] The Court of Appeal refused permission to appeal the above decision on the basis there was no real prospect of success. The Fee Agreement was fair and reasonable within the meaning of s.57(5) of the Solicitors Act 1974.

The High Court has held that the additional amount which can be awarded under CPR r.36.17(4)(d) should be calculated as a percentage of the basic monetary award but should not be applied to any award of interest. The court awarded a liquidator £360,000, plus statutory interest at 3% above base rate. The defendant was also ordered to pay all the costs on the indemnity basis. The court expressed the view that this was a case that should never have been defended. The liquidator had beaten its own Part 36 offer of £325,000 inclusive of interest and the judge also awarded an enhanced rate of interest of 10% above base rate on the sum awarded from the end of the relevant period until the date of judgment, interest at 10% above base rate on the costs and the additional amount allowed under CPR r.36.17(4)(d).[101]

5–19   In *Mohammed v Home Office*[102] however, the judge noted that there was conflicting High Court authority on the approach to CPR r.36.17(4)(d)(i); namely *Watchorn v Jupiter Industries Ltd* above and *Bolt Burdon Solicitors v Tariq*.[103] In *Watchorn* the judge assessed the additional amount as 10% of the net award, whilst in *Bolt Burdon* the court assessed the additional amount as 10% of the award including interest. Having considered each decision the judge concluded:

> "27. In my judgment, the proper construction of CPR r.36.17(4)(d)(i) is clear. In calculating the additional amount, the court should take into account the gross

---

[100] *Bolt Burdon Solicitors v Tariq* [2016] EWHC 1507 (QB); [2016] 4 W.L.R. 112; [2016] 4 Costs L.O. 617 Spencer J.
[101] *Husky Group Ltd, Re*; also known as *Watchorn v Jupiter Industries Ltd* [2014] EWHC 3003 (Ch); [2015] 3 Costs L.O. 337 HHJ Purle QC.
[102] *Mohammed v Home Office* [2017] EWHC 3051 (QB); [2018] 1 W.L.R. 1780; [2017] 6 Costs L.R. 1089 Edward Pepperall QC.
[103] *Bolt Burdon Solicitors v Tariq* [2016] EWHC 1507 (QB); [2016] 4 W.L.R. 112 Spencer J.

award that would have been made but for Pt 36. That is the sum that the court was about to award when taken to the Pt 36 offer. Such assessment therefore includes basic interest, whether awarded pursuant to contract (as in Bolt Burdon) or to the court's discretionary power, but excludes any enhanced interest awarded under CPR r.36.17(4)(a)."

The additional amount was not allowed in a case where, having made a Part 36 offer just before trial, the claimant beat her offer and sought payment of the additional amount under CPR r.36.17(4)(d). The court declined to make such an order, because she had raised a matter of fundamental importance to her case only in the course of opening, and other important information was disclosed only on the eve of the trial.[104]

Costs consequences

In a claim for damages for an accident at work, the defendant accepted liability and made a Part 36 offer for "£18,500 net of CRU and inclusive of interim payments in the sum of £18,500". The defendant also stated that the offer was made "without regard to any liability for recoverable benefits". The claimant obtained judgment for £29,550 made up of £4,000 general damages and the balance for loss of earnings. A CRU certificate was issued for £16,262. This was subsequently revised down to £6,760 because some of the benefits paid were not attributable to the accident. At first instance the recorder decided that the claimant had failed to beat the defendant's Part 36 offer. On appeal, the court held there was no contradiction between the concept of the offer being made "net of CRU" and it's being made "without regard to any liability for recoverable benefits". The natural meaning of "net of CRU" was "remaining after all necessary deductions of benefits".

The words "without any liability for recoverable amounts" did not mean that the court was to have no regard to the amount of recoverable benefit when deciding whether the claimant had obtained a judgment more advantageous than the offer. The offer was for £18,500 leaving aside any liability in respect of recoverable benefits once such liability had crystallised. The real measure of whether, after the CRUs revised certificate was issued, the claimant had bettered the offer, was whether the total payment he actually received was more or less than the amount of the offer. On that basis the claimant had beaten the Part 36 offer.[105]

The Court of Appeal has dealt with a case where the claimant had failed to beat the defendant newspaper's Part 36 offer at trial. At first instance the judge found that the newspaper's wrongdoing was far more extensive than it was prepared to admit and concluded that, since the newspaper had made limited admissions and had denied any liability until shortly before the trial, the claimant had some justification for proceeding. The claimant could not

5–20

---

[104] *Feltham v Bouskell* [2013] EWHC 3086 (Ch); [2014] 1 Costs L.O. 29 Charles Hollander QC.
[105] *Crooks v Hendricks Lovell Ltd* [2016] EWCA Civ. 8; [2016] 1 Costs L.O. 103.

recover his costs from the defendant but the judge did not order him to pay the defendant's costs using his powers under CPR r.36.17. On appeal by the defendant the court found that the trial judge had correctly decided that, where a claimant rejected a Part 36 offer because it reasonably wished to have the facts investigated at trial, that did not normally make it unjust for the normal costs consequences to follow; there had to be some further element: implicitly unjustness. The onus was on the person who had failed to beat the offer to show that it would be unjust for the normal consequences to apply. The appeal was dismissed.[106]

The court has considered the correct application of CPR r.36.17(4). It was agreed between the parties, following judgment at the end of a split trial on liability in favour of the claimant, that the judgment the claimant was awarded was more advantageous than the offer that he had made and which had been rejected. It was also agreed that Pt 36 is to be read as a self-contained code and not to be confused with contractual notions or general costs discretion under Pt 44 or non-Part 36 offers such as Calderbank type offers. The cases which support that proposition are *Gibbon v Manchester City Council*[107]; *Fox v Foundation Piling Ltd*[108]; and *Coward v Phaestos Ltd*.[109] The claimant had made an offer to settle of 80% of the damages to be awarded in the split trial case. The defendant did not accept the offer within the relevant period so that CPR r.36.17 applied. The judge in his draft costs order awarded indemnity costs to run throughout. He also ordered interest on those costs but at a lower rate than the maximum, from the end of the relevant period. The judge expressly made no order under CPR r.36.17(4)(a) (interest on the whole of or any part of any money awarded) or under CPR r.36.17(4)(d) (an additional amount not exceeding £75,000). Counsel for the claimant argued that the judge did not have the power to take that course given that Pt 36 was not only a complete code but was "as it were a menu all of whose courses must be delivered". It was argued that the judge was not free to choose between the relevant features of sub-rule (4) or to find that to apply one would be unjust and to apply another would not. The judge held, reading the plain language of the rule, that he was required to consider each stage of the sub-paragraph and ask whether the application of the particular sub-paragraph to this case with its own particular circumstances would be unjust. Having heard the argument, the judge amended his draft order so that the provision that the defendant should pay the claimant's costs relating to the issue of liability on the indemnity basis should be restricted expressly to the costs incurred or recoverable after the expiry of the relevant period.[110]

Where claimants were awarded damages of £2,000 having sought £3.7million, and the defendant had made two Part 36 offers, each far in excess

[106] *Yentob v MGN Ltd* [2015] EWCA Civ 1292; [2015] 6 Costs L.R. 1103.
[107] *Gibbon v Manchester City Council* [2010] EWCA Civ 726; [2010] 1 W.L.R. 2081.
[108] *Fox v Foundation Piling Ltd* [2011] EWCA Civ 790; [2011] C.P. Rep. 41.
[109] *Coward v Phaestos Ltd* [2014] EWCA Civ 1256; [2015] C.P. Rep. 2.
[110] *RXDX v Northampton BC* [2015] EWHC 2938 (QB); [2015] 5 Costs L.R. 897 Sir Colin Mackay.

of the amount awarded, ordinarily this would have entitled the defendants to its costs from the last date of acceptance of the first Part 36 offer, with the claimants entitled to their costs until that date, applying CPR r.36.17(3). Since the claim was exaggerated and opportunistic, the court made no order for costs until service of Further Information, and thereafter the defendants recovered all of their costs on an indemnity basis (plainly significant in a case where costs had been budgeted).[111]

The High Court held, on appeal, that the provisions of CPR r.36.17(4) apply equally in provisional assessment proceedings where a successful claimant's Part 36 offer has been made. This is in spite of the wording of CPR r.47.15(5) imposing a cap on the recoverable costs.[112] On appeal the Court of Appeal held:

5–21

> *"38.CPR r.47.20(4) provides expressly that Pt 36 shall apply to the costs of a detailed assessment subject to four express modifications which are irrelevant for these purposes. No mention is made of CPR Pt 47.15(5) and it is not modified in any way. It seems to me that if it had been intended that that rule was to be disapplied in the case of an assessment of costs on the indemnity basis under CPR r.36.17(4)(b) there would have been an express reference to it in either or both of the provisions or in r.47.20(4). There is nothing in any of those rules to suggest that r.47.15(5) should be disapplied or modified."*[113]

The appeal was allowed. For a discussion of this topic see **Ch.8, Qs 28** and **29**. The court is willing to impose sanctions on a defendant who seeks to avoid its liabilities and abuse the court's process. The defendant had sought an adjournment on the grounds that the Malaysian receiver needed time to decide whether or not to defend the summary judgment proceedings. The judge found that it could not be right that, if a defendant decided to petition for his own bankruptcy, at a time when he did not have to, the court must forget about the defendant and focus instead on the receiver. That would allow any defendant to avoid or delay proceedings. Further, an adjournment would serve no purpose from the Malaysian receiver's point of view. The judge also found that there was no real prospect of a successful defence and no other compelling reason for a trial. The judge awarded:

5–22

- The capital sums invested by the claimants through the defendant, together with interest at a rate "in the region of 20%", being the sort of return expected on the claimants' investment.
- The claimants' costs on the indemnity basis, given that the defendant's conduct in these proceedings had been "nothing short of abusive" and he had failed to beat the claimants' Part 36 offer.
- An additional amount under CPR r.36.17(4)(d). Although the judge had jurisdiction to award up to £75,000, he considered a more "modest" sum

---

[111] *Beattie Passive Norse Ltd and another v Canham Consulting* Ltd (No. 2 Costs) [2021] EWHC 1414 (TCC) (Fraser J).
[112] *Lowin v W Portsmouth & Co Ltd* [2016] EWHC 2301 (QB), [2017] C.P. Rep. 1; [2016] 5 Costs L.O. 719 Elisabeth Laing J.
[113] *W Portsmouth and Co Ltd v Lowin* [2017] EWCA Civ 2172; [2018] 1 W.L.R. 1890; [2018] 2 All E.R. 896; [2018] 1 Costs L.O. 1.

appropriate, bearing in mind that the Part 36 offer was in relation to a simple application for summary judgment, rather than, say, a lengthy trial, and that the interest rate already awarded was high.[114]

Where a claimant had made a Part 36 offer under the rules prior to 6 April 2015 and obtained judgment for almost three times the amount of the offer, the court held that it was not appropriate to reduce the costs award, because, although the claimant had not succeeded on every single issue, it had been overwhelmingly successful on the points which mattered most in terms of financial recovery. The defendant was ordered to pay costs on the standard basis up to the date upon which the court considered it was in a position to take an informed view of the quantum of the claim. Thereafter the defendant was ordered to pay costs on the indemnity basis together with enhanced interest for the same period at the rate of 8%.[115]

The Court of Appeal has dealt with the tension between the provisions of CPR Pt 45 IIIA (CPR r.45.29B) and Pt 36 (CPR r.36.21) where a claimant obtains judgment at least as advantageous as her Part 36 offer. The particular appeals were dealt with under the rules as they were before 6 April 2015, but the Master of the Rolls made it clear that the underlying provisions remain the same.

The question for the court was whether CPR r.36.17(4) Costs consequences following judgment, applies where a claimant makes a successful Part 36 offer, or whether the recoverable costs are limited to the fixed costs set out in Table 6 of CPR r.45.29C.

CPR r.45.29B provides: "the only costs allowed are—(a) the fixed costs in CPR r.45.29C; (b) disbursements in accordance with rule 45.29I". CPR r.36.21 was introduced to prescribe the costs consequences following judgment in section IIIA cases. While it modified some aspects of CPR r.36.17 in fixed costs cases, it left CPR r.36.17(4) unmodified.

In the two appeals before the court, one, *Broadhurst*, had been limited to the fixed costs in Table 6 whilst in the other, *Smith*, the judge had not limited the costs to Table 6.

The court was referred to the Explanatory Memorandum to the 2013 Amendment Rules:[116]

"... If a defendant refuses a claimant's offer to settle and the court subsequently awards the claimant damages which are greater than or equal to the sum they were prepared to accept in the settlement, the claimant will not be limited to receiving his fixed costs, but will be entitled to costs assessed on the indemnity basis in accordance with rule [CPR r.36.17]."

---

[114] *Bataillon v Shone* [2015] EWHC 3177 (QB) HHJ Waksman QC.
[115] *Thai Airways International Public Co Ltd v KI Holdings Co Ltd* [2015] EWHC 1476 (Comm); [2015] 3 Costs L.R. 545 Leggatt J. The subsequent appeal was dismissed by the Court of Appeal.
[116] Civil Procedure (Amendment No.6) Rules (SI 2013/1695).

The Master of the Rolls giving judgment with which the other members of the court agreed said:

> "23 CPR r.45.29B does not stand alone. The need to take account of Pt 36 offers
> in section IIIA cases was recognised by the draftsman of the rules. Indeed, CPR
> r.36.14A [36.21] is headed 'costs consequences following judgment where section
> IIIA of Part 45 applies'. CPR r.45.29F (8) provides that, where a Pt 36 offer is
> accepted in a section IIIA case, 'CPR r.36.10A [36.20] will apply instead of this
> rule'. And CPR r.45.29F(9) provides that, where in such a case upon judgment
> being entered the claimant fails to obtain a judgment more advantageous than
> the claimant's Pt 36 offer, 'CPR r.36.14A [36.21] will apply instead of this rule'.
> CPR r.45.29F does not, however, make provision as to what should happen where
> the claimant makes a successful Pt 36 offer.
> 25 The effect of CPR r.36.14 [36.17] and r.36.14A [36.21] when read together
> is that, where a claimant makes a successful Part 36 offer, he is entitled to costs
> assessed on the indemnity basis. Thus, CPR r.36.14 [36.17] is modified only to
> the extent stated by CPR r.36.14A [36.21]. Since CPR r.36.14(3) [36.17(4)] has
> not been modified by CPR r.36.14A [36.21], it continues to have full force and
> effect. The tension between CPR r.45.29B and CPR r.36.14A [36.21] must, there-
> fore, be resolved in favour of CPR r.36.14A [36.21].
> 31 Where a claimant makes a successful Pt 36 offer in a section IIIA case, he will
> be awarded fixed costs to the last staging point provided by CPR r.45.29C and
> Table 6B. He will then be awarded costs to be assessed on the indemnity basis in
> addition from the date that the offer became effective. This does not require any
> apportionment. It will, however, lead to a generous outcome for the claimant."[117]

More advantageous

Sub-paragraph 72 (vii) of the judgment in *Multiplex Construction (UK) Ltd v Cleveland Bridge UK Ltd* (dealing with the effect of *Carver v BAA*) should be disregarded.[118] *Carver* was effectively reversed by the rule change in previous CPR r.36.14(1A) (now CPR r.36.17(2))—a change that was recommended by Lord Justice Jackson in his *Review of Civil Litigation Costs: Final Report*. The judge making a costs order under CPR r.44.2 is exercising a broad discretion, not just deciding who the winner on each issue was, but taking into account the conduct of the parties and all the circumstances of the case. The judge is the best person to exercise that discretion having been immersed in the trial details.

5–23

In a successful claim for dilapidations, it was common ground that there was no offer under CPR Pt 36 which had any automatic costs consequences. The defendant had however made a Part 36 offer by letter dated 23 December 2011 in the sum of £1,000,000. When interest was added to the sums awarded

---

[117] *Broadhurst v Tan* [2016] EWCA Civ 94; [2016] 1 W.L.R. 1928; [2017] 2 All E.R. 60; [2016] C.P. Rep. 22; [2016] 2 Costs L.O. 155.
[118] *Hammersmatch Properties (Welwyn) Ltd v Saint-Gobain Ceramics & Plastics Ltd;* [2013] EWHC 2227 (TCC); [2013] B.L.R. 554; 149 Con. L.R. 147; [2013] 5 Costs L.R. 758; [2013].

of £900,000 and £20,320.40 up to 13 January 2012, the last date for acceptance of the Part 36 offer, the sum awarded to the claimant exceeded the defendant's Part 36 offer by £3,637.90, which represented a very small percentage of the sum offered.

The court noted that previous CPR r.36.14, had been amended on 1 October 2011, by the insertion of CPR r.36.14(1A) (now CPR r.36.17(2)). The claimant had not failed to obtain a judgment more advantageous than the defendant's Part 36 offer and therefore CPR r.36.14 (CPR r.36.17) did not apply. Ramsey J stated:

> *"The Pt 36 Offer made in this case could be said, in principle, to come within the wording of CPR r.44.2(4)(c). It is an admissible offer to settle and is not an offer to which costs consequences under Pt 36 apply. However I do not consider, even in a case such as this, where [the claimant] has only received a very small amount more than the sum which [the defendants] offered in its Pt 36 Offer, the court should approach CPR r.44.2(4)(c) on the basis that this could lead to an order that a claimant should pay the defendants' costs. In my judgment, to do so would be to seek to use the provisions of CPR r.44.2(4)-(c) to give a similar effect to a Pt 36 Offer and thereby introduce the same uncertainty into Pt 36 Offers which are near to but below the sum awarded, as led to the criticism of Carver and the subsequent amendment introduced in CPR r.36.14(1A) [now r.36.17].*
>
> *In my judgment the principle in sub-paragraph (vii) of [72] in Multiplex, derived as it was from Carver, is no longer a principle which applies to Pt 36 and should not be applied as a special near miss rule through CPR r.44.2(4)(c). If there is an unreasonable refusal to negotiate then that is a matter which comes within the circumstances which the court can take into account under CPR r.44.2(4) and sub-paragraph (a) in particular. I am doubtful that, on analysis, a 'near miss' offer can generally add anything to what otherwise would be conduct in the form of unreasonable refusal to negotiate . . ."*

The court considered issues of conduct by both parties and the relative success and failure on various issues. In the light of those circumstances the court assessed costs by reference to the factors in CPR r.44.2(4)(a) and (b). The claimant was awarded 80% of its costs.[119]

5–24   At a trial on quantum, the claimant succeeded in beating the defendant's Part 36 offer. The judge when considering what order for costs to make, took into account, as a matter of discretion, the Part 36 offer which had been beaten. Eder J made it clear that he was not introducing a "near miss" rule for Part 36 offers by the back door. In the judge's view the circumstances indicated that the claimant had insisted unreasonably on a higher figure than that offer, the claim had been much exaggerated and delays regarding disclosure

---

[119] *Hammersmatch Properties (Welwyn) Ltd v Saint-Cobain Ceramics & Plastics Ltd* [2013] EWHC 2227 (TCC); [2013] B.L.R. 554; 149 Con. L.R. 147; [2013] 5 Costs L.R. 758 Ramsey J. See also *JLE (by her mother and litigation friend, ELH) v Warrington & Halton Hospitals NHS Foundation Trust* [2019] EWHC 1582 (QB); [2019] 1 W.L.R. 6498; [2019] Costs L.R. 829.

and evidence had caused the defendant real difficulties in taking appropriate precautions to protect its position.[120]

The claimant appealed. The Court of Appeal held that it could not be misconduct simply to pursue a claim greater than the amount accepted by the defendant; something more was required to render pursuit of the claim unreasonable. The main judgment had not described the claim or any part of it as exaggerated. Significant parts of the business interruption claim had failed, but that did not mean that it had been exaggerated.

At first instance the claimant had been awarded 70% of its costs up to 21 days after the defendant's offer and was also ordered to pay the defendant's costs of the assessment of damages. The claimant had therefore been penalised twice for the same shortcoming. There was no basis on which it was appropriate to deprive the claimant of its costs after the offer, still less to require it to pay the defendant's costs. Its failure to succeed on all its claim was adequately reflected in the deduction of 30% of its costs (at [31]).[121]

There are numerous reported cases where offers which did not comply with CPR r.36.5 have been held not to be Part 36 offers. In these circumstances however, the court is not precluded from considering the fact that an offer has been made as part of the circumstances which it is required to take into account when considering what order for costs to make.[122] The court has held that Pt 36 should be construed as designed to protect defendants from claims being pursued, on the basis that a claimant might be able to persuade a defendant to pay more than the legal entitlement, or to pay the legal entitlement more quickly than would otherwise be the case, where the costs of contesting the entitlement would not be worth incurring. Part 36 is not intended to reward in costs, claimants who pursue their claims on such a basis.[123]

In a case where the claimant had achieved judgment against the defendant which was more advantageous than the proposal set out in its Part 36 offer, the defendants argued that it would be "unjust" to apply the previous CPR r.36.14(3)(b) and (c) (now CPR r.36.17(4)(b) and (c)). It was argued that the claimant had only succeeded as a result of material that had come to light since the Part 36 offer had been made. The argument was rejected by the Court of Appeal on the basis that the defendants were experienced litigators in the field and must have appreciated that there was a very serious risk that there would be a significant recovery above the interim payment which had already been made. The defendants had enough information to evaluate the Part 36 offer which they had rejected.[124]

5–25

In personal injury proceedings, the court, having found in favour of the claimant, ordered that the costs should be on the standard basis, save that the

---

[120] *Sugar Hut Group Ltd v AJ Insurance* [2014] EWHC 3775 (Comm); [2015] 2 Costs L.R. 179 Eder J.
[121] *Sugar Hut Group Ltd v AJ Insurance* [2016] EWCA Civ 46; [2016] C.P. Rep. 19.
[122] For example, *Rowles-Davies v Call 24–7 Ltd* [2010] EWHC 1695 (Ch); (2010) 160 N.L.J. 1043 Bernard Livesey QC; *Carillion JM Ltd v PHI Group Ltd* [2012] EWCA Civ 588; [2012] C.P. Rep. 37; [2012] 4 Costs L.O. 523.
[123] *D Pride & Partners v Institute for Animal Health* [2009] EWHC 1617 (QB); [2009] 5 Costs L.R. 803 Tugendhat J.
[124] *Bent v Highways and Utilities Construction (Costs)* [2011] EWCA Civ 1539; [2012] 2 Costs L.O. 127.

costs attributable to dealing with the evidence of the defendant's expert witnesses should be assessed on the indemnity basis. The defendant contended that it had made a written offer on costs, with a better outcome than the claimant had obtained. The court held that it was not possible to conduct a preliminary assessment of costs to establish arithmetically whether the defendant's offer was better on a pound for pound basis than the outcome achieved by the claimant. The justice of the case required the defendant to pay the claimant's costs of the oral hearing, together with the costs of the subsequent dispute as to costs of that hearing on the standard basis.[125]

5–26   In proceedings relating to a claim for breaches of a design and build contract where the claimant succeeded both in substance and in reality but was awarded significantly less than the amount claimed, and the defendant had made a Part 36 offer and had done better than that offer at trial, the court held that the claimant had failed completely on the element of its claim that was the largest in money terms and took the most time and effort regarding expert evidence and the trial itself. It had also failed substantially on two other large value elements in its claim. Overall, however, the claimant's conduct of the case was not unreasonable or deliberately exaggerated. The failure to accept the Part 36 offer did not merit indemnity costs. The claimant had been in a position to undertake its own assessment and valuation of the case at the time of the offer and was in a position to know that the result of independent tests significantly weakened the major elements of its claim, and that there were real risks that if it went to trial it would not recover more than was on offer. On that basis, the defendant was ordered to pay 80% of the claimant's costs up to a date 21 days after the offer was served with the reduction being the appropriate amount having regard to the claimant's partial lack of success. The claimant was ordered to pay 80% of the defendant's costs thereafter.[126]

Whilst CPR r.36.17 does not state in terms that it applies to the situation where a claimant does not accept a defendant's Part 36 offer and then fails altogether at trial, it appears that such situation is covered because the claimant has failed to obtain a judgment more advantageous than a defendant's Part 36 offer, and so CPR r.36.17(1)(a) applies. CPR 36.17(3) does not entitle a defendant whose Part 36 offer is not beaten to indemnity costs and an application for indemnity costs will simply fall to be decided under CPR r.44.2 in the usual way but the fact that the defendant has made a Part 36 offer may be taken into account in the exercise of that discretion. The Court of Appeal has held that where a defendant had thus beaten its own offer, the court should consider whether the claimant's conduct in refusing the offer took the case out of the norm so that indemnity costs should be ordered and the relevant question is whether at any stage a claimant would have concluded that the offer represented a better outcome than the likely outcome at trial.[127] Where

---

[125] *Williams v Jervis* [2009] EWHC 1838 (QB) Roderick Evans J.
[126] *Blackpool Borough Council v Volkerfitzpatrick Ltd* [2020] EWHC 2128 (TCC), HHJ Stephen Davies.
[127] *Lejonvarn v Burgess* [2020] EWCA Civ 114; [2020] 4 W.L.R. 43; [2020] Costs L.R. 45.

a claim had been dismissed as having a fundamentally false basis and the counterclaim had been partially successful but there had been a finding of dishonesty by the defendants, it would be unjust not to award the defendants (as Part 36 offerors) the CPR r.36.17(4) enhancements for the period after the effective date, and so from that date the claimant was ordered to pay 75% of the defendants' costs of the claim and counterclaim (as it was before the effective date) but on the indemnity basis plus interest at 10.1% per annum plus the additional amount of £75,000.[128]

Costs in the case and Pt 36

In a libel action brought by three claimants against three defendants in respect of emails sent in January and July 2012, the claimants each accepted offers of settlement which had been made by the third defendant. At the same time, the claimants gave notice of discontinuance of their claims against the first and second defendants.

5–27

The court had to determine the appropriate final orders in respect of damages and costs to give effect to the settlements and the discontinuance. The main issues were: whether such costs orders as were made against the claimants should be on the standard or the indemnity basis; whether the claimants should be jointly and severally liable for costs ordered in favour of the third defendant; and whether—and if so to what extent—costs and damages due to the claimants should be set-off against costs due to the third defendant. There was also an issue in respect of the effect of an order for costs in the case in respect of the third defendant's strike out application.

The court explained:

> *"The 'general effect' of an order for costs in the case is that 'the party in whose favour the court makes an order for costs at the end of the proceedings is entitled to that party's costs of the part of the proceedings to which the order relates': PD44 paragraph 4.2. Here, that general rule cannot be very readily applied; at the end of the proceedings the court has made orders for costs in favour of each party, save for [one].*
>
> *The action has concluded by settlement via Pt 36 and without prejudice save as to costs offers. All the claimants have obtained judgment for damages. [Two of the claimants] have recovered substantial damages, sums which on [the third defendant's] case are the maximum they could possibly have obtained. Yet it is said that they are the losers because their recovery is but a fraction of what they claimed. Views could differ about that conclusion, in this case and in others. It is easy to see that if [that] criterion were adopted there could often be lengthy argument as to which party has in reality 'won'.*
>
> *A simpler and better criterion is to hand for a case like this, which is to have regard to when in the proceedings the relevant costs were incurred and which party has obtained an order for costs in relation to that phase of the proceedings.*

---

[128] *Ahuja Investments Ltd v Victorygame Ltd* [2021] EWHC 2730 (Ch).

> *As a starting point I would suggest that acceptance of a Pt 36 Offer, which will ordinarily lead to an order for the costs up to the relevant date, should also carry with it any costs incurred within that period which are the subject of an order for costs in the case. Equally, if an offer is accepted 'out of time' and an order is made, in the ordinary way, for the offeree to pay costs since the expiry of the relevant period that order should carry with it any costs incurred in that period which are the subject of an order for costs in the case."*

What the judge found to be highly unreasonable conduct by claimants following their acceptance of the settlement offers justified awarding the defendant costs on the indemnity basis from the expiry of the offers' acceptance period. The claimants were jointly and severally liable for those costs incurred by continuing their common case after the offers. The court ordered the third defendant to pay the two claimants' costs of the strike out application.[129]

Cases in which the offeror's costs have been limited to court fees

5-28   Where, because of failure to file a costs budget on time or otherwise, the offeror is limited to applicable court fees, "costs" means, in respect of the costs subject to any such limitation, 50% of the costs assessed without reference to the limitation together with any other recoverable costs (see **Ch.4, Q78** for further consideration of this).

RTA Protocol and EL/PL Protocol offers to settle

5-29   Section II of Pt 36 applies to an offer to settle where the parties have followed the RTA Protocol or the EL/PL Protocol, and started proceedings under Pt 8, in accordance with CPR PD 8B (the Stage 3 procedure). Parties may make an offer to settle in whatever way they choose, but any offer which is not made in accordance with Section II will not have any costs consequences.

A Protocol offer under Section II must be set out in the Court Proceedings Pack (Form B) Form, and contain the final total amount of the offer from both parties. The offer is deemed to be made on the first business day after the Court Proceedings Pack is sent to the defendant.

A Protocol offer is treated as exclusive of all interest, and has costs consequences only in relation to the fixed costs of the Stage 3 procedure (as provided for in CPR r.45.18), not in relation to the costs of any appeal from the final decision in those proceedings. The amount of a Protocol offer must not be communicated to the court until the claim is determined. Any other offer to settle must not be communicated to the court at all.[130]

Costs consequences following judgment

5-30   CPR r.36.29 applies where on any determination by the court, the claimant obtains judgment against the defendant for an amount of damages that is:

---

[129] *Ontulmus v Collett* [2014] EWHC 4117 (QB) Warby J.
[130] CPR rr.36.24 to 36.28.

(a) less than or equal to the amount of the defendant's Protocol offer;
(b) more than the defendant's Protocol offer, but less than the claimant's Protocol offer; or
(c) equal to or more than the claimant's Protocol offer.

Where (a) applies, the court must order the claimant to pay the fixed costs in CPR r.45.26, and interest on those fixed costs from the first business day after the deemed date of the Protocol offer under CPR r.36.26. Where (b) applies, the court must order the defendant to pay the fixed costs in CPR r.45.20.

Where (c) applies, the court must order the defendant to pay interest on the whole of the damages awarded at a rate not exceeding 10% above base rate for some or all of the period, starting with the date specified in CPR r.36.26, the fixed costs in CPR r.45.20, interest on those fixed costs at a rate not exceeding 10% above base rate, and an additional amount calculated in accordance with CPR r.36.17(4)(d).

Deduction of benefits

For the purposes of (a) above, the amount of the judgment is less than the Protocol offer where the judgment is less than the offer once deductible amounts identified in the judgment are deducted.

5–31

Late acceptance

It has been suggested that in the case of a claimant's offer which is accepted late, CPR r.36.17 can be extended to analogous situations to justify awarding the claimant costs on the indemnity basis after the end of the relevant period in order to reward the claimant and penalise the defendant for failing to accept in good time.

5–32

In the case of late acceptance in fixed costs cases, CPR r.36.20(4) provides for what will happen where the defendant's offer is accepted late, but there is no provision for late acceptance of a claimant's offer in a fixed costs case in the rules. This may mean one is thrown back on CPR r.36.13(5) so the claimant will be awarded costs until date of acceptance but since costs is not given a particular meaning in this context, the general rule in CPR r.45.29B probably applies which means that the claimant will only be entitled to fixed costs plus disbursements.

It has also been suggested that it is arguable that a claimant would be entitled to indemnity costs by reference to the overriding objective because the parties are not on an equal footing if the claimant does not receive a benefit.

CPR r.36.8 provides:

> "(1) *The offeree may, within seven days of a Part 36 offer being made, request the offeror to clarify the offer.*
> (2) *If the offeror does not give the clarification requested under paragraph (1) within seven days of receiving the request, the offeree may, unless the trial has started, apply for an order that the offeror do so.*

> (3) If the court makes an order under paragraph (2), it must specify the date
> when the Part 36 offer is to be treated as having been made."

One may speculate that, where the request is genuine, the court may allow a further 21 days from the point that clarification is provided.

There is clearly an imbalance against claimants in Pt 36 because they only get the automatic benefits in the small number of cases which go to trial. This could be addressed judicially except in the case of fixed costs cases where a rule change is needed. In fixed costs cases, if the claimant accepts a Part 36 offer after the end of the relevant period but within the same stage, there are no costs implications in reality (because the costs are fixed for each stage).

Arguments about whether a party is entitled to indemnity costs often cost more than the increase (from standard costs to indemnity costs) is worth. However, this will change when fixed costs are extended.

A former soldier, who suffered from PTSD claimed damages from the Ministry of Defence. The defendant made a Part 36 offer which was not accepted within the 21-day relevant period. The offer was not withdrawn. The claimant made it clear that without further information he could not properly consider the offer made. Some three months later, a joint expert report was received which clarified matters. The claimant changed his solicitors and, three months after the joint expert's report, the claimant accepted the defendant's Part 36 offer. Three days later the claimant changed his mind and instructed his solicitor to cancel his acceptance of the offer, since he was unhappy with the settlement figure and felt under duress. The trial date had already been vacated. The defendant sought its costs from the expiry of the relevant period until the notice of acceptance. The court held that the offer had been accepted and that Pt 36 applied. The court was required to order the defendant to pay the claimant's costs until the expiration of the relevant period unless it was unjust to do so, pursuant to CPR r.36.17(5). The joint experts report was of great significance in resolving the different positions concerning quantification of the claimant's loss. It was not realistic to hold that the offer could have been evaluated within the relevant period before the expert's report had been received, allowing the claimant a reasonable period to evaluate the claim after receipt of the report, the window for acceptance was extended until 21 days after the expert's report had been received. Thereafter, the claimant was ordered to pay the defendant's costs until the date of acceptance.[131]

In a personal injury claim, the claimant accepted the defendant's Part 36 offer late. On the facts the court could find no reason to depart from the usual costs rule following late acceptance, namely that the claimant should be awarded his costs up to the date on which the relevant period expired and for the claimant to pay the defendant's costs from the date of expiry

---

[131] *Momonakaya v Ministry of Defence* [2019] EWHC 480 (QB); [2019] 1 Costs L.R. 101, Peter Blair QC.

of the relevant period to the date of acceptance.[132] A company shareholder who had petitioned for relief based on his allegation that a director of the company had breached his duties was entitled to costs on the indemnity basis where the director had delayed for more than two years before accepting a CPR Part 36 offer. The offer was accepted only two weeks before trial, after the shareholder had obtained late disclosure of documents that undermined the director's defence in material respects and damaged his credibility. The court held that the respondent had conducted his defence and acted in the proceedings with a significant level of unreasonableness or otherwise inappropriate conduct that took the matter out of the norm and justified an order for costs on the indemnity basis.[133] The court took account of the following factors. First, the respondent knew that the petitioner was funding the petition on a CFA basis. Walking away from a case after two years of knowing that one party was funding the litigation on such a basis, and taking advantage of that funding position, could amount to significant unreasonable conduct. Second, the respondent had rejected a Part 36 offer made over two years before the trial. Third, he accepted that offer close to the trial and did the equivalent of walking away from the action. Fourth, given that he knew that the petitioner was applying for indemnity costs to be made against him, it was significant that the respondent had failed to give reasons why he delayed for so long before accepting the Part 36 offer. Fifth, the respondent had let the petitioner incur additional costs in making the applications for disclosure, which would have been unnecessary if he had given full and frank disclosure in the first place, and costs in amending the petition. Sixth, it had transpired that the respondent had hidden his interest in a further third party to whom the company had made an unrepaid loan.[134]

Costs of detailed assessment proceedings

CPR r.47.20(4) clarifies that the provisions of Part 36 apply to the costs of detailed assessment proceedings with certain modifications. Where an offer to settle is made whether under Pt 36 or otherwise, it should specify whether or not it is intended to be inclusive of the costs of preparation of the bill, interest and VAT. Unless the offer makes it clear that the position is otherwise, it will be treated as being inclusive of all those matters.[135]   5–33

In a clinical negligence case, the defendant accepted the claimant's Part 36 offer of £475,000 to settle the costs. The claimant then made a £52,000

---

[132] *Campbell v Ministry of Defence* [2019] EWHC 2121 (QB), [2020] Costs L.R. 13; Lambert J.
[133] See *Excelsior Commercial & Industrial Holdings Ltd v Salisbury Hamer Aspden & Johnson (Costs)* [2002] EWCA Civ 879; [2002] C.P. Rep. 67. *Excelsior* is the authority which sets out the basis for an order for costs on the indemnity basis.
[134] *Rees v Oliver* [2019] EWHC 922 (Ch), Chief ICC Judge Briggs.
[135] CPR r.36.5(4) provides: A Part 36 offer which offers to pay or offers to accept a sum of money will be treated as inclusive of all interest until—
(a) the date on which the period specified under CPR r.36.5(1)(c) expires; or
(b) if CPR r.36.5(2) applies, a date 21 days after the date the offer was made.
A further sub paragraph was added by the Civil Procedure (Amendment) Rules 2021:
(5) A Part 36 offer to accept a sum of money may make provision for accrual of interest on such sum after the date specified in paragraph (4). If such an offer does not make any such provision, it shall be treated as inclusive of all interest up to the date of acceptance if it is later accepted. This provision came into force on 6 April 2021.

Part 36 offer in relation to the costs of assessment, which she bettered by £6,120 at the assessment and so sought the usual benefits of beating the offer. The costs judge held that a Part 36 offer cannot be made in relation to the costs of detailed assessment proceedings. If it could, this would open the way potentially to an indefinite cycle of Part 36 offers and new detailed assessment proceedings.[136]

In detailed assessment proceedings, the receiving party made a Part 36 offer to settle for £152,500. At the detailed assessment the bill was allowed at £173,693 which was more advantageous to the receiving party than the Part 36 offer. The costs judge declined to award the 10% additional amount stating that in circumstances where there had been a significant reduction in the claimant's bill, it would be unjust to reward the claimant with the additional amount prescribed by CPR r.36.17(4). On appeal, the court found that the costs judge was in error in relying on the degree of reduction on assessment. That approach penalised the appellant for making a reasonable Part 36 offer. It was the terms of the Part 36 offer not the level of the sums claimed in the bill of costs which were to be considered. Accordingly, the appellant was entitled to the additional award.[137]

5–34   In proceedings for detailed assessment, the paying party wrote to the receiving party, setting out what they described as Part 36 offers, which were stated to be open for 21 days, and offered a proportion or fixed sum in respect of the receiving party's costs. The offers were rejected, and the paying party made a further offer in respect of a third receiving party, if the other receiving parties were willing to accept the Part 36 offers. These offers were accepted, but the costs hearing still took place because the paying party contended they were entitled to costs in respect of the period from the expiry of the 21 days referred to in the original offers, until the point when the offers had been accepted. The court made no order for the costs in respect of that period. The court held, on the facts, that the earlier offer was not a Part 36 offer, because it specifically excluded the offerors from recovering all of their costs, and it could not, by its very terms, comply with CPR r.36.10(1) (now CPR r.36.13(1)).

The subsequent offer was indistinguishable from that in *C v D*,[138] and the subsequent offer should be treated as a Part 36 offer, particularly since all the parties treated the offers as having been made under Pt 36. The overriding objective, and common sense, suggested that an offer which was expressed to be a Part 36 offer, and which otherwise appeared to comply with Pt 36, had to be given substantially the same effect as a Part 36 offer. The offer which was accepted was significantly better than the original offer, and the allocation of liability for costs for the period between the expiry of the 21 days and

[136] *Best (Administratrix of the Estate of Phyllis Stuck, Deceased) v Luton & Dunstable Hospital NHS Foundation Trust* [2021] SCCO, 29 January, Costs Judge Leonard.
[137] *Cashman v Mid-Essex Hospital Services NHS Trust* [2015] EWHC 1312 (QB); [2015] 3 Costs L.O. 411 Slade J.
[138] *C v D* [2011] EWCA Civ 646; [2012] 1 W.L.R. 1962; [2012] 1 All E.R. 302; [2011] C.P. Rep. 38; 136 Con. L.R. 109; [2011] 5 Costs L.R. 773.

acceptance was a matter for the judge's discretion, without the presumption in favour of the paying party inherent in CPR r.36.10(4) and (5) (now CPR r.36.13(4) and (5)). The right order to make was that each party should bear its own costs from the expiry of the 21 days.[139]

In detailed assessment proceedings, the claimant receiving party made a Part 36 offer to accept £82,000 "exclusive of interest". On assessment, the costs of the action were assessed at £91,807. It was the defendant's case that an offer "exclusive of interest" was not an offer within Part 36. In a lengthy judgment, the court referred to CPR PD 47 para.19:

> "*Where an offer to settle is made, whether under Part 36 or otherwise, it should specify whether or not it is intended to be inclusive of the costs of preparation of the bill, interest and VAT. Unless the offer states otherwise, it will be treated as inclusive of these*".

In the circumstances of a detailed assessment, interest would be payable on the costs and the costs of the detailed assessment proceedings, but that would be added automatically by virtue of the Judgments Act 1838 and did not need to be claimed. It was prudent of the solicitors to specify that the offer was exclusive of interest, otherwise the effect of the Practice Direction would be that the offer would be treated as being inclusive of interest (at least until the conclusion of the relevant period). The validity of the Part 36 offer was not affected by the inclusion of the words "exclusive of interest".[140]

Section 2 Settlement other than under Pt 36

Encouragement to engage in ADR

In Chapter 36 of his Final Report Jackson LJ recommended that there should be a serious campaign (a) to ensure that all litigation lawyers and judges are properly informed about the benefits which ADR can bring and (b) to alert the public and small businesses to the benefits of ADR. 5–35

There is constant pressure from the judiciary and court users for greater use of ADR. The Jackson ADR Handbook is now in its second edition, written by three distinguished authors under the banner of the Judicial College, the Civil Justice Council and the Civil Mediation Council.

The book deals with the general principles of alternative dispute resolution (ADR) as well as the range of ADR options. These include: offer and acceptance (offers other than under Pt 36); negotiation; mediation; early neutral

---

[139] *Howell v Lees-Millais* [2011] EWCA Civ 786; [2011] 4 Costs L.O. 456.

[140] *Evelyn Horne v Prescot (No.1) Ltd* [2019] EWHC 1322 (QB), [2019] 1 W.L.R. 4808; [2019] Costs L.R. 279; Nicol J. The minutes of the November 2020 meeting of the CPRC indicate that a Part 36 offer should not be permitted to exclude interest and a proposed drafting solution by way of an amended PD 47.19 was agreed. This change was made by the 217th Practice Direction update in force 1 April 2021. "19. Where an offer to settle is made, whether under Part 36 or otherwise, it should specify whether or not it is intended to be inclusive of the cost of preparation of the bill and VAT. An offer which is made otherwise than under Part 36 should specify whether or not it is intended to be inclusive of interest. Unless the offer states otherwise it will be treated as being inclusive of all of these. (A Part 36 offer is treated as inclusive of interest: see CPR 36.5(4).)"

evaluation; expert evaluation; adjudication; and arbitration. All of these processes may be used in connection with the resolution of costs disputes.

The CJC issued its interim report on the future role of ADR in civil justice on 17 October 2017.[141] The CJC working group on ADR published its final report in November 2018.[142] It sets out 24 recommendations, many of which are directed at introducing more forceful methods to encourage parties to use ADR. The final report recommends a number of ways to raise awareness of ADR in the public arena, the establishment of a judicial ADR liaison committee and a website to provide a single online offering containing information about the different types of ADR available. It also supports increased regulation of mediators via the Civil Mediation Council, along similar lines to regulation of family mediators by the Family Mediation Council. At that time the CJC did not consider it appropriate to introduce into civil litigation generally any form of compulsory mediation or pre-action mediation, information and assessment meetings, which are currently used in the family courts.

Instead, the report set out a series of reforms to current civil procedure to reinforce a presumption that ADR should be attempted in any case which is not otherwise settled and to penalise more rigorously parties for unreasonably failing to do this. These included:

- Questions on the claim form (and possibly the defence) regarding the use of ADR.
- Improving the current wording on the directions questionnaire on ADR.
- More focus on ADR at the case management conference and potential sanctions at this stage for failing to engage in ADR (for example, recording the recommendation of a costs penalty on the file).
- Urgent reform of the Halsey list of acceptable reasons for refusing to mediate, which the report considers are currently too generous to the refusing party.
- For the future, the report recommends further consideration be given to introducing a "notice to mediate" system, based on the British Columbia model, whereby if one party issues a formal invite to another to mediate, a mediation will kick into action, with a mediator automatically appointed from a court approved roster in the absence of agreement.[143] At the end of 2019 the Civil Justice Council set up the Judicial Liaison Committee to look into and, if possible, implement the CJC's Report on ADR published a year earlier. It does not appear to have a website but has published a set of minutes.[144]

---

[141] *https://www.judiciary.gov.uk/publications/cjc-invite-submissions-on-the-future-role-of-adr-in-civil-justice/.*
[142] *https://www.judiciary.uk/wp-content/uploads/2018/12/CJC-ADRWG-Report-FINAL-Dec-2018.pdf.*
[143] With acknowledgements to The Practical Law Company.
[144] *https://www.judiciary.uk/wp-content/uploads/2020/07/2-SUMMARY-MINUTES-Jan-2020-Judicial-ADR-Liaison-Committee.pdf.*

At a meeting on 5 March 2021, the Civil Procedure Rule Committee (CPRC) discussed the aims of the ADR Committee which is intended to provide the judiciary, the ADR community and the professions with a dedicated forum for the discussion and exchange of information regarding ADR in the civil justice system. Part of its function is to consider the CPR and the encouragement of ADR at all levels of the civil justice system and whether ADR should be mandatory.

In 2021, the CJC revisited the issue of compulsory ADR. It published *Compulsory ADR* (June 2021)[145] in July 2021, in which it concluded that compulsory alternative dispute resolution (ADR) was compatible with Article 6 of the European Convention on Human Rights, and was, therefore, lawful (the "legality" question). On the "legality" question, the report considers relevant case law including decisions of the European Court of Human Rights, as well as *Halsey v Milton Keynes General NHS Trust* [2004] EWCA Civ 576, and provides examples where, to a greater or lesser extent, litigants are already being compelled to use ADR. Any form of ADR which is not "disproportionately onerous" and does not "foreclose the parties' effective access to the court" will be compatible with art.6. It follows that an order for participation in an ADR process that was disproportionality expensive, took an excessively long time, or was otherwise burdensome, would obstruct access to the court and breach art.6. The issue of sanction requires "special consideration". The report considers how a court order which requires participation in ADR should be enforced, and the sanction where participation in ADR is a required procedural step. The report examines how, in what circumstances, the type of case, and at what stage, compulsory ADR should be imposed (the "desirability" question). Factors to consider include the cost and time burden on the parties, whether the parties need or have access to legal advice, and the stage of proceedings where ADR may be required. The report concludes that introducing further compulsory elements of ADR will be lawful and "potentially an extremely positive development". Where participation requires no expense (for example, through the parties' answering questions in an online process), it is "very unlikely" that its compulsory nature will be controversial. If certain types of ADR, such as mediation, are to be compulsory, more regulation is required. As to next steps, more work is needed to determine the types of claim and the situations in which compulsory ADR would be appropriate. In response, Sir Geoffrey Vos, Master of the Rolls and Chair of the CJC and Head of Civil Justice, endorsed the report, which "opens the door to a significant shift towards earlier resolution of claims". In his view, ADR should no longer be viewed as "alternative"; the focus should be on "resolution" rather than "dispute". He also highlighted the HMCTS court reform programme in delivering online justice, where "all kinds of dispute resolution interventions will be embedded within that online process".

---

[145] *https://www.judiciary.uk/wp-content/uploads/2021/07/Civil-Justice-Council-Compulsory-ADR-report-1.pdf.*

On 13 July 2021, the Civil Mediation Council (CMC) published its response to the CJC's report "Compulsory ADR". The CMC welcomed the CJC's report calling it a "significant development" and called for ADR to be put "at the centre of the civil justice process". The CMC agreed with the CJC's conclusion that non-compliance with an order to engage in ADR should attract the same sanctions as, for example, non-compliance with an order for disclosure. The CMC downplayed the argument that mediation involves disproportionate or extra costs, stating that 80% of mediated cases settle on the day or shortly afterwards, resulting in notable time and costs benefits. In any event, failure to settle at mediation is not a waste of time and costs because the issues may have been narrowed for subsequent litigation. The CMC cautioned against what it perceived to be an implication in the CJC's report that mediation could be carried out "on the cheap" and emphasised that not all judges are necessarily equipped to become mediators unless they are properly trained and accredited.

On 3 August 2021, the government launched a major call for evidence "Dispute resolution in England and Wales" and sought feedback on how disputes in the civil, family and administrative jurisdictions might best be settled away from the court room. On 3 November 2021, the CMC published its response and on 26 November 2021, the Law Society published its response to the government's call for evidence and its response to the CJC's report, "Compulsory ADR".

On 13 July 2021, the Ministry of Justice published: A guide to civil mediation.[146]

On 28 October 2021, Sir Geoffrey Vos, MR, gave a speech at the European Association of Judges for Mediation (GEMME) lecture entitled: "Mediated interventions within the Court Dispute Resolution Process." He advocated for change in court-based dispute resolution and envisaged an online system comprising three tiers. He called for ADR to be integrated digitally within dispute resolution. He asked the CJC to prepare advice on how the online dispute resolution space could work best, with an emphasis on resolution rather than dispute, with an expectation of sharing the report in 2022. He stated that there is a forthcoming CJC report which will recommend that small claims worth less than £500 should be subject to mandatory mediation. If the small claims are not resolved consensually, they should be resolved by the judge on the papers without oral evidence or submissions.

5–36   On 12 September 2017, the European Parliament adopted a resolution on the implementation of the EU Mediation Directive (2008/52/EC). The resolution provided that EU member states should step up their efforts to encourage the use of mediation in civil and commercial disputes. The Commission should assess the need to develop EU wide quality standards and consistency in the provision of mediation services while taking into account the fundamental right of access to justice and differences in mediation cultures. The

---

[146] *https://www.gov.uk/guidance/a-guide-to-civil-mediation.*

Commission should assess the need for member states to create and maintain national registers of mediated proceedings. The European Parliament requested that the Commission undertake a detailed study on the obstacles to the free circulation of foreign mediation agreements across the EU and on various options to promote the use of mediation as an effective and affordable way of solving domestic and international conflicts. The Commission should find solutions to extend the scope of mediation to other civil or administrative matters. In the case of family law, mediation might require the implementation of appropriate safeguards to limit the risks for weaker parties and prevent any possible abuse of process.

The Cross-Border Mediation (EU Directive) (EU Exit) Regulations 2019

The Exit Regulations came into force after the end of the transition period on 31 December 2020. These Regulations revoke the Cross-Border Mediation (EU Directive) Regulations 2011 and the Cross-Border Mediation Regulations (Northern Ireland) 2011, subject to saving and transitional provision.

5–37

The 2011 Regulations partially implemented Directive 2008/52/EC of the European Parliament and of the Council of 21 May 2008 on certain aspects of mediation in civil and commercial matters in the United Kingdom.

These regulations also make amendments to provision which implemented the Mediation Directive relating to limitation periods. The regulations enable the continued application, with modification, of the provision amended by Sch.1 to mediations begun before exit day.

In relation to international mediations, on 26 June 2018, the 51st session of the United Nations Commission on International Trade Law (UNCITRAL) approved final drafts for The Singapore Mediation Convention on the Enforcement of Mediation Settlements and accompanying Model Law. The aim of the Convention is to formulate and implement an international framework for the enforcement of mediated settlements, similar to the way in which the New York Convention acts as a framework for the enforcement of arbitral awards. Also, on 2 October 2018, the Centre for Effective Dispute Resolution (CEDR) reported that the Convention had been published. It was signed in Singapore on 7 August 2019, and will come into effect six months after ratification by at least three United Nations states.[147] In May 2021, the then Lord Chancellor, Robert Buckland QC MP, gave a speech at London International Disputes Week in which he said, amongst other things, that the government would shortly begin a public consultation on whether the UK should join the Singapore Mediation Convention; a prospect which in the Lord Chancellor's view would promote international mediation and help maintain the UK's position as a dispute resolution hub.

---

[147] *http://www.uncitral.org/pdf/english/commissionsessions/51st-session/Annex_I.pdf.*

Unreasonable refusal to engage in ADR

5–38   The Court of Appeal has firmly endorsed the advice given in the ADR Handbook to the effect that, as a general rule, silence in the face of an invitation to participate in ADR is itself unreasonable, regardless of whether a refusal to engage in ADR might have been justified. There might be rare cases where ADR is so obviously inappropriate that to characterise silence as unreasonable would be pure formalism, or where the failure to respond was a result of a mistake, in which case the onus would be on the recipient of the invitation to make that explanation good. The court stated that the reasons for extending the guidelines set out in *Halsey v Milton Keynes General NHS Trust*[148] were: first, because an investigation of the reasons for refusing to mediate advanced for the first time at a costs hearing, perhaps months or years later, posed forensic difficulties for the court concerning whether those reasons were genuine. Second, a failure to provide reasons for refusal was destructive of the objective of encouraging parties to consider and discuss ADR. Any difficulties or reasonable objection to a particular ADR proposal should be discussed so that the parties could narrow their differences. Third, it would also serve the policy of proportionality. The court held it would be perverse not to regard silence in the face of repeated requests for mediation as anything other than a refusal. A finding of unreasonable conduct by a refusal to mediate did not produce an automatic result in terms of a costs penalty. The judge has a broad discretion.[149]

A defendant police commissioner who successfully defended proceedings was found to have refused to engage in the alternative dispute resolution process without adequate justification. The court found that the claimants could have obtained some level of damages. There were issues of fact to be resolved from which both parties ran the risk of adverse findings. The defence was not so strong as to have justified a refusal to engage in ADR. The commissioner did not make any offers to settle before ADR was suggested and ADR would not have delayed the trial of the action. The commissioner was awarded two-thirds of his costs.[150]

As discussed above,[151] the CJC has recently expressed the view that compulsory ADR is compatible with art.6 of the European Convention on Human Rights. The CJC indicated that it would be helpful if the issue could be revisited by an appellate court or legislature as soon as possible and stated that the view of the authors is that the firm view expressed in *Halsey* about art. 6 has proved to be the "beginning of a debate rather than a conclusion"[152]: Lord Dyson in *Halsey* expressed the view that "compulsion of ADR would be

---

[148] *Halsey v Milton Keynes General NHS Trust* [2004] EWCA Civ 576; [2004] 1 W.L.R. 3002; [2004] 4 All E.R. 920; [2004] C.P. Rep. 34; [2004] 3 Costs L.R. 393.
[149] *PGF II SA v OMFS Co 1 Ltd* [2013] EWCA Civ 1288; [2014] 1 W.L.R. 1386; [2014] 1 All E.R. 970; [2014] C.P. Rep. 6; [2014] B.L.R. 1; 152 Con. L.R. 72; [2013] 6 Costs L.R. 973.
[150] *Laporte v Commissioner of Police of the Metropolis* [2015] EWHC 371 (QB); [2015] 3 Costs L.R. 471 Turner J.
[151] See 5–35.
[152] Compulsory ADR: para.56.

regarded as an unacceptable constraint on the right of access to the court and, therefore, a violation of article 6."[153]

Discretion under CPR 44.2

When the court exercises its discretion under CPR r.44.2, it has to have regard to all the circumstances including the conduct of the parties both before and during the proceedings. "Conduct" includes a refusal to agree to ADR. The factors to be taken into account include: the nature of the dispute; the merits of the case; the extent to which other settlement methods have been attempted; whether the costs of ADR are disproportionately high; whether any delay in setting or attending the ADR would be prejudicial; and whether ADR has a reasonable prospect of success.[154]

5–39

A settlement agreement recorded that the respondent would pay the debt of US$1.5 million to the appellant by a certain date, failing which he would pay an extra $1,000 per day. The respondent failed to pay and the "$1,000 per day" clause became operative. Some time later, the parties reached a number of other agreements.

The appellant appealed against a judge's findings regarding the effect of agreements reached between them. The issue on appeal was the extent to which a forbearance to raise a defence later found to be without legal merit could constitute sufficient consideration to support an agreement between the parties. The Court of Appeal held that forbearance to raise a defence later found to be without legal merit could constitute sufficient consideration to support an agreement between the parties. The validity of the consideration had to be judged at the time the agreement was made. Even if the defence, at that time, raised a doubtful or undecided point, it would be valid consideration as long as the person intimating it believed it and intended to pursue it. There was a public policy in favour of holding people to their commercial bargains.[155]

The advantages of ADR

The advantages of ADR include: lower costs (provided that the ADR process is entered into sufficiently early); the speed of resolution of the issues; the choice of forum and process; the flexibility of process (the parties may agree how they wish to proceed; a wider range of issues/outcomes may be considered; and shared future interests may be protected. In mediation, the parties may choose the mediator and the process is entirely confidential. In litigation there will usually be a winner and a loser with damages and costs being paid by one party to another. In ADR the parties may have been unable to agree

5–40

---

on the contentious issues but may wish to maintain a potentially lucrative business relationship.

In particular litigation the defendant argued that its contract with the claimant contained a valid, binding and applicable ADR clause that prescribed a mandatory escalation and mediation procedure prior to the commencement of proceedings. The defendant applied to stay the proceedings which the claimant had commenced, pending referral of the dispute to mediation.

The court summarised the principles applicable where a party seeks to enforce an ADR provision by means of an order staying proceedings as follows:

> *"(i) The agreement must create an enforceable obligation requiring the parties to engage in alternative dispute resolution.*
> *(ii) The obligation must be expressed clearly as a condition precedent to court proceedings or arbitration.*
> *(iii) The dispute resolution process to be followed does not have to be formal but must be sufficiently clear and certain by reference to objective criteria, including machinery to appoint a mediator or determine any other necessary step in the procedure without the requirement for any further agreement by the parties.*
> *(iv) The court has a discretion to stay proceedings commenced in breach of an enforceable dispute resolution agreement. In exercising its discretion, the Court will have regard to the public policy interest in upholding the parties' commercial agreement and furthering the overriding objective in assisting the parties to resolve their disputes."* [32].

In concluding, on the facts, that the proceedings should be stayed, the court stated further:

> *"There is a clear and strong policy in favour of enforcing alternative dispute resolution provisions and in encouraging parties to attempt to resolve disputes prior to litigation. Where a contract contains valid machinery for resolving potential disputes between the parties, it will usually be necessary for the parties to follow that machinery, and the court will not permit an action to be brought in breach of such agreement.*
> *The Court must consider the interests of justice in enforcing the agreed machinery under the [contract]. However, it must also take into account the overriding objective in the Civil Procedure Rules when considering the appropriate order to make."* [58]–[59].[156]

Offers other than Part 36 offers

5–41   It is open to either party in litigation to make offers which do not comply with the requirements of Pt 36. These may be open offers or offers without prejudice save as to costs. The latter are generally known as Calderbank offers,

---

[156] *Ohpen Operations UK Ltd v Invesco Fund Managers Ltd* [2019] EWHC 2246 (TCC); [2020] 1 All E.R. (Comm) 786; [2019] B.L.R. 576, O'Farrell J.

which arose in the Family Division where there was no provision for payment into court, but the parties could be at risk as to costs, particularly in respect of financial arrangements.

In detailed assessment proceedings, the paying party made a Calderbank offer in respect of the receiving party's costs, which incorporated various conditions relating to a second action between the parties. The costs judge accepted that the receiving party was incapable of accepting the offer because its insurers had conduct of the second action, but determined that the receiving party could have accepted quantum and either varied the conditions, or sought a hearing to determine set-off. On appeal the court held that the offer was linked to conditions that made the firm unable to accept it. To rely on the offer for Calderbank purposes, it had to be an offer that was acceptable on its stated terms, not one that contemplated further attempts to negotiate. The effect of the costs judge's reasoning was to place the burden on the firm as the receiving party to negotiate a settlement of the offer's conditions or make a counter offer. That did not reflect the wording of the CPR or the nature of a Calderbank offer, namely that it was either acceptable or not.[157]

In deciding what order to make about costs the court is required to have regard to all the circumstances including the conduct of all the parties, whether a party has succeeded on part of its case and if not wholly successful, the extent to which that party has succeeded and any admissible offer to settle which is drawn to the court's attention and which is not an offer to which the costs consequences of Pt 36 apply. The question of who was the successful party will often be determined by who ultimately wrote the cheque at the end.[158] In a subsequent case, however, the court gave judgment on a claim for damages arising out of a restriction of competition contrary to TFEU Preamble Art.101. The court held that the claimant had sustained losses as a result of the operation of a cartel and was entitled to damages. In a subsequent judgment, the court dealt with the question of costs. The claimant submitted that the party who writes the cheque at the end of the day is the unsuccessful party and the party receiving the cheque is the successful party. Marcus Smith J stated:

> "4. I confess that I am not sure that the definition of success is so easy a concept, at least in this case. In this case, there was, from the outset, a binding finding against ABB. I refer to the Commission's decision which found the existing existence of the cartel which found that ABB was party to that cartel and which found that the BritNed Interconnector was a cartelised project pursuant to that cartel. In a very real sense, therefore, quantum was substantially the only issue before the Court.
>
> Absent one of the two factors that I list below, it was, one might well say, inevitable that ABB would be writing a cheque to BritNed. It does not, therefore,

---

[157] *Hugh Carwright & Amin v Devoy-Williams* [2018] EWHC 1692 (QB); [2018] 4 Costs L.O. 437 Nicola Davies J.
[158] *Day v Day (Costs)* [2006] EWCA Civ 415; [2006] C.P. Rep. 35. But see now: *BritNed Development Ltd v ABB AB, ABB Ltd* [2018] EWHC 3142 (Ch); [2018] 6 Costs L.O. 807, Marcus Smith J.

axiomatically follow that simply because a payment was ordered in this case, that ABB was the loser."

The two factors were, first, that it was open to the court to find there was no overcharge and no loss to *BritNed* at all (a contention which failed), although the outcome of the litigation in monetary terms was closer to ABB's case than to *BritNed*'s. The second factor was the existence of a Part 36 offer. ABB had made a Part 36 offer which was withdrawn after trial but before judgment. The existence of the offer was no more than a factor to be taken into account in the court's decision as to costs. The judge continued:

"12. In terms of who writes the cheque, it is clear. . . that BritNed is the winner. Against this, however, a number of points must be noted:
1. In terms of expectation, BritNed was substantially the loser in this case when measured by reference to its own Part 36 offer of €135m. BritNed recovered under 10% of this amount. . .
2. What is more, ABB made an offer, which remained open throughout the trial, that BritNed failed to beat.
3. The case on overcharge advanced by BritNed substantially failed. . .
4. It was a consequence of the failure, in relative terms, of BritNed's overcharge claim that the lost profit claim failed. So far as the regulatory cap issue was concerned, it might have to be said that that was something of a score draw for the parties. On the fourth issue, BritNed lost on the compound interest claim, but in terms of the time spent, this was a relatively minor issue."

The court went on to reject making an issues-based costs order. The overcharge claim had been central to *BritNed*'s case and their analysis was not accepted, whereas ABB's analysis was. The court indicated that if it were to award *BritNed* its costs, it would be on the basis of a discount of 40% to reflect the relative failure on the overcharge claim. The court also had to take into account the withdrawn Part 36 offer, and concluded that the existence of the offer was not enough, when quantification was so difficult, to reverse the incidence of costs. Accordingly, ABB was not awarded its costs, but the court considered that the making of a commercial offer early on that was not beaten by *BritNed* meant that it would be unjust for ABB to pay any of *BritNed*'s costs. Each party had to bear its own costs.[159]

Defendants appealed against a costs order which provided that they should pay 75% of the claimants' costs of their claim and that the claimants should pay the costs of the defendants' counterclaim. The Court of Appeal held that the defendants' initial offer did not have the costs consequences of a Part 36 offer because it had been withdrawn, in accordance with the version of the rules then in force. Nevertheless it was to be taken into account by the judge as a factor when exercising his general discretion on costs under CPR r.44.2. The court concluded that the judge at first instance had appreciated that the

---

[159] *BritNed Development Ltd v ABB AB, ABB Ltd* [2018] EWHC 3142 (Ch); [2018] 6 Costs L.O. 807, Marcus Smith J.

claimants had not in the end beaten the defendants' original offer. The court therefore rejected the submission that that was a material factor that he had failed to take into account. The issue was whether the claimants had acted unreasonably in rejecting the offer. The judge had decided that at that stage of the litigation, before disclosure and the exchange of witness and expert evidence, the offer had not been one that was easy for the claimants to accept; implicitly holding that the claimants had acted reasonably. Furthermore, although both sides had expressed a willingness to mediate, the claimants had taken active steps but the defendants had dragged their feet and mediation was abandoned. The case had clearly been suitable for mediation and there was a real prospect that it would have achieved a result. The judge was entitled to take the view that most of the blame for the failure to mediate lay with the defendants and to reflect that in his costs order.[160]

In professional negligence proceedings against a firm of solicitors, the firm made an offer which was not a Part 36 offer, on the basis that the Financial Services Compensation Scheme would meet 90% of the liability and the solicitors would pay the shortfall. The claimant bank subsequently made a Part 36 offer but, shortly before trial, purported to accept the original offer made by the solicitors. The court held that since the solicitors' offer was not a Part 36 offer, the impact on it of any counter-offer had to be addressed by reference to common law principles. On that basis, the subsequent Part 36 offer was a counter-offer with the result that the solicitors' offer was rejected and no longer available for acceptance. The matter, accordingly, had to proceed to trial.[161]

In litigation concerning an easement, the defendants offered to settle but did not deal with the question of costs, nor did they respond to enquiries about this. The offer was time limited and it lapsed. Shortly before trial the defendants made an identical offer which the claimant did accept. The question of costs then came before the judge at first instance who ordered the defendants to pay the claimant's costs up to the date of the expiry of the first offer and the claimant to pay the defendant's costs thereafter. On appeal, the court held that the justice of the case meant that the appropriate order was no order for costs after the date of expiry of the first offer. There was no good reason for the claimant not to have accepted the first offer, equally there was no good reason for the defendants to have withdrawn it rather than letting it stand. Taking into account all the circumstances including the conduct of both parties, the costs order was partially overturned.[162]

The appellants (Crest Nicholson) and the first respondent (Great Dunmow), had entered into a contract, for the sale of land owned by the first respondent. The contract was conditional on the fulfilment of certain conditions. By cl.6.2 of the contract, the parties were to appoint a valuer to ascertain the "Assumed

---

[160] *Thakkar v Patel* [2017] EWCA Civ 117; [2017] 2 Costs L.R. 233.
[161] *DB UK Bank Ltd (t/a DB Mortgages) v Jacobs Solicitors* [2016] EWHC 1614 (Ch); [2016] 4 W.L.R. 184 Andrew Hochhauser QC.
[162] *Patience v Tanner* [2016] EWCA Civ 158; [2016] 2 Costs L.R. 311.

Value" of the property. Clause 6.2.2 provided that the valuation date would be "the Challenge Expiry Date or (if later) the date of valuation". The second respondent (Stephen Downham) was appointed as the valuer.

Each party instructed its own expert. The two experts made different assumptions in relation to the valuation date, and produced significantly different valuations. The valuer maintained that the statement of agreed facts was merely a record of the views of the parties' own experts, and that the correct valuation date was the Challenge Expiry Date. The first respondent sought a determination as to the correct valuation date. The judge declared that on a true construction of the contract, the valuation date was the Challenge Expiry Date, but that the effect of the agreement in the statement of agreed facts about the correct valuation date was contractual and therefore binding, so that the valuation date was the date on which the valuer issued his determination. He decided that the jurisdiction of the court to decide the issues of construction and the effect of the statement of agreed facts was not excluded by the contract and that the valuer had no jurisdiction to issue a binding decision on the construction of cl.6.2.2.

In allowing the appeal the Court of Appeal stated that there was no reason in principle why the parties to a contract could not bind themselves to a specified method for making any subsequent variation to the contract. The scope and nature of an expert's jurisdiction was determined by the contract between the parties. The task of a valuer, set by the words of the contract, was to ascertain the assumed value of the property at the correct date. There was nothing in terms which gave the valuer the jurisdiction to determine what was the correct of two alternative dates, or to exclude the rights of the parties to refer that question of construction to the court.[163]

In detailed assessment proceedings following a successful clinical negligence claim, the defendant NHS Trust made a Calderbank offer which was reinstated on three occasions. In the final reinstatement, the offer contained a variation that the claimant would pay the defendant's costs of the detailed assessment from the date when the offer was first made. The claimant did not respond to that offer. At the detailed assessment hearing, some 12 months after the original offer, it became clear by lunchtime on the second day that the claimant would recover less than the offer. The claimant's solicitors sent an email to the defendant's solicitors, stating:

> "We write further to the offer in your letter of 27 September 2018 and to [your] email ... of [again 19] August 2019 reaffirming the offer, to confirm that the Claimant will accept that offer and will pay the Defendant's reasonable costs of detailed assessment."

The costs judge found that the claimant had validly accepted the offer.

On appeal, the court pointed out that in detailed assessment proceedings the Part 36 procedure was available to be used. However, the appellant had

---

[163] *Great Dunmow Estates Ltd v Crest Nicholson Operations Ltd* [2019] EWCA Civ 1683; [2020] 2 All E.R. (Comm) 97.

chosen to use the Calderbank offer approach. A Part 36 offer could only be accepted once the hearing had commenced with the court's permission. There was, however, no provision in Part 36 that such an offer lapsed at the door of the court. Nor was there an absolute bar on acceptance post-commencement. It was therefore not open to the appellant to argue that a Calderbank offer lapsed at the door of the court. None of the Calderbank offers had an absolute time limit. The appellant was aware throughout that it could withdraw the offer made, but decided not to do so. The appeal was dismissed.[164]

Fraud and dishonesty in making offers

Where parties in family proceedings had entered into a consent order com- 5–42
promising the wife's financial claims, it subsequently came to light that the husband had failed to disclose arrangements being made to float a software company in which he had a substantial shareholding. The judge at first instance found that the husband's evidence had been dishonest but did not set aside the consent order as the initial public offering had not taken place and was not likely to do so in the future. This decision was upheld by the Court of Appeal but overturned by the Supreme Court. The Supreme Court endorsed the broad approach to dishonesty that "fraud unravels all". The court emphasised the fundamental principle that parties have a duty to provide full and frank financial disclosure to one another and the court in financial remedy proceedings. The court and the parties must have all relevant information before them to enable an informed decision to be made about what constitutes a fair financial outcome.[165] This principle will clearly apply in all negotiated settlements.

In proceedings where a freeholder and leaseholders sued a number of defendants, the freeholder was unsuccessful and the leaseholders were successful. The court was required to determine which were the successful parties for costs purposes. The claimants maintained that, given the overall success of the claim, there should be no adverse costs order against the freeholder because, although it had been a separate claimant in law, it had not litigated the case for its own commercial benefit and had sought nothing additional to what the leaseholders were seeking.

The court held that the first claimant's involvement had been to enable the claimants as a group to succeed. Commercially, there was no difference between its claim and those of the other claimants. The circumstances in which it had been brought and pursued did not justify awarding D1 and D3 their costs of defending it as well as depriving the claimants of the costs of bringing it. A fair and proportionate result was to discount the claimants' costs by 7.5%.

---

[164] *MEF (a Protected Party by his Mother and Litigation Friend, FEM) v St. George's Healthcare NHS Trust* [2020] EWHC 1300 (QB), Morris J.
[165] *Sharland v Sharland* [2015] UKSC 60; [2016] A.C. 871; [2015] 3 W.L.R. 1070; [2016] 1 All E.R. 671.

With regard to D2, the claimants had failed to beat D2's offer. They had never convincingly addressed the difficulties of their case. The offer had clearly been intended as a means of enabling the claimants to extricate themselves from a claim they were likely to lose. Their overwhelming interest should have been to obtain a financial recovery. Claimants in fraud cases could not justify refusing a good offer just because it did not contain an admission or apology. D2's costs had to be discounted to reflect the fact that it vigorously contested the deceit issue against damning contrary evidence. The costs relating to deceit and reliance were roughly equal to each other. The claimants were ordered to pay D2's costs from expiry of D2's offer. A time-based order was the better course because it reduced the cost and complexity of any detailed assessment while producing the same overall result as a percentage-based order.

D1 and D3 had made a number of unreasonable stipulations in their offer. Faced with no reply from the claimants, they should have considered making a more straightforward offer or a Part 36 offer. The fact that there were multiple claimants, each with their own individual claims was no obstacle to doing that. The court would take account of the claimants' relative lack of success against D1 and D3 by discounting the claimants' costs by a further 12.5%, making a total reduction of 20%.[166]

Negotiation

5–43   Negotiation needs no explanation. It is the method by which the majority of civil cases are still settled. Negotiation may be between the parties themselves; between their lawyers; between experts, reporting back to the lawyers/clients; or any combination of the above.

Mediation

5–44   Mediation is conducted by an independent third party (who is normally an accredited mediator) who is independent of the parties and whose function it is to try to bring the parties together so that a settlement or compromise may be achieved. It is a confidential process, which can usually be arranged to take place within a reasonably short timescale. Lord Justice Jackson, in Ch.36 of his Final Report, stated:

> *"Mediation is not, of course, a universal panacea. The process can be expensive and can on occasions result in failure. The thesis of this chapter is not that mediation should be undertaken in every case, but that mediation has a significantly greater role to play in the civil justice system than is currently recognised."*

There are several types of mediation, the most usual being facilitative and evaluative. In facilitative mediation the mediator tries to help the parties reach a position with which they can live. There is often a matter of pride which prevents a party from compromising for fear of appearing weak. The cloak of confidentiality helps in this regard.

---

[166] *Zagora Management Ltd v Zurich Insurance Plc* [2019] EWHC 257 (TCC), HHJ Stephen Davies.

Evaluative mediation requires a rather more robust approach by the mediator. The writer has found that although one starts out on the facilitative track one finds that one ends up going down the evaluative route. Each party ultimately asks: "What do you think would happen on assessment?" or "What do you think it is worth?"

Many mediation agreements contain a clause to the effect that if the parties fail to agree, the mediator may be asked to give a non-binding opinion as to the final outcome.

The main benefits are that a neutral third party may be able to help each side see the strengths and weaknesses of its case. A skilled mediator may help parties step outside the adversarial framework and entrenched positions so the mediation may work even where a negotiation has failed. A skilled mediator may make possible offers and concessions look more acceptable. A robust and experienced mediator can help to find a way forward even in a relatively intractable dispute. The structure of a mediation allows a lawyer and a client time to review offers and options in a way which may not be possible in negotiation. Mediation can be used to allow a party to make a statement about something of particular personal importance. Experience suggests that mediation generally achieves good success rates and party satisfaction.

The mediator needs to be selected with care as regards expertise, experience etc. to ensure the parties have confidence in the process. The most obvious advantages of mediation are that, provided the parties are able to agree the process, a mediation can be set up quickly rather than having to wait nine to 12 months for a court hearing. The parties may choose their mediator. Parties are not permitted to choose the judge where a matter proceeds to litigation. The process is confidential, whereas in the absence of a specific order, all hearings in courts are in public.

The Court of Appeal has addressed the question of ADR in greater detail.[167] The court indicated that the burden was on the unsuccessful party to show why there should be a departure from the general rule on costs, in the form of an order to deprive the successful party of some or all of his costs on the grounds that he refused to agree to ADR. A fundamental principle was that such a departure was not justified unless it had been shown that the successful party had acted unreasonably in refusing to agree to ADR. In deciding whether a party had acted unreasonably the court should bear in mind the advantages of ADR over the court process and have regard to all the circumstances of the particular case. The factors that could be relevant include:

(i) the nature of the dispute;
(ii) the merits of the case;
(iii) the extent to which other settlement methods have been attempted;
(iv) whether the costs of ADR are disproportionately high;

---

[167] *Halsey v Milton Keynes General NHS Trust* [2004] EWCA Civ 576; [2004] 1 W.L.R. 3002; [2004] 4 All E.R. 920; [2004] C.P. Rep. 34; [2004] 3 Costs L.R. 393.

(v) whether any delay in setting up and attending the ADR would have been prejudicial;
(vi) whether the ADR had a reasonable prospect of success.

Where failure to mediate was due to the attitudes taken on either side it was not open to one party to claim that the failure should be taken into account in the order as to costs. A party who agreed to mediation but then took an unreasonable position in the mediation was in the same position as a party who unreasonably refused to mediate. That was something which the court should take into account in its costs order.[168]

Where a party reasonably considered that it had a strong case and where a party was faced with an unfounded claim and wished to contest it rather than buy it off, the court should be slow to characterise that as unreasonable conduct. The fact that a party reasonably believed that it had a watertight case might well be sufficient justification for refusal to mediate.[169]

In determining costs at the conclusion of litigation, a successful defendant's refusal to enter into mediation because it had believed that the claimant's case was hopeless and that the claimant had proposed mediation as a tactic designed to extract a nuisance payment, had not been unreasonable and no adjustment was therefore made to the defendant's costs.[170]

The court has to look beyond the polarised positions of the parties. A skilled mediator might be able to find middle ground by analysing the parties' position and making each reflect on its own and the other's position. By bringing other commercial arrangements or disputes into the discussion or by finding future business opportunities, a mediator might find solutions that the parties had not considered. On the facts of the particular case, the defendant's refusal to mediate had deprived the parties of the opportunity of resolving the case without a hearing, as had the claimant's failure to accept the defendant's offer. The fair and just outcome was that neither party's conduct should modify the general rule on costs. The claimant was accordingly ordered to pay the whole of the defendant's costs on the standard basis.[171]

5–45 In *Garritt-Critchley v Ronnan*[172] the defendants accepted the claimant's Part 36 offer just before judgment was to be given following a four-day trial. The judge did not criticise the late acceptance of the Part 36 offer but penalised the defendants in costs because he considered that they had been wrong in consistently refusing to mediate. The defendants had refused to mediate because they were confident of their position and believed that the parties were too far apart. The judge stated that the claim involved a question of fact which was a classic case for mediation and parties did not know whether they

---

[168] *Carleton (Earl of Malmesbury) v Strutt & Parker (A Partnership)* [2007] EWHC 424 (QB); 118 Con. L.R. 68; [2008] 5 Costs L.R. 736 Jack J.
[169] See *Halsey* (above) and *Daniels v Commissioner of Police of the Metropolis* [2005] EWCA Civ 1312; [2006] C.P. Rep. 9.
[170] *Parker Lloyd Capital Ltd v Edwardian Group Ltd* [2017] EWHC 3207 (QB); [2018] 6 Costs L.R. 1235 Lavender J.
[171] *Northrop Grumman Mission Systems Europe Ltd v BAE Systems (AL Diriyah C41) Ltd* [2014] EWHC 3148 (TCC); [2015] 3 All E.R. 782; [2014] T.C.L.R. 8; 156 Con. L.R. 141; [2014] 6 Costs L.O. 879 Ramsey J.
[172] *Garritt-Critchley v Ronnan* [2014] EWHC 1774; [2015] 3 Costs L.R. 453.

were too far apart until they sat down and explored settlement. Mediation also costs less than trial.[173] If the defendants had accepted the claimant's last offer of mediation, the difference in costs might have been almost £100,000. The judge applied *Halsey*, which held that in deciding whether a party had acted unreasonably in refusing ADR, the court should bear in mind the advantages of ADR over the court process and have regard to all the circumstances of the particular case.[174]

A defendant in person who unsuccessfully opposed a grant of probate in favour of the claimants, having lost at trial, argued that he should not have to pay the claimant's costs as they had initially refused to mediate. The court held that a successful party's unreasonable refusal to mediate might warrant a reduction in the amount of costs. In the instant case, however, the claimants had subsequently changed their attitude to mediation, but it did not take place because the defendant was not ready to take part. There was, therefore, no reason why the defendant should not face the usual order as to costs. The order was made on the standard basis since, although the defendant should not have challenged the will, the case did not cross the threshold for ordering costs on the indemnity basis. An order for payment on account was also made. Another issue was whether the claimant's counsel was entitled to a separate brief fee in respect of the defendant's late application to amend his defence to include a claim for forgery. The court did not specifically disallow the claim for a separate brief fee, but directed the costs judge to pay particular attention to the matter and to consider whether there would be any element of double recovery.[175]

In a building dispute the claimant made a Part 36 offer to settle, and also suggested mediation. At trial the judge awarded damages which were less than the claimant had claimed, and less than their Part 36 offer. The judge made no order for costs up to the expiry of the period for acceptance of the Part 36 offer, and ordered the claimant to pay the defendant's costs thereafter. The Court of Appeal held that the judge had erred fundamentally in his appreciation of the significance of the claimant's Part 36 offer. There was nothing in Pt 36 which stated that an offeror was to be prejudiced as to costs because she expressed her willingness to accept less than her formal claim. An order for no order as to costs did substantial justice between the parties. The claimant was the winner but only just. On an issues-based approach she had failed on three issues, but succeeded on one issue which had taken a substantial amount of time. The defendants' rejection of offers to enter into settlement negotiations or mediation was unreasonable, and conduct which ought to be taken into account.[176]

5–46

---

[173] Unless the mediation fails.
[174] In *Reid v Buckinghamshire Healthcare NHS Trust* [2015] EWHC B21 Master O'Hare in the SCCO ordered the losing defendant to pay the costs of detailed assessment from the date they unreasonably refused an offer of mediation.
[175] *Murray v Bernard* [2015] EWHC 2395 (Ch); [2015] 5 Costs L.O. 567 Mann J.
[176] *Rolf v De Guerin* [2011] EWCA Civ 78; [2011] C.P. Rep. 24; [2011] B.L.R. 221; [2011] 5 Costs L.R. 892.

While mediation is not compulsory, it is now well established that the courts may robustly encourage parties to embark on it and an unreasonable failure to do so places a party at risk of being penalised in costs. This decision is a reminder that refusing mediation is a high-risk strategy, and lawyers and their clients should consider their position carefully.

In holiday litigation, 205 claimants who had suffered misfortune, ranging from poor quality through minor illness to serious illness, sought their costs from the defendant holiday company. On assessment, the Master (using the *Lownds* test) found the overall base costs to be disproportionate and applied the test of necessity. The defendants appealed on the basis that the necessity test had not been applied with sufficient rigour. The defendants argued, among other things, that the quality only (as opposed to illness) claimant should either recover no costs at all or be restricted to the costs of using the ABTA Scheme. The judge on appeal found that if, at the detailed assessment stage, a defendant wished to rely on the availability of an industry-specific ADR Scheme (i.e. the ABTA Scheme), which was referred to in the relevant contract but was not binding and did not expressly oust the court's jurisdiction, the defendant had to make that clear in its pre-action protocol response. The defendant had not done so. It did not admit liability and robustly contested the claims. Furthermore, the company had not responded to the claimants' offer of ADR. The appeal was dismissed.[177]

In *Briggs v First Choice Holidays and Flights Ltd*[178] an interim costs certificate was refused where group litigation costs were not reasonable and proportionate. The master found that some of the claimants should have pursued their claims via industry-specific mediation. On appeal the court held that the cost judge's decision that it was inherently unreasonable for claimants to enter into conditional fee agreements rather than a voluntary arbitration scheme went too far. The holidaymakers had been entitled to litigate, but the costs judge had been entitled to reduce the success fee from 67% to 43%, as the fee had been based on a factual inaccuracy.[179]

Where a claimant had made serious and consistent allegations of fraud against defendants, which allegations had been entirely abandoned without explanation, the defendants were entitled to costs on the indemnity basis. The claimant had been guilty of conduct which was "out of the norm". The judge did not consider it appropriate to take the defendants' refusal to mediate into account when assessing costs, because she stated that where allegations of fraud and serious wrongdoing were made, proceedings were intrinsically unsuitable for mediation. In her view, this would be penalising the defendants for insisting on their right to have their reputations vindicated through the trial process.[180]

---

[177] *TUI UK Ltd v Tickell* [2016] EWHC 2741 (QB); [2016] 6 Costs L.O. 941 Elisabeth Laing J.
[178] *Briggs v First Choice Holidays and Flights Ltd* unreported 23 September 2016 SCCO.
[179] *Briggs v First Choice Holidays* [2017] EWHC 2012 (QB); [2017] 4 Costs L.R. 595 Singh J.
[180] *PJSC Aeroflot – Russian Airlines v Leeds (Trustees of the Estate of Berezovsky) (1) Desai Representative of the Estate of Nikolay Glushkov (2) Forus Holding SA – SPF (3) Forus Leasing SA (In Liquidation) (4) Forus Finance Ltd (5)* [2018] EWHC 1735 (Ch); [2018] 4 Costs L.R. 775 Rose J.

Where a claimant successfully claimed damages for personal injuries against a religious group and its trustees, the court had to decide whether the trustees should pay all of the claimant's costs on the indemnity basis in view of their refusal to engage in ADR and, secondly, the amount of enhanced rate of interest applicable to damages and costs from a particular date, pursuant to CPR r.36.17(4). The court had given a direction in the standard form that at all stages the parties had to consider settling by ADR and any party refusing to engage in ADR proposed by another had to serve a statement giving reasons within 21 days of the proposals. The claimant's solicitor suggested a Joint Settlement Meeting, but the defendant trustees stated they had no authority to negotiate settlement of her claim. On 9 July 2019, the claimant made a Part 36 offer to accept £62,750, which was rejected by the trustees. The court held that the trustees should have served a witness statement explaining why they had refused to participate in the Joint Settlement Meeting. Their failure to do so was unreasonable conduct. The Part 36 offer showed that the claimant was willing to settle the case for less than she was ultimately awarded. The court found that there was every reason to think that if the trustees had engaged with the proposal for a Joint Settlement Meeting at an earlier stage, that willingness would have become known. The court ordered the defendants to pay costs on the indemnity basis from the date of their unreasonable refusal to engage in the settlement meeting. On the facts, the court awarded enhanced interest of 4% above base rate.[181]

Where an action for wrongful termination of employment failed, the court disallowed a proportion of the first defendant's costs for failure to engage in mediation. It was held that the first defendant's refusal to mediate following the claimant's invitations to do so was unreasonable. The parties were therefore denied the opportunity fully to canvass and engage with the underlying issues pre-issue. There was no evidence that mediation would have prejudiced the first defendant's trial position. The first defendant had lost sight of the court's observations in *Halsey v Milton Keynes General NHS Trust*.[182] The court was satisfied that at each stage a mediation would have had realistic prospects of success. The court disallowed 50% of the first defendant's costs from pre-issue up to the point when the first defendant made a settlement offer and then 20% from the date when it refused to mediate for a second time. In respect of the second defendant, the court disallowed 20% of its costs on the basis that costs had been wasted due to the way the second defendant had advanced its case in applying for a late amendment to its defence.[183]

---

[181] *BXB v Watchtower & Bible Tract Society of Pennsylvania (1) Trustees of the Barry Congregation of Jehovah's Witnesses (2)* [2020] EWHC 656 (QB), Chamberlain J.
[182] [2004] EWCA Civ 576.
[183] *Wales (T/A Selective Investment Services) v CBRE Managed Services Limited* [2020] EWHC 1050 (Comm), HHJ Halliwell.

The "without prejudice" rule and mediation

5-47   The Court of Appeal upheld a decision that without prejudice (WP) statements made by the defendant at mediation were admissible to oppose the claimant's claim to set aside the parties' settlement[184]. It confirmed that the statements were admissible under the second exception to the WP rule in *Unilever plc v Procter & Gamble Co* [1999] EWCA Civ 3027 (which provides that evidence of WP negotiations is admissible to show that an agreement concluded during the parties' negotiations should be set aside for misrepresentation, fraud or undue influence). The claimant had alleged that the defendant was complicit in a fraud on the claimant by the claimant's agent and therefore knew that, in committing the claimant to the settlement, the claimant's agent was acting in breach of fiduciary duty and without authority. The defendant pleaded that, pre-settlement, the claimant had known about, and ratified, the impugned transactions, because the defendant had mentioned them in their mediation position papers. However, the lower court had erred in holding that the sixth exception (the so-called Muller exception) had also applied in the present case.

In a family case, the High Court dismissed a father's case for disclosure of the notes of the mediator and refused permission for the father to file a statement from the mediator in proceedings under the 1980 Hague Convention.[185] The father sought to disclose discussions from the mediator on the basis that they were relevant to the defences he was seeking to establish in the 1980 Hague Convention proceedings. The father argued that in the absence of the disclosure that he would be inhibited in establishing that facts advanced by the mother were untrue and he would, thereby, be denied a fair trial. The judge noted that the without prejudice rule is subject to exceptions. In Children Act 1989 proceedings, statements made by either party during meetings or communications for the purpose of conciliation cannot be used in evidence except where a statement indicates that the maker has caused, or is likely to cause, serious harm to a child. Even then the trial judge retains a discretion as to whether to admit the evidence; the public interest in protecting the child's interests must outweigh the public interest in preserving the confidentiality of conciliation.[186] The narrow exception did not apply in this case because the father was not seeking disclosure in order to safeguard a child but to further the interests of justice and uncover the truth. The decision highlights the sanctity of the conciliation privilege and the very limited circumstances in which it will be lifted unless the parties agree to waive privilege.

Mediation in the Commercial Court

5-48   The Commercial Court normally strongly encourages the parties to attempt to resolve their dispute by ADR. The parties are required to co-operate with

---

[184] *Berkeley Square Holdings Ltd v Lancer Property Asset Management Ltd* [2021] EWCA Civ 551.
[185] *SG v SW* [2020] EWHC 3379 (Fam).
[186] *Re D* [1993] Fam 231.

each other by exchanging the names of three mediators, who are available to conduct the mediation by the date fixed by the court. If the parties cannot agree, the court will give directions. In the event that the mediation fails the parties are required to explain why the mediation failed.

Early Neutral Evaluation

Early neutral evaluation (ENE) is carried out by an independent person, who   5–49
is normally experienced in the particular field of the issue under dispute. That
person may be appointed by one or all parties.

The *Technology and Construction Court Guide* and the *Commercial Court Guide*
both deal with ENE.[187] In *Seals v Williams*,[188] Norris J concluded that the wide
jurisdiction provided by CPR r.3.1(2)(m), to the effect that the court can make
any order to manage cases and further the overriding objective, provided the
power to order ENE. This did not therefore require the consent of the parties.
Following this, CPR r.3.1(2)(m) was amended to read:

> *"Except where these rules provide otherwise, the court may . . . (m) take any other
> step or make any other order for the purpose of managing the case and furthering
> the overriding objective, including hearing an early neutral evaluation with the
> aim of helping parties to settle the case".*

The court has the power, pursuant to CPR r.3.1(2)(m) to order early neutral
evaluation, even though one party has not consented to it. The rule does not
impose the limitation to the effect that the consent of all parties is necessary,
since that would be contrary to the overriding objective.[189] This rule is not
limited to Chancery proceedings but is of general application. It is expected
that its use in appropriate cases in the Chancery Division, the Queen's Bench
Division and the County Court is likely to become increasingly common. To
date there is no dedicated ENE Practice Direction. General guidance (excluding the need for party consent) can be obtained from the TCC and Admiralty
and Commercial Court Guides.

ENE is intended to be an advisory and evaluative process. ENE can take
place within the court system in which case it is usually carried out by a
judge. There is no requirement for proceedings to be in progress, any party
may appoint an independent third party to carry out an ENE. It is of course
preferable and more conducive to settlement if all the parties can agree to the
appointment.

Expert Evaluation

Expert evaluation may take different forms. This may be an evaluation similar   5–50
to early neutral evaluation or a determination. As the name implies one or

---

[187] See *Technology and Construction Court Guide* paras 7.5.1–7.6.4; the *Admiralty and Commercial Court Guide*, paras G2.1–G2.6.
[188] *Seals v Williams* [2015] EWHC 1829 (Ch); [2015] 4 Costs L.O. 423 Morris J.
[189] *Pauline Lomax v Stuart Lomax (Executor of Allen Lomax, deceased)* [2019] EWCA Civ 1467; [2019] 1 W.L.R. 6527; [2019] Costs L.R. 1431.

more neutral experts are appointed by the parties to evaluate or determine the issues between the parties. The evaluation/determination may be agreed to be binding between the parties or merely advisory, leaving the parties to proceed further if they so decide. Expert evaluation/determination is most commonly employed in cases of a technical nature (e.g. costs). The way in which matters proceed will be governed primarily by the terms of the contract by which the expert is appointed. The parties will usually agree that the determination will be final and binding and this is ordinarily recorded in the contract. The contract may state that the determination is final and binding in the absence of "manifest error". If the manifest error exception is included in the contract, recourse to the court is permitted in limited circumstances and the test is whether there are "oversights and blunders so obvious and obviously capable of affecting the determination so as to admit of no difference of opinion."[190] On the question of bias, an expert does not satisfy the independence requirement if the expert has a connection with one of the parties, an interest in the outcome or some other connection with the property that is the subject of the litigation which, viewed objectively, would create a real risk that the expert might act partially. It was appropriate to apply the test of apparent bias in assessing whether an expert had been independent at the date of the appointment. A fair minded and informed observer would have to consider the possibility of unconscious bias. Such an observer was likely to reject any blanket assertion that e.g. a prior valuation of the same property would necessarily impact on the subsequent valuation to the extent of encouraging the valuer to produce conformity between the two valuations. It would be necessary to take into account the distance in time between the two valuation dates and any other intervening events. The observer would also start from the position that an experienced valuer with a significant professional reputation was likely to act professionally so that if some information caused the valuer to doubt the accuracy of the earlier valuation, he would notify his previous clients, rather than compromising his duties.[191]

Adjudication

5–51   Adjudication usually takes place in a specialist commercial field where the parties prefer a system adapted to the needs of their industry or business. It is most frequently used in construction disputes. It is used to resolve specific issues and is usually agreed by the parties to a contract as a means of resolving disputes which may arise by a process agreed to be binding on the parties.

Construction industry adjudication is a creature of statute which requires all construction contracts to have a provision for adjudication.[192] The statutory requirement is for adjudication by an independent third person who

---

[190] *Veba Oil Supply & Trading GmbH v Petrotrade Inc (The Robin)* [2002] 1 All ER 703; [2001] 12 WLUK 110. Applied in *Flowgroup PLC (In Liquidation) v Co-operative Energy Ltd* [2021] EWHC 344 (Comm); [2021] Bus LR 755; [2021] 2 WLUK 311.
[191] *Re Maximus Securities Ltd* [2016] EWCA Civ 1057.
[192] Housing Grants Construction and Regeneration Act 1996 s.108.

produces a decision on the dispute which is binding on an interim basis until finally determined as appropriate by the court, arbitration, or agreement. The adjudicator is required to give a decision within a limited time. The decision is enforceable through the courts and appeal is only possible on the grounds of lack of jurisdiction or breach of the rules of natural justice.

In a construction dispute, the defendant made an open offer in the sum found by the adjudicator. The claimant believed it was entitled to more than the adjudicator had found and brought court proceedings. The claimant did not accept the offer and it was withdrawn. The claimant company applied for judgment on the basis that the offer was a formal admission of liability under CPR r.14.1. The court held that the open offer contained a package of terms that the claimant could accept or reject. It would run contrary to the basis of the offer if the claimant could accept part of it as being an admission of liability but then reject other terms. The court had to encourage the making of offers which was in accordance with the overriding objective. If a party were able partially to accept an offer and to reject other parts which ensured that the litigation continued, the purpose of making offers would not be met. The defendant's offer letter did not refer to CPR r.14.1, nor did it admit the truth of the claimant's case. It did not in any way admit that any of the defendant's points were bad. To be a formal admission under CPR r.14.1, it needed to be clear and unequivocal. The alleged admission was neither. The claimant had had to seek clarification and had been told that there was no admission in respect of early payment discounts. If there had been any admission at all, it was in respect of the sums identified by the adjudicator which was the opposite of the claimant's case.[193]

In May 2019 the Professional Negligence Bar Association (PNBA) introduced a revised adjudication scheme. Under the amended pre-action protocol for professional negligence cases which was introduced in May 2018, claimants are obliged to consider adjudication and give reasons if they believe it is not suitable. They can be penalised on costs if their behaviour is unreasonable.

It is suggested that among the advantages of adjudication are that cases are "done and dusted" within 56 days of appointment of an adjudicator and there is generally no need for an oral hearing. There is no longer any financial ceiling for adjudications.

The earlier limitation of cases to solicitors has now gone and any non-medical professionals may be involved, such as accountants, independent financial advisers and architects.

The PNBA scheme is entirely voluntary. Like building disputes, enforcement of adjudications is by summary judgment in the courts.

---

[193] *Dorchester Group Ltd (t/a Dorchester Collection) v Kier Construction Ltd* [2015] EWHC 3051 (TCC); [2016] C.I.L.L. 3753 Coulson J.

Arbitration

5–52   Arbitration is effectively a trial process outside the court system. Arbitrations may be domestic or international. They may be conducted under the Arbitration Act 1996 or under the rules of any of the numerous arbitration providers. In many commercial contracts there are clauses providing terms for arbitration should a dispute arise. Arbitrators may be appointed by agreement between the parties or, if no agreement is possible, by the President of the relevant professional body. If the arbitration requires three arbitrators, each side usually nominates one arbitrator and the third will be appointed by a neutral person e.g. the President of the professional body.

The agreement to arbitrate may be made before or after the relevant dispute has arisen. There is a strong public policy in favour of upholding arbitration agreements, which is supported by the idea that an arbitration clause in a contract is separable from the rest of the substantive contract[194] and so continues to apply even if the substantive contract is avoided. Where court proceedings are commenced in breach of an arbitration agreement, the defendant may apply to the court to stay those proceedings.[195]

It is worth looking at some of the provisions of the Arbitration Act 1996: ss.1, 4, 61 and 63. It is clear from the extracts below that the terms of any arbitration agreement are very much in the hands of the parties. Apart from the mandatory provisions (which are basically common sense), the terms may be agreed in whatever form the parties wish. The Act provides certain long stop provisions, e.g. in s.61, the powers of the Tribunal where the parties have not agreed:

> *"1. General principles.*
> *The provisions of this Part are founded on the following principles, and shall be construed accordingly—*
> *(a) the object of arbitration is to obtain the fair resolution of disputes by an impartial tribunal without unnecessary delay or expense;*
> *(b) the parties should be free to agree how their disputes are resolved, subject only to such safeguards as are necessary in the public interest;*
> *(c) in matters governed by this Part the court should not intervene except as provided by this Part.*
> *. . .*
> *4. Mandatory and non-mandatory provisions.*
> *(1) The mandatory provisions of this Part are listed in Sch.1 and have effect notwithstanding any agreement to the contrary.*
> *(2) The other provisions of this Part (the 'non-mandatory provisions') allow the parties to make their own arrangements by agreement but provide rules which apply in the absence of such agreement.*
> *(3) The parties may make such arrangements by agreeing to the application of institutional rules or providing any other means by which a matter may be decided.*

---

[194] Arbitration Act 1996 s.7.
[195] Arbitration Act 1996 s.9.

(4)   It is immaterial whether or not the law applicable to the parties' agreement is the law of England and Wales or, as the case may be, Northern Ireland.

(5)   The choice of a law other than the law of England and Wales or Northern Ireland as the applicable law in respect of a matter provided for by a non-mandatory provision of this Part is equivalent to an agreement making provision about that matter.

For this purpose an applicable law determined in accordance with the parties' agreement, or which is objectively determined in the absence of any express or implied choice, shall be treated as chosen by the parties.

. . .

61. Award of costs.

(1)   The tribunal may make an award allocating the costs of the arbitration as between the parties, subject to any agreement of the parties.

(2)   Unless the parties otherwise agree, the tribunal shall award costs on the general principle that costs should follow the event except where it appears to the tribunal that in the circumstances this is not appropriate in relation to the whole or part of the costs.

. . .

63. The recoverable costs of the arbitration.

(1)   The parties are free to agree what costs of the arbitration are recoverable.

(2)   If or to the extent there is no such agreement, the following provisions apply.

(3)   The tribunal may determine by award the recoverable costs of the arbitration on such basis as it thinks fit.

If it does so, it shall specify—

> *(a)   the basis on which it has acted, and*
>
> *(b)   the items of recoverable costs and the amount referable to each.*

(4)   If the tribunal does not determine the recoverable costs of the arbitration, any party to the arbitral proceedings may apply to the court (upon notice to the other parties) which may:

> *(a)   determine the recoverable costs of the arbitration on such basis as it thinks fit, or*
>
> *(b)   order that they shall be determined by such means and upon such terms as it may specify.*

(5)   Unless the tribunal or the court determines otherwise:

> *(a)   the recoverable costs of the arbitration shall be determined on the basis that there shall be allowed a reasonable amount in respect of all costs reasonably incurred, and*
>
> *(b)   any doubt as to whether costs were reasonably incurred or were reasonable in amount shall be resolved in favour of the paying party.*

(6)   The above provisions have effect subject to s.64 (recoverable fees and expenses of arbitrators).

(7)   Nothing in this section affects any right of the arbitrators, any expert, legal adviser or assessor appointed by the tribunal, or any arbitral institution, to payment of their fees and expenses."

There are no budgeting requirements in arbitration, unless the parties agree. This is unlikely to happen, although commercial clients are bound to want to keep strict control of expenditure. There should be no problems of the sort generated by *Mitchell v NGN Ltd*[196] and *Denton v TH White*.[197]

5–53   In a claim under s.68 of the 1996 Act (Challenging the Award: serious irregularity), the award was set aside in part, as sought by the claimants. The court dealt with the costs of the claim, having found that the claimants were the successful party. The claim was not very complex, factually or legally. The substantive hearing occupied one and a half days. The hearing bundle was contained within five lever arch files, plus bundles of authorities. The total costs were £1.2 million, and the judge was of the view that costs had been incurred by both sides without any regard for what might be a reasonably sufficient and proportionate work effort for advising upon, preparing and presenting the case.

The judge declined to attempt a summary assessment of the costs and ordered detailed assessment on the standard basis. He made the following comments:

"i)   *I regard it as prima facie surprising that the costs claimed should be more than c.30% of the actual totals (say, £180,000 on each side);*

ii)   *had the costs been of that order, most probably I would have assessed them summarily in an amount equal to a high percentage, perhaps 75%, of the sum claimed;*

iii)   *if the order were for either side to recover costs in full (subject to detailed assessment), the payment on account I would order would therefore be £135,000."*

The defendants were ordered to pay 80% of the claimants' costs and an interim payment of £110,000.[198]

Questions and answers

Section 1 Pt 36

A. Circumstances in which Part 36 offers can be made (CPR r.36.2)

Q1. Is there anything in CPR Pt 36 or the Privy Council Rules which prevents a Part 36 offer being made in costs proceedings before the Privy Council? (CPR r.2.1).

5–54   CPR r.2.1 states that the rules apply to all proceedings in the County Court, the High Court and the Civil Division of the Court of Appeal. There is no mention of the Privy Council. The Judicial Committee (Appellate Jurisdiction)

---

[196] *Mitchell v News Group Newspapers Ltd* [2013] EWCA Civ 1537; [2014] 1 W.L.R. 795.
[197] *Denton v TH White Ltd* [2014] EWCA Civ 906; [2014] 1 W.L.R. 3926.
[198] *RJ, L Ltd v HB* [2018] EWHC 2958 (Comm); [2018] 6 Costs L.R. 1347 Andrew Baker J.

Rules 2009 (SI 2009/224) set out the procedure before the Judicial Committee but make no mention of Pt 36 or anything equivalent to it. A party wishing to make an offer may make a Calderbank type offer. CPR r.43(1) of the 2009 Rules provides:

> *"the Judicial Committee may make such orders as it considers just in respect of the costs of any appeal, application for permission to appeal or other application to or proceeding before the Judicial Committee".*

The Judicial Committee Practice Direction dealing with costs states:

> *"To the extent that the Judicial Committee (Appellate Jurisdiction) Rules and Practice Directions do not cover the situation, the rules and Practice Directions relating to Parts 44 to 47 of the Civil Procedure Rules are applied by analogy at the discretion of the Costs Judge, with appropriate modifications for appeals from foreign jurisdictions. The legal principles applied are those also applicable to assessments between parties in the High Court and Court of Appeal in England and Wales."*[199]

Q2. i. Can a valid Part 36 offer be made in a small claim prior to the proceedings being allocated to the small claims track?
ii. Would a Part 36 offer made in pre-action correspondence as a claimant's offer be invalidated if the proposed defendant then issued a claim relating to the same subject matter and therefore the offeror became the defendant?
iii. If, pre-action, D makes a Part 36 offer and C makes a Part 36 counter-offer, can C accept D's offer, provided it has not been withdrawn?
iv. Can a claimant's Part 36 offer to accept payment in instalments, for example, four equal monthly instalments commencing 28 days after acceptance, be a valid Part 36 offer?
In a debt claim, can a defendant make a valid Part 36 offer to provide the claimant with something other than money (for example a painting) in full and final settlement of the dispute?
v. Can a defendant make a Part 36 offer that is subject to the claimant providing certain evidence in respect of quantum?
vi. Would a defendant's Part 36 offer continue to be valid after the original claimant has died and been replaced by a family member?
These miscellaneous questions do not fit readily into any of the categories below and so are dealt with here.

5–55

i.   CPR r.27.2(1)(g) states that Part 36 does not apply to small claims. Prior to allocation, however, the claim is technically not a small claim. Rule 36.2(2) states "(2) Nothing in this Section prevents a party making an offer to settle in whatever way that party chooses, but if the offer is not

---

[199] Judicial Committee PD 8 para.1.4.

made in accordance with rule 36.5, it will not have the consequences specified in this Section." Having said that the offeree is unlikely to accept the offer pre allocation, since once allocated Part 36 will not apply and the costs consequences will not follow. A better option would be to make a Calderbank offer. See also Q64.

ii. A Part 36 offer may be made at any time, including before the commencement of proceedings. (CPR 36.7(1). A Part 36 offer remains in force unless it is withdrawn in accordance with CPR r.36.9 or CPR r.36.10. The offer would certainly not be invalidated because the other party commenced proceedings. Pre-proceedings each party may consider itself "the claimant", but, until proceedings are commenced, the position of each party is merely one of having an interest in the issue under dispute. The costs consequences may change once the proceedings have begun but the court has the power to depart from the prescribed result if "it considers it unjust" to apply that result, see e.g. CPR r.36.17.

iii. Yes, see answer ii above. It is frequently the case that opposing parties make offers. Such offers remain available to be accepted until they are withdrawn or an offer is automatically withdrawn in accordance with its terms.

iv. Although CPR r.36.2(2) states "Nothing in this Section prevents a party making an offer to settle in whatever way that party chooses, . . . "Rule 36.5(4) states "(4) A Part 36 offer which offers to pay or offers to accept a sum of money will be treated as inclusive of all interest. . ." This appears to envisage an offer to pay or accept a single sum of money. It seems therefore that the offer should be in terms of the claimant being willing to accept £x. This could be accompanied by a letter explaining that if the defendant accepted the offer, the claimant would be willing to accept payment in instalments.

v. With regard to the debt claim, offering a painting would seem to fall within the provisions of the rule, in that there is nothing explicitly in the rules that prevents it. It seems most unlikely, however, that a court would ever regard a failure to accept a painting, even if apparently valuable, as against a much lower value claim, as being within Part 36. What the D could offer is to pay a sum of money, but then, try to agree under CPR.r.36.14(6), that payment will be made on the sale of a painting.

vi. It is not clear how a valid Part 36 offer could be made conditional on the claimant providing evidence of quantum. The rules set out in answer iv above apply. This is a situation in which it would be better to set out the offer in a letter "without prejudice save as to costs".

vii. Much depends on the wording of the retainer. For example the Law Society's Model CFA 2014 (currently being revised) states in its conditions

> *"This agreement automatically ends if you die before your claim for damages is concluded. We will be entitled to recover our basic charges up to the date of your death from your estate. If your personal representatives wish to continue*

your claim for damages, we may offer them a new conditional fee agreement, as long as they agree to pay the success fee on our basic charges from the beginning of the agreement with you."

In any event, where a party to litigation dies it is necessary, if the litigation is to continue, to substitute someone else in place of the deceased person in accordance with Part 19 and to obtain permission to carry on.

Q3. If a defendant makes a Part 36 offer which does not take into account its counterclaim and the offer is then accepted, what happens to the counterclaim? (CPR r.36.5).

In proceedings where there is both a claim and counterclaim, what are the costs consequences of the defendant/counterclaimant making a zero Part 36 offer? If accepted by the claimant, will the defendant/counter-claimant have to pay the claimant's costs—or the other way round?

In proceedings involving both a claim and a counterclaim, is it possible to make a valid Part 36 offer to settle on the basis that both parties discontinue proceedings without paying anything to the other?

CPR r.36.2(3)(a) clarifies that Part 36 offers can be made in respect of counter-   5–56
claims and other additional claims. When making an offer in a case concerning a counterclaim or other additional claim, it is important to make clear whether it is intended to be a claimant's or a defendant's offer. A counter-claiming defendant may wish to make a claimant's offer i.e. where the offer is to accept some payment on the counterclaim; or a defendant's offer i.e. where the offer is to pay some money on the claim. Such an offer may take the other adverse claim into account: see CPR r.36.5(1)(d) to (e).[200]

It is not clear from the second question whether the defendant is making a claimant's offer in respect of the counterclaim or a defendant's offer in respect of the claim. If it is a claimant's offer, the defendant to the counterclaim may wish to accept it but will not wish to pay the costs on acceptance; it seems therefore that the offer should not be accepted and then for the counterclaim defendant to argue that it would be unjust for the normal consequences to follow under CPR r.36.17(4). If it is a defendant's offer in respect of the claim, the claimant would have no reason to accept it.

In respect of question three CPR r.36.2 states "(2) Nothing in this Section prevents a party making an offer to settle in whatever way that party chooses, but if the offer is not made in accordance with rule 36.5, it will not have the consequences specified in this Section."

"Counterclaim" is defined by the CPR glossary as "a claim brought by a defendant in response to the claimant's claim which is included in the same proceedings as the claimant's claim". A counterclaim is treated for certain purposes as if it were a claim (CPR r.20.3). CPR r.36.2(3) provides that a Part 36 offer may be made in respect of the whole, or part of, any issue that arises

---

[200] *Van Oord UK Ltd v Allseas UK Ltd* [2015] EWHC 3385 (TCC); [2016] 1 Costs L.O. 1 Coulson J.

in a claim, counterclaim or other additional claim. It must state whether it takes into account any counterclaim (CPR r.36.5(1)(e)). CPR r.36.14(3) provides that if a Part 36 offer which relates to part only of the claim is accepted, the claim will be stayed as to that part upon the terms of the offer. The question which has to be decided is whether the counter-claim is "part only of the claim" or is a claim in its own right. Whilst the rules provide for a Part 36 offer to take into account the existence of a counterclaim if so desired, there is no requirement to do so and it is accordingly arguable that a counterclaim is a claim in its own right and would continue notwithstanding any Part 36 offer accepted in respect of the claim. The options for a party making a Part 36 offer, where a counterclaim exists, depend upon the facts of the case. What if the D accepts responsibility for a certain value of the claim, but is not in a position to value the counterclaim? e.g. PI liability apportionment agreed. D wants to avoid risk of a *Medway Oils* order at the end, but the counterclaim is much more serious and medical prognosis evidence not available whereas C's claim is capable of quantification. Why not make a Part 36 offer in respect of the claim excluding the counterclaim as the counterclaim costs are going to be much larger later? Alternatively, the counterclaim and the claim may arise out of entirely freestanding matters and, again, the counterclaim may not be capable of quantification yet. Why not cap the costs liability on the freestanding claim rather than run the risk of a percentage order that may not reflect far higher costs of the counterclaim? It is certainly arguable that a counterclaim is a claim in its own right for Pt 36. If so desired, a party making a Part 36 offer should ensure that the offer takes into account the counterclaim; or the party may make an offer without prejudice save as to costs, i.e. a Calderbank offer.

Where a defendant had made what purported to be a claimant's Part 36 offer in respect of the defendant's counterclaim, "the proceedings in respect of which" it was made included the claim and the proposed counterclaim, but were not restricted only to the counterclaim. A Part 36 offer may be made before the commencement of proceedings under CPR r.36.7 so the fact that the defendant's counterclaim had not been formulated or pleaded did not of itself matter.[201]

On the other hand: where an offer was expressed to relate to an additional claim which the defendants had set out in draft Amended Particulars of Claim the judge at first instance held that the claim was not yet part of the claim for the purposes of CPR r.36.5(1)(d) therefore the offer was not a Part 36 offer and the normal costs consequences did not apply. Although the claimant argued that it was possible to make a Part 36 offer before the commencement of proceedings and the references to the whole or part of a claim should be taken to include references to a claim that had not yet been brought but which was brought after the offer was made, the judge held that Pt 36 is a highly prescriptive and self-contained code and it would not be right to

---

[201] *AF v BG* [2009] EWCA Civ 757; [2010] 2 Costs L.R. 164.

add in further provisions on the basis that it would have an analogous effect to an existing express provision.[202] On appeal by the claimant, the Court of Appeal held that the position before proceedings commenced was different to that once they had been commenced. Once proceedings were underway, there would be pleadings in existence and the CPR regulated the proceedings. It would not be right to construe the Rules in a way that ignored the certainty and clarity which the pleadings provided and to interpret CPR r.36.10(2) as if the proceedings had not yet begun. It would introduce unnecessary uncertainty if claims or parts of claims or issues were given a wide definition, not anchored in pleadings. The words "claim", "part of a claim" and "issue" referred to those which had been pleaded, not to those which had mainly been intimated but never pleaded. Where there was a proposed amendment to a claim, it was not a "claim" within the Rule until the amendment had been allowed. The appeal was dismissed.[203]

It appears, however that the Court was not referred to the decision in *AF v BG* above.

The Court of Appeal had to decide whether a Part 36 offer was valid if it was made by a defendant in respect of both the claim and the proposed counterclaim which had yet to be pleaded, or if it contained provisions for interest to accrue at a particular rate after the expiry of the relevant period. In the proceedings, the claimant sued the defendant for damages for defective and incomplete work of refurbishment. Before serving its defence and counterclaim, the defendant made a Part 36 offer, indicating that it would accept £100,000 in settlement of both the claim and its unissued counterclaim. The offer was stated to include interest until the expiry of the relevant period, but that thereafter interest would be added at 8% per annum. The claimant rejected the offer and at trial the judge found sufficiently in favour of the defendant to conclude that it had beaten its own offer. The claimant was ordered to pay a proportion of the defendant's costs.

On appeal, the claimant/appellant relied on the decision in *Hertel v Saunders*.[204] This argument was rejected. As a result of CPR rr.20.2 and 20.3, a counterclaim was treated as a claim and nothing in Pt 20 excepted Pt 36 from those provisions. CPR r.36.2(3)(a) provided that a Part 36 offer might be made in respect of the whole or part of or any issue that arose in a claim, counterclaim or additional claim. CPR r.36.7 provides that a Part 36 offer may be made at any time, including before the commencement of proceedings. It therefore could not be right to say that a Part 36 offer could not be made in relation to an un-pleaded counterclaim. The court considered *AF v BG*[205] and also *Van Oord UK Ltd v Allseas UK Ltd*.[206] With regard to *Hertel*, this was held not to be directly relevant, since it did not address the issues in the case before

---

[202] *Hertel v Saunders* [2015] EWHC 2848 (Ch); [2015] 5 Costs L.R. 825 Morgan J.
[203] *Hertel v Saunders* [2018] EWCA Civ 1831; [2018] 1 W.L.R. 5852; [2018] 4 Costs L.R. 879.
[204] *Hertel v Saunders* [2018] EWCA Civ 1831; [2018] 1 W.L.R. 5852; [2018] 4 Costs L.R. 879.
[205] *AF v BG* [2009] EWCA Civ 757; [2010] 2 Costs L.R. 164.
[206] *Van Oord UK Ltd v Allseas UK Ltd* [2015] EWHC 3385 (TCC); [2016] 1 Costs L.O. 1.

the court and was primarily concerned with the effects of CPR r.36.10(2), which was no longer in the CPR, and the effect of which had been reversed.

With regard to interest after the relevant period had expired, the inclusion of such a provision would not render the Part 36 offer invalid. There was nothing in CPR r.36.5 to preclude the inclusion of such provisions. CPR r.36.2(2) makes it clear that a party may make an offer to settle in whatever way that party chooses. If there were no ability to provide for interest to run from the end of the relevant period, the offeror would not be compensated for any delay between the end of the relevant period and subsequent acceptance of the offer. The appellant's argument, that the ability to include provisions as to interest might lead offerors to make offers in such terms as to inhibit settlement, was rejected. Since interest after the end of the relevant period was ignored for the purposes of the CPR r.36.17 assessment, it was also to be ignored for the purposes of determining whether a Part 36 offer was valid. The court pointed out that if the offeree found such a provision unpalatable it could make its own Part 36 offer in the same terms, but without the provision for interest.[207] Note that with effect from 6 April 2021, CPR r.36.5(5) provides that a Part 36 offer may make provision for accrual of interest after the relevant period has expired and that if an offer does not make such provision, it shall be treated as inclusive of all interest up to the date of acceptance, if it is later accepted.

Q4. If C makes a Part 36 Offer which relates only to its claim, not to D's counterclaim, and C beats that offer at trial, but D recovers a larger sum under its counterclaim (and is ultimately the net recipient), would D have to pay C's costs because C has beaten its Part 36 offer, or would C have to pay D's costs because D is the net recipient of the litigation?

5–57 Where there is a claim and a counterclaim and both the claim and the counterclaim have succeeded, on detailed assessment the rule is that the claim is treated as if it stood alone, and the counterclaim bears only the amount by which the costs of the proceedings have been increased by it. In the absence of special directions by the court there should be no apportionment.[208] It is, however, within the judge's discretion to order the apportionment of the costs of a claim and counterclaim equally.[209] If there is likely to be a difficulty in relation to dividing the costs between the parties it seems that it is open to the court to state what the apportionment should be.

In this case the claimant has made a successful Part 36 Offer and is entitled to its costs in accordance with CPR r.36.17. The defendant, having succeeded in its counterclaim will be entitled to its costs of the counterclaim subject to the rule in *Medway Oil*. Both parties will be awarded an amount of costs which can then be set off.

---

[207] *Calonne Construction Ltd v Dawnus Southern Ltd* [2019] EWCA Civ 754; [2019] 1 W.L.R. 4793;[2019] Costs L.R. 309.
[208] See *Medway Oil & Storage Co v Continental Contractors* [1929] A.C. 88; [1997] Costs L.R. (Core Vol.) 5, HL and *Cartonneries De Thulin SA v CTP White Knight Ltd (Costs)* [1999] F.S.R. 922, Neuberger J.
[209] *Milican v Tucker* [1980] 1 W.L.R. 640; [1980] 1 All E.R. 1083; (1980) 124 S.J. 276, CA.

Q5. Our client is a defendant/Pt 20 claimant and is considering a Part 36 offer in respect of the Pt 20 claim. Will the usual costs consequences of a Pt 36 claimant offer apply, even if our client offers to accept the majority of liability in respect of the Pt 20 claim?

What is the position with respect to a Pt 20 defendant making a Part 36 offer to the Pt 20 claimant and what are the cost consequences? For example, would a Pt 20 defendant be liable to the Pt 20 claimant for not only the Pt 20 claimant's costs of the Additional Claim but also for the Pt 20 claimant's costs of defending the underlying claim? Would the Pt 20 claimant's costs also include the underlying claimant's costs as well?

CPR r.36.2(3) makes it clear that a Part 36 offer may be made in respect of the whole, or part of, or any issue that arises in a claim, counterclaim or other additional claim. Rules 20.2 and 20.3 provide that counterclaims and other additional claims are treated as claims and references to a claimant or a defendant include a party bringing or defending an additional claim. If the client's Part 36 offer is accepted, the usual costs consequences will apply. 5–58

With regard to the second question, this will inevitably be fact sensitive. The Part 36 offer is in respect of the Pt 20 claim only and the normal costs consequences will apply, but depending on how the claim itself is resolved, the court may order a Pt 20 defendant to reimburse the defendant in the action any costs which it has to pay to the claimant, by means of a Sanderson or Bullock order. There is really no clear answer to this in the rules, therefore a Pt 20 defendant might prefer to make a carefully drafted Calderbank offer in order to achieve certainty as to its potential liability if the offer is accepted.

Q6. If a claimant is a litigant in person but a solicitor then makes a Part 36 offer on the claimant's behalf without filing and serving a notice of acting, does this constitute a valid Part 36 offer?

If proceedings are ongoing, must a solicitor be on the court's record to make a valid Part 36 offer on behalf of the solicitor's client?

Can a trainee solicitor sign a Part 36 offer without invalidating the offer? If the solicitors for Party A made a Part 36 offer on behalf of A, then came off the record and the new solicitors for Party A do not appear to be aware of the Part 36 offer, does the firm acting for the opposing party have a duty to bring the Part 36 offer to the court's attention on the question of costs?

It depends on the wording of the offer. If it purports to come from the solicitors on behalf of the litigant in person, there is a difficulty because the solicitors are not on the record and ostensibly have no authority to act. If, however, the offer is drafted as coming from the litigant and the solicitors have acted as no more than a post box, there should be no difficulty. 5–59

A trainee solicitor is in the same position as any other member of the solicitors' firm. Any offer letter would normally be signed in the name of the firm rather than the individual. Most trainees would, in any event, have their letters checked before they went out. Provided that the trainee has authority to sign on behalf of the firm, there is no difficulty. From the offeree's point of view an offer signed in the name of the firm is, on its face, a valid offer. There would be no reason to challenge it. If the offer was unauthorised but was accepted by the offeree, that would be an internal problem for the solicitors' firm.

With regard to the last question, one may presume that the new solicitors have access to the previous solicitors' papers, but whether or not that is so it would be reasonable to expect the new solicitors to enquire if any offers have been made or, if that is not apparent from the papers for the previous solicitors to point it out. Failure by either firm of solicitors to establish the true position, may amount to negligence. As to whether there is a duty on the offeree's solicitors to bring it to the attention of the new solicitors, there is no strict duty, but any judge would, upon being made aware that the information had not been passed on, take an extremely poor view of the offeree's solicitors.

B. Content requirements for Part 36 offers (CPR r.36.5)

Q7. Can a valid Part 36 offer include settlement terms which (if accepted), impose conditions; require a defendant to do something other than pay money; or provide for interest to run after the end of the relevant period?

Can a Part 36 offer include a sum for future loss? In this case, the future loss is in the form of continuing loss of rental income? (CPR rr.2.1, 36.2(2), 36.5(4).

5–60   CPR r.36.2(2) states:

> *"Nothing in this Section prevents a party making an offer to settle in whatever way that party chooses, but if the offer is not made in accordance with Rule 36.5, it will not have the consequences specified in this Section."*

CPR r.36.5 sets out the form and content of a Part 36 offer. Provided therefore that CPR r.36(5) is complied with, the terms of an offer may be in whatever terms the offeror chooses. See *Calonne Construction Ltd v Dawnus Southern Ltd*, in **Q3** above.

With regard to the second question: there seems to be no reason why the claimant should not put forward an offer on a without prejudice save as to costs basis.

In relation to detailed assessment PD 47 para.8.3 provides "The paying party must state in an open letter accompanying the points of dispute what sum, if any, that party offers to pay in settlement of the total costs claimed. The paying party may also make an offer under Part 36."

Q8. The topic of making offers and content requirements attracted the largest number of questions as it did in the previous editions.
(i)   I act for a defendant in proceedings in which summary judgment has been awarded in my client's favour. Indemnity costs have been awarded to my client and the costs are to be summarily assessed.

The summary assessment is to take place at a separate hearing from that in which judgment was awarded. Can I make a Part 36 offer to the claimant in relation to the payment by him of my client's costs?

(ii) We act for a defendant who has accepted the claimant's Part 36 offer to settle the claim. The defendant has paid the settlement sum under the Pt 36 Agreement to the claimant, and the costs are now being assessed. Can the claimant make another Part 36 offer in relation to those costs, given that the defendant is already liable for the assessed costs under the original Pt 36 Agreement?

(iii) Can a claimant make a Part 36 offer to accept nothing (zero pounds)?

(iv) Is it possible to make a pre-action Part 36 offer and then commence legal proceedings before the relevant period has expired? If B makes a pre-issue Part 36 offer to A in relation to an unpaid invoice, is there a risk that A may issue proceedings, incurring solicitors and possibly counsel's fees, and then accept the offer before the end of the relevant period, so that B has to pay A's costs? If so, presumably this is something that should be explained to B?

(v) Is it possible to make a valid Part 36 offer with a set figure payable in respect of costs? I want the offer to be inclusive of a set amount of costs, but the costs are not fixed, and I do not want them to be subject to standard assessment.

(vi) Can a pre-action Part 36 offer be valid if it states that each party must bear its own costs? If the defendant makes a Calderbank offer that includes a condition that the claimant pays the defendant's costs or even that both parties pay their own costs, is there any reason why the claimant cannot reject the offer but then make exactly the same proposal in the form of a Part 36 offer? Would it make any difference if the Part 36 offer was exactly the same except that it did not refer to the costs consequences?

(vii) Will a claimant's Part 36 offer still constitute a valid offer if it is for an unliquidated amount (such as, for example, the settlement sum being 50% of a deceased person's net estate)? Can an offer to accept a percentage of the equity in a property (rather than a set amount of money because the value/sale price of the property is not known) be a valid Part 36 offer? Where A and B are in dispute in relation to a piece of land owned by A, can B make a valid Part 36 offer to acquire A's land? I am conscious that a Part 36 offer should be an offer to pay a single sum of money (CPR r.36.6), but what if that single sum of money is in the form of an offer to purchase something from the opponent? I note the payment timescale set down by CPR r.36.14(6) but if the offer was an offer to pay money in return for land, clearly it may not be possible to conclude the transfer within 14 days of acceptance.

> (viii) **Can a defendant's Part 36 offer be valid where the defendant does not have the finances to pay the amount contained in the offer?**
>
> (ix) **Can confidentiality terms be included in a Part 36 offer and if so, will that affect the costs consequences if the claim does not settle?**
>
> (x) **Where a defendant has made a Part 36 offer in proceedings, and the claimant then makes a Part 36 counteroffer, and neither offer is accepted, what are the costs consequences?**

5–61   (i) and (ii) CPR r.47.20(4) makes it clear that the provisions of Pt 36 apply to the costs of detailed assessment proceedings with certain modifications. However, there is no similar provision expressly applying Pt 36 to summary assessments. The position is considered in detail in **Ch.8, Q7**.

Where an offer to settle is made under Pt 36 or otherwise, it should specify whether or not it is intended to be inclusive of the costs of preparation of the bill, interest and VAT. Unless the offer makes it clear that the position is, otherwise, it will be treated as being inclusive of all those matters.[210]

(iii) CPR r.36.2(2) quoted in **Q3** above sets out the underlying provision which applies to all these questions. If a claimant makes a Part 36 offer to accept nothing, the defendant is unlikely to accept it (because of the costs consequences) and would argue that the claimant is seeking to discontinue the action without having to bear the defendant's costs under CPR r.38.6.

(iv) When a Part 36 offer is made, CPR r.36.5(c) states the offer must specify a period of not less than 21 days within which the defendant will be liable for the claimant's costs if the offer is accepted. If proceedings are commenced before the end of the relevant period, the accepting defendant would have a very strong argument for saying that they should not have to pay the costs relating to the commencement of proceedings.

With regard to the second question, the position should certainly be explained to B. Whenever the offer is accepted CPR r.36.13(1) provides:

> *"where a Part 36 offer is accepted within the relevant period the claimant will be entitled to the costs of the proceedings (including their recoverable pre-action costs) up to the date on which notice of acceptance was served on the offeror."*

So some costs will inevitably be payable. Depending on the facts it may be possible to argue that commencing proceedings and obtaining counsel's opinion was disproportionate and unreasonable.

(v) and (vi) The Court of Appeal has held that a term as to costs is not within the scope of a Part 36 offer. The original draftsman of Pt 36 had not

---

[210] CPR r.36.5 (4) A Part 36 offer which offers to pay or offers to accept a sum of money will be treated as inclusive of all interest until—
(a) the date on which the period specified under CPR r.36.5(1)(c) expires; or
(b) if CPR r.36.5(2) applies, a date 21 days after the date the offer was made. PD 47 para.19. (the Practice Direction appears to conflict with the rule, but it has not been amended.) The court, in *King v City of London Corp* ([2019] EWCA Civ 2266; [2020] 1 W.L.R. 1517; [2020] 3 All E.R. 643; [2019] Costs L.R. 2197), held that PD 47 could not control the interpretation of Pt 36. It supplemented Pt 47 not Pt 36. Moreover, PD 47 dated from 2013, whereas the version of Pt 36 engaged here was introduced in 2015.

intended terms as to costs to be included in a Part 36 offer as the wording of the rule was inconsistent with the term as to costs being part of such an offer. Given that CPR r.36.1(2) (now CPR r.36.2(2)) clearly states that nothing in Part 36 prevents a party making an offer to settle in whatever way the party chooses, the claimant is still entitled to make an offer which includes the terms to costs and the court will have regard to that in exercising its discretion in relation to the costs between the parties at the end of the case. The terms of CPR r.36.2(2) do not permit a party to include a term as to costs in the hope of securing an order for costs on the indemnity basis.[211]

Where parties had entered into a consent order providing for the claimant's reasonable costs to be paid on the standard basis, subject to detailed assessment if not agreed, the judge on appeal from a district judge (who had decided that the costs of the road traffic accident personal injury claim, following acceptance of the defendant's Part 36 offer, were to be determined under the fixed costs regime in Section IIIA of CPR Pt 45), found that the consent order was incompatible with an award of fixed costs and that the judge below had been wrong to vary what the parties had agreed.[212]

On appeal to the Court of Appeal it was held that the offer letter did not offer to pay conventional rather than fixed costs. Whilst CPR r.36.5(1)(c) did not impose an obligation on the offeror to say which rule applied: CPR r.36.20, which dealt with costs consequences of a Part 36 offer where Pt 45 Section IIIA applied, or CPR r.36.13, dealing with costs consequences of a Part 36 offer in other cases. A simple reference to CPR r.36.13 probably would not suffice to take the case out of the fixed costs regime. It was clear from the letter that the appellant was intending to make an offer to which Pt 36 applied. The letter would not have contained a Part 36 offer if it proposed anything other than the fixed costs regime: if a party to a claim that no longer continued under the protocol offered to pay costs on a basis that departed from Pt 45, the offer was incompatible with Pt 36 and could not be an offer under that part.[213] The respondent relied on the fact that CPR r.45.29B provided for the fixed costs regime to apply "for as long as the case is not allocated to the multi-track". The court held that the more natural interpretation could be that, where a case was transferred from the fast track to the multi-track, the fixed costs regime ceased to apply prospectively, not in relation to past costs.[214] The fixed costs regime was designed to ensure that both sides began and ended the proceedings with the expectation that fixed costs was all that would be recoverable.[215]

The court suggested that defendants wishing to make a Part 36 offer on the basis that the fixed costs regime would apply would be well-advised to refer

---

[211] *Mitchell v James (Costs)* [2002] EWCA Civ. 997; [2004] 1 W.L.R. 158; [2003] 2 All E.R. 1064.

[212] *Adelekun v Lai Ho* unreported 18 October 2018 County Court at Central London, HHJ Wulwik. Reversed 2019] EWCA Civ 1988, see also [2020] EWCA Civ 517.

[213] See *Mitchell v James (Costs)* [2002] EWCA Civ 997; [2004] 1 W.L.R. 158; [2003] 2 All E.R. 1064.

[214] See *Qader v Esure Services Ltd* [2016] EWCA Civ 1109; [2016] 6 Costs L.O. 973.

[215] *Hislop v Perde* [2018] EWCA Civ 1726; [2019] 1 W.L.R. 201; [2018] 4 Costs L.O. 515.

in the offer to CPR r.36.20 and not CPR r.36.13, and to omit any reference to the costs being "assessed", or assessment "on the standard basis" in any offer letter or consent order drawn up following acceptance of an offer.[216]

Where a purported Part 36 offer contained a term as to costs which was not in accordance with the provisions of CPR r.36.13 (if the offer were accepted on the terms of the offer letter, the claimant would pay the defendants' costs up to the end of the relevant period, whereas under CPR r.36.13 the claimant would pay the defendants' costs only up to the date of acceptance within the relevant period) the offer was held not to be an effective Part 36 offer.[217] In a different case the Judge rejected the submission that the claimant's pre-action Part 36 offer was ineffective because it specified that there would be no liability for costs.[218]

A purported Part 36 offer, which contained a term as to costs, was held not to amount to a Part 36 offer and did not carry the costs consequences of such an offer.[219] The court also stated obiter that had the letter amounted to a Part 36 offer, the claimants would have obtained a judgment more advantageous to them than that proposed in their offer. However, because the court's decision dealt with the beneficial entitlement to the net proceeds of a sale, this did not amount to a sum of money awarded within the meaning of CPR r.36.17(4)(a), nor a "sum awarded to the claimant" within the meaning of CPR r.36.17(4)(d). An asset which belonged beneficially to a particular party was not a "monetary award".[220]

(vii) See the answer to **Q7**, above. In respect of the first question the answer to this is yes, although it might be difficult for the trial judge to assess whether the offer was at least as advantageous as the judgment.

The third question proposes an offer which appears to fall foul of CPR r.36.6 by attaching to it conditions which themselves might fall foul of other provision of Pt 36 (e.g. time for payment). In the circumstances it would seem sensible to make the offer in the form of a Calderbank letter.

(viii) Provided that the defendant is not bankrupt, there appears to be no reason why a Part 36 offer should not be made. The reason we now have Part 36 offers rather than payments into court is largely because the NHSLA could not afford to make the payments into court. The introduction of Part 36 offers enables the NHSLA and other defendants with cash flow difficulties to make offers in the hope of settling claims and, unless the defendant is dishonest, it will hope to be able to raise the money to settle the case should the offer be accepted.

(ix) It is quite possible that such an offer would not comply with CPR r.36.5 and would, therefore, not have the Pt 36 costs consequences. In any event, if

[216] *Ho v Adelekun* [2019] EWCA Civ 1988; [2019] Costs L.R. 1963.
[217] *James v James (Costs)* [2018] EWHC 242 (Ch); [20181] Costs L.R. 175 HHJ Paul Matthews.
[218] *Bottrill v Thompson (t/a Witness Statement Bottrills)* [2017] EWHC 3815 (Comm) HHJ Waksman QC.
[219] See *Mitchell v James (Costs)* [2002] EWCA Civ 997; [2004] 1 W.L.R. 158; [2003] 2 All E.R. 1064 and *French v Groupama Insurance Co Ltd* [2011] EWCA Civ 1119; [2011] 4 Costs L.O. 547.
[220] *Knight v Knight* [2019] EWHC 1545 (Ch); [2019] Costs L.R. 1459, HHJ Paul Matthews.

the offeree wants to accept the money offer, but cannot agree to the inclusion of a confidentiality clause, is not the best thing for the offeree to communicate this to the offeror to cover its position in costs generally—by making its own Part 36 offer for just the money element of the offer? If the claim does not settle following a Part 36 offer which included confidentiality terms, the matter would presumably continue to judgment and the normal costs consequences would follow.

(x) CPR r.36.17 sets out the costs consequences following judgment: where upon judgment being entered: a claimant fails to obtain a judgment more advantageous than a defendant's Part 36 offer; the court must, unless it considers it unjust to do so, order that the defendant is entitled to: costs (including any recoverable pre-action costs) from the date on which the relevant period expired; and interest on those costs.

Where judgment against the defendant is at least as advantageous to the claimant as the proposals contained in a claimant's Part 36 offer; the court must, unless it considers it unjust to do so, order that the claimant is entitled to: interest on the whole or part of any sum of money (excluding interest) awarded, at a rate not exceeding 10% above base rate for some or all of the period starting with the date on which the relevant period expired; costs (including any recoverable pre-action costs) on the indemnity basis from the date on which the relevant period expired; interest on those costs at a rate not exceeding 10% above base rate; and provided that the case has been decided and there has not been a previous order under this provision, an additional amount, which shall not exceed £75,000, calculated by applying the prescribed percentage to an amount which is: (i) the sum awarded to the claimant by the court; or (ii) where there is no monetary award, the sum awarded to the claimant by the court in respect of costs.

Amount awarded by the court	Prescribed percentage
Up to £500,000	10% of the amount awarded
Above £500,000	10% of the first £500,000 and (subject to the limit of £75,000) 5% of any amount above that figure

CPR r.36.17(5) sets out the factors which the court must take into account in deciding whether it would be unjust to make the orders set out in the rule.

CPR r.36.17(7) and (8) set out certain exceptions to the rule.

Q9. Where there's more than one claimant, in his Part 36 offer must the defendant apportion the settlement sum he offers between each claimant?

I'm trying to find out if there is a case or any legislation that states that Part 36 offers to more than one claimant need to be apportioned between the offerees? For example, if a Part 36 offer of £50,000 is made to two

claimants, do you have to specify that it's 50/50 for each, or, say, 70% for one and 30% for the other (CPR r.36.5)?

5–62   CPR r.36.5 states that a Part 36 offer must:

"(d) state whether it relates to the whole of the claim or to part of it or to an issue that arises in it and if so to which part or issue; and (e) state whether it takes into account any counterclaim."

If there is more than one claimant the offeror may make a blanket offer leaving the claimants to sort out the apportionment, or make it clear how the offer is intended to be apportioned. CPR r.36.2 makes it clear that an offer to settle may be made in whatever way the party chooses, provided it complies with CPR r.36.5.

Similarly, in relation to the second question, the Part 36 offer does not need to be apportioned. The claimants can be left to agree the division between themselves. If, however, there is a reason for dividing the offer into particular percentages, it would be better to make two separate offers which can be accepted or rejected by each claimant separately.

Q10. In a case where there is no counterclaim and the claimant makes a Part 36 offer, does that offer need to state whether it takes into account any counterclaim given that there is no counterclaim in existence? (CPR r.36.5(1)(e)).

5–63   If the offeree were to argue that the Part 36 offer was invalid in that it failed to indicate whether it took into account any counterclaim, this would be, to say the least, a pedantic argument since there is no counterclaim in existence. In *C v D*[221] the Court of Appeal held that where an offer has been made which has been presented as a Part 36 offer and otherwise complied with the required form, the courts would not readily interpret it in a way which would prevent it from being a Part 36 offer.

C. Time when a Part 36 offer may be made or accepted

Q11. i. What is the position when a Part 36 offer is made pre-action and accepted after the issue of proceedings, but before the proceedings have been served on the defendant, where service has been reserved for up to four months?
ii. After our client (the claimant) issued proceedings, the defendant filed an acknowledgement of service and then accepted the claimant's pre-action Part 36 offer. What is the best way to record the settlement—is there any reason why we cannot use a Tomlin Order?

---

[221] *C v D* [2011] EWCA Civ 646; [2012] 1 W.L.R. 1962; [2012] 1 All E.R. 302; [2011] C.P. Rep. 38; 136 Con. L.R. 109; [2011] 5 Costs L.R. 773. See also *Essex County Council v UBB Waste (Essex) Ltd (No. 3)* [2020] EWHC 2387 (TCC), Pepperall J para 5.06 above.

iii. **If a Part 36 offer is expressly rejected (in writing), can the party then change their mind and accept the Part 36 offer (within the relevant period)? (CPR r.36.7)**
iv. **Where a defendant makes a pre-action Part 36 offer, the relevant period expires, the claimant issues proceedings and only then does the claimant accept the Part 36 offer, will the claimant be entitled to its pre-action costs?**

i. CPR r.36.7 permits a Part 36 offer to be made at any time including before 5–64 the commencement of proceedings. If the offer is not made in accordance with CPR r.36.5, it will not have the consequences specified in Section I of Pt 36. If the offer is not a valid Part 36 offer CPR r.44.2 requires the court to consider any offer to settle, that does not have the costs consequences set out in Section I, in deciding what order to make about costs.

CPR r.7.2(1) provides that proceedings are started when the court issues a claim form at the request of the claimant. The fact that the proceedings have not been served or that service has been reserved for a period is immaterial. The purpose of Pt 36 is to enable and encourage parties to settle cases at an early stage, without the need for a trial.

In a claim where, before proceedings, the defendants' solicitors sent a cheque for the amount claimed plus 1% interest, they then refused to pay any costs, stating that there was no obligation on them to do so. This led the claimant to commence proceedings. The defendant pleaded tender before claim and paid the money into court under CPR r.37(2). The defence of tender failed at first instance and in the Court of Appeal. At trial, the claimant was awarded more than the amount in court in respect of the original claim but an additional £30,000 claim was struck out. The master held that the claimant was not entitled to bring proceedings so as to recover his pre-action costs.

On appeal, the court held that the defendants acted unfairly in adopting the position of refusing to pay the claimant any of his pre-action costs. It must have been obvious to the defendants that a proper investigation would have been required before allegations of fraud and negligence were to be advanced against a reputable, professional firm and that such an investigation would incur significant costs. It was open to the defendants to choose to run the technical, tactical course that they did, seeking to rely upon the wording of the CPR in relation to a tender before claim, but in the circumstances where costs must necessarily have been incurred in complying with the PAP, the defendants must have realised that the risk in adopting this course was that interest and costs would mount whilst they maintained that denial. The claimant had made a number of Part 36 offers all of which he had beaten. Accordingly CPR r.36.17 applied.[222]

ii. With regard to the second question, once proceedings have been commenced, the Part 36 offer should be accepted in accordance with CPR

---

[222] *John Ayton v RSM Bentley Jennison* [2018] EWHC 2851 (QB); [2018] 5 Costs L.R. 915 May J.

r.36.11(1), i.e. by serving written notice of acceptance on the offeror. The acceptance of the offer in that way means that a costs order will be deemed to have been made on the standard basis (CPR r.44.9(1)(b)). In those circumstances, it should not be necessary to resort to a Tomlin Order.

iii. With regard to the third question, CPR r.36.11(2) provides that a Part 36 offer may be accepted at any time (whether or not the offeree has subsequently made a different offer) unless it has already been withdrawn. Accordingly, if the offer is still in existence (not having been withdrawn), it will still be open for acceptance. The question envisages accepting the Part 36 offer within the relevant period. Should the offeror purport to withdraw the offer by serving notice, before the expiry of the relevant period, of the withdrawal of the offer, the offeror's notice has effect on the expiry of the relevant period. If the offeree has served notice of acceptance of the original offer before the expiry of the relevant period, the acceptance will have effect unless the offeror applies to the court for permission to withdraw the offer: within seven days of the offeree's notice of acceptance; or, if earlier, before the first day of trial. The court may give permission for the original offer to be withdrawn if satisfied that there has been a change of circumstances since the making of the original offer and that it is in the interests of justice to give permission (see CPR r.36.10).

iv. CPR r.36.13 (4)(b) provides: where a Part 36 offer which relates to the whole of the claim is accepted after expiry of the relevant period; the liability for costs must be determined by the court unless the parties have agreed the costs. Rule 36.13(5) explains: where the parties cannot agree the liability for costs, the court must, unless it considers it unjust to do so, order that—

(a) the claimant be awarded costs up to the date on which the relevant period expired; and
(b) the offeree do pay the offeror's costs for the period from the date of expiry of the relevant period to the date of acceptance.

It appears therefore that the claimant would be entitled to its costs up to the expiry of the relevant period, but not thereafter.

Q12. Will a Part 36 offer still have effect if it is made during a stay of proceedings which were for reasons other than to allow for settlement of the case? (CPR r.36.7).Whilst I understand that accepting the Part 36 offer will stay the proceedings in accordance with CPR r.36.14(1), when will the stay come into force? Will the claim be automatically stayed upon deemed service of the notice of acceptance of the Part 36 offer? Can a party to litigation make a Part 36 offer during a period of stay of the claim? If it can, then when does the relevant period commence and end, and can that offer be accepted within the period of stay?

5–65 With regard to the first question the Rules appear to be quite clear. CPR r.36.7(1) provides "A Pt 36 offer may be made at any time ..." and CPR r.36.11(2) provides that a Part 36 offer may be accepted at any time (whether or not the offeree has subsequently made a different offer), unless it has already been withdrawn. Depending upon the terms of the stay, it may be necessary to apply to the court for permission to proceed.

As to the stay following acceptance of a Part 36 offer: a Part 36 offer is accepted by serving written notice of acceptance on the offeror (CPR r.36.11(1)); on acceptance the claim will be stayed (CPR r.36.14(1)). Rule 6.26 sets out the deemed dates of service.

The *White Book* 2021 states at para.3.1.8 "The term "stay" is defined in the Glossary (see Section E). The making of a stay imposes a halt, not only upon proceedings, but also upon the expiration of any time limit in those proceedings which had not expired when the stay was imposed. An order staying proceedings applies to every step otherwise required by the CPR, including the obligation to serve a claim form issued before the stay was imposed. When the stay is lifted, or the stay expires, the position as between the parties is the same as it was at the moment that the stay was imposed. The parties (and the court) pick up where they left off at the time of the imposition of the stay".[223]

Q13. Where a party (represented by solicitors) has served a Part 36 offer by email (when you have neither expressly nor by implication confirmed that you accept service by email), are you under any obligation to inform that party that you do not accept service by email? Where a Part 36 offer has been made, is there a duty or an obligation on the offeree, to bring to the attention of the offeror, any potential defects which may render the offer non-compliant with CPR Pt 36?

CPR r.36.7(2) states that a Part 36 offer is made when it is served on the offeree. Service of documents is governed by Pt 6. Rule 6.20(1)(d) provides that a document may be served by "fax or other means of electronic communication in accordance with Practice Direction 6A". CPR PD 6A (Service within the United Kingdom) para.4.1 provides that the party who is to be served or the solicitor acting for that party must previously have indicated in writing to the party serving (a) that the party to be served or the solicitor is willing to accept service by fax or other electronic means and the email address to which it must be sent. Sufficient written indication is taken to be an email address set out on the writing paper of the solicitor acting for the party to be served "but only where it is stated that the email address may be used for service". CPR PD 6A para.4.2 states:

5–66

> "Where a party intends to serve a document by electronic means ... that party must first ask the party who is to be served whether there are any limitations to the recipient's agreement to accept service by such means (for example, the format in which documents are to be sent and the maximum size of attachments that may be received)."

---

[223] *Grant v Dawn Meats UK* [2018] EWCA Civ 2212.

The Court of Appeal has held that a master had been wrong to validate service of a claim form retrospectively under CPR r.6.15(2) where the defendant's solicitors had allowed the validity of the claim form to expire before alerting the claimant to the fact that service had been ineffective. A solicitor's professional duty did not require him to draw attention to mistakes made by the other party in circumstances where the mistake was not of his making and arose in a situation not calling for a response.[224]

The High Court has held that where a landlord emailed a Part 36 offer without complying with PD 6A.4, this was a procedural error and remediable under CPR r.3.10 or CPR r.6.28. The lease guarantor sought to avoid Pt 36 enhancements by arguing that the emailed offer was invalid. The High Court held that the 2007 change to CPR r.36 which required that a Part 36 offer be served, not merely received, did not preclude the application of CPR r.3.10 which gave the court discretion as to whether a procedural defect should invalidate a Part 36 offer. Whilst the unexplained breach of CPR r.6 should not be taken lightly, the offer was received in December 2020 and no complaint was made about service until November 2021, and no prejudice was alleged to flow from the fact of service by email. The defective service was taken into account, however, as a factor which made it unjust to award any additional amount under CPR r.36.17(4)(d) or to exceed the judgment rate when awarding interest; but the landlord was awarded interest at the judgment rate from the end of the relevant period, indemnity costs from the same date and interest on costs at 5% above base rate.[225] In light of this decision, if the recipient of an emailed Part 36 offer does not object at the time, defective service may not be sufficient to obviate the Pt 36 enhancements, whether entirely or in part.

Q14. What would the costs consequences be if a claimant makes a Part 36 offer to settle less than 21 days before the trial date, the trial is then postponed by a month and the claimant obtains a judgment at least as advantageous as the offer at the postponed trial? Would the Pt 36 costs consequences apply and if so, from what date? Alternatively, would the court consider the offer when deciding what order to make about costs under CPR r.44.3 (as would otherwise have been the case)? Is the court's permission required to accept a Part 36 offer after a summary judgment application hearing has been heard (but before the handing down)? CPR r.36.11(3)(d) provides that the court's permission is required to accept a Part 36 offer if a trial is in progress but summary judgment does not fall under the definition of "trial".

5–67   A Part 36 offer may be made at any time (CPR r.36.7(1)). If the offer is made less than 21 days before the start of the trial (as is the case here) there is no requirement to specify a relevant period. The question does not make clear

---

[224] *Woodward v Phoenix Healthcare Distribution Ltd* [2019] EWCA Civ 985.
[225] *London Trocadero (2015) LLP v Picturehouse Cinemas Ltd* [2021] EWHC 3103 (Ch) (Robin Vos).

whether the offer was time limited or completely open. Assuming that the offer was not time limited, upon judgment being given which is at least as advantageous to the claimant as the offer, the provisions of CPR r.36.17(4) will apply subject to CPR r.36.17(7) which provides that CPR r.36.17(4) does not apply to an offer made less than 21 days before the trial "unless the court has abridged the relevant period". This does not appear to have happened in the instant case. Accordingly, the court is required to consider the offer in accordance with CPR r.44.2 in deciding what order to make about costs. It could also be argued that if the trial has not started because e.g. it was put off to another date, then it has not complied with CPR r.36.5, in that it has not specified a relevant date. Accordingly by a different route it can only be a CPR r.44.2 offer if it is an admissible one.

With regard to the second question Pt 24 deals with summary judgment. CPR r.24.1 states "This Part sets out a procedure by which the court may decide a claim or a particular issue without a trial." It is therefore clear that proceedings for summary judgment are not "a trial" and r.36.11(3)(d) does not apply. See para.5–09 above.

Q15. We (the claimant) have made a Part 36 offer on Form N242A sent via email to the defendant's solicitor. This has not been acknowledged by the defendant's solicitor, and the timescale has expired. The defendant's solicitors have not formerly said that they accept service via email but also have not said that they have not in response. We have previously served via email our directions questionnaire and draft directions without complaint. Is it still a valid offer? Would it be prudent to reiterate the offer (adjusting the time for acceptance) and sending via post?
See the answer to Q12 above, if there is any doubt about the matter it would clearly be prudent to reiterate the offer and send it by post.

5–68

D. Part 36 and asking for clarification (CPR r.36.8)

Q16. Where there is a Part 36 offer, what is the position where the offeree seeks clarification of the offer? Should I ask my opponent to clarify his badly drafted unclear Part 36 offer?
A pre-action offer was made and the 21-day relevant period is yet to expire. The other side have asked if a 14-day extension to the relevant period can be agreed. This would extend the relevant period as contained within the initial Part 36 offer. Can you extend the relevant period in a pre-action Part 36 offer before the relevant period has expired?
My claimant client has made a Part 36 offer. Clarification has been sought by the defendant on two points. The defendant has also requested a further 14 days from the date of response to the request for clarification, in which to respond to the Part 36 offer. Is there any reason to refuse the extension of time for reply, i.e. will this affect the validity of the offer or costs protection? (CPR r.36.8).

5–69   Under CPR r.36.8 the offeree may, within seven days of an offer being made, request the offeror to clarify it. If the offeror does not give the clarification requested within seven days of receiving the request, the offeree may, unless the trial has started, apply for an order that the offeror do so. If the court makes an order, it must specify the date when the Part 36 offer is to be treated as having been made. Where there had been a settlement agreement of the substantive claim, one party asserted that the other was in repudiatory breach and terminated the agreement. The party against whom breach was alleged, claimed damages from the other. The defendant (later the appellant) made a Part 36 offer of £200,000. The offer stated that it did "not take into account any counterclaim". The claimant (later respondent) requested clarification as to whether it was intended to bring a counterclaim and the defendant stated that he did not intend to. The claimant sought further information about the valuation of the claim but that was not provided.

The claimant refused the offer and issued proceedings, and the defendant filed a defence and added a counterclaim. The claimant then served a Part 36 offer which offered to accept £185,000 and stated that it "took account of the entire claim and counterclaim". The defendant accepted that offer outside the 21 day period to avoid an automatic costs order.

The defendant sought an order that the claimant pay his costs from 21 days after the first Part 36 offer. The claimant sought an order that the defendant pay her costs up to the date of his acceptance. At first instance the master held that she could not regard the offers as being on similar terms, as the claimant was proposing to settle the claim and counterclaim, thereby bringing finality, whereas an acceptance of the defendant's offer would not necessarily have done so. In light of the fact that the first Part 36 offer did not state whether it took into account any counterclaim, as required by CPR r.36.2, (now CPR r.36.5) she declined to "order otherwise" pursuant to CPR r.36.10(4) (now CPR r.36.13(4)) and ordered that the defendant pay the claimant's costs of the claim.

On appeal the court held that the master had taken account of the clarification but had concluded that it did not modify it and she was entitled to that view as a matter of law. However, in construing the first Part 36 offer, the subsequent clarification had to be taken into account. The master had failed to adopt that approach and should have seen that, had the respondent (claimant) accepted the first Part 36 offer, the appellant (defendant) would have been bound. The master had wrongly construed the first Part 36 offer as excluding any counterclaim without having regard to the whole of the correspondence. The first Part 36 offer had been modified in correspondence so as to encompass any counterclaim.

The counterclaim that had later been brought was not in fact a discrete claim but no more than a claim for a declaration as to the repudiation of the settlement agreement and therefore no more than a mirror image of the defence. The fact of the later counterclaim did not therefore alter the court's conclusion. Even if the first Part 36 offer had been capable of comparison with the second, the respondent had not initially acted unreasonably in refusing it. She had made reasonable requests for information that the appellant had not thought were relevant. The purpose of the Pt 36 regime was to encourage early settlement and allow the offeror costs if their offer was not accepted within 21 days. The appellant's letter and first Part 36 offer clearly explained the valuation of the respondent's claim. It was reasonable for the respondent to seek further clarification. However, she had misunderstood the valuation. There was no doubt that that misunderstanding had been corrected by the appellant and the respondent had received all the information needed to understand the official valuation shortly after the original offer.

The further information that the respondent requested was not relevant and it was not unreasonable of the appellant not to provide it. The respondent's questions had been answered by the letter accompanying the first Part 36 offer and she could have made an informed decision on that basis. It was not unreasonable conduct for the appellant to refuse to give further information and his actions were not unreasonable or obstructive. It would be unjust for the appellant to pay costs past the 21-day period following the first Part 36 offer.[226]

Whilst Pt 36 requires an offer to state whether it includes a counterclaim or not, provided the position is clear or is made clear by way of clarification, it therefore appears the court will give effect to the offer.

CPR r.36.9 deals with withdrawing or changing the terms of a Part 36 offer. Such an offer can only be withdrawn or its terms changed if the offeree has not previously served notice of acceptance. After the expiry of the relevant period, the offeror may withdraw the offer or change its terms without the permission of the court. Where the offeror changes the terms of a Part 36 offer to make it more advantageous to the offeree, as in this case, the improved offer will be treated not as the withdrawal of the original offer; but as the making of a new Part 36 offer on the improved terms. The relevant period will then be 21 days, or such longer period (if any) identified in the written notice of the change of terms.

Q17. Can you still ask for clarification of a Part 36 offer under CPR 36.8(1) (or otherwise) outside of the seven days specified therein? Are there any consequences for a late request? For example, would you be prohibited from then applying for a court order under CPR 36.8(2)?

It is hard to see that the time limit could not be extended by agreement or Court order, and there would then have to be analogous provision as to CPR r.36.8(2) and CPR r.36.8(3); but the later the request were left, the harder it is to see that the court would grant an extension.

---

[226] *Bailes v Bloom* unreported 23 November 2015 QBD Simler J.

E. Withdrawing or changing terms of Part 36 offers (CPR rr.36.9, 36.10)

Q18. Where a claimant made a pre-action Part 36 offer which was rejected and now that proceedings have been issued wishes to make a Part 36 offer that is more advantageous to the defendant, what is the position with regard to the original offer? If the claimant equals or beats the offer at trial when are indemnity costs likely to be awarded from: the earlier offer date or the one which supersedes it? (CPR r.36.9(5)) Can a notice of withdrawal of a Part 36 offer be included in a letter containing a further Part 36 offer, or should the notice be set out in separate correspondence?

5–70   CPR r.36.9 provides that a Part 36 offer can only be withdrawn or its terms changed if the offeree has not previously served notice of acceptance. Changing the terms of an offer is done by serving written notice of the change of terms on the offeree. The offer must specify a period not less than 21 days within which the defendant will be liable for the claimant's costs if the offer is accepted but that provision does not apply if the offer is made less than 21 days before the start of a trial.

CPR r.36.9(5) provides:

> "*Where the offeror changes the terms of a Pt 36 offer to make it more advantageous to the offeree (a) such improved offer shall be treated, not as the withdrawal of the original offer; but as the making of a new Pt 36 offer on the improved terms; and (b) subject to Rule 36.5(2) the period specified under CPR r.36.5(1)(c) shall be 21 days or such longer period (if any) identified in the written notice referred to in paragraph (2).*"

Under CPR r.36.17(4)(b), if the judgment against the defendant is at least as advantageous to the claimant as the proposals contained in the Part 36 offer, the court must, unless it considers it unjust to do so, order that the claimant is entitled to costs on the indemnity basis from the date on which the relevant period expired. The relevant period for the purpose of this question would seem to be that attaching to the changed offer.

If the offeree serves notice of acceptance before the expiry of the relevant period, that acceptance has effect unless the offeror applies to the court for permission to withdraw the offer or to change its terms within seven days of the offeree's notice of acceptance; or, if earlier, before the first day of trial. Where the offeror makes such an application, the court may give permission for the original offer to be withdrawn or its terms changed if satisfied there has been a change of circumstances since the making of the original offer and that it is in the interests of justice to give permission (CPR r.36.10).

As to when the acceptance takes effect if the offeror's application is unsuccessful, the answer may be fact sensitive but the starting point must be the date of the notice of acceptance. This has the slightly odd result that the case will then be deemed to be settled and stayed from a date before the hearing of the offeror's application.

With regard to the second question, there seems to be no reason why a notice of withdrawal and a new Part 36 offer should not be made in the same letter, provided that it is made clear that two separate things are happening.

Q19. My client is a defendant in a multi-track claim. Following service of the defence, the claimant made a Part 36 offer to accept a settlement sum of roughly X% of the claim. In response, we made a Calderbank offer to pay a sum that reflected X% of the claim and a contribution to a proportion of the costs. In light of our defence, we hoped the claimant would accept our offer. Instead, the claimant has withdrawn the offer (by letter within the relevant period). My questions are:

(i) **Can they withdraw their offer within the relevant period without permission of the court?**
(ii) **Having withdrawn their offer, do they lose the costs protection of that offer?**

If an offeror serves a notice of withdrawal of a (pre-claim) Part 36 offer before expiry of the relevant period, does that notice take effect immediately to make the Part 36 offer incapable of acceptance, or does the withdrawal notice take effect only after the relevant period has expired, thereby meaning that the Part 36 offer remains capable of acceptance by the offeree during the relevant period?

At the first CMC, we intend to ask the court to allow for the claim value to be increased. Are we, in the meantime, allowed to make a Part 36 offer to the defendant, stating a figure which is above the current claim value?

As to the rules surrounding the withdrawal of a Part 36 offer, either generally or within the relevant period, see the answer to **Q17** above.

5–71

With regard to the making of a Part 36 offer in excess of the amount currently claimed, the defendant will almost certainly either reject the offer or seek clarification. The options would appear to be to wait until you have the permission to amend the claim or at least to explain to the defendant in an accompanying letter the reason why the offer is set at a higher level.

Q20. What is the position where a Part 36 offer is withdrawn at the same time as the claimant purports to accept it? (CPR rr.36.9, 36.10)

The rules governing the withdrawal of offers are CPR rr.36.9 and 36.10. The following decision still holds good. An NHS Trust made a Part 36 offer to a claimant which stated that if it was accepted within 21 days, the Trust would be responsible for the claimant's costs. The offer pointed out that it could be withdrawn before the expiration of that period with permission of the court. Before the expiration of the relevant period the Trust obtained permission to

5–72

withdraw its offer but did so without serving any notice or evidence on the claimant who had accepted the offer on the day it was withdrawn. Leggatt J held that an application should not be made without notice unless that would enable the respondent to take steps to defeat the purpose of the application or there had been no time to give notice before the urgent assistance of the court was required. It was wrong in principle for the Trust to make its application for permission without notice to the claimant and for the court to entertain the application. It was all the more wrong to conceal from the claimant the grounds on which the order had been made. The making of orders which determined questions of substantive rights between the parties without notice could only be justified if that party had the right to apply to set aside the order. The test to be applied, when considering whether to grant a party permission to withdraw a Part 36 offer, was whether there had been a sufficient change of circumstances to make it just to do so.[227] The only new circumstances which could make it just were circumstances which the Trust was able and willing to make known to the claimant at the time of serving notice of withdrawal.[228]

Under CPR r.36.10(3), where the offeree serves notice of acceptance of the offer before the expiry of the relevant period and the offeror applies to court for permission to withdraw or change its terms within seven days of the offeree's notice (or, if earlier, before the first day of trial), the court will only give permission if satisfied that there has been a change of circumstances and that it is in the interests of justice.

Q21. The defendant has made a Part 36 offer which it wishes to vary following a query from the claimant. There are still 20 days left in the "relevant period". What are the costs consequences of this and does the relevant period commence again once a varied Part 36 offer is made?

5–73   Where the offeree has not previously served notice of acceptance, and the offeror has served notice of changes in the terms of its offer, to be less advantageous to the offeree, before the expiry of the relevant period, if the offeree does not serve the notice of acceptance of the original offer by the expiry of the relevant period, the offeror's notice has effect on the expiry of that period; if the offeree serves notice of acceptance of the original offer before the end of the relevant period, that acceptance has effect unless the offeror applies to the court for permission to withdraw the offer or to change its terms within seven days of the offeree's notice of acceptance, or, if earlier, before the first day of trial. If such an application is made, the court may give permission for the original offer to be withdrawn or its terms changed if satisfied that there has been a change of circumstances since the making of the original offer and that it is in the interests of justice to give permission (CPR r.36.10). Where the

---

[227] *Cumper v Pothecary* [1941] 2 K.B. 58; [1941] 2 All E.R. 516.
[228] *Evans v Royal Wolverhampton Hospitals NHS Foundation Trust* [2014] EWHC 3185 (QB); [2015] 1 W.L.R. 4659; [2015] 1 All E.R. 1091; [2014] 6 Costs L.O. 899, Leggatt J.

offeror seeks permission of the court to change the terms of its Part 36 offer to be less advantageous to the offeree before expiry of the relevant period, the permission of the court must, unless the parties agree otherwise, be sought by making a Pt 23 application which must be dealt with by a judge other than the trial judge or at a trial or other hearing provided that it is not to the trial judge (CPR PD 36 para.2).

If the offeree does not accept the original offer within the relevant period of the original offer Pt 36 is unclear about the relevant period for the changed offer. CPR r.36.9(3) says it takes effect on notice of the change. Whether this means a fresh relevant period starts and should be specified is not dealt with. The tone of the rule suggests not, but it seems unlikely that it should fall within the relevant period originally given as the variation may be served on the last day of that relevant period leaving the offeree one day to consider. This uncertainty is compounded by CPR r.36.10(2)(a) (where the offeror changes the terms of a Part 36 offer to make it more advantageous to the offeree) which suggests the variation has effect at the end of the original relevant period. It would be advisable for the offeror to specify a "new" relevant period on the variation and that as CPR r.36.10 is the specific rule in the context of this question, that period can only run from the expiry of the original relevant period. Where the offeror changes the terms of a Part 36 offer to make it more advantageous to the offeree: such improved offer is treated, not as the withdrawal of the original offer; but as the making of a new Part 36 offer on the improved terms; and the relevant period specified under CPR r.36.5(1)(c) will be 21 days or such longer period (if any) identified in the written notice.

Q22. If a Part 36 offer is not withdrawn, it continues to run. However, would this Part 36 offer be seen to be rejected if the other side makes its own Part 36 offer?

If the matter goes to trial and the judge finds that an amount is due which is more than the claimant's original Part 36 offer but less than the varied offer, what are the implications? Do the Pt 36 costs consequences still follow, based on the original Part 36 offer, or is it only the increased figure that is relevant, meaning that there would be no Pt 36 costs consequences? The Court of Appeal has held that the provisions of Pt 36 state clearly how an **5–74** offer may be made, how it may be varied and how it may be accepted. Unlike ordinary common law principles, they do not provide for an offer to lapse or become incapable of acceptance on being rejected by the other party. Once made, a Part 36 offer remains open for acceptance until the start of the trial or its withdrawal in accordance with CPR r.36.9(4). Where a party makes several offers in different terms, a later offer does not revoke or vary an earlier offer and all of them may be capable of acceptance at any one time.[229]

---

[229] *Gibbon v Manchester City Council* [2010] EWCA Civ 726; [2010] 1 W.L.R. 2081; [2011] 2 All E.R. 258; [2010] C.P. Rep. 40; [2010] 5 Costs L.R. 828.

Paras (3) and (4) of CPR r.36.7 do not apply to a Part 36 offer: which has been changed so that its terms are less advantageous to the offeree where the offeree has beaten the less advantageous offer.[230]

F. Part 36 offer acceptance requirements (CPR rr.36.11, 36.12)/Disclosure of Part 36 offer (CPR r.36.16)

Q23. Where there has been a split trial or a trial of preliminary issues, what is the position with regard to Part 36 offers which may have been made? (CPR r.36.12)
Can a defendant accept a Part 36 offer after the claimant has won a liability trial, bearing in mind CPR r.36.12, and what would the costs consequences be?

5–75   Where there has been a trial but all the issues in the case have not been determined,[231] any Part 36 offer, which relates only to parts of the claim or issues that have already been decided, can no longer be accepted. Subject to that proviso, and unless the parties agree, any other Part 36 offer cannot be accepted earlier than seven clear days after judgment is given or handed down in such trial.[232]

Where an offer, which relates to the whole of the claim, is accepted after the expiry of the relevant period, the court must, unless it considers it unjust to do so, order that the claimant be awarded costs up to the date on which the relevant period expired, and, that the offeree pay the offeror's costs for the period from the date of the expiry of the relevant period to the date of acceptance. In considering whether it would be unjust to make such orders the court must take into account all the circumstances of the case including the matters set out in CPR r.36.17(5) (see costs consequences following judgment, above). The claimant's costs include any costs incurred in dealing with the defendant's counterclaim if the Part 36 offer states that it takes the counterclaim into account.[233] CPR r.36.16 deals with restrictions on disclosure in such cases.

It is open to the court to depart from the normal costs rule in CPR r.36.13(5). Where a young boy had suffered frontal lobe damage in a road traffic accident, it was material that the inherent uncertainty in prognosis would have resolved well before the limitation period expired so that the child did not need to commence proceedings before the position was clear. The defendant had made a pre-action Part 36 offer in full and final settlement; the claimant accepted the offer after the date of its expiry. The court approved the settlement, but at first instance it was held that the defendant should be entitled to its costs from the date of acceptance. The Court of Appeal held that the judge's conclusion did not give weight to the particular features of the claimant's

---

[230] CPR r.36.17(7).
[231] Within the meaning of CPR r.36.3(e).
[232] CPR r.36.12.
[233] CPR r.36.13(5) to (7).

case, the consequence of omitting to give weight to the matters that were in the claimant's favour was that the normal rule dominated when it should not have done. In the circumstances it was unjust to make the normal costs order, and the claimant was awarded his costs throughout.[234]

There was previously no general rule that in the case of a split trial the court should ordinarily reserve the costs until the end of the case. Mr Justice Eder stated that there was an urgent need for the rule to be reviewed and possibly reformulated in order to address the question of split trials. In the particular case, due to the substantial level of costs, costs were reserved.[235] In response to these concerns, with effect from 6 April 2015, paras (3)(d) and (4) were added to CPR r.16. There is now no restriction on telling the trial judge at the end of a preliminary trial (a) about the terms of any Part 36 offers relating only to issues that have been decided (CPR r.36.16(3)(d)); and (b) about the existence (but not the terms) of any other Part 36 offers (CPR r.36.16(4)).

In a different case, the judge decided that success on the preliminary issue did not mean that the claimant would ultimately establish any claim in contract at all, and the incidence of costs should therefore be the same as if it had been tried as part of that claim. The judge did not think that this was a reason for departing from the general rule. The defendants had asked for a preliminary issue. They did so because it was thought to be helpful to the parties, and to the court, for the question of proper law to be determined as a discrete issue. The judge agreed, but the corollary of this was that the question did not arise as part and parcel of the trial but was tried separately. That necessarily involved a separate hearing with separate preparation and the incurring of separate costs on that issue. It is in general a salutary principle that those who lose discrete aspects of complex litigation should pay for the discrete applications or hearings which they lose, and should do so when they lose them rather than leaving the costs to be swept up at trial.[236]

In a split trial case the court decided that where there was a split liability/quantum trial, the appropriate course was to address costs only after quantum had been resolved, because it was only then that the court could determine who had been successful and whether the Part 36 offer affected the costs order that should be made; given the findings on liability, there would have to be a further hearing for an account of profits and/or an inquiry as to damages.[237]

The Court of Appeal has clarified that where a Calderbank offer, rather than Part 36 offer, has been made covering the whole dispute in a split trial, the court is not bound to treat the offer as equivalent to a Part 36 offer and defer ruling on costs until all stages of the litigation have concluded.[238]

---

[234] *SG (A Child) v Hewitt (Costs)* [2012] EWCA Civ 1053; [2013] 1 All E.R. 1118; [2012] 5 Costs L.R. 937.
[235] *Ted Baker Plc v Axa Insurance UK Plc* [2012] EWHC 1779 (Comm); [2012] 6 Costs L.R. 1023 Eder J.
[236] *Merck KGaA v Merck Sharp & Dohme Corp* [2014] EWHC 3920 (Ch) Nugee J.
[237] *Lifestyle Equities CV v Sportsdirect.com Retail Ltd (No.2)* [2018] EWHC 962 (Ch) HHJ Pelling QC.
[238] *McKeown v Langer* [2021] EWCA Civ 1792. See discussion above at 5–12.

Q24. My client received the Part 36 offer on Monday 14 August. The relevant period stated in the offer is "within 21 days of service" what is the final date for accepting the offer and how is it calculated?

5–76   CPR r.36.3(g) defines "the relevant period" as meaning, where the offer is made not less than 21 days before trial, a period of not less than 21 days (as specified in CPR r.36.5(1)(c)) or such longer period as the parties agree. Such an offer is accepted by serving written notice on the offeror in accordance with CPR r.36.11(1). The original calculation of time is governed by CPR r.2.8 to which reference should be made. See also CPR r.6.26 which provides that a document, other than a claim form, served within the UK in accordance with these rules or any relevant practice direction is deemed to be served on the day shown in the table in the rule.[239]

Q25. What are the costs consequences when a defendant accepts a claimant's Part 36 offer after the end of the relevant period? Is the defendant liable to pay indemnity costs from the end of the relevant period to the date of acceptance?

5–77   Where a Part 36 offer which relates to the whole of the claim is accepted after the expiry of the relevant period; the liability for costs must be determined by the court unless the parties have agreed the cost. Where the parties cannot agree the liability for costs, the court must, unless it considers it unjust to do so, order that the claimant be awarded costs up to the date on which the relevant period expired; and the offeree pay the offeror's costs for the period from the date of expiry of the relevant period to the date of acceptance (CPR r.36.13(4) and (5)). In considering whether it would be unjust to make the orders specified above, the court must take into account all circumstances including (a) the terms of any Part 36 offer; (b) the state in the proceedings when the Part 36 offer was made, including in particular how long before the trial started the offer was made; (c) the information available to the parties at the time when the Part 36 offer was made; (d) the conduct of the parties with regard to the giving of or refusal to give information for the purposes of enabling the offer to be made or evaluated; and (e) whether the offer was a genuine attempt to settle the proceedings (CPR rr.36.13(6) and 36.17(5)). The starting point will always be costs on the standard basis (see further para.5–33 above).

Q26. In a case where a Part 36 offer has been accepted out of time and costs were reserved during the proceedings in favour of the paying party, can the paying party reopen the issue of the reserved costs in an application to the court (on the basis that the proceedings on the acceptance of the Part 36 offer are stayed)?

---

[239] See also *Essex County Council v UBB Waste (Essex) Ltd (No. 3)* [2020] EWHC 2387 (TCC), Pepperall J para 5.06 above.

CPR PD 44 para.4.1 provides that the court may make an order about costs at any stage in the case. The table within PD 44 para.4.2 explains that where costs are reserved, the decision about costs is deferred to a later occasion, but if no later order is made, the costs will be costs in the case. There seems no reason why the paying party should not make an application to the court but may very well find itself in difficulties since the purpose of Part 36 offers and their acceptance is to bring proceedings to an end. That is why the acceptance of a Part 36 offer results in the claim being stayed.

Q27. In an employer's liability claim, the claimant made a pre-action Part 36 offer. Proceedings have now been issued. The defendant wishes to accept the claimant's offer (still not withdrawn) even though it would mean accepting it well after the end of the relevant period. Will the claimant's entitlement to costs be limited to EL fixed costs as per CPR r.45.29E? I understand that the claimant is entitled to indemnity costs under *Broadhurst v Tan* if the matter goes to trial and the claimant beats its own offer. Is that correct?

The judgment of the Court of Appeal in *Broadhurst v Tan* is dealt with at para.5–22 above. CPR r.36.13(4) deals with the costs consequences where a Part 36 offer is accepted after expiry of the relevant period i.e. the liability for costs must be determined by the court unless the parties have agreed the costs (see **Q25** above). Although *Broadhurst v Tan* deals with the costs consequences following judgment, it seems highly likely that the court would follow that decision in the circumstances set out in the question. See, however, the discussion of *W Portsmouth and Co Ltd v Lowin*[240] in **Ch.8 Q28**.

It is not possible for a claimant whose offer has been accepted late, but before trial, to rely on the decision in *Broadhurst v Tan*[241] to obtain indemnity costs. CPR r.36.20 makes it plain that it is the only rule which applies to the costs consequences of accepting a Part 36 offer in fixed costs cases. The interaction between the fixed costs regime and Pt 36 differs where the claimant is successful after trial and where a Part 36 offer is accepted before trial. On the correct interpretation of the Rules, in a fixed costs case, CPR r.36.20 applies where an offer is accepted late and CPR r.36.13 does not apply at all.[242]

Q28. We act for a claimant in a personal injury case where the defendant accepted the claimant's Part 36 offer out of time at a late stage in the proceedings. My interpretation of CPR r.36.13 is that we cannot commence assessment without an order from the court. The defendant's

5–78

5–79

---

[240] *W Portsmouth and Co Ltd v Lowin* [2017] EWCA Civ 2172; [2018] 1 W.L.R. 1890; [2018] 2 All E.R. 896; [2018] 1 Costs L.O. 1.

[241] *Broadhurst v Tan* [2016] EWCA Civ 94; [2016] 1 W.L.R. 1928; [2017] 2 All E.R. 60; [2016] C.P. Rep. 22; [2016] 2 Costs L.O. 155.

[242] *Hislop v Perde: Kaur v Committee (for the time being) of Ramgarhia Board Leicester* [2018] EWCA Civ 1726; [2019] 1 W.L.R. 201; [2018] 4 Costs L.O. 515.

interpretation is that we can if the parties can agree who is liable for costs and on what basis. What is your view?

5–80 Rule 36.13(4) provides that where a Part 36 offer which was made less than 21 days before the start of a trial is accepted; or a Part 36 offer which relates to the whole of the claim is accepted after expiry of the relevant period; a Part 36 offer which does not relate to the whole of the claim is accepted at any time, the liability for costs must be determined by the court unless the parties have agreed the costs. Where the parties cannot agree the liability for costs, the court must, unless it considers it unjust to do so, order that the claimant be awarded costs up to the date on which the relevant period expired; and that the offeree pay the offeror's costs for the period from the date of expiry of the relevant period to the date of acceptance (see further, Q25 above).

Rule 44.9 provides that where a right to costs arises under CPR r.36.13(1) or (2) (claimant's entitlement to costs where a Part 36 offer is accepted); a costs order will be deemed to have been made on the standard basis. This provision does not apply where a Part 36 offer is accepted before the commencement of proceedings. The circumstances described in the question do not fall within CPR r.36.13(1) or (2), there cannot therefore be a deemed order. This means that even if the parties agree the incidence of costs under CPR r.36.13(4) they will need a consent order to enable the court to assess the costs.

Q29. CPR r.36.16(2) provides that the existence and terms of a Part 36 offer must not be disclosed to the trial judge until the case has been decided. However, are we allowed to disclose the fact of a Part 36 offer in an interim application going before a district judge or master? If a defendant accepts a claimant's Part 36 offer, is the claimant required to keep the details of the settlement confidential?

5–81 A Part 36 offer is treated as being "without prejudice except as to costs". The fact that such an offer has been made must not be communicated to the trial judge until the case has been decided. This restriction does not apply where:

(i)   The defence of tender before claim has been raised;
(ii) The proceedings have been stayed following the acceptance of a Part 36 offer;
(iii) The offeror and offeree agree in writing that it should not apply; or
(iv) Although the case has not been decided, any part of it or issue in it has been decided, and the Part 36 offer relates only to parts or issues which have been decided.

Where a part or issue has been decided, the trial judge may be told whether or not there are Part 36 offers other than those relating to the parts or issues which have not been decided, but must not be told any of the terms of the other offers unless any of the above exceptions apply to them.[243]

---

[243] CPR r.36.16(1)–(4).

Where there is an application or interim hearing before a judge, other than the trial judge, the restriction does not apply. It is permissible to tell the judge of the existence of an offer, but there should be no need to disclose the amount or terms of the offer. If by any mischance the judge hearing the interim application is subsequently listed as the trial judge, the problem should be pointed out to the listing office so that a different judge may be appointed.

CPR r.36.16 does not apply to the situation where a Part 36 offer has been accepted. It refers to a Part 36 offer being made and for that fact to be withheld from the judge. Once an offer has been accepted, there is no longer an offer, there is a binding compromise and Pt 36 makes no reference to that situation. But that does not mean that the material may be freely referred to. It has to be relevant, and if there is a possible prejudice from its disclosure, it is within the court's discretion to prevent it. However, the prejudice would have to be very heavy to outweigh its relevance.[244]

Once a claimant's Part 36 offer has been accepted there does not appear to be any reason why the claimant should keep the matter confidential, unless there are features of the case, which we have not been told about, which means confidentiality has to be observed.

G. Costs consequences of acceptance of a Part 36 offer (CPR r.36.13)

Q30. What is the procedure for recovering costs in an action that settles without proceedings as a result of the acceptance of a pre-action Part 36 offer? (CPR r.36.13)
What is the procedure for enforcing a Pt 36 settlement if proceedings have never been issued? In this case, a Part 36 offer was made and accepted without issuing proceedings. The defendant has now reneged on the settlement.
Where a defendant accepts a claimant's pre-action Part 36 offer before proceedings are commenced, is the claimant entitled to recover its legal costs and, if so, how should the claimant enforce payment of those legal costs, bearing in mind CPR r.44.9(2)?
My opponent owes me quite a lot of money. I made a pre-action Part 36 offer, which my opponent accepted, but he has not complied with that settlement. No proceedings have been commenced. To obtain a County Court Judgment, must I commence proceedings?
Under CPR r.36.13, where a Part 36 offer is accepted within the relevant period, the claimant is entitled to the costs of the proceedings, including their recoverable pre-action costs, up to the date on which notice of acceptance was served on the offeror. CPR r.44.9(1)(b) states that where a right to costs arises under CPR r.36.13(1) or (2), a costs order will be deemed to have been made on a standard basis; but CPR r.44.9(2) states that para.1(b) does not apply where a Part 36 offer is accepted before the commencement of proceedings. If the

5–82

---

[244] *Richard v BBC* [2018] EWHC 2504 (Ch) Mann J.

costs cannot be agreed, there is no doubt about the claimant's right to costs including the pre-commencement costs and the appropriate procedure is to issue costs only proceedings in accordance with CPR r.46.14. When the order for costs to be assessed is made, the normal procedure for detailed assessment under Pt 47 applies. As to interest, CPR r.36.5(4) provides that a Part 36 offer which offers to pay or offers to accept a sum of money will be treated as inclusive of all interest until the relevant period expires. CPR r.36.14(5)(b) provides that any stay arising on the acceptance of a Part 36 offer will not affect the power of the court to deal with any question of costs (including interest on costs) relating to the proceedings.

The Court of Appeal has dealt with the question whether a Part 36 offer may exclude interest. In the particular case the parties had agreed the substantive claim with costs to be assessed if not agreed. During the detailed assessment proceedings the receiving party made an offer, said to be under Pt 36, to accept £50,000 in full and final settlement of his costs, exclusive of interest. The bill was assessed at £52,470 excluding interest. The receiving party claimed that the assessed figure was more advantageous to him than his offer and so CPR r.36.17(4) should apply.

At first instance and on appeal the offer was found not to be a valid Part 36 offer.

On appeal to the Court of Appeal it was held that a Part 36 offer could not generally exclude interest. The court rejected the appellant's arguments that Pt 36 allowed an offer to be limited to part of a claim, and the principal sum and a claim for interest on that principal sum were both "parts of" a claim within the meaning of CPR r.36.2(3). The court also rejected his submission that CPR r.36.5(4) was not mandatory. The appellant relied on CPR PD 47 para.19, which provided that an offer to settle made under Pt 36 should specify whether or not it was intended to include interest. The court held that PD 47 could not control the interpretation of Pt 36. It supplemented Pt 47 not Pt 36. Moreover, PD 47 dated from 2013, whereas the version of Pt 36 engaged here was introduced in 2015.[245]

Analysis of CPR rr.36.2(2) and 36.5 indicated that CPR r.36.5(4) was mandatory. Part 36 proceeded on the basis that interest was ancillary to a claim, not a severable part of it. A Part 36 offer had to be inclusive of all interest; interest could not be hived off. CPR r.36.5(4) stated that an offer to accept a sum of money had to be treated as inclusive of "all interest". Those words applied to every species of interest, as confirmed by CPR r.36.17(6).[246]

---

[245] The Civil Procedure (Amendment) Rules 2021 amend rule 36.5, by inserting — "(5) A Part 36 offer to accept a sum of money may make provision for accrual of interest on such sum after the date specified in paragraph (4). If such an offer does not make any such provision, it shall be treated as inclusive of all interest up to the date of acceptance if it is later accepted." Practice Direction 47 has been amended by the 127th update as follows: "19. Where an offer to settle is made, whether under Part 36 or otherwise, it should specify whether or not it is intended to be inclusive of the cost of preparation of the bill and VAT. An offer which is made otherwise than under Part 36 should specify whether or not it is intended to be inclusive of interest. Unless the offer states otherwise it will be treated as being inclusive of all of these. (A Part 36 offer is treated as inclusive of interest: see CPR 36.5(4).)"

[246] The reference to "interest" in that provision encompassed interest under the Judgments Act 1838 s.17 and the County Courts Act 1984 s.74: *Hertel v Saunders* [2018] EWCA Civ 1831; [2018] 1 W.L.R. 5852 and *Horne v Prescot (No.1)*

It was inconceivable that CPR r.36.5(4) was meant to turn an offer specifically stated to be exclusive of interest into one including interest. That would grossly distort the offeror's intentions. This offer was to be treated as one which did not comply with Pt 36.[247]

CPR r.44.9(2) merely states that where a Part 36 offer is accepted before the commencement of proceedings, a costs order will not be deemed to have been made on the standard basis. Assuming that both the offer and acceptance comply with Pt 36, there will be in existence an enforceable contract. If, however, the offeree cannot be persuaded to perform its side of the bargain, it would be necessary to commence Pt 7 proceedings. It would also be necessary to include in the claim a claim for reasonable pre-commencement costs.

Q31. I act for a proposed claimant in a dispute where legal proceedings have yet to be issued. The proposed defendant has served a Part 36 offer by Form N242A which states that the defendant will be liable for the claimant's costs in accordance with CPR r.36.13. CPR r.36.13 states the claimant will be entitled to the costs of proceedings including their recoverable pre-action costs. Does this mean my client can only recover pre-action costs as part of the costs of any proceedings? If this is so, can we agree that the pre-action costs are recoverable and if so, if the amount cannot be agreed can we issue costs only proceedings pursuant to Pt 8A to have the court adjudicate upon costs? (CPR r.36.13)

Part 8 Costs Only proceedings are the way forward. CPR r.36.13 depends on there being extant proceedings. With that in mind, if parties make a pre-issue settlement, they might consider making it a term of the settlement that the usual CPR Pt 36 consequences will follow. Alternatively, a party could make an offer to settle outside the terms of Pt 36, offering to pay the other party's reasonable costs. It may be possible to bring costs-only proceedings under CPR r.46.14. See also **Q29** above.

5–83

In a road traffic case where a Part 36 offer had been made and accepted before proceedings had been issued, the claimant contended that a deemed order for costs would have arisen providing a sufficient basis for commencing a detailed assessment. The court held that an order for costs:

". . . cannot exist in a vacuum divorced from any substantive proceedings, and accordingly an order for costs cannot be deemed to have been made under rule [44.9(1)(b)] if a Part 36 offer is made and accepted before any proceedings have been commenced."

The court stated:

"18. On the face of it, the procedure in rule [46.14 (Costs Only Proceedings)] is apt to refer to cases that fall within Part [36.13(1)] as well as to those that do

---

Ltd [2019] EWHC 1322 (QB); [2019] 1 W.L.R. 4808 considered.
[247] *King v City of London Corp* [2019] EWCA Civ 2266; [2020] 1 W.L.R. 1517; [2020] 3 All E.R. 643; [2019] Costs L.R. 2197.

> *not . . . it provides for Section II of Part 45 to take precedence in cases to which it applies: see rule [46.14(5) and (6)]. In my view the mechanism provided by rule [46.14] is intended to apply both to cases settled through the operation of Part 36 and to those settled without recourse to it."*

The court commented that it was not easy to see why a claimant who proceeds under CPR r.46.14 should be subject to a more restrictive costs regime, than one who started proceedings under Pt 7 to recover his costs:

> *"The whole purpose of introducing Section II of Part 45 was to impose a somewhat rough and ready system in a limited class of cases . . ."*

If the claimants' argument was correct, the acceptance of a Part 36 offer would always result in an order for costs on the standard basis in low value road traffic accident cases which would undermine the fixed costs regime and provide a powerful incentive for defendants not to make Part 36 offers in such cases. The court concluded that, subject to any agreement between the parties to the contrary, neither could recover more or less by way of costs than is provided for.[248]

Q32. If a defendant accepts a claimant's Part 36 offer after proceedings have been issued, is a consent order to dispose of the proceedings necessary?
I understand that generally speaking, there is no need for there to be a consent order if a settlement results from acceptance of a Part 36 offer. Am I right? If so, are there any significant exceptions from this general proposition? (CPR r.36.13(1)).
Where a Part 36 offer is accepted to settle a dispute, should the parties also draw up and sign a separate settlement agreement or enter into a consent order?
Is there any benefit in a defendant making a Part 36 offer in relation to costs after the claimant has discontinued the claim? If a defendant accepts the claimant's Part 36 offer, can the claimant require the defendant then to enter into a separate settlement agreement?

5–84 No, the notice of acceptance is all that is required. Under CPR PD 36 para.3.1 a copy of the acceptance must be filed at court. CPR r.36.14(1) provides that the claim will be stayed.

In the event that a defendant accepts a claimant's Part 36 offer, CPR r.44.9(1)(b) provides that where a right to costs arises under CPR r.36.13(1) or (2), a costs order will be deemed to have been made on the standard basis. This provision does not apply where the Part 36 offer is accepted before the commencement of proceedings. The existence of the deemed order for costs enables the claimant to commence detailed assessment proceedings under Pt 47.

---

[248] *Solomon v Cromwell Group Plc* [2011] EWCA Civ 1584; [2012] 1 W.L.R. 1048; [2012] 2 All E.R. 825; [2012] C.P. Rep. 14; [2012] 2 Costs L.R. 314.

Where a Part 36 offer is accepted within the relevant period the claimant will be entitled to the costs of the proceedings (including their recoverable pre-action costs) up to the date on which notice of acceptance was served on the offeror (CPR r.36.13(1)), there is therefore, normally, no need for a separate agreement. If there are matters outstanding following acceptance of the Part 36 offer it may be too late to do anything about it since the proceedings will have been stayed automatically.

Q33. CPR r.36.2 provides that a Part 36 offer may be made in a counterclaim or additional claim, and it includes a reminder that CPR r.20.2 and CPR r.20.3 provide that counterclaims and other additional claims are treated as claims. With that in mind, if a defendant makes a Part 36 offer in relation to its counterclaim, which is accepted within the relevant period (RP), does that mean that the defendant is automatically "entitled to the costs of the proceedings" (that is, the costs relating to both the original claim and the counterclaim) under CPR r.36.13(1)? (CPR r.36.13(7)).

There have been numerous questions covering more or less the same ground. 5–85 This question is directed at a situation where the offer is made by a defendant. All that changed when Pt 36 was reformed was that the rules made explicit what was already implicit: a defendant can make an offer on their counterclaim because it is treated as being a claim under CPR Pt 20. The answer to the question is that the defendant recovers the costs of their counterclaim, no more and no less.

To try to help with the evident confusion among practitioners, the CPRC drafted some guidance notes to Form N242A.

Note 5 reads as follows:

"In summary, Part 36 provides that: A party making a defendant's offer is offering something to settle their opponent's claim, counterclaim, additional claim, appeal, cross-appeal or costs assessment proceedings and to accept a liability to pay costs. A party making a claimant's offer is offering to accept something to settle their own claim, counterclaim, additional claim, appeal, cross-appeal or costs assessment proceedings on terms that their opponent pays their costs."

Coulson J in the TCC dealt with this situation.[249] A defendant contractor was sued by a sub-contractor for £10 million damages and interest on the basis of disruption and prolongation. The defendant counterclaimed in relation to interim payments made in relation to the claims. The judgment resulted in the claimant having to repay the defendant almost £2.8 million.

The defendant had made and beaten a Part 36 offer and the question arose whether this was a claimant's Part 36 offer attracting the enhancements in CPR r.36.17(4).

---

[249] *Van Oord UK Ltd v Allseas UK Ltd* [2015] EWHC 3385 (TCC); [2016] 1 Costs L.O. 1 Coulson J.

The court held that the offer was a defendant's Part 36 offer. Although the Court of Appeal in *AF v BG*[250] (see **Q3** above) had held that the offer was a claimant's offer, that case could be distinguished. The defendant's offer did not say expressly that it was a claimants' offer; it did not offer to accept an amount of money in settlement of claim and counterclaim (instead, it offered to pay an amount to the claimants); it offered to pay the claimants' costs; further, it did not spell out the enhanced consequences of non-acceptance. Instead, the offer had all the hallmarks of a defendant's Part 36 offer. It offered to pay a sum in settlement of the litigation (taking into account the counterclaim). The defendant stated that the claimants could retain the sums already paid. The defendant offered to pay the claimants' costs up to the date of acceptance, for a maximum period of 21 days after the date of the offer. And when the offer letter stated that "for the avoidance of any doubt" the defendant would seek an order that the claimants pay its costs from the date of the expiry of the offer if the claimants failed to do better than the offer at trial that was classically in accordance with a defendant's Part 36 offer. No separate, stand-alone counterclaim had been asserted by the defendant at the time of the offer, and no sum was set out in the offer as representing the liquidated amount of any such counterclaim. The court made an award of costs on the indemnity basis since the claim should not have been pursued.

The CPR do not give a great deal of guidance in relation to Part 36 offers where there is a counterclaim. Nothing in s.1 of Pt 36 prevents a party making an offer to settle in whatever way that party chooses, but if the offer is not made in accordance with CPR r.36.5, it will not have the consequences specified in the section. A Part 36 offer may be made in respect of the whole, or part of, or any issue that arises in—(a) a claim, counterclaim or other additional claim (CPR r.36.2(3)). A Part 36 offer must (a) be in writing; (b) make clear that it is made pursuant to Pt 36; (c) specify a period not less than 21 days within which the defendant will be liable for the claimant's costs in accordance with CPR r.36.13 (costs consequences of acceptance of a Part 36 offer) or CPR r.36.20 (costs consequences of acceptance of a Part 36 offer where Section IIIA of Pt 45 applies); (d) state whether it relates to the whole of the claim or to part of it or to an issue that arises in it and if so to which part or issue; and (e) state whether it takes into account any counterclaim (CPR r.36.5(1)). Subject to certain exceptions (explained in para.5–13 above), where a Part 36 offer is accepted within the relevant period, the claimant will be entitled to the costs of the proceedings (including their recoverable pre-action costs) up to the date on which notice of acceptance was served on the offeror (CPR r.36.13(1)). The claimant's costs include any costs incurred in dealing with the defendant's counterclaim if the Part 36 offer states that it takes it into account (CPR r.36.13(7)).

The topic of offers in claim and counterclaim has also been examined by the Court of Appeal. A landlord sued a tenant for rent arrears and the parties

---

[250] *AF v BG* [2009] EWCA Civ 757; [2010] 2 Costs L.R. 164.

agreed that approximately £6,000 in arrears were due. The landlord also claimed for physical damage to the property and consequential loss of rent both of which claims were disputed. The tenant counterclaimed for breach of the covenant of quiet enjoyment and for the landlord's failure to address the property's state of disrepair which far outweighed any sum claimed by the landlord. The landlord made what purported to be a Part 36 offer offering to withdraw the claim for the rent arrears if the tenant also discontinued the disrepair claim with each party paying its own costs. The offer specified a relevant period under CPR r.36.5(1)(c) of 21 days, but did not state that the tenant would be liable for the landlord's costs if the offer was accepted.

At trial the landlord was awarded the rent arrears and interest amounting to £16,000. The tenant was awarded damages for discomfort and inconvenience in the sum of about £7,000. The tenant was ordered to pay the costs of the landlord's claim on the standard basis until the date of the offer and on the indemnity basis with 8% interest after expiry of the relevant period. On appeal to the Court of Appeal, the court held that Pt 36 had been carefully drafted and meant what it said. The court held that the landlord's offer had not complied with CPR r.36.2(2)(c) (now CPR r.36(5)(1)(c)) which was a mandatory requirement that the offer specified a period within which the defendant would be liable for the claimant's costs. The offer had only specified the relevant period. Notwithstanding the fact that it was the tenant's counterclaim which determined the issue, the landlord and the tenant had been claimant and defendant respectively for the purposes of the rule. Accordingly, Pt 36 did not apply, the correct approach was under CPR r.44.2 under which the unsuccessful party would generally pay the successful party's costs. The court did not encourage issue-based costs orders and an appellate court would normally be slow to intervene with costs orders made by judges who were best placed to have a feel for the case. In the instant case, the judge at first instance had taken a mistaken starting point. Where much time had been taken by a party unsuccessfully taking numerous points, the court could give less weight to the fact that on balance that party had been ultimately successful. The case had not only been about the amount of equitable set off versus the rent arrears. The landlord had sued for substantial damages and had failed on many issues. The judge had insufficiently considered the parties' conduct and partial successes. The tenant had substantiated his allegation as to the state of the property and had been entitled to vindicate his claim even if the damages awarded were small. The landlord's offer had been very realistic and the tenant should have considered it more. The tenant had however received no response to his many requests for mediation. No dispute was too intractable for mediation and silence towards an invitation to engage an alternative dispute resolution was in itself unreasonable.[251] The tenant had won more issues than the landlord even if the latter had succeeded financially. A fair and

---

[251] See *PGF II SA v OMFS Co 1 Ltd* [2013] EWCA Civ 1288; [2014] 1 W.L.R. 1386. [2014] 1 All E.R. 970; [2014] C.P. Rep. 6; [2014] B.L.R. 1; 152 Con. L.R. 72; [2013] 6 Costs L.R. 973.

balanced approach was to make no order as to costs. The fact that the landlord had incurred costs of £85,000 and the tenant of £100,000 made a stronger case as was possible that there should be some form of limitation on the costs recoverable in such cases.[252]

Q34. Where a defendant entered into a consent order agreeing to pay costs on the indemnity basis in respect of the claimant's application for summary judgment on part only of its claim, and the defendant then made a Part 36 offer in full and final settlement of the whole claim, if the claimant accepted the Part 36 offer within the relevant period, would the defendant pay the claimant's costs on the standard basis pursuant to CPR r.36.13 or would the summary judgment costs still have to be paid on the indemnity basis in accordance with the consent order?

5–86   Whilst the acceptance of a Part 36 offer gives rise to a deemed order for costs of the proceedings on the standard basis, pursuant to CPR r.44.9, this is subject to any prior orders of the court or agreement between the parties in respect of costs relating to any specific part of the proceedings. Where there is such a prior agreement or order, then the right to costs arises by virtue of that prior order or agreement and not by virtue of CPR r.36.13. The prior order or agreement is not displaced. In the example given, the claimant would still be entitled to the costs of the application on the indemnity basis. The remainder of the costs of the proceedings would only be payable on the standard basis.

Q35. The defendant has accepted our Part 36 offer within the relevant period, and has requested a statement of our client's costs. Is there a set format for a Pt 36 statement of costs?
We act for a potential claimant in a defamation matter, which is still at the pre-action stage. We made a claimant's Part 36 offer to the defendant's solicitors, who have requested details of the claimant's costs so that they may consider the Part 36 offer. Is the claimant obliged to provide details of his costs before the defendant accepts the Part 36 offer?

5–87   There is no set format for such a statement and the defendant merely wants to know how much you are seeking but equally they will need sufficient detail to understand how you arrive at the figure. In multi-track cases utilising the first page of Precedent H ought to provide the necessary information or if that does not provide sufficient detail, Precedent Q.

With regard to the question whether the claimant is "obliged" to provide details of his costs, the defendant will want to know what the potential liability for costs is if the offer is accepted. An attractively low Part 36 offer could be accompanied by a wholly disproportionate claim for costs. So, although the claimant is not obliged to disclose details of the likely costs, if the objective is to settle the proceedings as soon as possible, it would seem sensible to provide the details of the costs requested.

---

[252] *NJ Rickard Ltd v Holloway* [2015] EWCA 1631; [2017] 1 Costs L.R. 1.

Q36. I act for a defendant on a claim against him that was valued by the claimant at £25,000. We are near to trial and the claimant has now made a Part 36 offer seeking just £250 plus costs (which he claims are circa £6,000). If I accept the £250 offer, can I challenge the claimant's right to costs given the vast discrepancy between what he valued his claim at and what he settled for? Or will I be stuck with paying costs subject to assessment? My client has received a Letter of Claim and wishes to make a Part 36 offer of under £10,000. If the claimant accepts the offer will my client be liable only for the claimant's fixed costs as the offer is below £10,000? See also Q64. *O'Beirne v Hudson*[253] was a personal injury action which settled   5–88
prior to allocation for £400 general damages and £719 hire charges which was concluded by a consent order providing that the defendant should pay the claimant's "reasonable costs and disbursements on the standard basis". On assessment the district judge held that the order was for costs to be assessed on the standard basis and none of the fixed costs regimes, including the small claims track regime applied. She was reversed on appeal in the County Court. The Court of Appeal held that the district judge was not free to rule that the costs would be assessed on the small claims track basis, but, when making the assessment, was entitled to take into account all the circumstances in accordance with CPR r.44.4(1) including the fact that the case would almost certainly have been allocated to the small claims track if allocation had taken place. Although it was not open to the district judge to vary the original order, or to assess by reference to the small claims track, it was quite legitimate to give items in the bill anxious scrutiny to see whether the costs were necessarily and reasonably incurred, and thus whether it was reasonable for the paying party to pay more than would have been recoverable in a case which should have been allocated to the small claims track.

H. Other effects of acceptance of a Part 36 offer (CPR r.36.14)

Q37. Is it possible to obtain an order for a payment on account of costs under CPR r.44.2(8), once a Part 36 offer has been accepted?
Claimants appealed against the refusal of their application for an interim   5–89
payment on account of costs following the defendants' acceptance of a Part 36 offer.

The principal issue in the appeal was whether there is jurisdiction to order an interim payment on account of costs pursuant to CPR r.44.2(8) where a Part 36 offer has been accepted within the relevant period. In those circumstances, CPR r.36.13(1) provides that the claimant is entitled to the costs of the proceedings (including recoverable pre-action costs) up to the date on which the notice of acceptance is served. Costs are to be assessed on the standard basis if not agreed: CPR r.36.13(3). A costs order to that effect is deemed to have been made: CPR r.44.9.

---

[253] *O'Beirne v Hudson* [2010] EWCA Civ 52; [2010] 1 W.L.R. 1717.

Teare J, who heard the application at first instance, found that the same question had been determined in the negative in *Finnegan v Spiers (t/a Frank Spiers Licensed Conveyancers)*[254] and that it was the only decision of the High Court on the point. That being so, the judge stated that judicial comity required a subsequent court to follow the earlier decision unless it was convinced that the previous judgment was wrong. He concluded that it was not possible for him to say that he was convinced that Birss J had been wrong and that, in the circumstances, it was his duty to follow the previous decision.

In *Finnegan v Spiers* Birss J held that an application for an interim payment was correctly refused on the basis that the court had neither the power nor discretion to make such an order. He held that under CPR r.44.9(1)(b) a costs order was be deemed to have been made on the standard basis. The correct analysis was that the place to find the court's ability to make a payment on account order, after acceptance of a Part 36 offer, was in Pt 36 itself. However, such an ability was absent from Pt 36 and there was no reason to read CPR r.44.2(8) in such a way as to make a payment on account applicable when a Part 36 offer was accepted.

On 5 August 2019 the Senior Costs Judge made an order that the claimants were entitled to an interim costs certificate in the sum of £225,000. The claimants, however pursued their appeal since they wanted to have the order for costs at first instance reversed, an order for the return of the money they had been ordered to pay on account and to be awarded their costs of the appeal, if successful.

The court went on to hold that Birss J was wrong to conclude that one can only look to the terms of CPR Pt 36 itself to find the jurisdiction to order an interim payment of costs. Although CPR Pt 36 is described as a "self-contained procedural code" there is nothing in the terms of CPR Pt 36 which suggests that it is entirely freestanding and that all costs consequences of the acceptance of a Part 36 offer are to be found within it. Express reference is made in CPR r.36.13, for example, to CPR r.44.3(2) and to CPR r.44.9.

Once it is seen that that the terms of CPR Pt 36 itself do not form an exclusive code as to the costs consequences of Part 36 offers, it is necessary to determine whether there is a tension or conflict between CPR rr.36.13 and 44.2(8). The court was referred to *Lowin v W Portsmouth & Co Ltd*,[255] *Broadhurst v Tan*,[256] *Solomon v Cromwell Group Plc*[257] and *Hislop v Perde*.[258] In each of those cases there was an apparent tension or conflict between two provisions of the CPR. The court held that once one has concluded that it is possible to look outside CPR Pt 36 itself, there is no conflict or tension between CPR rr.36.13(1) and 44.2(8) at all.

---

[254] *Finnegan v Spiers (t/a Frank Spiers Licensed Conveyancers)* [2018] EWHC 3064 (Ch); [2018] 6 Costs LO 729, Birss J.
[255] *Lowin v W Portsmouth & Co Ltd* [2017] EWCA Civ 2172; [2018] 1 W.L.R. 1890.
[256] *Broadhurst v Tan* [2016] EWCA Civ 94; [2016] 1 W.L.R. 1928.
[257] *Solomon v Cromwell Group Plc* [2011] EWCA Civ 1584; [2012] 1 W.L.R. 1048.
[258] *Hislop v Perde* [2018] EWCA Civ 1726; [2019] 1 W.L.R. 201.

Since the court had found that there was a jurisdiction to make an order for an interim payment on account of costs, there was no good reason why the jurisdiction should not be exercised. It was appropriate, therefore, to order a payment on account of £225,000.[259]

Q38. In a claim by a claimant (C) against two separate defendants (D1 and D2), where separate allegations are advanced against each defendant, if C makes a Part 36 offer to settle the whole of his claim which is addressed to both D1 and D2 as "the offeree", and only D1 accepts the offer, is the claim against D2 stayed, even though D2 did not accept the offer? (CPR r.36.14)

Where a claimant brings personal injury proceedings against two defendants and then makes a Part 36 offer to one of those defendants, which that defendant accepts, what are the costs consequences in respect of the other defendant?

Can a claimant make a Part 36 offer to multiple defendants? In particular, how should the offer be structured? What would the costs consequences be for the defendants and would there be any discontinuance implications for the claimant?

Can a claimant make one Part 36 offer to multiple defendants in different claims where there is cross-over in terms of the defendants, and the trial of the claims will occur at the same time? For example, is there an issue in making a Part 36 offer which relates to more than one claim, bearing in mind the wording of CPR r.35.5(1)(d) (which refers to "the claim")?

I am the claimant in a £300,000 court claim. Later today I will make a £100,000 Part 36 offer to the defendant to settle the claim. Is it a bad idea for me to make, at the same time, a (less generous) £200,000 Part 36 offer to the defendant to settle the claim?

The answer to the first question will depend on the exact wording of the offer.   5–90
CPR r.36.14 is clear:

> "(1) If a Part 36 Offer is accepted the claim will be stayed.
> (2) In the case of acceptance of a Part 36 Offer which relates to the whole claim the stay will be upon the terms of the offer."

Since the offer to settle in this question was an offer in respect of the whole claim, which has been accepted, it must follow that the whole claim is stayed. Had the offer been differently worded, CPR r.36.14(3) would apply "if a Part 36 offer which relates to part only of the claim is accepted the claim will be stayed as to that part upon the terms of the offer".

CPR r.36.15 deals with acceptance of a Part 36 offer made by one but not all defendants. The rule does not cover the circumstances described in this question.

---

[259] *Global Assets Advisory Services Ltd v Grandlane Developments Ltd* [2019] EWCA Civ 1764; [2020] 1 W.L.R. 128; [2020] 2 All E.R. 282; [2019] Costs L.R. 1597.

With regard to the other questions where there are multiple defendants the court has held that: the mere fact that an offer has been withdrawn does not necessarily deprive the offer of effect on the question of costs. On the particular facts, the defendant should have accepted the offer when it was available or should have appreciated the costs risk and taken protective steps by making a realistic Part 36 offer itself. The fact that the offer was withdrawn two or months before trial did not make it unjust to order that the claimant should get all their costs from 21 days after the offer was made. Prior to that, the defendants were ordered to pay 60% of the claimant's costs and the claimant ordered to pay 40% of the defendant's costs.[260] In the case of a claim against two defendants which was settled against only one defendant, the claimant has a choice whether to continue an action against the second defendant or to discontinue. A normal consequence of discontinuance is that the discontinuing party becomes liable for the other party's costs. Depending on the circumstances, it may be possible to apply to the court to alter the effect of the deemed Order under CPR r.44.9(1)(c) and it might also be possible to obtain a *"Bullock"* Order (see *Bullock v London General Omnibus Co*).[261] As to this, see the *White Book* 2020, para.44.2.28.

So far as the possibility of making one Part 36 offer to multiple defendants in different claims, this does not appear to be possible (because of the wording of CPR r.36.5(1)(d)) but, in any event, even if it were possible, it would be very risky in terms of costs. Thus, in one action it is possible to make a Part 36 offer to all the defendants, leaving them to decide how to apportion their liability between them, and even to make Part 36 offers to individual defendants with the attendant problems of discontinuance described above.

With regard to the suggestion that the claimant should make a £100,000 Part 36 offer to the defendant, together with a £200,000 offer (described as less generous), it is difficult to understand the thinking behind this strategy. If the defendant were persuaded that it was appropriate to accept the £100,000 offer, there is clearly no chance of the defendant deciding to accept the higher figure. Presumably the idea is to put pressure on the defendant on the basis that if the lower figure is not accepted, the defendant may still not beat the higher figure at trial. Great care would need to be taken because the lower offer would remain open to be accepted.

Q39. Can you have two Part 36 offers open at the same time? My client made an offer last year but wants to make another offer now without withdrawing the first offer. Will making a separate offer mean he loses the costs consequences of the first offer if we get to trial and the first one is not beaten?

---

[260] *Owners and/or Bareboat Charterers and/or sub-bareboat charterers of the ship Samco Europe v Owners of the ship MSC Prestige* [2011] EWHC 1656 (Admlty); [2011] 2 C.L.C. 679 Teare J.
[261] *Bullock v London General Omnibus Co* [1907] 1 K.B. 264 CA. See also: *IT Protect Ltd (In Liquidation), Re. Also known as Bramston (1), Harris (2) (as Joint Liquidators of IT Protect Ltd) v Pye (1), Mantague (2)*, [2020] EWHC 3001 14 October (Ch); Judge Barber.

It is certainly possible to have two Part 36 offers open at the same time. A   5–91
claimant who sought damages for personal injuries and associated losses
appealed against the costs order following the quantum trial. Two relevant
Part 36 offers were made by the defendant: the first offer was made on 25
January 2016 a long time before the trial. The offer was for a gross amount
of £50,000, which remained open until 15 February 2016. The offer letter
concluded:

> *"For the avoidance of doubt, if the claimant fails to obtain a Judgment more
> advantageous than the offer made in this letter then the defendant will seek an
> Order that the claimant should pay both parties' costs from 15 February 2016."*

The offer was not accepted.

The second offer was made on 7 February 2017, it was for a gross amount of
£30,000. The first offer was withdrawn. The second offer remained open until
1 March 2017, the day before the trial began. Again the offer letter stated:

> *"For the avoidance of doubt, if the claimant fails to obtain a Judgment more
> advantageous than the offer made in this letter then the defendant will seek an
> Order that the claimant should pay both parties' costs from 1 March 2017."*

The offer was not accepted.

The judge awarded £17,000 general damages and £5,488.32 special damages
which, together with interest totalled, £23,315.13. This was not a QOCS case
because it pre-dated the QOCS provisions. The judge stated that he did not
think that the second offer had any relevance. He awarded the defendant the
costs from the 15 February 2016 and the claimant was awarded her costs up
to that date.

On appeal the court held that it was difficult to see how the second offer
could be regarded as irrelevant. It had the effect of the more or less automatic
right of the defendant to its costs of the trial: CPR r.36.17(3)(a). Whatever the
relevance of the first offer, it could not have that effect: CPR r.36.17(7)(a). The
judge was found to have misdirected himself in respect of the second offer
and the claimant was awarded her costs up to 1 March 2017. She was ordered
to pay the defendant's costs thereafter.[262]

**Q40. Where a defendant has failed to comply with a Part 36 offer that has
been accepted, is it possible for the claimant to disclose the Part 36 offer
to the court when seeking judgment on the Pt 36? (CPR r.36.14) How do
you enforce an acceptance of a Part 36 offer of settlement served by a
claimant on a defendant in circumstances when the defendant has not
paid having accepted the claimant's Part 36 offer of settlement?**
**If a debtor, who pre-action (recently) accepted the creditor's Part 36 offer,
now refuses to pay what has been agreed, must the creditor commence
court proceedings to enforce the agreement?**

---

[262] *Ballard v Sussex Partnership NHS Foundation Trust* [2018] EWHC 370 (QB); [2018] 2 Costs L.O. 227 Foskett J.

5–92   If the defendant has made a Part 36 offer which is accepted, there would be no difficulty in producing this to the court, should the need arise. See *Richard v BBC*[263] and Q28.

If the defendant's default is in respect of costs, the notice of acceptance is a deemed order under CPR r.44.9 and a costs order will be deemed to have been made on the standard basis.

The court has no discretion under CPR Pt 3 to extend the 14-day time limit for payment of a Pt 36 sum under CPR r.36.14(6). The claimant had accepted the defendants' Part 36 offer some months after the expiry of the relevant period but the defendants did not pay the sum in accordance with CPR r.36.14(6). When the claimant sought an order for payment, the defendants applied to extend the time for payment pending determination of the party's costs claims. The court found that the time limit could only be disapplied by the parties' written agreement. Furthermore the court had no power under Pt 3 to order payment of the sum into court as security for the defendants' costs. The court ordered the defendants to pay the sum and the claimant to make a payment on account of the defendants' costs (from the expiry of the relevant period until the date of acceptance).[264]

Rule 36.13 (1) provides "where a Part 36 offer is accepted within the relevant period the claimant will be entitled to the costs of the proceedings (including their recoverable pre-action costs) up to the date on which notice of acceptance was served on the offeror."

The right to costs should result in a default of final certificate which is, in itself an order to pay and so is also enforceable.

Rule 36.14, so far as relevant, provides:

"(1) If a Part 36 offer is accepted, the claim will be stayed.

(2) In the case of acceptance of a Part 36 offer which relates to the whole claim, the stay will be upon the terms of the offer.

(3) If a Part 36 offer which relates to part only of the claim is accepted, the claim will be stayed as to that part upon the terms of the offer.

(4) If the approval of the court is required before a settlement can be binding, any stay which would otherwise arise on the acceptance of a Part 36 offer will take effect only when that approval has been given.

(5) Any stay arising under this rule will not affect the power of the court—
    (a) to enforce the terms of a Part 36 offer; or
    (b) to deal with any question of costs (including interest on costs) relating to the proceedings.

(6) Unless the parties agree otherwise in writing, where a Part 36 offer that is or includes an offer to pay or accept a single sum of money is accepted, that sum must be paid to the claimant within 14 days of the date of—
    (a) acceptance; or

---

[263] *Richard v BBC* [2018] EWHC 2504 (Ch) Mann J.
[264] *Titmus v General Motors UK Ltd* [2016] EWHC 2021 (QB) Laing J.

(b) the order when the court makes an order under rule 41.2 (order for an award of provisional damages) or rule 41.8 (order for an award of periodical payments), unless the court orders otherwise.

(7) If such sum is not paid within 14 days of acceptance of the offer, or such other period as has been agreed, the claimant may enter judgment for the unpaid sum.

(8) Where—(a) a Part 36 offer (or part of a Part 36 offer) which is not an offer to which paragraph (6) applies is accepted; and

   (b) a party alleges that the other party has not honoured the terms of the offer, that party may apply to enforce the terms of the offer without the need for a new claim."

Q41. May a defendant who is a protected party acting by her litigation friend make a joint Part 36 offer with three other defendants? Is it possible to avoid the obligation under CPR r.36.14(6) to pay out within 14 days? (CPR r.36.14(6))

A defendant who is a protected party may, provided the litigation friend has 5–93 been properly advised, make a joint offer with other defendants. Whether this is a wise thing to do depends upon the circumstances of the case and the interrelationship of the defendants, since if the offer is accepted and the other defendants default on payment, the protected party could find herself liable for the whole of the offer and the costs. Any acceptance of the protected party's Part 36 offer would require court approval under CPR r.21.10.

The court has no discretion to extend the 14-day time limit for payment of a Pt 36 sum under CPR r.36.14(6). The time limit can only be disapplied by the party's written agreement. See *Titmus v General Motors UK Ltd.*[265]

Q42. What is the position where a claimant's Part 36 offer is accepted pre-action and the defendant subsequently fails to abide by the terms of the offer and does not make payment? CPR r.36.14 suggests that the claimant may enter judgment, however I suspect that this relates to matters where a claim has already been issued. If that is so, would the claimant in this case be able to commence a Pt 8 claim (incurring the lower court fee) in order to obtain judgment on the basis of non-compliance of an accepted Part 36 offer? Would it be more suitable to record the acceptance under a Tomlin Order which the claimant could rely on to seek judgment?

As the question points out the matter is governed by CPR r.36.14. Given that 5–94 proceedings have not been started and there can be no stay of the proceedings, even so CPR r.36.14(5) provides that any stay under this rule will not affect the power of the court to enforce the terms of a Part 36 offer or to deal with any question of costs relating to the proceedings. CPR r.36.14(8) deals with the situation where a Part 36 offer is accepted and the other party has not

---

[265] *Titmus v General Motors UK Ltd* [2016] EWHC 2021 (QB) Laing J.

honoured the terms of the offer. The accepting party may apply to enforce the terms of the offer without the need for a new claim. If the claim were for costs only, Pt 8 proceedings could be commenced in accordance with CPR r.36.14. Where, as here, both the damages and costs are outstanding, it will be necessary to commence Pt 7 proceedings reciting the acceptance of the Part 36 offer and the other party's default.

I. Part 36 offers in multi-party disputes (CPR r.36.15)

Q43. If one of two defendants with joint and several liability makes a Part 36 offer, what are that defendant's costs implications assuming that before the offer he would have been jointly and severally liable for all of the claimant's costs? Can two defendants together make a valid single Part 36 offer to the claimant? Where a claimant makes a Part 36 offer in a claim involving two defendants, stating they will accept an amount from D1 only to settle the whole claim, and this is accepted by D1, is the claim stayed because it is in full settlement of the whole claim, even where there is no address/name in the offeree box and the offer is only accepted by D1? Or can the claimant still continue the claim against D2?

5–95   CPR r.36.15 deals with acceptance of a Part 36 offer made by one or more but not all defendants. The rule goes on to provide that if the defendants are sued jointly or in the alternative, the claimant may accept the offer: if the claimant discontinues the claim against the defendant who has not made the offer and that defendant gives written consent to the acceptance of the offer. If the claimant alleges that the defendants have a several liability, the claimant may accept the offer and continue with the claim against the other defendant if entitled to do so. Otherwise, the claimant must apply to the court for permission to accept the Part 36 offer.

There is nothing in the rules to prevent two defendants together making a valid single Part 36 offer to the claimant. This is frequently done and it is for the defendants to work out between themselves in what proportion they will contribute to the amount offered.

With regard to the third question, if the claimant accepts an offer from D1 to settle the whole claim, it is difficult to see on what basis the claimant could proceed against D2. The claim will have been stayed on acceptance of the offer and is, to all intents and purposes, over. Some help may be derived from this decision: Joint liquidators of a company obtained judgment against one of two respondents which exceeded their Part 36 offer. At trial, the liquidators were awarded an amount greater than their Part 36 offer and the claim against the second respondent was dismissed. The liquidators sought a costs order requesting the full consequences under CPR r.36.17(4). The respondents argued that the Part 36 offer had been made jointly to the respondent and not severally, and it had not been open to the first respondent to accept it without the second respondent also doing so, and so it would be unjust for the costs consequences to apply. The court accepted that the first respondent could not accept the offer without the second respondent also doing so. Acceptance by the second respondent would have made her liable for paying damages and costs for which she was not liable. Had the first respondent accepted the offer, it would have rendered him liable for all the costs, including those regarding an unsuccessful claim against the second respondent. These factors took the case out of the norm and it would be unjust for the costs consequences in CPR r.36.17(4) to apply. An issues-based order and detailed assessment would be impractical and disproportionate. A percentage order was appropriate. The first respondent was ordered to pay 50% of the liquidators' costs. The second respondent was entitled to all her costs on the standard basis.[266]

Q44. Can a Pt 20 defendant make a Part 36 offer? We have a case where the claimant is suing the first defendant (D1), the claimant is also suing the second defendant (D2), and D1 is suing D2, who they brought in as a Pt 20 defendant. D2 wishes to make a Part 36 offer, but is it possible for one Part 36 offer to encompass both claims?
How can you best use Pt 36 in multi-party disputes? We act for Party A in an action against Party B. Party B has issued Pt 20 proceedings against Party C. Our client wishes to resolve the claim by making a Part 36 offer to settle the entire action, including the Pt 20 proceedings, on terms that my client will accept a small sum in settlement from Party B, and that Party B will discontinue against the Pt 20 defendant (who is a Litigant in Person (LiP) and therefore has no costs consequences). There is a connection between Party A and Party B (CPR r.36.2(1), CPR rr.36.5, 36.15).
It is open to anyone who is a party to make an offer; and there is no restriction on the terms of the offer provided it complies with CPR r.36.5 (see below). In the first question both C and D1 are suing D2, so there seems no reason why one offer should not encompass both claims.

5–96

In the second question there is apparently no *lis* between claimant and Party C. The offer that claimant wishes to make appears to be "If you B will pay me a modest amount and discontinue against C, the matter can end there." Party C will obviously not object if proceedings are discontinued against him. The offer would therefore be between claimant and B, (it would be sensible to inform C of the offer being made to B).

CPR r.36 2(1) states:

"Nothing in this Section prevents a party making an offer to settle in whatever way that party chooses, but if the offer is not made in accordance with rule 36.5, it will not have the consequences specified in this Section."

CPR r.36.5 sets out the form and content of a Part 36 offer necessary to comply with the rule. If the offer does not comply with CPR r.36.5, CPR r.44.2 requires the court to consider an offer to settle that does not have the costs

[266] *IT Protect Ltd (In Liquidation), Re. Also known as Bramston(1), Harris(2) (as Joint Liquidators of IT Protect Ltd) v Pye(1), Mantague (2)*, [2020] EWHC 14 October (Ch); Judge Barber.

consequences set out in Pt 36 in deciding what order to make about costs. Given the complex nature of the claimant's proposed offer it might be more sensible to set it out in the form of a Calderbank offer which could be sent to all parties.

Q45. Our client is a defendant to a multi-party disease claim. For commercial reasons they would like to make a Part 36 offer for their portion of the claim and costs only. In what circumstances would CPR r.36.15 apply to a disease claim such as this? And if the offer were accepted by the claimant how would the court deal with the "common costs"?

5–97   It is not clear from the question whether the NIHL claim is proceeding under the protocol or not. If the claim concludes within the process, the fixed costs will apply. If the claim does not conclude within the protocol, but is subject to Pt 7 proceedings, the fixed costs regime in Pt 45 Section IIIA does not apply to disease claims and the general rules governing costs will apply. So far as the approach to common costs is concerned, the court (Patten J as he then was) has had to consider how to divide the common costs of action in a case where the trial judge had ordered the defendant to pay the claimant's costs of the action, save for three specific items of costs. Patten J stated:

> *"3. The CPR make no special provision for dealing with costs of this type and some of the difficulties in the assessment of these costs arise directly from a common failure by judges to appreciate the complexities which can be created by orders which seek to split the responsibility for costs between the parties other than by an order for the payment of a simple percentage or proportion of the total costs bill."*

The parties agreed that the costs order did not differ materially in its terms from the type of order considered by the Court of Appeal in *Cinema Press Ltd v Pictures & Pleasures Ltd*[267] which in turn applied the earlier decision of the House of Lords in *Medway Oil & Storage Co v Continental Contractors Ltd*.[268] Patten J decided:

> *"50. The decision in Medway applied in Cinema Press establishes that on a taxation of common costs ... it is appropriate to attribute part of a composite fee to the items of work which the fee was intended to cover ... The same goes for the time spent on preparing parts of witness statements which deal separately and exclusively with [a particular] issue. But what the decision in Medway does not do is to authorise the [Costs Judge] in a case like the present, to apportion the costs of work all of which is relevant to both claims."*

The judge concluded:

> *"57. .... Instead the Costs Judge must analyse all the work done and claimed for in accordance with the Medway principles set out."*[269]

---

[267] *Cinema Press Ltd v Pictures & Pleasures Ltd* [1945] K.B. 356; [1945] 1 All E.R. 440.
[268] *Medway Oil and Storage Co Ltd v Continental Contractors Ltd* [1929] A.C. 88; [1997] Costs L.R. (Core Vol.) 5.
[269] *Dyson Technology Ltd v Strutt* [2007] EWHC 1756 (Ch); [2007] 4 Costs L.R. 597 Patten J.

In proceedings which were compromised a Tomlin Order was drawn up which provided, among other things, that the third defendant would pay the claimant's costs of the action against the third defendant only. The order made it clear that the costs to be paid related exclusively to the professional negligence claim against the third defendant, and did not encompass any costs incurred by the claimant in respect of any dispute with the first and second defendants. There was no order for costs as between the claimant and the other defendants. The third defendant subsequently argued that the claimant was only entitled to costs against it of work carried out only against it, and if the work was carried out in relation to the claims against all three defendants, then such costs were not recoverable. In respect of the common costs, the court held, by reference to the authorities including *Medway Oil and Storage Co Ltd v Continental Contractors Ltd,*[270] that although common costs cannot be apportioned in such a case, there may be scope for them to be divided. The court held that in so far as common costs could be attributed to the claim against the third defendants, they represented costs which related exclusively to the professional negligence claim against the third defendant within the meaning of the consent order. In respect of common costs which were not susceptible to division, those costs would not relate exclusively to the claim against the third defendant. The court ordered that the third defendants were not liable for any common costs except to the extent that those costs fell to be attributed to the claim against them by division (rather than apportionment).[271]

Q46. i. We are one of two defendants in High Court proceedings. The claimant's solicitors have made a Part 36 offer to us which states, "We are prepared to settle the entire proceedings on the following terms". Those terms are payment by our client of £200,000. Obviously, if accepted, costs would also be payable. The same letter has also been sent to the other defendant. Can either of the defendants accept the offer and thus settle the entire proceedings, and then agree between them how to divide up the payment?

ii. Our client issued a claim against two defendants who are jointly and severally liable for the entire debt stemming from a hire agreement. We would now like to make a Part 36 offer to the defendants. Should that offer be in the form of a joint Part 36 offer, given there is joint and several liability, or separate Part 36 offers for the full amount addressed to each of the defendants?

iii. I am acting for two defendants who have instructed me to make a Part 36 offer to the claimant. Will I be required to complete a separate Part 36 form for each defendant? The claims against each are identical.

iv Can three out of four defendants make a joint Part 36 offer apportioning the liability as between them?

---

[270] *Medway Oil and Storage Co Ltd v Continental Contractors Ltd* [1929] A.C. 88; [1997] Costs L.R. (Core Vol.) 5.
[271] *Hay v Szterbin* [2010] EWHC 1967 (Ch); [2010] 6 Costs L.R. 926 Newey J.

v. In a negligence claim against multiple defendants each considered to have caused the resulting harm in varying ways, can a Part 36 be offered to each defendant for different amounts according to their alleged liability? What are the consequences of doing so (including in terms of costs should one accept and the other decline, or if both accept)?

5–98   i. and ii. The first two questions raise virtually the same point. In the first case, it is open to either defendant to accept the offer and then to agree how the damages should be split with the co-defendant. The danger with this is that the co-defendant may not wish to accept the offer and may refuse to contribute. It would therefore be sensible to agree with the co-defendant that one defendant will accept the offer and then the two defendants will agree how to split the liability.

In the second question given that liability is joint and several a single offer should suffice.

iii and iv. The third and fourth questions concern offers by more than one defendant. There is no reason why all the defendants should not make a single offer to the claimant to settle. CPR r.36.15 explains what happens on acceptance of a Part 36 offer made by one or more, but not all, defendants:

> "(1) This rule applies where the claimant wishes to accept a Part 36 offer made by one or more, but not all, of a number of defendants.
>
> (2) If the defendants are sued jointly or in the alternative, the claimant may accept the offer if—
>
> (a) the claimant discontinues the claim against those defendants who have not made the offer; and
>
> (b) those defendants give written consent to the acceptance of the offer.
>
> (3) If the claimant alleges that the defendants have a several liability to the claimant, the claimant may—
>
> (a) accept the offer; and
>
> (b) continue with the claims against the other defendants if entitled to do so.
>
> (4) In all other cases the claimant must apply to the court for permission to accept the Part 36 offer."

Although it would theoretically be possible to make separate offers to separate defendants, it would potentially be difficult for a claimant accurately to apportion blame. Far better to make an offer to all the defendants and leave them to a) decide whether or not to accept the offer and, b) how to divide liability between them. The answers to questions i and ii above amplify the position.

J. Calculating whether judgment more advantageous than Part 36 offer (CPR r.36.17)

Q47. Can an admissions payment improve the value of Part 36 offer? (CPR r.36.17)

5–99   In proceedings where the defendant made a Part 36 offer totalling £35,000 and subsequently made an admission of part of the claim amounting to £17,504 at trial, the defendant argued that the total value of the Part 36 offer was in fact £52,504 (£35,000 plus £17,504). That argument was rejected at first instance. On appeal the Court of Appeal held that the true analysis of the relationship between the Part 36 offer and the admission payment was first, the Part 36 offer was an offer to settle the entirety of the landlord's claim for £35,000, no more and no less. There was nothing in the correspondence concerning the admission payment referring to the Part 36 offer. Second, the admission payment was plainly made on the basis that it was a payment on account following admission against the landlord's entire claim. Third, the admission payment was liable to be taken into account as a part payment in advance of the £35,000 that would have been due and payable to the claimant if the Part 36 offer had been accepted. Accordingly, the defendant had obtained a judgment more advantageous than the value of the Part 36 offer.[272]

The Court of Appeal has more recently explained that a payment on account after a Part 36 offer will, unless the appropriate notice is given, reduce the Part 36 offer by the amount of the payment:

"27. Therefore, I consider that the reasoning in Macleish is equally applicable to any payment on account of a claim as it is to an 'admissions payment'. The second payment of £10,000 in this case was not simply some unattributed payment but, . . . a payment for the works and thus on account of the works or on account of the claim . . . where such a payment is made, there is a presumption of law that it is also on account of the earlier Pt 36 offer as Briggs LJ found at [23]. The contrary conclusion would lead to the absurd results he identified in that paragraph.

28. It seems to me that if the paying party wishes to prevent the presumption from operating, it is incumbent on that party either to state expressly at the time the payment is made that it is not intended also to reduce the amount of the earlier Pt 36 offer or to provide clarification to that effect promptly after the payment was made . . .

29. This conclusion does not lead to uncertainty which is inimical to the purpose of Pt 36 . . . If the paying party wishes to avoid the operation of the presumption on the basis that a payment is a voluntary interim payment or not intended to reduce the amount of an earlier Pt 36 offer, it should say so. If it does not do so and a payment on account of the claim is made without any such qualification, then parties will know where they stand. The analysis in [23] and [24] of Briggs LJ's judgment in Macleish will apply and the presumption will operate.

30. Furthermore, I do not consider that the application of Briggs LJ's analysis to all payments on account of a claim . . . has the effect of cutting across the Pt 36 regime. Given that the presumption operated as a matter of law, there was no need for the defendant to serve a notice of change in the terms of the Pt 36 offer pursuant to CPR 36.9(2). In other words, an unconditional payment on account of the sums claimed in the proceedings, made after the date of a Pt 36 offer, results in the amount of the Pt 36 offer being correspondingly reduced unless the payer

---

[272] *Littlestone v MacLeish* [2016] EWCA Civ 127; [2016] 1 W.L.R. 3289; [2016] C.P. Rep. 26; [2016] 2 Costs L.O. 275.

makes it clear to the other party, at any time prior to judgment or acceptance of the Pt 36 offer, that it is not to be so treated." Per Flaux LJ.[273]

Q48. When considering whether a claimant has failed to obtain a judgment more advantageous than a defendant's Part 36 offer how do you deal with any interest element that the judge awards the claimant at trial? Assuming that the defendant's offer was inclusive of interest until the expiry of the relevant period do you compare that figure with the principal sum that the judge awards at trial plus any interest awarded too up to the date of judgment? Or can you argue that for the purposes of working out whether the judgment is more advantageous you should only take into account the principal sum awarded and interest up to the date of expiry of the Part 36 offer? (CPR r.36.17)

5–100   CPR r.36.5(4) provides that a Part 36 offer which offers to pay or offers to accept a sum of money will be treated as inclusive of all interest until the date on which the relevant period expires; or, if the offer is made less than 21 days before the start of the trial, a date 21 days after the date the offer was made. When the judge gives judgment, any interest awarded in the judgment is part of that judgment. There appears to be no basis upon which, when considering whether or not the judgment is more advantageous, one should only take into account the principal sum awarded and ignore the interest element. See now CPR r.36.6(5) in force from 6 April 2021, and dealt with at para **5–06** above.

Q49. At the end of a trial, is the defendant likely to be awarded an indemnity costs order as a result of the claimant failing to obtain the judgment more advantageous than the defendant's Part 36 offer?

5–101   Where on judgment a claimant fails to attain a result which is more advantageous than a defendant's Part 36 offer, the court must, unless it considers it unjust to do so, order that the defendant is entitled to costs (including any recoverable pre-action costs) from the date on which the relevant period expired; and interest on those costs (CPR r.36.17(1)(a) and (3)). The effect of the rule is that the defendant would be entitled to costs on the standard basis. If, however, the court could be persuaded that this would be unjust, it might be possible to persuade the court to award costs on the indemnity basis. The court awarding costs on the indemnity basis should be satisfied that there is something in the conduct of the action or the circumstances of the case which takes the case out of the norm in a way which justifies an order for indemnity costs.[274]

Q50. Can a claimant in a boundary dispute make a Part 36 offer to realign a boundary to a certain position or does a Part 36 offer always have to have a quantifiable financial value? If the offer does not have to have a

---

[273] *Gamal v Synergy Lifestyle Ltd* [2018] EWCA Civ 210; [2018] 1 W.L.R. 4068; [2018] Costs L.R. 185.
[274] *Excelsior Commercial & Industrial Holdings Ltd v Salisbury Hammer Aspden & Johnson* [2002] EWCA Civ 879; [2002] C.P. Rep. 67.

quantifiable financial value, and it is not accepted, how does the court measure whether the offer was beaten at trial?
There appears to be no reason why a valid Part 36 offer to realign a boundary   5–102
should not be made in a boundary dispute CPR r.36.2:

> *"(2) Nothing in this Section prevents a party making an offer to settle in whatever way that party chooses, but if the offer is not made in accordance with CPR r.36.5, it will not have the consequences specified in this Section.*
> *(CPR r.44.2 requires the court to consider an offer to settle that does not have the costs consequences set out in this Section in deciding what order to make about costs.)"*

The difficulty may arise after judgment in deciding whether or not the judgment is "as least as advantageous". Clearly it will be fact sensitive.
The correct approach in determining whether a judgment award is more advantageous than a Part 36 offer is:

> *". . . to ensure that the offer or the Judgment sum is adjusted by eliminating from the comparison the effect of interest that accrues after the date when the relevant offer could have been accepted."*[275]

Some help may be derived from the judgment in *AB v CD*[276]:

> *"22 . . . In my judgment the offer must contain some genuine element of concession on the part of the claimant, to which a significant value can be attached in the context of the litigation. The basic policy of Pt 36 is to encourage the sensible settlement of claims before trial, or even before the issue of proceedings (see CPR r.36.3(2)(a) which provides that a Pt 36 offer may be made at any time, including before the commencement of proceedings). The concept of a settlement must, by its very nature, involve an element of give and take. A so-called 'settlement' which was all take and no give would in my view be a contradiction in terms.*
> *23 In the usual way, the concession offered by the claimant will be something that it is in the claimant's power to give up at the time when the offer is made. However, I do not think that this is an invariable requirement. I see no reason in principle why the concession offered may not also relate to an advantage or form of relief which the claimant would only be able to obtain at or after trial, provided that obtaining it would be of significant value to the claimant, and the agreement to forego the opportunity to obtain it is not merely an empty gesture. Furthermore, it is necessary to have regard to the principles stated by Moore-Bick LJ in Gibbon v Manchester City Council at paragraph [40], where he said that 'a party faced with a Pt 36 offer ought to be entitled to evaluate it by reference to a rational assessment of his own case (including the risk of incurring unrecoverable costs if he presses on). He should not have to make a significant allowance for the court's view of factors that are inherently difficult to value . . .'"*

---

[275] *Purrunsing v A'Court and Co* (A Firm) [2016] EWHC 1528 (Ch); [2016] C.I.L.L. 3861 HHJ Pelling QC. See also *Blackman v Entrepose UK* [2004] EWCA Civ 1109; [2005] C.P. Rep. 7; [2005] Costs L.R. 68.
[276] *AB v CD* [2011] EWHC 602 (Ch) Henderson J.

See also *R. (MVN) v London Borough of Greenwich*[277] and **Q58** below.

In the end it would be up to the trial judge to decide, in the light of the judgment, whether the result was at least as advantageous as the claimant's offer. A Calderbank offer may well avoid such difficulties.

K. Part 36 and costs consequences (CPR rr.36.17, 36.20, 36.21)

Q51. Where a defendant has made a Part 36 offer for settlement of the claimant's costs, and the claimant has rejected that offer but fails to beat/ meet it at trial: (a) is there a cap on how much the claimant has to pay to the defendant? (b) Is the cost consequence awarded as a percentage of the settlement offer or as a percentage of the value of the claim?

5–103   The matter is covered by CPR rr.36.17(3) and 47.20, to which reference should be made. There is no cap, as such, on the amount that the claimant has to pay the defendant. The amount is determined by the tests of reasonableness and proportionality. The costs consequences bear no relation to a percentage of the offer or a percentage of the claim. Recent authorities make it clear that there is no "near miss" principle in Pt 36. CPR r.36.17(2) provides:

> *"For the purposes of [CPR r.36.17(1)], in relation to any money claim or money element of a claim, 'more advantageous' means better in money terms by any amount, however small, and 'at least as advantageous' shall be construed accordingly."*

Q52. In a case where the claimant makes a Part 36 offer less than 21 days before trial, would the claimant still recover the additional 10% damages if he/she obtains a judgment at least as advantageous as the offer? (CPR r.36.17)

5–104   Under CPR r.36.17(1)(b), where judgment against the defendant is at least as advantageous to the claimant as the proposals contained in a claimant's Part 36 offer, the court must (subject to what appears below) unless it considers it unjust to do so, order that the claimant is entitled to various items and interest on costs including the additional amount. CPR r.37.17(7)(c) however, provides that that provision does not apply to a Part 36 offer made less than 21 days before trial, unless the court has abridged the relevant period. There is no indication in this case that the relevant period has been abridged and accordingly the additional amount is not payable.

There does not appear to be any authority as to the circumstances in which the court would abridge the relevant period, although in *PGF II SA v Royal & Sun Alliance Insurance Plc*[278] the court, in refusing to abridge the relevant period since the offer related only to a very small part of the overall costs of the litigation, stated:

---

[277] *R. (MVN) v London Borough of Greenwich* [2015] EWHC 2663 (Admin) Picken J.
[278] *PGF II SA v Royal & Sun Alliance Insurance Plc* [2010] EWHC 1981 (TCC); [2014] 1 W.L.R. 1386; [2014] 1 All E.R. 970; [2014] C.P. Rep. 6; [2014] B.L.R. 1; 152 Con. L.R. 72; [2013] 6 Costs L.R. 973.

"The position might have been different if there had been a Pt 36 offer which would resolve the whole dispute between the claimant and the defendants".

Q53. Can you explain how an award of costs on the standard basis (e.g. under CPR r.36.17(3)(a)) differs from an award of costs on the indemnity basis (e.g. under CPR r.36.17(4)(b)) in circumstances where a costs budget is in place? The definition of "standard basis" and "indemnity basis" appear to be hard to reconcile with the concept of costs budgets, because there should be no doubts about reasonableness to resolve in anyone's favour if the costs are within the court-approved costs budget. (CPR r.36.17(4))
See **Ch.4 Qs 93** and **94** on this topic.

5–105

Q54. Is it appropriate to award a lower additional amount under CPR r.36.17(4)(d) than the prescribed amount because the proceedings were determined early, for example, as a result of summary judgment being given, rather than going to full trial?
Defendants will not always be penalised. Where a claimant's Part 36 offer which had been refused, but not bettered at trial, expired days before the trial commenced and the defendants had not received its witness statements until the final day of the expiry of the offer, the High Court ruled that making a defendant who rejected a Part 36 offer pay an additional 10% of the sum awarded for costs, pursuant to CPR r.36.17(4)(d), would introduce a "penal" element and be unjust. The ruling was made after an injunction had been granted to the claimant restraining the defendant from joining another company before the end of his 12-month notice period.[279]

5–106

Q55. How do the Court of Appeal decisions in *AJ Insurance v Sugar Hut, Hammersmatch Properties (Welwyn) Ltd v Saint Gobain Ceramics and Plastics Ltd*, tie together with the Court of Appeal decision in *Coward v Phaestos*? It's not clear to me why a party who makes a Part 36 offer should be deprived of the benefits of CPR r.44.2, as interpreted by the Court of Appeal in *Coward v Phaestos*.
The answer is that Pt 36 is a self-contained code. There is no overlap with Pt 44. Part 36 is to be read as a self-contained code and not to be confused with contractual notions or general costs discretion under Pt 44 or non-Part 36 offers such as Calderbank type offers.[280] See also **Q47** above.

5–107

Q56. Do you agree that it may be difficult to decide who has obtained the more advantageous result in a detailed assessment? Also, does CPR

---

[279] *Elsevier Ltd v Munro* [2014] EWHC 2728 (QB); [2014] 5 Costs L.O. 797 Warby J. See also *Feltham v Bouskell* [2013] EWHC 3086 (Ch); [2014] 1 Costs L.O. 29 Charles Hollander QC; and see: *Bataillon v Shone* [2015] EWHC 3177 (QB) HHJ Waksman QC. See **para.5–22** above.
[280] *RXDX v Northampton BC* [2015] EWHC 2938 (QB); [2015] 5 Costs L.R. 897 Sir Colin Mackay.

r.36.17(4)) about enhancing claimants' recovery by 10% apply in detailed assessments? (CPR r.36.17)

5–108   Where a Part 36 offer has been made in detailed assessment proceedings, it will be for a specified amount. When the bill is totalled at the end of the detailed assessment there should be no difficulty in ascertaining whether or not the offer has been beaten. The power of the court under CPR r.36.17(4) to award interest not exceeding 10% above base rate on the sum awarded; to award indemnity costs; to award interest on those costs at a rate not exceeding 10% above base rate; and, an additional amount in accordance with CPR r.36.17(4)(d) is certainly exercisable. In detailed assessment proceedings, the receiving party made a Pt 36 offer to settle for £152,500. At the detailed assessment the bill was allowed at £173,693 which was more advantageous to the receiving party than the Part 36 offer. The costs judge declined to award the 10% additional amount stating that in circumstances where there had been a significant reduction in the claimant's bill, it would be unjust to reward the claimant with the additional amount prescribed by CPR r.36.17(4). On appeal, the court found that the costs judge was in error in relying on the degree of reduction on assessment. That approach penalised the appellant for making a reasonable Part 36 offer. It was the terms of the Part 36 offer not the level of the sums claimed in the bill of costs which were to be considered. Accordingly, the appellant was entitled to the additional award.[281]

In proceedings for detailed assessment where the receiving party beat its own Part 36 offer by just under £7,000, the costs judge at first instance found it would be unjust to award an additional amount where the offer was beaten by a small margin. Such an order would result in a disproportionate "bonus" of £40,000. On appeal, it was held that unless a rule, on its true construction, made it clear that the exception of injustice was to be applied to every case across the board, then the court had jurisdiction to consider it unjust to award some, but not necessarily all, of the orders in CPR r.36.17(4). The costs judge had not been entitled to take into account the amount by which the Part 36 offer had been beaten. CPR r.36.17(2) made it clear that "better in money terms" meant better "by any amount however small". The burden was on the party who failed to beat the offer to show injustice which was a formidable obstacle to the obtaining of a different order.[282]

In proceedings where appellant had claimed restitution of certain payments made towards annual wireless telegraphy licences issued by the respondent, the appellant had obtained a judgment more advantageous than its unaccepted Part 36 offer. The judge at first instance had awarder enhanced relief under CPR r.36.17(4)(b) and CPR r.36.17(4)(d) but declined to award enhanced

---

[281] *Cashman v Mid-Essex Hospital Services NHS Trust* [2015] EWHC 1312 (QB); [2015] 3 Costs L.O. 411 Slade J.

[282] *JLE (A Child by a Litigation Friend ELH) v Warrington and Halton Hospitals NHS Foundation Trust* [2019] EWHC 1582 (QB); [2019] 1 W.L.R. 6498; [2019] Costs L.R. 829, Stewart J. The minutes of the November 2019 meeting of the CPRC noted: "The 'all or nothing' approach lacks flexibility but may be more consistent with the underlying policy of Part 36. . . It was recommended that the CPRC leaves the decision in *JLE* in place and this was agreed."

interest on the principal sum awarded and on costs under CPR r.36.17(4)(a) and CPR r.36.17(4)(c).

On appeal the Court of Appeal held, relying on *JLE (A Child) v Warrington and Halton Hospitals NHS Foundation Trust*,[283] that it would be unusual for the circumstances to yield a different result for only some of the consequences. The judge's reasoning was that such an award would have been disproportionate given the very high nature of the offer and the other benefits awarded did not bear scrutiny.

The judge had taken account of irrelevant considerations, contrary to clear statements of principle in the authorities, and had failed to take account of his discretion about the rate of interest. Additional interest of 1.5% per annum would be awarded, making the total interest payable 3.5% above base rate, on both the principal sum and costs, from the relevant date.[284]

Q57. Further to a judgment, if costs in a matter are then settled using a Part 36 offer and thereafter the judgment is appealed successfully, how are costs calculated? That is to say, is the Pt 36 settlement ignored or do costs only run from the date of that settlement?

CPR r.52.20 deals with the court's powers on appeal i.e. the appeal court has all the powers of the lower court and may affirm, set aside or vary any order or judgment made or given by the lower court, make various other orders including a costs order. When making a costs order the court will exercise its discretion in accordance with CPR r.44.2. Where the appeal is successful, the court has the power to set aside the order for costs in the court below. It is not clear from the question whether the Part 36 offer in the lower court was made by the defendant who was ultimately successful on appeal or by the claimant who was ultimately successful. The appeal court in making the order for costs is required to take into account "all the circumstances" but it could well be that the Pt 36 settlement would be found to be of no effect and any money paid under it would have to be returned.

5–109

L. Part 36 and IPEC, Pt 45, Section IV

Q58. How does the cap on damages in the IPEC apply where there is also a claim for costs? (CPR r.36.17(4))

In the Intellectual Property Enterprise Court (IPEC) the cap on the maximum value permitted for a claim for damages on an account of profits is £500,000. A claimant in IPEC proceedings obtained judgment for an amount well in excess of its rejected Part 36 offer. The question was whether the "additional amount" payable by the defendant under CPR r.36.17(4) should be treated as further damages (subject to the £500,000 cap) or whether it was a separate payment unaffected by the cap. The court held that it appeared to be clear

5–110

---

[283] [2019] EWHC 1582 (QB), [2019] 1 W.L.R. 6498.
[284] *Telefonica UK Ltd v Office of Communications*, [2020] EWCA Civ 1374.

from the note to CPR r.36.14 in the *White Book* and the authorities there mentioned that the "additional amount" had nothing to do with compensating a claimant for any wrong committed by the defendant in the substantive dispute. It was solely intended to serve as an incentive to encourage claimants to make and defendants to accept appropriate Part 36 offers.[285]

M. Genuine attempt to settle (CPR r.36.17(5))

Q59. We represent a client in a case where we feel that the client is bound to succeed. We are considering making a claimant Part 36 offer to settle at 100% liability plus costs. This would save the defendant the time and cost of preparing for trial and the trial itself. Will this succeed? What is a genuine effort to settle under Pt 36? (CPR r.36.17)
Can a claimant's Part 36 offer to accept the amount claimed and interest at the rate pleaded be a valid Part 36 offer? Would it make any difference if the claimant had stated that it intended to file an application to amend its claim and increase the amount sought?

5–111   CPR r.36.17(5)(e) was added to deal with the problem of claimants making very high settlement offers (often as much as 95% of the value of the claim) not in a genuine attempt to settle the claim but to place the defendant at risk of indemnity costs pursuant to CPR r.36.17(4). "A genuine attempt to settle proceedings" is not defined further in the rules. The question will always be fact sensitive and will arise only when the court is considering whether or not it would be unjust to make the normal order.

In the light of the decision below caution is advisable with what you propose.

Prior to a trial, one of the issues in which was the claimant's age (i.e. whether the claimant was a child), the claimant made what purported to be a Part 36 offer stating that the defendant should accept the claimant's age and agree to pay the claimant's costs. The claimant was successful at trial and the issue arose as to whether the indemnity costs and interest on costs consequences set out in CPR r.36.17(4) should apply in view of the terms of the offer made. The defendant argued that the offer made by the claimant was not a genuine offer to settle as understood by CPR r.36.17(5)(e) and that it would be unjust to make the order sought. The defendant's counsel relied on *AB v CD*[286] and also *East West Corporation v DKBS*[287] arguing that there was no give and take involved in the offer made. It was a total capitulation offer. It did not assist the claimant to contend that the Part 36 offer was genuine because had the defendant accepted it, it would have gained by saving the costs of the hearing. There was no obvious answer to the matter in issue in the present case and the court's jurisdiction in disputed age cases was inquisitorial

---

[285] *000 Abbott v Design and Display Ltd* [2014] EWHC 3234 (IPEC) HHJ Hacon; on appeal [2016] EWCA Civ 98, the substantive decision was reversed, but no criticism was made of the approach to costs in the IPEC.
[286] *AB v CD* [2011] EWHC 602 (Ch) Henderson J.
[287] *East West Corp v DKBS* [2002] EWHC 253 (Comm); [2002] 2 Lloyd's Rep. 222 Thomas J.

not adversarial.[288] The court held that the claimant's offer was not a give and take offer, as the claimant was offering to take "nothing short of what he was claiming in the proceedings". It was not a settlement offer in any real sense but a "tactical ploy". It did not constitute a concession on the claimant's part but, had the defendant accepted the offer, the defendant would have saved costs. Accordingly, the claimant failed to obtain an order for enhanced interest, indemnity costs, enhanced interest on those costs and an additional amount under CPR r.36.17(4). Instead the defendant was ordered to pay costs on the standard basis.[289]

It is difficult to see how an indication that the claimant is going to seek to increase the amount of the claim would affect the issue of whether the offer is a genuine attempt to settle. Although under CPR r.16.3(7) the statement of value in the claim form does not limit the power of the court to give judgment for the amount which it finds the claimant is entitled to, which might suggest that the claimant can offer to accept more than it has claimed.

N. Part 36 and set-off (CPR r.36.22).

Q60. Where a claimant accepts a defendant's Part 36 offer after the expiry of the relevant period, can the defendant's costs for the period after the end of the RP to the date of acceptance be offset against the amount of the Part 36 offer? (CPR r.36.22)

Where a Part 36 offer which relates to the whole of the claim is accepted after expiry of the relevant period, the liability for costs must be determined by the court unless the parties have agreed the costs (CPR r.36.13(4)). The court's powers as to set-off as to costs are at CPR r.44.12.   5–112

Where a party entitled to costs is also liable to pay costs, the court may assess the costs which that party is liable to pay and either set-off the amount assessed against the amount the party is entitled to be paid and direct that party to pay any balance; or delay the issue of a certificate for the costs to which the party is entitled until the party has paid the amount which that party is liable to pay. And see *Lockley v National Blood Transfusion Service*.[290] Where, by operation of CPR r.36.14(6)(a), a claimant is entitled to be paid the offered sum within 14 days, he is entitled to such payment without set-off against an unquantified costs liability (*Cave v Bulley Davey*).[291]

The set-off of costs against costs in cases to which QOCS applies is, however, very limited. The Supreme Court has held that, as a matter of construction, CPR r.44.14 does not operate as a total ban on set-off of opposing costs orders under CPR r.44.12, but it does impose a monetary cap, beyond which enforcement is not possible, requiring that the monetary value of any set-off by the defendant should not exceed the monetary amount of the claimant's orders

[288] See *R. (CJ) v Cardiff* [2011] EWCA Civ 1590; [2012] P.T.S.R. 1235.
[289] *R. (MVN) v London Borough of Greenwich* [2015] EWHC 2663 Admin Picken J.
[290] *Lockley v National Blood Transfusion Service* [1992] 1 W.L.R. 492; [1992] 3 Med. L.R. 173.
[291] *Cave v Bulley Davey (A Firm)* [2013] EWHC 4246 (QB) HHJ Seymour.

for damages and interest. The decision of the Court of Appeal in *Howe v Motor Insurer's Bureau* (Costs) [2020] Costs L.R. 297; [2017] 7 W.L.U.K. 84 is no longer good law. The Supreme Court did indicate that it was for the Civil Procedure Rule Committee to consider whether their interpretation best reflected the purposes of QOCS and to amend the rule if not.[292] Crucially, where there is no court order for damages and interest, because a Part 36 offer has been accepted by a claimant, or made by the claimant and accepted by the defendant, set-off is not available at all, because there is then no court order for damages and interest as required by CPR r.44.14(1).[293]

O. Relief from sanctions where Part 36 offer may be affected (CPR r.3.9)

Q61. My firm needs to serve an expert's report out of time. The defendants are objecting to relief from sanctions. How does this affect potential Part 36 offers? (CPR r.3.9)

5–113   It depends on the particular facts of your case but this decision may help. The claimant applied to serve its expert report late, accepting that it was out of time and that the default was serious and without good reason. The issue for the court was whether it was appropriate to grant the claimant relief from sanctions. The defendant submitted that there would be prejudice if relief were granted as the date for making a Part 36 offer giving rise to costs consequences had passed. The defendant had already seen the expert report in draft and it was reasonable to suppose that it would be similar to the final version of the report. Therefore if the defendant was influenced by the report to make a Part 36 offer, it would most probably have done so before service of the final report. The court found that there was minimal prejudice to the defendants and granted relief from sanctions on very strict terms including that the claimant could not recover from the defendant any of its costs relating to the expert's report.[294]

P. Part 36 and detailed assessments (CPR rr.44.2 and 47.20)

Q62. If we make a successful Part 36 offer will we recover all our costs? (CPR r.44.2). Please explain the decision in *Webb v Liverpool Womens' NHS Foundation Trust*.[295]

5–114   The existence of a Part 36 offer does not, in principle, insulate the offeror from a proportionate costs order. The fact that there has been a Part 36 offer does not mean that the court is unable to make an issue based or proportionate costs order. Part 36 is a self-contained regime and the rule itself makes no

---

[292] *Ho v Adelekun* [2021] UKSC 43; [2021] 1 W.L.R 5132; [2021] Costs L.R. 927. See also **Ch.6** *Qualified One-Way Costs Shifting* on set-off.
[293] *Cartwright v Venduct Engineering Ltd* [2018] EWCA Civ 1654; [2018] 1 W.L.R 6137; [2018] 4 Costs L.O. 495.
[294] *Art & Antiques Ltd v Magwell Solicitors* [2015] EWHC 2143 (Ch) Klein J.
[295] *Webb v Liverpool Womens' NHS Foundation Trust* [2015] EWHC 449 (QB); [2015] 3 Costs L.O. 367.

reference to such orders. Nevertheless, insofar as such an order is necessary to avoid injustice, it is permissible for the court to make it.

In *Webb*, the claimant, who had suffered injuries at birth, sued the NHS Trust for failing to perform a caesarean section and secondly for managing the delivery inappropriately. The trial judge upheld the first allegation but rejected the second. The claimant was awarded damages on a full recovery basis. She had earlier made a Part 36 offer to settle for 65% of the damages claimed. The judgment was more advantageous to her than the offer. She accordingly sought all her costs on the indemnity basis. At first instance, the judge had made an issue based costs order and reduced the costs accordingly. On appeal to the Court of Appeal, the court held that the judge could not properly have deprived the claimant of her costs relating to the second allegation incurred before the effective date. The two allegations had been part of one event i.e. the claimant's birth. It was not unreasonable for her to pursue the second allegation. It was not unusual for a claimant to succeed on some but not all allegations in personal injury cases. There was no reason to deprive the claimant of any part of her costs. In deciding what order for costs to make the only discretion was that conferred under Pt 36. The discretion under CPR r.36.17 related both to the assessment of costs and to the determination of what costs were to be assessed. It was not unjust for the claimant to be awarded all her costs. The judge below had not taken into account the fact that the trust could have avoided all the trial costs.[296]

Q63. Is it possible to make a Part 36 offer in detailed assessment proceedings on terms that acceptance of the offer will not only settle the costs issue, but also compromise an outstanding appeal being pursued by the paying party?

This may be a step too far. Although a Part 36 offer may be made in whatever way that party chooses, you appear to be trying to settle two separate issues with one offer. The sensible course would seem to be to make a Calderbank offer, which the court may take into account under CPR r.44.2(4)(c).

5–115

Q64. When the question of costs is being decided is it possible for a party to refer to without prejudice correspondence in order to establish that the other party did not respond to Part 36 offers? (CPR r.44.2). Can without prejudice correspondence and Part 36 offers be disclosed to a mediator?

A defendant who had been found liable for misusing the claimants' confidential information made two Part 36 offers during the course of an inquiry as to damages. The claimants did not respond to either offer and made no counter-offer. When the court was dealing with the costs of the inquiry the defendant criticised the claimants' conduct and served a witness statement which referred to an exchange of without prejudice correspondence between

5–116

---

[296] *Webb v Liverpool Women's NHS Foundation Trust* [2016] EWCA Civ 365; [2016] 1 W.L.R. 3899; [2017] 2 All E.R. 313; [2016] C.P. Rep. 30; [2016] 2 Costs L.R. 411.

solicitors attempting to settle the question of costs. The claimants sought an order to strike out those passages which referred to the without prejudice correspondence.

The court stated that there was a strong public policy justification for denying the ability to rely on without prejudice correspondence at any stage in the proceedings including costs assessment. Where a without prejudice offer was made the recipient was free to make a without prejudice response. The response might be to make a counter-offer, ask for more information, reject the offer or simply ignore it. All these responses were protected by privilege. The fact that the claimants were seeking costs on the indemnity basis did not amount to a waiver of privilege but was based on criticism of the defendant's conduct.[297]

Q65. Where a Part 36 offer is accepted in a small claim that has not yet been allocated to the small claims track, is it the case that the fixed costs regime will generally apply? Is the claimant entitled to its costs if it accepts a pre-action Part 36 offer where the case would be allocated to the small claims track if it went to court? (CPR r.46.13)

5–117   CPR r.46.13(3) is a new provision following the Jackson Reforms and the decision of the Court of Appeal in *O'Beirne v Hudson*.[298] The rule provides that where the court is assessing costs, on the standard basis, of a claim which concluded without being allocated to a track, it may restrict those costs to the costs that would have been allowed on the track to which the claim would have been allocated if allocation had taken place. The position is further explained in CPR PD 46 para.8.2. The Court of Appeal has since decided that in relation to CPR r.46.13(2) (Allocation and Re-Allocation), the court has power to backdate the re-allocation for costs purposes if the court is satisfied that there were good reasons for doing so.[299]

Q66. What are the costs consequences if a pre-action protocol is not followed?

5–118   In a noise-inducted deafness hearing, the claimant who brought the proceedings against two former employers failed to follow the pre-action protocol which allowed for the recovery of fixed costs and disbursements only. The claim against one of the employers was subsequently dropped and the claim was settled under Pt 36 before the commencement of proceedings. At first instance it was held that the claim should have been brought under the Pre-action Protocol for Low Value Personal Injury (Employer's Liability and Public Liability) Claims and that pursuant to CPR r.45.24, the claimant was only entitled to the fixed costs and disbursements under the Protocol. On appeal, it was held that the interpretation of CPR r.45.24 was wrong and a provisional

---

[297] *Vestergaard Frandsen A/S v Bestnet Europe Ltd* [2014] EWHC 4047 (Ch); [2015] 1 Costs L.R. 85 Iain Purvis QC.
[298] *O'Beirne v Hudson* [2010] EWCA Civ 52; [2010] 1 W.L.R. 1717; [2010] C.P. Rep. 23; [2010] 2 Costs L.R. 204.
[299] *Conlon v Royal Sun Alliance Insurance Plc* [2015] EWCA Civ 92; [2015] C.P. Rep. 23; [2015] 2 Costs L.O. 319.

assessment of the costs was ordered pursuant to CPR r.47.1. The defendant appealed to the Court of Appeal who found that the claimant had not used the Protocol because there were initially claims against two defendants. All the new style Pre-action Protocols were expressly designed to apply where there was only one defendant. Accordingly, although the claim should have been made under the Protocol but was not, the focus therefore shifted to the CPR. The case was settled following acceptance of a Part 36 offer. CPR r.36.13(1) and (3) applied. Since the Protocol had not been used, CPR r.36.20 did not apply and would not have applied in any event, because CPR r.45.29A(1) did not apply to disease claims. The starting point was that the claimant was entitled to its costs assessed in accordance with the usual rules. CPR r.45.24 dealt with the costs consequences of failure to comply or electing not to continue with the relevant Protocol. The absence of proceedings and a judgment meant that CPR r.45.24 did not apply. Taking together paras 2.1, 3.1 and 7.59 of the Protocol, if a claim should have been started under the Protocol but was not and it was unreasonable that the claim was not so started, then by operation of the Pt 44 conduct provisions, the claimant should be limited to the fixed costs that would have been recoverable under the Protocol.[300] The defendant could rely on the conduct provisions in Pt 44. The appeal was allowed in part on the basis that the Protocol should have been used, its non-use was unreasonable and pursuant to the Pt 44 conduct provisions, the claimant would usually be entitled to recover only the fixed costs and the disbursements permitted by the Protocol.[301]

Q. Part 36 offers made after issue but before service

Q67. We have a matter which settled following acceptance of a Part 36 offer after the issue of proceedings but prior to service. Proceedings were never served, and the time for service has now expired. We take the view that we can commence detailed assessment proceedings without Pt 8 proceedings, despite the fact that proceedings were never served. We refer to CPR r.46.14(1)(c) which says that Pt 8 proceedings are required if no proceedings have been "started". Do you agree, or do you believe that we would need to issue Pt 8 proceedings for an order for costs before commencing assessment? (CPR r.46.14)

Rule 7.2 states: "(1) Proceedings are started when the court issues a claim **5–119** form at the request of the claimant." In your case proceedings have started and so you may proceed to assessment without having to commence Pt 8 proceedings.

---

[300] See *O'Beirne v Hudson* [2010] EWCA Civ 52; [2010] 1 W.L.R. 1717; [2010] C.P. Rep. 23; [2010] 2 Costs L.R. 204.
[301] *Williams v Secretary of State for Business, Energy & Industrial Strategy* [2018] EWCA Civ 852; [2018] 4 W.L.R. 147; [2018] 2 Costs L.R. 391.

Q68. What is the requirement for open offers in detailed assessment proceedings meant to achieve and how will they co-exist with Part 36 offers? (CPR 47 PD 8.3)

5–120   CPR 47 PD 8.3 sets the matter out clearly:

> *"The paying party must state in an open letter accompanying the points of dispute what sum, if any, that party offers to pay in settlement of the total costs claimed. The paying party may also make an offer under Part 36."*

Lord Justice Jackson's objective in inserting this requirement was to ensure that the parties were not in fact arguing over an insignificant amount of money. It is clearly open to the paying party to make an open offer of 0%. This would presumably only be done if there were an arguable point of principle which might well result in the receiving party recovering nothing. There is no requirement that the open offer and any Part 36 offer should be in the same terms.

If a paying party fails to make an open offer as required by the Practice Direction, it would clearly be within the power of the costs judge to strike out the points of dispute or if that were felt to be too draconian, to rely only on the written points of dispute and not permit any further oral argument.

The Court of Appeal expressly considered provisions of the CPR which contain mandatory language, but where no sanction is provided for any failure to comply in *Altomart v Salford Estates (No.2) Ltd*.[302] The court accepted the proposition that there might be implied sanctions which were capable of engaging CPR r.3.9 and equally there might be cases not analogous with CPR r.3.9 and where it was a matter for the court to determine the consequence of non-compliance. It is clear that the open offer does not form part of the points of dispute (it merely accompanies that document) and therefore it is difficult to see how any argument suggesting that the points of dispute should be struck out would find favour (indeed there is a risk it would be seen as an attempt to turn the rules into "tripwires" and invoke possible costs sanctions). Perhaps a more measured approach would be to identify the failure to comply to the paying party promptly, suggesting a short period for rectification, and, in default of compliance reserve the position to the question of costs of the assessment, if relevant, under "conduct" within CPR r.47.20(3)(a).

Section 2 Settlement other than under Pt 36

R. Calderbank offers

Q69. i. How are Calderbank offers treated in relation to costs? (CPR r.44.2(4))
Our opponent, the claimant, has sent us a letter headed "Without prejudice save as to costs", offering on that basis to accept 98% of the amount

---

[302] *Altomart v Salford Estates (No.2) Ltd* [2014] EWCA Civ 1408; [2015] 1 W.L.R. 1825; [2016] 2 All E.R. 328; [2015] C.P. Rep. 8; [2014] 6 Costs L.R. 1013.

claimed. (I'm not sure whether he's also demanding costs.) There has been controversy in recent years about whether a Part 36 offer in such terms would be a valid one because it's debatable whether it's a true offer: but what do you think the position would be in the law and practice of Calderbank offers?

ii. If an offer is marked "Calderbank Offer" but not "Without Prejudice Save as to Costs" or similar, is it still only admissible in relation to costs or is it effectively an open offer?

iii. If a claimant responds to a defendant's Calderbank offer by serving a Part 36 offer on the defendant, can the claimant still then accept the Calderbank offer before the deadline stated in the Calderbank offer?

i. With regard to Calderbank offers, the situation is obviously going to be fact **5–121** sensitive. Bear in mind that under CPR r.44.2(4)(c) the court is required to take into account any admissible offer to settle made by a party which is drawn to the court's attention, and which is not an offer to which costs consequences under Pt 36 apply.

The Court of Appeal has made it clear that the effect of a Calderbank offer is not to be assessed by analogy with the terms of CPR r.36.17(2) which defines a "more advantageous" judgment as one that is "better in money terms by any amount, however small" than the relevant offer. Parts 36 and 44 of the CPR are separate regimes with separate purposes. Part 36 is a self-contained procedural code which specifies particular consequences in the event that such offers are not accepted. Those consequences include features which go far beyond that which might be ordered by way of costs under Pt 44. Whilst Pt 36 is highly prescriptive and highly restrictive of the exercise of any discretion by the court, Pt 44 confers on the court a discretion in almost the widest possible terms. It contains no rules as to the way in which the court has to have regard to offers and there is no equivalent to the "more advantageous" test in Pt 36.[303]

ii. Whilst it would clearly be sensible to mark a Calderbank offer "without Prejudice save as to costs" it should, in most circumstances be clear to the offeree that "Calderbank offer" bears the same meaning

iii. Since a Calderbank offer is not a Part 36 offer, common law principles apply. The Part 36 offer would be a counter-offer with the result that the Calderbank offer would no longer available for acceptance See *DB UK Bank Ltd (t/a DB Mortgages) v Jacobs Solicitors*[304] in **Q67.**

Q70. i. Can a Calderbank offer be made in the course of an expert determination?

ii. What effect does a non-Part 36 offer have on costs in a case on the small claims track considering that there is no costs award?

---

[303] *Coward v Phaestos* [2014] EWCA Civ 1256; [2015] C.P. Rep. 2; [2014] 6 Costs L.O. 843.
[304] [2016] EWHC 1614 (Ch); [2016] 4 W.L.R. 184 Andrew Hochhauser QC.

iii. If a defendant makes a Calderbank offer without clarifying the position regarding costs other than to state that the "normal rules apply", what is the position regarding costs and how should a claimant respond? Where costs only proceedings are issued by the paying party in the Senior Court Costs Office for the assessment of costs and a Calderbank offer made by the receiving party is accepted by the paying party, who is entitled to the costs of the Part 8 proceedings? The rules as to the liability for costs of detailed assessment proceedings are contained in CPR r. 47.20. Generally, the receiving party is entitled to the costs of detailed assessment proceedings but the court may make a different order. Whether the court will do so will depend on the individual circumstances of the case. Part 36 also applies to the costs of detailed assessment proceedings.

iv. If you wish to withdraw a Calderbank offer, should this be done in open correspondence or should the letter be written on a "without prejudice save as to costs" basis?

v. Where you have received a Calderbank offer, can you make a counter-offer under Part 36 for the same amount?

5–122 i. Because Calderbank offers are not hedged about by rules in the same way as Part 36 offers, they can be used far more flexibly. The offer is made "without prejudice save as to costs" meaning that the court will not consider the offer until the end of the case when costs come to be decided. Accordingly, there appears to be no reason why a Calderbank offer should not be made in the course of an expert determination.

ii. Under CPR r. 27.14(2) no costs are payable on the small claims track save for certain exceptions including "(g) such further costs as the court may assess by the summary procedure and order to be paid by a party who has behaved unreasonably". Rule 27.14(3) makes it clear that "A party's rejection of an offer in settlement will not of itself constitute unreasonable behaviour under paragraph (2)(g) but the court may take it into consideration when it is applying the unreasonableness test." It follows therefore that such an offer will have little effect on costs, unless, in the particular circumstances of the case, it can be shown that the other party has behaved unreasonably.

iii. A Calderbank offer is an offer made "without prejudice save as to costs". So that if the offer is not accepted the offer will be produced to the Judge to decide what order for costs to make. In this case, if the offer is accepted "the normal rules apply". It is not clear what the offeror means by this, but CPR r. 42.2 states "(2) If the court decides to make an order about costs—

(a) the general rule is that the unsuccessful party will be ordered to pay the costs of the successful party; but (b) the court may make a different order." The sensible course would be to clarify what the offeror means by the words used, since, if for instance, they are intended to mean that each side should bear its own costs, the offer may be unattractive and not worth accepting.

iv. Given that the original Calderbank offer is made Without Prejudice save as to costs, it would be sensible to withdraw the offer on the same basis. If the withdrawal were contained in an open letter it would be apparent to the

Court that there had been an offer (the details of which the court does not know) which has now been withdrawn. The offeree would also complain that you had disclosed without prejudice information (the existence of the offer) to the judge

v. It would certainly be possible to make a Part 36 offer in the same terms as a Calderbank offer received from the opposing party, but it is difficult to see what the advantage would be.

As the court held in *DB UK Bank Ltd (t/a DB Mortgages) v Jacobs Solicitors*[305] since the Calderbank offer was not a Part 36 offer, the impact on it of any counter offer had to be addressed by reference to common law principles. On that basis, any subsequent Part 36 offer would be a counter-offer with the result that the Calderbank offer would be rejected and no longer available for acceptance. If the Part 36 offer is in the same terms as the Calderbank offer, the court, in considering what order for costs to make under CPR r.39.13 or CPR r.36.17, would have regard to CPR r.44.2(4)(c) as part of consideration of all the circumstances and the conduct of the parties and would almost certainly find that it was "unjust" to make the normal order. The obvious question is: Why not accept the Calderbank offer thereby saving both time and costs?

Q71. If a party has only put "without prejudice" on certain correspond-ence can they then retrospectively reserve their client's rights by sub-sequently adding "without prejudice save as to costs" to additional correspondence? In other words, can they retrospectively add "save as to costs" to the original letter?
"The contents of the "without prejudice correspondence will not be admis-   5–123
sible to establish any admission relating to the [party's] claim."[306] The without prejudice rule which prevents statements being made in a genuine attempt to settle from being put before the court is intended to encourage parties to reach settlement without the fear that any admission made during the course of negotiations may be put before the court by the opponent. If the correspondence in the question related to an attempt to agree the costs of the proceedings, the addition of the words "save as to costs" would seem to add very little. If however there is any doubt about it, there is no reason why the party who has omitted those words should not repeat the offer including the previously omitted words. The court is likely to view the whole exchange of correspondence to ascertain the extent of the without prejudice privilege.

Letters marked "Without Prejudice Save as to Costs" which referred to earlier without prejudice settlement negotiations did not fall within a recog-nised exception to the Without Prejudice rule. The court held that the first letter could be characterised as an offer to vary the existing Without Prejudice

---

[305] [2016] EWHC 1614 (Ch); [2016] 4 W.L.R. 184 Andrew Hochhauser QC.
[306] Per Lord Griffiths in *Rush & Tompkins Ltd v Greater London Council* [1989] A.C. 1280; [1988] 3 W.L.R. 939; [1988] 3 All E.R. 737; 43 B.L.R. 1; 22 Con. L.R.114. And see *White Book* 2019 para.31.3.40.

Agreement covering the settlement negotiations. That offer had been accepted by the applicants. In essence, the parties had agreed to treat the settlement negotiations as if they had always been conducted without prejudice, save as to costs. The effect of this was that everything said and done in the context of the mediation was admissible for the purpose of argument on costs.[307]

In a partnership dispute an arbitrator awarded the claimant 70% of its costs up to the date of the expert report, on the basis that it had succeeded in the arbitration but additional costs had been incurred because it had been slow to provide the defendant with information, and all of its costs thereafter. The defendant challenged the costs decision on the grounds that the arbitrator should have taken into account an offer he had made in November 2015 to settle for an immediate payment of £65,000. The arbitrator determined that he was entitled to take into account the offer and subsequent correspondence that had been marked "without prejudice". He considered that the defendant had beaten the November offer, but only in terms of value, that neither party had gained much from the arbitration process and that each side should bear their own costs. The claimant argued that the arbitrator was wrong to hold that he had a discretion to take into account without prejudice communications and that it could be inferred that the November offer was covered by the without prejudice rule because it was an offer to settle a live dispute.

The court referred to *Willers v Joyce*, above, and held that since the offer had been written in an attempt to settle a live dispute it should be treated as having been written on a without prejudice basis so far as the substantive dispute was concerned, but it could be referred to on the issue of costs. There was no underlying public policy justification that prevented communications not expressly marked without prejudice from being referred to on the issue of costs. There was no reason, where parties had not chosen to label communications expressly without prejudice, why the law should imply an agreement that it should be treated as without prejudice rather than without prejudice save as to costs. Therefore, the arbitrator had been entitled to consider the November offer on the issue of costs.[308]

In proceedings where a claimant had brought an action against five defendants and reached a settlement agreement with the third defendant, that agreement was not protected by without prejudice privilege or litigation privilege and had to be produced unredacted for the inspection of the other defendants, notwithstanding it had incorporated details of the claimant's communications with the third defendant prior to the settlement being reached.

The Court of Appeal held that in considering whether the privilege applied, the issue was the purpose of the relevant communication. In the particular case, the relevant communication was the settlement agreement. The purpose of that communication was not to negotiate, it was to conclude a settlement

---

[307] *Willers v Joyce and Nugent Executors of Albert Gubay (Deceased) v De Cruz Solicitors* [2019] EWHC 937 (Ch); [2019] Costs L.R. 781, Andrew J.
[308] *Sternberg Reed Solicitors v Harrison* [2019] EWHC 2065 (Ch); [2020] Ch. 223; [2020] 2 W.L.R. 176; [2020] 1 All E.R. (Comm) 681; [2019] Costs L.R. 1489, HHJ Hodge QC.

of the dispute between the claimant and the third defendant on the terms set out in the settlement agreement. It was therefore not covered by without prejudice privilege.

For litigation privilege to apply, the relevant communication had to have been made for the sole or dominant purpose of conducting adversarial litigation in progress or in contemplation.[309] On the face of the settlement agreement, the antecedent communications were incorporated into the agreement by the claimant so as to obtain the benefit of the third defendant's representations and warranties that he had disclosed a full and frank account of all the confidential information he had supplied to the second defendant. Therefore, the claimant would be able to sue the third defendant if those representations and warranties were inaccurate. Accordingly, the antecedent communications were incorporated to "police" the settlement agreement, which was a different purpose to the purpose of evidence-gathering that had informed the making of the antecedent communications. It followed that the dominant purpose condition was not satisfied, and litigation privilege did not apply.[310]

Q72. Is a simple consent order or judgment for the payment of money registrable in the Register of Judgments, Orders and Fines?
The website of the Registry of Judgments, Orders and Fines (*https://rojof.org.uk/*) explains: 5–124

> *"Registry Trust Limited is a not for profit company which operates the Registry of Judgments, Orders and Fines for England and Wales on behalf of the Ministry of Justice. All the information on the register is public information and anybody may have access.*
> *The register is divided into four sections:*
> *—Section one includes county court money judgments, administration orders and some child support liability orders*
> *—Section two includes High Court money Judgments after 6th April, 2006*
> *—Section three includes Fines registered by Local Justice Areas after 6th April, 2006*
> *—Section four includes enforced Tribunal Awards after 1st April, 2009."*

In the case of a judgment there would appear to be no difficulty; a consent order may however need some consideration. If the consent order is a Tomlin order, then the provision for payment of money will be in the schedule. As such, there is no judgment or order for payment of those monies. It is therefore not a judgment debt and will not be registered as such.

If, however, instead of a Tomlin the parties agree a consent order for payment of a judgment sum (i.e. in effect submit to the court making an order in those terms) then it is a judgment order and a judgment debt and will be registered.

---

[309] See: *Three Rivers DC v Bank of England* [2004] UKHL 48; [2005] 1 A.C. 610.
[310] *BGC Brokers LP v Tradition (UK) Ltd* [2019] EWCA Civ 1937.

Practical Law have issued a note on the issue which may be helpful at: *https://uk.practicallaw.thomsonreuters.com/a-024-9097?transitionType=Default&c ontextData=(sc.Default)&firstPage=true&bhcp=1.*

Q73. In respect of CPR r.44.14(1) relating to QOCS, can an order for costs be made up to the extent of any damages when a Calderbank offer has been made, or does this Rule only apply when a Part 36 offer has been made (i.e. this Rule does not apply to Calderbank offers)?

5–125 For a discussion of this question, see Ch.6 para.6–35.

Q74. I'm the claimant in a claim to which QOCS applies and in which the defendant has recently made a generous Part 36 offer. If I don't accept the offer and, at trial, my claim fails completely—will I have to pay the defendant's costs?

5–126 For a discussion of this question, see Ch.6 para.6–36.

S. ADR and Mediation

Q75. Does anyone/any kind of company (for example) have to use ADR because the law says so? If so we would be grateful if you would direct us to that law or illuminate what kind of people MUST use ADR. Do I have to mediate? Does a "mediation first" clause in a framework agreement with a supplier prevent our client from issuing court proceedings for injunctive relief requiring the supplier to urgently release their equipment etc?

5–127 In short: Yes. The Alternative Dispute Resolution for Consumer Disputes (Competent Authorities and Information) Regulations 2015 (SI 2015/542)[311] as amended implements the provisions of Directive 2013/11/EU of the European Parliament and of the Council of 21 May 2013 on alternative dispute resolution for consumer disputes. Regulation 2(3) of the amending regulations substitutes a new coming into force date for Pts 4 and 5, the effect of which is to postpone the commencement of the trader information requirements until 1 October 2015.

"Consumer" and "trader"

"Consumer" means an individual acting for purposes which are wholly or mainly outside that individual's trade, business, craft or profession.

"Trader" means a person acting for purposes relating to that person's trade, business, craft or profession, whether acting personally or through another person acting in the trader's name or on the trader's behalf.[312]

This includes those providing legal services.

---

[311] Note that the Legislation UK website states "Exit from the EU: There may be changes and effects to this Legislation not yet recorded or applied to the text".

[312] Alternative Dispute Resolution for Consumer Disputes (Competent Authorities and Information) Regulations 2015 (SI 2015/542) reg.3.

Schedule 1 lists the Competent Authorities: the Financial Conduct Authority; the Financial Ombudsman Service; the Legal Services Board; and the Office for Legal Complaints. Others may be added from time to time.

The Regulations provide:

"Consumer information by traders

19.—(1) Where, under an enactment, rules of a trade association, or term of a contract, a trader is obliged to use an alternative dispute resolution procedure provided by an ADR entity or EU listed body the trader must provide the name and website address of the ADR entity or EU listed body—

  (a) on the trader's website, if the trader has a website; and

  (b) in the general terms and conditions of sales contracts or service contracts of the trader, where such general terms and conditions exist.

(2) Where a trader has exhausted its internal complaint handling procedure when considering a complaint from a consumer relating to a sales contract or a service contract, the trader must inform the consumer, on a durable medium

  (a) that the trader cannot settle the complaint with the consumer;

  (b) of the name and website address of an ADR entity or EU listed body that would be competent to deal with the complaint; and

  (c) whether the trader is obliged, or pre-pared, to submit to an alternative dispute resolution procedure operated by an ADR entity or EU listed body.

(3) The trader information requirements set out in paragraphs (1) and (2) apply in addition to any information requirements applicable to traders regarding out-of-court redress procedures contained in any other enactment.

Consumer information by online traders and online marketplaces regarding the ODR platform

19A.—(1) Where under an enactment, rules of a trade association, or term of a contract, an online trader is obliged to use an alternative dispute resolution procedure provided by an ADR entity or EU listed body, the trader must—

  (a) provide a link to the ODR platform in any offer made to a consumer by email; and

  (b) inform consumers of—

    (i) the existence of the ODR platform; and

    (ii) the possibility of using the ODR platform for resolving disputes.

(2) The information in (1)(b) must also be included in the general terms and conditions of online sales contracts and online service contracts of the trader, where such general terms and conditions exist.

(3) An online trader must on its website—

    (i) provide a link to the ODR plat-form; and

    (ii) state the online trader's email address.

(4) An online marketplace must provide a link to the ODR platform on its website.

(5) The online trader requirements set out in paragraphs (1) to (3) apply in addition to the trader information requirements set out in regulation 19.

(6) The online trader and online marketplace requirements in paragraphs (1) to (4) apply in addition to any information requirements regarding out-of-court redress procedures contained in any other enactment.

(7) In this regulation—

'online marketplace' has the meaning given in Article 4(f) of the Regulation (EU) No 524/2013 of the European Parliament and of the Council of 21 May 2013 on online dispute resolution for consumer disputes and amending Regulation (EC) No 2006/2004 and Directive 2009/22/EC;

'online sales contract' means a sales contract where the trader, or the trader's intermediary, has offered goods on a website or by other electronic means and the consumer has ordered such goods on that website or by other electronic means;

'online service contract' means a service contract where the trader, or the trader's intermediary, has offered services on a website or by other electronic means and the consumer has ordered such services on that website or by other electronic means;

'online trader' means a trader who intends to enter into online sales con-tracts or online service contracts with consumers."

A "Mediation First" clause in a valid contract is enforceable, but there may be circumstances, e.g. in the case of perishable goods, when an application to the court would be successful in order to preserve the goods, the subject of the contract.

Q76. Are there any limitation issues to consider if a stay is ordered by the court for ADR to be considered?

5–128   The court has power under CPR r.3.1(2)(f) to stay the whole or part of any pro-ceedings or judgment either generally or until a specified date or event. "The making of a stay imposes a halt upon proceedings and also halts the expi-ration of any time limit in those proceedings which had not expired when the stay was imposed".[313] The imposition of a stay presupposes that the pro-ceedings have already been commenced within the limitation period. *Phillips v Symes*[314] below is an example of the court imposing a further limit in an attempt to focus the parties' minds on negotiating an appropriate settlement.

In *Phillips v Symes*, the court ordered a stay on terms where there was a long-standing dispute and there had been numerous hearings before the court and at least 60 applications during the course of the litigation. Peter Smith J stated:

"48. I did not think it appropriate that the court should be left holding this unfin-ished litigation indefinitely for one or other of the parties to pick it up in an uncer-tain date in the future when it suited them. The time has come in my view for the court to impose deadlines for the bringing of claims".

The court ordered the proceedings to be stayed for two years and that if no application were made to commence any proceedings in respect of any of the

---

[313] The *White Book* 2019 para.3.1.8.
[314] *Phillips v Symes (Stay Order)* [2006] EWHC 1721 (Ch) Peter Smith J.

subject matter in the particular partnership action, they should be debarred from bringing any further claims.

There is nothing to prevent a party applying for a stay to enable negotiations to take place. See also **para.5.41** and following above.

Q77. If there is an expert determination clause in a contract, can a party still make an application for pre-action disclosure?
CPR r.31.16 deals with disclosure before proceedings start. CPR r.31.16(3) explains: 5–129

> "(d) disclosure before proceedings have started is desirable in order to—
> (i)   dispose fairly of the anticipated proceedings;
> (ii)   assist the dispute to be resolved without proceedings; or
> (iii) save costs."

Such an application is necessarily made before proceedings have commenced, it therefore depends on the wording of the contract whether such an application is excluded by the requirement for expert determination.

T. Mediation and unreasonable refusal

Q78. Can you give examples when it is reasonable to refuse to mediate? Are parties using the court's sanctioning of parties for unreasonable refusal to mediate tactically particularly in detailed assessments? To avoid such costs orders and keep the idea and costs of mediation sensible, is it sensible to agree to mediate but make it clear that both sides should bear their own costs. What is the latest position on costs consequences for failure to use ADR? We act for a proposed defendant. The court fee alone and preparation of the particulars of claim are likely to be expensive. Given there are no limitation issues and the parties are almost certain to agree to mediation after commencement of proceedings in any event, can we insist on mediation prior to commencement of proceedings? It seems slightly absurd that a claimant can ignore an invitation to mediation before commencement of proceedings (which will consequently only have the effect of increasing the defendant's costs) and then agree at a later date. Who pays for the mediation? What do I need to do in relation to mediation to protect my position on costs?
This topic is discussed at para.5–41 above. It is normal in a mediation for the   5–130
parties to agree to split the cost of the mediator's fee, room hire, etc. and for each side to bear its own costs.

Some additional cases are set out below.

Following the decision in *PGF II SA v OMFS Co 1 Ltd*[315] the Court of Appeal decided that a failure to engage in mediation, even if unreasonable, did not

---

[315] *PGF II SA v OMFS Co 1 Ltd* [2013] EWCA Civ 1288; [2014] 1 W.L.R. 1386; [2014] 1 W.L.R. 1386; [2014] 1 All E.R. 970; [2014] C.P. Rep. 6; [2014] B.L.R. 1; 152 Con. L.R. 72; [2013] 6 Costs L.R. 973.

automatically result in a costs penalty. The judge at first instance had concluded that it was not unreasonable for the claimant to have declined to mediate. His solicitor had considered that mediation had no realistic prospect of success and would only add to the costs. The case also raised quite complex questions of law which made it unsuitable for mediation.[316]

A party should not be able to obtain a tactical or costs advantage where, in substance, the principles of a pre-action protocol had been complied with. In a case where the claimant had sent a letter of claim under the protocol containing a clear summary of the facts setting out the basis on which the claim was made and identifying the principal contractual terms and statutory provisions relied on and the nature of the relief sought, the defendant was held to be well aware, before the proceedings were commenced, what the nature of the claim was against it. The defendant had been given every opportunity to attend meetings, to discuss matters and to settle the dispute. When the claimant, who had been seeking a contribution from the defendant in respect of other proceedings, settled those proceedings, the defendant had sought an order for costs against the claimant on the basis that the pre-action protocol had not been fully complied with.[317]

Where a claimant sued a main contractor in respect of goods sold to a subcontractor, subject to a retention of title clause, the claimant offered to submit to mediation which was rejected. The claim was for £70,000, the defendant made a Pt 36 payment of £6,000 and judgment was ultimately given for £387. The defendant sought an order for costs on the indemnity basis and the claimant argued there should be no order for costs for the period during which the defendant had failed to provide the claimant with information on its payments to the sub-contractor and because of the refusal to mediate. The court held that the defendant's rejection of mediation was unreasonable, as there would have been reasonable prospects of resolving the matter, at least until the Pt 36 payment. The court held that the defendant's conduct deprived the parties of the opportunity to resolve the case at minimal cost. The claimant was granted its costs up to a particular date and the defendant its costs thereafter.[318]

Although the fact that the court could not order disclosure of without prejudice negotiations against the wishes of one of the parties, could mean that the court would not be able to decide whether a party had been unreasonable in refusing mediation, it was always open to a party to make open or Calderbank offers of ADR, and the other party could respond to such offers either openly or in Calderbank form. If a party gave a good reason why it thought ADR would not serve a useful purpose, that was one thing, if it failed to do so, that was a matter which the court might consider relevant although not conclusive in exercising its discretion as to costs. The reasonableness or

---

[316] *Gore v Naheed* [2017] EWCA Civ 369; [2017] 3 Costs L.R. 509.
[317] *TJ Brent Ltd v Black & Veatch Consulting Ltd* [2008] EWHC 1497 (TCC); 119 Con. L.R. 1 Akenhead J.
[318] *P4 Ltd v Unite Integrated Solutions Plc* [2006] EWHC 2924 (TCC) [2007] B.L.R.1 Ramsey J.

otherwise of going to ADR could be fairly and squarely debated between the parties, and under the Calderbank procedure, made available to the court when the question of costs came to be considered.[319]

The serving of a winding up petition in respect of a debt which was genuinely disputed on substantial grounds, amounted to an abuse of process, which would normally result in the petition being struck out with costs on the indemnity basis. In the particular case, however, there had been unreasonable behaviour on both sides. The company applying for the strike out had refused mediation in respect of the underlying dispute and in respect of the costs of the petition. The applicant company was awarded its costs until the point at which its own behaviour became unreasonable. Thereafter, there would be no order for costs.[320]

In a clinical negligence case, the defendant health trust's conduct of the litigation was held to be out of the norm. It had made various offers to settle, but ultimately the claimant made a Part 36 offer to accept 95% of the full value of her claim. This offer was rejected two days before the expiration of the relevant period. The defendant did not respond to invitations to alternative dispute resolution. Its witness statements, expert's reports and joint statements were served late. The claimant had to apply to the court to order the defendant to comply with certain case management directions. The Part 36 offer had not lapsed and was not withdrawn. The defendant accepted it over 12 months after the offer had been made. The costs payable by the defendant from the end of the relevant period until the date of acceptance were ordered to be paid on the indemnity basis.[321]

Q79. Where a claim is stayed for mediation, and following the mediation, a claimant's Part 36 offer is made and accepted, will the claimant be entitled to their costs of the mediation (in other words, will they be treated as costs of the "proceedings")?

See Q77 above. This depends on the mediation agreement. If a party making a Calderbank offer wishes to depart from the costs terms of the mediation agreement, that would need to be made clear. It is hard to see that a Part 36 offer could do this.

Q80. When we suggest mediation on behalf of clients we are often met with a variety of reasons why there should be no mediation. Have you any suggestions?

Parties may be reluctant to mediate for various reasons. The following are some common misconceptions and ideas to address them:[322]

> Mediating is a sign of weakness. Mediation is, in fact, usually a sign of

5–131

---

[319] *Reed Executive Plc v Reed Business Information Ltd (Costs: Alternative Dispute Resolution)* [2004] EWCA Civ 887; [2004] 1 W.L.R. 3026; [2004] 4 All E.R. 942; [2005] C.P. Rep. 4; [2004] 4 Costs L.R. 662.
[320] *Lakehouse Contracts Ltd v UPR Services Ltd* [2014] EWHC 1223 (Ch) Henderson J.
[321] *Holmes v West London Mental Health Trust* [2018] 4 Costs L.R. 763 HHJ Gore QC.
[322] With acknowledgements to Thomson Reuters Practical Law.

strength; the strength of knowing what the lawyer and the client want to achieve, and pursuing that objective through a negotiated outcome. The key to negotiating from a position of strength is the ability to identify what the client and the opponent really need to achieve. The CPR including the Pre-Action Protocols and the Practice Direction—Pre-Action Conduct require parties to consider mediation before commencing proceedings. Failure to comply with this can lead to costs sanctions. Referring to this may help to focus the parties' minds.

In *Jane Laporte v Commissioner of Police of the Metropolis*,[323] a police commissioner was found to have failed, without adequate justification, to have engaged in the alternative dispute resolution process, despite successfully defending the proceedings and, after taking into account the factors listed in *Halsey*, that was to be reflected in the costs order made.

Lawyers and clients can negotiate directly so mediation is unnecessary. There can be barriers to effective communication when negotiations are direct (between lawyers or between clients). The intervention of a neutral third party can change the dynamics and help to overcome these barriers. The mediator can use several techniques to manage the negotiating process, free up communications, encourage a problem-solving approach or brainstorming of options, and overcome deadlock. Parties tend to be unwilling to disclose information about their view of the case to an opposing party during direct negotiations.

Direct negotiations have failed so mediation will not succeed. Direct negotiations may become positional, with each party assuming entrenched and unrealistic positions and becoming increasingly defensive. A mediator can focus each party on a problem-solving approach, directing energy away from threats, attacks, or challenges to the credibility or good faith of a party in the dispute, towards a focus on the issues to be resolved and the potential implications of a failure to settle the problem.

The mediator is just a messenger. A mediator's task is considerably more sophisticated. It includes coaching, developing strategies and reality testing. The mediator is an active participant in the mediation process, and will use a range of techniques to engage people in the process and encourage them to consider a range of settlement options.

You cannot mediate until full disclosure is provided. Lawyers especially tend to argue that early mediation, before the disclosure process has been completed, is not appropriate. In practice, mediation simply requires knowledge of enough information (about the facts and the relevant law) for the lawyer to be able to advise the client on:

- the strengths and weaknesses of the case;
- the alternatives to settlement; and
- any options for settlement of the dispute.

---

[323] *Laporte v Commissioner of Police of the Metropolis* [2015] EWHC 371 (QB); [2015] 3 Costs L.R. 471 Turner J.

The earlier that mediation takes place and an agreement is reached, the lower the costs will be.

Mediation will be a waste of time and money if the case does not settle at mediation. Even a failed mediation can help to narrow the issues and increase the likelihood that the case will settle without the need for trial. The parties will certainly have a better understanding of each other's positions and perspectives, and the potential barriers to settlement. A failed mediation can also generate options and opportunities that can be discussed after the mediation. In practice, a large proportion of cases that do not settle during a mediation settle shortly afterwards.

Mediation only delays the progress of litigation. Agreeing to attempt mediation does not stop court proceedings unless the parties agree and the court stays the proceedings. Awareness of the implications of failing to reach settlement during the mediation (for example, in terms of the costs and management time that would be incurred going to trial) can help to focus the parties' minds, and encourage them to engage positively in the mediation process.

The courts are alive to the fact that parties may agree to mediation without any intention of trying to reach a settlement, but merely to avoid being criticised and suffering a costs sanction later in the proceedings.

Q81. There must be drawbacks to mediation—what are they?
There are possible drawbacks to mediation. A successful conclusion may   5–132
depend, to a certain extent, on the abilities of the mediator. Costs may be increased if the mediation fails. The mediator may need to handle the parties with some skill and firmness if a party tries to misuse the process, for example to obtain an unjustified offer in a weak case. Mediation may simply not work if the parties are deeply antagonistic. One can reach a point where each side complains that the other is "not engaging". Sometimes this is true and it becomes clear that one or possibly both parties have come to the mediation with the view that they are willing to negotiate provided that the other side will agree to everything they seek. Trying to get it through to them that a successful settlement may involve some pain on both sides is sometimes very difficult. The process may be more difficult where one or both parties are not represented or not fully advised in advance. Some mediators say that the presence of lawyers can prevent settlement, because the lawyers are programmed to litigate not to compromise. The situation is even worse when the parties are lawyers arguing about their own costs. There are no winners or losers in mediation and it can be difficult to get this altered mind-set across to the parties and their lawyers.

Q82. We act for a claimant in a consumer dispute. Our client is funded by a legal expenses insurance policy. We have yet to issue proceedings. Mediation is now proposed and we are hoping to mediate in the near future. The defendant has confirmed they are part of an Ombudsman scheme and suggested that the claimant refer to the Ombudsman. We

do not consider the dispute is appropriate for the Ombudsman. The only arbiter capable of deciding this is a judge. However, the client's legal expense insurer may require us to use the Ombudsman. My question is whether the Ombudsman service is deemed to be "ADR" and whether refusal to refer to the Ombudsman may be criticised by the court?

5–133   An Ombudsman scheme is a form of ADR i.e. it is an alternative to court proceedings. See *TUI UK Ltd v Tickell* and *Briggs v First Choice Holidays and Flights Ltd* at para.5–42 above. Where legal expenses insurers require a policyholder to use an ADR scheme, this could well affect the level of cover if the policyholder refuses to do as the insurer requests.

An investor complained to the Financial Ombudsman Service about the way an investment had been administered. The complaint was upheld and the administrators, a company, applied to the court for permission to appeal against the Ombudsman's decision under s.69 of the Arbitration Act 1996. The investor was the respondent to the application and the Financial Ombudsman Service intervened. The application was refused since the Ombudsman's decision was not the result of an arbitration agreement and was not an arbitration award. Both the respondent and the Financial Ombudsman Service sought their costs. The court held that before an unsuccessful party was ordered to pay costs to two parties, there had to be some good reason or circumstances justifying making such an order. The court held that this was not a case where the FOS needed to be represented in order for the appropriate arguments to be put before the court. The FOS's interest was not of sufficient force to make it appropriate to order the applicant to pay not only the respondent's costs but also the FOS's costs. The FOS was a public body. It had incurred costs in establishing the position in its general interest and there was no prejudice if an order for payment of its costs was not made.[324]

Q83. We are considering making a pre-action disclosure application for specific documents that would assist in resolving a contractual dispute. All voluntary requests have been met with silence, as have our requests for a mediation. The contract has a dispute resolution clause that requires the parties to use mediation in the event of a dispute, and failing that, expert determination. We are aware that pre-action disclosure will be refused by the court where the parties have agreed/are contractually required, to use arbitration in the event of a dispute on the basis that court proceedings are not anticipated. Firstly, would the same apply where expert determination is required? Secondly, would the same apply where mediation is required in circumstances where our multiple requests have been met with silence?

5–134   Dealing with the second question first—silence in response to a request for mediation. The Court of Appeal has held that it would be perverse not to

---

[324] *Berkeley Burke Sipp Administration LLP (Applicant) v Charlton* [2017] EWHC 2396 (Comm); [2018] 1 Lloyd's Rep. 337 Teare J.

regard silence in the face of repeated requests for mediation as anything other than a refusal.[325] See **Q74** and **para.5–40** above.

Where the contract between the parties envisages the use of expert determination in the event of mediation failing, it would seem that the court would be unlikely to interfere with the terms of the contract since the parties have agreed to use expert determination rather than making an application to the court.

Q84. I am acting for a party where we are agreed in principle to mediate. My client is a couple who are both legal and beneficial owners of the property which is the subject of the dispute. The other party is an individual who advances a beneficial interest in the property. The other party intends to bring his three (adult) children to the mediation. None of the children are parties to the dispute nor have any standing in it, save that they might give witness evidence if court proceedings follow. Is there any guidance available about whether it might be reasonable to insist that just the parties to the dispute attend, bearing in mind matters such as confidentiality? Might it be considered that, since the children might end up being witnesses in any subsequent litigation, it is reasonable for them all to attend?

The point about mediation is that it is controlled by the parties and it is up to 5–135
them what they put into the mediation agreement. Sir Rupert Jackson deals with mediation at some length in Chs 13 and 14 of *The Jackson ADR Handbook*. If there is a principled objection to extraneous people attending the mediation, they can, by agreement, be excluded. Such people may, however, help to bring about a settlement. If, on the other hand, your opponent thinks there is strength in numbers, it should be pointed out that this is not an adversarial situation and there will be no winner or loser at the end of it.

Q85. If particulars of claim were served on a without prejudice basis for the purpose of a mediation, is the other side allowed to refer to it in order to defend an application, e.g. for pre-action disclosure? A settlement in principle was agreed during a negotiation, although mediation continued in correspondence in order for the defendant to establish funding of the settlement sum agreed, during which time the claimant continued to incur costs. The defendant subsequently withdrew the settlement offer and stated he no longer wished to continue with the mediation process. Is there anything the claimant can do—for example, is there any scope for waiver of without prejudice privilege on the basis of delay and/or perjury, blackmail or other unambiguous impropriety and/or breach of contract and/or interim wasted costs to be sought?

---

[325] *PGF II SA v OMFS Co 1 Ltd* [2013] EWCA Civ 1288; [2014] 1 W.L.R. 1386 [2014] 1 W.L.R. 1386; [2014] 1 All E.R. 970; [2014] C.P. Rep. 6; [2014] B.L.R. 1; 152 Con. L.R. 72; [2013] 6 Costs L.R. 973.

5–136   A mediation is confidential and remains so after it has taken place. In addition to that the particulars of claim were served on a without prejudice basis. Attempting to refer to the particulars on an application for pre-action disclosure would clearly prejudice the other side. It may well be that when proceedings are issued the particulars will look very different to those disclosed during the mediation.

With regard to the second question it appears that the settlement in principle was never put into an enforceable agreement. In effect the mediation was unsuccessful. The whole process is confidential and it is not possible to apply for a waiver of without prejudice correspondence. There is no contract, therefore there can be no breach. Issues of perjury, blackmail and the like are criminal in nature and it is difficult to see how they could be raised in a civil court given the confidentiality of the mediation process.

Q86. If a settlement offer is made at a mediation but is not accepted, is it automatically withdrawn when the mediation comes to an end (in the absence of an express agreement to keep it open)?
Absent an express agreement, the offer lapses when the mediation ends.

U. Options when all issues resolved except costs

Q87. Can you please advise on the available options where the parties to an ongoing case have essentially agreed on every issue other than costs. It is at an early stage (just post-CCMC). Both sides are saying that the other should pay their costs. Both parties are alleging that the other's conduct has been in breach of the pre-action protocol. Because of the circumstances it is uncertain which party (if any) will be deemed to have "won" the case. What are the options available to the parties? It doesn't seem correct that the main case should proceed as everything other than costs is essentially agreed. I believe that costs only proceedings are not available where it is not decided as to who is paying who's costs. So, for example, could the parties make an application to end the current proceedings and just deal with costs, or go straight to assessment?

5–137   Where proceedings are already in existence, costs only proceedings are not available. Where the parties have agreed the substantive issues between them, there appears to be no reason why an application should not be made to the court to decide the one remaining issue namely which party should be liable for the costs. The decision in *M v Croydon*[326] is authority for stating that there would be cases where the link between the claim and the agreed relief was so clear that the claimant could properly be treated as the successful party for the purpose of an award of costs. However the claim had to be causative of the relief claimed. It is not possible to go straight to assessment since there is

---

[326] *M v Croydon LBC* [2012] EWCA Civ 595; [2012] 1 W.L.R. 2607.

no authority to assess i.e. there is no judgment or order under which the costs can be assessed. The question asks what the options available to the parties are and these, of course, include mediation and expert evaluation. The prospects for a successful mediation seem good given that the parties have managed to agree all the other issues.

Q88. We have a matter in which our client has successfully sued for professional negligence. The opponent made a Part 36 offer which was accepted and the damages settled. The issue remaining is our costs. The Part 36 offer included an offer to pay reasonable expenses. Having assessed our costs schedule the opponent has made a Part 36 offer significantly less than our costs. How does one challenge the offer made by the opponent for costs? This is a matter in which we do not want this to go to court for a detailed assessment but would certainly want a better offer than is currently being made.

It is not possible to "challenge the offer made by the opponent" since it is entirely up to the opponent what offer they are prepared to make. The options include a counter-offer and one would normally allow the matter to proceed to detailed assessment where the costs judge would deal with the costs of the assessment as well as the assessment itself. Given that the questioner does not wish to go for a detailed assessment, expert evaluation and/or mediation are the obvious answers.

5–138

Q89. Are you aware of any cases where a refusal to mediate a small claims track claim has resulted in the court making an adverse costs award against the refusing party? It is settled that refusal to accept an offer which is not beaten at trial is not "unreasonable behaviour" for the purposes of CPR Pt 27 and will not lead to adverse costs consequences, but it is unclear what effect, if any, refusal to mediate might have on the usual "no costs" rule.

There do not appear to be any reported cases on this point. The reason for this may well be that the small claims track was originally intended to be lawyer free and to have a (virtually) no costs regime. If all parties indicate on their directions questionnaire that they agree to mediation, the claim will be referred to the Small Claims Mediation Service. It is a moot point whether refusal to accept mediation would follow the decision in *Dammermann v Lanyon Bowdler LLP*[327]: for the purposes of deciding whether an appellant had behaved unreasonably within CPR r.27.14(2)(g) in pursuing an appeal in a small claims track case, the test was whether the conduct permitted of a reasonable explanation. If so, the course adopted might be regarded as optimistic and as reflecting on the judgment of the appellant and/or his legal advisers, if it led to an unsuccessful result, but it was not unreasonable.

5–139

---

[327] *Dammermann v Lanyon Bowdler LLP* [2017] EWCA Civ 269; [2017] C.P. Rep. 25; [2017] 2 Costs L.R. 393.

Q90. Are you permitted to recover costs under the CPR which were incurred during a temporary stay of proceedings, for example the costs of an unsuccessful mediation, at the end of proceedings?

5–140   The answer to this question depends upon the terms of the mediation agreement. The starting point is that each party is liable to pay its own costs and expenses in relation to an ADR process. There is no loser pays rule in relation to mediation. If the mediation fails and the matter is decided by the court, the court will exercise its discretion under CPR r.44.2 but will be bound by any contractual agreement between the parties relating to the costs and expenses of mediation. The other aspect of the question is whether one is permitted to recover costs incurred during a temporary stay of proceedings. Each case will be fact sensitive but the fact that proceedings have been stayed carries with it the expectation that no work will be done during the period of the stay, which may be e.g. to await a final prognosis in a personal injury case.

Q91. We recently acted for the respondent in a hearing in the Mercantile Court. At the end of the hearing the judge ordered the parties to agree costs, failing that to file written submissions on costs for a summary assessment. The parties have exchanged offers marked "without prejudice save as to costs" but failed to reach agreement. It is precisely the costs that we are now dealing with. Are we permitted to mention these offers in our written submissions on costs?

5–141   The words without prejudice save as to costs indicate that the offers contained within the correspondence are not to be disclosed to the court until the question of the costs themselves arises. In this case, the court has decided the substantive matter and has (presumably) ordered one party to pay the other's costs. When the written submissions are put before the court, the judge will need to know the amount sought by the receiving party and the amount offered by the paying party and the underlying reasons. It is clearly relevant to that decision for the judge to know what offers each side has made. If, however, the offers are Part 36 offers different considerations apply. See para.**5–14**.

Q92. The claimant sued for professional costs above the small claims limit. Judgment was entered in default of acknowledgment. The claimant then served a Part 36 offer for less than the default judgment. Would the correct procedure to recover the Pt 36 costs be to issue an application on notice for the additional sum claimable under Pt 36?

5–142   It is not at all clear why the claimant, having obtained judgment, then decided to make a Part 36 offer for less than the judgment. Surely the appropriate procedure would be to take steps to enforce the judgment. It is not clear whether the defendant has accepted the Part 36 offer but if so, the appropriate procedure would be to take steps to enforce the accepted offer. Another answer is that if this was a fixed sum claim, then CPR r.45 Section

I applies and there are fixed commencement and entry of judgment costs anyway.

Q93. Are failed "without prejudice" settlement discussions protected when the dispute then moves to mediation and the rules governing that mediation process explicitly expect previous settlement discussions and proposals to be disclosed to the mediator?
All mediations are confidential. The mediator will talk to each party separately and anything said to the mediator will be confidential, save to the extent that the party authorizes the mediator to pass information or an offer/counter offer to the other side. In the case in point, the questioner may prefer not to mention the without prejudice discussions to the mediator, but the opposing side may well do so. The mediator would not say that s/he was aware of the discussions. There seems little point in not putting the mediator fully in the picture. One may protect the without prejudice discussions as between oneself and the mediator; but you have no control over what the opponents may say.

V. Assessing costs in arbitration

Q94. What is the proper approach to assessing costs in an arbitration?
The form of words used in s.61 of the 1996 Act is derived from the rules of the Supreme Court which were in force between 1986 and 1998. RSC Ord.62 r.3(3) states:

> *"If the Court in the exercise of its discretion sees fit to make any order as to the costs of any proceedings, the Court shall order costs to follow the event, except where it appears to the Court that in the circumstances of the case some other order should be made as to the whole or any part of the costs."*

Section 63(5) of the Act states that the successful party shall be allowed a reasonable amount in respect of all costs reasonably incurred. Again, the wording is very similar to RSC Ord.62 r.12 (in force between 1986 and 1998) which reads:

> *"(i) On the taxation of costs on the standard basis there shall be allowed a reasonable amount in respect of all costs reasonably incurred and any doubt which the taxing officer may have as to whether the costs were reasonably incurred or were reasonable in amount shall be resolved in favour of the paying party and in these rules the term 'the standard basis' in relation to the taxation of costs shall be construed accordingly."*

It is clear that the Parliamentary Draftsman was ensuring consistency between the Rules and the 1996 Act.

As to the correct approach to deciding whether costs have been reasonably incurred and are reasonable in amount, RSC Ord.62 Appendix 2 (in force between 1986 and 1998), para.1 provides:

5–143

5–144

"Amount of Costs

1.(1) The amount of costs to be allowed shall . . . be in the discretion of the taxing officer.

2. In the exercise of his discretion the taxing officer shall have regard to all the relevant circumstances, and in particular to:

   (a) the complexity of the item or of the cause or matter in which it arises and the difficulty or novelty of the questions involved;

   (b) the skill, specialised knowledge and responsibility required of, and time and labour expended by, the solicitor or counsel;

   (c) the number and importance of the documents (however brief) prepared or perused;

   (d) the place and circumstances in which the business involved is transacted;

   (e) the importance of the cause or matter to the client;

   (f) where money or property is involved its amount or value;

   (g) any other fees and allowances payable to the solicitor or counsel in respect of other items in the same cause or matter but only where work done in relation to those items has reduced the work which would otherwise have been necessary in relation to the item in question."

Under Appendix 2 to RSC Ord.62, the taxing officer is required to have regard to "all the relevant circumstances" and in particular to the seven headings set out above. Conduct of the parties should be considered as part of "the relevant circumstances", when assessing the reasonableness of costs. Reasonableness, rather than proportionality, is the proper test to apply in assessing the costs of an arbitration under the 1996 Act.

If the arbitration is not proceeding under the 1996 Act it will depend entirely on the rules of the arbitral body which has been chosen and the terms of the arbitration agreement itself.

CHAPTER 6

Qualified One-Way Costs Shifting

Introduction

The introduction of a system of one-way costs shifting (QOCS) in personal injury litigation in April 2013 was the subject of close and detailed scrutiny and debate during Sir Rupert Jackson's review. Amongst its primary attractions was that it was seen to provide a possible solution to the problem and costs of the "indefensible" regime of after-the-event insurance (ATE) in such cases,[1] particularly given that claimants were perceived as being successful in the majority of personal injury claims.

6–01

In clinical negligence claims, where the perceived success rate of claimants was lower, the relatively higher costs of ATE premiums in such cases provided a counterbalancing justification for the consideration of one-way costs shifting.

Accordingly, the firm recommendation was that a system of one-way costs shifting should be introduced in all such cases with the specific aim of reducing the costs of personal injury litigation, in particular by removing the need for ATE. One-way costs shifting was part of a package, therefore, along with the restrictions in recoverability of ATE introduced by s.46 of the Legal Aid, Sentencing and Punishment of Offenders Act 2012 (LASPO).

Sir Rupert Jackson, however, was alive to the need to deter frivolous or fraudulent claims and to encourage acceptance of reasonable offers, aims which would be undermined by wholesale protection for claimants from the risk of adverse costs orders no matter what. Accordingly, the proposed system of one-way costs shifting was to be qualified to address these requirements, hence QOCS.

To avoid undue complexity and impracticality, QOCS was to be introduced for all personal injury claims, rather than merely being restricted to low-value claims or claims run on conditional fee agreements (CFAs). In fact, the definition in CPR r.44.13(1) makes clear that QOCS applies (at least in part) not merely to a "pure" personal injury claim, but to any proceedings which include such a claim, though CPR r.44.16(2)(b) then allows an order for costs against a claimant to be enforced, with the leave of the court, where "a claim is made for the benefit of the claimant other than a claim to which this section applies". This rule resulted in considerable argument as to its precise scope and application in practice. It was the subject of some judicial consideration in 2017 and 2018—see the cases of *Jeffreys*, *Siddiqui* and *Brown* below. The issues of principle as to the construction and interpretation of the rule were then resolved in the Court of Appeal decision on the second appeal in

---

[1] Final Report, pp.184 and 188.

Brown in 2019.[2] Issues of practical application remain, but as *Brown* makes clear, these are matters for the exercise of judicial discretion on the facts of the individual case.

When introduced, the only absolute exception to QOCS in personal injury claims was for cases where a claimant had entered into a pre-commencement funding arrangement (PCFA). Further partial or conditional exceptions exist within the rules (considered below).

6–02   Sir Rupert Jackson's proposal was for a system which provided a "broadly similar degree of protection against adverse costs" to that which applied to publicly funded litigants through what was then s.11 of the Access to Justice Act 1999.[3]

The proposal involved a broad test, based on the test applicable under s.11, whereby the costs ordered against a claimant in such cases would not exceed:

". . . the amount, if any, which is a reasonable one for him to pay having regard to all the circumstances including (a) the financial resources of all parties to the proceedings; and (b) their conduct in connection with the dispute to which the proceedings relate."

The proposal would firstly have allowed the courts to address concerns in relation to frivolous and fraudulent claims. Secondly, it would have ensured that QOCS could be limited where the claimant's means were such that it would be unjust not to require the claimant to pay costs. It would also have allowed for the possibility of a "football pools" type application, whereby a defendant who was initially not permitted to enforce a costs order might, in limited circumstances, reapply to do so where the claimant's finances subsequently and substantially improved.

However, whilst Sir Rupert Jackson's general proposal for a system of qualified one-way costs shifting was adopted, his proposed resource-based test was not and a more rigid approach, which does not include any limitation by reference to the claimant's financial resources, was introduced and is considered further below.

In order to address Sir Rupert Jackson's second concern, that of incentivising claimants to make Part 36 offers despite QOCS protection, Sir Rupert Jackson proposed the 10% increase in general damages which did come into effect, in relation to cases where there was no PCFA,[4] as a result of the Court of Appeal's decisions in *Simmons v Castle*.[5]

The post-April 2013 rules
6–03   The rules are set out in CPR Pt 44 Section II and CPR PD 44 para.12.1.

---

[2] *Jeffreys v Commissioner of Police for the Metropolis* [2017] EWHC 1505 (QB); [2018] 1 W.L.R. 3633, *Siddiqui v University of Oxford* [2018] EWHC 536 (QB); [2018] 4 W.L.R. 62 and *Brown v Commissioner of Police of the Metropolis* [2018] EWHC 2046 (Admin); [2018] 4 Costs L.R. 897 and [2019] EWCA Civ 1724; [2019] Costs L.R. 1633.
[3] Now s.26 of LASPO—see Final Report, p.189.
[4] As defined in CPR r.48.2.
[5] *Simmons v Castle* [2012] EWCA Civ 1288; [2013] 1 W.L.R. 1239 (only the second and definitive judgment is cited).

The scope of the rules

The rules apply to all proceedings which include a claim for damages for per-   6–04
sonal injuries or a claim under the Fatal Accidents Act 1976 or the Law Reform
(Miscellaneous Provisions) Act 1934 (CPR r.44.13(1)). This includes claims
arising out of clinical negligence (see the broad definition of "claim for personal injuries" in CPR r.2.3). Pre-action disclosure applications are specifically
excluded (CPR r.44.13(1)) and it is open to argument whether other pre-action
applications are similarly excluded (see further the discussion in relation to
the case of *Waterfield*[6] below).

Although there will often be little doubt as to whether a claim includes a
claim for damages for personal injuries, there will be the occasional situation
where the issue is open to argument. The point arose in *Howe v Motor Insurer's
Bureau*[7] in relation to claims under the untraced drivers scheme. After very
careful consideration, Mr Justice Stewart concluded that such a claim— a rare
event since the untraced drivers agreement contains its own internal resolution procedure—was not a claim for damages for personal injury because the
claim was made under express secondary legislation and independently of
any need to establish a civil wrong. The need to establish such a wrong was
an essential part of a civil claim and absent the same, the claim fell outside
the definition of a "claim for damages" and therefore QOCS. However, the
Court of Appeal disagreed.[8] Whilst concluding that treating "damages" in
CPR r.44.13 as including compensation payable under the regulations was a
departure from the strict and literal meaning of the words, it was more consistent with the policy objective of the introduction of QOCS to treat them as
the same. The claimant was, therefore, entitled to QOCS protection. Whilst
the main *Howe* decision was undoubtedly important both to the individual
claimant and to other claimants bringing claims under the scheme, the real
import in *Howe* lay in two different points.

The first was the emphasis placed on the need to satisfy the perceived
policy objectives of protecting what, in loose terms, could be described as
"personal injury claimants", even if this meant doing a degree of generous
interpretation of the strict wording of the rules. The QOCS rules have required
the courts to adopt a similar purposive approach to their construction on a
number of occasions.

The second point of significance lay in the second judgment in *Howe*,
dealing with the consequential decisions concerning the costs of the appeal
and the first instance proceedings. It was this decision which dealt with the
issue of set-off, a point of far wider implication for the operation of the QOCS
rules in all cases. This remained a contentious point until resolved by the
Supreme Court in a different case in 2021 (and may yet be addressed further
by the Civil Procedure Rule Committee (CPRC)).

---

[6] *Waterfield v Dentality Ltd* [2020] 11 WLUK 223 (unreported elsewhere).
[7] *Howe v Motor Insurer's Bureau* [2016] EWHC 884 (QB); [2016] 1 W.L.R. 2751.
[8] *Howe v Motor Insurer's Bureau* [2017] EWCA Civ 932; [2018] 1 W.L.R. 923.

QOCS does not apply to proceedings "ancillary" to personal injury claims—that is to say claims such as Civil Liability (Contribution) Act 1978 claims by a defendant to a personal injury action against a third party alleging that that third party was responsible for the claimant's injuries, even where such claims are brought as Pt 20 claims within the claimant's personal injury action. "Proceedings", in CPR r.44.13, is intended to refer to the claimant's claim for damages for personal injury[9], though this is probably wide enough to include proceedings – or parts of proceedings – which are an intrinsic part of the personal injury claim itself (such as proceedings, or parts of proceedings, to resolve issues of costs between claimant and defendant).[10]

There is no express exception to the application of QOCS for appeals (arising from claims within the scope of CPR r.44.13). The second edition of this book therefore boldly asserted that QOCS therefore applies to such appeals. The point was, in fact, argued in *Parker v Butler*[11] where Mr Justice Edis reached the same conclusion. That conclusion was then further supported by both the second *Howe* decision[12] and the Supreme Court's decision in *Plevin*[13] which, whilst, not strictly a decision on QOCS, made clear that the general distinction between first instance and appellate proceedings which arises in some costs contexts[14] does not apply when considering issues relating to funding arrangements arising out of the 2013 reforms. The issue was then put beyond doubt by the Court of Appeal's decision in *Wickes Building Supplies Ltd v Blair (No.2: Costs)*[15] in which the Court held that any appeal which concerned the outcome of the claim for damages for personal injuries, or the procedure by which such a claim is to be determined, was part of the "proceedings" under CPR r.44.13 and therefore within the compass of QOCS protection. This interpretation applied even where (as in that case) the court was dealing with a second appeal, the appeal was brought by the defendant to the original claim and the court had declined to exercise its discretionary powers to limit recoverable costs under CPR r.52.19. Accordingly, an appeal in a personal injury claim remains a proceeding (or part of a proceeding) which includes a claim for damages for personal injuries and QOCS applies, even though the appeal may, at the same time, be different proceedings for other purposes, such as the question of whether a first instance scheme of fixed costs automatically applies to the appeal).

An interesting potential variant on the question of what proceedings QOCS applies to arises in the context of approval hearings involving children and patients. Clearly, where such approval is sought in the context of ongoing substantive proceedings the approval is likely to be seen as part of the substantive personal injury proceedings and QOCS would apply. The same

---

[9] *Wagenaar v Weekend Travel Ltd* [2014] EWCA Civ 1105; [2015] 1 W.L.R. 1968 at [34]–[46].
[10] See, in this regard, paras 6 and 7 of *Ho v Adelekun* [2021] UKSC 43.
[11] *Parker v Butler* [2016] EWHC 1251 (QB); [2016] 3 Costs L.R. 435.
[12] *Howe v Motor Insurers' Bureau* [2017] EWCA Civ 932; [2018] 1 W.L.R. 923.
[13] *Plevin v Paragon Personal Finance Ltd* [2017] UKSC 23; [2017] 1 W.L.R. 1249.
[14] See *Hawksford Trustees Jersey Ltd v Stella Global UK Ltd* [2012] EWCA Civ 987; [2012] 1 W.L.R. 3581.
[15] *Wickes Building Supplies Ltd v Blair (No.2: Costs)* [2020] EWCA Civ 17, [2020] 1 W.L.R 1246.

would probably apply to any appeal arising out of the approval hearing (for example a costs or procedural point, an appeal on substantive issues being unlikely). More arguable may be the position where the substantive matter was concluded without the issue of proceedings. In such a situation, approval is sought pursuant to CPR r.21.10(2) and CPR r.21.10(2)(b) provides that, in that situation, *"the sole purpose of the proceedings is to obtain the approval of the court . . ."*. It appears at least arguable that, in this situation, the proceedings for approval and, in particular, any appeal from them might not therefore be a "claim for damages for personal injuries" and QOCS might not apply to them.

This would, however, appear to be entirely against the policy behind the introduction of QOCS. It may be a result of the almost impossible task of ensuring that there is no apparent conflict between each and every aspect of the CPR when the rules are amended, rather than reflecting any positive intention that applications for approval in unissued claims— intended to protect both the vulnerable claimant and the defendant—and appeals therefrom should be excluded from QOCS. Given the general approach taken by the higher courts to such matters seen in cases such as *Howe*, *Plevin* and *Budana*,[16] it may reasonably be expected that the Court of Appeal would adopt a similarly purposive approach here and would not allow any infelicitous drafting to prevent the application of QOCS in such circumstances.

Importantly, there is no restriction on the application of QOCS by reference to the date on which proceedings were brought. Although the new rules only came into effect on 1 April 2013, they apply from that date to all costs orders in all claims involving a claim for damages for personal injury (subject to one exception below), whether or not proceedings were issued prior to 1 April 2013.

This had the somewhat unheralded, but apparently intended, effect that not only did defendants who were involved in litigated personal injury claims which had been issued prior to 1 April 2013 find that the risks the claimant faced in the claim had shifted mid litigation,[17] but that even in claims which had concluded prior to 1 April 2013 and where the defendant had obtained a costs order in its favour, its ability to enforce that costs order was restricted by virtue of QOCS.

This effect was tolerably clear from the face of the rules, and any doubt was removed when this was affirmed by the Court of Appeal's in *Wagenaar*, where Vos LJ considered that the rules were clearly intended to operate "retrospectively" in this way.[18] In personal injury cases, at least, this potential unfairness to defendants is mitigated by the fact that the majority of claimants in such cases are likely to have had some form of pre-April 2013 funding arrangement and will therefore be excluded from QOCS, as explained in the following section. It was no doubt the assumption that this would be the case

---

[16] *Budana v Leeds Teaching Hospitals NHS Trust* [2017] EWCA Civ 1980; [2018] 1 W.L.R. 1965.
[17] Although from the claimant's perspective this may often have been theoretical since many such claimants in pre-April 2013 issued cases will have been insulated against adverse costs orders by virtue of ATE insurance.
[18] *Wagenaar v Weekend Travel Ltd* [2014] EWCA Civ 1105; [2015] 1 W.L.R. 1968 at [29]–[30].

in general, bar occasional exceptions, and that therefore this retrospectivity would be of little relevance in practice, that informed the drafting and obviated the need for yet further transitional arrangements.

6–05 There is therefore only a single operative transitional provision,CPR r.44.17,which provides that QOCS does not apply where the claimant has entered into a PCFA as defined in CPR r.48.2.

The definition of PCFA broadly covers CFAs (but not any other kind of retainer) or ATE policies entered into before 1 April 2013 in relation to the matter that is the subject of the proceedings in which the cost order is made.[19]

Accordingly, where a claimant has entered into either a CFA or has taken out ATE in respect of the claim before 1 April 2013, QOCS is not available at all. There may be cases where the claimant has taken out one, but not the other (for example has entered into a CFA pre-April 2013 but did not take out ATE, perhaps because none could be found before the deadline). In such cases, it may seem harsh that the claimant is denied QOCS protection when QOCS was intended, primarily, to be a quid pro quo for not taking out ATE and the claimant has not taken ATE. However, such apparent injustices in individual cases are arguably an inevitable consequence of broad-based procedural reform and once again the drafter appears to have favoured simplicity and clarity of drafting for the majority over seeking to cater for potential injustice in isolated and exceptional cases.

It appears that QOCS will be lost even where the claimant has not entered into a PCFA, but has erroneously told the defendant that they have, at least if the defendant relies on that representation. Such was the effect of HHJ Lopez's judgment in *Price v Egbert H Taylor and Co Ltd*.[20] In that case, the judge ruled that the claimant was estopped from denying that he had a pre-April 2013 CFA with success fee in place, even where the evidence appeared to be that he did not. QOCS was lost.

It is the author's understanding that the decision in *Price* was subject to appeal to the Court of Appeal, but was then disposed of without a substantive hearing and therefore without the benefit of any further guidance. The correctness of the *Price* decision—as a matter of principle—remains open to argument until such further guidance is given, though with the passage of time and the reducing relevance of the transitional arrangements it may be that this issue is never authoritatively resolved and becomes of academic interest only.

6–06 In addition to arguments such as that in *Price* there was an initial flurry of arguments concerning whether a claimant who had entered into a pre-April

---

[19] There are technical complexities to the definitions which are addressed in the section on funding arrangements. Note that the taking out of a post-31 March 2013 ATE policy does not affect the availability of QOCS, even where part of that ATE premium may remain recoverable in principle between the parties in a clinical negligence claim pursuant to the Recovery of Costs Insurance Premiums in Clinical Negligence Proceedings Regulations 2013 (SI 2013/739). Note also that by virtue of the definitions in CPR r.48.2, where the case is in one of the categories where there is a LASPO "exemption", allowing for continued between the parties recoverability of success fees and ATE premium, then QOCS will not apply. The only such category which involves claims which will also satisfy the definition of being *"personal injury claims"* is a mesothelioma claim. Accordingly, a mesothelioma claimant who funds their case by way of CFA (with a potentially recoverable success fee) or ATE policy (even if taken out after April 2013) will not have the benefit of QOCS.
[20] *Price v Egbert H Taylor and Co Ltd* unreported 16 January 2016 County Court (Birmingham).

2013 PCFA—and who would therefore not be entitled to QOCS—could later disavow that arrangement in order to make himself or herself eligible for QOCS. The reasons why this might be attractive are obvious. If the claimant, for example, had a CFA with his or her solicitors, but had been unable to obtain ATE insurance pre-April 2013, and it later became apparent that the claim would fail, then by terminating and setting aside the CFA the claimant would be able to obtain adverse costs protection. At the same time, the solicitors would be no worse off since, under the CFA, they would not have been entitled to payment anyway if the claim failed. Such an approach, however, smacked of an abuse of the QOCS provisions and in *Catalano*[21] the Court of Appeal confirmed that by virtue of having entered into a pre-LASPO CFA providing for recoverable success fees—or at the very least once services had been provided under the original CFA—the QOCS protection was lost for good and could not be revived in this way. Some of the potentially significant secondary consequences of the *Catalano* decision are discussed in **Ch.2** (Funding).

As noted, the passage of time means that there are ever fewer cases still to be resolved where the case commenced with a PCFA. As such, the transitional provisions are of diminishing relevance and importance, though may still be important in the limited number of remaining such cases, particularly since such cases are likely to be the higher value, more complex claims and more robustly contested claims with the effect that there may be a greater chance of the claim ultimately failing (and some form of costs protection being required) and the costs in such cases may be substantial.

Some issues in relation to the transitional provisions remain. One such concerns the position where the claimant commences the claim with a PCFA, but then dies after 1 April 2013. In such cases, the original CFA may well automatically end (there was a clause to this effect in the standard Law Society personal injury model up to 2014[22], though differently drafted agreements may have different provisions). The personal representatives may wish to pursue a Law Reform (Miscellaneous Provisions) Act 1934 claim, possibly together with a Fatal Accidents Act 1976 claim, and an issue may arise as to whether (i) those personal representatives should be regarded as pre-LASPO claimants, so as to be able to recover any success fee under any new CFA they enter into, even though post-LASPO and/or (ii) they should be regarded as post-LASPO Claimants, despite the original PCFA in respect of the claim, and therefore be entitled to QOCS.

Consistent with cases such as *Budana* and *Plevin*, and provided that the particular claimant whose case comes before the court is not viewed as having attempted to "play" the system, the court is likely to wish to ensure that the claimant does not fall through the gaps between the pre and post-LASPO schemes and is in one camp or the other for both the purposes of QOCS and

[21] *Catalano v Espley-Tyas Development Group Ltd* [2017] EWCA Civ 1132; [2017] C.P. Rep. 42.
[22] The Law Society model CFA was last updated in 2014 and is not currently published since it is in process of being reviewed. A revised version is due to be published "in due course" – no precise date has been given.

recovery of additional liabilities. In *Morgan v Singh*[23], that was effectively what happened. The personal representatives entered into a post-LASPO CFA. When the claim failed, they were held to be entitled to QOCS in respect of the costs of the claim, despite the deceased claimant having originally entered into a PCFA. QOCS was held to be intended to protect the particular claimant – and here the claimant, the personal representative, was a post-LASPO claimant. Whilst QOCS is directed to particular "proceedings" (see *Catalano*) and here the proceedings were the same as those started by the pre-LASPO deceased claimant, ultimately CPR r.44.14 prevents costs orders being enforced against "the claimant" unless "the claimant" has entered into a PCFA in respect of those proceedings. Here, the claimant – the personal representative – had not.

The effect of the rules

6–07 It is an important, and often misunderstood, part of the operation of QOCS that QOCS does not prevent the making of a costs order against a personal injury claimant. Any question of whether to make such an order falls to be decided on "usual" principles by reference to CPR r.44.2.

By the same token, it is a mistake for a claimant to regard QOCS as a guarantee of an award of costs in their favour in a successful case. The court's discretion under CPR r.44.2 remains entirely untrammelled and unaffected by QOCS and regardless of the impact of QOCS, a claimant may still find they are not awarded their costs, or are only awarded a percentage of those costs, where they have won if their conduct or other circumstances warrant it.

The effect of QOCS is limited to the defendant's ability to enforce against the claimant any costs order that has been made in its favour.

In practice, however, it can be anticipated that the presence of QOCS, as with the presence of adverse costs protection for publicly funded litigants, will, in certain circumstances, have an effect on the frequency with which defendants seek adverse costs orders where the option might otherwise be open to them to do so. This is particularly so given the absence of a "football pools" or "lottery win" provision allowing the defendant to return to seek enforcement of an order is an otherwise impecunious claimant's resources drastically improve and, in particular, in light of the Supreme Court's decision in *Ho*, considered below. As noted, financial resources (present or future) are (probably) immaterial to any question of the application of QOCS. If there is no reasonable prospect of being able to enforce the order, why incur further costs arguing for such an order?

Because the QOCS rules operate on enforcement of orders, where a claim comes within the scope of CPR Pt 44 Section II, any issue of the enforcement of any costs order (including interim orders) against a claimant is deferred until after the conclusion of the proceedings, including after any agreement or assessment of costs (CPR r.44.14(2)). Note, this does not mean that the assessment or agreement itself is deferred, merely the enforcement. Assessment

---

[23] Sheffield County Court, HHJ Robinson, unreported.

still takes place at the usual time and must be concluded before any issue of enforcement, and therefore whether QOCS prevents enforcement, falls to be considered. However, again in practice it is to be anticipated that in many cases parties will wish to deal with any question of whether QOCS applies and, if so, to what extent, before spending time and money on the assessment of costs that might never be payable. The reported cases suggest that, in appropriate cases, the courts do not object to dealing with issues as to the principled application of QOCS at an appropriate stage, without first requiring the assessment of the costs.

Where there are interim awards of costs, which may well take place at a time when the application of QOCS (or any exception to it) is yet to be decided, a defendant would be well advised in most cases to pursue an order for interim costs and the summary assessment of any such costs as if QOCS did not apply. To assume QOCS applies, and thereby to allow the opportunity to obtain such an order to pass, would be to risk losing an entitlement to costs which might be of benefit either (i) to set-off against any damages or interest (or possibly costs—see below) awarded to the claimant if the claim succeeds, even if QOCS applies and/or (ii) to seek against the claimant in the event QOCS is disapplied for some reason.

If such an order is obtained, a claimant might wish to consider obtaining a stay of enforcement of the order in light of the default provision that payment is due within 14 days (CPR r.44.7). However, this is probably unnecessary, since the QOCS rules themselves operate as an effective stay preventing enforcement save in the express terms set out in the rules and therefore it would be an unwise defendant that sought to enforce—by way of seeking immediate payment—an interim costs order in such circumstances unless, perhaps, it wished to do so as a way of "flushing out" any questions as to the applicability of QOCS in a given case.

Whether the wording of CPR r.44.14(2) also supports the argument that the assessment of costs is not to be regarded as separate "proceedings" within the meaning of that word for the purposes of QOCS is open to argument. On one view, detailed assessment is an ancillary part of the substantive proceedings, not a discrete proceeding in its own right. However, it could also be argued that the use of the word "and" in CPR r.44.14(2) suggests that the costs proceedings are distinct. Arguably, this would be consistent with the view taken by the Court of Appeal in *Crosbie v Munroe*[24] that Pt 8 costs proceedings are distinct proceedings from the "main proceedings", though caution must be exercised in reading across the Court's construction of one set of rules to a more recent set of rules introduced for a very different purpose. The Supreme Court's decision in *Ho* arose out of what the Supreme Court described as "an assessment dispute" and the Court in that case was not troubled by any argument that QOCS did not apply because the costs order in the defendant's

---

[24] *Crosbie v Munroe* [2003] EWCA Civ 350; [2003] 1 W.L.R. 2033.

favour was made in the assessment dispute and not in the substantive personal injury dispute.

6–08   The basic operation of the rules, where QOCS applies, may be summarised as follows:

(i) Any adverse costs order made against the claimant may be enforced in full to the extent that it does not exceed the amount of any order for damages and interest made in the claimant's favour (CPR r.44.14(1)). Emphasis should be placed on the term "order" in the later part of that sentence since, as is considered further below, it is now clear that the defendant may only enforce against damages and interest awarded to the claimant in a court order and not any damages or interest payable under a Tomlin order or by way of acceptance of a Part 36 offer.[25]

(ii) Where the claimant's claim has been struck out on the basis that it: (i) disclosed no reasonable grounds; or (ii) was an abuse of process; or (iii) the conduct of the claimant or someone acting on his behalf (and with the claimant's knowledge of their conduct) was likely to obstruct the just disposal of the proceedings, then the costs order may be enforced in full (CPR r.44.15(1)). In such a situation, of course, the claimant will not have been awarded any damages, so this provision simply allows full enforcement of any costs orders made in the defendant's favour in the proceedings against such assets as the claimant may have (or the use of the order as a mechanism for rendering the claimant bankrupt), as if QOCS did not exist.

(iii) Where the claimant's claim has been found, on the balance of probabilities, to have been "fundamentally dishonest", then the order for costs may be enforced to its full extent but only *"with the permission of the court"* (CPR r.44.16(1)). This, of course, covers a number of possibilities. The claim may have failed, but not been struck out per CPR r.44.15, in which case the defendant will need permission to enforce the costs order. The claim may have succeeded and some damages may have been awarded, but the claim may still be found to have been fundamentally dishonest, in which case the defendant can enforce without permission to the extent of the damages and interest awarded (assuming they are awarded under a court order), but requires permission to enforce any further. This latter position is considerably less likely following the introduction of s.57 of the Criminal Justice and Courts Act 2015, with effect from the 13 April 2015 (and only applying to claims issued on or after that date). This requires the court to dismiss any claim in its entirety where the claimant has been fundamentally dishonest in relation to it or a related claim, even though the primary claim has succeeded in whole or part. The only qualification is that the court has a discretion not to do so if it considers that to do so would cause substantial injustice.

Accordingly, in respect of post-April 2015 claims, where the claimant has been fundamentally dishonest, the claim as a whole is likely to be dismissed and the claimant is likely to be denied QOCS protection in whole or part.

---

[25] See *Cartwright v Venduct Engineering Ltd* [2018] EWCA Civ 1654; [2018] 1 W.L.R. 6137 discussed further below.

There may still be a benefit to defendants in seeking to strike out such claims as being abusive or on the basis that the claimant's conduct is obstructing just disposal, since this will give rise to an automatic disapplication of QOCS in its entirety, removing any question of judicial discretion.

(iv) Where the claim is brought in whole or part for the benefit of a person other than the claimant or a dependant in a Fatal Accidents Act case, or where the claim is only in part a personal injury claim, the defendant may enforce the order up to the full extent with the permission of the court (CPR r.44.16)—see further below. Again, in such cases, the defendant will be entitled to enforce in part without permission if damages have been awarded, but needs permission to go beyond the level of damages and interest (if any).

Each of these provisions warrants further examination.

CPR r.44.13

The key question that has arisen in relation to CPR r.44.13 is whether "proceedings" within that section encompasses a counterclaim to a personal injury claim. For example, if there is an accident between two cars and both drivers are injured. Driver 1 brings a claim against Driver 2. Driver 2 counterclaims. Both claim for damages for personal injury. In that situation, does QOCS apply both to the costs of the claim and the costs of the counterclaim so that Driver 1 (the "claimant" on the basis that they issued first) is protected by QOCS not merely against the risk of paying Driver 2's costs of defending Driver 1's claim (if Driver 1 loses), but also against the risk of paying Driver 2's 'claim' costs of pursuing his (Driver 2's) counterclaim? By the same token, is Driver 2 (the defendant) protected by QOCS at all—and if so, to what extent? If the protection is different, is it necessary to rush to be the "claimant" in order to ensure maximum protection? What if only one of the two parties has a claim for damages for personal injury?

There have been conflicting decisions in this regard at County Court appellate level but, as yet, still no authoritative decision of Court of Appeal level or higher. In *Ketchion v McEwan*,[26] the claimant had brought a claim for financial losses but no personal injuries arising from the accident. The defendant counterclaimed including a claim for damages for personal injuries. The claimant succeeded. The defendant was held to be entitled to QOCS protection in respect of all of the claimant's costs on the basis that the matters were all part of the same "proceedings" and that those proceedings included a claim (the defendant's claim) for damages for personal injuries—even though that claim had been brought by the defendant as a counterclaim, not the claimant.

In *Waring v McDonnell*,[27] the circuit judge reached the contrary view, expressly disagreeing with the decision in *Ketchion*. It was held that there were two claims—and therefore two proceedings for the purpose of QOCS. Each must be looked at separately. In *Waring*, both parties had suffered personal

6–09

---

[26] *Ketchion v McEwan* [2018] 6 WLUK 625.
[27] *Waring v McDonnell* [2018] 11 WLUK 203.

injury (though that point makes no difference to the principle). The claimant's claim succeeded, the defendant's failed. The defendant relied on *Ketchion* to claim QOCS protection in relation to the claimant's claim for costs in respect of his claim. However, the court held that in relation to that claim the defendant was not an unsuccessful "claimant" but instead a losing defendant. He was a claimant in respect of his counterclaim, but that had failed. Applying *Wagenaar*, the judge concluded that "proceedings" was synonymous with "a claim" so that the QOCS regime protected the defendant in his capacity as claimant in the "additional claim", but not in his capacity as defendant to the original claim.

The decision in *Waring* was recently and expressly followed by a third circuit judge, HHJ Gargan, in the case of *Sutcliffe v Ali*[28]. In that case, as in *Waring*, there were two claims, each including claims for damages for personal injury, one being brought as a counterclaim to the other. Once again, the claimant's claim (and defence of the counterclaim) succeeded. Analysing both *Waring* and *Ketchion* and applying a purposive approach to construing the rules, the judge concluded that it was more consistent with the principles underpinning the QOCS reforms that the defendant was indeed a defendant – and therefore did not have the benefit of QOCS – in relation to the costs of the claim, but that he did so in relation to his own, unsuccessful, claim (in respect of which the judge indicated that there would be "no order" for costs.

The cogent judgment of HHJ Gargan does, however illustrate the difficulties of navigating a purposive approach through the choppy waters of the rules. In identifying applicable propositions by reference to authority, the judge noted that they required him both to not construe the word 'proceedings' in its widest sense, but equally not to give it "an overly narrow construction". The key point ultimately appears to be that whether the construction should be a wide or narrow one (or should be perceived as being overly wide or narrow) depends on the ultimate question of whether the likely practical outcome resulting from that construction is perceived as serving the policy objective said to underpin QOCS.

The reasonings in *Sutcliffe* and *Waring* are directly in direct conflict with that in *Ketchion*. Weight of numbers alone is not determinative None of the cases appear to have been subject to further appeal (or at least one which has led to judgment). As stated in previous editions, the reasoning in *Waring (and now Sutcliffe)* would appear to be the more compelling and more consistent with the intended purpose of the QOCS regime – and the fact that the reasoning in *Ketchion* has now been considered and disagreed with in two subsequent judgments adds weight to that conclusion.

An interesting issue in relation to CPR r.44.13 arose towards the end of 2020 in the case of *Waterfield*.[29] In *Waterfield*, the (personal injury) claimants had applied for a group litigation order, prior to issuing proceedings. The

---

[28] Middlesborough County Court, 15 January 2021.
[29] *Waterfield v Dentality Ltd* [2020] 11 WLUK 223 (unreported elsewhere).

application was refused. The question was whether QOCS applied to prevent the defendants enforcing the costs order that was made in their favour in respect of the application. The judge held that it did not, because "proceedings" under CPR r.44.13 was held not to encompass pre-action applications. There was no claim form for damages for personal injury and therefore no proceedings which including such a claim before the court. The court noted that pre-action disclosure proceedings were expressly excluded from the scope of QOCS (CPR r.44.13) – though the fact of such express exclusion of one type of pre-action application could also have been said to support the argument that this was only necessary because such applications are otherwise assumed to be included in the QOCS protection. The judgment in *Waterfield* is thorough and carefully reasoned. However, as with other issues in this area, it concerns interesting issues of the construction of a rule against wider policy considerations and the point is certainly open to contrary argument. There does not appear to have been a second appeal. The issue is one which would merit further consideration or definitive resolution by the CPRC. In many of these areas, there is no "right" answer, since much is dictated by a perception of underlying policy. Access to justice – for both claimants and defendants – may well be better served by definitive clarification of the rules than continued argument.

CPR r.44.14

In relation to the basic operation of QOCS by restriction on enforcement (CPR r.44.14), one of the key questions since 2013 has been what is meant by "enforcement". The defendant's right to "enforce" a costs order in its favour is restricted. It is restricted to the limit of damages and interest awarded to the claimant by way of order of the court. There is no mention of the claimant's costs.   6–10

Before turning to the issue of set-off of costs against costs where QOCS applies, however, it is important to again emphasise that the ability of a defendant to set off its costs against the claimant's damages (say where a Part 36 offer is accepted late or not bettered or where the claimant wins on only some issue, or where the claimant wins but is subject to an adverse interim costs order) is limited to an ability to set costs off against damages and interest ordered by the court. If the award of damages and interest is not in a curial order of the court, the defendant cannot set its costs off against them. So, where the claimant is awarded damages by way of settlement, recorded in an agreement, or in a schedule to a Tomlin order, or by way of acceptance of a Part 36 offer, there is no order of the court and nothing against which the defendant may enforce any costs award in its favour. This perhaps surprising outcome has been authoritatively confirmed by the Court of Appeal in *Cartwright* (above). The Court of Appeal recognised that it cannot have been the intention of the rule-makers to prevent a successful defendant enforcing their entitlement to costs against the claimant's damages, but were unable to construe the rules to contrary effect.

Although it might have been anticipated, in those circumstances, that the rules would be amended to return matters to what appeared to be the intended position, the minutes of the CPRC in December 2019 recorded that the decision had been taken not to do so. The lacuna sub-committee concluded that the Court of Appeal's interpretation of the rules was "logical" and that it remained open to the parties to decide between them how to conclude a case – and therefore whether the awarded damages and interest may be subject to any set off under the QOCS rules. Whether, in practice, defendants truly enjoy the necessary freedom of contract in such circumstances that the sub-committee refers to and would be able, in practice, to "demand" a court order rather than accepting a Part 36 offer, for example, is a moot point given that it now appears that the rule is not to be amended.

Anecdotally, it appears that some on both the claimant and defendant side have not yet fully appreciated the effect of this decision and continue to dispose of cases without fully appreciating the effect of the way in which the case is settled or disposed of. The form of settlement or disposal may make a crucial difference.

Cartwright also resolved the question of whether a defendant who successfully defends a claim may set off its costs against damages awarded to a claimant against and payable by a different defendant in the same claim. The short answer is that the defendant could do so—but only, as noted, provided those damages were subject of an order of the court.

Returning to the question of the potential set-off of costs against costs, QOCS does not allow a defendant to enforce a costs order save through CPR r.44.14. However, is a set-off of costs against costs enforcement? The very section of the CPR which precedes QOCS deals with the ability of a party to "set-off" one costs order against another. Is a set-off enforcement? If it is not, then it would appear that the QOCS rules do not prevent a defendant setting off its costs against any costs awarded to the claimant, in addition to enforcing the costs order to the extent of damages awarded (subject, of course, to the total limit of the costs awarded to the defendant). If, however, a set-off of costs against costs does amount to enforcement, then the defendant's rights are limited to those under CPR r.44.14.

6–11   In *Vava*,[30] Andrew Smith J declined to allow a set-off of one costs order against another in circumstances where parties had entered into a QOCS-type contractual arrangement (but where QOCS did not in fact apply). He did so on the grounds that it would be "unfair" in the circumstances to do so.

In April 2017, in *Darini and Olsoy v Markerstudy Group*,[31] the circuit judge on appeal heard full argument and concluded that QOCS did not permit a set-off of a defendant's costs against interlocutory costs which had been awarded to an otherwise unsuccessful claimant. There was no second appeal in *Darini*. The issue was ripe for detailed appellate consideration.

---

[30] *Vava v Anglo American South Africa Ltd* [2013] EWHC 2326 (QB); [2013] 5 Costs L.R. 805.
[31] *Darini and Olsoy v Markerstudy Group* unreported 24 April 2017 County Court (Central London).

However, the issue then was addressed by the Court of Appeal in the second, unreported, judgment in *Howe*. In that case, the argument as to set-off had not formed part of the appeal. It only arose as part of the consequential argument as to costs of the appeal and therefore the Court of Appeal only dealt with the point relatively shortly and without the benefit of the full argument that counsel in that case would no doubt have deployed on a full appeal. Nevertheless, the court dealt with the issue and its judgment was binding on lower courts. The court concluded that QOCS did not prevent a set-off of costs against costs. In *Faulkner*[32], with some apparent judicial reluctance, the court held that it was bound to follow the decision in *Howe* and not the lower appellate decision in *Darini*. Despite this, the court then went on to hold, on the facts, that it was not an appropriate case in which to exercise the discretion to allow the set off.

The issue was then revisited in the case of *Ho v Adelekun*.[33] Again, as with *Howe*, the issue only arose as part of the consequential issues in the appeal on other issues and was therefore, in effect, a first instance hearing. The matter was argued at greater length than in *Howe*. The court rejected an argument that *Howe* had been decided per incuriam and therefore held that it was bound by the decision in *Howe*. However, without stating that it would definitely have reached a different conclusion had it been able to do so, the court concluded that there were "powerful arguments" on both sides and the terms of the judgment suggest that the court would have been minded to reach the contrary conclusion had it been free to do so. In the circumstances, the court took the unusual step of granting permission to appeal to the Supreme Court.

The matter was definitively resolved, subject to any amendment to the rules, by the Supreme Court's decision in *Ho*.[34] Although the Supreme Court expressed some concern about being asked to resolve issues of procedural law, a matter it regarded as essentially being the domain of the CPRC and the Court of Appeal, faced with two conflicting Court of Appeal decisions it did so and did so unanimously for the claimant. CPR r.44.14 operated by imposing a monetary cap on the extent to which a defendant was able to enforce a costs order against a personal injury claimant. That cap was the amount of damages (and interest) awarded to the claimant by court order. It did not include costs awarded to the claimant. Accordingly, if (as in *Ho*) the relevant damages and interest were nil (because per *Cartwright*, they had been paid by settlement and not court order), there was nothing the defendant could enforce its costs order against. It could not "set off" its costs against the costs awarded to the claimant, since that would – for the purposes of the QOCS rules – amount to enforcement. The claimant therefore had to be paid her costs and the defendant was unable to diminish those by the costs due to it. *Howe* was expressly overruled.

---

[32] *Faulkner v Secretary of State for Business, Energy & Industrial Strategy* [2020] EWHC 296 (QB), [2020] 1 W.L.R 2906.
[33] [2020] EWCA Civ 517, [2020] Costs LR 317.
[34] [2021] UKSC 43.

The decision in *Ho* is undoubtedly one of the most significant decisions in respect of QOCS since its introduction, particularly when stood alongside *Cartwright*. The practical effect is that a defendant's ability to give practical effect to a costs order in its favour in a QOCS case is very limited. It may be able to do so by diminishing or extinguishing the damages awarded – for example following an effective Part 36 offer – but only in practice if the matter goes to judgment or, for some other reason, the damages are awarded by order and not settlement. It may be able to do so if the case is struck out, or is fundamentally dishonest or another exception applies. However, in all other cases and in particular in cases where there are costs orders going both ways (for example where the claimant succeeds but loses an interim issue) not only will the defendant be unable to recover the costs awarded to it, but it will also be required to pay the claimant's full (assessed) costs.[35]

Once again – as for example with the retrospective effect of QOCS – this may simply be an example of the balancing act required in order to achieve the desired policy objectives. Whatever the position, for present purposes *Ho* is clear and definitive. The CPRC has been carefully monitoring the *Ho* case. its November 2021 minutes recorded that a decision on whether to consider the matter further had been deferred pending the wider work necessary in relation to the proposed expansion of fixed recoverable costs and "until the policy imperative on QOCS is known".[36] This is understandable. The construction of the present rules on this point has now been definitively determined. Any reconsideration of the same could, therefore, only be driven by policy and the desire for a clear statement of what that policy is before deciding whether to make any amendment appears entirely logical.

In *Corstorphine*[37] the Court of Appeal had to address a further issue in relation to CPR r.44.14, namely whether a claimant was entitled to QOCS protection against the costs of two defendants who had been joined to the proceedings—initially by way of Pt 20 claim by the original defendant. The court held that the claimant was entitled to QOCS protection against their successful claim. His (pre-commencement) CFA, properly construed, did not cover the claim against the other two defendants. The proceedings against the other two defendants were to be treated as separate proceedings for QOCS purposes and in the absence of a PCFA in respect of those proceedings (which would have removed QOCS protection per CPR r.44.17) the claimant was entitled to QOCS protection.

---

[35] Whilst there may be a certain temptation on the part of defendants to seek to circumvent this by, for example, seeking to set off its costs against the claimant's at the time of the making of a costs order (so that, for example, the claimant is only awarded x% of his costs), there are difficulties with such an approach. Firstly, it would only applied to the limited number of cases where it is the court that is making the final costs order. Secondly, there are already judicial warnings against seeking to use the terms of the costs order to inhibit the protection the claimant would otherwise have by way of QOCS if the 'usual' costs orders were made – see, for example, the *Corstorphine* case (above) and the brief reference to arguments on this point at para. 45 in *Ho*.

[36] *https://assets.publishing.service.gov.uk/government/uploads/system/uploads/attachment_data/file/1039324/cprc-5-november-2021-minutes.pdf*.

[37] *Corstorphine v Liverpool City Council* [2018] EWCA Civ 270; [2018] 2 Costs L.O. 213.

Finally, in respect of CPR r.44.14, it may be material to note that CPR r.44.14 refers to the enforcement of costs orders "made against a claimant". It is, of course, possible in any proceedings that a court may make orders against non-parties, for example against litigation funders. CPR r.44.14 does not, prima facie, appear to address any question of the enforcement of such costs orders against such non-parties, whether in terms or principle or procedure. It may be open to argument whether attempts to seek and enforce such orders are contrary to the legislative purpose behind the QOCS regime, but at present there is no authoritative guidance on this issue.

CPR r.44.15

CPR r.44.15 requires relatively little further discussion. The categories of strike out referred to therein mirror those in CPR r.3.4(2)(a) and (b) and issues as to when such a strike out is appropriate are beyond the scope of this section. The only real gloss to note is that where the strike out is on the basis that the conduct of the proceedings was such as to be likely to obstruct the just disposal of the proceedings, then in order to disapply QOCS it is necessary, in addition, that the court concludes that such conduct was that of the claimant himself or that he knew of the relevant conduct on the part of the person so acting on his behalf. A defendant seeking a strike out on this basis in a personal injury claim should take care to ensure that this additional aspect is specifically addressed in any judgment given on the strike out (and ideally recited in the order).

6–12

However, the case of *Brahilika*[38] illustrates that the court may be prepared to apply a relatively wide interpretation of the conduct likely to obstruct the just disposal of proceedings. In that case, the relevant conduct was the failure of the claimant to attend trial, due to being on holiday (it not being known whether the holiday was booked before or after the trial date was fixed).

There are two further points to note in relation to CPR r.44.15. Firstly, in *Shaw v Medtronic Corevalve LLC*[39] Mr Justice Lavender noted a possible lacuna in the rule in that, having set aside permission for the claimant to serve proceedings on D1 and D3, thereby bringing the claims to an end in circumstances where but for such setting aside he would have struck them out, the QOCS rules did not allow for those defendants' costs to be enforced against the claimant. He invited the CPRC to revisit this issue. Such circumstances are likely to arise only rarely and whether the risk of such a situation occurring again is sufficient to warrant a change to the rule or is instead to be seen as simply one of those outlying possibilities which does not warrant adding an additional exception remains to be seen. The lack of an amendment to the rules in this regard in the following years suggest that the latter position pertains.

More pertinently in *Shaw*, Lavender J also had to address the question of whether a notice of discontinuance filed by the claimant in relation to his

---

[38] *Brahilika v Allianz Insurance Plc* unreported 30 July 2015 County Court (Romford).
[39] *Shaw v Medtronic Corevalve LLC* [2017] EWHC 1397 (QB); [2017] 3 Costs L.R. 491.

claim against D5—following the dismissal of the claims against the other defendants—should be set aside. If the notice stood, then the QOCS rules protected the claimant from enforcement of any costs order, absent (for example) a finding of fundamental dishonesty. CPR r.38.6 allows for such a notice to be set aside and, if set aside, D5 would seek to argue that the claim should be struck out, thereby allowing it to enforce its costs pursuant to CPR r.44.14. Indeed, D5 had made an application for the claim to be struck out before the notice had been filed. Despite this, Lavender J declined to set aside the notice. He accepted that it was not necessarily required that the defendant show that the filing of the notice had been an abuse, but nevertheless concluded that there were a number of reasons why the notice might have been filed and that it was not appropriate to set it aside. The claimant retained his protection.

In *Mabb*,[40] Mrs Justice May similarly refused an application to set aside a notice of discontinuance in order, on this occasion, to allow an appeal against a refusal to strike the claim out to proceed. The approach in principle followed a similar, though not identical, course to *Shaw*.

CPR r.44.16

6–13   CPR r.44.16 and the introduction of a test of "fundamental dishonesty" had given rise to much debate, which has been added to by the introduction of s.57 of the Criminal Justice and Courts Act 2015 (discussed further at paras 6–08 and 6–11 above).

What does "fundamentally dishonest" mean? "Dishonesty" is a concept the courts are extremely familiar with and there is clear judicial guidance as to the issues a court must consider in deciding in a personal injury context whether a claimant has been dishonest—though it is important to note that the test in CPR r.44.16 is directed to whether the claim—and not the claimant personally—is fundamentally dishonest.[41] More contentious is the "fundamentally" aspect, which has troubled parliamentarians in recent debates in relation to the use of the term in s.57 of the new Act.

There have been a number of first instance cases where the issue has arisen. Whilst such cases—as with *Brahilika* above—do not contain any binding statement of principle, they are useful to illustrate the approach the courts have been adopting. One of the most thoroughly argued earlier cases was that of *Gosling*,[42] which was a classic case of a successful, but dishonestly exaggerated, claim, though with an added complication that the claimant succeeded only against one defendant and discontinued against a second. In that case, the judge held that a claim was not fundamentally dishonest merely because the claimant had been dishonest in respect of some collateral matter or some minor, self-contained head of damage, but that where the dishonesty went to the root of a substantial part of the claim the test was made out.

---

[40] *Mabb v English* [2017] EWHC 3616 (QB); [2018] 1 Costs L.R. 1.
[41] See, for example, *Brighton and Hove Bus v Brooks* [2011] EWHC 2504 (Admin).
[42] *Gosling v Hailo & Screwfix Direct* unreported 29 April 2014 CC (Cambridge).

The case appears to confirm, a number of propositions. First, that CPR r.44.16(1) may apply where the dishonesty does not infect the entire claim, but goes only to a substantial part of it—the classic exaggerated claim case. Secondly, where the test in CPR r.44.16(1) is made out, the court is not bound to allow the defendant to enforce the costs order to its full extent, but is then given a discretion to decide to what extent to allow such enforcement.

Both propositions appear logical interpretations of the rule. *Gosling* was held to be a correct analysis of the meaning and scope of fundamental dishonesty by HHJ Hodge QC in *Meadows*[43] and a district judge's failure to follow it was criticised in allowing an appeal in *Rouse*.[44] Perhaps more importantly, the reasoning in *Gosling* was endorsed by the Court of Appeal in *Howlett v Ageas*[45] and has been followed in other appellate cases, such as *Pegg*,[46] a case where a first instance finding that the claimant had not been fundamentally dishonest was overturned on appeal.

The first proposition—that a claim may be seen as being fundamentally dishonest as a whole even where the dishonesty only relates to part of the claim—is, of course, supported by the approach taken in s.57 of the 2015 Act, requiring the dismissal of the entire claim even where there are elements of that claim in respect of which the claimant has not been dishonest (see s.57(3)). It is also consistent with the Court of Appeal's approach to the issue of fraud in personal injury claims, as seen in *Hayward v Zurich Insurance Company Plc*[47] where, despite the fortuitous outcome for the appellant, it is clear from the judgments that the court regarded the whole claim as being fraudulent, despite the fact that there was no doubt that the appellant had been injured and his dishonesty related to the claim that the injury was continuing and had not resolved.

The case of *Diamanttek Ltd v James*[48] appears to be consistent with this **6-14** analysis. In that case, the judge cited *Gosling*, without disagreement, but approached the matter (necessarily) from a slightly different perspective to conclude that a claim could still be "fundamentally dishonest" where a claimant had "not told the truth" about a key aspect, even where the judge has also concluded that the claimant was not himself a "dishonest person". The case may, perhaps, best be seen as one where the appellate judge is wrestling with a slightly unfortunate use of terminology at first instance and not one which derogates in any way from the analysis contained in *Gosling*.

The issue of fundamental dishonesty has probably given rise to more cases on the issue of QOCS than any other. However, the majority of these tend to concern first instance decisions as to whether, on the facts, the claim was a fundamentally dishonest one and they add little to the arguments of

---

[43] *Meadows v La Tasca Restaurants Ltd* unreported 16 June 2016 County Court (Manchester).
[44] HHJ Gosnell, *Rouse v Aviva Insurance Ltd* unreported 15 January 2016 County Court (Bradford).
[45] [2017] EWCA Civ 1696.
[46] *Pegg v Webb* [2020] EWHC 2095 (QB), [2020] Costs LR 1001.
[47] *Hayward v Zurich Insurance Com* [2015] EWCA Civ 327; [2015] C.P. Rep. 30
[48] *Diamanttek Ltd v James* unreported 8 February 2016 County Court (Coventry) the decision was of a circuit judge (HHJ Gregory) on appeal but has wrongly been reported in some quarters as being a decision of the Court of Appeal.

principle. They are not reviewed here, but are readily available online and may be of assistance to anyone making or facing such an application.

As noted, the matter did, however, come to the Court of Appeal's attention in the case of *Howlett*.[49] In *Howlett*, the key question was whether a judge could find the claim to have been fundamentally dishonest where fraud had not been pleaded in the defence to the claim. The simple answer to that question was "yes". The important question was whether the claimant was given adequate warning of the matters to be alleged against him or her and an opportunity to address them, rather than the strict way in which those matters were pleaded or presented. If the claimant had notice of the matters and they were properly put in issue, then a court is entitled to find the claim to be fundamentally dishonest for QOCS purposes. None of that, of course, should be taken to be an encouragement to attempts to "ambush" claimants with such allegations. Quite the opposite.

Master Davison's decision in *Mustard v Flower*[50] re-affirms, the point that a defendant does not need to plead fundamental dishonesty in order to be able to seek to disapply QOCS – or to argue fundamental dishonesty under s.57. In light of that, there is no need – and indeed it is not appropriate – to seek to plead fundamental dishonesty on a contingent or speculative basis (in *Mustard*, the defendant sought to amend its defence, in part, to do so on the basis that if the court found conscious exaggeration, the defendant reserved the right to argue fundamental dishonesty). The claimant must have sufficient notice and opportunity to deal with the issues that could lead a judge to a finding of fundamental dishonesty and the issues to be explored at trial that may lead to such a finding can and should be set out within the statements of case, but provided such issues are identified the defendant can await the judge's findings before taking the point further.

Again, however, the majority of cases settle rather than proceeding to trial. CPR PD 44 para.12 contains clear guidance in relation to arguments under CPR r.44.16(1) and in particular that where parties settle proceedings the court will not, "save in exceptional circumstances" order that issues relating to fundamental dishonesty be tried (para.12.4(b)) and that such issues should normally be determined at trial (para.12.4(a)). The logic is obvious and needs little explanation, but the point should not be overlooked by defendants. Settlement of a claim will usually be an effective bar to taking this point. If a defendant wishes to pursue the point, it should do so at trial.

A claimant cannot, however, escape such scrutiny (at least in relation to fundamental dishonesty) by discontinuing the claim (CPR PD 44 para.12.4(c))—and see the discussion of the same in *Rouse* (above).

The decision of *Alpha Insurance*[51] makes the obvious point that, in contrast to the position where the case has settled, in face of a discontinuance by a

---

[49] *Howlett v Davies* [2017] EWCA Civ 1696; [2018] 1 W.L.R. 948.
[50] [2021] EWHC 846 (QB).
[51] *Alpha Insurance A/S v Roche* [2018] EWHC 1342 (QB); [2018] 4 W.L.R. 92.

claimant (which therefore deprives the defendant of the chance of taking the point at trial) an application by a defendant under CPR PD 44 para.12.4(c) does not require the defendant to show exceptional circumstances. It is an unfettered discretion which must be exercised in accordance with the overriding objective—and importantly the public interest in identifying false claims.

It must be noted, however, that CPR PD 44 para.12.4(c) only applies to allow the court to consider matters despite a notice of discontinuance where the issue raised by the defendant is one of fundamental dishonesty. Where the claimant has served such a notice and the defendant, for example, seeks to contend that the claim, whilst not dishonest, was one that disclosed no reasonable grounds for being brought, for example, and would therefore have been struck out allowing for the automatic disapplication of QOCS under CPR r.44.15(1)(a), the defendant will face the burden of having to satisfy the court as to why the notice of discontinuance should be set aside pursuant to CPR r.38.4 to allow the defendant to then apply to strike the claim out. This has been addressed above by reference to the cases of *Mabb* and *Shaw*. As the further case of *Magon*[52] illustrates, the defendant may find such an application difficult and the court will usually (though not invariably) expect to see that there has been some kind of abuse of process warranting such a course. Such an application will be particularly difficult if, as in *Magon*, it is brought after the 28-day time limit for doing so under CPR r.38.4.

It would appear, therefore, that a deliberate procedural line has been drawn. Where the case is arguably fundamentally dishonest, the claimant is unlikely to be able to escape scrutiny and arguments as to disapplication of QOCS by discontinuing. However, where the claimant's case is said to be abusive or disclose no reasonable grounds for having been brought, but not alleged to be dishonest, then a claimant may (but not necessarily will) be able to respond to a strike out application by discontinuing the claim, preserving their QOCS position. This might be said to reflect the more general position. Claimants are to be protected from adverse costs orders in failed claims, but not where they have behaved dishonestly.

CPR r.44.16(2) contains further exceptions which permit orders for costs **6–15** against the claimant to be enforced, with the permission of the court and to the extent that it considers just. It applies in two sets of circumstances. The one which has received most judicial attention is the second (CPR r.44.16(2)(b)), namely where a claim is made "for the benefit of the claimant other than a claim to which this section applies". This is intended to cover claims where the beneficiary of the claim is the claimant, but the claimant's claim is only partially a personal injury claim (the classic example being a housing disrepair claim where there may be a claim for personal injuries as part of a wider claim).

By virtue of CPR r.44.16(2) the mere fact that procedurally, the claim as a whole is deemed a personal injury claim, because it includes a claim for

---

[52] *Magon v Royal Sun Alliance* unreported 26 February 2016 County Court (Central London).

damages for personal injury, does not appear to prevent the court disapplying QOCS, to the extent just.[53] Commonly, this is likely to be used so that the court can allow full enforcement of adverse costs orders in relation to that part of the claim which was not a personal injury claim, and is likely to be used in cases where the personal injury claim is viewed as being the more modest or less complex part of the claim. An example might be a professional negligence claim which included an ancillary claim for damages for personal injury.

This interpretation, foreshadowed in earlier editions, is consistent with the approach adopted by Mr Justice Morris in *Jeffreys*[54] in which he concluded that it was permissible to identify, in a broad-brush fashion, those parts of a claim which were a personal injury claim and those which were not and to disapply QOCS from the costs of the latter parts. It was not necessary for the non-personal injury elements to be part of a discrete "claim", nor for those parts to be on other side of some clear division. Permission for a second appeal was refused in *Jeffreys*.

A second attempt to obtain guidance on the issue came in *Siddiqui*.[55] Mr Justice Foskett followed the guidance in *Jeffreys*. Permission for a second appeal was again refused.

A third opportunity arose in *Brown*.[56] Once again, the approach in *Jeffreys* was expressly followed. This time the matter did proceed to the Court of Appeal. However, the court largely followed the *Jeffreys* approach. The Court did give some useful guidance to make clear that where the claim was one which was a claim for damages for personal injuries, but included a claim for consequential losses upon that injury, such as loss of earnings, the same would usually be regarded as a personal injury claim in whole for QOCS purposes. Similarly, the court made it clear that where the claim was primarily a personal injury claim, such that the non-personal injury elements were largely incidental and not causative of substantial additional costs, the Court would not usually welcome applications by defendants under CPR r.44.16. Beyond that, however the issue is one for judicial discretion.

In light of the Court of Appeal's decision in *Brown*, the 113th Practice Direction update provided that, with effect from 6 April 2020, Pt 44 PD para.12.6 was amended to make clear that the court will normally order the

---

[53] The precise ambit and operation of the interestingly worded CPR r.44.16(2)(b) is unclear. As noted, CPR r.44.13 provides that QOCS applies where a claim "includes" a personal injury claim. Rule 44.16(2)(b) might be thought to be intended to address those situations where there is only a modest personal injury element *"tacked on"* to a large claim, allowing the court, at its discretion, to allow "normal" costs enforcement in relation to the non-personal injury element. However, the wording is a little ambiguous and it is noted that the preceding subsection, CPR r.44.16(2)(a) expressly refers to an exception where "the proceedings include a claim [for the financial benefit of another]", yet CPR r.44.16(2)(b) does not say "where the proceedings include a claim other than a personal injury claim". This may be slightly lax drafting or it may be arguable that CPR r.44.16(2)(b) has a narrower operation and is only aimed at making clear that if a claimant brings two, distinct, claims (but perhaps arising from the same facts), the fact that QOCS is available for one does not necessarily mean it will be available for the other. The discussion set out above assumed the former.
[54] *Jeffreys v Commissioner of Police for the Metropolis* [2017] EWHC 1505 (QB); [2018] 1 W.L.R. 3633.
[55] *Siddiqui v University of Oxford* [2018] EWHC 536 (QB); [2018] 4 W.L.R. 62.
[56] *Commissioner of Police of the Metropolis v Brown* [2018] EWHC 2046 (Admin); [2018] 4 Costs L.R. 897.

claimant or, as it may be, the person for whose benefit a claim was made to pay costs notwithstanding the usual QOCS provisions where the claimant has been found to be fundamentally dishonest (CPR r.44.16(1)) or where the proceedings included a claim for the financial benefit of another (CPR r.44.16(2)(a)) but that the guidance that this will "normally" be the case no longer applies to mixed claims (CPR r.44.16(2)(b)), where the matter will be for the discretion of the court. This is to accommodate the guidance in *Brown* that where, in mixed claims, the non-personal injury element is essentially incidental the court will not normally be expected to disapply QOCS. The need for such a change was expressly identified by Coulson LJ in *Brown*.

CPR r.44.16(2)(a), which allows the court to disapply QOCS where the claim in whole or part is for the financial benefit of a third party, has also proven to be contentious.

The rule itself gives only limited guidance as to the circumstances where it will apply. The Practice Direction is more specific and provides examples of where the claim is "made for the financial benefit of a person other than the claimant", including credit hire claims and subrogated claims (PD 44 para.12.2).

Whilst this seems to be the clear intention of the rule-makers, there is likely **6–16** to be argument in the future as to whether or not claims, such as credit hire or subrogated claims are properly claims brought for the financial benefit of another party, a wording which appears to cut across the traditional and well established legal status of claims by such parties where the involvement of the third party is seen as being *res inter alios acta* (that is to say something which is considered not to be the court's business when considering the claim between the parties), particularly in the context of costs, save in particular and unusual circumstances.[57]

The fact that the "examples" are given in the Practice Direction rather than forming part of the rule might be said to provide greater scope for such arguments.

The clear intention of CPR r.44.16(2) is that where QOCS is disapplied in this situation, it is not the claimant that should suffer. CPR r.44.16(3) contains a clear point to the making of a costs order directly against the third party in such a circumstance, subject to consideration of the usual rules for such orders under CPR r.46.2. Whilst such a third party costs order would not remove the order against the claimant, it is to be anticipated that in such cases the court's likely approach would be to decline to allow enforcement (beyond damages and interest) against the claimant, but to make a third party costs order for the relevant sum or percentage or issues against the third party for whose benefit that part of the claim was brought, and CPR PD 44 para.12.5 clearly points in this direction, indicating that it will be "exceptional" that (further) enforcement will be allowed against the claimant. CPR r.44.16(2)(a) may perhaps,

---

[57] See the classic case of *TGA Chapman v Christopher* [1998] 1 W.L.R. 12; [1997] C.L.C. 1306 in the context of subrogated claims.

therefore, more properly be seen not as being a true exception to QOCS (since QOCS only prevents enforcement of costs orders against claimants), but in most cases merely a signpost to the continued existence of the court's ability to make non-party costs orders in appropriate circumstances.

In *Select Car Rentals Ltd v Esure Services Ltd*,[58] Mr Justice Turner made clear his conclusion that CPR r.44.16(3) did not introduce any new jurisdictional basis for the making of a non-party costs order, but was merely procedural and indicative of circumstances where it might be appropriate to make such an order. The fact that a third party, such as a credit hire company, promotes litigation for its own benefit in the knowledge that the claimant has the benefit of QOCS may be a factor which it may be appropriate to take into account in deciding whether to make a non-party costs order, but the issue of whether to make such an order rests on well-established principles which are outside the scope of this work. Turner J's analysis appears sound and whilst even more authoritative guidance or a clarificatory rule change would always be welcome, the position in this regard appears relatively settled. The non-party costs order made against a credit hire company in the case of *First Central Management Ltd v On Hire Ltd*[59] and the dismissal of the appeal in respect of the same is a further example of these issues in practice.

A wider use of QOCS

6–17   The Ministry of Justice (MoJ) published detailed proposals for the extension of a version of QOCS to publication and privacy claims, such proposals being put out to consultation which closed in November 2013. Although the original intention was for QOCS to be introduced in this area with effect from April 2014, no implementation date was given.

It is now clear from the Lord Chancellor's written statement in November 2018[60]—made on the same date as the Government finally published its response to the consultation—that QOCS will not in fact be extended to publication and privacy claims. Instead, whilst recoverable success fees have been abolished, the premiums for ATE insurance continue to be recoverable.

The Civil Justice Council (CJC)'s Working Group on the impact of the Jackson reforms also considered arguments for and against the extension of QOCS to other categories of cases which are said to be characterised by an asymmetric relationship between the parties, such as actions against the police and professional negligence claims against solicitors arising out of personal injury claims. Nuisance claims were also under consideration.

In its final report[61] the Working Group described the arguments in favour of extension to claims against the police as being "strong if not compelling" and noted that principled arguments to the contrary did not appear to have

---

[58] *Select Car Rentals Ltd v Esure Services Ltd* [2017] EWHC 1434 (QB); [2017] 1 W.L.R. 4426.
[59] Unreported, HHJ Roberts, Central London County Court, 13 July 2021.
[60] *https://www.parliament.uk/business/publications/written-questions-answers-statements/written-statement/Lords/20 18-11-29/HLWS1096/*.
[61] *https://www.judiciary.gov.uk/wp-content/uploads/2011/03/cjc-qocs-2016-report.pdf*.

been made out. It noted that claims against the police might give rise to particular issues about how to apply QOCS in "mixed claims" and that this issue merited further consideration both in the context of police claims and personal injury claims as a whole, as to which see above. This concern did not undermine what can only be seen as a whole-hearted recommendation for extension of QOCS to actions against the police. The MoJ has yet to provide a formal response.

The Working Group was more equivocal on the issue of extending QOCS to professional negligence claims arising out of personal injury claims, describing the arguments for such extension as being a "fair case" and noting a number of concerns about the practical effect of such extension, not least the risk of creating an expanded "secondary market" in the pursuit of such claims. The subject also gave rise to a need to consider wider issues such as the available alternative forms of funding for such claims. Again, the ultimate decision remains one for the MoJ.

There have been other calls for the wider extension of QOCS, most notably from Ramsey J,[62] including to actions against the police and from the Public Law Project, amongst others, calling for an extension to judicial review proceedings, primarily on the basis that ATE for such proceedings is rarely available[63] and for an extension to housing disrepair litigation. The delays and difficulties with the privacy and publication extension and the lack of response to the work undertaken by the CJC Working Group suggest that it may be some considerable time before any such extension might materialise. The House of Commons Women & Equalities Committee, in its Tenth Report of Session[64] called for QOCS to be extended to discrimination claims in the County Court, though there is no sign at this stage that that proposal is to be taken forward.

In February 2020, there was an unsuccessful judicial review of the Lord Chancellor's failure to extend QOCS to discrimination claims in the County Court[65] and, absent any successful appeal in that decision, it seems clear ther fore that any extension of the QOCS regime rests firmly in the hands of the MoJ.

In February 2019 the MoJ carried out its Post Implementation Review of LASPO.

Its initial assessment in relation to that Review[66] noted that in relation to personal injury cases *"there is nothing to suggest that QOCS is not working as anticipated"*—a view which does not necessarily reflect all of the issues highlighted above. The Review[67] further stated that, based on the evidence

[62] In his speech to the Compass Law Commercial Litigation Conference: *http://www.litigationfutures.com/news/extension-qocs-key-true-jackson-says-ramsey*.
[63] *https://publiclawproject.org.uk/wp-content/uploads/2018/08/180822-PLP-response-to-LASPO-Part-II-PIR-call-for-evidence.pdf*.
[64] 17 July 2019.
[65] *R (ex parte Leighton) v Lord Chancellor* [2020] EWHC 336 (Admin).
[66] *https://assets.publishing.service.gov.uk/government/uploads/system/uploads/attachment_data/file/719140/pir-part-2-laspo-initial-assessment.pdf*.
[67] *https://assets.publishing.service.gov.uk/government/uploads/system/uploads/attachment_data/file/777039/post-implementation-review-of-part-2-of-laspo.pdf*

received, the Government considered that, on balance, the reforms in Pt 2 of LASPO had successfully met their objectives. Notably, the evidence showed that, in a range of personal injury claims (including clinical negligence claims), costs had reduced by around 8–10% and early settlement had also improved. A definitive judgement on the impact on unmeritorious claims could not yet be made, but the claims volumes data, the changes in financial incentives to CFAs, the test of fundamental dishonesty for QOCS, and anecdotal stakeholder feedback, suggested there had been an overall decline in unmeritorious claims.

In response to calls to extend QOCS beyond personal injury claims, the Government said that it would wish to be satisfied that the risks that some of the benefits of the LASPO reforms would be undermined (including the shifting of costs back to defendants, an overall increase in costs and the potential for prolonging rather than settling litigation) had been addressed before considering the case for extending costs protection further. A continued process of review was promised, but any immediate changes were ruled out.

In relation to other areas, the initial response was that "*QOCS does not exist outside personal injury claims. There is still an ATE market (which operates, as pre-LASPO, on a deferred contingent basis) and parties can take out ATE insurance, paying the premium if the case is successful*". This does not immediately suggest that any widening of QOCS is imminent.

It would appear from the approach taken in relation to privacy and publication proceedings (which avoided an extension of QOCS) and in relation to other areas such as environmental claims (where a differing approach to costs protection has been introduced) that an extension of QOCS for use outside personal injury claims, save in very limited areas, is unlikely.

The proposed implementation of the extension of fixed recoverable costs in October 2022 appears to be perceived by the CPRC as an appropriate opportunity to seek further MOJ input on the application, and possibly any extension, of QOCS[68] and any further steps to provide clarification in this regard will be welcome.

Questions and answers

A. *The circumstances in which QOCS applies*

Q1. How will QOCS apply where a claim comprises both a personal injury and a non-personal injury element?

6–18   This was the subject of authoritative decision by the Court of Appeal in *Brown v Commissioner of the Police for the Metropolis,* as addressed in the text above. The rule expressly allows the court to disapply QOCS to the extent that it considers just where this situation arises (CPR r.44.16) and the Practice Direction

---

[68] See, for example, CPRC November 2021 meeting minutes *https://assets.publishing.service.gov.uk/government/uploads/system/uploads/attachment_data/file/1039324/cprc-5-november-2021-minutes.pdf.*

envisages that where this arises the court will normally order the claimant to pay costs notwithstanding that they exceed the level of damages and interest awarded (i.e. will allow enforcement beyond the limit in CPR r.44.14, which is what CPR r.44.16 expressly envisages). The matter is one for judicial discretion and judgment, as was made clear in *Brown* (above).

In practice, it is likely that the court will seek to identify the true nature of the claim. Where the personal injury claim was dominant and the "additional claim" a modest ancillary part which is unlikely to have significantly increased the costs then the court may decide not to allow any enforcement beyond CPR r.44.14. Where the "additional claim" was dominant, and the court may be reasonably satisfied that the defendant would have had to incur broadly the same level of costs to meet that claim alone, then the court may allow full enforcement. Perhaps more commonly, the court may seek to identify, by percentage, date or in some other way, the "additional claim" and allow enforcement in that regard accordingly. This approach, identified as the likely course in earlier editions, was essentially the approach adopted by Morris J in *Jeffreys* and by the courts in *Siddiqui* and *Brown* which expressly followed *Jeffreys* and were, in turn, approved by the Court of Appeal in *Brown*.

Given that the claimant in this scenario may well have already suffered some costs deduction against damages (CPR r.44.14) and given that the quantum of costs may have been assessed (CPR r.44.13(3)) the court may simply make an order that enforcement of a certain sum above the level of damages is unjust. The Court of Appeal is unlikely to be keen to interfere with a broad exercise of discretion here unless the outcome is manifestly unjust and it is difficult to give definitive guidance since the potential factual combinations are many and the overall decision will be one to be arrived at exercising a broad measure of what is just in all the circumstances. What is clear, however, is that it need not be "all or nothing".

Q2. Is QOCS excluded where the claimant has before-the-event insurance?
No. Provided the claim is within CPR r.44.14, and provided that the claim-   6–19
ant has not entered into a CFA or ATE prior to 1 April 2013 in relation to the claim, then the method of funding is irrelevant. QOCS is available.

This applies even where the claim was commenced prior to 1 April 2013— and even where the costs order was made prior to 1 April 2013 but has not yet been enforced. It is the presence of a funding model which contains provision for recoverable additional liabilities which leads to the loss of availability of QOCS. Whether the claimant is otherwise indemnified for the costs liability is irrelevant. To that extent, QOCS may serve to protect a claimant's insurer or indemnifier (be it BTE or ATE), rather than just the claimant.

Q3. Does QOCS apply to costs incurred prior to 1 April 2013?
Yes. Provided the claim is within CPR r.44.13 and provided the claimant has   6–20
not entered into a PCFA (CPR r.48.2), then QOCS applies and the defendant's

ability to enforce a costs order is restricted accordingly. Although there is scope for argument beyond that raised in *Wagenaar*, the Court of Appeal's decision in that case disposed of the primary argument that QOCS could not operate retrospectively in this way.

Q4. Is QOCS excluded where the claimant has entered into a PCFA, even if the claimant then is advised not to pursue the claim by the initially instructed solicitor but later does so under a post-April 2013 funding arrangement with a different firm?

6–21   In the first edition of this supplement, it was stated that these issues needed to be resolved, but that the wording of CPR rr.48.2 and 44.17 suggested that the answer to this is "yes". Some first instance decisions suggested to the contrary. However, in *Catalano*, above, the Court of Appeal confirmed that this was the position, provided at least some services had been provided to the claimant under the first CFA (or perhaps more accurately, simply provided that the claimant had entered into a PCFA in respect of those proceedings —the reference to work having commenced perhaps confusing the provisions in relation to a single CFA with those for a Collective CFA). The quid pro quo for this appears to be that if the claimant had entered into a CFA with the second solicitor, that CFA would be regarded as a PCFA, even though entered into post-April 2013, and the success fee would be recoverable. This latter part, identified in the dicta in *Catalano*, but not fully explained, would, if correct, involve an extremely generous and purposive approach to s.44(6) of LASPO and CPR r.48.1, but appears to be part of the general theme of recent cases on the transitional provisions, the thrust of which is that where the claimant is in the pre-LASPO camp for a particular case the claimant will remain in that camp, despite changes in his or her funding arrangements, unless there are very good reasons not to do so.

Q5. Can a personal injury claimant who had a pre-action CFA (entered into before 1 April 2013) with a 100% success fee, and who wishes to proceed with the claim with the benefits of QOCS protection, terminate the existing CFA, on the basis that the law firm will waive its success fee, and enter into a new post-Jackson CFA? Would the claimant then be able to benefit from QOCS, even though the pre-action base costs are covered under a CFA entered into before 1 April 2013? Alternatively, could the client and or the solicitor agree to end the existing CFA, but enter into a new, post-LASPO CFA, with any success fee payable by the client only, but with the CFA expressly covering all work done since first instruction and thereby benefit from QOCS?

6–22   Based on *Catalano*, the answer is generally no. Once services have been provided under the first CFA (or probably more correctly once the CFA has been entered into in relation to those proceedings on a pre-LASPO basis) the claimant is within CPR rr.48.2 and 44.17 and QOCS is lost for good. However, the question (perhaps understandably) does not appear to anticipate the dicta at

[27] of the judgment in *Catalano* which appears to suggest that the success fee under the new CFA might continue to be recoverable between the parties. This would be on the basis that the new agreement, despite plainly being a pre-April 2013 CFA, should be treated as a PCFA. This part of the judgment in *Catalano* is a little unclear and appears to go rather further than the court subsequently went in *Budana*. In *Budana*, the key point was that there was clear evidence that the solicitor and client intended the original CFA to continue if at all possible and, in such circumstances, the court concluded that the CFA, even if strictly novated, continued to be a PCFA. In *Catalano*, the plain intention was to end the original CFA and to enter into a new and expressly post-LASPO CFA. In such a situation it is more difficult to see how the new CFA should come to be treated as a PCFA, but that appears to be the conclusion that the court arrived at.

Given the circumstances of *Catalano*—a failed claim—the court did not need to go on to deal with success fee issues and hence this part of the judgment is not fully reasoned. No doubt in due course there will be a case where the claimant has swapped arrangements, as in *Catalano*, in order to try and secure QOCS out of a fear of the claim failing, but then in fact wins the claim. At that stage it may be necessary to explore in a little more detail whether the success fee under what was plainly intended to be a post-LASPO CFA continues to be recoverable between the parties.

Lastly on this issue, in light of *Price* (paras **6–05** and **6–06** above) if there has been such a change in the funding arrangements which might operate successfully in order to secure QOCS—for example where no services were ever provided under the original CFA (a possibility the Court of Appeal expressed some scepticism about but was not prepared to rule out entirely) and if the case is one where the defendant has previously been notified that the case was funded by a CFA with a success fee, it will be important to expressly inform that defendant that this is no longer the case if the claimant is not to risk losing QOCS despite having abandoned the recoverable success fee.

Q6. Does the *Catalano* case answer all the questions about whether a party can have QOCS protection if they have had a pre-commencement funding agreement?

Catalano provides an authoritative answer to the key question of whether a   6–23
claimant can abandon a PCFA in order to try and bring him or herself within QOCS. In general, the answer is "no". Although *Catalano* was dealing with the position in relation to a CFA, given the wording of CPR r.48.2 the answer would be the same where the claimant had entered into a pre-April 2013 ATE policy with an ostensibly recoverable premium, but later sought to resile from that in order to obtain QOCS. Whilst the latter situation is less likely (if the claimant had ATE, why would there be a need for QOCS), it might arise where, for example, a claimant had been able to obtain limited ATE cover pre-April 2013 but was unable to obtain top up cover post and realised that the level of ATE cover available was inadequate and QOCS would be preferable. In light

of *Catalano*, an attempt to cancel the pre-April 2013 policy to obtain QOCS protection would be likely to fail.

There are a few uncertainties left by *Catalano*, as identified at [27]–[29] of the judgment. In particular, the suggestion at [29] that a different conclusion might be arrived at if "the second CFA retrospectively discharged and extinguished the first agreement and replaced it with a second agreement" seems inconsistent not only with the remainder of that paragraph of the judgment but also with the judgment generally. The logic of the earlier part of the judgment appears to be that if the claimant had entered into a PCFA and if (in relation to a CFA) any services had been provided under it at all, then that was a situation which could not later be unravelled or changed in order to obtain QOCS. Such a position has the benefit of certainty—and at least part of the potential injustice that might be caused by such certainty is mitigated by the suggestion that any subsequent CFA would be regarded as still being a PCFA with a recoverable success fee. The court was sceptical about the possible exceptions it identified towards the end of its judgment and it may be that such exceptions are in fact more illusory than real.

Catalano also does not address the question of what the position is where the claimant is a different claimant—for example where a claimant with a PCFA dies and the claim is then continued by the personal representatives on an ostensibly post-LASPO CFA. At present, there is no authoritative decision on this point, though there is a first appellate decision in the case of *Morgan* to the effect that what is material is whether the particular claimant against whom the costs order is made had a PCFA.

Q7. Does the 10% uplift to damages as provided for in *Simmons v Castle*[69] apply in cases where the parties are publicly-funded?

6–24 Yes. The only exclusion from the uplift is in respect of those claimant who fall within s.44(6) of LASPO. A publicly-funded claimant does not.

Q8. Will QOCS apply where a personal injury claimant entered into a CFA pre-Jackson Reforms but did not enter into an ATE insurance policy until after the introduction of QOCS?

6–25 No. Whilst the broad intention behind the introduction of QOCS was to act as a quid pro quo for the loss of between the parties recoverability of ATE premiums, the transitional provision at CPR r.44.17 expressly provides that QOCS does not apply to proceedings where the claimant has entered into a PCFA. These are defined in CPR r.48.2. They include a CFA with a success fee. Accordingly, where either or both of a CFA with a success fee or an ATE policy have been entered into prior to the 1 April 2013, QOCS will not be available. *Catalano* is a clear example of such a situation.

---

[69] *Simmons v Castle* [2012] EWCA Civ 1288; [2013] 1 W.L.R. 1239.

Q9. Does QOCS apply to just personal injury? We have a commercial litigation matter for breach of contract so nothing to do with personal injury.

Yes, at present QOCS only applies to personal injury—see CPR r.44.13(1). The   6–26
main body of the text identifies some areas where QOCS might be introduced, whether in the same form as at present or in a revised form. It is not presently anticipated that general commercial litigation will be one of these areas and indeed any extension of QOCS at all seems unlikely in the near future.

Q10. Does QOCS apply to claims for damages for clinical negligence?

Yes—see the definition of a claim for personal injuries at CPR r.2.3(1).   6–27

Q11. Does QOCS apply to personal injury claims where the injury was sustained in a foreign jurisdiction and proceedings are to be issued in England?

If the claim is one where the English courts have jurisdiction and if the   6–28
claim is one involving a claim for damages for personal injuries, then there is no obvious reason why QOCS should not apply. Any award of costs to the defendant will be an award of costs by the English court applying the CPR and the provisions within those same rules which protected the claimant against enforcement of that award will equally apply.

Q12. Are detailed assessment proceedings caught by QOCS?

It is assumed that the reference here to detailed assessment proceedings is to   6–29
detailed assessment proceedings which follow a personal injury claim. There is no authoritative judicial determination directly on this point at this stage. On the face of the wording of CPR r.44.13 and 44.14 there are clearly arguments which may be put forward both for and against detailed assessment proceedings following a personal injury claim being regarded as part of the "proceedings which include a claim for damages for personal injuries" within CPR r.44.13. Ultimately, the issue is likely to be seen as one of purposive construction – see the approach taken by the Court of Appeal to the word "proceedings" in a QOCS context in *Wickes*.[70]

Considerable support for the proposition that QOCS does apply to detailed assessment proceedings following a personal injury claim may, however, be taken from the Supreme Court's judgment in *Ho*[71]. In *Ho*, which addressed the question of QOCS and set off, the potential set off had arisen within what the Supreme Court described as an "assessment dispute". The Court specifically referred to the potential for a defendant obtaining an order for costs in its favour within detailed assessment proceedings as being one of the key examples of where opposing costs orders "may occur in a single set of proceedings" – see paras 6 and 7 – and proceeded on the express basis, both by reference

---

[70] *Wickes Building Supplies Ltd v Blair (no. 2) (Costs)* [2020] EWCA Civ 17.
[71] *Ho v Adelekun* [2021] UKSC 43, [2021] 1 W.L.R 5132.

to the facts of the case and in considering the generally applicable principles, that this was a situation where QOCS applied. Of course, absent specific argument on the point this does not prevent the point being argued elsewhere. However, it is perhaps a strong indication that the correct construction of CPR r.44.13 treats detailed assessment proceedings as being part of the personal injury proceedings for the purposes of QOCS. Anecdotally, it is understood that this is how the position is treated in practice by some judges, though as noted, there are sensible counter arguments. See further **Qs. 17** and **36** in **Ch.8**.

B. QOCS and discontinuance

Q13. Where a claimant is currently subject to an "old style" CFA (pre-April 2013 where QOCS would not apply) but the client seeks the protection of QOCS, would the presence of the old-style CFA prevent the claimant ever obtaining the benefit of QOCS under the workings of CPR r.44.17? If the claimant was to continue as a litigant in person would she then obtain the benefit of QOCS?

6–30 On the strict wording of the transitional provision, CPR r.44.17 provides that the fact of the pre-April 2013 CFA (assuming it had a success fee) would mean that QOCS is not available. Cases such as *Catalano*, above, suggest that that strict wording will be applied and provided the claimant in this example had received the benefit of some services under the PCFA (the CFA that had been entered into prior to April 2013) in respect of the claim, then QOCS will not be available. A change in representation to become a litigant in person would not be likely to make any difference.

Q14. QOCS and security for costs—A personal injury claimant enjoys QOCS protection: however this can be displaced. If the defendant's defence rests on a basis which, if accepted, means that there is a serious risk of the claim being held to be fundamentally dishonest, is the defendant able to seek security for costs against the claimant despite their ostensibly QOCS-protected status. We are not aware of such an order having been made since QOCS was introduced: indeed the concept of QOCS would seem to be inconsistent with it. There are of course only limited grounds on which security for costs can be ordered. If the defendant could establish one, would there be a risk of such an order, at the court's discretion?

6–31 The first point to note is that an individual claimant in a personal injury case is not usually vulnerable to an order for security for costs under CPR r.25.12. It is rare for the gateway criteria under CPR r.25.13 to be satisfied in such a situation. Assuming, however, that such conditions were satisfied, the court would have a discretion to order security for costs if it was just to do so in all the circumstances of the case. In a previous edition of this supplement, it was stated that there was no authority as to the impact of QOCS on such an application. It was stated that with a company the core test is usually whether there is reason to believe that it will be unable to pay the defendant's costs if ordered to do so. If that was the applicable test, then QOCS would probably be of little relevance, since the hypothesis on which the court is operating is that of an adverse costs order being made and the defendant being able to enforce it, which assumes no procedural bar to doing so. However, the test for an individual is different and usually turns simply on establishing a threshold (for example proving that the claimant has taken steps in relation to their assets that would make it difficult to enforce an order for costs against them) and then an exercise of discretion. There does not appear to be any reason why, as part of that exercise of discretion and balancing the justice of the case the court could not take into account the possibility that QOCS would be available. Much will depend on the facts of the case. However, if the court formed the view that there was a substantial risk that if the defendant won, it would be because the claim had been found to be fundamentally dishonest, then the court would be unlikely to attach much weight to the question of QOCS (in the same way that an ATE policy without anti-avoidance provisions would be of little weight if the facts of the case suggested that if the claimant lost it would be likely to be as a result of findings which would give the insurer a basis for avoiding the policy). If, however, there are a range of possible outcomes and a finding of fundamental dishonesty is neither inherently required in order to dismiss the claim nor particularly likely then the prima facie availability of QOCS will probably be of much more weight.

Since that edition, the helpful judgment of Mrs Justice Lambert in *QL v PM*[72] was handed down. In that case, consistent with the above analysis, the judge concluded that since one of the grounds for disapplying QOCS was fundamental dishonesty and since the claimant had not made full disclosure and that there was evidence that the claimant had been transferring money abroad to seek to stifle any claim to adverse costs, there was a real prospect of both the court making a costs order against her and of the QOCS provisions being disapplied. Accordingly, the potential applicability of QOCS provisions did not stand in the way of making the order for security for costs.

Q15. The claimant has incurred costs unnecessarily in an unmeritorious claim. He has now served a notice of discontinuance and, as QOCS applies, is not liable for the defendant's costs (unless an exception applies). In the above circumstances, is it possible for the defendant to apply for a wasted costs order even though a notice of discontinuance has been filed by the claimant?

This question covers a number of issues.

6–32

Firstly, the assumption that the claimant is not liable, in principle, for the defendant's costs is wrong. CPR r.38.6 is not disapplied merely because QOCS applies. As discussed above, the defendant is entitled in principle to the same costs order whether QOCS applies or not. QOCS only addresses the

---

[72] *QL v PM* [2018] EWHC 2268 (QB).

enforcement of that order. Of course, as with publicly funded claims, it may be the case that the difficulties with enforcement mean that, save where the costs order is automatic (which, of course, it is under CPR r.38.6(1) unless the court orders otherwise), there will be cases where the defendant chooses not to spend money arguing for a costs order which serves little practical benefit. However, in the example given, the defendant will by default have a costs order in its favour.

As to exceptions, CPR PD 44 para.12.4(c) must not be overlooked. A claimant cannot (automatically) escape the risk of a finding of fundamental dishonesty by discontinuing the claim and if there is any suggestion in this particular case that the claim was dishonest, in whole or part, rather than merely being unmeritorious, then this may be worth investigating.

An interesting issue arises where the claim is one which was arguably abusive or in relation to which it could be argued that there were no reasonable grounds for bringing the claim, but the claimant has beaten the defendant to the punch by discontinuing the claim before an application could be heard to have the proceedings struck out. CPR PD 44 para.12.4(c) does not address this. Under CPR r.38.4 it would be possible to apply to have the notice of discontinuance set aside in order for the court to hear an application to strike out which, if successful, would allow for full enforcement of the costs order without permission. It earlier editions of this supplement it was stated that it was likely that the court would only permit this in exceptional circumstances—perhaps where a claimant has been repeatedly warned as to the abusive nature of the claim, but has persisted, but then responds to a formal application to strike out by discontinuing. Recent cases such as *Shaw* and *Mabb*, above, do not set the bar quite so high, but nevertheless indicate that the court will be reluctant to set aside such a notice (save in the CPR PD 44 para.12.4(c) situation).

Accordingly, the defendant is not left entirely without remedy in this situation (though in practice, whether even an enforceable costs order is of any value against an impecunious claimant is a question which must be considered), but faces a significant burden and must also act quickly if it wishes to raise matters, such as those under CPR r.44.15, to allow effective enforcement of a costs order in a discontinued case.

As to the possibility of seeking a wasted costs order, the ability to make such an application is not ousted by the fact of the discontinuance. Nor, prima facie, is it ousted by QOCS, since CPR r.44.14 is directed to costs orders made against the claimant, not other parties. However, as is the case with publicly funded claimants (see the guidance in *Symphony Group Plc v Hodgson*[73]) the court will be very astute to guard against the risk that the wasted costs application is motivated by an inability to recover costs against the claimant, rather than being a properly founded application for wasted costs against a solicitor. Wasted costs orders will not be made against a solicitor merely because they

---

[73] *Symphony Group Plc v Hodgson* [1993] 3 W.L.R. 830, 842; [1997] Costs L.R. (Core Vol.) 319.

acted for a claimant in respect of a claim which is doomed to fail, or because they acted on a CFA basis. The courts will assume, unless it can be established to the contrary, that the solicitor will have properly advised the client and will have been acting on instructions. The difficulties in overcoming the problems created by the privilege in the advice given by a solicitor to their client when pursuing wasted costs orders are well known and are likely to make such applications unattractive in these situations save in the clearest of cases.

Q16. If a case is subject to QOCS and the claimant serves a notice of discontinuance on a defendant, do they automatically become liable for the defendant's costs?

This is largely answered in the previous question. Absent a successful application by the claimant for the court to "order otherwise", the automatic effect of serving a notice of discontinuance is that the claimant is liable for the defendant's costs (CPR r.38.6). The claimant could ask the court to order otherwise and seek a different order in principle.   6–33

If the claimant does not, he or she is liable for the defendant's costs, but in a personal injury case, QOCS applies despite the discontinuance (the claimant is in no better or worse position than a losing claimant). The previous answer discusses the defendant's ability then to seek to enforce despite QOCS, for example by seeking to have the notice of discontinuance set aside so as to obtain a finding of fundamental dishonesty or to seek to have the claim struck out. Neither of these are easy courses.

At the risk of laborious repetition, much of the misunderstanding in this area comes from a failure to appreciate the difference between a defendant becoming entitled to a costs order in principle, which is nothing to do with QOCS, and the ability to enforce that order, which is where the QOCS rules apply.

Q17. I need to discontinue my client's proceedings against a number of defendants in an action. Obviously, when I file a notice of discontinuance, there will be a deemed order for costs against the claimant unless the court orders otherwise (CPR r.38.6(1)). However, my understanding of QOCS (from CPR rr.44.14, 44.15 and 44.16) is that an order for costs may only be enforced if the claim has been struck out (no court permission needed) or if it is fundamentally dishonest (court permission needed). We do not have sufficient time to obtain written consent from each and every defendant in a consent order but in any event consider that we would be QOCS protected even by serving a notice of discontinuance.

This is largely answered in the pre-preceding answer. A costs order will be deemed to be made against the claimant unless the court orders otherwise, pursuant to CPR r.38.6. Assuming the claim is within CPR r.44.13 and no other exception applies, then QOCS protection will be available. However, if the claim is one which might be said to have been brought in a "fundamentally   6–34 dishonest" fashion, the defendants will still be able to ask the court to grant permission to enforce some or all of the costs order.

There is also a risk that the defendants might be able to persuade the court to set aside the notice of discontinuance and ask the court instead to strike the claim out, to avail themselves of the exceptions under CPR r.44.15. Some discussion of the circumstances in which the same may be allowed and consideration of such case law as there is available to date is set out above.

Q18. CPR r.44 relating to QOCS states that it will not apply if the claimant has disclosed no reasonable grounds for bringing the proceedings. What is the position where during the course of the court proceedings medical evidence comes to light which is not supportive of causation which means the claim may have to be withdrawn/discontinued? At the time proceedings were issued it was believed there were reasonable prospects/grounds for bringing the claim. Would the claimant still have the benefit of QOCS or would they automatically be liable for the defendant's costs due to filing a notice of discontinuance?

6–35　It is necessary to distinguish between the liability in principle for the defendant's costs and the availability of QOCS. As is noted above, QOCS does not prevent adverse costs orders. It merely prevents enforcement of them. In the above situation, and unless the court orders otherwise or the parties agree separate terms, the claimant will be liable for the defendant's costs on discontinuance by virtue of CPR r.38.6.

There does not appear to be any suggestion that the claim was fundamentally dishonest. Nor does the question suggest that the need to discontinue has arisen in an attempt to defeat an extant strike out application. Accordingly, the more likely circumstances in which a defendant might try and/or possibly be able to set aside the notice of discontinuance do not seem to apply. The prime (if not sole) purpose of QOCS is to prevent claimants being required to pay adverse costs in failed claims. The circumstances referred to above—those of a claim which was properly brought, but which on closer and more detailed examination has been revealed to have limited prospects of success—are precisely those where QOCS is intended to apply and as a matter of generality the fact that this has been recognised sooner rather than later and the claim has been discontinued is likely to be something the court will recognise as a positive step. Provided there is no suggestion that the claim was flawed from the outset, or that it has been negligently presented, or that the defects could and should have been noted much sooner (any or all of which might encourage a defendant to try and set aside the notice of discontinuance or seek an alternative remedy such as wasted costs) the claimant in such a situation is likely to be able to rely on his or her QOCS protection.

Lastly, on this point, it is not correct to say that QOCS will not apply if the claimant has disclosed no reasonable grounds for bringing the claim. QOCS is only disapplied under CPR r.44.13 (in this connection) if the claim has been struck out on the basis that the claimant has disclosed no reasonable grounds for bringing a claim. Accordingly, a defendant cannot simply obtain a deemed order under CPR r.38.6 and then appear at, say, an enforcement hearing and argue that QOCS does not apply because the claim disclosed no reasonable grounds. The defendant would have to have the claim struck out first. If this has already occurred, then of course there would have been no need to discontinue. If it has not occurred before discontinuance, then the defendant's only recourse would be to seek to set the notice of discontinuance aside in order to try and have the case struck out. Some of the issues and difficulties in this regard are discussed in the main text above, by reference to the cases of *Shaw* and *Mabb*.

C. QOCS and settlement offers

Q19. In respect of CPR r.44.14 (1) relating to QOCS, can an order for costs be made up to the extent of any damages when a Calderbank offer has been made, or does this rule only apply when a Part 36 offer has been made (i.e. this rule does not apply to Calderbank offers)?

CPR r.44.14(1) is ostensibly unrelated to Pt 36 (or indeed Calderbank offers). 6–36
In any situation where the defendant has a costs order in its favour—whether this be an interim costs order due, say, to a disclosure application, a final costs order because of a claimant's failure to beat a Part 36 or Calderbank offer or indeed a costs order in favour of a defendant on detailed assessment, the order may be enforced, without the court's permission, to its full extent save where that full extent exceeds the aggregate amount the claimant was awarded by way of damages and interest and provided the damages and interest were awarded by way of a court order (see the *Cartwright* case discussed above).

In this regard, the often-used comment that, from a defendant's perspective, "Part 36 trumps QOCS" must be approached with some circumspection. Whilst it is correct that a Part 36 offer—or indeed a Calderbank offer—if effective, may lead to a costs order in the defendant's favour for part of the proceeding, that costs order itself is still subject to QOCS and therefore—absent any of the QOCS exceptions being made out—can only be enforced to the extent of damages and interest awarded to a claimant. Of course, Part 36 (or, where appropriate, the use of Calderbank) offers remain powerful tools for defendants in light of their ability to (i) deny a claimant their own costs after a particular date and (ii) obtain an adverse costs order which has the potential to diminish or extinguish the value of the claimant's claim. However, it would be an error to operate on the basis that the successful use of a Part 36 offer meant that the QOCS provisions did not apply.

At the risk of repetition, however, defendants must be alive to the point that settling a case by way of acceptance (by claimant or defendant) of a Part 36 offer or by way of Tomlin order does not give rise to an order for damages in the claimant's favour, within the meaning of CPR r.44.14. In such circumstances, if the defendant has a costs order in its favour, there are no damages or interest against which those costs can be set off.

Q20. I'm the claimant in a claim to which QOCS applies and in which the defendant has recently made a generous Part 36 offer. If I don't accept the offer and, at trial, my claim fails completely, will I have to pay the defendant's costs?

6–37   No, unless you fall within any of the exceptions in CPR rr.44.13 and 44.14 which are discussed above. If the claim was successful in part, but you failed to beat the defendant's Part 36 offer, then any damages and interest awarded could be reduced by payment of any adverse costs awarded. However, if the claim fails completely and unless the claim is found to have been fundamentally dishonest or falls within one of the other exceptions, then an adverse costs order is likely to be made against you, but that costs order will not be capable of enforcement (and will not register as an unpaid judgment for credit rating purposes, etc.).

Q21. What should practitioners do in the light of *Cartwright?* Should claimants not use Part 36 offers? Should settlements be recorded in Tomlin orders? If acting for the defendant, is it advisable to seek to bring a counterclaim even if there is little basis for it?

6–38   *Cartwright* turned on the question of whether the terms of settlement—recorded in a Tomlin order—amount to "an order for damages and interest made in favour of the claimant" in accordance with CPR r.44.14. If it did not, there was nothing for the defendant's costs to be set off against (or at least nothing by way of damages—the defendant could seek arguably seek a set-off of costs against costs—see *Howe* above – but that route is now blocked by the Supreme Court decision in *Ho*).

The Court of Appeal in *Cartwright* held that a settlement by way of Tomlin order was not an order of the court under CPR r.44.14. It expressly held that the acceptance of a Part 36 offer similarly did not give rise to an order of the court for damages and interest. CPR r.36.14 expressly provides that where a Part 36 offer is accepted, the acceptance is on the terms of the offer. Whilst a deemed costs order follows or whilst the court may be required to award costs if the acceptance is out of time, that order is an order as to costs and not damages and interest.

This is an unhelpful anomaly. The court accepted that it was unintended but could not find an acceptable way to construe the rules to avoid it and the CPRC has decided not to seek to amend the rules. Accordingly, the practical incidence of QOCS and, in particular, the question of whether the claimant's damages are vulnerable to set off will depend on whether the award of damages and costs is by way of court order or settlement by way of Tomlin order or Part 36 acceptance.

From a claimant's point of view, there is no need therefore to avoid the use of Part 36 offers. The Court of Appeal's decision clearly places an accepted offer in the same, more favourable, camp as Tomlin orders. There are, of course, clear benefits generally to the use of Part 36 offers by claimants in particular and the decision in *Cartwright* does not undermine those. Similarly,

Tomlin orders are an effective mechanism for recording settlements whilst allowing for a simpler route to enforcement. There is no reason from a claimant's perspective to seek to avoid these. Indeed, the decision in *Cartwright* should provide further encouragement to claimants to settle by way of Part 36 offer and/or Tomlin order. What is important is that a claimant, on settling a case, should ensure that the settlement is properly recorded. In particular, the prevalent practice on settlement, including on acceptance of Part 36 offers, of asking the court to make an order by consent should be avoided.

From a defendant's perspective, *Cartwright* is unhelpful. Whilst the position in relation to QOCS and counterclaims requires further clarification by rule change or higher authority, there appears to be both force and logic in the judgment in the case of *Waring v McDonnell*[74] to the effect that a counter-claiming defendant is not a claimant for the purposes of QOCS in respect of the claimant's claim, but would have QOCS in respect of his own claim, to the extent that it included a claim for damages for personal injuries.

D. QOCS and set-off

Q22. A claimant loses a personal injury claim and a costs order is made in the usual way but the judge also finds fundamental dishonesty and thus allows enforcement of the costs order totalling £7,000.00. The claimant appeals against the finding of fundamental dishonesty, but not the loss of the claim, and wins and so the finding of fundamental dishonesty is quashed and the claimant is awarded costs of the appeal of £12,000.00. The original order against the claimant in respect of the costs of losing the personal injury claim remains in place but is now unenforceable. Could the defendant, successful in the primary claim, set off the £7,000.00 owed to it, under the common law doctrine of set-off?

Following the decision of the Supreme Court in *Ho*, the answer to this is no.   6–39
Set off is not available since this would conflict with the express terms of CPR r.44.14. The claimant would be entitled to his or her costs and the defendant would not be able to set off the costs order in its favour or to otherwise enforce it, absent the application of one of the express exceptions in the QOCS rules, which do not appear to apply here.

E. QOCS and costs management

Q23. Do parties still have to costs budget where QOCS applies and, if so, is the agreeing of budgets in such cases likely to be more difficult?

In answer to the first part of the question, the answer is a simple "yes", assum-   6–40
ing the case is within CPR r.3.12. QOCS relates to enforcement only. Until a case is concluded, a defendant (and the court) will not know whether or not the case is one where there might be good grounds to seek a disapplication

---

[74] *Waring v McDonnell* unreported 6 November 2018 Brighton County Court.

of QOCS. In any event, the defendant may be in a position to enforce a costs order against damages without needing to seek to disapply QOCS. There are a wide range of situations where the defendant may be entitled to, and able to enforce, some or all of its costs. In any and all of these situations, the defendant will need to be able to quantify its costs and, if it has failed to file a costs budget, is likely to find those costs (at least post-the date on which a budget should have been supplied) limited to court fees only pursuant to CPR r.3.14 or to suffer some other form of costs penalty or reduction.

As to agreeing budgets in such cases, there is no reason in principle why the budget should be more or less difficult to agree. Costs management also applies, for example, in publicly funded claims, where a not dissimilar form of costs protection exists (and, in fact, QOCS protection is also available). In both types of case, the budgeting rules apply without amendment. In practice, there will be concerns in such cases that defendants will be inclined to underestimate their own costs (because they are unlikely to be recovering them in many cases, or recovering them in full even in cases where some success is achieved), with a view to painting the claimant's budgeted costs as disproportionate by comparison. Anecdotal evidence suggests that the courts are alive to such risks, both in cases generally and in cases where QOCS is likely to apply. Also, there is a risk that in such cases the perceived greater likelihood that the claimant will be recovering costs at the end of the case may make the defendant more inclined to take every opportunity to limit those costs, and therefore to take a more aggressive approach at the budgeting stage.

Anecdotally, it appears to be the case that the most regularly contested CCMCs relate to personal injury claims, including clinical negligence and there appears to be a greater willingness to agree budgets between the parties in commercial claims. Whether this has anything particularly to do with QOCS or is merely a reflection of the fact that personal injury has long been the hotbed of satellite costs litigation is a moot point.

F. QOCS—the future

Q24. Will QOCS be extended to other areas in due course?

6–41   In early editions of this work, it was stated that this seemed highly likely. However, it now appears that there is no immediate legislative appetite for any extension – see the commentary above. It remains highly likely that if the mesothelioma exemption from the loss of between the parties recoverability of additional liabilities is itself ended, then QOCS or some similar protection for such cases will be introduced at the same time, on the current lines. However, there is no sign of the mesothelioma exemption being ended in the immediate future.

The extension of QOCS to publication and privacy claims was anticipated, but it is now clear that a different approach was adopted in April 2019.

Other areas, in particular, claims against the police, may benefit from a QOCS extension and in those cases at least it is likely that any such QOCS regime would follow the current model. The extension to claims against the police, addressed in detail by the CJC Working Group (above) would appear to be the most compelling and also, perhaps, the simplest to introduce since it would slip relatively simply into the existing model (though such introduction might provide an opportunity to review some of the existing provisions). The calls for an extension to judicial review proceedings also merit attention given the perceived difficulties for claimants obtaining ATE insurance.[75]

However, the Government's post-LASPO implementation review, discussed in the main text above, does not suggest that any extension of QOCS, whether in these areas or others, is likely imminently.

---

[75] See Government urged to extend costs-shifting to JR.

Fixed Costs; Indemnity Costs; Litigants in Person

What lies ahead

As referred to in Chapter 1, Sir Geoffrey Vos MR's speech to the Association   7–01
of Costs Lawyers on 25 November 2021 highlighted the Government's
announcement of its intention to bring forward many of the remaining recommendations as to fixed recoverable costs made by Lord Justice Jackson in
his report reviewing Fixed Recoverable Costs, published in July 2017.

That report noted that the general rule that a winner is entitled to recover
costs from the losing party was a "recipe for runaway costs". The two control
mechanisms had previously been declared to be "costs budgeting" and "a
general scheme of fixed recoverable costs" ("FRC"). The July 2017 report had
for its purpose the development of proposals for extending the FRC. It recommended a grid of FRC for all fast track cases, and suggested a separate grid for
certain claims up to £100,000 which could be tried in three days or less, with
no more than two expert witnesses giving oral evidence on each side. It recommended a separate grid for clinical negligence claims with a financial value
of up to £25,000. It recommended a voluntary pilot scheme for business and
property cases up to £250,000 with streamlined procedures and capped recoverable costs up to £80,000, and if successful, to be rolled out more widely for
use in appropriate cases. It also recommended measures to limit recoverable
costs in judicial review claims by reference to protective costs rules reserved
for environmental cases.

The writing has been on the wall for some time. On 6 September 2021, the
Ministry of Justice ("MoJ") published the government's response to a 2019 consultation paper, Extending Fixed Recoverable Costs in Civil Cases: Implementing
Sir Rupert Jackson's Proposals. The government's response confirmed its intention to introduce fixed recoverable costs for claims up to £100,000.

It specifically proposes:

- Extending fixed recoverable costs to all civil cases in the fast track up to a
  value of £25,000 in damages, as originally proposed by Sir Rupert Jackson.
- Expanding the fast track to include intermediate cases valued between
  £25,000 to £100,000 in damages (where the trial should not last longer
  than three days with no more than two expert witnesses giving oral evidence for each party, and where the case can be justly and proportionately
  managed under an expedited procedure). This is subject to exceptions
  such as mesothelioma/asbestos, clinical negligence and intellectual property cases. Judges will exercise discretion to ensure that intermediate cases

are appropriately allocated. The existing multi-track court fees for these intermediate cases will remain, but the government will keep this under review.

- Allocating all fast track cases to one of four bands of complexity, as set out in existing fixed recoverable costs regimes for most fast track personal injury cases. The four bands were recommended by Sir Rupert Jackson in his proposals. Those bands are:
  - Band 1: RTA (non-personal injury, including credit hire), and defended debt claims;
  - Band 2: RTA, personal injury claims (including package holiday sickness claims) proceeding in the pre-action Protocol;
  - Band 3: RTA, personal injury claims (outside of the pre-action Protocol); EL and PL claims; housing disrepair claims; tracked possession claims, and other money claims; and
  - Band 4: Complex tracked possession claims, professional negligence claims, property disputes, EL claims (not including noise induced hearing loss), and other claims at or towards the top of the fast track (i.e. the present £25,000 "limit").

- Unsuccessful challenges to the band of the claim creating a costs liability with further penalty for unreasonable behaviour. No intermediate case should be allowed to exit from the proposed fixed recoverable costs regime, unless there are exceptional circumstances. The current provision in CPR r.45.29J, enabling a party to exit the fixed costs regime in the fast track in exceptional circumstances, will continue to apply.

- Ring-fencing fees for counsel in Band 4 and in noise induced hearing loss cases only.

- Implementing an uplift of 35% to Part 36 offers not accepted in time, alternatively an uplift of 50% in circumstances where a party has behaved unreasonably; a 25% uplift for each additional claimant in claims arising from the same set of facts; and a London weighting of 12.5%. Consideration will also be given to making a general provision for higher fixed recoverable costs and additional disbursements where claimants are vulnerable.

- Implementing a new process and separate grid for noise induced hearing loss fast track claims valued below £25,000.

- Costs budgeting for all "heavy" judicial review cases (where the costs of a party were likely to exceed £100,000), observing that cost budgeting was effective in creating greater costs certainty for all parties in other areas of civil litigation. Courts will have the discretion to make a costs management order, either on their own initiative or upon the application of either party involved. In the government's view, parties would be forced to carefully consider costs at the start.

In summary, the recommendations made by Sir Rupert Jackson in 2017 will largely be implemented, save for his recommendation of an "Intermediate

Track" – instead, the government proposes that those cases will fall into an expanded fast track for cases valued up to £100,000.

To implement these proposals, the government is to submit draft rules for consideration by the Civil Procedure Rule Committee. We await further developments regarding that. The government confirmed that the figures in the fast track and intermediate cases grids in Sir Rupert's report would be updated for inflation.

In the minutes of the CPRC for November 2021, the MoJ Costs policy representative reinforced the intention to implement the extension of the FRC, and to do so in October 2022. There is clearly much more detail to come, but familiarity with the existing provisions has become even more important.

In the meantime, 31 May 2021 saw the introduction of a new Pre-Action Protocol for Personal Injury Claims Below the Small Claims Limit in Road Traffic Accidents for accidents occurring after 31 May 2021 ("the RTA Small Claims Protocol") and a new PD 27B which provides a tariff for the recovery of experts' fees in greater detail than, albeit in similar format to, the existing PD 27; and, The Whiplash Injury Regulations 2021 also came into force which set out a tariff for the amount to be awarded for pain, suffering, and loss of amenity payable in relation to one or more whiplash injuries and one or more minor psychological injuries suffered on the same occasion.

In order to implement the whiplash reforms, it was necessary to amend the CPR to, among other things, increase the small claims track limit for RTA personal injury claims from £1,000 to £5,000 for accidents on or after 31 May 2021. This change means that the majority of whiplash claims will no longer be subject to the fast track rules, where legal costs are recovered under the "loser pays" principle, subject to qualified one-way costs shifting, but to the small claims track rules where only limited costs are recoverable.

Any claim started under PD 27B will be treated as allocated to the small claims track and therefore its costs regime applies. The claimant will be able to recover the fees for a fixed cost medical report or medical records. The defendant has to pay for a further medical report, in addition to the first fixed cost medical report, if the claimant requests and justifies it. The court may also order that the defendant pay the cost of any police accident report incurred by the claimant.

For cases which exit the Official Injury Claim (OIC) Portal and where proceedings are started, the fixed recoverable costs provisions as set out in section IIIA of CPR 45 will normally apply.

At first sight, the tariff appears to be considerably lower than the awards routinely made by the courts following the guidance of the Judicial College. The Civil Procedure (Amendment No.2) Rules 2021 came into force on the same date, and provide, amongst other things, amendments to Pt 45 with the addition of a new Section IIIB in readiness for the claims falling under the new Pre-Action Protocol.

The scene for what lies ahead for fixed costs appears to be set to be tariff driven with less costs recoverable than before.

Background

7–02   Presently, Pt 45 of the Civil Procedure Rules deals with fixed costs and is divided into sections. The topics dealt with are as follows:

Section I	Fixed Costs in the normally accepted sense, i.e. costs which are payable in a given set of circumstances
Section II	Road Traffic Accidents—fixed recoverable costs
Section III	Pre-Action Protocol for Low Value Personal Injury Claims in Road Traffic Accidents and Low Value Personal Injury (Employers' Liability and Public Liability) Claims
Section IIIA	Claims Which No Longer Continue Under the RTA and EL/PL Pre-Action Protocols and Claims to Which the Pre-Action Protocol for Resolution of Package Travel Claims Applies-Fixed Recoverable Costs
Section IIIB	Claims which do not comply or do not continue under the RTA Small Claims Protocol
Section IV	Scale Costs for Claims in the Intellectual Property Enterprise Court
Section V	Fixed Costs: HM Revenue and Customs
Section VI	Fast Track Trial Costs
Section VII	Costs Limits in Aarhus Convention Claims

Section I

7–03   Section I of Pt 45 sets out the amounts which are to be allowed in respect of legal representatives' charges in cases to which it applies unless the court otherwise orders. Any appropriate court fee will be allowed in addition to the costs set out in Section I. The fixed costs provisions apply where-

(a) the only claim is a claim for a specified sum of money exceeding £25 and certain circumstances apply;[1]

(b) the only claim is a claim where the court gave a fixed date for the hearing when it issued the claim and judgment is given for the delivery of goods, and the value of the claim exceeds £25;

(c) the claim is for the recovery of land, including a possession claim under Pt 55, whether or not the claim includes a claim for a sum of money and

---

[1] The provisions apply where: (i) judgment in default is obtained under CPR r.12.4(1); (ii) judgment on admission is obtained under CPR r.14.4(3); (iii) judgment on admission on part of the claim is obtained under CPR r.14.5(6); (iv) summary judgment is given under Pt 24; (v) the court has made an order to strike out a defence under CPR r.3.4(2)(a) as disclosing no reasonable grounds for defending the claim; or (vi) CPR r.45.4 applies.

the defendant gives up possession, pays the amount claimed, if any, and the fixed commencement costs stated in the claim form;

(d) the claim is for the recovery of land, including a possession claim under Pt 55, where one of the grounds for possession is arrears of rent, for which the court gave a fixed date for the hearing when it issued the claim and judgment is given for the possession of land (whether or not the order for possession is suspended on terms) and the defendant:

    (i)   has neither delivered a defence, or counterclaim, nor otherwise denied liability; or

    (ii)   has delivered a defence which is limited to specifying his proposals for the payment of arrears of rent;

(e) the claim is a possession claim under Section II of Pt 55 (accelerated possession claims of land let on an assured shorthold tenancy) and a possession order is made where the defendant has neither delivered a defence, or counterclaim, nor otherwise denied liability;

(f) the claim is a demotion claim under Section III of Pt 65 or a demotion claim is made in the same claim form in which a claim for possession is made under Pt 55 and that demotion claim is successful; or

(g) a judgment creditor has taken steps under Pts 70 to 73 to enforce a judgment or order. No sum in respect of legal representatives' charges will be allowed where the only claim is for a sum of money or goods not exceeding £25.[2]

The provisions of CPR r.45.3 operate to apply the costs fixed by Section I of Pt 45 when the defendant is liable only for fixed commencement costs, unless the court otherwise orders. The court refused to exercise its discretion to allow more than the fixed costs, on the particular facts of one case, stating, among other reasons: **7–04**

"... *this Court has recognised the importance of a summary and prompt procedure to secure enforcement of adjudicators' decisions properly reached".*

"A party which makes a 'without prejudice save as to costs' offer is not entitled in some way to have it responded to or to assume that threatened proceedings against it will or might be withheld. It would be different if the without prejudice correspondence had revealed some agreement by which the claimant undertook, at least temporarily, not to issue proceedings ... It would not be fair to limit a successful claimant which complied with the steps called for in the rule and the [TCC] Guide".

The claimant was justified in issuing proceedings and the Pt 24, summary judgment, application following a threatened defence and an unqualified admission on the part of the defendant after issue.[3]

---

[2] CPR r.45.1(1)–(5) and see PD 45 paras 1.1–1.3.

[3] *Amber Construction Services Ltd v London Interspace HG Ltd* [2007] EWHC 3042 (TCC); [2008] B.L.R. 74; [2008] 5 Costs L.R. 715 Akenhead J.

7–05   Where the claimant has claimed fixed commencement costs under CPR r.45.2; and judgment is entered in a claim (to which CPR r.45.1(2)(a) or (b) applies) in the circumstances specified in Table 2, the amount to be included in the judgment for the claimant's legal representative's charges is the total of the fixed commencement costs; and the relevant amount shown in Table 2 depending on the particular type of judgment.[4]

The remainder of Pt 45 Section I contains rules covering: the amount of fixed commencement costs in a claim for the recovery of land or a demotion claim; costs on entry of judgment in a claim for the recovery of land or a demotion claim; miscellaneous fixed costs; and fixed enforcement costs.[5]

7–06   In an unusual departure from fixed costs, the High Court was concerned with a case where the claimant sought continuation of an interim charging order in respect of a claim to enforce an adjudicator's decision in a construction matter. The judgment sum in question was £185,000 odd plus interest plus costs of some £34,000. The applicant submitted that there was authority[6] for the proposition that in construction adjudications fixed costs are rarely going to be justified. In the instant case, the defendant was resident in the British Virgin Islands and had raised no defence or put anything forward to indicate why the interim charging order should not be made final. A number of other interested parties, such as the mortgagee and tenants of the subject property, had all been properly served but none of them had come forward with a reason why the order should not be made final. The court made the order final and considered the claimant's application for costs outside of the fixed costs regime. The court endorsed the decision in *Amber Construction Services Limited* for the proposition that the adjudication system would be undermined if a defaulting party could cause the creditor to run up substantial legal costs in the knowledge that when they seek to enforce their rights they are going to be left short because they will only recover fixed costs. However, the mere fact that the instant case was a construction adjudication case was not the reason for departure from the fixed costs regime. The instant case was one in which enforcement had not been straightforward. Personal service in the BVI, rather than the defendant nominating service, had necessarily caused additional cost and that rendered it unjust to limit the claimant to fixed costs.[7]

Section II

7–07   Section II of Pt 45 sets out the costs allowable in proceedings relating to certain road traffic accidents. The provisions apply to road traffic accident disputes,[8] where the accident giving rise to the dispute occurred on or after 6 October 2003. The fixed costs provisions are intended to meet the case where the

---

[4] CPR r.45.4.
[5] CPR rr.45.5–45.8.
[6] *Amber Construction Services Ltd v London Interspace HG Ltd* [2008] 5 Costs Law Reports at 715, per Akenhead J.
[7] *Blacknest Gate Limited (Formerly Fresh Lime Construction) v Seymour Realty Ltd*[2020] EWHC 3878 (TCC), per HHJ Kramer, sitting as a judge of the High Court.
[8] "Road traffic accident", "motor vehicle" and "road" are defined in CPR r.45.9(4).

parties have been able to agree damages within certain limits but have been unable to agree the amount of costs. The agreed damages include damages in respect of personal injury, damage to property, or both. The total value of the agreed damages must not exceed £10,000 or be within the small claims limit.[9] The provisions of this section do not apply where the claimant is a litigant in person, or where Sections III or IIIA of Pt 45 apply.[10]

Except where an application to exceed the fixed recoverable costs is made the only costs which are to be allowed are fixed recoverable costs calculated in accordance with CPR r.45.11; and disbursements are to be allowed in accordance with CPR r.45.12.[11]

The court will only entertain a claim for costs greater than the fixed recoverable costs if it considers that there are exceptional circumstances making it appropriate to do so. Failure to achieve an amount 20% greater than the amount of the fixed recoverable costs, will result in an order that the defendant pay to the claimant the lesser of the fixed recoverable costs and the assessed costs.[12]

Section III

Section III deals with the fixed costs that apply to low value personal injury   7–08 claims arising out of road traffic accidents, employers' liability and public liability. Where the relevant pre-action Protocol has not been complied with, CPR r.45.24 will apply to the costs consequences. In compliant cases, Section III sets out the applicable fixed costs.

The RTA Protocol Scheme

The provisions of the RTA Protocol apply to a claim for damages exceed-   7–09 ing £1,000, but not exceeding £10,000, arising from a road traffic accident occurring on or after 30 April 2010, and before 31 July 2013, or a claim for damages not exceeding £25,000 arising from a road traffic accident occurring on or after 31 July 2013. Claims which fall within the scope of the scheme must follow the process, although a claimant is entitled to settle directly with an insurer/defendant without using the process. The process may be adopted by agreement for claims arising from an accident prior to the implementation date, but the claimant's solicitor will only be allowed the fixed recoverable costs applicable to the process.

Changes have been made to the RTA Protocol, principally for the purpose of introducing a new regime in respect of the costs allowed for medical reports in claims to which the Protocol applies and which fall within the definition of "soft tissue injury claim" in para.1.1(16A) of the Protocol. A "fixed cost medical report" is defined as a report in a soft tissue injury claim which is from a medical expert who, save in exceptional circumstances:

---

[9] CPR rr.45.9(2), 26.8(2) sets out how the financial value of a claim is assessed for the purposes of allocation to track.
[10] CPR r.45.9(3).
[11] CPR r.45.10.
[12] CPR rr.45.13, 45.14.

> *"(a) has not provided treatment to the claimant, (b) is not associated with any person who has provided treatment and (c) does not propose or recommend that they or an associate provide treatment"* (Protocol para.1.1(10A)).

Paragraph 1.1(A1)(a) and (b) reads as follows:

> *"(A1) 'Accredited medical expert' means a medical expert who*
> a) *prepares a fixed cost medical report pursuant to paragraph 7.8A(1) before 1st June 2016 and, on the date that they are instructed, the expert is registered with MedCo as a provider of reports for soft tissue injury claims; or*
> b) *prepares a fixed cost medical report pursuant to paragraph 7.8A(1) on or after 1st June 2016 and, on the date that they are instructed, the expert is accredited by MedCo to provide reports for soft tissue injury claims."*

In para.1.1(16A) of the Protocol, a "fixed cost medical report" is defined as a report in a soft tissue injury claim which is from a medical expert who, save in exceptional circumstances:

> *"(a) has not provided treatment to the claimant, (b) is not associated with any person who has provided treatment and (c) does not propose or recommend that they or an associate provide treatment"* (Protocol para.1.1(10A)).

7–10   The rules and practice directions are unusual, in that they relate to work done in accordance with the RTA and EL/PL Protocols, rather than (except in relation to stage 3) to proceedings in court. The case will no longer continue under the Protocol if there is fraud at any stage, and under stage 1 if there is no admission of liability or there is an allegation of contributory negligence; or under stage 2 if damages cannot be agreed. Stage 3 applies where quantum cannot be agreed; application is then made to the court to determine the quantum.

The Protocol applies where: a claim for damages arises from a road traffic accident where the CNF is submitted on or after 31 July 2013; the claim includes damages in respect of personal injury; the claimant values the claim at no more than the Protocol upper limit; and, if proceedings were started the small claims track would not be the normal track for that claim.[13]

7–11   A low value RTA claim proceeding within the protocol did not automatically exit the Protocol when the personal injury element of the claim was settled. The Protocol was carefully designed to whittle down the disputes between the parties as the case passed through the various stages. CPR r.8.1(3) could not be used to subvert the Protocol process. Where a district judge, faced with a claim where the only outstanding issue was the claim for car hire charges, decided that the claim was not suitable to continue under the Stage 3 procedure but should continue under CPR Pt 7, the Court of Appeal held that

---

[13] RTA Protocol 4.1. In *JC and A Solicitors Ltd v Iqbal* [2017] EWCA Civ 355; [2017] C.P. Rep. 32; [2017] 3 Costs L.O. 377, the Court of Appeal dealt with the position under the RTA Protocol before its amendment in July 2013, and decided that the defendant had no right to repayment of stage 1 fixed costs where the claimant took no steps to pursue the claim after the conclusion of stage 1.

the district judge had not been entitled to make that order. The cost which the district judge's order caused the parties to incur were totally disproportionate to the sum at stake (the amount in dispute being £462).[14]

A claimant suffered personal injury in a road traffic accident. The claimant instructed solicitors and submitted a Claim Notification Form (CNF) in accordance with the Pre-Action Protocol for Low Value Personal Injury Claims in Road Traffic Accidents via the online portal. The defendant admitted liability.

The initial prognosis by a physician, suggesting that the symptoms would resolve in 12 months, was too optimistic. An orthopaedic surgeon took the view that the symptoms would take two years to resolve. This was subsequently revised to five years. There were also other conditions which resulted in psychiatric evidence being served.

The claimant requested an interim payment of £1,000 and then gave notice to the defendant that the claim was exiting the portal as the payment had not been made. This was incorrect as the payment had been made within the prescribed 10-day period.

The claimant commenced Pt 7 proceedings and the defendant admitted liability but disputed causation and quantum. The case was allocated to the multi-track and budgets were exchanged. After the CCMC the defendant made an increased Part 36 offer of £20,000 which the claimant accepted.

At detailed assessment the costs judge found, following the claimant's concession, that sending the notification to exit the portal, when not entitled to do so, amounted to unreasonable conduct within the meaning of CPR r.44.11. Having reviewed the facts and the authorities, the costs judge found:

> *"61. Given my conclusion that this case would always have exited the Protocol at some stage, it seems to me that the costs incurred would essentially have been the same as were actually incurred. To the extent that the departure would have been at a different time, I do not consider that to be sufficient to demonstrate any prejudice to the Defendant. In those circumstances, it would be inappropriate to limit the Claimant's costs in the manner contended for by the Defendant under rule 44.11. Instead, the Claimant should be entitled to such reasonable and proportionate costs as he can justify at a detailed assessment on the standard basis."*

The defendant appealed, arguing that the claimant's costs should be restricted to fixed costs under CPR r.45.18. The court on appeal reviewed the authorities cited before the costs judge and added *Surrey v Barnet and Chase Farm Hospitals NHS Trust*,[15] which was not cited in the court below, and found that these supported the costs judge's reasoning. The appeal court also found that CPR r.44.11 gives the court a discretion to be exercised judicially on the facts of the case before it. It is up to the costs judge to make the appropriate decision on the facts and arguments raised. The appeal was dismissed.[16]

---

[14] *Phillips v Willis* [2016] EWCA Civ. 401; [2016] C.P. Rep. 28; [2016] 3 Costs L.R. 473.
[15] *Surrey v Barnet and Chase Farm Hospitals NHS Trust* [2018] EWCA Civ 451; [2018] 1 W.L.R. 5831, [2018] 2 Costs L.O. 141.
[16] *Ryan v Hackett* [2020] EWHC 288 (QB), [2020] Costs L.R. 177; Stewart J.

The Pre-action Protocol for Low Value Personal Injury (Employers' Liability and Public Liability) Claims

7–12   This Protocol deals with low value personal injury employers' liability and public liability claims. An employers' liability claim is a claim by an employee against the employer for damages arising from a bodily injury sustained by the employee in the course of employment, or a disease that the claimant is alleged to have contracted as a consequence of the employer's breach of its duty of care in the course of the employee's employment, other than a physical or psychological injury caused by an accident or other single event. A public liability claim is a claim for damages for personal injuries arising out of a breach of duty of care made against a person other than the claimant's employer, or the claimant's employer in respect of matters arising other than in the course of the claimant's employment, but it does not include a claim for damages arising from a disease that the claimant is alleged to have contracted as a consequence of breach of statutory or common law duties of care, other than a physical or psychological injury caused by an accident or other single event.[17]

The protocol sets out the behaviour which the court expects of the parties prior to the start of proceedings where a claimant claims damages not exceeding £25,000 in an EL or PL claim.[18] The EL/PL Protocol applies where either the claim arises from an accident occurring on or after 31 July 2013, or in a disease claim where no letter of claim has been sent to the defendant before that date. The claim must include damages in respect of personal injury and must not exceed the upper limit of £25,000 on a full liability basis, including pecuniary losses but excluding interest. The claim must not be one in which the small claims track would be the normal track (i.e. the claim must be for more than £1,000). The Protocol ceases to apply to a claim where at any stage the claimant notifies the defendant that the claim has now been re-valued at more than the upper limit.[19] The protocol does not apply to a claim:

(i)   where the claimant or defendant acts as personal representative of a deceased person;

(ii)   where the claimant or defendant is a protected party[20];

(iii)   in a public liability claim where the defendant is an individual;

(iv)   where the claimant is bankrupt;

(v)   where the defendant is insolvent and there is no identifiable insurer;

(vi)   in the case of a disease claim, where there is more than one employer defendant;

---

[17] EL/PL Protocol 1.1.
[18] EL/PL Protocol 2.1. The Civil Procedure Rules 1998 enable the court to impose costs sanctions where this Protocol is not followed.
[19] EL/PL Protocol 4–4.2.
[20] As defined in CPR r.21.1(2).

(vii)   for personal injury arising from an accident or alleged breach of duty occurring outside England and Wales;

(viii) for damages in relation to harm, abuse or neglect of or by children or vulnerable adults;

(ix)   which includes a claim for clinical negligence;

(x)   for mesothelioma; or

(xi)   for damages arising out of a road traffic accident.

The fixed costs in CPR r.45.18 apply in relation to a claimant only where a claimant has a legal representative.[21]

The protocol procedure for both RTA and EL/PL is highly prescriptive and any further commentary would in effect be a mere repetition of the protocols and rules.   **7-13**

A claimant who had been injured in an accident at work sued his employers. He submitted a claim under the Protocol for Low Value Personal Injury (Employers' Liability and Public Liability) Claims. The defendant admitted liability. The parties failed to agree damages under the Protocol and the claimant filed a claim under CPR PD 8B. The district judge ordered the defendant to pay damages. The claimant appealed on the grounds that the district judge had erred in allowing the claim to continue under the Protocol. The appeal was allowed. The defendant appealed to the Court of Appeal, which held that the circuit judge had been wrong. The parties agreed that the claimant should pay the costs. The issue was that the respondent claimant considered that CPR rr.45.17 to 45.19 (fixed costs) applied to the costs of the appeal, while the appellant defendant considered that CPR r.52.19 applied.

The Court of Appeal held that CPR r.52.19(1) gave an appeal court a specific discretion to limit the recoverable costs of the appeal in "any proceedings in which costs recovery is normally limited or excluded at first instance". Accordingly, the fixed costs regime applicable to proceedings at first instance under the Protocol did not apply to the costs of an appeal. Instead, the appellate court had a discretion to limit the costs recoverable. The court declined to exercise that discretion. The claimant had made a claim under the Protocol and the defendant had properly complied with the procedural requirements. The claimant's appeal had been wholly unmeritorious and led the defendant to incur unnecessary additional costs. The defendant was entitled to its costs of both appeals.

As to enforcement, any appeal which concerned the outcome of a claim for damages for personal injuries, or the procedure by which such a claim was to be determined, was part of the "proceedings" under CPR r.44.13. That interpretation applied even where (a) the court was dealing with a second appeal; (b) the appeal was brought by the defendant to the original claim; and (c) the court had declined to exercise its discretionary powers to limit recoverable

---

[21] EL/PL Protocol 4.3, 4.4.

costs under CPR r.52.19. Accordingly, the costs order would not be enforceable against the respondent claimant.[22] See also **Ch.6 para.6–04**.

Section IIIA

7–14   Section IIIA applies where a claim is started under either the RTA or EL/PL Protocol, but no longer continues under the relevant protocol or the stage 3 procedure; and to claims to which the Pre-Action Protocol for Resolution of Package Travel Claims applies. This section does not apply to a disease claim which is started under the EL/PL Protocol.[23]

Section IIIB

7–15   Section IIIB is a new section which has been added with effect from 31 May 2021. It applies to claims which have failed to comply with or failed to continue under the RTA Small Claims Protocol. If the court finds the claimant to have acted unreasonably – in (i) valuing the claim so that the application of the RTA Small Claims Protocol was avoided; (ii) electing not to proceed following notification from the defendant that if proceedings were issued, the small claims track would be the normal track for the claim; (iii) any other way that causes the process in the RTA Small Claims Protocol to be discontinued; or (iv) not complying with the RTA Small Claims Protocol at all despite the claim falling within its scope – then the court may order the defendant to pay no more than the fixed costs and disbursements allowed in accordance with PD 27B.[24]

The Pre-Action Protocol for Resolution of Package Travel Claims

7–16   The Protocol describes the behaviour the court expects of the parties prior to the start of proceedings where a claimant claims damages valued at no more than £25,000 in a package travel claim. If, at any stage, the claimant values the claim at more than the upper limit of the fast track, the claimant should notify the defendant as soon as possible. The aims of the Protocol are to: encourage the exchange of early and full information about the claim; encourage better and earlier pre-action investigation by all parties; enable the parties to avoid litigation by agreeing settlement of the dispute before proceedings are commenced; enable the parties to narrow the issues in dispute before proceedings are commenced; and, support the proportionate and efficient management of proceedings where litigation cannot be avoided.[25]

7–17   The Court of Appeal has decided the question whether a disposal hearing, listed for the quantification of damages payable after judgment under CPR PD 26 para.12.2(1)(a) is or is not a trial within the meaning of CPR r.45.29E(4)(c).

---

[22] *Wickes Building Supplies Ltd v William Gerarde Blair (No.2) (Costs)* [2020] EWCA Civ 17; [2020] 1 W.L.R. 1246; [2020] Costs L.R. 31.
[23] CPR r.45.29A. Nothing in Section IIIA prevents the court from making an order under CPR r.45.24 (Failure to comply or electing not to continue with the relevant Protocol-costs consequences).
[24] CPR Pt 45, Section IIIB, rr. 45.29M and 45.29N.
[25] The full text of the Protocol is at *White Book* 2021 Vol.1 para.C17–001 ff.

The issue turned on the special definition of "trial" for the purposes of EL/PL Protocol cases in CPR r.45.29E(4)(c). An identical definition applies in cases started under the RTA Protocol. Many EL/PL Protocol cases are dealt with at disposal hearings and if such a hearing constitutes listing for trial, the fixed costs recoverable are at a higher rate than would otherwise be the case where there is a settlement between the date of listing and the date fixed for the disposal hearing.

Lord Justice Briggs, who gave the leading judgment, stated:

> "6. The issue with which this appeal is concerned is not fact sensitive. It is common ground that whenever an EL/PL Protocol case is listed for a disposal hearing after Judgment for damages to be assessed, under Part 26 PD12.2(1)(a), and is then settled before the date listed for that disposal hearing, then either the first or the third column in Table 6D Part B must be applicable so as to determine the fixed costs. The second column will not be applicable, since there will not have been a 'date of allocation under Part 26', because listing for disposal is an alternative to allocation to a track . . . ."

In the particular case, a customer visiting a garage was injured when a spanner was dropped on his hand. The claimant's solicitors entered his claim through the portal in September 2013. The defendant garage did not respond and the claim was withdrawn from the portal in October. Liability was, however, admitted in correspondence in November by the defendant's insurers. Although medical evidence and details of special damages were submitted to the insurer, nothing was agreed and proceedings were issued in April 2014. The defendant failed to acknowledge service and default judgment was obtained in May 2014. The case was transferred from the County Court Money Claims Centre to the County Court at Birkenhead for assessment of damages. The matter was listed for a disposal hearing in September 2014.

The case then settled and a Tomlin Order was filed with the court in July 2014, recording the terms of settlement. There was no agreement as to costs and the claimant's bill was provisionally assessed by the district judge in December 2014. The defendant requested an oral review confined to the issue of which column, within Table 6D Pt B, applied.

Having rehearsed the arguments, Briggs LJ stated:

> "12. In my judgement, listing a case for a disposal hearing following Judgment pursuant to Part 26 PD12, is listing for trial, for the purposes of triggering column 3 in Table 6D Part B where a case which originated in the EL/PL Protocol settled after listing. My reasons follow.
>
> 13. First listing a case for 'disposal' means exactly what it says. The purpose of doing so is, so far as possible, finally to dispose of the case at first instance. A default or other judgment for damages to be assessed leaves that assessment outstanding, as the last stage in the final disposal of the proceedings. For that

purpose, it matters not whether the judgment has been obtained by default (as here) or on an application for summary judgment on liability, judgment on admissions, or after a liability only trial: see generally Part 26 PD12(2).

14. The fact that it may be impossible to tell, prior to the disposal hearing itself, whether it will prove to be final in that sense, or merely the occasion for giving Directions, cannot be conclusive against listing of a disposal hearing triggering column 3 of Table 6D Part B because that table is concerned with settlement prior to trial. If the possibility of a disposal hearing being used for the giving only of Directions were to be admitted, then it is hard to see how listing could ever be a trigger for the application of column 3 following a settlement. Even the hearing date of a full trial may turn into a hearing for Directions if it proves impossible or unjust to do otherwise than permit an adjournment.

15. Secondly, the fact that a disposal hearing might prove to be uncontested is, again, neither here nor there. It is common ground that, even after a Judgment in default, the Defendant may attend and oppose the Claimant's case as to quantification of damages at the disposal hearing. Again, if the possibility that such a hearing might prove to be uncontested were sufficient to prevent its listing being a trigger for the application of column 3, then that possibility exists at all kinds of final hearing, including traditional trials.

16. Thirdly, as DJ Campbell emphasised, listing for a disposal hearing is the trigger for the Claimant (and any other party which wishes to take an active part at that hearing) to prepare and serve the requisite evidence . . .

17. Fourthly, there is a useful pre-history to the formulation 'final contested hearing' in Part 45.29E(4)(c). Part 45.15 deals with the success fee percentages applicable in road traffic accident claims. By Part 45.15(6)(b), as it was before April 2013, a reference to 'trial' was a reference to the final contested hearing. This rule was introduced in 2004. Lamont v Burton [2007] 1 WLR 2814 was about a road traffic accident claim which had concluded at a disposal hearing. It was taken for granted in this court (rather than determined after argument) that the disposal hearing had been a trial for the purposes of Part 45.15. I consider it very likely that, when it adopted the same definition of trial in 2013 for the purposes of fixed costs in the EL / PL Protocol cases, the Rule Committee had the analysis in Lamont v Burton well in mind."

The appeal was dismissed.[26]

7–18   The Court of Appeal has considered, in respect of claims started under the RTA Protocol, whether the fixed costs regime continues to apply to a case which no longer continues under the RTA Protocol but is allocated to the multi-track after being issued under Pt 7. Lord Justice Briggs gave the leading judgment[27]. He pointed out that the court was required not merely to interpret the relevant provisions of Section IIIA of CPR Pt 45 together with the relevant provisions of the RTA Protocol but also to consider whether they

---

[26] *Bird v Acorn Group Ltd* [2016] EWCA Civ 1096; [2017] 1 W.L.R. 1915; [2017] C.P. Rep. 8; [2016] 6 Costs L.O. 959.
[27] *Qader v Esure Services Ltd* [2016] EWCA Civ 1109; [2017] 1 W.L.R. 1924; [2017] 4 All E.R. 865; [2017] C.P. Rep. 10; [2016] 6 Costs L.O. 973.

suffered from an obvious drafting mistake which could be put right so as to bring them into compatibility with the intention of the CPRC. The EL/PL Protocol had a very similar fixed costs regime and although the appeals before the court concerned cases within the RTA Protocol, it was expected that their outcome would affect the interpretation and application of the similar and overlapping provisions in Pt 45 about the EL/PL Protocol. The judge reviewed the provisions of the fixed costs regime including Table 6B. Briggs LJ stated:

"*14 . . . The formulation of the detailed tabular provisions for the recovery of fixed costs in relation to claims started but no longer continuing under the relevant protocols was developed upon an assumption that, if Part 7 proceedings were issued, they would in due course be allocated to the Fast Track, if not determined at a disposal hearing following judgment for damages to be assessed . . .*
15 . . . claims for an amount for more than £25,000, or claims likely to require a trial lasting longer than one day or the deployment of multiple expert witnesses, are normally allocated to the multi-track. Plainly, they involve the expenditure of costs on a scale which will be higher, and often much higher, than that requisite for the determination of claims in the fast track."

Briggs LJ gave three examples of cases likely to be allocated to the multi-track rather than the fast track:

(i) Where a claim originally thought to be worth no more than £25,000 is revalued at a substantially higher level;
(ii) Because of the exclusion of vehicle related damages from the valuation of a claim for the application of the RTA Protocol, where the aggregate of the non-vehicle related damages is a little below £25,000 but the claim then ceases to continue within the Portal because liability is in issue, the ensuing Pt 7 claim may include a claim for vehicle related damages as well which, particularly in the case of credit hire charges for a luxury car, could put the claim well in excess of the £25,000 damages ceiling for a "normal" fast track claim. Whilst that fact alone would not necessarily mean multi-track allocation, the risk of such allocation remains real;
(iii) Where a claim is properly started in the RTA Protocol but is met by an allegation that the claim has been dishonestly fabricated. Such proceedings are inherently likely to be pursued and defended on the basis that no stone is left unturned and therefore at very substantial cost.

There was a problem because there was nothing in CPR r.45.29 which expressly limited the fixed costs regime applicable to cases started but no longer continuing under the relevant Protocol to fast track cases, or which excluded the fixed costs regime when a case was allocated to the multi-track. CPR r.45.29J provides for relief in exceptional circumstances, but only by permitting the court to conduct an immediate summary assessment or make an order for detailed assessment neither of which appear apposite at the case management stage when allocation takes place. CPR r.45.29J appears to offer a measure of relief only at the end of a trial or other resolution of the proceedings.

Under CPR r.45.29J, if the court considers that there are exceptional circumstances making it appropriate to do so, it will consider a claim for an amount of costs (excluding disbursements) which is greater than the fixed recoverable costs set out in the Rules. On such an application, the court has noted that Section IIIA of Pt 45 expressly provides that ex-Protocol cases remain subject to the fixed costs regime, save where the court allocates a case to the multi-track. "Exceptional circumstances" had to be evaluated against those cases covered by Section IIIA. The court referred to the decision of Coulson LJ in *Hislop v Perde*[28] where he had said: "It goes without saying that a test requiring 'exceptional circumstances' is already a high one".[29]

In *Qader*, the judges at first instance and on appeal were persuaded that CPR r.45.29 clearly provided that fixed costs should apply notwithstanding allocation to the multi-track. In the conjoined appeal of *Khan v McGee*, the district judge allocated the case to the multi-track but took the view that this disapplied the fixed costs regime and directed filing of costs budgets and adjourned the case to a CCMC. Briggs LJ concluded:

> "35 After more hesitation than my Lords I have come to the conclusion that section IIIA of Part 45 should be read as if the fixed costs regime which it prescribes for cases which start within the RTA protocol but then no longer continue under it is automatically disapplied in any case allocated to the multi-track, without the requirement for the claimant to have recourse to Part 45.29J, by demonstrating exceptional circumstances. . . ."

Briggs LJ then set out his reasoning at some length and went into the history of the making of the fixed costs scheme continuing:

> "54 In the present case the Rule Committee's apparent failure to implement the continuing intention of the Government, in response to stakeholder concerns, to exclude multi- track cases from the fixed costs regime being enacted for cases leaving the RTA and EL/PL protocols seems to me to satisfy all three of Lord Nicholls' preconditions [see Inco Europe Ltd v First Choice Distribution[30]]. The intended purpose of the fixed costs regime in this context was that it should apply as widely as possible (and therefore to cases allocated to the Fast Track, and to cases sent for quantification of damages at disposal hearings), but not to cases where there had been a judicial determination that they should continue in the multi-track. The intended restriction on the ambit of the fixed costs regime is clear, and the only reason for that restriction not being enacted in section IIIA of Part 45 appears to be inadvertence, rather than a deliberate decision by the rule committee to take a different course . . .

---

[28] *Hislop v Perde* [2018] EWCA Civ 1726; [2018] 4 Costs L.O. 515.
[29] *Ferri v Gill* [2019] EWHC 952 (QB); [2019] Costs L.R. 367, Stewart J.
[30] *Inco Europe Ltd v First Choice Distribution* [2000] 1 W.L.R. 586 at 592; [2000] 2 All E.R. 109.

. . . 56 The best way to give effect to that intention seems to me to add this phrase
to Part 45.29B, after the reference to 45.29J:
'. . . and for so long as the claim is not allocated to the multi-track. . .'"[31]

The wording has been corrected, as recommended by Briggs LJ, by the Civil
Procedure (Amendment) Rules 2017 (SI 2017/95) r.8.

In a claim for damages following a road traffic accident, the defendant   7–19
appealed against a decision ordering him to pay the claimant's costs on the
indemnity basis under CPR r.45.29J.

The claimant had commenced proceedings but the appellant defendant
asserted that neither he nor his vehicle was involved. The claimant made a
Part 36 offer which the defendant did not accept, and the case was allocated
to the fast track. Some time later the defendant accepted the Part 36 offer. A
judge accepted the claimant's application that the defendant should pay his
costs on the indemnity basis under CPR r.45.29J, on the basis that the defendant's dishonesty amounted to exceptional circumstances. The judge found
that the alleged dishonesty went to the heart of the defendant's case, and that
there would be no need for an oral hearing to decide the issue: the defendant
had had an opportunity to put in evidence and had chosen not to. He found
the dishonesty proven.

On appeal the court held that it was not accurate to say that the defendant
had not filed any witness evidence. He had done so in the course of the case.
The judge had failed to address the evidence that the defendant had adduced
earlier in the proceedings, and had erred in concluding, without testing that
evidence, that the defendant had been dishonest, and in using that conclusion as the basis of his finding that there were exceptional circumstances justifying an award of indemnity costs. It would have been clearer for both parties
if there had been a discussion at the directions hearing about the nature of
the hearing that would ultimately be required. Transparency might have been
achieved by the claimant making clear as he left the Part 36 offer open that if
it was accepted an application under CPR r.45.29J would follow.[32]

In respect of applications for pre-action disclosure (PAD) in claims which
started but no longer continue under the EL/PL Protocol the Court of Appeal
had to decide whether the fixed costs regime under Section IIIA of Pt 45
applied to such application. CPR Pt 46, Section I makes specific provision
(distinct from the general rules about costs) for the costs of PAD applications
both in the High Court and the County Court departing from the ordinary
general rule under CPR r.44.2, namely: that the unsuccessful party pays. Lord
Justice Briggs, who again gave the leading judgment stated:

"30. In my judgment the fixed costs regime plainly applies to the costs of a PAD
application made by a claimant who is pursuing a claim for damages for personal

---

[31] *Qader v Esure Services Ltd* [2016] EWCA Civ 1109; [2017] 1 W.L.R. 1924; [2017] 4 All E.R. 865; [2017] C.P. Rep. 10; [2016] 6 Costs L.O. 973.
[32] *West v Olakanpo*, [2020] EWHC 27 November (QB), Robin Knowles J.

> *injuries which began with the issue of a CNF in the portal pursuant to the EL/ PL Protocol but which at the time of the PAD application, is no longer continuing under that protocol . . .*
>
> *31. The starting point is that the plain object and intent of the fixed costs regime in relation to claims of this kind is that, from the moment of entry into the portal pursuant to the EL/PL Protocol (and, for that matter, the RTA Protocol as well) recovery of the costs of pursuing or defending that claim at all subsequent stages is intended to be limited to the fixed rates of recoverable costs, subject only to a very small category of clearly stated exceptions. To recognise implied exceptions in relation to such claim related activity and expenditure would be destructive of the clear purpose of the fixed costs regime which is to pursue the elusive objective of proportionality in the conduct of the small or relatively modest types of claim to which that regime currently applies.*
>
> *32. That conclusion is, in my view, expressly prescribed by the clear words of Part 45.29A(1) and 45.29D. In particular, paragraph D provides that the fixed costs and disbursements prescribed by the regime (in paragraph 29E and I respectively) are 'the only costs allowed'. Although this is subject to paragraphs F, H and J they are each part of the fixed costs regime, even though they permit different or enlarged recovery in certain precisely defined circumstances.*
>
> *. . .*
>
> *35. For those reasons it seems to me entirely apposite for a PAD application to fall within the description of interim applications in Part 45.29H, as being 'an interim application . . . in a case to which this section applies . . .'"*

It had become apparent during the submissions that insurance backed defendants were frequently failing in their protocol disclosure obligations, unless a PAD application was made. Counsel for the appellant argued that including the costs of such applications within the fixed costs regime would largely deprive such applications of their value as a spur to proper compliance. In respect of this submission, Briggs LJ stated:

> *"39. But in my judgment the answer to this submission lies not in subjecting the fixed costs regime to an implied exemption for PAD applications which exposed recalcitrant defendants to an altogether higher but variable level of recoverable costs liability, to be determined by assessment. Rather the answer lies in the availability of an application under Part 45.29J, if exceptional circumstances can be shown or, for the future, in recognition by the Rule Committee that the fixed costs regime needs to be kept under review, and defects in it remedied by adjustment of the fixed allowances where they can be shown to be justified."[33]*

7–20   The Court of Appeal has considered this question: where a person gives notification of a claim under the Protocol but thereafter dies before its conclusion and the notified claim then, without legal proceedings being issued, proceeds to settlement between the deceased's personal representative and the

---

[33] *Sharp v Leeds City Council* [2017] EWCA Civ 33; [2017] 4 W.L.R. 98; [2017] C.P. Rep. 19; [2017] 1 Costs L.R. 129.

defendant's insurers, are the costs and disbursements payable by the defendant to be calculated by reference to Section IIIA (or, as the case may be, even Section III), or by reference to Section II of Pt 45?

The defendant contended for Section IIIA costs whereas the claimant contended for the mostly more generous Section II costs.

The claim arose out of a road traffic accident and which was submitted by CNF through the Portal. The CNF was acknowledged but as there was no admission of liability, the claim exited the Portal. Within a week of the claim's exit, the claimant died to due to matters unrelated to the accident. The claim fell silent until about two-and-a-half years later when the claimant's solicitors gave notice of their intention to instruct a medico-legal expert. The letter giving notice indicated that the claimant was now deceased. A medico-legal report was obtained and served. The defendant insurer made a Part 36 offer which was accepted the same day. As the parties disagreed as to the applicable costs regime, Part 8 proceedings were issued.

The claim was first dealt with by a Regional Costs Judge who found in favour of the claimant. The defendant appealed to a Circuit Judge but the appeal was dismissed. The defendant appealed again to the Court of Appeal. The tension arose because:

(i)   the Protocol defines "claim" as a claim made prior to the start of proceedings under the process set out in the Protocol;
(ii) the Protocol defines "claimant" as the person starting a claim;
(iii) the Protocol states that it does not apply "... where the claimant ... acts as personal representative of a deceased person";
(iv) the Protocol provides that once a claim exits the process it cannot subsequently re-enter.

The Court of Appeal noted the provisions of the Law Reform (Miscellaneous Provisions) Act 1934, s.1(1) which causes a pre-existing cause of action to survive death and also noted the jurisprudence which treated Pt 45 and the Protocol as being comprehensive and not readily subject to judicial amplification or implication.

The appellant defendant argued that because of the non-admission, the claim had exited the Portal and it could not re-enter thereafter. The claim was properly within the Protocol as the claimant's death had occurred after the CNF had been issued. The claim that came to be settled was the claim that had been started by the claimant, albeit vested in the executor. Such an interpretation was said to be consistent with the certainty of the scheme as a whole.

The respondent claimant argued that the claim that came to be settled was not the claim that had been issued by the claimant through his CNF. The claim that had been settled had been the claim of the executor and a purposive interpretation would support that finding but the reasoning of the circuit judge had been correct otherwise the costs outcome would be so different depending on whether a prospective claimant died a day before a CNF could be issued or died a day after a CNF was issued.

The Court of Appeal dismissed the appeal and considered the Circuit Judge to have been correct. Sir Nigel Davis found that the word "claim" in the Protocol was not being used in a formal sense but rather used as a descriptive of a demand for damages prior to the start of any legal proceedings. The term "claimant" was used throughout the Protocol to refer to the person who was involved in the road traffic accident. As a result, costs fell to be assessed by reference to Section II.[34]

7–21   The remainder of Pt 45 IIIA deals, among other things, with: the application of fixed costs and disbursements—RTA Protocol; the amount of fixed costs—RTA Protocol; the application of fixed costs and disbursements—EL/PL Protocol; and the amount of fixed costs—EL/PL Protocol[35]; and claims to which the Pre-Action Protocol for Resolution of Package Travel Claims applies.[36] Where the order for costs is made in a claim to which the Pre-Action Protocol for Resolution of Package Travel Claims applies, the order shall be for a sum equivalent to one half of the applicable Type A and Type B costs in Table 6A. The Section also deals with: disbursements; claims for an amount of costs exceeding fixed recoverable costs; failure to achieve costs greater than fixed recoverable costs; and costs of the costs-only proceedings of detailed assessment. If it considers that there are exceptional circumstances making it appropriate to do so, the court will consider a claim for an amount of costs (excluding disbursements) which is greater than the fixed recoverable costs referred to in CPR rr.45.29B to 45.29H. Failure to achieve an amount 20% greater than the amount of the fixed recoverable costs, will result in an order for the party who made the claim to be paid the lesser of the fixed recoverable costs; and the assessed costs.[37]

7–22   In a road traffic accident claim involving a child, the Court of Appeal dealt with the question whether the cost of instructing counsel to advise on settlement under CPR r.21.10(1) and PD 21 para.5.2 was a disbursement reasonably incurred, due to a particular feature of the dispute within the meaning of CPR r.45.29I(2)(h). The court held that the fact that the claimant was a child was nothing to do with the dispute itself. Like age or linguistic ability or mental wellbeing, these characteristics were not generated by or linked to the dispute. "Particular features" related to matters such as how the accident happened, whether the defendant was to blame, the nature, scope and extent of the injuries and their consequences. The cost of counsel's advice was incurred because it was an almost mandatory requirement in such cases involving children. Accordingly, counsel's fee did not fall within the costs exception in

---

[34] *West v Burton* [2021] EWCA Civ 1005.
[35] CPR r.r.45.29–45.29E.
[36] CPR r.r.45.29–45.29E.
[37] CPR r.r.45.29I–45.29K.

CPR r.45.29I(2)(h). Counsel's fee was not recoverable as a disbursement, it was covered by the prescribed fixed costs.[38]

A RTA claim proceeding under CPR Pt 45 Section IIIA was listed for trial and on the day the parties were granted further time for negotiation and the matter settled, the claimant being awarded damages and costs. A recorder refused to award the fixed trial advocacy fee on the basis that the case had settled before the final contested hearing had commenced. On appeal, Coulson J held that the case had not settled prior to the date of trial and the costs should have been dealt with under Section C of Table 6B. It did not strain the language of the rule to conclude that the case was disposed of at trial albeit by way of settlement rather than judgment. There were sound policy reasons for concluding that the interests of justice would be better served if the advocate were not penalised financially for negotiating a settlement at the door of the court.[39]

7–23

In two appeals before the court, one, *Broadhurst*, had been limited to the fixed costs in Table 6 whilst in the other, *Smith*, the judge had not limited the costs to Table 6.

7–24

The court was referred to the Explanatory Memorandum to the 2013 Amendment Rules:

"... *If a defendant refuses a claimant's offer to settle and the court subsequently awards the claimant damages which are greater than or equal to the sum they were prepared to accept in the settlement, the claimant will not be limited to receiving his fixed costs, but will be entitled to costs assessed on the indemnity basis in accordance with rule [36.17]."*

The Master of the Rolls giving judgment with which the other members of the court agreed said:

"23 *Rule 45.29B does not stand alone. The need to take account of Part 36 offers in section IIIA cases was recognised by the draftsman of the rules. Indeed, rule 36.14A [36.17] is headed costs consequences following judgment where section IIIA of Part 45 applies . . .. Rule 45.29F (8) provides that, where a Part 36 offer is accepted in a section IIIA case . . . rule 36.10A [36.20] will apply instead of this rule . . . And rule 45.29F(9) provides that, where in such a case upon judgment being entered the claimant fails to obtain a judgment more advantageous than the claimant's Part 36 offer, 'rule 36.14A [36.21] will apply instead of this rule . . . Rule 45.29F does not, however, make provision as to what should happen where the claimant makes a successful Part 36 offer.'*
25 *The effect of rules 36.14 [36.17] and 36.14A [36.21] when read together is that, where a claimant makes a successful Part 36 offer, he is entitled to costs assessed on the indemnity basis. Thus, rule 36.14 [36.17] is modified only to the extent stated by 36.14A [36.21]. Since rule 36.14(3) [36.17(4)] has not been*

---

[38] *Aldred v Cham* [2019] EWCA Civ 1780; [2020] 1 W.L.R. 1276; [2019] Costs L.R. 1683. The claimants sought permission to appeal this decision to the Supreme Court. Permission was refused by the Court of Appeal, the renewed application to the Supreme Court was also refused.
[39] *Mendes v Hochtief (UK) Construction Ltd* [2016] EWHC 976 (QB); [2016] C.P. Rep. 33; [2016] 3 Costs L.O. 429, Coulson J.

modified by rule 36.14A [36.21], it continues to have full force and effect. The tension between rule 45.29B and rule 36.14A [36.21] must, therefore, be resolved in favour of rule 36.14A [36.21].

31 Where a claimant makes a successful Part 36 offer in a section IIIA case, he will be awarded fixed costs to the last staging point provided by rule 45.29C and Table 6B. He will then be awarded costs to be assessed on the indemnity basis in addition from the date that the offer became effective. This does not require any apportionment. It will, however, lead to a generous outcome for the claimant."[40]

Section IV

7–25   Section IV of Pt 45 sets out the scale costs for claims in the IPEC. The provisions do not apply where the court considers that a party has behaved in a manner which amounts to an abuse of the court's process or the claim concerns the infringement or revocation of a patent or registered design, the validity of which has been certified by a court in earlier proceedings.[41]

The court will make a summary assessment of the costs of the party in whose favour any order for costs is made. CPR rr.44.2(8), 44.6(b) and Pt 47 do not apply to Section IV.[42] The court will reserve the costs of an application to the conclusion of the trial when they will be subject to summary assessment.

Save where a party has behaved unreasonably the court will not order a party to pay total costs of more than £50,000 on the final determination of a claim in relation to liability; and £25,000 on an inquiry as to damages or account of profits. The amounts above apply after the court has applied the provision on set-off in accordance with CPR r.44.12(a). The maximum amount of scale costs that the court will award for each stage of the claim is set out in CPR PD 45. The amount of the scale costs awarded by the court will depend on the nature and complexity of the claim. Subject to assessment, the following may be recovered in addition to the amount of the scale costs set out in CPR PD 45: court fees; costs relating to the enforcement of any court order; and wasted costs. Where appropriate, VAT may be recovered in addition to the amount of the scale costs and any reference in Section IV to scale costs is a reference to those costs net of any such VAT.[43]

Where a party has behaved unreasonably the court may make an order for costs at the conclusion of the hearing. Where the court makes a summary assessment of costs it will do so in accordance with Section IV of Part 45.[44]

7–26   The court (IPEC) was required to determine whether the cap on costs of £50,000 under CPR r.45.31(1)(a) was inclusive of VAT. The court held that the headings of Section IV of Part 45 and CPR r.45.31 both suggested that the term "scale costs" was used to apply to both total and stage costs. The definition in CPR r.45.30(4) was such that this did not allow for any alternative

---

[40] *Broadhurst v Tan* [2016] EWCA Civ 94; [2016] 1 W.L.R. 1928; [2016] C.P. Rep. 22; [2016] 2 Costs L.O. 155.
[41] CPR r.45.30(1) and (2).
[42] CPR r.45.30(3).
[43] CPR r.45.31.
[44] CPR r.45.32 and CPR r.63.26(2) costs of applications.

interpretation of "scale costs". This led to the conclusion that a party claiming VAT on its costs could only recover a total of £50,000, including VAT. Subject only to CPR r.45.32 (Summary Assessment of the Costs of an Application Where a Party has Behaved Unreasonably) or where there had been exceptional circumstances.[45]

The court could only depart from the overall caps on costs and scale costs in truly exceptional circumstances. It was, however, possible not to apply scale costs for one or more of the earlier stages of the claim provided that the total award remained within the overall cap. Under CPR r.45.30(2), the overall IPEC cap could only be lifted where the court considered that a party had behaved in a manner which amounted to an abuse of process; or the claim concerned a registered right whose validity had been certified in earlier proceedings.[46] The court has an overriding discretion under CPR r.44.2 to award costs outside the cap in a truly exceptional case. In the instant case, the claimant's conduct had not been ideal but was not close to an abuse and was not truly exceptional. The overall cap of £50,000 was not disturbed. The general discretion to lift one or more of the caps on stage costs could be exercised in less than truly exceptional circumstances if the result was that the overall cap on total costs was left undisturbed. The defendants were awarded an extra £5,000 above the IPEC application cap.[47]

In patent infringement proceedings, the court found in favour of the 7–27 defendants in respect of the claimant's claim for misrepresentation and the defendants' counterclaim for royalties.

The claimants' claim of unjustified threats of patent infringement proceedings remained undecided. The defendants sought their costs in relation to the decided issues. The claimants argued that the assessment should be adjourned until the remaining allegations had been dealt with. The court held that the word "claim" in CPR r.45.31(1)(a) referred to a single set of proceedings. Accordingly, the court could not assess costs until all the issues including the threat allegation had been resolved.[48]

In a case in the IPEC, the claimant made a Part 36 offer (under the previous 7–28 version of Pt 36) the terms of which were to settle the claim against the first defendant if he consented to an injunction and paid £5,000 damages, additional damages and interest. The judgment against the defendant was more advantageous to the claimant than the offer. In the course of the judgment, the judge referred to *000 Abbott v Design & Display Ltd*[49] and quoted from the judgment of Lord Dyson MR in *Broadhurst v Tan* (see above). The court concluded that there would be no injustice in the claimant being awarded the further relief set out in CPR r.36.14(3) (CPR r.36.17(4)) and following the

[45] *Response Clothing Ltd v Edinburgh Woollen Mills* [2020] EWHC 721 (IPEC), HHJ Hacon.
[46] See *FH Brundle v Perry* [2014] EWHC 979 (IPEC); [2014] 4 Costs L.O. 576 HHJ Hacon.
[47] *Skyscape Cloud Services Ltd v Sky Plc* [2016] EWHC 1340 (IPEC); [2016] E.T.M.R. 40 HHJ Hacon.
[48] *Global Flood Defence Systems Ltd v Johann Van Den Noort Beheer BV* [2016] EWHC 189 (IPEC); [2016] 1 Costs L.R. 137 HHJ Hacon.
[49] *000 Abbott v Design & Display Ltd* [2014] EWHC 3234 (IPEC).

third and fourth grounds set out by Lord Dyson in his judgment, concluded that CPR r.36.14(3)(b) (CPR r.36.17(4)(b)) overrides the provisions of CPR r.45.31 (the amount of scale costs in the IPEC). Accordingly, neither the staged costs nor the overall cap applied to an award of costs under CPR r.36.14(3)(b) (36.17(4)(b)).[50]

7–29   At the opening of a patent trial, the judge refused the claimants permission to rely on an argument raised in their skeleton argument, since it had not been pleaded or sufficiently raised in the claimants' expert report. The claimants subsequently applied to adjourn the trial and for permission to serve a re-re-Amended Reply and Defence to Counterclaim and for further expert evidence to be served. The judge granted the adjournment on the basis that to refuse the claimants the possibility of defending their patent where there might be a sound argument which might establish that the patent was valid, notwithstanding that there was cited prior art, would result in very serious prejudice to the claimants. So far as prejudice to the defendants was concerned, if there were an adjournment, this was limited to the costs thrown away. In making the order for costs, the judge indicated that neither the IPEC overall costs cap nor any stage cap would apply in relation to the costs thrown away by the adjournment.[51]

Section V

7–30   Section V of Pt 45 sets out the amounts which are to be allowed in respect of HMRC charges in specified cases, unless the court orders otherwise.[52] This Section applies where the only claim is a claim conducted by an HMRC officer in the County Court for recovery of a debt, and the Commissioners obtain judgment on the claim. Any appropriate court fee will be allowed in addition to the costs set out in Tables 7 and 8 and the claim may include a claim for fixed commencement costs.[53]

Table 7 sets out the fixed costs on commencement of the County Court claim conducted by an HMRC officer. Table 8 sets out fixed costs on entry of judgment in a County Court claim conducted by an HMRC officer. The total to be included in the judgment for HMRC charges is the total of the fixed commencement costs, and the amount in Table 8 relevant to the value of the claim. In cases where the only claim is for a specified sum of money, and the defendant pays the money claimed within 14 days after service of the particulars of claim, together with the fixed commencement costs stated in the claim form, the defendant will not be liable for any further costs unless the court orders otherwise.[54]

---

[50] *Phonographic Performance Ltd v Hagan* [2016] EWHC 3076 (IPEC); [2017] F.S.R. 24 HHJ Hacon.
[51] *Technetix BV v Teleste Ltd* [2018] EWHC 1941 (IPEC), HHJ Hacon.
[52] CPR r.45.33. "HMRC charges" are claimed as "legal representative's costs" on relevant court forms and means the fixed costs set out in Tables 9 and 10 of Section V.
[53] CPR r.45.33(3)–(6).
[54] CPR rr.45.34, 45.35 and 45.36 and Tables 7 and 8.

Section VI

Section VI of Pt 45 governs the amount of fast track trial costs and their **7–31**
application. "Fast Track trial costs" means the cost of a party's advocate for
preparing for and appearing at the trial. It does not include any other disbursements, or any VAT payable on the advocate's fees. The "trial" includes a
hearing where the court decides an amount of money or the value of goods.
"Trial" does not include the hearing of an application for summary judgment,
or the court's approval of a settlement or other compromise by, or on behalf
of, a child or protected party.[55]

Section VII—costs limits in Aarhus Convention claims

Section VII of Pt 45 limits the amount of costs recoverable in Aarhus **7–32**
Convention claims.[56]

The Civil Procedure (Amendment) Rules 2017 (SI 2017/95) introduced an
entirely new version of Section VII. The amendments in relation to Section
VII and in respect of orders to limit the recoverable costs of an appeal in an
Aarhus Convention claim under CPR r.52.19A (see below), apply in relation
to Aarhus Convention claims commenced on or after the 28 February 2017.

> "45.41(2)(a) . . . "Aarhus Convention claim" means a claim brought by one or
> more members of the public
> (i) By judicial review or review under statute which challenges the legality of any
>   decision act or omission of a body exercising public functions and which is
>   within the scope of Article 9(1) or 9(2) of the UNECE Convention on Access
>   to Information, Public Participation in Decision Making and Access to Justice
>   in Environmental Matters done at Aarhus Denmark on the 25th June 1998;
>   or
> (ii) By judicial review which challenges the legality of any such decision act
>   or omission and which is within the scope of Article 9(3) of the Aarhus
>   Convention."

The Civil Procedure (Amendment No.3) Rules 2019 (SI 2019/1118), which
came into force on the 1 October 2019, amended CPR r.45.41(2) by substituting a new paragraph (a):

> "(a) "Aarhus Convention Claim" means a claim brought by one or more members
> of the public by judicial review or review under statute which challenges the legal-
> ity of any decision, act or omission of a body exercising public functions, and
> which is within the scope of Article 9(1), 9(2) or 9(3) of the UNECE Convention
> on Access to Information, public participation in decision making and access to
> justice in environmental matters done at Aarhus, Denmark, on 25 June 1998
> ('the Aarhus Convention')."

---

[55] Under CPR r.21.10; CPR r.45.37(1) and (2) and CPR PD 45 paras 4.1–4.3.
[56] An Aarhus Convention claim means a claim for judicial review of a decision, act or omission all or part of which is
subject to the provisions of the UNECE Convention on Access to Information Public Participation in Decision Making
and Access to Justice in Environmental Matters done at Aarhus, Denmark on 25 June 1998, including a claim which
proceeds on the basis that the decision, act or omission or part of it is so subject—CPR r.45.41(2).

Section VII does not apply to appeals other than appeals brought under s.289(1) of the Town and Country Planning Act 1990 or s.65(1) of the Planning (Listed Buildings and Conservation Areas) Act 1990 which are, for the purposes of Section VII, to be treated as reviews under statute.[57]

Where a claimant, who is a member of the public, has stated in the claim form that the claim is an Aarhus Convention claim, and, filed and served with the claim form a schedule of the claimant's financial resources, which is verified by a statement of truth and provides details of:

(i) the claimant's significant assets, liabilities, income and expenditure; and
(ii) in relation to any financial support which any person has provided or is likely to provide to the claimant, the aggregate amount which has been provided and which is likely to be provided.

CPR rr.45.43 to 45.45[58] do not apply, provided that the claimant has stated in the claim form that, although the claim is an Aarhus Convention claim, the claimant does not wish those rules to apply. If there is more than one claimant, CPR rr.45.43 to 45.45 do not apply in relation to costs payable by or to any claimant who has not filed and served a schedule of the claimant's financial resources etc. as set out above or has stated that the claimant does not wish those Rules to apply or is not a member of the public.[59]

Limit on costs recoverable from a party in an Aarhus Convention claim

7–33   A claimant or defendant in an Aarhus Convention claim may not be ordered to pay costs exceeding, in the case of a claimant, £5,000 where the claimant is claiming only as an individual or not as, or on behalf of, a business or other legal person; or £10,000 in all other cases. In the case of a defendant the amount is £35,000.

Where there are multiple claimants or multiple defendants, the amount set out above (subject to any direction by the court) apply in relation to each claimant or defendant individually and may not be exceeded irrespective of the number of receiving parties. These provisions are subject to cases where CPR rr.45.43 to 45.45 do not apply to a claimant (under CPR r.45.42) or to cases in which the court varies the limit on costs recoverable (under CPR r.45.44).[60]

7–34   The Court of Appeal has held that on the claimant's application for permission to apply for statutory review in planning proceedings being refused, a court could grant a costs order in favour of multiple defendants and interested parties who had served Acknowledgements of Service and Summary Grounds of Dispute. There was no limit, in planning cases, to the number of parties

---

[57] CPR r.45.41. CPR r.52.19A makes provision in relation to costs of appeals in Aarhus Convention claims.
[58] CPR r.45.43 Limit on costs recoverable from a party in an Aarhus Convention claim. CPR r.45.44 varying the limit on costs recoverable from a party in an Aarhus Convention claim. CPR r.45.45 challenging whether the claim is an Aarhus Convention claim.
[59] CPR r.45.42.
[60] CPR r.45.43.

who, served with a claim form, could recover their reasonable and proportionate costs of preparing and serving an Acknowledgement of Service and Summary Grounds if a judge refused permission to allow the claim for judicial review to continue.[61] Under the Aarhus cap, CPR r.45.43 limits the claimant's costs exposure. Costs should not be subject to a lower cap than the £10,000 because the claim failed at the permission stage. The cap applied to the costs incurred by the successful defendant or interested party at whatever stage the costs assessment was being done. The cap allowed claimants costs certainty from the outset. Defendants and interested parties knew that they had to deploy their arguments as early as possible because they faced expensive litigation with little costs protection if permission were granted.[62]

Varying the limit on costs recoverable from a party in an Aarhus Convention claim

In relation to the court's powers under CPR r.45.44 to vary the limit on costs 7–35
recoverable from a party in an Aarhus Convention claim, the Administrative Court held there would be a significant deterrent effect on meritorious claims if there were no certainty at the outset in relation to a claimant's potential cost liabilities. Disputes about the level of costs caps should be raised at the point of acknowledging service and a decision on cost capping made at an appropriately early stage in the proceedings. Later variation applications should not be made without good reason.

The court has the power to vary the amounts set out above and may remove altogether the limits on maximum costs liability. The court may do this only on an application made in accordance with the rules governing an application to vary and if it is satisfied that to do so would not make the costs of the proceedings prohibitively expensive for the claimant; and where the variation would reduce the claimant's maximum liability or increase that of a defendant without the variation, the costs of the proceedings would be prohibitively expensive for the claimant. This provision mirrors the requirements for applications for costs capping orders in judicial review claims which are not Aarhus Convention claims.

CPR r.45.44 sets out when proceedings are to be considered prohibitively expensive as follows: if the likely costs of the proceedings (including any court fees payable by the claimant) either exceed the financial resources of the claimant; or are objectively unreasonable having regard to:

(i)   the situation of the parties;
(ii) whether the claimant has a reasonable prospect of success;
(iii) the importance of what is at stake for the claimant;
(iv) the importance of what is at stake for the environment;

---

[61] See *R. (Mount Cook Land Ltd) v Westminster City Council* [2003] EWCA Civ 1346; [2004] C.P. Rep 12.
[62] *Campaign to Protect Rural England v Secretary of State for Communities and Local Government; Maidstone BC; and Roxhill Developments Ltd (Interested Party)* [2019] EWCA Civ 1230, [2020] 1 W.L.R. 352.

(v) the complexity of the relevant law and procedure; and
(vi) whether the claim is frivolous.

When the court is considering the financial resources of the claimant, it has to have regard to any financial support which any person has provided or is likely to provide to the claimant.

The court may only vary the costs caps (or remove altogether the limits on liability) on an application by a claimant or defendant. An application to vary a costs cap (or remove a limit) must be made at the outset and determined by the court at the earliest opportunity; and an application may only be made at a later stage in the process if there has been a significant change in circumstances.

The rules[63] provide: that an application to vary must:

- if made by the claimant, be made in the claim form and provide the claimant's reasons why, if the variation were not made, the costs of the proceedings would be prohibitively expensive for the claimant;
- if made by the defendant, be made in the acknowledgment of service and provide the defendant's reasons why, if the variation were made, the costs of the proceedings would not be prohibitively expensive for the claimant; and, be determined by the court at the earliest opportunity.

The above rule is subject to the proviso that an application to vary may be made at a later stage if there has been a significant change in circumstances (including evidence that the schedule of the claimant's financial resources contained false or misleading information) which means that the proceedings would now: be prohibitively expensive for the claimant if the variation were not made; or, not be prohibitively expensive for the claimant if the variation were made.

Such an application must: if made by the claimant: be accompanied by a revised schedule of the claimant's financial resources or confirmation that the claimant's financial resources have not changed; and, provide reasons why the proceedings would now be prohibitively expensive for the claimant if the variation were not made; and, if made by the defendant, provide reasons why the proceedings would now not be prohibitively expensive for the claimant if the variation were made.[64]

Challenging whether the claim is an Aarhus Convention claim

7-36   Where a claimant has stated in the claim form that the claim is an Aarhus Convention claim and complied with CPR r.45.42(1) (and subject to the exceptions in CPR r.45.42(2) and (3)), CPR r.45.43 (Limit on recoverable costs) will apply unless the defendant has denied in the acknowledgement

---

[63] CPR r.45.44.
[64] CPR r.45.44. Rule 39.2(3)(c) makes provision for a hearing to be in private if it involves confidential information (including information relating to personal financial matters) and publicity would damage that confidentiality.

of service that the claim is an Aarhus Convention claim and has set out the grounds for such a denial and the court is determined that the claim is not an Aarhus Convention claim. Where the defendant denies the claim is an Aarhus Convention claim, the issue must be determined at the earliest opportunity. If the court holds that the claim is not an Aarhus Convention claim it will normally make no order for costs in relation to those proceedings; if it holds that it is such a claim, it will normally order the defendant to pay the claimant's costs of those proceedings on the standard basis and that order may be enforced even if this would increase the costs payable by the defendant beyond the amount stated in CPR r.45.43(3) or any variation of it.[65]

Orders to limit the recoverable costs of an appeal in Aarhus Convention claims

A new CPR r.52.19A has been added to Pt 52 which provides that in an appeal   7–37
against a decision made in an Aarhus Convention claim to which CPR rr.45.43 to 45.45 apply, the court must consider whether the costs of proceedings will be prohibitively expensive for a party who was a claimant; and if they think it will be, make an order limiting the recoverable costs to the extent necessary to prevent this. When considering the financial resources of a party, the court must have regard to any financial support which any person has provided or is likely to provide to that party.[66]

Fast Track

A claimant will not lose the protection of the rules because it is a public   7–38
authority. It was not appropriate to refer to the Convention to place a gloss on the ordinary and natural meaning of "claimant" in PD 45.[67] "Environment" was to be given a broad meaning. A decision granting authorisation to carry out surveys, both non-intrusive and intrusive, related to the environment, especially when that was given a broad meaning. Accordingly, the claim benefited from the protection of the Convention.[68] The availability of protective costs orders for environmental cases falling within the Aarhus Convention had been deliberately limited to judicial review claims and did not extend to statutory appeals or applications. Accordingly, it was not appropriate for the court to exercise its discretion to grant cross protection in respect of an application to quash planning permission under the Town and Country Planning Act 1990 s.288, as this would side-step the limitation deliberately enacted in the CPR to give effect to a convention which had not been directly incorporated into domestic law. Legislative action was necessary to remedy CPR r.45.41's non-compliance with the Convention (it applied only in relation to judicial review proceedings).[69]

---

[65] CPR r.45.45.
[66] CPR r.52.19A.
[67] *R. (HS2 Action Alliance and London Borough of Hillingdon) v Secretary of State for Transport* [2015] EWCA Civ 203; [2015] 2 Costs L.R. 411.
[68] *R. (Dowley) v Secretary of State for Communities and Local Government* [2016] EWHC 2618 (Admin); [2016] A.C.D. 129 Patterson J.
[69] *Secretary of State for Communities and Local Government v Venn* [2014] EWCA Civ 1539; [2015] 1 W.L.R. 2328.

7–39   Several individuals and a Parish Council failed in judicial review proceedings in respect of planning permission granted by the Borough Council. The Borough Council sought costs of £15,000 and argued that the individual claimants should pay the costs in the amount of £5,000 and the Parish Council in the amount of £10,000. The Administrative Court held that where a claimant is ordered to pay costs in an Aarhus Convention claim, the amount ordered must not exceed £5,000 where the claimant claimed only as an individual; and otherwise must not exceed £10,000. The individual claimants fell into the first category and the Parish Council into the second. It was accordingly appropriate to consider the liability of the two sets of claimants separately and to award costs against each up to the maximum of the respective costs cap.[70]

Costs on the indemnity basis

The basis of assessment

7–40   Where the court assesses costs, whether by summary or detailed assessment, it will, (subject to any statutory provisions relating to, e.g. legal aid costs) assess those costs on either the standard basis or the indemnity basis. In either case the court will not allow costs which have been unreasonably incurred or which are unreasonable in amount. Where the court is assessing costs on the standard basis it will in addition only allow costs which are proportionate to the matters in issue and will resolve any doubt which it may have as to whether costs were reasonably incurred or reasonable and proportionate in amount in favour of the paying party. Where the amount of costs is to be assessed on the indemnity basis there is no proportionality requirement[71] but the court will resolve any doubt which it may have as to whether the costs were reasonably incurred or were reasonable in amount in favour of the receiving party.[72] Where the court makes an order about costs without indicating the basis upon which costs are to be assessed or purports to make an order on a basis other than the standard or indemnity basis the costs will be assessed on the standard basis.[73]

The Commercial Court has held that where costs are being awarded in accordance with contractual provisions and those provisions expressly provide that the costs should be limited to "reasonable attorney fees", the costs were confined to costs on the standard basis. The issues were whether: (1) the letter of indemnity provided a contractual right to indemnity costs; (2) indemnity costs should be awarded because the claimant obtained judgment for a greater amount than it had offered in its Part 36 offer, which the defendant should have accepted; (3) the claimant should recover only some of its costs due to

---

[70] *R. (Botley Parish Action Group) v Eastleigh BC* [2014] EWHC 4388 (Admin) Collins J.
[71] Save that in CPR r.1.1(2)(f), it is stated, "Dealing with a case justly and at proportionate cost includes, so far as is practicable . . . (f) enforcing compliance with rules, practice directions and orders." There is therefore now an argument that some element of proportionality may attach to costs on the indemnity basis. This point does not appear to have been argued to date.
[72] CPR r.44.3(1)–(3).
[73] CPR r.44.3(4).

the conduct of two individuals during the proceedings; (4) a payment on account should be ordered, and if so in what amount. The court held that the successful claimant was not entitled to costs on an indemnity basis, as neither its letter of indemnity with the unsuccessful party nor the fact that the unsuccessful party had refused its Part 36 offer supported such an order in the circumstances. The claimant was awarded costs on the standard basis, with a 10% reduction because two of its employees had withheld important information during the litigation and trial.[74]

When the court may order costs on the indemnity basis

The court awarding costs in its discretion on the indemnity basis should be **7-41** satisfied that there is something in the conduct of the action or the circumstances of the case which takes the case out of the norm in a way which justifies an order for indemnity costs.[75] Following *Excelsior Commercial & Industrial Holdings* it is appropriate to award costs on the indemnity basis where the conduct of a party has taken the situation away from the norm. It is not always necessary to show deliberate misconduct, in some cases unreasonable conduct to a high degree would suffice. The claimant's refusal of two reasonable offers to settle would have been enough in itself to warrant an order on the indemnity basis.[76]

The Court of Appeal has given a definitive decision on the correct approach to the award of costs on the indemnity basis.

In proceedings in the TCC for breach of contract and/or negligence, the **7-42** defendant made a Part 36 offer in the sum of £25,000 three weeks after the start of proceedings, which was not accepted. The defendant was an American-qualified architect, who was a friend and former neighbour of the claimants. Gratuitously, she provided assistance to the claimants when they wanted to undertake major landscaping works in their garden. There was a falling-out which led the claimants to commence proceedings against the defendant.

After a five-day trial, the judge concluded that the defendant had in fact provided very few services and had not been negligent in providing any of them. The claim failed in its entirety. The trial judge refused to award the defendant costs on the indemnity basis on the basis that the claimants conduct had not been such as to justify indemnity costs. The defendant appealed.

---

[74] *Euro-Asian Oil SA v Abilo (UK) Ltd* [2016] EWHC 3340 (Comm); [2017] 1 Lloyd's Rep. 287 Cranston J. However, this decision was not followed in *Alafco Irish Aircraft Leasing Sixteen Ltd v Hong Kong Airlines Ltd* [2019] EWHC 3668 (Comm). See also *Criterion Buildings Ltd v McKinsey & Co Inc (United Kingdom)* [2021] EWHC 314 (Ch) (17 February 2021), considered below.

[75] *Excelsior Commercial & Industrial Holdings Ltd v Salisbury Hammer Aspden & Johnson* [2002] EWCA Civ 879; [2002] C.P. Rep. 67. In *Suez Fortune Investments Ltd v Talbot Underwriting Ltd; The Brillante Virtuoso* [2019] EWHC 3300 (Comm); [2019] Costs L.R. 2019, Teare J, the court reviewed the authorities relating to the award of costs on the indemnity basis. The judge stated: "*11. In the light of the wide nature of the discretion to order costs on the indemnity basis I accept the submission made by counsel for the Underwriters that there may be an 'aggregation of factors' which justify an order for costs on the indemnity basis, one of which may be unreasonable conduct though not to a high degree. What matters is whether, looking at all the circumstances of the case as a whole, the case is out of the norm in such a way as to make it just to order costs on the indemnity basis. That is the approach in Excelsior; see also ABCI v Banque Franco-Tunisienne [2003] EWCA Civ 205 at paragraph 70 per Mance LJ.*"

[76] *Franks v Sinclair (Costs)* [2006] EWHC 3656 (Ch); [2007] W.T.L.R. 785 David Richards J.

The Court of Appeal explained:

"4. The appellant's costs were presented to the judge in the eye-watering amount of £724,265 (and even that was incomplete, because it excluded some items such as the costs of the earlier appeal). She sought assessment on an indemnity basis. The respondents argued, and the judge agreed, that costs should be assessed on the standard basis. The appellant's appeal against that decision on costs, together with the respondents' notice, raised three distinct issues:

a)   Whether this was a case in which the respondents' pursuit of what were said to be 'speculative, weak, opportunistic or thin claims' could properly be described as out of the norm such as to warrant an order for indemnity costs.

b)   Whether the respondents' failures to accept and subsequently to beat the appellant's Part 36 offer, made at a very early stage in the proceedings, also meant (either separately or taken cumulatively with the pursuit of these particular claims) that an order for indemnity costs was warranted.

c)   The relevance, if any, of the fact that the appellant's approved costs budget was said to be £415,000, but that any assessment on the indemnity basis would start at the appellant's actual costs figure of not less than £724, 265."

With regard to points a) and b) above the Court reviewed the relevant authorities (see [37]–[43] of the judgment) and concluded:

"43. In short, therefore, taking the CPR and these authorities together, the position is that, in contrast to the position of a claimant, a defendant (such as the appellant in the present case) who beats his or her own Part 36 offer, is not automatically entitled to indemnity costs. But a defendant can seek an order for indemnity costs if he or she can show that, in all the circumstances of the case, the claimant's refusal to accept that offer was unreasonable such as to be 'out of the norm'. Moreover, if the claimant's refusal to accept the offer comes against the background of a speculative, weak, opportunistic or thin claim, then an order for indemnity costs may very well be made. That is what happened in Excelsior."

Adding, in respect of speculative, weak, opportunistic or thin claims:

"45.There are a number of cases where costs have been awarded on an indemnity basis because of the weakness of the claimant's underlying claims: see by way of example Wates Construction Limited v HGP Greentree Alchurch Evans Limited [2006] BLR 45. In my summary of these principles in Elvanite Full Circle Limited v AMEC Earth and Environmental (UK) Limited [2012] EWHC 1643 (TCC), I referred to Wates as an example of a 'hopeless' claim, because on the facts of the case, that is what it was. I did not intend by that shorthand to indicate any sort of gloss on the conventional description of claims which were 'speculative, weak, opportunistic or thin' giving rise to the possibility of indemnity costs."

The court allowed the appeal in relation to the conduct of the respondents, considering that the pursuit of the claims from 7 May 2017 onwards was out of the norm such as to justify an order for indemnity costs. It also considered that the respondents' failures to accept and then to beat the appellant's Part 36 offer was a separate and stand-alone element of their conduct which was out of the norm, separately justifying an award of indemnity costs or, in the alternative, justifying such an order, when taken together with the nature of the claims pursued by the respondents. The court limited the indemnity costs to the period after they had had time to digest an earlier Court of Appeal judgment of April 2017, i.e. 7 May 2017. It was unreasonable that the respondents did not accept the Part 36 offer once they knew that a particular part of their case was not open to them. An order for indemnity costs was held to be necessary and appropriate here because, this situation was very similar to *Excelsior*: namely the pursuit of speculative/weak claims against the background of an offer that was unreasonably refused and subsequently not beaten.

The court dealt with the relevance of the costs budget as follows:

"8.2 The Applicable Principles

89. The figure produced by an approved cost budget mechanism (CPR r.3.12-r.3.18) is a different thing to the final assessment of costs following the trial. The former is prospective; the latter is retrospective. True it is that, in many cases, the approved costs budget will be the appropriate starting point for the final costs assessment. But that does not detract from the underlying proposition that they are different figures produced by different considerations with different purposes.

90. If there is an order for indemnity costs, then prima facie any approved budget becomes irrelevant. In Denton and Others v TH White Limited [2014] EWCA Civ 906, Lord Dyson MR and Vos LJ said at paragraph 43:

'If the offending party ultimately loses, then its conduct may be a good reason to order it to pay indemnity costs. Such an order would free the winning party from the operation of CPR r.3.18 in relation to its costs budget'.

91. A similar comment can be found in the more recent decision of Warby J in Optical Express Limited and Others v Associated Newspapers Limited [2017] EWHC 2707 (QB), a case where indemnity costs were ordered after a Part 36 offer had been accepted out of time. Warby J said at paragraph 52:

'52. In any case, it is legitimate to describe the claimants' conduct as highly unreasonable and such as to justify an order for assessment on the indemnity basis. The continued pursuit of the pleaded claim after time for acceptance of the Part 36 offer expired can properly be characterised as wholly disproportionate to the value of the claim. It is fair to say that the claimants have forfeited their right to the benefit of a proportionate assessment of the defendant's costs, and to the benefit of the doubt on reasonableness.'

92. The absence of an overlap between the cost budgeting regime on the one hand, and an order for indemnity costs on the other, was explained in detail by HHJ Keyser QC (sitting as a judge of the High Court) in Kellie v Wheatley and Lloyd Architects Limited [2014] 5 Costs LR 854; [2014] EWHC 2886 (TCC). He said:

'17 . . . As the passages set out in paragraph 14 above make clear, costs management orders are designed to set out the probable limits of the costs that will be proportionately incurred. It is for that reason, and not because of any quirk of

drafting, that r. 3.18 refers specifically to standard assessment and not to indemnity assessment. Proportionality is central to assessment on the standard basis and it trumps reasonableness; cf. Motto v Trafigura Ltd [2011] EWCA Civ 1150, per Lord Neuberger of Abbotsbury at [49]. However, proportionality is not in issue if costs are to be assessed on the indemnity basis; see r. 44.3(3). I therefore find it difficult to see why logical analysis requires importing the approach in r. 3.18 into assessment on the indemnity basis. The first reason given by Coulson J[5], at [29], has force if at all only if an approved or agreed budget does indeed reflect the costs that the receiving party says it expects to incur. However, the present case is an example precisely of the proper use of costs management in approving a budget at a lower figure than that proposed by the receiving party, on the very ground of proportionality. To suppose that the imposition of a budget under Part 3 would create some sort of presumption as to the limits of reasonable costs would be to ignore the fact that the approval of costs budgets is done on the basis of proportionality, not mere reasonableness. The matters referred to in connection with the first reason may, accordingly, justify having regard to the amount of costs the receiving party expected to incur, but they do not justify applying the r. 3.18 analogously to assessment of costs on the indemnity basis. Similarly, the second reason, stated at [30], seems to me, with respect, to go further than is justified by the costs management regime. When a costs management order is made, the parties know that costs within the approved budget are likely to be considered proportionate, and costs in excess of the approved budget are likely to be considered disproportionate; in either case, the burden of justification lies on the party seeking a departure from the approved budget. But the costs management regime is not intended to give litigants an expectation that they will not incur a liability for disproportionate costs pursuant to an order for costs on the indemnity basis; any such expectation must rest on a party's own reasonable and proper conduct of litigation. It is no objection to an order for costs on the indemnity basis that it is likely to permit the recovery of significantly larger costs than would be recoverable on an assessment on the standard basis having regard to the approved costs budget; that possibility is inherent in the different bases of assessment, and costs on the indemnity basis are intended to provide more nearly complete compensation for the costs of litigation. I accept, of course, that a party seeking to recover disproportionate costs on an assessment on the indemnity basis is required to show that those costs were reasonably incurred; though that requirement is subject to the provisions of r. 44.3(3). That does not, however, justify the analogous use of r. 3.18, which has three disadvantages. First, it is both unnecessary and contrary to the rationale of that rule. Second, it tends to obscure the fact that the nature of the justification required of a receiving party is quite different under the two bases of assessment. Third, and consequently, it risks the assimilation of the indemnity basis of assessment to the standard basis, which is not justified by the costs management regime in the CPR. In my judgment, the proper way of addressing the concern identified by Coulson J in Elvanite at [30] is, first, by ensuring that applications for indemnity costs are carefully scrutinised and, second, by the proper application of the well understood criteria of assessment in r. 44.3(3) to the facts of the particular

*case. It might also be remembered that, even if there exist grounds on which an
award of indemnity costs could properly be made, such an award always remains
in the discretion of the court.'*

*93. I respectfully agree with that analysis. In principle, the assessment of costs
on an indemnity basis is not constrained by the approved cost budget, and to the
extent that my obiter comments in Elvanite or Bank of Ireland v Watts[77] suggested
the contrary, they should be disregarded.*

. . .

*96. Secondly, for the reasons explained in Section 8.2 above, there is as a matter of
principle no overlap between a costs budget, which will have been approved on the
basis of a projected series of figures for costs that were assessed as reasonable and
proportionate, and the actual costs to be assessed by reference to the indemnity
basis (where reasonableness might still be an issue, but proportionality is not).
Thus, even if there had been an approved budget figure, it could not affect whether
or not the court should make an order for indemnity costs."[78]*

In group litigation concerning the anti-depressant *Seroxat*, the claimants sub-   7–43
mitted to judgment in the defendants' favour two working days before the
trial of the first generic issue. The defendants had consistently asserted that
the claimants' approach to the assessment of "Defect" under the Consumer
Protection Act 1987 was untenable. The court concluded that the duty to run
the claimants' case had rested throughout on the claimants' legal team, whose
responsibility was to evaluate and re-evaluate the merits of the action as the
litigation unfolded. The claimants were ordered to pay the defendants' costs
on the indemnity basis. Following both *Lejonvarn v Burgess* (above) and *Gee v
Depuy International Ltd* [2018] EWHC 1208 (QB).[79]

A successful claimant beat its Part 36 offer and the parties agreed an   7–44
order including the damages and interest, and also the additional amount
payable under Part 36. The defendants, however, resisted an order for costs
on the indemnity basis. The defendants' argument was that the claimant's
costs budget was approved in March 2018 when the claim form indicated
that the total value of the claim would exceed £50,000 but would not exceed
£100,000. The total damages, interest and additional amount was £19,746.37.
The defendants argued that an order for costs on the indemnity basis would
preclude the costs judge from having regard to proportionality and that it
would be unjust to make such an order for that reason, since the costs budget
had been based on an inflated valuation of the claim. During the course of
the proceedings, a direction had been given that all parties had to consider
settling by any means of alternative dispute resolution. The defendants had
indicated that it did not intend to engage in settlement negotiations and
remained confident in the strength of its defence. The court held that the

---

[77] *Elvanite Full Circle Ltd v Amec Earth & Environmental (UK) Ltd* [2013] EWHC 1643 (TCC); [2013] 4 All E.R. 765; [2013] 4 Costs L.R. 612; Coulson J.

[78] *Lejonvarn v Burgess* [2020] EWCA Civ 114. See also *Shearer v Neal [2020] EWHC 3272 (Comm)* Deputy Master Hill, QC) Indemnity costs awarded against debtor following non-compliance with order for an examination.

[79] *Bailey v GlaxoSmithKline UK Ltd* [2020] EWHC 1766 (QB), Lambert J.

reasons given for refusing to engage in mediation were inadequate. The court stated:

> *"No defence, however strong, by itself justifies a failure to engage in any kind of alternative dispute resolution."*

The fact that costs on the indemnity basis did not involve a consideration of proportionality was part of the incentive for parties to make and accept Part 36 offers.[80]

7–45   Where a claimant successfully claimed damages for personal injuries against a religious group and its trustees, the court had to decide whether the trustees should pay all of the claimant's costs on the indemnity basis in view of their refusal to engage in ADR and, secondly, the amount of enhanced rate of interest applicable to damages and costs from a particular date, pursuant to CPR r.36.17(4). The court had given a direction in the standard form that at all stages the parties had to consider settling by ADR and any party refusing to engage in ADR proposed by another had to serve a statement giving reasons within 21 days of the proposals. The claimant's solicitor suggested a Joint Settlement Meeting, but the defendant trustees stated they had no authority to negotiate settlement of her claim. On 9 July 2019, the claimant made a Part 36 offer to accept £62,750, which was rejected by the trustees. The court held that the trustees should have served a witness statement explaining why they had refused to participate in the Joint Settlement Meeting. Their failure to do so was unreasonable conduct. The Part 36 offer showed that the claimant was willing to settle the case for less than she was ultimately awarded. The court found that there was every reason to think that if the trustees had engaged with the proposal for a Joint Settlement Meeting at an earlier stage, that willingness would have become known. The court ordered the defendants to pay costs on the indemnity basis from the date of their unreasonable refusal to engage in the settlement meeting. On the facts, the court awarded enhanced interest of 4% above base rate.[81] The power to award costs on the indemnity basis may extend to the manner in which a party's expert had prepared and given evidence. In the particular case the defendants were ordered to pay the claimant's costs of having to recall its own expert, on the indemnity basis.[82] In another case involving an expert who was "inexperienced and overenthusiastic" the claimants, having put forward a figure at which they were prepared to settle, refused to settle at that figure when the defendants offered it. No explanation for the refusal was given. Akenhead J awarded costs on the indemnity basis against the claimants. Because of the claimants' unwillingness to accept the amount offered by the defendants in settlement, an enormous amount

---

[80] *DSN v Blackpool Football Club Ltd* [2020] EWHC 670 (QB); [2020] Costs LR 359, Griffiths J.
[81] *BXB v Watchtower & Bible Tract Society of Pennsylvania (1) Trustees of the Barry Congregation of Jehovah's Witnesses (2)* [2020] EWHC 656 (QB), Chamberlain J.
[82] *Siegel v Pummell* [2015] EWHC 195; [2015] 3 Costs L.O. 357 Wilkie J.

of time, costs and court resources had been wasted, and the defendants were entitled to costs on the indemnity basis.[83]

The Court of Appeal has held that there should be no general principle applicable to all applications under CPR r.31.22 (concerning subsequent use of disclosed documents) to the effect that indemnity costs would be awarded against the applicant. There are many different kinds of such applications and the general rules as to costs ought to be applicable to them as to any other application before the courts. On the facts of the case the judge at first instance had ample grounds for awarding indemnity costs in the circumstances. The applicant's application was one which was extraneous to the existing proceedings. It required a huge amount of effort from the respondent in terms of liaison, checking and legal consideration. The respondent had been fully entitled to resist the application in the public interest. These factors took the case outside the norm. An order for costs on the indemnity basis was justified.[84]

Following its successful damages claim against the respondents, the appellant company appealed against a decision to award costs on the standard basis. The company had already been awarded its trial costs on the indemnity basis which the respondents failed to pay by the relevant date. This led to means hearings which the respondents did not attend or produce any documentary evidence. Suspended committal orders were made and an application to stay based on an allegation of fraud by the respondents was dismissed as totally without merit. The judge at first instance did not regard the respondents' behaviour as "exceptional" since many debtors behaved in a similar way. Costs were awarded on the standard basis. The Court of Appeal, relying on *Excelsior* held that the "critical requirement" was that there had to be "some conduct or some circumstance which takes the case out of the norm". As a result of the respondents' behaviour the appellant was needlessly put to considerable trouble and expense. That was not "reasonable conduct of proceedings" or behaviour that the court should in any way sanction or encourage. The respondents were ordered to pay costs on the indemnity basis.

It was unfortunate that the judge used "exceptional" to describe the circumstances that might justify an order for indemnity costs. Whatever the precise linguistic analysis, "exceptional" was apt, as a matter of ordinary usage, to suggest a stricter test and was best avoided. It would be preferable if judges expressly used the test of "out of the norm" established by *Excelsior*.[85]

In a case of severe brain damage at birth the claimant achieved a judgment significantly more advantageous than his offer (which was not a Pt 36 compliant offer). The judge ordered that the defendant should pay the claimant's costs incurred as from 11 June 2015, (the date upon which the defendant rejected the claimant's offer), including the trial costs, on the indemnity basis.

7–46

7–47

---

[83] *Igloo Regeneration (General Partner) Ltd v Powell Williams Partnership* (Costs) [2013] EWHC 1859 (TCC); [2013] 5 Costs L.O. 746 Akenhead J.
[84] *Tchenguiz v Serious Fraud Office* [2014] EWCA Civ 1471; [2015] C.P. Rep. 9.
[85] *Whaleys (Bradford) Ltd v Bennett* [2017] EWCA Civ 2143; [2017] 6 Costs L.R. 1241.

The judge gave two reasons for her decision. The first was that the defendant had failed "to enter into meaningful negotiations in a collaborative way and to seek a sensible compromise in a quantum only trial" in a manner which "was unreasonable, especially in light of the self-evident weaknesses in their care and occupational therapy evidence". The second reason was that the judge regarded the nature of the case advanced by the defendant and as put to Mr and Mrs Cocking in the witness box as unsustainable and entirely inappropriate in the context of the case.

On appeal to the Court of Appeal the court held the defendant's conduct in negotiations should not attract any sanction in costs.

> "A judge should . . . be very slow to entertain a discussion as to whether parties to litigation have negotiated in a reasonable manner. Such an enquiry opens up the prospect of undesirable and wasteful satellite litigation, as the reasonableness of a negotiating stance may and almost certainly usually will depend upon a careful evaluation of the respective states of knowledge of the parties. The Pt 36 regime is designed precisely to obviate this kind of enquiry."

7–48   So far as the defendant's conduct of the trial was concerned the court took a different view. The case put against the claimant's mother and her husband was that they had dishonestly set out to mislead the professional advisers by exaggerating the difficulties involved in the claimant's care, and that their evidence at trial was in these respects similarly dishonest. It was suggested to them that they had been motivated by greed rather than by the interests of the claimant. The judge was very critical of the evidence given by the defendant's experts in the field of care and occupational therapy, saying that the evidence of the care expert was both "illogical" and "unrealistic". The judge found the evidence of the occupational therapy witness to be "wholly unrealistic" and, "extraordinary and . . . wholly out of kilter with awards made in this area". The defendant's appeal was dismissed.[86]

Following an order that unless the appellant rendered a final bill for work done in underlying proceedings it would not be permitted to serve further bills, the appellant failed to comply in time, and sought relief from sanctions. The application was refused and the appellant sought to appeal against that decision. It filed an appellant's notice. The notice indicated that permission to appeal was not required, but did not give any details of the circumstances in which permission had been obtained. Some months later it re-filed an appellant's notice indicating that it needed permission. It did not apply for an extension of time to apply for permission to appeal, so its notice was returned by the court. It refiled the notice, seeking an extension of time but again stating that permission to appeal was not required. The court ordered the appellant to file its evidence. The appellant sent a letter with copies of its earlier notices and correspondence. At the subsequent hearing, the court ordered the appellant to file a witness statement setting out why it was seeking

---

[86] *Manna v Central Manchester University Hospitals NHS Foundation Trust* [2017] EWCA Civ 12; [2017] 1 Costs L.O. 89.

to appeal against the master's decision, why it should be granted an extension of time, and why it had failed to comply with the order to file evidence. The appellant provided a witness statement. The court held that the witness statement did not comply with the order. It referred to the underlying merits of the appeal but did not address the defects in the appellant's notice regarding the requirement for permission to appeal. No attempt was made to explain why the notice had been filed in that form, and why it was not rectified for several months. As a result the appeal was struck out. No extension of time was justified. The appellant, as a solicitors' firm, knew the rules. It had given no explanation of why the original appellant's notice had not been accompanied by the grounds of appeal or the order under appeal, or why the appellant had proceeded as though permission to appeal was not required. It was appropriate to order costs against the appellant on the indemnity basis. Its conduct of the appeal had been lamentable, taking the case out of the ordinary, especially with regard to its approach to the question of permission to appeal. There was no justification for having repeatedly asserted that permission was not required.[87]

Where a bank's claim for professional negligence failed after it had refused **7–49** three offers to settle (two under Pt 36), the court held that it had not been a claim which was or should have been regarded as hopeless from the outset. On the contrary, it had been a case which had been supported, at least in part, by expert evidence and the detailed witness statements of those involved in the relevant events at the bank. For those reasons, the court was not persuaded that the bank's failure to beat the offers justified an order for indemnity costs. The court had been heavily critical of the bank's expert quantity surveyor. The judge stated:

> *"I consider that the costs of the defendant's QS expert, should be assessed on an indemnity basis, as should the costs of and occasioned by [the claimant's expert's] oral evidence at the trial. Beyond those two specific exceptions, and for the reasons that I have given, I consider that the appropriate order in this case is that costs should be assessed on the standard basis."*[88]

In a case which appeared at first sight to bear the hallmarks of entirely conventional proceedings in professional negligence against structural engineers for design failings in respect of foundations for two blocks of housing in a development in Sussex, a closer analysis revealed a far more atypical claim. Two claimants brought the claim against the defendant. The second claimant had its claim dismissed in its entirety and the first claimant was awarded damages in the sum of £2,000 in respect of a far larger pleaded claim of approximately £3.7m. The damages awarded represented the court's apportionment of quantum rather than being an award of nominal damages. Fraser **7–50**

---

[87] *Haider Kennedy Solicitors v Momson* unreported 30 October 2017 Ch.D.
[88] *Governors and Company of the Bank of Ireland v Watts Group Plc* [2017] EWHC 2472 (TCC); [2017] B.L.R. 626; 174 Con. L.R. 84; [2017] 5 Costs L.R. 899 Coulson J.

J in the TCC found that there were three fundamental aspects to the proceedings that were unusual:

(i) the foundations for the two blocks that were constructed by the specialist subcontractor were not in fact the foundations as ultimately designed by the defendant;
(ii) the buildings that had been constructed were so defective for other reasons (not connected with their foundations) that they had to be demolished in any event;
(iii) the party responsible for the construction of those buildings had its engagement terminated by the first claimant prior to completion.

The defendant had made two Part 36 offers (£50,000 and £110,00), both of which were far in excess of the amount awarded. The first Part 36 offer having been manifestly in excess of the damages awarded was the basis for the defendant's claim for costs. Whilst the usual consequences would have entitled the claimant to its costs up to the end of the relevant period, the defendant sought an order for all of its costs for the whole action from its commencement, to be assessed on the indemnity basis, it being averred that the usual consequences would be unjust within the definition of CPR r.36.17. The court considered the proper approach set out in the editorial note to the rule in the White Book 2021 at 36.17.3 and the guidance from *Lejonvarn*[89] as to the inter-relationship between Pt 36 and Pt 44. It observed numerous features which taken together took the case outside of the norm, including:

(i) the claimants wholly ignored (if not disguised) the factual causation issue which lay at the heart of the claim;
(ii) the quantum of damages was so small by comparison to the sum claimed as to be derisory;
(iii) the claim was supported by the claimant's appointed structural engineering expert, whose approach to his task left much to be desired;
(iv) the claimants refused opportunities to narrow the issues and wholly ignored a notice to admit facts served by the defendant;
(v) the claimants were plainly unreasonable not to have accepted the first Pt 36 Offer.

The court considered the features described by Tomlinson J in *Three Rivers*[90] (which included also features described by Gloster J in *European Strategic Fund*

[89] *Lejonvarn v Burgess* [2020] EWCA Civ 114.
[90] *Three Rivers District Council (2) Bank of Credit and Commerce International SA (in liquidation) v The Governor and Company of the Bank of England* [2006] EWHC 816 (Comm), per Tomlinson J, namely, where a claimant chooses to pursue speculative, weak, opportunistic or thin claims, he takes a high risk and can expect to pay indemnity costs if he fails. Examples of circumstances taking the case out of the norm included where a claimant:
• advances and aggressively pursues serious and wide-ranging allegations of dishonesty or impropriety over an extended period of time;
• advances and aggressively pursues such allegations despite the lack of any foundation in the documentary evidence for those allegations and maintains the allegations without apology to the bitter end;

Ltd[91]). It found the instant claim to have been plainly exaggerated, wholly opportunistic, unjustified and extremely thin as to quantum. Quantum was entirely far-fetched, and wholly irreconcilable with the contemporaneous documents. The failure to engage with the causation issue was wholly unreasonable and considerably out of the norm. The justice of the case demanded that the claimants should not recover any of their own costs. As the defendant had been found to be negligent in certain respects, the court ordered 'no order as to costs' up to the date of the expiry of the relevant period of the first Partt 36 Offer, and ordered the claimant to pay the defendant's costs thereafter on the indemnity basis. [92]

In a claim brought by a property owner for unpaid service charges against a former tenant said to amount to over £2m, the High Court found for the claimant and considered an application for indemnity costs said to arise out of the lease between the parties. The claimant contended that the defendant had covenanted to pay all the lawyers' costs of proceedings to recover arrears of service charge. Those clauses referred to expenses "properly incurred" by the landlord, and "all costs, charges and expenses which the landlord may from time to time incur." The court found that "proper costs" was not the same as "costs properly incurred" in that something may be a "proper cost", in the sense that it would be appropriate in some circumstances to incur it, and yet not "properly incurred", in the sense that the circumstances pertaining were not such as to make it appropriate to incur it. The court held further that the word "proper" should not make all the difference anyway, given that no improper cost can have been reasonably incurred, and yet the assessment of costs on the indemnity basis is restricted to costs which have been not unreasonably incurred. As a result, the court found that the contract was consistent with an indemnity costs award and ordered indemnity costs.[93]

7–51

Litigants in person

Prior to 1975, litigants in person who were successful in proceedings could recover only their out-of-pocket expenses.[94] The Litigants in Person Fees and Expenses Act 1975 and the Rules of Court made subsequently, enable litigants in person to recover some payment for the time which they expend in

7–52

- actively seeks to court publicity for its serious allegations both before and during the trial;
- turns a case into an unprecedented factual inquiry by the pursuit of an unjustified case;
- pursues a claim which is to put it most charitably thin, and in some respects far-fetched;
- pursues a claim which is irreconcilable with the contemporaneous documents;
- commences and pursues large scale and expensive litigation in circumstances calculated to exert commercial pressure on a defendant and during the course of the trial of the action the claimant resorts to advancing a constantly changing case in order to justify the allegations which it had made, only then to suffer a resounding defeat.

[91] *European Strategic Fund Limited v Skandinaviska Enskilda Banken AB* [2012] EWHC 749 (Comm), per Gloster J, namely that indemnity costs would be ordered in circumstances where the claim was (i) speculative involving a high risk of failure; (ii) grossly exaggerated in quantum; (iii) opportunistic; (iv) conducted in a manner that has paid very little regard to the proportionality or reasonableness giving rise to the incurring of substantial costs on both sides; (v) pursued on all issues at full length to the end of the trial.

[92] *Beattie Passive Norse Ltd (2) NPS Property Consultants Ltd v Canham Consulting Ltd (No. 2 Costs)* [2021] EWHC 1414 (TCC).

[93] *Criterion Buildings Ltd v (1) Mckinsey & company Inc (United Kingdom) (2) Mckinsey & Company Inc* [2021] EWHC 314 (Ch), per HHJ Paul Matthews, sitting as a judge of the High Court.

[94] *Buckland v Watts* [1970] 1 QB 27 CA.

conducting litigation. CPR r.46.5 is so worded that it is possible for a litigant in person to recover payment for legal advice as well as payment for time spent in conducting the litigation. There is an absolute cap on the amount recoverable by the litigant in person, namely two-thirds of the amount which would have been allowed if he had been legally represented, plus disbursements reasonably expended. The Court of Appeal has decided that in principle a litigant in person is entitled to his time for researching his case at the rate fixed by statute, subject to a cap of two thirds of what he would have recovered if he had been legally represented.[95]

In certain specified proceedings, where any costs of a litigant in person are ordered to be paid by another party to the proceedings or in any other way, there may be allowed on the assessment or other determination of the costs sums in respect of any work done and any expenses and losses incurred by the litigant in or in connection with the proceedings to which the order relates.[96] This provision applies to civil proceedings as follows:

(a)   in England and Wales in the County Court, in Northern Ireland in a county court, in the Family Court, in the Senior Courts or in the Supreme Court on appeal from the High Court or the Court of Appeal;

(b)   before the Lands Tribunal for Northern Ireland;

(ba) before the First-tier Tribunal or the Upper Tribunal; or

(c)   in or before any other court or tribunal specified in an order made under s.1 of the Litigants in Person (Costs and Expenses) Act 1975 by the Lord Chancellor.[97]

A litigant in person who does not fall within the provisions of the 1975 Act may claim only out of pocket expenses, although these may include fees and expenses charged by a solicitor to a litigant to equip him to argue a case in person.[98] There is no provision for the costs of litigants in person in criminal proceedings. Proceedings before the VAT Tribunal are also excluded. The Court of Appeal has held that the power to award costs for tribunal hearings is confined to sums recoverable at common law.[99]

7–53   Following an unsuccessful claim for judicial review of a public procurement process the court held that costs should follow the event. The claimant had lost completely and was liable to pay the costs. There was no principle to support the suggestion that it was entitled to costs until disclosure. Despite the extraordinary amount of time it had taken to bring the case to trial, there was no basis for anything other than the ordinary order that the claimant should pay the defendant's costs. Following disclosure, the claimant

---

[95] *R. (Wulfsohn) v Legal Services Commission* [2002] EWCA Civ 250; [2002] C.P. Rep. 34; [2002] 3 Costs L.R. 341.

[96] Litigants in Person (Costs and Expenses) Act 1975 s.1(1).

[97] The scope of the Act has been extended to the Employment Appeal Tribunal by the Litigants in Person (Costs and Expenses) Order 1980 (SI 1980/1159) and to Magistrates' Courts in England and Wales in relation to civil proceedings before these Courts by the Litigants in Person (Magistrates' Courts) Order 2001 (SI 2001/3438).

[98] *Buckland v Watts* [1970] 1 Q.B. 27; [1969] 3 W.L.R. 92; *Malloch v Aberdeen Corp* [1973] 1 W.L.R. 71; [1973] 1 All E.R. 304. See also *Commissioners of Customs and Excise v Ross* [1992] All E.R. 65; [1990] S.T.C. 353.

[99] *Nader (t/a Tryus) v Customs and Excise Commissioners* [1998] S.T.C. 806 CA, and see *Customs and Excise Commissioners v Ross* (1990) 2 All E.R. 65; [1990] S.T.C. 353 Simon Brown J.

should have known that it had been treated in precisely the same way as other bidders and that its claim was hopeless. The litigation had been conducted in an abysmally slow and haphazard fashion and the claimant had been in breach of orders of the court and the CPR. The claimant had also engaged in unjustified personal attacks on the other side and had made an application to commit for contempt of court although it had not been pursued. The claimant's conduct in pursuing judicial review challenge after disclosure was unreasonable on a number of bases and justified the award of indemnity costs once the claim had failed completely.[100]

A mother of a patient who lacked capacity defended an allegation by the local authority that she had been mismanaging the patient's disability living allowance, acting without representation and was thus a litigant in person. Rule 19.6(7) of the Court of Protection Rules 2017 disapplies CPR r.46.5 among others. The Court of Protection is not a senior court under s.1(1) of the Senior Courts Act 1981 and Sch.6 to the Mental Capacity Act 2005 (Minor and Consequential Amendments) did not add the Court of Protection to the long list of court to which the 1975 Act applies) and, accordingly, the Litigants in Person (Costs and Expenses) Act 1975 does not apply. This led to an injustice in the mother's case. A serious allegation had been made against her which she had to defend; her conduct had been reasonable and she had lost earnings in defending her reputation. The local authority was urged to pay her reasonable expenses and to make an ex gratia payment to her. The court expressed the view that the rules needed to be reviewed and revised so that the court could award the litigant in person costs in such a case.[101]   **7-54**

The official receiver, acting without a solicitor in disqualification proceedings, is a litigant in person, and is not limited to disbursements merely because he is salaried. Where costs over and above disbursements have been incurred these are pecuniary in nature and amount to pecuniary loss. The costs will be assessed in accordance with CPR r.46.5.[102]   **7-55**

The court has no power to award costs to a litigant in person in respect of assistance given by a non-legally qualified acquaintance. "Legal services" refer to services that are legal and provided by or under the supervision of a lawyer. Any payment made by the litigant to the assistant is not recoverable because it is not a disbursement which would have been made by a legal representative. The assistance being given was not expert assistance within CPR r.46.5(3)(c).[103]   **7-56**

Tugendhat J commented in *Mole v Hunter*,[104] that reform of the rules was unnecessary to deal with the effect that litigants in person were increasingly having on the courts. In his view, reform was unnecessary because the court already had sufficient power to manage cases effectively where one or more   **7-57**

---

[100] *Hersi & Co Solicitors v Lord Chancellor* [2018] EWHC 946 (QB) Coulson J.This decision was not followed by the Court of Appeal in *Sofer v Swiss Independent Trustees SA* [2020] EWCA Civ 699.
[101] *Hounslow LBC v A Father* [2018] EWCOP 23 district judge Eldergill.
[102] *Re Minotaur Data Systems Ltd* [1999] 1 W.L.R. 1129; [1999] 3 All E.R. 122; [1999] 2 Costs L.R. 97.
[103] *United Building and Plumbing Contractors v Kajla* [2001] EWCA Civ 1740; [2002] All E.R. (D) 265.
[104] *Mole v Hunter* [2014] EWHC 658 (QB).

parties were litigants in person. In this way it could, to a certain extent, ameliorate the procedural problems that litigants experienced. Notwithstanding this view, a new CPR r.3.1A (unrepresented parties) was introduced with effect from 1 October 2015 which imposes a positive obligation on the court to take certain steps where at least one party is unrepresented. These include: adopting a formal procedure appropriate to furthering the overriding objective; and, where necessary, questioning witnesses. The new rule, in making explicit the court's power to adapt its procedure to deal with a case justly and at proportionate cost for litigants in person, provides useful clarity. With effect from 6 April 2019, CPR PD 32 27.7 provides that, where a claimant is unrepresented, the court may direct that another party must prepare and produce the trial bundle.

7–58   In a case where the claimants were litigants in person, the defendant applied for an order that they should file a costs budget. The court held that the question was whether there was a significant benefit to the defendant in the filing of a costs budget by the claimants, when weighed against the difficulties faced by litigants in person in seeking to estimate the costs necessary to be inserted into the budget in a way which made the figures realistic. On the facts, it was not appropriate to direct the claimants to file a budget as the cost estimates relating to disclosure and witness statements were so unpredictable.[105]

7–59   In litigation which had been running seven years, both parties, incapable of compromise, bombarded the court with endless applications, so that the judge had to make orders that neither party could make an application without the leave of the court. The Court of Appeal held that justice cannot be done through a torrent of informal, unfocused emails. Neither the judge nor the court staff can, or should, be expected to field communications of this type. Judges must be entitled, as part of their general case management powers, to put in place, strict directions regulating communications with the court and litigants should understand that failure to comply with such directions will mean that communications that they choose to send, notwithstanding those directions, will be neither responded to nor acted upon.[106]

7–60   In an action for libel and malicious falsehood the defendant was in contempt of court by breaching injunctions which prohibited him from publishing further defamatory statements about the claimant. The claimant applied to have the defendant committed for contempt. The defendant was neither present nor represented, as was the case when the injunctions were granted. He had been served with the injunctions and with the committal application and supporting evidence. He had been repeatedly invited to seek legal advice and told that legal aid was available for contempt proceedings. However, he had decided not to engage with the court process. The court held that not proceeding would be unfair to the claimant and contrary to the overriding objective. It was open to the instant court to decide on the penalty in his

---

[105] *CJ and LK Perk Partnership v Royal Bank of Scotland* [2020] EWHC 2563 (Comm), HHJ Mark Pelling QC.
[106] *Agarwala v Agarwala* [2016] EWCA Civ 1252; [2017] 1 P. & C.R. DG17.

absence. The defendant was given still more time so that he could consider the court's findings and their implications, and decide whether to participate in the hearing on penalty, which would take place later that week.[107]

The Court of Appeal refused to entertain an application under CPR r.52.9A (now CPR r.52.19) (Orders to limit the recoverable costs of an appeal), as the application had not been made as soon as practicable, as was required under CPR r.52.9A(4) (now CPR r.52.19(4)). The fact that the defendant applicant was a litigant in person, and was ignorant of his rights, did not mean it was not practicable for him to make the application. There were not, nor ought there to be, special rules for litigants in person. The applicant's original claim should never have been brought, nor ought he to have appealed the Employment Tribunal's rejection of it. The fact that the other party had appealed the decision of the EAT would not have come as a surprise to the applicant. It would be unjust not to make an order for costs of the appeal against the applicant.[108]   **7–61**

The appellant litigant in person applied for an order under CPR r.6.15(2) that steps he had taken to bring his claim form to the respondent's attention should count as good service. At first instance the district judge found that there were no indulgences granted to litigants in person and there was no obligation on the solicitors to notify him, before the claim form expired, of their challenge to service. The district judge concluded that there was no "good reason" to exercise discretion under CPR r.6.15 to permit service by alternative means. The appellant's appeal against that decision was dismissed, the judge finding that there was no good reason why the appellant had not served the claim form during its validity. Before the Court of Appeal it was found that technical game-playing by defendants would count against them. The respondent's conduct could not, however, be criticised. The appellant had received correspondence with the correct address for service, had been told from the outset that an extension would not be granted, and had been reminded that service was still awaited. The appeal was dismissed.[109]   **7–62**

In December 2016 the Supreme Court granted the appellant leave to appeal. The grounds of appeal were essentially that the complexities of the CPR were such that a litigant in person could not be expected to cope with them or fully to understand their import. The hearing before the Supreme Court took place in November 2017.

Judgment was handed down on 21 February 2018, when, by a majority of three to two, the appeal was dismissed.[110] The court held that:

---

[107] *Pirtek (UK) Ltd v Robert Jackson* [2018] EWHC 1004 (QB) Warby J. See also *Country Cars of Bristol Ltd v County Cars (SW) Ltd* [2018] EWHC 839 (IPEC) HHJ Hacon, where defendants, who were unrepresented at the time, served but did not file the acknowledgement of service and defence. The judgment in default was set aside.
[108] *JJ Food Service Ltd v Zulhayir* [2013] EWCA Civ 1304; [2014] C.P. Rep. 15.
[109] *Barton v Wright Hassall LLP* [2016] EWCA Civ 177; [2016] C.P. Rep. 29.
[110] *Barton v Wright Hassall LLP* [2018] UKSC 12; [2018] 1 W.L.R. 1119. See also *Reynard v Fox* [2018] EWHC 443 (Ch) HHJ Paul Matthews, where the claimant argued that it would be unjust if his claim were to be struck out because he was a litigant in person and "didn't have a detailed knowledge of insolvency regulations." *Barton* was followed.

"Unless the rules and practice directions are particularly inaccessible or obscure, it is reasonable to expect a litigant in person to familiarise himself with the rules which apply to any step which he is about to take." [18].

Neither did the court accept that CPR r.6.3 and CPR PD 6A (Service within the Jurisdiction), to which Mr Barton did not in fact refer, were inaccessible and obscure. They did not justify his assumption that the opposing solicitors would accept service by email unless they said otherwise. Mr Barton had made no attempt to serve in accordance with the rules [21]. Having issued the claim form at the very end of the limitation period, and having made no attempt to serve it until the very end of its period of validity, he could have only a very limited claim on the court's indulgence under CPR r.6.15(2). By comparison, validation of service would prejudice the defendant by depriving them of an accrued limitation defence [23]. The appellant's argument under ECHR art.6 was dismissed as having no merit. The two dissenting judgments were on the basis that:

"30. In a case where . . . all those three purposes of the rules about service by email have been achieved, that is in my judgment capable of being, at least prima facie, a good reason for validating service under rule 6.15 . . . .I mean a sufficiently good reason provided that there are not, on a full review of the circumstances, adverse factors pointing against validation sufficient to outweigh the full achievement of those purposes."[111]

7–63   Where a company, represented by one of its directors, appealed against a winding-up order, the court dismissed the appeal, stating that while the court had a general duty to assist litigants, it was responsible for deciding what that duty required in any particular case. The fact that a litigant was acting in person was not in itself a reason to disapply, or excuse non-compliance with, procedural rules, orders or directions. *Barton v Wright Hassall*, above, followed. On the facts, the company should not be given special treatment by reason of its status as a litigant in person at first instance. Its director was an articulate and knowledgeable layman who had been able to put together sensible written arguments and bundles for the hearings. The position of the represented party and the public generally had also to be considered. Every indulgence given to a litigant in person placed an additional burden on the represented party and the court system.[112]

7–64   The court ordered a defendant litigant in person to pay the claimant's costs on the indemnity basis, given the defendant's unreasonable conduct. The

---

[111] See also: *Baynton-Williams v Baynton-Williams* [2019] EWHC 2179 (Ch), Master Clark. A litigant in person was given permission to rely on a witness statement which he had filed late and not served on the claimant. The claimant's solicitors should have checked the court file, which included the statement, and they had wrongly told the litigant in person that there was an absolute bar to him relying on the late statement, when in fact he could have applied for an extension of time. The expert had not understood or adhered to the requirements of his role. He had drawn an unjustified distinction between the documents he was given by the claimant's solicitors and the information in the defendant's email.
[112] *EDF Energy Customers Ltd (formerly EDF Energy Customers Plc) v Re-Energized Ltd* [2018] EWHC 652 (Ch); [2018] B.P.I.R. 855 HHJ Paul Matthews.

judge noted that "being a litigant in person does not excuse poor conduct, particularly it does not excuse making and maintaining baseless allegations of fraud, which only increase the temperature in litigation, and make it more difficult to compromise any aspect of a claim" (para.31). The court considered that the offers by the litigant in person to mediate were not relevant, as mediation would not have been successful due to his stance.[113]

A master had dealt with an application to strike out a claim under CPR   **7–65** r.3.4(2) as though it were an application for summary judgment under CPR r.24.2. The claimant, who was acting in person, was not told by the master that he was treating the application in that way, and nor did he expressly consider the fairness to her of dispensing with the procedural requirements of Pt 24. She appealed against the striking out of her claim disputing the validity of a will, and sought permission to amend her particulars of claim. The court, on appeal, held that as a litigant in person the claimant was entitled to have proper notice of the fact that the defendants were applying for summary judgment. The master had conducted a mini-trial contrary to the guidance in *Three Rivers DC v Bank of England*.[114] This amounted to a serious procedural irregularity which rendered the striking out unjust. Had the procedural and substantive consequences been explained to the claimant at the hearing, it was likely that she would have obtained an adjournment so that she could seek legal advice. Had she done so, it was likely that her claim would have been reformulated. The appeal proceeded by way of a re-hearing and was allowed.[115]

The Court of Appeal declined to amend a direction requiring the oppo-   **7–66** nent of a litigant in person to take responsibility for preparing bundles of documents for itself and the litigant for the substantive hearing, with a condition that the litigant could file a further bundle if she believed anything material to the issues had been omitted. The litigant had been uncooperative over the bundles and had twice returned copies to the opponent, and the court directed that the opponent should try once more and that the appellant should accept them.[116]

In *Ndole Assets Ltd*[117] Coulson J held that service of the claim form and the   **7–67** particulars of claim was a reserved legal activity under the Legal Services Act 2007, s.12. However, where a litigant was acting in person, service could be effected either by the litigant or by an agent acting on his behalf. This decision does not sit easily with *Gregory v Turner*[118] where the Court of Appeal had to consider whether the grant to an unqualified person, of an enduring power of attorney conferred a right to conduct litigation on a litigant in person's

---

[113] *Liu v Matyas* [2020] EWHC 2923 (Ch), Deputy Master Linwood.
[114] *Three Rivers DC v Bank of England* [2001] UKHL 16; [2003] 2 A.C. 1.
[115] *St Clair v King* [2018] EWHC 682 (Ch) Andrew Sutcliffe QC.
[116] *Kaur v Leeds Teaching Hospitals NHS Trust* [2018] EWCA Civ 311. See also *Axnoller Events Ltd v (1) Nihal Mohammed Kamal Brake (2) Andrew Young Brake* [2021] EWHC 1706 (Ch) where represented parties who had provided, in accordance with a court order, soft copy trial bundles to litigants in person at a time when they were themselves represented, were not required to supply a hard copy without charge.
[117] *Ndole Assets Ltd v Designer M&E Services UK Ltd* [2017] EWHC 1148 (TCC); [2017] 1 W.L.R. 4367, Coulson J.
[118] *Gregory v Turner* [2003] EWCA Civ 183; [2003] 1 W.L.R. 1149.

behalf. The court held that under the Courts and Legal Services Act 1990 s.27(2)(d) and s.28(2)(d) a right of audience and a right to conduct litigation was conferred on a person who was a party to the proceedings and would have had those rights "in his capacity as such a party" if the 1990 Act had not been passed. However, those rights did not extend to an agent of a party to the proceedings; accordingly the unqualified person had no right to conduct litigation on the litigant's behalf and he did so only by the exercise of the court's discretion.

On appeal the court held that the principles set out in *Gregory v Turner* (above) meant that the judge's reasoning could not stand. The formal service of a claim form on a defendant fell within the "conduct of litigation" for the purpose of the 2007 Act. It was therefore a reserved legal activity which could only be performed by a statutorily authorised person or by an exempt person. And CSD (the agents acting for the litigant) were neither. This approach led the court to consider the apparent problem that the same might be said of process-servers or postal employees. Further what if the litigant in person, if an individual, asked a family member to deliver the claim form or, if a company, asked an employee to do so: was the conclusion compelled that such a family member or employee was to be adjudged to have committed an offence? Such a conclusion was unacceptable. Substance had to prevail over form. A pragmatic solution was the correct solution, i.e. one that distinguished between those who merely perform an administrative or mechanical function in connection with service of documents and those who undertake, or who have assumed, legal responsibility with regard to service as prescribed by the rules.[119] Process-servers and the like were not within the statutory prohibition: they were simply engaged in the "mechanical" activity of actually delivering the claim form. Delivery, for these purposes, was not to be equated with service of a claim form as prescribed by the rules. The service of a claim form by a person who was not an authorised or exempt person for the purposes of the Act did not mean that the service was invalid, so long as they were simply engaged in the "mechanical" activity of actually delivering the claim form.[120]

Striking out

7–68   In *Chambers v Rooney*[121] Walker J explained to the claimant litigant in person:

> *"B. Striking out heads of claim: value to a litigant in person*
> *17 Striking out decisions can, among other things, bring to an end parts of a claim which are unsound in law. Parts of a claim with no real prospect of success can also be brought to an end by using the summary judgment procedure. Bringing to an end such parts of a claim can be of particular value to litigants in person. . . .*

---

[119] The Court suggested that this accorded with the acceptance by the court in *Agassi v Robinson (Inspector of Taxes) (Costs)* [2005] EWCA Civ 1507; [2006] 1 W.L.R. 2126; [2006] 1 All E.R. 900; [2006] 2 Costs L.R. 283 in [43] of the judgment that the statutory prohibition did not extend to "what might be termed purely clerical or mechanical activities."

[120] *Ndole Assets Ltd v Designer M&E Services UK Ltd* [2018] EWCA Civ 2865; [2019] B.L.R. 147.

[121] *Chambers v Rooney* [2017] EWHC 285 (QB) Walker J.

18 There is a real danger that litigants in person may press on with parts of a claim which seem to them to demonstrate how badly the other side has behaved but for which there is no legal basis. Similarly, there may be parts of the claim for which, despite the strong suspicions or firm belief of the litigant in person, there is plainly no factual basis.

19 It will generally be of great assistance for litigants in person if these parts of the claim are struck out . . ..However where a strike-out application succeeds against litigants in person, or the court of its own motion strikes out part of a claim by litigants in person, then litigants in person have a benefit that they would not otherwise have received. The relevant part of the claim has been examined by the judge, and disposed of at an early stage.

20 Litigants who are represented have lawyers who can give them expert advice about the legal and factual merits of the case. Litigants in person often lack such advice. For litigants in person, a potential advantage of a strike-out decision against them is that it may, to an extent, remedy that lack. Among other things:

> *(1) The physical and mental resources required when undertaking the tasks of preparing for and conducting a trial are all too easy to underestimate . . ..The tasks of preparing and conducting a trial impose huge pressures on litigants in person. By striking out the relevant part of the claim, the court saves the litigant in person from the burden of preparing, and fighting at trial, parts of the claim which the strike out procedure has identified in advance as being bound to fail.*
>
> *(2) Striking out such parts of the claim will also benefit the litigant in person in relation to possible costs consequences . . ..Under our civil procedure system litigants in person are potentially exposed to an order that they must pay those costs . . ..This is because costs orders running to tens of thousands of pounds may be made against them in relation to parts of the claim which have failed at trial. Litigants in person have often found themselves facing ruin by attacking their opponents on too many fronts, with costs orders against them vastly outweighing any such amounts as may have been awarded in their favour . . .. Nevertheless, because it was a claim which was bound to fail, the striking-out order minimises the pain and protects litigants from being at risk of an order that they pay future costs of the part of the claim in question.*

21 When parts of the claim are struck out the natural reaction of the litigant in person is disappointment. However the course to be taken by litigants in person— and indeed by litigants who are represented—is to stand back and review the case. For litigants in person, a decision striking out parts of the claim will generally be a clear indication that they have been fighting on too many fronts, and that they need to stop wasting time and energy on parts of the claim that are bound to fail.

22 A strike out decision can sometimes assist litigants in person in other ways. Well before trial all litigants need to review the case. Things that litigants in person need to have in mind are discussed in chapter 15 of the Handbook for Litigants in Person. All litigants in person should pay careful attention to what is said in that chapter. Particularly relevant for present purposes is section K of that chapter. . . ."

McKenzie Friends

7-69   On 12 July 2010 the Master of the Rolls and President of the Family Division handed down a Practice Note,[122] which applies to civil and family proceedings in the Court of Appeal (Civil Division), the High Court, County Courts and the Family Proceedings Court in the Magistrates' Courts. The Note is issued as guidance, not as a Practice Direction, and sets out to remind courts and litigants of the principles set out in the authorities.

Litigants have the right to have reasonable assistance from a lay person (McKenzie Friends), but McKenzie Friends have no independent right to provide assistance. They have no right to act as advocates or to carry out the conduct of litigation.

McKenzie Friends may:

(i)   provide moral support for litigants;
(ii) take notes;
(iii) help with case papers; and
(iv) quietly give advice on any aspect of the conduct of the case.

A McKenzie Friend may not: (a) act as a litigant's agent in relation to the proceedings; (b) manage litigants' cases outside court, for example by signing court documents; or (c) address the court, make oral submissions or examine witnesses. The Practice Note points out that while litigants ordinarily have a right to receive reasonable assistance from McKenzie Friends, the court retains the power to refuse to permit such assistance. It may do so where it is satisfied that, in a given case, the interests of justice and fairness do not require the litigant to receive such assistance.[123]

The following factors should not be taken to justify the court refusing to permit a litigant receiving such assistance: (i) the case or application is simple or straightforward, or is for instance a directions or case management hearing; (ii) the litigant appears capable of conducting the case without assistance; (iii) the litigant is unrepresented through choice; (iv) the other party is not represented; (v) the proposed McKenzie Friend belongs to an organisation that promotes a particular cause; and (vi) the proceedings are confidential and the court papers contain sensitive information relating to a family's affairs.

7-70   A litigant may be denied assistance of a McKenzie Friend because its provision might undermine or has undermined the efficient administration of justice. Such circumstances might include:

(i)   the assistance is being provided for an improper purpose;
(ii) the assistance is unreasonable in nature or degree;
(iii) the McKenzie Friend is subject to a civil proceedings orders or a civil restraint order;

---

[122] *Practice Note (Sen Cts: McKenzie Friends: Civil and Family Courts)* [2010] 1 W.L.R. 1881; [2010] 4 All E.R. 272.
[123] Conversely, in *Ravenscroft v Canal and River Trust* [2016] EWHC 2282 (Ch) Chief Master Marsh permitted an almost illiterate party to appoint a McKenzie Friend to act as his advocate in circumstances where his near illiteracy and emotional involvement with the issues meant that he was unlikely to be able adequately to represent himself.

(iv) the McKenzie Friend is using the litigant as a puppet;

(v) the McKenzie Friend is directly or indirectly conducting the litigation; and

(vi) the court is not satisfied that the McKenzie Friend fully understands the duty of confidentiality.

The Note points out that McKenzie Friends do not have a right of audience or a right to conduct litigation, and it is a criminal offence to exercise rights of audience or to conduct litigation unless properly qualified and authorised to do so. The court may grant such rights to a McKenzie Friend on a case-by-case basis, but the courts should be slow to grant any application from a litigant for a right of audience or a right to conduct litigation to any lay person, including a McKenzie Friend. The court should only be prepared to grant such rights where there is good reason to do so, taking into account all the circumstances of the case. Such grants should not be extended to lay persons automatically or without due consideration. They should not be granted for mere convenience.

When a Civil Proceeding Order under s.42 of the Senior Courts Act 1981 was made against a vexatious litigant, it should be standard practice to include a paragraph prohibiting the vexatious litigant from acting as a representative or McKenzie Friend. If a litigant was to be prevented without leave of the court from bringing cases himself, the case was stronger to prevent him from appearing as a representative.[124]   **7–71**

A request to grant a right of audience had to be justified and that depended on the circumstances.[125] Where the proposed advocate was someone who had set himself up as an unqualified advocate and held himself out as providing advocacy services, the court would make such an order only in exceptional circumstances. The defendant's McKenzie Friend had not mentioned that he had unsuccessfully applied to the Solicitors Regulation Authority to have his indefinite suspension terminated. There was no good reason to grant him rights of audience. It would be wrong in principle as it would undermine the role of the Solicitors Disciplinary Tribunal.[126]   **7–72**

Litigants may enter into lawful agreements to pay fees to McKenzie Friends for the provision of reasonable assistance in court, or out of court by, e.g. carrying out clerical or mechanical activities such as photocopying documents, preparing bundles, delivering documents to opposing parties or the court, or the provision of legal advice in connection with court proceedings. Such fees cannot lawfully be recovered from the opposing party. Even where the court has granted a McKenzie Friend the right to conduct litigation, fees said   **7–73**

---

[124] *Attorney General v Vaidya* [2017] EWHC 2152 (Admin) Bean LJ and Goss J.

[125] See *Clarkson v Gilbert (Rights of Audience)* [2000] C.P. Rep. 58; [2000] 2 F.L.R. 839; [2000] 3 F.C.R. 10, CA.

[126] *Azumi Ltd v Zuma's Choice Pet Products Ltd* [2017] EWHC 45 (IPEC) Douglas Campbell QC. For an example where a McKenzie Friend was granted the right to address the court, see *The Secretary of State for Business, Energy and Industrial Strategy v Rajgor* [2021] EWHC 1239 (Ch), where the defendant had had several retinal detachments of one of his eyes in the preceding months and needed the assistance of his wife to have the contents of various documents read out to him and needed the support of his wife from time to time to speak for him.

to be incurred by a McKenzie Friend are, in principle, recoverable from the litigant for whom the work was carried out, but cannot lawfully be recovered from the opposing party. Where a McKenzie Friend is granted a right of audience, the fees incurred by the McKenzie Friend are, in principle, recoverable from the litigant on whose behalf the right is exercised, and are also recoverable, in principle, from the opposing party as a recoverable disbursement.

7-74   The court has power to deny a litigant a McKenzie Friend, if to allow it would undermine the administration of justice, especially where the assistance was for an improper purpose or the McKenzie Friend was subject to a civil proceedings order. Such an order was made following a Crown Court recorder's findings that the respondent had attempted to deceive the court and had wasted public funds.[127]

7-75   Since the guidance, which summarised the case law as it stood in 2010, was introduced there has been a significant increase in the number of both Litigants in Person and McKenzie Friends. The Judicial Executive Board issued a consultation paper: *Reforming the Courts' approach to McKenzie Friends*. The consultation closed on 9 June 2016. On 15 September 2017 it was reported that the judiciary is set to reassess proposals for regulating the McKenzie Friend sector after a large number of responses to a consultation on banning fee recovery. In February 2019 the Lord Chief Justice issued the Consultation Response to *Reforming the Courts' approach to McKenzie Friends*. The response recommends:

> "*The question of the reform of the courts' approach to McKenzie Friends is one on which, as the consultation demonstrates, there are varying strongly held views. The growth in McKenzie Friends has coincided with the period following the enactment of the Legal Aid, Sentencing and Punishment of Offenders Act 2012. The government has been reviewing the impact of the changes to the availability of legal aid. JEB conclude that the growth in reliance on McKenzie Friends, and particularly fee-charging ones, should be considered in the context of the impact of those changes. It is for the government to consider appropriate steps to be taken to enable LiPs to secure effective access to legal assistance, legal advice and, where necessary, representation.*
>
> *The role of the judiciary is to apply the law concerning the provision of legal assistance, the right to conduct litigation and rights of audience according to the law established by the Legal Services Act 2007, the common law and precedent.*
>
> *The JEB remain deeply concerned about the proliferation of McKenzie Friends who in effect provide professional services for reward when they are unqualified, unregulated, uninsured and not subject to the same professional obligations and duties, both to their clients and the courts, as are professional lawyers. The statutory scheme was fashioned to protect the consumers of legal services and the integrity of the legal system. JEB's view is that all courts should apply the current law applicable to McKenzie Friends as established by Court of Appeal authority.*

---

[127] *Attorney General v Carruthers* [2016] EWHC 3830 (Admin) Simon LJ, Cox J.

The Lord Chief Justice and JEB refer this consultation response and the annex summarising the views expressed in the consultation, to the Lord Chancellor. Question 7 in the consultation paper concerns the provision of a Plain Language Guide for LiPs and McKenzie Friends. JEB support the view that a plain language guide could be produced by a non-judicial body for the assistance of LiPs. The judiciary continues to support the promotion of public legal education which would be aided by such a guide.

Finally, the Lord Chief Justice and JEB note that the current Practice Guidance on McKenzie Friends has not been revised or updated since it was issued in 2010. To ensure that it properly reflects the current case law, it should now be updated and re-issued."

Questions and answers

A. Fixed Costs

Small Claims Track
Q1.i. On the small claims track if a party makes an application but then wishes to withdraw it, are there any fixed costs which the applicant must make to the respondent? And is the position any different if the applicant and the respondent jointly agree that the application can be withdrawn? I am trying to check whether withdrawing an application in the small claims track could have costs consequences for the applicant, but I can find nothing on-point in the CPR. What fixed costs are defendants entitled to in a small claim?
ii. If a prospective claimant has two separate causes of action against the same defendant, one of which is for approximately £8,000 with good prospects of success, and the other which is for over £11,000 but has a much lower chance of success, can the prospective claimant choose to forego its right to recover the larger claim in the interest of pursuing only the smaller claim in the small claims track to limit its costs exposure? For the avoidance of doubt, the claimant would be completely foregoing its intention to pursue the larger claim – it would not attempt to recover that claim at any point in the future (it is appreciated that to do so would likely be an abuse of process).
i. CPR r.27.14(2) is specific: The court may not order a party to pay a sum to another party in respect of that other party's costs, fees and expenses, including those relating to an appeal, except those set out in the rule. Paragraph 27.14.1 of the *White Book* 2021 states:

7–76

"This rule must be read in conjunction with para.7 of the Practice Direction which accompanies Pt.27. The costs recoverable in a small claims case are restricted but this is not a true 'no costs' rule. This is because the costs provisions of the CPR at Pts 44 to 48 still apply, other than where the specific provisions of Pt 27 override these. Accordingly, if the court makes a costs order under CPR r.44.2, there is

> *still the scope for the following costs to be awarded in addition to the expenses at r.27.14(2)(d) and (e):in most small claims, court fees and any fixed costs on issue are payable if the claimant is successful (r.27.14(2)(a) and (c));in proceedings for an injunction a sum not exceeding £260 made be ordered (r.27.14(2)(b) and CPR PD27 para.7.2);expert fees not exceeding £750 (r.27.14.(2)(f) and CPR PD27 para.7.3(2));costs assessed summarily where a party has behaved unreasonably and is ordered to pay them (r.27.14(2)(g));stage 1 and stage 2 costs in certain claims under the Low Value Personal Injury Protocols (r.27.14(2)(h));the costs of any approved transcript reasonably incurred in an appeal (r.27.14(2)(i)) costs under a contractual provision (see Chaplair Ltd v Kumari [2015] EWCA Civ 798."* See Q8.

Thus, if the court is of the view that any of the above apply an order for costs may be made in favour of either party as appropriate.[128]

7–77   ii. If a claimant has two separate causes of action it is entirely open to the claimant to choose to pursue one action and not the other. It is suggested that pursuing the second action at some point in the future would be likely to be an abuse of process, but, although the parties are the same, if there are two distinct causes of action it is difficult to see how subsequent proceedings could amount to an abuse, unless both causes of action arose from the same set of facts.

Q2. Is there a leading authority on costs orders on the small claims track?

7–78   The small claims track is generally not costs-bearing save for the exceptions set out in CPR r.27.14 which includes unreasonable conduct costs (CPR r.27.14(g)). The scope for making a costs order on the small claims track is set out in the rule. That is best referred to rather than case law.

Q3. We act for the defendant in a small claims track matter. Parties instructed a joint expert to prepare a report. In respect of costs, if our client loses at trial we believe the claimant would only be entitled to: the claim amount, fixed costs under Pt.45, any court fees (including issuing fee and trial fee) and then any interest awarded by the court. Please can you confirm that the claimant would not be entitled to recover the cost of the expert report, which was split jointly between the parties.

7–79   The full exceptions to the no-costs rule in the small claims track are set out in CPR r.27.14. CPR r.27.14(f) provides that a sum may be ordered in relation to expert fees and CPR PD 27A at para.7.3 provides that such sum shall not exceed £750. The court is likely to consider any express basis upon which the parties instructed the expert (firstly through court order failing which any agreement between the parties), alternatively resort to its discretion in all the circumstances as to the recoverability of such fees as between the parties.

---

[128] See *Dammermann v Lanyon Bowdler LLP* [2017] EWCA Civ 269; [2017] C.P. Rep. 25; [2017] 2 Costs L.R. 393.

Q4. My question is regarding applying for contractual costs on default judgment. We are planning on requesting a default judgment as the defendant has failed to file an acknowledgment. Returning the notice of issue with the "request judgement section completed", however, does not give an option to set out the contractual costs we have incurred; whereas we are seeking to recover costs from the tenant based on the contractual provisions under the lease. What is the best way to recover costs in full?

Costs which are payable under a contract are payable in accordance with the terms of the contract unless the court orders otherwise. These provisions do not apply to a contract between a solicitor and his client.[129]

7–80

Rule 44.5 only applies if the court is assessing costs payable under a contract. It does not require the court to make an assessment of such costs; or require e.g. a mortgagee to apply for an order for those costs where there is a contractual right to recover out of the mortgage funds.

Most of the authorities relate to the costs of mortgagees. The leading authority is *Gomba Holdings (UK) Ltd v Minories Finance Ltd (No.2)* [130] in which the Court of Appeal set out a number of principles to be applied:

(i)   an order for the payment of costs of proceedings by one party to another is always a discretionary order under s.51 of the Senior Courts Act 1981;

(ii) where there is a contractual right to the costs, the discretion should ordinarily be exercised so as to reflect that contractual right;

(iii) the power of the court to disallow a mortgagee's costs sought to be added to the mortgage security, is a power that does not derive from s.51 but from the power of the courts of equity to fix the terms on which redemption will be allowed;

(iv) a decision by a court to refuse costs in whole, or in part, to a mortgage litigant may be a decision in the exercise of the s.51 discretion, or a decision in the exercise of the power to fix the terms on which redemption will be allowed, or a decision as to the extent of the mortgagee's contractual right to add his cost to the security, or a combination of two or more of these things. The pleadings in the case and the submissions made to the judge may indicate which of the decisions has been made;

(v)   a mortgagee may not be deprived of a contractual or equitable right to add costs to the security merely by reason of an order for payment of costs made without reference to the mortgagee's contractual or equitable rights and without any adjudication as to whether or not the mortgagee should be deprived of those costs.

---

[129] CPR r.44.5.
[130] [1991] Ch. 26; [1990] 3 W.L.R. 780; [1990] E.G. 19 (CS) and see PD 44 paras 7.1–7.3.

For a case in which a claimant bank brought proceedings for possession which it later discontinued see *Cooperative Bank Plc v Phillips*.[131] The court held that the bank was not entitled under the loan agreement to recover from the defendant any costs incurred by it which were unreasonable in amount or unreasonably incurred. In the case in the question an application for judgment in default would result only in recovery of the fixed costs. It would therefore be necessary to make an application to the court for recovery of the costs under the contact.

It is possible that the question is intended to refer to the case where the claimant has a contract with the defendant that includes a right to indemnity basis costs and so the questioner is asking a practical question as to how a claimant in such a situation can request a judgment in default in a specified claim whilst preserving a right to those costs (the request for judgment in default in that situation – Form N225 – refers to the legal representative's costs on issuing the claim and on entering the judgment in default, providing one box for the answer, in other words assuming the insertion of the fixed costs). If so, it seems that the answer lies in CPR r.45.1, the court must order otherwise to disapply the fixed costs. Instinctively, one would expect the claimant to file the N255 in the usual way, but to complete the costs boxes (as they should have the costs box on issue) 'to be assessed – contractual costs' and to make an application at the same time, supported by evidence, for an order for costs to be assessed.

Q5. I am looking to find any practice directions or case law on the recovery of contractual legal costs recovery in the fast track.

7–81   CPR r.44.5 sets out the provisions applicable where costs are payable under a contract. CPR PD44, para.7 supports CPR r.44.5, and there is a presumption of reasonableness as to such costs being incurred and their amount. These provisions reflect the principle in *Gomba Holdings (UK) Ltd v Minories Finance Ltd (No2)* [1993] Ch 171, [1992] 4 All ER 588, CA. Common examples of contractual costs are found in mortgages and landlord and tenant contracts. A more recent example of the latter can be found in *Chaplair Ltd v Kumari* [2015] EWCA Civ 798.

Q6. I have a client who has instructed me to issue a money claim against a debtor. In the contract that formed the basis of the agreement, there is a clause for an indemnity to cover legal costs if the debtor defaults on payment – which it has. Pre-action correspondence to recover the debt has failed. Should that pre-action work, including the drafting of the particulars of claim, be included in the main claim amount, or separately as costs to be assessed by the court?

7–82   The statement of case should claim for costs pursuant to the contract, as to which see CPR r.44.5.

---

[131] [2014] EWHC 2862 (Ch); [2014] 5 Costs L.R. 830, Morgan J.

Q7. When there is a contractual entitlement to costs, on an indemnity basis, in relation to a debt claim, should one include the costs incurred to the date of issue of a claim within the main claim amount?
Losses which can be particularised ought to be, and it should be stated that the loss is ongoing.　　7–83

Q8. In relation to entering judgment following strike out for failure to comply with a court order (we are pre-allocation but the value of the claim is under £10,000), I assume that my client will be unable to claim its full costs of the claim due to its financial value? In addition, I have reviewed the circumstances where fixed costs may be claimed on entering judgment in CPR Part 45 and cannot see that these cover entering judgment pursuant to CPR r.3.5. Does this mean that my client cannot claim any legal costs at all (save the fixed costs on issue) when we submit the request for judgment?
Where judgment is entered under CPR r.3.4(2) on the grounds that there has been a failure to comply with a rule, practice direction or court order, the court may make any consequential order it considers appropriate. Such an order should contain an order for costs. If the order is for costs on the standard basis, it is likely to be met with the argument that it should be treated as a small claim, although it has not been allocated. As to that see: *O'Beirne v Hudson*[132] and Q9 below.　　7–84

Q9. If a claimant issues a small claim but fails to pay the court fee for the hearing so the matter is struck out by the court, can you claim costs for the wasted time spent in preparing and filing the witness evidence and responding to the claim? In a small claims RTA, does the litigant in person claimant have to use the portal and form RTA1 or will a letter before action and commencement in the small claims track suffice? Do the fixed fees in CPR rr.45.2 and 45.4 apply to a money claim over £10,000? If not, why not?
It is presumed that the first question comes from the defendant. It would clearly be open to the defendant to claim its costs under CPR r.27.14(2)(g).　　7–85

With regard to the second question: If the value of the claim is such that, if proceedings were started the small claims track would be the normal track for the claim, then the claim is outside the scope of the RTA Protocol pursuant to para.4.1 and the Protocol does not apply. A claimant using the Protocol in such circumstances would be at risk of a subsequent order that the costs should be limited to small claims track costs on a retrospective basis—see *O'Beirne v Hudson*.[133]　　7–86

---

[132] *O'Beirne v Hudson* [2010] EWCA Civ 52; [2010] 1 W.L.R. 1717; [2010] C.P. Rep. 23; [2010] 2 Costs L.R. 204.
[133] *O'Beirne v Hudson* [2010] EWCA Civ 52; [2010] 1 W.L.R. 1717.

CPR r.27.14(h) provides that:

"The court may not order a party to pay a sum to another party in respect of that other party's costs, fees and expenses, including those relating to an appeal, except— . . .

> *(h) the Stage 1 and, where relevant, the Stage 2 fixed costs in rule 45.18 where—*
>
> > *(i)   the claim was within the scope of the Pre-Action Protocol for Low Value Personal Injury Claims in Road Traffic Accidents ("the RTA Protocol") or the Pre-action Protocol for Low Value Personal Injury (Employers' Liability and Public Liability) Claims ("the EL/PL Protocol");*
> >
> > *(ii)   the claimant reasonably believed that the claim was valued at more than the small claims track limit in accordance with paragraph 4.1(4) of the relevant Protocol; and*
> >
> > *(iii) the defendant admitted liability under the process set out in the relevant Protocol; but*
> >
> > *(iv)   the defendant did not pay those Stage 1 and, where relevant, Stage 2 fixed costs;".*

Accordingly, unless the claimant reasonably believes, at the time of starting the claim, that its value is above the small claims limit and that the claim otherwise is within Protocol scope, the Portal should not be used and the claim should be notified in the conventional fashion.

For a road traffic accident which occurred after 31 May 2021, pursuant to the new RTA Small Claims Protocol, para.2.2 makes it plain that the Portal is to be used by an unrepresented claimant to obtain any medical report in support of their claim and it is therefore implicit that the Portal should be used to make a claim by a litigant in person.

7–87   With regard to the third question, CPR r.45.1(2) sets out the amounts which, unless the court orders otherwise, are to be allowed in respect of legal representatives' charges. Paragraph 45.1.2 of the *White Book* 2021 states:

"In para.1.1 of Practice Direction 45 it is explained that, under r.27.14, costs which can be awarded to a claimant in a small claim include the fixed costs payable under Pt 45 attributable to issuing the claim. The fixed costs are the sum of (a) the fixed commencement costs calculated in accordance with Table 1 of r.45.2, and (b) appropriate court fee or fees paid by the claimant (above para.1.2)."

Both Table 1 under CPR r.45.2—Amount of fixed commencement costs in a claim for the recovery of money or goods; and Table 2 under CPR r.45.4—Costs on entry of judgment in a claim for the recovery of money or goods, provide for cases over £5,000.

Q10. i. The client has now received a bill of costs in the sum of £7,000.00. Can it now argue that costs are not payable as it would have been a small claims track matter and therefore Part 36 offers are excluded from it in line with CPR r.27.2?

ii. Are the fixed commencement costs in a claim for the recovery of money or goods set out in CPR r.45.2 only applicable to small track claims? Or do they also apply to fast track claims?

iii. If a case is originally a Small Claims matter and the value of the claim is a small claims matter but, due to various reasons the matter is re-tracked to the fast track and then to the multi track at a later point, are the costs which have been incurred in respect of the small claims element irrecoverable given that costs are not claimable on the small claims track?

iv If there is a matter in dispute which is just over the £10k limit, and is allocated to the fast track but subsequently settled for less than £10,000.00 by way of a Part 36 offer. Will fast track cost consequences still apply?

i. CPR r.27.14 (Costs on the small claims track) states "(1) This rule applies to any 7–88 case which has been allocated to the small claims track." Rule 46.11(2) (Costs on the small claims track and fast track) inserts the proviso "Once a claim is allocated to a particular track, those special rules shall apply to the period before, as well as after, allocation except where the court or a practice direction provides otherwise." Accordingly, CPR r. 27.2(1)(g) has no application as the case has not yet been allocated. This is a case where the principles laid down by the Court of Appeal in *O'Beirne v Hudson*[134] will apply.

ii. CPR r. 45.2 provides for fixed costs in circumstances where judgment has 7–89 been entered upon an admission, summary judgment or strike out, or where the claim is conceded. The rule does not envisage that the claim will have been allocated and there is no qualification by allocation as to the applicability of the fixed fees.

iii. CPR r.46.13 provides the complete answer to this question: 7–90

"(1) Any costs orders made before a claim is allocated will not be affected by allocation.
(2) Where—
   (a) claim is allocated to a track; and
   (b) the court subsequently re-allocates that claim to a different track, then unless the court orders otherwise, any special rules about costs applying—
     (i) to the first track, will apply to the claim up to the date of re-allocation; and
     (ii) to the second track, will apply from the date of re-allocation.
(3) Where the court is assessing costs on the standard basis of a claim which concluded without being allocated to a track, it may restrict those costs to costs that would have been allowed on the track to which the claim would have been allocated if allocation had taken place."

iv. See the answer to iii above, once the case is allocated to the fast track, the 7–91 fast track rules apply. CPR r.36.13 provides "(1) Subject to paragraphs (2) and

---

[134] *O'Beirne v Hudson* [2010] EWCA Civ 52; [2010] 1 W.L.R. 1717; [2010] C.P. Rep. 23; [2010] 2 Costs L.R. 204.

(4) and to rule 36.20, where a Part 36 offer is accepted within the relevant period the claimant will be entitled to the costs of the proceedings (including their recoverable pre-action costs) up to the date on which notice of acceptance was served on the offeror." Paragraph (2) relates to offers for only part of a claim and paragraph (4) deals with: where (a) a Part 36 offer which was made less than 21 days before the start of a trial is accepted; or (b) a Part 36 offer which relates to the whole of the claim is accepted after expiry of the relevant period; or (c) subject to paragraph (2), a Part 36 offer which does not relate to the whole of the claim is accepted at any time. In such cases the liability for costs must be determined by the court unless the parties have agreed the costs. Rule 36.20 relates to personal injury claims.

Fast Track and Multi Track

Q11. Does a child approval hearing for a fast track PI claim attract fixed costs for "hearing" or is it as D has argued not a contested hearing and therefore not eligible for hearing costs? D has argued as the matter settled post issue but pre allocation it is eligible for pre allocation fixed costs only as quantum was agreed at that stage. But we have said an approval hearing was required and therefore hearing costs are due.

7–92   Assuming that any of the RTA or EL/PL Protocols is engaged, then Stage 3 becomes operative. CPR PD 8B.1 sets out the scope of the procedure which includes at (2) the scenario where a settlement has been agreed between the parties but approval of the court is nevertheless required (in accordance with CPR Pt 21). In such circumstances, the hearing is a "Settlement hearing" (per CPR PD 8 at para.3.3). CPR r.45.16 extends the scope of Section III in CPR Pt 45 to claims that started under CPR Pt 8 "the stage 3 Procedure". As a result, a Stage 3 fee in accordance with CPR r.45.18 will apply.

Q12. Our client is being threatened with legal proceedings for an unpaid sum under a contract for £31,000. It should be noted that liability for this sum is denied. The claimant is attempting to intimidate our client into accepting an offer of £10,000 to settle the matter, on the basis that this will therefore fall within the small claims track and only fixed costs will be recoverable. What options do we have available to us as a potential defendant to have this matter allocated to a different track which will allow a greater level of recoverable costs?

7–93   The court will allocate the claim to a track, when all parties have filed their directions questionnaires; or, when giving directions. CPR r.26.7(1) provides that in considering whether to allocate a claim to the normal track for that claim the court will have regard to the matters mentioned in CPR r.26.8(1); i.e:

(a)   the financial value, if any, of the claim;
(b)   the nature of the remedy sought;
(c)   the likely complexity of the facts, law or evidence;

(d) the number of parties or likely parties;

(e) the value of any counterclaim or other Pt 20 claim and the complexity of any matters relating to it;

(f) the amount of oral evidence which may be required;

(g) the importance of the claim to persons who are not parties to the proceedings;

(h) the views expressed by the parties; and

(i) the circumstances of the parties.

It is for the court to assess the financial value of a claim.

Q13. Form N1C provides that upon a defendant receiving a claim they may: (a) pay the total amount i.e. the amount claimed, the court fee, and solicitor's costs (b) admit that he owes all or part of the claim and ask for time to pay or c) dispute the claim. An unrepresented defendant has paid (outside of 14 days but before judgment entered) the full sum claimed plus the fixed costs on the claim and interest. They have not sent an admission form as they say that they took the first option as set out on the Form N1C. It is my understanding that an admission should have been filed stating the date of payment, but I do have some sympathy for the defendant as the Form N1C does appear to suggest that no admission is needed if payment is made. Do you have any thoughts on this? The significance is that the claimant has now applied for costs on the basis that payment was made outside of the 14 days and therefore they should not be limited to fixed costs. In your view is the claimant entitled to its costs above and beyond the fixed rate on the claim form and should an admission now be filed by the defendant?

Form N1C is quite clear: "You must reply within 14 days of the date it was served   7–94
on you." And later: "If you do not reply judgment may be entered against you."
CPR r.3.1A deals with how the court should deal with a litigant in person. It
appears from the question that the defendant has paid the full amount due,
albeit outside the 14-day time limit. The claimant's application is likely to be
badly received as being disproportionate and a waste of the court's time.

**Q14. i. We are filing a request for judgment in default (Form N225). We act for the claimant and the defendant filed and served an acknowledgement of service but failed to file and serve a defence. The claim relates to unpaid commission of £25,000. The debt was originally disputed in the acknowledgment of service. In terms of costs, we are aware that our costs for filing Form N225 will be fixed (£35). Will our costs for issuing the claim be fixed costs? As a side note, the court allocated this case to the multi-track.
ii. We act for the claimant in a matter. We have obtained default judgment against the defendant, after previously making an unaccepted Part 36 offer. My query is, are we able to recover our costs pursuant to Pt 36 or Pt 45?**

iii. If your claim is for a sum in excess of say £25,000 and you wish to obtain default judgement and costs to be assessed in the absence of agreement, can you do this on a request or must C make an application?
iv. If I have issued a claim for over £40,000 and the defendants then fail to acknowledge the claim and I make a request for judgment, would fixed costs still apply? Would this still be the case where I incurred costs over £4,000? If Fixed Costs do apply, what grounds would I potentially have in trying to persuade the court to apply discretion and how would I go about making such an application?

7–95   i. CPR r.45.1 states:

> *"(1) This Section sets out the amounts which, unless the court orders otherwise, are to be allowed in respect of legal representatives' charges.*
> *(2) This Section applies where—*
> > *(a) the only claim is a claim for a specified sum of money where the value of the claim exceeds £25 and—*
> > *(i) judgment in default is obtained under rule 12.4(1); . . .*
> *(4) Any appropriate court fee will be allowed in addition to the costs set out in this Section.*
> *(5) The claim form may include a claim for fixed commencement costs."*

It is not clear from the question if fixed commencement costs have been claimed in the claim form. Assuming that such a claim has been included CPR r.45.2 provides:

> *"(1) The amount of fixed commencement costs in a claim to which rule 45.1(2) (a) or (b) applies—*
> > *(a) will be calculated by reference to Table 1; and*
> > *(b) the amount claimed, or the value of the goods claimed if specified, in the claim form is to be used for determining the band in Table 1 that applies to the claim.*
> *(2) The amounts shown in Table 4 are to be allowed in addition, if applicable."*

Then CPR r.45.4:

> *"Where—*
> *(a) the claimant has claimed fixed commencement costs under rule 45.2; and*
> *(b) judgment is entered in a claim to which rule 45.1(2)(a) or (b) applies in the circumstances specified in Table 2, the amount to be included in the judgment for the claimant's legal representative's charges is the total of—*
> > *(i) the fixed commencement costs; and*
> > *(ii) the relevant amount shown in Table 2."*

And finally, CPR r.45.7:

> *"Table 4 shows the amount to be allowed in respect of legal representative's charges in the circumstances mentioned."*

It is a question of going to each of the relevant tables and selecting the fee from the appropriate box.

ii. The second question relates to an unaccepted Part 36 offer. Presumably 7–96 the judgment in default is at least as advantageous to the claimant as the proposals in the claimant's Part 36 offer. The editorial note in the *White Book* 2021 at para.36.17.1.1 refers to a Court of Appeal authority[135] for the proposition that the words "...upon judgment being entered" should not be interpreted narrowly. "Judgment" is undefined in Pt 36 and undefined in the Glossary to the CPR. Conversely, "default judgment" is defined at CPR r.12.1 as a "judgment without trial". The CPR therefore includes a "default judgment" as a type of "judgment", perhaps unsurprisingly given its name. In these circumstances, it appears that costs are recoverable pursuant to Pt. 36.

iii. With regard to the third question, the normal position is that fixed costs 7–97 apply; see CPR r.45.4. CPR r.12.9 deals with the procedure for obtaining a default judgment for costs only. This presupposes however that the defendant has paid the claim but is refusing to pay the costs.

iv. The answer to this question (subject to rule 45.1 "unless the court orders 7–98 otherwise") is set out within CPR r. 45.4 – Costs on entry of judgment in a claim for the recovery of money or goods, see above. The rule contains no power for the court to increase the fixed costs. The only option (other than CPR r.45.1) would therefore appear to be rule 44.11 – the Court's powers in relation to misconduct. So far as relevant the rule provides

> *"(1) The court may make an order under this rule where—*
> > *(b) it appears to the court that the conduct of a party or that party's legal representative, before or during the proceedings or in the assessment proceedings, was unreasonable or improper.*
> *(2) Where paragraph (1) applies, the court may—*
> > *(b) order the party at fault or that party's legal representative to pay costs which that party or legal representative has caused any other party to incur."*

Q15. We act for the claimant in a personal injury claim. The case was settled on the basis that the defendant agreed to pay the claimant's costs on a standard basis to be assessed if not agreed. I understand that there has been a recent court decision that determined that by reason of the procedure adopted by the claimant when issuing the claim, the defendant only had to pay fixed costs. However, there is a private agreement between the claimant and the defendant that the defendant pays standard costs. Can the parties contract out of a fixed costs regime?
In the event that a Part 36 offer is accepted by a defendant in a low value personal injury claim (where QOCS and fixed costs regime apply), would the claimant be entitled to recover under the Pt 36 regime only its fixed costs or the entirety of its costs on an indemnity basis? Further, if the

---

[135] *Crooks v Hendricks Lovell Ltd* [2016] EWCA Civ 8; [2016] Costs 1 L.O. 103.

defendant chooses to make a Part 36 offer and it is accepted, would the defendant only have to pay the claimant's fixed costs or its actual costs (on the standard basis)?

7–99   Yes. The first question seems to be on all fours with *O'Beirne v Hudson*. A personal injury action, which settled prior to allocation for £400 general damages and £719 hire charges, was concluded by a consent order providing that the defendant should pay the claimant's "reasonable costs and disbursements on the standard basis". On assessment the district judge had held that the order was for costs to be assessed on the standard basis, and none of the fixed costs regimes, including the small claims track regime, applied. The Court of Appeal held that the district judge was not free to rule that the costs would be assessed on the small claims track basis, but, when making the assessment, was entitled to take into account all the circumstances in accordance with CPR r.44.4(1), including the fact that the case would almost certainly have been allocated to the small claims track if allocation had taken place. Although it was not open to the district judge to vary the original order, or to assess by reference to the small claims track, it was quite legitimate to give items in the bill anxious scrutiny to see whether the costs were necessarily and reasonably incurred, and thus whether it was reasonable for the paying party to pay more than would have been recoverable in a case that should have been allocated to the small claims track.[136]

More recently the Court of Appeal has dealt with the situation where D had agreed to pay reasonable costs to be assessed on the standard basis and the court dealt with the argument as to whether parties could contract out and, if so, how.

Where parties had entered into a consent order providing for the claimant's reasonable costs to be paid on the standard basis, subject to detailed assessment if not agreed, the judge on appeal from a district judge (who had decided that the costs of the road traffic accident personal injury claim, following acceptance of the defendant's Part 36 offer, were to be determined under the fixed costs regime in Section IIIA of CPR Pt 45), found that the consent order was incompatible with an award of fixed costs and that the judge below had been wrong to vary what the parties had agreed.[137]

On appeal to the Court of Appeal it was held that the offer letter did not offer to pay conventional rather than fixed costs. Whilst CPR r.36.5(1)(c) did not impose an obligation on the offeror to say which rule applied: CPR r.36.20, which dealt with costs consequences of a Part 36 offer where Pt 45 Section IIIA applied, or CPR r.36.13, dealing with costs consequences of a Part 36 offer in other cases. A simple reference to CPR r.36.13 probably would not suffice to take the case out of the fixed costs regime. It was clear from the letter that the appellant was intending to make an offer to which Pt 36 applied. The letter would not have contained a Part 36 offer if it proposed anything

---

[136] *O'Beirne v Hudson* [2010] EWCA Civ 52; [2010] 1 W.L.R. 1717; [2010] C.P. Rep. 23; [2010] 2 Costs L.R. 204.
[137] *Adelekun v Lai Ho* unreported 18 October 2018, County Court at Central London, HHJ Wulwik.

other than the fixed costs regime: if a party to a claim that no longer continued under the Protocol offered to pay costs on a basis that departed from Pt 45, the offer was incompatible with Pt 36 and could not be an offer under that part.[138] The respondent relied on the fact that CPR r.45.29B provided for the fixed costs regime to apply "for as long as the case is not allocated to the multi-track". The court held that the more natural interpretation could be that, where a case was transferred from the fast track to the multi-track, the fixed costs regime ceased to apply prospectively, not in relation to past costs.[139] The fixed costs regime was designed to ensure that both sides began and ended the proceedings with the expectation that fixed costs was all that would be recoverable.[140]

The court suggested that defendants wishing to make a Part 36 offer on the basis that the fixed costs regime would apply would be well-advised to refer in the offer to CPR r.36.20 and not CPR r.36.13, and to omit any reference to the costs being "assessed", or assessment "on the standard basis" in any offer letter or consent order drawn up following acceptance of an offer.[141]

The second question is not entirely clear, in that it does not state whether **7–100** the Part 36 offer is accepted within or without the relevant period. CPR r.36.13 sets out the costs consequences of acceptance of a Part 36 offer, but that is subject to CPR r.36.20. If the claim no longer continues under the RTA Protocol pursuant to CPR r.45.29A(1) and the claimant's offer is accepted within the relevant period CPR r.36.20(2) applies:

"(2) Where a Part 36 offer is accepted within the relevant period, the claimant is entitled to the fixed costs in Table 6B, Table 6C or Table 6D in Section IIIA of Part 45 for the stage applicable at the date on which notice of acceptance was served on the offeror."

The rule appears to apply whether the offer is made by the claimant or by the defendant.

CPR r.36.20(4) states:

". . . where a defendant's Part 36 offer is accepted after the relevant period—
(a) the claimant will be entitled to the fixed costs in Table 6B, Table 6C or Table 6D in Section IIIA of Part 45 for the stage applicable at the date on which the relevant period expired; and
(b) the claimant will be liable for the defendant's costs for the period from the date of expiry of the relevant period to the date of acceptance."

Rule 36.20(5) provides:

"(5) . . . where the claimant accepts the defendant's Protocol offer after the date on which the claim leaves the Protocol—

---

[138] See *Mitchell v James (Costs)* [2002] EWCA Civ 997; [2004] 1 W.L.R. 158.
[139] See *Qader v Esure Services Ltd* [2016] EWCA Civ 1109; [2016] 6 Costs L.O. 973.
[140] *Hislop v Perde* [2018] EWCA Civ 1726; [2018] 4 Costs L.O. 515.
[141] *Ho v Adelekun* [2019] EWCA Civ 1988; [2019] Costs L.R. 1963.

> (a) the claimant will be entitled to the applicable Stage 1 and Stage 2 fixed costs in Table 6 or Table 6A in Section III of Part 45; and
>
> (b) the claimant will be liable for the defendant's costs from the date on which the Protocol offer is deemed to have been made to the date of acceptance."

It is not possible for a claimant whose offer has been accepted late, but before trial, to rely on the decision in *Broadhurst v Tan*[142] to obtain indemnity costs. CPR r.36.20 makes it plain that it is the only rule which applies to the costs consequences of accepting a Part 36 offer in fixed costs cases. The interaction between the fixed costs regime and Part 36 differs where the claimant is successful after trial and where a Part 36 offer is accepted before trial. On the correct interpretation of the Rules, in a fixed costs case, CPR r.36.20 applies where an offer is accepted late and CPR r.36.13 does not apply at all.[143]

Q16. On an application for possession of residential property, following the service and expiry of a s.8 notice, my understanding is that fixed costs apply in the event the proceedings are undefended. However, is the successful claimant that obtained a possession and money order (for arrears) and fixed costs able to bring fresh proceedings (for breach of contract) against the tenant to recover the balance of the solicitors' costs that he has incurred in bringing the possession proceedings but not recovered? The tenancy agreement provides that all costs associated with recovering rent will be payable by the tenant. I am aware of the following case where, under the small claims track, legal costs have been awarded, above the fixed costs usually permitted, as they were claimed under a contractual obligation (a clause in a lease) *Chaplair Ltd v Kumari* [2015] EWCA Civ 798 (27 July 2015). Are there any appeals/cases since that have set a different precedent, where the legal costs have been limited to the fixed costs in small claims cases, even when there was a contractual obligation?

7–101   This appears to be covered by CPR r.44.5—amount of costs where costs are payable under a contract, and the relevant case law. A claim brought by a landlord for recovery of unpaid rent and service charges was allocated, by consent, to the small claims track. The claim was successful. In the lease there was a contractual right to recover the costs of proceedings. At first instance the district judge awarded costs to the landlord but held that there was no power to award costs other than CPR r.27.14 fixed costs. On appeal to the circuit judge, the appeal was successful and the defendant appealed to the Court of Appeal. The court refused to grant permission on that particular issue as the law on the point was well established: where there was a contractual right to costs, the court should normally exercise its costs discretion to reflect

---

[142] *Broadhurst v Tan* [2016] EWCA Civ 94; [2016] 2 Costs L.O. 155.
[143] *Hislop v Perde: Kaur v Committee (for the time being) of Ramgarhia Board Leicester* [2018] EWCA Civ 1726; [2019] 1 W.L.R. 201; [2018] 4 Costs L.O. 515.

those rights; CPR r.27.14 should be read as being subject to CPR r.44.5 which gives effect to the general principle set out above and which was not excluded from CPR r.27 by CPR r.27.2. The rule making power cannot, in any event, set aside or overrule a contractual entitlement which would be necessary for CPR r.27.14 to have an exclusionary effect.[144] Separate proceedings for the costs are not required.

With regard to the second question, the decision in *Chaplair v Kumari* is still good law.

7–102

Q17. Are there any fixed costs we can charge for making an Order for Sale Claim?

CPR r.45 Section I sets out the proceedings covered by fixed costs. An application for an order for sale is not among them. Applications for charging orders are subject to fixed costs (CPR r.45.8, Table 5). There seems to be no reason why the normal costs rules should not apply. This means that costs will be summarily assessed at the end of the hearing (see para.1 of the sample forms of order for sale at Appendix A to CPR PD 73). Consequently, the applicant should file and serve a statement of costs being claimed at least 24 hours before the hearing. The costs of a successful application for an order for sale will be paid out of the proceeds of sale of the property: see paras 1 and 7 of the sample forms of order for sale at Appendix A to CPR PD 73 (Charging Orders, Stop Orders and Stop Notices).

7–103

B. Fixed costs and multi-party situations (where fixed costs may not apply equally)

Q18. Where a claim is made against more than one defendant, one of whom admits the debt and judgment is obtained under CPR r.14.4(3), while the other defendant does not respond and judgment in default is obtained under CPR r.12.4(1), is the claimant entitled to two sets of fixed costs given that there are two defendants and judgment has been obtained on two different bases? (CPR r.45.1)

Can two or more claimants both claim fixed costs i.e. two or more sets?
Section I of Pt 45 deals with fixed costs. CPR r.45.1(2) states:

7–104

> "*this section applies where (a) the only claim is a claim for a specified sum of money where the value of the claim exceeds £25 and [judgment is obtained under one of a number of provisions]*".

From the wording of the rule it would appear that only one set of costs is recoverable. There has been a single claim against two defendants and judgment has been obtained against each defendant. The defendants are presumably jointly and severally liable but the judgment debt would be recovered

---

[144] *Chaplair Ltd v Kumari* [2015] EWCA Civ 798; [2015] C.P. Rep. 46.

only once and logic dictates that only one set of costs is recoverable. There does not appear to be any authority on the point.

Similarly, if there are two claimants there is presumably one claim, and they should have only one legal representative. There does not appear to be any basis upon which a claim for two sets of fixed costs could be founded.

Q19. What is the court's approach to legal costs for a general claim on the fast track before trial, e.g. costs of a summary judgment application or other interim application? Are costs of those not fixed and subject to summary assessment? Do judges routinely summarily assess such costs?

7–105   CPR r.45.1 provides that, unless the court orders otherwise, the costs to be allowed in respect of legal representatives' charges shall be those set out in the Section. CPR r.45.1 does not refer to "trial costs" as if to distinguish those costs from other costs that may arise in any given claim. Therefore, the position is that if the fixed costs regime does apply, the costs of any summary judgment or interim application will be swept up by the fixed costs regime, unless the court orders otherwise. This approach is endorsed by the Court of Appeal in *Sharp v Leeds City Council* [2017] EWCA Civ 33.

Successful parties on interim applications should therefore consider whether to apply for costs outside of the fixed costs regime upon conclusion of the application.

Cases which fall within Section IIIA (at CPR r.45.29), namely claims which no longer continue under the RTA, EL/PL Pre-Action Protocols and claims to which the Pre-Action Protocol for Resolution of Package Travel Claims applies, are governed by CPR r.45.29H in relation to interim applications and, in the event of an order for costs being made, those costs are to be for a sum equivalent to one half of the applicable Type A and Type B costs in Table 6 or 6A.

Where costs do come to be summarily assessed, judges do routinely summarily assess costs and on an interim application it would be usual for this to be done at the conclusion of the application.

C. Getting the court to order more than fixed costs

Q20. If a fast track hearing is to be decided in writing with another hearing to decide costs at a later date:
1. Can another statement of costs be filed?
2. Can a new or revised costs bundle be filed?
3. Does the fast track fixed trial cost apply to both hearings or to each hearing?

7–106   CPR Pt 45 Section VI deals with the amount of costs which the court may award as the costs of an advocate for preparing for and appearing at the trial of a claim in the fast track.

> *"'trial' includes a hearing where the court decides an amount of money or the*
> *value of goods following a judgment under Part 12 (default judgment) or Part 14*
> *(admissions) but does not include —*
>
> (i)   *the hearing of an application for summary judgment under Part 24; or*
> (ii)   *the court's approval of a settlement or other compromise under rule*
>   *21.10.*
>
> *'fast track trial costs' means the costs of a party's advocate for preparing for and*
> *appearing at the trial, but does not include—*
>
> (i)   *any other disbursements; or*
> (ii)   *any value added tax payable on the fees of a party's advocate."*

It would seem that the costs hearing is merely an adjourned part of the fast track trial and therefore only one set of costs may be awarded.

The court may not award more or less than the amount shown in the table except where—(a) it decides not to award any fast track trial costs; or (b) CPR r.45.39 applies, but the court may apportion the amount awarded between the parties to reflect their respective degrees of success on the issues at trial. See CPR rr.45.37 to 45.40. And see **para.7–13** above.

As to filing another statement of costs and/or a revised costs bundle, this may be permissible but is unlikely to impress the judge.

Q21. Can you/how do you get more than fixed costs? Can you give some guidance/authorities regarding when the court will order otherwise than fixed costs under CPR r.45 in a case where the fixed costs provisions should otherwise apply?
Is it possible for costs be assessed when requesting default judgment or are only fixed costs allowed pursuant to CPR r.45?
CPR rr.45.13, 45.14, 45.29J and 45.29K contain the relevant provisions. Fixed   7–107
costs apply unless a party can persuade the court that there are exceptional circumstances. The court will only entertain a claim for costs greater than the fixed recoverable costs if it considers that there are exceptional circumstances making it appropriate to do so. Failure to achieve an amount 20% greater than the amount of the fixed recoverable costs, will result in an order that the defendant shall pay to the claimant the lesser of the fixed recoverable costs; and the assessed costs. CPR rr.45.29J and 45.29K contain broadly similar provisions. The most likely reason for being able to persuade the court is that the opponent's conduct has been such as to require the receiving party to do far more work (remember the 20% requirement) than was ever envisaged when the rule was drafted.

Q22. What is the relationship between fixed costs and assessed costs and fixed costs and Pt 36? i.e. what happens if they overlap?
My client made a pre-action Part 36 offer to settle a contractual debt. The recipient failed to respond, and proceedings were subsequently issued. Since the defendant did not file an acknowledgment of service or a

defence, we intend to apply for default judgment on behalf of our client. Will our client still have the costs benefit of the Part 36 offer? If so, how does that work in practice? Presumably when applying for default judgment we can only include fixed costs?

7–108   Ideally there should be no overlap between assessed costs, fixed costs and Pt 36 costs. See *Broadhurst v Tan*[145] discussed above, where the court held that the tension between CPR r.45.29B and CPR r.36.21 must be resolved in favour of CPR r.36.21.

CPR r.44.6 deals with assessed costs:

"(1) Where the court orders a party to pay costs to another party (other than fixed costs) it may either—
   (a)   make a summary assessment of the costs; or
   (b)   order detailed assessment of the costs by a costs officer,
unless any rule, practice direction or other enactment provides otherwise.
(Practice Direction 44—General rules about costs sets out the factors which will affect the court's decision under paragraph (1).)
(2) A party may recover the fixed costs specified in Part 45 in accordance with that Part.
Rule 44.1(1) defines fixed costs: 'fixed costs' means costs the amounts of which are fixed by these rules whether or not the court has a discretion to allow some other or no amount, and include—
   (i)   the amounts which are to be allowed in respect of legal representatives' charges in the circumstances set out in Section I of Part 45;
   (ii)   fixed recoverable costs calculated in accordance with rule 45.11;
   (iii) the additional costs allowed by rule 45.18;
   (iv)   fixed costs determined under rule 45.21;
   (v)   costs fixed by rules 45.37 and 45.38."

Part 36 is a self-contained code:

"36.1 (1) This Part contains a self-contained procedural code about offers to settle made pursuant to the procedure set out in this Part ('Part 36 offers').
(2) Section I of this Part contains general rules about Part 36 offers.
(3) Section II of this Part contains rules about offers to settle where the parties have followed the Pre-Action Protocol for Low Value Personal Injury Claims in Road Traffic Accidents ('the RTA Protocol') or the Pre-Action Protocol for Low Value Personal Injury (Employers' Liability and Public Liability) Claims ('the EL/PL') and have started proceedings under Part 8 in accordance with Practice Direction 8B."

It is not possible for a claimant whose offer has been accepted late, but before trial, to rely on the decision in *Broadhurst v Tan*[146] to obtain indemnity costs.

---

[145] *Broadhurst v Tan* [2016] EWCA Civ 94; [2016] 1 W.L.R. 1928; [2017] 2 All E.R. 60; [2016] C.P. Rep. 22; [2016] 2 Costs L.O. 155.
[146] *Broadhurst v Tan* [2016] EWCA Civ 94; [2016] 1 W.L.R. 1928; [2017] 2 All E.R. 60; [2016] C.P. Rep. 22; [2016] 2 Costs L.O. 155.

CPR r.36.20 makes it plain that it is the only rule which applies to the costs consequences of accepting a Part 36 offer in fixed costs cases. The interaction between the fixed costs regime and Pt 36 differs where the claimant is successful after trial as opposed to a Part 36 offer being accepted before trial. On the correct interpretation of the Rules, in a fixed costs case, CPR r.36.20 applies where an offer is accepted late and CPR r.36.13 does not apply at all.[147]

With regard to the second question, CPR r.45.1 states "(1) This Section sets out the amounts which, unless the court orders otherwise, are to be allowed in respect of legal representatives' charges." Under CPR r.45.4, however, where the claimant has issued a claim including fixed commencement costs under CPR r.45.2 and judgment in default is entered, the costs are fixed as per the table, unless the court orders otherwise in accordance with CPR r.45.1(2).   **7–109**

For the purpose of this answer it is assumed that the claim is above the Small Claim limit. If possible, the claimant should wait to issue until after the expiry of the relevant period and should not claim fixed costs on the claim form. Whether it is enough, on the request for judgment in default form, simply to enter "costs to be assessed pursuant to 36.17" or whether a Part 23 application is necessary, will depend on what the local court requires. Any application must be accompanied by a copy of the Part 36 offer.

It could be argued that the "specific" of CPR r.36.17 must override the "general" of CPR r.45.1 and that unless the court orders otherwise the claimant should get the CPR r.36.17 benefits. There is nothing to indicate that "judgment" in CPR r.36.17 only means judgment after trial and prima facie it appears to apply to the entry of any kind of judgment. There does not appear to be any reason why you could not ask the court to "order otherwise" in order to give effect to CPR r.36.17 or, in the alternative, why CPR r.36.17 should not trump CPR r.45.1 in any event.

Q23. A fast track trial has been vacated and is to be determined on written submissions with a paper determination. Would Counsel's preparation of written submissions here constitute a "fast track trial cost" pursuant to CPR r.45.37 or would these costs be recoverable in the usual way? I have a client who has a claim which is shortly to be allocated to the fast track with a value of £23,000. I am aware that fast track trial costs are capped, but I can find little to no reference to costs incurred which do not relate to the preparing for and attendance at Trial. Please would you confirm your view on the position.

None of the authors of this work have ever heard of a fast track trial being disposed of on written submissions. If it were to happen it would be an extremely rare and unusual event. The case would be likely to involve a dispute where the facts are agreed and the case is on submissions only about the law. It seems however, that this could only be done by agreement of the parties and with   **7–110**

---

[147] *Hislop v Perde: Kaur v Committee (for the time being) of Ramgarhia Board Leicester* [2018] EWCA Civ 1726; [2019] 1 W.L.R. 201; [2018] 4 Costs L.O. 515.

the court being prepared to undertake the trial in this way. It has to be said that there is no equivalent to CPR r.27.10 in the fast track and there has to be a query about the jurisdiction to undertake this. The simple answer would be: do not agree to this process and insist on the right to a hearing.

CPR r. 45.37(2) states "fast track trial costs" means the costs of a party's advocate for preparing for and appearing at the trial". In this scenario, counsel has to prepare but does not appear at a hearing. Section VI of Part 45 is silent as to what is to happen in these circumstances. By analogy, CPR r.36.3(d) states "a trial is 'in progress" from the time when it starts until the time when judgment is given or handed down." Although this is not in Part 45 the court is unlikely to adopt a different meaning for "trial", although in the given scenario, it is at least arguable that the meaning of "trial" should be extended to the preparation of written submissions and judgment, that being the unusual method chosen to deliver a concluded outcome to the claim.

Rule 45.39 gives the court power to award more or less than the amount of fast track trial costs. As to awarding more, CPR r.45.39(3) provides for an additional amount (limited to two-thirds of the amount payable for that claim) where a separate trial of an issue is considered necessary. It seems to be intended to provide for the "unusual". Whether the circumstances could be said to fall within this criteria would again depend on how liberal an interpretation was given to the word "trial".

It is arguable that the word "trial" used in Section VI is not being used in a formal sense but rather used as a descriptive of the mechanism of a concluded outcome, and the Court of Appeal could be said to have been so creative analogously.[148] But this particular point seems to be uncharted territory at the current time.

7–111   With regard to the second question, CPR r.45.37 deals with the scope of the rule:

"(1) This Section deals with the amount of costs which the court may award as the costs of an advocate for preparing for and appearing at the trial of a claim in the fast track (referred to in this rule as "fast track trial costs").
(2) For the purposes of this Section—
"advocate" means a person exercising a right of audience as a representative of, or on behalf of, a party;
"fast track trial costs" means the costs of a party's advocate for preparing for and appearing at the trial, but does not include—
(i)   any other disbursements; or
(ii)   any value added tax payable on the fees of a party's advocate; and
"trial" includes a hearing where the court decides an amount of money or the value of goods following a judgment under Part 12 (default judgment) or Part 14 (admissions) but does not include —

[148] *See West v Burton* [2021] EWCA Civ 1005, considered above at 7–19, as to the interpretation of the word "claim" in the RTA Protocol.

(i)   the hearing of an application for summary judgment under Part 24; or
(ii)   the court's approval of a settlement or other compromise under rule 21.10."

It will be seen that the rule deals only with the FastTrack Trial costs. It may well be that the litigation is being conducted under one of the other Sections in Part 45. If so that part will govern the amount which may be recovered.

Q24. After a fast track trial, can you explain in detail to what extent costs of the proceedings may be fixed and whether some costs may be subject to assessment. (Also whether the court can order otherwise than fixed costs where they would otherwise apply for example if a party asks for costs to be assessed because circumstances are unusual/exceptional.) (This is just for an ordinary claim ie not one to which fixed costs apply generally because of the provisions of CPR r.45)
CPR Pt 28 sets out the general provisions for cases allocated to the fast track.   7–112
CPR Pt 28.2(5) limits the court's power to award trial costs (being the costs of the person exercising a right of audience) in accordance with Section VI of CPR Pt 45.

Further Sections of CPR Pt 45 set out the fixed costs regimes applicable to the costs of legal representatives' charges (i.e. other than trial costs) in many cases allocated to the fast track. Where the fixed costs regimes of CPR Pt 45 do not apply, the default general rules about costs in CPR Pt 44 will apply in that the court has a discretion as to whether costs are payable by one party to another, the amount of such costs and when they are to be paid (CPR Pt 44.2). Where a fixed costs regime does apply, the court nevertheless retains a discretion in specified circumstances: see CPR rr.45.1(1); 45.13; 45.19(2B); 45.22(6); 45.24; 45.25(4); 45.29(J); and 45.39.

Q25. Is the position this for a fast track claim – not portal claim?:
After trial, regarding fast track trial costs (as defined in CPR 45) fixed costs only. No possibility of getting order otherwise for those costs. Regarding other costs (ie not falling within the definition of fast track trial costs) costs not fixed and subject to summary assessment
Pre-trial applications – no costs fixed even if the application was similar to a trial and there was advocacy. If costs order made, all costs subject to summary assessment.
For claims to which a fixed costs regime do not apply, then the trial costs are   7–113
indeed fixed in any event by Section VI in CPR Pt 45. As for the legal representatives' costs, as those costs are not caught by a fixed costs regime, they fall to the court's discretion pursuant to CPR r.44.2 and will be the subject of summary assessment, failing which detailed assessment.As for pre-trial applications, claims caught by Section IIIA do have fixed cost provisions as set out above. In other claims which are not so caught, the default provision of CPR

r.44.2 would apply and if costs were awarded, they would most likely be the subject of summary assessment.

Q26. In proceedings in the IPEC where costs are awarded against a party for unreasonable behaviour does the stage costs cap in Pt 45 apply?

7–114   A claimant who had behaved unreasonably in proceedings in the IPEC was ordered to pay the defendant's costs of the claimant's failed application for permission to re-amend its particulars of claim under CPR r.63.26(2). The court held that CPR r.45.31 imposed the overall cap on total costs. The Rule allowed for an exception to the overall cap where costs were awarded for unreasonable behaviour in the course of an application. The wording of CPR rr.45.31 and CPR r.45.32 were too clear to permit the conclusion that costs awarded against an unreasonable party were free of the stage caps on costs, accordingly the caps applied. The court would exercise its discretion on costs to lift a stage cap only in truly exceptional circumstances if the result was that the overall cap on total costs was left undisturbed. The defendants between them were entitled to their costs of the claimant's application up to a maximum of £3,000 permitted under the stage caps of Pt 45.[149]

Claimants, who were successful in a trademark infringement action in IPEC, argued that the defendants' conduct of the proceedings was such that the scale costs should be disapplied, and costs should be awarded on the indemnity basis.

The court found that the defendants' conduct was an abuse on both limbs of Lord Diplock's guidance in *Hunter v Chief Constable of the West Midlands Police*,[150] because: it was manifestly unfair to the claimant and it had, inevitably, brought the administration of justice into disrepute amongst right thinking people by seeking to obscure the truth from the court and, in so doing, preventing the court from fully and justly assessing damages from the infringements.

The costs cap was disapplied; the court stating:

"24 I did not make this decision lightly. I accept and understand that the costs cap is a key feature and benefit of litigation in IPEC, and that certainty about the application of the Scale Costs Scheme is extremely important to facilitate access to justice for litigants in lower value intellectual property claims. However, where there is an abuse of the processes of the court, as Lord Diplock guides us, the court has a duty to identify it. If the court does not protect the integrity of the court processes to ensure that it meets the overriding objective to deal with cases justly and at proportionate cost, who will?

---

[149] *Akhtar v Bhopal Productions (UK) Ltd* [2015] EWHC 154 (IPEC); [2015] F.S.R. 30 HHJ Hacon.
[150] *Hunter v Chief Constable of the West Midlands Police* [1982] A.C. 529.

25 Litigants in IPEC must understand that conduct which amounts to an abuse of the processes of the court will cause them to lose the benefit of the protection that the Scale Costs Scheme gives them."[151]

Q27. Does CPR r.46.5 apply to litigants in person on the small claims track? What costs can a litigant in person recover on the small claims track?

Costs on the small claims track are governed by Pt 27. Essentially the costs are   7–115
limited to the fixed costs attributable to issuing the claim plus certain exceptional items set out in CPR r.27.14(2):

"The court may not order a party to pay a sum to another party in respect of that other party's costs, fees and expenses, including those relating to an appeal, except:

(a) *the fixed costs attributable to issuing the claim which:*
    (i) *are payable under Part 45; or*
    (ii) *would be payable under Part 45 if that Part applied to the claim;*

(b) *in proceedings which included a claim for an injunction or an order for specific performance a sum not exceeding the amount specified in Practice Direction 27 for legal advice and assistance relating to that claim;*

(c) *any court fees paid by that other party;*

(d) *expenses which a party or witness has reasonably incurred in travelling to and from a hearing or in staying away from home for the purposes of attending a hearing;*

(e) *a sum not exceeding the amount specified in Practice Direction 27 for any loss of earnings or loss of leave by a party or witness due to attending a hearing or to staying away from home for the purpose of attending a hearing;*

(f) *a sum not exceeding the amount specified in Practice Direction 27 for an expert's fees;*

(g) *such further costs as the court may assess by the summary procedure and order to be paid by a party who has behaved unreasonably;*

(h) *the Stage 1 and, where relevant, the Stage 2 fixed costs in r.45.18 where:*
    (i) *the claim was within the scope of the Pre-Action Protocol for Low Value Personal Injury Claims in Road Traffic Accidents ('the RTA Protocol') or the Pre-action Protocol for Low Value Personal Injury (Employers' Liability and Public Liability) Claims ('the EL/PL Protocol');*
    (ii) *the claimant reasonably believed that the claim was valued at more than the Small Claims Track limit in accordance with paragraph 4.1(4) of the relevant Protocol; and*
    (iii) *the defendant admitted liability under the process set out in the relevant Protocol; but*

---

[151] *Link UP Mitaka Ltd trading as Thebigword v Language Empire Limited, Yasar Zaman;* [2018] EWHC 2728 (IPEC); [2018] 6 Costs L.R. 1279, HHJ Melissa Clarke.

> (iv) *the defendant did not pay those Stage 1 and, where relevant, Stage 2 fixed costs; and*
>
> (i) *in an appeal, the cost of any approved transcript reasonably incurred."*

CPR rr.46.11 and 46.13 make provision in relation to orders for costs made before a claim has been allocated to the small claims track. Once a claim is allocated to a particular track, those special rules shall apply to the period before, as well as after, allocation except where the court or a practice direction provides otherwise. Any costs orders made before a claim is allocated will not be affected by allocation.

Q28. Following the decision in *Chaplair v Kumari*, it is clear that a landlord can recover costs of proceedings under a leasehold indemnity in its favour irrespective of whether the claim would fall within the fixed costs regimes of the small and fast tracks. What is the position in relation to residential possession claims under CPR Pt 55, to which the fixed costs regime under CPR Pt 45 applies?

7–116 The position in *Chaplair v Kumari* is set out in the answer to Q17.[152]
So far as possession claims under Pt 55 are concerned the *White Book 2021* states (at 55.7.8)[153]:

> *"Fixed costs apply to certain types of possession claims—unless the court orders otherwise. CPR r.45.1 provides that fixed costs apply where—*
> *The defendant gives up possession and pays the amount claimed (if any) and the fixed commencement costs;*
> *One of the grounds for possession is arrears of rent, the court gave a fixed date for hearing, a possession order is made (whether suspended or not) and the defendant has either failed to deliver a defence or the defence is limited to specifying proposals for payment of arrears; and*
> *The claim is brought under the accelerated procedure (Pt 55 Section 2) against an assured shorthold tenant, a possession order is made and the defendant has neither delivered a defence nor otherwise denied liability.*
> *The claim is a demotion claim or a demotion claim is made in the same claim form in which a possession claim is made and the demotion claim is successful."*

It is certainly arguable that, provided the "indemnity" costs provision in the Landlord and Tenant agreement is properly drafted, CPR r.44.5 should apply. It might in fact be easier to persuade the court to "order otherwise" under CPR r.44.5(2) rather than get into a discussion about whether the contractual terms should take precedence.

---

[152] *Chaplair Ltd v Kumari* [2015] EWCA Civ 798; [2015] C.P. Rep. 46.
[153] Note CPR r.55.A1 – Coronavirus—temporary provision.

Q29. Does the court fee that was paid by the claimant (when commencing proceedings) count towards the normal £10,000 small claims track claim limit?
No. The court fee is an item of cost whereas the limit is a reference to the claim for damages.

7–117

Q30. Is it correct that the London weighting (12.5%) only applies where a claim is subject to fixed costs? in a claim that is not subject to fixed costs (pre 2013 personal injury), I understand it would not apply but a success fee would apply. Is that right?
The fixed costs regime recognises an uplift for London and is commonly referred to as "London weighting". The justification for it is largely based on the fact that the cost of living and the cost of business overheads are generally speaking more expensive in London than elsewhere in the country. This sort of "weighting" has been reflected in the guideline hourly rates which inform a judge when conducting a summary assessment. Success fees are entirely unrelated.

7–118

Q31. I am dealing with a small claims where the claim is for £500.00 but I am a little confused regarding fixed costs and court fee and what can be claimed as fixed costs. Part 45 Fixed costs on rule 45.1 states where the value of the claim exceeds £25 but does not exceed £500 fixed cost is £50 where the claim form is served by the court or by any method other than personal service by the claim or £60 where the claim form is served personally by the claimant and there is only one defendant. Rule 45.3 states a defendant is only liable for fixed commencement costs where the only claim is for a specified sum of money (£500) (b) the defendant pays the money claimed within 14 days after being served with the particulars of claim, together with the fixed commencement costs stated in the claim form, the defendant is not liable for any further costs unless the court orders otherwise. It is my understanding that both the fixed costs of £50 and the court fee of £50 can be claimed if the defendant is liable. Is that correct?
Yes. CPR r.45.1(4) provides that "Any appropriate court fee will be allowed in addition to the costs set out in this Section."

7–119

Q32. Are there likely to be more cases on escaping fixed costs by virtue of exceptional circumstances?
From time to time, yes. Exceptionality will be, more often than not, case-specific, but some general illustrations can be found in the case of *Lloyd v 2 Sisters Poultry Ltd (Costs)* [2019] EW Misc 18.

7–120

Q33. A client has brought a professional negligence counterclaim and subsequently lost. The other side is now claiming they have bettered a Part 36 offer but marginally so. The firm which brought the original

proceedings and defended the counterclaim are basing their costs at their usual hourly rate to clients. Are there any provisions or authority stating there must be a reduced hourly rate when defending themselves i.e. only the cost to the firm not including profit?

7–121   CPR r.36.17(2) provides that "more advantageous" means better in money terms by any amount, however small. The so called "near miss" approach has gone. The successful claimant is entitled to its costs in the normal way. The point being raised by the question appears to be: can solicitors acting on their own behalf charge full costs? Where an action is brought against a solicitor who defends it in person and obtains judgment, he is entitled, upon assessment, to the same costs as if he had employed a solicitor, except in respect of items which the fact of his acting directly renders unnecessary.[154] The Court of Appeal has considered whether that principle has survived the introduction of the CPR. Chadwick LJ stated:

> "20 . . . The position of a practising solicitor who chooses to represent himself in his firm name, or (where in partnership) to be represented by his firm, remains unaltered by the provisions of CPR r.48.6 [now r.46.5]. His costs are allowed (or not as the case may be) by virtue of, and in accordance with the principle established in the London Scottish Benefit Society case.
>
> . . .
>
> 24 . . . A partner who is represented in legal proceedings by his firm incurs no liability to the firm; but he suffers loss for which under the indemnity principle he ought to be compensated, because the firm of which he is a member expends time and resources which would otherwise be devoted to other clients. The only sensible way in which effect can be given to the indemnity principle is by allowing those costs. And, as I have sought to explain, that is the solution which for over 100 years the courts have adopted as a rule of practice."[155]

See also *Robinson v EMW Law* at **Q42** below and further at **Q47** below.

D. Fast Track Trial Costs

Q34. Is the indemnity basis applicable in cases where there is an abuse of process or where a party has been guilty of unreasonable conduct? When can you get indemnity costs rather than fixed costs?

7–122   Section 51 of the Senior Courts Act 1981 provides quite simply that: "subject to the provisions of this and any other enactment and to Rules of Court" the costs of and incidental to all proceedings in the High Court shall be in the discretion of the court. When considering whether to make an order for costs on the indemnity basis the trial judge has a wide discretion but it is critical that

---

[154] *London Scottish Benefit Society v Chorley* [1884] 12 Q.B.D. 452 CA.
[155] *Malkinson v Trim* [2002] EWCA Civ 1273; [2003] 1 W.L.R. 463; [2003] 2 All E.R. 356; [2003] C.P. Rep. 11; [2003] C.P.L.R. 99; [2002] 3 Costs L.R. 515.

there be some conduct or circumstance that takes a case out of the norm.[156] Such factors include the high-risk situation where a claim is speculative, weak, opportunistic or thin, and where a claimant commenced and pursued large-scale and expensive litigation in circumstances calculated to exert unfair and commercial pressure on a defendant to renegotiate what had become a commercially unattractive contract. The fact that one party lost resoundingly, does not automatically mean that the other should be awarded costs on the indemnity basis. On the facts, an order for costs on the indemnity basis was not made although it had not been unreasonable for the successful party to seek such an order.[157] The Companies Court, in applying the decision in *Excelsior Commercial and Industrial Holdings Ltd*[158] ordered the claimant to pay the costs of an unfair prejudice petition on the indemnity basis where the petition had been an abuse of process and should never have been brought, and where the claimant had no basis for defending the company's claim for breach of duty as a director and employee. The costs of both actions had been increased significantly by virtue of the claimant's highly aggressive tactics in the conduct of the litigation. Overall, the case constituted a departure from the norm, which made it just to order costs to be paid on the indemnity basis.[159]

7–123 A different court ordered an unsuccessful claimant to pay costs on the indemnity basis and to pay interest on the costs from one year before the commencement date of the trial because of the claimants' unreasonable conduct in that the case had changed constantly throughout the course of the proceedings and the claimant had produced wholly unacceptable volumes of documentation.[160]

7–124 In another example, where claimants had sued their former financial advisor, the defendant, before serving its defence, applied for summary judgment. Four months later the application was withdrawn. The court had to decide the question of costs. There was nothing sufficiently unusual about the case to justify departing from the general rule that the unsuccessful party should be ordered to pay the successful party's costs. The court went on to make an order on the indemnity basis because the defendant was not justified in seeking summary judgment before filing the defence. The application constituted conduct which was sufficiently "out of the norm" within the meaning in *Excelsior* and other authorities.[161]

7–125 Where a party applied without notice for a worldwide freezing injunction but had failed to give full and frank disclosure of material factors, this could have resulted in the injunction not being granted even if it would otherwise have been just and convenient to do so. On the facts of the particular case an

---

[156] *Excelsior Commercial & Industrial Holdings Ltd v Salisbury Hammer Aspden & Johnson* [2002] EWCA Civ 879; [2002] C.P. Rep. 67.

[157] *Obrascon Huarte Lain SA v Government of Gibraltar* [2014] EWHC 1028 (TCC); [2014] B.L.R. 484 Akenhead J.

[158] *Excelsior Commercial & Industrial Holdings Ltd v Salisbury Hammer Aspden & Johnson* [2002] EWCA Civ 879; [2002] C.P. Rep. 67.

[159] *Re Flex Associates Ltd* unreported 15 February 2010 (Ch.D.) David Donaldson QC.

[160] *ABCI (formerly Arab Business Consortium International Finance & Investment Co) v Banque Franco-Tunisienne (Costs)* [2002] EWHC 567 (Comm) HH Judge Chambers QC.

[161] *The Libyan Investment Authority v Goldman Sachs International* [2014] EWHC 3364 (Ch) Rose J.

injunction was granted but the applicant was penalised by an order for costs on the indemnity basis.[162]

7–126   In proceedings to recover a spread betting debt, the defendant had dishonestly alleged that he had had no previous experience of spread betting and had sought to hide his dishonesty by failing to give proper disclosure of documents. He had rejected a Part 36 offer. A bankruptcy order was made against him. The advancement of an untruth, compounded by a failure to give disclosure, amounted to unreasonable behaviour by the defendant which would have added to the claimant's costs. An order for costs on the indemnity basis was justified. The Part 36 offer had represented a real and substantial benefit that the defendant should have opted to take. In those circumstances it was appropriate to summarily assess costs with 3% interest, running from 21 days from the date of the Part 36 offer.[163]

7–127   Liquidators who had litigated the same issues unsuccessfully in other jurisdictions discontinued without explanation four days into a six-week trial. Their conduct was out of the norm, and they were ordered to pay costs on the indemnity basis.[164]

7–128   A bank succeeded against the first defendant in a claim over guarantees given to the bank, but failed against the second defendant, his wife. The defendants had counterclaimed alleging that the bank's enforcement process was part of a fraudulent scheme to acquire the companies' assets at an undervalue. That counterclaim was dismissed. Given the findings as to the first defendant's dishonesty, the bank was entitled to costs on the indemnity basis. It was out of the norm for the first defendant to rely on an implausible defence throughout the proceedings, particularly where it involved allegations of such dishonesty. He had also sought publicity for his case. The defendants failed entirely in relation to their counterclaim and the bank was entitled to its costs, subject to any deduction by reference to its conduct in connection with certain issues or issues on which it failed.

One issue did occupy a considerable amount of time, and the court considered that the claimants had no real basis to contest it, and should not have done so. The dispute tended to confuse and obscure the real issues; and it might even have been that this was part of the intention of the defendants by counterclaim. The court also commented adversely about the "chorus of false evidence", and "a thoroughly disturbing tendency on the part of the claimants and their associates to put forward sworn evidence which they consider advances their case and a propensity to require their subordinates to subscribe to and support the version of events thus put forward regardless of its truth".

The bank's actions did not affect the court's decision, but a material discount was warranted. The bank was entitled to 75% of their costs in the counterclaim assessed on the standard basis.[165]

---

[162] *U&M Mining Zambia Ltd v Konkola Copper Mines Plc* [2014] EWHC 3250 (Comm) Teare J.
[163] *CMC Spreadbet Plc v Khan* [2017] EWHC 2008 (Ch) Andrew Baker J.
[164] *Hosking v Apax Partners LLP* [2018] EWHC 2732 (Ch); [2019] 1 W.L.R. 3347; [2018] 5 Costs L.R. 1125, Hildyard J.
[165] *Bank St Petersburg PJSC v Arkhangelsky* [2018] EWHC 2817 (Ch); [2018] 6 Costs L.R. 1303 Hildyard J.

Q35. What is the position of litigation funders in relation to orders for costs, particularly orders for costs on the indemnity basis?
Where claimants funded by third party litigation funders lost the claim,   **7–129**
the litigation funders were ordered to pay the costs of the defendant on the
indemnity basis up to the limit of their investment. Christopher Clarke LJ
stated:

> *"Justice requires that when the case fails so comprehensively, not merely on the
> facts but because it was wholly bad in law, the funder should, subject to the Arkin
> cap, bear the costs order to be paid by the person whom or which he has unsuc-
> cessfully supported, assessed on the scale which the Court thinks it just for that
> person to pay in the light of all the circumstances, including but not limited to
> that person's behaviour and that of those whom that person engaged."*

The judge stated that the funder should, absent special circumstances, follow
the fortunes of those from whom he himself hoped to derive a small fortune.
To do otherwise would be unfair to the defendants and their personnel. To
make an order for indemnity costs would not be to penalise but to recom-
pense. Christopher Clarke LJ further stated:

> *"If it serves to cause funders and their advisors to take rigorous steps short
> of champerty, i.e. behaviour likely to interfere with the due administration of
> justice—particularly in the form of rigorous analysis of law, facts and witnesses,
> consideration of proportionality and review at appropriate intervals—to reduce
> the occurrence of the sort of circumstances that cause me to order indemnity costs
> in this case, that is an advantage and in the public interest."*[166]

The funders appealed, some arguing that they should not have been ordered
to pay costs on the indemnity basis, others arguing that they should not have
been ordered to pay costs at all. The Court of Appeal held that it was appropriate that the commercial funders, who had funded a hopeless action, should
pay the successful defendants' costs on the indemnity basis even though they
themselves were not guilty of any discreditable conduct or conduct which
could be criticised. An argument arose as to whether additional security
ordered to be paid should count towards the Arkin cap. The court specifically
declined to revisit the Arkin cap or to comment on it (at [28]) but dealt with
the argument in this way:

> *"39. In order to resolve these arguments it is simply necessary to return to first
> principles. As emphasised in Dymocks, the rationale for imposing a costs liability
> upon a non-party funder is that he has funded proceedings substantially for his
> own financial benefit and has thereby become 'a real party' to the litigation. It is
> ordinarily just that he should be liable for costs if the claim fails. The pragmatic
> solution reached in Arkin, and accepted by the funding community, is that the*

---

[166] *Excalibur Ventures LLC v Texas Keystone Inc (Defendants and Costs Claimants) and Psari Holdings Ltd (Costs Defendants)* [2014] EWHC 3436 (Comm); [2014] 6 Costs L.O. 975 Christopher Clarke LJ.

funder who finances part of a claimant's costs of litigation should be potentially liable for the costs of the opponent party to the extent of the funding provided, i.e. invest one in the pursuit of the common enterprise and bear the risk of liability in that same amount in the event of failure, in which event by definition the initial investment is already lost. I see no basis upon which a funder who advances money to enable security for costs to be provided by a litigant should be treated any differently from a funder who advances money to enable that litigant to meet the fees of its own lawyers or expert witnesses. Both the provision of security for costs, if ordered by the court, and the payment of the litigant's own lawyers and experts, are costs of pursuing the litigation which, if not met, will result in the litigation being unable to proceed. I do not understand why contribution to different categories of the costs of pursuing the litigation should attract different regimes. All the sums advanced are used in pursuit of the common enterprise and for the benefit of all of the funders."[167]

7–130   A claimant fought and lost, and was ordered to pay £3.9million towards the defendant's costs. The claimant had been funded by a commercial funder, which argued that its total liability should be limited to the overall maximum that it had provided to the claimant, namely £1.2million. The court held that the decision in *Arkin v Borchard Lines Ltd (Costs Order)*[168] was not to be taken as having intended to lay down a rule or guideline to be applied mechanistically in every case involving commercial funders. The court held on the facts that it would not be just to apply the *Arkin* cap in the funder's favour. Among other factors, the application of the *Arkin* cap would insulate the funder from the Indemnity Costs Order which arose from the way in which the claim was pursued. This was a factor which had not been present or considered in *Arkin*. The funder had been closely focused on its own self-interest in funding the litigation with no correlation between the amount of its investment and the claimant's exposure to costs. The claimant's access to justice had been less important to the funder than its return on its commercial investment. The funder was ordered to pay costs incurred after the date of the Funding Agreement.[169]

7–131   Following this decision the Court of Appeal addressed the Arkin question. In insolvency proceedings, a creditor obtained Judgment against the owner of a company for the amount due under a personal guarantee. Proceedings were commenced to recover the costs of enforcing the guarantee and the Judgment. The defendant counter-claimed, alleging that the creditor had interfered in the administration and was vicariously liable for the Administrators' failings. She entered into a funding arrangement with a third party funder in which they agreed to advance £2.5million, but in return would recover a "Funder's Profit Share" in addition to the repayment of the £2.5million if the litigation

---

[167] *Excalibur Ventures LLC v Texas Keystone Inc* [2016] EWCA Civ 1144; [2017] 1 W.L.R. 2221; [2017] C.P. Rep. 13; [2016] 6 Costs L.O. 999.
[168] *Arkin v Borchard Lines Ltd (Costs Order)* [2005] EWCA Civ 655; [2005] 4 Costs L.R. 643.
[169] *Davey v Money* [2019] EWHC 997 (Ch); [2019] 1 W.L.R. 6108;[2019] Costs L.R. 399, Snowden J.

was successful. The defendant was obliged by the funding arrangement to obtain ATE insurance, but failed to do so. The funder therefore revised the agreement by reducing its funding to £1.25 million, expecting to be protected by the "Arkin cap". Judgment was entered in favour of the creditor and administrator, and the funder was joined as a party for the purposes of costs and ordered to pay their costs on the indemnity basis. The court refused to apply the Arkin cap. The Court of Appeal observed that Arkin had been decided when third party funding was still nascent and Conditional Fee Agreements and ATE insurance were relatively new at the time of that case. These were all now much more established so that a funder should be able to protect his position by ensuring that it or the claimant had ATE cover. This did not mean that the Arkin approach was redundant, but it did not represent a binding rule and judges did not necessarily have to adopt it when determining the extent of a commercial funder's liability for costs. Judges retained a discretion and might consider it appropriate to take matters other than the extent of the funding into account, including considering the funder's potential return. The more a funder stood to gain, the closer it might be thought to be the "real party" ordinarily ordered to pay the successful party's costs. In the case under appeal, the funder stood to receive in return a profit amounting to more than five times what it had spent before the defendant had any prospect of keeping anything for herself. The judge was entitled to have regard to the extent that the Arkin cap would leave the creditors and administrators out of pocket. It was inevitable that they would incur costs greatly in excess of the funding provided by the funder, but there was no protection of ATE cover. The funder's waiver of the requirement for the defendant to obtain ATE insurance very much increased the other side's costs exposure. The appeal was dismissed.[170]

Q36. Does an order for indemnity costs mean that a party can escape penalty for failing to update a costs budget?/Does an order for indemnity costs mean that parties may recover costs outside budgets without having to show good reason?

Have the courts shown more or less willingness to make indemnity costs orders over the last few years or are there no trends; it just all depends on the case?

The apparent confusion caused by the decision in *Elvanite Full Circle Ltd v Amec Earth & Environmental (UK) Ltd*[171] has been clarified by the Court of Appeal in *Lejonvarn v Burgess*.[172] The topic is discussed at some length at para.7–43, and in Chapter 4 at 4–20 and **Q93 and Q94**.   7–132

Q37. What is the position if the losing party has won on certain issues and lost on others?

---

[170] *Chapelgate Credit Opportunity Master Fund Ltd v James Money (1) Jim Stewart-Koster (Joint Administrators of Angel House Developments Limited) (2) Dunbar Assets Plc (3)* [2020] EWCA Civ 246.
[171] [2013] EWHC 1643 (TCC); [2013] 4 All E.R. 765; [2013] 4 Costs L.R. 612; Coulson J.
[172] [2020] EWCA Civ 114.

7–133   CPR r. 44.2 states:

> *"(2) If the court decides to make an order about costs—*
> (a)   *the general rule is that the unsuccessful party will be ordered to pay the costs of the successful party; but (b) the court may make a different order."*[173]

CPR r.44.2(6) sets out examples of the orders which the court may make and which includes "(f) costs relating only to a distinct part of the proceedings". Such orders are thankfully rare as the process of detailed assessment for a cost judge facing such an order becomes extremely complex.

Claimants who had been unsuccessful at trial were liable to pay all the costs of the successful defendant, to be assessed on the standard basis, where the evidence showed that the no-loss defence and the limitation defence run by the defendant were not discrete issues and where they had made no identifiable difference to the costs incurred by either party.[174]

Q38. Can you get indemnity costs after late acceptance of Part 36 offer?
7–134   This topic is dealt with in **Ch.5 para.5–32** and following.

Q39. I note that indemnity costs are recoverable in the event the claimant makes a valid Part 36 offer, goes to trial and then matches or does better than its Part 36 offer at trial however if the claimant was making a Part 36 offer to two parties (1) an individual and (2) a company, please could you advise as to whether the claimant will be able to claim indemnity costs in full from each party?
7–135   If the claimant obtains a judgment that is "at least as advantageous" than the claimant's CPR Pt 36 offer made to two parties, then the claimant will be entitled, amongst other things, to costs on the indemnity basis from the date on which the relevant period expired. The order for costs will determine whether the costs are to be recovered against one or both parties, and whether that is to be on a joint or several basis. There is no prospect of double-recovery. The claimant's costs can only be recovered once irrespective of how many parties may be responsible.

E. Litigants in Person

Q40. The defendant was represented by solicitors but then served a notice of change stating that the defendant shall be acting in person. Must the defendant provide an alternative address for service in the UK? Is

---

[173] See also *Various Claimants v WM Morrison Supermarkets Plc*[2018] EWHC 1123 (QB); [2018] 3 Costs L.R. 531, Langstaff J. The defendant was ordered to pay the claimants 40% of their costs where the claimants had lost on their case of direct liability, but succeeded on vicarious liability.
[174] *Kellie v Wheatley & Lloyd Architects Ltd* [2014] EWHC 2886 (TCC); [2014] B.L.R. 644; [2014] 5 Costs L.R. 854 HHJ Keyser QC.

a defendant litigant in person entitled to write direct to the claimant, rather than to the claimant's solicitor, to try to agree a settlement? The situation in the first question is governed by CPR r.42.2, which, so far as relevant, provides:

7–136

> *"(1)   This rule applies where—*
> ...
> > *(c)   a party, after having conducted the claim by a solicitor, intends to act in person.*
> *(2)   Where this rule applies, the party . . . must—*
> > *(a)   file notice of the change; and*
> > *(b)   serve notice of the change on every other party and, where paragraph (1). . .*
> > *(c)   applies, on the former solicitor.*
> *(3)   The notice must state the party's new address for service.*
> *(4)   The notice filed at court must state that notice has been served as required by paragraph (2)(b). . ."*

With regard to the second question, it may be difficult to prevent a litigant in person from communicating direct with the claimant. The LiP may not be aware that the correct method is to communicate with the claimant's solicitors. Also the LiP may think that arranging a settlement direct may save time and money. One way of dealing with such a situation is to advise the claimant to pass any communication to the solicitors to deal with and not to attempt to respond to the approach. It is not unknown for liability insurers to approach claimants direct (before they have instructed solicitors) in order to try and settle at a level which the insurer thinks is appropriate.

7–137

Q41. i. Is it correct that LiPs need not prepare costs budgets even though they can potentially recover some costs from their opponents?
ii. Where a litigant in person has brought a claim against a legally represented defendant and, after the CCMC, the litigant in person decides to engage legal representation, does the former litigant in person now need to serve a costs budget?
iii. Where a litigant in person only instructs solicitors after the CCMC, what happens if those solicitors and their client choose not to file a costs budget? Will the client be entitled to an assessment of costs if successful at trial?
As to the first question, the answer is yes. CPR r.3.13 states:

7–138

> *"(1)   Unless the court otherwise orders, all parties except litigants in person must file and exchange budgets—*
> > *(a)   where the stated value of the claim on the claim form is less than £50,000, with their directions questionnaires; or*
> > *(b)   in any other case, not later than 21 days before the first case management conference.*

> (2)   In the event that a party files and exchanges a budget under paragraph (1),
> all other parties, not being litigants in person, must file an agreed budget
> discussion report no later than 7 days before the first case management
> conference."

The fact that the LiP has not prepared a costs budget does not affect the litigant's entitlement to costs in an appropriate case.

The *Chancery Guide* states that the court may direct a LiP to serve a budget in an appropriate case (para.17.13).

Legally represented parties involved in proceedings with a LiP still have to file a costs budget of their costs and preferably try to agree it with the LiP. Rule 3.13 states "(6) Even though a litigant in person is not required to prepare a budget, each other party (other than a litigant in person) must provide the litigant in person with a copy of that party's budget."

7–139   With regard to the second question, CPR r.3.13 also states:

> "(3) The court—
> (a) may, on its own initiative or on application, order the parties to file and
> exchange costs budgets in a case where the parties are not otherwise required
> by this Section to do so;
> (b) shall (other than in an exceptional case) make an order to file and exchange
> costs budgets if all parties consent to an application for such an order."

As the solicitors have been instructed after the CCMC, the time for filing a budget has passed. It would be sensible for the new solicitors to try to agree with their opponents whether or not a budget is necessary. Failing that it would be sensible to apply to the court for directions.

7–140   With regard to the third question, if the solicitor and client choose not to file a costs budget, the client will not ordinarily be penalised for that choice in circumstances where the first CCMC has passed and at the material time the client was a litigant in person. However, when the solicitor is instructed, the other party might apply for the court to budget costs or the court could order it of its own volition.Further and more detailed consideration of these issues is set out in **Ch.4, Q2.**

Q42. If a solicitors' firm is representing itself in litigation, would it need to file a cost budget on the basis that it is deemed to be a litigant in person?

7–141   Not by default, but the court may order it to do so.

Q43. Can a LiP include printing and stationary costs on the statement of costs on the fast track? In a fast track trial, what are the costs that a successful litigant in person could recover?

7–142   CPR r.46.5(4) provides:

> "The amount of costs to be allowed to the litigant in person for any item of work
> claimed will be—

(a) where the litigant can prove financial loss, the amount that the litigant can prove to have been lost for time reasonably spent on doing the work; or

(b) where the litigant cannot prove financial loss, an amount for the time reasonably spent on doing the work at the rate set out in Practice Direction 46."

CPR r.46.5 (2) states:

"The costs allowed under this rule will not exceed, except in the case of a disbursement, two-thirds of the amount which would have been allowed if the litigant in person had been represented by a legal representative."

Subject to those constraints a LiP may include a claim for printing and stationary costs. Not being solicitors they will not have an hourly rate which takes into account such overheads.

Q44. Is there a way of protecting a defendant's position in terms of legal costs on a claim brought by an individual claimant who appears to have no prospect of success and who is a LiP?
The obvious solution, if it can be achieved,[175] is an application for security: 7–143

"25.12
(1) A defendant to any claim may apply under this section of this Part for security for his costs of the proceedings.
(Part 3 provides for the court to order payment of sums into court in other circumstances. Rule 20.3 provides for this section of this part to apply to Part 20 claims).
(2) An application for security for costs must be supported by written evidence.
(3) Where the court makes an order for security for costs, it will—
(a) determine the amount of security; and
(b) direct—
(i) the manner in which; and
(ii) the time within which the security must be given."

The court will make an order for security if it is satisfied, having regard to all the circumstances of the case, that it is just to do so, one or more of the conditions set out below applies or an enactment permits the court to require security for costs. The conditions to be fulfilled before the court will make an order for security are:

"(a) the claimant is—
(i) resident out of the jurisdiction; but
(ii) not resident in a State bound by the 2005 Hague Convention, as defined in section 1(3) of the Civil Jurisdiction and Judgments Act 1982;

. . .

---

[175] Difficult with individual claimants as there is no ground for obtaining security from an impecunious individual as opposed to an impecunious company.

(f)   the claimant is acting as a nominal claimant (other than as a representative claimant under Part 19) and there is reason to believe that he will be
unable to pay the defendant's costs if ordered to do so."

Note that this changed as from 1 January 2021 following Brexit.

The Civil Procedure Rules 1998 (Amendment) (EU Exit) Regulations 2019[176]
(CPR Regulations) were made on 7 March 2019 and made changes to the CPR at
the end of the transition period (31 December 2020).[177] Paragraph 8 of the CPR
Regulations amend CPR r.25.13 (conditions to be satisfied for security for costs).

Under CPR r.25.13(2)(a)(ii) security for costs is, at the time of writing,
available where the claimant is resident outside the jurisdiction, but is not
resident in a state which is a contracting party to the Brussels Convention,
a state bound by the 2007 Lugano Convention, a state bound by the Hague
Convention, or a Regulation State (which is defined in s.1(3) of the Civil
Jurisdiction and Judgments Act 1982 as an EU member state).

This is amended to delete the requirement that the claimant is not resident in a state which is a contracting party to the Brussels Convention, a
state bound by the 2007 Lugano Convention or a Regulation State because
on 31 December 2020 the domestic legislation implementing the Brussels
Convention and the 2007 Lugano Convention will be amended and the
Recast Brussels Regulation will cease to apply.

The requirement that the claimant is not resident in a state bound by the
Hague Convention, however, will remain, so security for costs will continue
to be unavailable against claimants in EU member states in relation to claims
to which the Hague Convention applies (that is, claims in respect of which
the English court has jurisdiction pursuant to an exclusive choice of court
agreements within the scope of the Hague Convention).[178] Transitional and
saving provisions (para.20 of the CPR Regulations) provide that in respect of
claims issued before 31 December 2020, CPR r.25.13 will continue to apply on
and after that date as if the amendments had not been made.

**Q45. In claim for £11,500 in total and allocated to the fast track, a defend-
ant LiP incurred no costs other than his time until the claimants had
incurred over £25,000 aggressively litigating their claim. Would it then
be considered proportionate for the LiP, who believes he has a strong
defence, to seek counsel to verify his defence and to incur costs (not trial
costs) of £8,000 to maximise his chances of succeeding in his defence?**

7–144   CPR r.46.5 is so worded that it is possible for a LiP to recover payment for
legal advice as well as payment for time spent in conducting the litigation.
Just because the claimant has spent so much does not make the defendant's
costs proportionate. For example, if the claimant wins it does not mean it will

---

[176] SI 2019/521.
[177] See Legal update, Civil Procedure Rules 1998 (Amendment) (EU Exit) Regulations 2019: Brexit SI.
[178] See Practice note, Hague Convention on Choice of Court Agreements.

recover the sum it has spent. There is really insufficient detail about the case to be more specific.

Q46. What is the position of a solicitor or barrister acting on his or her own behalf?
We are acting for the claimant in court proceedings which have been listed in the multi-track. The defendant is a solicitors' firm. My understanding is that they are acting as a LiP as no notice of acting has been filed. Does that sound right and, if they are considered to be acting in person, what costs, if any, are they entitled to claim?
If the claimant is a firm of solicitors and they are representing themselves, can they claim costs on the basis of their normal charging rates as solicitors, even though they are, essentially, a litigant in person?
It is a question of fact whether a solicitor in sole practice is acting for himself/ **7–145** herself as a true LiP or, is, instead, represented by himself/herself in the firm name. It was held to be relevant that the underlying litigation concerned a claim for professional fees with allegations of negligence and breach of duty since those were matters arising out of the solicitor's practice as a solicitor and not out of the course of his private life.[179]

In proceedings where the claimant was a solicitor who had, at the same **7–146** time, practised as a costs draftsman until July 1999, the court had to decide whether or not she was a LiP before 26 April 1999 and also whether she was a LiP after that date under the CPR. The question depended upon the criteria used to define the term "practising solicitor". Prior to 26 April 1999, the court found that the claimant was undoubtedly a practising solicitor from a regulatory point of view under the Solicitors Act and the Rules of Practice, but she was not a practising solicitor who was able to charge for her time for the purposes of RSC Ord.62 r.18(6) and the rule in *London Scottish Benefits Society v Chorley*.[180] The court therefore held that she was only entitled to recover costs for that period as a LiP. With regard to the period after 26 April 1999, it was accepted by the claimant that if a court found that she was not a practising solicitor for the purposes of RSC Ord.62 CPR r.18 then she was unable to take advantage of CPR PD 46 para.3.2. The court held that this provision was designed to do no more than preserve the rule in *London Scottish Benefits Society*. The criteria remained the same.[181]

A solicitor, who left one firm and joined another as a consultant, settled **7–147** litigation with his former firm on favourable terms. The firm he had joined as a consultant had acted on his behalf throughout the litigation. On detailed assessment, the costs judge found that since the firm had not sent a client care letter and charged the work done by the solicitor himself at its usual rate, disallowed those costs. On appeal, the court found that the engagement to

---

[179] *Hatton v Kendrick* [2002] EWCA Civ 1783; [2003] C.P. Rep. 32.
[180] *London Scottish Benefits Society v Chorley* [1884] 13 Q.B.D. 872.
[181] *Joseph v Boyd & Hutchinson* [2003] EWHC 413 (Ch); [2003] 3 Costs L.R. 358 Patten J.

act did not have to be by way of a written retainer. The new firm had been on the record from the outset. It did not matter that the client care letter had not been sent until the proceedings were well underway, nor that it was not retrospective. There was no agreement that the solicitor would not be liable for the firm's costs in any circumstances. The presumption in *R. v Miller (Raymond Karl)*[182] came into play. The solicitor could recover his costs for the work he did under the principle in *London Scottish Benefit Society v Chorley*,[183] which applied equally to a practising solicitor who instructed another firm to act for him, but who relieved that firm of part of the work required by doing it himself. The solicitor was making a claim for expenditure in terms of measurable skill and labour, and was entitled to recover on the basis that his carrying out the work himself meant that he did not have to pay another solicitor to do it. The amount payable was to be assessed on the basis of a reasonable rate for the services which he carried out.[184]

7–148   In *JH v CH & SAP (Costs: the Chorley principle, Litigants in person)*[185], however, the evidence was that the solicitor never instructed her firm to act for her and had never been personally liable for any of their fees. The firm agreed. They did not suggest that they were acting for the solicitor but asserted, that she was acting for the applicant in her capacity as an employee of the firm. The judge did not accept that proposition.

> "24   In all the reported cases the solicitor litigant was acting through his own practice or firm or had instructed a third-party firm and "relieved the firm of some of the work by doing it himself". The essential point to be drawn from them is that the solicitor party was not acting in person, was not a true litigant in person. There is no case that I have been taken to which permits a true litigant in person to recover costs at a professional rate without being able to establish personal loss."

7–149   Where a barrister had successfully defended herself in disciplinary proceedings was initially awarded £120 per hour for the work which she had done on her case, the Bar Standards Board appealed arguing that she should receive only the £18 an hour (then) prescribed for a LiP. That argument was rejected by the Administrative Court which ruled that the hourly rate should be cut to £60 per hour taking into account the fact that the barrister was not practising at the time. On appeal to the Court of Appeal, the court held that it had not been open to the Administrative Court to fix the rate of £60 even though it had been reached by agreement between the parties. Under s.31(5) of the Senior Courts Act 1981, a court upholding a judicial review can only substitute its own decision if "without the error there would have been only one

---

[182] *R. v Miller (Raymond Karl)* (1983) 1 W.L.R. 1056.
[183] *London Scottish Benefit Society v Chorley* (1884) 13 Q.B.D. 872.
[184] *Robinson v EMW Law LLP* [2018] EWHC 1757 (Ch); [2018] 4 Costs L.O. 477 Roth J.
[185] [2020] EWCOP 63. In *Poole v Scott-Moncrieff and Associates LLP* (17 November 2020) (SCCO), Master Rowley found that where practising solicitors represent themselves, there was "no distinction in principle between a solicitor in practice on their own account, or in partnership, or as here acting on their own account as a consultant".

decision which the court or tribunal could have reached". The court ordered the barrister to pay 60% of the BSB's judicial review costs.[186]

Q47. Upon acceptance of a defendant's pre-action Part 36 offer, can a LiP recover costs that he has incurred seeking advice from solicitors who are not on record as acting? To what extent can litigants in person claim for costs of legal services that they received and paid for? How can you challenge large costs claims made by a litigant in person for experts and agents fees?

The first two questions are covered by the same answer: CPR r.46.5 provides: 7–150

"(3) The litigant in person shall be allowed—
(a)   costs for the same categories of—
    (i)   work; and
    (ii)   disbursements,
which would have been allowed if the work had been done or the disbursements had been made by a legal representative on the litigant in person's behalf;
(b)   the payments reasonably made by the litigant in person for legal services relating to the conduct of the proceedings; and
(c)   the costs of obtaining expert assistance in assessing the costs claim."

Practice Direction 46 states:

"3.1 In order to qualify as an expert for the purpose of rule 46.5(3)(c) (expert assistance in connection with assessing the claim for costs), the person in question must be a—
(a)   barrister;
(b)   solicitor;
(c)   Fellow of the Institute of Legal Executives;
(d)   Fellow of the Association of Costs Lawyers;
(e)   law costs draftsman who is a member of the Academy of Experts;
(f)   law costs draftsman who is a member of the Expert Witness Institute."

CPR r.46.5(3)(b) provides for the recovery of the costs of legal services relating to the conduct of the proceedings. There seems to be no reason, therefore, why those costs cannot be recovered in accordance with the rule.

In answer to the third question, the challenge is made in either detailed or summary assessment in accordance with CPR r.46.5. This is dealt with at para.7.51.

Q48. I have been instructed on a matter where a LiP has filed poor particulars of claim. We do not want to issue a strike out application as we believe that the court is likely to be lenient. Do you have any guidance on

---

[186] *R. (Bar Standards Board) v Disciplinary Tribunal of the Council of the Inns of Court and Sivanandan* [2016] EWCA Civ 478; [2016] 1 W.L.R. 4506; [2016] 3 Costs L.R. 633.

requesting further and better particulars and whether this should be done in the defence or through the Part 18 procedure?

7–151 See *Barton v Wright Hassall LLP*[187] at **para.7–60** above. The Supreme Court has made it clear that it is up to LiPs to read the rules and comply with them. It depends on the contents of the Particulars of Claim, whether a request for Further and Better particulars would be more appropriate than a Pt 18 request.

Q49. Are there any rules relating to recovery of costs, where the party is a LiP, but uses a barrister through direct access?

7–152 The Direct Access Scheme (now known as the Public Access Scheme)[188] is a useful device for reducing costs, particularly in cases of a technical nature where a solicitor would otherwise be no more than a conduit between, e.g. a specialist tax practitioner and a specialist tax barrister. The scheme has however produced a difficulty in that a taxpayer being advised by members of the Institute of Taxation and by counsel under the Direct Access Scheme appealed from a decision of the Commissioners and thence to the Court of Appeal where the taxpayer was successful. Although it was conceded that the taxpayer was entitled to his costs, there was considerable argument as to the extent of those costs. The Court of Appeal found that the tax payer had been acting as a LiP (although he had in fact taken no active part in the proceedings), that counsel's fee was recoverable since it was a disbursement which would have been made had solicitors been instructed but that the fees of the tax advisers were not recoverable save to the extent that they may have been acting in an expert capacity.[189]

7–153 Services provided by a lawyer qualified in another jurisdiction did not constitute "legal services" for the purposes of CPR r.46.5(3)(b). There was no material difference between the position of a lawyer qualified in another jurisdiction and the specialist tax advisers in *Agassi v Robinson (Inspector of Taxes) (Costs)*.[190] The service provider had valuable knowledge and expertise but was not authorised to conduct litigation and was not subject to the wasted costs jurisdiction of the court.[191] On appeal the Court of Appeal held that although CPR r.46.5(3)(b) did not state so expressly, it could be seen from the case law that "legal services" had to be "provided by or under the supervision of a lawyer". A foreign lawyer lacking a qualification in the jurisdiction could not be regarded as a "lawyer" or, providing "legal services" for the purposes of CPR r.46.5(3)(b), since what mattered in that context was expertise in the law and procedure governing the relevant proceedings, namely that of England and

[187] *Barton v Wright Hassall LLP* [2018] UKSC 12; [2018] 1 W.L.R. 1119.
[188] Guidance on public access rules is available at the Bar Standards Board website: *https://www.barstandardsboard.org.uk/media/1666529/2_the_public_access_scheme_guidance_for_lay_clients.pdf*.
[189] *Agassi v Robinson (Inspector of Taxes)* [2005] EWCA Civ 1507; [2006] 1 W.L.R. 2126; [2006] 1 All E.R. 900; [2006] S.T.C. 580; [2006] 2 Costs L.R. 283.
[190] *Agassi v Robinson (Inspector of Taxes)* [2005] EWCA Civ 1507; [2006] 1 W.L.R. 2126; [2006] 1 All E.R. 900; [2006] S.T.C. 580; [2006] 2 Costs L.R. 283.
[191] *Campbell v Campbell* [2016] EWHC 1828 (Ch); [2016] 4 Costs L.R. 687 David Foxton QC.

Wales. The LiP was not entitled to recover the costs of work undertaken on his behalf by the foreign lawyer.[192]

In construction litigation brought by the employer, the defendant contrac- **7–154** tor, who had acted with the assistance of claims consultants, was successful. The contractor claimed the costs incurred by the claims consultants. It was common ground between the parties that the contractor was acting as a LiP for the purposes of CPR r.46.5. The court held that *Agassi v Robinson* was not authority for a general proposition that costs of claims consultants or other consultants who gave advice and support in litigation could never be recovered. The relevant question was whether, in the particular instance, the costs of a claims consultant were recoverable as a disbursement; the question was answered by establishing whether those costs would have been recoverable as a disbursement had it been made by a solicitor. It was necessary to recognise that a solicitor might well normally not carry out work himself but rely on a specialist, even though the work might be "solicitor's work". There were distinct features of adjudication and adjudication enforcement proceedings that could and should be taken into account in considering what disbursements would be recoverable if made by solicitors and which were consequently recoverable by a LiP. Costs incurred by claims consultants assisting a LiP would usually be recoverable in adjudication enforcement proceedings, assuming that the same consultants had represented the party in the adjudication. The costs of the claims consultant were recoverable as disbursements.[193]

The Public Access Scheme Guidance for Lay Clients dated February 2018 explains: the purpose of the Guide is to explain how the public access scheme works and to show how members of the public ("lay clients") can use it to instruct barristers.

Q50. Is it possible for the court to make an order for costs on the indemnity basis against a litigant in person?
Section 51 of the Senior Courts Act 1981 gives the court full power to deter- **7–155** mine by whom and to what extent the costs are to be paid. In appropriate circumstances therefore, it is entirely open to the court to make an order for costs on the indemnity basis against a litigant in person. In family proceedings, the father made committal applications against two CAFCASS officers and the mother's solicitor. The judge found the application to be fundamentally flawed with no real prospect of success. The mother's solicitor had written to the father at an early stage on an open basis setting out the grounds of the defence all of which had succeeded. The court found that the father's very serious allegations had no evidential basis and the application having fatal procedural defects and no real prospect of success ought therefore to be

---

[192] *Campbell v Campbell* [2018] EWCA Civ 80; [2018] 1 W.L.R. 2743; [2018] 2 All E.R. 567; [2018] 1 Costs L.R. 51.
[193] *Octoesse LLP v Trak Special Projects Ltd* [2016] EWHC 3180 (TCC); [2017] B.L.R. 82; [2016] 6 Costs L.R. 1187, Jefford J; and see *NAP Anglia Ltd v Sun-Land Development Co Ltd (Costs)* [2012] EWHC 51 (TCC); [2012] B.L.R. 195; 141 Con. L.R. 247; [2012] 4 Costs L.O. 485, Edwards-Stuart J.

regarded as an abuse of process. The mother's solicitor had incurred significant costs and the father was ordered to pay those costs on the indemnity basis.[194]

Q51. Is it possible for a firm of solicitors which is an LLP to be regarded as a LiP for the purpose of a costs assessment?

7–156   CPR r.46.5(6) states:

> *"For the purposes of this rule, a litigant in person includes:*
>
> *(a)   A company or other corporation which is acting without a legal representative; and any of the following who acts in person (except where any such person is represented by a firm in which that person is a partner):*
>
> > *(i)   A barrister*
> >
> > *(ii)   A solicitor*
> >
> > *(iii) A solicitor's employee*
> >
> > *(iv)   A manager of a body recognised under section 9 of the Administration of Justice Act 1985; or*
> >
> > *(vi)   A person who for the purposes of the 2007 Act is an authorised person in relation to an activity which constitutes the conduct of litigation (within the meaning of that Act)."*

A defendant solicitor was ordered to pay the claimant's costs following his unsuccessful application for summary judgment. The claimant was a limited liability partnership of practising solicitors. They had represented themselves and instructed counsel (the court did not deal with the significance of the instruction of counsel). At first instance, the defendant asserted that the claimant partnership was a LiP and that the costs should accordingly be limited. The costs judge did not accept that argument and the defendant appealed. The judge held that as the claimant was "a company or other corporation" which was acting with a legal representative, it was not a LiP under CPR r.46.5(6)(a). The defendant argued that the claimant was a LiP under CPR r.46.5(6)(b)(v). The judge held that the rule had no sensible foundation if "person" included a corporation. The judge queried why the rule should exclude from the definition of a LiP an ordinary solicitors' partnership acting by one of its own solicitors (which was the effect of the rule) while including an LLP also acting by one of its own solicitors. Companies and corporations were dealt with comprehensively in CPR r.46.5(6)(a) whereas CPR r.46.5(6)(b) dealt with several categories all of whom were natural persons. The judge further pointed out that in the rules individuals were described as acting in person but a company was described as acting "without a legal representative".[195]

---

[194] *H v Dent (Costs)* [2015] EWHC 2228 (Fam); [2016] 2 F.L.R. 566 Roberts J.

[195] *EMW Law LLP v Halborg* [2015] EWHC 2005 (Ch) HHJ Purle QC. Affirmed on appeal [2017] EWCA Civ 793; [2018] 1 W.L.R. 52; [2017] C.P. Rep. 30; [2017] 2 B.C.L.C. 442; [2017] 3 Costs L.R. 553.

Q52. To what extent will the court grant some leeway to a LiP who fails to comply with a rule practice direction or court order? Do solicitors owe special duties when dealing with a LiP? Is there an extra duty on solicitors to give full and frank disclosure when dealing with a LiP? Is the solicitor for a claimant required to ascertain whether the defendant LiP is a protected party who lacks capacity to conduct the proceedings?

When the party on the other side is an LiP, and they make a non-compliant Part 36 offer, is the solicitor acting for the represented party under a duty to advise the opponent LiP of the content requirements of a Part 36 offer?

Under CPR r.3.1A (Case Management—Unrepresented Parties) the court must, when exercising any powers of case management, have regard to the fact that at least one party is unrepresented and is required to "adopt such procedure at any hearing as it considers appropriate to further the overriding objective".

7–157

In proceedings to assess the damages for the claimants in a child abuse case, the personal representative of the original defendant wrote to the court stating that she could not afford legal representation, she also said that she did not intend to attend the trial, but asked that her witness statement and arguments set out in the counter-schedules of loss be taken into account. The court had to consider the applicability of CPR r.3.1A. The judge did not think that CPR r.3.1A(5) was limited to occasions when the LiP was present. The provisions of the overriding objective result in CPR r.3.1A (5) being engaged even when the unrepresented party is not present.

"15 ... The Judge, must be astute to avoid descending into the forensic arena in such a manner or to such an extent that it might appear that he has abandoned his role as an impartial arbiter. On the other hand, in seeking to put to the Claimants and their witnesses the matters properly raised by the unrepresented absent Defendants, there is little point in doing so in such a manner that the exercise is of little or no forensic value."

The judge concluded:

"17 In my judgment, even where the unrepresented party is not present, but where it is clear the unrepresented party has indicated matters which are of concern to that party, it is proper for a Judge to explore those matters with relevant witnesses for the represented party. In this case there are relevant matters which have been raised in the Counter-Schedules of loss, the witness statement of CW and also in the letter written by her to the Court.

18 In one sense, it may be thought that these observations do not go any further than the right of a Judge to seek clarification of matters adduced in evidence by a Claimant in a case where the Defendant has not attended, whether represented or not. The Claimant still has to prove his case to the satisfaction of the Judge. However, there will be cases, of which this is one, where there are matters raised by the unrepresented party which go beyond matters of clarification which

> *it would be proper for the Judge to explore on behalf of the absent unrepresented party. This is what I have attempted to do in this case, in a manner intended to achieve and maintain the delicate balance to which I have already referred."*[196]

7-158 Similarly, where a LiP had not shown any good reason for not having attended the final day of the trial of her employment claim, the court refused to set aside the judgment dismissing her claim under CPR r.39.3(3).[197]

7-159 The answer to these questions will always be fact sensitive and the cases below give examples of the different approaches the court may take. Where a defendant LiP failed to file an appeal bundle in breach of an unless order as a result of which her appeal was struck out, the court refused an application for relief from sanctions under CPR r.3.9, holding, in applying the *Denton* test, that the failure to file an appeal bundle was a significant breach. The process of registering a foreign judgment (which was the subject matter of the appeal) was meant to be swift and seamless but the process had been awkward and delayed. The court was bound to treat the default as serious and significant. In giving judgment, the court emphasised that not all LiPs should be treated the same. The court could take into account the needs of a LiP who was impecunious or unable to speak the language. In the instant case, the defendant was a sophisticated person with sufficient access to resources to protect her interest. There was no good reason for her breach. Although the court would not usually take into account the underlying merits of the claim when making case management decisions in considering all the circumstances under CPR r.3.9, the court found that it was entitled to take into account the merits of the underlying proceedings and to conclude that the defendant had no right to delay registration of the foreign judgments further.[198]

7-160 In a case where proceedings had been brought against four defendants, one of the defendants owned and controlled another defendant. Judgment was entered against all four defendants. The LiP did not attend as a result of ill health. She appealed, arguing that she and her company should never have been parties to the proceedings and that her application to strike out the claims had not been dealt with by the court at first instance. Two days before the appeal was due to be heard, the LiP realised she only had permission to appeal the judgment and costs order made against her in her personal capacity and not against the company. She applied for permission to file an appeal notice on behalf of the company at the appeal hearing itself. The Court of Appeal applied the three stage test in *Denton v TH White* and found that the delay was serious and significant. The explanation was that the LiP did not realise that she also needed to appeal separately on behalf of the company. The court held that the circumstances were "truly exceptional" and it was just to extend the time. A judgment against the company could, at least in theory,

---

[196] *LXA, BXL v Mrs Cynthia Willcox as Personal Representative of the Estate of Edward Willcox, Deceased; Mrs Cynthia Willcox* [2018] EWHC 2256 (QB) HHJ Robinson.
[197] *Buckley v Greenwood Academies Trust* [2018] EWHC 2441 (Comm) HHJ Waksman QC.
[198] *Akcine Bendore Bankas Snoras (in Bankruptcy) v Yampolskaya* [2015] EWHC 2136 (QB) Green J.

result in proceedings against the litigant in person under the Disqualification of Directors' legislation. The facts relating to the company were exactly the same as those relating to the litigant personally and the claimant was fully aware that both were, for the purposes of the litigation, to be regarded as one and the same.[199]

A LiP sought an adjournment of her trial for two weeks because she was **7–161** dissatisfied with the specific disclosure provided by the defendant, and wished to argue that this affected her ability to prepare for trial, and that, as a LiP, she needed more time to consider the newly disclosed material and to amend her skeleton argument. The court refused her application holding that if it became apparent during the trial that further information was required this could be dealt with by the trial judge. An adjournment of the trial would have a very considerable impact. The defendant had already incurred substantial costs which would be lost or duplicated if the trial were adjourned and the adjournment would not be for two weeks but for several months, and given that the proceedings had commenced in 2007, it was in the interests of both parties that the issues be determined. The documents which had been disclosed were "relatively peripheral" to the case. The date of trial was put back by four days to give the litigant some further time in which to consider the new material and finalise their skeleton argument.[200]

In a case where only quantum was in dispute, the court directed that **7–162** there should be a meeting of experts on a specified date. The meeting did not take place because the claimant LiP fell out with his expert and had not paid his fees. The defendant applied to extend the time for the meeting and obtained an order that unless the experts met by the new date, the claimant's expert evidence should be struck out. The claimant's application to set aside the order and vacate the trial date and for new directions on expert evidence was dismissed. The judge held that the claimant was responsible for the expert ceasing to act, given his criticism of the expert's opinion and the non-payment of his fees. Also, it was not appropriate for the claimant to indicate that he would look to the expert for any shortfall in the sums he sought to recover. The judge considered the *Denton* principles and decided that the non-compliance with the relevant order was serious and significant and was the claimant's fault. It was not fair, just or reasonable in all the circumstances for relief to be granted.[201]

Where a LiP made 11 applications, all of which were wholly without merit, **7–163** the court granted an application for an extended civil restraint order against the LiP. The defendant complained that the courts had never looked at the merits of her case and that she was a LiP who did not understand the procedure. In giving judgment the judge stated:

---

[199] *Kishenin v Von Kalkstein-Bleach* [2015] EWCA Civ 1184.
[200] *El-Demellawy v European Bank for Reconstruction and Development* [2015] EWHC 3291 (QB) Hickinbottom J.
[201] *Sargeant v UK Insurance Ltd* [2015] EWHC 3304 (QB) Picken J. See also *Brand and Goldsmith v Berki* [2015] EWHC 3373 (QB) Jay J.

> "...if it is otherwise appropriate to make a civil restraint order, the fact that the litigant is a litigant in person who does not understand procedures and gets things wrong is precisely supportive of making a civil restraint order rather than not making one. [The litigant in person] needs to understand that by making a civil restraint order ....she does not lose any rights at all. If she has an application or an appeal or a claim that has any merit the judge who hears or deals with an application for permission to launch such an application, appeal or claim will make an order permitting her to proceed. The civil restraint order is only a filter to preclude the making of unmeritorious applications".[202]

7-164   The question about mental capacity really answers itself. The only people qualified to give an opinion as to capacity are medical practitioners who specialise in that area. Solicitors simply do not have that facility. Added to that the LiP is the opposing party and there are limits to the way in which the claimant's solicitor may approach them. If there are serious doubts, the matter should be brought to the attention of the court which will then, if appropriate, give directions.

7-165   As to the third question, there is no strict duty to inform the LiP that the offer is non-compliant, but given that an LIP is involved, any judge, upon being made aware that the information had not been passed on, would be likely to take an extremely poor view of the offerees' solicitors.

Q53. What is the position where someone has issued a claim using Money Claims Online, has detailed £13,000 in outstanding invoices, but has paid the court fee for a claim of up to £10,000? This person stated in the claim form that the amount claimed is £10,000. The person is a LiP who wishes for the court to award an amount of up to £10,000 rather than pay a higher court fee to claim £13,000 (though this is not set out in the claim form). The defendant has claimed that this is an abuse of process and the claim should be struck out.

7-166   On the face of it, if the claimant has limited the claim to £10,000 and paid the appropriate fee, there is nothing wrong, unless or until the claimant tries to increase the value of the claim, which might then be regarded as an abuse of process. Solicitors acting in some 30 claims for negligence indicated in pre-action correspondence that each claim was for hundreds of thousands of pounds. When the claim forms came to be issued, however, the value was stated to be considerably lower and a lower level of court fees was paid. Before the claims were served, the claimants amended their claims to the higher actual amounts and paid the balance of the larger court fees. On the defendant's application for an order striking out the claims, the court found that the solicitor's actions constituted an abuse of process but that it would be disproportionate to strike out the claims, although the possibility of costs sanctions was left open. The court held that the claimants could not be regarded as

---

[202] *KL Communications Ltd v Fu* [2015] EWHC 2026 (IPEC) Warren J.

having paid the appropriate fee in circumstances where the act of payment was an abuse of process.[203]

Q54. Are there any restrictions, beyond the obstacle of cross-examination, which would prevent a person acting as a representative on behalf of a LiP and also acting as their independent witness in a civil court matter?
On 12 July 2010 the Master of the Rolls and President of the Family Division handed down a Practice Note,[204] which gives comprehensive guidance on the use of McKenzie Friends (see para.7–69 above). A person given permission to appear as a McKenzie Friend could clearly not be an "independent witness". Permission would not be granted for such a person to take on both roles. 　7–167

Q55. Is it possible for a company to be represented by a McKenzie Friend?
Hildyard J found that a company may be represented by a McKenzie Friend under rights of audience granted in exceptional circumstances. Although there was no direct authority on the point, the court could rely on its power to regulate its own proceedings and in circumstances where otherwise the body corporate would have no one capable of speaking for it, to prevent a failure of the administration of justice. The judge relied on Sch.3 of the Legal Services Act 2007 and on the Courts and Legal Services Act 1990 both of which assumed and recognised that the courts had such jurisdiction even if it was not conferred expressly. The litigation concerned the attempt by the claimant bank to wrest a large group of companies in the Russian Federation from the control and ownership of the defendants. An application for disclosure by the defendants had been admirably argued on their behalf by their McKenzie Friend. 　7–168

The company referred to CPR r.39.6 (Representation at Trial of Companies or Other Corporations) which provides:

"A company or other corporation may be represented at trial by an employee if:
(a)　The employee has been authorised by the company or corporation to appear at trial on its behalf; and
(b)　The Court gives permission."

The judge stated in relation to a helpful note on the applicable framework for a McKenzie Friend provided by counsel for the claimants:

"It suggests the conclusion that, given that CPR r.39.6 does now allow an employee of a body corporate, duly authorised to do so by it, to appear at trial on its behalf with the permission of the Court, the Court does have the jurisdiction to allow a body corporate the assistance of a McKenzie friend, and in appropriate

---

[203] *Lewis v Ward Hadaway* [2015] EWHC 3503 (Ch); [2016] 4 W.L.R. 6; [2016] 1 Costs L.O. 49, John Male QC. Not followed in *Atha & Co Solicitors v Liddle* [2018] EWHC 1751 (QB); [2018] 1 W.L.R. 4953 Turner J. (The appeal was dismissed.)
[204] *Practice Note (Sen Cts: McKenzie Friends: Civil and Family Courts)* [2010] 1 W.L.R. 1881; [2010] 4 All E.R. 272.

(and exceptional) circumstances to allow that McKenzie friend the right of audience on an ad hoc basis."[205]

Q56. Will the court order interim payments to enable LiPs to obtain legal representation?

7–169   Defendant LiPs who had left Russia and were in France (for their own safety) issued a counterclaim for $80 million. The eight-week trial had already been adjourned twice.

The defendants argued that without legal representation a fair trial was not possible and would not be ECHR art.6 compliant. They sought a further adjournment and an interim payment to enable them to instruct representatives.

The court found that it had to be satisfied that there were good case management reasons for making an interim payment and that if the matter went to trial the defendants would obtain judgment for a substantial sum.[206] In ordinary circumstances the notion that an interim payment should be made to fund a legal costs was fanciful, but there was the extraordinary factor in the instant case of the allegation that there would otherwise be an unfair trial. The counterclaim was complex and would require expert evidence. The prospect of identifying a separate issue with sufficient cohesion to be safely heard within five days, and deciding before then that the defendants would obtain judgment, was remote in the extreme. It would not be consistent with the court's judicial obligations, nor would it be fair to the bank, to order an interim payment.

The jurisdiction to award costs before the determination of an issue was normally confined to cases where there was a "common fund", such as in trust, company or matrimonial proceedings. The court was unlikely to exercise it outside of those circumstances to make one party fund another in a substantial amount going beyond disbursements reasonably required for the trial, and the application for costs was refused.

A definition of a fair trial was impossible and unwise. It was not impossible to afford the defendants proper access to the legal process and proper adjudication of claims. It was relevant that the defendants had voluntarily chosen England as a jurisdiction when they must have known of their travel difficulties, and that they had always encouraged the court's expectation that they would attend the trial, either themselves via video link or through their McKenzie Friend. (See the question above.[207])

---

[205] *Bank St Petersburg PJSC v Arkhangelsky* [2015] EWHC 2997 (Ch); [2016] 1 W.L.R. 1081 Hildyard J. With effect from 6 April 2019, CPR PD 39A was deleted by the 104th Update – Practice Direction Amendments. As a result, the guidance on the court's approach to the CPR r.39.6 exception was removed.
[206] See *Revenue and Customs Commissioners v GKN Group* [2012] EWCA Civ 57; [2012] 1 W.L.R. 2375; [2012] 3 All E.R. 111; [2012] S.T.C. 953; [2012] C.P. Rep. 20.
[207] *Bank St Petersburg PJSC v Arkhangelsky* [2015] EWHC 2997 (Ch); [2016] 1 W.L.R. 1081.

Q57. A LiP has sent numerous emails and letters persistently threatening to bring action against my client if we do not settle but, despite repeated requests to do so, has not provided any evidence to substantiate his claim. We have attempted to engage but are limited in what we can respond to due to his lack of evidence. As a result a small costs bill has run up. Is there any way in which these costs can be recovered from the proposed claimant in view of the fact that his claim appears to have been completely without merit?

Given that there are no proceedings in existence, the court is not seized of the matter and has no jurisdiction to make an order for costs. A letter informing the litigant that unless or until evidence is provided your client will not consider the claim and that further communications will not be responded to, may either spur the litigant into issuing proceedings (which you can then apply to have struck out) or give up.

7–170

Q58. We act for a claimant in residential possession proceedings on the ground of trespass (N5 claim form submitted). The defendant is a LiP, and has repeatedly ignored court directions, submitted witness statements the day before a hearing, had an ambulance called to the court mid-hearing (which meant the court halted the hearing) and now, the evening before a fast track hearing, he has emailed me to say he won't be attending tomorrow for medical reasons. What is the best course of action to stop this abuse of the court process and preferably to bring these costly proceedings to a close?

This sounds like a problem for the case managing judge to get a grip of. An application for an unless order requiring the defendant to comply with direction by a certain date or be stuck out, should bring matters to a head.

7–171

Q59. I am dealing with a LiP on the other side. She has asked us to acknowledge that her husband may act as her representative in future correspondence. Do I now have to correspond with her husband or do I continue to deal with the LiP herself? I act for a client who is pursuing a claim against a LiP. The LiP is of majority age and I have no concerns about their capacity. I have received correspondence from the LiP permitting me to correspond with one of their family members in relation to this matter and then subsequent correspondence from that family member which asks various questions in relation to my client's case and which I suspect will be used for the purposes of the litigant in questions defence. Are there any conduct implications in corresponding with the family member (assuming that the LiP is also copied in to all correspondence)?

Provided that the legal representative is acting in accordance with CPR r.3.1A and the conduct which that rule requires, there should be no problem in communicating with a person nominated by the litigant, so long as the litigant is copied in to all correspondence.

7–172

Q60. What can a claimant do if a defendant LiP sends an email to the court expressly referring to a "without prejudice save as to costs" letter from the claimant to the defendant? What can be done where a LiP refers to without prejudice communications in a statutory demand? Can a wasted costs order be made against a LiP?

7–173 Hobhouse J, as he then was, stated: "The trained legal mind will have no difficulty [in putting such distractions] to one side." A letter to the court, copied to the LiP pointing out what has happened, should ensure that the judge puts the matter out of his/her mind, or if that proves impossible, that the matter is passed to another judge without the offending document.

During the course of the trial of a personal injury action, in which the claimant was acting in person, he revealed the contents of the defendant's "without prejudice save as to costs" letter, despite the judge's efforts to warn him that the letter was "without prejudice" and that he should not introduce it. He had also been warned before trial by the defendants' counsel. The judge withdrew from the case and adjourned the trial. The claimant was ordered to pay the costs of the two-day trial "thrown away", and to pay interim costs of £11,000 within four months, failing which the claim would be struck out. That sum represented around 10% of the costs already incurred by the defendant.

On appeal, the Court of Appeal held that whilst LiPs would always attract the court's assistance, they were not and could not be a privileged class, relieved of their obligations under the CPR. Judges would show common sense and often flexibility, but in the end had to enforce the Rules, and have a proper eye to the legitimate interests of the other parties to litigation, including as to costs. The appellant's conduct, even as a LiP, satisfied the test in *Ridehalgh*,[208] and the judge had been correct to order the appellant to bear the resulting wasted costs.[209]

Q61. We are currently preparing Form N260 on behalf of our client (claimant), ahead of a hearing where assessment of costs will take place. There was a period of time at the beginning of this case where the claimant acted as LiP. Is it best practice to state what the claimant's costs were during that period, together with the amount of legal fees incurred by us (including disbursements) on the same Form N260?

7–174 CPR PD 47 para.5.8 states:

> "*Where it is necessary or convenient to do so, a bill of costs*[210] *may be divided into two or more parts, each part containing [background information; items of costs claimed; summary showing the total costs claimed on each page of the bill.] Circumstances in which it will be necessary or convenient to divide a bill into parts include the following—*

[208] *Ridehalgh v Horsefield* [1994] Ch. 205, [1994].
[209] *Ogiehor v Belinfantie* [2018] EWCA Civ 2423; [2018] 6 Costs L.R. 1329.
[210] Form N260 is here treated as akin to a bill of costs although they are not the same.

(1) Where the receiving party acted in person during the course of the proceedings (whether or not that party also had a legal representative at that time) the bill must be divided into different parts so as to distinguish between;
> *(a)   the costs claimed for work done by the legal representative; and*
> *(b)   the costs claimed for work done by the receiving party in person."*

It would certainly be appropriate to include the claimant's costs when acting as a LiP with your Form N260. It may be more convenient to set out the claimant's costs on a separate sheet rather than try and complete the boxes on the form. The claimant will probably not have the information which the form requires.

CHAPTER 8

Assessments of Costs and Payments on Account of Costs

Introduction

The overall intentions of the 2013 reforms in respect of the process for deter- 8–01
mination of "between the parties" costs were to reduce the issues and lessen
the time, and therefore the cost, expended upon this stage of a claim, recognising that in many cases the "costs of the costs" had become unreasonable and disproportionate. These aims were achieved by a combination of
changes—some introducing entirely new concepts and procedures and some
being simply variations of what already existed. They were:

- Costs management, designed, in part, to reduce the costs in dispute at
  the conclusion of a claim and reduce for the need for/the scope of assess-
  ments. This has been considered in **Ch.4.**
- The introduction of the further fixed costs schemes considered in **Ch.7**
  removing any need for assessments.
- Improvements to the summary assessment regime.
- A more efficient detailed assessment hearing process.
- The introduction of provisional assessments.
- A change of approach to payments on account of costs.

It is the last four of these upon which we shall concentrate in this chapter.
As a preliminary point to so doing, we should note that the last year has
seen the publication of the updated Senior Courts Costs Office Guide, the
revision of the Guide to Summary Assessment and the Civil Justice Council
Final Report on Guideline Hourly Rates. In addition, the Master of the Rolls
has made public (for example in speeches at The Association of Costs Lawyers
annual conference and at the Civil Justice Council: National Forum on Access
to Justice for Those Without Means) that, amongst other costs issues, he has
already charged the Civil Justice Council with further work on guideline
hourly rates.

Summary assessment

One of the options outlined by Jackson LJ in his preliminary report[1] was 8–02
to abolish summary assessments altogether. He rejected this, describing the
procedure as:

---

[1] *Review of Civil Litigation Costs: Preliminary Report*, May 2009.

> *"a valuable tool which has made a substantial contribution to civil procedure, not least by deterring frivolous applications and reducing the need for detailed assessment proceedings."*

Instead, the process was altered in 2013, but only slightly, and the emphasis on proportionality in this context was designed to encourage more summary assessments in place of detailed assessments. Subsequently, there has been little further amendment. The most significant has been the unsuccessful trialling of amendments to Form N260, to introduce Forms N260A (for interim applications) and N260B (for trials in costs managed cases) under a pilot scheme set out at CPR PD 51X (see para.8–05 below for more detail on the pilot). The procedure for assessing costs by summary assessment is found at CPR r.44.6 and CPR PD 44 para.9 and is the same whichever version of Form N260 is used.

The court is charged with considering a summary assessment whenever it makes an order about costs that does not provide for fixed costs. The general rule is that a court will undertake a summary assessment at the end of a fast track trial and at the conclusion of any other hearing which has lasted not more than a day (including appeals), unless there is good reason not to do so. We say that this is the general rule because this is the wording used in CPR PD 44 para.9.2. However, this is preceded by the requirement at CPR PD 44 para.9.1 that "whenever a court makes an order about costs which does not provide only for fixed costs to be paid the court should consider whether to make a summary assessment of costs". There is a further steer to a summary assessment when appropriate at the end of a multi-track trial in CPR PD 29 para.10.5. There is an issue about whether only the judge who has conducted the trial/hearing and made the relevant award of costs order may undertake the summary assessment. In *Transformers and Rectifiers Ltd v Needs Ltd*[2] the court concluded:

> *"I consider that, in appropriate circumstances, another judge may be able summarily to assess the costs arising out of a hearing conducted (or an order made) by another judge. I do not consider that there is any binding authority under the current version of the CPR to the contrary."*

In fact, CPR r.44.1, to which no reference was made, does provide that a summary assessment "means the procedure whereby costs are assessed by the judge who has heard the case or application". Despite the comment above, in *Transformers and Rectifiers Ltd* the court was only expressly considering the position in a more limited context, namely after a disposal of an application "on the papers". This is considered in more detail in the question and answer section of this chapter below (see **Q7** below).

The parties must file and serve statements of costs not less than two days before a fast track trial and 24 hours before the time fixed for any other hearing.

---

[2] *Transformers and Rectifiers Ltd v Needs Ltd* [2015] EWHC 1687 (TCC); [2015] 3 Costs L.R. 611.

The slight changes to the process in 2013 were:

(i)   a new N260 statement of costs;
(ii) the requirement to serve a statement of costs in advance applies to Detailed Assessment hearings and the summary assessment of the costs of those proceedings.

Form N260 was updated again in June 2015 and there is currently the possibility of further revisions following two recommendations made to the Civil Rules Procedure Committee in the Civil Justice Council Guideline Hourly Rates Final Report April 2021. These are as follows:

1)   To require the receiving party to specify the location – i.e. the office to which a fee earner is, or is predominantly, attached – of the fee earner(s) for whose work claims are made; and
2)   To replace, in the "Description of fee earners" section of the form, the word "(grade)" with "(GHR grade)".

i. The post-March 2013 N260—statement of costs

One of the major criticisms of the previous version of the N260, particularly   8–03
where the summary assessment was of the entire costs of a claim, as distinct from a discrete application, was the lack of information that it contained. The post-March 2013 N260 ensures that the assessing judge has more detail by introducing a breakdown of the time spent on documents. CPR PD 44 para.9.5(3) is no more prescriptive than its predecessor and only requires that "the statement of costs should follow as closely as possible Form N260". However, given the increased emphasis on enforcing practice direction compliance in the overriding objective at CPR r.1.1(2)(f), it is a bold practitioner who uses a "homemade" variation, as there is likely to be little sympathy, rather the prospect of some sanction, if the form used does not provide the information necessary in clear terms. Practical experience nine years on suggests both that there are bold practitioners and that there is little sympathy.

ii. The requirement to serve a statement of costs in advance of detailed assessment hearings

Rule changes made by omission of previous provisions are often overlooked as   8–04
they are harder to spot. The provision previously found at s.45.3 of the Costs Practice Direction was removed in April 2013. Parties seeking the costs of a detailed assessment must comply with the provisions of CPR PD 44 para.9.5(4) and file and serve an N260 24 hours before the assessment (see **Q3** below).

Forms N260A and N260B

A valid criticism of N260 has been that it does not match the budget phases of   8–05
Precedent H, making ready comparison impossible and summary assessment challenging, if not out of the question, at the conclusion of a costs managed

case. In his Final Report, Sir Rupert Jackson looked forward to the day when time capture recording systems would lead to "a new software system . . . which will be capable of generating bills of costs at different levels of generality". That day arrived for detailed assessments with the mandatory use of the "new bill" for all work undertaken after 6 April 2018 other than the exceptions set out in CPR PD 47 para 5.1(a)(i)-(ii) (see para.**8–08** below). However, this did not address the difficulties posed on a summary assessment. In recognition of this, the CPRC introduced a two-year voluntary pilot of new Forms N260A and N260B originally scheduled to run from 1 April 2019 until 31 March 2021. This pilot period was extended for a further year until 31 March 2022. The Civil Procedure Rules Committee minutes from May 2021 revealed that the take up by practitioners using these forms had been low and a focused consultation was launched. The outcome was revealed in the December 2021 minutes. There was insufficient evidence to justify continuing the pilot. As a result, it will not be extended and ends on 31 March 2022. However, the CPRC minutes suggest that further work is anticipated on the existing Form N260 "to improve usability".

The change of emphasis

8–06 A decision as to whether to undertake a summary assessment or to order a detailed assessment is a case management decision. The overriding objective applies to all case management decisions and requires the court to consider the proportionality of its decision. Notwithstanding the "costs cap" in the provisional assessment regime (see below), there can be little argument that a summary assessment requires significantly less resource, both in costs and in court time, than a detailed assessment. Accordingly, there should now be an increased number of summary assessments than prior to April 2013. The likelihood of this being the case is enhanced by the fact that many of the multi-track cases that might previously have gone to a detailed assessment will have been subject to costs management orders and, absent "good reason", the court will only be troubled by the non-budgeted costs (see **Ch.4** for further consideration of this) reducing the scope of, and the time needed for, a summary assessment, and by the introduction of Form N260B to facilitate comparison between budget and sum claimed.

Parties wishing to seek summary assessment at the end of trials/hearings that exceed one day should ensure that Form N260 is available to the court and has been served so that this is a realistic option for the court if time permits (even if summary assessment does not take place, the form can, in appropriate cases, then be referred to as the basis for a payment on account). It may be sensible to fie and serve a Precedent Q to enable easy comparison between budget and spend. Whilst there is sometimes resistance to a summary assessment where the costs are substantial, it is interesting that para.F13.2 of *The Business and Property Courts of England & Wales: The Commercial Court Guide 11th Edn* envisages summary assessments of the costs of interim applications where the statement of costs of the receiving party is no more than £250,000, but requires parties to be prepared for the court to undertake such an assessment even "for a heavy application where the costs exceed that amount". This increased emphasis on the court to undertake summary assessments is illustrated by the provision at CPR 57AB PD 2.59, that, save in exceptional circumstances, the court will undertake such an assessment at the conclusion of cases proceeding under the Shorter Trials Scheme (which means summary assessment of cases where there has been up to a four-day trial). Although CPR r.3.12 does not apply to this scheme (unless the parties agree otherwise), the costs schedules that the parties are required to enable the trial judge to undertake a summary assessment must provide detail of the costs attributable to each phase of Precedent H. In other words, the parties must record their time under appropriate discrete phases in the same way they would have to if subject to the costs management regime. (For useful commentary on the summary assessment process within the Shorter Trials Scheme see *Insulet Corporation v Roche Diabetes Care Ltd.*[3])

Detailed assessment hearing process

In Ch.45 of his Final Report, Sir Rupert Jackson set out a number of recommendations designed to produce a more efficient and proportionate detailed assessment process. One, provisional assessment, is considered separately below. The others were:

8–07

- A new format of user friendly bill that is inexpensive to prepare and ultimately can be linked to the same time capturing system that can prepare client costs estimates and Forms H for costs budgeting.
- Shorter and more focused Points of Dispute and Replies.
- Compulsory offers.
- The cross-application of CPR r.36 to detailed assessment proceedings generally and the requirement upon the paying party to make an open offer.
- Clarity on the date from which time runs to appeal decisions made in the detailed assessment.
- Paper assessments when only disbursements are in issue.

Save in respect of the first of these recommendations, for which a voluntary pilot operated in the SCCO for two years from 1 October 2015 and in respect of which the use of a new form of bill became mandatory for all costs incurred after 6 April 2018 in almost all CPR r.7 multi-track claims, (see para.8–08 below for more detail), the remainder were introduced in April 2013 by the following provisions:

- CPR PD 47 para.8.2 requires Points of Dispute to be "short and to the point". If a Reply is served (and it remains optional) it must be limited to points of principle and concessions (CPR PD 47 para.12.1).

---

[3] *Insulet Corporation v Roche Diabetes Care Ltd* [2021] EWHC 2047 (Pat).

- Under CPR PD 47 para.8.3 the paying party must make an open offer to accompany the Points of Dispute.
- CPR r.47.20 expressly applies the provisions of CPR r.36 to detailed assessment proceedings (it is worth noting that any CPR r.47.20 offer does not need to be the same as the open offer).
- CPR r.47.14(7) makes it plain that where the assessment takes place at more than one hearing, the time for appealing does not run until the conclusion of the final hearing (presumably this also means that where there is only one hearing, but over many days, the time for appealing any decision, regardless of which day it was made upon, does not run until the conclusion of the assessment).
- CPR PD 47 para.5.7 contains provisions for limited bills and paper assessments where the only dispute between the parties concerns disbursements.

Apart from the implementation of the recommendations above, the introduction of provisional assessment and the requirement to file and serve a Form N260 24 hours before the assessment hearing (see above), the procedure for detailed assessments largely remains as it was prior to April 2013, with certain discrete variations in respect of electronic bills (see para.**8–08** below) and the addition of proceedings in the Senior Courts Cost Office to the Electronic Working Pilot Scheme under CPR PD 51O (see para.**8–09** below). However, there have been two other subsequent significant procedural amendments to detailed assessment proceedings—one to address the difficulties posed on an assessment of costs in a case subject to a costs management order prior to the introduction of a new form of bill or where its use is not required, to facilitate comparison between any budgeted sum and the sum claimed on assessment for a particular phase and to identify those costs outside CPR r.3.18 which remain for assessment on the basis of reasonableness and proportionality, and the other to provide certainty as to the correct proportionality test to apply where the transitional proportionality provisions apply under CPR r.44.3(7)—see **Ch.3** and, in particular, **Q1** for more detailed consideration of these arrangements and **Q22** below considering the clarification provided by the Court of Appeal in respect of the treatment of additional liabilities. The specific provisions dealing with these two significant procedural amendments apply from 6 April 2016 and are as follows:

- CPR r.47.6 and PD 47 para.5.8(8) combine (as CPR r.47.6(1)(c) refers to the requirements of the PD) to provide that where a costs management order has been made and the costs are to be assessed on the standard basis (so CPR r.3.18 applies see **Ch.4**), the bill must be divided into separate parts so as to distinguish between the costs claimed for each phase of the last approved or agreed budget, and within each such part the bill must distinguish between the costs shown as incurred in the last agreed or approved budget and the costs shown as estimated. To make the comparison even easier CPR r.47.6(1)(c) (again by cross-reference to CPR PD 47), requires the bill to be accompanied by a breakdown of the costs claimed for each phase of the proceedings (this does not apply to electronic bills where, unless the format of the bill already provides the requisite information, for example in identifying the costs within each phase, the bill should incorporate a summary in a form comparable to the "Funding and Parts Table" in Precedent S to provide the information that would otherwise be provided by its division into parts—CPR PD 47 para.5.A3). An amendment from October 2015 introducing CPR PD 47 paras 5.2(f) and 13.2(m) already required the paying party to serve and file a breakdown of the costs claimed for each phase of the proceedings. CPR PD 47 para.5.1A refers to Precedent Q in the Schedule of Costs Precedents to CPR PD 47 as a model form of such a breakdown. It is important to note that both the breakdown and the division of the bill are required (the latter does not replace the former)—except where the costs are to be assessed on the indemnity basis, where, curiously, the breakdown is still required, as there is no limitation in CPR PD 47 para.5.2(f) to standard basis assessments, but, understandably, the bill does not need to be divided into separate parts for each phase, as CPR PD 47 para.5.8(8) expressly only applies to standard basis assessments (see **Ch.4, Qs 94** and **95** for further consideration of this).

- CPR PD 47 para.5.8(7) provides that in any cases commenced on or after 1 April 2013, where the bill is to be assessed on the standard basis and covers costs for work done both before and after that date, the bill must be divided into parts so as to distinguish between costs shown as incurred for work done before 1 April 2013 and costs shown as incurred for work done on or after 1 April 2013 (see comments in previous bullet point about electronic bills—CPR PD 47 para.5.A3).

The Electronic bill

The 92nd update to the CPR amended CPR r.47.6   8–08

> *"to provide for the filing of electronic and/or paper versions of the bill of costs, if appropriate, and to direct users to the relevant practice direction supplementing Part 47 (Practice Direction 47)."*

The practice direction at CPR PD 47 para.5.1 makes clear that the electronic bill (Precedent S) must be used in respect of all costs recoverable between the parties for work undertaken after 6 April 2018 in all Pt 7 multi-track claims except those:

- in which proceedings are subject to fixed costs and scale costs; or
- in which the receiving party is unrepresented; or
- where the court has ordered otherwise.

In cases not caught by the mandatory requirement to use the electronic bill parties may use it or may still present paper bills. CPR PD 47 paras 5.A1–5A4 specify that:

- the electronic bill must be in the spreadsheet format reached by the link at 5.A2 or a spreadsheet format that contains the information that can be found in Precedent S and which is set out at 5.A2(a)–(e);
- the existing provisions of PD 47 paras 5.7–5.21 continue to apply to electronic bills save where they are inconsistent with the form and content of Precedent S;
- where work, for which recoverable costs are sought, was undertaken both on and before and after 6 April 2018, a party may serve and file either a paper or electronic bill in respect of the work done before 7 April 2018 and must serve and file an electronic bill for work done after 6 April 2018. (One might assume that in such a situation it will be easier to produce the entire bill electronically as part of it has to be in that form anyway. However, this may depend upon the degree of detail of the time recording of the work before 6 April 2018).

A party serving or filing an electronic bill must also serve and file a hard copy in a manageable paper format as per the pdf version of Precedent S. This should be done at the same time as "providing" to the paying party and filing at court the full electronic spreadsheet bill by email or other electronic means (CPR PD 47 para.5.1A). This provision is disapplied in respect of electronic bills filed at the Costs Office using Electronic Working under Practice Direction 51O (see para.8–09 below). CPR PD 47 para.5.1B provides, instead, that:

> "*Whenever an electronic bill is filed at the Costs Office using Electronic Working (see Practice Direction 51O)—*
> (a) *a copy of the full electronic spreadsheet version and a pdf version must be uploaded; and*
> (b) *the electronic bill must not be filed at court by any other means.*"

The wording of CPR PD 47 para.5.1A raises the issue of whether the requirement to file a copy at court arises on the commencement of detailed assessment proceedings (which would result in the court receiving the bill prior to any request for a detailed assessment hearing)—see **Q10** below for consideration of this issue. On a more practical level the requirement for service begs the question of where the paying party has no known email address—see **Q11** below on this point.

The provisions relating to electronic bills apply to provisional assessments, although the requirement to file an additional copy of the bill at CPR PD 47 para.14.3(c) only applies to any paper bill.

Inevitably the electronic bill contains the same certificate as to accuracy as the paper bill. However, as most of the information within the bill will be reliant upon the accuracy of the time recording (and this is likely to be electronic in most cases), then for the person signing the bill to be confident in so doing, it is an imperative that proper systems for attributing time appropriately between phases, tasks and activities are implemented. Whilst obvious, it is also vital that a check is done to ensure that the spreadsheet is self-calculating accurately. Do not simply assume this to be the case.

The electronic working pilot (CPR PD 51O)

The electronic working pilot scheme at CPR PD 51O was introduced with effect from 16 November 2015. It is currently due to run until 6 April 2023. As of 7 October 2019, it was extended to operate in the Senior Courts Costs Office as follows:

8–09

- to detailed assessment proceedings in which the request for a hearing is filed on or after 7 October 2019;
- to applications filed on or after 7 October 2019; and
- to proceedings started in the Costs Office on or after 7 October 2019.

(Note also the Practice Note issued by the Senior Costs Judge on 1 October 2019.)

It is important to note that the provisions of CPR Pt 47 still apply to proceedings within the pilot. From the 7 October 2019 until 19 January 2020 the pilot was voluntary for represented and unrepresented parties. From 20 January 2020, the pilot has been mandatory for represented parties starting and/or continuing any relevant claims, detailed assessment proceedings or applications.

There can be no substitute for parties familiarising themselves with the detail of the pilot, but in summary only, PD 51O makes provision for:

- registration for an account;
- creation of a new file;
- uploading of documents;
- payment of fees;
- continuation of proceedings within the pilot that started outside it;
- the practicalities of filing;
- sealing of documents;
- service of documents;
- calculation of time periods;
- transfer of proceedings;
- applications;
- case and costs management and other directions;
- statements of truth;
- trial bundles;
- inspection of documents, whether electronically or otherwise; and
- security of information and documents stored.

Provisional assessment

In his final report, Sir Rupert Jackson recommended the introduction of provisional assessment under a pilot scheme. The pilot took place in certain courts

8–10

in respect of bills for £25,000 and under. In the April 2013 amendments, the scheme was extended to all courts and applies to any "between the parties" bill where the costs claimed are £75,000 or less (see **Qs 21** and **22** for consideration of what is included in this sum).

A provisional assessment is one undertaken by the court on the basis of papers filed, without an oral hearing and any attendance by the parties. There is a limited opt-out provision found at CPR r.47.15(6), under which the court may at any time consider the bill unsuitable for provisional assessment and may list for hearing with the procedure for a detailed assessment hearing then applying.

The procedure is set out at CPR r.47.15 and PD 47 para.14. It can be divided into four stages as follows:

(i) Pre-assessment.
(ii) The assessment.
(iii) After the assessment excluding an oral hearing.
(iv) Oral hearings and appeals.

(i) Pre-assessment

8-11 The title given to CPR r.47 relates exclusively to detailed assessment. There can be no doubt that a provisional assessment is a form of detailed assessment. CPR PD 47 para.14.2 and 14.3 expressly identify the many provisions of the detailed assessment process with CPR r.47 and its PD that apply equally to provisional assessments. For the avoidance of doubt, these include the time periods for commencement of detailed assessment proceedings and the time for requesting a detailed assessment hearing. As a result, it is not surprising that many of the procedural provisions relating to the request for an assessment borrow heavily from those for detailed assessment hearings. CPR PD 47 paras 13.2 and 14.3(b)–(e) prescribe the documents that must be filed with the request itself. However, there is some confusion as to what, if any, further documents must be filed and when. Some have taken CPR PD 47 para.14.2(2) disapplying CPR PD 47 para.13.11 to mean that the receiving party does not file further documents in support of the bill. Others point to CPR r.47.15(3) and (4) as requiring supporting documents. This is supported by the fact that CPR PD 47 para.13.12 applies to provisional assessments. This apparent conflict is considered at **Q24** below. What is clear is that the court retains the power to direct the filing of any further documents which the court considers that it needs to reach a decision (CPR PD 47 para.13.13).[4] Note that, unlike the position for detailed assessment hearings, the receiving party must file any "without prejudice save as to costs" and CPR Part 36 offers (in a sealed envelope marked "Part 36 or similar offers", but which does not reveal which

---

[4] Note that in the SCCO only para.13 of the Hearings and Detailed Assessments in the Senior Courts Costs Officer Judge July 2020, issued for the foreseeable future as a result of the Covid-19 pandemic, provides that "the receiving party will not be required to file papers in support of the bill unless expressly requested by the court".

party/ies have made the offers). The rationale is obvious – parties are not present to draw the attention of the court to any relevant offers as they would be at the end of a detailed assessment. CPR PD 47 para.14.3(d) is clear that all offers must be filed, but only those made under CPR Pt 36 or which are "without prejudice save as to costs" should be in a sealed envelope. In other words, the open offer required under CPR PD 47 para.8.3 should not be in the sealed envelope, but should be available for the assessing judge to view.

(ii) The assessment
Strictly there is no requirement either for the court to fix a date for a provisional assessment or to give notice of it as CPR PD 47 paras 13.4 and 13.6 do not apply (which might explain the logic behind CPR PD 47 para.13.11 not applying, but 13.12 applying—see para.**8–10** above) and the parties are not permitted to attend the assessment. The only obligation on the court is to use its best endeavours to undertake the assessment within six weeks of receipt of the request.[5] In practice in the SCCO and the County Court, non-attended hearing dates are being allocated—in other words, the judge has time specifically allocated in the list to deal with a provisional assessment even though no parties attend. Some come with a further order that should the court be able to undertake the assessment at an earlier date it will do so without notice to the parties. The rationale behind these orders is understandable. The costs judges and the District Bench simply cannot accommodate these assessments in addition to other work requirements and so discrete time is made available within lists. However, should lists go short and there not be other work, then the further order enables the court to undertake these assessments earlier than listed.

CPR r.47.15(4) is clear that the assessment is based on the information in the bill, the supporting papers and the contentions in Form G (the Points of Dispute and any Reply to it). Documents filed beyond those required by the rules (e.g. lengthy skeleton arguments) and not by specific requests from the court, may be ignored by the assessing judge. The rules specify what documents must be considered and there is no obligation on the assessing judge to look at further documents filed unbidden (particularly when the time set aside for the assessment will not have been based on consideration of unrequested paperwork).

(iii) After the assessment
After the assessment the court will return the Form G (and the bill or any other documents, if decisions have been recorded on these). Whilst CPR PD 47 para.14.4(2) suggests that the court's decisions will be on the Form G, the decisions may be on that, may be on the bill or on a separate document—for example where the court is giving a written judgment on a substantive point and there is insufficient room to do this on the bill or Form G. On this point parties would be well advised, when not filing electronically in an alterable

8–12

8–13

---

[5] CPR PD 47 para.14.4(1).

form, to allow sufficient space for the judicial decision—too often a lengthy Point and Reply are followed by an utterly inadequate box for the reasoned determination. Some judges are requesting that Form G is filed electronically in an alterable form so they may type the decisions (to avoid the problems of deciphering handwriting) and so it is possible to expand the decision box for there to be sufficient space for these to be recorded.

The parties must agree the amount at which the court has assessed the bill within 14 days of receipt of the Form G and any other documents recording decisions. Any party wishing to challenge any aspect of the provisional assessment must file and serve a written request for an oral hearing within 21 days. If no request for an oral hearing is filed and served within that period then, save in exceptional circumstances, the provisional assessment is binding.

Practice varies on how costs of the provisional assessment itself are assessed where there is no challenge to the assessment. Some courts make costs orders when conducting the provisional assessment on alternative bases depending on whether any offers prove to be relevant. This becomes more complicated when the bill, or part of it, is subject to the proportionality cross-check under CPR r.44.3(2)(a) after the court has determined what is the reasonably incurred and reasonable in amount sum and even after it has made some proportionality rulings on discrete items as it undertook the reasonableness assessment. (See **Q26** below.)

The costs of the assessment are subject to the provisions of CPR r.47.20 and the general rule is that the receiving party is entitled to the costs. CPR r.47.15(5) caps the maximum costs the court will award to either party (other than the costs of drafting the bill and excluding court fees and VAT) at £1,500 (subject to CPR r.47.20(4)—see **Q28** and analysis of the decisions in *Lowin v W Portsmouth & Co Ltd*[6] below).

(iv) Oral hearings and appeals

8–14 Any written request for an oral hearing must identify the item(s) challenged and provide a time estimate for the hearing of the challenge(s). On receipt of the notice, the court will then fix a date for the hearing, giving notice of at least 14 days to the parties.

The party requesting the oral hearing will pay the costs of that hearing unless it achieves an adjustment in its favour of 20% or more of the sum provisionally assessed or the court orders otherwise. This potential costs penalty clearly is designed to preclude minor challenges. On a bill where the costs are limited to £75,000 anything other than a challenge to an item of substance is unlikely to result in a 20% adjustment. There is limited guidance in CPR PD 47 para.14.5 as to when the court may order otherwise, indicating that conduct and offers will be taken into account. As yet no authorities have

---

[6] *Lowin v W Portsmouth & Co Ltd* [2016] EWHC 2301 (QB); [2017] C.P. Rep. 1 and *W Portsmouth and Company Ltd v Lowin* [2017] EWCA Civ 2172; [2018] 1 W.L.R. 1890.

emerged to supplement this guidance. (See **Q29** for consideration of the position where a CPR r.47.20 Part 36 offer is relevant.)

It is worth reiterating that a request for an oral hearing, as opposed to an application for permission to appeal, is the correct procedure to challenge any decision made on a provisional assessment. The case of *PME v The Scout Association*[7] serves as a warning that if a party wishes to appeal determinations made by an Authorised Costs Officer on a provisional assessment pursuant to CPR rr.47.21–47.24, that may only be in respect of decisions that were challenged under the right to request an oral hearing. Even though the provision at CPR r.47.24 refers to a "re-hearing", the court concluded that this can only apply to decisions made at a hearing (and in the provisional assessment process, the only hearing from which to seek a re-hearing is the oral hearing). By cross-application, it would seem that any appeal from a judge on a provisional assessment, would be similarly limited. Whether this will result in parties taking a scattergun approach to points challenged in an oral hearing, so as to preserve more points for a possible appeal, remains to be seen. The December 2021 minutes of the CPRC presage revisions to CPR PD 47 to reflect this decision.

A final word

Those keen to ensure that they comply with all relevant rules in the light of   **8–15**
the more robust compliance regime now in place may find it a relief that CPR
PD 47 para.14.2(2) does not require compliance with CPR PD 47 para.13.9 as
this provision does not seem to exist.

Payment on account

Prior to April 2013 where the court made an order that a party was to pay costs   **8–16**
it could order a payment on account of those costs pending an assessment.
There was no presumption that it would do so, as was made clear in *Blackmore
v Cummings*.[8] The April 2013 reforms reversed this by the introduction of
CPR r.44.2(8), which provides that where the court makes a costs order and
provides for a detailed assessment of those costs, then it will order a reasonable sum on account of those costs, unless there is good reason not to do so
("good reason" is considered in **Q41** below). The vexed issue of payments
on account under deemed orders has finally been resolved by higher court
intervention. The suggestion that the wording of CPR r.44.2(8) precluded payments on account other than at the time of making the costs order, so excluding both subsequent applications in those cases and any applications under
deemed costs orders, has been rejected. In *Global Assets Advisory Services Ltd v
Grandlane Developments Ltd*[9] the Court of Appeal concluded that:

---

[7] *PME v The Scout Association* [2019] EWHC 3421 (QB); [2019] Costs L.R. 2003.
[8] *Blackmore v Cummins* [2009] EWCA Civ 1276; [2010] 1 W.L.R. 983.
[9] *Global Assets Advisory Services Ltd v Grandlane Developments Ltd* [2019] EWCA Civ 1764; [2019] Costs L.R. 1597.

- there can be no reason to conclude that the power contained in CPR r.44.2(8) can or should only be exercised by the judge who has heard the substantive proceedings; and
- no distinction is to be drawn between those orders for costs that are deemed and those that are not. As per [18] of the judgment "in both circumstances something should be paid without delay."

(This topic is dealt with in more detail in **Q42** below.)

In pursuit of proportionality of process, the court is likely to adopt a robust procedure when determining the amount of any payment on account. In *Kazakhstan Kagazy Plc v Zhunus*[10] Leggatt J (as he then was) was asked to list a half-day day hearing to determine the amount of any payment. In dealing with the matter without a hearing he concluded:

"The third request made in the claimants' letter is that, if the court intends to make an order for a payment on account of costs, a half day hearing should be fixed for this purpose for which the claimants would wish to instruct a specialist costs counsel. Not only is this request contrary to the terms of the order agreed by the claimants for the matter to be dealt with on paper, but to incur the costs of a half day hearing to argue about the amount of a payment on account of the costs of a two day hearing would be utterly disproportionate and wasteful."

The quantification of the amount of the payment on account (including the relevance of budgeted costs) is considered at **Qs 38** and **39** below.

Questions and answers

Summary and detailed assessment

Q1. At the end of a fast track trial or any other hearing lasting no longer than one day, but in a case or application to which fixed costs apply, should a party seeking costs have filed and served Form N260?

8–17   The simple answer is that in fixed costs cases there is no requirement to serve/ file Form N260. This is because CPR r.44.6 provides that:

"(1) Where the court orders a party to pay costs to another party (other than fixed costs) it may either –
(a) make a summary assessment of the costs; or
(b) order detailed assessment of the costs by a costs officer,
unless any rule, practice direction or other enactment provides otherwise.
(Practice Direction 44 – General rules about costs sets out the factors which will affect the court's decision under paragraph (1).)
(2) A party may recover the fixed costs specified in Part 45 in accordance with that Part."

---

[10] *Kazakhstan Kagazy Plc v Zhunus* [2015] EWHC 404 (Comm); 158 Con. L.R. 253.

This is supported by CPR PD 44 para.9.1, which provides:

"Whenever a court makes an order about costs which does not provide only for fixed costs to be paid the court should consider whether to make a summary assessment of costs."

However, there will still be instances where a party seeking costs in a fixed costs case ought still to file a Form N260. Examples are where a disbursement which is sought to be recovered is not fixed within the scheme (e.g. CPR r.45.29I(2C)) or where a party seeks to persuade the court to exceed the fixed recoverable costs, as if successful the court may then summarily assess the costs (CPR r.45.29J(2)(a)).

Q2. Who is able to sign the certification on the statement of costs? Who can sign a costs statement within a firm of solicitors? Has the certification altered as a result of the 113th update to the Civil Procedure Rules? Is proper certification, whether of a statement of costs or a bill of costs important?
CPR PD 44 para.9.5(3) provides that the statement of costs must be signed.   **8–18**
It specifies that this must be by the party or the party's legal representative. "Legal representative" is defined in CPR r.2.3 as meaning:

- a barrister;
- a solicitor;
- a solicitor's employee;
- the manager of a body recognised under s.9 of the Administration of Justice Act 1985; or
- a person, who for the purposes of the Legal Services Act 2007 is an authorised person in relation to an activity which constitutes the conduct of litigation (within the meaning of that Act).

The form of the certification has not been altered by the amendments made to "statements of truth" by the 113th CPR update, nor was there any recommendation that it should be in the Civil Justice Council report of Guideline Hourly Rates (although it suggested other changes to Form N260). For Forms N260 and N260A the certification remains:

"The costs stated above do not exceed the costs which the is liable to pay in respect of the work which this statement covers. Counsel's fees and other expenses have been incurred in the amounts stated above and will be paid to the persons stated."

Although the question deals with the certification of a statement of costs, it is worth making the general point that the decision in the case of *Barking, Havering & Redbridge University Hospitals Trust v AKC* (a protected party by Litigation Friend MCK)[11] albeit considering the signature on a bill for detailed

---

[11] *Barking, Havering & Redbridge University Hospitals NHS Trust* [2021] EWHC 2607 (QB).

assessment, is a timely reminder that the court regards certification as an important matter, citing the comment from *Bailey v IBC Vehicles Ltd*[12] that certification "is no empty formality". There is every reason to suppose that the court views the certification on statements of costs for summary assessment in the same way.

Q3. What is the position when Form N260 is either served/filed late or not at all?

8–19   CPR PD 44 para.9.6 maintains the previous position—namely that a failure to file and serve Form N260 without reasonable excuse will be taken into account when the court determines what order to make about costs of the claim or hearing (as appropriate) and about the costs of any further hearings/ assessments which the failure may necessitate (so the failure is relevant both to the award, as well as the amount, of assessed costs).

The leading pre-April 2013 authority on this provision is *MacDonald v Taree Holdings Ltd*.[13] The appellate court held that despite the use of the word "must", the provision is not mandatory and the judge had been wrong to refuse the successful party's application for summary assessment of his costs on the grounds that he had not served a statement of costs upon the respondent 24 hours in advance. The court made a distinction between cases where there had and had not been factors aggravating the failure to serve a statement. If there were no aggravating features, then a party should not be deprived of all his costs. The court should take the matter into account, but its reaction should be proportionate. In these cases, the court was presented with three options as follows:

- Whether it would be appropriate to have a brief adjournment for the paying party to consider the statement and then to proceed to a summary assessment of the costs. In such a case the "sanction" was that the judge should err in favour of awarding a lighter figure.
- Whether the matter should be stood over for a detailed assessment.
- Whether the matter should be adjourned for summary assessment at a later date or for summary assessment to be dealt with in writing.

8–20   Does this approach survive the April 2013 reforms? In *Webb v E-Serv*,[14] albeit in an entirely different context of considering the time period to renew a request for permission to appeal, Turner J held that the word "must" did convey a mandatory requirement. If this applied to a failure to comply with the provisions of CPR PD 44 para.9.5 a party otherwise entitled to a costs order may not secure it as that provision makes the preparation, lodging and serving of a statement of costs a condition precedent to applying for costs

---

[12] *Bailey v IBC Vehicles Ltd* [1998] 3 All ER 570.
[13] *MacDonald v Taree Holdings Ltd* [2001] C.P.L.R.439; [2001] 1 Costs L.R.147 Neuberger J.
[14] *Webb Resolutions Ltd v E-Surv Ltd* [2014] EWHC 49 (QB); [2014] 1 Costs L.R. 182 Turner J.

(CPR PD 44 para.9.5 refers to the fact that a party intending to seek costs must prepare a written statement and CPR PD 44 para.9.5(4) states that this must be filed and served the prescribed amount of time before the hearing).

Whilst, reported cases until 2019 suggested that the court was still resisting complete disallowance of costs, the case of *R (on the application of) Kuznetsov v London Borough of Camden*[15] comes as a stark reminder that a failure to comply may result in no award of costs. In that case, Mostyn J issued a clear warning to those appearing before him:

> "*It is my practice in such circumstances, where the court is charged with a duty to bring closure by summary assessment, and where there is a positive duty to file a Form N260, the legal advisers having failed to do so they, having made that bed, must lie in it and they will not get an award of costs.*" para.39

However, in *Wheeler v Chief Constable of Gloucestershire Constabulary*,[16] neither party had filed a statement of costs in advance of an appeal. The upshot for the successful party was an order for costs to be the subject of a detailed assessment, but with the receiving party to pay the costs of those proceedings.

In contrast, in *Kingsley v Orban*,[17] where the successful party had filed and served a statement late and the first instance court had pressed on and assessed those costs without any concession to the late service, the appellate court looked at whether there were aggravating factors, determined there were not, but that the first instance court ought to have adjourned for a short period to allow the paying party time to consider the statement before proceeding to assess, and allowed the paying party to raise further points on appeal (all of which failed). However, it is worth mentioning that the judgment makes no reference to the decision in *Wheeler*, instead determining that there was no reason not to apply *MacDonald*.

A halfway house was adopted by Akenhead J in *Group M UK Ltd v Cabinet Office*,[18] where a statement of costs was served only three hours before the handing down of a judgment when costs would be considered and, even then, that N260 did not contain the breakdown of time spent on documents. Akenhead J applied the *Denton v TH White*[19] "three-stage" test to the breaches, concluding that the breaches were serious, that there was good reason for them and that it would be wholly disproportionate to allow no costs and, instead, imposed a "delay discount" of £2,240 as a sanction for what he described as a breach "at the lower end of serious".

8–21

Reference is made at para.8–03 above to some parties using "homemade" versions of Form N260. A regular omission from these is a breakdown of the document time. Whilst there is no authority on this, it is conceivable that the court may regard the *Group M UK Ltd* "sanction" approach as of application

---

[15] *R (on the application of) Kuznetsov v London Borough of Camden* [2019] EWHC 3910 (Admin).
[16] *Wheeler v Chief Constable of Gloucestershire Constabulary* [2013] EWCA Civ 1791.
[17] *Kingsley v Orban* [2014] EWHC 2991 (Ch) Nugee J.
[18] *Group M UK Ltd v Cabinet Office* [2014] EWHC 3863 (TCC); [2014] 6 Costs L.R. 1090 Akenhead J.
[19] *Denton v TH White* [2014] EWCA Civ 906; [2014] 1 W.L.R. 3926.

in such a situation—and disallow all or part of the document time (the sanction being directly linked and limited to the breach). In *Changing Climates Ltd v Warmaway*[20] when confronted by a "home-made" statement of costs that was not in N260 format, the court concluded that it could only adopt a broad brush looking at overall costs, observing that:

> "*The problem…I have with this schedule is that that detail* [the detail under the correct headings in N260] *is not given and it is much harder for the court to assess, and for defendant to make detailed submissions as to, whether something is reasonable or proportionate in amount in the absence of the level of detail you would expect and the categorisation in the usual form.*"

Inevitably decisions will be case specific. For example, whilst it may be appropriate to adjourn some cases for a detailed assessment where there is failure to file and serve a statement, if this failure were to occur in respect of a discrete application where the costs would be minimal, the court may take the view that an adjournment for a subsequent summary or detailed assessment in such a case would, applying the overriding objective, be disproportionate (even if the receiving party had to pay the costs of the assessment, as court time would have to be allocated to this). In such a case the court may determine that the successful party forfeits the right to a costs order on the application or as in *R. (SRA) v Imran*,[21] where no statement of costs was produced, make only a notional costs award. Dove J explained this as follows:

> "*However, it does seem to me that the respondent having been successful, I should assess costs. And I am going to do so in a notional figure of £5,000. That is the best I can do. Adding to the costs of the proceedings by ordering detailed assessment seems to me to be quite disproportionate.*" At [42].

Avoid the uncertainty and the risk—comply both with the form of the costs statement and the provisions for service and filing of it!

Q4. Does the requirement for a breakdown of time spent on documents on the Form N260 mean that the court will deal with challenges to this on an item-by-item basis or will the court make one overall assessment of time spent on documents?

8-22   Notwithstanding the additional information provided in the documents schedule to the costs statement, the process remains a summary assessment. As such it would be inappropriate to expect the court to resort to micromanagement. The schedule to N260 was not introduced to turn summary assessments into quasi detailed assessments. Indeed, in his Final Report Jackson LJ indicated that he thought the "old" N260 was adequate in respect of interim applications. His concern was that:

---

[20] *Changing Climates Ltd v Warmaway* [2021] EWHC 3117 (TCC).
[21] *R. (SRA) v Imran* [2015] EWHC 2572 (Admin); [2015] A.C.D. 134.

"... in respect of summary assessments at the end of a trial or appeal, I consider that Form N260 provides insufficient information. The court is assessing not only costs related to the trial or appeal, but also the costs of the whole pre-trial process. In the short term, I recommend that a revised and more informative version of Form N260 be prepared for use in connection with summary assessments at the end of trial".

Whilst we would expect the court to entertain submissions that the document time is unreasonable by reference to some examples from the schedule, the court is extremely unlikely to determine disputes over individual items in the schedule—rather it will use the schedule to inform the decision over the total document time that is reasonable or the total time for a particular task, e.g. drafting statements.

A useful illustration of a summary assessment of a costs managed case using Form N260 is *Slick Seating Systems v Adams*.[22] The trial judge had also case and costs managed the case throughout. In fact, he concluded that an award of indemnity costs was appropriate (and duly assessed those summarily), but his approach amply illustrates the benefits of costs management as he was able to avoid a detailed assessment (as would probably have been the outcome prior to the costs management regime) and undertake the simplest of summary assessments as follows:

"By running this case with a costs budget, I approved a budget of a grand total of £359,710.35 pence for doing this case through to trial. In my judgment that budget was proportionate to what was at stake: the £4.4 million sum that I have just awarded. The claimants have laudably kept within that budget and have exercised due control over their activities and expenditure in an exemplary fashion. The statement of costs on 13.5.13 (which is today) is favourably compared with the costs estimate of 22.5.12. The form is signed by the partner of the solicitors and a member of the client company as well, Mr Beasley; the grand total is £351,267.35 pence. In my judgment that is a sum which is, looking at each of the phases, within the budget that was set and the claimants are to be commended with controlling the budget throughout this particular period.
That will be the sum that I would award to be paid within 14 days without the need for detailed assessment, detailed assessment becoming otiose ..."

Even where there is an argument on "good reason" it may still be possible to dispose of this at a summary assessment, avoiding the costs, time and delay of an assessment. Precisely this occurred in *Sony Communications International AB v SSH Communications Security Corp*.[23]

It is worth giving thought to those multi-track cases that may be suitable for summary assessment at the case management stage. This is so any appropriate orders may be made (such as for the filing and service of Forms N260

---

[22] *Slick Seating Systems v Adams* [2013] EWHC 1642 (QB); [2013] 4 Costs L.R. 576 HH Judge Simon Brown QC.
[23] *Sony Communications International AB v SSH Communications Security Corp* [2016] EWHC 2985 (Pat); [2016] 4 W.L.R.

and Precedents Q in cases in which that would not automatically occur—e.g. trials over one day) and so that the trial timetable provides time for the exercise, should the court accede to the request to conduct a summary assessment.

Q5. How does the proportionality cross-check at CPR r.44.3(2)(a) work in the summary assessment process that is already one undertaken with a broad brush?

8-23   In *Morgan v Spirit Group Ltd*,[24] the Court of Appeal made the obvious point that the court must undertake either a summary or detailed assessment of the costs. The judge had not done so. Instead, in a paragraph, the judge had simply determined a proportionate figure and added something to that to allow for the existence of what he had, erroneously, described as "a contingent fee agreement". Summary though the assessment is intended to be, the court concluded that what had taken place here was not a summary assessment. So, summary though the procedure may be, it must still recognisably be an assessment.

These comments resonate loudly under the post-March 2013 regime, where the court is required to undertake an assessment of what is reasonably incurred and reasonable in amount for those items reasonably incurred and then step back and apply the proportionality cross-check under CPR r.44.3(2)(a). Even though the Court of Appeal in *West v Stockport NHS Foundation Trust*[25] concluded that it is possible for the assessing judge to deal with the proportionality of a particular item of costs whilst undertaking line by line reasonableness, it accepted that reasonableness and proportionality are conceptually different. If the summary assessment is too summary, then the court will struggle to draw a distinction between the determination of what is reasonable and the determination of what is proportionate. The court must undertake the determinations of reasonableness and proportionality applying identifiably different factors, as to do otherwise makes the flawed assumption that the conclusions always elide. They do not. Whilst they will in some cases, they will not in others. There will be cases where the reasonable costs fall within what is proportionate (in which case the court need do no more than articulate that, having considered the factors at CPR r.44.3(5) and/or any "wider circumstances" under CPR r.44.1(1), the reasonably assessed costs are also proportionate), but there will also be cases where the reasonable costs are not proportionate (in which case the court then determines the figure that is proportionate and assesses the recoverable costs in that sum—see **Ch.3** on proportionality for more detail as to how the court will undertake this exercise).

Q6. Albeit in a family context, does not the case of *SB v MB (Costs)*[26] suggest that summary assessment is confined to fast track trials and other hearings lasting a day or less?

---

[24] *Morgan v Spirit Group Ltd* [2011] EWCA Civ 68; [2011] 3 Costs L.R. 449.
[25] *West v Stockport NHS Foundation Trust* [2019] EWCA Civ 1220; [2019] Costs L.R. 1265.
[26] *SB v MB (Costs)* [2014] EWHC 3721 (Fam).

In *SB v MB (Costs)* Hayden J declined to undertake a summary assessment as   **8–24**
to do so was "likely to fall foul" of what was para.13.2 of the Costs Practice
Direction. In fact, the relevant provisions he identified of what was para.13.2
(namely that this was not a fast track trial and that the hearing had exceeded
one day) are in the same terms as what now appears at CPR PD 44 para.9.2(a)
and (b). However, it is clear that the possibility of "falling foul" of the Practice
Direction was not determinative. Hayden J had already identified that there
were elements of costs which would require consideration beyond the time
and information available to the court that day. As such there was no need for
the court to consider the application of the "general rule" at what is CPR PD
44 para.9.1 and was Costs PD para.13.1 and the other steers referred to above
illustrating that CPR PD 44 para.9.2 is not an inflexible straitjacket (e.g. CPR
PD 29 para.10.5).

**Q7. Does the decision in *Transformers and Rectifiers Ltd v Needs Ltd*[27]
mean that summary assessments of the costs (a) of applications, whether
disposed of either at a hearing or on the papers and, (b) after trials, may be
conducted by a judge other than the one who dealt with the application/
trial?**

As set out at para.8–02 above, CPR r.44.1 seems clear that if there is to be a   **8–25**
summary assessment after a hearing or a trial, this can only be undertaken by
the judge who conducted the hearing or trial. Strictly this definition does not
seem to apply where an application is disposed of on the papers, as was, in
fact, the case in *Transformers and Rectifiers Ltd*. This is because CPR r.23.8 makes
it clear that the court may "deal" with an application without a hearing. In
this situation the less prescriptive provisions of CPR PD 44 para.9.7 apply.
Applying these the court reached its conclusion by noting the substitution
of the word "may" in the current version instead of the word "must" in the
previous versions in the phrase "may give directions as to a further hearing
before the same judge" and interpreted this as permissive of a summary assessment by another judge, stating that:

> "The provision at paragraph 9.7 of the PD is permissive: if time does not permit
> the summary assessment then and there, it may be heard later by the same judge.
> Equally, therefore, it may be heard by another judge."

If this interpretation is correct and any judge may deal with the summary
assessment at a further hearing, then what purpose do the words "by the same
judge" serve in CPR PD 44 para.9.7? The alternative construction, and one
that makes use of the words "by the same judge" purposeful, is that where a
summary assessment is appropriate, but not possible immediately upon disposal of an application, the word "may" is permissive of a choice, between
either a summary assessment at a later date before the same judge or of a
detailed assessment.

---

[27] *Transformers and Rectifiers Ltd v Needs Ltd* [2015] EWHC 1687 (TCC); [2015] 3 Costs L.R. 611.

Q8. If an award of costs is made, but the summary assessment of them is deferred to a later date (for example if there is not sufficient time for this to take place immediately at the end of the hearing to which it relates), can a CPR Part 36 offer be made in respect of the costs by either party?

8–26   First, we must make two general points:

- In an ideal world this situation should not arise as time estimates should be sufficient for the disposal of the substantive matter, the award of any costs and, if the decision is to undertake a summary assessment of those costs, that assessment (save in the Shorter Trials Scheme—see **para.8–06** above). However, even with the best case and hearing management this situation still arises.
- If the situation arises because the receiving party did not comply with the requirement to file and serve Form N260 when required, in time or at all, then this question becomes superfluous if the court has already made an order that the defaulting receiving party pays the costs caused by having to reconvene for a later summary assessment (see **Q3** above).

However, the position is not straightforward if there is a simple order that, for example, A is to pay B's costs of the claim/hearing, to be assessed by summary assessment before the judge who conducted the trial/hearing at a date to be fixed (which is sufficiently far enough ahead to enable time for a valid CPR Part 36 offer to be put—see CPR rr.36.3(g) and 36.5).

The argument in favour of CPR Pt 36 applying is purely procedural. CPR r.36.2(3) states that:

"(3) A Part 36 offer may be made in respect of the whole, or part of, or any issue that arises in—
(a)a claim, counterclaim or other additional claim; or
(b)an appeal or cross-appeal from a decision made at a trial."

The determination of the amount of costs in a summary assessment under a costs order is a part of, or an issue that arises in, a claim.

The procedural arguments against CPR Pt 36 applying are that:

- The costs consequences in CPR r.36.17 are expressly stated to apply where judgment is entered. This is not the language of an assessment of costs. At the end of a summary assessment an order for payment of costs is made.
- Similarly the wording of CPR r.36.13(4)—in particular references to "the claim" and to "trial" do not resonate with the language of an assessment of costs.
- This language disconnect is supported by the fact that to apply CPR Pt 36 to detailed assessment proceedings: (i) the CPR has to make express provision for this to take place (see CPR rr.47.20(4) and (7))—and we pause to ask why this is necessary if CPR Pt 36 automatically cross-applies to detailed assessments anyway? And (ii) CPR r.47.20(4)(a)–(e) has to set out

various definitions (including the meaning of "judgment being entered") without which the provisions of CPR Pt 36 would make no sense in this context. There are no similar procedural provisions in respect of summary assessment (understandable as the rule makers, no doubt, intended these to be undertaken at the end of the trial/hearing in which the costs order had been made).

- Even though appeals are expressly included within the CPR Pt 36 regime (see CPR r.36.2(3) set out above) as the terminology of appeals does not sit happily with that of a claim/counterclaim or additional claim, CPR r.36.4(2) sets out an enabling definitions table. As stated in the bullet point above, there is no such provision to equate the terminology of CPR Pt 36 with that of a summary assessment.

- The requirement to file and serve costs statements two days before a fast track trial and 24 hours before any other hearing suggests that the rule makers did not envisage CPR Pt 36 applying to summary assessment, given that this would not permit offers to be made that allow the "relevant period" for acceptance.

We are of the view that as CPR Pt 36 is a self-contained procedural code, that summary assessment is not expressly brought within this rule (in the way detailed assessment is under CPR r.47.20) and that the language of summary assessment does not sit happily with the language of CPR Pt 36 enabling any easy implied inclusion, then CPR Pt 36 does not apply to a summary assessment.

In *Best v Luton & Dunstable Hospital NHS Foundation Trust*,[28] the court declined to apply Part 36 after a summary assessment of the costs of a detailed assessment (in other words, when it was asked to deal with the costs of the costs of the costs!). It did so on the basis that the costs of a detailed assessment are not an "issue that arises in the claim", making it clear that a summary assessment of such costs is not an independent claim (as opposed to the detailed assessment proceedings themselves which are under CPR r.47.20).

The process for summary assessment of costs in the Shorter Trials Scheme may provide an opportunity for further authority on this point, if it is required, depending upon whether there is time between the parties filing and exchanging schedules of their costs and the subsequent summary assessment, for CPR Part 36 offers to be made (see para.8–05 above for consideration of summary assessment within this scheme). We say if it is required, because the Minutes of the Civil Procedure Rules Committee for April 2021 reveal that the Association of Costs Lawyers has raised the matter and it is, at the time of writing, still being considered by the Costs Sub-Committee. The December 2021 minutes of the CPRC reveal that it considered the case of *Best* and concluded that there was no need for any rule changes and that the omission of the costs of the detailed assessment proceedings themselves from the Part 36 regime was deliberate. The CPRC consulted the Senior Costs

---

[28] *Best v Luton & Dunstable Hospital NHS Foundation Trust* [2021] EWHC B2 (Costs).

Judge who confirmed that "he and the other costs judges he has consulted, consider that the decision in *Best* is probably correct" and that he recalls that the intended scope of Part 36 "was not intended to address the costs of the detailed assessment process."

Q9. Should a party making an application that, if successful, will dispose of the claim (e.g.to strike it out) file Form N260 to cover the costs of the entire claim as well as Form N260 to cover just the costs of the application?

8–27   Yes. If the court strikes out a claim, then under CPR r.3.4(3) it may make any consequential order it considers appropriate. Presumably the successful party will ask the court to award that party its costs of the claim, to include the costs of the application itself. If the hearing has taken no more than a day, then the rules dictate that there will be a summary assessment and so Form N260 for the entirety of the costs is required. As the court may not strike out the case, but might still award the applicant its costs of the application, it would be prudent to file and serve a separate Form N260 in respect of the application costs alone.

Q10. Does a party commencing detailed assessment proceedings also need to file a copy of the bill at court at the same time?

8–28   This question arises out of perceived uncertainty in CPR PD 47 para.5.1A, which expressly deals with the requirements when commencing detailed assessment proceedings under CPR r.47.6. CPR PD 47 para.5.1A provides:

> *"Whenever electronic bills are served or filed at the court, they must also be served or filed in hard copy, in a manageable paper format as shown in the pdf version of Precedent S. A copy of the full electronic spreadsheet version must at the same time be provided to the paying party and filed at the court by e-mail or other electronic means."*

The second sentence has been understood by some to suggest that the requirement to file and serve arises even where only service has taken place under the terms of the first sentence, as it contains no "or" qualification.

Our view is that:

- the use of the word "or" in the first sentence clearly indicates that the filing of the bill in hard copy is only required when the bill is filed in electronic form;the second sentence merely clarifies what must be provided and how it must be served if an obligation arises under the first sentence either to file or to serve.[29]

In other words, the second sentence does not require a party to file the bill, when it has only served it on the paying party.

---

[29] A view shared by the Senior Costs Judge, albeit as a "personal view" and whilst recognising that there might be a case for clarifying the second sentence of CPR PD 47 para.5.1A.

It is worth remembering that CPR PD 47 para.5 comes under the heading "Commencement of detailed assessment proceedings: rule 47.6" and that the rule itself refers only to service and not to filing—echoed by CPR PD 47 para.5.2, which refers only to service on the commencement of detailed assessment proceedings. The specific procedural provisions upon requesting a detailed assessment hearing are found at CPR PD 47 para.13.2 and include the filing of a copy of the bill (CPR PD 47 para.13.2(b)). At that stage the requirements under CPR PD 47 para.5.1A become relevant.

It might have been clearer had the references to filing a bill been removed from CPR PD 47 para.5 and inserted instead under CPR PD 47 para.13 or, at least, had there been cross-referencing between paras 5 and 13 to remove the anomaly of something not required under CPR r.47.6 featuring under the section of the PD accompanying that specific part of the CPR.

As a more general point on filing, the provisions of CPR PD 47 para.51B require a party filing an electronic bill under the electronic working pilot (CPR PD 51O see para.8–09 above), to upload both a spreadsheet and a PDF version, but not to file it by any other means.

Q11. How can a receiving party comply with the obligation to serve the new bill electronically if the paying party has not previously agreed to electronic service or has no method of receiving the bill electronically?
The starting point must be whether, in fact, there is an obligation to serve   8–29
the bill electronically. CPR PD 47 para.5.1A imposes an obligation upon the receiving party to provide the full spreadsheet bill electronically (whether by email or some other electronic means). Does "provide" equate to "serve" in this context? Our view is that it does not as this section of the PD uses both words, suggesting that the semantic distinction is made deliberately. Although CPR PD 47 para.5A.4, dealing specifically with transitional provisions, expressly requires service of the electronic bill, this does not appear to add anything as compliance with this service obligation falls within CPR PD 47 para.5.1A as that provision applies "whenever electronic bills are served or filed at court". Whether our interpretation of the provision is correct or not the requirement "to provide" is still mandatory, so, in practical terms, is there any difference? It seems to us that this can only be looked at in terms of the consequence of non-compliance. No prescribed outcome is specified for breach of the obligation, so that will be a matter of judicial discretion. It is hard to imagine that any sanction imposed will be different from one that relates to a failure to serve, as whether the requirement is to serve or provide, the intent is that the paying party receives the bill in spreadsheet form and a failure to provide prevents that happening.

In the light of the conclusion above it is important to understand the procedural requirements that govern an obligation to "provide" electronically. CPR r.6.20(1)(d) governs electronic service of documents other than the claim form and specifies that this is in accordance with the provisions of CPR PD 6A. The relevant provisions of CPR PD 6A at paras 4.1 and 4.2 are that:

"4.1. . .where a document is to be served by fax or other electronic means—
(1) the party who is to be served or the solicitor acting for that party must previously have indicated in writing to the party serving—

(a)   *that the party to be served or the solicitor is willing to accept service by fax or other electronic means; and*

(b)   *the fax number, e-mail address or other electronic identification to which it must be sent; and*

(2) the following are to be taken as sufficient written indications for the purposes of paragraph 4.1(1)—

(a)   *a fax number set out on the writing paper of the solicitor acting for the party to be served;*

(b)   *an e-mail address set out on the writing paper of the solicitor acting for the party to be served but only where it is stated that the e-mail address may be used for service; or*

(c)   *a fax number, e-mail address or electronic identification set out on a statement of case or a response to a claim filed with the court.*

4.2 Where a party intends to serve a document by electronic means (other than by fax) that party must first ask the party who is to be served whether there are any limitations to the recipient's agreement to accept service by such means (for example, the format in which documents are to be sent and the maximum size of attachments that may be received)."

However, it is here that the strict semantic distinction may be relevant. If provision is not service, then it is arguable that CPR PD 6A paras.4.1 and 4.2 strictly do not regulate the obligation under CPR PD 47 para.5.1A. If that is correct, then provision to an email address or other electronic communication address absent agreement of the recipient to accept service at it may be sufficient. However, as the position is far from clear, then until there is clarity on the point, and as the obligation to provide is mandatory, paying parties may consider it prudent to adopt counsel of caution under CPR PD 47 para.5.1A and ensure compliance with CPR PD 6A paras.4.1 and 4.2. In so doing it seems from this that the following possibilities arise:

i)   Where the paying party has previously agreed to service of documents by electronic means, then the receiving party must still contact the paying party prior to provision to comply with CPR PD 6 para.4.2.

ii)   If the receiving party is aware of a method for electronic service of the paying party, but there has either been no written indication that it will accept service in that form, or it has expressly declined so to do, then a specific request seeking written agreement to provision of the spreadsheet bill by this method and raising the issue in CPR PD 6 para.4.2 must be made. The paying party should also be asked to provide written confirmation of an alternative method of electronic provision if it declines to accept by the method identified by the receiving party.

iii) If the receiving party is unaware of any method by which electronic provision may be effected on the paying party, then the receiving party should contact the paying party asking it to identify a method by which it will accept electronic provision, confirming any restrictions under CPR PD 47 para.4.2.

In each scenario, the receiving party should afford the paying party a specified reasonable period to respond and provide the information required. Given the mandatory wording of CPR PD 47 para.5.1A it seems sensible that the request should also state that in the absence of a satisfactory response (including one that there is no available method of electronic provision) within that period, then the receiving party will have to apply to the court prior to commencement of the detailed assessment proceedings, to dispense with the requirement to provide the bill electronically. A paying party unable to provide a method for electronic provision would be well advised to consent to such an application.

For assessment proceedings commenced within the electronic working pilot, para.8.2 of CPR PD 51O is clear that:

> "*Unless the Court orders otherwise, any document filed by any party or issued by the Court using Electronic Working in the Rolls Building Jurisdictions, B&PC District Registry, the Central Office of the Queen's Bench Division or the Costs Office, which is required to be served shall be served by the parties and not the Court.*"

Q12. When is use of the electronic bill mandatory? Is use of the electronic bill required in Judicial Review claims?
CPR PD 47 para 5.1 sets out when the electronic bill must be used. This is when: 8–30

> "*(a) the case is a Part 7 multi-track claim, except—*
>   (i)   *for cases in which the proceedings are subject to fixed costs or scale costs;*
>   (ii)   *cases in which the receiving party is unrepresented; or*
>   (iii) *where the court has otherwise ordered; and*
> (b) *the bills of costs relate to costs recoverable between the parties for work undertaken after 6 April 2018 ('the Transition Date').*"

Obvious though it may be, it is worth noting that the procedural provision makes no distinction between bills that will fall within the provisional assessment regime and those that will proceed to a detailed assessment hearing.

CPR r.54.1(2)(e) provides that the CPR Pt 8 procedure applies to claims for Judicial Review. Accordingly, Judicial Review claims do not fall within the definition of those cases where use of the electronic bill is mandatory.

Q13. Who is responsible for the costs of providing the breakdown required in a model form like Precedent Q?

8–31   If an electronic bill is used, then so long as the electronic bill provides fully the information required by Precedent Q that document becomes superfluous (CPR PD 47 para.5.2(f)). However, if the information is not so provided and Precedent Q is required as a free-standing document, then this forms part of the bill preparation item. As such, subject to the receiving party being awarded the costs of the assessment, then it should recover the reasonable and proportionate costs of preparation of the form. However, if time has not been recorded in a fashion that leads to easy allocation to a particular phase, what is reasonable and proportionate may be the source of some argument— (the same point applies to bill preparation time, including in respect of electronic bills if the time recorded post-6 April 2018 is not clearly allocated and results in increased bill preparation time).

Q14. Does the requirement to file and serve a statement of costs under CPR PD 44 para.9.5 apply to cases in which a costs management order has been made? Does the answer differ depending upon whether the hearing to which the costs relate is listed for more than one day?

8–32   Costs managed cases are not excluded from the provisions of CPR PD 44 para.9. As the provisions of para.9 apply to costs managed cases, then the general rules at para.9.2 introduces the distinction between cases/hearings that last no longer than one day. However, this does not prevent a party seeking a summary assessment in a costs-managed case, even if the case/hearing lasts in excess of a day (see the provision at para.9.1).

However, parties should be astute to the fact that if there are interim applications that are made in a costs-managed case, but these were reasonably not included in the budget, then the costs of such applications will be dealt with outside of the budget. In this situation parties, seeking costs in a hearing lasting no longer than a day, must file and serve a statement of costs in accordance with para.9.5(3) in the usual way.

Q15. Is a party limited to claiming published Guideline Hourly Rates on a summary assessment? Given the move to remote working as a result of the Covid-19 pandemic, is the Guideline Hourly Rate that where the work has been done by individual fee earner, if that is different from the rate for the location where the solicitors' firm on the court record is based? Are the new Guideline Hourly Rates retrospective?

8–33   The rates are guideline rates only. As a result, parties may, and routinely do, insert other rates. It is then up to the court to determine the hourly rate. It does so by reference to the factors at CPR r.44.4(3).

The rates have been updated following the recommendations made in Civil Justice Council Final report on Guideline Hourly Rates in April 2021 ("CJCFR"), which were accepted by the Master of The Rolls. The new rates, and the revised guide to summary assessment were implemented from 1 October 2021. When seeking rates above the guideline figures on a summary assessment the following provisions of the revised guide merit consideration:

- The guideline figures are intended to provide a starting point for those faced with summary assessment (para.28).
- In substantial and complex litigation an hourly rate in excess of the guideline figures may be appropriate for grade A, B and C fee earners where other factors, for example the value of the litigation, the level of the complexity, the urgency or importance of the matter, as well as any international element, would justify a significantly higher rate. It is important to note (a) that these are only examples and (b) they are not restricted to high level commercial work, but may apply, for example, to large and complex personal injury work. Further, London 1 is defined in Appendix 2 as "very heavy commercial and corporate work by centrally based London firms". Within that pool of work there will be degrees of complexity and this paragraph will still be relevant (para 29). This provision has been deliberately extended from its predecessor to include grades B and C fee earners.

On the other side of the coin, those seeking to argue that a receiving party should recover less than the guideline rate should note that the fact that para.29 of the revised guide does not mention a reduction in rate "was not an oversight by the working group. The reasons why a possible reduction are not specified is (a) if a costs judge considers that the work does not warrant a Grade A-C fee earner, the usual way of reflecting this is by allowing the work done at the rate of a lower grade fee earner, though (b) the judge always has a discretion to allow a lower rate than GHR" (para.8.9 of the CJCFR).

The question concerning remote working is one that the change in working practices as a reaction to the Covid-19 pandemic has highlighted. It was an issue considered by the Civil Justice Council working group in its Consultation Report in January 2021. It concluded as follows:

"Another suggestion was that the report be paused because of the effect Covid-19 was having on the business models of solicitors' firms. It was not within our remit to pause the review. Nor did we believe it to be necessary or appropriate. We have taken this factor into account in our recommendation for a further review within a relatively short period of time." (Para.3.2)

When accepting the Civil Justice Council recommendations, the Master of the Rolls announced that there will be a further review of guideline hourly rates, reporting within two years. He has already charged the Civil Justice Council with working on this. The expectation is clear, that by then the long-term impact that Covid-19 has had on working arrangements should be clear and consideration will need to be given then to how, if at all, this will be acknowledged in the application of rates.

The CJCFR was clear in rejecting arguments seeking to limit the retrospective effect of the updated rates, saying only that "the new rates...should be used on summary assessments which are carried out after the [implementation]date" Para.10.2 of the CJCFR. As already stated, the implementation date was 1 October 2021. However, there is a caveat to this. It is important to remember that these rates are not "fixed fees", and so they do not operate as an exception to the indemnity basis. As a result, solicitors hoping to rely upon the increased rates (as the rates for all grades of fee earner in each band were increased) must ensure that their solicitor client rates at least match the updated rates for the periods for which they claim them (see **Q2** above identifying the certification required on a statement of costs).

Q16. What are "good reasons" to depart from budgeted costs at a detailed assessment? Does a reduction in the hourly rate of incurred costs at assessment amount to a "good reason" to depart from budgeted costs under CPR r.3.18?

8–34   "Good reason" (including in respect of hourly rates) is covered in Ch.4 at para.4–20 and in Qs 96–98. Note the position in respect of costs management orders in respect of agreed incurred costs considered in **Ch.4** at **Q90**.

Q17. Does QOCS apply to the detailed assessment procedure, where the claimant has been successful in proceedings which included only a claim for personal injury, but failed to beat a relevant CPR Part 36 offer at detailed assessment and has been ordered to pay the defendant's costs of assessment procedure?

8–35   The answer appears to turn on a question of interpretation, namely whether the detailed assessment procedure is part of the proceedings under CPR r.44.13(1). Whilst there is an increasing body of case law relating to various issues associated with QOCS, there has not been a reported authority directly on this point. However, the Court of Appeal in *Brown v Commissioner of Police of the Metropolis* considered the correct interpretation of "proceedings" and "claims" for the purpose of Section II of CPR Pt 44. Whilst this was in the context of determining the application of QOCS in mixed claims under CPR r.44.16(2)(b), the court gave what it described as a "sensible and straightforward interpretation of the rule", in these terms:

> "What is the proper interpretation of the words 'other than a claim to which this Section applies'? It seems to me quite clear. 'This Section' is the Section of the CPR setting out the QOCS regime. Rule 44.13(1) identifies the three types of claim which are covered by that regime: they are claims for damages for personal injury. Thus, if the proceedings also involve claims made by the claimant which are not claims for damages for personal injury (that is to say, claims 'other than a claim to which this Section applies'), then the exception at r.44.16(2)(b) will apply."

Does this assist in answering the question posed? At first blush, it does. Claimants bringing proceedings to claim for personal injury, seek costs consequential upon success in such a claim. They include the claim for costs in the prayer for relief at the end of the claim form and particulars of claim. As such, the claim for costs is part of the claim for personal injury and is brought within proceedings to which the QOCS protection from enforcement applies (subject to set-off under CPR r.44.14(1) against damages and interest that will apply in the context of this question, as it is put on the basis that the claimant has been successful in the claim for damages). Further support may be gleaned for this interpretation from the case of *Serbian Orthodox Church – Serbian Patriarchy v Kesar & Co*[30]. Albeit when dealing with the issue of service (and in particular whether the service of notice of commencement of costs assessment proceedings was to be equated with service of originating process for the purposes of CPR r.6.15), the court concluded:

> " I accept that the detailed assessment of costs is a distinct phase of the proceedings, with a distinct process for commencement. However, I do not accept that this is equivalent to the commencement of originating process…The commencement of "detailed assessment proceedings" is the next step in the proceedings…"

Recently, the Supreme Court in *Ho v Adelekun*,[31] which considered the issue of set-off within the QOCS regime specifically referred to the potential for a defendant obtaining an order for costs in its favour within detailed assessment proceedings as being one of the key examples of where opposing costs orders "may occur in a single set of proceedings" (see paras 6 and 7). The court proceeded on the express basis, both by reference to the facts of the case and in considering the generally applicable principles, that this was a situation where QOCS applied. However, there was no argument on the point.

Notwithstanding the above, the wording of CPR r.44.14(2) appears to support the contrary view:

> "44.14(2) Orders for costs made against a claimant may only be enforced after the proceedings have been concluded and the costs have been assessed or agreed."

The use of the word "and" suggests that the process of assessment or agreement of costs is in addition to, and separate from, the proceedings, which conclude at the end of the substantive dispute involving one of the types of claim in CPR r.44.13(1). On this strict construction basis the rule seems to point to the conclusion that QOCS protection does not apply to the costs of the detailed assessment process. However, clearly there is no authority directly on point and there are strong arguments both ways. However, the semantic interpretation of the CPR r.44.14(2) gains further support from these rule provisions:

- CPR Pt 47 (Procedure for assessment of costs and default provisions), which in r.47.1 clearly identifies the necessity of the "proceedings" being

---

[30] *Serbian Orthodox Church – Serbian Patriarchy v Kesar & Co* [2021] EWHC 1205 (QB).
[31] *Ho v Adelekun* [2021] UKSC 43, [2021] 1 W.L.R 5132.

concluded before the assessment procedure may commence, making it clear that the detailed assessment procedure is not part of the proceedings:

> *"47.1 The general rule is that the costs of any proceedings or any part of the proceedings are not to be assessed by the detailed procedure until the conclusion of the proceedings, but the court may order them to be assessed immediately."*

- CPR r.47.20(7) which, albeit in the context of consideration of CPR Pt 36, expressly provides that detailed assessment proceedings "are to be regarded as an independent claim". That independent claim is clearly for costs and not for personal injury damages.
- The acceptance in *Parker v Butler*[32] that "not every step in proceedings (broadly defined) which began with a claim for personal injuries is included in the definition of the word 'proceedings' as used in CPR r.44.13"—although it is accepted that *Parker* decries attempts to exclude appeals from the QOCS regime, stating that this "would do nothing to serve the purpose of the QOCS regime", and the same might be said of the separation of the substantive claim and the costs of the substantive claim.

Albeit in costs-only proceedings, Sharpe LJ concluded in *Tasleem v Beverley*[33] that:

> *"The bringing of Part 8 costs-only proceedings is not the commencement of, or part of, the detailed assessment proceedings, albeit it is a necessary preliminary to that process if there are no underlying proceedings in existence. This is because detailed assessment proceedings are distinct from the proceedings whether under Part 7 or Part 8 which have given rise to the costs order (see CPR rule 47.6(1))"*

Also, in costs-only proceedings, but phrased in far wider terms, a distinction was drawn in *Crosbie v Munroe*[34] between the proceedings for the substantive remedy and, thereafter, and quite separately, the subsequent proceedings for the assessment of the costs liability of the paying party:

> *"Until the time the substantive claim is settled, the 'proceedings' relate to liability and the amount of any compensation. After the substantive claim is settled, the 'proceedings' relate to the assessment of the costs the paying party has to pay."*

This may all be a moot point where it matters not by what route the claimant has to pay any costs of the detailed assessment (namely where the damages are such that QOCS protection would not prevent off-setting in full anyway against damages and it is only the route by which the court reaches this outcome that turns on the construction of "proceedings"), but, where there is insufficient to off-set, this argument is pertinent.

(See **Ch 6 Q12** for further consideration of *Ho* in this context.)

---

[32] *Parker v Butler* [2016] EWHC 1251 (QB); [2016] 3 Costs L.R. 435.
[33] *Tasleem v Beverley* [2013] EWCA Civ 1805; [2014] 4 Costs L.O. 551.
[34] *Crosbie v Munroe* [2003] EWCA Civ 350; [2003] 3 Costs L.R. 377.

Q18. Is there any sanction if a paying party fails to make an open offer under CPR PD 47 para.8.3? Is a party permitted to make an open offer of nil under CPR PD 47 para.8.3?

On the face of it no sanction applies to this provision. However, the Court 8–36 of Appeal expressly considered provisions of the CPR which contain mandatory language, but where no sanction is provided for any failure to comply in *Altomart v Salford Estates (No.2) Ltd.*[35] The court accepted the proposition that there might be implied sanctions which were capable of engaging CPR r.3.9 and equally there might be cases not analogous with CPR r.3.9 and where it was a matter for the court to determine the consequence of non-compliance.

Accordingly, it seems that if a paying party wishes to rely on an open offer made after the service of the Points of Dispute, where no such offer accompanied that document, then, by implication the court should approach this as analogous to an application for relief from sanction. The outcome of any applications made by "receiving parties" for some sort of sanction are far less predictable. It is clear that the open offer does not form part of the Points of Dispute (it merely accompanies that document) and therefore it is difficult to see how any argument suggesting that the Points of Dispute should be struck out will find favour (indeed there is a risk it will be seen as an attempt to turn the rules into "tripwires" and invoke possible costs sanctions). Perhaps a more measured approach is to identify the failure to comply to the paying party promptly, suggesting a short period for rectification, and, in default of compliance reserve the position to the question of costs of the assessment, if relevant, under "conduct" within CPR r.47.20(3)(a).

The question of whether a party complies with the obligation under CPR PD 47 para.8.3 by making an open offer of "nil" is an interesting academic one. However, as a matter of practice the answer is clearly "yes, it does comply". This is because the Practice Direction requires an open offer of "a sum, if any . . ." The logic is obvious. Clearly the rules cannot compel a party to offer money when its primary position is that nothing is due (e.g. there is no valid retainer). However, expect the court to scrutinise carefully the reasons for such an offer to prevent an abuse of process (most challenges to the indemnity principle are standardised and not based on any information leading to a dispute.)[36] A better approach may be to make an open offer of "nil" with reasons, but also to add an open offer in the event that the primary case fails. This way the parties may narrow the dispute by agreeing the costs, subject to resolution of the primary issue. Adopting this approach lends some credence to the primary point (in that it is not being advanced simply to avoid giving a figure) and is clearly proportionate, in that it is a genuine attempt to narrow the issues. Given that those advancing a potential knockout primary point in Points of Dispute invariably go on to raise other points in more traditional

---

[35] *Altomart v Salford Estates (No.2) Ltd* [2014] EWCA Civ 1408; [2014] 6 Costs L.R. 1013.
[36] As per CPR r.47 PD 13.2(i).

fashion, in the event that their primary case fails, it should not add any cost to calculate what qualified open offer to make as a secondary position.

Q19. Precedent S only includes certain defined contingencies within its phases—namely applications. Does this not make budget/spend comparison on other budgeted Precedent H contingencies more difficult, time-consuming and expensive?

8–37   Whilst the headline figures for contingencies will appear in the summary of budget v bill on worksheet 10 of Precedent S, the detail is more difficult to analyse. This is because the phase code for contingencies, P11, only covers various types of applications (see worksheet 15).

What of contingent work budgeted unrelated to the costs of an application? If the contingency budgeted relates to one of the named phases, and it occurs, presumably the work is included within that phase. However, when one looks at the task codes (and, indeed, the activity codes) within the phases it becomes apparent that using those alone, it will be impossible within the phase to identify the work attributed to the original phase budget and that attributed to the contingency. It seems that to check the attribution of costs in the worksheet 10 summary one must look at the description of the individual items of work on worksheet 14 in the hope that it is sufficiently specific to enable division between the phase and the contingency. If the contingency does not relate to work that can be linked to an existing phase, then where does that appear in the bill, as there is no phase code that enables categorisation?

However, the new bill is a work in progress. Use is bound to result both in improvements and the emergence of practical solutions. It is a shame that there was not greater uptake of the SCCO pilot, to provide the learning experience at an earlier stage.

Wholly unrelated to the questions above, is the oddity that 20 years after the terminology changes introduced by the introduction of the CPR in 1999, Precedent S refers to "interlocutory" as well as "interim" applications.

Q20. If a bill is served in a case which has been costs managed and the bill is divided into the required parts under CPR PD 47 para.5.8(7), but no Precedent Q or equivalent has been served, can the receiving party request a default certificate if Points of Dispute are not served within the time specified under CPR r.47.9(2)?

8–38   The answer seems obvious. In such a situation the receiving party is not entitled to a default costs certificate (save where the qualification in the brackets in CPR PD 47 para.5.2(f) applies and this is considered in the final paragraph of this answer). However, the question raises some interesting points, which highlight inconsistent wording in the CPR and what may be a theoretical flaw with Form N254. Neither makes us reconsider our conclusion and we use the word "theoretical" because we assume that a party in breach of a requirement of the CPR would not take advantage of an omission in a prescribed court form to circumvent the consequence of that breach.

CPR r.47.6(1) provides that detailed assessment proceedings are commenced when the receiving party serves on the paying party the notice of commencement, a copy of the bill or copies of the bill of costs as required under CPR PD 47 and, where required under CPR PD 47, a breakdown of the costs claimed for each phase of the proceedings (Precedent Q or equivalent). This is reinforced by CPR PD 47 para.5.2 which sets out all the documents that must also be served on commencing detailed assessment proceedings and which is, in fact, more extensive than the requirement in CPR r.47.6. Accordingly, it seems clear that a failure to serve Precedent Q or an equivalent breakdown, means that detailed assessment proceedings have not been commenced. Inevitably, as a result, any request for a default costs certificate is inappropriate.

The procedural inconsistency of wording is that CPR r.47.9 refers to the obligation to serve Points of Dispute being triggered by service of the Notice of Commencement and not to the Notice of Commencement and other specified documents. Whilst this creates scope for argument that a failure to serve specified documents does not prevent a request for a default costs certificate if the notice of commencement is served, this must be a specious argument, as it does not negate the fact that where there has been a breach of the requirements of CPR r.47.6(1)(a)–(c) there are no detailed assessment proceedings.

The oddity of Form N254 is that it does not make any reference to all the documents mentioned in CPR PD 47 para.5.2, instead simply requiring confirmation that the receiving party has served the notice of commencement, the bill and a copy of the document giving the right to detailed assessment on the paying party. If a receiving party has simply served the three documents referred to in the preceding sentence, then strictly it can properly sign the certificate on Form N254. If it does so and files this, then even if it has not served the other documents required on the paying party under CPR PD 47 para.5.2, the court will issue a default costs certificate as an administrative exercise as there will be no way for it to know that not all required documents have been served.

The qualification to which we have referred in the first paragraph above, is that no separate breakdown in Precedent Q or equivalent is required where an electronic bill is used and this information is fully provided within that bill. In Precedent S there is a page entitled Summary of costs as claimed vs amounts in last approved/agreed/submitted budget (p.10 of Precedent S) that does provide the requisite breakdown.

B Provisional Assessment

Q21. Does the £75,000 limit for provisional assessment include or exclude VAT?

This is a purely procedural point. CPR r.47.15 and its PD provisions describe the limit of £75,000 as being in respect of costs. The definition of "costs" in CPR r.44.1 does not include a reference to VAT (albeit that this is not an exhaustive list)—in fact, VAT is defined separately in the same rule.

8–39

Accordingly, it seems that the £75,000 limit does not include VAT and refers to the total profit costs and disbursement sum. There is also a clear logic to this. Why should one bill fall within the scheme and one not where the difference is the VAT and one party is VAT registered and the other is not where the non-VAT sums claimed are equal? Notwithstanding this, some practitioners are not completing the provisional assessment part of Form N258 and are requesting detailed assessment hearings where the total sum only exceeds £75,000 because of the VAT.

Q22. Does the £75,000 limit for provisional assessment include "additional liabilities" (where the transitional provisions still permit recovery of these between the parties)?

8–40   In a different context, in *BNM v MGN Ltd*[37] the Court of Appeal concluded that the post-31 March 2013 definition of costs in CPR r.44.1(1) does not include additional liabilities. However, the upshot of *BNM* was not that recoverable additional liabilities were not costs at all, but rather that they were costs, but under the pre-April 2013 rules, as what was CPR r.43.2(1)(a) included "additional liabilities" in the then definition of costs. This might suggest that as additional liabilities are still costs, then they should be included for the purpose of determining whether the "costs" are £75,000 or less. However, the current CPR r.44.1 expressly applies to Pts 44 to 47 unless the context requires otherwise. On that basis, it is the current definition of "costs" that determines what is included when determining whether the limit under CPR r.47.15(1) has been exceeded. If this interpretation is correct, then bills that may total significantly in excess of £75,000 due to high percentage success fees or costly insurance premiums will fall within the provisional assessment scheme. This has not been our experience. Certainly, in editions prior to *BNM*, we had taken the view that additional liabilities were included when calculating costs for the purpose of the cap. It may be that this is an occasion when the court will have to grapple with the qualification "unless the context otherwise requires" in CPR r.44.1(1), although with the reducing numbers of cases in which additional liabilities remain recoverable it may be that this is already a vanishingly thin occurrence.

Q23. There seems to be a feeling that a receiving party who does not serve Replies to the Points of Dispute is at a disadvantage at a provisional assessment. Should receiving parties serve Replies in this situation as a matter of course?

8–41   CPR r.47.13, which makes Replies optional, and CPR PD 47 para.12, which requires Replies to be limited to points of principle and concessions, both apply to provisional assessment by virtue of the provisions of CPR PD 47 para.14.2. Accordingly, the court ought not to be penalising a party who complies with these provisions. Indeed, the reverse is true and the court ought to

---

[37] *BNM v MGN Ltd* [2017] EWCA Civ 1767; [2017] 6 Costs L.O. 829.

be astute not to entertain replies that contain "general denials, specific denials or standard form responses". Replies should not be filed as a matter of routine and there should be no disadvantage to the receiving party as a result.

By the same token, paying parties should not serve "extended" Points of Dispute in an attempt to make up for the fact that there will be no opportunity for oral submissions. CPR PD 47 para.8.2 is unambiguous—Points of Dispute must be "short and to the point".

Useful guidance on these twin requirements has been given in the case of *Ainsworth v Stewarts Law LLP*.[38] Although this was a case involving a solicitor-client assessment, the Court of Appeal had to consider the form that Points of Dispute under CPR PD 47 para.8.2 should take. Its conclusion, which applies equally to "between the parties" assessments was that the provision:

"... *makes it absolutely clear that points of dispute should be short and to the point and, therefore, focussed. Furthermore, sub-paragraphs (a) and (b) leave no doubt about the way in which the draftsman should proceed. General points and matters of principle which require consideration before individual items in the bill or bills are addressed, should be identified, and then specific points should be made 'stating concisely the nature and grounds of dispute.' ... Common sense dictates that the points of dispute must be drafted in a way which enables the parties and the court to determine precisely what is in dispute and why. That is the very purposes of such a document. It is necessary in order to enable the receiving party, the solicitor in this case, to be able to reply to the complaints. It is also necessary in order to enable the court to deal with the issues raised in a manner which is fair, just and proportionate.*" [37] and [38]

Q24. What papers should a receiving party file in support of a bill for a provisional assessment?[39]

The challenge of what documents to file and when to do so is considered at para.8–10 above. It may be that any uncertainty arises out of the use of different terms in CPR r.47.15 — "supporting documents" and "supporting papers". The starting point must be CPR r.47.15 (3) and (4). The former provides that the court will undertake a provisional assessment on receipt of, amongst other things, the relevant supporting documents specified in PD 47 and the latter provides that the court will undertake the provisional assessment based on the information contained in the bill and supporting papers and contentions set out in Precedent G. Reference to "supporting papers" leads to CPR PD 47 para.13.12, which does apply to provisional assessments under CPR PD 47 para.14.2(2), and which identifies "papers to be filed in support of the bill". This lists the following documents:

8–42

---

[38] *Ainsworth v Stewarts Law LLP* [2020] EWCA Civ 178.
[39] Note the question and reply are predicated on the basis that the assessment is not in the SCCO. In respect of assessments in the SCCO see para. 8–11 above and Hearings and Detailed Assessments in the Senior Courts Costs Office Practice Note by the Senior Costs Judge, July 2020.

- Instructions and briefs to counsel arranged in chronological order together with all advices, opinions and drafts received and response to such instructions.
- Reports and opinions of medical and other experts.
- Any other relevant papers.
- A full set of any relevant statements of case.
- Correspondence, file notes and attendance notes.

In other words, the "papers to be filed in support of the bill" are exactly the same whether the bill proceeds by way of a provisional assessment or at a detailed assessment hearing.

The reference to relevant supporting documents in CPR r.47.15(3) is because the obligation on the receiving party requesting a provisional assessment extends further than simply filing the papers in support. The receiving party must also file the documents referred to in CPR PD 47 para.14.3, namely:

- A copy of the open letter from the paying party with the offer that accompanied the Points of Dispute under CPR PD 47 para.8.3 (experience suggests that in practice this is rarely, if ever, included).
- The documents referred to in CPR PD 47 para.13.2.
- An additional copy of the bill, including a statement of the costs claimed in respect of the detailed assessment drawn on the assumption that there will not be an oral hearing following the provisional assessment.
- The offers made (with those made "without prejudice as to costs" or under Part 36 in a sealed envelope).
- A completed Form G.

Where there is a difference between supporting papers in provisional assessments and in respect of bills proceeding to a detailed assessment hearing is the timing for filing these. In the former the combination of CPR r.47.15(3) and CPR PD 47 para.14.4(1) suggests that all the documents, including the papers in support must be filed with the request for the assessment (an alternative construction of these provisions would seem to mean that the court need do nothing, and certainly not undertake a provisional assessment, unless and until it has received both the N258 and all the supporting documents). In the latter the time for filing the papers in support is governed by CPR PD 47 para.13.11.

Q25. Is there a sanction if the receiving party fails to file the required documents with the request for provisional assessment and can this be rectified? If so how?

8–43   What is the position if a receiving party fails to file the documents required by the rules or by specific order? One possible answer adopting the approach to CPR r.47.15(3) and CPR PD 47 para.14.4(1) in the way considered in the brackets in the penultimate paragraph of para.8–42 above, is that the court simply does not undertake the provisional assessment unless and until there is compliance. As the court does not now simply let matters sit in abeyance, the likelihood is that if the court did decide that receipt of all documents was a precondition of there being a provisional assessment, it would make an "unless order" providing for a period within which the breach should be remedied and, in the absence of compliance, the bill would be assessed at nil.

However, what seems to be happening is that the court is listing and undertaking the provisional assessment. What happens then if there has not been compliance? This was precisely the position that confronted the court in *Mehmi v Pincher.*[40] The Points of Dispute raised a dispute about the receiving party's liability to pay costs to his solicitor. In breach of CPR PD 47 para.13.2(i) the receiving party failed to file the requisite documentation in respect of his retainer agreement. The assessing judge provisionally assessed the costs at nil. The claimant requested an oral hearing and applied for relief from sanction under CPR r.3.9. These were listed together and the relief application was taken first. The court concluded that the decision was a sanction and so CPR r.3.9 applied, dismissed the application for relief and upheld the nil assessment as a result. On appeal the court concluded that the PD itself did not prescribe an explicit sanction for non-compliance and nor could one be implied. Instead, as part of the assessment of costs, the court had simply concluded that on the available evidence there was a breach of the indemnity principle and so assessed the costs at nil, rather than imposing that assessment outcome as a sanction for non-compliance. The appeal was allowed and the matter was remitted for the oral hearing, with an indication that CPR PD 47 para.13.13 could be used by the court to afford the receiving party another opportunity to file the missing documentation.

In addition, the court highlighted in the judgment a standard order in use in that court to address routine non-compliance with CPR PD 47 para.13.2(i). That order provided for:

- an adjournment of the provisional assessment to a later date;
- the use of CPR PD 47 para.13.13 to make an "unless order" requiring compliance, with default resulting in an assessment at nil and an adverse costs order; and,
- prospective reduction of 50% of any costs of the provisional assessment to which the receiving party might subsequently become entitled if there was compliance with the "unless order", presumably in recognition of, and as a sanction for, the original non-compliance with CPR PD 47 para.13.2.

---

[40] *Mehmi v Pincher County Court* unreported 20 July 2015 (Liverpool) HHJ Wood QC.

This decision raises three interesting procedural issues, as follows:

(1) Does the reference to "any document" in CPR PD 47 para.13.13 include documents that the receiving party ought to have filed anyway under the mandatory requirement at para.13.2? In strict terms there can be no doubt that where there is a dispute about retainer, the actual retainer documents are understandably necessary to enable the court to reach its decision on this issue—falling within the wording of the provision. Similarly, the rule refers to "any" and not "any further" document. However, it seems illogical that one element of a specific procedural provision makes the filing of identified documents mandatory, whilst another element affords an unfettered opportunity for the court to disregard this without any involvement of either party.

(2) CPR PD 47 para.13.2 is mandatory—it uses the word "must". There is a body of post-March 2013 authority in different contexts e.g. time for renewing a request for permission to appeal at an oral hearing (under what was CPR r.52.3(5))[41] and applying promptly to set aside judgment in default (CPR r.13.3(2)),[42] suggesting that even though no sanction is prescribed, the word "must" means that when considering any extension of the time permitted for compliance with CPR PD 47 para.13.2(i), the court should still consider the three stages set out in *Denton v TH White Ltd*.[43] Accordingly, either if the court of its own volition engages CPR PD 47 para.13.13 to remedy a breach of the requirements of 13.2 (ignoring the question posed in (1) above and assuming that it can do so), or whether it requires the receiving party to apply retrospectively to extend the time period for compliance with 13.2, the ultimate decision requires a reasoned judgment.

(3) Is it proportionate to adjourn the provisional assessment to permit late compliance with the filing obligation? The court will have lost the time already set aside and will have to allocate a further provisional assessment listing. The alternative is that the court proceeds with the assessment and is likely to conclude that the retainer is not proved and assess the costs at nil and leaves it to the receiving party to decide whether to apply for an oral hearing and an extension of time within which to comply with CPR PD 47 para.13.2(i)—a route that may (as opposed to definitely will) lead to further court time being expended. It is right to record that the court in *Mehmi* did implicitly consider this in the broader context of managing a large court where the issue had been occupying significant resources and explicitly felt an adjournment preferable to the "more cumbersome process of the inevitable oral review".

---

[41] *Webb Resolutions Ltd v E-Surv Ltd* [2014] EWHC 49 (QB); [2014] 1 Costs L.R. 182.
[42] *Mid East Sales Ltd v United Engineering & Trading Company (PVT) Ltd* [2014] EWHC 1457 (Comm); [2014] 4 Costs L.O. 605.
[43] *Denton v TH White Ltd* [2014] EWCA Civ 906; [2014] 1 W.L.R. 3926.

One unarguable certainty is that compliance with the documentary filing requirements avoids many "interesting procedural issues".

Q26. How does the court deal with the proportionality cross-check after a provisional assessment where the assessed bill is returned to the parties to do the arithmetic?[44]

With more cases now falling under the new proportionality provisions of CPR r.44.3(2)(a) rather than the old *"Lownds"* provisions (see **Ch.3— Proportionality**), this has become a pertinent issue. It is unlikely that the court will calculate the total of the bill immediately after assessing what is reasonably incurred and reasonable in amount (not only because CPR PD 47 para.14.4(2) places the responsibility for agreeing the total sum at the door of the parties—and that is not amended in the light of the introduction of electronic and self-calculating bills—but also because of the time it may take to do this in non-electronic bill cases and just in case the court makes an arithmetical mistake—even spreadsheets may sometimes not format properly and so self-calculate incorrectly).

8–44

There are two schools of thought, namely:

(i) The court returns the bill, the Form G and any separate rulings to the parties to do the arithmetic, but adds an order as follows (or in similar terms):

> *"The proportionate sum pursuant to CPR r.44.3(5) factors is £x. If the reasonably incurred and reasonable in amount costs exceed £x when the bill is recalculated then anything over £x is disproportionate and the bill is provisionally assessed at £x. If the reasonably incurred and reasonable in amount costs are less than £x when the bill is recalculated then those costs are proportionate and the bill is provisionally assessed in the recalculated sum."*

This completes the provisional assessment and time for requesting an oral hearing is triggered by this order.

(ii) The court requires the parties to confirm the recalculated sum after assessing what was reasonably incurred and reasonable in amount, together with any submissions on proportionality. This is then referred back to the assessing judge to determine proportionality. Having done so the bill is then returned to the parties provisionally assessed in the recalculated sum, if it was proportionate, or, provisionally assessed in a lower figure (being the sum determined proportionate) if the recalculated sum was disproportionate. The provisional assessment is only completed for the purpose of the time for requesting an oral hearing at this stage.

---

[44] We remain of the view that the proportionality cross-check under CPR r.44(3)(2)(a) should be done as a separate exercise after the reasonable costs have been determined notwithstanding the suggestion that this is not necessarily the case in *May v Wavell* unreported 22 December 2017 County Court (Central London)—see **Ch.3** at para.3–03 and **Q13** above.

The decision of the Court of Appeal in *West v Stockport NHS Foundation Trust*[45] that any proportionality reductions must be by categories of costs, specific periods of costs or particular parts of the profit costs, creates difficulties with both these approaches that had adopted a global proportionality assessment. Whilst a global assessment of proportionality is still an appropriate starting and finishing point, if the reasonably assessed costs are determined, by that route, to be proportionate, it can only be the starting point, and not the finishing point, if the reasonably assessed costs are higher than that global proportionality assessment. This is because the court may only, then, consider reductions to achieve global proportionality, by reference to categories of costs, periods of costs and parts of costs.

It remains to be seen how courts undertaking provisional assessments will adapt their practices to apply the *West* approach. However, a very real concern for the court (in terms of allocation of time) and the parties (in terms of additional work within a capped costs scheme) is that the court will need more from the parties than simply compliance with CPR PD r.47.14.4(2) and the provision of the total figure in which it has assessed the bill, if it is to consider proportionality reductions by reference to categories of costs and specific periods or parts of costs. Our view is that with electronic bills, the court is likely to rely upon the self-calculated figures for reasonable costs after determination of those, assuming the bill to be correctly formatted—which is, of course, the responsibility of the receiving party anyway under CPR PD 47 para.5.A2(d)—and move immediately on to an overall determination of proportionality and if that leads to the requirement for reduction look to the detail of the bill to identify categories, periods or parts that are disproportionate. In the remaining non-electronic bills, then parties are likely to find specific orders made for provision of more detail after the determination of the reasonable costs, simply to enable proportionality to be considered.

Q27. Does the costs cap include or exclude success fees (where the transitional provisions still permit recovery of success fees between the parties)?

8–45   Until the decision of the Court of Appeal in *BNM v MGN Ltd*[46] we had confidently stated that the costs cap may include both base costs and success fees, with the qualification that combined they cannot exceed £1,500. We gave the following examples to illustrate this:

- If the base costs are assessed at £750 and the success uplift is allowed at 100%, then both base costs and success fees are recoverable in full, as together they do not exceed the cap.
- If the base costs are assessed at £1,000 and the success uplift is allowed at 100%, then the base costs are recoverable in full, but only £500 of the success fee is recoverable.

---

[45] *West v Stockport NHS Foundation Trust* [2019] EWCA Civ 1220; [2019] Costs L.R. 1265.
[46] *BNM v MGN Ltd* [2017] EWCA Civ 1767; [2017] 6 Costs L.O. 829.

- If the base costs are assessed at £1,500 and the success uplift is allowed at 100%, then the base costs are recoverable in full, but none of the success fee is recoverable.

However, for the reasons set out in **Q22** at para.**8–40** above, the decision in *BNM*, albeit not on this point and in which this issue was not considered, has compelled both further consideration and a different conclusion. If, as *BNM* decided, additional costs do not fall within the CPR r.44.1(1) definition of costs and the current definition of "costs" applies to the use of this word in CPR r.47.15(5) (as CPR r.44.1(1) states that it does, "unless the context otherwise requires"), then the cap does not include success fees. As a result, it appears that success fees are recoverable (subject to reasonableness and proportionality) even if the combination of costs under CPR r.44.1(1) and the success fees exceed £1,500. We suspect that this is not the way most had interpreted and applied the cap prior to *BNM*. It may be that this is another occasion when the court will have to grapple with the qualification "unless the context otherwise requires" in CPR r.44.1(1), but again on the basis that with the reducing numbers of cases in which additional liabilities remain recoverable it may be that this is already a vanishingly thin occurrence.

Q28. Can the court make an award of indemnity costs under CPR r.36.17(4)(b) in provisional assessment proceedings and, if so, what, if any effect does this have on the costs cap of £1,500.

The starting point is that CPR r.36.17(4) is relevant in provisional assessments by virtue of CPR PD 47 para.14.2, which applies CPR r.47.20 to these proceedings. There is no doubt that the result of these provisions is that the court must make an award of indemnity costs to the receiving party who has made an effective offer under CPR r.36.17(1)(b) in a provisional assessment unless the court considers it is unjust to do so (CPR r.36.17(4)). However, how does an order for indemnity costs interact with the cap on costs at CPR r.47.15(5)?

8–46

In a previous edition we noted that hot on the heels of the decision in *Broadhurst v Tan*,[47] which provided that an award of indemnity costs to a claimant under CPR r.36.17(4)(b) in a fixed costs regime case under CPR r.45 permits escape from that regime, came the case of *Lowin v W Portsmouth & Co Ltd*[48] and the apparent answer to this question. In this case, on the first appeal, the court concluded that an effective CPR Part 36 offer made by a receiving party meant that it was no longer constrained by the costs cap in CPR r.47.15(5). The court determined that as CPR PD 47 para.14.2(1) applies CPR r.47.20 and, therefore, by cross- application CPR Pt 36 to provisional assessments, had the rule-makers not intended the award of indemnity costs under CPR r.36.17(4)(b) to include the possibility that the receiving party would receive in excess of the cap, the rule would expressly say so.

---

[47] *Broadhurst v Tan* [2016] EWCA Civ 94; [2016] 1 W.L.R. 1928.
[48] *Lowin v W Portsmouth & Co Ltd* [2016] EWHC 2301 (QB); [2017] C.P. Rep. 1.

However, we ventured to suggest that this argument had not run its course, suggesting that there were valid arguments to permit the contrary conclusion, namely that:

(i) There was nothing in the provisions of CPR r.47.15, 47.20 or 36.17(4) or the practice direction to CPR r.47 which provided that the £1,500 cap does not apply when there is an award of indemnity costs under CPR r.36.17(4).

(ii) There is a distinction between fixed costs (as in *Broadhurst*) and a cap (as in *Lowin*). In a fixed costs regime the award of indemnity costs under CPR r.36.17 is purposeless unless the claimant escapes the fixed costs regime as the end outcome is still the prescribed fixed cost sum. Under a cap there remains the possibility that an award of indemnity costs may make a difference e.g. if the reasonable and proportionate costs of a provisional assessment on the standard basis are less than £1,500, but with the removal of proportionality considerations the costs on the indemnity basis are higher than the costs that would have been awarded on the standard basis.

(iii) The decision would have the undesirable effect of reducing the incentives on parties to keep the costs of a provisional assessment as low as possible in recognition of the cap.

The first appeal decision of Laing J was, itself, appealed. In *W Portsmouth and Company Ltd v Lowin*[49] the Court of Appeal decided that whilst an award of indemnity costs could be made in respect of the costs of provisional assessment, costs assessed under such an award could not exceed the cap in CPR r.47.15(5). In reaching this conclusion the Court of Appeal determined that:

- Capped costs cannot be equated with fixed costs (this decision of Laing J was not subject to appeal).
- *Broadhurst* (above) is not directly applicable to the capped costs regime of provisional assessments.
- There is no tension between the provision of CPR r.36.17(4)(b) that enables a party to have an assessment on the indemnity basis and CPR r.47.15(5) that caps the costs, as the cap does not prevent an assessment on the indemnity basis, but simply inhibits the amount that may be recovered.
- CPR r.47.20(4), which applies CPR Pt 36 to detailed assessments, does not disapply the provisions of CPR r.47.15(5) and nor do the provisions of either CPR r.47.15(5) itself or r.36.17(4)(b). The Court of Appeal concluded that "there is nothing in any of those rules to suggest that rule 47.15(5) should be disapplied or modified."[50]

---

[49] *W Portsmouth and Company Ltd v Lowin* [2017] EWCA Civ 2172; [2018] 1 W.L.R. 1890.
[50] *W Portsmouth and Company Ltd v Lowin* [2017] EWCA Civ 2172; [2018] 1 W.L.R. 1890 at [38].

- The conclusion that the cap applies even where costs are awarded on the indemnity basis "is also consistent with the policy behind both CPR r.47.15 and Pt 36. It does not undermine the intention to encourage the quick and cheap resolution of the assessment of costs in cases in which the costs claimed are £75,000 or below."[51]

Accordingly, the answer is that an award of costs on the indemnity basis may be made by application of CPR r.36.17(4)(b) in the usual way (unless it is unjust to do so), but that the costs assessed under such an award may not exceed the cap.

As the Court of Appeal was keen to stress, it is worth remembering that whilst a claimant making a valid CPR r.36 offer in these circumstances may still be subject to the costs cap, the other consequences under CPR r.36.17(4) (a), (c) and (d) apply without restriction.

Q29. What happens in respect of the costs where at an oral hearing a party does not achieve an adjustment in its favour of 20% or more, but the adjustment made does make a CPR Part 36 offer relevant under CPR r.47.20?

This question is best answered by reference to specific examples. Example A is where the receiving party makes a Part 36 offer to accept £10,000. The bill is provisionally assessed at £9,500. The receiving party seeks an oral hearing at which the bill is increased to £10,100. In example B the paying party makes a Part 36 offer to pay the receiving party £10,000. The bill is provisionally assessed at £10,500. The paying party seeks an oral hearing at which the bill is reduced to £9,900. In neither example is there a relevant Part 36 offer by the other party. In both examples, the party requesting the oral hearing has not achieved an adjustment in its favour of 20% or more of the sum provisionally assessed (in example A the adjustment is 6.3% and in example B the adjustment is 5.7%). However, in both examples, the figure assessed after the oral hearing means there is a relevant Part 36 offer.

It is important to note that the question raises the costs of the provisional assessment generally and not just the costs of the oral hearing. They raise separate issues and need to be considered individually.

8–47

The costs of the oral hearing

CPR r.47.15(10) provides a general rule that the party requesting the oral hearing pays the costs of and incidental to that hearing. There are two qualifications to this general rule. The first is where the party requesting the oral hearing sees an adjustment in its favour of 20% or more. In neither of our examples has this been achieved. The second is if the court orders otherwise.

Which CPR provision prevails—CPR rr.47.15 or 47.20 (and by implication CPR r.36.17))? In the 2nd Edition of this text, we suggested that CPR r.47.15

8–48

---

[51] *W Portsmouth and Company Ltd v Lowin* [2017] EWCA Civ 2172; [2018] 1 W.L.R. 1890 at [40].

had to be the relevant provision, but that the CPR Part 36 offer would be relevant as an offer under CPR PD 47 para.14.5 (but as an offer generally and not as a CPR Part 36 offer with its prescribed consequences) when the court considered whether it should order otherwise. In the 3rd Edition we re-considered the position in the light of the decision of Laing J in the first appeal in *Lowin*[52] (above in **Q28**) and had to conclude (albeit reluctantly) that CPR Pt 36 applied. However, the subsequent judgment of the Court of Appeal overturning the decision of Laing J and the reasoning adopted by Asplin LJ suggests that:

- there is no tension between CPR Pt 36 and CPR r.47.15(10);
- had the rule-makers intended to disapply CPR r.47.15(10) in a situation where there is a relevant CPR Part 36 offer then this would be stated in CPR r.47.15(10) itself or in r.47.20(4) or PD 47 para.14(5).

This is not a situation analogous to the general rule in CPR r.44(2), which is overridden where there is a relevant CPR Part 36 offer as:

- CPR r.44.2 is a general rule only, subject to exceptions and overridden by the freestanding provisions of CPR Pt 36. Under CPR r.47.15(10), the wording is mandatory, "any party which has requested an oral hearing will pay the costs of and incidental to that hearing" unless one of only two situations arise—the adjustment of 20% or more in its favour or the court otherwise orders.
- The guidance at CPR PD 47 para.14.5 on what the court should take into account when considering whether to depart from the order indicated in CPR r.47.15(10) is specific and refers to offers generally (and in doing so without distinguishing between CPR Pt 36 and other admissible offers, makes it clear that CPR Pt 36 is not free-standing for this purpose).
- Neither CPR r.47.15(10) nor CPR PD 47 para.14.5 specify that the departure from the order indicated for an offer made under CPR Pt 36 carries the prescribed consequences under that rule.

Accordingly, the answer to the question appears to be that the order indicated in CPR r.47.15(10) remains the starting point, that a relevant CPR Part 36 offer may be a reason for the court to exercise its discretion to make an order other than the order indicated, but that CPR Pt 36 does not apply as a free-standing provision and so an offer made under its provisions is treated no differently in this exercise of the discretion to any other admissible order and it does not carry the prescribed consequences of a relevant offer under CPR Pt 36.

---

[52] *Lowin v W Portsmouth & Co Ltd* [2016] EWHC 2301 (QB); [2017] C.P. Rep. 1.

The costs of the provisional assessment (excluding the oral hearing)
Rule 47.20 applies to the provisional assessment itself and when determining   **8–49**
the costs of that procedure (excluding the costs of the oral hearing) the court
simply looks at the end result. In our example A, the receiving party, has
obtained an outcome more advantageous than its offer and so CPR r.36.17(1)
(b) and (4) apply. In our example B, the receiving party, has failed to obtain an
outcome more advantageous than the paying party's CPR Part 36 offer and so
CPR r.36.17(1)(a) and (3)) apply. As explained in **Q28** above, whilst an order
for indemnity costs may still be made under CPR r.36(17)(4)(b), the amount
assessed under such an order is still subject to the cap on costs set out in CPR
r.47.15(5).

**Q30. Does the costs cap at CPR r.47.15(5) include the additional amount
under CPR r.36.17(4)(d) as applied by CPR r.47.20?**
The "additional amount" under CPR r.36.17(4)(d) is not defined in CPR   **8–50**
r.36.17, CPR r.47.20 or elsewhere in the rules. Perhaps of more significance
is that the phrase does not appear in the definition of costs in CPR r.44.1. In
these circumstances it is certainly arguable that it is a sum outside the cap.
This interpretation would make sense of the word "additional" and also give
effect to the purpose of CPR r.47.20, namely to encourage settlement by the
threat to the paying party of a heightened liability if a reasonable proposal is
not accepted. This view is supported by the decision in *OOO Abbott v Design
and Display Ltd*,[53] where it was argued that the "additional amount" counted
towards the £500,000 cap in the Intellectual Property Enterprise Court. HHJ
Hacon held that the "additional amount" had nothing to do with compensation, but was solely to do with a procedure to serve as an incentive to encourage claimants to make appropriate offers. In other words, "additional amount"
is not defined because it is simply that, an additional amount. Whilst HHJ
Hacon re-considered the decision under CPR r.36.17(4)(b) in *Phonographic
Performance Ltd v Hagan*,[54] the conclusion under CPR r.36.17(4)(d) remained
unaltered.

**Q31. How does the £1,500 cap operate in respect of cases that are dealt
with under the provisional assessment provisions, but where there are
interim applications, e.g. to set aside a default costs certificate, for an
interim costs certificate or for relief from sanction?**
It is important to stress that the costs cap of £1,500 at CPR r.47.15(5) is the   **8–51**
maximum amount that the court will award to any party as the costs of the
assessment.

If there is an application to set aside a default costs certificate, then it seems
that cannot be an application made within the assessment, as by definition,
at that time, there is a default costs certificate with the costs of the assessment

---

[53] *OOO Abbott v Design and Display Ltd* [2014] EWHC 3234 (IPEC) HHJ Hacon.
[54] *Phonographc Performance Ltd v Hagan* [2016] EWHC 3076 (IPEC); [2017] F.S.R. 24.

proceedings dealt with under CPR r.47.11. As such, any application to set aside a default costs certificate appears to be a free-standing application and the costs under any award of costs fall to be assessed (one would expect summarily) there and then as costs of that discrete application.

Similarly, an application for relief from sanction—presumably in connection with the late service of a Reply to the Points of Dispute—seems to be a free-standing application. It is not part of the assessment process set out in CPR r.47. As such it follows that any costs awarded on such an application would not be costs of the assessment and would be entirely separate from the cap. Indeed, in both this scenario and that relating to default costs certificates, it is conceivable that the costs of these applications will be awarded to a different party than the one which is awarded the costs of the assessment.

It is arguable that there is no jurisdiction for the court to issue an interim costs certificate in a provisional assessment. This is because CPR r.47.16(1), which enables the court to issue such a certificate, relates to cases where the receiving party has filed a request for a detailed assessment hearing. The very nature of the provisional assessment regime dispenses with hearings save where the court determines that the matter is unsuitable for the regime and lists a hearing or, after the assessment on paper, when a party requests an oral hearing. Having said this, CPR PD 47 para.14.2 applies CPR r.47.14(1) to the provisional assessment regime and the wording of that provision refers to a "request for a detailed assessment hearing". In reality, the point is unlikely to arise as CPR PD 47 para.14.4(1) provides that the court will use its best endeavours to undertake the provisional assessment within six weeks of receipt of the request. This is reinforced in para.13.2 of the SCCO Guide 2021, which states that any application for an interim costs certificate in a case proceeding to a provisional assessment will not be listed for hearing before the date fixed for the provisional assessment unless there is some good reason for an early listing.

Q32. Is the amount of the bill or the sum in which it is assessed in a provisional assessment likely to inform how much of the capped fee is awarded, e.g. does a bill of £70,000 justify an award of a higher proportion of the £1,500 than a bill of £20,000?

8–52   There is no straightforward answer to this. The cap is not set as a sliding scale. On a standard assessment it will depend entirely upon what the court determines is the reasonable and proportionate sum in any given case. Value alone does not determine this. There may be complex points of principle raised for determination within the assessment of a £20,000 bill that do not arise in a bill of £70,000. This links to the factors defining proportionality at CPR r.44.4(1) and factors relevant to the assessment of costs at CPR r.44.4(3).

Q33. Can the court make more than one award of costs for the provisional assessment and, if so, is the total amount apportioned between the

parties limited to £1,500 or may there be separate awards to each party, each with a cap of £1,500?

CPR r.47.20 applies to the principle of the award of costs of the assessment   8–53
proceedings. As such there is a general rule (47.20(1)(a)) that the receiving
party will recover the costs of the assessment. However, this is immediately
qualified to permit the court to make some other order in respect of all or part
of the costs of the assessment (CPR r.47.20(1)(b)). Rule 47.20(3) then lists specific considerations, amongst all the circumstances, that the court must take
into account and CPR r.47.20(4) applies CPR Pt 36. It is clear from this that
the court may decide to make more than one costs award in the assessment
(perhaps taking into account when a CPR Part 36 offer was made). However,
when considering this the court must consider the terms of CPR r.44.2(6) and
(7). This may lead to two awards of costs for separate and specific periods or
one award, but of a specified percentage only.

If the court does make awards of costs to more than one party to the assessment, the wording of CPR r.47.15(5) seems clear—the maximum it will award
to "any party" is £1,500. So, if there are two parties who both receive costs
awards for certain specified periods of the assessment, it appears that each
may recover up to £1,500. However, given the amount of work required in
the provisional assessment process, it seems unlikely that a reasonable and
proportionate amount would see the combined costs exceed £1,500 by much
(save if it was a case where there is still a success fee recoverable between the
parties).

Q34. Does the £1,500 cap on costs under CPR r.47.15 include costs incurred in "Costs Only Proceedings" under CPR r.46.14?

It would seem not. The argument that the costs of the CPR r.46.14   8–54
process are not costs of the substantive claim and so, by definition,
must be costs of the provisional assessment (relying on the judgment of
Brooke LJ in *Crosbie v Munroe*[55]) and included within the £1,500 limit, was
dealt a fatal blow by the Court of Appeal in *Tasleem v Beverley*.[56] As Sharp LJ
concluded:

> *"The bringing of Part 8 costs-only proceedings is not the commencement of, or
> part of, the detailed assessment proceedings, albeit it is a necessary preliminary
> to that process if there are no underlying proceedings in existence. This is because
> detailed assessment proceedings are distinct from the proceedings whether under
> Part 7 or Part 8 which have given rise to the costs order (see CPR rule 47.6(1))."*[57]

Accordingly, any costs awarded under CPR r.46.14 are entirely separate from
the costs cap in CPR r.47.15. Of course, the outcome of the provisional assessment may inform what award of costs the court makes on the CPR r.46.14

---

[55] *Crosbie v Munroe* [2003] EWCA Civ 350; [2003] 1 W.L.R. 2033.
[56] *Tasleem v Beverley* [2013] EWCA Civ 1805; [2014] 1 W.L.R. 3567.
[57] At [18].

proceedings—for example, the paying party may have made an offer before those proceedings in a sum that exceeds the receiving party's subsequent recovery on the assessment. For this reason, it may be inappropriate for the court to decide who is entitled to the costs of the CPR r.46.14 proceedings until after the assessment of the costs of the substantive proceedings has taken place. An appropriate order may defer the award of costs until the conclusion of the detailed assessment (whether by provisional assessment or not) and, if that is by settlement, give liberty to either party to restore for this purpose. The court will then deal with the award and any consequent summary assessment.

This may seem an obvious conclusion as the simple fact is that CPR r.47.15 states that it only applies to certain "detailed assessment proceedings" and CPR r.46.14 proceedings are not detailed assessment proceedings (as is clearly apparent from the title "Costs only Proceedings"). If further support was needed, it can be found in CPR r.44.1 where "detailed assessment" is defined as a procedure for determining the amount of costs under CPR r.47. "Costs only Proceedings" may enable a party to start detailed assessment proceedings, but they do not determine the amount of costs—obvious until one remembers that in *Crosbie*, Brooke LJ had concluded that:

> "... assessment proceedings cover the whole period of negotiations about the amount of costs payable through the Part 8 proceedings to the ultimate disposal of those proceedings, whether by agreement or court order".[58]

However, the Court of Appeal in *Tasleem* specifically considered *Crosbie* and took the view that it served only to support its conclusions.

The costs of detailed assessments (whether provisional or at a hearing) and additional amounts

Q35. Can a CPR Part 36 offer be made in detailed assessment proceedings? If so, is there any special wording to bear in mind when making a CPR Part 36 offer in detailed assessment proceedings? If a defendant is entitled to costs from which provisions of CPR r.36(17) may it benefit if it makes a CPR Part 36 offer in the assessment of its costs?

8–55   CPR r.47.20(4) makes it plain that CPR Pt 36 applies to detailed assessment proceedings. Accordingly, any party wishing to make such an offer in those proceedings must comply with the requirements of CPR Pt 36. CPR r.47.20(4) makes some modifications, but these are of terminology and are designed to ensure that CPR Pt 36 can easily be cross applied to a detailed assessment (CPR r.47.20(a)–(e)). It is important to note that following the decision of the Court of Appeal in *King v City of London Corp*[59] CPR PD 47 para.19 has been amended so that it mirrors the provision in CPR r.36.5(4) to provide that an

---

[58] At [34].
[59] *King v City of London Corp* [2019] EWCA Civ 2266; [2019] Costs L.R. 2197.

offer intended to be under CPR r.36, relying on r.47.20(4), will be treated as inclusive of interest. An offer made other than under CPR r.36 must specify whether or not it is intended to be inclusive of interest.

The modifications of terminology make the receiving party "the claimant" when considering the consequences of an applicable Part 36 offer. Accordingly, a defendant in whose favour a costs order has been made, becomes the receiving party in the assessment proceedings. As a result, if it makes an appropriate Part 36 offer in respect of those costs, then unless the court considers it is unjust to do so, the defendant may benefit from the consequences set out in CPR r.37.17(4).

Q36. Under CPR r.36.17(4)(d) can a party recover the additional sum on a detailed assessment by operation of CPR r.47.20 if it has already received an additional amount in respect of the substantive award in the claim?
This question raises a semantic issue that arises when considering the subtle   8–56 qualification that appears at the beginning of CPR r.36.17(4)(d) with the words "Provided that the case has been finally decided and there has not been a previous order under this sub-paragraph" and the wording of CPR r.47.20(7) which provides that:

> *"For the purposes of rule 36.17, detailed assessment proceedings are to be regarded as an independent claim."*

Is a case finally decided before the costs of that case have been resolved and, is "a claim" the same thing as "a case"? The plot thickens when CPR r.47.1 is considered. At first blush, this seems to suggest that detailed assessment comes after a final decision. However, this rule talks of a final decision in "the proceedings". Are proceedings the same as "a claim" and/or "a case"? None of these three descriptive terms are defined in CPR r.2 or in the Glossary at the end of the CPR. However, as the only purpose of CPR r.47.20(7) seems to be to distinguish detailed assessment proceedings from the substantive litigation, the scales appear to weigh in favour of answering "yes" to the question posed. This interpretation and conclusion is supported by the fact that CPR PD 47 para.1.1 clearly identifies a final decision as being of all the substantive issues other than costs and sits happily with the semantic interpretation we identified in answering **Q17** above, that detailed assessments are separate proceedings and not subject to the QOCS regime. if this is correct, it does raise the interesting question of whether the claimant is able to recover an additional amount on both the costs of the provisional assessment and the costs of any oral hearing (see **Q29** above). The logical conclusion is that as the provisional assessment and an oral hearing following it are both component parts of one set of detailed assessment proceedings, then only one CPR r.36.17(4)(d) award may be made. However, they are clearly separate components (CPR r.47.15(7) refers to an oral hearing "when a provisional assessment has been carried out" and there are clearly different starting points for the award of costs for each (CPR r.47.20(1) and CPR r.47.15(10)). As such it seems that the costs of each must be dealt with separately which would suggest that only one may attract the additional amount.

Q37. Is the determination of disbursements under the procedure set out at CPR PD 47 para.5.7 a provisional assessment?

8–57 Strictly this procedure is included within CPR r.47.14 and not CPR r.47.15, although the way in which it is to be dealt under CPR r.47.14 (as set out at CPR PD 47 para.13.5) resonates more with the provisional assessment procedure:

> "*Unless the court otherwise orders, if the only dispute between the parties concerns disbursements, the hearing shall take place in the absence of the parties on the basis of the documents and the court will issue its decision in writing.*"

It seems that this is a free-standing procedure. It has its origins in Jackson LJ's *Review of Civil Litigation Costs: Final Report*, December 2009.[60] Although in the report the procedure was discussed in terms of disbursement only disputes in fast track cases where the profit costs are subject to a fixed fee regime, CPR PD 47 para.5.7 contains no such restriction and the procedure is, therefore, available in appropriate multi-track cases as well.

As the procedure is not a provisional assessment and a paper disposal is expressly provided for, without the oral hearing review process, it seems that any challenge to the outcome must be by appeal in the usual way.

One practical difficulty is the assessment of the costs of the assessment itself. Logically (and for reasons of proportionality) one would expect this also to be undertaken as a paper exercise with the parties filing statements of costs for summary assessment and offers in sealed envelopes. As the exercise is not a provisional assessment the fee cap in CPR r.47.15(5) does not apply, although it is difficult to imagine a situation where the court would allow more than that cap anyway where the disputed disbursements do not exceed the provisional assessment costs limit of £75,000.

As an aside this short form procedure is advocated by Sir Rupert Jackson in his *Review of Civil Litigation Costs: Supplemental Report Fixed Recoverable Costs*[61] as a mechanism to be used in fast track cases, where the claim does not go to trial and so there is not a summary assessment, for the resolution of any arguments within his proposed extension of fixed recoverable costs regimes. It remains to be seen whether this procedure makes its way into the rules, now that the Ministry of Justice has decided to press ahead with the introduction of Sir Rupert's recommendations and is working with the Civil Procedure Rules Committee on implementation.

---

[60] *Review of Civil Litigation Costs: Final Report*, December 2009 Ch.45 para.5.2.
[61] *Review of Civil Litigation Costs: Supplemental Report Fixed Recoverable Costs* para.5.22.

C Payments on account

Q38. Is there any rule of thumb as to what proportion of the costs claimed the court will order as a reasonable sum by way of payment on account?
There never has been any genuine "rule of thumb". *Mars UK Ltd v Teknowledge*   **8–58**
Ltd (Costs)[62] is often cited as authority for the proposition that two-thirds of the sum claimed is an appropriate amount. In fact, the route by which the payment on account was reached in that case is far from straightforward and does not endorse any specific percentage as a general rule.

The decision is fact-specific in each case. This is a point reiterated by Clarke LJ in *Excalibur Ventures LLC v Texas Keystone Inc*[63] when ordering 80% of the sum claimed on account stating:

"What is a reasonable amount will depend on the circumstances, the chief of which is that there will, by definition, have been no detailed assessment and thus an element of uncertainty, the extent of which may differ widely from case to case as to what will be allowed on detailed assessment."

He went on to tender this approach to payments on account, which reinforces the case-specific nature of the determination of amount:

"A reasonable sum would often be one that was an estimate of the likely level of recovery subject, as the costs claimants (sic) accept, to an appropriate margin to allow for error in the estimation. This can be done by taking the lowest figure in a likely range or making a deduction from a single estimated figure or perhaps from the lowest figure in the range if the range itself is not very broad."

In *Rallison v North West London Hospitals NHS*,[64] a clinical negligence claim settled for £450,000 (where a much larger sum had been sought) and where the claimant sought a payment on account of costs of £574,000 and the defendant was offering £250,000, the court stressed that determination of the likely level of recovery at assessment necessarily involved consideration of proportionality of the costs claimed (other than, of course, in cases where the award of costs is on the indemnity basis as proportionality does not arise). The court awarded a payment of £306,763 on account.

However, the advent of costs budgets appears to be both assisting and simplifying the process by creating greater certainty over likely recovery on any subsequent assessment because part of the costs are budgeted as reasonable and proportionate already and absent "good reason" under CPR r.3.18 will be the sums recovered on assessment for that part of the costs. In *Elvanite Full Circle Ltd v AMEC Earth & Environmental (UK) Ltd*,[65] Coulson J (as he then was) used the budget set as the basis for a determination of the reasonable sum to be paid on account stating, "the costs management order is likely to be the

---

[62] *Mars UK Ltd v Teknowledge Ltd (Costs)* [1999] 2 Costs L.R. 44; [2000] F.S.R. 138 Jacob J.
[63] *Excalibur Ventures LLC v Texas Keystone Inc* [2015] EWHC 566 (Comm).
[64] *Rallison v North West London Hospitals NHS Trust* [2015] EWHC 3255 (QB); [2015] 6 Costs L.O. 771.
[65] *Elvanite Full Circle Ltd v AMEC Earth & Environmental (UK) Ltd* [2013] EWHC 1643 (TCC); [2016] 4 W.L.R. 186 Coulson J.

benchmark for the costs to be recovered", and based the payment on account on the conclusion that the receiving party's costs were unlikely to be much under the budgeted sum. This is a view that he repeated in *Bank of Ireland (Governors and Company of) v Watts Group Plc*,[66] stating "that is because such a figure is also the starting point (and very possibly the end point, too) of the costs judge's assessment", referring to CPR r.3.18. Accordingly, it may be that in the absence of an indication that the budget is to be subject to some fundamental challenge under "good reason to depart from the budget" under CPR r.3.18, a starting point will be the budgeted sum. Indeed, in *Thomas Pink Ltd v Victoria's Secret UK Ltd*,[67] Birss J (as he then was) concluded that the advent of costs budgets had altered the position. The budget was £678,000. The claimant sought £644,000 as a payment on account and the defendant proposed £350,000 (which the court accepted was "the sort of figure one would have expected to have awarded"). However, having posed the question whether the costs budgeting rules have a significant impact on orders for payments on account, Birss J concluded that:

> *"The sum sought by the claimants is essentially the budgeted sum at the time they asked for it. It seems to me that the impact of costs budgeting on the determination of a sum for a payment on account of costs is very significant although I am not persuaded that it is so significant that I should simply award the budgeted sum. Bearing in mind that unless there is good reason to depart from the budget, the budget will not be departed from, but also taking into account the vagaries of litigation and things that might occur and the fact that it is, at least, possible that the assessed costs will be less, although no good reason why that is so has been advanced before me, I will make an award of 90% of the sum in the claimants budget (£644,829.10) rounded up to the nearest thousand."*[68]

The deduction of 10% from the budgeted costs was endorsed by Coulson J in *MacInnes v Gross*,[69] who put it in more general terms when making a reduction of that amount, stating this to be "the maximum deduction that is appropriate in a case where there is an approved costs budget".

In the light of the decision in *Harrison v University Hospitals Coventry and Warwickshire NHS Trust*,[70] namely that the court will not depart from budgeted costs without good reason and the clear acceptance that the court may only make costs management orders in respect of incurred costs under CPR r.3.15(2)(c), it seems logical that the court should approach the quantification of a payment on account in a costs managed case as follows:

---

[66] *Bank of Ireland (Governors and Company of) v Watts Group Plc* [2017] EWHC 2472 (TCC); [2017] B.L.R. 626.
[67] *Thomas Pink Ltd v Victoria's Secret UK Ltd* [2014] EWHC 3258 (Ch); [2015] 3 Costs L.R. 463 Birss J.
[68] At [60].
[69] *MacInnes v Gross* [2017] EWHC 127 (QB); [2017] 2 Costs L.R. 243 at [28].
[70] *Harrison v University Hospitals Coventry and Warwickshire NHS Trust* [2017] EWCA Civ 792; [2017] 1 W.L.R. 4456.

- By adopting the *Thomas Pink Ltd/MacInnes v Gross*[71] approach as a starting point in respect of those costs subject to a costs management order (and this would include under CPR r.3.15(2)(c) even though it does not fall within CPR r.3.18 in terms of specified consequences, as it seems unlikely the court would not order on account those costs that had been agreed by the paying party).
- By adopting the *Mars UK Ltd/Excalibur Ventures LLC* and *Excalibur Ventures LLC v Texas Keystone Inc* approach to non-costs managed costs.

This approach was adopted by the court in *Cleveland Bridge UK Ltd v Sarens (UK) Ltd*,[72] in which the court highlighted that separate considerations arise when considering budgeted and non-budgeted costs when determining a payment on account:

"*I also accept that insofar as the costs budget can properly be regarded as 'approved' it is appropriate to take the approved figure (which will be the esti-mated/budgeted costs) as the starting point when seeking to determine an appro-priate payment on account in respect of those costs and the maximum deduction in such a case should be 10%. . . However, I do not accept that this is necessarily the approach that the court should adopt to incurred costs, which are, by defini-tion, not approved costs, . . . As to these, it seems to me that (consistent with the approach taken in cases where there is no approved costs budget) the court must determine in every case, a reasonable sum by reference to an estimate which will be dependent upon the circumstances, including the fact that there has as yet been no detailed assessment and thus there remains an element of uncertainty, the extent of which may differ widely from case to case, as to what will be allowed on detailed assessment. . . Accordingly, in my judgment, a reasonable sum in respect of incurred costs will often be one that is an estimate of the likely level of recovery subject to an appropriate margin to allow for error."*

Q39. Does the court consider the proportionality of costs sought when ordering a payment on account?
Yes it does. See the answer to **Q38** above and, in particular, the decision in **8–59** *Rallison v North West London Hospitals NHS.*[73] In fact, this case was one to which the pre-1 April 2013 proportionality test applied (see **Ch.3**). The fact that proportionality now trumps both necessary and reasonable costs under CPR r.44.3(2)(a) only serves to increase the importance that the court will attach to proportionality when considering payments on account in cases governed by that provision.

---

[71] The approach of Coulson J (as he then was) to the relevance of budgeted costs in *MacInnes* were cited with approval by Davis LJ in *Harrison* in these terms: "*In that case, in the context of considering an interim payment on account of costs, Coulson J in terms said, at paragraph 25, that the significance of CPR 3.18 'cannot be understated' and meant that, where costs are assessed, the costs judge 'will start with the figure in the approved costs budget.' . . . I agree with those observations of Coulson J.*"
[72] *Cleveland Bridge UK Ltd v Sarens (UK) Ltd* [2018] EWHC 827 (TCC); [2018] 2 Costs L.R. 333.
[73] *Rallison v North West London Hospitals NHS* [2015] EWHC 3255 (QB); [2015] 6 Costs L.O. 771.

In *Dana Gas PJSC v Dana Gas Sukuk Ltd*[74] the court made repeated reference to the payment on account being linked to the reasonable and proportionate costs in allowing about 23% of the overall costs claimed as a payment on account. The receiving party had sought 60% on account. This case serves as a useful reminder that the determination of what is a reasonable sum on account will depend on the circumstances, which may vary widely from case to case.

Q40. Must a party have filed a Form N260 (or equivalent statement of costs) if it wishes to seek a payment on account of costs?

8–60   In *Astonleigh Residential v Goldfarb*[75] the court concluded that the CPR contained no requirement that a party seeking a payment on account had to have produced a statement of costs to inform the court's decision. Of course, in most CPR Pt 7 multi-track claims the court will have the better detail of a costs management order to inform its decision (see **Q38** above). It seems inevitable that in the absence of either a budget or a statement of costs, the court is likely to be conservative in determining the amount of any payment on account.

Q41. When may a departure from the general rule at CPR r.44.2(8) be justified?

8–61   There may be facts particular to a case that render a payment on account inappropriate. As an example, in *Rawlinson & Hunter Trustees SA v ITG Ltd*[76] the court was asked either to order an immediate detailed assessment of an interim costs order or, if it was not prepared to do so, to order a payment on account of costs. In fact, it declined to do either for the same reasons—namely that the claimant might later secure a costs order against the defendant, may have difficulties in enforcing that and, if it had already paid costs would have lost the chance to set-off what if owed against what it was due. Further examples can be found in both *Pepe's Piri Piri Ltd v Muhammad Ali Junaid Food Trends Ltd (Now Dissolved)*[77] and *Hincks v Sense Network Ltd (Costs)*.[78] Both illustrate that the decision to depart is fact-specific. In the former, the receiving parties were LiPS, had not, therefore, filed any Precedent H and had provided no costs information at all to assist the judge in determining an appropriate sum. In the latter, apart from an unsuccessful attempt to stay the execution of any award on account as it was said that would stifle an appeal, the court refused to award a payment on account of costs that exceeded the budget, refusing to accept at this interim stage, that the costs judge would have good reason under CPR r.3.18 to depart from the budget.

---

[74] *Dana Gas PJSC v Dana Gas Sukuk Ltd* [2018] EWHC 332 (Comm); [2018] 2 Costs L.O. 189.
[75] *Astonleigh Residential Care Home Ltd v Goldfarb* [2014] EWHC 4100 (Ch).
[76] *Rawlinson & Hunter Trustees SA v ITG Ltd [2015]* EWHC 1924 (Ch).
[77] *Pepe's Piri Piri Ltd v Muhammad Ali Junaid Food Trends Ltd (now dissolved)* [2019] EWHC 2769 (QB); [2019] Costs L.R. 1881.
[78] *Hincks v Sense Network Ltd (Costs)* [2018] EWHC 1241 (QB); [2018] 3 Costs L.R. 511.

Q42. Can a payment on account of costs be ordered under CPR r.44.2(8) other than at the hearing awarding the costs?
This question arises out of the wording of CPR r.44.2(8). That wording seems   8–62
to suggest a clear temporal link restricting the court's jurisdiction to the time
of the award of costs. On the face of it, there is a certain logic to this interpretation. It is the awarding judge who best understands the issues of the case
enabling a determination of what payment on account is reasonable. This sits
happily with the provision that only when there is more detail about the costs
(in the form of a bill, Points of Dispute and, possibly, a Reply) can an interim
costs certificate be requested. This suggests that detailed information about
the case is a prerequisite to interim payments of costs, whether by a payment
on account or an interim certificate.

Of course, adopting such an approach automatically excludes payments on
account in cases where there has been a deemed costs order (see CPR r.44.9).
It was within the confines of a deemed costs order that the Court of Appeal
considered any temporal restrictions in *Global Assets Advisory Services Ltd v
Grandlane Developments Ltd*[79] (see para.**8–16** above). In this case, the receiving party's entitlement to costs arose under a deemed costs order under CPR
r.44.9, following the acceptance of a CPR Part 36 offer within the relevant
period. At first instance, the court adopted the approach taken in *J P Finnegan
v Frank Spiers T/A Frank Spiers Licensed Conveyancers*,[80] in which the court had
concluded that CPR r.44.2(8) did not apply in respect of deemed orders consequential upon acceptance of a Part 36 offer within the relevant period, on
the basis that Pt 36 and not Pt 44 spelt out the consequences of acceptance
and those did not include a payment on account of costs. This conclusion was
rejected by the Court of Appeal, with Asplin LJ making wider observations
about deemed orders generally and payments on account as follows:

> *"I can see no reason why the power to make an order under CPR r 44.2(8) should
> be restricted to circumstances in which the court has physically made the order
> as opposed to circumstances in which an order of the court is deemed to have
> been made. In both circumstances, it is the court which has ordered the party to
> pay the costs and accordingly, it seems to me that the circumstances fall within
> the wording of CPR r 44.2(8). A deemed order is no less an order of the court. . .
> Furthermore, the rationale for ordering a payment on account of costs is the
> same whether or not the order for costs is an order which is deemed to have been
> made. . ."*

> *". . . there is no conflict or tension between CPR r 36.13(1) and CPR r 44.2(8)
> at all. It is not necessary to determine which provision must prevail. The former
> entitles a party to its costs of the proceedings on a particular basis and is com-
> plemented or supplemented by the latter which creates the jurisdiction to order a
> payment on account of those costs."*

---

[79] *Global Assets Advisory Services Ltd v Grandlane Developments Ltd* [2019] EWCA Civ 1764; [2019] Costs L.R. 1597.
[80] *J P Finnegan v Frank Spiers T/A Frank Spiers Licensed Conveyancers* [2018] EWHC 3064 (Ch); [2018] 6 Costs L.O. 729.

Putting the final nail in the coffin of arguments that CPR r.44.2(8) contains a temporal link, limiting the award of a payment on account to the time of the substantive decision, the court rejected the notion that only the trial judge could entertain applications for interim payments:

> "*It seems to me that the current wording [of 44.2(8)] cannot form the basis for a distinction between cases in which the application for an interim payment is heard by the trial judge and those in which it is not. It seems to me that it applies whether or not the trial judge hears the application for an interim payment. If the judge hearing the application considers that there is good reason not to make the order, the terms of CPR r 44.2(8) enable him to decline to do so.*"

The court made the obvious point that if the court hearing the application considers there is a good reason not to order a payment on account, then it should not do so. A good reason might include uncertainty over, or paucity of information concerning, the detail of the substantive dispute. This, however, is an exercise of discretion and not a question of whether there is jurisdiction to make an order at all.

Q43. Where there is a judgment on liability, but quantification of the claim is incomplete, can a party obtain a payment on account of quantum costs?

8–63   The answer appears to be yes, provided that the court first makes an order for costs, as, by definition, a payment on account of costs can only be of those costs to which a party is entitled under an order for costs. In *X v Hull & East Yorkshire Hospitals NHS Trust*,[81] there had been an order approving a liability settlement in 2012, which also included a provision for the defendant to pay the claimant's costs to that date. The claimant subsequently instructed other firms of solicitors. The current solicitors sought a payment on account of the costs of the quantum exercise, as the final prognosis remained unclear and it was agreed that final determination was unlikely to be possible until 2022. Two payments on account of costs under the 2012 order had been made, one of which included a sum to the current solicitors, albeit that their involvement post-dated the liability settlement. Notwithstanding the opposition of the defendant, the court concluded that it had jurisdiction to make a costs order in proceedings that were ongoing and to order a payment on account under that order. It should be noted that in this case there was a judgment on liability, no Part 36 offers and significant sums had been paid on account, making it virtually a certainty that the claimant would recover costs to the date of the order.

When considering a similar request based on *X v Hull and East Yorkshire Hospitals NHS Trust*, the court in *RXK v Hampshire Hospitals NHS Foundation Trust*[82] tentatively suggested that the following information should be provided to support such an application:

---

[81] *X v Hull & East Yorkshire Hospitals NHS Trust* unreported 25 February 2019 (HHJ Robinson).
[82] *RXK v Hampshire Hospitals NHS Foundation Trust* [2019] EWHC 2751 (QB).

- the type of funding agreement and details of any payments made under that agreement;
- whether any Part 36 or other admissible offer has been made, and if so, full details of the offer;
- details of any payments on account of damages made to date;
- a realistic valuation of the likely damages to be awarded at trial;
- a realistic estimate of the quantum costs incurred to the date of the application;
- any other factor relevant to the final incidence of costs, such as the possibility of an issue-based costs order, arguments over rates or relevant conduct;
- the likely date of trial or trial window.

Q44. Can continuation with a claim/defence be made conditional upon compliance with an order for a payment on account of costs?

Yes, it can. In *Ogiehor v Ogiehor*,[83] a trial of a personal injury case, the claimant, representing himself, had disclosed to the court the existence and amount of an offer made "without prejudice as to costs". As a result, the trial had to be adjourned, the claimant was ordered to pay the wasted costs associated with the abortive trial and payment of these was made a condition of being able to continue the claim. One of the two grounds of appeal was whether "in making payment of the interim sum a pre-condition to the case continuing, the judge erred in principle." The court referred to the provisions of CPR r.3.1(3) and (5), the Court of Appeal, reminding itself that:

8–64

> *"the condition must be one which is capable of being complied with and an impecunious party should not be ordered to pay into court a sum of money that they are completely unable to raise".*

The court was satisfied that the trial judge had taken account of the claimant's ability to pay and had been entirely justified in making continuation with the claim conditional upon payment of the interim costs order.

---

[83] *Ogiehor v Ogiehor* [2018] EWCA Civ 2423.

The Effect of the Jackson Civil Justice Reforms on Solicitor-Client Costs

Introduction

The Legal Aid, Sentencing and Punishment of Offenders Act 2012 (LASPO)   9–01
and associated secondary legislation, together with the reforms to the Civil
Procedure Rules introduced in April 2013, have had a significant effect on the
conduct of litigation and on the scope of costs recovery between the parties.

Apart from the imposition of a number of statutory caps on the levels of
success fees (in personal injury claims) and on the levels of the "payments"
under the now more widely available damages-based agreements (DBAs)[1],
and some relatively minor procedural amendments, those changes do not
directly address the question of solicitor-client costs. The fundamental legal
principles underpinning the ability of a solicitor to charge a client and the
ability of a client to dispute those charges are unaffected. The law in this
regard emanates from a combination of statutory provisions (primarily ss.56–
75 of the Solicitors Act 1974) and common law and it is doubtful that amendments to the CPR alone would have the standing to alter those principles.

However, a number of the key changes undoubtedly have a substantial indirect and practical impact on the question of costs as between the solicitor and
the client. In some areas of reform, such as costs budgeting, it appears that the
attempt indirectly to exercise a degree of control on solicitors' charges to their
clients was intentional. In others, for example in relation to proportionality and the substantial increase in solicitor-client disputes concerning success
fees arising from the removal of between the parties recovery, the effect was
perhaps less intentional, but nevertheless has been significant.

Those key changes will be considered in turn. It is beyond the scope of this
chapter to consider in detail the established legal principles relating to assessment of solicitor-client costs, which are addressed in detail in a number of
substantial works, beyond by way of brief overview and consideration of how
those principles have been, or may be, affected by the Jackson Civil Justice
Reforms. Risk management and law firm management are also outside the
scope of this book. However, by pointing out where issues arise as a result of
the Jackson reforms, this chapter aims to give readers a clear steer in relation
to issues that they may need to consider carefully and, if appropriate, seek
further guidance on. Once again, the plea is also repeated, as it has been in
every edition of this work, for properly codified statutory reform in this area.
The substantial growth in solicitor-client costs disputes, and in particular the

---

[1] See further **Ch.2** in relation to DBAs and other funding arrangements.

mushrooming of grossly disproportionate disputes concerning very modest sums of costs in low value personal injury claims since 2013, merely shines further light on the fact that the Solicitors Act 1974, encrusted with many years of caselaw passed down from it's almost identical and venerable predecessors, causes more problems than it cures and is long overdue for reform.

None of this is to suggest that one side or the other in such disputes is invariably right or wrong – clients require proper consumer protection just as solicitors should be able to be reliably paid their fees for work done and pursue defaulting clients. The present regime, however, does not provide a clear, practical or proportionate remedy for either of those aims and instead causes a huge waste of cost and court time as well as substantial uncertainty for all sides. It is perhaps an unfortunate irony that solicitors may be criticised within Solicitors Act proceedings for not properly explaining to their clients what their rights to assessment are, when the very difficulty in understanding and explaining those rights and their many associated intricacies is a consequence of the unsatisfactory nature of the regime itself. The Senior Costs Judge, at the 2021 Costs Law Reports conference, called (once again) for a review and simplification of the system in Part III of the Solicitors Act 1974, a call he had also made back in 2018 when he called for a review of the "Byzantine" system. Reform is long overdue. Given that the scheme is contained in primary legislation there is only a limited amount the Costs Judges – and those judges who find themselves hearing such cases on appeal – can do to resolve the problems without government intervention.

The passage of almost nine years since the introduction of the LASPO reforms has indeed seen a considerable increase in solicitor-client disputes, particularly in the area of low-value personal injury claims where the loss of between the parties recoverability of success fees means that clients now frequently face deductions from damages in a way which was much less common with such cases with pre-LASPO funding arrangements. One consequence has been to remind solicitors in such cases that the basic principles of solicitor-client costs—the rendering of statute bills, the potential for an assessment under the Solicitors Act 1974—apply just as much to acting for clients with such claims as they do in the areas where solicitor-client disputes were perhaps more common in the past. In particular, the mere fact that the solicitor looks primarily to the opponent for payment of some or all of the solicitor-client costs should not be allowed to obscure the fact that between the parties costs are paid in the client's name. The solicitor's right to payment rests on its charging and billing arrangements with the client, and not simply on the fact that costs are recovered between the parties. In addition, the increased use of fixed costs between the parties, costs management and the revised test of proportionality have all served, to a greater or lesser extent, to increase further the situations where the solicitor looks to the client for payment of a shortfall. All these points serve to emphasise the need for the solicitor to have a proper understanding of their own contractual and billing arrangements and the provisions relating to solicitor-client assessments.

One of the inadvertent consequences of the reforms was that they shone a bright spotlight on issues surrounding changes in funding, for example concerning the reasonableness of a switch from public funding to a case being funded with a conditional fee agreement (CFA). A combination of anecdotal evidence and a number of reported decisions[2] indicate that in the run-up to 1 April 2013 there were a substantial number of cases where such changes took place. In such cases, where the claimant is awarded costs, opponents have an incentive to challenge the circumstances of such changes in order to try and avoid payment of any additional liabilities or even to identify some technical defect which might allow them to avoid paying costs altogether. Whilst the basic test for the reasonableness of such a change was set as long ago as 2002,[3] the particular combination of circumstances following the reforms has led to the parameters of those principles being closely examined and tested. In many such cases, one of the key issues in dispute will be the quality of the advice provided to the client about the change in funding and the between the parties cases may well have a marked effect on and implications for more general issues about the quality of the advice to be given to clients about costs and funding options generally. See, in particular, the cases of *Herbert v HH Law Ltd*[4] and *Belsner v Cam Legal Services Ltd*[5] discussed further below. Whilst the number of such cases diminishes over time, those remaining cases where there is an issue as to a change in funding to a pre-April 2013 model with additional liabilities are likely to be the larger and more complex cases where the costs and the related additional liabilities will be substantial indeed.

A brief overview

There is a fundamental distinction between costs on a solicitor-client basis   9–02
and costs between the parties. The latter are payable as a result of any costs order or agreement between the parties and are subject to the very broad discretion conferred on the court by s.51 of the Senior Courts Act 1981 and any rules of procedure made thereunder.

However, costs on a solicitor-client basis are (usually) payable as a result of the contract between the solicitor and the client. Subject to specific statutory and procedural restrictions, the key determining factor therefore is the terms of the contract between the solicitor and client.

As with any other form of costs payable under a contract where the liability is a contractual one, such costs are usually payable on the indemnity basis, unless the contract otherwise provides (see CPR r.44.5 for the position in relation to costs payable under contracts generally).[6]

---

[2] See, for example, *Hyde v Milton Keynes NHS Trust* [2015] EWHC B1 (Costs) (appellate judgment [2017] EWCA Civ 399); *Proctor v Raleys Solicitors (A Firm)* [2015] EWCA Civ 400; [2015] P.N.L.R. 24; *McDaniel & Co (A Firm) v Clarke* [2014] EWHC 3826 (QB); [2014] 6 Costs L.R. 963; and the combined cases in *Surrey v Barnet and Chase Farm Hospitals NHS Trust* [2018] EWCA Civ 451; [2018] 1 W.L.R. 5831.

[3] See *Sarwar v Alam* [2001] EWCA Civ 1401; [2002] 1 W.L.R. 125.

[4] *Herbert v H Law Ltd* [2019] EWCA Civ 527; [2019] 1 W.L.R. 4253 discussed further below.

[5] [2020] EWHC 2755 (QB).

[6] The introduction of the concept of indemnity basis assessment of costs between the parties only came much later, with the introduction of the concepts of "standard" and "indemnity" basis in 1986.

Accordingly, the starting point is that a solicitor-client costs dispute is a contractual dispute and is subject to any limitations within that contract.

However, as noted, there are numerous statutory, common law and procedural restrictions imposed which fundamentally change the character of the claim as between solicitor and client. These exist primarily as a combination of a recognition of the peculiar position of solicitors and the court's supervisory jurisdiction over them and a form of what would, in modern parlance, be termed "consumer protection".

These provisions may be analysed in three main categories.

Nature of retainers

9–03   Firstly, provisions which govern the nature of the contract that a solicitor may enter into with a client are primarily restrictive—that is to say, they limit the nature of the arrangements beyond what would be permitted in an ordinary commercial context.

These arrangements, in turn, fall primarily into two main categories, namely those relating to what is termed "non-contentious business" and those relating to contentious business. As to what is and is not contentious business, there is a very circuitous definition of both at s.87 of the Solicitors Act 1974, whereby contentious business is defined as business done "in or for the purposes of proceedings begun before a court or before an arbitrator . . . not being business which falls within the definition of non-contentious business" and non-contentious business is defined as "any business done by a solicitor which is not contentious business". The key point to note is that work which would have been classed as non-contentious business will be classed as contentious business provided that that work was done with a view to proceedings being begun and proceedings were in fact begun.[7]

If further guidance on this issue is required, the most comprehensive recent consideration of the issues is to be found in Chief Master Hurst's judgment in *Tel-Ka Talk Ltd*.[8]

The primary statutory provisions in this regard are s.57 of the Solicitors Act 1974, which, at subs.(2) sets out the very broad nature of the arrangements that a solicitor may lawfully enter into with their clients in relation to non-contentious business (a non-contentious business agreement, or NCBA), including what might be described as contingency, or outcome-based arrangements, and specifies the requirements for such arrangements, and s.59 which sets out the ability of solicitors to enter into a contentious business agreement (CBA) with clients.

It is important to note that both CBAs (Contentious Business Agreements) and NCBAs with clients are merely optional and that it is not necessary for a solicitor-client retainer in respect of contentious business, for example, to take the form of a CBA—though the exemption of NCBAs from the effects of ss.58

---

[7] See *Re Simpkin Marshall Ltd* [1959] Ch.229.
[8] *Tel-Ka Talk Ltd v HMRC* [2010] EWHC 90175 (Costs).

and 58AA of the Courts and Legal Services Act 1990 is an important reason why such agreements should be considered in appropriate circumstances.

Mr Justice Mann's judgment in *Wilson v the Specter Partnership*[9] should not be overlooked in this context, not least in that it makes clear that whether something is a CBA or not (and the same reasoning would apply to an NCBA) depends not on the label put on it by the parties, but on its terms and whether it satisfies the essential requirements for such an agreement. The essential requirement identified by Mann J, for a CBA at least, was that of certainty. See also Master Brown's decision in *Whitaker v Richard Slade & Co Plc*[10] which emphasises that there is a distinction between a client agreeing to pay a sum in settlement of their solicitor's claim for costs (which may just be a conventional contractual compromise) and a CBA.

The distinction remains important—and the subject of disputes. It can have both procedural and substantive implications. See, for example, the judgment of HHJ Kelyn Bacon QC, sitting as a Judge of the High Court, in *Healys LLP v Partridge*[11] where a "debt" claim by the solicitors was transferred from CPR Pt 7 to CPR Pt 8 on the basis that it was based on a CFA which was held to be a CBA. Under s.61 of the Solicitors Act 1974, a CBA could not found a cause of action, at least unless and until the court had decided whether it could be enforced and whether it was fair and reasonable.

The Court of Appeal in *Hollins v Russell*[12] indicated, at para.93, without detailed argument on the point, that a CFA will generally be a CBA and it is notable that s.59–61 of the 1974 Act were specifically amended by the Courts & Legal Services Act 1990 (the same act that introduced CFAs) to bring agreements providing for remuneration by hourly rate within the scope of CBAs[13].

This does not mean that all CFAs are CBAs, as the judge in *Healys* made clear. However, in that case there was no statement in the CFA that it was not a CBA (though the judge was careful to make clear that this may not have been determinative anyway).

This issue continued to trouble the courts in 2021 – and once again, the fact that it remains such a difficult issue to identify whether something is or is not a CBA (which is fundamental in then identifying what rights the client has) is a further example of the need for reform in this area. *Cardium Law Ltd*[14] is a further example of a CFA being considered to be a CBA. In *Acupay Systems LLC v Stephenson Harwood LLP*[15], Master Leonard rejected an argument that a CFA was a CBA on the essential basis that, whilst following *Wilson* the fact that the description a document gives itself is not necessarily determinative,

---

[9] *Wilson v the Specter Partnership* [2007] EWHC 133 (Ch); [2007] 6 Costs L.R. 802.
[10] *Whitaker v Richard Slade & Co Plc* unreported 31 October 2018 SCCO.
[11] *Healys LLP v Partridge & Partridge* [2019] EWHC 24871 (Ch); [2019] Costs L.R. 1515.
[12] [2003] EWCA Civ 718, [2003] 1 W.L.R. 2487.
[13] They had previously been held to be insufficiently certain generally to be CBAs – see Lord Denning in *Chamberlain v Boodle & King* [1982] 3 All ER 188.
[14] *Cardium law Ltd v Kew Holdings Ltd* [2021] EWHC 1299 (Ch).
[15] SCCO, 25 June 2021.

where the parties have clearly agreed that the CFA is not a CBA such an agreement may – and in this case did – determine the issue.

NCBAs appear to produce less controversy, at least in terms of their identification, though they do occasionally raise interesting points. The effectiveness (for the solicitor) of a NCBA, when properly used can be seen from the case of *Bolt Burdon v Tariq*,[16] one of the very few reported appellate cases relating to the modern use of such arrangements. The DBA type contingency fee arrangement entered into there was upheld by the court in full. The judgment is a useful reference point for anyone considering the use of such an agreement as to the sort of challenges that might be raised and the legal tests that apply.[17]

In contrast to s.57 (NCBAs), s.59 (in relation to CBAs) expressly provides that nothing in that section shall give validity to (inter alia) any agreement by which the solicitor retained stipulates for payment only in the event of success (a "conditional" fee), or by way of a percentage of recovery (a "contingent" fee).

This reflects the proposition that s.59 does not prohibit such arrangements but equally is not to be taken to permit them, in contrast to s.57 which does expressly permit, for example, payment by way of a percentage for non-contentious business.

9-04   The restriction on such arrangements in contentious business comes not from the Solicitors Act 1974 therefore but from the common law prohibition on champertous arrangements, which could have been overridden by the statutory provision at s.59 of the 1974 Act, but expressly was not. That common law prohibition has, however, been relaxed by express statutory provisions in s.58 of the Courts and Legal Services Act 1990 (permitting CFAs that comply with the requirements of ss.58 and 58A) and then more recently (since April 2013) by s.58AA of the same Act permitting DBAs that comply with the requirements of that section.

It has been authoritatively recognised judicially that any question of any relaxation of the ability of solicitors to enter into such arrangements is a matter to be decided upon by Parliament and not a matter for incremental judicial expansion.[18]

Any conditional or contingency fee agreement relating to contentious business which does not comply with the statutory requirements is unenforceable, either by operation of the express provisions of those sections or the common law and the solicitor is unlikely to be able to rely on a quantum meruit to remedy the situation.[19]

---

[16] *Bolt Burdon Solicitors v Tariq* [2016] EWHC 811 (QB); [2016] 2 Costs L.R. 359.
[17] A more salutary tale for the solicitor may be found in *Ejiofor v Legal Ombudsman* where Wynn Williams J upheld the Legal Ombudsman's decision that the solicitor refund the majority of a 20% contingency fee where the solicitor was found to have known that the risk of a substantive dispute was small and that the amount of work he would undertake was substantial. The contrasting judgments in *Bolt Burdon* and *Ejiofor*—albeit reflecting very different facts—also highlight the alternative remedies available to a client. The remedies under the Solicitors Act 1974 are not the only remedy.
[18] See Lord Neuberger MR (as he then was) in *Sibthorpe & Morris v LB Southwark* [2011] EWCA Civ 25; [2011] 1 W.L.R. 2111 at [40]–[41].
[19] See *Awwad v Geraghty* [2001] Q.B. 570.

If a solicitor enters into an unlawful and unenforceable retainer with their client, the likely effect is that the solicitor will not be entitled to payment of any fees for the work done, even if the solicitor's work was not done as the conducting solicitor, but is still seen as the provision of litigation services[20] (see, for example, *Rees v Gateley Wareing (A Firm)*).[21] However a solicitor in such a case may still be able to retain sums that the client has already paid, assuming there has been no complete failure of consideration.[22]

Both ss.58 and 58AA contain provisions (subss.(5) and (9)) making clear that the statute does not limit the right to enter into a conditional or contingency fee agreement for non-contentious business—save in respect of employment matters. Accordingly, the position remains that, as between solicitor and client, the nature of arrangements that may be lawfully entered into, and the formality requirements that must be complied with in relation to those arrangements, are substantially more restrictive where the subject matter of the retainer relates to contentious business rather than non-contentious business.

A number of issues relating to the ability of solicitors to "transfer" retainers, whether by assignment or otherwise, arose following the reforms. These commonly arose in a between the parties context, though since they were based on an attempt by opponents to take advantage of the indemnity principle at their heart was a contention that the retainer between one or other of the firms of solicitors involved and their client had "failed" in some way. This issue is addressed in some detail in the chapter on funding (**Ch.2**) and is not separately addressed here.

Entitlement to payment

The second category of provision relating to a solicitor's entitlement to payment from their client concerns the way in which a solicitor should bill or otherwise require payment from that client in order to be able validly to claim fees from the client.

9–05

Again, the primary provisions are to be found in the Solicitors Act 1974 and again, the primary effect is to impose a series of obligations and restrictions which differentiate the position from that of a normal contractual relationship.

Firstly, in relation to CBAs and NCBAs, the broad effect is that they determine the client's liability without right on the client's part to a full assessment of the fees payable under them. However, they are subject to an ability on the court's part to set aside the agreements if they are considered to be unfair or unreasonable.[23] The decision of the Senior Costs Judge in *Vilvarajah*[24] is an important reminder of the court's power under s.61 of the Solicitors Act 1974

---

[20] See ss.57 and 61 respectively.
[21] *Rees v Gateley Wareing (A Firm)* [2014] EWCA Civ 1351; [2015] 1 W.L.R. 2179.
[22] See *Aratra Potato Co v Taylor Joynson Garrett* [1995] 4 All ER 695.
[23] For modern consideration of the court's approach to these tests, see the *Bolt Burdon* case above.
[24] *Vilvarajah v West London Law Ltd* [2017] EWHC B23 (Costs).

(and the similar power in relation to NCBAs under s.57 of the 1974 Act) to examine a CBA and to set it aside and order an assessment of costs in appropriate circumstances.

Where such agreements provide for remuneration by hourly rate (rather than, for example, by fixed sum), the time spent on the case is capable of assessment despite the agreement being an NCBA or CBA.

Importantly, in relation to CBAs, the statute expressly provides that a claim may not be brought on a CBA, but that either party to it may apply to the court to enforce or set aside the agreement (s.61). Accordingly, as the court held in *Healys LLP v Partridge*, a CBA cannot found a debt claim. Instead, if the solicitor wishes to enforce it, it must be subjected to the scrutiny of the court under s.61 as to its fairness and reasonableness.

The Act also provides the basic requirements for the form of a solicitor's bill of costs for both contentious and non-contentious business (s.69). A bill complying with s.69 (known as a "statute" bill) is a fundamental requirement before a solicitor can bring an action to recover his costs. Errors in the form of a bill are not infrequently a flaw in such actions.[25] The statutory requirements have been amplified in case law such that it is now well established that a statute bill must be reasonably complete, must have a sufficient narrative[26] (though what is sufficient may be fact dependent and may not be a bar if the client is held to have sufficient knowledge of the relevant matters in any event) and should contain a satisfactory breakdown of the fees claimed.[27]

9–06 An express exception to the latter exists in relation to contentious business where a solicitor may deliver a "gross sum" statute bill (s.64), though if this option is chosen certain additional rights to request further detail and/or challenge the bill are conferred on the client. It also appears to be the case that "gross sum" bills are permitted in non-contentious business (though the issue is not expressly addressed in the statute). It is certainly the view of the Law Society that this is the case (indeed, the expectation appears to be that a gross sum bill will be the norm in non-contentious business)[28]. It should be noted that the Solicitors Act 1974 s.57 expressly provides that in non-contentious business a solicitor may agree with their client to be remunerated by a "gross sum", but this is different from the question of billing and whether a solicitor is entitled to, or, as a matter of fact, has, delivered a gross sum bill to their

---

[25] See, for example, *Vlamaki v Sookias & Sookias* [2015] EWHC 3334 (QB); [2015] 6 Costs L.O. 827 in which it was held that a claim for assessment was premature since the solicitor's bills were not statute bills. Accordingly, the client's remedy was to seek an order under s.68 of the Solicitors Act 1974 for delivery of a final bill, and not to seek detailed assessment. That decision was followed by the Senior Costs Judge in *Rahimian & Scandia Care Ltd v Allan Janes LLP* [2016] EWHC B18 (costs). The two cases illustrate that the point may be deployed by either solicitor or client, but it is usually the client that will seek to make use of the point, to try and avoid the time limits under s.70 of the 1974 Act that would otherwise apply if the bills were statute bills.

[26] See *Garry (A Firm) v Gwillim* [2002] EWCA Civ 1500; [2003] 1 Costs L.R. 77 at [59]–[60].

[27] A recent appellate example of a solicitor being held to have fallen down in this regard is *Bloomsbury Law Solicitors v Macpherson* [2016] EWHC 3394 (QB); [2016] 6 Costs L.R. 1227. A far starker example, where the solicitor's claim was held to be dishonest such that he was ordered to repay all sums paid was *Alpha Rocks Solicitors v Alade* [2016] 4 Costs L.R. 657. Although part of the latter case deals with issues relating to statute and non-statute bills, the case was so far outside the norm that it is useful only as an illustration of the existence of improper practices rather than as any guide to the matters which are addressed in this chapter.

[28] *https://www.lawsociety.org.uk/en/public/for-public-visitors/using-a-solicitor/paying-for-a-solicitor.*

client in circumstances where the basis of charging is, for example, the more conventional hourly rate basis.

There have been a number of important judgments in recent years concerning what is and what is not a valid statute bill.

In *Parvez*,[29] one of the raft of disputes arising from deductions of damages in low-value claims, the solicitor had sent the client a letter informing her of the deductions to be made to her damages. It had also drafted a Bill of Costs, which was on the file when sent to the client's new solicitor, but which had never been sent to the client. Mr Justice Soole held that this was not a bill of costs, nor had it been delivered as such. It is for a solicitor to decide whether and when to bill the client and unless and until a document was sent to the client as a demand for payment it could not be considered to be a bill.

In the case of *Slade*,[30] the point was even more technical, but was of fundamental importance to many solicitors' practices. The question was whether, in order for a solicitor's bill to be a valid statute bill under the Act, that bill must include disbursements for the relevant period it covered in addition to profit costs. It had been held below that it was inconsistent with the proper operation of the Solicitors Act 1974 for the disbursements to be billed separately. This would have meant that any solicitor's bill which did not include all profit costs and disbursements for the relevant period was not a statute bill. This was contrary to common practice. The Court of Appeal overturned the decision and re-established that it was permissible for a bill to be for either profit costs or disbursements (or both) and still be a valid statute bill, provided it was clear what it was intended to cover.

In the case of *Sprey*,[31] the court addressed the question of whether invoices for discounted fees rendered on an interim basis during the conduct of a case, in a case conducted on a discounted CFA, could be seen to be statute bills. The answer—on appeal—was that they could not. The true effect of the agreement was that the client's liability was created on success or failure of the case (or in any other circumstances where the agreement ended) and that was when the solicitor was entitled to render a statute bill. The case is of assistance, but the judgment is clear that it turns primarily on the construction of the particular contract. It does not mean that it is impossible to have a discounted CFA where the interim bills for the discounted fees (payable in any event) are statute bills. However, it would be necessary for the agreement to make this clear. A second appeal to the Court of Appeal, which was due in December 2018, appears to have been compromised.

In *Patel*,[32] the court had to consider whether a solicitor's bill had been adequately paid (see further below concerning the importance of this when seeking an assessment). The court confirmed that, for the purposes of s.70 of the 1974 Act, payment mean payment of the entire bill. Part-payment was

---

[29] *Parvez v Mooney Everett Solicitors Ltd* [2018] EWHC 62 (QB); [2018] 1 Costs L.O. 125.
[30] *Richard Slade & Co v Boodia* [2018] EWCA Civ 2667; [2018] 5 Costs L.R. 1185.
[31] *Sprey v Rawlinson Butler LLP* [2018] EWHC 254 (QB).
[32] *Patel v French LLP* [2020] EWHC 1079 (QB), [2020] Costs LR 523.

not sufficient to trigger any limitation on the client's rights to challenge the bill under the Act. Furthermore, the Court confirmed that payment into client account is not payment under the Act. Payment does not take place until the sums are (properly) transferred to the office account.

The rendering of a statute bill, whether on an interim or final basis—and therefore the issue of whether a bill is or is not a valid statute bill—is important because it is the delivery of the bill that triggers the client's right to assessment of the costs claimed in the bill. There are strict time limits which apply, whereby the client's right to such an assessment reduces from an absolute right (s.70(1)), to a discretion on the court's part, which may be subject of conditions (s.70(2)), to a situation where either the client may have to show "special circumstances" to obtain an assessment or the court's power to order a statutory assessment may be removed completely (s.70(3)).

A statute bill is also important because, unless the solicitor-client agreement it is usually the delivery of a statute bill that triggers the solicitor's right to retain monies from the client and to transfer them from client to office account. It is not uncommon for a solicitor to discover, in the course of contested solicitor-client assessment proceedings, that what they had considered to be statute bills are not, in fact, statute bills and that the belief that the solicitor had in the right to finally retain monies (because they had billed the client and the bills had not been contested within the statutory time limits) is misplaced. Procedural difficulties aside, the common consequence of such an outcome is that that solicitor will have to render a final statute bill or bills to the client and the client will then be able to exercise their statutory rights to challenge the costs in those bills. See the latter part of the *Winros* judgment for an illustration of the difficulties that can arise in such a situation[33].

Although the failure of a client to take timely action to seek assessment following the rendering of a valid statute bill may result in a loss by the client of the rights to assessment, it is important to note that where the costs within a particular bill are unpaid (in whole or part) and the solicitor sues the client for the unpaid costs the client is likely to have the additional remedy of a common law right to dispute the quantum of the claimed fees, and therefore obtain an effective assessment, regardless of the time limits in s.70.[34] This is one reason why questions of whether the bill has been paid or not, if so when it was paid (and, of course, whether the bill is a valid statute bill in the first place) may be important. See *Patel* (above).

---

[33] *The Winros Partnership v Global Energy Horizons Corporation* [2021] EWHC 3410 (Ch).
[34] See *Turner & Co v O Palomo SA* [2000] 1 W.L.R. 37; [1999] 4 All E.R. 353. However, it is important to note in this context that a common law assessment is not precisely the same thing as an assessment pursuant to s.70 of the Solicitors Act 1974 and, in particular, that s.70(9) of the Act—which applies a robust presumption that the client will be awarded the costs of the assessment if the bill is reduced by 20% or more—does not apply. See in particular *Ahmud & Co v Macpherson* [2015] EWHC 2240 (QB); [2016] 3 Costs L.R. 443. In such a case, the client should rather follow the approach in more conventional litigation of seeking to make Part 36 offers in order to achieve a measure of adverse costs protection. Further, it is at least in principle open to the Court to determine that the client has not identified adequate reasons to warrant a common law assessment—see *Re Park* (41 Chd) 326 at pp.333–334.

The recent decision of HHJ Gosnell in *Erlam*[35] provides some helpful context to earlier decisions as to whether a solicitor must not merely advise a client in general of their rights under the Solicitors Act 1974 to seek an assessment when rendering a statute bill, but must go further and explain the implications of a bill being a self-contained bill, particularly in so far as the time limits for seeking assessment are concerned. The judge's conclusion is that there is no such further obligation – though the conclusion is carefully couched in terms which indicate that the judge did not necessarily think that the absence of such an obligation was a good thing.

The necessary form of a statute bill aside, perhaps the key issue which arises in solicitor-client disputes is that in order to be able to render a statute bill on anything other than a final basis (that is to say other than when the work has been fully completed) there either must be an express or implied agreement allowing the solicitor to render "interim" statute bills,[36] or the court must be able to identify a "natural break"[37] in the matter at which it was appropriate to render a statute bill. If neither of these apply, then any interim bill will be merely an "on account" bill, at best and will neither give the solicitor a right to sue for payment, nor trigger the time limits for the client's rights to assessment.

Solicitor-client assessment and disputes

The third set of provisions relate to the procedure for resolving solicitor-client   9–07
disputes. As already noted, s.70 of the Solicitors Act 1974 sets out a set of time limits which apply to a client's right to assessment, such time limits generally being triggered by the delivery of a statute bill.

The basic principle is that a client may apply (usually by way of Pt 8 claim or by defence to a debt claim by the solicitor) for an assessment of any bill or series of bills within these time limits and subject to being able to satisfy any applicable test (such as special circumstances). Although such applications are almost always made by the client, a solicitor is entitled to apply for an order for assessment of his own bill.

As noted, an application for assessment under the Act is usually by way of Pt 8 claim (see CPR r.67). However, it may be made by way of application in response to a debt claim by the solicitor. There can, occasionally, be something of a rush to issue, with the solicitor wanting to bring a debt claim to place pressure on the former client and, perhaps, have the matter heard in a particular forum and the client instead seeking assessment under Pt 8[38]. As the case of *Badaei v Woodwards*[39] shows, where the issues are really ones con-

---

[35] *Richard Slade & Co. Plc v Erlam* [2022] EWHC 325 (QB).
[36] There is substantial case law in this area. See *Re Romer & Haslam* [1893] 2 Q.B. 286 at 293 for the fundamental principle.
[37] For example, see *Re Hall & Barker* (1878) 9 Ch. D. 538.
[38] The case of *Carpmaels & Ransford Llp v Regen Lab SA* [2021] EWHC 845 (Comm) doesn't give rise to any new legal principle, but is an interesting example of how the approach in the Commercial Court on a Pt. 7 debt claim may differ from that in the costs courts on a Pt.8 claim.
[39] *Badaei v Woodwards Solicitors* [2019] EWHC 1854 (QB); [2019] Costs L.R. 1253.

cerning the validity of retainers, bills of costs or the assessment of those costs and lengthy evidence and cross-examination is not required, the court will usually accept that detailed assessment is the appropriate process and allow a Pt 8 claim to proceed if that was issued before the debt claim. See further the recent case of *Jones v Richard Slade & Co*[40] in which the costs judge held that issues concerning undue influence (which went to whether a supposed compromise on costs payable to the solicitor was binding such as to prevent an assessment of the solicitors' costs) were appropriate to be heard in the SCCO.

Where such an assessment is ordered, as a matter of discretion or right, prior to April 2013, old CPR r.48.8 applied. Until April 2013, CPR r.48.8 confirmed that any assessment was to be on the indemnity basis. However, it also went further. In addition to the two key general indemnity basis principles (that is to say: (i) the fact that a test of proportionality does not apply; and (ii) that where a doubt persists as to whether an item was reasonably incurred or reasonably in amount the benefit of the doubt will be given to the receiving party[41]), old CPR r.48.8 confirmed:

(i) that where the costs were incurred with the express or implied approval of the client they shall be presumed to be reasonably incurred;
(ii) that where the amount of the costs was expressly or impliedly approved by the client, the amount shall be presumed to be reasonable; but that
(iii) where they are of an unusual nature or amount and the solicitor did not tell the client that as a result they might not be recovered in full between the parties, they are presumed to have been unreasonably incurred.

This latter point (CPR r.48.8(2)) was an important point and had the ability to have a particular impact in the context of "unusual" disbursements. It is a significant gloss on the general application of the indemnity basis. The importance of its re-iteration post April 2013 has been highlighted in recent caselaw and is addressed further below.

9–08   Although CPR r.48.8 did not strictly apply on a "common law" assessment, the general practice of the courts appears to be to treat such an assessment in a similar, although possibly more broad brush, fashion to a statutory assessment and in particular to approach the assessment on an indemnity basis, given the contractual nature of the liability.

Old CPR r.48.10 (there was no CPR r.48.9) and CPR PD 48 para.54.1 provided a set of more practical guidance as to the mechanics of the conduct of a solicitor-client assessment (these provisions survived the reforms largely unchanged and the April 2013 amendments are considered below).

The key remaining statutory provision to note at this point is s.70(9) of the Solicitors Act 1974. This applies a very specific provision for determining liability for costs of the solicitor-client assessment, known as the "20% rule".

---

[40] [2021] EWHC B28 (Costs).
[41] See now, CPR r.44.4(2) and (3).

Where the bill (or that part of the bill which has been referred for assessment see s.70(5)) is reduced by one-fifth (20%) or more, the solicitor pays the costs of the assessment.[42] Otherwise, the client pays the costs.

This is subject to the court being able to make a different order where it considers there are "special circumstances", a situation which appears to have been open to greater argument in recent years, particularly where one or other party has made an effective offer.[43] The Court of Appeal has confirmed that where part or all of a bill is disallowed because of some problem with the solicitor's retainer with the client—rather, for example, than the more common reason that the costs claimed in that part were unreasonable—the 20% rule still applies to the whole bill. Accordingly, provided the client reduced the bill by more than 20%, whether that was because of the retainer problem or because the costs were unreasonable, the client would benefit from the presumption of being awarded his costs unless there were special circumstances which warranted another order.[44]

The 20% rule does not apply on common law assessments, for the obvious reason that such an assessment is not conducted under s.70 of the Act. In a common law assessment, the costs are in the court's discretion under CPR 44.2, as in any other dispute for unpaid fees. The relevance of offers is likely to be more straightforward in common law assessments, where usually discretionary or CPR Part 36 principles will apply, untrammelled by the statutory presumption applied by s.70(9) and the need to identify "special circumstances" to depart from its strictures.

Finally, in relation to costs, it is possible for a solicitor to agree with their client that the client shall pay the costs of any billing dispute on a particular basis (such as the indemnity basis). However, care must be taken with any such agreement, since it will be closely scrutinised and, in particular, as seen in the *Chevalier* case, such an agreement may be held to be unenforceable under the Consumer Rights Act 2015.[45]

Stepping back, it can be seen that both in terms of the nature of the retainer, the ability of the solicitor to bill the client and sue for its costs and the mechanism that is used to determine any such dispute, the position as between

---

[42] Save where the assessment was requested by the solicitor and the paying party did not attend the assessment.

[43] See for example *Angel Airlines SA v Dean and Dean Solicitors* [2008] EWHC 1513 (QB); [2009] 2 Costs L.R. 159.

[44] *Wilsons Solicitors LLP v Bentine* [2015] EWCA Civ 1168; [2016] Ch. 489. One issue left open by this case is whether the court should consider the 20% "rule" by reference to each individual statute bill which has been assessed or whether it can and/or should consider the totality of the bills. In both the cases dealt with in *Bentine*, the latter approach was adopted, though this seems to have been without demur by and/or at the request of the parties. This will often be eminently sensible where a number of statute bills are assessed as a result of a single application. The position is not helped by the fact that s.70(9) appears to have been drafted in anticipation of a single assessment in respect of a single bill—perhaps a historical legacy reflecting times when the idea of interim statute bills, rather than a single statute bill at the conclusion of the work, was far less common. Although the point is open to argument, it would seem difficult in principle to the court making a single costs order in respect of the assessment of a number of statute bills where those bills were the subject of a combined application. The "costs of the assessment" would relate to the assessment of all of the bills. However, in light of the wording of the statute, there would seem to be a strong argument that any such order would have to properly reflect the outcome in respect of each individual bill and whether the solicitor or client was the "winner" by reference to s.70(9).

[45] *Carmen Chevalier-Firescu v Ashford LLP*, 29 January 2021, Central London County Court.

solicitor and client is, and has long been, heavily modified from that which generally applies as between "trader" and "customer".

As is suggested elsewhere in this section, the changes introduced by the Jackson reforms and, in particular, the loss of recoverability of additional liabilities and the fact that some clients now face deductions from their damages for success fees and ATE premiums does appear to have sparked an increase in the number of solicitor-client disputes, particularly in cases of more limited value where such disputes were traditionally rarely seen.

Whether this is a short-term phenomenon remains to be seen. It has given rise, in the short term at least, to a flurry of first instance, and now appellate, decisions concerning the circumstances in which a client is entitled to a copy—or a further copy—of (part of) the former solicitor's file of papers. The leading case is the judgment of Mr Justice Soole in *Hanley v JC & A Solicitors*[46] in which he held that the court had no jurisdiction to make orders under either its inherent jurisdiction or s.68 of the Solicitors Act 1974 to order solicitors to deliver up documents that were their property. The precise details of the dispute rest on long-established legal principles and not directly out of the Jackson reforms and are not addressed further here.

Finally in this section, the availability of alternative remedies through the Legal Ombudsman should not be ignored,[47] perhaps particularly in the very sort of lower value cases which presently appear to be troubling the costs courts. The ability of the Ombudsman to provide enforceable rulings in relation to fee disputes which are binding on the solicitor, provided the client agrees to the ruling,[48] in circumstances where the Ombudsman will take into account, but is not bound by the decisions a court might make in similar circumstances,[49] and to order the payment of compensation in addition where appropriate,[50] in what is usually a no costs environment,[51] and where the client's complaint, though subject to some basic time limits,[52] is subject to less complicated restrictions than under the Solicitors Act 1974, arguably provides a far more flexible and effective and, from a solicitor's perspective, potentially more dangerous source of redress for a client. The Ombudsman has produced a guidance paper setting out what it regards to be "good service" in the costs context, which bears close reading by all involved in this area.[53]

Effect of the Jackson reforms

9–09   This will be considered under a number of headings. Many of these headings relate to issues which have been considered in detail elsewhere and only their effect on the solicitor-client position will be considered here.

---

[46] *Hanley v JCA Solicitors Ltd* [2018] EWHC 2592 (QB); [2019] 4 Costs L.R. 693.
[47] See the *Ejiofor* case mentioned above.
[48] Scheme Rules r.5.49.
[49] Scheme Rules r.5.37(a).
[50] Scheme Rules r.5.38(b).
[51] Scheme Rules r.5.39.
[52] Scheme Rules rr.4.4 and 4.5.
[53] *https://www.legalombudsman.org.uk/wp-content/uploads/2019/05/190509-An-Ombudsman-view-of-good-costs-service.pdf*.

Changes to the procedural rules in relation to solicitor-client assessments

"Old" CPR rr.48.8 and 48.10 no longer exist, but have been repeated in sub-stantially identical terms in current CPR rr.46.9 and 46.10, including the important provision, now at CPR r.46.9(3)(c) relating to the presumed unrea-sonableness of costs where they are of an unusual nature or amount and the client was not warned that they may not be recovered from the other party to litigation as a result.

For reasons which are not entirely clear, there has been a slight amend-ment to the wording such that where the rule used to provide that they were presumed to be unreasonable if the client was not warned that they might not recover "all of them", the rule now merely provides that they are pre-sumed unreasonable if the client was not warned that the costs "might not be recovered". This would appear to be merely a tidying up of the wording and is not presently thought to have been intended to introduce any substantive change.

The application of the presumptions, as enacted in almost identical form pre-April 2013, has already been referred to above. The power of the presump-tions should not be ignored by either side in such a dispute. Master McCloud's decision in *Archerfield* is a powerful illustration of how agreement by a client to costs being incurred might provide an effective bar to any attempt to later dispute those costs.[54] However, there are numerous instances of costs being presumed to be unreasonable because they have been held to be unusual in nature and the client was not warned that they "might not be recovered". As will be seen below, the important case of *SGI Legal LLP v Karatysz*[55] may have important implications for the question of how the courts should approach this particular presumption and, in particular, whether there is a requirement for the client to have given informed consent to the fact that the costs are unusual and may not be recovered.

Almost certainly the most significant solicitor-client costs case in 2020 (and still awaiting resolution in 2021) was that of *Belsner*[56], which directly con-cerned CPR r.46.9(2) and its interaction with the presumptions under CPR r.46.9(3). CPR r.46.9(2) provides that s.74(3) of the Solicitors Act 1974 applies to any solicitor-client assessment *"unless the solicitor and client have entered into a written agreement which expressly permits payment to the solicitor of an amount greater than that which the client could have recovered from any other party to the proceedings"*.

S.74(3) of the 1974 Act in turn provides that, in relation to contentious business done in the County Court, the amount that may be allowed on a

---

[54] *Mr H TV Ltd v Archerfield Partners LLP* unreported 21 October 2019.
[55] [2021] EWCH 1608 (QB), on second appeal in 2022.
[56] *Belsner v CAM Legal Services Ltd* [2020] EWHC 1755 (QB).

solicitor-client assessment shall not exceed the amount which could have been allowed in respect of the particular items on a between the parties basis.

Both CPR r.46.9(2) and s.74(3) are capable of being misunderstood. The first point to note is they only apply where the work is contentious business done in the County Court. The second is that neither s.74(3) nor CPR 46.9(2) mean that the solicitor-client assessment must limit the costs by proceedings to "assess" what would have been allowed in the County Court on a between the parties assessment and then applying that as a cap. Instead, s.74(3) is aimed at preventing the solicitor form being able to charge the client costs which could not have been recovered in the County Court, as a matter of principle, unless the client has agreed otherwise – see *Lynch*.[57] A classic example of this would be where the costs were fixed between the parties in the County Court.

In *Belsner*, the claim was an RTA "Protocol" claim, where the costs are indeed fixed. The solicitors sought to charge the client a success fee. Success fees are, of course, irrecoverable between the parties. The client had been told this. However, the quantum of the success fee was based on the solicitor's profit costs. Those profit costs substantially exceeded the profit costs which could have been awarded as fixed costs under the Protocol. Whilst, at the end of the case, the solicitor effectively "waived" any claim to profit costs over and above the fixed costs, this was not a term of the contract. Nor, it was said, did it cure the problem that the success fee (albeit capped under the CFA Order 2013) was initially calculated by reference to the full profit costs. The claimant disputed liability for the success fee. The solicitor relied on an alleged agreement under CPR r.46.9(2) which, it was said, showed that the claimant had agreed to be liable for costs greater than sums recovered. Whilst in general terms, this is indeed what the agreement appeared to provide, Lavender J held that this was insufficient.

Whilst he rejected a direct comparison to CPR r.46.9(3) and the idea that "informed consent" was required as a result, he went on to held that informed consent to the CPR r.46.9(2) agreement was needed for other reasons, in particular because of the "fiduciary relationship" between solicitor and client. Although the claimant had been given an estimate of her likely costs, she had not been told that that estimate was substantially higher than the likely fixed protocol costs and, accordingly, informed consent was lacking. As such, the solicitor could not rely on the alleged CPR r.46.9(2) agreement.

Belsner is an interesting case. Whilst the concept of informed consent to incurring prima facie unusual charges under CPR r.46.9(3) is now well understood, the judgment arguably breaks new ground in incorporating that into the requirements for a CPR r.46.9(2) agreement. It also raises interesting issues in its analysis that the solicitor is in a fiduciary relationship when negotiating its own terms of retainer with the claimant at the outset, as well as arguments as to whether or not a claimant who signs terms of business should be taken

---

[57] *Lynch v Paul Davidson Taylor (A firm)* [2004] EWHC 89 (QB).

to have read, understood and accepted those terms absent some form of mis-representation or other impropriety. A second appeal is due to be heard in the Court of Appeal in early 2022 and should provide an important further oppor-tunity for that court to examine the nature of the solicitor-client relationship.

In the meantime, the *Belsner* case is of considerable importance to solicitors when considering their terms of retainer, particular in relation to cases which, if issued, would be heard in the County Court and in any case where any or all aspects of the costs which might be recovered between the parties in the event of issue are fixed or otherwise limited by the CPR. This may include cases where costs recovery would be limited by virtue of CPR r.3.18 and the rules on costs management. Simply advising the client, in such cases, of the possibility of a shortfall costs liability is unlikely to be sufficient. It is likely to be necessary to provide the client with sufficient information for the client to be able to understand the likely practical effect of such a shortfall – whether by way of precise figures, percentages or in some other way that the potential impact can be understood.

Belsner stands alongside *Karatsyz* as the two most important pending appeals in this area. In *Karatsyz*, the issue concerned the presumption under CPR r.46.9(3)(c) that costs are presumed to have been unreasonably incurred if they are of an unusual nature or amount and the solicitor did not tell the client that, as a result, the costs might not be recovered from the other party. In that case – another fixed costs case – although the hourly rate was held to be unusual, the client had been told that the costs (on the basis of rate mul-tiplied by hours) would almost certainly exceed the recovered costs. This was held to satisfy the requirement in CPR r.46.9(3)(c)(ii) that the client be told that these costs might not be recovered. The key question was – did the client have to agree to this, on an informed consent basis (as, for example, with agreement or approval of costs under CPR r.46.9(3)(a)) or was it enough for the client simply to have been told this. On the wording of the rule, Lavender J held the latter – for this part of CPR r.46.9(3) informed consent was not required.

This case is also subject to a second appeal. It is to be hoped that the Court of Appeal will be able to pull the threads of both together and to provide comprehensive guidance both as to the requirements of CPR r.46.9 (2) and (3) as a whole, but also more generally in relation to the operation of s.70 of the 1974 Act, particularly in the context of low value claims for additional liabili-ties. Whilst such guidance would be very welcome, it is unfortunate that what should be relatively simple provisions for identifying the basis on which an assessment is to be conducted should require repeated argument and appeals.

Whilst not strictly related to the 2013 reforms, the Court of Appeal's deci-sion in *Ainsworth*[58] is a useful reminder of the importance of properly drafted Points of Dispute, whether in a solicitor-client context or between the parties. The *Ainsworth* decision was in the former context and whilst the decision was

---

[58] *Ainsworth v Stewarts Law LLP* [2020] EWCA Civ 178, [2020] 1 W.L.R 2664.

based on the requirements for Points of Dispute generally, as set out in CPR r.47 PD para.8.2, it is worth bearing in mind that there are important differences between the two processes, not least the degree of access to and knowledge of the solicitor's papers that the client usually has in such an assessment. Because of that greater knowledge of the detail, it is entirely understandable that the court expects considerable specificity in the Points of Dispute. Whether paying parties in between the parties assessments should be held to quite such a high standard, given that the drafter of the points of dispute will not usually have had access to any of the receiving party's papers, is an interesting argument.

Finally, in terms of procedure, the Court of Appeal has confirmed that the provision under CPR r.39.2(3) to order that a hearing may be held in private applies equally to solicitor-client assessments under the 1974 Act and the case illustrates and provides guidance as to the sort of circumstances in which such an order may be made.[59] It is highly unlikely that the courts will allow such orders to become commonplace in this context.

Costs budgeting

9–11   Costs budgeting is addressed elsewhere.[60] From a solicitor-client perspective, the most significant impact is likely to be that, where a costs management order is made reflecting either agreement between the parties or approval by the court after making revisions, there exists a clear restriction from that point onwards on the "future" costs that the client is likely to be able to recover from the opponent if the litigation succeeds and there may have been clear comments as to reasonableness or proportionality of the incurred costs or of the costs as a whole.

It is important that the client is made aware of that restriction and its effect and of any comments the judge has made which might affect the recoverability of costs. This is particularly so in County Court cases – see the discussion of *Belsner* above – but is a salutary lesson generally. In particular, where, as will commonly, though not always, be the case, the retainer between solicitor and client provides that the client's liability is not limited to costs recovered between the parties, it will be extremely important that the client is made aware of any likely shortfall in costs and is provided with an opportunity to provide an informed agreement to costs which fall outside the approved budget being incurred – or at the very least is informed of any costs which the court has considered to be unreasonable or disproportionate and which the client is unlikely to be able to recover from the opponent even if successful.

The practical approach to this is likely to differ from case to case (or at least type of case to type of case). However, as a minimum, it should be expected that at the outset the client will be told in clear, written, terms of the risk of a shortfall of costs even if the claim succeeds and costs are awarded, and of

---

[59] *Dechert LLP v Eurasian Natural Resources Corp Ltd* [2016] EWCA Civ 375; [2016] 2 Costs L.O. 327.
[60] See **Ch.4.**

particular types of costs which will not or might not be recovered. The obvious example, post-April 2013, is a success fee. Save for a limited class of cases, it is inexcusable not to tell the client, in clear terms, that, where a success fee will be charged, that success fee will not, in any circumstances, be recoverable from the opponent, even if costs are otherwise awarded and that the success fee will be payable by the client alone. The same point applies to the costs of setting up a particular form of funding, or of considering ATE insurance. More fact-dependent examples might include the risk of non-recovery of the costs of leading counsel, or of particular experts, or of the costs of an unusually large disclosure exercise or, returning to the issue of costs management, that the court has only approved a certain amount of future costs for a particular phase, but that for reasons stated the solicitor considers and/or the client requires that it may be necessary to incur additional costs which will not be capable of between the parties recovery at all even if the case succeeds absent either (i) establishing good reason under CPR r.3.18 or (ii) obtaining an order for indemnity basis costs. Further, that even in either of the last two situations, the costs will still be subject to assessment and are unlikely to be recovered in full.

Equally, the common warning in the past, that as a rule of thumb a between the parties recovery of, say, two-thirds (or 70%) of the costs was likely is now likely to be both inaccurate and insufficient, particularly in light of the "new" proportionality test (see further Ch.3). What the client needs to be made aware of is the risk of a substantial shortfall generally, of the risk of not recovering particular items of costs that might be incurred, and that the client has a choice, which they should be given reasonable information in order to make, as to whether such costs are to be incurred (whilst, where appropriate, being informed whether, and if so why, the solicitor considers that those costs are appropriate, desirable or necessary).

The decision in *Blyth v Nelsons*[61] illustrates the sort of difficulties that may arise. In that case, the firm had indicated to its client an intention to "honour" figures set out in a Precedent H. However, in due course the firm sought to charge the client more than those sums on the basis that this was not intended to be a binding cap on costs and that the assumptions on which the Precedent H had been changed had not met reality. Stewart J upheld the first instance decision that the statement of an intention to honour the Precedent H did not amount to a binding cap and more could be charged, though whether and to what extent the indication in respect of the Precedent H would be relevant on any detailed consideration of the extra costs is not addressed in the judgment.

More generally, it is clear that estimates (or a lack of such) provided by solicitors to their clients of likely solicitor-client costs remain a fertile ground for dispute in Solicitors Act assessments and that a failure to provide accurate estimates, to stick to estimates provided and/or to update those estimates as

---

[61] *Blyth & Blyth v Nelson Solicitors Ltd* [2019] EWHC 2063 (QB); [2019] Costs L.R. 1409.

things change may well result in a solicitor's remuneration being severely restricted, below what would otherwise have been regarded as reasonable.[62]

9-12   Reference has already been made to the presumptions which apply under what is now CPR r.46.9. A failure to make it clear to the client that a cost to be incurred is one which falls outside the budget (because, for example, it is not a recoverable cost or it is a cost not included on approval of the budget) may well result in that cost being seen as falling within CPR r.46.9(3)(a) and/or (b) or, in any event, may lead to the court being satisfied that it is unreasonable for the client to be held liable to pay that cost. By the same token, obtaining the client's express approval to the cost being incurred despite the probability of it being irrecoverable between the parties, because it is outside the approved budget, will give the solicitor the benefit of the CPR r.46.9(3)(a) and/or (b) presumptions.

It is, of course, in any event, good practice (and possible essential) to provide the client with clear and accurate costs estimates, see for example SRA Standards and Regulations 2019 Code of Conduct for individuals CPR r.8.7. This requires:

> *"You ensure that clients receive the best possible information about how their matter will be priced and, both at the time of engagement and when appropriate as their matter progresses, about the likely overall cost of the matter and any costs incurred."*

The SRA Standards and Regulations 2019 replaced the SRA Code of Conduct 2011. There are now two codes of conduct—one for individuals and one for firms—and the new rules are less prescriptive than before, leaving matters to the professional's judgement. Indicative behaviours which were guidance in the old Code have been stripped away. Rule 7.1 of the Code for Firms also applies that rule to firms.

Despite initial suggestions to the contrary (see, for example, HH Judge Simon Brown QC[63]), when CPR Pt 3 Section II was introduced it imposed no requirement to obtain the client's signature or to record in any other way the client's approval or agreement that the costs in the Precedent H budget submitted to the court were reasonable or proportionate or in any other way were an appropriate sum to expend on the case. In addition, oddly, there is also no requirement that the terms of any costs management order are served on the client. The provision in the pilot scheme in the Commercial Courts under CPR PD 51G para.6, which provided that the client should be notified with seven days of the budgeting hearing of the budget set by the court was also not carried through to the wider reforms.

---

[62] For recent examples of such disputes, see *Howard Kennedy LLP v Spartafield Ltd* [2019] EWHC 1218 (Ch); [2019] Costs L.R. 749, where the estimate was used as a "yardstick" even where the client had not relied on the estimate, and *Dunbar v Virgo* unreported 12 February 2019 SCCO. These issues are not new and rely primarily on pre-Jacksonian principles and accordingly are not addressed further here.

[63] HH Judge Simon Brown QC, "Costs control Costs management & docketed judges: are you ready for the big bang next year?" (2012) 6 April & 13 NLJ 498–499.

However, it was clearly an intention of the costs budgeting reforms that effective between the parties costs management, whilst not fixing the price between the solicitor and client,[64] would be in the interests of the clients.[65] In the absence of express provision in the rules on costs management, it seems that in practice this might be achieved by the courts, on any subsequent solicitor-client assessment, placing a high burden on solicitors who charge clients sums above the costs budget to show that the client received proper information in this regard and was given an informed choice as to whether to incur such costs, or at the very least was made aware when such costs were being incurred that they were unlikely to be recoverable between the parties.

Both caution and good practice suggest that where the costs budget which is prepared shows costs potentially claimable between the parties which are materially less than those the client is liable to pay, the client should be given clear prior information and explanation in relation to this. The party/party costs budget filed under CPR r.3.13 is the client's costs budget, not the solicitor's, and if the budget indicates any "limitation" on the costs which might be claimed, let alone recovered or allowed, between the parties then the client should be informed of this.   **9–13**

One way to address this might be by producing a modified budget for the client, showing the additional sums the client may be liable to pay.

It is important to remember that between the parties costs are not generally intended to be a full indemnity for the client. There will almost invariably be an element of costs incurred which simply are not and never would be recoverable between the parties (a classic modern example being the costs of arranging or considering various forms of funding).[66] In addition, it will be rare that the costs awarded on a between the parties basis cover the full costs which might have been reasonably incurred on the client's instructions. The fact that the indemnity basis is the default basis for solicitor-client assessments expressly recognises this.

Equally, and perhaps even more importantly in light of the "new" proportionality test, no test of proportionality applies on a solicitor-client basis.

It is, therefore, unrealistic to expect that costs budgets, subject to rigorous review on the standard between the parties basis, applying a test of proportionality, should be expected also to set the proper level of costs on a solicitor-client basis, or that such budgets should simply be used by solicitors as their costs estimates on a solicitor-client basis unless those solicitors genuinely wish to restrict the costs they might reasonably charge their clients.[67]

What the budgeting provisions do emphasise, however, is the fundamental importance of solicitors providing clients with clear and regular costs information both as to costs they may have to pay to their solicitor and costs they may recover from the other side if they are successful in their litigation (and

---

[64] See Judiciary: Lord Justice Jackson's paper for the Civil Justice Council conference, 21 March 2014, paras 5.2 and 5.7.
[65] See Final Report, p.415, para.7.3, for example.
[66] See *Motto v Trafigura* [2011] EWCA Civ 1150; [2012] 1 W.L.R. 657.
[67] For further discussion on this topic see Ch.3, Q16.

which they may have to pay the other side if they lose) and, in particular, of explaining in clear terms how and why the costs the client may be liable to pay may differ from the costs to be allowed between the parties. A simple statement that "if you are awarded costs against your opponent, the costs awarded are unlikely to cover our full costs" is no longer sufficient. A great deal more detail is now required—an explanation of the test(s) of proportionality (and the substantial uncertainty that it creates), of what costs budgeting means, of the various tests on assessment, the meaning of the retainer and so on. The standard, pre-April 2013, retainer letter wording of the type indicated above is no longer sufficient. The information provided needs to be tailored to the individual client and repeated at various intervals. With regard to the effect of costs budgeting, if the client is closely involved in the process and there is a process set up for what happens if the court does not allow costs, it is likely to make for less argument later.

Proportionality

9–14 This has been touched on above. The new test of proportionality, introduced by CPR r.44.3(5), was expressly intended to reverse the unsatisfactory test as clarified in *Lownds*[68] with a view to reducing the costs of litigation, at least where the assessment of costs is being carried out on a standard basis.

The precise effect of the "new" test is addressed elsewhere in this supplement. However, it seems clear that the new test, reinforced by the amendment to the overriding objective and in conjunction with the wider use of costs budgeting and of summary assessment, was intended to be a robust tool in the judicial armoury.

If "new" proportionality is to serve its intended purpose, the ultimate outcome seems to be that there will be a reduction in between the parties' costs.[69] Further, that this will, by the very nature of the test, be a somewhat subjective test, the precise effect of which will be difficult to predict in any given case.

Its impact may potentially be greater in cases of relatively modest value, though again this remains to be seen.

All of this means that there is likely to be a greater shortfall (or at least the risk of a greater shortfall) between the costs recovered between the parties and those for which the client is prima facie liable on a solicitor-client basis and that this shortfall will potentially be proportionately all the greater in the very cases where the successful client's damages are lower. However, because of the uncertainty surrounding proportionality, the actual amount of reduction is hard to specify.

This serves to emphasise further the points in the preceding section as to the increased need for clear and regularly updated guidance to clients as to any potential shortfall. Even if this is just in broad terms and all that can be

---

[68] *Lownds v Home Office* [2002] EWCA Civ 365; [2002] 1 W.L.R. 2450.
[69] See the notes in the chapter on proportionality as to how this new approach is taking effect in practice.

said is that there is likely to be a shortfall and no one can say for certain in what amount.

Whilst no test of proportionality applies on a solicitor-client assessment, a solicitor is obliged to discuss with a client, in a clear and accessible form, whether the potential outcome of a case is likely to justify the expense involved. Where a solicitor fails to provide clear information in this regard both at the start and during the case, and where the solicitor fails to warn the client, particularly in a low-value claim, that there may be a substantial shortfall, it may reasonably be anticipated that the courts will take an increasingly hard line towards solicitor-client assessments of the shortfall costs.

The wider effect of "Jackson"

The costs management reforms were intended to be part of a coherent package   9–15
of reforms aimed at not merely reducing the cost of litigation, but improving the process.

It is the express purpose of costs management that the court should manage not merely the costs to be "incurred by the parties" (note, not merely "recovered by" or "allowed to" the parties), but also the steps to be taken.

In this regard, the reforms extend beyond the introduction of costs management and seek to give the courts more robust powers in relation to case management generally. These include explicit powers to restrict expert evidence by reference to specific issues (CPR r.35.4), to limit the issues to be addressed by witnesses and the length and format of statements (CPR r.32.2) and to take a more focused, and where appropriate, restricted approach to disclosure (CPR r.31.5).

Although these matters do not necessarily directly impact on solicitor-client costs, they can arguably control spend. It is clearly an issue of vital importance that clients are made aware that, to the extent that there was before, there is no longer any guarantee of a system whereby the client can simply engage in "chequebook" litigation. Clearly, a client must be informed on occasions that, although it is open to the client to take a Rolls Royce approach to an aspect of litigation, the cost of doing so is unlikely to be recovered between the parties (for example, the instruction of a QC where the court considers it disproportionate). In addition, the client should be made aware that, whilst the solicitor may consider that a particular approach to the litigation is appropriate (for example the instruction of experts in a particular field), the court may disagree and is exhorted by CPR r.3.12 to take both case and costs management together.

Equally, there will increasingly be occasions where the client must be told that, however much it is prepared to spend, the cost will be to no benefit. This is not a question of recoverability but of restrictions on the client's options because of case management decisions. There is little point in the client engaging a number of costly experts if it is likely that the court will direct evidence from a single expert on limited issues only and the client must be warned of this increased risk before the cost incurred.

Case and costs management is looked at in more detail in **Ch.4.**

Fixed costs claims

9–16 An element of fixed costs, whether in relation to certain aspects of the costs (such as trial costs in fast track claims) or the whole of the profit costs (for example in low-value RTA claims) is an increasing part of the CPR and is a feature seems likely to apply much more widely in future.[70]

In principle, the ability of a solicitor to charge a client for work done is unaffected by the fact that the costs are fixed in whole or part on a between the parties basis, save to the extent that s.74(3) of the Solicitors Act 1974 and therefore CPR r.46.9(2) bites in respect of County Court claims. See the discussion in relation to *Belsner* and *Karatsyz* above. However, it is a clear and obvious point that, where the solicitor's retainer does not limit the costs payable by the client to those recovered between the parties, the client must be told in clear terms that the costs of the claim are, or might be, fixed and that, even if successful, there is likely to be a significant difference between the costs payable by the client and those recovered from the opponent. A failure to do so is likely to lead to an inability to recover any shortfall between the two. Further, to the extent that those costs might be regarded as unusual (whether because of the hourly rate charged or otherwise) the presumption in CPR r.46.9(3)(c) must be addressed and the client advised that, as a result, they may not be recovered.

It is important to remember that any arrangement whereby the costs to be charged to the client are limited to sums recovered between the parties is a species of CFA (a CFA "lite"), on the basis that it is *"an agreement . . . which provided for fees and expenses, or any part of them, to be payable only in specified circumstances,"*[71] even where it does not provide for a success fee, and therefore such an agreement must comply with s.58 of the Courts and Legal Services Act 1990 if it is to be enforceable.

Conversely, it should be remembered that between the parties costs are an entitlement of the client and are recovered in the client's name. In a fixed costs claim (and assuming that the indemnity principle is effectively disapplied), where the costs recovered between the parties exceed the sums the client is liable to pay under the retainer, the balance belongs to the client, not the solicitor. Accordingly, where fixed costs are likely to apply, the retainer should usually provide that if fixed costs apply, the sum charged shall (as a minimum, whether or not also as a maximum) be set at the level of the applicable fixed costs.

Further details in relation to Fixed Costs generally may be found in Ch.7.

Additional liabilities

9–17 Further details in relation to additional liabilities and funding options may be found in Ch.2.

---

[70] As to which, see the discussion on this topic in **Ch.7**.
[71] Courts and Legal Services Act 1990 s.58(2).

Save in limited circumstances addressed in other chapters, additional liabilities are no longer recoverable on a between the parties basis in relation to funding arrangements entered into on or after 1 April 2013 (or later dates for specific categories of proceedings identified in **Ch.2**).

In practice, particularly in the context of lower value personal injury litigation, prior to April 2013 it was rare for a client to be charged a success fee where that success fee was not recovered on a between the parties basis, save possibly where a small additional percentage was charged in respect of the delay in payment, as opposed to the risk of the claim winning or losing.

Whilst the charging of an unrecovered success fee to the client was more common in higher value and commercial litigation, it nevertheless remained relatively rare that such success fees ever became subject of a solicitor-client assessment.

The removal of between the parties recoverability is likely to see such success fees being challenged increasingly on a solicitor-client basis.

CPR r.46.9 expressly includes a provision (subs.(4)) stating that in such circumstances the success fee is to be assessed by reference to all the relevant factors as they reasonably appeared to the solicitor (or counsel) at the time the CFA was entered into or varied (i.e. the same test that applies on a between the parties assessment) though, as noted, on a solicitor-client assessment, the benefit of any residual doubt goes to the solicitor.

Accordingly, it will be at least as important as before that the solicitor keeps an accurate risk assessment in order to support any claimed success fee. Indeed, arguably the importance is increased since it is to be reasonably anticipated that the courts may take a harsher line towards the charging of success fees, particularly in lower value claims, where the success fee is being paid by a client or from a client's damages rather than by an opponent.

This point has been highlighted by the important case of *Herbert*.[72] In *Herbert*, the claimant had instructed solicitors in respect of a low-value RTA. The client had entered into a post-LASPO CFA, with a 100% success fee but capped by reference to classes of damages. He had also taken out a policy of ATE insurance, on his solicitor's advice.

On a solicitor-client assessment, the district judge reduced the success fee to 15% on the basis that the client had not "approved" the success fee simply by signing the CFA, but that something more was required in order for that consent to be informed. Absent approval, the success fee fell to be assessed. The solicitor stated that it charged a 100% success fee in all cases, but then capped by reference to damages. The court held that this was unreasonable and that the success fee must be assessed on an individual case basis. Doing so, no more than 15% was reasonable. The decision was upheld by Mr Justice Soole and, in turn, by the Court of Appeal.

---

[72] *Herbert v HH Law Ltd* [2019] EWCA Civ 527; [2019] 1 W.L.R. 4253. An additional, but important side note in *Herbert* was that the Court of Appeal made clear that the ATE premium was not a disbursement and was not therefore capable of assessment—and reduction—on the solicitor-client assessment. This therefore protects the solicitor from being left responsible (at least via this route) for the client's complaints about what they have paid for the ATE.

It is an important case on the point of "informed consent" and again emphasises the importance of the presumptions under CPR r.46.9. The judgment does not hold that setting the success fee on the basis that it will be same across the broad for all clients in a particular category of case is, per se, wrong or unreasonable. Rather, that if the solicitor is to do so and is to argue that the client has "approved" the success fee, then the client must be told that it was set on such a basis and not by reference to the facts of his individual case. If this is not done, there is no presumption of reasonableness and the success fee falls to be assessed, and must be justified, by reference to the facts of the individual case. Here, on that basis, the first instance judge was not wrong to decide that only 15% was reasonable.

Again, therefore, the emphasis is on the client being properly informed. If so, the client's rights are appropriately restricted. If not, the court will robustly scrutinise the costs claimed.

An important counterbalance to *Herbert* may be found in the decision on Mr Justice Saini in *Higgins*,[73] which contains an important analysis of a client's rights not merely by reference to the more conventional Solicitors Act 1974 route, but by reference to the Consumer Rights Act 2015 and arguments about clauses being onerous. It concerns a CFA based on the Law Society standard model and provides comfort to solicitors using such models that terms under them will not usually be regarded as being unusual or onerous.

9–18 Of course, in personal injury claims, success fees are subject to maximum limits by reference to percentages of certain types of damages (essentially general damages and past loss) recovered. Nevertheless, it should not be assumed that this "cap" on the maximum success fee chargeable will necessarily mean that the success fee cannot be challenged as long as it does not exceed that cap—as the *Herbert* case clearly shows.

For example, if the permitted classes of damages were £20,000 and the success fee, set at 100%, amounted to £5,000 (which is precisely 25% of the prescribed damages, and therefore the "capped" maximum), it would still be open to the client to argue that the 100% success fee was too high and should be reduced on assessment.

In earlier editions of this work, it was stated that it will therefore be important to ensure that the success fee is set at a reasonable level, that the reasons for doing so are properly recorded, and that the client is made fully aware that the success fee will not be recoverable between the parties but will fall to be paid by the client. This point has now been hammered home by *Herbert*.

A specific issue in this regard arose in relation to low-value personal injury claims involving children (and possibly protected parties), where, pursuant to CPR r.46.4, the general rule is that the court must order a detailed assessment of the costs payable by or out of any money belonging to a child or protected party.

In a number of cases, it had been held on such assessments that it is "unrea-

---

[73] *Higgins & Co Lawyers Ltd v Evans* [2019] EWHC 2809 (QB); [2019] Costs L.R. 1711.

sonable" to charge the child a success fee and to seek to deduct the same from the child's damages. The precise reasoning for this appears to be legally flawed—CFAs with success fees are a legitimate means of access to justice and the loss of recoverability between the parties was part of a package of reforms, including an increase in general damages, intended to offset (in part at least) the effect of lost recoverability.

This was a repetition of an early problem following the original introduc-   **9–19** tion of CFAs in 1995, when success fees were not recoverable, which was cured by a specific provision when the CPR was introduced in 1999 (CPR r.48.9(5)), but which was removed in due course because it was thought unnecessary following the introduction of between the parties recoverability of success fees. The short point is that the court should be able to reduce the success fee because it was set at an unreasonable level, but otherwise should not disallow such fees.

The position was, in part, addressed by virtue of the amendment to CPR r.21.12 with effect from 1 April 2015. Rather than the more simplified approach taken under the original 1999 regime, the amendment to CPR r.21.12 imposes limitations on the sums a Litigation Friend is entitled to out of any money recovered on behalf of a protected person.

A different approach is adopted depending on whether or not the damages awarded or agreed exceed £25,000. If they do not, the litigation friend's ability to recover costs will be limited to the (reasonable) success fee or sum payable under a DBA. If the sum awarded or agreed exceeds £25,000, a new CPR r.21.12(7) will limit the Litigation Friend's ability to recover costs to a sum not exceeding 25% of general damages and past pecuniary loss. Whether such restrictions are necessary given the ability of the court to scrutinise the reasonableness of costs and expenses and whether these restrictions will have an inhibiting effect on the willingness of individuals to act as Litigation Friends, or solicitors to act for protected persons, remains to be seen.

The decisions of Regional Costs Judge Lumb in the case of *A&M v Royal Mail Group*[74] may be seen as the courts seeking to explore the proper working of those new arrangements, both in terms of the new procedure and of how to approach the previously rarely asked question of how to assess the reasonableness of success fees which are to be paid out of the damages of child claimants. Two points to note emerge. The first is that the procedure provided for under CPR r.21 and the accompanying Practice Direction—including the provision of proper evidence of why the claimed success fee is said to be reasonable—is there to be followed and a failure to follow it may lead to losing the ability to claim the success fee. The second is that the courts cannot be expected to simply "sign off" on claims for success fees at a high percentage, particularly in low-value claims, or to allow a practice whereby a high percentage success fee is routinely applied simply because the client will then be "protected" by the 25% LASPO "cap". The correctness or otherwise of the particular decision

---

[74] *A&M v Royal Mail Group* unreported 27 August 2015 and 1 October 2015 County Court (Birmingham).

in *A&M* is less important than the message that claims for success fees on a solicitor-client basis, particularly from child or other protected party claimants, will require careful preparation and delicate handling.

Previous editions of this chapter highlighted a further problem with CPR r.21.12 and in particular the amendment introduced in 2015 by CPR r.21.12(1A). CPR r.21.12(1A) expressly provides that "costs recoverable under this rule are limited to . . . costs incurred by or on behalf of a child". This is despite the fact that the rest of CPR r.21.12 clearly and expressly refers to the recovery of costs incurred on behalf of a "child or protected party". Why CPR r.21.12(1A) sought to exclude costs incurred on behalf of a protected party from the ambit of the rule that otherwise appeared to allow such recovery was unclear. This matter was corrected by amendments in 2019 which made clear that CPR r.21.12(1A) applies only to cases involving children and the restrictions therein do not apply to cases where the Litigation Friend is acting on behalf of an adult protected party.

As part of the 2019 amendments CPR r.21 PD 21 para.11.1(A) was amended to provide that where an application is made for costs to be paid out of a child or protected party's damages, that application must be accompanied by a copy of the solicitor-client bill or a breakdown of the solicitor-client costs. This was a simple and sensible practical measure to assist the court in identifying what is being sought and whether it is reasonable. It further emphasises the need for solicitors—particularly those dealing with personal injury cases—to ensure that they have proper client billing practices in place.

Not all of the practicalities have yet been fully worked out. For example, the amendments have the helpful effect of allowing the court to conduct a summary assessment of solicitor-client costs at the approval hearing, thereby avoiding the need for a detailed assessment. However, CPR r.46.4(5) appears to limit this to where the sums claimed are only a success fee or DBA payment, not where there is a claim for "shortfall" profit costs or disbursements. Given that the court has to have a schedule of the costs anyway and will probably have to consider the level of profit costs as part of its decision in relation to the success fee, there does not appear to be any good reason why the court should not be able, in appropriate circumstances, to also summarily assess shortfall profit costs.

In considering these recommendations, the CPRC also noted that para.11.2 of the practice direction to CPR r.21 required the provision of a copy of the risk assessment relating to the success fee to be provided where the application for costs out of the protected party's damages relates to a success fee. There is an oddity here in that there is no strict statutory requirement to produce a risk assessment when entering into a CFA (indeed, although it seems to be considered that the obligation to do so ceased with the introduction of LASPO, in fact the strict statutory obligation to do so ended in November 2005 with the revocation of the Conditional Fee Agreement Regulations 2000). Nevertheless, the CPRC consider that it is sensible to maintain the provision in the practice direction. This may seem anomalous, but plainly is intended to send out a clear message—namely that whilst there is no statutory provision requiring a risk assessment when entering into a CFA, it is good practice to do so and not doing so may hamper the solicitor's ability to recover the success fee from the client. This is consistent with the court's emphasis in *Herbert*—above—on the need for the solicitor to be able to justify the success fee in the individual case. These clear indications should not be ignored.

Following the apparent increase in solicitors seeking shortfall costs from child or protected party clients, following the introduction of the Jackson Reforms, the SCCO in December 2021 produced a practice note on the "approval" of costs settlements and assessments under CPR r.46.4(2)[75]. The note is not considered in detail here, but in summary it takes a relatively narrow approach to the rules and practice direction which means that a solicitor seeking a shortfall from a child or protected party client (other than in relation to a success fee in the limited circumstances set out above) is likely to face a detailed assessment, on a solicitor-client basis – of its costs and, according to para.17 of the note, is likely to have to pay its own costs of that mandatory process (unless the child or protected party or their litigation friend or other representative has taken active opposition to the claim). Approval of the shortfall costs by the litigation friend will not remove the obligation to seek assessment nor apparently otherwise mitigate the court's scrutiny of the costs claimed. If this procedure is followed, it appears likely that solicitors will be less willing to seek such shortfall costs (not least because of the irrecoverable costs of doing so). Whether this will have any knock on effect on their willingness to accept instructions from such clients remains to be seen.

The introduction of DBAs has brought a relatively new aspect to solicitor-client assessments. Although such arrangements have always been possible in non-contentious business, they have been rarely used. Prior to the Court of Appeal's decision in *Zuberi v Lexlaw*[76] (discussed in detail in **Ch.2**) only a relatively limited number of DBAs appeared to have been entered into since April 2013. Whilst a number of interesting cases have arisen concerning DBAs, there is, as yet, no reported decision yet of a solicitor-client costs dispute in relation to the reasonableness or fairness of the percentage fee charged under such an agreement.[77] The closest is the relevant part of the decision in *Bolt Burdon v Tariq*, concerning a challenge by the client to a non-contentious business agreement which, in its operation, was similar in terms to a DBA. That agreement was upheld and the court awarded the solicitor the full amount of the contingent fee (which was very substantially more than the conventional hourly rate fee would have been for the work done to the point of settlement).

---

[75] https://www.associationofcostslawyers.co.uk/write/MediaUploads/News/SCCO_Practice_Note_-_Deductions_from_damages.pdf.

[76] [2021] EWCA Civ 16.

[77] DBAS, the regulations surrounding them and the reasons why were little used prior to the *Zuberi* decision are considered in depth in the **Ch.2**), along with the CJC Working Committee's Report, the Mulheron/Bacon proposals in this regard and some of the possible future amendments to the rules and regulations surrounding DBAs.

By far the most significant decision in this area was the Court of Appeal's early 2021 decision in *Zuberi v Lexlaw*, which is considered further in **Ch.2**. The issue in that case, however, was one of principle as to the ability to have a provision in such an agreement allowing for payment of conventional fees if the client chooses to terminate the agreement. We are still awaiting any disputes focussed more closely on, for example, the reasonableness of the percentage payment under such an agreement. Whilst ostensibly it could be said that if there is a signed agreement which states the percentage, then the scope for argument should be limited, the same could, of course, have been said of success fees under CFAs. As the case of *Herbert* shows, the argument is not likely to be that simple.

In contrast with the position in employment cases, there are no specific regulatory requirements for advice to the client prior to the entering into of a DBA and accordingly, given the nature of DBAs, there is substantial scope for argument at the conclusion of the case as to whether the fee claimed was "reasonable". Cases will be heavily fact dependent, but where a DBA is used there is a clear requirement for very clear information to be given to the client as to the basis on which any DBA fee is set, for clear records to be kept of cogent reasons for setting the fee at the level chosen and, perhaps above all, for clear written information to be given to the client about the difference between the DBA payment being charged and the basis on which fees might be recovered between the parties if the case is won.

Reference has already been made to the Legal Ombudsman, which has already expressed its critical view as to the lack of clarity of CFAs and its concerns as to the risks of the same with DBAs.[78] Solicitors should not underestimate the need to make the key facts in relation to CFAs and DBAs clear in plain and, if necessary, repeated terms. The reluctance, at least pre-*Zuberi*, to use DBAs in light of the poor drafting of the DBA Regulations 2013 should not obscure the fundamental need to ensure a consumer-focused approach to the drafting of such agreements and related documentation where they are used. The expansion in their use – which anecdotally is believed to be quite considerable – following the Court of Appeal's decision may well lead to a number of cases where the courts have to consider the reasonableness of the chosen terms of remuneration. It is notable that in *Zuberi*, the majority in the Court of Appeal was reassured in adopting the definition of "what is a DBA" that it did by the existence of the right to a solicitor-client assessment under s.70 of the Solicitors Act 1974 as a robust check on their misuse.

The introduction of DBAs, the changes to CFAs and the loss of recoverability between the parties of ATE insurance premiums, together with the likely changes in between the parties costs recovery, mean that the range of funding options available to a client and the permutations in any given case are greater than ever. Whilst the risks have always been present, they are greater than ever and the obligation to give a client proper advice in order to allow

---

[78] See Complaints in focus: "No win, no fee" agreements: *https://www.legalombudsman.org.uk/publications/no-win-no-fee/*.

the client to make an informed choice as to the appropriate funding option should not be ignored.[79]

Questions and answers

Q1. Have the "Jackson" reforms changed the basis on which I, as a solicitor, can charge my client?
Only to the extent that the scope of lawful arrangements has widened to include DBAs in contentious business. That apart, the ways in which you can agree with your client to pay you remain the same, though the Jackson reforms have had a material effect on whether certain major elements of those costs, primarily the success fee, can be recovered from an opponent.

    9–20

In personal injury claims, that loss of between the parties recoverability has resulted in a limit being imposed on the maximum amount of the success fee you can charge your client.

Those matters apart, it was beyond the scope of the reforms, for example, to change the indemnity basis for assessment of solicitor-client costs and that was neither their intention, nor is it their effect. The basic principle that such costs are to be assessed on the indemnity basis remains, and the core CPR provisions in relation to such an assessment, now at CPR r.46.9, remain unchanged.

However, the anticipated reduction in between the parties costs, combined with the changes in funding methods, including the loss of recoverability of success fees, means that there is likely to be a greater number of cases, in particular in low-value claims, where the solicitor seeks to charge a "shortfall" to the client where, in the past, such a shortfall might not have been charged.

This is likely to bring a more regular and greater scrutiny to such claims, either by the courts or by the Legal Ombudsman.

Accordingly, whilst the basis on which you can charge your client remains largely the same and whilst the basis on which such costs will be assessed has not changed, the practical effect is that, particularly in personal injury claims, it is likely to be far more common that the client will be asked to meet some of the costs out of their damages and both as a result of this and other changes it seems probable that claims for "shortfall" costs will be more regularly disputed than before.

Q2. Can you advise the client of the full range of funding options but then say but we as a firm do not offer X, or Y or only offer X or Y on this basis?

---

[79] See *David Truex (A Firm) v Kitchin* [2007] EWCA Civ 618; [2007] 4 Costs L.R. 587 (solicitor's claims for costs disallowed for failure to advise as to the availability of legal aid) and *McDaniel & Co v Clarke* [2014] EWHC 3826 (QB); [2014] 6 Costs L.R. 963 (solicitor's claim disallowed for failure to advice of availability of trade union funding) for two examples of the dangers.

9–21   Yes. This was a common situation with publicly funded cases (when public funding was more widely available).

A solicitor's duty is to consider, at the outset (i.e. at the time the client first seeks to instruct the firm) what forms of funding are reasonably available to the client and to advise the client accordingly. This includes advising the client that there may be other forms of funding available which the firm does not provide. This may include public funding or may, in certain circumstances, include other forms of funding such as CFAs or DBAs which the firm may not offer.

The SRA Codes of Conduct for Solicitors and Firms, part of the Standards and Regulations 2019, have deliberately slimmed down the list of obligations on a solicitor in this regard, such that they are instead encompassed within broader requirements. Nevertheless, it is expressly provided (para.8.7 of the Code for Solicitors) that a solicitor must ensure that clients receive the best possible information about how their matter will be priced and, both at the time of engagement and when appropriate as their matter progresses, about the likely overall cost of the matter and any costs incurred. This should not be treated as an exhaustive statement of the requirement.

The ultimate requirement is to treat the client fairly and to ensure that the solicitor complies with the duty to act in their best interests, even if that might mean advising them of a form of funding which the firm does not offer with the result that the client chooses to instruct a different firm.

Provided this is done, it is entirely proper to indicate that if the client wishes to instruct the firm the only terms which the firm is prepared to offer are the X or Y referred to.

Q3. My case is subject to costs management. Am I required to seek my client's approval to the budget and does the budget, if agreed or approved, limit the costs I can charge my client?

9–22   In answer to the first part of the question, no. There was some discussion of a requirement for the client to sign the budget, or the solicitor to confirm the client's agreement to the budget, but this did not make it into the final rules.

However, as a matter of practice, it is important that the client is aware of the likely costs of the claim and of how the costs which might be recovered from the opponent relate to the cost that the solicitor is likely to charge the client. It is also important that the client is made aware of how the likely costs of the claim might impact on the conduct of his claim. For example, if, as a result of the costs being seen to be disproportionate on a between the parties basis, the scope or extent of witness or expert evidence is likely to be restricted, the client needs to be made aware of the reasons for this and the options available to address it. See the discussion in relation to informed consent and cases such as *Belsner* and *Herbert* above.

The client should be receiving regular costs estimates and updates on a solicitor-client basis anyway and differences between these and the between the parties budget should be highlighted so that the client has an informed choice as to whether or not to incur the additional costs.

As to the second part of the question, again the answer is "no", unless the solicitor-client retainer is such that the costs chargeable to the client are limited to sums recovered between the parties. Even then, the final effect will not be known until the end of the case, when it is known whether the client has won, what costs order has been made, whether indemnity costs are awarded (CPR r.3.18) and whether, if the budget applies, the budget is to be departed from for any "good reason" (CPR r.3.18). In any event, the budget only "bites" on costs from the date of the budget (CPR Pt 3 PD 3E para.7.4).

Q4. Do the revised rules on Pt 36 apply in a solicitor-client assessment?

There is a lack of clarity in this regard. There is a primary statutory provision   9–23
dealing with the incidence of costs at the conclusion of a statutory assessment of solicitor-client costs, namely s.70(9) of the Solicitors Act 1974.

This provision cannot be, and has not been, displaced by CPR Pt 36 and continues to apply. However, that provision is subject to s.70(1), whereby the court can depart from the otherwise mandated outcome if there are "special circumstances" (as to which, see *Wilsons Solicitors LLP v Bentine*, above). It seems to be increasingly accepted that the making of effective offers by the parties to the assessment is capable in principle, dependent upon the particular facts, of amounting to a special circumstances, and this would appear to fit with the ethos of both the CPR generally and the Jackson reforms in encouraging the making of offers to compromise disputes at an early and less costly stage.[80]

Accordingly, the making of a Part 36 offer may, on the facts of a case, be capable of amounting to a special circumstance, but the automatic provisions of CPR rr.36.10 and 36.14 do not appear to apply because they conflict with s.70(9), which is a primary statutory provision of express application.

Whether a successful Part 36 offer therefore attracts any greater benefit than a Calderbank offer is open to argument. Given that the full rubric of Pt 36 cannot apply, and Pt 36 is intended to be a complete and self-contained code, it seems more likely that a successful Part 36 offer should be treated as an admissible offer under the court's general discretion under r.44.2(4)(c), assuming that the automatic consequences under s.70(9) do not apply.

In "common law" assessments (i.e. those which are based on a common law right to dispute the reasonableness of a claim for unpaid fees, rather than assessments under s.70 of the Solicitors Act 1974) Pt 36 would appear to apply and to be an important aspect of any such claim—see *Ahmud v MacPherson* (above).

Lastly, in relation to costs of solicitor-client assessments, the judgment of

---

[80] As an aside, similar principles developed under the CPR, such as penalising a party in costs for failing to negotiate also seem to be capable of being "special circumstances"—see *Allen v Colman Coyle LLP* [2007] EWHC 90075 (Costs).

Mr Justice Morris in the case of *Parissis*[81] should not be overlooked. It is a firm illustration of the risk to a solicitor of failing to provide a client with reasonable information as to the costs the client is being charged with and is instructive for any solicitor considering how to respond to a request by the client for further information.

Q5. Can we charge/recover for preparing the solicitor-client estimate?

9–24 It is assumed that this question refers to the costs of provision of costs information to the client rather than the costs of preparing a Precedent H for the purposes of between the parties costs management, which are limited by CPR PD 3E para.7.2.

The (reasonable) costs of preparing such a between the parties Precedent H will, of course, form part of the costs payable by the client.

Time reasonably spent advising the client in relation to their own costs, whether by way of costs estimates, funding arrangements or the like should ordinarily form a part of the charges payable by the client, at least in so far as such work is work undertaken once the client is, indeed, a client (see *Motto v Trafigura Ltd*[82]). However, there will be a limit on the extent to which such time is recoverable. It is to be expected that solicitors have systems in place which allow them to properly record, monitor and analyse time spent and the cost of these is an overhead. The court will not expect that, save in exceptional cases, the solicitor will have to spend substantial time providing an initial estimate or updating that in due course.

Q6. It is still not clear how solicitors should go about doing estimates of costs for their clients and the extent to which Precedent H is sufficient/ useful for this purpose. Can you express a view?

9–25 A solicitor must provide a clear explanation to a client of the solicitor's fees and best possible information about how their matter will be priced and, both at the time of engagement and when appropriate as their matter progresses, about the likely overall cost of the matter and any costs incurred (Code of Conduct for Solicitors 2019, para.8.7). All information must be provided in a way the client can understand (para.8.6).

Taking these requirements into account, best practice would require the provision of an estimate and costs benefit analysis at the start of any retainer, together with regular updates and revisions of the estimate, particularly when there are any material changes which might affect the likely costs or the costs benefit analysis.

Precedent H produced for the between the parties costs management process may be a useful tool in this process and it may well be that some solicitors develop a practice of using a Precedent H type model to provide costs estimates to their clients from the outset of cases, particularly following the

---

[81] *Parissis v Matthias Gentle Page Hassan LLP* [2017] EWHC 761 (QB); [2017] 3 Costs L.O. 269.
[82] [2011] EWCA Civ 1150.

introduction of J Codes. However, care must be taken to make the client aware of any differences between the amounts set out in the between the parties Precedent H and the sums that the client may be required to pay.

Where a budget is agreed or approved on a between the parties basis, the client should be made aware of any differences between the sums agreed or approved and those which were sought and as to the client's liability for such sums (if any).

The case of *Harrison v Eversheds LLP*[83] is a recent and illustrative example of the dangers to a solicitor in seeking costs in excess of an estimate without proper explanation and justification.

Q7. If a case is not costs managed, should the client still be sent Precedent H for solicitor-client purposes or a different type of estimate?
There is no rule-based requirement to do so. Nor is such a practice required   9–26
or imposed by the Code of Conduct for Solicitors and Firms or any similar practice requirements. It is a matter for the individual solicitor as to how to inform the client of any matters relating to the case and costs management of the client's case. However, for the reasons set out in the text above, it is important that the client should be made aware of any potential shortfall between the client's potential liability to costs and the likely recovery of those costs if the case succeeds. If the solicitor, in producing the Precedent H, intends to include a materially lower level of costs than those for which the client is likely to be liable then good and protective practice would include informing the client of this and the reasons for it. Similarly, if the Precedent H is then approved or agreed at a lower figure in relation to estimated costs, or if the court makes comments on the costs of any material kind, good and protective practice would be to inform the client of these matters. It is the client's costs which are being costs managed and a failure to inform the client of material information relevant to the likely between the parties recovery of those costs may result in the solicitor experiencing difficulties in recovering those costs himself from the client in due course.

In addition, the provisions of CPR PD 44 para.3 should not be overlooked. A Precedent H which has been filed may still be relevant on the assessment of costs, even where a costs management order is not made. Accordingly, if a Precedent H is produced, the client should be made aware of any effect this might have on the recovery of costs even if the matter does not proceed to a costs management hearing.

Of course, there are a number of scenarios where the rules do not require a Precedent H to be filed at all. In such cases, the solicitor should not overlook their duty to keep the client informed throughout the case both as to the level of costs incurred and as to the likelihood of any shortfall.

---

[83] *Harrison v Eversheds LLP* [2017] EWHC 2594 (QB); [2017] 5 Costs L.R. 931. See further *Kennedys LLP v Spartafield* (above).

Q8. Can a solicitor charge their client a lower amount than that stated in a costs budget, or a schedule or bill of costs?

9–27   Yes. A costs budget or costs management order has no direct effect on the amount the solicitor is able to charge their client. That amount may be more, or less, than the amount stated in the budget. However, if at the end of the case the solicitor agrees to limit the client's liability to a sum less than the amounts approved or agreed in a costs management order, then the client would be unable to claim the full amount in the approved budget from the opponent on any assessment, by virtue of the operation of the indemnity principle. In such circumstances, (i) the between the parties bill of costs produced would have to make clear any limit on the costs claimable on a between the parties basis as a result of any agreed limit on the client's liability and (ii) the effect of the indemnity principle would almost certainly be a "good reason" under CPR r.3.18 for the court to depart from the agreed or approved budget.

What is more common in practice is either that the solicitor and client enter into a CFA "lite" which allows for an attempt to recover the costs in full between the parties, but provides that the client's liability will be limited to the sum recovered, or that the solicitor seeks to recover the maximum possible amount of the client's costs liability to the solicitor on a between the parties basis. It is only once the amount of that recovery is known that the solicitor then decides whether to restrict or waive any claim for a shortfall from the client. See further the sections on Costs Management (**Ch.3**).

Q9. What should solicitors be bearing in mind for solicitor-client costs when the proposals for expansion of fixed recoverable costs are implemented? e.g. If the client is likely to recover a lesser sum between the parties, then the solicitor might want to charge less or ensure that solicitor-client retainer is tightened so that the solicitor can still charge and recover from the client a higher amount.

9–28   These are matters which it is important for the solicitor to consider in any case involving any element of fixed costs. For a variety of reasons, commercial or otherwise, the solicitor may wish to limit the charge to the client to the sums recovered. However, in doing so, the solicitor should be wary to ensure that he does not erroneously limit those costs. For example, a retainer which limited the client's liability to fixed costs would be unhelpful if the client was able to "escape" fixed costs, for example by an indemnity basis costs order. A better approach in such circumstance would be to use a suitably drafted CFA lite, limiting the client's liability to sums recovered.

As the question anticipates, however, it may well be that the desire is to make clear that the client may be liable for more than the fixed costs or sums otherwise recovered. There are myriad possibilities here. That liability might be unlimited, it might be capped as a percentage of damages, alternatively, the "shortfall" might be capped in some way, or there may be a fixed fee element or a range of other possibilities. The important points to note are that (i) the client must be made aware of the terms of any arrangement and in particular, the potential for any shortfall, (ii) such terms must comply with any applicable consumer legislation, (iii) where the retainer relates to business to be done in the County Court, the provisions of s.74 of the Solicitors Act 1974 (ostensibly restricting the solicitor-client liability to the amount which could have been allowed on a between the parties basis) should be expressly addressed and "disapplied" by written agreement if required and (iv) the client must be kept informed as the case progresses as to any matters which may affect the client's liability and the size or risk of any shortfall. Given the potentially significant widening of the scope of cases covered by fixed costs firms should take care to ensure their retainers for such categories of work are reviewed and may wish to review their business model in terms, for example, of the grade of fee earner used for types of work. In that regard, the Court of Appeal's decision in *Thomas v Hugh James Ford Simey*[84] concerning the scope of retainer and standard of care to be expected of a firm conducting high volume, low-value litigation was no doubt welcome news to many practitioners.

Q10. Do solicitors have to/should solicitors use software solutions for solicitor-client costs purposes?

There is no regulatory requirement to use such software solutions. However, the introduction of electronic bills (as to which see Ch.8) for between the parties assessments (as to which see the chapter on assessments) and a range of other reasons, from matters of internal efficiency, to the need to be able to provide clients with reliable costs information, to the need to be able to monitor reliably any disparity between the parties costs budgets and the client's liability, to the desire to be able to produce reliable interim statute bills containing sufficient information about the costs chargeable in any given period all point towards the greater use of bespoke software solutions for both time recording and costs analysis.

9–29

Q11. How have the courts been considering whether a switch of funding was reasonable? What is the best way for solicitors to advise regarding switching funding?

The leading case in this regard is *Surrey v Barnet*.[85] The issue is one of reasonableness and, as already noted, is based on pre-April 2013 principles. Put simply, the choice to change funding must be reasonable on a between the parties basis if the costs are to be recovered and, if, as often will be the case, the reasons for changing were based on advice by the solicitors, then it is that advice which must be reasonable. If the advice was not reasonable, then there will be a burden on the claimant to show that he or she would have made the same choice if the "proper" advice had been given. It is fair to say that, post-*Surrey*, claimants have struggled in many cases to recover success fees and ATE premiums where there was a pre-April 2013 change from

9–30

---

[84] *Thomas v Hugh James Ford Simey Solicitors* [2017] EWCA Civ 1303; [2017] 5 Costs L.O. 643.
[85] *Surrey (A Child) v Barnet & Chase Farm Hospitals NHS Trust* [2018] EWCA Civ 451; [2018] 1 W.L.R. 499.

legal aid to CFA, though there are some reported instances of success, the most recent of which appears to be *AB v Mid Cheshire*.[86] The reconsideration of some of these issues in the case of *XDE* essentially restated and affirmed the principles set out in *Surrey*.

As to advice to be given, in this particular context, the time has passed. The arguments concern recoverability of additional liabilities and the cases concern testing the advice that was given a number of years ago and a situation which will not arise in respect of new cases because of the removal of between the parties recoverability of additional liabilities. Nevertheless, insofar as guidance may be derived more generally as to how to advise the client, for example, about choices of funding or about incurring particular items of costs, the *Surrey* case fits neatly alongside cases such as *Herbert* in emphasising that it is important that the solicitor provide the client with clear information, in a way which is accessible to and understandable by the client, about what is being proposed and why. "Informed consent" is the key, and whilst this does not carry quite the same connotations as in the medical field, the important point is to provide the client with all reasonable information to understand the options they are being provided with. See also the requirements of the SRA Standards and Regulations particularly the Code of Conduct for individuals Rules rr.8.6–8.7.

Q12. Following *Herbert*, should 100% success fee retainers not be used?

9–31 There is no particular reason not to use 100% success fees post *Herbert*. The key problem in *Herbert* was the lack of informed approval by the client, because the client was not told that the firm had a practice of charging a 100% success fee to clients in all such cases. Had the client been told of this, the client could have chosen to accept this, to try and negotiate a different success fee, or to seek to instruct a different firm. Had the client chosen the former, then it may have been very difficult for the client to dispute the 100% success fee at the end of the case.

It should be borne in mind that, in personal injury cases, the recoverable success fee is further limited by the cap on the success fee, by reference to certain classes of damages, imposed by the CFA Order 2013. There is no immediately obvious reason why a solicitor could not seek to identify a particular business model whereby the client was charged a particular success fee, but the effect of the success fee was the mitigated by the cap (or by some other additional cap on the client's total liability). What is important is that the client is made properly aware of the basis on which he or she is to be charged and, if the charge is based on a wider business model rather than one peculiar to the client's own circumstances, that the client is told of this. See further the *Belsner* case where additional guidance from the Court of Appeal is likely. Provided the agreement is otherwise lawful, provided the advice and information to the client is reasonable and is properly recorded and provided the

---

[86] *AB v Mid Cheshire Hospitals NHS Foundation Trust* [2019] EWHC 1889 (QB); [2019] Costs L.R. 1197.

client agrees on an informed basis, then the solicitor will benefit from the presumption that the agreed fees are reasonable under CPR r.46.9.

Q13. Does the indemnity principle apply (and if so, to what extent) to CFAs and DBAs?
This issue is addressed in more detail in the chapter on funding (Ch.2). 9–32
However, the short answer is "yes", subject to some caveats. Firstly, if the agreement is what is termed a "lite" agreement, that is to say one where the client's liability is limited to sums recovered from the opponent in litigation (whether by way of costs or damages), it is well established that such an agreement does not breach the indemnity principle (or, if it does, that such breach does not prevent recovery of the costs).

Secondly, where the costs payable are fixed costs under the CPR, it has again been long established that the indemnity principle does not apply to payment of the "profit cost" element of those fixed costs (see the case of *Nizami*,[87] the relevant dictum in which has been approved by numerous Court of Appeal and High Court judgments in the subsequent 13 years). Indeed, it is difficult to see how the bulk systems of fixed costs now provided for in CPR Pt 45 III and IIIA and the relevant protocols could operate in practical terms if compliance with the indemnity principle was required in each case.

None of this, however, diminishes the obligation on a solicitor to ensure that their agreement is a valid, enforceable and lawful one. To do otherwise would leave them in breach of their Code of Conduct.

Q14. The law links party/party and solicitor-client costs in certain areas (e.g. see s.74(3) of the Solicitors Act 1974 regarding County Court work) and recent cases have required the client to have given "informed consent" if they are being expected to pay the solicitor more than they might recover. Are we seeing a connection between party/party and solicitor/client costs now more than ever? Is the requirement for transparency in relation to costs now being applied more than before to solicitor/client costs?
The short answer to the final part of the question is "yes". It is undoubtedly 9–33
the case, particularly in lower value claims where relatively modest sums of costs (in absolute terms) are deducted from damages, but those costs form a significant part of the damages recovered, that the courts have been far more involved in the consideration of the reasonableness of such sums on a solicitor-client basis than was the position before April 2013 when the arguments primarily occurred in between the parties assessments.

There has been no change in the law in this regard. However, the greater frequency of challenge and the focus on the hitherto relatively unexplored context of low-value claims means that there has been some interesting judicial clarification of the existing procedural and substantive law – see the

---

[87] *Nizami v Butt* [2006] EWHC 159 (QB); [2006] 3 Costs L.R. 483.

discussion on *Belsner* above. In County Court cases, the often misunderstood effect of s.74(3) of the 1974 Act introduces a further limitation. The net effect, in such cases, is that solicitors need to be increasingly careful in any such situation where "shortfall costs" are to be claimed from the client to ensure that the client has been given a clear and transparent explanation of their potential liability.

Q15. Does CPR 44.5 (amount of costs where costs are payable under a contract) apply to solicitor/client costs if the client has agreed to pay the solicitor's costs? What about if the costs are those of a former solicitor which the former client has agreed to pay but disputes the amount? And can costs only proceedings under CPR r.46.14 apply in that situation? Or does the Solicitors Act and CPR r.67 and CPR r.46.9 apply instead?

9–34   CPR r.44.5 does not directly apply, since it is a rule of procedure which must take second place to the express primary statutory provisions in s.70 Solicitors Act which govern the assessment of solicitor-client costs. Procedurally, s.70 is then supplemented by the express rules at CPR r.46.14 and those express rules would again displace (to the extent that they conflicted) the general rule in CPR r.44.5. In practice, however, little turns on this since the key effect of CPR 44.5 is to provide that costs payable under a contract will be payable on the indemnity basis unless the contract expressly provides to the contrary and it is well established that solicitor-client costs are payable on the indemnity basis in any event. Perhaps the key difference is that CPR r.46.9 then sets out some express further presumptions which then qualify this general position, but as noted there is no dispute that such further qualifications apply.

Q16. In the event that a retainer was entered into on a private basis providing for regular interim bills, but those bills were never rendered due to the client's impecuniosity, does *Thai Trading*[88] remain effective so as to allow the receiving party's solicitor to certify on a bill of costs that there has been no breach of the indemnity principle and so recover inter parte costs? This would be on the basis that there was an understanding between the firm and the client that there would be no charge unless the claim succeeds but when it is common ground that that understanding was never formalised in writing so as to satisfy s.58(3)(a) of the Courts and Legal Services Act 1990.

9–35   *Thai Trading* should not be regarded as good law in relation to the question of whether an unwritten agreement with a client for a conditional basis of charging is contrary to public policy and therefore unenforceable. In *Hughes*[89], *Thai Trading* (in which the respondents had been unrepresented) was expressly not

---

[88] *Thai Trading (A Firm) v Taylor* [1998] EWCA Civ 370.
[89] *Hughes v Kingston upon Hull City Council* [1999] QB 1193.

followed on the basis that it had been made without consideration of the House of Lords' decision in *Swain*[90].

Subsequent caselaw has made it plain that a CFA with a client which does not comply with the requirements of primary and secondary legislation is, as s.58 of the Courts & Legal Services Act 1990 makes clear, unenforceable (save possibly only if any breach of the requirements is immaterial) and that the ability to recover costs in such circumstances cannot be save by reliance on a quantum meruit[91], though the receiving party client may still be able to recover costs whichh they have actually paid to their solicitors (see *Aratra Potato Co*[92]), a position unlikely to arise in the instant scenario.

Much may, however, turn on the precise factual situation. The question refers to an "understanding". The indemnity principle has, at its heart, the question of whether the client is liable to pay the costs in question, not, for example, whether the client is able to or has paid those costs – see, for example, *R v Miller*[93]. There is a presumption the client is so liable and whilst this may be rebutted by evidence of an express or implied agreement that the client would never have to pay the costs in any circumstances, mere impecuniosity will not suffice, nor will the fact that the solicitor has not billed the client or has not pursued payment from the client pending attempts to recover from the opponent, or the fact that a third party is indemnifying the client. Accordingly, a mere understanding between solicitor and client that the solicitor will look to recover costs from the opponent and that the solicitor may decide not to pursue the client for any shortfall will not normally suffice to prevent between the parties recovery. However, a formal and binding agreement that the client will not in any circumstances be liable would do so.

Finally, it should be noted that CFA "lites" – that is to say CFAs where the client's liability to the solicitor for profit costs and/or disbursements is limited to sums recovered from the opponent by way of costs and/or damages – are a lawful exception to the indemnity principle. However, since they are a form of CFA they must be in writing and comply with the other statutory requirements in order to be enforceable.

Q17. A client agrees a normal hourly rate retainer to pursue an employment tribunal claim. The claim is for £350,000 gross (approximately £250,000 after any tax to be paid on the award). The claim is issued and defended. Ahead of the trial, the solicitors estimate that their overall time costs are likely to be in the region of £90,000 by the end of the trial. They propose to the client that, although entitled to recover their time costs in full regardless of outcome, they will in fact only seek to recover the full £90,000 in the event of substantial success (which they suggest is

---

[90] *Swain v Law Society* [1983] 1 AC 598.
[91] See *Awwad v Geraghty* [2001] QB 570.
[92] *Aratra Potato Co v Taylor Joynson Garrett* [1995] 4 All ER 695.
[93] [1983] 1 W.L.R 1056.

judgment for in excess of £200,000); that they would reduce their overall fees to £50,000 in the event of judgment between £100,000 and £200,000; and to £30,000 in the event of judgment up to £100,000). The client agrees. Do the DBA Regulations apply here? Is the agreement compliant from a regulatory standpoint?

9–36 It is debatable whether the agreement is a DBA. What it certainly is – if not a DBA – is a Conditional Fee Agreement. It is an agreement whichh provides for part of the fees to be payable only in specified circumstances. As such, it must comply with s.58 Courts & Legal Services Act 1990 and the CFA order 2013 in order to be enforceable.

Prior to April 2013, such an agreement would almost certainly have been regarded as being a CFA and not an unenforceable contingency fee agreement. The costs payable are not a percentage of the damages, but rather the conventionally calculated profit costs. It is simply that only some of them are payable in certain specified circumstances. The wording of s.58AA(3) of the 1990 admits of an argument that such an agreement is now a DBA, since the client is making a payment to the solicitor if the client obtains a specified financial benefit and the amount of that payment is arguably determined by reference to the amount of the benefit obtained. However, this is probably incorrect since it conflates the concepts of the measure of success being a trigger for the obligation to pay with that measure of success also being the measure of the payment due. Despite s.58AA, such an agreement is probably still better regarded as being a CFA. The amount of the fees is not determined by reference to the amount of the financial benefit – the amount of the fees is determined in the conventional way. It is merely that they are only payable in certain specified circumstances.

The agreement is probably, therefore, a CFA and should comply with the applicable legislation. Care must also be taken to ensure that the client provides an informed consent to any such agreement and that issues surrounding the variation of the existing contractual retainer are properly addressed.

Q18. When is a CFA a contentious business agreement?

9–37 See the commentary above. In *Hollins*[94] the Court of Appeal concluded that a CFA – or at least the CFA before it in that case – was a CBA – see paras 23 and 93. The general starting point appears to be that a CFA is likely to be a CBA, but that it is possible to agree with the client that it is not. As Master Leonard noted in *Acupay Systems LLC v Stephenson Harwood LLP*[95], a finding that a CFA is a CBA may often be to the client's detriment, since its statutorily prescribed effect is to limit the client's right to challenge the detail of the costs payable provided the CBA generally is not unfair or unreasonable. As he put it, it "sacrifices" the right to a detailed assessment. Nevertheless, the courts are sometimes keen to find agreements to be CBAs in the clients' interests where those

---

[94] [2003] EWCA Civ 718.
[95] SCCO, 25 June 2021.

rights have been sacrificed or foregone in any event (for example through passage of time) in order to provide the client with at least some ability to challenge the solicitor's remuneration.

As a general rule, it should be assumed a CFA is likely to be a CBA absent a clear, mutual agreement to the contrary.

Index

set-off, 6–39
settlement offers, 5–125—5–126,
  6–36—6–38
10% uplift where parties are publicly
  funded, 6–24
wasted costs orders, 6–32
wider use, 6–17, 6–41
Reasonableness
costs management, 4–70
proportionality, 3–14—3–16
Retainers
budgeted sum exceeding sum due under
  retainer, 4–96, 4–121
effect of termination on CFA, 2–48
solicitor and client costs, 9–03—9–04
RTA Protocol
see **Pre-action protocols**
Scale costs
IPEC claims, 7–25—7–29
Set-off
Part 36 offers, 5–112
qualified one-way costs shifting, 6–39
Settlement
see also **Part 36 offers**
alternative dispute resolution
  adjudication, 5–51
  advantages, 5–40
  agreement in principle to mediate,
    5–135
  arbitration, 5–52—5–53
  arbitration costs assessments,
    5–144—5–145
  Brexit, 5–37
  consumer disputes, 5–127
  contractual obligation to use ADR,
    5–134
  discretion, 5–39
  early neutral evaluation, 5–49
  encouragement, 5–35—5–36
  expert determination, 5–50, 5–129
  generally, 5–35—5–36
  limitation periods where stay ordered,
    5–128
  mediation, 5–44—5–48
  negotiation, 5–43
  ombudsman schemes, 5–133
  pre-action disclosure, 5–129
  questions and answers, 5–127—5–136,
    5–139—5–144
  refusal to use ADR, 5–130, 5–134,
    5–139
  temporary stay of proceedings, 5–140
  unreasonable refusal to engage, 5–38

without prejudice basis of particulars,
  5–136
Calderbank offers
  consent orders, 5–124
  generally, 5–41, 5–121
  offers in the course of expert
    determination, 5–122
  qualified one-way costs shifting,
    5–125—5–126, 6–36—6–38
  reference to offers in written
    submissions, 5–141
  registration of consent orders, 5–124
  'save as to costs' omitted from
    correspondence, 5–123
case management, 4–13
fraud and dishonesty in making offers,
  5–42
generally, 1–08
introduction, 5–01
negotiation, 5–43
offers to settle
  fraud and dishonesty, 5–42
  generally, 5–41
  questions and answers, 5–121—5–126
open offers, 5–41
options when all issues resolved except
  costs, 5–137—5–138
qualified one-way costs shifting,
  5–125—5–126, 6–36—6–38
questions and answers
  alternative dispute resolution,
    5–127—5–136, 5–139—5–144
  Calderbank offers, 5–121—5–126
  options when all issues resolved
    except costs, 5–137—5–138
Shorter trials scheme
costs management, 4–35
Small claims
fixed costs, 7–76—7–91, 7–115
Part 36 offers, 5–117
Solicitor and client costs
additional liabilities, 9–17—9–19
advising clients on funding options, 9–21
assessment
  changes to, 9–10
  generally, 9–07—9–08
basis of charging clients, 9–20
charging lower amount than stated in
  budget, 9–27
conditional fee agreements
  contentious business agreement, as,
    9–37
  indemnity principle, 9–32